EDIBLE FOREST GARDENS

EDIBLE FOREST GARDENS

❧ **VOLUME TWO** ❧

Ecological Design and Practice
for Temperate–Climate Permaculture

DAVE JACKE
with Eric Toensmeier

CHELSEA GREEN PUBLISHING COMPANY
WHITE RIVER JUNCTION, VERMONT

The field research for, and writing of, portions of this manuscript were undertaken under the auspices of the New England Small Farm Institute, Inc., Belchertown, Massachusetts.

RECYCLED PAPER STATEMENT

Chelsea Green sees publishing as a tool for cultural change and ecological stewardship. We strive to align our book manufacturing practices with our editorial mission, and to reduce the impact of our business enterprise on the environment. We print our books and catalogs on chlorine-free recycled paper, using soy-based inks, whenever possible. *Edible Forest Gardens* was printed on paper supplied by Marquis that is made of recycled materials and other controlled sources.

Project Editor: Collette Leonard
Developmental Editor: Ben Watson
Copy Editor: Cannon Labrie
Proofreader: Nancy Ringer
Indexer: Peggy Holloway
Designed by Peter Holm, Sterling Hill Productions

Printed in Canada.
First Printing, June 2005.

22 21 20   11 12 13
Printed on acid-free paper.

Library of Congress Cataloging-in-Publication Data
Jacke, Dave.
   Edible forest gardens / Dave Jacke with Eric Toensmeier.
      p. cm.
   Includes bibliographical references and index.
   ISBN 1-931498-80-6
   1. Edible forest gardens. 2. Edible forest gardens—North America. I.
Toensmeier, Eric. II. Title.
   SB454.3.E35J24 2005
   635'.0915'2—dc22

                        2004029745

Chelsea Green Publishing
85 North Main Street, Suite 120
White River Junction, Vermont 05001
(802) 295-6300
www.chelseagreen.com

To the herbaceous understory,
and
to the designer and forest dweller in all of us.

Edible Forest Gardens is complete in two volumes. *Volume One: Ecological Vision and Theory for Temperate Climate Permaculture* offers a holistic vision for forest gardening and explains the underlying ecological principles. *Volume Two: Ecological Design and Practice for Temperate Climate Permaculture* covers the practical considerations of forest gardening, including design, maintenance, and a uniquely valuable "plant matrix" describing hundreds of edible and useful species.

Volume One, ISBN 1-931498-79-2, $75
Volume Two, ISBN 1-931498-80-6, $75
Volumes One and Two as a Set, ISBN 1-890132-60-8, $150

www.chelseagreen.com
802-295-6300

CONTENTS

LIST OF WORKSHEETS, TABLES, AND FIGURES

WORKSHEETS

TABLES

FIGURES

PREFACE

When Eric and I met with Chelsea Green staff in the summer of 2004 and decided to make our one-volume book two volumes, I knew I was in for a challenging ride. Separating Siamese twins is never easy, even when the divisions seem clear. However, the difficulty of the reconstructive surgery needed in this second volume, particularly in chapters 3 and 4, was a surprise to me. Attempting to integrate diverse ecological theories with each other, and with a nonlinear design process in a linear format, while taking account of all the possible variations people may have was, perhaps, a bit ambitious. Without Cannon's copyediting comments and Eric's insistence I would never have undertaken the job of rewriting chapter 4 in particular. In the end, I am grateful for the critiques and suggestions made by both of these men, and for Eric's patient and determined reminders of what you, our readers, needed from us. Thank you again to Ben Watson; to Margo Baldwin for taking up the torch and being willing to risk the two-volume set; to Cannon for his drive for excellence; to Elayne Sears for the beautiful illustrations; to Peter Holm and cohorts for the great cover and design; and last but certainly not least, to Collette Leonard. Collette, you threw me a lifeline at a critical time, held on tight, let go at the right times, and did God knows what else to support the project. I don't know if or how I can ever repay you.

Intellectual forebears that also deserve credit include Walt Cudnohufsky and Don Walker, my teachers at the Conway School of Landscape Design; Christopher Alexander; David Perry; Gregory Bateson; Harris, Clark, and Matheny; Wes Jackson; Robert Kourik; Stuart Hill; Robert Hart; Martin Crawford; Bill Mollison; and David Holmgren. David Holmgren gave of his very limited and valuable time to review and comment—thanks. Thanks very much to Steve Breyer of Tripple Brook Farm, Michael McConkey of Edible Landscaping, Ken Asmus of Oikos Tree Crops, Lorraine Gardner and the folks at One Green World, Kermit Cromack at OSU, and Harvard Forest. Your photos made it all so much better. Jonathan Bates provided great pictures and worked with Eric to develop the case study design for their duplex in Holyoke, not to mention applying our ideas with Eric in their garden. My clients Geoff Mamlet and Hannah Bloch allowed me to put them off multiple times through their design project in support of this book. Thanks so much!

Many have offered listening ears and physical and moral support through the dark and stormy final passage: Eric, Martha Hills, Leslie and John, Bill and Cathy, Jono and Kemper, Peter, Justin, Jennifer S., Cecilia, Dr. Rich, Betsy T., Frank and Amy, Faith Priest, Gurumayi, all the other Siddha yogis, and oh so many others.

And finally, I come again to the family connections. Emily, you are so awesome. Thanks again, Mom. Thanks as well to Doug and Kim, Karen, Sue and Chris, and Peter and Michelle. You are all great. This book is an expression of our father's legacy in strange and ironic ways. I finished the second draft of the (one-volume) book on the anniversary of my father's death and completed the last draft of volume two on the anniversary of his birth. Truly, it is difficult to comprehend the hidden powers that weave through and synchronize our lives, but I offer my gratitude to them—and to my father—nonetheless. Thanks for your support from the other side.

SGMKJ
Dave Jacke
February 10, 2005
Keene, NH

Introduction:

A Forest Gardener's Tool Kit

Perhaps we seek to recreate the Garden of Eden, and why not? We believe that a low-energy, high-yield agriculture is a possible aim for the whole world, and that it needs only human energy and intellect to achieve this.

—BILL MOLLISON AND DAVID HOLMGREN, *Permaculture One*, 1978

The forest gardening vision brings humans and nature into a mutually enhancing embrace as co-creative participants in our shared health and evolution. In volume 1 we explored this vision as a practice that reintegrates humans with the natural world, and that both supports and requires a paradigm shift if we are to succeed. Forest gardening uses the overarching strategy of ecosystem mimicry to achieve this reintegration. Mimicry also helps us achieve our more practical goals of high, diverse yields of food and other products; a self-renewing, self-fertilizing, self-maintaining garden; and healthy ecosystem function. To mimic the forest, we must clearly comprehend the structure and function of our forest ecosystem models.

In volume 1, we therefore examined forest ecosystem architecture, social structure, underground economics, and vegetation dynamics. Our understanding of forest ecology supports the potential of the forest gardening idea, showing that mimicry of those structures and functions will help us achieve our goals. Numerous specific implications for design and management also arise from that understanding. However, these implications arise in a pattern that is not entirely useful or accessible to us as gardeners. We must organize these ideas in a way that is relevant to the specific issues gardeners face and provide strategies for success in a format gardeners can easily approach. We must do that without losing touch with the new worldview and understandings we want to embody. This is no small task.

The tools of a forest gardener differ from those of a vegetable gardener in significant ways. Our tools have much to do with design and planning, with thinking things through before we act. What do we need to know to design our forest gardens? How do we deal with weeds in this new gardening paradigm? How do we prevent and manage pests and diseases? What are the key points to consider in designing an overyielding polyculture? We must prepare the ground exceptionally well before planting, or we will be more likely to position our ecosystem for poor performance. What site preparation problems might we face, and how might we solve them? What are the key ideas we will need to keep in mind to manage our forest gardens well?

This volume of *Edible Forest Gardens* is essentially a "forest gardener's tool kit" designed to answer the above questions. As such, there are many tools in it, some of which you may not need—at least not right away. You will have to pick and choose which tools fit your needs in the moment, but you have them all available to you in case you need them.

We begin by taking the forest gardening vision to a deeper, more practical, and more specific level. Chapter 1 thus explains exactly how we mimic forest ecosystem structure and function, and as such it is an overview of forest gardening's conceptual and ecological foundations and its most essential strategies and techniques. However, these strategies and techniques are organized as a bridge between ecological theory and gardening practice, to provide easy reference as well as guidance for design and management problem solving. Those of you who have read volume 1 will find this chapter a useful catalog of the implications arising from the ecological analysis there, with a few new ideas thrown in for good measure. If you have not read volume 1, this chapter will get you up to speed on what it's all about. The chapter also foreshadows the rest of this volume.

Chapter 2 provides a different but related summary of forest gardening by offering patterns for design. This pattern language or "idea bank" provides visceral and visual building blocks with which you can create your forest garden. The patterns presented here embody much of what arose from our ecological analysis in volume 1. There is some overlap between these first two chapters, but their purposes are different, and we expect people to reach for each chapter at different times, in different ways, for different reasons. Take what you like and leave the rest.

Chapters 3 and 4 offer conceptual frameworks and step-by-step assistance for the process of designing your forest garden. These chapters present the most robust, full-fledged, all-out design process we can think of, with variations and options for different circumstances. Please do not think you have to do everything we suggest here; think of these chapters as a menu from which you can create your own meal "from soup to nuts." If you have a big appetite, great! If not, great! Pick and choose your design process from what we have on tap. Just remember that, as David Holmgren says, "Design is as natural as breathing, and, like breathing, most

of us can learn to do it better."[1] We hope what we offer will help you acknowledge and value your own inherent design genius as well as help you wield that genius with greater skill and humility.

Almost any site will present challenges to the designer that require either adaptive design or preplanting site preparation. Chapter 5 provides a comprehensive discussion of many of these challenges and how we can deal with them. Good site preparation can make an immense difference in the long-term productivity and health of growing plants, thereby making your design and planting investments yield a better return and reducing the work required to run the garden ecosystem. This information ties into the design work you will go through in chapters 3 and 4 and will help you get your forest garden off to a good start.

Proper garden establishment also helps maximize the yield of your garden. In addition, it minimizes losses resulting from poor planting and aftercare practices. Chapter 6 discusses how to stake out your design; acquire high-quality planting stock; organize for planting day; plant trees, shrubs, and herbs properly; and care for them afterward. As the saying goes, the devil is in the details, and the details of stock selection, plant placement, how you dig and refill holes, and how you lay mulch can make a huge difference in the survival of your plant allies. Use this chapter to take your planting practices to the next level.

Once your garden is planted and established, you enter the longest and most enjoyable phase of all: living with your forest garden. We wax poetic in this chapter only a little because we focus our discussion on the practicalities of management and maintenance. However, when we come around to the subject of coevolution, we begin connecting to the bigger potentials inherent in the forest garden for ourselves, our culture, and our world, and the potentials are great. Given what we know has worked, and given what we know is possible, who wouldn't wax poetic? A low-energy, high-yield agriculture *is* a possible aim for the temperate humid forest biomes of the world; the Garden of Eden *is* a practical prospect for any of us in our lifetimes—if we only apply our human energy and intellect.

The appendices follow our poetic interlude to provide solid grounding for applying our human energy and intellect to this task. There we offer design data for over six hundred useful and functional plants, as well as data on edible mushrooms, beneficial animal habitat requirements, and informational, organizational, and supply resources to aid your quest.

We hope that you find this second volume of *Edible Forest Gardens* a useful companion and tool kit on your journey, and that you will develop the tools you find here and share your developments with others. We humans are powerful beings that both see and create the world in our own image. May we find in ourselves the beauty, diversity, cooperation, dynamism, abundance, and promise that the forest garden embodies so we can remake our world in such a likeness.

1. Holmgren, 2002, page 15.

1

Issues and Strategies in Forest Garden Design and Management

Many things we currently think of as "maintenance" issues are actually system design issues. A great example of this appeared in a publication discussing minimizing pesticide use by designing and building landscapes differently.[1] Grasses and weeds grow at the base of the chainlink fences around tennis courts, but lawn mowers, string trimmers, and scythes cannot easily cut them there. Therefore, landscape contractors frequently use herbicides to make things look neat and trim. However, simply extending the tennis court's asphalt 6 inches (15 cm) outside the fence would allow one to run a lawn mower along the edge of the asphalt, make it look good, and eliminate the need for herbicides to meet one's aesthetic goals. Our disconnected contemporary suburban ecology presents a larger example of the work, waste, and pollution created by poor system design. Though it may help increase the gross national product and the employment rate, it isn't personally or ecologically sustainable. We have better things to do with our time, energy, and resources. Designing well reduces the costs, time, and toxins required to maintain the system; this fundamental idea stands behind forest gardening and ecological design in general. By understanding the principle of shifting the burden to the intervenor, and applying other ecological principles to our landscapes, we become designers and managers more than hard laborers.

Accordingly, this chapter examines how we can turn major forest gardening maintenance and management issues into design issues. It provides an overview of the practical approaches forest gardening takes to meeting our goals. In the process, it summarizes the design and management ideas arising from the ecological analysis of volume 1 in a pattern more directly appropriate to the needs of garden designers and managers. A natural result of doing so is that we also define the specific functions that make polycultures effective. The chapter details specific strategies to address the whole universe of forest garden design and management issues. We will occasionally refer you to patterns in the following chapter by number (e.g., "pattern #6"), and to other chapters in this volume and in volume 1 where you can find further information related to the topic at hand.

As we said in volume 1, at its simplest, edible forest garden design involves choosing plants and deciding when and where to place them in the garden. These seemingly simple choices must generate the forestlike structures that achieve our design goals. We must now revisit this idea. We must refine and articulate it to express more accurately what we are attempting to do as forest garden designers and managers. Figure 1.1 crystallizes the essential forest gardening task: using specific design elements to create particular ecosystem dynamics so the garden ecosystem yields our desired conditions.

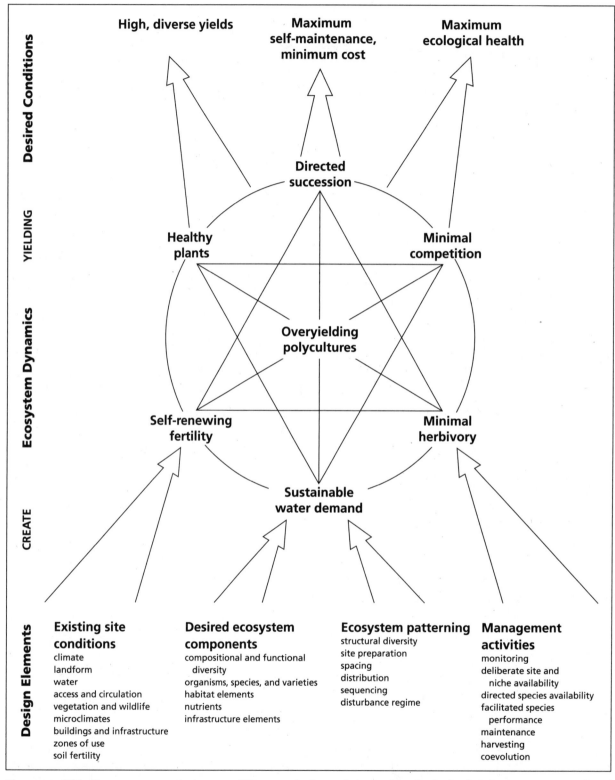

High, diverse yields

Maximum self-maintenance, minimum cost

Maximum ecological health

Desired Conditions

YIELDING

Ecosystem Dynamics

CREATE

Directed succession

Healthy plants

Minimal competition

Overyielding polycultures

Self-renewing fertility

Minimal herbivory

Sustainable water demand

Design Elements

Existing site conditions
climate
landform
water
access and circulation
vegetation and wildlife
microclimates
buildings and infrastructure
zones of use
soil fertility

Desired ecosystem components
compositional and functional
   diversity
organisms, species, and varieties
habitat elements
nutrients
infrastructure elements

Ecosystem patterning
structural diversity
site preparation
spacing
distribution
sequencing
disturbance regime

Management activities
monitoring
deliberate site and
   niche availability
directed species availability
facilitated species
   performance
maintenance
harvesting
coevolution

FIGURE 1.1. This diagram presents the essence of forest gardening and summarizes the fundamental strategies we employ in garden design and management. It also forms the basis for the structure of this chapter.

We know that, in general, we want to create high, diverse yields from a self-maintaining garden that creates maximum ecosystem health (your specific goals may vary). What identifiable ecosystem dynamics will generate these three conditions? There are seven. The most central of these, overyielding polycultures, results at least partly from the interaction between the other six: self-renewing fertility; sustainable water demand; minimal herbivory (that is, minimal varmints, pests, and diseases); minimal competition (from "weeds" and between crops); directed successions; and healthy plants. All of these ecosystem dynamics are emergent properties of the garden ecosystem; they arise from the interaction between elements at least as much as from the character of the elements themselves. They represent forest gardening's answer to the issues gardeners face, using ecosystem design strategies more than maintenance strategies (table 1.1).

In forest gardening, for example, we deal with plant nutrition through creating self-renewing fertility, not just fertilizing. We minimize herbivory by pests, varmints (large pests), and diseases through ecosystem design as much as possible, not only with direct pest suppression. Conventional gardeners and farmers often look at the issues of spacing and "weeds" separately, when in fact they are part of a single discussion concerning minimizing competition.

The forest gardening perspective puts all these issues into a less human-centered, more ecological context. It also relates these issues more fully to each other. For example, weeds also come into play in managing succession, but the intention is different. Rather than setting succession back as an unconscious result of weeding, we look at the question of how we direct succession where we want it to go, and what roles weeds play in that process. This is a complete turnaround. Then again, forest gardeners face some issues that conventional gardeners generally do not. Most gardeners do not even understand the concept of overyielding, or additive yields, while it is central to what we want to achieve. This con-

TABLE 1.1. Translation of typical gardener's issues to forest-garden ecosystem dynamics and desired conditions. This table will give you tips for where to look in this chapter for strategies related to the issues you face.

Typical Issues	Ecosystem Dynamics and Desired Conditions
fertilizing	self-renewing fertility
soil improvement	self-renewing fertility; healthy plants; sustainable water demand
weed control	minimal competition; directed succession
pest control	minimal herbivory
disease control	minimal herbivory
dealing with varmints	minimal herbivory
plant spacing	healthy plants; minimal competition; minimal herbivory; directed succession
what to plant	all ecosystem dynamics and desired conditions
when to plant	minimal competition; directed succession
where to plant	self-renewing fertility; sustainable water demand; minimal herbivory; minimal competition; directed succession; high, diverse yields; maximum self-maintenance, minimum costs
how to plant	healthy plants
growing healthy plants	healthy plants; self-renewing fertility; sustainable water demand; minimal herbivory; minimal competition
watering and irrigation	sustainable water demand
harvesting	overyielding polycultures; high, diverse yields; maximum self-maintenance, minimum cost
maximizing yields	overyielding polycultures; high, diverse yields
minimizing labor and costs	maximum self-maintenance, minimum cost

textual shift is necessary if we are to fully enter the paradigm shift required to completely succeed in creating designed ecosystems that carry more of the burden of their own maintenance.

What design elements do we use to create these seven ecosystem dynamics? Are we designing only with plants? Obviously not. The site and its inherent resources are fundamental, as are our desired plants, other desired organisms, and their key habitat elements. In addition, we must consciously design the patterns of the ecosystem and our management activities. We use these direct physical elements and actions to create our structural and functional mimics of forest ecosystems. To these physical elements and actions, we apply ecological design principles and processes to develop site-specific strategies for our own forest gardens.

This chapter will offer generalized design and management strategies for achieving each of the three desired conditions and creating each of the seven ecosystem dynamics, using the design elements at our disposal (as shown in figure 1.1). It lays the groundwork for understanding how the design and management principles, processes, and practices discussed later serve the forest gardening purpose. We intend this chapter to be an accessible reference and guide that links all the discussion in the first volume of *Edible Forest Gardens* with the design and management chapters that support and follow through on the ideas presented. We begin with an overview of the design elements with which we work and then address strategies for each ecological dynamic and desired condition.

DESIGN ELEMENTS

When we design forest gardens, we apply design principles and processes to understanding and planning the design of physical elements, as well as our management-activity patterns. What are these design elements? How do they influence the ecosystem dynamics of our forest gardens? What strategies might we need to apply to these design elements to achieve our goals? What processes and principles might we apply to the design of these elements? Words in bold italics in the following signify design elements listed under the four headings in figure 1.1.

EXISTING SITE CONDITIONS

Your forest garden site is the palette upon which you paint. It consists of relatively discrete components, including *climate, landform, water, access and circulation, vegetation and wildlife, microclimates, buildings and infrastructure, zones of use,* and *soil fertility.* The site's character, conditions, and resources influence every aspect of your forest garden, from the effect of soil fertility on yields and on competition between plants, to weed problems from the soil seed bank, to the existing pests, diseases, and varmints with which you will have to deal, and much more. Site selection is therefore one of the critical first steps in forest garden design. Once we have chosen a site, we need to understand the site conditions as well as we can so we can determine site preparation strategies, species selections, planting patterns, and management activities. The existing vegetation holds many clues to help us design effective polycultures, so we need in-depth understanding of it as well.

The first key strategy here is to choose your site carefully, keeping in mind the implications the site holds for your gardening efforts, from successional dynamics and weeds, to site problems you might want to avoid, to what crops you can grow. Do not minimize the importance of this step; it can prevent major problems and much work. Remember, however, that clearly articulating your specific design goals is a necessary first step. Your goals will directly guide your site selection process to its optimal outcome.

Once you have selected a site, you need to analyze it and assess what it will mean for your design. Site analysis and assessment (A&A) work is critical to developing a good design; people often do it poorly, if they do it at all. Site A&A guides all aspects of your design, from site preparation to species selection, patterning, and management. Analysis and assessment will help you decide whether you will mostly leave the site be and adapt to it (adaptive design), modify it to create more conducive growing conditions for your desired plant species (site preparation), or use a combination of different strategies for different patches. Once you understand the climate, soils, light, water, and other factors with which you have to work, you can determine the available niches you will fill with selected species.

Deeply understanding the existing vegetation is a critical part of site A&A. Some existing species you may want to keep, while others may require removal. You should know this ahead of time. In addition, the existing plants will help you learn more about your site, its soil and moisture conditions, and what species will work well there. Existing vegetation A&A can also help you develop ecological analogs. Finally, the vegetation surrounding your garden site also affects your garden's manageability, the amount of work required to direct succession effectively, and the proximity of beneficial animals to your garden. To understand all of these factors, we recommend characterizing your vegetation during site A&A, as well as analyzing the niches of existing species and assessing habitat quality in your neighborhood. Chapter 3 details all of these critical design processes.

DESIRED ECOSYSTEM COMPONENTS

The desired ecosystem components—the living organisms and nonliving ingredients we pull together to perform specific desired functions—are the most concrete and malleable of the design elements. By incorporating diverse ecosystem components, all performing multiple functions, we can realize benefits of diversity such as provision of niches, reduction of competition, increased productivity and yield, functional interconnection, stability and resilience, reduced herbivory, and elegance and beauty. Select your ecosystem components with both compositional and functional diversity in mind.

We create *compositional diversity* starting with diverse *organisms, species, and varieties*. Diversity at each of these taxonomic levels has the best potential to foil pests and create functional interconnection. Keep in mind that the most important beneficial interactions occur between kingdoms of organisms (for example, between plants and nitrogen-fixing bacteria, or plants and fungi), rather than within kingdoms (such as between plants and plants). Our concept of "diversity" should also include diversity of taxonomic families and genera. The different families and orders of plants usually represent groups with similar adaptations, biochemistry, and species niches. Therefore, using different taxa at these higher levels helps fill more community niches. In addition, pests and diseases often prey upon different members of the same family (e.g., many rose family plants, such as apples, roses, and juneberries, get the same fungal and bacterial diseases). So, using a mix of plant families in your garden is a good idea, as is including multiple genera and species. For example, Martin Crawford's 2-acre (0.8 ha) forest garden in Devon, England, has 31 families of woody plants in the canopy alone, and the garden as a whole includes over 450 species. In addition, varietal diversity or genetic diversity within a species is particularly important for warding off pests and diseases.

In addition to diverse organisms, we need to include diversity in the nonliving components, such as *nutrients, habitat elements*, and *infrastructure elements*. The need for diverse nutrients and nutrient sources is obvious. These include materials like compost, a variety of mulches, and soil amendments like greensand or rock phosphate as needed. They will also include fertilizers like compost tea and fish or seaweed emulsions. We do not recommend chemical fertilizers due to their effects on the soil food web. After testing your soils and subsoils you can decide what you need and where. This may vary from patch to patch.

Some desired organisms and species we deliberately introduce into the garden. Others we attract by providing good habitat. In both cases, we need habitat elements to meet the food, water, and shelter needs of beneficial organisms. Habitat elements include many things already found in forest gardens, like mulch and plants, and also more specific things like miniponds, dead wood, dead flower heads, and brush and rock piles. Including such elements expands the pest control and other services of wildlife by filling more community niches. See appendix 5 for detailed information on the ecological roles and required habitat elements of a wide range of beneficial organisms.

Infrastructure includes such things as paths, sheds, compost and mulch piles, irrigation equipment, rhizome barriers, and the like. We need to select and design these based on our functional requirements and our site analyses and assessments.

Despite all the above, random compositional diversity is not likely to work optimally for us. We therefore strive for diverse ecosystem components that work together as a functional unit; thus we seek *functional diversity* in all four of its aspects. We must work directly with the multiple functions of organisms and nonliving elements by understanding their species niches. We want to fill all the important community niches so our gardens have diversity of function. We must fill each community niche with diverse organisms and species so the system provides redundancy of function. Finally, we must link the needs and yields of the various parts of our garden ecosystem so we create functional diversity—diversity that works. Creating mutual-support and resource-sharing guilds helps us achieve these ends. Key design processes help us do these things: niche analysis, guild-build, ecological analogs, and polyculture design.

ECOSYSTEM PATTERNING

The design element of ecosystem patterning deals with the architecture of the garden and its environs. *Structural diversity* is variation in a habitat's architecture both above- and belowground. It includes variations in soils, microclimates, and the density and patterning of plants (*Lumpy Texture*, pattern #39), as well as a stand's age structure. Structural diversity at a larger scale also includes between-habitat diversity, which results from having different habitats within and around the garden. This

means having sunny glades, dense tree stands, open savanna, thickets, lawns, brushy edges, and the like.

Variation in these structural features both within and between habitats provides niches for a wider array of plant species. It also increases both bird and arthropod diversity, which aids in balancing food webs above- and belowground. Understanding and designing these patterns confers many of the same benefits as diversity in general, including more niches, less competition, reduced herbivory, higher yield and productivity, stability, resilience, and opportunities for functional interconnection, as well as beauty. Structural diversity arises from the existing site patterns, as well as our design and management activities.

In natural systems, ecosystem patterns result from variations in site conditions and in disturbance and succession patterns. These variations occur in a patchwise manner. Patterns also develop in response to plant adaptations for defending against herbivory and parasitism, facilitating alliances with other species, reducing competition, or increasing competitive advantage. In designed systems, ecosystem patterning arises from five key design and management activities: site preparation work; plant spacing; plant distribution; plant sequencing; and the disturbance regime. We want our patterning activities to increase structural diversity. How can we achieve this?

Succession studies show that patches are fundamental organizational units in natural ecosystems. Patches help create structural diversity. They occur in multiple dimensions. In space, they occur vertically, horizontally, and at different scales. In time, patches appear and disappear through seasonal and multiyear cycles, sequencing, and successions. In kind, patches occur in dimensions that include patterns of resources like nutrients, water, light, pollen, nectar, crop plants, mulch types, and so on; variations in vegetation density; and differences in disturbance types, severity, intensity, and frequency. To create structural diversity, we should respond to and mimic this patchy reality.

Site analysis and assessment should reveal foundational resource patterns in your garden. You can build upon these foundations by designing your guilds, polycultures, and management patterns in related patch patterns, choosing species appropriate for the patch conditions present. You can also respond to the existing patterns by altering them through *site preparation*. Either way, you then design the *spacing, distribution,* and *sequencing* of ecosystem elements, and your *disturbance regimes*, to create patch patterns appropriate to the resource patterns and your desired conditions. You can use patterns such as those shown in chapter 2 to help you determine the spacing, distribution, and sequencing of the design elements in your garden.

Site preparation includes anything you do before planting to alter site conditions to your liking. We include it as an ecosystem pattern because site preparation alters the above- or belowground structure of the site. Chapter 5 covers site preparation challenges and solutions in detail. Designing site preparation is a critical part of forest garden design. If you do robust site analysis and think ahead, you should have to do site prep only once, and it should dramatically increase your forest garden's productivity and ease of maintenance. Not resolving soil and weed problems before planting your forest garden can cause more work than site prep would have required; it can also cause reduced garden productivity or even failure of the system or some of its components.

Plant spacing is one of the most crucial issues in forest garden design. This is particularly true for trees and shrubs, because they are harder to move than herbaceous plants, and because they so strongly affect shade in the understory. Planting too close together increases competition and maintenance, decreases yields, and can shorten the life spans or bearing life spans of plants. In addition, as pointed out in volume 1, chapter 3, density defines plant community character, so consider the character of the community you want to create when you are thinking about how far apart you will plant. Chapter 4 discusses spacing in greater detail.

A number of functional issues influence distribution design, that is, plant patterning. For example, many fruiting plants must be reasonably close to a cross-pollinator, while nitrogen fixers and dynamic accumulators should be in close proximity to the plants we intend them to assist. On the other hand, we should scatter plants intended to provide nectar for beneficial insects everywhere in the garden, preferably in clumps. Examining the evolved dispersal mechanisms in plants will help us understand their natural distribution patterns and may help us surmise the reasons for their distribution. We need to mimic any of these patterns that align with our purposes. For instance, the long-distance dispersal by animals of large-fruited tree seeds is a way for the tree's offspring to evade their parent's pests and diseases. Planting apples and similar fruit trees scattered among other species would mimic their natural pattern and should reduce insect and disease problems compared to large monoculture orchard blocks. Chapter 2 discusses numerous examples relating to distribution patterns and community character and function. Chapter 4 discusses distribution and patterning in guild and polyculture design, as well as polyculture patterning based on the architecture, behavior, required management regime, and the spacing needs of plants.

Sequencing is the patterning through time of events of any kind, for example, disturbance events, fertilization, mulching, the introduction of species into a patch, or other activities. Sequencing is an aspect of directed succession (discussed more fully later). It is an important design element in relay plantings, instant successions, gap dynamics, and so on. It may relate to the designed dominance pattern of species in a patch, either in a seasonal cycle or through a successional sequence. Good sequencing, such as thoughtful crop maturity timing, improves the flow of work in the seasonal round. Good timing can reduce labor; for example, catching weed problems in the early stages can prevent the need to expend twenty times more energy in control efforts later on. We must consider the sequencing of bloom times for beneficial-insect nectary plants if we want to keep beneficials in the garden year-round. It is often necessary to create calendars and timelines to work out sequencing patterns in our designs. Sequences are not necessarily cyclic or regular patterns.

In contrast, disturbance regimes frequently are cyclic or recurring patterns. Disturbance can reset the successional clock or set the stage for it to move in a new direction by affecting the legacies of the postdisturbance system. The type, pattern, frequency, intensity, and severity of disturbance shape the structural diversity of the ecosystem. We need to design the disturbance regimes for our forest garden patches to maintain the diversity we desire. Matching the disturbance, maintenance, and management requirements of species we plant together in a polyculture patch simplifies management and should improve plant health and yield. Growing perennial root crops harvested each year within the feeder-root zone of shallow-rooted trees wouldn't make much sense. Nor would it make sense trying to grow a long-term medicinal crop with such annually disturbed root crops: ginseng, for instance, needs seven or more years to reach maturity. These are extreme examples to make the point, but the idea can get much more subtle. Polyculture patches of medicinals harvested in early fall under trees bearing fruit in late fall make sense. You can harvest the herbs, cut them back and mulch them in preparation for winter, and leave the space clear for fruit harvest a few weeks later.

Designing your disturbance regimes occurs at various stages of the design process. It starts with noticing the disturbance regimes already occurring on the site during site analysis. It continues with niche analysis of existing and desired species, by noting what disturbance, maintenance, and management the various species need. Your schematic garden design may use disturbance regimes as part of its organizing concept, for example, by locating less-disturbed patches farther from accessible parts of the garden and more-disturbed patches closer to

pathways. Once you have laid out your proposed disturbance patterns, you design patches and successional scenarios, select species, and build guilds and polycultures with disturbance regimes in mind.

MANAGEMENT ACTIVITIES

Once we have selected the site and its ecosystem components, patterned the garden, and planted it, management is what we have left to steer the system.

People don't usually think of management activities as design elements. Management and maintenance have mainly been just "things we do" habitually after a garden is installed. However, treating management activities as legitimate objects of design gives us the opportunity to eliminate this work or make it easier to do. It helps us think through what tools and techniques we will use, and how they might affect garden design. Designing management activities also helps us plan our seasonal workflow and make sure we know how to keep track of the garden ecosystem and direct its development. How will we monitor the garden to follow its progress and changes? How will we deliberately manage site and niche availability to keep succession on its preferred track? How will we direct species availability and species performance? What kinds of maintenance will we need to do? How might we coevolve with our garden over time? Clearly, we cannot and will not think all this through in complete detail before we plant. Nevertheless, we should consider it in our design process to a reasonable degree. Chapter 7 discusses these topics more thoroughly, but we offer an overview here.

Once you plant your forest garden, *monitoring* begins. You can do much frequent, ongoing observation while you wander the paths and nibble. However, we also recommend mapping what you planted where and observing plant and polyculture performance and behavior. Record other changes in your garden over time, too, such as soil development. You will also need to monitor for weeds, pests, and diseases. Monitoring helps you learn and keeps you ahead of the curve so you can prevent problems or stop them from getting out of hand.

Deliberate site and niche availability is about controlling the initial conditions of succession, primarily through designed disturbances. Other strategies also play a role in this: filling niches through community design and proactive planting, managing resources to prevent invasion by unwanted species, and site selection and design (see table 1.6 later this chapter). Once we have set a successional direction through site preparation and garden planting, deliberate site and niche availability should fall to the background as a strategy. Sometimes, however, we need to make sites or niches available as part of a planned succession or to keep weeds from heading the system in a direction we don't want. We must also take advantage of natural disturbance events when they occur, turning them into deliberate opportunities for ecosystem change or making sure we redirect the community back toward our previous intentions.

Directed species availability simply means making sure that the species taking advantage of the available sites and niches in your garden are species you desire. The primary method of achieving this is proactive planting: putting in place plants or plant propagules (seeds, cuttings, or whatever) whenever a site or niche becomes available. This certainly includes planting into your newly mulched garden. It might also mean popping something into the space vacated by a weed or a desired plant that did not survive. If you don't act quickly, rest assured that nature itself will seize the opportunity. In addition to proactive planting, though, we must also manage the vegetation or other features in or around the garden to deal with seed or underground rhizomes attempting to colonize open niches.

The art of encouraging the species you desire and discouraging those you don't is what *facilitated species performance* is all about. This is the core of all good gardening, and many factors come into play here (again, see table 1.6). In forest gardening, we try to do most of our work on this issue *before*

planting. It comes down to good site selection and design; good site preparation; good resource management (especially fertility and water); good species selection and community design (that is, architecture, guild, and polyculture design); and good soil food web management. The rest of this volume covers these topics in depth.

In chapter 2 of volume 1 we discussed the differences between management (planning and guiding change) and *maintenance* (the grunt work of keeping the garden running). Of course, the whole point of forest gardening is to reduce maintenance to a minimum, but we'll still have some to do. We should use maintenance work as an opportunity to look for design solutions to the work we do. How can we prevent the weed problems we are dealing with? What are the life cycles, natural enemies, and habitat requirements of the pests we confront? We also need to beware of creating additional problems from the manner and timing of our maintenance activities, for most of them qualify as disturbances of one kind or another. We can often reduce future maintenance by following our maintenance interventions with "mop-up operations," such as proactive planting or mulching after weeding. Timing our interventions differently can have the same effect. For example, summer pruning reduces fruit tree growth the following year, reducing the need for additional pruning and making monitoring, pest management, and harvesting easier. Chapter 7 focuses on the kinds of maintenance we're likely to encounter.

Harvesting is often a form of designed disturbance, particularly for root crops, but also for leaves. Design your forest garden so that the patches you harvest thrive with this disturbance. You can also consciously direct the succession in the patch following the harvesting disturbance. Designated pathways minimize damage to vegetation and the soil profile structure during harvest. Make sure that your paths are wide enough, and that they provide access to all parts of all planting beds without forcing you to step on and compact the growing bed soil.

Coevolution with your forest garden is a long-term process. It includes our learning from and refining our forest gardens, as well as breeding and selecting new varieties. It is possible to design this coevolutionary process to some degree. Plant breeding and selection benefit from conscious design, as do personal and group learning.

ECOSYSTEM DYNAMICS

Ecosystem dynamics are certain system characteristics or "behaviors" associated with specific interactions between ecosystem components. These interactions and characteristics arise in the forest garden through mimicking ecosystem structure and function, and through careful selection of the components themselves. What follows is our attempt at providing clear and specific guidance for how to embody forest ecology in designed gardens so that these ecosystem dynamics arise from the structures we create and functions we employ.

As we said earlier, forest gardening puts the basic problems gardeners face into an ecological context. We must therefore reframe these issues in that context. How do we deal with weeds? That is an issue of minimizing competition, as well as one of directing succession. How do we deal with varmints, pests, and diseases? This question is really about minimizing herbivory (except, of course, *our* herbivory!). Fertilization? Self-renewing fertility. Irrigation? Sustainable water demand. Maximizing yields? This gardener's issue is both a desired condition *and* an ecosystem dynamic: creating overyielding polycultures is a dynamic central to forest gardening, and one that helps achieve high, diverse yields.

Ecosystem dynamics help us achieve our three primary design goals indirectly. We design a garden ecosystem that generates these dynamics so the system itself is responsible for exhibiting the qualities of high yields, maximum self-maintenance, and maximum health. The interrelationship between the ecosystem dynamics is therefore what achieves our goals. We also have direct means of achieving these goals (which we'll deal with in the following section). Combining direct and indirect measures helps ensure success, while minimizing our labor and energy inputs. Similarly, we have direct and indirect means of creating our ecosystem dynamics. Interactions between garden ecosystem components help create these dynamics, as do particular qualities of the garden components themselves.

The subsections that follow examine these ecosystem dynamics in some detail, offering guidance for creating them both directly and indirectly. What are these ecosystem dynamics? What traditional gardening issues nest inside them? How do they help us achieve our three goals? What strategies, patterns, principles, and design processes will help our gardens generate these dynamics? We'll begin with "healthy plants" and work our way counterclockwise around the circle in figure 1.1, ending with "overyielding polycultures."

HEALTHY PLANTS

Everything we do in the forest garden is designed to create healthy plants. For the most part, we can easily discern how the other ecosystem dynamics help create plant fitness. Healthy plants support our goals and the other ecosystem dynamics in similarly obvious ways. We'll mention two points in this regard that may be a bit less obvious. Healthy plants resist herbivory more effectively because they have the resources to resist, and they can recover more easily. Likewise with competition: healthy plants better resist the negative effects of competition and can compete better themselves. However, in ideal conditions, plants will not compete because they have plentiful resources, and plentiful resources help create healthy plants.

The principle of stress and harmony states that stress is the denial of needs, not allowing inherent functions or forcing unnatural function, while harmony is the meeting of needs, allowing natural functions and preventing forced function (see volume 1, page 129). This principle plays a large role in plant vigor, urging us to reduce plant stress, meet plant needs, and allow natural plant functions. Most of the strategies below relate to this principle. What design strategies help us create healthy plants?

Right Plant, Right Place:
Match Plant Needs to Site Conditions

By choosing species that will thrive in the conditions we have (or will create), we lay the foundation of plant health. We must therefore consider soil texture, fertility, pH, and moisture regime, as well as current and anticipated light levels and climate and microclimate conditions (figure 1.2).

Create Loose, Deep, Fertile, Healthy Soil

Good soil is a key prerequisite for healthy plants. The deeper the soil, the more room plant roots

have to roam and meet their own needs without ongoing intervention. If your soils are compacted, shallow, or poorly drained, you may have to improve conditions before planting. Fertility is an obvious health requirement, but some plants require richer soils than others do. We must therefore match our soil preparation work in each patch with the plants we will plant in it. A healthy soil food web has numerous benefits, as discussed in volume 1, chapter 5. All you have to do in most cases is add organic matter, provide perennial plant roots, and stop tilling, all of which forest gardeners do anyway. However, site preparation may be necessary to create the conditions a healthy soil food web requires.

One of the most important ways to maintain loose, deep soil is to define clear pathways, and use them exclusively for getting around the garden,

FIGURE 1.2. Dealing with microclimate factors in garden design is essential. Strong prevailing winds rush across this hillside in Wales. All of the trees shown were planted at the same time, but those to the left had windbreak protection, while those to the right did not. The difference in growth rate and survival is tremendous. Ragman's Lane Farm, Gloucestershire. *Photo by Dave Jacke.*

avoiding walking on planting beds as much as possible (see pattern #24, *Definite Pathways*). Soil compaction is one of the biggest banes to healthy soil, reducing its fertility, its root penetrability, its soil food web health and numbers, its ability to soak up and hold rainfall, and so on. Defined paths concentrate the impact of human feet and cart wheels, keeping planting bed soil in top shape. Paths allow you to use the garden even when the soil is wet without fear of destroying soil structure. They also help us organize the garden, defining patches and zones of use. Make them wide enough to accommodate carts or wheelbarrows as well as humans (see pattern #29, *Pathway Width*).

Maximize Harmony in Polycultures

Design your polycultures so each species can express its natural form, habit, and behaviors; this maximizes harmony and minimizes stress. To do this, pay attention to proper plant spacing and place species in an appropriate successional context. Also, design your polycultures so they mix species with complementary forms, habits, and behaviors (especially rooting patterns) and complementary needs for light, nutrients, and other resources. This minimizes competition between them by partitioning resources. You can also maximize harmony by mixing species in polycultures that form mutual-support guilds, thereby embodying the principle of functional interconnection (see volume 1, page 29). Finally, you can minimize plant stress and your work by designing patches so all species within them have compatible management and disturbance requirements. Chapter 4 discusses succession and polyculture design.

Prepare the Ground Well prior to Planting

Removing weeds and improving soils before planting creates the conditions for your plants to thrive. Even if it takes one or two years of site preparation before you can plant, it is probably worth it. Also, make sure to plan and install your irrigation or other water systems in advance.

Use Healthy, Resistant Stock and Plant Carefully

Whenever possible, choose species and varieties that resist the pests and diseases known to live in your region. Your site analysis and assessment will help you determine which pests and diseases you need to defend against. Planting disease-free plants with healthy root systems gives your forest garden a major head start on creating healthy plants in the long run. Chapter 6 has a complete discussion of how to evaluate and select planting stock, as well as how to plant properly. Poor planting can do serious damage to a plant's long-term prospects. Proper planting techniques give your plants the chance to establish themselves quickly and strongly and to perform to their optimum.

Use Proper Plant Spacing

Proper plant spacing provides multiple benefits for healthy plants. It reduces competition, allowing plants to thrive. It also provides better air circulation, and this reduces many fungal and bacterial diseases caused by excess moisture. As author-farmer Gene Logsdon says, "Sunshine is the best fungicide."

Design and Manage for Minimal Pest and Disease Problems

Once you accept that there will always be a certain population of pests in your forest garden, you can set out to keep their populations low by designing for structural and compositional diversity, a healthy soil food web, and incorporation of food, water, and shelter for beneficials. Ongoing monitoring and ecological pest, disease, and varmint control will help keep herbivore populations manageable once your garden is up and running.

SELF-RENEWING FERTILITY

The forest-gardening approach to fertility emphasizes strategies employed in the design phase that should reduce the need for work and expensive inputs later on down the line. Many basic characteristics of forest gardens support self-renewing fertility by their very nature: perennial plant roots provide consistent root-zone resources to the soil food web; lack of tilling allows undisturbed development of the soil organism community; consistent mulch provides stable food resources for the decomposers and a stable soil environment for everyone who lives down there; and so on.

While all of the following strategies are important for creating self-renewing fertility, this section provides in-depth information on nitrogen-fixing and dynamic accumulator plants.

Use Site Analysis and Assessment and Niche Analysis

To create self-renewing fertility, you must begin with a careful assessment of your soils. Make sure to assess nutrient levels in both your topsoil and your parent materials so you can determine long-term fertility prospects and needs (see chapter 5 in volume 1 for a discussion of the role of parent materials). Also, evaluate the soil profile so you can identify possible problems of compaction, high water tables, and other factors that may influence the plants' belowground resources. Desired species niche analysis (chapter 3) tells you which soil conditions your plants prefer. The site and niche analyses will guide you in developing a garden design and a site preparation plan that will in turn determine how to use the strategies listed below.

Maximize Root Penetration of the Soil Profile

Making sure that plants can get their roots deep into the soil profile gives them the greatest access to the most soil resources. It allows plants to absorb nutrients leaching into the deep soil and those released by weathering of the parent materials. This aids nutrient recycling and conservation and ultimately enriches and deepens the topsoil as the plants drop leaves on the surface and their roots die throughout the soil profile.

Create Healthy Soil Food Webs

With proper care, subterranean microherds and fungal allies offer tremendous nutritional benefits to our plants. To receive these benefits we must treat them well by minimizing compaction, adding organic matter, and minimizing tillage and other forms of soil disturbance. Perennial plants help sustain a year-round root-zone soil food web capable of storing more nutrients than can the decomposer food web by itself. Mycorrhizas are especially important and beneficial for plants and for nutrient storage and transport (see chapter 5 in volume 1 for information on the ecology and cultivation of mycorrhizas).

Fertilize the Way Nature Does: From the Top Down

By mimicking natural fertilizing processes we enable the ecosystem to develop nutrient processing pathways that will run properly even when we aren't around to do the work. This means using nutrients in the form of organic matter and rock powders whenever possible, and applying them appropriately. Though it may be slower, feeding the soil from the surface with organic materials creates the biological infrastructure the ecosystem needs to function properly. Placing organic matter or compost deep in the soil profile, however (say, in the bottom of a planting hole), can make matters worse: less oxygen is available deeper down, so the organic matter often decomposes anaerobically. This in turn can kill roots and beneficial soil organisms. Mulching and fertilizing the soil surface allows leaching, plant roots, and decomposers to act naturally, reduces disturbance to the soil profile, and works in harmony with natural soil-building processes.

Apply Mulch, Compost, and Amendments Appropriately

Mulch is one of the most critical components of forest gardens. A mimic of the litter layer found on forest floors, mulch has numerous benefits. It is not without its drawbacks—notably the cozy habitat it provides slugs and voles—and one must apply it to an appropriate depth.

Compost provides organic matter and nutrients and also inoculates the soil with beneficial organisms.

However, compost is usually expensive. It is best mixed into the soil during site preparation or used as a topdressing after planting, if the soil needs much help. Never fill tree-planting holes with compost, as it can lead to "pot-bound" roots and anaerobic soil conditions. Always mimic natural soil profile structures by spreading compost on the soil surface, or at most mixing it into the topsoil, then covering it with mulch.

Some perennial gardeners pull back their mulch, add 1 to 2 inches (2.5 to 5 cm) of compost to their gardens, and then remulch—every year. This certainly creates a healthy garden, but it is not self-maintaining, self-renewing fertility by a long shot. If the soil is in rough shape, yearly additions of compost might make sense until the plants get well established and serious nutrient cycling and conservation get going in the ecosystem. Otherwise, an early boost, followed by mulch, should be enough. It can take five to seven years, or more, for forest gardens to firmly establish their own nutrient cycles. However, with good design using fertility-building plants, the garden will get there eventually, making its own compost every year with no effort on your part.

For greater amounts of nutrients, and to make up for serious nutrient deficiencies, you can use a wide variety of organic soil amendments. Again, we should most often use these as an early system-establishment boost until the garden cycles get going. In areas with some combination of high rainfall, warm winters, nutrient-poor parent materials, and degraded topsoils, you may need to add amendments every few years to account for leaching losses, even after the nutrient cycling and conservation system gets going.

Create Lush Vegetation and Abundant Organic Matter

Plants and organic matter play key roles in the anatomy of self-renewing fertility, cocreating a dynamic, nutrient-conserving system. More vegetation means more water transpired from the soil, which reduces nutrient leaching. It also means more nutrients built into biomass, which then becomes organic matter. More organic matter means more cation exchange sites and, thus, more room in the soil to store nutrients.

Emphasize Aggrading, Midsuccession Habitats

The aggradation phase of succession (see chapter 6 of volume 1) is when ecosystems exhibit the greatest control over nutrient flows. The aggradation phase is also when the ecosystem most rapidly converts the greatest amounts of nutrients and sunlight into biomass and builds other forms of natural capital. Emphasizing the aggradation phase will therefore maximize nutrient conservation, storage, and recycling. This means creating midsuccession habitats ranging from oldfield mosaics to sun-loving pioneer-tree woodlands. Since most of our best crop trees and shrubs are competitor-strategist plants adapted to such environments, we are in luck. We just need to build the complete ecosystem with diverse components to make it work. Patterns in chapter 2 that will help you create midsuccession environments include #12, *Minithickets;* #13, *Oldfield Mosaics;* #14, *Woodland Gardens;* #16, *Gaps and Clearings;* #19, *Copses;* and #20, *Forest Edges.*

Diversify the Leaf Litter to Aid Nutrient Cycling

Research has shown that diverse forms of litter on the forest floor aid nutrient cycling in the litter layer and topsoil. Diverse litter provides for better decomposition and diversity in the decomposer food web. Therefore, using various kinds of mulch and planting plants that provide diverse kinds of litter will improve self-renewing fertility.

Grow Your Own Mulch

You can dedicate an area of your landscape to growing plants that produce prodigious amounts of organic matter and that regrow when cut, so you can use them as mulch sources. You can place this "mulch garden" around or downhill of your compost or manure piles to catch nutrients that leach away from the piles. Or place it in an area where runoff from neighboring lawns or gardens carries nutrients onto your land. The mulch garden will also catch and filter any toxic substances that wash onto your land, but it will provide you with a usable product nonetheless. In addition, you can create patches of mulch plants in various places throughout your garden, such as at the back of planting beds in harder-to-reach zones. Ideal plant candidates for mulch gardens include species that act as nitrogen fixers or dynamic accumulators and woody species that coppice, such as willows, alders, hazels, and so on.

Use Nitrogen-Fixing Plants

Nitrogen is one of the most important plant nutrients and often a limiting factor to plant growth. We can import nitrogen from off-site in many forms, such as blood meal, fish fertilizers, and other amendments. In forest gardening, we seek to reduce off-site inputs as much as possible by populating our ecologies with plants that "fix" nitrogen from the atmosphere.

Nitrogen fixation results from a symbiotic relationship between certain types of plants and bacteria. If the right strain of bacteria is in the soil near roots from the right species of plant, a "beneficial infection" of the roots occurs. Nodules form on the roots and provide sites for an exchange—the bacteria fix atmospheric nitrogen into a plant-usable form, and in return, the plants provide the bacteria with carbohydrates.

The amount of energy this exchange requires means that most of these plants can fix nitrogen only in full sun, or something close to it. As a result, the vast majority of nitrogen-fixing plants act as pioneer species in succession and do best in open, disturbed sites. They can colonize low-fertility sites because they provide their own fertilizer. Nitrogen fixers typically exhibit many adaptations characteristic of pioneer species, including a tendency toward successfully spreading their seed around; that is, they can be weedy. They are often among the first on the scene after a dis-

turbance. For instance, witness the success of the actinorhizal nitrogen fixer autumn olive (*Eleagnus umbellata*) as it takes advantage of numerous disturbed sites throughout eastern North America. Some actinorhizal species can stick it out longer in the successional sequence than most legumes and hence can grow in shadier situations.

Numerous studies have shown that nitrogen fixers make nitrogen available to surrounding plants through decomposition of leaf and twig litter. Root dieback can account for up to 50 percent of the nitrogen released. The nitrogen provided thus becomes available slowly, through decomposition, and is much less vulnerable to leaching away than are chemical fertilizers. This is particularly appropriate for tree crops, since too much nitrogen can cause fast, weak growth that is susceptible to late dormancy and winterkill as well as disease and insect problems. Easily available nitrogen fertilizer also tends to hold back succession, supporting competitor-strategist and ruderal plants.

These soil-building functions allow other, less tolerant species to recolonize and move the system toward a rich, diverse, and complex ecosystem. The nitrogen added to the ecosystem in early succession is critical for the long-term productivity of mature successional stages. At a community level, nitrogen fixation tends to decline with successional age due to decreasing sunlight availability.

Researchers recently demonstrated that nitrogen-fixing trees and shrubs can fix amounts of nitrogen similar to such standbys as clover and alfalfa (90 to 150 lbs/ac/yr, or 100 to 170 kg/ha/yr). Interplanting with nitrogen fixers can increase the yields of orchard trees and the growth rates of timber trees.[2]

Martin Crawford has done excellent research on the use of nitrogen-fixing trees and shrubs to provide the nitrogen requirements of fruit, nut, and berry crops. He has estimated ratios between the canopy area of mature nitrogen fixers to the canopy area of crop trees that provide the complete nitrogen requirements of the crop trees. He breaks tree crops into three categories based on nitrogen requirements, as

TABLE 1.2. Nitrogen demand by perennial crops, and the canopy area of nitrogen fixers required to meet crops' nitrogen demand. These ratios assume nitrogen-fixation rates of 90 lbs of nitrogen (N) per acre per year. *Crawford, 1998.*

Nitrogen Demand	Sample Crops	Canopy Area Ratio (N-fixer area:crop area)
High	blackberry, chestnut, citrus, plum, walnut	1:1 50% nitrogen fixers
Moderate	apple, apricot, bamboo, black currant, filbert, gooseberry, hazel, medlar, mulberry, peach, pear, persimmon, quince	6:10 38% nitrogen fixers
Low	bayberry (*Myrica*), blue bean (*Decaisnea*), cherry, dogwood (*Cornus*), elderberry, hawthorn, honey locust, juneberry, mountain ash (*Sorbus*), plum yew (*Cephalotaxus*), raspberry, strawberry tree (*Arbutus*), sumac (*Rhus*), viburnum, *Xanthoceras, Zanthoxylum*	2:10 17% nitrogen fixers
Very Low	fig, angelica tree (*Aralia*), linden and basswood (*Tilia*), magnolia, nut pine, red currant, spicebush (*Lindera*)	0:10 no nitrogen fixers

shown in table 1.2.[3] The canopy-area ratios shown in table 1.2 assume that the nitrogen fixers will generate about 90 pounds of nitrogen per acre (100 kg/ha) per year. This is a conservative average for most of the trees and shrubs studied.

In urban and suburban areas, polluted rainfall can deposit more nitrogen than the low-nitrogen-demanding crops need, up to half the nitrogen moderate-demand crops need, and 40 percent of what high-demand crops need. Cut your nitrogen-fixer ratio as appropriate in these regions until we clean up the air. Appendix 3 includes a table listing all the nitrogen fixers from the Plant Species Matrix.

Use Plants as Nutrient Pumps: Dynamic Accumulators

Dynamic accumulators are another kind of fertility-improving plant. Their roots reach down into and extract nutrients from the subsoil for their own use. The nutrients become available in the topsoil as the plants' foliage and roots decompose and leaching from their tissues occurs. Like nitrogen fixers, many of these plants colonize disturbed sites because their dynamic-accumulator abilities allow them to survive in nutrient-poor environments. Including dynamic accumulators in your garden is a useful strategy for creating self-renewing fertility.

Integrate these plants throughout the forest garden to offer their benefits to adjacent polyculture members. They also work well at the backs of beds, with crop plants in the more easily accessed zones. In England, many forest gardeners grow large patches of comfrey, nettles, and other important accumulators in "pockets of production" or mulch gardens outside their forest gardens. They then cut these plants for mulch or compost them. They also make them into fermented "teas" by submerging a large bunch of cut plants in a barrel of water until the leaves decompose into a slimy liquid, or the water turns a dark color (it also ferments and usually smells pretty bad). Once the tea is ready, you can water your garden with your own "green gold." Even if plants are not dynamic accumulators, you can use them to make such teas; rhizomatous weeds such as quackgrass are good candidates for drowning this way, since their roots can so readily grow even after being pulled. These techniques allow you to grow much of your own fertilizer. Of course, many dynamic accumulators also make fine edibles or perform multiple other functions.

Little research has been done on dynamic accumulators. The species listed in appendix 3 represent only those for which information was available. It is highly likely that many more plant species are accumulators. Some plants that concentrate heavy metals are being used commercially to remove toxins from water and soils. Could we select and breed plants for improved accumulation of subsurface minerals, so they become improved sources of fertilizer for forest gardens? Only time and effort will tell.[4]

SUSTAINABLE WATER DEMAND

When dealing with the practical issues gardeners face, water is key. It is one of the most critical resources for plants. Adequate water is crucial for proper fruit set and optimum growth. On the other hand, too much water can lead to stressed and disease-prone plants—unless they are adapted to wet sites. The following brief treatment applies what we have learned in our other discussions to how we create sustainable water demand in our forest gardens, and the best ways to meet that demand.

Establishing sustainable water demand involves creating a garden whose need for water is balanced with the available supply. A garden that exhibits this characteristic does not rely on large quantities of pumped irrigation for its sustenance but instead makes optimal use of rainfall and runoff and on-site water storage. When we irrigate, we irrigate conservatively.

Analyze the Site's Water Conditions

Water issues come into play in a number of ways during site analysis and assessment. Rainfall data, on both quantities and timing, are critical, of course. One must also evaluate watershed sizes, flow patterns, and characteristics, whether these be roof areas or lands uphill of the garden. Noting wet and dry spots in the landscape, as well as the location of water lines, ponds, streams, culverts, and other water features, will also help guide your design decision making. Soil factors come into play as well, particularly with regard to compacted soils, high water tables, soil profile structure, and so on.

Improve the Soil Profile

If your site analysis indicates problems in the soil profile, it is definitely worth taking the time and effort to correct these before planting, if possible. Breaking up compaction, poking through restrictive soil layers, modifying runoff flow patterns, or creating mounds to provide more rooting depth are among many possible responses to poor soil conditions. The goal here is to provide the greatest possible rooting depth and the greatest possible amount of water storage in the soil. That way, you can maximize the ability of plants to meet their own needs without needing irrigation or other efforts on your part. Chapter 5 discusses a number of techniques we can use to achieve these ends, such as backhoe loosening, double digging, deep ripping (chisel plowing), mound planting, pits and mounds, radial trenching, raised beds, soil staking, and subsurface drainage systems.

Get Water in the Ground: Increase Infiltration

The preceding point about storing the greatest possible amount of water in the soil may need some clarification. In permaculture circles, we talk about increasing the number of water "storages" on a site to improve productivity. Water storages include things like lakes, ponds, wetlands, water tanks, and the soil. Of these, the soil is usually the cheapest place to store water; water tanks are the most expensive. Soil storage is the cheapest because the pore spaces are generally already there waiting to be filled. Storing water in the soil puts it right where the plants need it, eliminating the cost of irrigation infrastructure. In some cases, we need to improve the soil's ability to hold water by improving the soil profile first, but in most cases, all we need to do is to fill the existing pore spaces. Of course, if your soils are already overly wet, you have the opposite problem and this does not apply to you.

Many techniques help us increase runoff infiltration, some involving earthworks, others not. Earthworks entail any technique where we move earth to reshape the land for a particular purpose. Earthworks for increasing infiltration include infiltration swales, mounds, pits and mounds, and check logs (see chapter 5). These techniques are particularly important on sloping ground, where rain has less time to soak in and runs off more readily. We can also increase infiltration by simply laying out pathways, planting beds, tree lines, and hedgerows along the land's contour, or level, across the slope. Another critical part of increasing infiltration is to improve the soil's ability to absorb water by improving soil aggregation.

Improve Soil Aggregation

Soil aggregates are "crumbs" composed of mineral particles and organic matter, created by the action of soil organisms. Crumbs of different sizes provide pore spaces of different sizes. This diversity of crumb and pore-space sizes makes the soil more able to absorb water, to hold it, and, paradoxically, to drain well and provide better aeration. Improving soil aggregation requires adding organic matter and creating a healthy soil food web. Plant roots do both these things. Mycorrhizas are critical components of the soil food web for creating aggregates, and for improving plants' ability to absorb water and withstand drought. Chapter 5 in this volume and chapter 5 in volume 1 discuss more ways to create a healthy soil food web. Mulch is a key aspect of adding organic matter, with research showing that mulching improves soil aggregation.

Conserve Soil Water: Mulch

Besides its other multiple benefits, mulch also conserves water in the soil. It keeps the soil cool, reducing direct evaporation losses. It also reduces runoff speeds, thereby increasing infiltration. The effects of mulch on soil aggregation also help the soil to absorb and hold more water. Just be careful not to pile it on too deeply. When mulch is deep, small rainstorms wet the mulch but not the soil, and you can find yourself surprised by wilting plants when you least expect it.

Match Vegetation Density to Water Availability

Lush, dense vegetation requires more water than sparse vegetation does, all other things being equal. Therefore, it makes sense to match the density of our plantings with how much water is available in the ecosystem. In dry soils and climates, we should plant more thinly; in moister areas we can plant more densely. We can plant irrigated patches more densely than unirrigated patches. This is fine as a rule, but it is hard to put in practice given the variations in weather and the huge gray area between wet and dry and between dense and sparse. However, the awareness of this rule is a good tool as we design our gardens and can help us as we decide what zones of water use we will designate in our gardens.

Design Zones of Water Use

We can design our gardens to create zones of water use (see pattern #8) based on how much water plants need and how we supply it to them. We can designate a zone for weekly irrigation for crops that really need it, zones for irrigation only during drought conditions or during fruit ripening, and zones that never receive irrigation. We can locate each of these zones based on their proximity to water resources and infrastructure. We then choose our plants, our planting density, and our management activities for each zone as appropriate. In this way, we maximize the effectiveness of our infrastructure while minimizing its cost and using our water resources efficiently.

Choose Deep-Rooted Plants

Deep-rooted plants can avail themselves of water deep in the soil profile. They therefore deal more effectively with unirrigated or minimally irrigated landscapes than do shallow-rooted plants. Combining plants with deep and shallow roots can help reduce competition for water by partitioning the soil profile.

Choose Species Appropriate to the Water Regime

Clearly, we also need to choose our crop species to match the moisture conditions in our soils, unless we plan to irrigate. Otherwise, we will create a system under stress, and plant health, yields, and self-maintenance will suffer. This is especially true at the extremes of wetness and dryness. Many dry- or wet-tolerant plants will grow fine in moist conditions. However, while that may be the case, plants specifically adapted to moist conditions often outcompete dry- or wet-tolerant plants in moderate conditions. Species native to your immediate area are likely to be adapted to your conditions. Tables 1.3 and 1.4 list a few especially dry- and wet-tolerant crops. The Plant Species Matrix rates the moisture tolerance of each species, many of which are also tolerant of such moisture extremes.

Irrigate Conservatively

If you choose to irrigate your forest garden, design your irrigation system to use the minimal amount of water possible. This typically means using drip irrigation. Drip irrigation conserves water by putting it right where you and your plants want it, on the soil in the root zone. Typical spray irrigation is highly inefficient, since water evaporates as it flies through the air and it sprays everywhere, even on pathways. Also, spraying water onto plant leaves can increase the incidence of disease. And in addi-

tion, research indicates that spray irrigation favors early-succession ruderal and competitor species. This may not be in our best interest as forest gardeners. Drip irrigation should help minimize this successional effect and help us favor the plants we want in the successional process.

MINIMAL HERBIVORY

Herbivory is the consumption of plant matter or plant products for one's own sustenance. That means that we humans are herbivores, as are rodents, deer, fungal and bacterial diseases, fungal and bacterial plant mutualists, and insect pests. *Minimal herbivory*, then, means minimal herbivory by organisms that damage our plants or that compete with us for their yields. Minimal herbivory is an ecosystem characteristic caused by interactions between system components, as well as by the characteristics of the components themselves. It deals with the typical gardener's problems of pests, varmints, and disease.

TABLE 1.3. Selected dry-soil-loving species. These species hail from deserts, prairies, pine-oak forests, and other arid areas. Form: H = herb, S = shrub, T = tree.

Latin Name	Common Name	Form	Functions
Achillea millefolium	yarrow	H	dynamic accumulator, insectary, nectary, ground cover
Astragalus crassicarpus	groundplum milk vetch	H	native, nitrogen fixer, sweet edible pods
Baptisia spp.	wild indigo	H	native, nitrogen fixer
Caragana arborescens	Siberian pea shrub	S	hardy nitrogen fixer
Castanea mollissima	Chinese chestnut	T	edible nuts
Castanea pumila	chinquapin	S	native, edible nuts
Coreopsis verticillata	thread-leaved coreopsis	H	native, nectary, ground cover
Cytisus decumbens	prostrate broom	S	ground cover, nitrogen fixer
Diospyros virginiana	American persimmon	T	native, excellent fruit
Lupinus perennis	wild lupine	H	native, nitrogen fixer
Pinus koraiensis	Korean pine	T	edible nuts
Prosopis glandulosa	honeypod mesquite	S	edible pods, nitrogen fixer
Quercus macrocarpa	bur oak	T	native, "sweet" acorns
Quercus prinoides	dwarf chestnut oak	S	native, "sweet" acorns
Rosmarinus officinalis	rosemary	S	excellent culinary
Thymus spp.	thyme	S	excellent culinary
Vaccinium angustifolium	lowbush blueberry	S	edible berries, native, ground cover
Zizyphus jujuba	jujube	T	edible fruit

TABLE 1.4. Selected wetness-loving species from the Plant Species Matrix. The following plants tolerate or prefer wet feet, wet meadows, swamps, floodplain forest, and other wetlands and seasonally wet spots. A number of other useful species for running or deep still water are not included in appendix 1, such as wild rice (*Zizania latifolia*), wild lotus (*Nelumbo lutea*), arrowhead (*Sagittaria latifolia*), cattail (*Typha* spp.), and a tremendous diversity of wetland insectary plants (in the *Aster* and *Solidago* genera, among others). Moist, shady areas are also optimal for mushroom production. Form: B = bamboo, H = herb, S = shrub, T = tree.

Latin Name	Common Name	Form	Functions
Alnus spp.	alders	S	nitrogen fixer, many native species
Amelanchier spp.	juneberry	S	berries, many native species
Arundinaria gigantea	canebrake bamboo	B	native bamboo, edible shoots
Camassia spp.	quamash, wild hyacinth	H	native, edible bulbs, forms giant colonies in wet meadows
Crataegus spp.	mayhaw	T	edible fruit, excellent for jams
Dentaria spp.	toothwort	H	native ground cover, spicy rhizomes
Houttuynia cordata	tsi, hot tuna	H	edible ground cover
Lobelia cardinalis	cardinal flower	H	native, attracts hummingbirds
Matteuccia struthiopteris	ostrich fern	H	native, edible "fiddleheads"
Mentha spp.	mints	H	culinary, tea, dynamic accumulator, nectary, ground cover
Nasturtium officinale	watercress	H	edible, dynamic accumulator
Quercus bicolor	swamp white oak	T	native, edible "sweet" acorns
Quercus macrocarpa	bur oak	T	native, edible "sweet" acorns
Sambucus canadensis	elderberry	S	edible flower, berries, native, nectary
Vaccinium corymbosum	highbush blueberry	S	native, excellent berries
Vaccinium macrocarpon	cranberry	S	native, edible berries

Numerous manuals can tell you how to control herbivory organically through direct intervention and controls (see appendix 7). Such information will probably be useful for most forest gardeners. However, we wish to emphasize the concept of pest control by design. The following strategies should minimize your need to use the direct controls described in other references.

Know Your Herbivores

Site analysis and assessment is an essential element in devising strategies for dealing with varmints, pests, and diseases. Your site conditions and regional pest situations will tell you what problems you are likely to face. Once you know what these challenges might be, you can select resistant varieties, undertake helpful site preparation, build fences, or devise whatever other strategies you think necessary. Sometimes, you'll need to research the specific life cycles, habitat needs, and natural enemies of the pest organisms. Then you can make your garden inhospitable to them, or hospitable to their natural

enemies, by design or through management. You should also have a backup plan ready for direct intervention and control in case of emergency.

Use Large-Scale Defenses for Large Organisms

Those of us with varmint problems—such as deer, porcupines, mice, rabbits, woodchucks, other humans, and the like—need to respond at a scale similar to the varmints we face. Garden location is a key factor in dealing with many of these, potentially preventing problems before they even begin. Keeping the forest garden close to your home will make humans, deer, and many other varmints less likely to try your delicacies. Domestic dogs and cats can work wonders in this regard as well. Fences, walls, and electric fences are other direct design methods to diminish competition for our food.

Some people have created multifunctional "chicken moats" around their gardens. These consist of two parallel fences 6 feet (2 m) or more high and 4 feet (1.3 m) or more apart surrounding the garden (figure 1.3; you'll also need a chicken house and other accou-

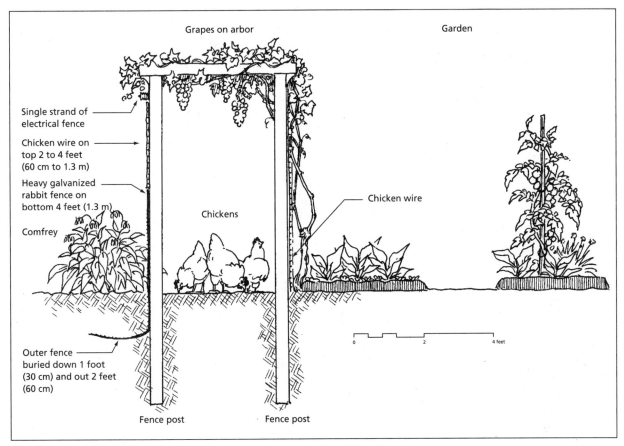

Grapes on arbor

Garden

Single strand of electrical fence

Chicken wire on top 2 to 4 feet (60 cm to 1.3 m)

Heavy galvanized rabbit fence on bottom 4 feet (1.3 m)

Comfrey

Chickens

Chicken wire

Outer fence buried down 1 foot (30 cm) and out 2 feet (60 cm)

Fence post

Fence post

0　2　4 feet

FIGURE 1.3. A "chicken moat" such as this surrounding your garden can perform multiple functions, including the exclusion of large varmints such as rabbits, woodchucks, and deer, as well as holding back rhizomatous weeds from outside the garden. Planting comfrey or other dynamic accumulators outside the moat allows the chickens to graze the comfrey through the fence while preventing the birds from killing it. The plants also absorb runoff laden with chicken manure for cycling back into the garden or the birds. See the text for a full discussion of functions and design details. This idea comes from Joe Jenkins of western Pennsylvania.

treements, but we'll leave those aside here). This acts as both a chicken run and a varmint and rhizomatous weed barrier. With enough chickens, the moat interior will be essentially bare earth: the birds will eat or scratch into oblivion any plant that pokes up its head. Deer are unlikely to jump over two 6-foot (2 m) fences 4 feet (1.3 m) or more apart, and a single strand of electric fence along the top of the outside fence will stop climbing varmints. If you bury the bottom of the outside fence 1 foot (30 cm) vertically and 2 feet (60 cm) to the outside horizontally you will discourage diggers like rabbits and woodchucks. In the meantime, you can toss your garden weeds and excess into the moat to feed the chickens. You can

also throw seedy mulch such as hay or straw in there for them to glean and fertilize with their manure before you use it as a rich, newly seed-free mulch. Placing a pergola over the top of the fences multiplies your growing area for vining plants such as hardy kiwis and grapes. It also further discourages deer from trying to take the plunge while offering shade and winged-predator protection for the chickens. Multiple functions indeed!

Many other creative ideas akin to the chicken moat are possible. Turning problems into opportunities like this is what permaculture is all about; see appendix 7 for references to permaculture resources with more similar ideas.

Create Compositional and Structural Diversity

The first rule of minimizing herbivory by insects and smaller organisms is to use compositional and structural diversity in your garden. We discuss this above, under "Desired Ecosystem Components" (page 9) and "Ecosystem Patterning" (page 10), as well as in volume 1, chapter 3. However, let us review the highlights to drive them further home.

We know that each of the following structural and compositional diversity strategies used alone reduces herbivory. If we use all of them in our forest gardens, creating a compositionally and structurally diverse ecosystem in diverse ways, pest populations are less likely to explode out of control.

Diverse Organisms, Species, and Varieties

Using diverse organisms, species, and varieties is the foundation of diversity in the garden. Diversity at all these taxonomic levels provides diversity of function and diversity of susceptibility, tolerance, and response to pest and disease attack. It is best to attract diverse insects and birds to your garden than to try to reduce diversity and keep out every organism except your crops. It is better to grow multiple species of winter storage fruit than to rely just on apples in case one crop gets hit hard by herbivores. It is better to grow seven apple varieties rather than only one to minimize the chances of a runaway pest or disease problem.

Lumpy Texture

Lumpy vegetation texture tends to increase bird and insect diversity and to balance the food web with more insectivore species, regardless of the compositional diversity present. We should therefore create lumpy texture (see pattern #39) by design and with our management practices. We need lumpy texture to extend vertically as well as horizontally for maximum effect. Lumpy texture helps spiders greatly, and these generalist predators are critical to maintaining pest population balance.

Plant Polyculture Patches

Diverse patterning of plants—mixing them up rather than planting them in monoculture blocks—makes it harder for herbivores to find their preferred food sources. It forces them to spend more time moving, searching, and exposing themselves to predators, rather than feeding and reproducing. You can achieve this by planting in overlapping scatters, drifts, and clumps, in regular patterns, or in random mixtures. Polyculture by its very nature helps reduce pests and diseases in crops.

We also know from volume 1 that disturbance and succession take place in a patchwise manner, and that ecosystems are therefore organized in patches. Patches occur at various scales, involving habitats at the largest scale, trees at a somewhat smaller scale, shrubs at another, and herbs at another. These patches nest inside each other, one tree patch containing many herb and shrub patches, for example. We mimic this structure by designing nested, interwoven, and overlapping patches of habitats and plant species mixtures within which to grow our crops. We call these polyculture patches (see pattern #44).

Use Resistant Species and Varieties

One of the easiest ways to avoid herbivory is to plant species that are rarely bothered by pests or diseases (like pawpaws, persimmons, and hardy kiwis). There are also delicious, resistant varieties of susceptible species (like scab-resistant apples and blight-resistant hazels). If you decide you must grow apples or other highly susceptible crops, research the pests and diseases prevalent in your area, and track down resistant varieties. Appendix 1 in volume 1 ("Forest Gardening's Top 100 Species") profiles many good resistant species.

Maintain a Healthy Soil Food Web

In addition to its benefits to plant health, the soil food web plays specific roles in minimizing herbivory. A healthy root-zone food web is critical to defending plants against belowground herbivores.

Numerous fungi, predatory nematodes, and other organisms there outcompete or consume soil-borne diseases and root-feeding herbivores. The soil food web also provides food for many aboveground beneficials, particularly birds. This maintains high populations of birds so they are on hand in case of an aboveground pest outbreak.

Create Healthy Leaf-Surface Food Webs

Recent research indicates that healthy leaf-surface food webs can prevent many pests and diseases. Acid rain and other pollutants can damage these food webs, while healthy plants and the use of high-quality compost tea as a foliar spray support and rejuvenate them. Compost tea sprays can effectively prevent fungal and bacterial leaf diseases, including toughies like *Botrytis*.[5]

Grow Healthy Plants

Healthy plants fend off pest and disease attacks more effectively and recover more quickly. They have the resources to create chemical defenses that unhealthy plants do not. All of the strategies mentioned earlier therefore apply to minimizing herbivory. This creates mutually reinforcing feedback in the garden ecosystem, an upward spiral of good health and minimal herbivory that provides higher yields and maximal self-maintenance.

Space Plants Properly!

This point bears repeating because we've seen it done poorly so many times: proper plant spacing is highly critical to healthy plants and minimal disease problems. Good air circulation and sunshine into the interior of susceptible species is vital. Minimal competition from good spacing makes for healthier plants.

Provide Specific Habitat Elements for Beneficial Organisms

We can attract numerous predatory and parasitoid organisms to our gardens to manage pest populations for us—if we provide the specific habitat elements the beneficials require. These organisms include insects, spiders, snakes, toads, birds, bats, and more. Their specific habitat requirements therefore vary tremendously, though there are common threads. See feature article 1, "Beneficial Wildlife Habitat Principles," for a full discussion.

Carefully Design Your Insectary Plant Guilds

Beneficial insects are particularly important to reducing herbivory in our gardens because, unlike most birds and mammals, they usually don't need acres of territory to survive. Our small gardens can provide most or all of the habitat requirements of numerous beneficial insects. Beyond the more general approaches to increasing insect diversity discussed above, we can greatly increase populations of beneficial insects in our landscapes by meeting their specific food and shelter requirements. Plants that meet beneficial insects' food or shelter needs are known as insectary plants. While some insects have habitat needs besides insectary plants, the following discussion will focus on designing nectary plant guilds that provide nectar to beneficial insects.

We are most concerned here with two kinds of beneficial insects. Predatory insects catch and eat pests. The larvae of syrphid flies, also known as hover flies, for example, devour large numbers of aphids. Parasitoid insects, on the other hand, lay their eggs on or inside the eggs, larvae, or adults of pests. When parasitoid eggs hatch, the young devour the pest in a grisly feast. Each parasitoid species usually specializes in parasitizing a particular host species. One well-known group of parasitoids is the tiny wasps of the genus *Trichogramma*, which lay their eggs in caterpillars.

Both these kinds of insects need nectar sources to fuel their search for prey or hosts. Different insects, however, have different kinds of mouthparts, and this influences which flowers they can use. Parasitoid and specialist predatory insects usually have biting mouthparts and are often tiny.

Feature Article 1:
Beneficial Wildlife Habitat Principles

Many references on attracting wildlife to your backyard exist, but attracting just any old wildlife to your garden is not forest gardening. In fact, some wildlife species we probably do *not* want in our forest gardens: deer, rats, and cedar waxwings (frugivorous, or fruit-eating, birds), for example. In forest gardening, we want to attract specific wildlife species to do specific jobs in our gardens, that is, to fill specific community niches. We might like to keep out species that would compete with us for the food we are growing for ourselves. It's a nice ideal, anyway.

This article focuses on putting together the elements required to attract *desired* wildlife to your forest garden. It summarizes basic principles, offers representative information on selected beneficial animal species and groups, and lets you research other specifics elsewhere. *Beneficial wildlife* means beneficial mammals, birds, reptiles, amphibians, arthropods, and soil organisms. Probably the biggest lesson of this exploration is that simply by creating a forest garden, rather than something else, you are creating a haven for many forms of beneficial wildlife. With a little more thought and attention to detail, you can improve the habitat you create tremendously and focus your efforts on attracting the wildlife that you want and need to minimize your labor in forest garden maintenance.

Basic Principles

The first principle of attracting beneficials to your garden is to stop spraying pesticides! Virtually all agrochemicals, including organic agrochemicals, have unintended undesirable consequences, and such disturbances will set back the successional development of your garden's food webs. Enough said? Let's hope so.

All wildlife have four basic needs: food, shelter, water, and enough space in an appropriate environment. Not all beneficials need all these needs met in the same location, though most do. Nonetheless, providing all the elements a desired species needs increases the chances it will visit, choose to stay, and survive that choice from generation to generation. Even birds, the most movable parts of the forest garden, are habitual: once they find a place that meets their needs, they will stick around. Migrating birds often return to areas where they can expect to find food, water, cover, and space. When they visit, they will perform useful services for you just by being who they are, acting out their fundamental strategies for survival. It is these fundamental strategies that can guide us in putting together the parts of the ecosystem we need for the system to function as a whole. If we can fill all the key community niches in the forest-garden food web by attracting the right wildlife, then we'll minimize our work maintaining the system. We'll discuss this part later. First, though, let us review the four basic needs of beneficial wildlife.

Food

Animal food requirements vary seasonally as individuals mature, breed, bear young, prepare for winter, and age. Protein needs tend to increase in spring and early summer when most animals breed and feed young. Most beneficials rely heavily on animal foods during this season. Birds and mammals need more carbohydrates in late summer and fall to build reserves for hibernation, migration, or winter austerities. The insectivorous animals we want in our forest gardens need winter food if they are active year-round residents. Most of the latter switch at least partially from animal to plant foods in winter due to reduced prey availability. This means that providing winter grub is critical to ensuring the summertime balance of our gardens. Therefore, plant extra seeds, fruits, and berries, particularly winter fruits for winter residents, but also late summer and early fall crops for migrants, in return for the pest management services you gain. Many shrubs hold berries into the winter for birds to eat later on, and many of these are fruits less palatable to humans. For the late summer and fall carbohydrates the migrants need, you may just have to plant more of everything and make your offerings with gratitude. Don't forget the lesson from chapter 4 in volume 1 about how feeding the soil food web feeds the aboveground ecosystem. Unbeknownst to us, many, many foodstuffs that keep our garden allies alive and well arise from the soil ecosystem.

The other thing to remember in this regard is diversity. Volume 1's chapter 4 also discusses the "herbivore hump" in food web structure: no matter how much plant diversity you have, there will virtually always be higher herbivore diversity to eat the plants. However, the greater the plant diversity, the greater, too, is the predator diversity to help control the herbivores. Providing high plant diversity gives the predators more food in general and increases the numbers and kinds of predators in the ecosystem. Pest populations therefore remain a lower proportion of the whole insect population in the garden. This does not, however, mean that diversity for diversity's sake is the way to go. We need functional diversity when possible, or diversity with a purpose: diverse plantings that perform specific functions. Providing food for specific animals is one of those functions. Providing shelter is another possible function.

Shelter

Shelter takes numerous forms, depending on what animal needs shelter for what purpose at what time of year. Cover from predators is a year-round concern for all species, especially when breeding or raising young. Most, if not all, species need protection from heat, cold, and other climatic conditions when these become extreme. Shelter can also mean hibernation sites, estivation sites (summer hibernation, as in some reptiles and amphibians), daily or nightly resting or roosting sites, and hiding places allowing ambush of prey. Each function may require different shelter characteristics for each species, though there is often plenty of overlap.

Overwhelmed? Don't worry. Your garden will meet many beneficials' requirements simply by being a forest garden rather than something else. The rest you can develop over time. Simply relinquishing a need for "order" and "tidiness" in your garden will make a huge difference. Why?

Order and tidiness by definition reduce structural diversity in ecosystems. Structural diversity provides shelter for many animals for many purposes. Common structural elements for shelter include:

- loose soils, or manure, mulch, or sawdust piles for burrowing;
- thick mulch or leaf litter of diverse origins (woody and nonwoody, from various species);
- rocks, rock piles, logs, stumps, and woody debris on and in the ground;
- patchy, layered, and variably dense herbaceous and shrubby vegetation, including ground-cover plants, grassy hummocks (predaceous beetles love grassy hummocks), brushy areas, and thickets;
- patchy, variably dense canopy vegetation;
- evergreen plants in all vegetation layers;
- perches at varying heights, including at ground level and in ponds or pools;
- standing dead trees, ideally with holes in them;
- dead herbaceous seed heads, ragged perennial clumps, and hollow plant stems where spiders

and other friends can hold winter slumber
parties;

- living trees of varying sizes and ages, both
  whole and hollow, but especially trees larger
  than 10 inches (26 cm) in diameter, in which
  many beneficial birds like to nest;
- loose or rough bark on living or dead trees;
- nest boxes, bat houses, and earwig hotels (a
  plant pot stuffed with straw hanging upside
  down in a tree); and
- water, especially water with aquatic plants,
  woody debris, rocks, and mud in it.

Including all or many of the above elements in
your forest garden will provide shelter to many
species for many purposes. Using the data in
appendix 5 will help you focus your efforts to provide shelter for the beneficials you most want in the
places you most want them. See also "Food and
Shelter Plants for Beneficials" in appendix 3.

Water

Water in the garden is one of the least understood,
most overlooked, and most critical elements, both
functionally and aesthetically. Installing a garden
pool or pond seems daunting to many, and it isn't
always easy, but it is usually not very difficult. The
benefits are enormous if the installation is done
with care to meet the needs of your garden allies.
Most animals drink water, birds and others bathe in
it, many beneficials lay eggs and grow up in it, and
frogs take shelter in it. It reflects the sky. It makes
delightful sounds. It conjures desirable states of
mind. From temporary pools in spring, to full-
blown ponds, to miniature created wetlands, to bird
baths, and everything in between, water in the
garden can take many forms and meet many
wildlife needs in a garden or landscape of any size.
Save the wet habitats you have. Add more. You are
unlikely to regret it.

Any pond or pool you create should have shallowly sloping banks down to and into the water on
at least one side to make access by amphibians, rep-

tiles, birds, and small mammals safer and easier.
Rocks and woody debris sticking partially out of the
water surface provide insects with safe access, too.
Dripping or running water attracts birds much more
quickly than a still pool. Even if you have a typical
birdbath on a pedestal, give it a dripping hose and
you should see more birds than before. That pedestal
is a good thing, as well, for it keeps the birds a little
safer from predators while they are performing their
ablutions. Aquatic plants add beauty to the garden,
but they can also offer safe access to the water, as
well as cover in the water for frogs, aquatic insects,
amphibian eggs, and so on. Mosquitoes like water,
too, so design your pond or pool to support at least a
few frogs or minnows if possible to keep the mos-
quito larvae under control. Most water gardening
books can help you there.

An Appropriate Environment

Enough space in an appropriate environment
involves many different factors for each species, not
all of which we necessarily know. The vertebrates
and arthropods tables in appendix 5 provide some
information to guide you here for selected beneficials. A species' preferred habitat types will tell you
what vegetation types, soil types, moisture regimes,
relative elevation, and so on it prefers or survives in,
if we found that information. Home ranges or territories will indicate whether your site, or your neighborhood, has enough of that habitat to create the
appropriate environment for the species. Many other
factors may affect a species' survival; these tables are
only a beginning guide. Research the wildlife more
thoroughly to ensure your success. And don't forget:
animals, like plants, don't read books! Their behavior
may differ, so give things a try even if the data indicates it may not work.

What we do know, however, can take us far. Part
of creating an appropriate habitat is to arrange the
food, shelter, and water resources that beneficial
wildlife need in an optimal way. Salamanders often
will not cross barren or open areas near their
breeding grounds, for example. In this case, if you

want salamanders in your forest garden, you will probably have to provide cover for the animals across the barren area. According to some reports, placing a pool in the forest garden may not work for at least some salamander species, as they can be so loyal to ancestral breeding grounds that they will not begin using a new pond until it is twenty to fifty years old! On the other hand, a friend of ours made a pond and had salamanders in it the first spring. Frogs may take up residence in a new pond in a matter of days or hours. If that pond is in or near your forest garden, and there is good cover between the two, you can rest assured that your amphibian friends are on duty at night helping balance your garden's food web.

Filling Community Niches: Guilds and Strategies

This is where hard-core forest garden design most differs from simple landscaping for wildlife. It is also cutting-edge application of ecological theory. Can we consciously create a garden ecosystem where most if not all of the key community niches are filled by intentionally planted or "cultivated" plant and animal species? Choosing and planting plants for their ecological functions is relatively easy. The animal component is much harder, more fluid, and less in our control, but we can give it a shot anyway. Even partial success is success nonetheless, and the more species we have filling those niches, the less work we'll have to do in the long run.

The most critical piece of information we need to "design" the food web of our gardens is the basic species-niche strategy of the animal species in which we are interested. Knowing an animal's basic niche strategy tells us what community niche the species fills, and therefore what services it provides to its community and what resource-partitioning guild it is in (these are all different facets of the same thing; see chapter 4 in volume 1 for a discussion of these concepts). Is it gleaning insects off twigs and leaves in the upper or lower canopy, off the bark and

branches, or on the ground? Does it screen the air for flying insects or ambush them in flight? It would obviously be good to have species doing all these things, or indeed more than one species doing each, wouldn't it?

Such information is not easy to come by. With that in mind, appendix 5 provides niche strategy information for as many of the beneficial animals as possible. The tables there also summarize what habitats each species or group prefers, specific habitat elements each needs, and any other design criteria we could find, including territory sizes. With this information, you can try to meet the needs of species filling every possible beneficial community niche, if you so desire.

While listing and meeting the various needs of all your desired species may sound overwhelming, many beneficials have similar specifics. The "Beneficial Animal Habitat Elements" table in appendix 5 shows who benefits from particular habitat elements, and what specific design requirements those elements should follow to meet their needs. This allows you to focus your efforts on what will help the most, and to see who else you might help along the way if you are trying to help a particular species.

Plants are one of the main resources that wildlife depend upon, for food, shelter, and appropriate habitat conditions. The Plant Species Matrix in appendix 1 indicates which of the plants included are excellent wildlife plants. However, appendix 1 does not say what specific wildlife benefits the selected plants offer (food or cover, for whom, and in what season). You can find that information in the "Nectary Calendar" and "Food and Shelter Plants for Beneficials" tables in appendix 3. Other plants not included in appendix 1 are also excellent wildlife plants; you'll have to find that information elsewhere (see appendix 7). Just be careful, because many plants that some people consider great for wildlife are also opportunistic.

Good luck, and have fun attracting beneficial wildlife to your garden!

FIGURE 1.4. The flowers of the native cow parsnip (*Heracleum sphondylium*, formerly *H. maximum*) exemplify the umbels or multiple florets of Apiaceae plants. The huge (up to 8 inch/20 cm) flowers of this species provide abundant nectar for specialist and generalist predator insects through the spring. The plant is enormous, growing up to 10 feet (3 m) high. Its tender roots are cooked like parsnips, and its dried seeds make a decent condiment. However, contact of the sap with the skin can cause photodermatitis. *Photo by Eric Toensmeier.*

FIGURE 1.5. Most plants in the aster family (all with daisylike flowers) can provide nectar to specialist predators in the garden, including many natives like this New England aster (*Aster novae-angliae*). *Photo by Dave Jacke.*

Specialists therefore need small flowers with short tubes, which we call specialist nectary plants. Some predatory insects are nectarivorous in their adult forms and predatory in their larval stages. These have sucking mouthparts that can access the same flowers that pollinators use for nectar, which we call generalist nectary plants. Many beneficials need pollen as a protein source to help them rear young, so pollen plants are another important insectary guild component. Finally, many other plants provide overwintering habitat, egg-laying (oviposition) sites, or preferred foliage habitat, meaning beneficials congregate on the leaves for one reason or another. Scores of these insectary plants also fill other functions for the forest gardener.

Foremost among nectary plants are those in the Apiaceae, or parsley family. They used to be called the Umbelliferae, because they produce "umbrellas" of countless tiny flowers, collectively called umbels (figure 1.4). You have probably seen Queen Anne's lace (*Daucus carota*), a classic member of this family.

Umbels offer nectar for long periods because the tiny flowers mature at different times. This family also features scores of edible, medicinal, and ornamental plants, including common crops such as dill, carrots, parsnips, celery, parsley, cilantro, and many more. Unfortunately, some Apiaceae are deadly poisonous, and members of this family are often difficult to tell from one another, so be careful.

The Asteraceae, or composite family, is also important to beneficials. Any plant with daisylike flowers is probably a nectary member of this family (figure 1.5). Numerous other plants are nectaries as well, including many members of the mint (figure 1.6) and saxifrage families, as well as flowering onions (*Allium* spp.). The foliage of a subfamily of the legumes, the Papilionoideae, also appears to attract beneficials. The indications are that insects like the biochemicals produced by these pea family species.[6]

Insectary habitat is an area in need of much research—we have found relatively few studies on this topic, but the ones we have found offer interesting possibilities for design. See the Plant Species Matrix and the "Food and Shelter Plants for Beneficials" table in appendix 3 for more detailed insectary species information. Many more insectary

FIGURE 1.6. Mint family plants such as wild bergamot (*Monarda fistulosa*) provide nectar for generalist insect predators and pollinators as well as some specialist predators and parasitoids. This species also provides a flavorful tea and offers culinary and medicinal uses. While this photo was taken in a bur oak savanna in Wisconsin, wild bergamot can grow in a variety of early- to midsuccession environments. *Photo by Dave Jacke.*

garden. The "Nectary Calendar" table in appendix 3 will help you make your own nectary guilds, as discussed in chapter 4.

Planting patterns for insectary plants are somewhat of a guessing game. The typical flying or walking distances of the various beneficial insects are mostly unknown and probably vary significantly. We should therefore scatter low-maintenance insectary plants throughout our forest gardens to ensure good pest control by our insect allies. Small clusters of different nectary plants should help the insects keep moving around and still not be far from an energy source. The ideal would be to mix nectary and other habitat species in among crops, but this is not always best for crop management. Borders and islands including both food and shelter plants should work well, too. On the other hand, many crop species are also insectary, so mixing them is easy!

Countless common wild plants and weeds also offer insectary benefits, such as goldenrods and asters. When analyzing and assessing your site, make sure to record the species already present and see whether they are in one of the key plant groups: families Apiaceae, Asteraceae, or Lamiaceae or subfamily Papilionoideae of the Fabaceae. You can also just watch the flowers on a nice day to see who visits them. You sometimes have to wait until late afternoon when the sun is at a low angle to see the tiniest parasitic wasps. In any case, your own

species are not included in our appendices—in fact, the Asteraceae and Apiaceae are among the largest plant families in the world, and all of their species provide nectar for beneficials.

The key goal for nectary guild design is to have both specialist and generalist nectary plants blooming throughout the growing season (see table 1.5). This supports a steady population of predators and parasitoids, as well as pollinators, in your

Latin Name	Common Name	Other Uses & Functions	A	M	J	J	A	S	O
Chrysogonum virginianum	green and gold	ground cover, native	•	•	•				
Viburnum trilobum	highbush cranberry	edible fruit, wildlife food, native	•	•	•				
Tiarella cordifolia	foamflower	ground cover, native		•	•				
Levisticum officinale	lovage	edible leaves and "celery"		•	•	•			
Sambucus canadensis	elderberry	edible flowers and fruit, native		•	•				
Myrrhis odorata	sweet cicely	culinary herb, delicious seeds		•	•	•			
Coreopsis spp.	tickseed	ground cover, native		•	•	•	•		
Solidago odora	sweet goldenrod	tea, native			•	•	•	•	
Sium sisarum	skirret	edible roots			•	•			
Aster novae-angliae	New England aster	beautiful native						•	•

TABLE 1.5. A simple specialist-nectary plant guild with flowering times.

observations of the local flora will help you fill your insectary guilds with useful plants adapted to your own site conditions.

Play with Aromatic Pest Confusers

Gardening lore suggests that strong-scented plants can help confuse pests in their quest to find food. While we were not able to find any hard scientific data to support this hypothesis, many of these odiferous species are well suited for forest gardens. These include the many perennial onions (*Allium* spp.), *Artemisia* spp., and numerous members of the mint family, including thyme (*Thymus* spp.), lemon balm (*Melissa officinalis*), bee balm (*Monarda* spp.), sage (*Salvia* spp.), rosemary (*Rosmarinus officinalis*), mints (*Mentha* spp.), and mountain mints (*Pycnanthemum* spp.). Again, scattering these plants, particularly upwind of crops, will spread the scents best.

Use Intermediate Disturbance Regimes

The intermediate disturbance hypothesis discussed in chapter 6 of volume 1 states that intermediate levels of disturbance maximize species richness. Putting this hypothesis into practice should maximize species diversity in the insect and bird communities, not just in the plant community. Intense or severe disturbance should cause insect- and bird-species richness to decline because fewer species tolerate it. Too little disturbance will allow competitive exclusion to reign, and that decreases diversity, too. This relates to all kinds of disturbance, from mowing and shearing to clearing and tilling.

Practice Good Sanitation

Good sanitation is the byword of organic crop production, and it is no different in forest gardens. For herbivore-resistant species it may have less importance, but for the fruits and nuts most people love the same rules apply: standard sanitation practices are good things to know about, if not to always follow. For example, raking up leaves that harbor scab spores is a typical chore for apple growers, as is picking up worm-infested fruits that drop off the

trees during the summer. However, these practices represent much work, and you should make sure you know what sanitation practices your desired crops will require in your region to see whether you really desire to grow them after all.

You can also look at the standard practices and seek ways to design them out or to reduce the work required. Some growers let chickens or sheep graze their orchards on rotation to eat fruit drops during the summer. Michael Phillips, an organic orchardist, applies lime to fallen apple leaves in the fall to inhibit scab spore growth. He then chops the leaves with a flail mower or other device and lays compost on top. Thus, both leaves and scab fungi decompose over the winter, cutting down on scab disease the following year.[7] These steps also reduce winter vole damage, by pulling the leaves away from the tree trunks, and improve soil nutrition and pH.

Each fruit species has its own set of sanitation considerations, depending on the pests and diseases at issue. We must design our forest garden guilds, polycultures, and disturbance and management regimes with sanitation in mind. Otherwise, we will only cause problems for ourselves down the road. Under susceptible fruits, we may need to grow shorter ground covers or crops that we can harvest and then mow or scythe. This will facilitate picking up drops or raking up leaves. Designing growing beds and paths so movable electric fencing can easily surround each tree or tree group can allow controlled livestock rotations under and around specific trees for the same purpose. And so on. Just make sure you protect your trees from browsing livestock; goats, for example, can rapidly strip bark off trunks and will even jump up to grab and nibble branches, causing much damage. Of course, all this is reason to focus on disease-resistant species such as persimmons, pawpaws, and hardy kiwis, rather than apples, peaches, and grapes, but we all have our preferences. If you want to grow susceptible species, just make sure you design with sanitation in mind.

Use Targeted Organic Controls, Not Broad-Spectrum Interventions

Occasionally a particular pest or disease does get out of hand, and you may feel a need to intervene to limit crop damage. In this case, use targeted controls for the specific pest species rather than broad-spectrum controls if you can. Broad-spectrum chemicals, even "organic" ones like pyrethrum and rotenone, are more likely to damage the ecosystem and throw it out of whack. Targeted controls affect fewer members of the food web, and hopefully just the one population that is the apparent problem. The latter therefore allow the system to continue its balancing act more effectively and to recover from the intervention more quickly. Broad-spectrum damage to the food web can actually make pest problems worse over the long run. Try to limit the number of times you spray, too, especially with broader-spectrum controls. This also helps limit unintended damage. Good monitoring is therefore critical: "nipping problems in the bud" takes less frequent and intensive intervention compared to stopping a headlong rush or an all-out flood of pests. Also remember that you need some pests around to keep your beneficials happy and well fed. Set thresholds to determine how much damage to fruit or leaves is acceptable, and monitor to see when you should take action. See chapter 7 for more on pest management.

Minimal Competition

Understanding the ecology behind competition assists us in reducing its negative effects and using it creatively to achieve our own ends. Competition occurs when two or more organisms require the same resource at the same time, and supplies of that resource are limited. Competition can therefore come from unwanted "weeds" or from interactions between desired species. It may arise in relation to any number of resources, from light, water, and nutrients to pollinators, herbivore predators, and management attention.

Competition reduces yields and increases stress. Minimizing competition between desired species reduces plant stress and allows crops to focus their energies on growth, defense against herbivores, and reproduction. It also improves our chances of creating the other ecosystem dynamics we want, particularly overyielding polycultures, healthy plants, minimal herbivory, and directed succession. Self-renewing fertility and sustainable water demand help us create minimal competition in our forest gardens.

On the other hand, the theory of community invasibility (volume 1, feature article 5) discusses the probability that new species are able to "invade" a new environment when resource limitations are lifted, through either disturbance or variations in resource availability caused by other factors. This means that to prevent weed problems we have to design competition *into* the system. We therefore have an apparent paradox to resolve: ultimately, what we want is to competitively exclude unwanted species, while simultaneously minimizing competition between desired species. The strategies below discuss how to do this.

Know Your Resources and Competitors

Site analysis and assessment, along with garden inhabitants analysis and assessment, once again comes to the fore. We need to understand the resource conditions we are dealing with, and who is going after those resources, if we are to design and manage effectively. Is the limiting resource in your forest garden likely to be light, water, or nutrients? Which preexisting plants on-site—or in the neighborhood waiting to blow in—will be likely to present the greatest management challenges? Chapter 3 will help you answer these questions.

Manage Resource Limitations

Managing resource limitations is one of the keys to creatively using competition to achieve our ends.

In most cases, we should work to improve the availability of water and nutrients, providing all of these that our crops need, and then some. Self-renewing fertility and sustainable water-demand strategies will help us achieve these ends. We may need to provide water and nutrient supplements in the early stages to help our crops get established. We may need to provide periodic supplements of one or both these resources over the long run in soils with poor parent materials and topsoils, on dry sites, or in rainy climates where nutrient leaching is elevated. Ultimately, though, we would hope to create a system that meets its own needs in this regard as much as possible, one that provides these elements in abundance or demands no more than nature offers. We should also try to design guilds and polycultures that fully use the available water and nutrients (see below).

Meanwhile, limiting unwanted plants requires limiting at least one resource. In most cases, the best resource to manage this way is light. We do this by maximizing the use of light by desired species: completely filling the available light niches with useful plants through guild and polyculture design, plant spacing, and management. Completely filling the niches available for water and nutrients will also help.

Site Preparation:
Minimize Unwanted Plants at the Start
As discussed in volume 1, chapter 6, disturbance influences the succession that follows by affecting the legacies from the previous system. If our garden site has a legacy of unwanted plants, our best opportunity to deal with them is to eradicate them at the start, and make sure they cannot come back. While this may take time initially, it saves a tremendous amount of work and time over the long run.

We generally recommend at least one year of tilling and cover cropping before planting a forest garden to both improve the soil and reduce weed competition. We also recommend using the sheet mulch technique to suppress weeds and give your plants the best chance of becoming the dominant species in the garden ecosystem.

Install Rhizome Barriers
Many of the most problematic weed species are expansive plants that spread by rhizomes or stolons and can pop up far from their nearest shoots. Once you eliminate these plants from your garden site, you must keep them out at the edges of your garden or all your weeding work can go up in smoke. Sometimes we also have desired species that spread the same way, and we need to keep them under control or they will turn into a problem, too. We therefore need to include some kind of rhizome barrier in our design plan (see pattern #52, *Expansive Plant Containers*).

Use Proper Plant Spacing!
The fact that plant spacing keeps showing up as a strategy for different reasons tells us how important it is. To limit weed growth, we should use mature crown diameters as the foundation distance for plant spacing. If weed competition is intense, we may want to plant a little more closely than that or underplant with ground covers or other functional plants to use the light fully. To keep competition between desired plants to a dull roar, we should modify the "crowns touching" spacing based on limiting factors, aboveground architecture, and rooting patterns, among other things (see "Plant Spacing," page 301). We also need to keep an eye on the limits to plant density of any particular site: too much living biomass with too few resources will generate intense competition, and plants will die or die back.

Partition Resources in Your Polycultures
Species with the same or similar niches compete the most because they seek the same resources at the same time in the same way. Mixtures of plants compete with each other the least when they partition resources. When designing polycultures, therefore, we can reduce competition between our desired species by mixing species with divergent niches. These can be niches in time, space, or kind. For example, spring ephemeral plants avoid compe-

tition by using light and nutrients earlier in the season than anyone else. Different summer green plants mature at different times during the growing season, so the timing of their maximal use of nutrients, water, and pollinators probably varies, too. Shallow-rooted trees probably compete less with taprooted trees than with other shallow-rooted trees, and plants in different vegetation layers compete less with each other than do plants in the same layer. Plant architecture—that is, form, size, habit, and rooting pattern—is therefore a good indicator of niche, and we should mix plants that have varying and compatible architectures.

At the same time, we can reduce the chances that an unwanted species will invade by attempting to fill all the niches for the most important resources. For example, if roots from desired species occupy all the horizons of the soil profile, unwanted species have fewer opportunities to retrieve needed nutrients and water. A dense ground cover of shade-tolerant plants under the tree canopy will make less light available for weeds.

These two strategies are essentially the same thing. Partitioning niches with useful plants reduces competition between the desired species *and* inhibits weeds by filling more of the available niches. Not only that, but we should be able to plant plants with dissimilar root patterns or light requirements more closely together. This would theoretically allow us to increase plant density while minimizing increased competition, further reducing opportunities for weed colonization.

An important aspect of partitioning nutrient resources in your polycultures is to include plants that fix nitrogen or act as dynamic accumulators. At best, this increases nutrient resources for the whole system. At the least, though, it reduces the nitrogen fixer's competition with its neighbors for nitrogen or the dynamic accumulator's competition with its neighbors for whatever nutrients it accumulates.

Use Ground Covers

A ground cover, for the purposes of this book, is a plant that functions to densely cover the ground, occupying niches that weeds would otherwise colonize. Use of ground covers is essentially an application of the principle of competitive exclusion (volume 1, page 133). Hence, the best ground covers grow quickly, shade the soil surface completely, and remain vigorous and self-repairing indefinitely. They therefore prevent weed seed germination by shading and at least slow down many perennial weeds, if not outcompeting them to extinction.

Ground covers are gaining popularity as lawn substitutes because of their low maintenance requirements once established. They offer a great way to cover large areas and suppress weeds, and they are especially important for larger forest gardens. Most of the nut trees, for example, cover large spaces and will require an extensive herbaceous layer beneath them. Low-maintenance, long-lived ground covers can take up the space while providing other benefits, whereas some of the more finicky perennial vegetables like perennial broccoli and asparagus would wear out the gardener on that scale.

Ground covers can be shrubs, herbs, grasses, ferns, or other plants. Most fall into one of two categories: running ground covers, which spread indefinitely, and clumpers, which grow to a certain width and no further. In addition, ground covers may be mat-forming or sprawling. Mat formers are dense plants that create solid carpets and may run or clump. Sprawling ground covers are vines of various types that, along with running ground covers, are often vigorous. They can overwhelm small or delicate perennials. For best performance, use a polyculture of ground covers, including a mix of clumpers, runners, and mat formers.

In addition to suppressing weeds, many ground-cover species perform other important functions, including erosion control, soil building, and ornament. For appendices 1 and 3, we have selected from thousands of ground-cover species those that either are excellent at this one purpose or have additional important functions.[8] See also feature article 3, "Ground-Cover Polycultures."

Turn Unwanted Plants into Useful Crops

Unwanted plants are virtually inevitable in any garden. If a weed is able to establish itself, our garden has (or had) an unfilled niche. At this point, we need to stop and consider the options. We usually pull things out without thinking, when we can sometimes save that effort by researching the plants that arrive unbidden to see whether they have uses or functions we might want. If the weed turns out to be useful as an insectary plant or edible, for example, then you might decide to keep it. If the weed is a dynamic accumulator, you might want to turn it into a nutrient pump by continually cutting it back and using it for mulch.

Even if a weed doesn't offer one or more of these functions, we can still make use of the information its presence provides. How did the plant get there? What resources is it using? What is its architecture? What useful species can we substitute for the weed that will offer us benefits and fill the same niche? Figure out these things, then pull the plant, turn it into compost or compost tea, and replace it with the alternative as soon as possible.

Fill Weed Gaps Immediately

We should always follow disturbance with proactive planting if we want to maintain control of the successional process. The best strategy for guiding postdisturbance succession is to plan your revegetation before the disturbance occurs, get all your materials together beforehand, and implement it immediately afterward. Whenever you pull an unwanted plant out of the ground, make sure to replant the disturbed space or mulch it heavily to prevent more weeds from establishing themselves there. As the bulldozer drives away from the construction site, begin planting and mulching if you can. This gives you greater influence over species availability and plant performance, as well as soil nutrient flows.

Use the Cropping Principle

"Cropping" a group of competing plants reduces their competition and helps maintain plant diversity. This is known as the cropping principle (see volume 1, page 134). Cropping maintains diversity because it prevents the competitive exclusion principle from operating. Pruning, shearing, fire, grazing, and harvesting are all forms of cropping in forest gardens.

In polycultures of plants that share the same niches, cropping is the only way to prevent the polyculture from losing diversity due to competitive exclusion. So, if a patch contains one or more vigorous plants, you will have to hack them back sometimes to keep them from outcompeting their neighbors. However, you must be mindful to use intermediate disturbance and intermediate disturbance frequency. If you don't crop enough you will not reduce competition; if you crop too much, you will reduce plant health or the stand's ability to suppress weeds. If a polyculture includes vigorous dynamic accumulators or nitrogen fixers that you harvest regularly for mulch, you can lean on the cropping principle and worry less about mixing plants with dissimilar niches.

Manage Problem Plants outside the Garden

The availability of plant propagules to an open site or niche is one of the three primary causes of succession (see table 1.6). Given that fact, we must sometimes manage plants outside of our gardens if we are to minimize our problems with weeds inside the garden. Rhizome barriers are one way to prevent rhizomatous weeds outside from entering the garden. What of the airborne invaders?

Highly dispersive plants that spread by wind- or animal-borne seed can be a major weed problem. Sometimes we have to manage these plants to prevent them from spreading their progeny where we don't want them. We can cut plants before they produce seed or take out the plants entirely. Sometimes a hedge, windbreak, or fence can stop too much windblown seed from entering the garden. Animal-borne seed is hard to stop by managing the animals, especially if they are birds. Reducing the number of bird perches in the garden can help, but dealing with the seed source is more likely to be effective.

Create Self-Managing Successions

Any time we create a disturbance in the garden, we create an opportunity for unwanted plants to establish themselves. Therefore, to minimize opportunities for weeds to get a foothold, we should design a successional pathway that requires the fewest interventions along the way. Instant successions would seem the optimal solution, because we plan the whole successional sequence and plant it all at once. This is not to say that relay plantings are out of the question, just that they carry more risk of weeds because they are likely to require more disturbances along the way.

DIRECTED SUCCESSION

Directed succession is, not surprisingly, just that: the intentional guidance of changes in community composition over time. Traditional farmers and gardeners direct succession all the time, but they usually direct it backward, to a secondary succession origin, and then let it go forward for only one year. Either that or they continually disturb the system using mowing, cutting of hay, or grazing so the community doesn't change much over time. Under these conditions, knowing the principles behind directing succession is unimportant, for the practices and their outcomes are well known. However, forest gardening brings us into an unfamiliar territory where we must go back to essentials if we are to apply ourselves intelligently to the situations we will face. Designing and managing succession in forest gardens is a new art and science. Good theory will support us in making better choices along the way.

Few conventional gardening issues nest inside the topic of directing succession, except for the fact that guiding which plants join the community when is fundamental to any agricultural enterprise. Weed management enters this discussion from a different angle than before, however. Earlier we talked about weeds as competitors for the resources we would prefer our desired plants to get. Here weeds represent potential diversions from our desired successional pathway.

Directing succession helps us achieve our three primary goals of high, diverse yields, maximal self-maintenance, and maximum ecological health in several ways. By limiting opportunities for unwanted plants to take over, we help ensure the yields we desire. Through intelligent design and management we hope to create a self-directed succession, one that requires few interventions from us once we set it up and get it going. This reduces our maintenance work. Ecological health arises from the fact that intervening less frequently and less intensively allows the system to build ecological capital. An aggrading ecosystem generates many benefits both within and outside the aggrading area. Within the system, food webs develop and diversify, and increases occur in soil nutrients, soil organic matter, biomass, biodiversity, plant and animal health, and system stability and resilience. At a larger scale, we find that we get better water quality, cleaner air, less erosion, and more wildlife. These ecosystem benefits feed back to the other two goals, supporting higher, more diverse yields and maximal self-maintenance.

The strategies discussed below arise from table 1.6 (reprinted from volume 1, chapter 6), which summarizes what we call the unified oldfield theory. The law of vegetation dynamics (volume 1, page 280) lays out three primary causes of succession: site or niche availability; varying species availability to the site or niche; and varying species performance once there. Each primary cause of community change has a corresponding succession guidance approach: deliberate site and niche availability; directed species availability; and facilitated species performance. We use these three intuitively obvious approaches to succession guidance all the time, but we often use them unconsciously. Making them explicit and conscious should make our succession design and management efforts more

TABLE 1.6. A unified oldfield theory: the causes of plant succession and means of succession management. The importance of each contributing process or condition and defining factor will vary from time to time and place to place. *Modified from Pickett and McDonnell, 1989, and inspired by Luken, 1990.*

Causes of Community Change	Contributing Processes or Conditions	Defining Factors	Guidance Strategies D = Design M = Management	Succession Guidance Approaches
Site or niche availability	Disturbance	• Kind of disturbance • Scale and size • Pattern • Intensity and severity • Timing and frequency	D: site selection and design M: designed disturbance	Deliberate site and niche availability
	Niche availability	• Timing and quantity of resources available: light, water, nutrients, pollinators, etc. • Resource use and niche overlap of species present (their niche, size, form, density, pattern, vigor, resource demand, etc.)	D: community design M: designed disturbance M: proactive planting M: resource management M: soil food web management	
Differential species availability (propagule survival and dispersal)	Propagule pool	• Size of pool • Nature of propagule (species; seed, bud, advance regeneration; size, weight; etc.) • Propagule viability over time • Disturbance regime and land use and management pattern, as they affect propagule viability • Preexisting species (e.g., soil seed bank)	D: site selection D: species selection M: designed disturbance M: proactive planting M: soil food web management	Directed species availability
	Propagule dispersal	• Landscape structure and pattern • Dispersal agents' behavior and ecology (wind, animals)	D: site selection and design D: community design M: designed disturbance M: proactive planting	

(continued next page)

focused and effective. Yet these approaches stand at the most general level of the hierarchy. We need more specific strategies that will affect (1) the processes or conditions contributing to each cause of succession and (2) the specific factors that define them (as laid out in table 1.6).

Table 1.7 summarizes the design and management strategies related to each of the three main succession guidance approaches. The discussion below briefly explores each strategy, beginning with the design strategies. Chapter 4 discusses these design strategies further. Table 1.8 lists techniques associated with each succession management strategy. Chapters 5, 6, and 7 provide more information affecting succession management. Table 1.6 and volume 1's chapter 6 provide the background for this whole discussion.

Carefully Select and Design Your Site
When you choose a specific forest garden site, you choose a set of climate, water, soil, and other conditions that influence the course of succession. Each site also has an existing flora, a use and disturbance history, and tendencies toward a particular disturbance regime and a certain set of random stresses and events.

Always evaluate the options before choosing your forest garden site. You may find that one site has an intractable weed problem, for example, or that it has a history of severe wind events that could damage your crops. One site may receive unwanted seed deposits from neighboring trees or intense perennial-weed rhizome pressure, while others will be free of such influences or may receive seed or rhizome pressure from more easily managed species. Understand the resource conditions and

(table 1.6, continued)

Causes of Community Change	Contributing Processes or Conditions	Defining Factors	Guidance Strategies D = Design M = Management	Succession Guidance Approaches
Differential species performance (colonization, vigor, persistence, and reproduction)	Resource availability and environmental conditions	• Nutrient, water, and light availability • Topography • Microclimate • Soil character	D: site selection and design D: community design M: designed disturbance M: resource management M: soil food web management	Facilitated species performance
	Random environmental stresses	• Climate cycles and extremes • Site history and prior occupants • Pollution events	D: site selection and design	
	Plant tolerances, requirements, and capacities	• Germination requirements • Growth and assimilation rates and timing • Soil, water, and climate tolerances and requirements	D: species selection	
	Life history and strategy	• Energy and biomass allocation pattern (ruderal, competitor, stress tolerator), form, and habit • Life span and reproductive timing and mode	D: species selection	
	Herbivory (including disease and predation)	• Plant defenses, resistance, and vigor • Climate cycles and variation • Community architecture and texture • Population cycles and food-web interactions	D: species selection D: community design M: designed disturbance M: soil food web management	
	Competition	• Competitors' identity, niche, numbers, and relative size and vigor • Resource supplies • Competition intensity and for what resources • Competitors' herbivores and mutualists • Competitors' environmental tolerances and conditions	D: species selection D: community design M: designed disturbance M: proactive planting M: resource management M: soil food web management	
	Mutualism (and facilitation)	• Partners' identity, niche, numbers, and vigor • Level and kind of support • Partners' predators, herbivores, and allies • Partners' environmental tolerances and conditions	D: species selection D: community design M: designed disturbance M: soil food web management	
	Inhibition (plus allelopathy and self-poisoning)	• Soil conditions • Prior occupants and current neighbors • Soil food web composition • Fungal:bacterial balance	D: species selection D: community design M: designed disturbance M: soil food web management	

other legacies present, and consider how they will influence your site-preparation needs, the species you'll plant, their performance, the rate of succession, and your maintenance workload.

Similarly, your site design influences most of the same factors and may ameliorate undesirable conditions. Windbreaks, irrigation or drainage systems, rhizome barriers, and even roads and paths can alter climate, microclimate, water, and soil conditions, as well as the patterns of animal- and wind-borne seed dispersing into your site.

Select Species Prudently

Once plants have occupied an available site or niche, plant performance reigns as the core ecological process determining the path of succession. Therefore, plant species selection largely determines the course of designed successions, because our

TABLE 1.7. Guiding succession: design and management strategies that influence the processes or conditions contributing to each primary cause of succession.

	Design Strategies	Management Strategies
Deliberate Site Availability		
Consciously creating new sites for plant establishment, or altering the character of sites to prevent establishment.	• site selection and design	• designed disturbance
Directed Species Availability		
Influencing the availability of seeds, buds, rhizomes, suppressed plants, or other propagules that may establish themselves in sites made available by disturbance.	• site selection and design • species selection • community design	• designed disturbance • proactive planting
Facilitated Species Performance		
Supporting optimal performance of desired species and reducing performance of unwanted species. Performance includes germination, establishment, growth, resilience, survival, and reproduction.	• site selection and design • species selection • community design	• designed disturbance • proactive planting • resource management • soil food web management

species choices determine the characteristics of the plants in a succession, and consequently how they will perform in the conditions they encounter and create. Species selection also affects social interactions in the community, and the resulting propagule pool. Though species selection forms part of the community design process, its importance justifies separating it from the patterning of those species in space and time as a succession guidance strategy.

We can group the eight contributing processes or conditions that determine species performance into three categories: (1) site conditions (resource availability; random environmental stresses); (2) plant species characteristics (plant tolerances, requirements, and capacities; life history and strategy); and (3) social interactions (herbivory; competition; mutualism; inhibition). This trio of factors forms the basis for the species selection process, along with desired uses (food, fuel, fiber, fodder, fertilizer, farmaceuticals, and fun) and needed ecosystem functions (insectary and fertility plants, ground covers, and so on).

Site conditions, desired functions, and human uses act as filters limiting our species choices to adapted plants that fulfill our goals. Within that set of species, we arrange plants in time by successional phase based on life history (mainly life span and reproductive age) and strategy (ruderal, competitor, or stress tolerator; form; and habit). Then we select among the plants for each stage of our designed succession based on physical and social characteristics (size, niche charac-

teristics) to arrange plants in space (polycultures and patches). One can clearly see the connection to community design in this selection process. Such a process fits the plants together in time and space so they perform optimally, giving us a stronger lead in the successional dance.

Design the Plant Community Well: Architecture, Guilds, and Polycultures

Plant-community design affects plant performance directly and indirectly through social interactions, changing environmental conditions, and the demand for and supply of resources. The growth forms, size, spacing, patterning, and resource needs of the species occupying a patch determine whether a site or niche is available for another plant to occupy. If no site or niche is available, the relative performance of species will determine vegetation dynamics. If a site or niche is available, new species may enter the community to change the dynamic.

Community layering, density, and species composition determine the demand for light, water, and nutrients relative to supply, and therefore the availability of these resources. For instance, the dense canopies of multistemmed shrubs dominate light resources in stable shrublands so completely that trees cannot establish themselves. Ground covers do the same thing against herb-layer weeds. Excessive vegetation density can create demand for water or nutrients in amounts exceeding supply, especially in poor or dry soils. This can slow succession, set the system up for a disturbance such as a fire, dieback gap, or major insect attack, or create an opportunity for species tolerant of resource limitation to succeed where others fail, changing the course of succession.

The community's texture and patchiness influence the abundance and diversity of insects and birds, and hence the amount of herbivory. The patterning and diversity of species influence these animals, too, and influence competition, mutualism, and inhibition as well. The architecture of the community also affects wind flow and animal behavior, which in turn affects seed-dispersal patterns. Calm wind areas tend to receive higher deposits of windblown seed, and sites with good bird perches receive both seed and nutrient deposits.

The community's social structure largely determines which plants benefit the most from social interactions. Guild and polyculture design affect the whole food-web structure, especially insect populations, which in turn influences plant performance. Competition and cooperation between species can strongly influence plant performance, and hence the course of succession.

Use Designed Disturbances

Designed disturbance powerfully alters the direction of vegetation change, which is why we use it so much. It affects virtually all successional processes—all three primary causes—to one degree or another. Designed disturbance includes many different techniques and strategies, all with different effects on different ecosystems at different times. The effects also vary depending on the intensity, frequency, duration, scale, and pattern of each disturbance. Designed disturbances include site preparation and planting activities (chapters 5 and 6), as well as management and maintenance activities (chapter 7). Table 1.8 provides a comprehensive list of designed disturbances, as well as the other succession management strategies and techniques.

Effectively disturbing vegetation requires clear objectives. Important designed-disturbance objectives include making new sites available for colonization, altering the initial flora and propagule pool for a following succession, and changing the availability of nutrient, water, and light resources. Disturbances can also reduce competition and maintain plant diversity. By altering vegetation texture and structure, disturbances influence patterns of herbivory, disease, predation, and seed dispersal. Knowing when *not* to act and carefully considering how to achieve specific desired effects with minimal side effects are probably the hardest aspects of designing disturbances. In addition, we need to look at the long term and envision for each vegetation patch disturbance regimes (frequency, timing, intensity, scale, pattern, and kind) that will direct succession and create or maintain desired architecture. Disturbance regimes also figure prominently in the evolution and breeding of plants. Chapter 7 covers more specifics on these points and discusses the major disturbance strategies we use in forest gardening. We should most often follow designed disturbances with proactive planting if we want to retain the lead in the successional dance. We should also consider our disturbances in the context of pattern #30, *Patch Disturbance and Regeneration*.

Many natural events and human activities may result in vegetation disturbance and alteration of the successional pathway: heavy storms, severe droughts, animal activities, cars compacting wet soil, and so on. Remaining attuned to possible disturbance events in our gardens will help us head off problems and take advantage of opportunities, turning unplanned disturbances into design and management opportunities.

Plant Proactively

Proactive planting is the deliberate dispersal or placement of chosen species propagules at sites made available through disturbances, made evident through observation, or revealed by the growth of unwanted plants. Farmers and gardeners proactively plant after planned disturbances all the time, but we need to expand the idea to include planting after unintentional and naturally occurring or random

TABLE 1.8. Succession management strategies and techniques.

Designed Disturbance

Deliberately making sites available how, when, and where desired; affecting propagule
viability and dispersal; affecting plant performance; altering soil conditions; preventing competitive exclusion.

Site Preparation & Planting Actions:
- scraping: bulldozing, grading, stumping
- compacting
- decompacting: deep ripping or chisel plowing, backhoe loosening, double digging, radial trenching
- filling, mounding, raised beds, pits, trenching, swaling
- clearing: may include trimming, weeding, burning, animals, mowing, scraping, cultivation; canopy openings, gaps in various layers, ground vegetation disturbance
- cultivation: plowing, tilling, disking, hoeing, raking
- animals: animal tractors, grazing, browsing, trampling, scratching
- multiple cover crops
- weeding: digging, pulling, hoeing, grubbing, girdling, woody weed extraction, herbicides (flaming, hot water, solarization, chemicals)
- rhizome barriers
- prescribed burning, slash and burn
- soil staking, check logs
- mulching: spot, temporary, topdressing, sheet, deep, smother mulch

Management & Maintenance Actions:
- harvesting
- biological controls, trapping, spraying
- limited cultivation: hoeing, raking
- mulching: spot, temporary, topdressing, sheet, deep, smother mulch
- trimming: pruning, thinning, shearing, cutting, coppicing, pollarding
- weeding: digging, pulling, hoeing, grubbing, girdling, woody weed extraction, herbicides (flaming, hot water, solarization, chemicals)
- clearing: may include trimming, weeding, burning, animals, mowing, scraping, cultivation; canopy openings, gaps in various layers, ground vegetation disturbance, soil disturbance
- mowing: scythe, sickle, flail or rotary mower, string trimmer
- animals: animal tractors, grazing, browsing, trampling, scratching
- prescribed burning, slash and burn
- draining, flooding

Proactive Planting

The planned dispersal and establishment of chosen species at sites made available through
disturbances or into open niches revealed through observation or by the growth of unwanted plants.

- complete area coverage: dense broadscale planting
- nuclei that merge: layering, facilitated rhizome spread, facilitated self-sowing
- patch, spot, or in-fill plantings
- instant successions, nurse crops, relay plantings
- seeding: broadcast, drilling, frost seeding, undersowing, facilitated self-sowing
- transplanting: bare root, containers, balled-and-burlapped, divisions, whole-plant transplants, wildflower sod

Resource Management

Manipulating key plant resources (light, water, and nutrients) to favor
or inhibit particular plants and therefore change the course of succession.

Nutrients/pH:
- dynamic accumulators
- mulch: compost, raw organic matter
- foliar feeding
- liquid or powdered soil fertilization
- liming, wood ash, prescribed burning
- adding sulfur, vinegar drench

Water:
- raising water table
- lowering water table
- irrigating, draining, flooding
- mulching

Light:
- mulching
- pruning, clearing, selective thinning
- grazing, browsing, or not
- mowing
- burning

Heat:
- black plastic mulch
- wood ashes on soil surface
- stone mulch
- rocks, masonry, ponds to absorb heat

Air:
- soil compaction or loosening
- CO_2 enrichment

Stored Energy (in Plants):
- pruning (timing, intensity)
- thinning fruit, flowers
- harvesting

Soil Food Web Management

Managing the soil food web to slow or speed succession or to favor some plants over others.

- soil management: tilling vs. not, bare vs. mulched, green vs. brown manures, etc.
- provide food for wanted microbes: use plants to alter fungi:bacteria ratio; mulch, soil staking, or other carbon for fungi; sugars or green matter mixed into soil for bacteria; etc.
- avoiding chemical fertilizers, pesticides, and fumigants
- good fungal or bacterial compost
- inoculation: compost tea, soil inoculation, native fungi transplants, commercial mycorrhizal inoculum

events as well. Combining proactive planting with thoughtful community design will minimize the need for further intervention to maintain the system's successional direction.

The most critical time to take the lead in the succession dance is immediately after a disturbance, no matter what caused it. The most resources are then available, and the members of the propagule pool then most actively attempt to get ahead in the initial flora marathon. The first plants out of the box after the starting gun have a major advantage, so if we want that advantage for our chosen plants, we need to take the lead. The biggest mistake we can make is to let undesirable plants take over after a disturbance, for it either dooms desired species to mediocrity at best or requires another disturbance, or two or three or more, to turn the tide in our plants' favor.

Proactively planting chosen species on available sites immediately after a disturbance reduces or eliminates available niches for unwanted plants and sets the course of succession in our intended direction. It actively alters the propagule pool by adding consciously chosen plants in a form or life stage chosen for optimum establishment and performance (seeds, rooted cuttings, potted plants, balled-and-burlapped individuals, "sods" of herbaceous polycultures, and the like). It turns competitive exclusion to our advantage and strongly shapes the following successional pathway.

The key to proactive planting is to design and implement the disturbance *and the planting* as a single, continuous activity. Order the seeds or plants and have them on hand, along with your mulch materials, so you can put them in the ground immediately as the bulldozer leaves the building site, for example. Keep a certain amount of plant stock on hand to fill in when unexpected disturbances occur, and try to fill every hole you make when weeding with a chosen plant. As our forest gardens mature we will have extra plants around, and the propagule pool will begin to fill with seeds and roots of desired species. Hence, the need for proactive planting should decrease.

Manage Resources

Manipulating vital plant resources (nutrients, water, and light) in different ways favors different plants and therefore changes the course of succession. For example, competitor-strategist plants outcompete stress-tolerant plants when nutrients are abundant. Researchers have observed that soluble fertilizers support grass and forb dominance and inhibit woody species, perhaps because early-succession ruderal and competitor-strategist plants take up soluble fertilizers and turn them into plant biomass more rapidly. Soluble fertilizers may also favor bacteria-dominated soils, which woody plants tend not to like. Forest garden successions will probably benefit from fertilization with mulch, since mulching tips the soil food web into fungal dominance, favoring later-succession shrubs and trees. Similarly, altering soil pH selects for species adapted to the pH conditions created.

While moisture regimes tend to moderate during succession, drastic changes in a site's water regime may act as a disturbance that can set succession back. If we install drainage on wet sites with existing wet-tolerant plants, the existing species will be susceptible to competitive exclusion by plants adapted to drier conditions.

Experimental evidence suggests that broadcast irrigation favors grasses over later-succession forbs and woodies, thereby slowing succession. Hence, manipulating moisture regimes on a system-wide basis may not speed succession. If we are going to irrigate, we should use drip irrigation to aid individual plants instead; the success of individual plants will foster the successional process we have designed. Otherwise, we should probably either let nature take its course or just keep adding organic matter. This will improve the moisture regime over time as the soil improves.

The third key resource in succession management is sunlight. The understory tends to get shadier as succession goes on. Designed disturbances can alter this progression if you want more sun: pruning branches, making gaps or clearings, or thinning the canopy or middle layers of vegetation. If you want to establish shade-loving plants at a sunny location early on, you'll have to use special measures such as shade structures or fast-growing nurse plants you can cut down after a slower-growing canopy establishes itself. Pioneer trees such as pin cherry, black cherry, poplar, and birch can serve this function. However, relay plantings of shade-tolerant plants when conditions are right will have the best chance of success for the least effort.

Clearly, these resources interact: increasing sunlight can warm the soil and speed decomposition, making more nutrients available for both plants and leaching. This would favor plants that are more competitive. If you wanted the increased sunlight without the increased nutrient availability and losses, you would have to shade the soil with mulch, plants, or something else to keep it cool.

Manage the Soil Food Web

The soil food web affects plant performance, and therefore succession, by altering the availability of nutrients and water. Plants with the proper mycorrhizal associates and other root-zone microbes will have better nutrition than those without. Similarly, plants with the right soil allies will resist disease, recover from herbivory, compete, and resist inhibition more effectively than those without. All these factors will improve the associated plants' performance and strengthen their role in the vegetation dynamic. The longevity and viability of seeds and other propagules depend upon soil food web conditions also. Seeds of grasses and other early-succession herbs may need bacteria-dominated soil to germinate successfully. Managing the soil food web should shift the kinds of weeds we encounter.

The fungal-bacterial balance of the soil food web can influence plant performance and survival. For example, most trees and many shrubs struggle to find a niche in grasslands. This may be partly due to bacterial soils creating nitrate-nitrogen, whereas most woodies prefer nitrogen in the form of ammonium. Obviously, to spur succession by planting woodies in a grassland will require altering the soil food web to a more fungal condition, using mycorrhizal inoculation, soil staking, carbonaceous mulch, or fungal composts (see chapter 5).

Combine Strategies

The succession guidance strategies above direct you to specific actions you can use to influence the ecosystem's path. Combining these specific actions helps marshal all the relevant forces to direct succession the way you want.

For example, managing the initial flora is a key task before planting a forest garden. A standard strategy combining several modes of influence includes a series of cultivations (designed disturbances) and plantings of cover crops (proactive plantings) that will outcompete weeds and improve the soil over a year or two. If you don't have the time or equipment this strategy requires, you can cut back the vegetation (designed disturbance), inoculate and plant your woody plants (proactive planting and soil food web management), and sheet-mulch with weed barriers, mulch, and compost (resource management and soil food web management) to limit unwanted plants and fertilize desired species. Once the site is sheet-mulched, you can plant herbaceous species to fill the remaining niches (proactive planting and community design). Indeed, these two strategies are common forest-gardening fare because they work in many situations. However, understanding the underlying basis for these typical strategies will help you modify them, or create other strategies, to meet your specific site conditions, resources, and succession-management needs. See chapters 5 and 6 for more practical examples of specific succession-management strategies.

OVERYIELDING POLYCULTURES

Overyielding or additive yielding occurs when two or more crops growing in polyculture produce higher yields than equal areas of the same crops grown separately. This can occur because one or more of the crops yields more per unit area when grown in a polyculture. Overyielding can also result from polycultures where the yield of each crop per unit area is *lower* than when grown in monoculture, but the total system yield is higher because the yields add together—and you have many different crops to tally. Additive yielding is crucial for achieving high, diverse production from our forest gardens, which is one reason that "Overyielding Polycultures" sits in the middle of the ecosystem dynamics in figure 1.1. We might call it one of forest gardening's holy grails. However, we have much clearer guidance for how to create this ecosystem dynamic than King Arthur's knights had for their quest.

Unthinking mixing of species can lead to competition, stress, and lower yields for all crops concerned. Since a forest garden is, by definition, a polyculture, we just can't have any unthinking mixing of species, then, can we? What specific objectives must our polycultures achieve to create overyielding? A polyculture is most likely to overyield when:

- it has more resources available to it, either because the mixture more fully uses available resources or because one or more species increases the availability of a scarce resource; and
- pests, diseases, climate fluctuations, and other stresses affect the polyculture less because it is more stable and resilient.

Every ecosystem dynamic discussed above also helps generate an overyielding polyculture. Plant health, self-renewing fertility, sustainable water demand, minimal herbivory, minimal competition, and directed succession are prerequisites. In the following subsections we articulate the basic strategies that will increase both the resources available to a polyculture and the polyculture's stability and resilience in the face of stress.

Design Polycultures for Greater Resource Access

The basic approach here is to diversify the different strategies used by plants in the polyculture to access vital resources. Instead of using only flat-rooted trees, we use flat-, heart-, and taprooted trees to gain complete penetration of the soil profile and all the resources available in it. We use perennials with different root patterns to do the same. Useful crops growing in the partial shade below a tree-crop canopy will obviously increase total system yields, most likely without reducing tree-crop yields. This approach builds what we call a resource-sharing or resource-partitioning guild.

We have talked about resource-partitioning guilds throughout this chapter. Creating these guilds has multiple benefits including reducing competition, increasing diversity, and increasing yields, as well as the secondary effects of decreasing herbivory, increasing system resilience, and so on. Making sure you design your resource-sharing guilds to fully use the available resources is central to creating overyielding polycultures. You therefore need to make sure your polycultures include plants with diverse forms, habits, root patterns, shade tolerance, and so on.

Design for Greater Resilience and Stability

A plant community's resilience and stability in the face of stress result from functional interconnection between members of the community, as well as diversity of function and redundancy of function within the community. Functional interconnection arises when the inherent products, yields, or behaviors of one member meet the inherent needs of another member. Diversity of function involves making sure that all community niches are filled, that all the functions a community needs to remain viable and stable get performed. Redundancy of function develops from making sure that more than one species fills each of the important community niches. This provides a fail-safe: if one species drops out of the system, others will be there to keep the community working.

Resource-sharing guilds create redundancy of function. As long as the resource being shared reflects a key community niche, resource-sharing guilds will build stability into your forest garden. For example, making sure you have generalist nectary plants flowering throughout the whole growing season will help ensure that you have pollinating insects present at all times. In this case, the pollinators are the shared resource, and the plants partition the growing season to avoid competition for pollination services.

Diversity of function and functional interconnection arise from creating mutual-support guilds and providing habitat for beneficial animals. Mutual-support guilds entail interactions between species from different levels in the food web, such as nectary plants attracting wasps that lay their eggs in herbivores of your crops. We can assume that herbivores will find our forest gardens, because we are providing them with habitat just by planting plants. What we must do is provide habitat for the beneficial animal allies that will help fill the predator niches in the ecosystem. In some cases these are plants, as discussed above in "Minimal Herbivory" (page 23). We must also supply other physical elements to meet the needs of the allies we want to attract (see appendix 5). Limiting disturbance and intervention in the system also allows the community to develop diversity and redundancy of function on its own.

In essence, this entire book aims toward creating overyielding polycultures using resource-sharing and mutual-support guilds. The great thing is that virtually all of the strategies we have discussed for each of the ecosystem dynamics are mutually supportive. The same strategies apply to all of the dynamics, and each of the dynamics supports the creation of all the others. In other words, each of the strategies we employ to create our forest gardens is multifunctional, just like the plants we intend to use in the garden itself. The fact that the principles of design for forest gardening apply to the act of design itself should give us heart. It supports the validity of the principles and their application in realms outside of forest gardening. If we learn them here, we can apply them successfully in any realm.

In the meantime, we still have a job to do: to create a forest garden with high, diverse yields, maximal self-maintenance, and maximal ecological health. We know that the ecosystem dynamics we have been discussing help achieve these goals, but there are also direct design and management actions we can take to fulfill these goals. Let us look at these next.

DESIRED CONDITIONS

The phrase *desired condition* may seem strange to some when the word *goal* might do just as well. Why use it then? Simply because it is more accurate and has less cultural baggage. Stating a goal as a desired condition, putting it in present tense, helps us discern whether the condition is actually something we want. It helps us state our goals more clearly as a result. It also serves as an affirmation, changing our consciousness and focusing our attention on the present-moment reality. If the statement of desired condition resonates inside of us, then the effort of creating that desired condition will flow from a deep inner place and result in a participatory paradigm. Meanwhile, a "goal" is often stated when we are trying to impose something on ourselves or another. Imposition implies separation; separation instigates intervention. This is cultural baggage we can—and must—do without.

As with the ecosystem dynamics covered in the previous section, we have at our disposal direct and indirect strategies for creating our desired conditions. The indirect strategies include primarily the ecosystem dynamics we have already discussed. Therefore, this section will focus on additional strategies that help us directly create our desired conditions in the forest garden.

High, Diverse Yields

We want our forest gardens to produce an abundance of useful products. We want them to produce a variety of foods, diverse in their timing of harvest, their nutritional value (proteins, carbohydrates, vitamins, and minerals), in their character (nuts, fruits, berries, greens, shoots, roots, mushrooms), and in their habitat requirements. Ideally, a sweeping range of other products would also grow in our gardens, meeting many of our needs besides food—medicines, fuel, fiber plants, animal food, dyes, flowers, and so on—if we want them. The diversity is relatively easy. High yields are more challenging to achieve.

We discussed overyielding in the previous section. With careful selection of design elements and attention to creating ecosystem dynamics in your design, you should be well on your way to high, diverse yields. However, there are a few other tricks to ensuring a plenitude of things to eat throughout the growing season.

Choose a Forest Garden Site with Habitat Diversity

Habitat diversity is a form of structural diversity that radically increases the potential for organism and species diversity. A forest garden site that has more than one kind of soil, has different microclimates, or combines wet, moist, and dry spots will present more potential for variation in crop species, varieties, and seasons as well as kinds of yield. Habitat diversity also includes variation in slope aspect, elevation, disturbance history, vegetation type, and soil texture, structure, consistence, fertility, pH, depth, and parent material.

Create an Outdoor Living Room

Forest gardens work best when we live in them a lot. When we place our gardens out of sight and out of mind, we miss opportunities for harvesting and management that would be obvious and easy if the gardens were right in our face. We will therefore get higher yields, and more kinds of yields, if we design our forest gardens as outdoor living rooms (see pattern #6). The social and emotional "yields" from a beautiful forest garden can take on great importance beyond the food.

Choose High-Yielding Species and Varieties

This is an obvious strategy for creating a high-yield garden. Just be careful that the species and varieties you choose do not also have high-maintenance requirements, as high-yield varieties often do! You should decide whether you want to emphasize high yields per amount of labor invested or high yields per acre; many cultivars do not meet this double test.

Choose Crops with Diverse Yields in Time, Space, and Kind

Remember, we are talking about yields including food, fuel, fiber, fodder, fertilizer, "farmaceuticals," and fun. For food, we are talking about several general categories. Forest gardens will provide bountiful early spring harvests of greens and shoots. Most of these take on much stronger flavors later in the season, making them less desirable then. Berries begin in early summer and, if planned well, can last far into autumn. Larger fruits begin in mid- to late summer and continue into the fall, while nuts tend to mature late. Late fall and early spring are the prime times for harvesting root crops and mushrooms. Throughout the growing season, there will be minor harvests of flowers, leaves, seeds, and various tasty nibbles. By planting a mix of greens, roots, fruits, and nuts, we can spread out the season of harvest considerably. This diversity also creates variety in space and by kind, providing redundancy that helps ensure a yield no matter what the weather. We should also choose crops that grow in different habitats. For instance, both sun-loving and shade-loving greens taste good, and both will provide additional diversity of harvest.

As for crops other than food, this is up to you. Forest gardens can certainly provide them easily, and they can fill in gaps in the garden that weeds or ground covers would otherwise fill. Our Plant

Species Matrix (appendix 1) focuses on food plants, so you will probably have to research the other uses on your own. However, the effort should be well worth it.

Fit Yields to Niche

The yields we ask from a plant should relate to its niche requirements. Many plants with edible greens, for example, do fine in partial shade, even producing larger leaves to compensate for lower light levels. Growing fruit crops in the shade, however, is less likely to result in a happy experience, unless the plant is adapted to that condition—as some varieties of gooseberry and currant (*Ribes* spp.) appear to be.

Create Redundant Yields

The principle of redundancy (volume 1, page 150) suggests that we should not put all our eggs in one basket but should make sure our most critical needs get met in more than one way. However, we should not think about redundancy in a simplistic manner. Think about your essential needs in the most fundamental sense: it's not having more than one source of eggs, it's having redundant sources of protein. It isn't having more than one source of apples; it's having multiple sources of fruit for storage, fresh eating, pies, juice, or whatever. Redundancy of function is the key.

Create Mostly Midsuccession Environments

Midsuccession environments have the highest net primary productivity in deciduous forest biomes. Such environments provide us the best opportunity for high yields from forest mimics (see patterns #12, 13, 14, 16, 19, and 20 in chapter 2). In addition, our most fully developed fruit and nut crops are midsuccession species. Finally, the characteristics we tend to breed into perennial crops shift plants toward characteristics typical of competitor-strategist midsuccession species and away from characteristics typical of stress-tolerant late-

succession species. Making sure our forest garden consists primarily of midsuccession habitats will therefore most likely give us the highest yields.

Ensure Adequate Yields by Planting Extra

Though this may be incredibly obvious to some, it bears stating anyway: plant more food than you need. That way, unexpected herbivory or drought will give you just the right amount! You can give away the extra food, compost it, or feed it to your chickens or pigs, if you have them. Whatever you do, though, if you have an excess of fruits or nuts do not leave them lying around, as doing so can invite more pest or disease problems the following year.

Create Pockets of Production

Most forest gardens will consist primarily of polyculture patches containing mixtures of useful and functional plants. However, small pockets of monoculture production sometimes make sense. Perhaps you have only one crop that needs a certain management regime, such as fall-fruiting raspberries that you mow to the ground after harvest is complete. You may want a patch where you know you will get lots of asparagus while you test various polycultures that include asparagus to see how they work. Or you just don't want to bother playing with polyculture techniques, but you still want the benefits that polyculture offers.

Small patches of monoculture within a context of polyculture patches should still confer many of the same benefits of polyculture patches. We call these small monocultures "pockets of production" (see pattern #45). We should ensure, however, that the monoculture patches remain a small portion of the whole forest garden: certainly less than one-half, perhaps less than one-third, depending on the crops and their pests and diseases in the region. Surround each pocket of production with polyculture patches, especially patches containing insectary plants and habitat elements for the predators of the monoculture crop's pests.

Plan for Pollination

Pollination is crucial for the formation of fruits, nuts, and seeds. Therefore, make sure to plant adequate pollenizers for plants that require cross-pollination, especially if your neighborhood does not have abundant members of your desired species. See the tables for fruits and nuts in appendix 2 for information on pollination needs. Many nursery catalogs also give information on the pollination requirements of specific varieties. See pattern #48, *Cross-Pollination Clusters,* for one way to resolve the seeming paradox of having to plant cross-pollinators near each other, but wanting to mix species to complicate the lives of herbivores.

Planting generalist nectary flowers to attract predators also provides flowers for pollinators. This is critical to ensuring pollination in your garden, particularly if poor pollinator habitat surrounds your garden. You also need to supply nesting habitat for native pollinators. This generally entails providing dry, bare soil or leaving dead stalks for insect nesting and overwintering. You may also want to introduce pollinators such as orchard mason bees. For more information, see the tables on food and habitat for beneficials in appendix 5. Of course, you may also be interested in raising honeybees. This activity is quite compatible with forest gardening.[9]

Grow Mushrooms

Growing mushrooms is one of the most exciting and effective means of maximizing forest garden productivity. This kind of gardening is new territory for most of us; we can only hit a few highlights in this book. A number of mushroom cultivation methods are available for a range of edible and medicinal species, using a variety of substrates and cultivation methods (see pattern #37, *Gourmet Decomposers,* for a basic discussion). We also strongly suggest you read Paul Stamets's book *Growing Gourmet and Medicinal Mushrooms* for more information, including instructions and cautions.

MAXIMUM SELF-MAINTENANCE, MINIMUM COST

Along with overyielding polycultures, a completely self-maintaining garden is likely to remain another holy grail of forest gardening; it is something we can approach but may never achieve. Maintenance is the grunt work of keeping a system running: getting materials where they are needed when, making sure important processes take place, keeping the gears well oiled. Self-maintenance is when the system does this work itself, without the need for our labor or mechanical energy. For example, generating self-renewing fertility should mostly eliminate the need for fertilizing once the system is up and running. The other ecosystem dynamics discussed earlier will have similar benefits for creating this highly desirable condition.

Maintenance is one of the biggest costs of any system. Energy-efficient homes, for example, cost marginally more to build but save tremendous amounts of money over the long haul. Gardens share a similar story: reducing maintenance drastically reduces costs over the long run, and investing more up front in good design and installation maximizes the ultimate payout. However, up-front costs are still a significant factor. We'll talk here about how to minimize all these costs and to maximize self-maintenance, in ways beyond what the ecosystem dynamics have to offer.

One thing we should remember throughout this discussion is that many times we have trade-offs to make. One is whether we will spend time or spend money. When we say "minimizing cost," we mean reducing the money outlay in most cases. Some of the ideas below will reduce both the time and the money requirements for maintenance, but for most up-front investments, we will be trading time for money.

A second trade-off is the choice of whether to maximize yields or to maximize self-maintenance and minimize costs. Many tactics to increase yields cost more up front or require more maintenance. Some ways to decrease costs and maintenance decrease yields. Each of us will have to do our own calculus on which way to lean when such a trade-off exists. We attempt to focus here on strategies that will not cause such trade-offs to occur.

Make Mistakes on Paper

Designing on paper allows you to experiment with many ideas without money or labor invested. You don't want to have to move large trees a few years down the road because they will grow up into a power line, for example. Make sure you are clear about the key issues of site selection, site modification, and the location and spacing of large plants before you break out the shovel or backhoe. Make sure to design the infrastructure well (pathways, irrigation lines, fencing, and so on). These are places where people often make big mistakes that are hard to fix and cost effort or money continuously down the years. Sketch things out or stake them out on-site. Walk through your sketch or stakes imagining how you will get trucks in and out, if necessary, how you will pump your septic tank, what you'll do if you have to redo your foundation, and other long-term possibilities. Plant spacing is particularly important to plan in advance. Many a forest garden has suffered long-term productivity declines and increased maintenance needs from poor plant spacing. One of the points of design is to make, and catch, as many mistakes as possible before you create your design on the ground. It costs you time and effort up front but saves you immeasurably down the line.

Adapt to or Modify Site Conditions?

We must choose whether to adapt to challenging site conditions or to modify the site on a case-by-case basis. Modifying site conditions can cost significant time and money, or it may not, depending on the conditions present. However, it often radically increases garden productivity over the long run, especially if it involves improving adverse soil conditions such as compaction or low fertility. Research has shown that, within a few years, fruit trees planted after even two years of soil-improving cover crops surpass the growth and yield of non-cover-cropped trees planted two years earlier. Sometimes, however, adapting to the site conditions is cheaper and faster and does not have as big an impact on productivity over the long run. It may involve only a change of crops and letting go of attachments to favorite species you want to grow. For example, you could lime acid soils to achieve a more neutral pH, or you could instead plant acid-loving plants like chestnuts, blueberries, and nut pines. You could install irrigation on a dry site or simply plant drought-tolerant species.

We encourage you to think through all the options carefully; impatience and short-term thinking all too often win out in the decision-making process. However, as mentioned, the up-front costs often leverage major productivity increases. Furthermore, acting on impatience yields only once, in the immediate moment, whereas patient preparation can yield benefits for decades. See chapter 5 for a discussion of various site challenges and how you can adapt to or modify them.

Design Your Site to Minimize Work

We talked about this obvious strategy for maximal self-maintenance and minimal costs in the first paragraph of this chapter. Many times, all it takes is forethought, not more money or time. During the design phase, we strongly recommend you integrate the following patterns in particular into your garden:

• Zones of use are an aspect of the "zones and sectors" (see pattern #7) of permaculture fame. The basic idea is that we should locate landscape elements that need frequent attention or that yield most frequently in positions close to our most frequented places in the homestead: near the main door, along the main path, near the kitchen, within view from the most prominent windows. Landscape elements that need infrequent care or yield only periodically can go farther away, in more physically and visually inaccessible locations.

- We often need to import large quantities of mulch, manure, compost, or other materials to spread around our forest garden, especially in the early years. Moving this material involves a tremendous amount of work. Hence, we suggest you plan ahead for this and designate a place for a strategic materials depot (see pattern #25).
- Narrow paths can be a major problem in a garden (see figure 1.7). Think through your pathway width (see pattern #29) in all parts of your garden early in your design. Think in three dimensions, too: tree crowns hanging into paths are less of a problem when the branches are high than when they are low.
- Consider widening your paths at key places to create nodes for short-term storage of mulch piles, full carts, plants-in-transit, or tools while allowing you to get by without tripping over things (see pattern #26, *Paths and Nodes*).
- When natural systems must transfer matter or energy across a membrane or boundary, they usually evolve a sinuous, folded, highly convoluted pattern that maximizes the surface area of contact between the two substrates that the boundary separates. Keyhole beds (see pattern #28) have a similar function: the transfer of energy and materials in the form of work, food, attention, mulch, fertilizer, and water between pathways and planting beds. Keyhole beds[10] maximize bed space and minimize path space, while providing excellent access.
- When we scatter crop plants away from each other within a context out of harmony with their needs, we increase the amount of work we must do to care for them and increase their stress at the same time. Fruit trees scattered in a grassy field are a common illustration of this. However, if we cluster plants with similar requirements near each other, we form a nucleus where we can create an environment suitable to the crops. At the same time, we have

FIGURE 1.7. Eric Toensmeier emerges from one of the narrower sections of path in Robert Hart's forest garden. Robert's narrow paths created a delightfully foresty atmosphere but made walking in the garden in wet weather uncomfortable; increased the likelihood of disease transmission through the garden; and made working in the garden more difficult, especially with carts or wheelbarrows. Design your pathway widths consciously! *Photo by Dave Jacke.*

less distance to travel to care for the same number of plants and reduce the infrastructure and materials we need to irrigate them, mulch them, fertilize them, and so on. Such cluster planting (see pattern #47) can take many forms.

Many other ideas exist that can reduce the amount of work it takes to maintain a forest garden. Most of the ideas above come from the literature on permaculture, which is replete with many more such examples. We suggest familiarizing yourself with this literature, and keeping your eyes open for ideas from other quarters.

Eliminate or Reduce Irrigation

Irrigation is one of the biggest costs, both up front and on an ongoing basis, for any garden. Quality irrigation equipment is usually the best value, since cheap materials fail much more frequently, but even so, good equipment can be expensive. Pumping water takes large amounts of energy. Designing, setting up, and maintaining an irrigation system takes much time and effort, particularly in cold climates where the system needs winterizing. On the other hand, irrigation may be a necessity on your site or in your climate, or it may provide sizable gains in yields. In any case, it makes sense to design your garden to minimize or eliminate the need for irrigation. This is especially true if minimizing costs is your focus, but it even makes sense when your priority is high yields. Many strategies help us do this. See "Sustainable Water Demand" (page 21) for pointers. Again, the literature on permaculture offers many ideas for reducing the need for and increasing the efficiency of irrigation.

Propagate Your Own Plants

This is one of the best ways to save money on your forest garden. Plants, particularly herbaceous perennials, will be one of your highest budget items. The number of perennials it takes to fill the spaces below large trees is simply staggering. Many means of propagation exist, each suitable for different species.

The grafting of woody plants is an ancient and deeply satisfying art. Learning to graft not only saves money but also allows you to graft developed varieties onto wild seedlings or existing trees. Rooting cuttings is another gratifying technique. You may need a small greenhouse or perhaps a misting setup for optimal growth of cuttings, but you would be surprised how much you can do in a simple nursery bed or cold frame.

Growing herbs from seed is especially thrifty. A packet of good King Henry seeds (*Chenopodium bonus-henricus*) costs $2.50 and contains, let's say, fifty seeds. Fifty good King Henry plants, assuming you could even find them, would probably run about $5 each, or $250, if not more. Keep in mind that propagating requires quite a bit of effort—you are replacing money with labor. However, even when considering the cost of pots and potting soil, growing from seed makes financial sense. If you want a specific variety, however, growing from seed will not result in offspring with identical characteristics. For this reason, fruits and nuts are generally best propagated vegetatively, while most herbs are fine to start from seed. In addition, once you have mature perennials you can divide them to multiply your plants each year.

We can often acquire free plants from friends and neighbors; just beware of pests and diseases coming along for the ride. Buying smaller plants also helps save money. In fact, small woody plants often recover from transplant shock more rapidly than larger ones. Within a few years they can overtake larger plants that were planted at the same time

We generally recommend against collecting wild plants, particularly from pristine environments, for we humans have done enough damage to natural areas already. However, you can collect small portions of seeds and cuttings from wild plants, and you can dig wild specimens from areas destined for "development." On the other hand, we have removed small sections of rhizome from large, healthy colonies in healthy woods on rare occasions. Use your best judgment, and always make sure to leave the vast majority of wild stock in the wild.

Choose Wildling Crops

The warnings about wild-collected plant stock notwithstanding, we do recommend choosing plants that are less domesticated than most crops when doing so meets your productivity criteria. However, this does not necessarily mean completely undomesticated species.

A number of useful plants provide excellent crops but have undergone less selection and breeding than have apples, pears, peaches, and so on. These include persimmon, pawpaw, saskatoon, native grapes (e.g., Concord or muscadine), hardy kiwis, groundnut, Jerusalem artichoke, and blueberries, among others. Less-developed crops such as these may have "imperfections" or "flaws" relative to developed varieties. However, developed varieties often have had their naturally evolved disease and pest defenses bred right out of them. In many ways, plants in the middle ground of development are optimal for the forest garden. They can provide improved characteristics for us yet still retain some of their natural defenses, adaptations, and genetic diversity. In the case of blueberries, some recent cultivars represent backcrossing of developed varieties with wild stock. These "half-high" blueberries are hardier and have better flavor than most of the usual cultivars.

Some forest garden species have undergone no domestication at all. Many of these wild species are great nonetheless, and we recommend planting them. These include sugar maple, ramps, sweet goldenrod, ostrich fern, wood nettle, stinging nettle, juneberries, camass, chinquapin, violets, native honeysuckle (*Lonicera villosa*), and a number of native and nonnative plums and cherries. Some wildlings do need selection for better flavor and productivity, though; for example, some juneberries taste great, while others are not as good. Even so, such wildlings tend to need less maintenance than cultivars, and growing seedlings of a species provides you with genetic diversity to help reduce the rampancy of any diseases and pests that do occur. However, when we say wild species, we mean *nursery-propagated* wild species; beware of "nursery-grown" plants that may have been dug from the wild, grown in the nursery for a year, and then sold to you. The latter practice contributes to the destruction of wildlands.

Choose Self-Renewing Crops

This strategy is worth repeating, despite the fact that it is an underlying theme of this whole book. Using perennials and self-sowing annuals reduces our workload tremendously. It is a direct strategy for creating self-maintenance. However, let us take it a step further: self-renewing crops can also mean those that need no attention from us to bear year after year. While apples and other fruits need pruning to maintain their productivity over time, crops such as mulberries, persimmons, and pawpaws need less pruning or none at all, yet they bear anyway. Ostrich ferns keep making fiddleheads, despite our complete neglect. Elderberries and juneberries keep on fruiting without our help. Picking such low-input species provides the least amount of work for a yield. Granted, some small amount of tweaking (pruning or other effort) can dramatically increase yields for some of these crops, but if your primary goal is maximal self-maintenance, you should emphasize these species. See "Forest Gardening's Top 100 Species" (volume 1, appendix 1) for a listing of the best crops and their relative maintenance requirements.

Let Go of Fruit Perfectionism

A large percentage of conventional agriculture's effort and resources goes toward making "perfect" fruit, blemish-free vegetables, and so on. If we simply relax our standards of perfection, we can get by with far less work and far fewer chemicals—organic or conventional. For highly pest- and disease-susceptible crops like apples and peaches, you may want to redefine what "attractive" fruit looks like. Minor cosmetic imperfections generally don't affect flavor or nutrition. They do affect our sense of visual beauty, and perhaps ease, but the latter is counterintuitive: we should probably feel less easy about eating perfect, chemical-doused fruit than scabby unsprayed apples. Many imperfect fruits are fine for fresh eating, and those that aren't usually work great for processing in one form or another, whether for canning, drying, or juicing or in sauces, pies, jams, or jellies. Letting go of the rigidity of perfectionism in any form takes emotional work, but it is worth the sanity it provides in the end.

Group Plants by Disturbance and Maintenance Needs

This is another expression of the idea behind zones of use and keyhole beds. The difference here is that we need also to think about the kinds of disturbance or maintenance our plants need, not just how often they need disturbance or maintenance. Root crops are a clear example; mixing root crops harvested annually with species that need to mature for several years before harvest obviously would not work well. We also need to think about the vigor of plants; planting highly vigorous species together will allow them to grow more compatibly with each other and as a result will probably mean less frequent shearing or cutting back. It will also be easier to cut back the whole patch than to have to choose which plants in a patch to cut and to cut around those that don't need it. Grouping fruit trees that all need the same kaolin clay or dormant oil treatment will make the spraying faster and more efficient than if they are scattered among other species. While this latter advice may contradict our earlier advice about mixing trees to confuse pests, the two are not always mutually exclusive. What this strategy asks of us is that we think through the maintenance and disturbance regimes our crops will require. You may have to choose which strategy to prioritize if there is a conflict.

Scavenge Materials

In every neighborhood, there is a wealth of free materials available that we can creatively use for our own ends. In Eric's town, people put bags of leaves out for collection on the curb—free mulch that someone else has already gathered for you! Local power-line clearing contractors will often happily dump huge loads of fresh wood chips you can use for mulch and mushrooms. Cardboard for sheet mulching is particularly easy to come by. Appliance stores are usually delighted to let you take home huge refrigerator boxes, saving the owners the fees for having them hauled away and giving you the most cardboard with the fewest seams to seal against weeds. Other needs may include the essential and multipurpose five-gallon bucket, thick plastic for smothering mulches, and materials for rhizome barriers. You may also be able to find nice wood for mushroom production when a neighbor takes down some trees or a tree blows over. Your rural neighbors may have goats, pigs, or chickens that you could use in clearing land or for other designed disturbances. The possibilities are almost endless, and the benefits many and varied. This is, however, another instance where you often have to invest time for the sake of saving money.

Beware of Opportunist Species

All plants disperse themselves; otherwise they wouldn't survive. Likewise, all plants must expand to some degree for the same reason. However, we should be wary of plants that are especially good at one or both of these behaviors. While these behaviors may offer benefits when we are attempting to cover large areas of bare soil or to recapture a damaged urban environment for food production, in most forest garden situations they can quickly become a nuisance. Therefore, the "Nuisances" column in the Plant Species Matrix (appendix 1) provides data on dispersive and expansive plants.

Before using these plants, consider their means of expansion or dispersal, and plan accordingly. Always check your species choices against the "Watch List" chart in appendix 4 and the "Nuisances" column in the Plant Species Matrix. Good rhizome barriers can turn a potential expansive nuisance like mint or bamboo into an excellent and "well-behaved" crop. Dispersive plants are somewhat harder to control. Consistent maintenance can prevent problems there, too, though once that maintenance ends, the problem is still there to spread. Though you may think a highly dispersive plant that provides edible fruit is a good idea, not all your neighbors will necessarily agree with you. For instance, goumi (*Eleagnus multiflora*) is a relative of autumn olive and Russian olive, two plants considered invasive by many biologists. Goumi has been developed as a crop in Russia, and good varieties are now available. Whether goumi will be a dispersive nuisance is a question that is impossible to answer definitively at this point: the behavior of its relations appears to indicate dispersiveness, but some dispute these claims because the large areas planted with *Eleagnus* species may have more to do with its spread than the plants' fecundity.

MAXIMUM ECOLOGICAL HEALTH

When we use our design elements to create the ecosystem dynamics shown in figure 1.1, we create a healthy ecosystem. Aldo Leopold defined ecosystem health as "the capacity of the land for self-renewal." Creating these ecosystem dynamics will renew the land, building natural capital in the forms of improved soil fertility and soil structure; increased biodiversity and ecosystem stability and resilience; improved rainfall retention; reduced soil erosion and runoff; and so on. The wider benefits for our neighborhoods are legion: more wildlife habitat, increasingly balanced food webs, and better air and water quality, among others. Growing our own food also has multiple benefits for the planet. Reducing our dependence on destructive industrial agriculture reduces the use of fossil fuels, pesticides, and herbicides, along with their attendant impacts on water and air pollution, biodiversity destruction, and global climate change. It also reduces our contribution to the loss of soil and wild habitat in farming areas. Conventional agriculture is one of the most destructive forces on the planet. Our home-scale efforts have many unseen effects in distant places.

When we ponder what direct strategies we can use to maximize ecosystem health, there are not that many beyond creating the ecosystem dynamics discussed earlier. A healthy ecosystem appears to be an emergent property of forest gardens, arising as a direct result of their intrinsic character. Let us review a few additional strategies anyway, looking at what you might do if maximum ecological health was the focus of your design, rather than a side benefit.

Use as Few Chemicals as Possible

Chemical fertilizers and pesticides are, at least in most cases, a no-no for ecological health. Chemical fertilizers can easily kill many members of the soil food web, they burn organic matter, and large amounts leach away without any beneficial effects except on the fertilizer company's bottom line. Research also indicates that highly available fertilizers push succession backward, aiding and abetting early-succession plants with ruderal strategies. We most likely want to move our gardens away from such plants toward later-succession competitors and stress tolerators. Pesticides have similar problems, often imbalancing the food web, which can then create the "need" for chemical intervention again—and again, and again.

One-time chemical interventions can be useful—if they are part of a long-term strategy that prevents the ecosystem and the gardener from becoming addicted. Still, most chemical agents have inert ingredients of which we must be wary, not to mention the active ingredients themselves. Recent revelations about toxic waste that contains lead, arsenic, cadmium, mercury, and dioxin being sold as home fertilizer—and the US Environmental Protection Agency going along with it—should raise serious alarm bells.[11] Organic controls and fertilizers are much more likely to be free of such agents, but they still represent a dependence on the industrial system, with its attendant environmental and social justice problems. No garden is an island.

Be Wary of Opportunistic Plants

There is widespread and growing concern these days about the spread of what most people call "invasive exotic" species. Our discussions of this topic in volume 1 revealed many unanswered and even rarely asked questions about the whole topic and leave us with concerns about the way the issue is being framed in the pubic discourse. Given that the term *invasive* puts all the responsibility on the species so-called, for example, when there is no way that the process of "invasion" can result only from species characteristics, we have chosen to call these species *opportunists* in this book (see the glossary for a definition). In any case, we do know that some species have inherent characteristics that lend themselves to greater risk of taking major advantage of the opportunities we humans have created for their dispersal and expansion. Given that the ecosystems of which we are part are *all* disturbed by human activity in one way or another, such *dispersive* (spreading rapidly by seed) and *expansive* (spreading vigorously by vegetative growth) plants are worth our wariness. However, this does not necessarily mean we should never plant them or make use of them.

Our recommendation is that we forest gardeners make an effort to use native plants whenever possible to meet our design needs and fill our garden-ecosystem niches. This will help right the imbalances we have created and that opportunist species are exploiting mightily. However, when you need a plant to perform a function or offer a use that natives cannot provide, or an exotic does the job much more effectively, we believe you can then look to nonnatives for your garden. Choose plants that have little evidence of being highly dispersive or expansive whenever possible. Not only will this limit whatever problems the species could cause the local environment, but it will also save you hassle—dispersive and expansive plants can make large amounts of work for us if we want our gardens to be a certain way.

On the other hand, some species that are useful and productive crops are known opportunists (such as five-leaved akebia, *Akebia quinata*, and autumn olive, *Eleagnus umbellata*; see appendix 4's "Watch List") or have relatives that are considered opportunists, such as goumi (*Eleagnus multiflora*). Before using such species, carefully consider their behavior and site tolerances, as well as the possible downsides to their spread in your neighborhood and garden. Species that are expansive but not dispersive and that are growing in conditions near the limits of their moisture tolerance, for instance, present a different kind of situation than those that are expansive, dispersive, and persistent growing under ideal circumstances.

As another example, autumn olive, *Eleagnus umbellata*, is a large, attractive, nitrogen-fixing shrub planted en masse along highways throughout the United States. It produces small fruits that birds love to eat, with seeds that then drop wherever the birds go. Many consider it invasive. Some doubts about this attribution exist since one can imagine that massive plantings in disturbed environments would create strong seed pressure and opportunities for species establishment for many species. Autumn olive has some named selections and varieties that produce tasty, nutritious, and beautiful fruit, reportedly with anticancer properties. If the species is already in our neighborhood in large numbers, it is hard to imagine that planting a few improved varieties could do much harm. If there isn't any autumn olive already nearby we might not want to plant it. In fact, as a general rule, if we live in or near a healthy wild area with few or no opportunists, we should avoid planting anything that might threaten the integrity of the healthy ecosystem. Also, we should do what we can to increase the populations of native plants and other threatened species in every garden, every region, and the world at large.

Build an Ark:
Create Habitat for Threatened Species and Varieties
The debate over native plants and exotic species raises many questions from many angles about their use in the garden and landscape. However, we do know that native plants and their habitats are under assault by human activities. If you want to focus on ecological health in your forest garden, you can "build an ark" for threatened species. You might decide to focus on native or useful species in this regard, or not.

Many medicinal plants, such as the natives goldenseal (*Hydrastis canadensis*) and ginseng (*Panax quinquefolia*), have been severely overharvested in the wild and are now threatened with extinction. Even some nonnative medicinals have this problem and deserve a fair chance to grow. Propagating species such as these in your forest garden accomplishes two things: it prevents you from buying the medicinal, reducing pressure for overharvesting, and it multiplies the plants and their habitat, thereby reducing their chances of extinction. The group United Plant Savers has a complete list of threatened medicinal species and information on how to grow them (see appendix 7).

Besides medicinals, a number of wild species are losing habitat and have good forest garden functions. Many provide beneficial insect habitat—any species in the Asteraceae or Apiaceae, for example. Some of these plants are likely dynamic accumulators or perform other useful functions, too, but we need more research to determine this. Natives are especially of concern, since they used to grow "in these parts," though many nonnatives also face habitat loss or possible extinction in their native habitats. In addition, there are many excellent, obscure, and ancient food plants that deserve preservation and use, such as skirret (*Sium sisarum*) and good King Henry (*Chenopodium bonus-henricus*).

We should think not only about threatened species but also about threatened varieties. Many heirloom apple varieties have been falling by the wayside over the past few decades—and many people have been working to save them. These time-honored varieties offer home gardeners a wide range of interesting flavors and colors and useful characteristics such as disease resistance, storability, or suitability for specific purposes such as drying, pie making, cider, applesauce, and so on.

If building an ark is an interest of yours, then go for it! Our attitude is that *any* threatened species deserves room to grow, regardless of its utility to humans or place of origin. Choose the plants or varieties of interest to you, and start growing them.

We need many amateurs doing this work, for the government and nonprofits cannot do it alone, if they are doing it at all. Home gardeners can do much to help the situation.

Avoid Intervening in Healthy Habitats

We forest gardeners have a special responsibility and challenge. The idea of forest gardening holds many possibilities for application in varied environments. Among these are healthy forests, or habitats that may have experienced little recent human intervention. Yet the ideas and tools of forest gardening can easily tempt us to insert ourselves into situations we would be better off leaving alone.

Before we go plunging headlong into mucking around in healthy habitats of any kind, we need to take stock of both the ecosystem in question and ourselves. What are our motivations? How long are we committed to engaging with this ecosystem? Where do we stand in relation to the ecosystem? Do we see ourselves as part of it or outside of it? If we have a short-term commitment or see ourselves outside the system, then we are likely to be intervening rather than participating. We must understand the ecosystem well and take responsibility for our actions if we are to do justice to the situation.

We urge extreme caution here and recommend focusing your forest-gardening efforts on places needing the healing touch of human hands. We are more likely to mess up relatively healthy landscapes, and the world needs less of that. Working and playing in damaged habitats is more likely to leave the planet in better shape than we found it. In fact, this idea has even been canonized as the principle of site repair by Christopher Alexander and his cohorts (see pattern #5). As Alexander has written, "We must treat every act of building as an opportunity to mend some rent in the existing cloth."[12] Forest gardening is an excellent way to do this, and its potential for healing both the land and ourselves is immense. Thank you for taking up the opportunity to do this valuable work.

SUMMARY

The ideas in this chapter represent the underlying strategic foundations of forest gardening, the invisible structure of the forest-gardening idea. Forest gardening proposes mimicking the structure and function of forest ecosystems as a way of achieving three primary goals or desired conditions. We must configure physical design elements so they generate our desired conditions as a natural outgrowth of specific ecosystem dynamics. Only then will we minimize our labor to run the system. Figure 1.1 summarizes the functions or ecosystem dynamics we must create if we are to achieve this.

It is worth restating the fact that, though the intent here is to design our way out of the typical issues that gardeners face, the gardener's classic strategies will still be necessary to some degree. Pulling weeds is likely to remain a useful technique in forest gardening, as will spraying for insect pests, irrigating, fertilizing, and all the other things gardeners do. We expect, however, that using the strategies discussed in this chapter will significantly reduce the need for such direct interventions. In some cases it may eliminate them, at least for periods of time. If Charlie Headington and Martin Crawford's experiences are any indication, then that last sentence is likely an understatement (see chapter 7 and the case studies in volume 1).

When we step back and look at the strategies proposed in this chapter as a whole (table 1.9), we see that very few of them are direct interventions.

All these indirect approaches to solving problems go against the grain of typical American or Western command-and-control culture. This is part of the paradigm shift we all must go through. If we want to design a system that maintains itself, we have to give up the control our emotional conditioning drives us to take. We have to learn how to let the system do things on its own. We have to learn to design and cultivate conditions and whole systems, not just plants. We have to let go of a monoculture-minded focus on one thing—yield— as an outcome and see the character of the ecosystem as an equally valuable outcome.

Another, and a final, insight from a review of table 1.9 is that many of the strategies are discussed more than once in the chapter. This means that the principle of multiple functions applies to the design process as well as to the forest garden and its design elements. When we apply a strategy for one reason, it supports the creation of the other ecosystem dynamics. This mutually reinforcing structure is part of the magic of both natural ecosystems and forest gardens. Once we get the system going, it begins generating a positive spiral of increased system health, higher yields, and greater self-maintenance as the strategies support each other in creating the ecosystem dynamics. This is great reason for hope, not only for our forest gardens, but for the world. If we can get these lessons in our gardens, then we can learn to apply them at a larger scale for the betterment of the planet and all its inhabitants.

1. Daar, 1993.
2. Crawford, 1998.
3. Crawford, 1998.
4. To learn more, check out Martin Crawford's 1995 series "Fertility in Agroforestry & Forest Gardens" in *Agroforestry News* and Robert Kourik's *Designing and Maintaining Your Edible Landscape Naturally* (1986). Lawrence Hills's *Comfrey: Past, Present, and Future* (1976) is an excellent guide to this "king of dynamic accumulators."
5. Soil Foodweb Inc., www.soilfoodweb.com. Also see www.growingsolutions.com.
6. Nentwig, 1998.
7. Phillips, 1998, page 97.
8. For further reading, we recommend Martin Crawford's *Groundcover Plants* (1997d) and David MacKenzie's *Perennial Groundcovers* (1997).
9. We suggest reading *The Forgotten Pollinators* (Buchman and Nabhan, 1996) to open yourself to the fantastic and overlooked world of pollination ecology.
10. Mollison, 1988; Mollison and Slay, 1994.
11. Williams and Williams, 2002; see also www.safefoodand fertilizer.org.
12. Alexander et al., 1977, page 510.

TABLE 1.9. Summary of design issues and strategies.

Ecosystem Dynamics:

- **Healthy Plants**
  - Right plant, right place: match plant needs to site conditions
  - Create loose, deep, fertile, healthy soil
  - Maximize harmony in polycultures
  - Prepare the ground well before planting
  - Use healthy, resistant stock and plant carefully
  - Use proper plant spacing
  - Design and manage for minimal pest and disease problems

- **Self-Renewing Fertility**
  - Use site analysis and assessment and niche analysis
  - Maximize root penetration of the soil profile
  - Create healthy soil food webs
  - Fertilize the way nature does: from the top down
  - Apply mulch, compost, and amendments appropriately
  - Create lush vegetation and abundant organic matter
  - Emphasize aggrading, midsuccession habitats
  - Diversify the leaf litter to aid nutrient cycling
  - Grow your own mulch
  - Use nitrogen-fixing plants
  - Use plants as nutrient pumps: dynamic accumulators

- **Sustainable Water Demand**
  - Analyze the site for water conditions
  - Improve the soil profile
  - Get water in the ground: increase infiltration
  - Improve soil aggregation
  - Conserve soil water: mulch
  - Match vegetation density to water availability
  - Design zones of water use
  - Choose deep-rooted plants
  - Choose species appropriate to the water regime
  - Irrigate conservatively

- **Minimal Herbivory**
  - Know your herbivores
  - Use large-scale defenses for large organisms
  - Create compositional and structural diversity
  - Use resistant species and varieties
  - Maintain a healthy soil food web
  - Create healthy leaf-surface food webs
  - Grow healthy plants
  - Space plants properly
  - Provide specific habitat elements for beneficial organisms
  - Carefully design your insectary plant guilds
  - Play with aromatic pest confusers
  - Use intermediate disturbance regimes
  - Practice good sanitation
  - Use targeted organic controls, not broad-spectrum interventions

- **Minimal Competition**
  - Know your resources and competitors
  - Manage resource limitations
  - Site preparation: minimize unwanted plants at the start
  - Install rhizome barriers
  - Use proper plant spacing
  - Partition resources in your polycultures
  - Use ground covers
  - Turn unwanted plants into useful crops
  - Fill weed gaps immediately
  - Use the cropping principle
  - Manage problem plants outside the garden
  - Create self-managing successions

- **Directed Succession**
  - Carefully select and design your site
  - Select species prudently
  - Design the plant community well: architecture, guilds, and polycultures
  - Use designed disturbances
  - Plant proactively
  - Manage resources
  - Manage the soil food web
  - Combine strategies

- **Overyielding Polycultures**
  - Design polycultures for greater resource access
  - Design for greater resilience and stability

(continued next page)

(table 1.9, continued)

Desired Conditions:

• High, Diverse Yields
  - Choose a forest garden site with habitat diversity
  - Create an outdoor living room
  - Choose high-yielding species and varieties
  - Choose crops with diverse yields in time, space, and kind
  - Fit yields to niche
  - Create redundant yields

  - Create mostly midsuccession environments
  - Ensure adequate yields by planting extra
  - Create pockets of production
  - Plan for pollination
  - Grow mushrooms

• Maximum Self-Maintenance, Minimum Cost
  - Make mistakes on paper
  - Adapt to or modify site conditions
  - Design your site to minimize work
  - Eliminate or reduce irrigation
  - Propagate your own plants
  - Choose wildling crops

  - Choose self-renewing crops
  - Let go of fruit perfectionism
  - Group plants by disturbance and maintenance needs
  - Scavenge materials
  - Beware of opportunist species

• Maximum Ecological Health
  - Use as few chemicals as possible
  - Be wary of opportunistic plants

  - Build an ark: create habitat for threatened species and varieties
  - Avoid intervening in healthy habitats

❧ 2 ❧

A Forest Garden Pattern Language

> Landscape has all the features of language. It contains the equivalent of words and parts of speech—patterns of shape, structure, material, formation, and function. All landscapes are combinations of these.
>
> —Anne Whiston Spirn, *The Language of Landscape*

> The elements of this language are entities called patterns. Each pattern describes a problem which occurs over and over again in our environment, and then describes the core of the solution to that problem, in such a way that you can use this solution a million times over, without ever doing it the same way twice.
>
> —Christopher Alexander et al., *A Pattern Language*

When we are children, we must learn to speak several new languages. Body language comes first, along with tones of voice and emotions, then spoken words, and finally written ones. Most of us, however, have grown up in a culture so disconnected from nature that the language of landscape did not get passed down to us in the ways that it used to be. Even those of us blessed with the ability to read or compose with the language of landscape may have some new vocabulary to learn in the following pages.

This chapter summarizes and consolidates many of the ideas and directions that arise from the ecological analysis presented in volume 1. It crystallizes many issues and ideas unique to forest garden design. It serves as both a resource for design ideas and inspiration and a springboard into the following "how-to" chapters.

We will do our best to explain the essence of pattern languages here. However, the best explanations exist in two other books, *The Timeless Way of Building*, by Christopher Alexander, and *A Pattern Language*, by Alexander and several other architects and associates. We drew inspiration from these two works in developing our pattern language for forest gardening. Alexander expresses a deep philosophical viewpoint and a specific method of design and construction that we find compelling. Our task is not to explain that viewpoint or those methods here. We simply intend to summarize what a pattern language is and where ours comes from and to present our "pattern-language-in-process" to you. First, though, let us split a few hairs.

In chapter 3 of volume 1 we spoke of patterns *in* and *of* the forest. In this sense, pattern means "a natural or chance configuration," as a naturalist or ecologist might speak of the distribution patterns of plants, habitats, and resources in the landscape. In this context, pattern is a result of natural processes, and it shapes those processes as well. We will use this definition again in this volume's chapter 3 as we discuss deriving meaning from these inherent landscape patterns during site analysis and assessment.

Patterns also lie sleeping within our design goals and objectives. We can investigate our goals to see what elements—what relationships among elements—lie latent in our intentions, waiting to be awakened and expressed. Some of these patterns arise directly from our goals, while others arise from the relationship between the goals and the site. We might call the former "configurations of desire" or "intention patterns," while the latter, called "solution directions," are patterns we might choose to develop in our landscapes.

Designers of different stripes use the word *pattern* in a variety of ways. Bill Mollison of permaculture fame refers to natural patterns, but he also speaks of patterns as geometries that achieve certain purposes in design. The palette of possible design patterns extends far beyond the clumped, regular, and random distributions of plants in a forest. Design pattern results from purpose, as well as process and landscape, as we solve problems and achieve goals by "patterning" the landscape in certain ways.

Mollison's use of the word as a verb indicates the importance he places on pattern understanding in permaculture:

> For the final act of the designer, once components have been assembled, is to make a sensible pattern assembly of the whole. Appropriate patterning in the design process can assist the achievement of sustainable yield. . . . It is this patterning that permits our elements to flow and function in beneficial relationships. The pattern *is* design, and design is the subject of permaculture.[1]

Though we may quibble with his placement of patterning at the end of the design process, we agree that pattern plays a central role in design.

Not all designers see or use the term the way Mollison does. For some, patterns are simply examples, templates, or models that demonstrate how to solve specific design problems. "Patterns can range from solutions to single requirements to complex prototypes that respond to many desires."[2] We can then peruse our catalog of patterns and choose those that fit our goals best. Unfortunately, this approach can lead to "cookie-cutter" projects, as designers impose patterns upon the natural and cultural landscape. We see the sad results of such unthinking and unfeeling design work all around us in the suburban and commercial sprawl of North America and elsewhere today. Experientially, these places are dead zones.

In response to such soulless environments, architect Christopher Alexander and his associates created a new sense of the word *pattern*. They attempted to take the idea of patterns as models back to the point that they become universal archetypes in the sense we will explain below. They did this by studying many cultures, always seeking the furtive, flickering essence of what brings built environments to life. The entire goal of patterns, in their view, is to express "the quality that has no name," to bring health, wholeness, and beauty back to the built environment. They sought the soul behind each pattern and brought together networks of patterns into a "pattern language" with which we can write poetry in the landscape. The pattern is merely a touchstone that helps us find the place inside ourselves that knows how to create environments that live, or places with soul. Using these patterns, building them into our landscapes, encourages health, beauty, and wholeness to live more fully in each of us.

In this chapter, we present patterns for forest garden design in the form of a pattern language. These patterns range in quality from simple examples or models to, we hope, patterns clear and compelling enough to rank as full-fledged archetypes. Before we present our patterns, let us further define patterns and pattern languages in Alexander's sense.

WHAT IS A PATTERN LANGUAGE?

In summary, both ordinary languages and pattern languages are finite combinatory systems which allow us to create an infinite variety of unique combinations, appropriate to different circumstances, at will.

—CHRISTOPHER ALEXANDER ET AL.,
A Pattern Language

A pattern language is like any language: you select from the language which pieces you want to use to achieve your particular ends. Instead of words and phrases, though, this language uses patterns as the elements we combine to speak our minds, compose a poem, create a forest garden. Like any language, a pattern language not only contains elements that you may combine but also, ideally, has rules for how to combine them. However, we're getting a bit ahead of ourselves. Let's first examine what characteristics define a pattern in this context.

PATTERNS

In the context of pattern languages, patterns have a number of different qualities and functions. We discern when a configuration of elements is a pattern by discerning whether it exhibits these qualities or functions. Good patterns live. Patterns in Alexander's sense of the word resolve conflicting forces within the environment and within us. They manifest uniquely each time. Patterns solve problems and they give instructions for how to solve them. They also feel good.

Good Patterns Live

Patterns form living wholes, and they are parts of living wholes: they are like atoms that form molecules, which form cells—yet they are all of these. They respond to their context, and they change it. They support the life and beauty of the worlds within and around them, including us. They are stable, yet they evolve and grow with circumstances and culture. They are eminently practical, yet they are also aesthetic and experiential. Patterns may be expressed by things or by the relationships between things, though they are not the things themselves. They are sets of relationships in time and space that define, facilitate, or change the flows, functions, or spaces where events or the relationships among elements occur.

Consider the ripples in a patch of wind-blown sand. This pattern is a recognizable and constant pattern, because it is a truth about the laws that govern sand and wind. The same can happen in a garden, where the plants, and wind, and animals are perfectly in balance. . . . And just this also happens in patterns from the human realm. Their quality does not depend on purpose, but on their intrinsic stability. . . . In short, saying these patterns are alive is more or less the same as saying they are stable. . . . A pattern lives when it allows its own internal forces to resolve themselves.[3]

Patterns Resolve Conflicting Forces

"As an element in the world, each pattern is a relationship between a certain context, a certain system of forces which occur repeatedly in that context, and a certain spatial configuration which allows these forces to resolve themselves."[4] These conflicting forces have the potential to tear down or weaken the health and life of systems. Resolving these forces well allows their energy to generate harmony, not conflict.

Patterns Manifest Uniquely Each Time

Patterns are like principles, in the sense that they contain such deep truths about a design problem or situation that their expression remains adaptable to circumstance. The forces that patterns resolve tend to recur in certain contexts, like the wind and the sand, but the exact configuration of the forces is never the same. The patterns respond to the unique system of forces in each context, expressing themselves uniquely each time. Because patterns are like principles, a pattern can express itself a thousand times and each expression will be unique. This is one reason why they are "alive."

Patterns Solve Problems and Give Instructions

As Kevin Lynch states in his classic book *Site Planning*, "Few site problems are totally without precedent," and patterns serve as a "direct bridge" to design solutions for these recurring problems.[5] Since a problem, a question, and an intention are three different ways of saying the same thing, we can say that *patterns solve problems, answer questions, and express intentions*. In forest gardening, we seek patterns that create increased opportunities for yield, reduce work, make maintenance easier, and generate system health and self-regulation.

Patterns not only exist in time and space as a set of relationships among things (once created) but also are instructions for how to generate themselves. "As an element of language, a pattern is an instruction, which shows how this spatial configuration can be used, over and over again, to resolve the given system of forces, wherever the context makes it relevant. . . . [A pattern is] both a description of a thing which is alive, and a description of the process which will generate the thing."[6]

Good Patterns Feel Good

We each have inside of us an internal guidance system that tells us when things are good for us, and when they are not. When the forces in and around us remain unresolved, we feel uncomfortable at best, and unhealthy at worst. When we find ourselves in environments where the forces in and around us are resolved and in harmony, we feel alive, whole, and healthy. We can use this internal guidance to help us select and create the patterns that we build around us. When we do so, we are using a pattern language. The best forest-garden patterns make our lives easier and our gardens more productive, and they increase our sense of aliveness and well-being, too.

Good patterns by themselves are not enough, though. Good patterns expressed in the right context in the right way feel good, look good, and work well. What rules govern the grammar of pattern languages? How do we know how to put them together?

PATTERN LANGUAGES

Christopher Alexander argues that pattern languages are inherent in human culture, but that they have largely been an unconscious phenomenon.

In traditional culture, these patterns exist as independent entities within your mind, but it is not necessary for you to recognize them as separate atomic units, nor to know them by name, nor to be able to speak about them. It is no more necessary than it is for you to be able to describe the rules of grammar of the language which you speak. However, in a period where languages are no longer widely shared, when people have been robbed of their intuitions by specialists, when they no longer even know the simplest patterns that were once implicit in their habits, it becomes necessary to make patterns explicit, precisely and scientifically, so that they can be shared in a new way—explicitly, instead of implicitly—and discussed in public.[7]

In the case of a pattern language for forest gardening, we are creating a language for new forms from both old patterns and new ones, natural patterns and human ones. Making these new patterns explicit allows us to share, test, refine, and add to them.

The Structure and Rules of Pattern Languages

A pattern language has the structure of a network. . . . However, when we use the network of a language, we always use it as a sequence, going through the patterns, moving always from the larger patterns to the smaller. . . .

—CHRISTOPHER ALEXANDER ET AL.,
A Pattern Language

Patterns occur at different scales in time and space. These patterns nest within each other by scale and relate to each other through their context and function. In *A Pattern Language*, Alexander and his cohorts talk about towns, buildings, and construction. They present their patterns as a sequence in order of descending scale, grouped by function. We have done the same thing with our forest garden pattern language. The sequence of patterns provides both an index to the patterns and a summary of the language.

When we use the pattern language as a design tool, we choose which patterns to use for the object we are building, whether it be a forest garden, a planting bed, a porch, or a house. "Every site design problem will demand a particular combination of patterns, some unique, others applicable elsewhere."[8] But the language does not contain the full universe of patterns from which we can draw. It only suggests patterns; it only suggests links. We all have pattern languages in our heads and hearts and patterns in our environment to which we can look for inspiration or guidance. The patterns we choose for our project, our project-specific pattern language, will determine the character of that which we create: its functions, its shape, and its look and feel. "For this reason, of course, the task of choosing a language for your project is fundamental."[9]

We have integrated the selection of patterns for your garden design into the design processes detailed in the following chapters, and pattern selection is indeed a fundamental part of the design process. Yet we have created this pattern language not only as a resource for designing your garden. It is also a crystallization of design ideas and "directives" derived from the ecological analysis presented in volume 1. It summarizes patterns that we have seen, have tested, or have deduced from the ecological information we have presented there. It represents problems, questions, and intentions in forest garden design. In this sense, we hope that our pattern language spurs your own creativity, questioning, problem solving, goal setting, and play. These patterns are design shorthands, quick mimics, images to inspire, ploys to play with, grist for the mill. We hope you will find in them ideas that you can use directly or that you can use as springboards to create or discover your own patterns.

Finding and Creating Patterns

Alexander's *A Pattern Language* lays out 253 patterns that result in towns, buildings, and construction that express the aliveness native to humanity and that reconcile the social, cultural, and internal forces that act upon us in our daily lives. A number of those 253 patterns deal with gardens and outdoor spaces (such as those shown in table 2.1); however, most concern aesthetic, social, or experiential aspects of design. None of them deals with anything like forest gardening in practical or ecological detail. So how do we generate patterns for ourselves? First we need to understand the inherent structure of patterns.

TABLE 2.1. Relevant patterns from *A Pattern Language*. When we refer to these patterns in our pattern language, they are designated with "APL" before the pattern number. *All patterns listed here are from Christopher Alexander et al., 1977,* A Pattern Language, *courtesy Oxford University Press.*

APL	1	Independent Regions
APL	3	City Country Fingers
APL	98	Circulation Realms
APL	104	Site Repair
APL	105	South Facing Outdoors
APL	106	Positive Outdoor Space
APL	111	Half-Hidden Garden
APL	114	Hierarchy of Open Space
APL	120	Paths and Goals
APL	121	Path Shape
APL	125	Stair Seats
APL	126	Something Roughly in the Middle
APL	127	Intimacy Gradient
APL	134	Zen View
APL	163	Outdoor Room
APL	168	Connection to the Earth
APL	169	Terraced Slope
APL	170	Fruit Trees
APL	171	Tree Places
APL	172	Garden Growing Wild
APL	173	Garden Wall
APL	174	Trellised Walk
APL	175	Greenhouse
APL	176	Garden Seat
APL	177	Vegetable Garden
APL	178	Compost
APL	241	Seat Spots
APL	243	Sitting Wall
APL	245	Raised Flowers
APL	246	Climbing Plants
APL	247	Paving with Cracks between the Stones
APL	248	Soft Tile and Brick

Alexander describes the specific, consistent structure of patterns in *The Timeless Way of Building*:

> Each pattern is a three-part rule, which expresses a relationship between a certain context, a problem, and a solution. Patterns can exist at all scales. And a pattern may deal with almost any kind of forces.[10]

We must be able to draw a pattern simply, and it must have a communicable name, so we can share it with others and discuss it in an explicit manner. Probably the biggest challenge we face is being able to state the pattern so that it is flexible, yet specific; loose, but narrow in its definition; precise, but variable in its application. Our task is to define a fluid field of relationships that is applicable to specific contexts and a specific problem or set of forces.

We can derive patterns from nature. We can derive patterns by observing what works well, or poorly, in our built environments, other people's gardens, or books and magazines. We can deduce them from goal-setting and problem-solving processes or from our sense of the forces that we need to resolve in a particular situation. Some of our patterns arose through the process of thinking about links from patterns we had already generated.

Alexander describes in *The Timeless Way of Building* the process of abstracting a pattern from an old Danish house in a way that may be helpful; the fundamentals follow. If you find yourself in a specific garden or other place that "works," that feels alive to you, that you want to use as a basis for abstracting a pattern, you must do three things. First, define the physical feature(s) of the place that seem worth abstracting. Base this judgment on your own observation of the space, its features, and what makes it so special. What is the essence of what makes the place work so well? Second, define the problem the pattern solves or the field of forces that this pattern resolves. Finally, define the range of contexts where this problem or field of forces exists, and where this pattern might therefore be useful.[11]

A preexisting pattern language is a good guide to what a pattern is and how to define one for yourself. Ultimately, though, your inner senses will be the best guide to this work. Pay attention to your inner voice as you go through the process, for when you experience an "aha" moment you will have found something worthwhile. The key points to remember are that the best patterns generate a sense of aliveness, and that *patterns solve problems*.

A FOREST GARDEN PATTERN LANGUAGE

What follows represents only the beginning of developing a pattern language for forest garden design. We hope and expect this language to evolve as people play, practice, and learn. We do not pretend or intend this language to be exhaustive or complete at this time but present what we feel are some essential patterns for forest gardens. In addition, we present a few ideas intended to shake up the usual patterns that prevail in our current culture's pattern language, though we have not tested many of these ideas for practicality. This language is not prescriptive or proscriptive, merely suggestive or strongly suggestive. Take what you like and leave the rest.

Some of the patterns we present derive from other references, including Bill Mollison and Christopher Alexander, as noted. Some patterns here are similar to those found elsewhere but serve a slightly different purpose or represent "convergent evolution" of ideas that come from observation and deduction. You may find other potentially useful patterns scattered throughout Mollison's *Permaculture: A Practical Guide for a Sustainable Future* and other books, though they do not follow the useful structure set out by Christopher Alexander.

The pattern language below begins at landscape scale and proceeds downward through site, garden, and element scales (table 2.2). We further separate patterns *of* the garden from patterns *in* the garden. At each scale, a number of different kinds of pat-

TABLE 2.2. Summary of the edible-forest-garden pattern language

Patterns at the Landscape Scale

Fit the forest garden site into the larger context so that it helps create these larger patterns, and these larger patterns support each forest garden site.

1 Productive Landscape Mosaic	2 Islands and Corridors

Patterns at the Site Scale

Fit the forest garden into the living, breathing, working landscape of the site so that it generates the greatest ease, health, and diversity.

3 Patterns That Arise	6 Outdoor Living Rooms
4 Habitat Diversity	7 Zones and Sectors
5 Site Repair	8 Zones of Water Use

Patterns of the Garden

Define the garden's fundamental structure using a more or less formal geometry, …

9 Dynamic Patches	10 Mandalas

… or by patterning the forest garden so that it mimics natural ecosystem architecture and composition, …

11 Temporary Shrublands	15 Mature-Forest Forest Gardens
12 Minithickets	16 Gaps and Clearings
13 Oldfield Mosaics	17 Forest Gardens in the Woods
14 Woodland Gardens	18 Shifting-Mosaic Forest Gardens

… or by applying forest-gardening principles to the cultural landscape, maintaining or mimicking aspects of that landscape, but transforming it at its essence.

19 Copses	21 Microforest Garden
20 Forest Edges	22 Suburban Landscape Mimic

Patterns *in* the Garden

Define the landform and circulation patterns before defining vegetation patterns.

23 Pits and Mounds	26 Paths and Nodes
24 Definite Pathways	27 Rootlike Path Geometries
25 Strategic Materials Depot	28 Keyhole Beds
	29 Pathway Width

Determine your establishment, reestablishment, and management patterns.

30 Patch Disturbance and Regeneration	33 Relay Plantings
31 Instant Successions	34 Disturbance and Maintenance Regimes
32 Nuclei That Merge	

Define the overall structural goals that help you select the organisms, species, and varieties you want.

35 Diversity of Life Forms	40 Layers of Harvest
36 Extraordinary Edibles Everywhere	41 Staggered Harvests, Clustered Harvests
37 Gourmet Decomposers	42 Nectaries Always Flowering
38 Three-Layer Minimum	43 Native Species
39 Lumpy Texture	

Define species placement patterns within the larger patterns defining the structure of the garden as a whole.

44 Polyculture Patches	49 Ground-Cover Carpets
45 Pockets of Production	50 Drifts, Clumps, and Scatters
46 Flower-Petal Beds	51 Functional Plants Throughout
47 Cluster Planting	52 Expansive Plant Containers
48 Cross-Pollination Clusters	

Garden Elements

Embellish and enrich the garden you have created with specific elements that bring higher diversity and functionality.

53 Living Soil	56 Mulch
54 Habitat Elements	57 Dead Wood
55 Fruitful Footpaths	

terns present themselves, each dealing with different issues or topics. These patterns appear in relevant groupings, each group leading off with a statement that tells you how to use the patterns in the group or how they function in design. Some patterns solve practical problems. Others simply present natural architectural patterns that we might want to mimic. Thematic patterns present design concerns to remember in the midst of all the other issues with which garden designers must contend. Finally, some deal with primarily aesthetic or experiential aspects of garden design.

Obviously, these categories overlap. However, we have attempted to focus our attention here on patterns that fit within the first three categories: practical problem solvers, natural architectural patterns, and thematic design concerns. We have generally avoided including patterns that fit primarily in the aesthetic category (though some in table 2.1's list of relevant patterns from *A Pattern Language* do). The exceptions to this rule include a few aesthetic patterns that help us create forest gardens as *living spaces*, rather than as icons of ecological righteousness held at arm's length. Only as living, lived-in spaces can we participate in our forest gardens as we must if we are to reintegrate ourselves into the landscape.

Each pattern below has a number denoting its place in the pattern language, which helps us refer to the patterns and discuss how they relate to each other. We begin discussion of each pattern with a statement of the context for the pattern, that is, where and when this pattern is likely to apply. This is followed by a boldface statement of the problem or question the pattern addresses, the intention behind it, or an observation that forms the seed of the pattern. We then describe the pattern and most often provide a graphic depiction of the pattern to help you visualize its physical expression.

PATTERNS AT THE LANDSCAPE SCALE

Fit the forest garden site into the larger context so that it helps create these larger patterns, and these larger patterns support each forest garden site.

Forest gardens and related ecosystems play a critical role in defining the character of their region, community, and landscape. The arrangement of these habitats in the landscape at large increases or reduces the viability of the habitats themselves.

1. Productive Landscape Mosaic

This pattern helps create greater regional self-sufficiency by bringing food production closer to home and diversifying its nature and character.

> **When sterile, unproductive, and monocultural landscapes dominate the built environment, local ecosystems and culture suffer.**

When food production occurs far away, alienation from the land, poor health, and instability threaten the community's integrity and sustainability.

> **Generate mosaics of productive and beautiful habitat throughout and around cities, towns, and suburbs by creating a full range of healthy and useful ecosystems on public and private lands (figure 2.1).**

These include restored wild habitats, perennial polycultures, and forest gardens of all kinds and sizes, as well as conventional farmlands and gardens. The nature, size, and shape of the elements in the mosaic, and the relationships between them, should balance habitat and life-form diversity with habitat and life-form redundancy.

2. Islands and Corridors

Within a *Productive Landscape Mosaic* (#1), the patterning of habitats is a critical element of biological stability. When patchy mosaics (contiguous areas of different habitats) aren't possible, another pattern is necessary to maintain biological viability.

> **When forest gardens exist as isolated "biological islands," especially small ones, they have difficulty maintaining plant, insect, and animal diversity, as well as ecosystem health and stability.**

Ecologists have noted that isolated chunks of habitat behave like islands in the middle of the ocean. Smaller islands tend to have lower biodiversity, stability, and resilience and higher rates of extinction, while larger islands have the opposite. Islands that exist in chains or near large land masses have even higher diversity, stability, and resilience and even less extinction. The size of the habitats and their connections to other similar habitats allow genetic diversity within plant and animal popula-

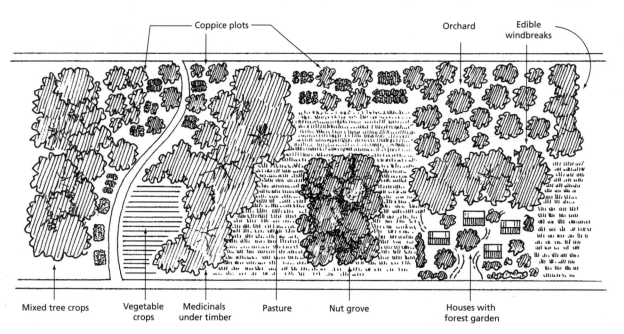

FIGURE 2.1. Productive landscape mosaic.

tions to remain high and allow individuals to move from one habitat to another as conditions change over time. If wild habitat patches amid "developed" urban and suburban habitats act similarly, then the same will be true of our forest gardens.

Whenever possible, link your forest garden to other biologically rich habitats by locating your garden near them or by providing corridors that connect to them (figure 2.2).

If you cannot do either of these, then make your forest garden as large, biologically rich, and fertile as you can to attract and hold beneficial species and cross-pollinators. If many rich habitats surround you, then interconnect them to create a network of healthy habitats. You can create the connections with simple unmown strips of vegetation or by planting good wildlife trees, shrubs, and herbs in the corridor.

Ecologists have distinguished two kinds of corridors: line corridors and strip corridors.[12] Line corridors are so narrow that they do not have an interior habitat distinct from

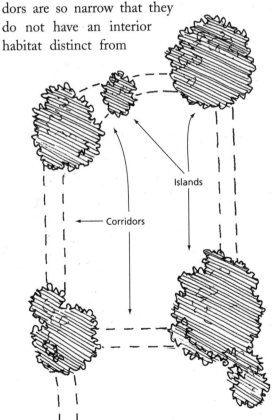

FIGURE 2.2. Islands and corridors.

that of their edges. The interiors of the wider strip corridors, though, are different from their edges. Measurements of herbaceous species abundance have indicated that the critical width that distinguishes strip corridors from line corridors is about 40 feet (12 m). Use strip corridors if you want to facilitate the movement of shade-tolerant plants or woodland creatures.

PATTERNS AT THE SITE SCALE

Fit the forest garden into the living, breathing, working landscape of the site so that it generates the greatest ease, health, and diversity.

Where to locate your forest garden on your site is a critical choice. The following group of patterns helps us make that decision.

3. Patterns That Arise

This pattern is different from the other patterns in this language because it does not describe a specific configuration of elements that solves a problem. Rather, it describes a process of design that helps us understand the patterns inherent in a specific site that we are designing. It therefore applies to every design project.

Every site expresses unique patterns of soils, microclimates, habitats, and other qualities and forces that we need to understand and work with in a conscious way.

We must understand the interdependent factors of any landscape as a whole system if we are to interact with that landscape with integrity and wisdom. Keen, comprehensive, and detailed observation of the site is the only way to achieve the kind of understanding we are talking about. Within the unique patterns specific to any site we will find the exact form of our goals in healthy relationship to the land. If we ignore these patterns, we end up imposing ourselves on and intervening in the landscape, not participating with it in a process of unfolding.

This pattern is a specific process of design, not a particular configuration of physical elements. Design your

forest garden in the context of clear self-understanding concerning what you seek to create, and design in concert with the landscape patterns that rise to consciousness through holistic understanding of that landscape.

The first part of this directive leads us to articulate our goals clearly and consciously. The second part urges us to undertake a process we call site analysis and assessment. These two streams of information converge to help us see and feel the patterns that arise from our interaction with the land. Please see chapters 3 and 4 for more information on how to design, but keep in mind always that the patterns of our designs arise from the inherent qualities of ourselves and our land.

4. Habitat Diversity

Various kinds of diversity within a site or a landscape help generate healthy and stable systems. The fundamental base of diversity is habitat diversity.

Monotonous habitats offer limited opportunities for diverse, self-sustaining species assemblies.

When your site has only one soil type, one level of soil moisture and fertility, one kind of disturbance regime, and an unvarying vegetation structure, the limited niches available allow only a certain set of plants and animals to live there. This can limit the ability of the ecosystem to maintain itself because it cannot create a diverse social struc-

ture. Conversely, diverse habitats within a site lend themselves to diverse gardens, species, and crops and a higher probability of healthy ecosystem structure.

Create diverse habitats in and around your forest garden by selecting a site with varied topography, wetness, soil types, microclimates, and vegetation structure, or by modifying the site to create such variation (figure 2.3).

Then take advantage of this diversity using diverse species and organisms to create diverse architecture in the varied habitats.

5. Site Repair

This is the only one of all the patterns from Alexander's *A Pattern Language* relevant to forest gardeners that we feel is important enough to repeat here. Please take heed.

Some pieces of land contain extremely damaged or sick ecosystems, while some have extremely beautiful places. Some contain both of these extremes. However, every piece of land contains areas that are relatively more beautiful and healthy and areas that are less so. In which of these places should we put our gardening efforts?

People often build or garden in the most beautiful spot on their land, leaving the rest of the site to its own devices.

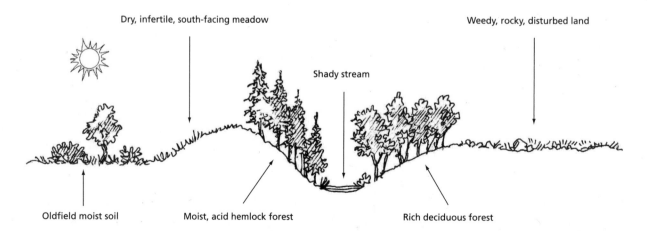

Dry, infertile, south-facing meadow

Weedy, rocky, disturbed land

Shady stream

Oldfield moist soil   Moist, acid hemlock forest   Rich deciduous forest

FIGURE 2.3. Habitat diversity.

How many times have we seen people tear apart a beautiful piece of land to create something less beautiful than what was originally there? Often in these cases, a nearby piece of land lies already damaged and in need of healing. Unfortunately, as Alexander states, "when the construction begins on the parts of the land that are already healthy, innumerable beauties are wiped out with every act of building."[13] Meanwhile, the places that truly need our attention get neglected. The result is that every piece of land gets worse instead of better. When we think about where to build our forest gardens we should consider that they can be forces for healing, but they may actually create a net loss of beauty and health if we aren't careful.

> **Leave the most beautiful, healthy, precious, and comfortable places on your site alone. Build and garden in those areas that need the most repair and attention.**

"We must treat every act of building [or gardening] as an opportunity to mend some rent in the existing cloth."[14] Placing our forest gardens in damaged areas will increase the liveliness and beauty of the planet as we bring human care and attention to bear. Putting forest gardens in landscapes that are already healthy is more likely to mess things up than to add value.

6. Outdoor Living Rooms

With an understanding of the site, based on the patterns above, we now add to the mix a consideration of the level of interaction we intend to have with our forest garden. The kind of forest garden you create will be determined, in large part, by how much time you intend to spend there, how much maintenance you can and want to give it, and what kind of water resources you can offer it. The following patterns help you make those choices and arrange the other uses of the site in appropriate fashion.

> **Those forest gardens that function best are lived in most.**

Some parts of every plot of land lie in areas integral to the functioning and activity of the site. Other areas may as well not exist for their human inhabitants. We have seen forest gardens plunked down in the middle of nowhere, disconnected from the life and activities of a site. Inevitably, these gardens go downhill, or at least require much conscious effort to maintain. Worse yet, their gardeners miss the whole point of forest gardening: to become participants in the ecosystem in a very real and deep way. If you aren't spending time in your forest garden, you aren't getting to know it intimately, learning its rhythms and character, picking up the subtle cues that will teach and guide you.

> **Design your forest garden so that it looks, acts, and feels like an outdoor living room.**

Put it close by, near the door or along a main path, where you can easily see, care for, live in, and interact with it on a frequent, if not daily, basis (figure 2.4). Place the garden so you can see into it from key windows inside the house: Dave loves being able to watch garden goings-on as he washes dishes, for example, or to look out the window as he ponders what to make for dinner. Make the garden easy to get to from the kitchen. Position it so main

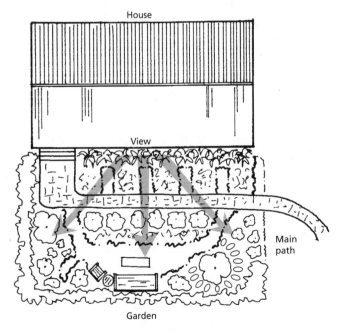

FIGURE 2.4. Outdoor living rooms.

outdoor pathways go through it, so you walk into and through the garden as a matter of course in your day: on the way to and from the car, the compost pile, the chicken yard, the outhouse, or wherever.

Make the garden enjoyable to spend time in. Design it so that at least some of your daily activities—reading, eating, talking to friends and family, cooking—can comfortably and naturally occur there, or in places that allow you to watch your forest garden and its animal inhabitants. Make the garden work as an outdoor social space for the family and groups of friends, and as a place for private time alone or in twos, or for children to do homework with fresh, healthy, homegrown food at their fingertips. Think about how to make the location work in different seasons, creating microclimates for people to enjoy in every part of the day and year, wet or dry, warm or cold, sunny or not. The more you live in the garden, the more it will live in you, both as food transformed into your body and as a psychic and social space.

7. Zones and Sectors

This pattern, along with *Site Repair* (#5) and *Outdoor Living Rooms* (#6), guides the layout of a site and the location of your forest garden. Bill Mollison and David Holmgren have developed this basic idea well, and we recommend you read their various treatments of it.[15]

> **Plants or animals that require frequent care or yield frequently often don't get the attention they need because they are "out of sight, out of mind," far from the eyes and hands of those responsible for them. In addition, we need to deal appropriately with forces and factors that radiate into or out from the site.**

When we place our garden out in "the back forty," we lose touch with it, we miss opportunities to receive the garden's benefits, and things don't get managed as well as they should. Yet only those elements that require daily care need to be close at hand, whereas crops that yield once a year, for example, can be sited farther away. Zoning the landscape by frequency of access saves labor and increases yields with little or no investment except thoughtful attention.

In addition, each site has forces that radiate from the center outward or toward the center from the outside, such as sun, winds, views, water, access, and the like. We need to manage these "radial energies" for maximal energy conservation and site productivity: we need to mitigate cold winds and summer sun and facilitate the energies of cooling summer breezes, winter sun, desirable views, and so on.

> **Organize your site and locate your forest garden based on the patterns of circulation, land-use intensity, frequency of use, and "radial energies" of the landscape.**

Conceptually, these zones of land-use intensity are a series of concentric circles that range from intensively managed and used to wild, with different management strategies for each (figure 2.5 and tables 2.3 and 2.4). In reality, however, the pattern of zones skews to orient around the paths and nodes of the site and to relate to views from inside the house (figure 2.6). The radial energies in question vary from site to site, but many are similar for every site, such as sun and wind sectors.

How one uses zones and sectors may be made clear from the following example. Let's say you

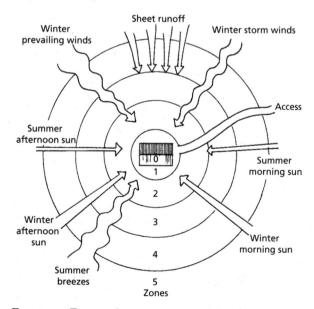

FIGURE 2.5. Zones and sectors, conceptual diagram.

TABLE 2.3. Permaculture zones of use: how various design factors change from zone to zone as distance from the core of a homestead or farm increases. Zone 5 is wild and unmanaged. *Adapted from Mollison, 1990.*

Factor or Strategy	Zone 1	Zone 2	Zone 3	Zone 4
Main objects of design	House climate, domestic sufficiency	Small domestic stock and orchard	Main crop, animal forage, stored products	Wild-harvesting, forage, pasture, forestry
Plant strategies	Complete sheet mulch, fenced areas, nursery production, high-value transplants	Patch and spot mulch, tree guards, cluster planting, high-value transplants, layering	Soil conditioning, green manure, seeding, low-value transplants, selected wildlings	Soil conditioning only, selected wildlings, guided natural regeneration
Pruning and trees	Very intensive; cup, espalier, trellis; fully dwarfing or semi-dwarfing stock, multi-grafted trees	Pyramid and built trellis; semidwarf and full-size trees, grafted and selected stock; intensively managed; short-rotation coppice	Selected seedlings for later grafts; managed by browse, fire, other extensive techniques; medium-rotation coppice	Natural regeneration, thinned to selected individuals, biological enrichment, long-rotation coppice
Water provision	Rainwater tanks, wells, pipes, high-pressure systems, wind pumps, intensive irrigation networks, filtration	Earth tanks, wells, low-pressure systems, solar pumps, some pipes, extensive irrigation	Runoff infiltration, ditches, swales, gravity pressure only, ponds for water storage and fire control, flood irrigation	Storage in dams, rivers, or soils, gravity pressure only, flood irrigation or none
Structures	House, attached greenhouse, home storage, food storage, integration	Detached greenhouse, barn, poultry, small-stock housing	Feed store, field shelters, windbreaks	Field shelter grown as hedgerow, woodlots, windbreaks

TABLE 2.4. Forest-garden zones of use: suggested changes in forest garden design characteristics as distance from the core of a homestead increases. Many smaller sites will not have enough room for zones 3 and 4. Zone 5 is wild, unmanaged landscape.

Factor or Strategy	Zone 1	Zone 2	Zone 3	Zone 4
Intensity of use	Highly intensive	Intensive	Extensive	Semi-wild
Site preparation	Complete modification, e.g., double digging, complete sheet mulch	Major modification, e.g., complete or patch sheet mulch, pits and mounds	Adapt and improve, e.g., cover crops, spread manure or compost, spot mulch	Totally adaptive, e.g., intersperse hardy species with existing vegetation
Sample patch themes	All-edibles polyculture; shoots 'n greens guild; tea-plant patch; feastable flowers	Best crop polyculture; pockets of production; berry-nut scrub; perennial three sisters; all-edible underwood	Nut and fruit groves; mulch-plant patches; fertilizing herbal fallow; ground-cover glade	Feral crop jungle; nectary meadow; wild edible woodland; expansive species unleashed
Species selection	High-care, frequent-yield, high-value foods, medicinals, culinaries; rare or delicate species (disease- or pest-prone)	Grafted trees, quality perennial vegetables, trellised species, highly multifunctional plants	Larger nut and fruit trees, mass-planted functional herbs, expansive plants, ground covers	Seedlings, tough native and naturalized species, forage crops, fertility plants, other ecosystem support plants
Disturbance and management	Constant intensive disturbance and management; daily monitoring; ongoing mulching, irrigation, fertilizing, pest management	Frequent intensive disturbance and management; periodic irrigation, fertilizing, pest management; early-phase mulching	Frequent broadscale, patch, and spot disturbance and management; resilient species; minimal irrigation, pest management, and fertilizing	Occasional/infrequent broadscale, patch, and spot disturbance

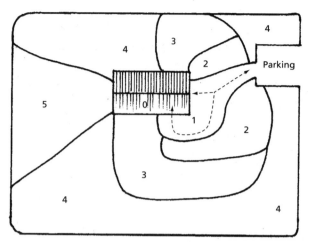

FIGURE 2.6. In actual reality, zones are not concentric but skew to relate to paths, doors, and views from inside the house (zone 0).

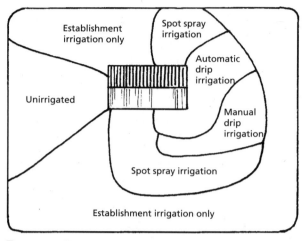

FIGURE 2.7. Zones of water use.

wanted to figure out the best location to place Korean nut pines on your site. These evergreen trees yield in the fall and need little care other than harvesting. Therefore, they can go in a zone farther from the house, say zone 4. As evergreens, they would not be beneficial to the design in the sun sector, but they would perform multiple functions if placed in the cold-wind sector. Another plant, such as the Mediterranean perennial herb rosemary, is one that you might use on a daily or weekly basis, that needs a hot microclimate for best performance in summer, and that doesn't like moisture or wind in the winter. You would therefore most likely place it in the afternoon-sun sector in zone 1 or perhaps 2.

8. Zones of Water Use

While zoning land-use intensity we must consider the availability of water.

> **Water is frequently the most limiting nutrient in horticulture, and it can be rather expensive.**

Irrigation can increase yields, stabilize them from year to year, and prevent serious losses in drought years. Whether a plant requires or benefits from irrigation is a critical factor in plant selection and placement.

> **Pattern your gardens, plants, and management based on the availability of water.**

Locate your most-irrigated zones where they can get the most attention and use (figure 2.7). Concentrate your water-needy plants in areas where water is most easily and cheaply available. Zones of water use might include areas with an automatic irrigation system, areas watered by hand on an as-needed basis, spots receiving roof runoff or where land runoff concentrates, and completely unirrigated zones. Your design, plant selection, and management should reflect these patterns.

Patterns *of* the Garden

With the location of the forest garden based on the patterns above, we can determine the form and structure of the garden as a whole or, if it is a large garden, of its various habitats. You can define the fundamental structure of the garden by using a more or less formal geometry, by mimicking natural ecosystem architecture and composition, or by applying forest-gardening principles to the cultural landscape—maintaining or mimicking aspects of that landscape, but transforming it at its essence. We have grouped the patterns that follow into these three categories.

Define the garden's fundamental structure using a more or less formal geometry …

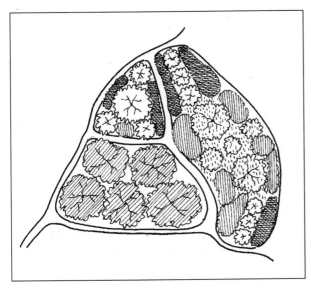

FIGURE 2.8. Dynamic patches.

Natural ecosystems usually do not exhibit formal geometries but consist of irregular and overlapping patches as their basic, integrating structural pattern. We can choose irregular patches to structure our forest gardens, or we can structure patches into one of many possible geometric patterns (we discuss only one here). Whether you use a geometric pattern or not, patches are a fundamental structural component of forests and of forest gardens.

9. Dynamic Patches

This pattern looks at patches in space as the basis for patch dynamics (for more information on patch dynamics, see volume 1, chapter 6). *Patch Disturbance and Regeneration* (#30) and *Disturbance and Maintenance Regimes* (#34) discuss the dynamics of patches in time.

What pattern can give the forest garden some structure and organization, especially if we are not going to use a formal geometry?

Patch-dynamics theorists base their research on the observation that the fundamental organizational units of any ecosystem, at many different scales, are patches. Patches derive from the underlying geology and soil patterns, varied light distribution, patterns of water flow and collection,

microclimates, and other environmental factors. Patches also develop from the random or non-random influences of disturbances and the subsequent successional processes, including plant dispersal mechanisms. When we gain awareness of the factors contributing to the patchiness of the natural world, we can then read the patches to understand the different influences in the environment. When we can read these influences, we can design in concert with those with which we must, and we can influence the rest effectively.

Structure and manage the garden as a set of overlapping, interconnected, and dynamic patches, each with its own influences, conditions, disturbance regime, and successional process (figure 2.8). These patches, taken together, create the habitat of the garden.

Before you do anything to start your forest garden, do a site analysis to recognize the patches that already exist on your site. Then, patiently and consciously develop your scheme for patterning the patches within your forest garden to create the habitat or habitats you desire based on the geometries you want to use in the garden. These may be irregular geometries, found geometries, natural ecosystem architectures, functional patterns of use and access, or geometries you imprint on the landscape. Consider the patches at every relevant design scale, from landscape to site to garden to growing-bed scale. Pattern the patches at each scale so that you create the kind of habitat you want, whether it is a dense canopy with an open understory or an old-field mosaic with many rooms of differing character.

Also, recognize that whatever patch structure you envision, design, and implement will change over time as the system undergoes succession; the character of the garden will change, and the plants will move on their own to meet their needs. Attempting to control the shifting patch patterns will result in more work, and you will have to choose between putting in the effort to maintain the patch structure you want or "going with the flow" and adapting to the changing patterns that the forest garden develops on its own.

10. Mandalas

"Man•da•la \ *n* [Sanskrit *mandala* circle] 1: a Hindu or Buddhist graphic symbol of the universe; *specif*: a circle enclosing a square with a deity on each side 2: a graphic and often symbolic pattern usually in the form of a circle divided into four separate sections or bearing a multiple projection of an image."[16] Mandalas are not the only geometric pattern you can use in forest gardening. We have derived this pattern from Mollison's permaculture books and present it to you because it seems particularly relevant.

> **Most geometries used by humans in Western culture bear little relation to natural forces and forms, often waste space, and express little meaning to most observers. Yet in some settings, wild or patchy gardens may not be socially sustainable or appropriate.**

The rectangular geometries used in Western culture for almost everything have their benefits. However, in gardens they are odd and out of place, conflicting with almost every natural pattern imaginable. Rectilinear gardens maximize the path area per unit of production area, thereby maximizing maintenance and reducing yield. This works well in large-scale commercial and industrial production, but not so well at a smaller scale, where it may push us toward fossil-fuel dependency as we find machines easier to apply to garden problems than a reasonable, creative, and informed design process. In addition, plants, animals, water, and landscape just don't operate in squares; they work in circles, spirals, branches, triangles, and other, often more irregular forms.

Since wild, free-for-all gardens may not be appropriate for some settings in our culture or may be undesirable to some gardeners, we need to give functional structure, geometric beauty, and perhaps even meaning to forest gardens in these situations. It would be nice to do this while minimizing the amount of space the garden takes up while at the same time maximizing its productive area.

> **Create mandalic patterns that express beauty, function, and meaning in small geometric spaces.**

The compact, often circular form of mandalas lends itself to functionally integrated uses. The circular form minimizes the surface area exposed to invasion from outside rhizomatous weeds and creates a sense of enclosure. The right pathway geometry inside maximizes growing-bed access, while minimizing path area. Compact and linked beds simplify irrigation and fertilization schemes. The geometry can respond to the forces and patterns of plants and their roots, microclimate factors, and so on. Use the geometry of the garden to express meanings of all kinds—spiritual, secular, or aesthetic in nature. We present one example in figures 2.9 and 2.10.

…Or define the garden's fundamental structure by patterning the forest garden so that it mimics natural ecosystem architecture and composition …

Most of the following "ecosystem mimic" patterns derive from the architecture of natural plant communities. A few derive from human habitats. They are not necessarily patterns in the typical sense of solutions to problems or resolutions of conflicting forces. They are patterns of architecture found in natural and cultural landscapes.

All patterns in nature are patterns of succession at any given moment, and the following patterns derive from various stages of succession. Consequently, few of these ecosystem mimics exist as stable elements of the landscape, even theoretically. This is especially true of *Temporary Shrublands* (#11), *Oldfield Mosaics* (#13), *Woodland Gardens* (#14), and *Gaps and Clearings* (#16). We can link some of these patterns into a successional sequence leading to *Mature-Forest Forest Gardens* (#15) or generating *Shifting-Mosaic Forest Gardens* (#18). By doing so we hope to mimic natural successions and guide them in the direction we want, to compress the time needed for succession to occur, and to replace the less useful natural species with selected useful species that fill similar niches. However, you may also maintain any of these as the desired end stage of succession; the right *Disturbance and Maintenance Regimes* (#34) can maintain any of these habitats indefinitely. The other patterns below, or at least their natural models, may stabilize for an extended time under the right conditions even without human-induced disturbance.

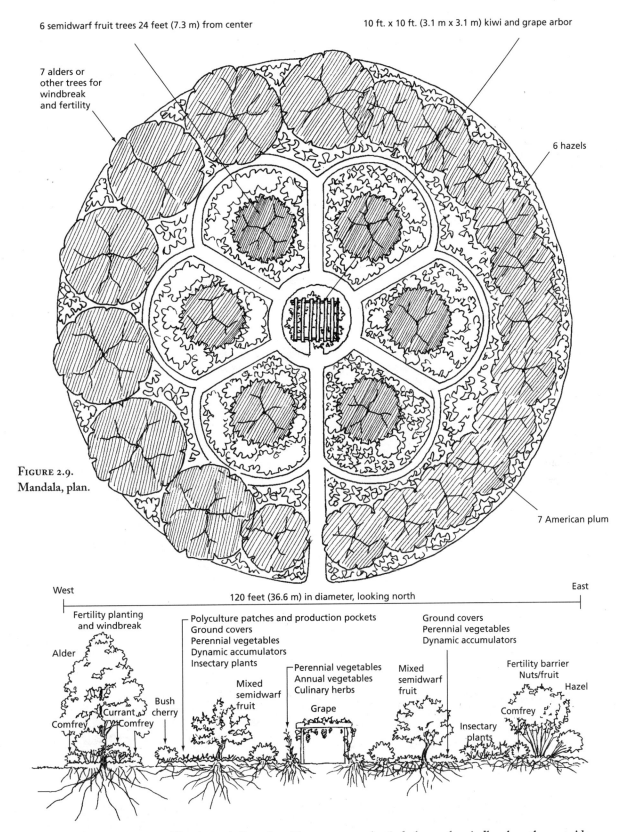

6 semidwarf fruit trees 24 feet (7.3 m) from center

10 ft. x 10 ft. (3.1 m x 3.1 m) kiwi and grape arbor

7 alders or
other trees for
windbreak
and fertility

6 hazels

FIGURE 2.9.
Mandala, plan.

7 American plum

West

East

120 feet (36.6 m) in diameter, looking north

Fertility planting
and windbreak

Polyculture patches and production pockets
Ground covers
Perennial vegetables
Dynamic accumulators
Insectary plants

Ground covers
Perennial vegetables
Dynamic accumulators

Alder

Perennial vegetables
Annual vegetables
Culinary herbs

Mixed
semidwarf
fruit

Fertility barrier
Nuts/fruit

Hazel

Mixed
semidwarf
fruit

Grape

Comfrey

Comfrey

Bush
cherry

Currant

Comfrey

Insectary
plants

FIGURE 2.10. Mandala, section. This design is for a site with strong westerly winds, hence the windbreak on the west side.

Not all the models for these patterns lend themselves to easy or particularly useful mimicry. We present them anyway, because we do not know what creative ideas you, our readers, may develop by bouncing off them. Other models from your local ecosystems may offer additional inspiration for your mimicry efforts. We first consider early and midsuccession habitats.

11. *Temporary Shrublands*

A shrubland consists of a habitat dominated by shrubs, but with less than complete shrub canopy closure (40 to 99 percent shrub-layer coverage, and less than 50 percent tree coverage). This pattern is most appropriate in midsuccession forest gardens.

Shrublands can be very productive habitats, yet they are unstable unless maintained by frequent disturbances.

Sun-loving shrubs thrive in midsuccession, especially after they have shaped the soil food web to their liking and have dominated light resources. Though the shrubs usually grow in clumps, at this stage the canopy may remain open enough that the shrubs do not compete heavily with each other, as they will if they reach the density of a thicket. Primary production is therefore at a peak, so the shrubs grow rapidly and can produce large quantities of fruit, nuts, or biomass. It would be effective to be able to use this stage of succession to generate useful products, and perhaps to maintain the stage for an extended time. Yet there is still a niche for taller woodies to exploit if they can gain a foothold, and this most often makes shrublands temporary unless we maintain them.

Essentially, the shrubland stage represents a race between the shrubs and the trees, as they each attempt to gain long-term control over the site. Meanwhile, the herb layer still contains remnant sun-loving grasses and forbs. Hence, typical shrub "orchards" (e.g., hazelnuts, juneberries, raspberries) allow light and room for herb- and ground-layer crops but require disturbance if they are not to succeed to woodland or forest. The disturbance we usually use is mowing, which also maintains the soil food web at the wrong fungal-bacterial balance for woody plants. How can we use shrubland habitats with minimal work while providing optimal soil habitat for the roots?

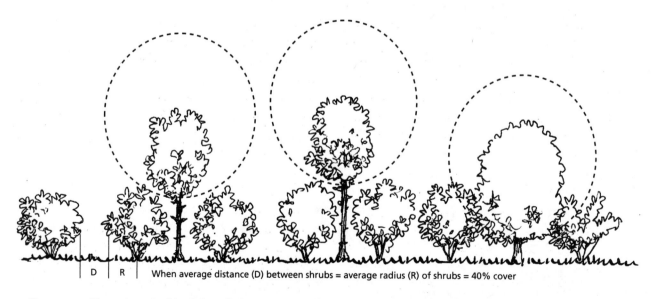

D | R | When average distance (D) between shrubs = average radius (R) of shrubs = 40% cover

FIGURE 2.11. Temporary shrublands have little tree cover and 40 to 99 percent shrub cover. Eventually trees grow to dominate, however. Closely spaced shrubs help "prune" trees growing in their midst to a more upright form.

Design shrublands as a temporary stage of succession, and control the direction of that succession by planting the succeeding trees, either with the shrubs or later on (figure 2.11).

Create open-canopied shrub orchards by planting shrub crops at distances equal to or less than their mature canopy radius, with useful ground-cover polycultures underneath. Interplant trees, or leave room for them, so they will eventually take over and shade out the shrub crops after a time. When you plant fruit or nut trees into the shrubland, you can use the shrub crops to help "prune" the trees to a central leader form by planting the shrubs closer together and forcing the trees planted in their midst to grow upward to get the most light.

12. Minithickets

Thickets are stands of shrubs with dense, 100 percent canopy coverage and interlocking shrub crowns. These are midsuccession habitats, but if designed well they should be able to hold back further succession with minimal maintenance.

If shrubs grow to completely dominate the canopy they can prevent trees from invading, thereby stopping succession indefinitely. However, we then cannot get access to harvest crops.

When shrub crowns grow to interlock, they shut off most of the light reaching the soil surface. This can prevent the germination and successful establishment of trees that might otherwise shade out the shrubs and lead to further tree invasion. Researchers have found that thickets can resist tree colonization for decades without any maintenance whatsoever after the initial work of establishment. Unless, of course, a disturbance makes sites available.

Yet the problem with thickets is that they are, well, thickets—impenetrable by humans as well as trees. How can we use the thicket as a model but still get access? Often during oldfield succession we find shrubs growing in a mound as they spread by root suckers or stolons from a central point (see figure 2.38, page 111). The center of the mound is higher because it is older, and the mound spreads down and

out from there. These minithickets often grow in patterns that would work for crop harvesting by hand, but are still dense enough to prevent tree invasion. We could use forms like these for low-maintenance production of nuts or fruits whether the shrubs we plant spread vegetatively or not.

Plant dense masses of shrubs that will crowd out trees and prevent succession, but plant them in star- or flower-shaped clusters that allow reasonable access.

Shrub spacing should be slightly less than full crown diameter at maturity (figure 2.12). Multistemmed shrubs that keep sending up new shoots from the root crown, such as hazel, will tend to last longer and resist tree invasion better than other forms. Placing multiple minithickets near each other can form a megathicket. Keep paths narrow to minimize light to the thicket floor.

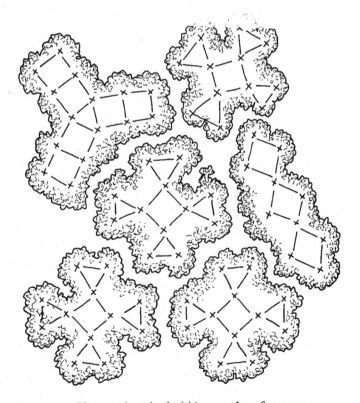

FIGURE 2.12. You can plant shrubs (x) in a number of patterns to create a minithicket, but try to provide access to each plant from at least two sides and keep the plant-to-plant distance (lines) consistent. As shown here, you can mass minithickets with narrow paths in between them to form a megathicket.

13. *Oldfield Mosaics*

Oldfield mosaics will be part of many forest gardens started from scratch. See "Oldfield Succession" on pages 88–90 in volume 1 and "Fungal–Bacterial Balance" on page 233 in volume 1 for a fuller discussion and illustrations.

> **Early- to midsuccession mosaics of trees, shrubs, and herbs constitute one of the most productive and beautiful habitats to mimic, but a multitude of forces can make this stage of succession difficult for woody plants.**

Heavy competition by early-succession grasses and forbs can prevent sites and niches from being available to invading woody plants. The bacteria-dominated soil food web of early succession reduces woody plant performance. Midsuccession shrubs overcome these factors by growing in clumps or mounds that spread by root suckers or stolons into the grassy territory and shade out their competitors. Pioneer trees often do the same, or they have simply adapted to bacterial soils, though they pull the soils into fungal dominance. Some trees invade

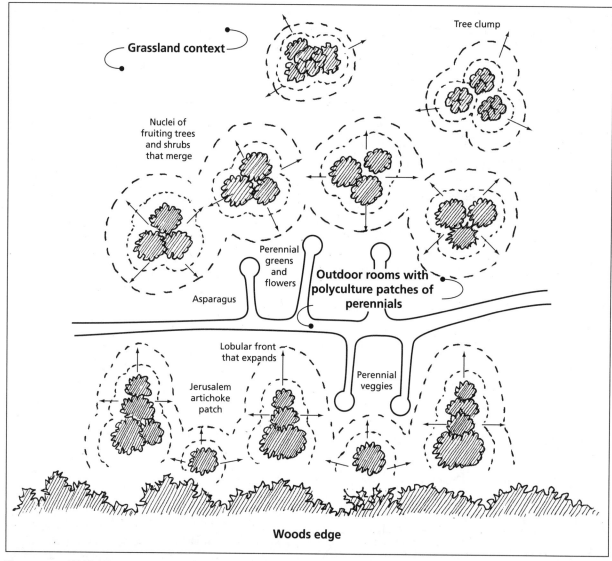

FIGURE 2.13. Oldfield mosaics consist of mixtures of shrubs and trees expanding into a context usually consisting of grasses and perennial herbs. The shrubs and trees often form natural "outdoor rooms" of great diversity and beauty.

through holes that develop as the shrub mounds age or that result from disturbances. The result of these forces and strategies is a complex mosaic of meadow, shrubs, and trees varying widely in density and overall pattern. In early stages, clumps of shrubs and trees scatter amid the meadow plants. These nuclei grow and converge to form masses of shrubs and trees with patches of remnant meadow.

Plant woody plants into grassy, bacteria-dominated soils in clumps, rather than as isolated individuals, to create a mosaic of annual and perennial herb patches with clumps or masses of shrubs and pioneer trees.

The coverage of the various habitats and species can vary widely, and the patterning of the system will vary with these various densities. The shrubs and trees may move into the meadow as a linear or lobular front, or scattered clumps may grow and merge. Arrange the shrub and tree clumps or masses to create sun traps and outdoor "rooms" with specific microclimates for particular crops or human uses (figure 2.13). Choosing stoloniferous, root-suckering, or running plants will allow you to layer the plants into adjacent areas or simply let them expand there on their own (table 2.5).

14. Woodland Gardens

Now we get closer to the realm of true forest gardening! Though woodlands contain trees sufficient

TABLE 2.5. Selected running and thicket-forming plants for oldfield mosaics and nuclei that merge; gc = ground cover, da = dynamic accumulator.

Latin Name	Common Name	Habit	Uses & Functions
Trees			
Asimina triloba	pawpaw	suckering	edible fruit, native
Diospyros virginiana	American persimmon	suckering	edible fruit, native
Prunus americana	American plum	suckering	edible fruit, native
Robinia pseudoacacia	black locust	suckering	nitrogen fixer, native
Toona sinensis	fragrant spring tree	suckering	edible leaves
Zizyphus jujuba	jujube	suckering	edible fruit
Shrubs and Bamboos			
Amelanchier stolonifera	running juneberry	running thicket former	edible fruit, native
Gaultheria shallon	salal	running thicket former	edible fruit
Hippophae rhamnoides	sea buckthorn	clumping thicket former	nitrogen fixer, edible fruit
Phyllostachys spp.	sweetshoot bamboos	running thicket former	edible shoots
Prunus angustifolia var. *watsonii*	sandhill plum	running thicket former	edible fruit, native
Robinia viscosa	clammy locust	running thicket former	nitrogen fixer, native
Rubus spp.	raspberry, blackberry	running thicket former	edible fruit, some native
Zanthoxylum piperitum	Japanese pepper tree	clumping thicket former	culinary spice plant
Herbaceous Plants			
Achillea millefolium	yarrow	running herb	specialist nectary, gc, da
Dennstaedtia punctilobula	hay-scented fern	running herb	gc, native
Glycyrrhiza spp.	licorice	running herb	nitrogen fixer, culinary/tea
Helianthus tuberosus	Jerusalem artichoke	running herb	edible roots, native
Mentha spp.	mints	running herb	generalist nectary, gc, culinary/tea
Passiflora incarnata	maypop	running herbaceous vine	edible fruit, native
Urtica dioica	stinging nettle	running herb	da, edible leaves

to create only 40 to 99 percent canopy coverage, trees still define the character of these mid- to late-succession ecosystems. Woodland gardens are likely to be the most common category of forest garden, but the possible variations within the theme are tremendous.

Woodlands offer the opportunity for the most varied, interesting, complex, and productive mosaics of trees, shrubs, and herbs.

Woodlands can exhibit a broad array of attributes. Widely spaced trees offer varied microclimates for understory shrub, herb, and vine crops. Denser tree cover focuses production on the tree crops, with less energy for the understory. Trees may be regularly spaced as in an orchard, more randomly scattered as individuals, or clumped with spaces between the clumps that keep total tree cover well below the density of a true forest (figure 2.14a–d). Each of these patterns of tree cover, within the broad framework of "woodland," creates a different environment with varied texture and possible species composition. We have much room to play in creating consistent broadscale habitats or highly varied mosaics where different areas serve different purposes and grow different crops.

Create a woodland garden by designing for overall tree canopy coverage of between 40 and 99 percent.

At 40 percent tree coverage, the average distance between tree crowns equals the average radius of each crown. Yet in the densest woodlands tree crowns do not interlock as they do in true forests.

Provide for multiple layers of crop vegetation in and around the trees in the varied light and shade conditions they create. Try to keep the woods unevenly aged. Vary the distances between trees to create *Drifts, Clumps, and Scatters* (#50) if you want more diversity of microhabitat. Keep spacing consistent if you want a consistent crop-planting pattern and more consistent conditions throughout your woodland garden.

15. Mature-Forest Forest Gardens

This pattern is similar to *Forest Gardens in the Woods* (#17), except that here we create the forest from

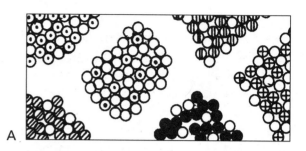

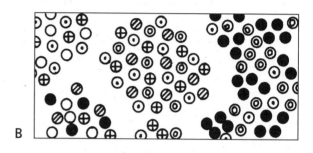

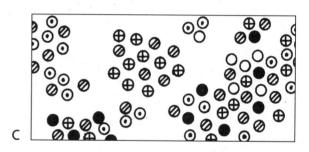

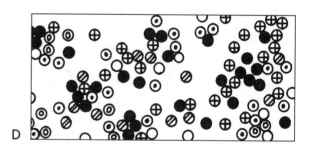

FIGURE 2.14A–D. Different patterns of tree distribution for woodland gardens encourage structural diversity. (a) Tight clumps of one or a few species with consistent spacing within and between clumps whose total cover value exceeds 40 percent. (b) Clumps of varied sizes and species mixtures, but with consistent spacing between trees. (c) Varied clump size and spacing between clumps. (d) Varied clump size, spacing between trees, and spacing between clumps. Similar patterns can be used for shrubs and herbs. *Adapted from Rodwell and Patterson, 1995.*

scratch, while there we plant into existing woods. This pattern relates to late-succession ecosystems and usually requires larger land areas than most suburban house lots have available.

Technically speaking, a climax forest consists of a canopy dominated by shade-tolerant species that replace themselves generation after generation. Theoretically, self-replacement generates landscape-scale stability and dynamic equilibrium; however, true climax forests are extremely rare. In the literal sense, we probably won't be able to create a climax forest garden, because the requirements for self-replacement, stability, and dynamic equilibrium are so challenging to meet. We may, however, create mature forests with deep shade using crop trees and useful understory plants.

Mature forest, by definition, creates a dense canopy with shaded layers below it. How can we make best use of such an architecture? What implications does this structure have for forest gardening, particularly at a small scale?

Trees create a forest when canopy coverage reaches 100 percent and their crowns interlock. As a result, the canopy intercepts the vast majority of the sunlight, making it the most productive layer in the community. However, the depth of shade in the understory depends on two things: the density of the tree crowns and the size and shape of the forest stand. Trees with thin crowns permit more light to the lower layers, while dense crowns block more. In addition, the density of the upper layers within the understory will influence the amount of light in the lower understory layers. Some British researchers who experimented with creating new woodlands believe that the minimum clump size necessary to create conditions suitable for shade-tolerant woodland understory plants is around 16,000 square feet (0.15 hectares/0.37 acres, a square about 130 feet/ 39 m per side or a circle 140 feet/42 m in diameter).[17] Stand shape and context are important, too: small, linear stands surrounded by open land permit more light to enter the stand from the sides than do large, round stands in the same context. The sea-

sonality of light levels on the ground plays a significant role in mature forest ecology as well.

We must, therefore, place very productive species within the canopy to make the most of the situation. The crops we grow in the lower layers must be those adapted to the levels of shade the architecture produces (see "With All These Layers ..." in volume 1, page 76). Many of the summer green herbs appropriate to shady conditions will be slow-growing edibles or medicinals from which we harvest large leaves, roots, or other storage organs. We can gather a large quantity of food and energy from edible mushroom production in shaded environments. We can gain highest yields from the ground and herb layers of shady forests using some of the many useful and delicious ephemerals that grow rapidly in spring before trees leaf out (such as ramps and spring beauties).

Finally, we must remember that a mature forest remains stable for long periods only at a landscape scale, and only if the stand has an uneven age structure. At small scale, the forest cycles through disturbance and succession, at least from gap dynamics if not from fires, storms, and the like. If you have a large site, design your mature-forest forest garden to contain diversely aged trees to create sustained and stable yields. If you have a small site, plan on moving through cycles of succession every number of years, depending on the life span of the canopy trees.

Create a mature-forest forest garden by designing for 100 percent tree-canopy coverage using very productive and useful tree species (fruits or nuts) of different ages (figure 2.15).

Select useful understory shrubs and herbs appropriate to the light conditions created by the canopy tree crown densities and the size and shape of the stand. Make sure to plant spring ephemerals to take advantage of early-season sunlight and yields.

16. Gaps and Clearings

The distinction between gaps, clearings, and glades is based mainly on the ratio of the diameter of the

FIGURE 2.15. Mature-forest forest gardens consist of mixed-age crop trees with 100 percnt canopy cover along with vines and shade-tolerant understory crops.

opening to the height of the surrounding trees. In glades, the largest of the three forest openings, the central space separates from the forest edge as a different microclimate and habitat. For this reason, in glades you have two spaces that you can treat somewhat separately, one as an open space and the other according to *Forest Edges* (#20). This pattern deals with smaller openings in forests or forest gardens where such a strong separation of edge and center does not occur, and the opening remains more or less a unitary whole. It applies in mature existing or created woods where you want a bit of early- or mid-succession habitat.

How can we use created or existing gaps and clearings for forest gardening?

Gaps and clearings form in mature forests even when they are unaffected by storms, fires, and other disturbances. You may either have access to or want to create a gap or clearing within existing woods for forest gardening (but see *Site Repair*, #5), or you may want to create a gap or clearing within a mature forest garden.

The light and microclimate conditions within gaps and clearings vary depending on many factors. The size, shape, and orientation of the opening determine the light, shade, temperature, moisture,

and fertility differences between the gap or clearing and its forest context.

With a diameter-to-height ratio (D:H) less than or equal to 2 (figure 2.16a and b), gaps are small enough that only shade-tolerant species can take advantage of them; the available soil nutrients do not increase much if at all compared to the forest; and the outgrowth of surrounding trees is a major factor influencing the longevity of the gap. In forests, it usually takes several gap-episode growth spurts for shade-tolerant trees to get into the canopy from sapling stages.

Clearings are larger (D:H from 2 to 4; figure 2.16c) and sunnier than gaps and tend to exhibit increased nutrient availability as well as longer-lasting soil moisture increases. Upgrowth from the floor takes on more importance in regenerating clearings than it does in gaps, offering us more opportunities to influence the successional process. Gaps tend to favor shade-tolerant species, while clearings can allow space and time for shade-intolerant trees to mature into the canopy.

In existing gaps or clearings, adapt your planting schemes to the conditions within the opening, especially light conditions. Create gaps or clearings of desired sizes and shapes in forests or gardens to create habitats for specific useful species.

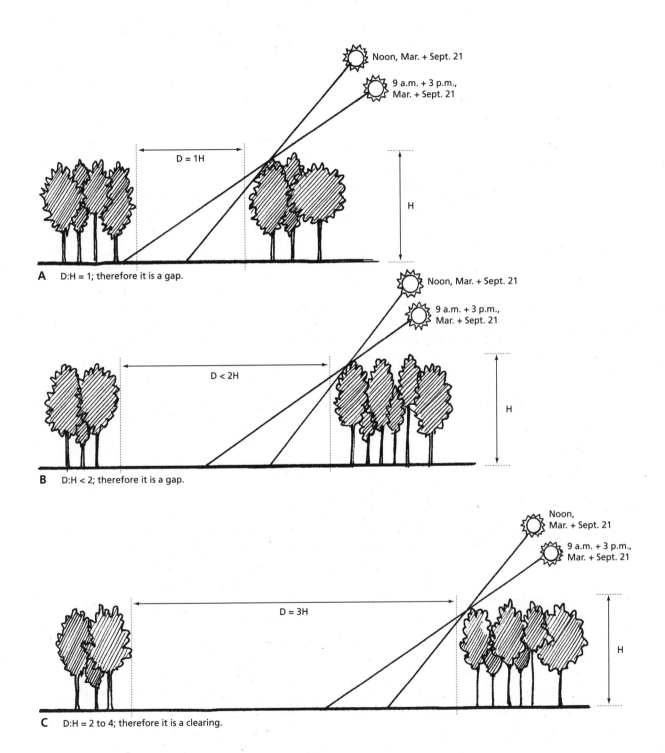

FIGURE 2.16A–C. Gaps and clearings: These sections show diameter-to-height (D:H) ratios with the sun at its locations for 40° north latitude at noon, 9 a.m., and 3 p.m. on March 21 and September 21. Gaps (a and b) have a D:H ≤ 2, while clearings (c) have a D:H of 2–4; gaps favor species that are more shade-tolerant than do clearings.

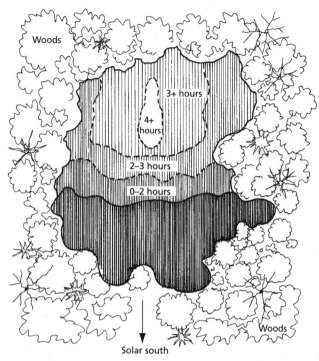

FIGURE 2.17. These shade patterns, mapped for a hypothetical gap, are typical for gaps. The poleward center of the gap gets the most sun, with less to the east and west and even less in the sunward direction. The edge nearest the sun gets no direct sunlight at any time during the growing season.

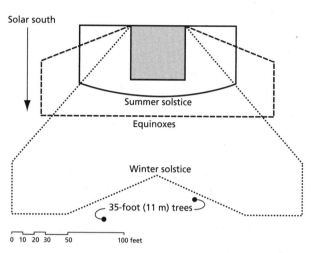

FIGURE 2.18. If you want to get full sun for six to eight hours on a given area, the shapes of the clearings you would need would be similar to these. This sketch assumes flat ground at 42° north latitude, a 50-foot-square (15 m) sunny zone (gray), and surrounding trees or other objects 35 feet (11 m) tall. The solid line shows the required clearing for eight hours of full sun on the summer solstice, when the sun is at its highest. The dashed-line area, if cleared, would offer eight hours of sun on the equinoxes. The dotted line shows the required area for six hours of full sun on the winter solstice.

Use gaps (D:H ≤ 2) for planting one or two shade-tolerant trees that you eventually want to grow into the canopy (such as pawpaws). You may need to maintain the gap or create new ones nearby to offer your chosen trees the opportunity to reach the canopy sooner. In the meantime, you may be able to get moderate production of fruiting shade- or partial-shade-tolerant plants such as raspberries, gooseberries, or currants, or healthy production from various shade-tolerant or partial-shade-tolerant edible and medicinal herbs such as some of the perennial onions (*Allium* spp.), spring cress (*Cardamine bulbosa*), or good King Henry (*Chenopodium bonus-henricus*). The poleward edge of a gap gets the most sun, but usually not more than four hours in late fall when trees most need the sun for fruit ripening (figures 2.16 and 2.17). Since gaps are relatively shady, you are less likely to have vigorous weed problems from ruderal or competitor-strategist plants. Significant coppice production can also occur in gaps, though less so than in clearings.

Clearings are more useful for more species, as long as you map out the patterns of shade and light within them or design your created clearing for maximum sun (figure 2.18). Many useful gap species can grow in the shadier parts of clearings, while the sunny side offers potential for many useful sun-loving plants. The edge of a clearing away from the sun tends to be the sunniest. The edges closer to the sun tend to get the most shade. The shape of the opening required for full sun varies depending on many factors, including latitude, height of surrounding objects, slope of the land, when you want the sun, and so on. However, linear openings oriented east–west tend to offer more sun in the center of the spaces, especially as latitude increases and the sun moves toward the equinoxes. For winter sunlight, the optimal opening shape tends toward a bent linear space or "solar banana," since the sun lies low and rises and sets closer to the equator.

17. Forest Gardens in the Woods

This pattern differs from *Mature-Forest Forest Gardens* (#15) because here we plant into existing woods, while there we create the woods as a forest garden. Use this pattern when you want to forest-garden with minimal impact on existing forest.

How can we forest-garden in existing woods without major disturbance to the forest?

Sometimes we have a situation where we don't want to rock the ecological boat too much. Given the damage forests have sustained since Columbus landed on this continent, we'd do well to leave our remaining woods alone. Yet we may want to garden in these woods, to increase the number and quantity of useful products we can derive from at least some of the forests we have left, and perhaps in the process to improve the ecological balance of our forest remnants.

Assess the structure of the existing woods to see what community niches may be missing, then fill in with useful plants, preferably native species (figure 2.19).

The fundamental essence of this pattern involves deep observation of the existing ecosystem so that our interventions or influences do not do any damage but, instead, enhance the system. This is very site-specific work and requires conscious, conscientious, and careful effort. Numerous useful shade-tolerant herbs thrive under closed or slightly open canopies, and these are often the most lacking in existing forest remnants due to historical land uses in the eastern United States. In patches with

FIGURE 2.19. Forest garden in the woods.

1 Giant Solomon's seal	4 Maidenhair fern	7 Pawpaw (young)	10 Sweet cicely
2 Ginseng	5 Oregon grape	8 Ramps	11 Violets
3 Jostaberry	6 Ostrich fern	9 Redbud	12 Wild ginger

more light, woodland shrubs such as gooseberries and currants can bear at least some fruit.

18. *Shifting-Mosaic Forest Gardens*

This pattern derives from the shifting-mosaic idea, the successor to classic climax in forest-succession theory (see volume 1, chapter 6). Though we know of no one who has planned for the long-term successional rotation of woody crops in this way, except perhaps the Native American agroforesters of centuries ago, it has some interesting possibilities. In any case, it expresses our view that *forest gardening includes all stages of succession at once in a diverse mosaic of interacting patches.* The pattern applies over long time scales and probably over large areas if the shifting mosaic will include true woodland or forest habitats in the mix.

> **How can we integrate all stages of succession into one forest garden such that we allow the process of succession to proceed yet still gain the benefits of mimicking the true nature of forest ecosystems?**

Recent research strongly indicates that climax in the classic sense does not occur even when a forest remains undisturbed for long periods. Instead, undisturbed forests may reach what researchers call a shifting-mosaic steady state: at a small scale, any given site within a forest cycles through succession to maturity followed by self-induced disturbance (gap dynamics), which leads to a renewed secondary succession. Meanwhile, at a landscape scale, the forest remains in a relative steady state because the proportions of the forest at the various stages of succession remain basically stable: 60 to 75 percent of the woods in middle succession, 20 to 30 percent in very mature stages, and the remaining 5 to 10 percent at early succession. This shifting-mosaic forest is much like a rotational arrangement of garden plots or farm fields: the location of any given crop (or stage of succession) shifts from year to year, but the total area covered by a given crop (or successional stage) remains the same. It allows species from all stages of succession to persist within forests in perpetuity.

Shifting mosaics can offer some of the same values that conventional crop rotations do: diversified vegetation architecture and composition, decreased disease and insect pest problems, improved soil fertility, and consistent, stable yields of crops from different habitats. The main challenges arise from the fact that shifting mosaics involve woody plants with longer and more varied life spans than conventional crops. The timescale of the woody-plant rotations (50 to 200 years) results in lopsided proportions of the various successional stages within the rotation compared to the even proportions of vegetable-crop rotations. However, the fact that shifting mosaics contain species from all stages of succession offers us the opportunity to create diverse habitats with varied species providing products from all stages of succession, all the time. That shifting mosaics tend to contain a majority of sites at mid- to late succession, where productivity is highest, is also a benefit.

> **Create a shifting mosaic of productive habitat patches at all successional stages that continually grow to maturity and then cycle back to the beginning of secondary succession.**

The shifting-mosaic forest garden can include all the previous ecosystem mimic patterns: *Temporary Shrublands* (#11), *Minithickets* (#12), *Oldfield Mosaics* (#13), *Woodland Gardens* (#14), *Mature-Forest Forest Gardens* (#15), *Gaps and Clearings* (#16), and *Forest Gardens in the Woods* (#17). In fact, it should always include many of these different patterns, with their locations shifting over time as succession proceeds and cycles back to the beginning (figures 2.20 and 2.21).

If we are trying to create a true rotation in the agricultural sense, then the proportions of the various stages of succession within the shifting mosaic would ideally remain constant, even though the specific site or patch where each stage is located would change over time. However, the different life spans of forest garden crops mean that the proportions of each successional stage in a forest garden will probably vary from those quoted above for natural forests. Those proportions also may not suit our

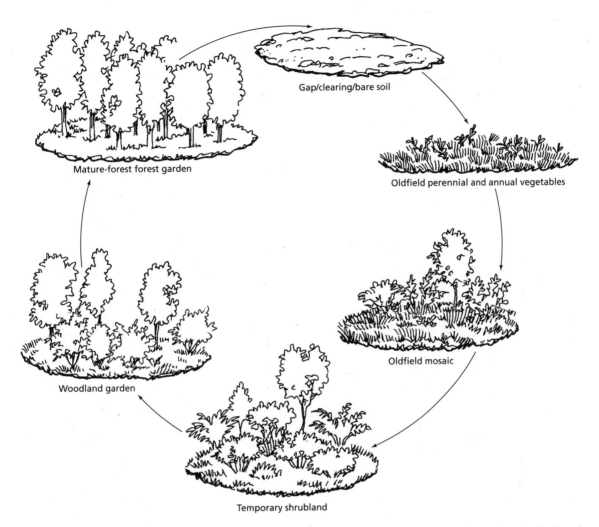

Gap/clearing/bare soil

Mature-forest forest garden

Oldfield perennial and annual vegetables

Oldfield mosaic

Woodland garden

Temporary shrubland

FIGURE 2.20. A possible cyclic successional pattern for one patch in a forest garden. Such a successional round can be the foundation of a shifting-mosaic forest garden.

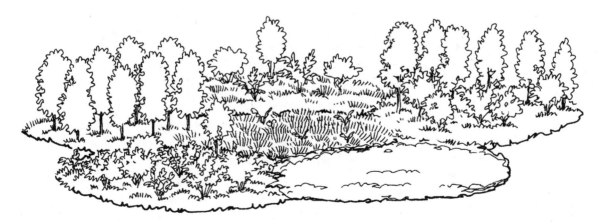

FIGURE 2.21. A shifting-mosaic forest garden combines all stages of a successional cycle like that shown in figure 2.21 at once, with different patches at different stages, all cycling through in concert.

food preferences and needs, at least for a few generations, until we fully develop a wide range of high-quality perennial food plants for every stage of succession, particularly starch and protein crops, as well as vegetables. Unlike the hypothetical shifting-mosaic steady state of forest ecosystems, therefore, this pattern does not require stable proportions of each stage. Shifting-mosaic forest gardens do not have to achieve equilibrium. This means that shifting-mosaic forest gardens can or will act more like the nonequilibrium systems of patch dynamics, and the proportions of each stage within the garden will vary over time, perhaps significantly. However, wooded or forested patches should probably dominate if we are to call it a forest garden!

The central idea here is that of a mosaic of patches, all going through cycles of succession, followed by disturbance to restart the cycle in a given patch. If you have a mosaic of patches—say a raspberry patch, a hazel thicket, a patch of woodland fruit trees with a useful understory, and a dense mixed-nut orchard—but you maintain each patch at a given stage of succession rather than allowing them to change and succeed to the next stage, that isn't a shifting mosaic.

To design a shifting mosaic, we need to have a grasp on the life spans of the various dominant crops that will govern the character of each stage of succession (see "Estimated Useful Life Spans of Selected Woody Species" in appendix 2). The problem is that this information is not very solid, partly because it varies so much depending on the conditions a given plant experiences during its life. However, we do know that nut trees tend to live much longer than fruit trees, and that fruit trees vary in their life spans, depending especially on the rootstock they grow upon. This makes sense because nut trees tend to be stress tolerators of late succession, while fruit trees tend to be competitive stress tolerators of middle succession.

Therefore, a general scheme for a patch within a shifting mosaic might follow a pattern like this:

- field (annual vegetables, weed control, soil preparation and improvement), to
- oldfield (sun-loving perennial vegetables and herbs, fertility plants), to
- shrubland and thicket (coppice, small fruits, shrub nuts, fertility plants) or oldfield mosaic (all previous stages), to
- woodland (fruit trees and coppice, plus understory herbs and vegetables, some fertility plants), to
- forest (nut trees and timber, with shade-tolerant understory edibles and medicinals), then
- back to some stage near the beginning, depending on where you want to take it and how much disturbance you want to give it.

Clearly, we can decide to intervene at the overmature phase of any of these successional stages to disturb and regenerate. In this way, we could take the patch back to any of the earlier stages or speed the patch to a later successional stage. But since the time spans of each stage will vary, all we can do is develop a scenario of what we might like to have happen (or maybe more than one scenario) and then act based on what makes sense given our scenarios and what is happening at any given time.

To encompass all the stages outlined above could require a minimum of as much as a half acre (2,000 sq. m) of reasonably fertile, deep-soiled land in a dense planting, though you might decrease this minimum with careful selection of only self-fruitful varieties of everything. It would also require numerous cycles through the early stages during one cycle of the nut-tree rotation. However, we can use these early stages not only to grow crops but also to slowly build soil fertility and improve soil depth and structure by those slow, natural means that forests are famous for. You can shorten the rotation period for first-round tree crops if they aren't performing as well as you might like by bringing along replacements in other patches before the old ones give out. You can shift the locations of stone and pome fruits from generation to generation to avoid specific replant disease and balance out nutrient demands on the soil. And you can adapt the scenario as you go over the years—you'll have plenty of time to decide what to do next!

…Or define the garden's fundamental structure by applying forest-gardening principles to the cultural landscape, maintaining or mimicking aspects of that landscape, but transforming it at its essence.

19. Copses

A copse is similar to a thicket architecturally, except the dominant plants are coppiced trees or shrubs cut on a rotation of nine to twenty-five years depending on species and use. Thickets can stop succession from proceeding unless disturbed, while copses stop succeeding because they *are* disturbed. The size of these permanent midsuccession habitats varies widely depending on what you intend to harvest from them. For more information on tools and craft products from coppice systems, see Raymond Tabor's 1994 book *Traditional Woodland Crafts.* Appendix 2 lists coppicing species.

How can we achieve high sustained yields of fuel, structural material, biomass, and animals, vegetables, and medicinals in a wooded ecosystem?

Gardening and other activities demand small-diameter wood for poles, posts, trellises, and other garden furniture. Forest gardening also demands large quantities of mulch, as well as biomass for mushroom production. It would be helpful if this biomass and mulch could also act as fertilizer. Many of us burn wood for fuel to heat our homes or just for occasional fires in the fireplace or campfires outdoors. Can we generate such products in a relatively small area, while providing room to grow at least some food and medicinal items as well?

Coppice systems can produce structural wood products of small to medium diameter for crafts, firewood, fencing, various garden uses, and even shoes and tools. Coppiced nitrogen-fixing or dynamic-accumulator species can generate large quantities of mulch products as fertility enhancers.

Oaks and other hardwoods sprout from the stump to produce biomass useful for mushroom production. The oscillation between dense canopy and open woodland floor creates good conditions for a number of useful species, including herbaceous plants and wild or domestic animals.

Grow densely packed, coppicing shrubs or trees that produce biomass and small-diameter wood on long rotations with a useful herbaceous understory beneath.

Establish plants or encourage wildlings as coppice "stools" (table 2.6). Several of these species fix nitrogen or accumulate minerals, which can create the kind of mulch we might desire in our gardens.

Dense packing of coppiced species is necessary for straight stems to grow, which makes for easier cutting and woodworking and helps keep brambles and other "weeds" under control. Cut the initial tree stems the first time when they are the same size at which you intend to cut them on an ongoing basis. If the initial stem gets too big, it does not

TABLE 2.6. Coppicing fruit-bearing and edible-leaved trees and shrubs. Some species may not produce nuts or fruit until sprouts are relatively old, but little data is available on this. Grafted trees, when coppiced below the graft union, will revert to the fruit quality of the rootstock (usually poor). See appendix 2 for more coppicing species.

Latin Name	Common Name	Food Use
Asimina triloba	pawpaw	fruit
Carya spp.	shagbark hickory, pecan	nuts
Castanea spp.	chestnut, chinkapin	nuts
Corylus spp.	hazel, filbert	nuts
Crataegus spp.	hawthorns, mayhaw	fruit
Diospyros spp.	persimmons	fruit
Fagus grandifolia	American beech	nuts
Ginkgo biloba	ginkgo	nuts
Gleditsia triacanthos	honey locust	pods
Malus spp.	apples	fruit
Morus spp.	mulberries	fruit
Prunus spp.	cherries, plums, etc.	fruit
Pyrus communis	European pear	fruit
Quercus spp.	oaks	acorns
Sorbus spp.	mountain ash	fruit
Tilia spp.	linden, lime tree	leaves
Toona sinensis	fragrant spring tree	leaves

FIGURE 2.22. Copses: A "coppice with standards" system includes a scattering of standard timber or nut trees with an understory of trees coppiced on rotations of five to twenty-five years, depending on the species and their intended uses. The coppice on the left was felled the previous winter and is rapidly regrowing. The stand on the right has grown for five seasons and could be felled again soon if needed. The two stands include five small timber trees.

coppice as well and the stump is more likely to rot after cutting. You may include "standards," or full-size trees, within your coppice lots, but do not allow more than about twelve standards per acre (thirty per hectare) or they will cast too much shade and reduce coppice production (figure 2.22).[18] These may be timber trees, nut trees, or both.

We can also use coppicing to keep typically large trees with edible leaves or fruit small and accessible. For example, mulberries (*Morus* species) usually grow to around 50 feet in height. If, however, you cut a stump a few feet high and let sprouts grow (coppicing on stumps well aboveground is called pollarding), you can cut these sprouts on a three- or four-year rotation, getting fruit from the three- and four-year-old branches while the other branches mature, and keeping the tree small. Coppicing also keeps commonly large nitrogen fixers such as gray, Italian, and Japanese alders (*Alnus incana, A. cordata,* and *A. japonica,* respectively) smaller and provides mulch and polewood, as well as releasing nitrogen from the roots when cutting occurs. A coppicing strategy may also help control opportunistic plants if they already exist on your site, providing mulch in the meantime.

20.   Forest Edges

Many cultural landscapes contain edges between forests and fields or lawns. Such edge environments offer a great opportunity for forest gardening.

Most forest edges in cultural landscapes are a sudden shift from woods to field, with no transitional space to speak of. This limits the potential for beauty and productivity at this useful edge environment.

The sudden transitions from woods to field we often find in our landscapes may feel and look clean and tidy, but they diminish the ecological health, productivity, and diversity of the landscape. As we have said, many of our crop plants are midsuccession species; woods edges are great environments for many of them. The richness of diverse edges is beautiful in many respects, while providing habitat for many wildlife species.

Develop a diverse and productive forest-edge community using a mixture of useful trees, shrubs, and herbs.

Essentially, this pattern represents a linear version of *Oldfield Mosaics* (#13). Forest edges can be nucleic, linear, lobular, or any combination thereof (figure 2.23). Plant crops, wildlife plants, insectary plants, soil builders, indeed the whole range of forest garden species.

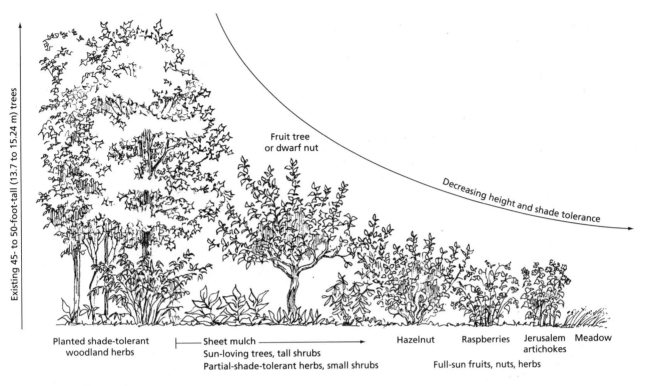

Existing 45- to 50-foot-tall (13.7 to 15.24 m) trees

Fruit tree or dwarf nut

Decreasing height and shade tolerance

Planted shade-tolerant woodland herbs

Sheet mulch
Sun-loving trees, tall shrubs
Partial-shade-tolerant herbs, small shrubs

Hazelnut   Raspberries   Jerusalem   Meadow
                                  artichokes

Full-sun fruits, nuts, herbs

FIGURE 2.23. Forest edges.

21. Microforest Gardens

This pattern is most appropriate for urban or small-lot suburban tracts, but it can also be used as a base pattern for *Nuclei That Merge* (#32).

How can we forest garden if we have only the tiniest of spaces in which to do it?

Technically, a forest is a large area of trees with interlocking crowns, and most forest gardens will not achieve the size and density to meet this guideline. But we can still apply forest-gardening principles to very small spaces with one, two, or three trees.

Use the principles of forest gardening in a small planting of trees, shrubs, and herbs that fits into a tight space (figure 2.24).

This planting should include guilds of insectary and soil-building plants when possible, as well as numerous high-value crops. Ideally, each plant will perform multiple functions to maximize the yields and health of the miniature ecosystem, and the plants will together serve as resource-sharing and mutual-support guilds.

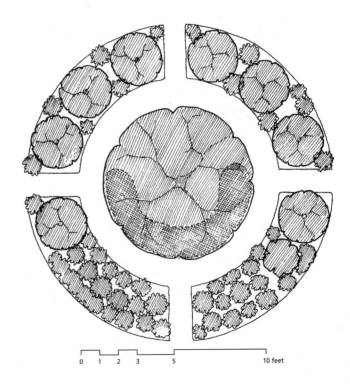

0 1 2 3   5   10 feet

FIGURE 2.24. Microforest gardens. For details, see figure 2.14 and table 2.1 in volume 1.

22. *Suburban Landscape Mimic*

This pattern is appropriate when you have nearby neighbors that talk, and what they say matters to you.

The architecture of typical suburban yards and gardens seems antithetical to the architecture of forest gardens. Or is it? How can we apply the principles of forest gardening to areas where social, legal, and aesthetic codes dominate our landscape design choices?

This topic is a whole book in itself. In many neighborhoods, aesthetic and social norms cause us to shy away from replacing our lawns with diverse edible plantings. We've even heard that some suburban communities have laws against vegetable gardening in front yards or regulating the allowable height of grass! Our culture's monoculture mindset runs very deep, and people can get quite emotional and even abusive if we don't conform. Though it seems insane (and probably is), it's a reality. What's a creative, playful, and innovative forest gardener to do? Isn't there a middle way that allows us to have our typical landscape and eat it too?

Pattern the landscape to take forms that look like typical suburban landscape elements, but apply the principles and patterns of forest gardening to them to shift or add to their ecological functions.

When we take apart a suburban landscape, we find landscape architectural elements we can easily adapt to forest gardening (figure 2.25). What follows is a list of some of these elements and the patterns in this chapter that relate to them:

- the landscape pattern overall: *Mandalas* (#10), *Oldfield Mosaics* (#13), *Woodland Gardens* (#14), *Gaps and Clearings* (#16);
- lawns: *Ground-Cover Carpets* (#49), *Expansive Plant Containers* (#52);
- perennial borders: *Nectaries Always Flowering* (#42), *Polyculture Patches* (#44), *Drifts, Clumps, and Scatters* (#50), *Mulch* (#56);
- trees with mulch circles around their bases: *Flower-Petal Beds* (#46);
- specimen trees: a number of useful trees are rather beautiful specimens; fruit trees in particular have abundant beautiful blossoms in spring;
- foundation plantings and privacy screens: *Minithickets* (#12);
- berms: *Pits and Mounds* (#23); and
- plant selection in general: *Extraordinary Edibles Everywhere* (#36), *Native Species* (#43).

Essentially, a suburban landscape may demand more formal patterning and clean lines, and therefore work, but we can still adapt these to fulfill our ecological and food production purposes. It may look like suburbia, but it sure tastes good! Just make sure, if you have an on-site sewage system (usually a septic-tank leach field), that you keep any woody plants at least 20 feet (6.1 m) from the leach field, or the roots may clog the leach field and cost you thousands of dollars for repair or replacement.

FIGURE 2.25. Suburban landscape mimic: This garden at Copia in Napa, California, includes a plum tree (*Prunus domestica*), a currant bush (*Ribes sp.*), borage (*Borago officinalis*), bronze fennel (*Foeniculum vulgare*), perennial kale (*Brassica oleracea*), and a ground cover of sweet woodruff (*Galium odoratum*) with a few coral bells (*Heuchera sp.*) mixed in. *Photo by Jonathan Bates.*

PATTERNS *in* THE GARDEN

Define the landform and circulation patterns before defining vegetation patterns.

People often ignore the effects of path layout on water flows, but they can be of great consequence in either positive or negative directions. Path layout also significantly influences our ability to work in and maintain our gardens.

23. Pits and Mounds

The pit-and-mound topography of old-growth forests is the model for this pattern, though Mollison's herb spiral and mulch-pit planting patterns also support the inspiration.[19] See Mollison's *Introduction to Permaculture* for more information. Such earthmoving has a place in many contexts for habitat diversification purposes.

> **Essentially flat sites, or those with unvarying soils, have few opportunities for habitat diversity, which is the foundation of other kinds of diversity. On extremely wet or dry sites, variation of topography can mean the difference between success and failure with many crops.**

The pits and mounds of old-growth forests generate the small-scale structural diversity that makes it possible for these woods to contain up to fourteen herb species per square yard, on average, and up to forty species per habitat. Pits and mounds develop in old growth when the rootballs of large trees turn on their sides as the trees fall and then decay. This piles up the topsoil in one place and exposes mineral soil elsewhere, raising the elevation of one area and lowering the elevation of another. You can imagine the diverse little environments throughout the pit and mound created by this arrangement. In our culture we tend to "make the rough places plain, and the crooked straight," thereby destroying such foundations of species diversity. Now we have the opportunity to recreate them!

Undulating topography is even more critical in extreme soil conditions. A few inches of additional dry soil can make all the difference in survival and production for some species in wet soils. The reduced evaporation and concentration of water in pits can do the same in dry conditions. Pits can even become catchments for blowing and drifting mulch and snow, improving poor or dry soils.

One additional advantage of undulating topography is that it increases the surface area available for planting. Mollison uses this idea in the famous herb spiral pattern. These spiraling cone-shaped planting beds generally rise 3 to 4 feet (1 to 1.3 m) high from a 5-foot-diameter (1.6 m) base. The flat area under the herb spiral is about 20 square feet (1.8 sq. m), while the surface area of the herb spiral is about 30 square feet (2.8 sq. m), half again as much as the original planting area, probably more. With pits and mounds, the planting area increases twice as much as that, because the surface area increases down into the pit as well as up into the mound. Long berms also increase the surface area, but not as much as do cone-shaped mounds.

> **Create pit-and-mound topography to diversify habitats in the herbaceous layer, improve tree and shrub survival and growth, and increase the surface area available for planting.**

You can do this on a small or large scale, depending on your inclination, tools, and willingness to invest time and energy. You can create pits and mounds in a variety of patterns (figures 2.26 and 2.27), by hand or by carefully using heavy equipment. Plant a variety of herbaceous species in the resulting microhabitats in a patchwise manner. You can also use the pits or mounds as a means of modifying the soil conditions for trees in marginal habitats—pits in dry areas and mounds in wet soils. Please read "Mounds, Mound Planting, and Pits and Mounds" in chapter 5 (page 347) for important details on mound design.

24. Definite Pathways

We have seen many forest gardens with few or no defined pathways. Besides discouraging wandering in the garden, indefinite paths create practical problems.

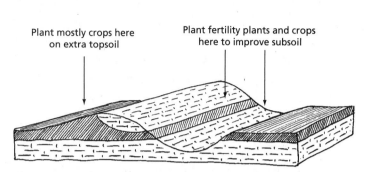

Plant mostly crops here on extra topsoil

Plant fertility plants and crops here to improve subsoil

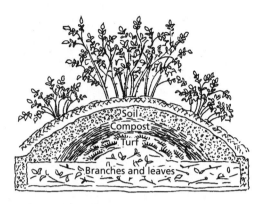

Soil
Compost
Turf
Branches and leaves

FIGURE 2.26. Pits and mounds: Hand-dug berms (left) end up with buried topsoil and exposed subsoil unless you move the top-soil out from under the berm first and then lay it on top. The former can increase habitat diversity, but you can also improve the exposed subsoil with amendments and plant dynamic accumulators. At right is a mulch mound as used by Robert Hart, consisting of coarse branches and leaves covered by layers of turf, compost, and soil and then planted. Such mounds are useful for creating drier habitats on wet soils. They eventually rot down to a low, rich, humusy mound.

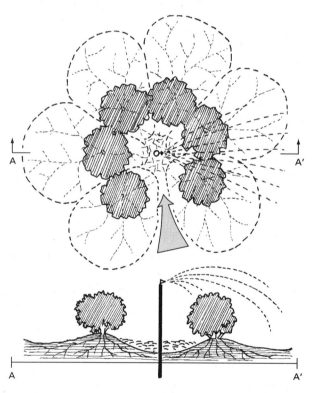

FIGURE 2.27. A circle-mound and mulch-pit planting scheme allows for easy watering with one spinning sprinkler. Placing a compost or mulch pile in the middle feeds the plants on the mound simply and well, as long as you leave access to the middle for dumping mulch and for maintenance and harvesting. Though the plants are spaced quite closely, their root areas will extend outside the circle, as shown.

Soil compaction is one of the major banes of healthy, living, productive soil.

The pressure of human feet, or worse yet, mechanized equipment, can squeeze the pore spaces right out of the soil. This reduces the amount of air and water the soil can hold and decreases the amount of habitat available for our soil-dwelling friends. Soil compaction can also decrease earthworm populations.[20] The more often compaction happens, the worse it gets and the faster it happens because the soil's ability to resist and bounce back from the pressure decreases. Wet soils compact more easily, too, as the water lubricates the soil particles. We need to stay off productive soils as much as possible, especially when they are wet. At the same time, we need to gain access to our plants to observe, care for, and harvest from them.

Create definite pathways and growing areas, clearly demarcated, that tell human visitors where and where not to walk (figure 2.28).

Design these pathways to maximize access to the growing beds and minimize the need to walk on them. The character of the two areas should be sufficiently different that the difference in function and use is clear at all times of year, especially when plants are dormant and soils tend to be the wettest. Use a change of elevation, surface treatment, and

FIGURE 2.28. Definite pathways improve garden function by directing traffic, thereby preventing compaction in growing beds, limiting damage to plants, and preventing disease transmission from plant to human to plant in wet weather.

plant cover type and density to establish this difference in character. In places where you do not need pathways frequently, use stepping-stones or some other "intermittent path" to designate access points and spread the weight of garden visitors on the soil.

25. Strategic Materials Depot

Forest gardens require large quantities of mulch, if not on an ongoing basis, then at least until the ground covers gain dominance of the ground layer. We must either bring in this biomass from the outside or generate it on-site, or both. *Copses* (#19) and *Functional Plants Throughout* (#51) help generate on-site materials. This pattern deals with handling the imported materials.

Moving around large quantities of mulch is one of the more difficult tasks in forest-garden establishment and management. Clearly, the location of the mulch piles is a key ingredient in determining how much work and time this will take.

Most of us do not want to look at our mulch piles all the time, nor do we want them in our way when we don't need them. Yet getting mulch to our site often requires a motorized vehicle, and we usually use garden carts to get it where we want it in the garden. And sometimes these mulch materials weigh an awful lot!

Early in your design process, decide upon the location of the strategic materials depot where you will gather, store, and dispense your bulk organic materials.

Place the depot where it is accessible by trucks and car trunks, preferably year-round, yet out of sight of key views and out of the way of main pathways (figure 2.29). Provide plenty of space to work around your piles, and to accommodate the occasional windfall of a utility crew with a large load of wood chips needing a place to drop their load. You may choose to put your household compost pile in the same location if it is near enough to the house. If you will be composting at the same site, make sure you have easy access to water to help care for the working piles. Ideally, you should also locate the depot to minimize your work carting the stuff around the garden. A central location is therefore good. In addition, locate the depot above the garden if you can so gravity helps you move materials, and you push only empty carts uphill. You will also likely need wider paths approaching the depot than you might want elsewhere in the garden, to accommodate carts.

26. Paths and Nodes

This pattern deals with making the pedestrian space of the garden practical and workable, but it does not suit everyone's aesthetic sensibilities.

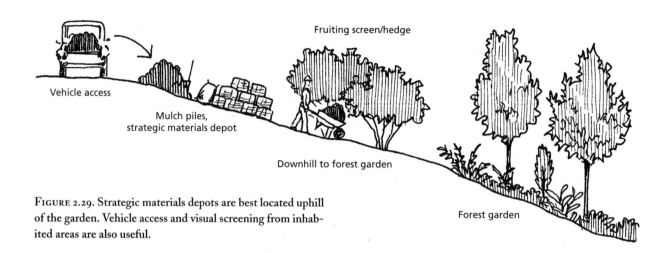

Fruiting screen/hedge

Vehicle access

Mulch piles,
strategic materials depot

Downhill to forest garden

Forest garden

FIGURE 2.29. Strategic materials depots are best located uphill of the garden. Vehicle access and visual screening from inhabited areas are also useful.

At the most practical level, the paths in a garden must conveniently connect related points of activity. They should also provide easy access to and from growing beds for people, carts, tools, and materials such as mulch and produce. We should use these two basic, practical functions of garden paths to define the framework of a garden path system in a way that makes working in the garden a joy, not a difficulty.

The first of these functions, connecting related points of activity, suggests that we look for *nodes*. Nodes include particular activities or places in the garden that require an area rather than a linear space, as well as destinations or points that we desire to get to and from. These may include the garden and building entrances, tool shed, *Strategic Materials Depot* (#25), greenhouse, sitting spots, hammock, and so on. We can divide these different activities into at least two categories of spaces: activity nodes and resting nodes.

Activity nodes are active work spaces that form the destination of one or more paths, that occur at the intersection of several paths, or that lie along a main path: entrances and exits, work spaces outside the greenhouse or around the compost pile, mulch storage and loading areas, water spigots, and so on. Resting nodes provide spaces for contemplation, resting, eating, sleeping, quiet conversation, observation, and so on. Resting nodes are best located on cul-de-sacs, or at least off main

paths, though keeping them in view of main paths is often a good idea.

Each of these nodes has certain requirements for its relative location, size, shape, and relationship to other garden features, depending on its function. If you haven't sited some of these within the garden yet, then siting them will be a strategic design issue. Their location will control, to some extent, the pattern of pathways in the garden. This is because "desire lines," or desired directions of movement, emanate from and to the various activity and resting nodes. Convenient connection between these nodes does not necessarily imply a straight-line path; however, the path should usually be relatively direct.

As for the second function of pathways listed above, it behooves us to remember that pathways are a working space. They must provide access to and through the garden without bottlenecks that make work difficult. Since we often have carts, and piles of weeds and mulch and brush, and still have to be able to get around while the carts and piles are lying there, we might want to think about a third kind of node. Let's call these "working nodes," since they are a work-saving feature.

Working nodes lie along paths to facilitate flow and prevent bottlenecks. These small open spaces have flexible uses to fit the need: cart turnarounds, cart pull-offs so you can walk by, temporary piles of weeds, mulch, and brush that don't block the path,

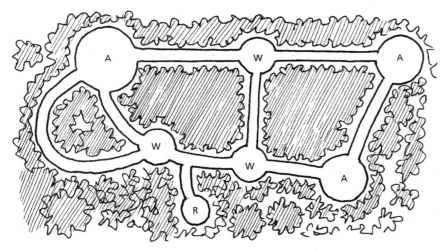

FIGURE 2.30. Paths and nodes. Nodes come in at least three basic types, including activity nodes (A), working nodes (W), and resting nodes (R).

a place to put transplants while they are in transit, and so on. We can design working nodes as specifically designed widenings of a path, but existing intersections work, too, widened or not as you like. The need for working nodes varies depending on how many people you have working in a garden at once and how big and densely vegetated the garden is. The pattern of intersections or the width of a path may obviate the need for specifically designed working nodes; then again, it may not.

Consciously design the pattern of nodes and paths in your garden for practical and aesthetic reasons (figure 2.30).

First locate and define activity nodes and resting nodes at logical and natural places within the garden, giving them a function, size, and shape and indicating any desire lines (figure 2.31). You can then connect these nodes with paths, either immediately or once you have considered other aspects of the site analysis and assessment. These straight or somewhat curved paths form the core framework of your path system. You may want to locate resting nodes after you have completed a basic layout of the activity nodes and connecting paths. This way you can locate resting nodes in quieter areas of the garden. Try to put resting nodes at the ends of spurs or cul-de-sacs so there is less activity around them, even when no one is resting there.

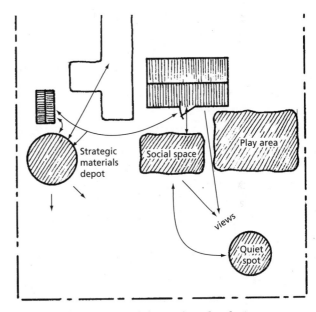

FIGURE 2.31. One way to define paths and nodes is to create an initial bubble diagram showing the locations of nodes and the "desire lines," or desired lines of foot travel, that lead to and from them. View lines may also be important.

Consider the location of working nodes as you lay out the rest of the path network. What intersections work well as turnarounds? Where might you want to have a pull-off or to be able to pile materials temporarily? In these places, slightly widen the path or intersection to make room for a wheelbarrow or mulch pile. But don't widen it too much; make it just big enough that you will be able to get around a pile or object parked there. Revise the locations of nodes as you refine the pathways and planting design. If your garden is very much a social space, vary the path shape to create social activity nodes.

27. *Rootlike Path Geometries*

Thinking of the path system in the way this pattern describes is appropriate in any garden where you will create definite pathways.

> **Pathways are like plant roots. Different path geometries work best in different situations, just as different plant root patterns work better in different environments. What factors tell us which path geometries work best in what situations?**

Pathways are like plant roots. Both structures organize and facilitate the flows of energy, materials, and water from one place to another. Some roots and paths act as storage zones, but others don't. Some live long and prosper, while others are temporary. Some far-flung outposts see little action, while others keep consistently busy. Both roots and paths must fit their particular circumstances to be adaptive. What basic principles underlie path geometry selection?

With roots, the character and distribution of key resources—light, soil, and water—determine the optimal pattern. For garden paths, vegetation is an additional key resource, and our choices about pathway geometry have a major influence on our ability to gain access to and maintain vegetation. Our design intentions and aesthetics, as well as landform, also influence our choices. Yet the patterns of roots remain good models for us to mimic in many cases, once we understand what makes them appropriate.

> **Mimic appropriate plant root patterns in your forest garden path layout.**

Determine the appropriate path geometry by assessing the resource patterns in your site, clarifying your design intentions, and consulting your sense of aesthetics.

We can distinguish, and will briefly discuss, at least four plant root and pathway patterns: radial, branching, rhizomatous, and networked (figure 2.32a–d). One additional pattern (*Keyhole Beds*, #28) deals not only with path geometry but also with planting-bed layout, so we discuss it separately. Each of these patterns has its uses. Plants frequently use these patterns in combination, and we probably will, too.

Radial patterns (figure 2.32a) arise from a central point and radiate outward in all directions. They may also radiate toward a center from the outside. Radial patterns become optimal either when a need exists at a point surrounded by resources or when a resource exists at a point, surrounded by needs. A tree stem is a point need, and its resources surround it. A fruit tree is a point resource, more or less, and we generally need access to it from all sides. Both situations suggest radial patterns. Radial paths around a tree also support the radial pattern of tree roots by minimizing soil compaction across roots (see *Flower-Petal Beds*, #46). The fact that plant roots radiate toward resource-rich areas, not necessarily in all directions, does not diminish the usefulness of radial geometries. It just skews them in various ways.

Branching patterns result from directional flow from dispersion to concentration, or vice versa, or both (see figure 2.32b). They result in a hierarchy of root or branch sizes from small and numerous in the dispersion zone to few and large near the concentration zone. This implies that small branches absorb and main trunks transport. However, in roots there is no clear separation of functions, just a difference of emphasis based on where the particular root sits in the root hierarchy. In gardens, main paths should mimic this by being wider and perhaps having a tougher surface since they get more traffic. Less-traveled paths can be smaller, gentler on the earth, and more numerous. This improves access to specific areas of the garden for gathering and dispersing resources in exchange with our plant and soil allies. A hierarchical structure to the path network aids the understanding, organization, movement, and use of diverse resources in the garden.

Plants use *rhizomatous* patterns most effectively when resources are patchy, especially when different

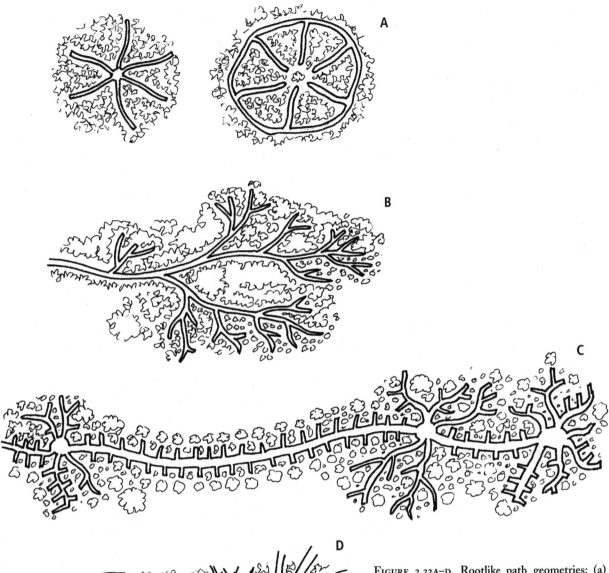

FIGURE 2.32A–D. Rootlike path geometries: (a) Radial geometries occur when a point need is surrounded by resources, or a point resource requires access from all sides. (b) Branching geometries concentrate dispersed resources or disperse concentrated ones. They tend to have a hierarchical structure and a point of access or egress. (c) Rhizomatous patterns connect patchy resources. They may have radial or branching geometries at points along the connecting link, and the connectors may have large-surface-area (keyhole) patterns. (d) Networked geometries offer omnidirectional flows for complex interaction. They may or may not have a hierarchy.

required resources don't overlap in one space. The resulting linear rhizomes have radial, branching, or networked root systems wherever the plant finds a cluster of resources. This pattern works well on sloping land, especially when occasional broad terraces occur. Even where terraces do not occur, the overall linear pattern of rhizomatous paths can crisscross a slope, directing water flows as well as people. Sometimes a rhizome will grow a continuous series of short rootlets along its length, which looks something like a linear path with *Keyhole Beds* (#28) along it (as shown in figure 2.32c).

Networks consist of various combinations of linear or curvilinear links or segments and the intersections between them. Sometimes nodes, or widened areas that provide room for materials storage, occur at the intersections. Interconnected loops can also create networks. We consider rectilinear grids a networked pattern.

The crucial element of networks is that they are definitely omnidirectional, not uni- or bidirectional as are branches. Networks may exhibit hierarchy like branches, or they may not. Plant roots don't often network, as far as we know. However, root networks can form when much root grafting occurs between trees, or in ephemeral root fans growing in forest duff. Networks definitely occur when you add mycorrhizas to the equation.

Networks occur most often when complex interactions between elements demand a lot of flexibility (figure 2.32d). So it is with path networks. They allow the multidirectional sharing or movement of resources or information, whether resources are scarce or abundant. The challenge of networks, especially when they are nonhierarchical and dense, is that you easily get lost or confused unless there is some form of organization besides a hierarchy. It is also harder to control or direct a flow of whatever kind that enters the network, whether it be a root virus killing root-grafted trees one after the other, excess runoff from a rainstorm causing erosion among garden beds, or something else.

28. Keyhole Beds

This pattern lays out another option for a specific path geometry as well as the patterning of plants within growing beds. It relates more to the end branches of paths, the primary edge zones of contact between people and garden, rather than the pattern of trunk lines that carry people and products from place to place. This pattern comes from the work of Bill Mollison in his various permaculture books.

Assuming we will have *Definite Pathways* (#24) in our garden, how do we maximize access to growing beds with minimal infrastructure in the smallest space? What natural patterns solve similar problems?

The interface between paths and garden beds is like a membrane, across which we move energy and materials in the form of fertilizers, mulch, and harvested products. Whenever there is a need to transfer materials and energy across a boundary in a small space, especially at low pressure, natural systems tend to create sinuous, undulating, folded patterns with large surface area, as in our lungs and intestines. An undulating or folded pattern efficiently compresses a large surface area of contact zone between paths and beds into a small space. Mollison calls this pattern a "keyhole bed" (figure 2.33).[21]

In many circumstances (but not all), keyhole beds compress more accessible growing space into a given area with less path area than do rectangular growing beds in a grid pattern. In addition, grids create more grids around them, whereas folded patterns can fit into spaces of many shapes and sizes easily and effectively. The challenge with keyhole beds is that they are not always accessible from all sides, unlike those gridded rectangles, unless you can place keyholes back-to-back. So how can we overcome this accessibility challenge with keyhole beds?

We have applied the principle of relative location to our sites at a large scale in *Zones and Sectors* (#7). We can apply the same principle at a small scale by zoning the plants in our growing beds according to frequency of use.

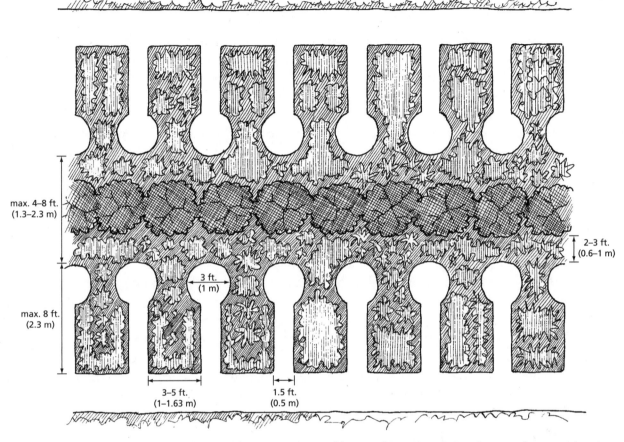

max. 4–8 ft.
(1.3–2.3 m)

2–3 ft.
(0.6–1 m)

3 ft.
(1 m)

max. 8 ft.
(2.3 m)

3–5 ft.
(1–1.63 m)

1.5 ft.
(0.5 m)

FIGURE 2.33. Keyhole beds mimic the large-surface-area patterns of lungs and intestines designed to transfer materials at low pressure across a membrane, like food and maintenance effort between path and growing bed. Beds patterned this way fit into oddly shaped spaces more effectively than grids can and usually offer a higher ratio of bed area per foot of path, too. Place less frequently used plants in back and oft-used plants in front. Beds should be a width equal to twice your easy-reaching distance, usually 3–5 feet (1–1.6 m).

Lay out your garden beds as keyholes, and zone the plantings in the beds based on frequency of access or use.

Provide short spurs off travel paths (no more than 6 to 8 feet, or 2 or so meters, long). End these spurs in small bulges big enough to sit down in (around 3 feet/1 m in diameter) so you can stay in one place and work on all sides of you without moving or stepping on the growing beds. Design the beds so the distance between keyhole paths equals twice the easy reaching distance from the keyhole paths (2 to 3 feet/0.6 to 1 m, depending on your age, agility, and ability; 4 to 6 feet/1.2 to 2 m

total). In this way you can reach from both sides to the center of the beds between keyholes.

Keyhole beds are about more than the configuration of the paths and beds, though. The pattern of plantings within the keyhole beds is also critical. The idea is to "zone" the planting beds by frequency of access, similar to the larger-scale pattern suggested in *Zones and Sectors* (#7). Place plants that need the most frequent care or that yield most frequently—such as culinary herbs and salad greens—in the front of the beds, near the path. Plants that need the least care or yield the least—such as insectary plants or mulch-producing species cut once per year—often go in back, away from paths. Provide stepping-stones into the backs of the beds, if desired. Otherwise, just walk on the beds once per year or so to harvest the less intensive crops back there. If you desire easy reach to all parts of every bed, place keyhole beds back-to-back, so the distance between the bulges at the ends of the spurs equals twice your easy-reaching distance.

The continuous planting beds that result from keyhole patterning also work extremely well with drip irrigation system layouts, unlike blocks of rectangular planting beds. Keyhole beds are a great idea in many contexts, but they are optimal in the "capillary zones" of the garden, where traffic is lighter than on main paths and the functional focus is the care of planting beds and plants, rather than getting somewhere. However, keyhole beds also work well along main paths.

29. Pathway Width

This pattern aids organization and good working conditions in the garden. It seems simple and obvious enough, but it's amazing how frequently it gets ignored.

Poorly sized pathways impede enjoyable and safe working and playing conditions in the forest garden. We need to balance this concern with a desire to maximize growing space.

How many times have you worked in a garden with cramped paths, where it was difficult to move or get anything done without tripping over yourself, your tools, or other people? How often have you walked through a garden pushing plants out of the way because they were growing into and blocking the path? Have you ever tried to use a garden cart in a path wide enough for a wheelbarrow at best? All of these situations are at least inconvenient, and at worst can cause unsafe working conditions or damage the plants we want to encourage. We have tripped over objects lying in narrow

paths or hidden under overgrowing plants more than once while carrying heavy objects. Walking through wet plants can spread disease from one place to another, which is certainly a problem even if you like the lush feeling of "overgrown" pathways.

Poorly sized paths commonly result from either lack of thought or unclear thinking about how wide to make paths and why. When people keep paths narrow, it is usually in their enthusiasm to fit as many plants into their garden as they can. Rarely are paths too wide, though it does happen. Obviously, we'd like to keep pathways as narrow as possible without compromising safe and enjoyable working and playing conditions. We also don't want them to hog too much space, which they can easily do. All it takes is a little forethought. What guidelines might we use?

Define pathway widths by the intensity of use the path will receive and the kinds of tools or equipment that will need to move through (figure 2.34).

A pedestrian requires about 2 feet (60 cm) of path width to walk comfortably. However, 2 feet barely accommodates a standard wheelbarrow and

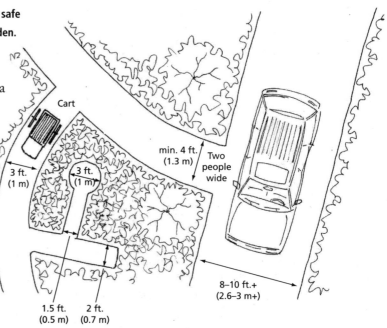

FIGURE 2.34. Pathway width.

will not accommodate a small garden cart, which requires at least 2.5 feet (75 cm), and more at corners and if you want to be able to get around the cart while it is parked. Larger garden carts require at least 3 feet (1 m), tractors between 4 and 8 feet (1.2 to 2.4 m), and trucks from a minimum of 6 feet (1.8 m) for small pickups to 7 feet (2.1 m) for "standard" large US pickups. Any regularly traveled vehicle path needs at least 10 feet (3 m) of width, if not 12 feet (3.6 m).

The least used "defined" paths can be simple stepping-stones through a garden bed, but these are not appropriate for frequent use or for wheelbarrows or carts. Pedestrian-only paths, such as short keyhole spurs, could be 2 feet (60 cm) wide, or perhaps 18 inches (45 cm) if infrequently used and space is tight. The smallest cart paths, including keyhole spurs longer than about 5 feet (1.6 m), should be 2.5 to 3 feet (75 to 100 cm) wide at minimum. None of these widths offer any space to get around a parked cart or another person working in the path. If you include working nodes in your path design this can be okay (see *Paths and Nodes*, #26), but otherwise widen the path by at least 6 inches (15 cm), and preferably a foot (30 cm).

When you start getting into two-way paths, or paths where a cart and a person will regularly pass each other, minimum path sizes should rise to at least 4 feet, if not 5 (1.2 to 1.5 m). Some designers recommend a 6- to 8-foot (2 to 2.6 m) minimum width for main paths. These are good widths for all main paths between major activity nodes, and they help set a path hierarchy and provide orientation to the path network as a whole—if you have enough space in your garden. Of course, space constraints and your aesthetic sensibilities also need to come into play in these decisions.

Determine your establishment, reestablishment, and management patterns.

Pattern and process are equally important in forest garden design. How we get where we want to go

will influence the design dramatically. The following group of patterns defines possible methods of establishing or altering the trajectory of forest gardens.

30. *Patch Disturbance and Regeneration*
Patch dynamics theory underlies this pattern. It adds more dynamics to pattern #9, which defines patches in space, by considering system establishment as patch disturbance and succession. We discuss disturbance as maintenance in *Disturbance and Maintenance Regimes* (#34).

What is the best way to redirect succession or change the structure or composition of a vegetated area with minimal soil nutrient losses due to disturbance?

Let's say that you have a well-established forest garden many years old, but that one area of that garden is getting old and less productive or isn't working out as you had hoped or planned. How could you deal with this situation such that you minimize the work of management now and in the future?

The area of concern in this question is a patch. The unified oldfield theory states three causes of succession: available sites or niches; differential species availability to a site or niche; and varied species performance (see table 1.6). We must manage these three general causes if we are to manage succession in our patch.

Changing the direction of an existing succession usually requires some form of disturbance, which will make sites and niches available. We must consciously design the disturbance—timing, kind, intensity, and severity—if we want to achieve specific successional goals; otherwise, we increase the chances of unintended consequences. Yet if we stop there, we will lose the leverage we have gained by designing the disturbance in the first place. The rules of initial floristic composition and competitive exclusion, among others, still apply. We need to further guide the succession by preferentially making desired species available to the disturbed area and supporting the high performance of those chosen plants. Only when we have firmly established the replacement species can we relax and let nature take her course—unless we are willing to let nature take whatever course she wants to take from the start.

In addition, we know that whenever a disturbance occurs, especially a soil disturbance, the soil community responds by rapidly releasing nutrients into the soil water. This speeds the revegetation of the site. However, though a large quantity of nutrients gets released within the first months after the disturbance, leaching can deplete this burst of available nutrients within less than two years. Whatever plants get to the site first after the disturbance will have the best shot at garnering these nutrients and gaining dominance over the sites and niches that have become available. If we want to manage plant establishment and performance— and the direction of succession—following a disturbance, we must get the plants we want to the site right away. Immediate revegetation is essential to recapturing these available nutrients before they leach away, and to directing the following succession with the least effort in the long run. *No* act of disturbance is complete until we have designed and implemented the follow-through that guides the following succession.

> **Establish consciously defined patches, and direct the following succession within them, using designed disturbances and immediate regeneration or establishment of desired vegetation (figure 2.35).**

Always consider disturbance and succession as a totality. Make conscious choices about which patches are to receive what treatments, and why: boundaries, goals, and timing. Consciously choose how and when to disturb, and how and when to support or influence regeneration in response to those disturbances. Never let disturbed soil go unplanted if you want to manage the following succession. Develop scenarios of where the vegetation will go: write down the scenario,

even if in brief notes, so you can refer to it later and evaluate the evolution of the system after your disturbance. We discuss designed disturbances further in chapter 7.

31. *Instant Successions*

Instant successions are probably most appropriate in secondary successions where soils already contain a variety of legacies from previous ecosystems. If soils are poor, more soil development may be necessary than instant successions can provide, and the ultimate productivity of the system could be lower than its true, fully developed potential. In such cases, long-term midsuccession environments with significant focus on building fertility will generate higher productivity in the long run. See also the discussion of instant successions in volume 1, chapter 2.

> **Natural successions may take decades to develop to anything like a climax or steady state, and the route the system takes to get there varies depending on**

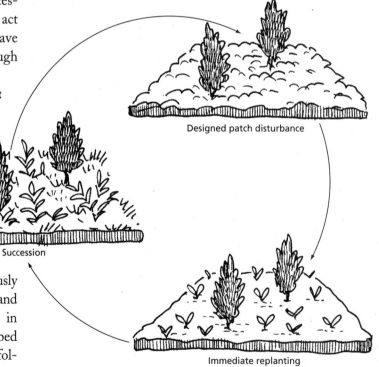

Designed patch disturbance

Succession

Immediate replanting

FIGURE 2.35. Patch disturbance and regeneration.

many factors. How can we guide successional change to arrive where we want sooner, through a more defined or designed pathway, and with the least work in management?

Ecosystem development is a complex business dealing with soil development, architectural development, and social development all at once. No wonder succession from field to forest generally takes a long time compared to a human life. If we could get a reasonably productive forest garden in less than a decade, that would be a good thing, wouldn't it?

A host of factors influence successional pathways and processes. However, the theory of initial floristic composition says that the plants present after a disturbance, the initial flora, will largely determine the successional pathway the system takes. Therefore, we must manage the initial flora of the site if we want to have the best chance of managing the successional path, species composition, and structure. We can do this in at least two ways: designed disturbance and competitive exclusion.

Many plants already live on any site before we get there and decide that we want to forest-garden. These preexisting plants, seeds, or other propagules have an advantage over any plants we might introduce and will strongly drive the successional path of the ecosystem. Hopefully, many of these inhabitants have uses or beauties we want to maintain and can work into our plans. However, it is likely not all will, and some have the potential to be at least a problem, if not a major nuisance, as part of the ongoing flora of the site. This is where designed disturbances come in, if necessary.

In addition, nearby species constantly disperse into our forest garden sites. This is where competitive exclusion comes in, and why the initial flora has the advantage. The best way to prevent invading plants from establishing is to fill all the available sites and niches immediately after a disturbance ends. If we fill the niches and sites with the plants we want for every stage of succession, we will have less work to do down the line, and (theoretically) the initial flora we install will guide the system in a fairly predictable direction.

Beginning with the end in mind, design a disturbance or series of disturbances to change the existing flora, and then densely plant patches or whole areas at one time with plants from every stage of your proposed or intended succession.

Though successional communities generally develop from the bottom up, moving forward through time, *we must design from the top down moving backward in time*. This is what we mean by "begin with the end in mind." Design the "climax" or horizon stage of your succession first (figure 2.36), and then work backward stage by stage in two- to five- to ten-year increments. Design the various layers at maturity and include them in the earlier planting schemes as younger plants as you work backward in time. When you get back to the first year, you will have a very complex planting plan (figure 2.37), but one that will take full advantage of the initial floristic composition concept to govern succession from the beginning to the "end" of your designed succession. Then plant all those plants at once, except any shade-requiring species. A timeline is a very useful tool in designing instant successions.

Pay attention to soil development needs in your instant succession plan. Make sure to include good mineral fertilizers, dynamic-accumulator and nitrogen-fixing plants, compost and mulch, and soil-microbe inoculants as needed based on your site analysis. Consider the architecture of each stage of succession, as well as the social structure.

32. Nuclei That Merge

Nuclei that merge are fundamental patterns that help create *Oldfield Mosaics* (#13).

How can we establish forest gardens when we don't have money, time, or energy for extensive broadscale plantings over large areas?

The density and diversity of forest garden plantings can rack up large time, energy, and money costs rapidly when applied to large areas. Not only do we have to design and prepare the ground, but

FIGURE 2.36. Instant-succession plan for the horizon habitat at twenty-five years. The bottom swale and associated plantings shown here are to be installed late in the successional sequence and do not appear in figure 2.37 below.

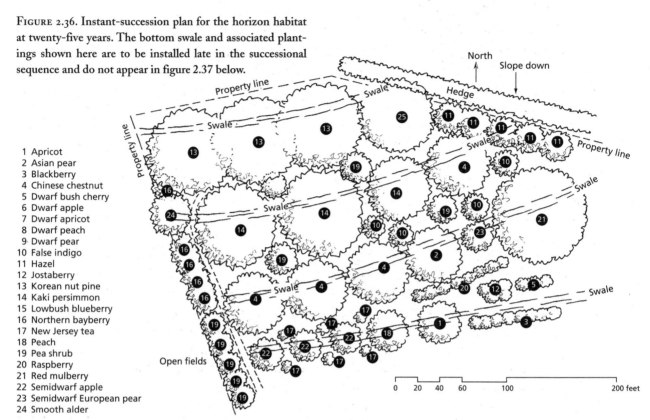

1 Apricot
2 Asian pear
3 Blackberry
4 Chinese chestnut
5 Dwarf bush cherry
6 Dwarf apple
7 Dwarf apricot
8 Dwarf peach
9 Dwarf pear
10 False indigo
11 Hazel
12 Jostaberry
13 Korean nut pine
14 Kaki persimmon
15 Lowbush blueberry
16 Northern bayberry
17 New Jersey tea
18 Peach
19 Pea shrub
20 Raspberry
21 Red mulberry
22 Semidwarf apple
23 Semidwarf European pear
24 Smooth alder

0   20 40 60   100   200 feet

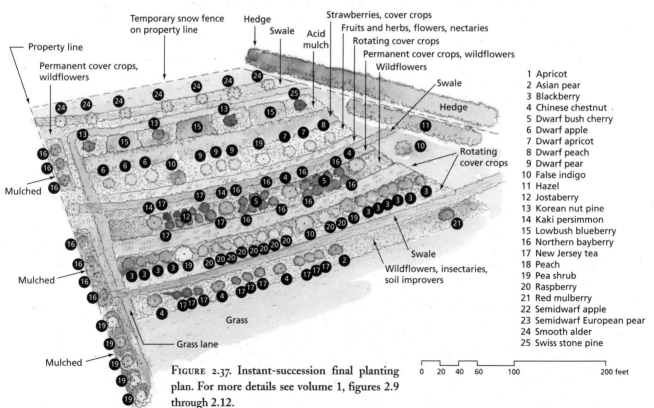

1 Apricot
2 Asian pear
3 Blackberry
4 Chinese chestnut
5 Dwarf bush cherry
6 Dwarf apple
7 Dwarf apricot
8 Dwarf peach
9 Dwarf pear
10 False indigo
11 Hazel
12 Jostaberry
13 Korean nut pine
14 Kaki persimmon
15 Lowbush blueberry
16 Northern bayberry
17 New Jersey tea
18 Peach
19 Pea shrub
20 Raspberry
21 Red mulberry
22 Semidwarf apple
23 Semidwarf European pear
24 Smooth alder
25 Swiss stone pine

FIGURE 2.37. Instant-succession final planting plan. For more details see volume 1, figures 2.9 through 2.12.

0   20 40 60   100   200 feet

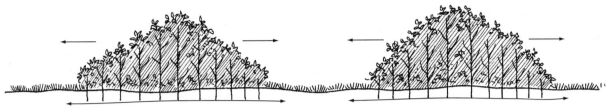

FIGURE 2.38. Shrubs that spread using rhizomes, stolons, or root suckers often develop beautiful mounded forms as they expand from their point of initiation in grassland habitats. These nuclei eventually merge or expand to form a thicket, either from one plant spreading on its own or when a number of such mounds converge.

the effort of planting and immediate after-care can be overwhelming if you aren't ready for it. Buying large numbers of perennials usually isn't cheap, and propagating them yourself isn't easy either (though it can be a lot of fun). Nor do we encourage the wholesale transplanting of wildlings out of forests or fields in your locale or anywhere else—we've done enough damage to these places already without ripping them apart for our backyard ecologies, and the survival rates aren't that high anyway. Nursery-propagated stock tends to transplant and grow better. So if we have a large area we want to turn into forest garden, what can we do?

We based this pattern on observations of oldfield successions where shrubs establish and then expand (figure 2.38), taking over the grasses and herbs until the nuclei of shrubs merge into a mass. Trees frequently express a similar pattern of expanding clumps that eventually merge into a mass of forest. Our successional nucleus mimics can be *Instant Successions* (#31), except that here you consciously select species that propagate vegetatively or from

seed. As your initial plantings grow, use this nucleus as a nursery to propagate more plants, then use these plants to establish more nuclei.

This strategy reduces the total amount of watering you need to do at any one time as plants establish themselves. It allows you to firmly establish each nucleus with few or no weed problems or dead plant gaps to refill before expanding your operation to other areas. It allows you to test various plants and plant combinations and to improve your design with each new experience. Finally, you can learn how much work each nucleus takes and gauge your final forest garden size on what you learn so you don't plant more than you can handle.

Plant perennial polyculture nuclei that expand and reproduce until they fill the available space (figure 2.39).

Design and plant a small, defined *Instant Successions* (#31) patch, located in a spot where it can slowly expand. As your plants grow, you can reseed, divide, and multiply the perennials and propagate the shrubs by layering or stooling. Propagate or buy and plant trees to create new

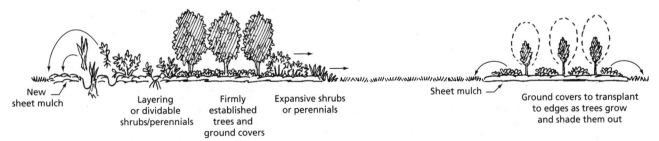

New sheet mulch

Layering or dividable shrubs/perennials

Firmly established trees and ground covers

Expansive shrubs or perennials

Sheet mulch

Ground covers to transplant to edges as trees grow and shade them out

FIGURE 2.39. Nuclei that merge can be created by planting a small nucleus of trees along with expansive shrubs and perennials, or shrubs or perennials that can be layered, divided, or used to generate seed stock. Once the nucleus is fully established, you can allow the plants to expand the nucleus or establish new nuclei by layering and dividing them. You can also transplant plants getting shaded out as trees grow. Creating several nuclei and expanding them until they merge can establish complete control over a large area at an ever-increasing rate.

nuclei as the other plants become available. Fit the nuclei into a predetermined plan of pathways and overall forest garden architecture, and refine the planting plan as you learn from your experiences with earlier nuclei.

33. *Relay Plantings*

You are likely to use this strategy in the later stages of your forest-garden successions.

> **All plants have their environmental preferences. Some desired species will not grow or will not grow well in certain environments until successional modifications or improvements take place.**

Various environmental conditions change radically over the course of succession, from temperature and moisture regimes to soil, light, and shade conditions. This is especially true in extreme situations such as on barren, infertile, or damaged soils, where limited legacies from earlier ecosystems can slow succession and hold down productivity for long periods. Obviously, in such extreme circumstances we would be wasting our time and energy trying to plant late successional species when the ecosystem is in an early succession condition.

We must, then, sometimes use a strategy of successive plantings as conditions change during succession, even if we use an *Instant Successions* (#31) strategy overall. We should use the successional process to modify environmental conditions in favor of plants we want to grow and plant those plants only when conditions are right. This may involve shade-loving plants that will not thrive until a decent canopy has developed. In other cases this will involve plants that prefer cool, moist, rich, humusy soils or the fungi-dominated soils of later succession. Many times these environmental changes must be synchronized for a plant to thrive. For example, mature forest plants such as ginseng probably will not thrive in a midsuccession thicket, even if shade conditions are about right, because the soil food web is very different from what they prefer.

> **If your site approximates primary succession conditions and needs major environmental modification, plan your succession as a series of steps with specific soil and environmental modification goals that, once achieved, will allow more useful or desirable plants to grow there (figure 2.40).**

In extreme conditions, the primary focus of your plan will need to be soil building for a number of years. Plant mostly prolific biomass-producing plants, dynamic accumulators, and nitrogen fixers, along with some edibles, to invest in creating legacies for the later ecosystem. As site conditions moderate and improve, establish clusters of new plants within the garden to begin the new stages of succession.

If your site is more of an early secondary succession environment, there will still be plants that you shouldn't try to include until after the system is established and conditions become more shaded, rich, and humusy. Hold back these plants until the time and conditions are ripe for them.

Instant-succession planting of sun-loving and partial-shade-tolerant crops

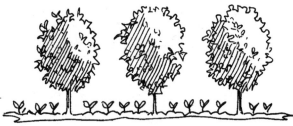
Patch disturbance and replanting of shade-tolerant crops

FIGURE 2.40. Relay plantings come in handy as conditions change during succession. For example, if you plant an instant succession with all sun-loving plants, the maturing trees will eventually shade out the sun lovers. If you patch-disturb and replant with shade tolerants, you will continue the successional relay race.

34. Disturbance and Maintenance Regimes

The phrase *disturbance regime* usually connotes the pattern of natural disturbances over time (their timing, kind, severity, and intensity) within a particular patch or habitat. We can use disturbances to establish a new ecosystem, to alter an existing ecosystem, or to maintain a system in a certain condition. Disturbance and maintenance regimes therefore include human-induced ecosystem maintenance patterns as well as natural disturbance patterns. This pattern integrates *Patch Disturbance and Regeneration* (#30) but focuses on maintenance disturbances and long-term course-setting disturbances, rather than system establishment.

The patterns of human and natural disturbance over time determine, to a large extent, the character and composition of plant communities within a patch or habitat, and their successional trajectory.

Every natural habitat tends to have a certain disturbance regime that helps create or maintain it, or that allows certain life forms to grow that wouldn't if disturbance occurred more frequently or severely. Human activities represent forms of disturbance, some of which we have designed to create and maintain certain habitat conditions. For example, many parts of the Midwestern prairie would have been forested before European colonization if it weren't for frequent fires set by the native peoples that prevented the success of trees. Forests and forest gardens, by definition, receive severe disturbances less frequently than vegetable gardens and meadows, or they wouldn't be forested.

Mentally framing our management and maintenance activities as forms of disturbance within an overall disturbance regime integrates them into the same continuum of ecosystem influences as natural disturbances. This helps us think outside the box of traditional maintenance habits. It allows us to see the bigger picture of the system-wide effects of our actions. It pulls the random events of nature and "acts of God" into our frame of reference and indicates how they may affect the future course of events. This helps us stay upright more effectively as we surf the waves of change that nature throws at us.

Disturbance and maintenance regimes can and do include disturbances and activities that occur on a daily, weekly, monthly, or yearly basis, as well as every other year, every five or ten years, or longer. Disturbance and maintenance regimes contain essentially three kinds of disturbances:

- frequent, ongoing, low-intensity disturbances that maintain the system or support its continued development in a certain direction;
- infrequent, intense natural disturbances that alter or set the course of succession; and
- infrequent, intense, human-induced disturbances that alter or set the course of succession.

We must think through the kinds of ongoing disturbances that our gardens require to guide succession or maintain the conditions we desire. This is especially true since forest gardens do not need the typical patterns of maintenance (e.g., weekly mowing) with which many of us are familiar. Frequent, low-intensity maintenance disturbances include pruning, mulching, weeding, cutting back overgrowth, spraying dormant oils, other pest management activities, harvesting, and so on. These are the kinds of activities we try to minimize by design (except the harvesting!), but which we will probably never completely eliminate while at the same time maintaining high yields. *Estimating the timing and time requirements of these activities is essential to making sure you aren't designing more than you can maintain.* In addition, understanding these activities will help you locate plants and elements within your garden (*Zones and Sectors*, #7), as well as the patterns of access they will require (*Rootlike Path Geometries*, #27; *Keyhole Beds*, #28; and *Flower-Petal Beds*, #46). Clearly, you won't have an accurate sense of this work until you have solid experience with your garden, but any try is better than nothing in this regard. These ongoing maintenance tasks can vary from patch to patch within the forest garden depending on what you are growing and how.

We don't often think of the longer-term, more infrequent events that determine the composition, form, and successional direction of forests and forest gardens. Yet infrequent, intense disturbances are fundamental influences on forest succession. Their timing and nature are key to the kind of impact they have, for they set the course of succession far into the future. These may be natural disturbances, or they may be human induced.

Natural disturbances of the infrequent, intense kind may include fires, drought, storms, flooding, and insect outbreaks. Most of these we instinctively tend to guard against or attempt to buffer our gardens from. Few of these have we learned to take advantage of in the way that at least some species in natural forests do. For instance, if an ice storm damages a tree in our forest garden, how can we respond to take advantage of that, to direct the impact of that disturbance on the understory as well as the canopy? Questions we might ask ourselves in any situation like this include: Does the disturbance affect only the ground layer, or does it affect the canopy, shrub, and low tree layers? Is the soil disturbed, or not? How and how deeply? What plants were distributing seed right before the disturbance, and which plants are distributing seed now? What neighboring plants might benefit? What other plants from elsewhere in the garden might usefully occupy the sites and niches now available? Observation and good questions will guide us to see how we can turn such events into opportunities. Ice storms create many small gaps in the forest canopy, or just a lessening of shade all around, for example, that we might take advantage of in our understory plantings. There is also often an abundance of mulch material available after such events.

We can also consciously design periodic disturbances as a tool to maintain, manage, or set the successional trajectories of our forest gardens. We must extend our thinking past the typical short frames of time reference in management and maintenance, into the realm of once per five years, once per decade, twice per century, and so on. This aspect of the disturbance and maintenance regime—planned *Patch Disturbance and Regeneration* (#30) at long intervals—is probably critical to low-maintenance forest garden management over the long run. Such disturbances generate implications for overall system design and maintenance. However, though succession theory very clearly points us in this direction, we have few specifics on practical uses and details in this regard, and much to learn. Here are a few ideas to consider:

- Restored prairies need to be burned every two or three years to maintain their diversity. Some forests get similar treatment on a natural basis. In volume 1, chapter 1, we discussed how Native Americans burned butternut groves on a three-year rotation for insect and disease control as well as increased yields. Do some of the other species we might consider for forest gardening, especially natives, have a similar need? We don't know at this point, but it is a good question to keep in mind.
- We need to decide how frequently we will cut the coppice in a coppice patch and how that influences the other uses we give the patch. If we are planting willow for mulch, we can cut every year. Sun-loving and partial-shade-tolerant plants may then be appropriate for the understory, with species selection depending on the seasonal timing of the willow cut. If we are growing stove-wood-size coppice (2 to 6 inches/5 to 15 cm in diameter) or oak logs for shiitake production (minimum 6 inches/15 cm in diameter), the rotation will be longer (five to fifteen years, depending on species, climate, and site), and a more shade-tolerant understory will be necessary.
- The disturbance regimes may be different for the different patches in a forest garden. We mentioned that the rotation period of the earlier stages of a shifting mosaic will be shorter

than for a nut orchard within a *Shifting-Mosaic Forest Garden* (#18), especially a small one. We may choose to patch-disturb and regenerate a set of eight patches in a staggered forty-year rotation, setting one back every five years to early secondary succession, then guiding it through annuals (five years), small fruits (fifteen years), and mixed hazels and semidwarf fruit trees (twenty years) so that each patch is always at a different stage or phase within a stage. This way each crop is unevenly aged and gets rotated out of its stage as it gets toward the end of its most productive life. In the meantime, the nut orchard will start out evenly aged and begin to differentiate in about a hundred years as it gets brought into the rotation piecemeal.

It may seem ludicrous to think this far in advance, but why not? A lack of this kind of thinking is one reason why our culture and environment are in such disarray. The long-term thinking we envision here is not "planning" in a tightly scripted or controlling sense of the word (we don't even know enough to attempt this, and probably never will), but more an imagining of possible scenarios and how we might create or respond to them. Imagining likely scenarios is a critical step in designing the near-term future, for we can consciously or unconsciously limit our long-term possibilities or open to them by design. The point is that we need to wrestle with the long-term view and make room for various scenarios we imagine are likely, but not expect that what we plan will actually be what happens. *It's not about planning, it's about possibilities.*

In a general way, sketch out the disturbance regimes for each garden patch, and the garden as a whole, as you design it.

What kinds of disturbance will need to happen how often to generate the kind of habitat and crops you want within the patch? What kinds of natural disturbances might occur, and how might you respond to them? Do you want to set up a long-term rotation for your forest garden? What might that

Box 2.1: The Oak Beams of New College, Oxford

by *Gregory Bateson*

I owe this story to a man who was I think a New College student and was head of the Department of Medicine at the University of Hawaii, where he told it to me.

New College, Oxford, is of rather late foundation, hence the name. It was probably founded around the late 16th century. It has, like other colleges, a great dining hall with big oak beams across the top, yes? These might be eighteen inches square, twenty feet long.

Some five or ten years ago [*as of 1980— ed.*], so I am told, some busy entomologist went up into the roof of the dining hall with a penknife and poked at the beams and found they were full of beetles. This was reported to the College Council, who met in dismay, because where would they get beams of that caliber nowadays?

One of the Junior Fellows stuck his neck out and suggested there might be on College lands some oak. These colleges are endowed with pieces of land scattered across the country. So they called in the College Forester, who of course had not been near the college itself for some years, and asked him about oaks.

And he pulled his forelock and said, "Well sirs, we was wonderin' when you'd be askin'."

Upon further inquiry it was discovered that when the College was founded, a grove of oaks had been planted to replace the beams in the dining hall when they became beetly, because oak beams always become beetly in the end. This plan had been passed down from one Forester to the next for four hundred years. "You don't cut them oaks. Them's for the College hall."

A nice story. That's the way to run a culture.

Reprinted courtesy of the Institute for Intercultural Studies, Inc., New York.

look like? Even if you don't want a rotation, how will you deal with the inevitable death of the dominant trees in your garden? What might come next?

We recommend that you at least sketch out on paper some sense of the tasks each patch of your forest garden will require each month, each year. This will give you a somewhat realistic sense of the time your garden will ask of you. Use this to adjust the size of your forest garden overall, to choose the location of each patch or crop according to *Zones and Sectors* (#7), and to guide your activities throughout the year.

Imagine the long-term future of your garden. Think beyond a static "climax"-forest viewpoint into a dynamic present-yet-to-be. If you want to gain the benefits of a shifting mosaic, try to work out a rotation scheme with the limited information now available (see "Estimated Useful Life Spans of Selected Woody Species" in appendix 2). Imagine your forest garden as a success, imagine it as a failure, imagine it as you grow old. How might you regenerate succession? What will the needs and issues be? How can you adjust the current design to make room for some of these eventualities and possibilities?

Consider the various kinds of natural disturbances that occur in your region. How might you respond to them? Think about the plants you would use to regenerate disturbed patches. How could you keep them growing in your garden on an ongoing basis so you can easily propagate them to fill gaps? What disturbance regime would generate the kind of habitat they require?

Define the overall structural goals that help you select the organisms, species, and varieties you want.

35. Diversity of Life Forms

Certain kinds of diversity help stabilize ecosystems and keep them healthy. This pattern focuses on the living elements of compositional diversity, while many other patterns deal with structural and functional diversity. It applies to every forest garden.

What kinds of beings, living together, form the foundations of community health and stability? Species diversity is good, but it's just the beginning.

Thousands upon thousands of microbe species live in forest soils. Meanwhile, only a hundred or so vertebrate species live in temperate forests. Yet all kinds of organisms are important to building healthy ecological communities, including insects of all kinds, birds, reptiles, amphibians, mammals, and everything else. Each group of organisms plays more than one essential role in keeping the community running in a sort of moving balance.

At the other end of the spectrum, the diversity of temperate forests is about as high as that of tropical forests when you include variation within the species as well as the number of species in the equation. This genetic diversity within species aids adaptation to highly variable and patchy environments as well as variable climates. It also helps prevent disease and insect outbreaks from devastating the whole species at one time, ensuring that some individuals will live on to keep the species going.

So we must provide for the immigration and naturalization of diverse kinds of organisms into our forest gardens if we want them to work well. We also must include diverse members within a species, meaning diverse varieties, to help ward off disease and increase the chance of stable yields for ourselves.

Create habitats for every kind of good organism you can think of in your forest garden, and bring them there if they aren't there already. Also, plant diverse varieties of any crops you grow to better protect yourself from disease and pest calamities.

36. Extraordinary Edibles Everywhere

So many of the patterns deal with things other than food that we have to include this pattern somewhere!

Healthy, delicious, and enjoyable food is a primary, primal, and practical motivation for creating and maintaining a forest garden. To maximize our benefit from the effort, food production should be able to occur in every niche of the forest garden. However, our developed crops and tastes can't yet fill every niche.

We all have our food preferences. In our current culture, we tend to eat a very narrow range of plant species (only about twenty species account for the vast majority of food consumption worldwide[22]). These plants represent a very limited set of growing conditions, habitats, and ecological niches. If we are to make maximum use of forest gardening, we'll have to expand our range somehow.

Many useful and delicious perennial crops remain underused, such as persimmons, ramps, currants and gooseberries, and so on. Meanwhile, other potentially valuable crops exist that need further development, including earthchestnut, skirret, and groundnut. Even if we grow only the tastiest perennial crops we will expand our dietary range dramatically from what most people in our culture eat. These crops can fill a variety of niches in forest gardens.

Beyond those boundaries, food plants exist for virtually every community niche in the forest garden ecosystem. Not all of them are delicious yet. Many need selection and breeding improvement. But that kind of work isn't always hard or only for specialists; anyone can play a role. We already have a range of valuable underused perennial crops to choose from (see volume 1, appendix 1, for a list of the "Top 100"). Before long, with concerted effort, we'll have a whole new range of crops to choose from. Let's grow these foods, eat them, and develop them.

Yet we must feel motivated to plant and manage our gardens. Therefore, we need to focus our efforts on growing crops that we enjoy and that are good for us. However, let us not do that to the exclusion of the other interesting, tasty, and potentially tasty species we can fit into our backyard ecosystems.

Focus your forest gardening on foods you enjoy, and find and grow a range of new and different food crops in all areas and niches of your forest garden.

Use the base of enjoyable foods to motivate you to experiment with other food crops. Expand your range of tastes, and improve the other crops that need it. Just by growing genetically diverse populations of marginal food species, we increase the chances of finding a better selection that can lead to a new crop. Therefore, grow at least some of your forest garden crops from seed, and select the best plants from those seedlings for future propagation efforts.

37. *Gourmet Decomposers*

Decomposers fill key community niches in forest food webs. Fungi strongly influence nutrient and energy flows, disease processes, and the structure of soil and soil food webs. Edible mushrooms can grow on varied substrates.[23] Appendix 2 provides a table of edible mushrooms and their niche characteristics to give you a start.

The vast majority of net primary plant production in forests passes through decomposers. How can we tap into this energy flow to feed ourselves?

Decomposer organisms process large amounts of organic matter each year, releasing nutrients and energy that run the bulk of the food web and energy economy of forest ecosystems. Fungi are a critical component of this community, since they are the only organisms that can break down the complex carbohydrates within woody materials. Many of these fungi are edible. Some of these edible fungi help fight disease in the ecosystem by competitively excluding disease fungi from fungal niches in the soil food web. Some produce biochemicals that promote plant health, too. Many edible fungi appear to have powerful medicinal effects on the human body, as well as being delicious and often easy to grow.

When inoculating an outdoor environment with mushroom spawn, the cultivator relinquishes much control to natural forces. There are obvious advantages and disadvantages to natural culture. First, the mushroom patch is controlled by volatile weather patterns. This also means that outdoor beds have the advantage of needing minimum maintenance. The ratio of hours spent per pound of mushrooms grown becomes quite efficient.... When cultivating mushrooms outdoors you have *entropy as an ally*. [Italics added][24]

Integrate food fungus production into your forest garden using logs, stumps, wood chips, straw mulch, manure piles, and enriched soils (see figures 2.41 through 2.47).

All mushrooms need moisture to thrive, so proper siting is important in locating your mushroom beds or logs. Established forest gardens, or even annual vegetable gardens, should work fine as long as there is sufficient vegetation to shade the inoculated mulch or logs and you keep things watered. Most mushrooms prefer shade, but some species, such as the king stropharia, can grow in sunny conditions. Charlie Headington had his shiitake logs placed in the shade of his garage right next to his garden pond and the main path from his house to his car. This kept the logs from drying out in the sun, made it easy to moisten them in the pond, and kept them in a primary view zone for ease of monitoring and harvest. That latter point is important: mushrooms sprout and mature fast, and they fade just as quickly. Put them somewhere prominent so you can harvest them at peak quality.

Purchase spawn from one of the sources listed in appendix 7, or create your own.[25] Spawn comes in several forms; sawdust, grain, and plugs are the three most common types. Each of these substrates is sterilized and then inoculated with pure cultures of the chosen species. When the fungi have completely colonized the substrate, it is shipped to you. Plug spawn is placed in holes drilled in logs or stumps—or old furniture, for that matter. You then seal the holes with wax to keep the plugs moist. You can also pack sawdust spawn into holes drilled into logs or stumps, or you can use either the wedge or the disk techniques as shown in figures 2.41 through 2.44. Once inoculated, the fungus will spread into the substrate and then begin fruiting. Many species can grow this way, including the mild and somewhat gelatinous wood ear mushroom (*Auricularia polytricha*) and the maitake mushroom (*Grifola frondosa*), also known as the hen-of-the-woods. The maitake tastes excellent but is tough

FIGURE 2.41. You can grow gourmet decomposers by a number of means, including by drilling a one- to three-month-old stump and putting in plug spawn. You can also stuff sawdust spawn into drilled holes, but it isn't as easy as using inoculated plugs. Once the holes are filled, cover them with wax to keep the spawn moist. *Adapted from Stamets, 1993.*

Sawdust spawn

FIGURE 2.42. If you cut a tree high off the ground, you can inoculate the tall stump using sawdust spawn and the wedge technique. *Adapted from Stamets, 1993.*

Spawn

FIGURE 2.43. You can use the spawn disc technique on either a freshly cut tree stump or a log planted in the ground. *Adapted from Stamets, 1993.*

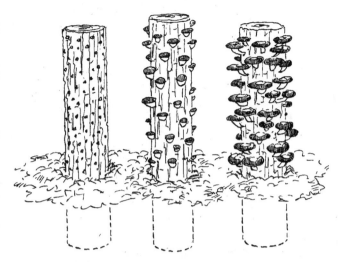

FIGURE 2.44. Planting inoculated logs in the ground helps keep the logs moist and spurs mushroom production. These logs were drilled and the holes filled with sawdust or plug spawn. Logs should be freshly cut to prevent contamination with wild fungi before inoculating. *Adapted from Stamets, 1993.*

FIGURE 2.45. Burying inoculated logs in sawdust or gravel is another way to keep them moist. *Adapted from Stamets, 1993.*

FIGURE 2.46. Many mushroom growers stack inoculated logs and cover them with a tarp, especially when doing commercial production. The stacks should be in full shade, ideally with water available to keep them moist. *Adapted from Stamets, 1993.*

and needs to cook for a long while, unlike most other mushrooms.

If your site has stumps on it, you can inoculate the stumps with edible or medicinal mushrooms and speed the stumps' demise while you eat (figure 2.41). You have to inoculate when the stump is fresh, however. If you wait more than one to three months, wild fungi from the neighborhood will have already taken over and your species will probably not make it. Leave a tall stump so you can inoculate it as shown in figure 2.42. You can also completely or partially bury inoculated logs to keep the wood moist (figures 2.43, 2.44, and 2.45). Just make sure you match the mushroom species with a suitable substrate, or vice versa; each species has its wood preferences (see appendix 2). The black poplar agrocybe (*Agrocybe aegerita*), for example, has a mild, porklike flavor and grows on stumps or in wood chips from hardwood trees such as maple, cotton-wood, willow, and, of course, poplar. If you prefer the taste of lobster, then try the lion's mane (*Hericium erinaceous*), which grows on stumps and logs of oak, beech, elm, maple, and other hard-woods. It is also the only species in our listing known to grow on walnut wood. If lobster doesn't turn you on, then the chicken-of-the-woods (*Laetiporus sulphureus*) is probably more to your liking. It really does taste like chicken!

Growing mushrooms on logs and stumps turns otherwise inedible products into food and medicine, as well as fertilizer. Many coppice-producing woody plants make great substrates for mushroom produc-tion, too. If you don't have a chipper, log production is a great way to make use of slash (see figure 2.46). If you do have a chipper, then you can turn your slash and brush into wood chips for mulch-bed mushroom production.

Growing mushrooms in mulch is a pretty simple affair. Again, though, your mulch must be fresh, or wild fungi will have already colonized the substrate. You can use straw, wood chips, or other woody organic materials, including waste paper, as a sub-strate. Place a layer of fresh substrate as mulch on

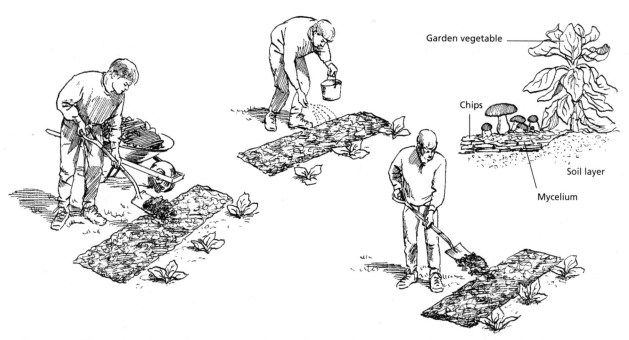

Garden vegetable

Chips

Soil layer

Mycelium

FIGURE 2.47. You don't need to use logs to grow mushrooms; fresh sawdust, wood chips, or other mulch works well, too, depending on the mushroom you are cultivating. Simply lay down moist mulch in a garden bed, sprinkle spawn over the top, and add more moist mulch on top of the spawn. Keep the mulch moist or the fungal mycelia will die back. *Adapted from Stamets, 1993.*

your garden bed, or along one edge (figure 2.47), and moisten it with water. Sprinkle your spawn material on top of the substrate. Ideally, you will use a 20 percent inoculation rate, that is, 1 gallon (4 l) of spawn would inoculate 5 gallons (20 l) of substrate. Cover the spawn with another layer of substrate, and moisten that. It's that simple! Keep the substrate moist. The fungus will colonize the substrate within one to eight weeks, depending on climatic conditions, the type of spawn, and the vigor of the inoculum. At that time you can either expand the patch again by a factor of five by inoculating more substrate with the patch you just created, or you can induce fruiting. One usually induces fruiting by providing shade and lots of water. You will soon be harvesting tasty and nutritious mushrooms for your kitchen. Production may be seasonal, however, with more fruits produced in the cooler and wetter spring and fall than in hot, dry summer weather.

Growing mushrooms in your garden mulch doesn't take up much additional space, if any. The labor requirements are relatively low once the bed is established, but you do have to nurse the culture along: cultivated mushrooms are not long-lived perennials in most cases. It's like keeping a yogurt culture alive by inoculating new substrate when necessary to keep the culture strong. You will therefore find that you'll have to reestablish beds and logs every so often, unless you choose species that are likely to naturalize and they actually do so. With the right conditions, a number of species will naturalize. Forest gardens are frequently the perfect environments for this process to occur. The garden oyster mushroom (*Hypsizygus ulmarius*), for instance, grows well in straw and garden debris as well as on logs and stumps. Can you guess what it tastes like?

We encourage you to find out more about mushroom cultivation. The potential benefits are enormous, and the subject is rife with possibilities and fascination. It's a whole new world of food growing perfectly suited to creating diverse, high-yielding, self-maintaining, self-fertilizing gardens. If you do it right, mushrooms could be one of the first harvests from your forest garden. You should also have a good field guide on mushrooms so you can positively identify any mushroom you are thinking of eating. Make sure you know any similar fungus species and the risks they pose to your health. With those stipulations in mind, have fun exploring. The diversity, flavor, and health value of mushrooms are mind-boggling.

38. *Three-Layer Minimum*

This pattern applies to every forest garden. It helps us define when a forest garden is a forest garden.

How many layers does it take to make a forest garden, or to make it ecologically healthy and stable?

This seemingly simple or semantic question cuts to the heart of several forest-garden design issues, even though at some level it can have only an arbitrary answer unless we are talking about specific situations. It seems reasonable to set a limit somewhere for how many layers of vegetation are necessary to make a stand of plants a forest or a forest garden.

Technically speaking, it takes only one layer of vegetation to create a forest: a dense, interlocking canopy of trees over 12 feet (3.7 m) above the ground.[26] However, foresters note that when a forest has only one or even two layers of vegetation, let's say only a canopy and an herb layer, the forest is not ecologically stable. There are no young or middle-aged trees to replace the canopy dominants when they die. The age structure is skewed to one age group, or maybe two. The system won't stay in good health or steady production for long. Not only that,

but the structural diversity of such a system is low. There are more likely to be insect pest imbalances because fewer niches exist for birds and predatory insects. The diversity of species is likely to be lower, too, because only two kinds of plants are present. At least some foresters have concluded that three layers are the minimum for a stand of trees to be considered a forest, at least a healthy one.

Design your forest garden with at least three layers of vegetation (figure 2.48).

These do not have to be continuous throughout the whole forest garden, but they should ideally interweave to some degree, stacking on top of one another in some way, so that they create habitats at different levels of the community. This will aid the diversification of bird and insect populations and increase opportunities for yield in the garden. Create these layers both by using plants of different life forms (tree, shrub, herb) and by diversifying the age structure of the system.

39. *Lumpy Texture*

This pattern is closely related to the previous pattern, *Three-Layer Minimum* (#38). However, here the concern is the patterns of the layers, not how many there are. It, too, applies to every forest garden.

Many forest gardens we have seen have a smooth, thick texture because the gardeners have tried to use all the layers, all the time. This creates numerous problems in the forest garden and does not truly mimic the structure of natural forests.

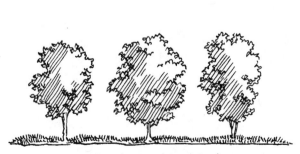

Not a forest garden: only two layers

Forest garden with at least three layers: canopy, shrub, herb

FIGURE 2.48. Three-layer minimum.

When all the layers of a forest garden are more or less evenly full across the whole garden, it tends to create what we have called "split-pea soup" texture. Rarely do we find this texture in natural forests, at least in those forests that have been able to establish a natural disturbance and regeneration regime. Pea-soup texture reduces air flow through the forest garden, thereby increasing the likelihood of disease. It makes it hard to work in the forest garden, to see or move through it. Too dense a stand of vegetation can even create higher stress in all the plants in the system because they may demand more water and nutrients than the site can handle. This can lower everyone's productivity and enjoyment of life. Pea soup minimizes variation in microenvironments, smoothing out patterns of light and dark and offering fewer niches in the community for birds and insects. In sum, pea-soup texture in the forest garden does not offer the pest- and disease-balancing benefits that "lumpy texture" does, nor does it truly mimic the structure of most healthy, natural forests.

Design planting density and layering patterns to create lumpy texture (figure 2.49).

Vary the layer locations and density in a clumpy, drifty, patchwise manner. In some places the herb layer may be dense and full with no shrub layer; in others the shrub layer will be dense with no herb layer; in still others, both will be thinly sprinkled with plants. The canopy can vary in density, too, creating light and dark patches on the forest floor to which the lower layers will respond.

40. Layers of Harvest

We use this pattern to generalize an idea about minimizing harvesting complications from Martin Crawford, in his article on ground-cover polycultures.[27] Use it when you are attempting to maximize yields from any or every patch and you are designing intensively and thoughtfully in an effort to get high yields with minimal effort.

It can get very challenging to harvest various products (berries, leaves, nuts, flowers) from plants in a dense polyculture when all the plants are the same height.

Let's say you had two ground covers growing in polyculture, each one with a height of between 6 and 12 inches (15 and 30 cm). One yields edible berries, the other medicinal leaves. Imagine trying to harvest the berries or leaves when the plants are growing all mixed in polyculture. We might characterize this situation as difficult, time-consuming, potentially frustrating, perhaps overwhelming, and probably unnecessary.

Segregate your harvestable products by layer, or by height within a layer, when growing plants in dense polycultures (figure 2.50).

FIGURE 2.49. Lumpy texture results from diversity in the structural patterning of vegetation throughout the layers (left). Contrast this with "split-pea soup" texture (right), where every layer is evenly full of vegetation.

For any polyculture patch, define the harvestable products, when they are available, and how you harvest them. Figure these factors into your polyculture design. For example:

The most useful method of reducing the complications of harvesting is to mix species which grow at distinct different heights. This could even allow for a commercial herb crop, for example, by growing a larger perennial herb like lemon balm (*Melissa officinalis*) with a low-growing running cover like ground ivy (*Glechoma hederaceae*), where the herb can be cut at say 25 cm (10 inches) above ground by hand or mechanically. A variation on the height difference scheme is to have the taller species deciduous in habit, with a summer "crop" to harvest, along with an evergreen lower species with an autumn or winter "crop": both species will be easily accessible and visible when they are required.[28]

41. Staggered Harvests, Clustered Harvests

If you intend to grow much or most of your own food, you need to consider what this pattern has to offer you. When we design a garden, we design our whole lives, for the implications for how we spend our time can be enormous.

Sometimes during harvest time we can get totally overwhelmed by the quantity of food we have to pick, eat, process, and store. Then again, work can be inefficient when we have to go out and pick a crop many times over days or weeks of ripening, rather than being able to harvest all at once.

Many gardeners forget to plan their harvests or their work during harvest when they select and buy the seeds for their vegetable garden. They then bear the consequences the following summer or fall when everything comes in at once or there are gaps in the food supply. Are the canning peaches coming in at the same time the Jerusalem artichokes need to be pulled and the nuts need to be cured and put away, not to mention all the vegetables that need to be harvested? Sometimes we can't prevent this, but with some thinking we can smooth out the work flow so it doesn't get overwhelming. Annual vegetables offer us new chances to make better choices every year as we learn how

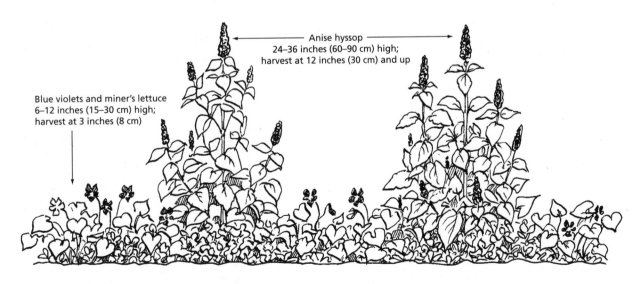

Anise hyssop
24–36 inches (60–90 cm) high;
harvest at 12 inches (30 cm) and up

Blue violets and miner's lettuce
6–12 inches (15–30 cm) high;
harvest at 3 inches (8 cm)

FIGURE 2.50. Create layers of harvest by separating harvested products by height within or between layers. Here we see anise hyssop (*Agastache foeniculum*), a 24- to 36-inch-high (60 to 90 cm) herb growing with a ground-cover polyculture of miner's lettuce (*Montia perfoliata*) and blue violets (*Viola sororaria*). Both of these ground covers are harvested using scissors for their edible greens and flowers and grow to a maximum of 12 inches (30 cm). Meanwhile, the anise hyssop can be harvested at 12 inches (30 cm) or higher.

these things work. Perennials aren't so forgiving: you make the choices once, and then bear the consequences year after year.

We must therefore make conscious choices concerning crop varieties and the implications these choices have for time of ripening, workloads, and food quantities. Do you want to have a steady supply of fruits throughout the year, with the consequent continuous flow of work in harvest, or would you rather have it come in all at once so you can do a major harvest workathon and get it all done at one time? Maybe you want to have a steady supply of table fruit and nuts throughout the year and two or three surges of produce for storage at different points to break up the total workload into manageable portions.

Think not only of spreading out or clumping the ripening of each kind of fruit (i.e., getting three varieties of pears that come in at different times through late summer and fall), but of all the other crops you have coming, too. Will the pears, peaches, raspberries, hazelnuts, kiwis, and chestnuts all come in at the same time and overwhelm your capacity to make use of them? Not only are we designing a whole ecosystem in forest gardening, but we are designing a whole household economy that needs to work for us, the human inhabitants of the garden.

Plan the timing and quantity of your harvests to even out supply or improve work efficiency.

Create a calendar of ripening for your forest garden to plan your workload, showing expected dates of ripening and expected quantities at maturity for each crop. Include on or with this calendar options for processing and approximate time to process the foods or other products that will need it. Use this to estimate your workload, knowing that weather and chance will influence actual times of ripening from year to year. Develop a scenario and strategy you think will work for you and your family, your lifestyle, and circumstances, as best you can, and then use that strategy to help you select species and varieties that fit.

42. *Nectaries Always Flowering*
If minimizing pest problems is important to you, then so is this pattern.

Beneficial predatory insects and pollinators require year-long energy sources if they are to stick around and do their job.

The location of nectary plants, scattered throughout the garden, is not the only critical factor in providing for our predatory and pollinating allies. The timing of their flowering is equally if not more important. We must ensure that beneficial insects can always find their energy sources during the growing season, or we will lose their services and have to replace them with our own labor.

Select a suite of nectary plants such that several species are flowering at all times of the growing season.

Create a calendar of bloom for nectaries, and select species so that their flowering times overlap by at least a week. Try to have at least two or three species flowering every week of the growing season for every niche of beneficial insects. This will add up to quite a few species! Don't forget to include your fruit trees as sources for pollinators when they are flowering. Then scatter these plants around the garden so that no part of the garden is without nectaries flowering at any time for any group, according to *Functional Plants Throughout* (#51).

43. *Native Species*
Many of us seek clear guidance on when and why to use native plants and why we might not want to. Here's a quick guideline. For more discussion see volume 1 and its feature articles on the topic.

We feel concerned about the loss of native species and the explosion of opportunist exotics, but many of our most desired and useful plants are not native. What should we do?

There's no escaping it: most Americans prefer to grow and eat plants that didn't originate anywhere on this continent, much less in their region or locale. However, few edible crops become opportunist exotics. It's the ornamental, wildlife food and shelter, and "soil conservation" plants that most often go wild. A number of opportunistic plants are quite useful in forest gardening, but we mostly don't recommend using them (see appendix 4, "The Watch List"). However, going to the extreme by refusing to use nonnative plants at all is problematic as well as unrealistic given the ecological, botanical, and epicurean realities we face. Most of us do not want to go that far but seek a reasonable middle ground.

Look to native plants to perform your desired garden functions first, before looking to nonnatives.

Weigh the functions and characteristics of the various species, giving reasonable priority to native plants. When deciding whether to use an exotic species, consider its means of dispersal, its vigor and persistence, whether it is already abundant in your locale, and whether a similar native can perform the same function(s) or not.

Define species placement patterns within the larger patterns defining the structure of the garden as a whole.

Repeating the same or similar patterns over a large area helps create order and improve work efficiency. Varying patterns helps create diversity. Used wisely, modular patterns can vary enough in their expression and relate well enough to the specifics of place that they don't end up as "cookie cutter" patterns but help create theme and unity through creative repetition.

44. *Polyculture Patches*

This is one of the key patterns for forest gardening. It offers structure that helps satisfy those of us who are looking for some organization within our forest gardens, rather than a wild free-for-all.

Patches of various sizes are the fundamental architectural units of forests and other ecosystems. Yet many forest gardens we have seen so far consist of random, evenly mixed polycultures throughout the whole forest garden, without consciously designed patches within them. This pattern, or lack of pattern, **results in overly complex arrangements that seem hard to understand, manage, and benefit from.**

Most of us in Western culture are used to landscape patterns defined by hard edges. Forests rarely express such patterns, tending instead to consist of seemingly random, irregular, fluid, overlapping, and interwoven plant distributions with feathered or indefinite edges. It is hard for most of us to see the structure within these patterns, but there is structure there: the structure of patches.

Each of these patches consists of a different architecture: a given set of layers, soil horizons, densities, plant distribution patterns, and diversities. They are ephemeral, undergoing change through succession. And they usually contain many species growing together as natural polycultures, often as resource-sharing or mutual-support guilds. We use patches as the basic structural unit of the forest garden, building the garden as a whole from various kinds of patches, many of which are polycultures.

In the context of forest gardening, polycultures are intentional species mixtures grown for specific purposes, in an attempt to create both resource-sharing and mutual-support guilds. Two species growing together have multiple interactions ranging from neutralism to cooperation to competition, all happening at the same time with respect to different resources, needs, and yields. Such pairwise relationships are already complex enough to try to understand and evaluate for their efficacy as useful polycultures. When we multiply this complexity by ten, twelve, or twenty species interacting throughout a forest garden, we have no hope of evaluating whether various polycultures will work to fulfill our purposes or to negate them. How can we simplify this complexity to increase the intelligibility of the forest garden without losing the benefits of high diversity?

The non patchiness we have seen in many forest gardens also seems to lend itself to more difficulty, not just in understanding what works, but in managing and harvesting crops. It is simply harder to get around in, work in, and enjoy the benefits of a garden that is so unstructured. If we don't have *some* understanding of what species mixtures work well, we are likely to be working harder and getting less yield than we otherwise might.

> **Plan and plant most of your forest garden patches as polycultures containing between two and seven plant species (figure 2.51).**

Design each polyculture patch based on the conditions, functions, architecture, and disturbance and maintenance regime you have discovered in or defined for it. Vary the polycultures (using different species mixes) enough at each scale to vary the architecture of the forest garden and generate structural

diversity. Also, use the different species in enough different mixes to see how they perform with each other so you can learn which polycultures generate useful guild combinations under your conditions. This will create a diverse habitat with lumpy texture, but with enough organization to make management, harvesting, observation, and learning easier.

We gain important benefits from knowing whether or not our polycultures work. Because of that and the multiple facets of interaction between species, it makes sense to limit the number of species we design into our polyculture patches, at least in the beginning. We suggest keeping your patches to between two and

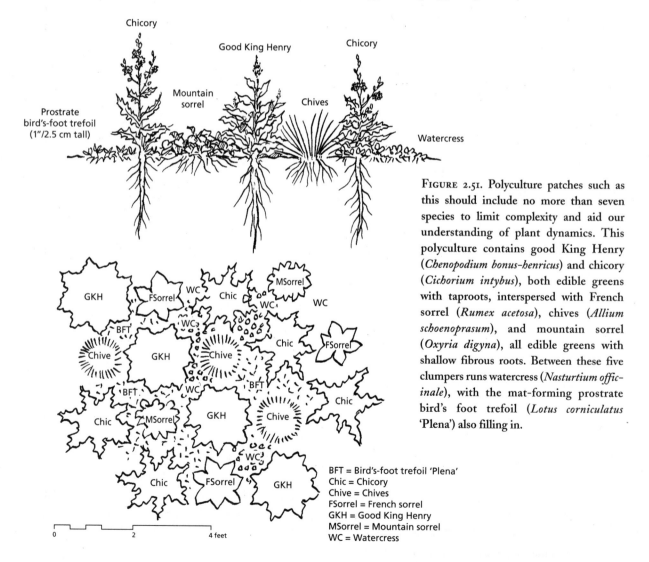

FIGURE 2.51. Polyculture patches such as this should include no more than seven species to limit complexity and aid our understanding of plant dynamics. This polyculture contains good King Henry (*Chenopodium bonus-henricus*) and chicory (*Cichorium intybus*), both edible greens with taproots, interspersed with French sorrel (*Rumex acetosa*), chives (*Allium schoenoprasum*), and mountain sorrel (*Oxyria digyna*), all edible greens with shallow fibrous roots. Between these five clumpers runs watercress (*Nasturtium officinale*), with the mat-forming prostrate bird's foot trefoil (*Lotus corniculatus* 'Plena') also filling in.

BFT = Bird's-foot trefoil 'Plena'
Chic = Chicory
Chive = Chives
FSorrel = French sorrel
GKH = Good King Henry
MSorrel = Mountain sorrel
WC = Watercress

seven species, starting at the low end and adding species as you learn what works and what niches each polyculture needs to have filled (see figure 2.51). Pick your species so that each is adapted to the conditions in the patch, but together they form both resource-partitioning and mutual-support guilds. You should probably design the canopy or overstory patches separately from and before the underlying layer patches because of the differences in scale and the influence of upper layers on conditions below them.

Polyculture patches may also be polycultures in time, not just in space. Spring ephemerals may dominate in May and June, while other species will do so later. These polycultures may then yield different products at different times.

45. Pockets of Production

This pattern eases the transition from the typical monoculture gardening most of us are used to doing to the complex polycultures we need to play with and learn about.

Polycultures can offer numerous benefits to agriculture, yet they represent a new strategy for most gardeners, and for virtually all common crops. How can we be sure to get decent production if we want the benefits, but we don't yet want to play with polycultures for a certain crop?

We have outlined the benefits of polycultures in many places in this book. Yet we have much to learn about polyculture production even for our common crops, much less the new and different ones we discuss. Which polycultures will produce higher yields than the crops grown separately, and under what conditions? How many crops can we plant in polyculture without making management too difficult? We can learn all these things, but it will take time. Even so, there will probably still be crops that we prefer to grow in monoculture for some reason. How can we do that without losing the ecological and other benefits we seek from polyculture production? Small pockets of monoculture in the midst of diverse plantings are not exactly monocultures, and they can make high production easier.

Plant pockets of monoculture crop production in the midst of diverse plantings to produce crops in quantity yet maintain a diverse habitat mosaic within the garden (figure 2.52).

Scatter these pockets of production within a diverse matrix of beneficial insectary plants, fertility plants, and crops grown in polyculture. *The matrix should be larger than the pockets for this pattern to work to its optimum,* so make sure the matrix is also productive habitat. Divide large areas of monocrop into several smaller pockets, and disperse these pockets to make pests and diseases work harder to find their hosts. This gives predators a better chance to find their prey. The size of the pockets should vary according to the size of the plants in the crop; for example, blueberry pockets might be tens of feet in diameter, while pockets of culinary herbs would be a few feet in diameter. To maintain the polyculture environment, pockets of production should remain a small proportion of the total forest-garden system—say, less than one-third.

46. Flower-Petal Beds

This pattern explores the radial pathways around a tree in more detail (see *Rootlike Path Geometries*, #27). It is most appropriate in small-scale forest gardens where management can be more intensive.

Many of a tree's inherent needs and preferences conflict with what makes our management tasks easier.

Maintaining a fruit tree requires access to the tree for pruning, monitoring and managing insects and diseases, picking up dropped fruit, and harvest. Meanwhile, tree roots prefer uncompacted, fungi-dominated soils. At the same time, we desire to plant polycultures that use space below the tree for production, nutrient accumulation, and beneficial-insect attraction. Also, diverse plant associates help create the guilds that meet the tree's needs for pollination, defense, nutrition, and so on, but these plantings can get in the way of managing a tree. Grass ground covers are easy to maintain, offer freedom of movement around the tree, and make picking up dropped fruit easy, but they create a

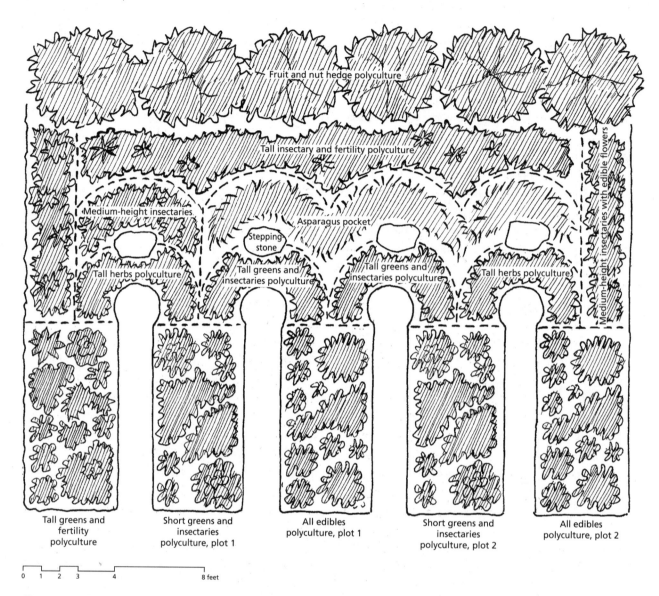

Tall greens and fertility polyculture

Short greens and insectaries polyculture, plot 1

All edibles polyculture, plot 1

Short greens and insectaries polyculture, plot 2

All edibles polyculture, plot 2

0 1 2 3 4 8 feet

FIGURE 2.52. Pockets of monoculture crop production should always be surrounded by polyculture patches, especially of insectary and other functional plants. In this design, a pocket of monoculture asparagus production is surrounded by polycultures of insectary plants, greens and insectaries, and herbs. Note the stepping-stones set back from the ends of the keyholes to facilitate harvesting the asparagus in the spring. Also note replicate trials of the same polycultures in the front beds.

highly bacterial soil and encourage soil compaction all around a tree's roots.

> Design the planting beds under and around each tree in the form of flower petals, with a ring path around the tree's crown and radial pathways into and away from the center of the tree (figure 2.53).

The ring path allows free movement around the tree yet minimizes compaction to a narrow band away from the fine feeder roots that extend past the crown's dripline. Locate the pathways toward the center between the tree's lower scaffold branches to minimize branch breakage and ease access to the trunk and branches. Allow the planting beds to become wider as they extend farther from the tree, using radial keyhole paths into these petals to gain access with minimal compaction. Then design the

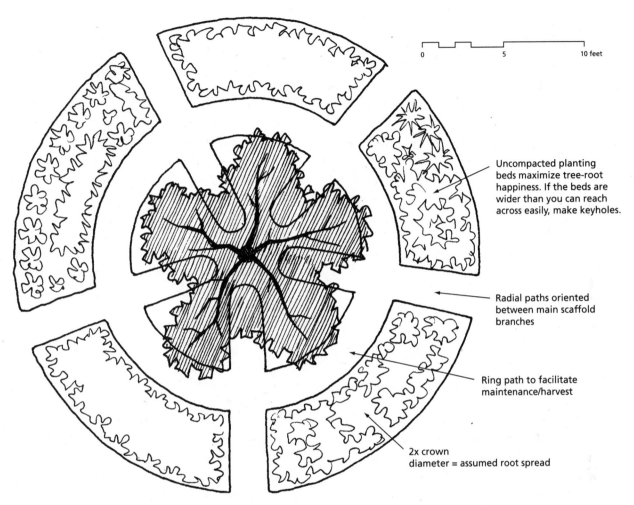

Uncompacted planting beds maximize tree-root happiness. If the beds are wider than you can reach across easily, make keyholes.

Radial paths oriented between main scaffold branches

Ring path to facilitate maintenance/harvest

2x crown diameter = assumed root spread

FIGURE 2.53. Flower-petal beds maximize the uncompacted soil available to tree roots while still providing access to the tree. Orient radial paths so they fall between major scaffold branches, and provide a ring path to facilitate maintenance. The outside diameter of the growing beds should reflect the estimated maximum spread of the roots as determined by soil conditions and the estimated crown diameter. Tree roots spread up to one and a half times the crown diameter in moist, fertile, deep soils, and up to three times the crown diameter in dry, infertile, or shallow soils.

planting beds to encourage the proper soil food web and loose soils the tree roots prefer, filling them with compatible guild species that support the tree in its functions or that generate products for your own direct use.

47. Cluster Planting

This pattern applies especially in the early phases of forest-garden planting and succession, when the differences between the habitats we have and those we are creating can be dramatic—at least for our plant and microbial allies. It derives in part from discussions in Mollison's permaculture books.

Plants generally prefer to grow in association with other compatible plants and their microbial friends. When we plant our green allies into hostile or stressful environments as scattered, isolated individuals, they suffer. They are also harder to care for easily and effectively.

Trees tend to prefer and create a fungi-dominated soil, while grass tends to prefer and create a bacteria-dominated soil. When we disperse trees

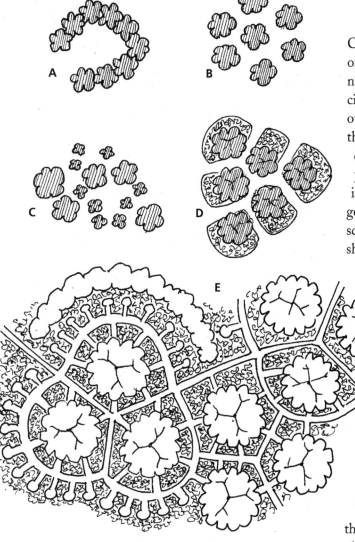

FIGURE 2.54A–E. A few possible patterns for cluster planting.

When planting into an environment different from that which the plant prefers, plant in clusters.

Clusters may include a number of individuals of one or more species of plants planted in any number of patterns (figure 2.54a–e). They can be circles of plants at a reasonable spacing from each other such that a single circular sprinkler can water the whole cluster. You may leave one end of such a circle open for access to the plants from inside, or you may leave enough space between plants to get inside the circle for management purposes. Other geometric shapes can work, such as triangles, squares, and so on. Clusters may also take irregular shapes depending on the species, their access and maintenance needs, and how the cluster must fit into the available space.

48. Cross-Pollination Clusters

Patterning the layout of different species within the forest garden demands understanding and balancing the dynamics of pests and pollination, among other things.

Many fruit and nut trees cannot pollinate themselves and need one or two different varieties of the same species nearby to produce. Yet we want to mix up our crops so they don't grow in blocks that offer pests and diseases concentrated habitat in which to thrive.

The pollination of flowers is an essential step in the production of seed and fruit in any flowering plant. "Self-fruitful" crops can pollinate themselves. "Self-unfruitful" species require pollen from a different variety to produce seed and fruit. Insects carry this pollen from one flower to another to cross-pollinate most fruit trees and shrubs. The wind does this job for most nuts. While we recommend that you plant self-fruitful varieties whenever possible, especially when you have small garden sites, doing so doesn't always meet your design goals and food preferences. Often we must plant more than one tree to get fruit, and sometimes we must plant three varieties for optimal fruit production.

Most discussions of cross-pollination in fruit-growing books recommend that cross-pollinators be

into a grassland, each tree finds itself in a hostile environment with few or no allies nearby. Not only is the soil environment counter to the tree's needs, but often the aboveground microclimate is, too. Harsh, drying winds and extreme temperatures buffet our friend, reducing its ability to grow and produce. In addition, if we want to water, mulch, or fertilize, a dispersed pattern of trees scatters our energies and focus and requires more hoses and equipment, so we spend more time on our horticultural tasks than we otherwise might.

planted right next to each other to ensure the best crops. However, planting single-species blocks like this supports the pests and diseases of those crops in finding and thriving on their hosts. To minimize pests and disease, we need to mix species together in polycultures so that pests must keep moving to find their hosts, thereby spending less time feeding and reproducing and more time exposing themselves to their predators. How can we achieve both of these objectives at the same time?

One solution is to graft different fruit varieties onto the same tree, creating multivariety trees that can cross-pollinate themselves readily. This works when you want to plant only one tree of a self-unfruitful crop species on your land, or with multiple trees that you want to scatter around your site. But some species are difficult to graft, or simply can't be. Nor does everyone know how to graft. In addition, if the grafted branch breaks or dies from disease, it will take time to get your pollenizer going again, during which time you won't get crops on that tree. What planting pattern can we use to obviate these problems, and to back up the multivariety tree strategy?

The key to a strategy rests on the observation that pollination distances of 50 feet (15 m; some say up to 100 feet or 30 m) work well enough if the ecosystem provides an abundance of pollinating insects. Edible forest gardens—organically managed and with pollinator habitat offered—should have no problem with that!

Create a polyculture consisting of interwoven, overlapping clusters of cross-pollinating plants.

For example, think of three semidwarf pear trees that cross-pollinate each other. Place them in a triangle where the distance between any two of the three trees is 50 feet (15 m). Then take three semidwarf peach trees and place them in a triangle with 50 feet (15 m) between them. Do the same with three cherries and three hazels. Overlap these triangles into each other so that no species stands next to another of its kind, but each is within 50 feet (15 m) of its pollenizers (figure 2.55). This is a cross-polli-

FIGURE 2.55. Cross-pollination clusters mix species to confuse pests but keep pollenizers within the maximum 50- to 100-foot (15 to 30 m) pollination distance from each other. This example uses overlapping triangles, but other geometries can work too.

nation cluster. Interwoven triangles such as this work well for creating the pattern, but you can use any other pattern you want.

All pollenizers should be within the maximum 50- to 100-foot (15 to 30 m) pollination distance of each other, but they should be separated from each other by at least one other plant of the same layer. The intervening plants may be other crop plants, insectary plants, dynamic accumulators, or nitrogen fixers. Make sure that the neighboring plants do not share pests and diseases, and that the chosen pollenizers flower at about the same time.

49. Ground-Cover Carpets

This pattern is most critical when you are dealing with large forest gardens where the amount of food you could grow in the understory overwhelms your ability to manage or use it. This pattern applies the competitive exclusion principle and ideas from the unified oldfield theory (table 1.6 and volume 1, chapter 6), as well as the principle of multiple functions.

> **How can we manage weeds when we don't continually disturb the soil to prevent their germination and spread? Can we do so in a way that gains us other benefits as well as reducing our workload?**

By definition, forest gardens will have less frequent disturbances than annual gardens, and perhaps still fewer than a perennial flower bed if we do it right (see *Disturbance and Maintenance Regimes*, #34). Since most human-created disturbances are some form of work, less disturbance is a good thing. However, this by definition means fewer opportunities to influence the composition of the plant community, and we may find ourselves contending with many uninvited plants if we aren't careful.

"Weeding" these uninvited guests, as we usually practice it, is simply another form of disturbance that only creates more available niches and sites for new plants to colonize. Herbicides have many undesirable consequences, though they have their uses in extreme circumstances, and they, too, leave niches open for other plants to take over. *Mulch* (#56) helps in many cases but isn't always appropriate or desirable, since it implies a need for more work and possible expense to keep finding more of it. How, then, can we keep plants we don't want out of our gardens, or at least keep them to something below a "dull roar"?

The principle of competitive exclusion states that when two plants have the same niche, whichever one has the advantage will compete the other to extinction unless the other has an escape. Ground-cover plants can outcompete other plants because they grow densely, smothering the soil surface with leaves and branches and cutting off light to new growth below. This suppresses the germination of weed seeds. If the ground cover is vigorous enough, it can even outcompete established weeds of other species, if not at least preventing their offspring from reestablishing. For this to work best, the ground covers need to have a head start, as discussed in *Patch Disturbance and Regeneration* (#30).

Weed suppression isn't the only function ground covers can fulfill. The flowers of many ground covers support beneficial insects. Many fix nitrogen or accumulate needed mineral nutrients. Some grow edible leaves, flowers, or fruits. Many are underused native plants that can help enrich our garden's diversity and support healthy ecosystems.

> **Plant dense carpets of ground-cover plants that fill the available niches for unwanted plants in the forest garden, suppressing weed germination and growth. Select species that also perform functions such as attracting beneficial insects, improving the soil, producing food, or increasing populations of native plant species.**

For example, 'Huntington's Carpet' rosemary (*Rosmarinus officinalis*) is a high-density ground-cover variety that grows about 1 foot (30 cm) high and also produces culinary greens. Another well-known multifunctional ground cover is white clover (*Trifolium repens*), a nitrogen fixer that also has edible flowers and provides nectar for generalist predators. Ground-cover carpets may be composed of a single-species monoculture or polycultures of two or more species. If you desire a polyculture, see feature article 3, "Ground-Cover Polycultures," to help you select the cohabitants and plant them at the proper spacing.

50. *Drifts, Clumps, and Scatters*

This pattern does not directly deal with a successional strategy but, rather, concerns the spatial distribution patterns of plants. These patterns influence the reproductive success of each species, the success of pollinators and plant pests, and the aesthetics of the planting design. It applies at both large and small scales.

> **Regular or geometric patterns aren't the only patterns in which we can place plants in the garden. What natural patterns of plant distribution can we mimic in our forest garden polycultures?**

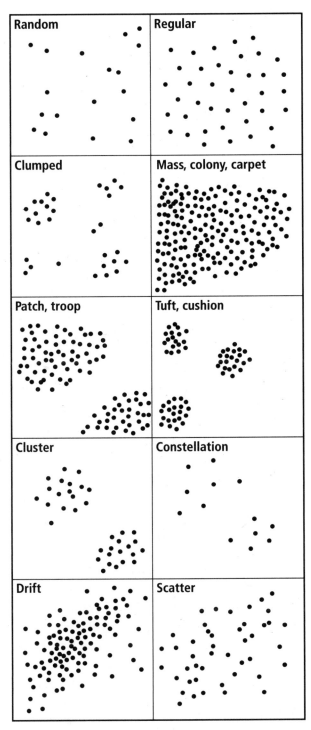

FIGURE 2.56. Plant distribution patterns.

Plants develop their own distribution patterns in natural systems (see figure 2.56). These patterns are innately determined to some degree, but they also depend upon the influences of the other plants a species grows with and the patterns of resources in the environment. When we observe the patterns of species distributions in nature, we find that most plants distribute themselves in one of three types of clustered distributions: drifts, clumps, or scatters. Clumps are the tightest, closest, and most defined groupings and range from masses to constellations. Scatters are the most open and fluid, with the least definite edges. Drifts are somewhere in between. These three patterns relate mostly to the plant's primary mode of dispersal into its environment.

Clumping plants tend to spread by heavy seeds that are few in number, by short rhizomes, stolons, or suckers, or by multiplication of buds or self-division, as is the case with chives and many other types of perennial onions. They can form pure or almost pure stands, with little room for other species within their clumps, or they may leave some space or time for others to show their faces. Clumps may in turn distribute themselves in clumps, drifts, or scatters.

Drifting plants spread primarily by seed or by longer runners, rhizomes, stolons, or suckers. Drifts (and scatters) leave plenty of room for other plants to interweave in time and space, so by definition, drifts tend to occur in polycultures. Drifts tend to be dense near their centers, with feathered edges as the density of a species thins to the outside.

Scatters form almost exclusively from seed-borne plants that grow singly, although some rhizomatous plants also look like scattered, isolated individuals when seen only from aboveground. Scattered plants by definition tend to exist within a context of different plants, rather than creating the environment around themselves as drifts and clumps tend to do.

You may discern within each of these three categories further subcategories of pattern. In any case, these patterns arise from plants for at least one

FIGURE 2.57. Drifts, clumps, and scatters of plants can overlap in complex polycultures as they do in nature. Here there are six different species distributed in different overlapping patterns.

reason, and it would behoove us to work out what functions these patterns perform for the plants, for it may save us time and effort. In addition, these patterns generate more visual fluidity in the landscape and may be aesthetically preferable to regular geometries in many cases.

Distribute plants, and allow them to distribute themselves, in patterns true to their means of dispersal for maximum effectiveness and beauty.

Observe the form and structure of each plant and discern its natural behaviors to determine what patterns might suit it best. Interweave these patterns when growing several species together to create beautiful and functional polycultures (figure 2.57).

51. *Functional Plants Throughout*

This is another pattern that applies almost universally to forest gardens, at least those where the gardener wants the garden to take more care of itself, rather than less.

Every place in the forest garden needs the functions of fertility plants and beneficial-insect attractors.

Beneficial insects need high-energy flower nectar, which enables them to fly around seeking prey to eat or upon which to lay eggs, or helps feed a pollinator colony and keep it strong year-round. Insect predators need the ability to scout the whole garden without worrying where their next meal is coming from. They need tiny flowers that produce nectar in quantity, and they need them everywhere, at least anywhere you want these insect allies to be. Pollinators need a variety of flowers depending on the pollinator species, and they need them especially in early spring, late summer, and fall to recover from and prepare for winter.

Nitrogen is the nutrient most frequently in short supply in the forest and the garden. Every plant needs nitrogen in sufficient quantity to produce well. The same goes for the other nutrients, especially those that are most liable to leach away into groundwater or that are most scarce in the soil. We need nitrogen fixers and dynamic accumulators everywhere in the forest garden.

Scatter mulch plants, nitrogen fixers, insectary plants, and dynamic accumulators throughout the forest garden, not just in a few pockets here and there.

Use these plants as part of virtually every polyculture, as *Ground-Cover Carpets* (#49), as shade plants, as hedges and barriers, as dividers between polyculture patches, and so on.

52. *Expansive Plant Containers*

Expansive plants, that is, those that spread vegetatively, can be a nuisance. This pattern helps deal with such species at a large or small scale. It does nothing for dispersive plants—those that spread by seed.

Some extremely useful plants, such as some bamboos, spread vigorously by underground rhizomes or suckers and outcompete other desirable plants. How can we contain them? To hold back an unwanted rhizomatous species, sometimes we don't need a strong container, just a significant barrier. What kind of barriers might we use?

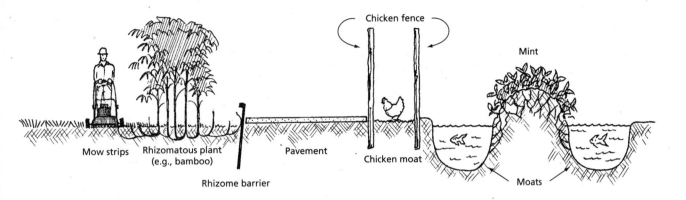

FIGURE 2.58. Expansive plant containers can take a variety of forms.

Growing expansive plants in polycultures or dealing with rhizomatous weeds outside our gardens can be extremely difficult or almost impossible. We need either to design environments that let these plants be who they are without interfering with our other plans or to work to manage them on an ongoing basis. Which do you think we prefer? The only exception to our choice might be if the rhizomes were a delicious edible and harvesting these rhizomes prevented their spread, as is true with many bamboos. However, the problem with management is that it doesn't always happen, and it always stops sometime. Then what happens? Do you really think you will go out there and rip out the plant after you've broken your leg or something? Even if you did, you probably wouldn't get it all, and it would come back. We say, prevent the plant's spread by design and save the hassle. Or don't use the plant at all.

Prevent the spread of expansive plants by surrounding them with inhospitable habitat, with physical barriers, or with barriers made of other plants (figure 2.58).

We can limit the spread of many rhizomatous plants using rhizome barriers. These are sheets of heavy plastic, metal, ferrocement, or other materials laid vertically in the ground to a depth of 12 to 18 inches (30 to 50 cm) or more, depending on the species you need to control. The most vigorous rhizomes, such as those from running bamboos (as opposed to clumping ones), require strong barriers with sealed seams buried vertically in the ground to 2 to 3 feet (60 to 100 cm) deep. See chapter 5 for details on rhizome barrier design and construction.

Expansive plant containers can take other forms, too. We may control less-vigorous rhizomatous plants simply by surrounding them with well-used and compacted pathways. Mown pathways can also act as rhizome barriers, but stop mowing and your barrier disappears. Pavement works as a rhizome barrier for most species, though we have heard that bamboos can sprout 20 feet (6 m) away on the opposite side of a road. Buildings usually work, too, depending on what kind of foundation they have and what plant it is. However, some trees can break foundations with their roots. On his North Carolina farm, Harvey Harmon grows aggressive mints on an island in a pond. This way he has his mints, and eats them too, but they cannot get out of control and take over his gardens. Certain plants can act as rhizomatous weed barriers when planted densely: "Blackberry edges have been reported as confined by comfrey, wormwood, *Coprosma repens*, pine, or cypress hedges."[29] Dave has seen poison ivy (*Toxicodendron radicans*) held at bay by the deep shade and allelopathic chemicals of Norway maple (*Acer platanoides*). Alternatively, you can surround the expansive plant on all sides with taller species that shade it out. Trenches can work, too, depending on the species you want to control, but most plants tend to grow down into and then out of the trench eventually.

GARDEN ELEMENTS

Embellish and enrich the garden you have created with specific elements that bring higher diversity and functionality to life.

53. *Living Soil*

This is another universal pattern, though how you achieve it varies depending on your garden's scale. See volume 1 for important information about the horizons, fertility, biology, and successional development of the soil (chapters 3, 5, and 6).

> **Living soil is the fundamental resource of the forest garden. Natural forests build living soils over many decades of successional development. How can we build and maintain living soils without waiting decades?**

Healthy forest soils contain rich reserves of nutrients and organic matter, provide living space for abundant and diverse soil food webs, and support large amounts of aboveground biomass. Living soil feeds not only plants but the whole ecosystem, including aboveground predators. Clearly this is a resource we must husband carefully and, ideally, develop quickly if our garden doesn't already live in this way. What key elements support this community?

Good soil texture, structure, and consistence (see feature article 2) form the foundation for soil health, because they influence the ability of water and air to move into and through the soil. If these factors are not ideal at your site, abundant organic matter improves the lot of almost any soil in this regard. However, organic matter belongs most abundantly on the soil surface: we should work with, not counter to, the functions of the natural soil profile. Nutritionally, the mineral content of bedrock and subsoil form the ultimate foundation

of fertility, even though healthy forests eventually become minimally dependent on these resources as they build the fertility of the topsoil.

A healthy soil food web offers many gifts to the gardener wise enough to return the favors. Dead organic matter feeds the decomposer food web, and the organisms in this web help build good soil structure as well as making nutrients available to plants and keeping them from leaching away. The soil food web also depends on the roots of plants to feed sugars and other exudates to microbes living in the plant root zones, which outnumber decomposers by many orders of magnitude. Mycorrhizas are of particular importance, but they are only one strand in the complete soil food web we should strive for.

Plants are the key link in self-renewing soil fertility. They create a system that generates long-term net gains of fertility in the topsoil by plugging nutrient leaks and increasing the size of nutrient containers. Deep-rooted perennial plants speed the fertility buildup, particularly those that fix nitrogen from the atmosphere or dynamically accumulate minerals from the subsoil.

These three key elements of living soil—soil structure, soil food webs, and plants—often need a little help from us in the beginning, especially on damaged, harsh, or infertile, dry sites. Ultimately, though, they should be able to fend for themselves if we get it right.

> **Build living soil quickly and for the long run by working with the inherent tendencies of the three key elements: soil structure, soil organisms, and plants.**

Prevent and mitigate soil compaction. Add plenty of organic matter consistent with the soil profile structure, both as a source of energy and nutrients and as a means of improving the air- and water-holding capacities of the soil. Inoculate the soil with a healthy balance of soil organisms using good composts, soil inoculants, and leaf mold. Maintain a diversity of plants in the ecosystem to create a diverse soil food web and keep the anatomy of self-renewing fertility working for you. Improve the nutritional profile of the soil with the judicious use of organic and natural amendments, and use nitrogen-fixing and dynamically accumulating plants. Minimize soil disturbance to promote continued health and stability of the living soil community.

54. Habitat Elements

Every species has specific needs, yields, and characteristics that define its species niche. Here we work to meet the needs of the beneficial organisms within the garden so they can help to maintain the balance of the system (see appendices 3 and 5 for details). Again, this pattern applies to virtually all forest gardens, though to each in different ways.

If our gardens don't meet the habitat requirements of beneficial wildlife, then the beneficials won't come to dwell in them. If our gardens are not home for these beneficials, then we will have to do their work, or the system will suffer.

Numerous beneficial organisms help maintain the balance of pest and disease populations in natural ecosystems. When ecosystems don't contain these organisms, important "jobs" in the community don't get done, and population imbalances become more likely. Either that, or we have to take over the job of maintaining balance, which we simply cannot do on our own very effectively.

Provide all the food, shelter, water, and other elements that beneficial wildlife need to dwell in your forest garden.

Beneficial wildlife that help maintain ecosystem balance come in all kinds, shapes, and sizes, from predatory, parasitoid, pollinator, and decomposer insects to reptiles (snakes and, in southern climates, lizards), amphibians (salamanders, toads, and frogs, especially tree frogs), birds (mainly the insectivorous ones, but also omnivores), and some of the mammals (bats and shrews). All of these wild beings need food, shelter, and water.

Food consists mainly of the insects and other beings we want to keep in check. However, beneficial insects need sources of flower nectar, and omnivorous birds need berries and perennial and annual seeds to supplement their insect diets. We should therefore make sure to provide them with extra berries and seeds beyond our own needs so we don't compete with them. They need summer sweet berries, fall berries rich in fat, and berries that dry "on the vine" for winter food.

Shelter means different things to different species. The diverse perennial plantings and mulch of the forest garden work fine for most insects for summer shelter and overwintering, as long as there is a good litter layer. Perennial borders, hedgerows, thickets, and deciduous and evergreen trees serve this function well, though many insects prefer specific plants for summer shelter or overwintering habitat. Many ground-dwelling residents like piles of loose rock, dead logs, brush piles, and mulch. Native pollinators like various specific habitats. Bird- and bathouses go a long way, too.

Small garden ponds with sloping sides and various objects sticking out of the water as landing sites for insects serve almost everyone as a water source. Bigger ponds hold more room for amphibians, who move into the garden during the summer and catch many insects.

55. Fruitful Footpaths

Any garden with definite pathways could make use of this idea, though it is easier to apply at small scale than at large.

The footpaths in the garden don't have to be barren of useful plants or devoted to only one purpose or function.

Garden paths often get left as single-purpose spaces without any benefit to the gardener except garden access. It doesn't have to be this way.

Design at least some paths to function for food production, beneficial-insect attraction, or soil improvement, not just as access ways.

TABLE 2.7. Trample-tolerant ground covers. Under a Foot Plant Company offers numerous foot-tolerant ground covers. Other uses include: aroma = aroma may confuse pests; DA = dynamic accumulator; inv. shelter = shelters beneficial invertebrates; spec. nectary = specialist insect nectar plant; gen. nectary = generalist insect nectar plant; ed. = edible

Latin Name	Common Name	Functions & Uses
Bellis perennis	English daisy	greens, medicinal, inv. shelter, spec. nectary
Carex pensylvanica	Pennsylvania sedge	gen. nectary, pollen, native
Chamaemelum nobile	chamomile	tea, medicinal, DA, inv. shelter, spec. nectary
Chrysogonum virginianum	green and gold	inv. shelter, spec. nectary, semi-evergreen, native
Clinopodium glabellum	smooth-leaved satureja	medicinal, gen. nectary, aroma
Coptis trifolia var. *groenlandicum*	goldthread	medicinal, evergreen, native
Dryas octopetala	mountain avens	nitrogen fixer, native
Epigaea repens	trailing arbutus	ed. flowers, medicinal, gen. nectary, evergreen, native
Fragaria chiloensis	beach strawberry	fruit, tea, DA, gen. nectary, wildlife
Gaultheria procumbens	wintergreen	fruit, tea, medicinal, DA, wildlife, evergreen, native
Houttuynia cordata	hot tuna, incl. 'Chameleon'	culinary, ed. flowers, medicinal
Linnaea borealis	twinflower	medicinal, evergreen, native
Lotus corniculatus 'Plena'	prostrate bird's-foot trefoil	nitrogen fixer, inv. shelter
Mentha requienii	Corsican mint	culinary, tea, medicinal, gen. nectary, aroma
Mitchella repens	partridgeberry	fruit, medicinal, wildlife, evergreen, native
Petasites japonicus	fuki	ed. stalks, medicinal, inv. shelter
Phlox subulata	moss pink	pretty, native
Potentilla anserina	silverweed	ed. roots, tea, medicinal, DA, gen. nectary, native
Satureja douglasii	yerba buena	culinary, tea, medicinal, DA, gen. nectary, aroma, native
Thymus spp.	thyme	culinary, tea, medicinal, gen. nectary, aroma
Trifolium repens	white clover	tea, ed. flowers, nitrogen fixer, DA, inv. shelter, gen. nectary
Waldsteinia fragarioides	barren strawberry	evergreen, native

Grow creeping edible plants between stones on well-used paths (table 2.7), or *Ground-Cover Carpets* (#49) that act as nectary plants, dynamic accumulators, or nitrogen fixers on less-traveled ways. The paths can function as part of a water-control system by directing runoff where you want it to go. You can mulch infrequently used paths with wood chips inoculated with *Gourmet Decomposers* (#37).

56. *Mulch*

Mulch should be applied in the early stages of almost every forest garden. How long you import mulch depends on how quickly the soil gains healthy, fertile status, how much time and energy you have, and how soon the garden starts mulching itself. Chapter 5 offers a detailed discussion of mulch, including its uses, advantages, and drawbacks.

"Bare soil is damaged soil."[30] Dead organic matter on the soil surface performs a wide range of important ecosystem functions that no other single garden element can perform.

Forests naturally generate a mulch layer of leaves and other litter that covers the soil surface. This organic matter represents a store of nutrients and energy that feeds the soil food web, and ultimately the whole ecosystem, releasing nutrients at a pace the ecosystem can handle without leaching. Mulch adds organic matter to the soil profile in a manner consistent with how the soil profile works. It modifies the soil microclimate, reducing water losses, temperature swings, and wet-dry and freeze-thaw cycling that can kill plants and destroy soil aggregates. The litter layer stops erosion and soil compaction by rainfall and footsteps. It reduces weed competition. Mulch increases the growth of fine roots and improves nutrient absorption in apples, chestnuts, and peaches, compared to grass or herbicided bare strips[31] (this is probably also true of other species).

Mulch also provides habitat for numerous organisms, most of them beneficial to ecosystem balance, from microbes to insects, reptiles, amphibians, birds, and mammals. Scientific studies have shown that mulch layers composed of diverse kinds of litter—leaves from a variety of plants, plus a mixture of various-size wood products—support higher fungal and bacterial biomass and a higher abundance of nematodes (most of which are beneficial). "In particular, abundance and diversity of omnivores and predators were significantly higher in complex litters."[32] Many predators and omnivores that dwell in the litter layer do their predatory work throughout all vegetation layers at different stages of their life cycle. We want higher levels of these organisms in our forest gardens to help balance pest populations of all kinds.

Finally, we probably also want our forest gardens to feel like a forest—mulch helps create this atmosphere.

Mulch, mulch, mulch!

Mix it up, but don't mix it in. Use more than one kind of mulch to develop a diverse litter layer on the soil surface throughout the forest garden: leaves, hay, straw, and woody material of all kinds, as well as good composts and manures. Leave the mulch on the surface rather than mixing it in to allow the mulch to do its work and save labor and energy. Leaving mulch on the surface promotes a fungi-dominated soil community, while mixing it in promotes a bacterial community. Mixing mulches into the soil can also cause short-term

nitrogen deficiency, as the microbes use nitrogen to break down the carbon in the mulch. Slowly decomposing mulches minimize this problem.

57. *Dead Wood*

Gone, but not forgotten, every forest garden should have some dead wood. Just keep it away from your house if you live in termite country.

Standing or lying dead wood adds structural diversity to the ecosystem, provides critical habitat for decomposers, insects, and animals, becomes a biological island of healthy soil organisms, and helps store water in your forest garden.

Old, rotten logs can hold large quantities of water essential to plant survival in drought (they sink their roots right into them). Numerous insects and microbes make their homes in old logs, not the least of which are fungi that often serve as mycorrhizal partners of nearby plants. Brush piles offer safe haven for numerous animals, including frogs, toads, reptiles, and birds (the rodents they attract can be a nuisance, we admit). As chunks of wood decay and mix into the soil, they add lumpy texture and structural diversity to the soil environment, fostering a fungi-dominated soil.

Leave standing dead trees, fallen logs, branches, and brush piles scattered throughout the forest garden.

Add to the population of dead wood as time goes on, too. Dead wood helps create *Living Soil* (#53) and forms one of the essential *Habitat Elements* (#54) for wildlife of all kinds. You can use dead wood to create *Definite Pathways* (#24), feed *Gourmet Decomposers* (#37), or define and separate *Dynamic Patches* (#9). Dead wood at key path corners can guide hoses and other objects moving along the pathway, keeping them from damaging plants inside the planting beds.

1. Mollison, 1990, page 70.
2. Lynch and Hack, 1984, page 116.
3. Alexander, 1979, page 120.
4. Alexander, 1979, page 247.
5. Lynch and Hack, 1984, page 116.
6. Alexander, 1979, page 247.
7. Alexander, 1979, page 246.
8. Lynch and Hack, 1984, page 116.

9. Alexander et al., 1977, page xxxviii.

10. Alexander, 1979, page 247.

11. Alexander, 1979, pages 246–76.

12. Luken, 1990, page 190.

13. Alexander et al., 1977, page 510.

14. Alexander et al., 1977, page 510.

15. Mollison and Holmgren, 1978, pages 49–59; Mollison, 1988; Mollison and Slay, 1994.

16. *Webster's New Collegiate Dictionary*. Springfield, MA: Merriam Co., 1981.

17. Harmer and Kerr, 1995, page 124.

18. Tabor, 1994, page 35.

19. Mollison, 1990, pages 96 and 117.

20. Li et al., 1997.

21. Mollison, 1990, page 90, and numerous other permaculture books.

22. Facciola, 1990, page iii.

23. See Stamets, 1993, for detailed cultivation information.

24. Stamets, 1993, page 22.

25. See Stamets, 1993, for guidance.

26. UNESCO, 1973, gives 5 m (about 16 feet) as their minimum height.

27. Crawford, 1997c.

28. Crawford, 1997c, page 9.

29. Mollison, 1990, page 422.

30. We know that we heard or read Bill Mollison saying this, but we don't know where.

31. Atkinson, 1980.

32. Ettema and Hansen, 1997.

⚬ 3 ⚬

Design Processes 1:
Overview, Goals, and Assessments

It takes a finger to point to the moon,
but woe to the person who mistakes the finger for the moon.

—BUDDHIST PROVERB

Planning is the substitution of error for chance.

—AUTHOR UNKNOWN[1]

A discovery is an accident meeting a prepared mind.

—ALBERT SZENT-GYORGY

Design is an elusive and enigmatic alchemy. Yet the magic of design lives, not in any design technique we might learn and use, but inside each one of us. The techniques serve only as touchstones to connect each of us to our own living creative process. Do not confuse the finger pointing to the moon with the moon itself.

The design process is an inherent part of every human being. We cannot teach you design. You have to discover your design process for yourself. In this chapter, we will offer a number of different fingers pointing to the moon in the hope that these fingers will help you see what we are pointing toward. Once you connect with your own inner knowing, listen to your own wisdom and guidance about how to proceed. If you get lost, you can always come back to the book, find a pointing finger that seems relevant, and look up.

We all design every day as we make choices in our lives: deciding what we want, assessing the best way to create it, and going for it. This happens so fast we don't realize we are doing it at least half the time. We intend here to slow this process down, take it apart, make it understandable, and put it back together again. We want to help you refine your design process, give you more design tools to choose from, and help you make choices more consciously, so you can make more mistakes. "Huh?" you say. "Make more mistakes?" Precisely.

Planning *is* the substitution of error for chance. Though that may sound pessimistic, it's actually a good thing. Many great innovations have come about by chance, but not *only* by chance. Our hope is that you will make your worst mistakes on paper so you won't make them on the ground. Then, when you plant your forest garden, you can make useful mistakes, the kind we can't anticipate because we don't know enough yet. A thorough design process increases the likelihood of you achieving your goals despite your mistakes, whether they are "good" mistakes or not. Even so, we can never eliminate chance from the process. Good design prepares you to benefit from your accidents by turning them into discoveries.

Like the forest, the design process is complex and multilayered, yet both have structure. Certain principles and "archetypal" activities undergird every effective design process, yet each trip through it is unique. This dual reality allows us to offer guidelines to speed you along the forest-garden design path and requires us to offer an array of techniques to fit different people, places, and situations. Use these tools as you see fit. Invent new ones as necessary. We hope you will find, as we have, that improving your design process improves your ability to observe, think, create, and be who you truly want to be.

Our discussion of forest-garden design processes begins in this chapter with an overview of the process. We will then discuss the initial stages of the process in detail: goals articulation, base mapping, and site analysis and assessment. These pieces lay the foundations for responsive and responsible ecological design. Chapter 4 completes the discussion with details on how to design the garden, from concept to details. We will offer examples of various pieces of the design process using a case study of a forest garden designed by Eric and his friend Jonathan in Holyoke, Massachusetts.

DESIGN PROCESS OVERVIEW

Three major sources of ideas and information feed the usual professional landscape design process: the client, the site, and the designer.[2] The client has final say on design decisions. The client's goals generate much of the design's drive and form. The site provides the context for the goals' fulfillment and strongly influences the means of achieving them, if not the goals themselves. The designer brings biases, values, themes, principles, and a body of work and knowledge to inform the design, express ideas, and shape the marriage of site and client.

Forest garden design, however, involves a qualitatively different set of site information from that of most other design processes: considering the nature of the garden's existing and potential inhabitants,

and the relationships between them, is fundamental to forest gardening. We need to consider the inhabitants' niche requirements, their interactions, and what combinations of species can reduce our workload and increase yields. People often undertake such a "garden inhabitants" analysis in a vague way. Here we propose doing so in a more conscious manner with clear objectives in mind.

Besides inquiring into these information sources, we must integrate our inquiry results into a coherent whole using an organizing idea, which we call a "design concept." We must design the details of that whole to a point where we can gather the materials, energy, and money necessary to create it, or at least identify logical first steps. Of course, we must implement the design on the ground. It's also always good to step back and evaluate our work every so often so we stay on track, especially at the "end" of the process. Thus, when we take apart an idealized forest-garden design process we can see six fundamental, interrelated actions:

- Goals articulation
- Site analysis and assessment
- Design concept development
- Design
- Implementation
- Evaluation

Exploring the designer's biases and values does not show up in this list. If the gardener and the designer are the same person, it isn't an issue. If the designer and the gardener are different people, then this is a relevant field of inquiry, usually when the client selects the designer. For the purposes of this book, we'll assume that the gardener and designer are the same person.

DESIGN AS DISCOVERY

Design is a process of discovery. The design lies inherent in the relationship between the goals and the site with its inhabitants; we don't create it out of thin air. The idea that design is a creative process, and that we create out of thin air, leads people to focus on the "design" phase to the exclusion of the other phases of the design process. Taking the design phase out of its context like this leads to errors—and arrogance. Ecological design processes inquire into the realities at hand to discover at least one harmonious pattern within those realities. If you have no idea what to do in the design phase, look for your directives by asking more questions of, and getting more answers from, the goals and the site. However, we need to ask our questions with a sense of direction.

The complex, multifaceted reality of every landscape and its inhabitants means we could analyze endlessly. We need a filter to guide our analysis, limit our scope, and assist us in deriving meaning from what we find. The goals fill this role, directing our attention to the most important aspects of the site. The analyses help us discover patterns, implications, and relationships within the goals and the land that guide our design choices. Frequently, with good goals articulation and site analysis, one or more designs simply "pop out" of the synthesized information, presenting themselves to our awareness. In a sense, then, "the design does us" rather than "us doing the design." A semilinear flow of goals articulation, analysis and assessment, and then design seems to help this process of discovery along. *Our goals guide the site analysis and assessment; the site analysis and assessment discovers the design.* We believe this to be a fundamental principle of design process. Yet it is not the whole picture.

DESIGN IS RATIONAL, INTUITIVE, AND MESSY

Design is fundamentally messy. We learn useful things when we take it apart and put order to it, but we also risk fooling ourselves into thinking that the process is clean, linear, and organized. To start, the goals evolve and change as you go, sometimes necessitating further site analysis in the midst of the design phase. Second, conscious and unconscious evaluation takes place frequently throughout. Third, the design concept can come at any time, or it may never come at all. Finally, a linear flow doesn't work for many people. Order, rationality, and linear thinking constitute less than half the way the world works.

We all have two sides to our brains. The left side functions mostly in a step-by-step, linear, rational, analytical, and verbal mode. The right side functions mostly in an overall-pattern-and-process, imaginative, synthesizing, and visual-spatial mode. Neither side is better than the other, despite our cultural left-brain bias. The whole is greater than the sum of its parts; if we neglect one aspect of ourselves, we lose more than half the value. Using both sides of our brains—and all parts of our beings—brings balance and wholeness to the gardens and lives we design. A good design process cycles through analysis and synthesis, verbal and spatial, linear and nonlinear. Working through rationality provides grist for the intuitive mill, a solid foundation for the heart's choices, and a loaf for Spirit to leaven. The idea is to inform your intuition, and then follow it. Leave room for inspiration, grace, and mystery by remaining flexible, not rigidly following an idealized design-process outline, even ours. Yet, balance that freedom and spontaneity with some sort of structure that creates an integrated flow or container, like a river within its banks. Using an integrated process can make good ideas better, or it may show them to be not so good after all.

When we say design is an "integrated process," we mean this: every piece is essential, and every piece relates to, feeds, and needs the others. The best way to "get" this integration is to design. Look for it as you go, then you'll know. "Dis-integrated" thinking usually causes people to get stuck. Solid links between the parts of the process keep things moving. If you do get stuck, look upstream or downstream and see if you can find there the source of your impasse or the passage to forward progress.

Don't get locked into the river as the only metaphor for the process, however. You can work on the six phases in a rough linear order, in a circular or spiraling order, or by simply bouncing back

Box 3.1:
Designing Your Design Process

The first step in your design process should be to design the design process! Plan the work, at least sketchily, and then work the plan. Before you can plan the work, however, you need to know what the work is. Therefore, we recommend you begin by reading this chapter and the next fully through so you get an overview of the whole process we outline, knowing that what we have written represents the most full-on, in-depth design process you could do. As you read you will surely be considering how much of what we discuss you are willing to do or feel capable of doing. Then consider some of the following factors:

How much time do you have to design your garden? How much do you enjoy thinking things through ahead of time? Are you a stickler for details or a seat-of-the-pants kind

TABLE 3.1. A range of on-paper design projects, their level of intensity, and their estimated times to design completion. One day equals eight hours.

TASKS	PROJECTS		
	Small (< 1/3 acre/0.1 ha), simple site, few species, clear intent	**Moderate size** (1/3–2/3 acre/0.1–0.25 ha) and complexity, many species, but simple succession	**Large size** (> 2/3 acre/0.25 ha), complex goals and site, many species, complex succession
Articulate Goals	Goals Articulation Summary exercise only; simple goals. 1–2 hours	All goals exercises plus summary; many goals. 2–6 hours	Outline process, with revisions; many goals and criteria. 1–2 days
Base Mapping	16 hours	16–24 hours	3–6 days
Analyze and Assess Site	Simple, quick, and sketchy. Three bubble diagrams and a simple summary. Existing- and desired-species niche analyses. 4–8 hours	Assess all topics with their own quick diagram. Complex summary. Existing- and desired-species niche analyses; varmints, pests, and diseases; ecological neighborhood. 12–18 hours	In-depth diagram for all topics. Complex summary. Existing- and desired-species niche analyses; varmints, pests, and diseases; ecological neighborhood; native ecosystem analyses. 3–5 days
Design Concept	A few options. 1–2 hours	Several options. 2–3 hours	Many options. 2–5 hours
Schematic Design	Few options and iterations. Single instant succession to a horizon. 4–8 hours	Several options and iterations. Several instant-succession nuclei that merge. 8–12 hours	Many options and iterations, group decision making; successional rotation schemes. 2–4 days
Detailed Design	Small number of species and guilds. 4–6 hours	Many species and guilds. 6–8 hours	Many species and guilds; crop timing and maintenance considerations. 1–3 days
Patch Design	Four or five patches of low to moderate complexity, with some repetition. 4–10 hours	Many patches of low to moderate complexity, with little repetition. 12–20 hours	Simple, broadscale patches plus complex intensive patches with rotational schemes. 2–4 days
TOTALS	4–7 days	8–12 days	14–21 days

of person, or somewhere in between? How energetic and persistent are you? How patient and able are you to sustain interest and enthusiasm in a project without knowing exactly where it is headed or without having to jump right into physically doing something? Be true to yourself here.

Are you designing alone or with other people? What skills do you and the others already possess, and what will you need help with in designing your garden? What do you want to learn in the process of designing your garden?

Do you like thinking on paper, or do you prefer figuring things out in the physical space you are working with? Do you tend to think and solve problems in a visual way, using words and sounds (such as thinking out loud or talking to people about things), or by physically moving yourself and objects around in space?

How clear are you about your goals? What scale and kind of forest garden are you thinking of designing? Are you designing only a forest garden, or do you need to design a whole landscape with a forest garden in it? How attached to a particular outcome are you?

How large and complex is your site, and how well do you know it? How well do you know the plants and animals that already live on your site and in your neighborhood, and what else do you need to learn? How well do you know the plants you intend to plant in your garden?

All of these factors and more will influence your choices about how intensively you want to design your forest garden, how much detail to put into your base map or even whether to use a base map at all, and so on. Thinking through these questions will help you pick out the pieces of the process that feel most important to you to do, and to gauge the depth at which to do the pieces you choose. That way you can fit the work to your needs and interests most effectively. Table 3.1 lays out a few different design project variations for different project circumstances, just to give you an idea of how much time it may take to do your design.

One of the most important factors in designing your design process relates to your forest-garden design approach: are you designing your forest garden primarily by building it from desired plants to create an ecosystem that works for them and their growing requirements, or are you starting with an ecosystem in mind that you want to create and looking for useful plants that will grow in that kind of ecosystem? We call these the "plants-to-ecosystem" and "ecosystem-to-plants" approaches. Which approach you use will determine your choice of exercises as you move through the design process, especially in the design phase. How you approach your goals articulation will influence your ability to use various design-phase exercises, so make sure to read and think through the design process information we offer from beginning to end before you start.

We recommend that you create for yourself a similar checklist of which design tasks you want to take to what level of detail, just to give you some sense of the road you have ahead. Estimating the time it will take is the most difficult part, so you can give that part a pass if you want. To help you choose your path through the design process, each section of this chapter and the next explain why you might want to do which pieces of the process, and why you might not. While all of this may feel overwhelming, most people find the design process interesting and fun, not to mention enlightening. There is much to learn about our landscapes, our garden allies, and ourselves in the process, so welcome to the adventure!

and forth between them in apparent random purposefulness as need arises. Ultimately, the order of events doesn't matter. Your process will work as long as you undertake each action to a depth sufficient to guide your design to a reasonable resolution in the time you have available, and you have integrated and balanced all the aspects of the design with each other. The design-process outline offered might not reflect what works for you. Use it if it works; don't if it doesn't. Think of this chapter as a menu. Keep all the key pieces in mind, follow your heart, gut, and nose, and you'll get a healthy, well-rounded meal.

Many of you will be designing not only forest gardens but also your whole landscape. Accordingly, this chapter presents a full-blown, full-scale version of the design process, with commentaries about each part. Not everyone will need to go to the depth we discuss. That's fine. Take what you like and leave the rest (see box 3.1, "Designing Your Design Process"). However, no matter what depth or path of design you choose, if you observe carefully you will see all six actions inherent in your work. Including the six actions in your process more consciously will help ensure that your forest garden harmonizes with its landscape context, exhibits many beneficial ecosystem properties, and truly represents who you are and what you want to create.

CLEAR INTENTIONS: ARTICULATING YOUR GARDENING GOALS

What specific things do you want to achieve in your forest garden? What do you want your forest garden to be? What crops do you want to grow, and what are their needs, preferences, and tolerances? Articulating your answers to these questions, both generally and specifically, represents a foundational task of the design process. Clear goals are essential to any forest garden designer interested in more than design by chance. Clear goals help us create

gardens that meet our specific needs, acting as a rudder to guide us to our destination.

Clear, well-articulated intentions also speed both the design and the implementation processes. They focus our work to understand the site, prevent wasted effort, and save us time. In addition, they help ensure we get all the information we need to make good decisions. Clearly articulated goals can keep us from bogging down in the design process, or they can get us out of quicksand we've gotten into.

Each forest gardener and his or her family or group will have a unique set of goals. The processes below will help you articulate your own unique goals, reveal their implications, and then use them to guide the rest of your design work. Before we get into details, though, we'll offer a few important commentaries.

ARTICULATION: GET IT DOWN, THEN GET IT GOOD

The word *articulate* has several meanings, including "to utter distinctly" and "to form or fit into a systematic whole." We use the word in both senses here. Ideally, your goals statement will express your values and goals distinctly, will lead naturally to a set of usable design criteria, and will form these into a systematic whole. We use the phrase *goals articulation* instead of *goal setting* to encourage you to look inside and discern your own truth rather than impose goals on yourself. Distinctly uttering your inner truth is what goals articulation is all about.

You can articulate goals in many different ways and to varying depths of inquiry (we'll offer two possible ways below). However, in all cases the first rule in goals articulation is "get it down, then get it good."[3] Get your ideas out on paper in rough form, then revise, restate, organize, and reality-check what you have generated. We get our goals down and then "get them good" for one reason, and one reason only: to carefully define the problems we want to solve, the questions we are asking, and the intentions we seek to fulfill.

CAREFULLY DEFINE THE PROBLEM, QUESTION, OR INTENTION

A question, a problem, and an intention are three different ways of saying the same thing. How we define a problem, question, or intention will define the universe of possible solutions, answers, or manifestations we find for it. If we ask, "How can we maximize yields of apples on a per-acre basis?" we will look in a certain set of directions. Asking "How can we get the most fruit per acre with the least input of energy, labor, and money?" sets our quest on a much different course. The boxes of our cultural conditioning and habitual thinking often limit our sense of the possibilities, and hence the questions we ask. Beware of limiting your goals to only what you believe is possible or that with which you are familiar.

We find it helps to think about goals in the abstract to some degree. Separate what you want from the specific site or landscape. Look behind the "things" you want to see what they do for you. Make sure you ask yourself why you want what you think you want; we often limit ourselves without even knowing we have done so. Freeing our goals from form at the outset and focusing on functions and purposes opens up creative possibilities and gets us closer to our deepest desires. Clear yet flexible knowledge of what we truly want is a powerful force. Be careful how you define your goals, because you will probably get what you ask for!

WRITE DOWN YOUR GOALS

The best way to articulate your goals is to write them down. Getting your thoughts on paper helps you evaluate their reality, coherence, and truth. It's easier to revise thoughts on paper than in your head, and it's also easier to revisit them to remind yourself what you are doing. Writing down your goals is especially important when more than one decision maker is involved, as it facilitates communication and usually decreases conflicts later in the process. What's more, *how* you write them down is almost as important as *that* you write them down.

STATE GOALS IN PRESENT TENSE AND ACTIVE VOICE AS DESIRED CONDITIONS

Read the following two goal sentences to yourself both silently and aloud, and feel how you respond to them, especially in your gut. Which feels more powerful and compelling? Which most effectively helps you discern its truth for you? Which feels more "heady" and which more grounded and embodied?

> Goal: to create a forest garden that will provide all the fruits and nuts my family will eat.
> Goal: my forest garden provides all the fruits and nuts my family eats.

Most people find the second sentence more powerful, compelling, grounded, and true. The first sentence may seem accurate, but most people have a harder time gauging whether it is really what they want. Why?

The first sentence uses the future tense. The second sentence is in present tense, as if the desired condition has already been achieved. It therefore possesses more presence and resonance, carries more weight, and feels more real. We can then compare the stated goal to our inner desires more effectively. We can better envision our intentions and therefore create them more easily. We tap into our creative core and inner guidance. The resulting touchstone fosters persistence as we interact with stubborn material reality.

Dave once worked with some folks who wanted to design an environmental education center. As he and his clients rewrote their goals in present tense together, one of them looked up with fear in her face and said, "That makes it seem so real!" Soon thereafter, they stopped the project and radically changed direction. Making it "seem so real" showed them what they really wanted—or didn't want. Though this meant less work for him, Dave considered it a successful design process. The question then becomes "What is your desired condition?" This asks you to put your goals in present tense. Yet present tense alone may not be enough to really nail down what you want.

A friend once wrote the following statement of core goals/values for her forest garden design:

As we design and implement our edible forest garden, we are realizing our long-held dream. Our well-being and self-sufficiency are increasing. We are developing a sense of place. We teach, demonstrate, and share our experiences, knowledge, and skills with and for others.

She used present tense exclusively here, yet passive voice makes the statement feel mushy and weak. Wordiness is promoted when passive voice is used in writing. Active voice fosters brevity, accuracy, and forcefulness. Here's how this friend modified the above:

As we design and cocreate our forest garden, we manifest our long-held dream. We increase our well-being and self-sufficiency. We experience and express our sense of place. We teach, demonstrate, and share our experience, knowledge, and skills with and for others.

This feels stronger and more grounded. It connected this person to her true desires and put her in the driver's seat. When she spoke actively, she also changed words to fit more closely her inner sense. Forceful, concise, and honest communication with ourselves and others results from increased use of the active voice.

Once you get your goals down, revise your goals statements into active, present tense "desired conditions" to get them good. Use this exercise to discern your true goals, and to better align your written statements with your inner truth. Let this work empower you to fully express yourself in the world.

GOALS EVOLVE THROUGHOUT THE DESIGN PROCESS

Our goals evolve as we evolve. Design changes us as we take in new information and discover new ideas. The analysis and assessment or design phases may tell you that certain objectives won't work, or they may present other possibilities you hadn't considered before. Writing down your goals makes this process of evolution more conscious. Keeping your goals statement handy and prominent as you work on your design project makes it easier to add to, subtract from, or radically change your goals. It takes effort to track changes in your goals during a design project. However, this effort almost always pays off. It prevents wasted effort, improves confidence, clarifies communication, and focuses your site analysis work. It also helps you create a clear vision, evaluate options more easily, and, ultimately, generate a design that truly fulfills your purposes.

HOW TO ARTICULATE YOUR GOALS: FOUR OPTIONS

Effective goals articulation results in a written statement that clearly defines the complete universe of what you want to achieve at an appropriate level of detail, stated as present-tense, actively-voiced desired conditions. We offer four processes for goals articulation below. The first two include a "basic" method for straightforward forest-garden design projects and a more involved "robust" method for complex projects, hard-core designers, or those who just want to do it a different way than the first. The basic method is clear-cut and well defined, while the robust method requires more thought, discernment, inner direction, and effort. Either of these methods will effectively define your goals, and one of them should form the foundation of your goals articulation effort. We also offer two additional exercises of which we think most people should do at least one: desired-species niche analysis and model ecosystem analysis.

Many of you have some sense of what plant species you want to grow. For most people and most forest-garden design projects, getting crystal clear on your desired species and their niche characteristics is essential to selecting your forest garden site, learning what you need to know about that site, and designing your forest garden well.

Desired-species niche analysis forms the foundation for designing the garden's social system in most of the possible methods of social structure design (see chapter 4). If you have any desired species showing up in your goals, do this exercise.

Some of you know that you want to design a certain kind of plant community or that you want to create a forest garden modeled after a certain kind of community. In this case, model ecosystem analysis is a critical part of your goals articulation process. It will help you define key design criteria that will guide your site analysis and design processes and will form the foundation of detailed design processes discussed in chapter 4. If you have a list of desired species and you know what kind of ecosystem you want to create or mimic, then you are in the lucky position of getting to do both exciting exercises!

In any case, we suggest that you read all four of these goals-articulation options to weigh which ones best suit your needs and interests. Please also read the section "Determine Analysis and Assessment Issues and Questions" on page 195 before creating your goals statement so you understand how you will use it there. We also suggest reading the first three sections of chapter 4 (up to "Design Phase How-To" on page 249) if you need help deciding whether to do desired-species niche analysis, model ecosystem analysis, or both.

Basic Goals Articulation

At the end of your goals articulation process you should have a written statement that clearly defines what you want to achieve. In the basic approach to goals articulation, you start by simply writing your Goals Articulation Summary statement. If your intentions are straightforward, you have a clear sense of your goals at the outset, and writing that summary the first time gives you a clear written statement and a sense of fullness and satisfaction, then you are finished with goals articulation! However, we recommend that you revise and refine your writing at least once, putting things in present-tense, active-voice

bullet points. If, on the other hand, your intentions are a little more complex, you aren't clear at the outset, or your first time through the summary exercise leaves you feeling a bit unsure of what you want, then you can play with the Specific Forest Garden Questions. You may then be better able to complete your summary. If you are dealing with the design of more than just a forest garden or want to think ahead about your site, then you may want to consider the Questions about Site Uses and Long-Term Issues before completing your summary.

Goals Articulation Summary

This exercise will help you summarize your essential forest garden goals and is the minimum required exercise in the goals articulation process. You will refer back to (and perhaps modify) the results of this work many times in your design process.

Think about your goals for your forest garden separate from your landscape as much as possible: What are your purposes, needs, and wants? Summarize in a list of bullet points the essential goals you have relevant to the following issues:

- Desired foods and other useful products (types and season) and specific "must-have" species.
- Other essential needs you want the garden to fulfill, whether spiritual, emotional, aesthetic, practical, or otherwise;
- Other (present and future) uses of the site with which the forest garden must be compatible.
- Desired successional stages and vegetation architecture or patterns.
- How your garden relates to the larger ecosystem and neighborhood context, e.g., are there functions you want the garden to perform to make the environment healthier or to improve your privacy, connection to neighbors, views, or other issues?
- Your sense of your basic approach to key issues such as:
  1. use of native, exotic, and opportunist species;

2. how much you want to adapt to or modify problematic site conditions;
3. your willingness to work for desired high-maintenance crops or to eat whatever you can grow with minimal effort; and
4. in what ways, if any, you want to experiment, and what you are not willing to risk.
• Your maintenance and establishment efforts and approximate total budget.

If you are doing this exercise after having done the other work in this section, summarize the details from your other work to respond to the bullet points above. What issues float to the top? Which pieces are the most essential aspects of your goals, the ones without which your garden cannot succeed? How can you frame brief statements that contain or include many points from your more detailed answers in the following two exercises?

After completing the bullet points above, write a brief statement, of three sentences or less, describing your overarching goals for your forest garden: What main purposes will your forest garden serve? What qualities will it have? What will it offer you? Besides setting out why you are creating this forest garden in the first place, these three sentences should encapsulate the goals that you have written in your bullet points. These sentences represent your garden's statement of purpose or mission statement. What is the fundamental reason for your forest garden's existence? The statement of purpose is different from your vision of the garden—the vision, also known as your design concept, expresses in a nutshell your sense of how you will fulfill your purposes in a specific time and place. What you are writing here should answer the question *why?* Your bullet-point responses should be in harmony with and express the details of the three-sentence summary, but the mission statement should express the wholeness or fullness of your goals. Remember to revise and rewrite your bullets and three-sentence summary in active-voice, present-tense terms. Table 3.2 offers an example

goals summary statement for our case study of Eric and Jonathan's forest garden.

We recommend that you read your bullet points and three-sentence summary out loud to yourself and to at least one other person to hear and feel it, and to receive responses and questions that may illuminate your goals. You will know you have a good goals summary when reading it brings a lift to your heart, energy to your body, or a smile to your face. If you find that your summary doesn't satisfy, then do the Specific Forest Garden Questions to help you get to more of the details that may help you bring completion to the goals articulation process. If your summary does satisfy, congratulations! Move on to the basic mapping section to continue your design work.

Specific Forest Garden Questions
Sometimes, to get the big picture clearly in our minds, we need to delve into details. The Specific Forest Garden Questions will help you get many details down on paper so you can then step back and see the big picture. These details will also allow you to be more specific in your garden design and to more accurately create your heart's desire. Use this exercise when you want a more thorough design process, when you aren't clear about your goals at the outset, or when your first attempt at your goals summary doesn't get you where you want to be. These questions focus on the forest garden only. Larger landscape issues are dealt with in the following exercise.

Start by reviewing the list of questions in table 3.3. Choose which ones speak the most to you, or for which you have answers leaping to mind, or that most repel you (often the questions we most avoid are the ones we most need to answer). Write brief answers to these questions on separate sheets of paper in bullet-point style. When you finish, review your answers, make any adjustments that make the answers more coherent with each other, and rewrite them in present tense and active voice. Then go back to the Goals Articulation Summary and

---

TABLE 3.2. Eric and Jonathan's goals summary.

Mission statement:

We intensively manage our urban forest garden as a backyard foraging paradise, a megadiverse living ark of useful and multifunctional plants from our own bioregion and around the world. The forest garden unifies the larger permaculture design for food production, wildlife habitat, and social spaces that encompasses the entire property.

Desired foods and other useful products:

- We eat fresh fruit from May to November from the gardens (with more of some things to store and process when possible).
- The forest garden provides greens, shoots, roots, and mushrooms in season.
- We also eat well from the greenhouse, fish farming, and aquatic vegetable and annual and tropical garden elements.

Other essential needs you want the garden to fulfill:

- The permaculture design for the property as a whole integrates the forest garden with space for a "patio," ponds and wetlands, a greenhouse, a tropical food garden, and annual garden beds, plus a private sitting area, tool and equipment storage, possibly a large water tank, and mulch and compost piles.
- Vehicle access down one of the alleys allows us to bring in materials.
- Our garden is an educational and demonstration site showing what forest gardens and urban permaculture can accomplish.

Desired successional stages and vegetation architecture or patterns:

- The garden is a mosaic of annual beds, oldfields, thicket/shrublands, and some shadier forested habitats, with the majority in midsuccession aggradation.

- We have different spaces with different "feels"—some wilder, some managed and manicured, some sunny and open, some shady, and some private.

How your garden relates to the larger ecosystem and neighborhood context:

- Our garden serves as a refuge in our biologically impoverished neighborhood, attracting and housing a great diversity of beneficial wildlife, particularly birds and invertebrates.
- We bring our dead and blighted backyard to life, creating a lush, semiprivate oasis that inspires our neighbors to plant their own.

Your maintenance and establishment efforts and approximate total budget:

- We establish our garden in phases using annual spring planting parties.
- We use pulses of work alternating with periods of less maintenance, but we do up to an hour a week in the forest garden, usually less.
- We spend about $1,000 a year during the establishment years.

Your basic approach to key issues:

- We choose the species in our garden based on their ability to fit a specific niche regardless of region of origin, although we go out of our way to incorporate underutilized eastern natives.
- To quickly maximize productivity, we choose to transform our small, infertile lot rather than adapt to it or slowly change it.
- We put in some extra work to grow apples and stone fruits, although more of our emphasis is on resilient, "pest-proof" species.
- We enjoy experimentation with breeding projects, novel species, and new polycultures, but we also make sure that we have reliable food production.

---

encapsulate the answers to these questions there. Make sure to save your answers to these questions for later reference.

Questions about Site Uses and Long-Term Issues
This exercise is for those dealing with designing a whole landscape, not just a forest garden, or with longer-term questions. It is also appropriate for those who are not sure where to put their forest garden in their landscape.

Use a separate sheet of paper to answer the questions in table 3.4 in brief bullet-point statements. Write down and answer any other questions that come to mind for you regarding your situation.

When you are finished, review and revise your answers as needed to create present-tense, active-voice statements. Then go back to the summary exercise and complete that with these points in mind. Make sure to save your answers to these questions for later reference.

Robust Goals Articulation:
Brainstorms and Outlines
The robust goals articulation process is more involved than the basic process discussed above. This method articulates your goals to the greatest degree of any technique offered here and takes the most time, effort, and self-inquiry up front.

TABLE 3.3. Specific forest garden questions. Use these questions to help you define your forest garden values, goals, and criteria in more detail than the Goals Articulation Summary exercise allows. Write answers to the questions you choose to answer on separate pieces of paper, preferably as bullet points rather than prose for ease of review. Revise your first draft into present-tense, active-voice statements for a second draft if you have time and energy.

Overarching and Specific Goals

- Why do you want a forest garden? What are you yearning for that you believe a forest garden will give you? What value does it offer you, or what values does it embody?
- What are you looking for in a forest garden? What specific and tangible benefits do you hope to gain? How will you know you have achieved your overarching goals?

Your Approach to Key Issues

- *Natives, exotics, and opportunists:* You could take a range of stances on the topics of natives versus exotics and opportunist species (commonly called invasives; see glossary). You may choose more than one of the following stances (a different stance for each vegetation layer or plant function, even) or one not listed here:
  - - you use only species believed native to your region, state, or county (which?);
  - - you look to natives first to fulfill your desired functions and uses;
  - - you use whatever species best fit your niches and desired functions and uses without regard to place of origin;
  - - you use only species that have no history or risk of opportunism;
  - - you use potentially opportunistic species, but not known opportunists;
  - - you use expansive species, but not dispersive species (see glossary); or
  - - you use opportunistic species if they are already present in your neighborhood, but you will not introduce new, potentially opportunistic species to your locale.
- *Adapt or modify:* As a general rule, do you select species and develop a design that works with the existing conditions of your site (e.g., choose drought-resistant species for dry sites), or do you modify your site to meet your design requirements (e.g., build swales, install irrigation, improve soils for a dry site), or something in between?
- *Work for valued crops, or eat what grows:* Some commonly desired crops such as peaches and apples require a fair amount of work to grow healthy crops. Are you willing to do the maintenance required for your preferred foods, do you want to choose resistant species and varieties even if they are less familiar, or some of both, or somewhere in the middle? If you are in the middle, can you define which crops are most important to grow or what kinds of work you are willing or unwilling to do?
- *Experimentation:* How experimental do you want to be? What specifically do you want to experiment with (kinds of plants or foods, topic areas, skill development)? What do you want to be sure of achieving? What don't you want to risk?

Desired Crops and Uses

- What kinds of foods do you like to eat (e.g., fruits, nuts, berries, shoots, leaves, roots, culinary herbs, edible flowers, mushrooms)? Are certain kinds of foods a priority?
- What specific crops do you want to grow (e.g., Asian pears, pawpaws, chestnuts, ginseng, Jerusalem artichokes, ramps, asparagus, tarragon)? You may want to review "Forest Gardening's Top 100 Species" (volume 1, appendix 1) or the species-by-use and species-by-function tables (appendices 2 and 3 in this volume) for ideas. List crops by categories such as trees, shrubs and bamboos, vines, herbs, and mushrooms.
- Approximately how much fruit do you eat in a year? How many nuts? Would you eat more of these if you were growing them and had them available?
- What medicinal herbs do you regularly use, or might you use? Condiment herbs?
- Do you want to process foods and herbs for storage (e.g., canning, drying, preserves, tinctures) or just use them fresh?
- Do you want your fruits and other produce to be spread throughout the season or lumped in batches of harvest? Specify timing if you can for different crop types, specific crop species, or crops for storage versus crops for fresh eating.
- What other uses and functions are important to you (e.g., cut flowers, ornamental qualities, butterfly or hummingbird plants, scented plants, chicken fodder)?

Desired Landscape Patterns

- What kind of environment do you hope to create? A shady forest, an open savanna, a wild oldfield mosaic, a tidy orchard? More than one? A sequence?
- Are there specific wild areas or gardens that you want to mimic? What is it about these places you want to bring to your garden?
- Review the patterns in chapter 2. What site patterns (#s 3 through 8) and patterns of the garden (#s 9 through 22) might you want to use? Do other patterns in the pattern language particularly speak to you? If so, list them.

Logistical and Budget Issues

- How many people will be maintaining the forest garden? Who? How much time per week on a consistent basis per person? How much time per week during "rush" work periods, such as planting and harvesting?
- Does anyone who will be working or playing in the garden have health or physical concerns that limit access to the garden or their ability to work? What and how?
- What kind of budget do you have for system establishment (time and money)? Do you intend all-at-once or piecemeal establishment (see pattern #s 30 through 34)?

TABLE 3.4. Questions about other site uses and long-term issues. Answer these questions on a separate sheet of paper to help you think about the other uses on your site now and in the future. They should help you determine the site, size, and location of your forest garden as well as some of its characteristics.

Is this house your permanent, year-round residence? Do you expect to move in the future? If so, how soon?

If this is not your year-round residence, what times of the year do you tend to be there? How do you plan on maintaining the landscape when you aren't there? Who will be responsible, if anyone?

Are the existing driveways and paved paths on-site adequate? Do they need expansion now or in the future? Can they be reduced in size? Will or do you need more area for parking, or for storage, of large equipment or recreational vehicles (tractors, boats, trailers, and such)?

Do you expect to increase the size of the house or septic system at any time in the future? If you have a septic system and decide to add bedrooms, you will need to increase the size of the septic system to accommodate the extra bedrooms.

Are the patios, decks, and so on adequately sized? Do you see any potential for expansion of these?

What activities occur outside around your house? Where do they occur, and what size, shape, and location of an area do these need? Are there any needs for lawn-sports areas (e.g., croquet), children's play areas, outdoor cooking, group gatherings, and so on? How many people, what size area, and how frequently?

Do you plan or want to leave room for major landscape elements such as a pool, pond, tennis or other game court, shed, greenhouse, and the like?

What other gardens might you have or like to have in the future?

What service area requirements are there now or might there be in the future, e.g., dog runs, clotheslines, compost and trash areas, septic tank pump-truck access, or gas and oil tanks?

However, it often saves tremendous amounts of time, effort, and confusion later on. Organizing and understanding your goals this way can generate flexible yet razor-sharp clarity about your intentions. It can also reveal and resolve hidden goals conflicts and greatly focus your analysis and design efforts. Perhaps the biggest benefit this method offers is the way of thinking and seeing it engenders. It is most useful for complex design projects that deal with issues beyond forest gardening alone, such as the design of whole landscapes or when the forest garden is the nexus for many overlapping needs, issues, opportunities, problems, and constraints.

Those who have a penchant for thoroughness and clear thinking are also likely to enjoy this process.

Robust goals articulation entails brainstorming many goals, needs, issues, problems, and desired values, qualities, functions, "things," and design criteria for your project. You then organize these ideas into an outline so they relate to each other in a functional way, so the reasons for every detail and the means of achieving every general goal are clearly expressed. Once you have a draft outline, we suggest ways of refining and filling out the outline to amplify and clarify what you have generated to increase its clarity, completeness, and coherence. We suggest reading through the entire series of tasks below so you understand the process as a whole before beginning.

Generating Ideas

You can generate goals ideas any number of ways. The simplest way to feed the process is to write short, catchy phrases in no particular order on index cards, sticky notes, or scraps of paper in response to the questions offered in table 3.5. You can also use the questions in tables 3.3 and 3.4, above. Choose those questions most appropriate to your situation, and modify them according to your liking or needs. In addition, you can generate such ideas using any of the techniques suggested in table 3.6 or even a technique of your own creation if responding to the tables doesn't suit you. Don't, however, do all of these different processes. Just pick the one, two, or three that work for you. Start with the most intriguing technique and stop when you sense you have enough material.

As you write each card or note, lay it out on a table or the floor or post it on the wall to stimulate your brainstorming. Writing each idea on a separate sticky note or card makes sorting and organizing the ideas easier in the next exercise, while still allowing you to see all the ideas (if you write large enough). If this is a household, family, or group project, it is much more important to post the ideas so all can see and bounce off them.

TABLE 3.5. Landscape-design brainstorm questions. Use these to help generate ideas that you will use to make a goals artic- ulation outline. These open-ended questions relate to whole site design, not just forest garden design, so use them for proj- ects involving more than just a forest garden. Spend a set amount of time, such as ten minutes or more, brainstorming on each of these topic areas and writing down each thought on a separate index card, sticky note, or paper scrap.

Qualities

Imagine that someone who has never before been to your place arrives and spends about twenty minutes wandering around your landscape when you have it well under way, speaking to you about topics other than the landscape. As your guest leaves your place, a third party stops him or her and asks for five words that express the qualities of the landscape the visitor just wandered through and unconsciously imbibed. What words would you want your visitor to say? What qualities do you want your landscape to express? (You can list more than five.)

Things

What objects do you want in your landscape? These can be living or nonliving. You can list particular plants you want here, too.

Goals

What do you want your landscape to do for you? What do you hope to achieve? Is there a specific look or feel or image you want to express or embody? See tables 3.3 and 3.4 for addi- tional questions to stimulate your thinking here.

Problems

What problems do you have with your landscape? Are there drainage problems, access problems, aesthetic problems, insect problems, or such?

Likes

What qualities, features, things, or patterns of your landscape do you particularly like already?

TABLE 3.6. Various goal-generating processes.

- Cut images out of books and magazines and write down things you like and don't like about what you see.
- Visit other people's gardens or wild places, or look at pictures of gardens or wild places, and write down things you like and don't like.
- Create a guided visualization for yourself, imagining yourself walking through, working in, or hanging out in your forest garden five or ten years from now, and then write or sketch what you see.
- Doodle little diagrams of your forest garden with notes around them.
- Think about the foods you eat and which ones you might like to grow.
- Order plant catalogs from various nurseries (appendix 7) or visit them on the Web and start a list of what you get excited about when you browse them.
- Keep a sheet of paper on your refrigerator or another handy spot, and keep adding to your list of garden or landscape wants, needs, hates, loves, problems and opportunities, and dreams and nightmares over the course of a few days or weeks.
- Interview various stakeholders in the project about their con- cerns, desires, goals, and ideas.

When brainstorming, a free flow of ideas is the most important thing at first. Don't worry how well stated an idea is, whether it is entirely accurate, or even whether it is silly or not. Just get ideas down. Use moderation in doing this; too much informa- tion can be a problem, as can too little. Also use nonattachment—just because you are writing ideas down in black and white doesn't mean they are in concrete. The key thing is to generate first and improve upon it later.

An example brainstormed list of forest garden goals and ideas for a four-person family on a small lot in a New England town is shown in table 3.7.

Sorting Ideas

After generating a reasonable number of ideas, gather them in one place and sort them. Posting the cards or sticky notes on a wall or spreading them out on a floor or table is the easiest way to organize. Keep blank cards or sticky notes nearby so you can name groups of ideas and add or clarify individual cards. Before we talk about how to actually sort the ideas, let's talk about the intentions behind the sorting process. Goals outlines are easier to create than to explain, but let's give explaining it a shot.

A goals outline organizes your ideas based on their level of specificity and their functional rela- tionships to each other. Most people's brain- stormed goals lists include a few vague ideas (e.g., "an abundant forest garden"), a few or no very spe- cific ideas (e.g., "10 bushels of apples per year"), and many ideas in a middle range of specificity (e.g., "a variety of fruit" or "fruit for processing, fresh eating, and storage"). The primary goals-outlining task is to organize your ideas so the links and relationships

TABLE 3.7. Sample brainstormed goals ideas for a four-person family on a small lot in New England (not our case study).

Qualities

peaceful	abundant
private	wildish
open	organized, coherent
enclosed	easy
sunny	safe, healthy
lush, green	flowing
colorful	

Things

vegetable garden	plums
orchard—various tree fruits	peaches
small lawn	raspberries
flowers	blueberries
shed	other fruits
kiwi trellis	nuts
birds, wildlife	herbs: edible, medicinal
sculpture	echinacea
sunny and shady benches	goldenseal
greenhouse (small)	ginseng
a nice front walk, paved	compost in logical place
apples	out-of-sight storage
pears	

Goals

fruits for a family of four	privacy (in yard, in garden, on
healthy food—organic, safe	"back deck")
low maintenance	some play space

Problems

hot in house in summer	boring landscape: grass
cold winter winds	too much mowing
driveway too big	too much shoveling of driveway
lack of privacy in yard	dirt driveway—dirt in house
(sunbathing, playing,	crowded apple trees
sitting in sun and	lead chips from peeling house
reading, sleeping,	paint
gardening with shirt off)	

Likes

east-facing deck: space, views to yard
quaint house charm
sunny yard
Nanking cherry hedge, dogwood hedge
quiet neighborhood (except Elm St.)

TABLE 3.8. A simple value, goal, and criterion outline.

VALUE: An abundant forest garden lives in our backyard.

GOAL: The forest garden produces a variety of fruits for processing, storage, and fresh eating.

CRITERION: At least 10 bushels of apples per year—3 for fresh eating and 7 for processing and storage.

---

between them become clear. Each level of specificity or generality plays an important role.

The vaguest, most general ideas represent overarching values or desired qualities we often find difficult to define ("abundant," "low-maintenance," "sustainable," or "beautiful"), but these lie at the core of who we are and what we want to create. These values drive our actions and choices, often unconsciously.

Moderately specific goals define overarching values in more detail. They serve the values, because they help create them. Goals are means; values are ends. To one person, "an abundant forest garden" might mean "produces a variety of fruits for processing, storage, and fresh eating," while to another it means "produces large quantities of nuts." To someone else, it might mean something completely different. Several goals usually define each overarching value in more concrete terms, but even these are usually not specific enough to design. What kinds of nuts? What kinds of fruit? And how much of each?

These questions further define the goals and eventually bring us to specific measurable or observable design criteria. Criteria assist us in creating and knowing we have created that which we seek. For example, we can translate "at least 10 bushels of apples a year" into a specific number of trees of a specific size when we design. Criteria guide us as we analyze, assess, and develop our designs. They ground the values and goals in the practical world. They begin to make clear the forms inherent within our goals. To design anything in physical form, you eventually have to define all of the following criteria: *what* it is, its *size*, its *shape*, its *location*, and its *relationship* to other design elements or goals.[4]

Hence, our values, goals, and criteria have an inherent structure and relationship to one another (see table 3.8). When our goals link our values to practical design criteria that make our values real, our direction and purpose are clear, internally consistent, and well aligned. Once this structure is clear,

TABLE 3.9. Revised goals outline based on the example in table 3.7 (not our case study).

Annual and perennial gardens provide safe and healthy foods and herbs for a family of four.

- Food production occurs in a clean and healthy environment
  - gardens away from lead-paint zones near house
  - car fumes and road runoff blocked from garden sites
- Intensive annual vegetable gardens focus on generating abundant fresh produce (minimal stored).
  - 600 to 1,000 sq. ft. (55 to 93 sq. m)?
  - can scatter some annuals within forest garden
- Forest garden provides fruit, nuts, perennial vegetables, and medicinals with minimal possible maintenance.
  - fruits—variety throughout season, some for storage
    - ~ berries: raspberries, blueberries, other unusual ones
    - ~ apples, pears, peaches, plums, and maybe some unusual ones
  - nuts: hazelnuts, chestnuts? what else can we grow?
  - perennial vegetables to supplement annual garden
    - ~ asparagus, onions, rhubarb, greens, edible flowers, Jerusalem artichokes, other less common stuff
  - medicinals: echinacea, goldenseal, flu and cold remedies
- Small greenhouse for winter vegetables and seed starting
  - 8 x 16 ft.(2.4 x 4.8 m)?
  - winter food production
    - ~ close to house (minimal shoveling)
    - ~ minimum of six hours of winter sun
    - ~ efficient, superinsulated? no additional heat
    - ~ winter-hardy vegetables, greens
  - seed starting
    - ~ electricity (for seedling heating)
- Prefer organic management if possible

A small public zone is beautiful by American standards, but most of the yard is rather private and beautiful by our standards.

- Enclosed and diverse private spaces create a sunny but open feeling
  - Landscape exhibits high diversity, but with a theme so there's unity
  - Minimal lawn area for play
  - Different spaces sunny at different seasons, times of day
  - Connected glades within trees for open/enclosed feeling

Maintenance effort is minimized to the extent possible.

- Willing to work on caring for moderately challenging fruit trees and other similar crops

The landscape helps keep the house warm in winter and cool in summer.

- winter winds blocked
- winter sun allowed
- summer sun blocked in afternoon on west wall and roof of house
- allow winter sun to neighbor's house

internally consistent, and well aligned, the design process moves rapidly and relatively easily. However, when our intentions and their structure are hidden, vague, or internally inconsistent, the design process bogs down, gets lost or confused, or erupts into conflict. Many arguments about design ideas really concern unspoken values, goals, or criteria conflicts. Vague, implicit, or internally inconsistent intentions can destroy or obstruct the process. Clear, explicit, coherent intentions generate a powerful creative force. In the goals-outline format, each succeeding level of the outline more fully defines what the higher outline levels mean in more detail. As you move down in the outline hierarchy (more and more indented), the bullets more specifically answer the question *how*—these are design criteria. As you move to the higher levels of the outline (less and less indented), you get more and more encompassing of goals and details, and you get answers to the question of *why*—these are values. Table 3.9 offers an example outline based on the earlier brainstorm list in table 3.7. This example is well on its way to completion and therefore includes ideas not in the original brainstorm list, because it is the result of the next exercise as well as this one, but it will give you a fuller idea of where you are headed.

To generate your outline, first sort your piles of cards or sticky notes into groups of related ideas based on their content. Any group may contain values, goals, or criteria. For example, one group may contain ideas related to aesthetic and social issues in the garden such as privacy, quiet reading spaces, and so on, while another may deal with very practical issues around what kinds of food you want. Determine what groupings to make based on the content of your cards. Some ideas may need to go in more than one group, so write more cards to make this possible. Sometimes you have to split an idea on one card into two or more cards to make this work. Sometimes you will find ideas appearing repeatedly in slightly different forms and can combine cards or lump them into the same group. These fine variations often hold important subtleties, however, so don't toss them without consideration.

After you sort the cards into related groups of ideas, try to discern the structure of values, goals, and criteria within each group. For each group of related ideas, separate general values and specific criteria. Which ideas "float to the top" or feel more encompassing and governing (values)? Which sink to the bottom (criteria)? Sometimes whole groups will float to the top, and others will sink to the bottom. Values often show up as single words that express qualities ("magical," "wild"), but not always. For example, in table 3.9, one of the values is "Maintenance effort is minimized to the extent possible." On the other hand, "things" tend to be criteria, for they are solutions to problems or manifestations of intentions that are often hidden or not well defined. Criteria are also always measurable or observable, while values are felt or experienced and hard to define. For instance, in table 3.9 species are listed as some of the more specific ideas in the outline. There will also be many cards that are somewhere in the middle range of specificity. Leave the criteria and the midrange goals aside for the moment while you work with the most general ideas.

You should find that many of the ideas on your cards are actually ways of creating a few core values. The core values are the most vague, most encompassing things or experiences you want. You need to determine your core values so you can make them the few major headings that lead the outline. Everything else flows from them. To find your core values, ask, "What am I really after here?" or "Why do I want these?" about each sticky note or index-card group in turn. The core values should stand alone, that is, they will be things you just want, things for which there is not really an answer to these questions, whereas all the other ideas are there as ways of creating the core values.

Once you have identified the most general ideas in each group of cards, begin to structure the ideas in each group. The basic question to ask is "What serves what?" Which specific ideas serve to create which less-specific ideas? Which goals serve which values, and which criteria serve which goals? This is where the structure will really begin to take shape. There may be several goals articulating a single value or several design criteria articulating a given goal. Several levels of goals may lie between a value and a criterion. You will likely have gaps between values and criteria or goals and criteria that you will need to fill with additional goals statements to make the link. You can do this now if they jump out at you, or you can wait until the next exercise. You may need to jettison ideas that don't fit or that were silly ideas that came out as part of the brainstorming process. However, before getting rid of anything look it over carefully to see whether there isn't some useful germ of truth buried in it somewhere.

Now look at the groups and see how they relate to each other. Do some of the groups fall under the core value of other groups? Try to keep the number of major values or top-level goals—the major headings of your outline (e.g., "an abundant forest garden")—under five, or the structure will become unwieldy and unintelligible. If you have more major headings than that, see if you can logically combine some to reduce the total number at the core that form your first level of headings. You will likely need to work back and forth from looking within groups of ideas to looking at the relationships between groups. This is not a linear process.

Basically, you just want to take all of your ideas and find within them a structure of values, goals, and criteria that resonates with your internal sense of what you want. Ultimately, you should find functional links between every group and every card, either among or implied by the ideas you have already generated. Each idea will relate to ideas above and below it in specificity, the more general values being articulated more and more as you follow the indentions in the outline. The structure usually has a branching pattern, not unlike tree roots, since the values tend to be few, the goals greater in number, and the criteria potentially the most numerous of all. Always remain attuned to your insides as you go through this process to discern whether your sorting and organizing choices feel right, to listen for questions and answers, and to connect to your internal guidance system. Move the cards around as much as necessary to create a structure that feels right and true to you. As you work, you should discover a growing sense of rightness or inner harmony as you whip your outline into shape and the connections become clearer.

Once your cards or notes are all organized—or are organized enough—write or type the structure you have created in cards on the floor, table, or wall in an outline form. Try to keep your goals outlines within two to five pages unless a project is large and complex.

"Organized enough" is a relative term whose meaning depends on you, your enjoyment of or tolerance for the process, your time availability, and the complexity of the ideas you generate. The work of outlining your design values, goals, and criteria is potentially the most difficult part of the design process if you decide to undertake it. However, people tend to get more lost more frequently and more completely later on if they don't undertake this goal-clarifying process to some reasonable degree. You will have to judge how much effort is reasonable for you and your project.

Revise Structure and Apply the "Wholeness Test"
Once you have typed it up, step back and evaluate your goals statement as a whole. Do some values or goals have many specifics while others have few? Does the structure feel whole and complete? If everything on your outline came true, would you feel satisfied? Are there goals missing? Can you eliminate anything without losing the essence? Listen to your heart and gut, and act accordingly.

The outline format allows you to look for holes in your goals using the "wholeness test." This form assumes that achieving all of the goals *at the next level of indention* below a value will fully create that value. Similarly, when you achieve all of the criteria one level below a particular goal, the goal should be

realized. To clarify this point, let's look at an example.

The simple value, goals, and criterion outline in table 3.8 (page 155) states one midrange desired condition that "the forest garden produces a variety of fruits for processing, storage, and fresh eating." The one criterion states that it produces "at least 10 bushels of apples per year—3 for fresh eating and 7 for processing and storage." If we achieve this criterion, will we have created the goal of producing a variety of fruits for processing, storage, and fresh eating? Probably not. Producing only apples does not create a variety of fruits, even if we use diverse apple cultivars. Either we must add and achieve more criteria to create that desired condition, or we must modify the goal above it so the outline has internal consistency. Similarly, producing a variety of fruits for processing, storage, and fresh eating may or may not feel like a complete expression of "an abundant forest garden" to you. Maybe you'd need to add other goals to fill out that level, such as those in table 3.10. Even this revised outline needs more criteria to flesh out the goals defining an "abundant forest garden" for these people. Even some of the most specific ideas in this example could use further definition to become measurable, observable, and designable.

You will likely have to add new goals to establish hidden links and make the outline feel whole and inclusive, or additional criteria may spring to mind to help you define more fully what your goals mean in physical reality. People often have key values with no goals or criteria defining them, criteria with no goals above them, or goals with no values at the top. To understand what value a goal holds or what goal a criterion serves (what problem these solutions attempt to solve), ask "Why? Why do I want that? Why does this idea show up here?" To get detailed design information from values and goals, ask *how, how much, how many, who, what,* and *where* questions. "What do you mean by 'an abundant forest garden'? What kind of abundance? How much? When? Where? Who will plant, maintain, and harvest it?" Sometimes you have to research these ques-

TABLE 3.10. Revised simple value, goal, and criterion outline, filled out based on applying the "wholeness test." Most of the goals stated here still need criteria to fully define them, but even so, this provides a pretty solid basis for site analysis and design.

- An abundant forest garden lives in our backyard.
  - The forest garden produces a variety of fruits for processing, storage, and fresh eating.
    - ~ At least 10 bushels of apples per year—3 for fresh eating and 7 for processing and storage.
    - ~ Other tree fruits should include pears, peaches, and plums, with openness to unusual varieties and species.
    - ~ Small fruits for fresh eating throughout the season.
      - * blueberries, juneberries, raspberries, currants, others
      - * small numbers of plants
      - * different varieties with varying maturity times for continuous harvest
  - The forest garden produces enough nuts for a family of four in a short time frame, without waiting many years for harvest.
    - ~ Shrubby nut crops provide 200 pounds of nuts per year.
      - * hazelnuts, filberts, chinquapins?
      - * how many plants?
  - The garden grows greens and herbs for fresh eating.
  - A small quantity of key medicinal plants provide basic health needs.
    - ~ Ginseng, goldenseal, echinacea

tions (how many bushels of apples *do* you eat in a year?), whereas answers to the *why* (value) questions always come from inside.

Inquiring toward general values helps properly align our goals with our values, so we don't run off in the wrong direction and end up dissatisfied by the successful fulfillment of the wrong goal. It also gains us flexibility. As we understand what we are really after, we open ourselves up to other possible ways of creating our values, and we can detach ourselves from our preconceived solutions. Inquiring toward specific design criteria helps us understand the implications of our goals and values and guides us in finding out what we need to know to design them into existence.

You may need to revise the structure and rewrite goals several times to bring the goals statement to a whole, clear, and complete place. It helps to sleep on it sometimes, to read parts of it aloud, to set it

down for a day or two and come back to it fresh. Other times it helps to set a time limit and stick to it, getting it as good as you can and then moving on. Rarely will any of us have the time or energy to do a completely finished goals outline. You do not need to have a criterion for every single goal. Do enough to give you a clear sense of what you are actually after, to seek out and modify any inherent conflicts in your thinking, and to add new ideas to what you already had in mind. The effort of putting our goals into this form alters the way we think about what we are trying to do, and that is one of the main intentions here. If you have gotten your brainstormed ideas onto paper and into some semblance of an outline like what we are talking about, you have done well. We hope and expect the effort has helped clarify your intentions and some of your questions. In any case, the work should make it easier to keep headed in the right direction as you move through the rest of the design process.

Desired-Species Niche Analysis

The species-niche concept outlined in chapter 4 of volume 1 provides a framework for analyzing forest garden plants. This means gathering information on the climate and soil tolerances, size and form, ecological functions, human uses, and key behaviors of these species so you can assess if, how, and where they fit into your forest garden plans. We focus here on your desired species; existing-species niche analysis is covered in the "Basic Site Analysis and Assessment" section later this chapter. The foundational ideas we will discuss below apply to all kinds of niche analysis, however. If you have no desired species listed in your goals, then the exercise discussed here does not apply to you, but we recommend reading the introductory remarks anyway. Niche analysis is a process we will use several times in the design process.

Over time, we gardeners and nature lovers build mental dossiers on the niche characteristics of our garden's plants and animals—and the wildlings we know—based on direct experience. Niche analysis is a poor substitute for this direct knowledge.

However, inexperienced and experienced gardeners alike can benefit from the niche-analysis technique. Most gardeners have not approached plants as ecosystem design elements the way we do in forest gardening. Getting your knowledge on paper, or gathering it from other sources, will help you design edible ecosystems more effectively, and it can spur the kind of observation needed to fill out such a dossier. Most importantly for now, desired-species niche analysis provides critical guidance for the site analysis processes that follow goals articulation.

For desired species in the goals articulation stage, niche analysis focuses on gathering the information you need to select a forest garden site and to analyze and assess it. For example, if you wanted to grow walnuts you might discover through this exercise that walnuts are taprooted, which might lead you to investigate the depth of your soils or to compare soil depths at various possible garden sites. If you have listed specific crops or other species you want to grow as part of your goals, then you need to evaluate the site in relation to these species. Knowing the niche characteristics of your desired plants helps you know what you must learn about your site, assess whether your desired crops are appropriate there, and investigate what you may need to do to improve your site to meet the plant's needs if there isn't a good match. Desired-species niche analysis is essentially a way of fleshing out additional specific site-selection and design criteria you need for the next phase of the design process.

Niche analysis also serves several other functions. The niche-analysis forms we offer here will help you create a more focused plant species palette for your project. Appendices 1 through 4 contain comprehensive tables containing much information about several hundred possible forest garden plants. As a designer, you need to select plants from these appendices (and elsewhere), learn about them, remember what you learn, refresh your memory, and have easy access to that information as necessary. Filling out the forms helps commit this species information to memory. It gets the necessary plant species information in one place. The forms are a handy reference on the chosen species. You can post your niche-analysis sheets on the wall or carry them around and refer to them quickly and easily during the project's design phase, indoors or out. The forms ease species sorting and selection and record those choices.

Feel free to copy this form out of this book (see worksheet 1). We intend you to print it on both sides of legal-size paper (8½ by 14 inches), so enlarge it as you copy to make more room to write. You can also compose a similar form on your computer so you can have an electronic copy, which will simplify your sorting process as you add species to the list. You may have specific functions or concerns that this form does not cover (dye plants, fibers, fodder, and so on), so feel free to modify it (we offer blank columns for that reason). Create a different way of recording and accessing niche-analysis information if you want. Engage with the information about the plants with clear intentions about what you seek to learn, and remain open to learning anything else useful along the way.

Begin your desired-species niche analysis by considering your goals, your desired functions and uses, and, of course, any species you listed in your earlier goals articulation work. Revise or add to the form in worksheet 1 to make space for recording information on your desired functions and uses. Prioritize your desired species as essential, important, or nice. Some of you may have a large number of desired species, but even if you don't, you should probably niche-analyze only your essential and perhaps your important species now—niche analysis is a lot of work, and we are mostly looking for site-selection and site-analysis guidance. Put your list of essential or important species on the worksheet, and start researching. For now, focus primarily on page 1 of the form: the habitat and site condition needs, tolerances, and preferences of your desired plants. You can add details concerning functions, uses, and behaviors to your niche analysis during the design phase, but of course if you come across that information now, put it on the form.

Worksheet 1: Desired-Species Niche Analysis for _____

Date _____

Sheet _____ Side 1

Genus	Species	Common Name	Family	USDA Zone	Preferences / Tolerances			Form	Habit/ Root Habit	Height x Width	Native to	Pref. Habitat or Successional Stage
					Light	Water	Soil					

Enlarge at 137% to make a legal-size (8½ by 14 inches) version for more room to write. This form may also be found on the Web at www.edibleforestgardens.com.

Worksheet 1: Desired-Species Niche Analysis for _____   Date _____   Sheet _____ Side 2

Species	Edible? (part)	Medicinal? (part)	N-fix or Dyn Acc?	Wildlife?	Invert. Shelter?	Nectary? (flwrg time)	Ground cover?	Other	Nuisances	Poison? (part)	Notes

Enlarge at 137% to make a legal-size (8½ by 14 inches) version for more room to write. You may also find this form on the Web at www.edibleforestgardens.com.

Species Niche Analysis for _____

Date _____

Sheet _____ **Side 3**

Species												Notes

Enlarge at 137% to make a legal-size (8½ by 14 inches) version for more room to write. You may also find this form on the Web at www.edibleforestgardens.com.

Use this book's appendices as a resource to start researching, but also look at plant catalogs, books, Internet resources, and so on. Fill in using your own knowledge and experience, as well. Different information sources may disagree on some points. If so, evaluate the sources and where they are located (their regional experience may differ) and see whether you feel more confident in one or another. You can also review three or four sources and take a preponderance of the evidence. You may need additional room on separate paper to write more notes about the ideal site conditions for your species.

As you look through the various references for data, other plants you haven't considered will probably catch your eye, but try not to get sidetracked into selecting more species at the moment unless something really strikes your fancy. Methodical species selection for building guilds and polycultures will happen during the design phase. You could certainly make a separate list of candidate species to consider later.

When you have completed the details of your niche-analysis work for each species, look over the group of plants as a whole and summarize what you see. Which habitats are common preferred environments for your species? Which site conditions predominate as needs? Which successional stages? Which species are outliers, needing quite different conditions than the rest? End the exercise by writing down a list of key site-selection criteria and site-analysis questions to which the work has led you. Grouping the species by habitat-type or site-condition similarity and noting what site conditions each group prefers may also bring you insights into where your goals are heading you.

Model Ecosystem Analysis

Model ecosystem analysis, like desired-species niche analysis, is a way to develop more and more distinct design criteria during goals articulation. It is most useful if you want to design a forest garden that mimics a specific kind of ecosystem, whether that ecosystem is a historical native ecosystem or an existing ecosystem in your region that contains both native and naturalized species. The intention is to derive habitat design criteria from the model ecosystem by analyzing the architecture, social structure, and site conditions of the model community.

First you must choose your model ecosystem. If you want to model your forest garden on a historical native plant community, find out what ecosystems and species grew in your region before European colonization. Relate the habitat information to your site to find out which species might have grown there previously and might grow well there now. Dry forest habitats have little relevance to a wet site, for example. Community colleges, state universities, and libraries usually have information on native plant communities, as do local nature centers, especially if they own land with remnant native ecosystems. For native plant communities, the best nationwide reference we have found for this so far, *The Landscape Restoration Handbook*, lists species characteristic of each vegetation layer for major potential natural vegetation types in the contiguous forty-eight states. Appendix 7 includes this and other references for native-ecosystem information, most of it fairly broadscale and only for "climax" communities. Solid, easily available information on earlier succession communities appears to be sorely lacking.

If you want to mimic an existing plant community that you know, then you may not to be able to find species lists and other useful records to help you. You will need to gather the species and habitat architecture data on your own using field guides and your wits. Seek out naturalists, botany clubs, or old-timers. Visit natural areas near you and identify, or get lists of, the plants growing there.

Once you get a species list from the model ecosystem, put the species on a desired-species niche analysis form and research the plants' taxonomy, tolerances and preferences, uses, and functions. Follow the directions in the desired-species niche analysis section to generate criteria to help guide your site analysis and assessment. Though we're using the desired-species niche analysis form and directions, we'll call this a model-species niche analysis because that is what it is.

Ideally, you will gather more information about the model community than just species lists, however. To design a habitat mimic, it is best to visit and observe the architecture of the model community. You need to assess the density, patterning, and diversity of each vegetation layer; list species in and note the architecture of various polyculture patches; and get a sense of the soil horizon structure on which the system grows. What kinds of patches do you see in the model habitat? What layers does each kind of patch have, and how dense are they? What species do they contain? What kinds of site conditions do they inhabit? Only with observations such as these can you get a clear sense of how to mimic the model in all of its architectural dimensions, not to mention assessing whether your site is appropriate for the endeavor. If you can get only species lists, you can still use this process to help design your forest garden. Try to make some inferences about architecture by identifying which species appear to have grown in which layers of vegetation.

Bring your model ecosystem analysis to a close by summarizing in writing what you learned about the ecosystem's architecture. Characterize the desired habitat of your forest garden in response to the model in terms of the five elements of architecture. Prioritize your model species list to identify the key species you want to use or find analogs for, and list the site conditions they require to help guide your site analysis.

With this work complete, you can select and map your site before analyzing and assessing it.

BASIC MAPPING FOR LANDSCAPE DESIGN

The design process described here and in the following chapter assumes you will develop your site analysis and assessment and your garden design using a "base" map of your site. Base maps form the basis for on-paper design. They show the relative size, shape, and location of key site features from a "bird's-eye view" in two dimensions. They show the site as is, without interpretation or future plans. Drawing the map at a proportional scale (such as 1 inch on the drawing equals 10 feet on the ground, or 1 cm = 1 m) makes measurements, relationships, and design options on the drawing correspond reasonably accurately to the reality on the ground.

Designing a landscape or garden on paper is extremely useful, potentially saving backaches, headaches, and heartaches. On-paper design gives you many benefits, including the ability to:

- get a conceptual overview of the site and the design;
- store and work with site analysis information;
- draw multiple options and compare them side by side;
- make mistakes on paper, catch them, and change them before making them on the ground; and
- store your design plan and refer to it years later to help you recall and understand your design choices.

For many, the challenge is getting to the point where you have in your hands a piece of paper with an accurate scale representation of the site.

Mapmaking lies outside the realm of most people's experience, though many have an intuitive understanding of it from using maps in their daily lives. The purpose of this section is to take the mystery out of mapping and give you the skills to create simple site plans for forest-garden site selection, site analysis, and design.

We have placed our discussion of base mapping after goals articulation because mapping the site is the next logical step for most people. These folks know where they plan to put their forest garden or are designing their whole site and thus need to map it all. Those of you who are unsure where your forest garden is going on your land may want to skip ahead to the site analysis and assessment discussion and read up through the "Site Selection" subsection; the discussion here does contain relevant information on making quick site maps for your purposes, but we suggest reading about site selection first. Nonetheless, virtually all of you will need all of the information in this mapping discussion at some point before undertaking your site analysis.

First Principles

Map making is logical, orderly, and understandable. As long as you work methodically, the process is easy and effective. A few fundamental principles, some simple geometry, and a few basic tools are all you need. We'll discuss two quick and dirty mapping methods here: triangulation and extensions with offsets. We have used these two methods alone and in combination to create dozens of base plans of all sizes for diverse purposes. Before we get into these methods, though, let's discuss first principles.

The Map Is Not the Territory

The first rule of mapping is to remember that maps are an abstraction of physical reality. The mapmaker is responsible for making the map as "real" as necessary, but not too real. Don't put too much on the map or you won't be able to read it; too much detail can make an otherwise good map hard to use. The point of mapping is to simplify reality so we have all the data we need, and little or nothing that confuses the issue. As a result, we must always use a map with the knowledge that it is not the territory, and we must consciously decide what the map's purposes are so we can do only the amount of work needed. We should also always use maps primarily to store and process information gathered from the site, not to replace intimate knowledge of the landscape.

In addition, the principle of "garbage in, garbage out" applies. Take your measurements and notes carefully, and keep the big picture in mind. Understand the process conceptually, and imagine how you will draw what you are measuring *as you measure it*. Remember that if something isn't on the map, it "doesn't exist," so choose your data points wisely. An inaccurate or incomplete map makes design work more difficult. Slow, methodical mapping often ends up being faster than quick, slapdash mapping, depending on your purposes.

What Is a Base Map?

Also known as a site plan or base plan, a base map is a drawing made for a defined purpose portraying a piece of ground and its critical site features at an appropriate scale with an acceptable level of accuracy. Let's take apart that last sentence to understand what it means for the mapping process.

A Drawing

First, a map is a drawing. In this book, we assume you will put pencil to paper to make your map. We will not cover computer mapping, though many of the principles are the same. If you want to use a computer, read this section but refer to other resources too.

We use two kinds of paper for drawing maps: tracing paper and vellum. We draw rough drafts on cheap, translucent tracing paper, and we put the final copy on better-quality vellum. Vellum is also translucent, allowing it to be taped down over the rough draft so you can trace the final copy more carefully. Vellum's higher quality means that it lasts longer and takes copying and handling more effectively. You can make copies of the vellum base plan on regular bond paper at the copy shop, but you can also make blueprints with vellum because light passes through it well. We avoid using costly mylar for maps in most cases. If your budget and convenience require, you can make your final base map on tracing paper. Just make sure to get copies made on bond paper to create a decent-quality original that will more likely stand the test of time.

We prefer technical pencils over regular pencils for drawing, simply because consistent and consciously chosen line weights make maps more readable. For your purposes, regular wooden pencils

Box 3.2: Tools of the Designer's Trade

Like any craft, landscape design requires its own set of specialized tools for a pleasant and effective work experience. Luckily, design can be a low-budget operation in this regard, at least for the part-timer or nonprofessional. No big computer programs or fancy equipment here. Dave started his design business with a door for a drafting table, and he still uses that door as a worktable over twenty years later! We've kept the list of recommended tools in the table 3.11 to a minimum but also offer a list of additional tools that will make your job easier.

The estimated cost of the minimum recommended tools stands at $30 to $50, plus tape measures and stakes. The cost of the longer tape measure (used for site mapping, on-site design, and staking out) varies considerably by length and quality of construction. We recommend at least a 100-foot (33 m) length, but we prefer a 200-footer (60 m) for our own design work. A retractable 25- or 30-foot (8 or 9 m) tape measure is easier for shorter measuring jobs, but it cannot replace the long tape when mapping. Stakes are useful in both design and final layout. You can make your own or buy them at widely varying cost. You can often pick up several dozen good stakes for free, and improve the beauty of your community in the process, by taking down political posters along roadsides the day after an election.

TABLE 3.11. Simple tools of the designer's trade.
Minimum Recommended
• Tracing paper: 12-, 18-, or 24-inch (30, 45, or 60 cm) roll.
• Graph paper: 8.5 x 11 inches (A4), maybe 18 x 24 inches (A2) or larger, with ten squares per inch.
• Engineer's scale (see figure 3.1) and a regular ruler. Use the ruler for drawing lines and the engineer's scale only for measuring distances on the map.
• Drawing surface: smooth surface, no seams, holds tape well, ideally with at least one straight edge.
• Masking tape: to hold drawings and overlays on the table aligned on top of each other.
• Circle-drawing template.
• Circle-drawing compass.
• Retractable 25- or 30-foot (8 or 9 m) tape measure.
• 50-, 100-, or 200-foot (15, 33, or 60 m) tape measure.
• Stakes and ribbon or flagging.
• Clipboard, paper, pen.
• Magnetic compass.
Also Helpful
• Drafting triangles.
• T-square.
• Technical and sketching pencils. Technical pencils should be distinctly different line weights, such as 0.3, 0.7, and 0.9 mm.
• Colored pencils.
• Photocopier that enlarges and reduces and can take 11- x 17-inch (A3) paper.

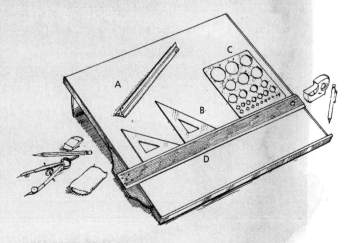

FIGURE 3.1. The basic tools of the designer's and mapmaker's trade make life as a designer much easier. (a) An engineer's scale is the tool used for map reading and plotting. It has six scales ranging from 1 inch = 10 feet to 1 inch = 60 feet (1:20 to 1:125 metric). These allow you to accurately read distances directly from the plan without doing math in your head. (b) Drafting triangles help you draw 30°, 45°, 60°, and 90° angles. (c) Circle-drawing templates make it easy to draw neat circles of exact sizes. This is handy when designing plant locations on a plan. (d) The T-square helps you draw parallel lines using the edge of your drafting table. You can get away without one of these if you use grid or graph paper with tracing paper on top of it.

should do fine. If you want to invest a little bit of money in technical pencils, get a set including 0.5, 0.7, and 0.9 mm pencils to give you distinct variations in line weights for different items on your plan. Just remember that technical-pencil line weights are consistent only when the pencil is held perpendicular to the drawing surface.

You will also need a suitable surface for drawing. Any good, clean, flat table without seams or cracks for the full size of your paper will do—the smoother, the better. You can smooth out rough surfaces by taping down one or more layers of tracing paper. You can also use a picture window, especially when tracing, but hands and backs tend to tire rapidly in the upright position.

Map Purposes

Defining the purpose of your map may seem extraneous, since it appears obvious. However, articulating your purposes will help you make a number of decisions about the size of the mapped area, what features to put on your map, and how accurate it must be. Is your map intended to help you design your whole landscape, to select your forest garden site, or just to design your forest garden? Do you intend to design just the canopy of your forest garden on paper, or do you want to go into more detail and design patches and the placement of specific herbaceous species? Will you design with stakes and string on-site and just use your map to record the design you develop that way, or will you use the map extensively to play with ideas and patterns before staking out? Think these things through before deciding what kind of map to make using the points that follow. The kind of map you make and what you put on it will frame your thinking throughout your design process, so these choices are critical. Ideally, the kind of design problems and site you face will govern the kind of map you create, not the reverse. Since this fundamental choice determines the whole way you will do your forest garden design, we believe everyone should clearly define their map purposes at the outset.

Follow up by defining the map's boundaries, features, scale, and desired accuracy.

One of the key choices you will have to make relating to map purposes is whether you need to select your forest garden site or design your whole landscape, or whether you need only to map the area you have chosen for your forest garden, or both. We suggest you read the "Site Selection" section later this chapter to help you make this choice, for it determines all the map characteristics discussed below, including map boundaries.

Map Boundaries

Maps represent "a piece of ground," which implies that you know the limits of the area you want to map. This is critical. You must make some design decisions before you even map the site, just to map it. Where will you put your garden? What factors will influence the design? Are there natural features that define the boundaries of the area you will use? Most often, for small sites, we use the property boundaries as the limits of mapping. However, sometimes features off the property, such as large trees, buildings, or road culverts have a major impact on design. Portraying offsite features on the plan allows you to assess their impact. Other times the property is larger than what you have the time, inclination, or need to map, and you must narrow your focus. In this case, you may need to create a larger-scale sketch plan of the whole site to help you figure out where to put your forest garden and therefore what area to map in more detail. In all cases, consider your goals and the natural and human boundaries of the site to define the area you will map.

It is usually good to map an area somewhat larger than you think you will actually use for your forest garden. This gives you flexibility to expand and change your garden as ideas develop during design. It also helps you relate your garden to the larger context. You can, however, put most of your data-gathering effort into the garden area and leave the rest of the map sketchier. You can fill in details at the edges later if needed. Just be aware that mapping an area larger than about one and a half acres (a 200- by 300-foot rectangle, or 0.75 hectares) may be faster and more accurate using other techniques (such as transit surveying). You can map large areas with the techniques below, but longer extension-line distances and more reference points for triangulation add complexity and room for more error. However, if you pick your reference points, take your measurements, and plot your data with additional care and attention to detail you should be fine.

Critical Site Features

Every map should show critical site features, including things like buildings, driveways, walkways, septic systems, boulders, utility lines, underground pipes, steep slopes, and so on (see table 3.12). All these features can and will influence the design of your landscape. Which features are critical and which are not depends partly on your map's purposes and scale. A quick sketch plan for site selection need only show the largest features, those that orient you to the physical reality on the ground and those that define spaces. For the garden-design base plan, the most critical site features are those

most permanent and hardest to change; those affecting site uses by needing access, casting shade, limiting plant choices, and so on; and those affecting pedestrian circulation, water movement, soil health, or your ability to manage vegetation. Put more features on the map than you think are critical at the outset, but don't go overboard. You can always add features to the map if you discover that something is more important than you thought it was earlier. In general, you should get more details in areas that need the most design attention or that have the most challenging design problems to solve.

After you've defined the mapped area, but before you start mapping, walk around and make a list of all the critical site features you want to put on your map. Start with the list in table 3.12, but use your eyes and mind to create your own list based on what features are important to you. You may need to research your land and house documents to locate your septic system or sewer lines or find a floor plan of your house. This is worth the effort. Knowing where your septic system lies is a critical piece of work: tree roots can destroy leach fields, costing thousands for replacement, not to mention the hassles and the destruction of your forest garden during the replacement process! If you have a property

---

TABLE 3.12. Site features often critical to put on a base map.

• buildings, sheds	• stone walls, retainers	• drainage ways, ditches
• features on buildings:	• walkways, paths, steps	• puddle zones
- doors, door stoops	• roads, drives, dirt tracks	• steep slopes
- windows	• parking areas	• ledge, rocks, boulders
- bulkheads	• clotheslines	• poor or good soil areas
- electric outlets and meter	• dog runs	• woods edges
- hose bibs, faucets	• septic tanks, leach fields	• edges of mown areas
- oil fill	• sewer and water lines	• trees, with trunk and crown diameters
- dryer vent	• wells	• shrubs, with centers and crowns marked
- downspouts	• irrigation lines, heads	• other key plants
- light fixtures	• utility poles, lampposts	• vegetation patch types
- chimneys	• gas tanks and lines	• garden beds
- roof overhangs	• culvert inlets and outlets	• bird bath, sundial, etc.
- roof peaks, valleys	• street sewer inlets	• arbors, pergolas
- alcoves, projections	• property lines and corners	• fences
- decks, patios	• manholes	• hedges
• old foundations	• drain pipes	

survey, see whether it shows iron pins or other monuments at property corners near your mapped area so your map can connect to these monuments. House floor plans can speed mapping dramatically, saving you a number of steps. Just make sure what was built is actually reflected in the drawings.

Appropriate Scale

"Appropriate scale" deals with the ratio of inches on the map to feet on the ground (or cm to m). For most garden designs, a scale of 1 inch on the map equals 10 feet on the ground (1" = 10') is ideal: conversions are easy, and most site features are large enough on the plan to be drawn effectively and accurately. If you have a small garden and want to design the herbaceous layers in detail, 1 inch equals 5 feet (1" = 5') might be more appropriate. For a sketch plan for garden site selection or overall site design, a scale of 1" = 10', 1" = 20', or 1" = 30' or more could be good, depending on the size of the area under consideration. In the metric system, scales of 1:125, 1:100, and 1:50 are most appropriate for small-scale garden design. The balance of our discussion will forgo metric equivalents for the sake of brevity.

Appropriate scale also depends on the paper size you are willing to handle. Measure the size of the total mapped area in the field to see what size paper you will need to show that area at a given scale. For example, an area of 50' x 100' would take up 5 inches by 10 inches at 1" = 10' scale, so it would easily fit on 11- x 17-inch paper. However, for a garden that small, 1" = 5' might be a better scale for design purposes and would take up only 10 x 20 inches, fitting on 18- x 24-inch paper. Both 11- x 17-inch and 18- x 24-inch sheets are easy and cheap to buy, handle, store, and copy, as long as the scale shows enough detail for your design purposes. We prefer to work on paper no bigger than 24 x 36 inches to keep costs and hassle to a minimum.

Always decide on your map's scale before you start gathering field data. This helps guide your data-gathering choices because you can estimate the size various objects will be on your plan, and whether it is worth trying to show them or not. For example, a 2-foot by 4-foot boulder would be tiny at 1" = 20' but a major feature on a map at 1" = 5'.

The tool to use for scaling, in most cases, is a triangular engineer's scale (see box 3.2 and figure 3.1). The engineer's scale provides six different scales from 1" = 10' to 1" = 60' for your map-reading pleasure. This tool reduces the effort, confusion, and errors resulting from using a regular ruler and doing conversions in your head. Each rule on the engineer's scale can represent any similar-scale ratio in factors of ten; e.g., you can use the ten scale to represent 1" = 1', 1" = 10', 1" = 100', 1" = 1,000', and so on. Architect's scales are similar to engineer's scales, but they are more complex and more confusing to use. They have eleven different scales on them, such as $\frac{1}{16}$ inch = 1 foot, $\frac{1}{8}$ inch = 1 foot, and so on. We won't try to explain how to use an architect's scale here. Make sure if you buy a triangular scale ruler that you get an engineer's scale, not an architect's scale.

In countries using the metric system, triangular scales come with six ratios starting at 1:20 and then rising from 1:25 to 1:125 in increments of twenty-five.

Acceptable Accuracy

For most garden design work, "acceptable accuracy" means that map measurements are within a foot or so of field measurements. To achieve this you can round measurements to the nearest half-foot during fieldwork. To design architectural features such as walks and patios, you probably want higher precision. Use a more detailed scale (e.g., 1" = 4' to 1" = 2' or ¼ to ½ inch per foot), and take your field measurements to the nearest inch.

Designing on Paper versus Designing On-Site

We noted a few of the many benefits of on-paper design earlier and strongly recommend that you make some sort of base map for your design process. However, on-paper design does have its limits. Some people have difficulty visualizing the physical reality a plan represents, or they simply take in and process information best through their body (kinesthetically), rather than visually. In addition, when you get to a certain scale of planting design detail, it becomes much more challenging to design on paper. Finally, at some point everyone will have to stop designing on paper and use stakes, string, and other tools to lay things out on the actual landscape before actually planting or building; some will choose to do this sooner rather than later. Obviously, you should adjust the level of detail in your mapping to match how far you will go in designing on paper.

The advantage of on-site design is that you get to design in real space, staking out paths and activity areas, locating trees and laying out beds, and so on. This gives you a feel for the elements' size and the experience of space they create in a direct, kinesthetic way. You can use stakes to show tree locations and then tie a pole or sapling the approximate height of the mature tree to the stake. A tape measure to estimate the crown diameter, along with a few more stakes, helps visualize the full tree's impact—such as how it might affect views, shadows, and so on. White string, rope, or an empty garden hose are great for playing with the shapes and sizes of planting beds, paths, patios, play spaces, and the like. You can also use white sand, lime, or old, useless Portland cement powder poured in lines on the ground to play with path locations and bed edges, but these can be hard to see and erase if you make many changes, or they can get lost in the rain if you ponder for too long. You can use sheets of cardboard, old carpet, or mulch to represent various objects or patches of plants (though the wind can present a problem here). Be creative with what you have. Simple movable objects of whatever kind can substitute for the real things you are designing in the landscape. Then you can play with ideas and make decisions on the spot, imagining and sensing the future you intend to create. It's like playing in a really big sandbox, so have fun with it!

Some people prefer to design on-site to the exclusion of designing on paper. That is certainly fine if it works best for you. However, this can actually be more difficult and time-consuming in the end, and less successful. While on-site design works fairly well for the design phase, especially the latter stages, the method works less well for site analysis, and lack of site analysis can lead to major design errors. It also takes more time to generate, evaluate, and go back to previous options on-site than on paper. Therefore, even if you want to do mostly on-site design, we recommend you create a rough base map for site analysis and then keep the map and a notebook handy to sketch ideas, take notes, and evaluate options during the design phase. Bubble diagramming and scheming on paper while walking the site works well, allowing you to work on the big picture and get the other advantages of on-paper design while still gaining the benefits of on-site experience. We generally recommend that the minimum on-paper design you do is to get your design through the schematic phase (see chapter 4) on paper and then shift to on-site mode to work on the details. This means you don't have to do as much base-mapping detail.

For those more interested in on-paper design, we still recommend you use on-site design techniques to help answer specific design questions and to refine your design in its later stages; remember, the map is a place to store and work with site data, not a replacement for on-site experience. So, walk the site as much as possible during the design phase, perhaps with a tape measure, hammer, and stakes handy to check your ideas and revise your sketches. No matter what, you should always use on-site techniques before you actually build things: staking out your design is the first step to building it, and it offers you a chance to make last-minute adjustments as you transfer your on-paper ideas into physical reality.

Considering all the above principles and points should prepare you to make and use your map effectively and efficiently. So, once you have considered and decided upon the points above, how do you go about making your base map? We will begin by briefly discussing how to make quick sketch plans for larger-scale, less-detailed work, such as garden site selection or projects where you will do mostly on-site design. However, the principles behind detailed mapping often apply to the larger-scale sketch plans, so most of you will need to know the fundamental processes for close-in mapping: measuring and plotting buildings; triangulation; and extensions with offsets.

Quick Sketch Plans for Site Selection

Some of you will need to make a quick sketch plan of your whole property to help you select your garden site. If, for example, you have a large site with few defining features, no distinct spaces, and no clearly optimal location for your forest garden, you may need to draw two maps—one sketchy, loose, and large-scale for site selection, and one tighter, more accurate, and smaller-scale for garden design once you have selected your site. Obviously, mapping the whole property in detail would take more work than is desirable if you need to design only part of the site in detail. So, how can you develop a rough sketch plan useful for quick and dirty site assessment without spending too much time on mapping? Before you try making a sketch plan for this purpose, we recommend you read the "Site Selection" section in this chapter to give you an idea of what your tasks will be. Then you can better gauge what kind of map you will need, if any.

Sometimes you can get away with a very rough map like what you would scratch into the dirt for someone—accurate scale and so on may not matter, as long as the sketch helps you think about the site in a useful way. Many times, though, you have to get just a bit more accurate to do your site selection work. You can often get a good start on a sketch plan by enlarging or reducing your property survey to a reasonable scale at a copy shop—if you have a property survey. Then you can add a few key features by pacing and eyeballing things based on sight lines between objects that are already on the plan, or by using triangulation and extensions with offsets as discussed below. Your town's tax assess-ment map of your property *may* work as a basis for a sketch plan, but don't count on it, as these maps are notoriously inaccurate.

Even without a property survey or assessor's map, you can make a simple sketch plan from scratch. The mapping process is essentially the same as we discuss below for close-in mapping—draw the house (if needed) and triangulate or make extensions with offsets from there. This can be done rather quickly and can act as a dry run for learning the mapping process for the close-in map. The main differences are that you plot many fewer data points to give you only enough details for a rough sense of the site, and you plot them at a larger scale—1" = 10', 1" = 20', or higher. If you know you will need a sketch of the house in plan view for both drawings, you may as well use the mapping process described below for both and just reduce the house sketch to an appropriate scale for the more general drawing. With that in mind, let's move on to the fundamental mapping methods of basic mapmaking.

Start at Your Doorstep: Map Your House

In most cases, landscape design sites already have buildings of one sort or another on them, and the main building is usually a home. In this case, the best way to start mapping is to make an accurate plan of the house to scale, showing all the relevant features on the house (figure 3.2). This is especially important as a first step when you are going to use the house corners as reference points for triangulation or the house walls as reference lines for extensions with offsets, as usually happens.

If you are one of the lucky few that has floor plans of your house from construction, you've likely saved much work. You will probably have to reduce your floor plans to the scale you will use for your map (a copy shop can help you), and you may have to consolidate information from several of the plans to one drawing (e.g., use the plumbing plan to put the outdoor faucets on the house outline). Also spend some time with a tape measure outside the

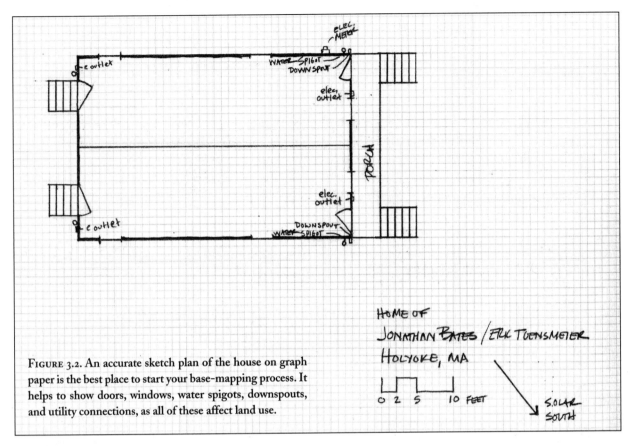

FIGURE 3.2. An accurate sketch plan of the house on graph paper is the best place to start your base-mapping process. It helps to show doors, windows, water spigots, downspouts, and utility connections, as all of these affect land use.

house double-checking measurements and making sure all the important features are on the drawing.

To make a plan of the house from scratch, you'll need a good tape measure (preferably a 100-footer/33 m or longer, but a 30-foot/9.1 m retractable usually works too), a clipboard with paper on it, and ten-squares-per-inch graph paper. A friend helps, too. Generally we note field measurements on the back of scrap-paper sheets held on a clipboard and plot the measurements on graph paper later. Start by making a rough overall sketch of the house in plan view, then put detailed measurements of each wall section on a separate sheet of paper. The overall house diagram gives you an overview of what you are doing and helps keep the separate wall-measurement diagrams organized.

When measuring the house, always start at one wall corner and measure all the way to the end of the wall, noting the distance of each feature on the wall from zero. *Never* measure the width of each

object separately (e.g., wall section, window, or door) and add the widths together to get the total length of the wall. If you do the latter you will add errors and end up with a highly inaccurate map. Make sure to include in your measurements all the fixtures and elements on the house shown in table 3.12. Once you measure one wall, turn the corner and start again at zero, measuring all the way to the end of that wall, noting the distance from zero of each feature, as before. We tend to work clockwise around the house, always starting zero at the beginning of each wall section. Such consistency reduces confusion and keeps the notes clear and aligned with our visual memories of what we did. This speeds plotting and increases accuracy.

We almost always plot the house on ten-squares-per-inch graph paper because it is easier than using drafting equipment to draw square corners and parallel lines, and because we usually use a scale of 1" = 10'. Even if you use a different scale, you can easily make conversions with ten-squares-per-inch graph paper. Of course, this also assumes that the house itself is square and the walls are straight, which is not always the case. If your lines do not close when you plot the house, add together the lengths of parallel walls on each side of the house from your notes to see whether the numbers agree. If they don't, you may have to measure the wall lengths again to see where you made an error. If the field measurements and your notes agree but the diagram still won't close, the house may not be square. Out-of-square houses are rare, but they exist, so check your math and measurements carefully. Older buildings, or those with multiple additions built at different times, are most likely to be out of square.

Once you have the house diagram, you can decide which of the other methods you want to use, or, if you want to use both, where you will use them.

Triangulation or Extensions with Offsets?

Triangles are the most stable geometric figures in nature. Squares, rectangles, pentagons, hexagons, and all other geometric shapes can retain the lengths of their sides but still change shape. Triangles cannot. That means the three points of the triangle are always stable in relation to each other, and that is why the primary method we use for mapping is called triangulation. In triangulation, we use triangles to establish the location of various points on the ground relative to two known reference points.

The extensions with offsets method extends the lines of building walls or some other object to create an extension line. You then measure along this extension line to the place where it intersects other objects. You can also create and measure offset lines perpendicular to the extension line to locate objects the extension line does not intersect. This means you need a building wall or other straight-line object with which to establish the extension line(s).

Extensions with offsets are faster and take less work than triangulation, but they usually result in

maps with lower accuracy because you have to eyeball the extension and perpendicular offset lines. Triangulation works better in areas with few or no human features that offer reference lines, for you can pick any two points to begin triangulating. In most cases, we use both methods in different areas for any one base map we create. Read the following sections through to help you understand each method before choosing which to use in what areas of your site.

TRIANGULATION

The basic idea behind triangulation is to begin with two reference points (also known as benchmarks) a known distance apart, and then to measure from each of those reference points to a series of other points (figure 3.3). This results in two measurements for each feature or point that you are locating. When you go back to your drafting table, first plot the two benchmarks. Then use a circle-drawing compass to locate the data points by drawing arcs from the reference points to find the intersection of the two distances. The process is very simple in concept and reasonably simple in practice. Here are a few pointers to make sure it works well.

Choose Two Reference Points

After you have defined your map purpose, boundaries, and scale, made a list of key features for the plan, and prepared a scale diagram of the buildings on-site, carefully choose your two triangulation benchmarks. These points should be prominent, easily recovered, within sight of each other, well placed, and a good distance apart.

Prominent, easily recovered benchmarks allow you to go back later to double-check, remap, or add something. Building corners and prominent rock corners or peaks are good points because they tend not to move very much. Ideally, the two reference points will allow you to measure in all or many directions from each point: the peak of a boulder, for example, will allow a tape measure to stretch out in any direction, whereas the corner of a building will limit in which directions you can measure. If you have a raw site with few permanent features, you can put a stake in the ground or a nail in a stump or tree to mark your reference points.

The two benchmarks should be within sight of each other and all the other points you need to put on the map. This makes it easy to measure distances and gives you visual memories that greatly help the plotting process. Since they are reference points, they will form the basis of the whole map. You will measure between the reference points and from *both* reference points to every other point you will map using triangulation.

The reference points should be well placed and a good distance apart. This means that ideal benchmarks are located so that most or all of the data points are at more than a 30-degree angle from the line between the reference points (see figure 3.6, page 178). The wide angle allows for greater accuracy, because the arcs from the points will intersect almost at right angles when plotted. Narrowly spaced reference points or data points within 30 degrees of the line between the reference points result in arcs that intersect more acutely, and it is harder to tell where the intersection point lies. The optimal distance between reference points depends on the scale of the map. At 1" = 10', reference points 100 feet apart would end up 10 inches apart on the plan, and this works well. However, at 1" = 100', they would be only 1 inch apart, making plotting more difficult. Note that the second sentence of this paragraph uses the word *ideal*, and cut yourself some slack on this point. Few sites allow you to choose ideal reference points for all data points.

Always take careful measurements between the two reference points. Name one reference Point A and the other Point B (or whatever), and write a complete description of their locations in your field notes so you can find them months or years down the road (this does happen sometimes!). Also take a magnetic compass bearing from one reference to another to give you an accurate north arrow for your

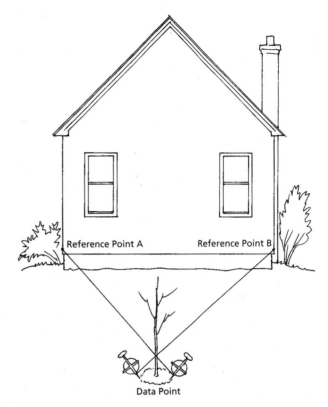

FIGURE 3.3. Triangulation begins with two reference points a known distance apart, in this case two corners of a house. You then measure from each reference point to your data points to create a triangle with sides of known lengths.

base plan. Mark the points in the field well so you can find them again later. Orange paint, flagging, nails, and stakes are all good ways of doing this.

Measure from Each Reference Point to Each Data Point or Feature

Pull out the list of features you want to map and begin measuring from Points A and B to each feature. By measuring from both reference points to each data point, you are describing a triangle unique to that data point. You already know the distance between the reference points, and now you have measured the other two legs of the triangle. It is a good idea to scuff the ground at each data point to help you remember the points to which you measured. Always complete the measurements to one data point from both benchmarks before moving to the next data point to avoid mixing up numbers. This is where friends come in. Things go much faster with two people with 100-foot (33 m) or longer tape measures, with a third person taking notes. The person who will plot the points should be the one who writes the notes. This minimizes communication and memory problems.

In your notes, make a table with three or four columns: the point name or number (if desired), a column for distance from Point A, a column for distance from Point B, and a column for notes and descriptions (figure 3.4). Write the distances in the appropriate columns, and describe each point in the notes. The description of each point should include enough information so that you can draw the object on the map when plotting, i.e., "south side of 12-inch sugar maple, branch spread approximately 30 ft."; "corner of 20-foot-wide driveway"; or "center of 4-foot-diameter boulder." You may also choose to take your field notes in a more graphic form, sketching out the reference points and the data points and drawing lines connecting them with the distances shown on the drawing. This works better for some people, but the drawings can get messy

and confusing unless you keep the number of data points per sketch to a minimum.

Picking your data points can be a bit of a puzzle. Remember those "connect the dots" drawings we did as children? Here's your chance to create one in reverse! Choose your data points so that when you connect the dots you create the shape of the feature you want, such as a driveway (figure 3.5). Locate data points at corners, and place several along smooth curves. For trees, especially large ones, it is good to measure to the same spot on the tree from both reference points and to write down which side of the tree you measured to and the trunk diameter, so you can plot it accurately. Make sure you measure from your reference points to the house in at least two or three places so you can properly locate the house relative to your reference points on the map. This is often not a problem, because we frequently use house corners as reference points.

If you find that you need to create second set of reference points to get additional areas, try to use at least one of the original reference points for the second set. If you can't do that, the new points should ideally both be within sight and measuring distance of the old set. *Measure from the first set of reference points to each of the new reference points, more than once if possible.* Compass bearings between them all wouldn't be a bad idea either. If you start a

Point	SE corner House Ref A	NW corner House Ref B	NOTES
Apple Sapling	32.5'	36.1'	Crown spread 3 ft
SW Corner Garden Bed	25.3'	46.3'	Outside corner of stone wall; Wall 1 ft thick
SE Corner Garden	15.4'	35.6'	Outside corner wall
Center Boulder	16.9'	40.7'	Boulder 4 ft dia.
Birdbath			

9/16/04

FIGURE 3.4. Since you measure to each data point from at least two reference points, you will need a field-notes sheet something like this. We recommend writing a good description of each data point on your notes so you can remember which site feature the numbers relate to. Think about how you will draw what you map as you take measurements so you can note helpful information on your notes and measure to good points.

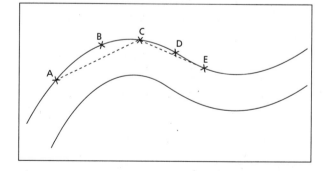

FIGURE 3.5. Choose your data points carefully so you can connect the dots appropriately. In this example, measuring only to points A, C, and E, while skipping B and D, will make drawing the edge of the pathway less accurate. Note that if the pathway is a consistent width you have to measure points only on one side of the path to be able to draw it well.

new set of benchmarks without being able to link them to the old set, you will have two map sections that you cannot accurately connect to each other. If you use house corners as reference points, the above doesn't apply, as long as you have an accurate drawing of the house.

Before you finish measuring, go back to your list of key features and check it twice. It isn't always easy to get friends together to help. If you have never done this mapping stuff before, it might be a good idea to do some plotting before you do all your measuring. That way you will better understand the whole process and will therefore take better measurements and notes. Having a table to plot upon out in the field near where you are measuring makes it easier, too, especially if you orient the paper and points on the plan to match the orientation of the actual landscape (i.e., the north arrow on the plan should point in the same direction as north in reality).

Plot the Points

Begin plotting the data by first taping tracing paper down on your drafting surface so it won't move as you work. Draw the two benchmarks to scale on your tracing paper. Think through where the reference points lie on the ground relative to the data points you measured to, and try to place the references on the paper so that you have enough room to plot all the other points without going off the page. Label the reference points clearly to help avoid confusion while plotting. If you used house corners as reference points, tape down your house plan and tape the tracing paper over it with enough room to extend all the lines you need without going off the page.

Use the engineer's scale to adjust the spread of the circle-drawing compass to the distance you measured from Point A to the first data point. Draw an arc with the compass from the proper reference point on the plan. Do the same for the first data point from reference Point B. Where the two arcs intersect is where the feature you measured to is located on the map (figure 3.6). Be careful that

you place the arcs in the right position: circles virtually always intersect in two places, so you might transpose the data points to the symmetrical position on the wrong side of the benchmarks. This is where your visual memory and spatial sense come into play, and why having the plan aligned to the same orientation as the land helps. You have to judge whether the data points you are plotting are ending up in about the right place. Sometimes it helps to draw both intercepts of the arcs so you can decide which is the right one. Once you are sure you have the data point in the right place, mark and label that feature, erase the arcs, and then plot the next data point.

As you add data points, connect the dots between points to begin drawing the map and help you stay oriented to the ground reality as you plot. For example, if you took several data points that indicate the edge of the driveway, connect these points to start drawing in the driveway. Drawing the map as you plot helps you find mistakes before you go too far astray and builds excitement and motivation as the map appears before your eyes.

Often, you need to go back out and remeasure points because of mistakes or things that don't look right on the plan. This is common, especially when you haven't had much experience with the process. Even if you find your plan looks familiar, it is a good idea to field-check the rough draft when you are done. Use the engineer's scale to measure a few distances between objects on the plan that you had not actually measured between when you gathered data. Then go outside to check whether the distance on the ground is the same as, or close enough to, what the map shows. If not, find the problem and fix it. If so, congratulations!

At some logical point in the process, if you haven't done so already, lay your tracing-paper rough-draft map over the scale diagram of the house you did earlier, and redraw the house on the same sheet of the tracing paper. You can do this before or after plotting, or before or after you field-check the map, whatever works best for you. If you have more than

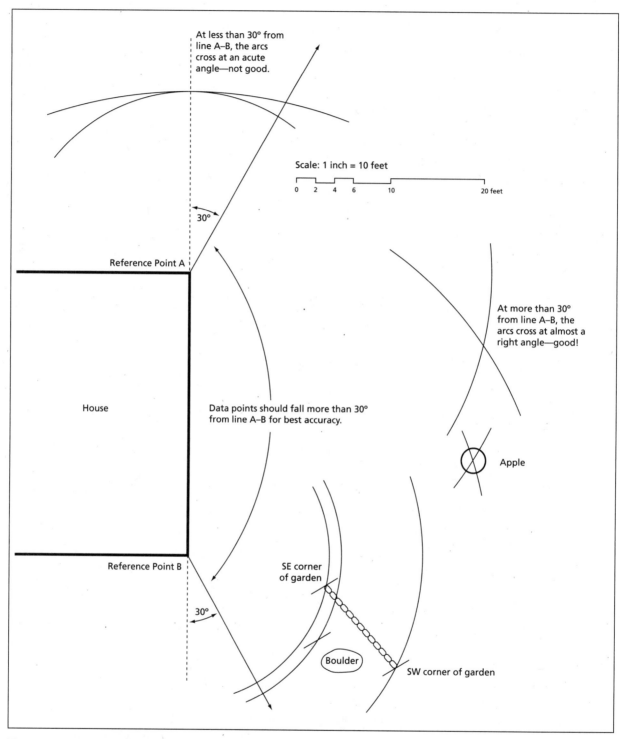

FIGURE 3.6. When plotting triangulation data, use a circle-drawing compass and your engineer's scale to draw arcs from each reference point to each data point at the scale you are using for your map. Be careful when choosing data points in the field that the arcs you will draw will cross at close to a right angle. When data points approach the line that runs through the reference points (the dashed line in the drawing above), the arcs cross acutely over a long distance, and it is hard to tell where to locate the object on the map.

one set of benchmarks, try to plot them on the same piece of tracing paper if you can. If you must use separate pieces of paper, then make sure each plotting diagram has enough common points of reference (at least three) that you can overlay one plot on the other and get them properly aligned.

If you also use the extensions with offsets method, plot that data on your tracing-paper rough draft too. Once you get all the data onto one sheet of tracing paper and field-check it, you can lay vellum over the tracing paper and redraw the map on vellum. Make sure you add a title block, north or solar-south arrow, and scale (see figure 3.2, page 173) to your final drawing. To get a north arrow when plotting, you can use a protractor or magnetic compass to plot magnetic north on the plan based on the compass reading you got between the two reference points or on one wall of the house.

EXTENSIONS WITH OFFSETS

As discussed earlier, extensions with offsets involve using the walls of buildings or other straight-line objects to create extension lines for mapping. By extending those straight lines out into the landscape around the building, we can measure where the extension lines intersect things we want on our map. We can also measure perpendicular to the extension lines to locate site features away from them (figure 3.7).

Setting Up the Extension Line
Once you have made your key choices about where to map, at what scale, and what features to put on the map, you need to decide which areas you can map using extensions and offsets. This depends on what objects in your mapped area have lines you can extend into the landscape.

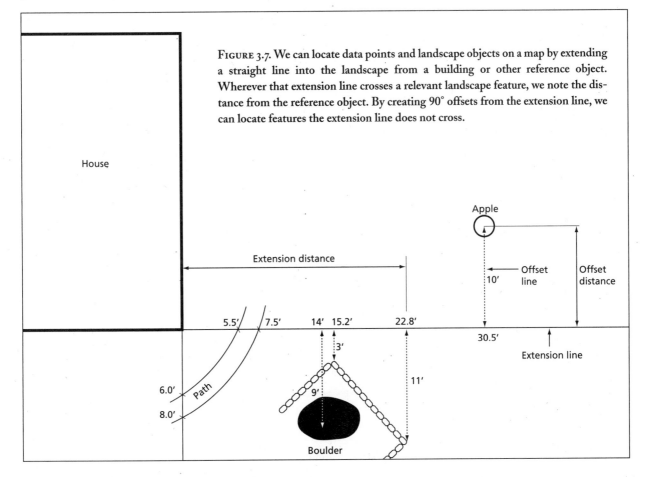

FIGURE 3.7. We can locate data points and landscape objects on a map by extending a straight line into the landscape from a building or other reference object. Wherever that extension line crosses a relevant landscape feature, we note the distance from the reference object. By creating 90° offsets from the extension line, we can locate features the extension line does not cross.

Building walls are the easiest lines to extend for setting up your extension lines. To do this, attach your tape measure to the building corner (or put a stake at the corner, or have someone stand there holding it), and then walk away from the building in line with the wall. Check your alignment with the wall by closing one eye and looking down along the building wall whose line you are extending. As you move your head slowly perpendicular to the extension line, you will notice that when your eye is too far outside the wall, you can see along the whole length of the wall. As you move your eye too far to the inside of the wall, the wall disappears behind the building corner. Your eye is in perfect alignment with the wall *just* when the length of the wall disappears at the edge of the building (figure 3.8). Lay out your 100-foot (33 m) or longer tape measure as an extension of the building wall to use as an extension line by placing it where the wall just

disappears from sight, with zero at the building corner. The tape is now your extension line.

If you don't have a building to use for extension lines, you can set up stakes in a 3-4-5 right triangle and eyeball between each of the pairs of stakes to set your reference lines (figure 3.9). A 3-4-5 right triangle has a 90° angle between the two short legs, and therefore the extension lines extending from the short legs of such a triangle will be perpendicular. This makes for easier plotting. To set up a 3-4-5 right triangle, first remember that in geometry $a^2 + b^2 = c^2$, so $3^2 + 4^2 = 5^2$, or $9 + 16 = 25$. If you create a triangle with sides of 3, 4, and 5 feet (or meters), you will create a triangle with one 90° angle. The same is true of a triangle where the sides are multiples of 3, 4 and 5, such as 6, 8, and 10 or 9, 12, and 15. So put a stake in the ground in a good place on your site, and put a second stake in the ground 6 feet away. Using two tape measures at

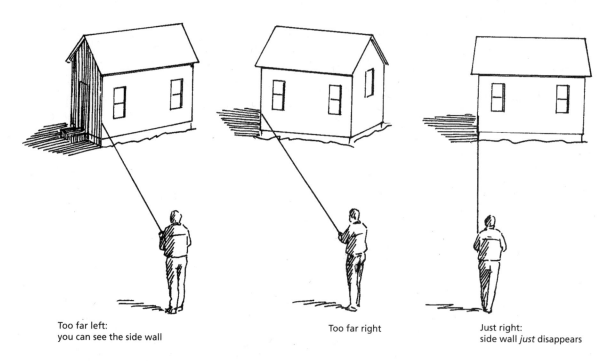

Too far left:
you can see the side wall

Too far right

Just right:
side wall *just* disappears

FIGURE 3.8. To create your extension line, attach your tape measure to the corner of the house and walk backward away from the building. Close one eye and sight down the wall of the house. Move your eye and body side to side relative to the wall you are extending. When you are too far to the outside of the wall, you will be able to see the wall. When you are perfectly lined up with the wall, the wall will *just* disappear from view. When you are too far to the inside, you won't see the wall either—you have to place yourself and your tape measure so that the wall *just* disappears from view.

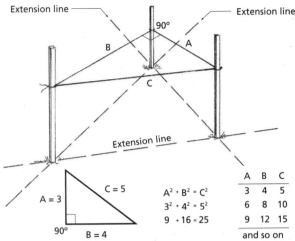

FIGURE 3.9. If you do not have an existing building to use for creating extension lines, you can create a reference from three stakes. Since any triangle having sides with the ratio of 3-4-5 is a right triangle, you can create three extension lines with known relationship to each other that you can easily plot on paper. Just put three stakes in the ground 3, 4, and 5 feet (or meters) apart, and you are all set. Or use any multiple of 3, 4, and 5, such as 6, 8, and 10 or 12, 16, and 20 and so on. Line up your tape measure up with two of the stakes and you have your extension line.

FIGURE 3.10. When creating offsets from the extension line, it is good to use a framing square or other tool to help you get a 90° angle for the offset line. This is especially true when the offset line exceeds 10 to 15 feet (3 to 5 m).

once, put a stake in the ground where the 8-foot and 10-foot marks intersect. Then you can stretch extension lines from each of the pairs of stakes in turn by extending the long tape measure so that it aligns with the two stakes, with zero at the stake where the line leaves the triangle.

Noting Features and Making Offsets

Once you have set up an extension line, you can note at what distance from zero the line intersects other objects, such as driveways, walks, edges of mown areas, trees, shrubs, planting beds, and the like. Again, make a diagram for each extension line on a separate sheet of paper and note the distance and what the line crosses (similar to figure 3.7).

Of course, many objects will lie in places other than where the extension line goes. For these, you need to make perpendicular offset lines with a second tape measure (figure 3.10). Have a friend take the zero end of the second tape measure to the object off the extension line, while you hold the

other end. Once your friend is in position, move your end of the tape along the extension line until the second tape is perpendicular to the extension line. Note down two distances: the distance from zero on the extension line where the second tape crosses, and the offset distance from the object to the extension line. Also note in which direction from the extension the offset line goes (north, south, east, west, or whatever), and describe the object or feature that the offset locates. It helps greatly if your notes are a graphic depiction of the extension, offsets, and objects, rather than just a list of numbers.

Usually you will extend more than one house wall or other extension line while mapping. Complete one extension line and all its offsets before moving to the next. Put notes for each extension line on a separate sheet of paper. Pick your data points carefully so you can connect the dots, as discussed above.

Minimizing Errors

The biggest challenge with extensions and offsets is getting the lines accurately laid out. A poorly aligned extension line spells doom for accuracy, and the same goes for an offset line that is not accurately placed 90° off the extension line. The longer a poorly aligned extension line is, the worse the error gets. The farther a poorly aligned offset goes from the extension line, the greater the error. Add both errors together and you can get into big trouble. So, to avoid these errors:

1. make sure the wall you are eyeballing is actually straight;
2. be very careful in aligning the extension line with the wall, checking it every so often to make sure the tape hasn't moved;
3. minimize the distance you extend the extension line (100 feet/33 m or less is good);
4. keep offset-line distances to a minimum (30 feet/9.1 m maximum, if that); and
5. use a magnetic compass, framing square, or other device to get the 90° angle for offsets, at least for long-distance offsets (more than 10 to 15 feet/3 to 5 m).

We also try to use extensions and offsets only in areas where accuracy is less important, when help for triangulation is not available, or when time is of the essence.

Plotting Extensions and Offsets

This part is fairly self-explanatory. If you extended the lines of the house walls, obviously you'll need to start with a scale plan that shows the house on it. If you extended lines from some other object, or a set of stakes as suggested above, then plot those things on the plan first, at scale. Draw your extension line using a ruler, use a drafting triangle against the ruler to get your 90° offsets and your scale to measure the distances, and bingo, you're on! Again, connect the dots as you draw to help check your accuracy.

After you have a rough draft, field-check the map as described earlier. Combine with triangulation data, connect the dots, and check your list of site features to make sure you have covered all the bases. Once you have a final rough draft, lay a clean sheet of vellum over the top and trace your final copy onto the vellum. Voilà!

Add a title block, north arrow, and scale to your final drawing. To get a north arrow if you have not done triangulation, take a compass bearing while looking down along a building wall or between two stakes that you used as one of your extension lines. When plotting, you can use a protractor to plot magnetic north on the plan.

SITE ANALYSIS AND ASSESSMENT

> We shall not cease from exploration
> And the end of all our exploring
> Will be to arrive where we started
> And know it for the first time.
>
> —T. S. Eliot, *Little Gidding*

> The perception of what is small is the secret of clear-sightedness.
>
> —Lao Tzu

When skillfully practiced, site analysis and assessment offers the designer vital insights, juicy connections, practical raw data, deep pattern understanding, and elegant design multifunctionality. It allows you to explore a place and know it for the first time in a methodical, spontaneous, and fascinating way that alters your perceptions of the landscape forever. Site analysis and assessment (A&A) does this not only by helping us perceive what is small, but by giving us a perspective that helps us see that *we* are small, that helps us see what is bigger than ourselves and our place in that bigger reality in a new way. The only way to have that experience is to actually do site analysis skillfully. With that in mind, we'll keep the theory to a minimum and then jump right into practical matters.

SITE ANALYSIS AND ASSESSMENT THEORY

The word *analysis* literally means "to break up." When we analyze something, we separate a whole entity into its component parts in our minds. We examine a system of interacting elements by looking at what elements compose the system and at the relationships between them. The word *assess* literally means "to sit beside" or "to assist in the office of a judge." When we assess something we determine its importance, size, or value. Assessment, therefore, is the act or an instance of giving weight or value to something.

Any landscape is a whole system composed of elements or parts. We can analyze these parts or characteristics—we can describe the site in terms of its soils, sun and shade patterns, water regimes, and vegetation architecture, for example. These parts and their relationships make up the "what" of analysis and assessment. Assessment gives meaning to the analysis by evaluating or weighing the parts. What do these parts and the relationships between them mean for this design? What is important here? What is unimportant? Assessment is therefore the "so what" of analysis and assessment. The process of analysis and assessment, then, answers the questions "what?" and "so what?"[5]

The natural thinking processes of analysis and assessment offer much value to design. Without analysis, assessment is shallow and broad, of little use for design or problem solving. Without assessment, analysis is meaningless. Good site analysis and assessment helps you discover the capabilities, limitations, and needs of the land, building a strong foundation for ecological design and management. It connects the goals to the site, ensuring continuity of purpose and generating a design responsive to its context and the needs of the land and gardener. Poor A&A leads to unresponsive design at best, irresponsible design or no design at worst. Thorough analysis and assessment eases the designer's burden, prevents things from getting stuck, and speeds design projects in innumerable ways.

Good Site Analysis and Assessment Is . . .

What makes a site analysis and assessment "good"? One answer derives from the meanings of the words *analysis* and *assessment* as applied to our direct experience of our mental process. When we analyze a site, we observe aspects of that piece of land. When we assess, we interpret those observations to give them meaning. Observation is the "what" of analysis, while interpretation is the "so what" of assessment. Maintaining a clear separation between observations and interpretations is essential to skillful site A&A. We even write them down differently, using a dot bullet at the beginning of each observation and an arrow at the beginning of each interpretation (see figure 3.11). Segregating observations and interpretations keeps our thinking clear, allowing us to evaluate and change our interpretations as necessary, and to make more than one interpretation from an observation.[6]

Good site analysis is focused, balanced, and comprehensive. Since we can analyze landscapes infinitely, we need guidance. Your design goals offer some of this guidance; remember, the goals guide the analysis and assessment, and the analysis and assessment discovers the design. For example, if you were interested only in tree crops, you wouldn't analyze and assess the site for its suitability for cultivated annual crops. However, do not use the goals as your sole guidance, for they generally reflect only our human agenda. Balance your agenda by listening to the land's needs as best you can, and respond appropriately. Below, we will offer ways to determine what questions to ask based on the need to understand the site on its own terms, not only your goals.

Good site A&A also engages both sides of the brain: linear and spatial, rational and intuitive, verbal and visual, analytic and synthesizing. Using both words and drawings helps achieve this (you may use other media, but we will focus on these two). You don't need to be an artist to do this work, and you don't need a bunch of expensive tools (see box 3.2). You simply need to express your thoughts and observations on paper in more than one way. We refer here to drawings using simple forms such as circles and arrows to record your observations of the site and its characteristics. Sketchy, reasonably messy drawings are good.

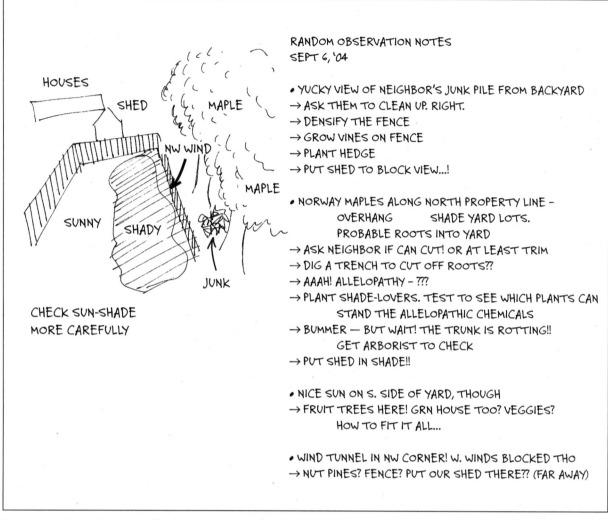

FIGURE 3.11. It is important to discern between your observations and your interpretations when doing site analysis and assessment. We suggest writing a bullet before each observation and an arrow before each interpretation to help keep yourself clear, as shown here. Notice that you can have many interpretations for each observation, and that the interpretations may conflict with each other. That is okay; write down any solution directions that come to mind anyway, but don't choose any one of them yet. Just keep the ideas coming and get them down on paper. *Sketch design by Dave Jacke, reproduced by Sterling Hill Productions.*

We also strongly encourage you to write directly on your drawings so that your thinking is more integrated in time and space.

Site A&A can generate a large quantity of information, even when it is reasonably focused. A good site analysis and assessment boils down the mass of observations and interpretations to their essence so you can use them effectively. Usually this results in a summary drawing that gathers the key information in one place. This summary lays the foundation for the decisions made in the design phase that follows.

Choosing Your Path through Site A&A

As said earlier, we can analyze and assess any site in infinite ways. Obviously none of us have infinite time for this work, so it is wise to think things through before you begin your site analysis.

TABLE 3.13. Optional site analysis and assessment exercises and their purposes.

Exercise	Purposes
Varmints, Pests, and Diseases Analysis	• Identify the pests and diseases of your main crops in your region; research strategies for design, species selection, and management to prevent problems; and identify relevant beneficial animals for these pests and their habitat needs. • Research local "problem" varmints and how to manage them.
Ecological Neighborhood Analysis	• Map healthy habitats in your neighborhood and evaluate them for habitat quality and linkage to your site. • Identify additional species for use, analogs, or possible problems. • Consider implications for how much and what kinds of habitat to create in your garden.
Native and Naturalized Species Analysis	• Identify historical and currently existing native and naturalized species in your region for direct use in your garden design, or for use as models for ecological analogs.

Site analysis and assessment serves at least two basic functions for forest gardeners: to help you select a site for your forest garden, and to help you design the forest garden. Some of you already know where you want your forest garden. Great! This simplifies your work. If you have more than one garden-siting option or no idea at all, the "Site Selection" section will help you make your siting decision. The section offers a few ways to select your site based on your goals and on the discreteness of the possible garden sites. Once you know where you want the garden, the other site A&A exercises we discuss will help you understand the site well so you can design it well.

Many possible paths exist through the analysis and assessment of your garden site, each with varying depths of investigation and areas of focus. We have segregated the options into the analysis and assessment work we feel everyone should do to at least a minimal level—the basic site assessment—and a set of optional tasks to take you deeper and focus you on issues appropriate to your circumstances.

The basic site assessment consists of random and thematic observation and interpretation exercises that offer a well-rounded view of what your garden site is made of and how that reality interacts with your design goals. We believe the essential structure of these exercises should vary little between forest gardeners, but that the specific questions and the amount of effort each of you puts into it should vary to suit your needs, interests, and time constraints. The "Basic Site Analysis and Assessment" section provides the questions and guidance you require to negotiate the process.

Table 3.13 lists the optional site assessment exercises and their purposes. To help you select which of these to undertake, consider two basic approaches to forest garden design: starting with the ecosystem as a whole and working into species selection (working from the ecosystem to the plants) versus starting with preferred species and designing an ecosystem to accommodate them (working from the plants to the ecosystem). These two approaches exist on a continuum. We expect most people will find themselves "working both ends toward the middle," but starting with a clearer sense of one end or the other. Look at your goals and read the following to see where you fall along this spectrum and which tasks relate to your situation. These approaches hold implications for the design-phase processes you might use as well, so it may behoove you to review chapter 4 and begin mapping out your work there, too.

Some of you already know what kind of ecosystem or garden character you want to create, or you have an existing ecosystem that you intend to modify slightly, but your sense of what species you want to grow is more open or vague. You can therefore define the character and qualities of that ecosystem so you can design it or adapt to it. Species selection will be driven by these parameters, as will the garden's architecture. This is typical of the way landscape architects work, where plant-species selection is one of the designer's last acts. Model ecosystem analysis is central to this approach, as it leads to design using ecological analogs and polyculture analogs. If you see yourself approaching forest garden design from ecosystem to plants and you did not analyze a model ecosystem during goals articulation, then do it as part of your site analysis. You need to have some design criteria for your mimic ecosystem to make your site analysis work best for you. Existing-species niche analysis (discussed in the "Basic Site Analysis and Assessment" section) can play a role in this approach. Native and naturalized species analysis is also a useful tool in ecosystem-to-plants design. It gives you a wider range of model species from which to choose for direct use or ecological analogs. Varmint, pest, and disease assessment is less important in this context. All of this work leads toward habitat mimicry and the related design processes described in chapter 4.

Many of you know what species you want to grow, while your criteria for ecosystem character are more open or vague. You can design a garden ecosystem to accommodate the plants, with the garden's character growing from putting together the ecosystem building blocks. Some ecologists would argue that ecosystems are actually constructed like this, as an expression of the characteristics of the individual species composing the whole. In this case, you can rely more on niche analysis of desired species (as discussed beginning on page 159) and existing species, as well as varmint, pest, and disease analysis, to help you understand both the site as it is and the garden ecosystem as you want it to be. You may want to analyze your ecological neighborhood to support developing your pest- and disease-management strategies, depending on the outcome of your varmint, pest, and disease work. Native and naturalized species analysis is less important in this case, though it is still helpful for finding useful, locally adapted native and naturalized species.

These analyses all lead toward guild-build and the related design process described in chapter 4.

Folks often have goals for both the ecosystem character and the garden's species. Some conflicts may arise from this fact, as certain species may not adapt to the desired ecosystem. All of the optional exercises will be useful for this situation, as will existing- and desired-species niche analysis. You'll have to prioritize if you want to reduce your workload here; the best way to prioritize is to shift your approach toward one or the other basic approaches to forest garden design.

SITE SELECTION

Forest gardens live and grow in one place for decades. The costs and benefits of choosing a good, fair, or poor forest garden site add up for a long time. It pays to invest effort on this choice up front.

Some of you will have sites small enough or visions large enough to consider your whole property a forest garden, even if it contains small areas of lawn or pavement as part of the habitat mosaic. In this case, you can skip this part of the process, create a base map of your whole site, and move into site analysis and assessment. If, however, you have a larger site or smaller-scale plans in mind, you may want to designate one area as forest garden, while other parts of your landscape have other functions and character. This subsection is for you. The processes described here will help ground your site selection in your goals and the site realities. The first step for site selection in all cases is to get clear on your site selection criteria. We then offer three ways to select your garden site, each requiring different amounts of effort and for sites of varied complexity.

Selecting your site before creating a base map reduces your mapping work to only the area you absolutely need. However, a sketch plan of your site can be useful in site selection, as well as in overall site planning. It's your choice whether to map a larger or a smaller area. Since site selection is less detailed work, you can easily create a simple sketch plan to help you select your site, as discussed earlier.

Once you have a sketch plan for site selection, determine your site selection criteria.

Determine Site Selection Criteria

Look for site selection criteria in your goals statement and desired-species niche analysis work (if any), and summarize them on a separate piece of paper. You may have clearly stated these already, or they may lie implicit in your goals. Look at each goal or list item and ask, "What does this imply about where I place my forest garden?" Compare the site selection criteria proposed in table 3.14 with your goals to see how they match. Try to determine the "what, size, shape, location, and relationship" of the whole forest garden based on your goals: its habitat character, sun-shade requirements, moisture requirements, access requirements; how many trees of what size and their general spacing; the garden's relationship to your house and other site functions (play spaces or eating areas, for example); and so on. If specific plants are essential to your garden vision, their requirements will help you determine these criteria. Also remember to use patterns #1 through #8 in chapter 2 as possible guiding ideas. You will probably have additional criteria. If you have numerous criteria, it would probably help to prioritize them as essential, important, or nice. Make sure also to consider where *not* to put your forest garden (see table 3.15).

Observe and Interpret Based on the Criteria

Sometimes the simple act of pulling together your site selection criteria will make it obvious where to put your forest garden. Other times it isn't that easy and you need to go further. With a list of site selection criteria in mind and on paper, the next task is to make observations of the site. Given well-defined criteria, your observations and interpretations usually make your siting decision quite clear. However, achieving that clarity may take a few tricks, and the process can take as little as a half hour, or four or more hours if things are complicated. We offer three site selection techniques for

---

TABLE 3.14. Key practical criteria for forest-garden site selection. Modify these, make them more specific, and add your own criteria, practical or not practical, as needed. "#" denotes patterns in chapter 2.

Essential Criteria

- *In close proximity to the gardener.* Place your garden near the house, especially the kitchen, so you walk by or through it often, can get to it easily, can see it from house windows, and so on. How close depends on what you want to grow and how you want to use the space. See #6, *Outdoor Living Rooms,* and #7, *Zones and Sectors.*

- *6 to 8 hours of sun per day* for overstory plants, especially in fruit-ripening season. This may not always be an essential criterion: some forest gardens may need or tolerate shade for certain crops.

- *Access to water.* Moist soils and easy irrigation are best, but one or the other can work alone. See #8, *Zones of Water Use.*

- *Access to nutrient and organic-matter resources.* This does not necessarily mean fertile soils (see below). You need the mulch, compost, and so on whether your soils are fertile or not.

Very Important Criteria

- *Deep, well-drained soils.* These offer more "leg room" than shallow soils (see "Deeply Rooted Trees Do It Better," volume 1, chapter 5) and more breathing space than wet soils. These can be more important than fertility, which we can build over time. If you must choose between two sites of about equal fertility, but with varying depth, take the deeper soils. If it's between one with infertile, deep soils and one with fertile, shallow soils, choosing deep soils and building fertility may be best, unless the deep soils are extremely poor.

- *Fertile soils.* These offer healthier, faster-growing plants with higher yields and less nutrient competition in the ecosystem.

- *A long-term forest garden site.* No expected future buildings, driveways, or other major disturbances in or near the garden.

- *Site repair* (see pattern #5). Leave the healthy and beautiful parts of the site alone, and build and garden in the areas that need care and attention. Watch for endangered species, unique or fragile habitats, or just beautiful places you should leave be. Notice barren, compacted, or eroding soils, sick plants, monocultured habitats, or other damaged areas you can nurture. This may conflict with choosing the best soils or other criteria.

Important Criteria

- *Links to other habitats* (see #2, *Islands and Corridors*).
- *Habitat diversity* (see pattern #4).
- *Lack of existing vigorous or opportunist weeds* (unless you choose to do site repair by removing them and gardening there).

varied situations, including, in order of complexity, quick evaluations, site-selection matrices, and criteria mapping. Each of these techniques is appropriate for different circumstances, though you may start with the simplest technique and then "graduate" to the next level if necessary.

Sometimes a property will contain several distinct, easily defined areas bounded by existing site features. Other properties will have no easily definable areas, and we must then consider a set of interacting characteristics and values that vary across the landscape. These two cases require somewhat different approaches to site selection. In either case, we recommend starting with the quick evaluation to see whether you can make your site selection with minimal effort.

Quick Evaluation

When you have distinct spaces you can simply define each area on a quick sketch or a copy of a site plan, or just go walk around each area, and then evaluate each one based on your criteria. This technique may not even require any mapping work if you can sketch a reasonable representation or know the spaces well enough that you can just make lists of their characteristics on a pad of paper. Writing down or bubble diagramming (see box 3.3) your observations and interpretations will help you select your site. Take your site criteria with you, and use them to direct your attention. Take notes. Distinguish between observations and interpretations. Note the pros, cons, and implications of each site. Consider the landscape as a whole, and the other activities and functions there, not just the forest garden itself. Think about all four seasons, too. For example, where does the snowplow push the snow? In all cases, listen to your gut and heart as you do this. In most cases, this will result in a clear choice of sites, or at least a narrowing of choices. If no clearly optimal site emerges, you can create a site-selection matrix to make finer distinctions in the value of each site.

When your landscape does not have distinct spaces, quick evaluations are more challenging but still possible. Use your criteria to heighten your awareness of what is happening on your site, and go into the space, sketch, bubble-diagram, and write. Trust your inner designer, and see what happens. If you find yourself mystified or not fully clear, then move to a more involved process. For landscapes with indefinite spaces, we suggest using criteria mapping.

TABLE 3.15. Some indicators of where not to put your forest garden.

- *Future construction zones.* Consider your own plans, and perhaps the most likely plans of future owners, for additional parking, house additions, garages, and so on. Think of equipment access and earthmoving as well as the actual construction itself.

- *On-site septic systems.* Some state regulators say that if woody plants grow within 10 feet (3 m) of your leach field, the roots will eventually destroy the septic system. Some commentators say even more distance is necessary, and the discussion in chapter 5 of volume 1 supports this conclusion. However, feeding your trees with wastewater is a good idea, so some balance between absolutely no tree roots in the leach field and some fine roots there makes sense. We can't say where that balance point lies.

- *Polluted areas.* Consider road runoff and fumes, pesticide runoff or spray drift from neighboring properties, runoff and contamination from your own vehicles, garages, storage sheds, and so on.

- *Poor soils.* This depends on what crops you want to grow. Shallow, infertile, or dry soils and soils with a high water table are less desirable for most woody crops.

- *Too much shade.* This also depends on the crops you want to grow.

- *Competing uses.* Children's soccer fields, annual vegetable gardens, overflow car parking during parties, piles of snow during the winter season, the area where you dump and process firewood every year, and other uses may make some areas unsuitable for forest gardening. However, many times you can find creative ways to integrate these uses into a forest garden, so don't automatically eliminate areas without thinking things through.

- *Aesthetic or social concerns.* Trees can block important views or solar access to buildings (we have more than once seen people forget this fact and plant trees in front of "solar" homes!); the kind of forest garden you want may not fit the character of your neighborhood and so may not be socially appropriate for your front yard or other public spaces; the kind of forest garden you want may not fit the tone you want to establish in your entry or arrival area; and so on.

Box 3.3: Bubble Diagramming

Bubble diagrams are a basic drawing tool for site analysis, design concepts, and schematic design. These simple, sometimes messy drawings boil down a site's functions, flows, and spaces to a meaningful essence using circles and arrows and a paragraph explaining what each one is, to paraphrase Arlo Guthrie. You can also use other simple geometries—such as stars, boxes, and triangles—to make the points the drawing needs to make. Bubble diagramming is like explaining something to someone by wiping clear a patch of dirt and drawing on it with a stick: "Here's the house, there's the property line, there's the wet spot and the steep slope. If we put the forest garden here, then the patio has to go there. . . ." With bubble diagrams, we use paper, pencil, and more detailed symbols than you can make with a stick in the sand, but they are still scratchy, sketchy, abstract drawings.

Bubble diagrams help us see the current reality more clearly by taking away the clutter and exposing the site's framework, its "bones," its layout, and its problems and opportunities. We've used bubble diagrams to design houses, kitchens, landscapes, and gardens, as well as towns and regions. We've used them to analyze and assess water flows and landforms, as well as microclimates, plant communities, and zones of use. They help find and express the big picture of what's happening on-site, and of what we want to have going on there, in a rough way. Bubble diagrams are about relationships, functions, and ideas, not about specific things, exact sizes, or detailed design. We're serious about the paragraphs, too. Write on the drawings to summarize or explain what the bubble diagram helps you see.

What you "bubble out" on a bubble diagram depends entirely on your drawing's purpose (figure 3.12). One bubble could represent the sunny, dry slopes, another the wet spot, and a third the frost pocket, with others showing various other microclimate subtleties. Bubbles could indicate the rough sizes and positions of the proposed driveway, lawn, "oldfield garden," thicket, and grove, while thick, solid black lines indicate the proposed main paths, thinner lines the secondary paths, and dotted lines the stepping-stone paths. Brief notes in each bubble could summarize the character of the space, or the species assembly that goes there. A star could denote each bench spot, and wiggly lines where you propose putting the water lines underground, with *W*s and dots for the water spigots. Get the idea? Invent your own graphic language to make notes and observations about whatever you are observing or pondering.

Use bubble diagrams whenever you need to think fast about the big picture without getting caught in too much detail, whether it's site analysis and assessment or design schemes and concepts.

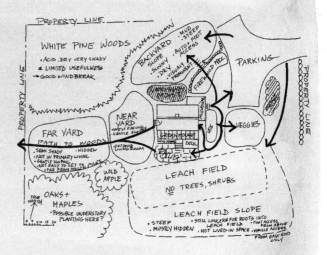

FIGURE 3.12. Bubble diagrams are simple drawings requiring little drawing skill that can convey much useful information about a site or its proposed uses. We use bubble diagrams in site analysis and assessment, as shown here with observations noted, as well as during many phases of site design.

The Site-Selection Matrix

A site-selection matrix is an array of rows and columns that allows you to evaluate different clearly defined sites against a set of selection criteria (table 3.16). We don't use it often, but we find a matrix handy when we can otherwise see no clear winners or need to evaluate many sites against a large number of criteria. A matrix allows you to choose one site over the others or to rank them in order of value. Matrices are fast and simple, support clear thinking, and usefully augment our intuition.

Make a chart with enough columns for the number of sites you have to evaluate, plus a wide column on the left. List the selection criteria in the left-hand column, one in each row. State all the criteria in positive terms, that is, a "yes" to each criterion is a desirable site. You can also state them all in negative terms, but if you state some negatively and some positively, things will get very confused. List the criteria in priority groupings: put all the "essential" criteria at the top, then the "important" criteria, then the "nice" criteria.

Go through each criterion for each site, and *quickly* decide or guess whether the site gets a wholehearted "yes" to each criterion, a wholehearted "no," or a "maybe, sort of." Be careful not to answer "maybe, sort of" if you just don't know. Use question marks instead. If you have many question marks, then you need to do some research or careful observation before you continue. We like to fill in each "cell" in the matrix with either a full black box if it gets a no, a gray or a diagonal half-black box if it's a maybe or sort of, and a blank box if it's a yes. This gives us a visual image of which site fulfills the most criteria.

If you don't get a clear visual answer, add up a score for each site by designating a yes as 2, a maybe as 1, and a no as 0. If it's still too close to call or a tie, add up the scores for the essential, important, and nice goals separately and see what that tells you. You can also give differing weights to your various goals based on their priority. Give each level of priority a multiplier, such as 3 for essential, 2 for

TABLE 3.16. A sample forest-garden site-selection matrix. White means the site meets the criterion, gray means maybe-sort of, and black means it does not meet the criterion. In the first total, white counts as 2 points, gray as 1, and black as 0. In the second total, the points above are multiplied by the criterion priority rating, with Essential at 3 points, Important at 2 points, and Nice at 1 point.

E, I, N	Criteria	Sites A	B	C	D
E	Min. 6 hours full sun				
E	Within 50 ft. of hose faucet				
E	Fertile, uncompacted soil				
I	Visible from kitchen window				
I	Whole space <75' from kitchen door				
I	Level with or downhill of mulch piles				
I	Site needs repair				
N	Nice views from garden				
N	Site has wind-protected space for sitting				
N	Neighbors cannot see into space				
	Criteria-only totals	12	14	10	14
	Criteria times priority totals	27	26	25	24

important, and 1 for nice. Then multiply the scores in each cell by the priority multiplier for its criterion and add up the scores for each site. Check to see whether sites receive high scores because they have a lot of nice and important criteria and no essentials, or because they have all the essentials but lack important or nice features.

Listen to your gut when you get an answer from the matrix. Other values can arise from within when you express things this way, and gut instincts may overrule the matrix process. Beware of the black-white thinking a matrix can foster; there may be excellent and creative ways to use more than one of the sites concurrently or sequentially in your design. Indeed, the clarity and simplicity of the matrix process may help you ponder how to do that and why! The information the matrix offers can inform your instincts so that you can more effectively follow them.

Criteria Mapping

When you do not have distinct areas you can map your criteria to find good forest garden sites.

Essentially what you must do is find the distinctions on the site that are not immediately obvious. This may entail further defining your criteria. A simple site sketch, if not a site plan, is useful for this, but you can also stake things out on the ground. In the latter case, you may need additional tools such as a tape measure, magnetic compass, or stakes and string to help you mark out the criteria. You can use a process of elimination, a process of selection, or, typically, both.

Start with a process of elimination. Which areas definitely have no potential as forest garden sites (see, for example, table 3.15)? Take a copy of your site sketch (not the original!) or put a piece of tracing paper over it, and simply blacken out or draw hatch marks over these areas. This may result in one or more remaining possible garden areas, which may or may not be optimal for forest gardening. Now see whether at least one remaining area meets your basic criteria for what it *is*, rather than what it is *not*. If the remaining areas are distinct, you can go back to the previous processes to select among these areas. If large, indefinite spaces still stare you in the face, you'll need a different method.

You can define the boundaries of good sites within undifferentiated spaces using observable, but seemingly invisible, characteristics. These include distances from doors; soil characteristics; sun patterns; view corridors; pedestrian, cart, and vehicular circulation patterns; and so on. With a little thought, you can delineate reasonable boundaries and guidelines based on your selection criteria, map them out, and see what patterns arise. Look at the essential criteria first, then the important criteria, and so on. Eventually a pattern should emerge to give you a sense of direction.

Let's say you want a 50-by-50-foot forest garden, and that convenient access and using the garden as an outdoor living room are essential. You decide, therefore, that the distance from the kitchen door is a key criterion, the optimal distance being between 25 and 75 feet, since you want a few intensive annual garden beds and a patio right by the door.

Sketch lines for the 25-, 50-, and 75-foot distances from the door on a piece of tracing paper over your site plan. That's the analysis. The assessment could use the same "yes-maybe-no" format as described for site-selection matrices to keep things simple. You decide that 25 to 50 feet is optimal (yes), and you leave that blank; and 50 to 75 feet is maybe, so it's hatched (figure 3.13). Similarly, proximity to

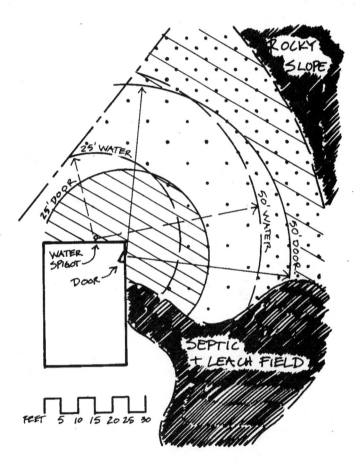

Figure 3.13. Mapping site selection criteria can help you define the spaces for various uses such as forest gardening. In this example, the definite no-go spaces for a forest garden are colored black, such as the leach field and a steep, rocky slope. Within the remaining space, you can map key site selection criteria such as distance from the kitchen door or the water spigot and views from key windows. The heavier the hatch marks, the less desirable the space is for your forest garden. Such a process, using your own criteria, can help you work out the best location for your forest garden when you have a large, featureless space within which to work. *Sketch by Dave Jacke.*

water is essential for easy maintenance. So on top of the previous pattern you overlay another, such that any space within 25 feet (one hose length) from the water spigot is a yes (clear), 25 to 50 feet is a maybe (light hatching), and anything beyond 50 is a no (heavy hatching). You then turn to another essential criterion defining your optimal forest garden site. You can plot distance from the mulch piles or strategic materials depot, soil variations, or views from the house on the plan by making observations, delineating assessment categories, and sketching out relevant areas on the plan or staking them out on-site.

As you define reasonable guidelines within the various criteria, then observe, weigh, and sketch on the plan (or mark on the ground) how they shape up, you define spaces that meet or don't meet the various criteria. By overlaying the various sheets of tracing paper on top of one another, or using various colors of pencil or marker on a copy or three of the plan, you can see which spaces fit which criteria. If your plan is accurate, you should be able to pace or measure these areas to define them on the ground, field-check your information, and come to a final decision.

Make sure to consider the aesthetics of the forest garden site and how it will define and change the sense of space and the uses of space in the landscape. You may need to balance mutually exclusive criteria against each other. If you have several areas of only moderate potential, you'll have to evaluate them in light of which criteria they meet and which they don't. In any case, this process of mapping out guidelines based on your criteria helps you differentiate within seemingly indefinite space, making the qualities of those spaces clearer so you can make conscious choices.

If no good sites emerge from any of these processes, reevaluate your goals in light of the information you have gathered. Chances are you can design some kind of forest garden practically anywhere, but you may not be able to design the one you envisioned. Which goals can still work?

Which are more important or less so? Can you create the same values but with different specifics and a different vision? Are there ways you can modify one or more of the sites to make them meet your or your plants' needs? Some areas you eliminated earlier may meet some of your essential or other criteria, so you may want to reconsider why you eliminated them in the first place. Examine your attachments and desires. Go deeper. Brainstorm radically different alternatives. You may need to play with ideas for how to design forest gardens that fit various less-than-ideal sites, and see which forest garden suits you and your land best.

Once you have selected your forest garden site, create a map of the site and its immediate surroundings before continuing your design process.

Basic Site Analysis and Assessment

Having chosen a forest garden site, every forest gardener should do at least a minimal amount of site analysis and assessment. What we discuss in this section represents that minimum core of observation and interpretation. Of course, each of you can investigate your forest garden site using this basic format to a greater or lesser degree—that is for you to decide. In any case, though, the basic site analysis and assessment process entails exploring all the components of the landscape, as well as the landscape as a whole, looking for the design implications of the land's character in the context of your goals. What components of the landscape shall we examine? We have derived the basic structure of our site analysis from the scale of permanence (box 3.4). Again, though, to avoiding getting lost in the infinitude of things we could analyze and assess, we need guidance. The first step of any site A&A process, therefore, is to derive directives for the process from your goals and the land. Then, before you observe and interpret on-site, it makes sense to gather information from off-site resources.

Box 3.4: The Scale of Permanence

Over many years cattle farming in the dry Australian hills, P. A. Yeomans developed the "keyline approach" to land planning as a way of radically increasing the health, fertility, and productivity of farmlands. Yeomans saw that some landscape elements are more permanent and harder to change than others. Since the wise man buys the tie to fit the suit, and not the other way around, he felt it made sense to consider and modify the more permanent landscape elements first and the more easily changed elements later.[7] The scale of permanence codified this insight (see table 3.17, first column).

Bill Mollison and David Holmgren adapted Yeomans's scale of permanence to a broader siteplanning context as they developed permaculture in the late 1970s[8] (see table 3.17, second column). We have modified the scale of permanence again as shown in the third column of the table.

No one person can significantly change the climate. We can alter landform, but only at great expense. Landform influences water-flow patterns more than the opposite. Most legal issues are hard to change, and water-flow patterns have much to do with determining how legal issues affect a given site. In addition, legal issues often define where access roads can be located. Placing roads and pathways based on landform and water-flow patterns minimizes problems and allows us to use roads and paths to direct water flows. Access patterns strongly influence our ability to manage vegetation and wildlife. Indeed, this is the key insight behind zone planning. Vegetation, water, and landform create the microclimate of local areas. We should adapt our buildings to their microclimate and the other more permanent features of the landscape. Our buildings determine the optimal zones of use within a site, which determine how to manage the soil. Aesthetic qualities are the most ephemeral landscape features.

On the other hand, land is not a linear, ordered system, and all these landscape elements interact with each other. Yet the scale still holds value and a slice of truth. It can guide the general order of landscape design and construction; we obviously must modify grading (landform) and drainage (water) before we plant vegetation, for example. It helps us stay on track and cover our bases as a checklist of topics for analysis and assessment. If we don't know where to start a design or we get lost, the scale can get us going. Memorize the scale of permanence so you can use it as an organizing framework to guide your design process, keep things moving, and make sure you get the basics covered.

TABLE 3.17. The scale of permanence revisited, with the earliest version at left and the latest at right. Changes from previous scales are italicized.

Yeomans' Scale[1]	Permaculture's Scale[2]	Our Scale
Climate	Climate	Climate
Landform	Landform	Landform
Water Supply	Water Supply	Water (*in general*)
Farm Roads	Farm Roads	*Legal Issues*
Trees	*Plant Systems*	*Access & Circulation*
Permanent Buildings	*Microclimate*	*Vegetation & Wildlife*
Subdivisional Fences	Permanent Buildings	Microclimate
Soil	Subdivisional Fences	Buildings & *Infrastructure*
	Soil	*Zones of Use*
		Soil (*Fertility & Management*)
		Aesthetics

1 Yeomans, 1958, pages 22–28.
2 Mollison and Holmgren, 1978, page 36.

TABLE 3.18. Site analysis and assessment topics derived from common forest-garden design goals. This comprehensive list may look overwhelming, but not everyone will need to know all of this for their site. Bold items are essential for virtually every design. Other items may be useful for many people, but not all.

Climate
plant hardiness zone
status of predicted future climate change
annual precipitation, seasonal distribution
latitude
wind directions: prevailing, seasonal variations, storms
growing degree days (important for ripening nuts)
average frost-free dates
chilling hours (important for fruit-tree dormancy)
extreme weather potential: drought, flood, hurricane, tornado, fire

Landform
slope (steepness, rise/run in percent)
topographic position (i.e., midslope, hill crest, valley floor, and so on)
bedrock geology: permeability, depth, nutrient content, acidity
surficial geology: type of parent material, permeability, depth, stoniness, nutrient content, acidity, suitability for various uses, and so on
estimated depth of seasonal high water table
estimated depth to bedrock, hardpan, or impermeable layers of soil
elevation
landslide potential

Water
existing sources of supply: location, quantity, quality, dependability, sustainability, network layout and features (e.g., spigots, pipes, filters)
watershed boundaries and flow patterns: concentration and dispersion areas, including roof runoff patterns, gutters, and downspouts
potential pollution sources: road runoff, chemical runoff from neighbors, etc.
flooding, ponding, and puddling areas
possible sources of supply: location, quantity, quality, dependability, sustainability, cost to develop
location of all on-site and nearby off-site culverts, wells, water lines, sewage lines, septic systems, old wells, and so on
erosion: existing and potential areas

Legal Issues
zoning setbacks for sheds and other buildings from property lines
some jurisdictions require trees and shrubs to be certain minimum distances from septic-tank leach-field systems
if your site contains or lies near streams, wetlands, or other water bodies, there may be regulations relating to site modification, vegetation management, erosion control, and so on that could affect your design
more and more jurisdictions are restricting the planting of "invasive" species
many areas restrict the planting of gooseberries and currants (*Ribes* spp.) or other species because of plant-disease concerns
some localities or neighborhood associations restrict the kinds of landscaping you can have on your lot or in your front yard

Access and Circulation
activity nodes, storage areas
pedestrian, cart, and vehicle access points and current and potential patterns
materials flows: mulch, compost, produce, firewood, laundry, and so on

Vegetation and Wildlife
see text for discussion of detailed species and ecosystem assessments
existing plant species: locations, sizes/quantities, patterns, uses, poisonousness, invasiveness, weediness, what they indicate about site conditions, etc.
ecosystem architecture: layers and their density, patterning, and diversity; resultant habitat conditions, light/shade, character, quality
habitat types, food/water/shelter availability

Microclimate
definition of various microclimate spaces
slope aspects (direction slopes face relative to sun)
sun/shade patterns
cold-air drainage and frost pockets
soil moisture patterns
precipitation patterns
local wind patterns

Buildings and Infrastructure
building size, shape, locations, doors and windows, existing and possible functions
permanent pavement and snow piles from plowing it
power lines (above- and belowground) and electric outlets
outdoor water faucet, septic system, well locations
location of underground pipes: water and sewer line, footing drain, floor drain and downspout drain lines, tile drains, culverts, other
fences and gateways

Zones of Use
property lines, easements, rights-of-way
existing zones of land and water use (see patterns #7 and #8)
well protection zones, environmental and other legal limits (e.g., wetlands regulations, zoning regulations, building setbacks)
current uses by neighbors and passersby
use history and impacts on land, current or future uses

Soil Fertility and Management
soil types: texture, structure, consistence, profile, drainage
topsoil fertility: at least pH, % organic matter, N, P, K, Ca
soil toxins: lead, arsenic, mercury, cadmium, asbestos, etc.
management history

Aesthetics / Experience of Place
outdoor rooms, walls: define spaces (walls, ceilings, floors), qualities, feelings, functions, features
arrival and entry experience: sequencing, spaces, eye movements, feelings
view lines and corridors: define them, inside and outside, existing and potential
visual integration: alignment of elements, unity and variety, compositions, textures, colors
private/public continuum, formal/informal continuum
"sense of place": unique elements of the site that express and connect you to the place, the neighborhood, the region
disharmonies: noise, views, visuals, feelings, spaces
existing overall feelings/qualities/experience

TABLE 3.19. Goal-derived site analysis and assessment questions for Eric and Jonathan's forest-garden design case study. These questions and topics came from table 3.18 and from reviewing their goals summary statement and asking, "What do we need to know about our site so we can design a forest garden to meet our goals?"

1. Climate
- Hardiness zone and frost-free dates.
- Wind directions.

2. Landform
- Bedrock and surficial geology.
- Slopes (for gravity-fed irrigation and drainage).

3. Water
- Existing water sources.
- Roof runoff catchment potential.
- Flooding, ponding, and puddling areas.

4. Legal Issues
- Can we have chickens or other livestock?
- Can we have a graywater system?
- Are there rules for locating a shed and a greenhouse? Do we need permits?

5. Access & Circulation
- Vehicle access and turnaround for delivering materials.
- Social spaces.
- Storage areas.
- Potential walking and cart access ways.

6. Vegetation & Wildlife
- Existing plant species.
- Current successional stage.
- Habitat quality in yard and neighborhood.
- Existing beneficial-organism populations.
- Can we improve our sun access by trimming our neighbor's shade trees?
- Weeds, pests, diseases, and varmints on-site or in the neighborhood.

7. Microclimate
- Where is the best greenhouse site?
- What areas of the garden receive sufficient sunlight for fruit and annual vegetable production?
- Sun and shade in the garden (by season).
- Microclimates.
- Soil moisture patterns.

8. Buildings & Infrastructure
- Nail down existing buildings (and neighboring buildings) on map.
- Location of fences.

9. Zones of Use
- What "dead spaces" are best suited to shed and compost/mulch storage?
- Existing nursery bed and garden area, greenhouse.

10. Soil Fertility & Management
- Just how bad are the soils, and what will we have to do to improve them?
- Soil types: texture, structure, consistency, drainage.
- Topsoil fertility.
- Contamination: lead!
- Recent construction, disturbance, and fill history.
- Damaged soils: especially compaction.

11. Aesthetics
- Views: from street down the alley, to hills from backyard, from house to garden.
- Public/private continuum.
- Blighted areas needing beautification.

Determine Analysis and Assessment Issues and Questions

Determining your site analysis questions is similar to looking for site selection criteria, as described earlier, but here we include more issues in more depth because the purposes are different. To guide our design work effectively we need to know a broader range of things in a more nuanced way than we need for site selection. We must seek our guiding questions not only from our goals, but also from the land itself.

Questions from Your Goals

Extract site A&A questions, issues, and topics from your goals by reading each goal and asking, "What do I need to know about the site so I can design this or achieve this goal?" Your desired-species niche analysis should also provide fodder for defining your site analysis questions. Table 3.18 offers an ample listing of site analysis and assessment topics for forest gardening to help you get started with your own list. The list of goal-derived site A&A topics for Eric and Jonathan's case study in table 3.19 came from the sample project goals in table 3.2 as well as table 3.18.

Don't worry if your list isn't complete. As you design you will discover where to investigate your site further. Get down as much as possible based on your goals, and then move on to consider what the land itself wants you to know and act upon.

TABLE 3.20. Site analysis and assessment topics derived from the land and our assumed sense of the land's "desire" for health, diversity, beauty, and so on.

Landform
steep slopes to avoid using

Water
erosion: existing and potential areas

sensitive waterways, wetlands, and seasonal wet areas: setbacks/protection areas

groundwater pollution sources (including pesticides and fertilizers)

excess pavement or other impervious surfaces preventing groundwater recharge

areas damaged or stressed by road runoff

Access and Circulation
too many roads/paths in the wrong places

rutted, eroding routes

areas where paths/roads concentrate runoff, risk erosion, or prevent infiltration

Vegetation and Wildlife
rare, endangered, and threatened species

opportunistic species

habitats or habitat elements to protect/create

unique or ancient trees

stressed, weak, diseased, or damaged trees

areas of especially low diversity (to diversify) or high diversity (to protect)

Buildings and Infrastructure
lead paint (especially exteriors)

old underground oil or gas tanks and the like

leaking septic tanks or sewer lines

stored toxins: old pesticides, other hazardous materials

Zones of Use
wild areas

Soil
damaged soils: e.g., bare, compacted, infertile, contaminated

soil toxins: e.g., lead, mercury, cadmium, asbestos, automotive oil, gasoline

Aesthetics/Experience of Place
beautiful, unique, or fragile natural features

beautiful, unique, or fragile habitats

blighted areas needing beautification

ugly features needing renovation or removal

Questions from the Site

What must you do in your design to support and heal the land? Ask this question and note the answers that come to mind, heart, and gut. Ponder the discussion below and add to your list of A&A questions. Review the site-derived topics and questions, too (see table 3.20). Follow through on the answers and you will manifest ecological values.

The principle of site repair (pattern #5, chapter 2) asks us to leave beautiful places alone and put our effort into improving damaged or unhealthy places instead. Though mainly a site selection issue, there are site design aspects to this principle. How can you support native plants and animals in your garden? Can your design reduce water pollution and erosion? Can you reduce energy use by shading or allowing solar access for buildings? Can you reweave remnants of the local ecological fabric?

When you integrate these site-derived topics into your goals-derived list, you will have a comprehensive agenda to guide your observations and interpretations. Now you can begin gathering information.

Gather Information Resources

Most of your site A&A information will come from direct observation. However, information from other sources can greatly aid your quest (see table 3.21).

The Natural Resources Conservation Service (NRCS) has created soil surveys of most counties in the United States (look in your phone book under "United States government Department of Agriculture"; other countries have similar services). These surveys contain a wealth of information about your region's climate, landform, geology, and soils. Using aerial photos as a base map, they locate each soil type in the county, discuss its parent materials, fertility, typical soil profiles, and so on, and rate its suitability for a variety of land uses. We strongly recommend these excellent resources, but we offer one caution.

Never rely *only* on the soil survey for your soils information. Dig and observe your own holes!

TABLE 3.21. Key off-site resources for site analysis and assessment. Book titles are italicized. For details on the resources mentioned here, see appendix 7.

To learn more about your region's climate:

- Plant hardiness zone maps. See appendix 6 for maps of North America and Europe.
- Also contact your state or provincial agricultural college or university.
- Contact your local weather-monitoring stations; local airports can often provide accurate local wind-direction information.
- Appendix 7 includes various publications on climate in the United States.

To learn more about your site's soils, landform, and more:

- The Natural Resources Conservation Service (NRCS) provides soils maps for the United States county by county. Visit http://soils.usda.gov/survey, or look under "United States government, Department of Agriculture" in the phone book.
- The National Soil Database (NSDB) is a database of Canadian soil, landscape, and climatic data. Visit http://sis.agr.gc.ca/cansis/nsdb.
- *Start with the Soil.* An excellent introductory guide to soils.

To learn more about legal issues you may face:

- Speak to your town or city about zoning regulations if you will erect any permanent structures as part of your design; your local conservation commission will have information concerning wetlands and waterways.
- Your state's cooperative extension service or county NRCS office should be able to direct you to relevant information relating to state or federal regulation of land use near waterways or septic systems.

To learn about the potential natural vegetation of your site:

- *Deciduous Forests of Eastern North America.* A survey of the vegetation of different regions of the eastern forest region.
- *Ecology of Eastern Forests.* A basic field guide to eastern forest types.
- *Landscape Restoration Handbook.* Lists native "climax" species for all regions of the continental United States.
- North American Native Plant Society. Can connect you with regional organizations. Visit www.nanps.org.

To learn to identify the species present on your site or in your neighborhood:

- *Newcomb's Wildflower Guide.* Wildflower and flowering-shrub identification guide for the eastern region.
- *Field Guide to Trees and Shrubs.* A guide to eastern woody plants.
- *Weeds of the Northeast.* Field guide to annual and perennial weeds.
- *Edible Wild Plants of Eastern North America.* Features tables describing useful plant species for a range of habitats and successional stages.
- *Garden Insects of North America.* Identification guide to the herbivores, predators, and pollinators in your garden.
- *Insect, Disease, and Weed ID Guide.* Identification of unwelcome organisms.
- *Mushrooms of Northeastern North America.* An excellent field guide to eastern mushrooms, including edibility.

Most soil survey maps show only soil types covering more than 2 to 3 acres (3 to 5 ha). Any soil different from the predominant type that covers less than 2 to 3 acres will not show on the map. Also, with the usual 80 percent accuracy, 20 percent of the time a given spot on the ground will be a different "included" soil type. So the map may say your 2-acre lot is one soil type, but it could be something different. Do not fear, though! When a survey discusses the soil types, it usually says which related soils are included, and under what conditions (i.e., in flatter, steeper, or wetter areas). So even if your soils vary from the map, its data goes a long way to helping you make good observations in the field, and especially to interpreting what you find.

You can usually get soil surveys free at your county NRCS office or borrow them at your local library. Some NRCS offices charge for them, but that's a crime, since we already paid for them with our tax dollars! If you live in an urban area, the survey may not show much useful information since urban areas tend to contain highly varied and disturbed soils. It is worth checking anyway, just to make sure. If nothing else, you can have an agent from the NRCS office come to your property to evaluate your soils and teach you about them. This, too, should be free of charge.

US Geological Survey topographic maps provide a good overview of where your site fits into the local landform and watershed, and if you can link to nearby natural areas for your forest garden's ecological balance. If you can't get a USGS topo map, then road maps may be useful, but these do not usually show landform very well.

If you need climate information, look first in your county soil survey. You can also get such information from local airports, colleges, universities, or radio or TV stations. See appendix 6 for a copy of the USDA's map of plant hardiness zones of the United States and Europe. Many climate resources are available on the Internet, as well, but these are often very broadscale and may not be as useful as more local resources.

Good plant, bird, and insect identification guides also come in handy. Check appendix 7 for details.

Observe and Interpret Your Site

Finally, we arrive at the core of site analysis and assessment! If your design pathway is linear, you should by now have completed a goals statement, a site plan, and a list of site analysis and assessment questions based on your goals and your sense of the site's needs, and you should have gathered all the off-site information resources you need. To proceed you should have available several copies of your site plan or several sheets of tracing paper to place over a copy of your site plan, a notepad and pen or pencil, a measuring tape, a compass, an eager mind, and an open heart and senses. A camera can also be quite useful. Before we proceed, let us make a few quick comments.

Guidelines for Site Analysis and Assessment

Let us reemphasize our recommendation to distinguish carefully between what you observe and how you interpret your observations. Use different kinds of bullets in front of each when you write notes in the field, as shown earlier in figure 3.11. Sometimes you have to write down your thoughts and then make the separation. It seems like extra work, but if we tangle our observations of reality with our interpretations, we can unknowingly paint ourselves into a conceptual corner.

Our interpretations often take the form of solutions to design problems, but we encourage you to state these as "solution-directions" instead. Solution-

directions are leadings or trends, not answers, and are more functional than physical. "Put a fence here" is a solution. "Block the public view into the private space" is a solution-direction. Jumping to solutions limits the creativity and multiple functionality of your design. A fence may block the public view, but a hazelnut hedge would do that and more. "Blocking the view" leaves more room for multiple-function solutions. Also, look for more than one solution-direction for each situation.

On the other hand, as we mentioned earlier, design ideas can arise at any time during the design process, even when you are following a linear course. Allow this natural process. At the same time, discipline yourself not to get caught up in design ideas yet. Remain focused on analysis and assessment. When you have finished your analyses and assessments you can look at all of the solution-directions as a whole, in context, see in what directions they lead, weigh them against each other, and choose a direction for the design. Then you can elegantly resolve many issues at once rather than using a piecemeal approach that may not hang together. It can be hard to hold a space of "not knowing" for a long period, but that is precisely what we are asking you to do. The wait is worth it. Therefore, when design ideas arise, note or sketch them and go back to the task at hand—observing and interpreting your site with an open mind.

We urge you to read the whole discussion of basic site A&A below before beginning. Plan your work. Review your guiding questions and prioritize. Set yourself some time limits if you want to manage your involvement at this stage. Giving yourself a limit of fifteen or thirty minutes for each of the scale of permanence topics is a fine way to get a quick but comprehensive view of what you are dealing with. More time is great, too, and lets you really soak up your site in a way many people have never tried before.

We discuss below two basic kinds of analysis and assessment exercises: undirected observation and thematic observation. We recommend you do both. Ready? This is one of the best parts!

FIGURE 3.14. Looking southeast from the far end of Eric Toensmeier's and Jonathan Bates's backyard in Holyoke, Massachusetts. This site, our design-process case study, has a new duplex that was built after the previous home burned down. Clearly, this site needs healing attention. The barn and arborvitae hedge to the south (right) are owned by the neighbor. *Photo by Eric Toensmeier.*

FIGURE 3.15. Looking northwest from the upstairs bedroom at Eric and Jonathan's backyard, we can see the area disturbed by construction in the near ground, some of which is underlain by the old house's foundation. The tree behind the chair on the right is one of the neighbor's two huge Norway maples that cast shade over the northern part of the yard. *Photo by Eric Toensmeier.*

Undirected Observation

Undirected observation is just what it sounds like: observing in a random, whatever-catches-your-attention way. This observation is not unbiased, but unconsciously biased, primed by the goals-articulation process. It can give you a quick "gestalt" of the site. When doing professional design, it is good to observe undirectedly first thing, before you know much about a client's site or goals. You can have such valuable first impressions only once! For example, what are your first impressions of our design-process case study site (figures 3.14 and 3.15)?

Set a time limit to these sessions, or don't. Start anywhere, even inside the house. Watch where your eyes rove and why, and where your eyes do *not* go and why. Where do your feet carry you, and what do *they* say? What piques your interest? What do you avoid? What site features, problems, opportunities, plants, animals, and patterns do you see, smell, hear, taste, or touch? What thoughts and feelings arise in response? As always, listen to your heart and gut, as well as your mind. Release your previous work on the project. Let your unconscious lead for a while to see what it brings you. Become a clear channel, and record what comes through. Take copious notes. Write down observations and interpretations. Make sketches.

Do undirected observation more than once. Integrate it into your daily life. Important information can come during these random moments, so write down or draw what comes even when walking the dog or leaving the house in a rush. Mindful chaos can be a great teacher!

Thematic Observations

Remember Edison's saying "Genius is 1 percent inspiration and 99 percent perspiration"? Perspire a bit with focused observations that will form a firm base for the project's design phase.

Thematic observation is also just what it sounds like: observation with a theme. If your theme is water in the landscape, focus your attention on that and only that. You can use just your senses to observe, or you can use specific tools such as shovels, rulers, or soil tests. We're entering territory where "analysis paralysis" can occur, so prioritize your list of A&A questions and set time parameters for yourself. How long it will take you depends on the area covered, its vegetation density, how fast you can observe, write, and sketch, how deeply you want to explore, and how much fun you are having, among other things.

Focus at least one session on each scale of permanence category, examined one at a time. Cover the whole area you have mapped, observing only those aspects related to the theme of your session. Take your list of questions, a site plan, a notebook, and any tools you may need. Devote at least one copy of your site plan or one or more pieces of tracing paper to each theme. Make bubble diagrams on the plan. Note your observations and what they mean relative to your goals on the plan or in your notebook. You can do an undirected thematic observation of the site for each topic area, then go around more methodically with your list of questions. You can also reverse that, using the undirected thematic observation to summarize your work on the theme.

The method suggested here results in one or more site sketches for each theme, each with bubbles and stars and notes and arrows all over them. It will help greatly if, before you close each thematic session, you pick out the three to five most important observations and interpretations from within the masses. Emphasize these graphically on the sketch and in writing before you move on to the next task.

As you work with each theme, remain focused on that theme. If something from another theme comes to mind, write it down and let it go. The work of integrating the themes comes later. Go for depth in each part of the analysis first, and generate the breadth later when you summarize. The following subsections discuss a few fine points of each A&A theme. Tables 3.17, 3.18, and 3.20 offer a road map.

Climate

The USDA plant hardiness zone map in appendix 6 contains critical climate information, offering basic guidance for plant-species selection. You'll also need to know winter and summer prevailing wind directions to think about their influence on your site's microclimate or design windbreaks. Data on average annual precipitation and its seasonal distribution and variation helps you estimate the length of drought conditions and design irrigation and roof-runoff collection systems. County soil surveys can usually give you this data.

Temperate-zone fruit trees each require a certain number of hours below 45°F during dormancy to grow and produce fruit abundantly. USDA plant hardiness zones 7 through 9 may not be cool enough to satisfy this need for some trees. Contact your local cooperative extension service for information.

Human actions affect global climate. Consider global climate-change scenarios for your region, and what you might do to adapt.

Landform

Determine your topographic position and elevation using a USGS topo map or your neighborhood knowledge. Topographic position and elevation affect plant choices and garden siting. Hilltops tend to be windy and cold, and valley bottoms frosty. Midslopes tend toward warmth and long growing seasons. Consider how the landform affects wind patterns. It may block, focus, or redirect prevailing winds.

The NRCS soil survey should discuss the impact of the bedrock and its overlying material on fertility, wetness, rooting depth, and so on. What kind of site preparation might this imply? Should you install raised beds, underdrainage, and wet-tolerant plants, or should you use drought-tolerant plants or irrigate? You may need deep soil samples to gauge the parent materials' fertility. Consider how you'll manage fertility based on this information.

Sketch the approximate locations of high and low points and steep slopes (see figure 3.16). How does steepness affect access patterns and land use? Poorly draining flat areas can be a problem, as can steep areas. Various site features have specific slope requirements (table 3.22), so you may want to estimate slopes by measuring the vertical rise and the horizontal run (rise/run x 100 = slope percentage; see figure 3.17). Slopes too steep to mow (25 percent slope or more) might be good forest garden sites.

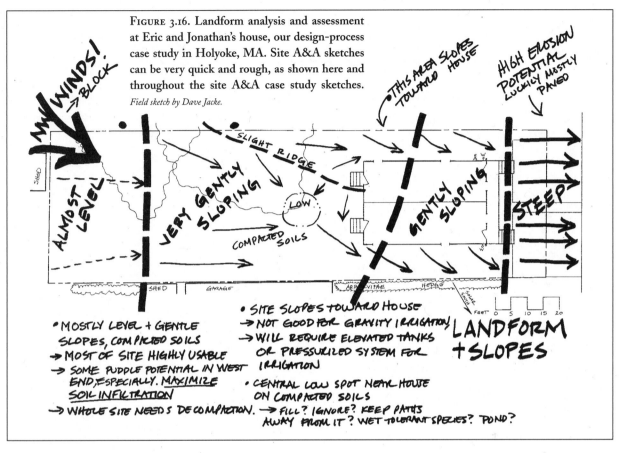

FIGURE 3.16. Landform analysis and assessment at Eric and Jonathan's house, our design-process case study in Holyoke, MA. Site A&A sketches can be very quick and rough, as shown here and throughout the site A&A case study sketches.

Field sketch by Dave Jacke.

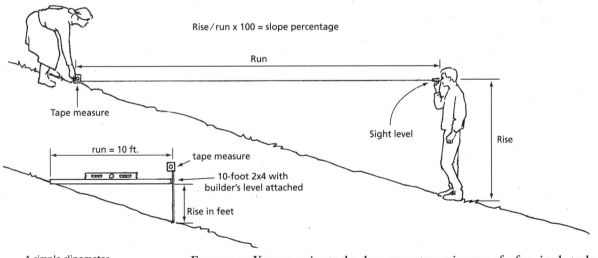

FIGURE 3.17. You can estimate the slope percentage using one of a few simple tools. A builder's level taped or wired to a straight board of known length along with a tape measure allows you to calculate slope percentage directly. Sight levels are small telescopes with a bubble in them that allow you to look in a level line. Used with a tape measure, they also allow you to estimate slope percentage directly. Making a simple clinometer with a protractor and nut hanging on a string allows you to estimate the degrees of slope, which you can then convert to slope percentage on a calculator or using a conversion table.

TABLE 3.22. Slope criteria for various site uses and functions, with angles of repose for earth materials. All outdoor areas, particularly paved surfaces, should have some slope unless you desire standing water and poor drainage. Minimum slopes should be increased in poorly drained soils. Slope percentage = rise/run x 100, e.g., 10 feet of rise in 100 feet of run = 10%. °s = approximate slope in degrees. Angles of repose are maximum slopes at which earthen materials will remain stable; mounds and banks should not exceed these slopes for safety reasons.

Use of Surface	Extreme Min. Grade %	Desirable Grade Range %	°s	Extreme Max. Grade %	°s
Auto circulation					
Driveways (longitudinal slope)	0.25%	1–10%	0.6–6	20%	11
Unpaved roads (longitudinal slope)	0.5%	1–8%	0.6–5	20%	11
Parking areas (longitudinal slope)	0.25%	2–3%	1–1.7	5%	3
Parking areas (cross slope)	0.5%	1–5%	0.6-3	10%	6
Pedestrian circulation					
Concrete sidewalk (longitudinal slope)	0.5%	1–5%	0.6–3	10%	6
Concrete sidewalk (cross slope)	1%	2%	1.7	4%	2.3
Service areas	0.5%	2–3%	1–1.7	10%	6
Pathways	0.5%	0.5–8%	0.3–5	10%	6
Paved sitting areas	0.75%	1%	0.6	3%	1.7
Lawn areas					
Recreation and play areas	1%	2–3%	1–1.7	5%	3
Lawn and grass areas	1%	5–10%	3–6	25%	14
Berms and mounds	1%	5–10%	3–6	25%	14
Mowed slopes	n/a	<20%	<11	25%	14
Planted slopes and beds	0.5%	2–5%	1–3	10%	6
Angles of repose for fill materials					
Dry sand				67%	34
Loose earth, firm clay				72%	35
Loose gravel, wet sand				77%	37
Boulders and cobbles				80%	39
Firm earth (undisturbed)				100%	45
Compacted clay, loose rock				150%	63

Water

Identify drainage-ways, puddles, dry spots, and watershed boundaries. Where does water come from, where is it held, and where does it go? Do walks, roads, and pathways put runoff in useful or problematic places? Where does the roof drain? Locate faucets, wells, and water lines on the plan. Identify potential water sources and possible water-pollution sources (road runoff, chemical runoff from neighbors, failing septic systems). Does the grade slope properly away from buildings? Should you regrade before planting? Do you need to fill somewhere, put in a swale (a level ditch that holds water) to let runoff seep into the ground, or put in a ditch (a sloping one) to prevent puddling or divert runoff? Note any water problems, opportunities, or solution-directions you see (figure 3.18).

Legal Issues

Legal issues are probably the least fun of anything on the scale of permanence, but they are a reality we must sometimes deal with. They mostly relate to property-line setbacks for built structures, setbacks of woody plants from septic-tank leach fields, and any landscaping regulations of your local government or neighborhood association. Some jurisdictions are beginning to regulate the sale and planting of species they consider invasive, and restrictions on planting

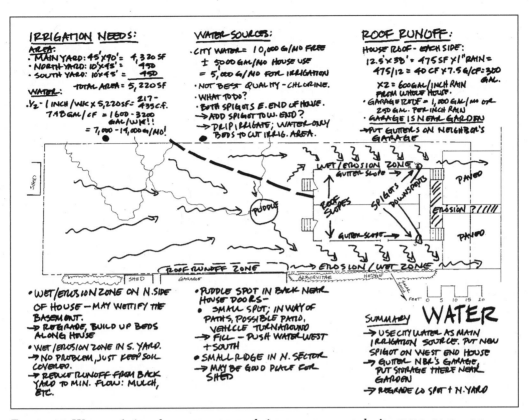

FIGURE 3.18. Water analysis and assessment at our design-process case study site. *Field sketch by Dave Jacke.*

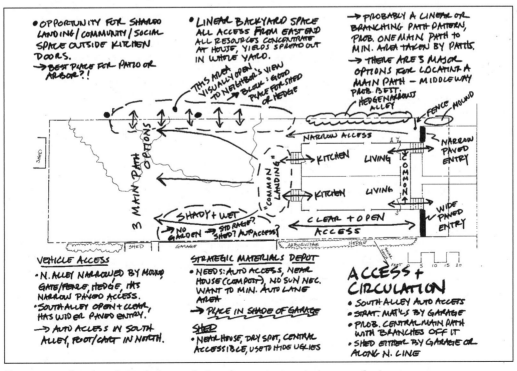

FIGURE 3.19. Access and circulation analysis and assessment at our case-study site. *Field sketch by Dave Jacke.*

species to prevent diseases of forest trees or farm crops are longstanding and occasionally forthcoming. Some regulations intended to protect wetlands and waterways may impinge on your ability to manage vegetation the way you want, or they may provide guidelines for how to alter vegetation or the soil surface in or near such water bodies. Many of you won't have to deal with such things, but it is a good idea to check. See table 3.21 for suggestions about where to find out about these things.

Access and Circulation

Identify existing paths, destinations, and activity nodes on your plan (figure 3.19). Are they well located? Do they cause or solve practical or aesthetic problems? Observe the overall circulation pattern. How does it affect your goals? Might additional access points serve you? Where do materials move on the site now? Do these flows work well, or not? Identify specific problems to solve or good patterns to build upon. Do changes in the circulation patterns come to mind? Can you reduce your work by changing the circulation pattern? One of Dave's former clients used to carry her laundry all the way around her house while going from house to washing machine to clothesline to house. Simply moving her clothesline near the garden cut that labor in half and made doing her laundry part of managing and enjoying her beautiful landscape.

Vegetation and Wildlife

Vegetation and wildlife analysis and assessment is potentially the most complex piece of any site A&A, especially for forest gardeners. We have separated some of the possible parts of vegetation and wildlife A&A from this subsection and placed them as separate exercises in the "Optional Site Analyses" section later in this chapter. For now and at minimum, use this thematic observation session to characterize habitats; observe the architecture of the community; identify existing plants; niche-analyze existing species for their site-indicator value, uses, and functions; note wildlife paths and safe havens;

and interpret all of these. This will inform you greatly about the site and how you will need to adapt to or modify it to suit your needs.

Architecture, Wildlife, and Plant Species. Make bubble diagrams showing the site's different habitats. In the process, add more existing trees, shrubs, and herbs to your base plan if necessary. Characterize the architecture of each habitat and the garden site as a whole: layers, density, patterning, and diversity (see figure 3.20; a section/elevation sketch like those that appear through many parts of this book may help here, in addition to a plan sketch). Does the site contain trees all the same age or of varied ages? What kinds of shade do they create? How "lumpy" is the texture? Does the patch structure of the existing vegetation reveal anything about soil or moisture patterns or the historical disturbance regime? What recent disturbances do you know about, and which will likely recur? How frequently? How intense and severe are these? How might they influence the community's successional pathway? Make sure to observe the habitats around your garden site as well as in it.

If you know the homes and movements of critters on your site, and it's relevant to your design, sketch them onto the diagram. Do deer tend to travel to or through your garden site? Do you have skunks, raccoons, neighborhood dogs, or other critters that live or go certain places? How do these realities relate to your goals? What might you do in your design about these things (see figure 3.21)?

If you want to go deeper, you can also characterize each habitat one at a time by looking at each layer and estimating how full it is. For example, does the canopy tree layer as a whole have less than 25 percent cover, 25 to 50 percent cover, 50 to 75 percent cover, or 75 to 100 percent cover? Which of these categories does the shrub layer fall into as a whole? The herb layer? The ground layer? What is the patterning of the vegetation in each layer; are the plants in masses, clumps, drifts, scatters, or single individuals? (See figure 2.56, page 133; table 3.5 in volume 1 provides written definitions.) What do these patterns and layer densities mean

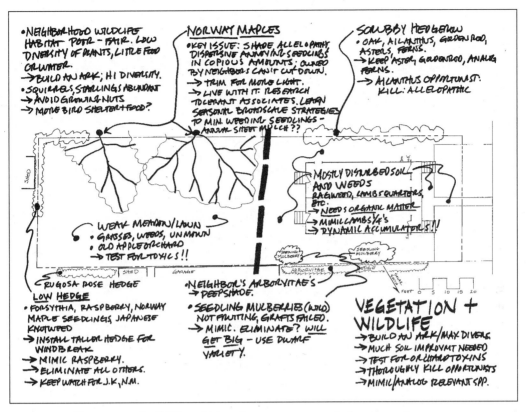

FIGURE 3.20. Vegetation and wildlife analysis and assessment at our design case study. *Field sketch by Dave Jacke.*

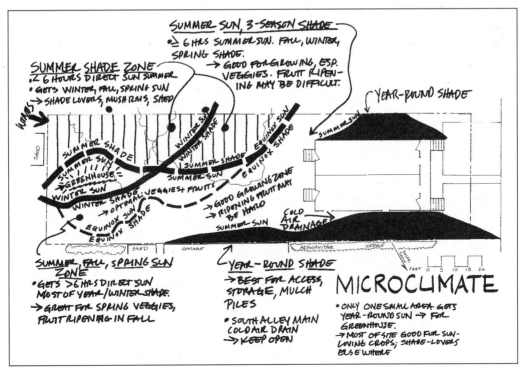

FIGURE 3.21. Microclimate analysis and assessment for our design case study. *Field sketch by Dave Jacke.*

for your garden design? What stage(s) of succession do the different habitats represent? Evaluate the plant legacies of the existing system: what is the initial flora at this time? Who will win out eventually? What plants may seed in from nearby? Is the community in an early stage of succession, with ruderals dominating, or is it a later stage, with competitor-strategist or stress-tolerant plants?

After observing and interpreting the vegetation as a whole, begin identifying species in each habitat; take a notebook, a good field guide or two, and if need be, someone who qualifies as a "plant geek." Go through each habitat and each vegetation layer in an orderly fashion. Make sure you look *around*, not just *in*, your forest garden site. You need to know what neighboring plants could influence your garden's successional pathway by seeding in once you reduce maintenance. Manicured landscapes may have more existing species than you realize. Stop mowing your lawn for a while to see who pokes their head out. A complete vegetation survey takes a full growing season to perform, which isn't feasible for everyone. Just catch what you can and move on. Identify the most abundant species first, and then seek out the less obvious plants.

Positively identify all plants with their scientific names (genus and species); otherwise you may research the wrong plants. Most wildflower guides use flower structure to organize their keys. The unique key in *Newcomb's Wildflower Guide* can often help you identify northeastern or north-central United States plants even when they aren't flowering. If an unidentified plant is abundant, take a sample of the lower and upper leaves, stem, and flowers. Put the sample in a plant press or a plastic bag in the refrigerator to show to a university professor, naturalist, or cooperative extension agent. Take notes or pictures, not a sample, of less abundant species. Make sure to identify ornamental species, as they are often opportunists! Most field guides include few ornamentals, so have a nursery or landscape person look at them if you don't know what they are.

Existing-Species Niche Analysis. We strongly recommend that you do existing-species niche analysis as a vegetation A&A exercise.[9] Understanding site indicators is the most basic use of existing-species niche analysis; some of these species may also have valuable ecological functions or direct human uses, or they may suggest useful relatives that will also grow well on your site. Some may be opportunistic or potentially weedy, suggesting that you should take preventive action before planting your garden. A record of the pre-existing ecosystem may offer clues about events in your garden years down the road. Existing-species niche analysis can help you select your forest garden species, determine site-preparation strategies, and give you baseline data for monitoring your garden's development. You can do this niche analysis only to use the existing plans as site indicators, or you can do a full-blown niche analysis looking for useful and functional species already on-site or for model species for ecological analogs during the design phase.

To do existing-species niche analysis, list the species you identify habitat by habitat and layer by layer on an Existing-Species Niche Analysis form (worksheet 2). Copy the form out of the book, enlarging it to legal size (8½ by 14 inches) to give you more room to write. Fill out at least the worksheet's first page concerning the plant's Latin name, habitat (disturbed soil, brushy edge, maple woods, and so on), growing conditions, health, and site-indicator value. You can use symbols like those in the Plant Species Matrix (appendix 1) to fill out the form. All the columns on the first page are relevant to determining what site indications a plant offers; just be careful how you use site indicators. For example, a plant that indicates high pH but that doesn't look healthy is not a high-pH indicator—especially if it is surrounded by acid-tolerant species. Even if the species you have on-site do not appear in tables 3.23 or 3.24 as site indicators, evaluating the plants' health and what kind of plants they are can give you gut-sense data

TABLE 3.23. Indicator plants. These species, when found growing wild in abundance on a site, frequently indicate certain conditions. Some, but not all, are restricted to the conditions indicated. For a more extensive list, see Kourik, 1986.

Latin Name	Common Name	Dry	Wet	Tilled	Abandoned	Low Nitrogen	High Nitrogen	Low Potassium	High Potassium	Low Phosphorus	High Phosphorus	Sand	Clay	Hardpan/Crusty	Acid	Alkaline	Low Fertility	High Fertility	Salty
Achillea millefolium	yarrow							●											
Alnus spp.	eastern native alders		●																
Amaranthus spp.	pigweed			●															
Amorpha canescens	leadplant	●														●			
Aristida dichotoma	poverty three-awn grass	●															●		
Artemisia vulgaris	mugwort				●														
Asplenium spp.	spleenworts (not ebony)															●			
Bellis perennis	English daisy												●		●				
Brassica spp.	mustards													●	●				
Capsella bursa-pastoris	shepherd's purse											●							●
Centaurea spp.	knapweeds								●						●				
Chenopodium album	lamb's-quarters			●														●	
Cichorium intybus	chicory			●									●					●	
Cirsium arvense	Canada thistle												●						
Comptonia peregrina	sweetfern	●										●			●				
Convolvulus arvensis	field bindweed											●		●					
Cyperus spp.	sedges		●																
Daucus carota	Queen Anne's lace				●							●				●	●		
Diospyros virginiana	American persimmon																●		
Iris versicolor	blue flag iris		●																
Kalmia latifolia	mountain laurel														●				
Opuntia compressa	eastern prickly pear	●																	
Plantago spp.	plantain		●	●									●		●				
Pteridium aquifolium	bracken fern							●		●					●				
Ranunculus acris	buttercup		●	●									●						
Rhus spp.	sumac				●														
Rumex acetosella	sheep sorrel	●										●			●				
Rumex spp.	docks		●												●				
Salicornia spp.	glasswort		●																●
Salix spp.	willows		●																
Scirpus spp.	bulrush		●																
Solanum carolinense	horse nettle			●		●						●							
Stellaria media	chickweed			●														●	
Symplocarpos foetidus	skunk cabbage		●																
Taraxacum vulgare	dandelion			●									●		●				
Trifolium arvense	rabbit's-foot clover	●				●					●				●				
Trifolium pratense	red clover					●			●										
Trifolium repens	white clover	●			●	●													
Tussilago farfara	coltsfoot	●											●		●				
Vaccinium angustifolium	lowbush blueberry	●													●				
Vaccinium macrocarpon	cranberry		●												●				
Verbascum thapsus	mullein				●										●		●		

TABLE 3.24. Native plants used as pH indicators in southern New England. The presence of one or more of these species in quantity indicates soils with the pH range shown. *Adapted from Jorgensen, 1978.*

pH 6 to 8	
Adiantum pedatum	maidenhair fern
Aquilegia canadensis	columbine
Asplenium spp.**	spleenworts
*Camptosorus rhizophyllus***	walking fern
Dicentra cucullaria	Dutchman's breeches
Geranium maculatum	herb Robert
Hepatica acutiloba	sharp-lobed hepatica
*Pellaea atropurpurea***	purple cliffbrake
Polystichum acrostichoides†	Christmas fern
Sanguinaria canadensis	bloodroot

pH 5 to 6	
Actaea spp.	baneberries
Aster spp.	wild asters
Caltha palustris	marsh marigold
Erythronium americanum	dogtooth violet
Geranium maculatum	wild geranium
Hamamelis virginiana	witch hazel
Hepatica americana	blunt-lobed hepatica
Lindera benzoin	spicebush
Osmunda claytoniana	interrupted fern
Polygala paucifolia	fringed polygala
Trillium erectum	red trillium

pH 4 to 4.5	
Cypripedium acaule	pink lady's slipper
*Epigaea repens**	trailing arbutus
*Gaultheria procumbens**	wintergreen
*Kalmia latifolia**	mountain laurel
Lilium philadelphicum	wood lily
Lygodium palmatus	climbing fern
Maianthemum canadense	Canada mayflower
Medeola virginiana	Indian cucumber root
Mitchella repens	partridgeberry
Rhododendron spp.*	azaleas
Vaccinium spp.*	blueberries

*No native members of the family Ericaceae (heaths), such as these, can tolerate lime. They can grow on limestone or marble only when there is a thick layer of acidic humus.

.**These small ferns nearly always grow only on limestone or marble rocks. Though commonly found near limestone and marble, ebony spleenwort can tolerate somewhat more acidic soil.

†Though it has a reasonably wide pH tolerance, Christmas fern indicates slightly acid soil when growing in large quantities.

about what is happening on the land, if not specific theories to investigate in other ways. At the very least, refer to the discussion of ruderal, competitor, and stress-tolerator plant strategies in volume 1, chapters 4 and 6, to help you assess the species' basic niche strategies.

What do your existing plant species say about your site's soils, moisture, fertility, ecology, disturbance history, and successional stage (see tables 3.23 and 3.24), both individually and as a group? Are there indications of their light, soil, moisture, or disturbance regime preferences or successional strategies? Do they seem like a potential weed problem? Do they grow singly or in masses, clumps, drifts, or scatters? How do they distribute themselves (windborne seed, runners)? Do you know of any uses? Note your observations on worksheet 2; you may need to make your assessments on separate sheets of paper. Refer to the appendices to see whether the species' uses, functions, and tolerances are listed. Refer to other books, catalogs, and Internet resources to see what you can learn (see appendix 7). Which are edible or medicinal? What potential problems do these plants have? Do some carry pests or diseases that might harm your crops? Don't rely on written information alone—your observations are important, too. Some species may have ecological functions or human uses no one has written up yet. What roles might these plants play in your edible ecosystem? Dig up a few individuals to examine the root systems, once you're sure the species is not endangered.

You'll need to decide which existing species to keep or replant (and why) and which to replace. Can you identify useful relatives of any of these plants that might also grow well? Complete your existing-species niche analysis by noting those you want to keep or use as models for ecological analogs, noting the functions you want the existing plants or their relatives to perform; page 2 of the worksheet provides space for these purposes. Also summarize the weed, nuisance, pest, and disease potential of the existing plants and any thoughts you have about

Worksheet 2: Existing-Species Niche Analysis for _____

Date _____

Page _____ Side 1

Genus	Species	Common	Family	Conditions Growing In			Native to	Habitat(s) Found In	Health	Site Indications
				Light	Water	Soil				

Enlarge at 137% to make a legal-size (8½ by 14 inches) version for more room to write. You may also find this form on the Web at www.edibleforestgardens.com.

Worksheet 2: Existing-Species Niche Analysis for _____ Date _____ Page ____ Side 2

Species	Edible? (parts)	Medicinal? (parts)	N-fix or Dyn Acc?	Wildlife?	Invert. shelter?	Nectary? flwr time	Ground cover?	Nuisance?	Poison?	Notes/Useful Relatives/ Management Strategies & Issues	Keep? Eco An?

Enlarge at 137% to make a legal-size (8½ by 14 inches) version for more room to write. You may also find this form on the Web at www.edibleforestgardens.com.

how to respond. This information may spur you to research other aspects of your site you hadn't been motivated to yet, such as compaction or nutrient deficiencies. Take particular note of any plants that are growing particularly well, for they or their relatives may be good candidates for your garden, or they may be your crop's competitors!

If you want to go deeper into vegetation and wildlife analysis and assessment, see the exercises in the "Optional Site Analyses" section later in this chapter.

Microclimate

Bubble-diagram the site's different microclimates on your site plan (see figure 3.21, page 205). Note shadiness, windy and calm zones, first and last snowmelt areas, frequent frost spots, and so on. If you don't know your site well you can still guess

based on topography, slope aspect, overall landscape configuration, and so on. For example, frost usually occurs on still, cold nights with clear skies, when cold air flows downhill like molasses. Cold air "ponds" made by "dams" across the slope such as buildings, fences, or hedges tend to get frost. Radiational cooling contributes, too, so cold-air ponds with clear sky above them make optimal frost sites. Slope aspect strongly determines microclimate and habitat diversity, especially in the understory (see figure 3.22). Soil moisture levels also influence microclimates, so consult your water A&A, and note particularly dry or wet spots, too. The crown-density estimates for the trees listed in table 3.25 can help you estimate how shady your site is if you have any of the trees listed there.

A "sector analysis" showing prevailing wind directions, the sun's location at key times, prime or

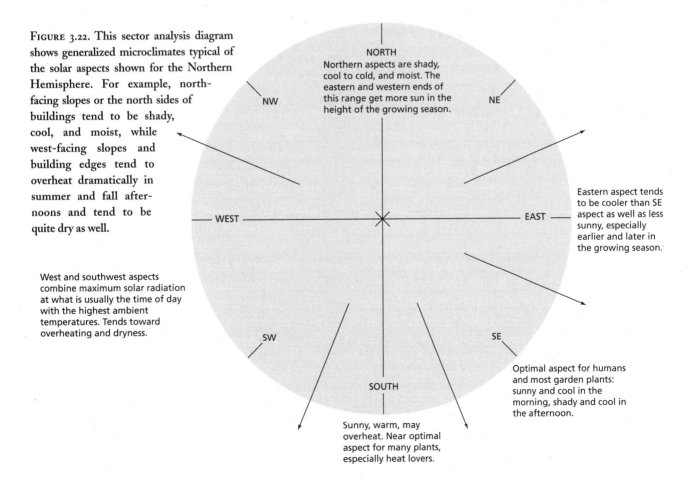

FIGURE 3.22. This sector analysis diagram shows generalized microclimates typical of the solar aspects shown for the Northern Hemisphere. For example, north-facing slopes or the north sides of buildings tend to be shady, cool, and moist, while west-facing slopes and building edges tend to overheat dramatically in summer and fall afternoons and tend to be quite dry as well.

West and southwest aspects combine maximum solar radiation at what is usually the time of day with the highest ambient temperatures. Tends toward overheating and dryness.

NORTH
Northern aspects are shady, cool to cold, and moist. The eastern and western ends of this range get more sun in the height of the growing season.

Eastern aspect tends to be cooler than SE aspect as well as less sunny, especially earlier and later in the growing season.

Optimal aspect for humans and most garden plants: sunny and cool in the morning, shady and cool in the afternoon.

Sunny, warm, may overheat. Near optimal aspect for many plants, especially heat lovers.

NW NE WEST EAST SW SE SOUTH

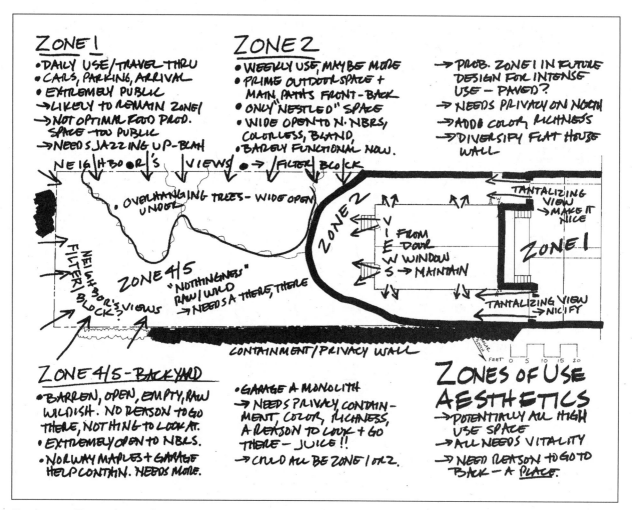

FIGURE 3.23. Zones of use and aesthetics analysis and assessment for our design case study. *Field sketch by Dave Jacke.*

ugly views in and out of the site, and so on helps determine microclimate patterns, among other things (see figures 3.22 and 2.5).

Microclimate interpretations deal mainly with plant-species selection and location, but they may also influence your choice of sites for windbreaks, shade trees, sheds, benches, social spaces, and so on. What aspects of the existing microclimates do or do not work for you? How does what exists compare to your goals? Do you want more or less sun, wind, or moisture somewhere? More microclimate diversity? Compare your microclimate analysis to your desired species.

Buildings and Infrastructure

Your site plan should already show the existing buildings in basic form. Make sure your plan shows all the relevant infrastructure: key doors, steps, and windows; electric lines, poles, and meters; oil fill spouts and gas tanks; underground pipes, culverts, street sewers, and septic-tank pump-out holes; and the like. Can the septic pumper, meter reader, or gas and oil delivery people do their job without damaging plants? Can you avoid digging up fruit trees to replace a water or septic line someday? Dave has more than once moved or pruned soon-to-be-large trees planted right under power lines. If you haven't plotted the location of your on-site

TABLE 3.25. Crown densities of selected native tree species when in leaf. Foliage and branching density are controlled primarily by genetic factors and are therefore somewhat predictable; however, pruning, poor health, or undesirable site conditions can reduce foliage and branching density. "Open Crown" species provide more than 50 percent openings in their canopies, with sparse branching, light foliage, and light shade. Species with "Moderate Crown Density" provide 33 to 50 percent openings in their silhouette. "Dense Crown" species provide 0 to 33 percent open space in their silhouette and cast deep shade. This table includes North American natives only, both useful species and common ornamentals. *Adapted and reprinted with permission of John Wiley & Sons, Inc., from* Native Trees, Shrubs, and Vines for Urban and Rural America, © *1988, Gary L. Hightshoe.*

Open Crown		Moderate Crown Density		Dense Crown	
Acer saccharinum	silver maple	*Acer rubrum*	red maple	*Abies* spp.	firs
Betula nigra	river birch	*Aesculus* spp.	buckeyes	*Acer saccharum*	sugar maple
Betula populifolia	gray birch	*Betula lenta*	black birch	*Amelanchier* spp.	serviceberries
Carya illinoinensis	pecan	*Betula lutea*	yellow birch	*Castanea dentata*	American chestnut
Carya ovata	shagbark hickory	*Betula papyrifera*	paper birch	*Cornus florida*	flowering dogwood
Carya tomentosa	mockernut hickory	*Carya cordiformis*	bitternut hickory	*Crataegus* spp.	hawthorns
Catalpa speciosa	northern catalpa	*Celtis occidentalis*	hackberry	*Fagus grandifolia*	American beech
Cornus alternifolia	pagoda dogwood	*Cercis canadensis*	redbud	*Halesia tetraptera*	Carolina silverbell
Diospyros virginiana	American persimmon	*Fraxinus* spp.	ashes	*Juniperus virginiana*	eastern red cedar
Gleditsia triacanthos	honey locust	*Liriodendron tulipifera*	tulip tree	*Malus ioensis*	prairie crabapple
Juglans cinerea	butternut	*Pinus resinosa*	red pine	*Morus rubra*	red mulberry
Juglans nigra	black walnut	*Pinus strobus*	white pine	*Picea* spp.	spruces
Pinus banksiana	jack pine	*Prunus virginiana*	chokecherry	*Quercus rubra*	northern red oak
Pinus flexilis	limber pine	*Quercus alba*	white oak	*Tilia americana*	American basswood
Pinus ponderosa	ponderosa pine	*Quercus bicolor*	swamp white oak	*Tsuga canadensis*	eastern hemlock
Pinus rigida	pitch pine	*Quercus coccinea*	scarlet oak	*Viburnum lentago*	nannyberry
Platanus occidentalis	sycamore	*Quercus ellipsoidalis*	northern pin oak		
Populus spp.	aspens	*Quercus marilandica*	blackjack oak		
Prunus pensylvanica	pin cherry	*Quercus palustris*	pin oak		
Prunus serotina	black cherry	*Quercus prinus*	chestnut oak		
Quercus imbricaria	shingle oak	*Quercus velutina*	black oak		
Quercus macrocarpa	bur oak	*Salix bebbiana*	Bebb willow		
Quercus meuhlenbergii	chinkapin oak	*Salix discolor*	pussy willow		
Quercus stellata	post oak	*Ulmus americana*	American elm		
Rhus spp.	sumacs				
Robinia pseudoacacia	black locust				
Salix amygdaloides	peachleaf willow				
Salix nigra	black willow				
Sassafras albidum	sassafras				
Sorbus decora	showy mountain ash				
Zanthoxylum americanum	prickly ash				

septic system yet, do it now. Keep woody plants 10 feet (3 m) or more away from the leach field unless you want to spend thousands on a replacement system after tree roots plug it! Consider possible future construction and construction access, too. Ponder the visual and practical relationship between the garden and the different rooms inside the house, especially the kitchen and living areas.

Zones of Use

Define your current zones of use based on the activities that occur (play areas, wild areas, dining areas), the destinations you visit (compost pile, wood pile), and how often you visit them (daily year-round, daily in the winter only, weekly, monthly; see figure 3.23). You can use the zone designations of permaculture (zones 1 through 5; see pattern #7, chapter 2), but what you really want to know is what specific functions occur where. Where do you go, and how frequently? Which areas do you visit most or least easily, just by the sheer layout of doors, gates, pathways, and functions? Visual access helps us know and manage our garden. Which areas do you look at most and least

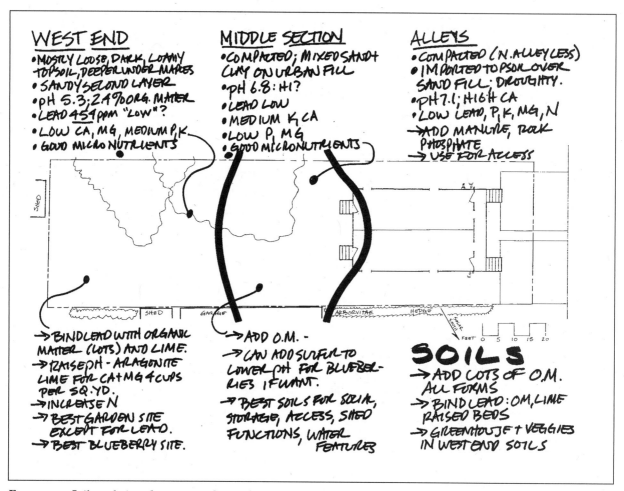

FIGURE 3.24. Soils analysis and assessment for our design case study. *Field sketch by Dave Jacke.*

often? Washing dishes affords a great opportunity to see what the birds, bees, and chipmunks are doing out there! What does the above imply about locating new landscape elements, the forest garden overall, or specific plants? Do any land-use pattern changes come to mind? Map where, how, and how often you irrigate to identify water-use zones. Are there any implications for zones of use?

Soil Fertility and Management

Landform A&A deals with geology and overall topography. Focus here on the top few feet of soil. Your county soil survey contains useful information, but dig your own soil pits and take soil samples to evaluate the soil profile, rooting and resource condi-

tions, and the soil food web. We cannot overemphasize the importance of digging soil pits! At least half of your plants' biomass will live belowground. Investigate the soil environment so you can adapt to it and modify it as necessary.

Before digging, wander the site looking at the soil from above, and map areas of similar soils (see figure 3.24). Does the vegetation change anywhere for no apparent reason? Can you tell where the ground feels different beneath your feet or to the touch? Where was the soil disturbed or trucked in, and where is it the native stuff? Which soils grow the healthiest plants? Which areas have rocks at or near the surface or have little topsoil? Which are the most fertile spots? Which are the most damaged and need the most site repair? Use this quick assessment to choose your hole-digging sites.

As you dig, consider the legacies you see: Is the soil closer to primary- or secondary-succession conditions? How much organic matter is there? Testing will help here, but your own observations are critical. How well aggregated is it? Consider whether soil drainage will slow succession or limit plant choices. Note soil profile characteristics by measuring the depth of the various horizons, and determine which horizon is which (see volume 1, chapter 3, "Soil Horizons"). The texture, structure, consistence, and color of each soil horizon (feature article 2) will help you determine whether the soil has a layer restrictive to the movement of water and the growth of plant roots. Note how many roots and critters you see at each level, whether there's any water entering the hole at a certain depth, and so on. Consider implications for species selection, plant spacing, irrigation needs, and site preparation and planting strategies. Record and keep your observations and interpretations. Note on a map where you dug your holes so you can dig holes in later years to note changes over time.

While you're digging, consider taking topsoil samples so you can estimate nutrient and organic matter levels using conventional soil testing. Test for lead, hydrocarbons, and other contaminants if you own urban or roadside property or old industrial, commercial, farm, or orchard land, or if you have an old house or barn that had or has lead paint. You can then devise fertility-management or toxics-mitigation plans. Testing the subsoil is not a bad idea either, for it can tell you what the underlying fertility "constitution" of your soil is like (see the discussion in volume 1, chapter 5, concerning self-renewing fertility for more information). However, not all soil-testing labs will understand *that* you are testing your subsoil, or why, nor will they necessarily know *how* to test subsoils.[10]

Evaluate the soil food web so you can redress any imbalances, receive the soil organisms' gifts, and manage fungal-bacterial balance for your plants.

Most gardeners know the following simple soil-health indicators:

- Fresh, green organic matter decomposes to half its weight in a month (assuming adequate water and temperatures). Woody material and the second half of fresh green materials take longer.
- Rain or runoff infiltrates rapidly when there is good soil structure. Poor infiltration, puddling (especially long-standing puddles), or surface mineral crusts signify unhealthy soils. The infiltration rate also depends on the soil type and the amount of water already in the soil, so consider these, too. Mineral crusts mean little churning or litter shredding is going on, and they probably also indicate a lack of organic matter (OM). Rotten-egg or other anaerobic smells also indicate poor soil-food-web health due to lack of oxygen. Good crumb structure suggests that aggregation is happening at all three scales (microaggregates, macroaggregates, and crumbs), meaning the bacteria, fungi, and big kids are all doing their jobs.
- You find many critters in the soil as you dig. Diverse and numerous large invertebrates (beetles, etc.) indicate healthy lower levels of the food web.

The dominant plants and the kind of organic matter they create roughly indicate the soil's fungal-bacterial (F:B) balance. Disturbed soils and grass or annual communities with mostly green (high-nitrogen) organic matter associate with bacteria-dominated soils. Herbaceous perennials with moderate-carbon OM enjoy a balanced F:B ratio. If shrubs and trees dominate, with their high-carbon OM, the soil is probably fungal or headed that way. Evergreens and very-late-succession forests tend toward extreme fungal dominance. Select species to match what you have, or plan to alter the F:B ratio to suit your crops.

Soil-food-web testing offers more data to guide action in support of optimal soil-food-web functioning (see appendix 7), though it is expensive.

Feature Article 2:
Reading Your Soil Horizons

Not only is the soil composed of horizons that constitute the soil's profile, but it also has small-scale particles that constitute the basic building blocks of the soil in each horizon. We can characterize those particles as a body using the terms *texture*, *structure*, and *consistence*. These three soil characteristics determine many physical and biological properties in every soil layer. A soil's color is a response to these physical and biological properties.

Knowing the texture, structure, consistence, and color of your soil will aid you greatly in learning how to live with and improve your soil. By digging a hole or two or three, noting these characteristics and how they change with depth, then pondering what you observe, you will learn what is going on in the belowground ecosystem to a large degree.

It is good to dig a hole at least 1 foot (30 cm) in diameter, preferably more, as far down as time and effort allow. Before looking at the profile, scrape away at one wall of the hole with a clean knife or trowel to expose fresh soil unmixed and unsmeared by the digging process. Measure the depth of each horizon from the surface, as well as its thickness, and note these on your clipboard. Then explore the texture, structure, consistence, and color of each horizon as discussed below. Once you have estimated the soil texture, structure, and consistence for each horizon, you can then evaluate whether each horizon constitutes a restrictive layer.

Texture

Soil texture results from the relative proportions of different-size mineral particles in the soil (see figure 3.25). Sand particles range in diameter from 0.05 to 2.0 mm, silt particles run from 0.002 to 0.05 mm, and clay particles fall below 0.002 mm (the period at the end of this sentence is about 0.33 mm, the size of medium sand). Sandy soils tend to be rather porous and droughty; clay soils tend to be heavy,

---

TABLE 3.26. Determine soil texture class by feel by moistening the soil well and rubbing it between your fingers. Test for ribboning in silty and clayey soils by holding a moist ball of soil in your palm and progressively squeezing it out between your thumb and the side of your index finger to "grow" a flat ribbon extending over the edge of your finger. *Source: NHWSPCC, 1984.*

Sandy Textures

1. Sand
   - Very gritty
   - Does not form ball
   - Does not stain fingers

2. Loamy Sand: may be modified with the terms *fine* or *coarse* (e.g., "coarse loamy sand") depending on the dominant size of sand particles
   - Very gritty
   - Forms easily broken ball
   - Stains fingers slightly

Loamy Textures

1. Sandy Loam: may be modified with the terms *very fine* or *fine* (e.g., "fine sandy loam") depending on the dominant size of sand particles
   - Moderately gritty
   - Forms fairly firm ball that is easily broken
   - Definitely stains fingers

2. Loam
   - Neither very gritty nor very smooth
   - Forms firm ball
   - Stains fingers but does not ribbon

3. Silty Loam
   - Smooth or slick "buttery" feel
   - Forms firm ball
   - Stains fingers and has a slight tendency to ribbon with a flaky surface

4. Silty Clay Loam
   - Moderately sticky, very smooth
   - Forms firm ball
   - Stains fingers and will ribbon out with some flaking on ribbon surface

Clayey Textures

1. Silty Clay
   - Sticky feel
   - Forms ball that, when dry, cannot be crushed with fingers
   - Stains fingers
   - Squeezes out at right moisture content into a long ribbon

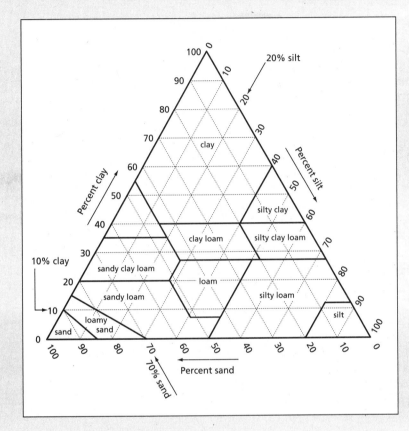

Figure 3.25. Soil texture classification according to the United States Department of Agriculture. Combine the percentages of sand, silt, and clay in your soil to find the soil texture.

divide by the total thickness of soil particles to estimate the soil's texture (see figure 3.25).

If your soil texture is not ideal, in almost all cases it is better, cheaper, and easier to add organic matter than to try adding clay to sandy soils or sand to clayey soils. Not only is organic matter lighter and cheaper (particularly if you grow it rather than buy it), but the earthworms and plants will do your digging for you.

Structure

Soil structure, in this case, refers to the arrangement of the soil particles and how they aggregate. Granular soils are just that, and they probably are the best structure to have. Massive soils are cemented into a large, usually impermeable mass. Blocky structure is similar to massive, except the blocks are smaller masses that can limit root growth and water movement if too compact. Platy structure consists of flat particles of silt and clay that bond together into (you guessed it) plates, though not necessarily round ones. Platy structure can also be root and water limiting unless it is a loose soil with plenty of sand. Simply looking at a soil sample and comparing the particles to those in figure 3.26 is usually all you need to do to figure out the soil structure. A 10x hand lens is useful for examining soil samples.

sticky, and poorly aerated; and silt soils are often fertile but structurally weak. Loam is an even mix of all three particle sizes and is the ideal soil texture: well drained yet moist, fertile yet strong, airy and light yet solid.

Though laboratory tests are the most accurate way of determining soil texture, you can estimate it well by feeling the moistened soil between your fingers and applying simple guidelines (see table 3.26). You can also do a simple "jar test" by putting soil into a straight-sided jar of water, shaking it up, and letting it settle over a period of several days to a week. The sand will settle out first, followed by the silt, and finally the clay over the last days. You can measure the thickness of each band of soil particles and

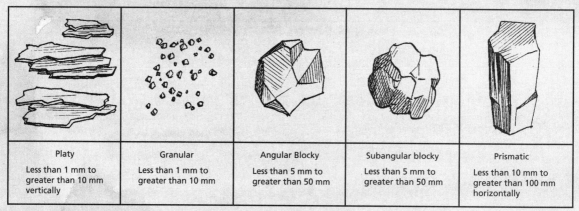

Platy	Granular	Angular Blocky	Subangular blocky	Prismatic
Less than 1 mm to greater than 10 mm vertically	Less than 1 mm to greater than 10 mm	Less than 5 mm to greater than 50 mm	Less than 5 mm to greater than 50 mm	Less than 10 mm to greater than 100 mm horizontally

FIGURE 3.26. Kinds of soil structure. Along with texture and consistence, structure determines the ease with which water, soil organisms, and plant roots can make their livings in the soil. Most of these particles are visible with the naked eye, but a 10x lens helps you see the structure greatly.

Consistence

Yes, soil scientists call it "consistence," which is related to *consistency*. How compact is the soil? Official terms to describe consistence range from *loose* to *friable* ("spongy") to *firm* to *very firm*. This characteristic, combined with texture and structure, affects the ability of water, air, roots, and organisms to move through the soil, and of water and wind to erode the soil. Simply squeezing a clod of undisturbed soil in your hand helps you determine the consistence of the different soil layers (table 3.27). You can use a knife to break a chunk of soil out of the side of your hole in each horizon without breaking up the clod to get an undisturbed sample in your hand. How easy it is to dig your holes will give you some idea of the soil's consistence, as well.

Color

Color is an indicator, not a determinant, of soil processes. Black or brown soils are high in organic matter (though nearer the tropics organic matter is not as dark as in cooler climates). If they are also loose and silty, they may be too high in organic matter, which can lead to waterlogging. Gray soils indicate lack of oxygen, usually because of frequent or constant wetness, while reds, reddish browns, and yellows indicate well-aerated soils, where the iron in the soil is oxidized or turned into rust. Yellow and olive-colored soils are higher in aluminum or manganese than iron. White or generally lighter-colored soils usually indicate a leached condition. Distinct patches or spots of varying color, called *mottles*, show up in parts of the soil profile that alternate between wet, low-oxygen, and well-drained, higher-oxygen conditions. Mottles indicate the average top of the seasonal high-water table and the probable limit of rooting depth.

With all of the above information estimated for each soil horizon, compare your results to table 3.28 to determine whether any of the horizons is restrictive to plant roots or water movement. If you do have one or more restrictive layers, where in the soil profile is it and why is it restrictive? Answering these questions and thinking through the implications will help you understand what your plants will have to deal with belowground, and what you might be able to do about it during site preparation. Think about the effects of your soil profile structure on water movement, irrigation needs, seasonal wetness, rooting depth, nutrient availability, plant spacing, plant stress, and plant species selec-

TABLE 3.27. Determining soil consistence by feel. Consistence is measured by the ease with which a clod can be crushed by the fingers, and it affects ease of root penetration and water movement. The terms commonly used to describe consistence relate to three standard moisture condition: dry, moist, and wet. *Source: NHWSPCC, 1984.*

Dry Soil Condition

1. Hard
   - Moderate resistance to pressure
   - Can be broken with difficulty between thumb and forefinger
2. Soft
   - Breaks into powder or individual grains under very slight pressure

Moist Soil Condition

1. Loose
   - Lack of cohesion by soil particles
   - Does not hold together in a mass
2. Friable
   - Crushes easily under gentle pressure between thumb and forefinger
   - Can be pressed together into a lump
3. Firm
   - Crushes under moderate pressure between thumb and forefinger, but resistance is distinctly noticeable
4. Very Firm
   - Crushes under strong pressure between thumb and forefinger
   - Barely crushable

Wet Soil Condition

1. Plastic
   - Readily deformed by moderate pressure but can be pressed into a lump
   - Will form a "wire" when rolled
2. Sticky
   - When wet, adheres to both thumb and forefinger
   - Tends to stretch somewhat and pull apart rather than pulling free

Any Moisture Condition

1. Cemented
   - Hard—soil particles bound together very strongly (this occurs most commonly in sand or sand and gravel material)
   - Little affected by moistening

TABLE 3.28. Clues to identifying restrictive soil layers using texture, structure, and consistence. Any combination of texture, structure, and consistence within the shaded areas may indicate a restrictive soil layer. *Source: NHWSPCC, 1984.*

General Texture	Structure	Moist Soil Consistence
Sandy	Single grain	Loose
Loamy	Granular	Friable
Clayey *	Platy*	Firm
	Prismatic*	Very firm*
	Blocky*	Cemented*
	Massive	

General Texture	Structure	Moist Soil Consistence
Sandy	Single grain	Loose
Loamy	Granular	Friable
Clayey*	Platy*	Firm
	Prismatic*	Very firm*
	Blocky*	Cemented*
	Massive	

General Texture	Structure	Moist Soil Consistence
Sandy	Single grain	Loose
Loamy	Granular	Friable
Clayey*	Platy*	Firm
	Prismatic*	Very firm*
	Blocky*	Cemented*
	Massive	

*Probably a restrictive layer based on this single property.

tion. See chapter 5 for more information on soil problems and how to deal with them.

When you examine these four characteristics of each layer of the soil profile, you can begin to understand the physical, chemical, and biological conditions in which your plant roots and soil microbes are living. Even if you think you don't understand, you will still get a gut sense of the reality underground that will feed into your design and management processes. Evaluate your soil profile before you start gardening, and keep doing it yearly to watch the changes take place. See the resources in appendix 7 if you want to explore this topic further.

Use testing or your observations to clarify the measures needed to prime the soil food web to its highest functioning by design, site preparation, or management (see chapter 5).

Aesthetics

Ah, the most ephemeral, yet for some people most important thing! We won't give a course in landscape aesthetics here, but we will offer a few aesthetic points to observe and interpret (see also table 3.18).

Define and observe the existing outdoor "rooms." What do you like and dislike about them? What do they need? Are the spaces formal, informal, or a mix? Do they exhibit unity and variety or disharmony? How? Do the boundaries and transitions between public and private spaces work? What character do the spaces have? What features are unique? Which are common? What kinds of themes exist there (color, texture, height, materials, and so on)? Are the forms you find there angular, rectilinear, linear, curvilinear, organic, or something else? What character and feelings do you experience (table 3.29)? How might your forest garden relate to these realities? What of the above do you want to keep, ameliorate, eliminate, or transform?

Note views to and from doors, windows, walkways, entrances, and exits as opportunities for accents and landscape tone setting. The arrangement of landscape elements can create visual integration, movement, or chaos. Do things create odd angles or uncomfortable spaces, or do they direct your eye and create desired qualities? Do the color and texture schemes make sense? What about the visual composition? Identify the aesthetic functions of plants or plant clusters: screening public views, summer flowers, scent, fall color, and so on. What do you want to change or keep?

If your forest garden will be near your home's entrance, consider the aesthetics of the arrival and entry sequence. Walk and/or drive the sequence, coming and going several times while paying attention to the obvious, the subtle, the practical, and the aesthetic. What feelings and qualities does the landscape evoke? Where do your eyes go and not go? What orients you to the site? Would newcomers feel lost, or would they know where they were going? Can you see the door of the house when you arrive? Are key functions missing, like a space to stand or sit and chat with guests as they arrive and leave? Is the transition from public to private space marked by changes in space, texture, color, and light? How might your forest garden relate to all of these?

Other Themes

You may have developed additional thematic categories based on your goals or the site. Assess these as well, creating notes and one or more sketches of your observations and interpretations.

If you have no other themes, or when you finish your other themes, your thematic site analysis and assessment is complete. By now you should have several site A&A sketches, potentially as many as one sketch for each theme or more, depending on how much time you spent and how much you got into the process. Each sketch should have both graphic and written information on it, and the set of sketches should cover all the themes and isues relevant to your project. If you are going to do additional analyses discussed below, move on to them. If not, skip down to the "Integration: Summarize Your Observations and Solution-Directions" section.

OPTIONAL SITE ANALYSES

With your basic site analysis and assessment complete, you now get to choose whether or not to complete one or more of the following optional analyses. Whether to do these or not depends mostly on your time investment, your patience and tolerance, and your desire to design in depth. You can certainly design a forest garden without doing any of the following exercises, though it will involve more guesswork if you do so. These exercises will definitely increase your understanding of your site and the possible species you can grow there, not to

TABLE 3.29. Words for landscape character (adjectives) and your subjective responses (feelings) to it. Use these in site analysis or to define what you want to create. *Modified from the handouts of Walt Cudnohufsky, Conway School of Landscape Design.*

Landscape Adjectives

active	forestlike	noisy	sloping
animated	formal	open	smooth
artificial	green	panoramic	soft
barren	hard/harsh	pastoral	spacious
bleak	hidden	peaceful	sparse
boring	hilly	picturesque	static
bright	historical	piecemeal	steep
broad	informal	placid	stiff
bushy	inhabited	pleasant	stony
chaotic	inspiring	polluted	straight
clean	insular	private	stuffy
colorful	intimate	public	suburban
contrasting	invigorating	quiet	sunny
cool	inviting	relaxing	tranquil
craggy	isolated	repulsive	undulating
crisp	jagged	rich	uniform
damp	light	rippled	unkempt
dark	lumpy	rocky	unspoiled
desolate	magical	rolling	urban
dynamic	majestic	rough	varied
enclosed	meditative	rugged	vast
eroding	monotonous	rural	warm
exciting	monumental	sculptural	well maintained
expansive	muted	secluded	wet
extensive	mysterious	shady/shadowy	wild
flat	natural	sheltered	windswept
flowing	nestled	simple	woodsy

Landscape Feelings

abandoned	confused	enchanted	intimidated
ambiguous	constrained	enclosed	isolated
angry	contented	envious	nostalgic
annoyed	defeated	exhausted	overwhelmed
awed	defensive	exposed	peaceful
bad	delighted	fascinated	precarious
betrayed	diminished	fearful	pressured
bored	distracted	frantic	protected
burdened	disturbed	gratified	refreshed
calm	dominated	happy	relieved
captivated	dubious	humbled	secure
challenged	eager	hurt	tense
charmed	elated	ignored	unsettled
childish	electrified	inspired	vulnerable

mention helping you fend off the challenges of competitor species in the ecosystem.

Earlier, in "Choosing Your Path through Site A&A," we discussed two fundamental approaches to forest-garden design: working from plants to ecosystem and from ecosystem to plants. Assuming you want to go deeper into the optional analyses than zero or the minimum, these approaches will influence your choice of which of the following exercises to do. We suggest you reread that section (page 184) before reviewing the exercises and deciding which ones to do. We will explain the value and purposes of each at the beginning of each exercise below.

Varmints, Pests, and Diseases

Consider the challenges you may face growing your desired crop species before finalizing your species list or engaging in much design. Find out what pests and diseases affect them in your region, and which "varmints," or potentially problematic wildlife, live nearby. How can you reduce these problems by design or management? You may want to change your desired species list after learning what you are up against! For example, growing apples can be demanding. They have the biggest pest and disease complex of almost any crop you can grow in North America. Pears have significantly fewer pests and diseases; persimmons have fewer still. Good species and variety selection radically reduces your pest- and disease-management work!

List the pests and diseases afflicting your desired species in your area, noting what kind of damage they do and how you can manage them (see table 3.30). Pests and diseases vary from crop to crop and region to region, so this book offers limited information on them. Many books discuss the pests and diseases associated with most conventional fruit, berry, and nut crops. A few discuss unconventional crops (see appendix 7). Also contact your state university, cooperative extension service, or state agriculture department to find out what pests and diseases afflict your desired crops in your locale, and how to manage them.

Wild plants can also host crop pests and diseases. Wild plums and cherries host black knot, a fungal disease creating rough, black swellings on the branches of cultivated and wild *Prunus* species (plums, cherries, apricots). Besides selecting resistant varieties and winter-pruning to prevent reinfection the following year, you may also need to remove wild cherries from the area (supposedly within a ¼-mile or 0.4 km radius!) to reduce the disease on your trees. Find out the alternate hosts of the pests and diseases so you can limit your exposure to such problems.

Find out which past pest and disease problems could come back and those that could move in from other regions. One commercial grower in the Pacific Northwest planted acres of hazelnuts but didn't plant varieties resistant to eastern filbert blight because the blight didn't exist there. Just before he got a crop, the blight killed every bush he had nurtured for several years. Think long term and large scale when planting long-lived crops. Many pests and diseases are on the move these days, not only because we humans are on the move, but because of climate change. Look to adjacent climates a bit warmer than yours to see what pests and diseases may come your way.

Your own observations are the best source of information on your friendly neighborhood varmints. You can safely assume that small rodents are eagerly waiting to chew on your fruit trees' trunks in the winter. Porcupines quickly do a lot of damage. Consider potential human varmints, too. Good design can minimize vandalism and theft in neighborhoods where they are a problem. Speak to other area gardeners or orchardists, neighborhood old-timers, the cooperative extension service, and your town or city's animal control officer to find out what "problem" species might be afoot. Local nature centers and naturalists are good sources, too.

Deer are an increasingly large problem in many suburban and rural areas, destroying any tasty vegetation they find. If they are a major problem where you live, think seriously about fencing your whole forest garden. If you are going to fence, do it before

TABLE 3.30. A sample varmint, pest, and disease matrix for our case study example of Eric and Jonathan's forest-garden design process. Other pests and diseases can be added to this list, and some strategies have yet to be added, but this is a beginning to the thinking process. They are putting much emphasis in their design on trouble-free species like pawpaw, persimmon, and hardy kiwi but are willing to take some of the steps listed to ensure yields of more conventional fruits.

Crops	Pest/Disease/Varmint	Possible Strategies
all woody plants	mice chew bark in winter	use tree guards and gravel mulch; remove organic mulch from trees' bases in winter; trap or poison; neighbors' cats
tubers	mice eat them in winter	plant plenty; harvest and replant in spring; mulch with wire screen?
all berries	birds eat fruit	plant plenty (many birds eat bugs too); plant yellow (vs. red) varieties to fool birds into thinking still unripe; use netting when bad; neighbors' cats
all nuts (hazel, pine, chinquapin)	squirrels eat nuts	plant plenty; use netting; trap; pray
rose family and other plants	Japanese beetles	inoculate ground with milky spore disease; trap; pray
pome and stone fruits (apple, pear, peach, plum)	plum curculio: can devastate an apple or plum crop	use kaolin-clay spray; knock bugs off branches in spring; run chickens under trees; grow dwarf varieties to ease management
pear, apple, juneberry	fireblight: devastating, especially to pears	resistant varieties; dwarf varieties for ease of monitoring; sterilize when pruning; monitor and remove cankers early
grape	black rot and other diseases	resistant varieties; proper pruning; good air movement among vines
raspberry	nasty viruses	purchase certified virus-free plants
apple, peach, other trees	borers: bore into stem and kill tree	monitor frequently and kill when present with a wire stuck into bore hole
perennial greens	leaf miners	grow lots; test to find resistant species and varieties
perennial brassicas	late-season aphids	reduce compost and nitrogen feeding?

you plant! Once deer know where good food is, they will go to extreme lengths to get to it. Shorter fences built before planting are often more effective than taller fences built after the deer have tasted the delicacies you have growing.

Research prevention and management strategies for the pests, diseases, and varmints you discover. What species and varieties can you select to resist them? What conditions foster and prevent them? What natural enemies do they have? Generate a list of the relevant beneficial insect, bird, and other species you want to encourage and their habitat requirements. See chapter 1 for a discussion on reducing pest and disease problems by design, and see appendices 5 and 7 for useful information and resources. For the varmints, consider whether you should fence your garden, and how, or if you should get a dog, attract owls and hawks, or buy a rifle, a freezer, and a big stew pot. What pest-management equipment should you get so you aren't caught up short when a crisis appears? Summarize your solution-directions for the pest challenges in one place, perhaps by adding to your goals statement. Add to or subtract from your plant-species list, if need be. You may find several different pest challenges leading you in similar directions design-wise.

Forewarned is forearmed. Learn the habits and habitat of your competitor critters so you can fend them off and keep them in balance before they get out of hand.

Your Ecological Neighborhood

If your forest garden is an isolated island, attracting and maintaining healthy populations of beneficial insects and birds will be difficult. How does your site fit into your ecological neighborhood? What nearby ecosystems can you visit as models or use as seed or soil inoculum sources? What ecosystems connect to your land, and what kind of habitat do they offer in support of diverse animal populations in your garden? Assessing your ecological neighborhood can be a very quick and simple affair if you know what to look for. Just eyeballing the surrounding landscape and taking a few notes if needed is a good minimum. You can also have fun making a simple neighborhood map if you choose. Since mapping is a bit more complex than the quick and dirty eyeball, we'll discuss the mapping process. If you don't want to use a map, that's fine—you can just walk around and get a sense of your neighborhood in less formal fashion—but do read on to get some sense of what to look for.

Maps can help illuminate land-use patterns and locate natural areas and corridors in your neighborhood. A USGS topographic map of your area is probably the best available tool for this, but any map showing watercourses and open versus forested lands will work. Get a photocopy or two of the map to draw upon, perhaps enlarging the relevant portion to make room for details and notes.

Think about and locate local natural areas on the map, not just the big chunks of wildness, but also the little chunks and the threads that connect them. Include any parks, odd corners, patches of woods, thickets, oldfields—or whatever—within about a half mile of your site. Wildish corridors often persist along streams, in wet areas, under power lines, and behind commercial establishments. Mark these places on your map (use pencil; you can use a color scheme to assess these areas later). Also note blank spots on the map to investigate or overlooked areas in your neighborhood.

Next, choose how you will assess the habitats in your ecological neighborhood. You can simply take them in at a gut level, or you can use a simple color scheme to evaluate them, such as in table 3.31. Don't get too technical about this evaluation; just make a rashly reasonable judgment about each place and move on. For example, Dave's neighbor's yard is mostly lawn, with two Norway maples and few flowering plants of any kind: poor bird and insect habitat. Down the street, a small seasonally wet area surrounded by several private lots contains floodplain forest with a gap or two (lumpy texture), a brushy edge zone, and a small wet meadow with diverse wildflowers, but no conifers or thickets. Unfortunately, more lots like the first neighbor's isolate it, so that makes it a fair habitat at best. If you lived next to it, you could make it a good habitat by extending the healthy ecosystem and linking it to the wildness on the other side of the lots.

With your maps and colored pencils in hand (if you are using them), visit the places your preview indicated. Having analyzed your existing and desired plant species niches, you should have a better idea of what plants you're seeing out there and their usefulness to beneficial insects or wildlife. Start by looking into your adjacent neighbors' yards and assessing their habitats. Does their land offer benefits to your forest garden? Do their brushy edges link your site to another nearby wild zone? Then expand your zone of inquiry to the broader area.

As you check out the neighborhood haunts, note what habitats you find where. Assess each habitat, watch the patterns develop, and consider the implications for your forest garden. How connected is your forest garden site to ecosystems that can lend community members to your efforts? What kinds of corridors make the links, and what kinds of wildlife are likely to travel them? How big are the gaps in the corridors? What opportunities for greater connection do you see? Are you going to be an island and therefore need to support populations of beneficials all by yourself? Are there habitats and resources nearby that you can lean on and link to? What insect- and bird-supporting resources are most lacking in your neighborhood? How lavish an environment must you create to attract and hold beneficial insects and birds?

This survey also offers an opportunity to learn more about the plants in your neighborhood. They may give you ideas about other useful species that like your environs, or they may warn you about potential weed or disease problems you might encounter. Also,

TABLE 3.31. A simple neighborhood habitat assessment scheme. We focus here on the question of what makes a good context for edible forest gardens, specifically beneficial insect and bird habitat. This table in no way presumes to say what is good wildlife habitat in general. We intend this only as a rough guide to help you evaluate whether the neighborhood is good forest garden context.

Basic Habitat Needs

	For beneficial insects:	For birds:
Food	• Flowering plants in the families Asteraceae (composites), Apiaceae (umbels, formerly Umbelliferae), and Lamiaceae (mints). • A vibrant, thriving insect community.	• A vibrant, thriving insect community; ongoing pest populations to keep the beneficials going. • Diverse, year-round plant-food sources, especially berries.
Shelter	• Overwintering sites: brushy areas, leaf litter, mulch, etc. Varies by invertebrate group; see appendix 5. • Varies by species; see appendix 5.	• Evergreens and conifers, thickets, brush. • Standing dead trees and snags.
Water	• Open water with debris, plants, and so on sticking out to allow them safe and easy access	• Open water with islands, shallows, and debris allowing them easy and safe access.
Disturbances	• Lack of pesticide spraying. • Patchy disturbances that create cycles of succession and lumpy habitat texture.	• Patchy, infrequent disturbances that create cycles of succession and lumpy habitat texture.

A Simple Habitat Assessment Scheme

Colors shown are the suggested color scheme for mapping.

Excellent (green)

• Any habitat containing year-round food, shelter, and water for insects and birds.
• Large (1 acre/0.4 ha or more) contiguous areas with a mosaic of three or more diverse habitats (e.g., forest, wetland, oldfield), including year-round water, isolated or linked to other habitats.
• Small habitats with food, shelter, and water for insects and birds, linked to other nearby habitats.
• Large areas of diverse flowering insectary plant communities, especially in the ground layer.
• Very lumpy community texture.

Good (yellow)

• Habitats with two out of three of food, shelter, and water for insects and birds.
• Large contiguous areas with two habitat types and only seasonal water.
• Small areas of three or more habitat types connected to other fair, good, or excellent habitats.
• Small, dense areas of flowering nectary plants.
• Lumpy community texture.

Fair (orange)

• Areas with one of three of food, shelter, and water for insects and birds.
• Small, diverse habitat areas (three or more habitat types), isolated.
• Large areas of one habitat type and few useful species.
• Areas of sparse flowering nectary plants.
• Little lumpy vegetation texture.

Poor (red)

• Areas of high chemical usage, pollution, or frequent intense disturbance.
• Monocultures.
• Little or no food, shelter, or water for insects or birds.
• Small, isolated, low-diversity areas.
• Barren areas, or very evenly textured vegetation.
• Few or no flowering nectary plants.

watch for particularly healthy communities that may offer seed sources or healthy soil ecosystems for inoculating your soil (see chapter 5).

Native and Naturalized Species Analysis

Native and naturalized species analysis fulfills the primary purpose of helping you find useful, locally native or naturalized plants not existing on-site. It supplements existing-species niche analysis by broadening the area within which you look for directly useful or model species. This work is most important if you will be developing ecological analogs or polyculture analogs, or if you live outside this book's primary region of interest.

Not everyone wants to limit their search to native plants. Nonnatives that have naturalized in your locale can also offer ideas for ecological analogs, if not an opportunity for direct use of the species. Most likely you will need to go out to find and identify naturalized species in your area; few people care to make lists of species in habitats dominated by them. Look in all the odd corners of the landscape where people do little or no management: woods edges, small stands of trees, abandoned lots, and so on. Don't ignore the healthy natural areas and their natives species, but don't necessarily ignore the nonnatives either.

Once you have species lists from relevant habitats, research the uses of the plants, starting with our appendices and then going further afield if you want. Let's hope some will work in your forest garden. Some species will be the same as or related to those from your earlier niche analyses, speeding your work. Fill out existing-species niche analysis forms for each species with potential value so you can discover its preferred conditions. Add good ones to your desired species list. Beware of potential opportunist species! Make sure you check your list against lists of "invasives" and consider the plant's means of dispersal before you choose to include it in your garden. If you decide to grow natives in your forest garden, make sure you buy only nursery-propagated plants ("nursery-grown"

plants may have been taken from the wild). Do not take plants from the wild unless the site you take them from is about to be developed or destroyed (see chapter 6 and appendix 7 for more information on procuring native plants).

INTEGRATION: SUMMARIZE YOUR OBSERVATIONS AND SOLUTION-DIRECTIONS

Analysis and assessment breaks the site apart so you can gain deep understanding of each piece of it. The last steps of site analysis and assessment integrate all the information you have gathered into a whole and feed the data back to your goals to begin integrating the goals and the site. These steps include synthesizing your thematic and undirected observations into a summary that offers comprehensive understanding, and then seeing how all this new site information affects your goals. You should do these steps to at least a minimal degree, even if you did a very brief site analysis and assessment.

Start with a fresh piece of tracing paper or a copy of your site plan, blank notepaper, and your goals statement. Refresh your memory by reviewing all your site A&A notes and sketches. Pin drawings on the walls or spread them all out on a table or the floor so you can take it all in. Look at the key observations and interpretations you summarized from each theme as you went along, but don't neglect the other ideas. What jumps out at you?

As with painting, start with the broad brush and then work to the details. What is the general drift of the information? Do the solution-directions all head the same way, or more than one way? Do some goals seem in conflict now that you have analyzed and assessed the site? Must your goals change, or can they manifest easily? You should start seeing connections between different themes and interpretations. If you put your thematic sketches on tracing paper, try overlaying two or more themes to see what patterns emerge. Combining key observations and interpretations on a new drawing can give you a sense of direction, too. Write directly on your drawings to keep both sides of your brain engaged and "on the same page." Keep sifting to find relevant patterns and evidence reinforcing or negating them as they emerge.

Look over the information you have about your site and then review table 5.2 (page 319) to see what site-preparation issues you face. Are any of your site conditions addressed in "A Rogue's Gallery of Challenging Site Conditions" (page 318)? Which adaptive and/or site-modification strategies from the "Hero's Gallery" (page 331) can address your challenges? Record both challenges and possible solutions to them on your summary drawing.

Your existing- and desired-species niche analyses, as well as the optional analyses you may have done, should help you see patterns in the species you have and have chosen. Organize your desired-plant lists by habitat, sun-shade tolerance, layer, or whatever makes sense to you if you haven't already. Do these species represent one or two successional phases, or the whole range of succession? How many of what kinds of species do you have? What does this mean for your forest garden? Do the listed plants meet all of your goals and objectives? Compare your desired species to what you know about your site or your desired ecosystem type. Do they match? What will you have to change on-site to fit the species? How? Is it feasible? Prune out plants that definitely will not grow on your site. Put plants that marginally fit your site or preferred habitat on a "B" list, keeping the rest on your "A" list as most likely to get planted, at least for now. Prioritize the species on your "A" and "B" lists as essential, important, or nice. This work provides a solid foundation for schematic design and further species selection. When you select more species depends on your temperament, your design-process flow, and how well you can control your plant enthusiasm! We recommend waiting until you get into the detailed design phase.

If you have completed a varmints, pests, and diseases analysis, consider your priority crops and which beneficials and beneficial-animal habitats are most critical. Which habitat elements have the most functions or are most essential for key benefi-

cials? List the goals or functions your species lists do and don't achieve to guide design-phase species selection. List some of the equipment you'll need to manage insects and diseases. You may see other ways to summarize the information you have gathered. In what directions does it lead your design, site preparation, and management?

What you want to end up with is a drawn *and* written summary of landscape patterns, guiding forces, conflicts, and solution-directions relevant to your design goals and the site's integrity (figure 3.27). *This is not a design drawing but a summary of the current reality and its implications.* Make a bubble diagram that shows the patterns of the site and how the different factors overlap. List key characteristics of each space on your site. Include only the essential and most important points—you can get the details from your thematic work when you need them. Generally it is good to get at least one key thought from each topic area onto your summary. Ultimately, your summary drawing should help you see the big-picture patterns of the site, and it should give you a sense of one, two, or three directions in which to head with your design as a whole. At the very least, it should illuminate quite clearly the key issues, problems, or challenges you face in your design, and it should give you good background on how to resolve them, if not clear direction. You may need a separate written document as well, but that is up to you, and depends in part upon which analysis work you did and how you summarize best.

Once you have completed your site analysis and assessment summary, briefly review and evaluate your goals statement. Is your vision possible? Do any values or goals need to change? What goals can you add now that you know the site better? Can you define more design criteria now? Add goals and criteria for site preparation, design, and management to your goals statement, such as preventing an existing plant from becoming a weed problem. Be careful not to write solutions into your goals, but to lay out your intentions for functions,

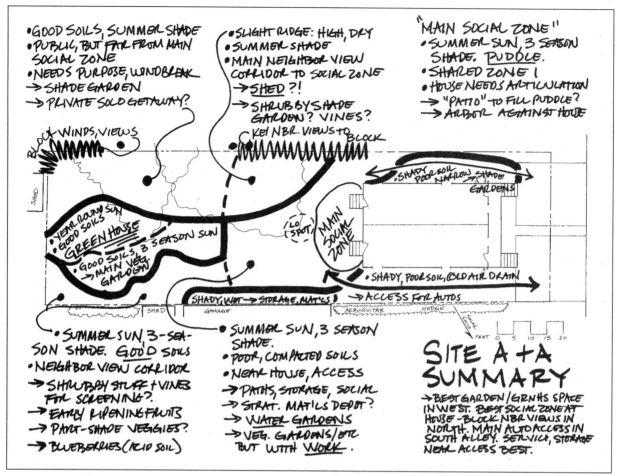

FIGURE 3.27. Site analysis and assessment summary diagram for our design case study. *Field sketch by Dave Jacke.*

uses, and character in terms of values, goals, and design criteria.

CHAPTER SUMMARY

If you have read all of the foregoing and completed all that work, congratulations! It is a long haul, we know. People often feel frustrated by this point in the design process, if not well before. You've done all this work and "have nothing to show for it." This feeling is to be expected. Things are building to a crescendo. You have held off on making a whole host of decisions, and the tension can be excruciating. Just breathe, and let go of the excess. Let the

rest of the tension feed you and your design process: it is a crucial ingredient to finding an optimal design solution. With good goals articulation and site analysis, designing can go quickly, with great clarity and confidence. The decisions sometimes almost appear to make themselves. While we call the next stage the "design" phase, goals articulation and analysis work are design, too, though implicitly so.

By this point, you will have built an incredible foundation of information upon which to build your forest garden design. You will know a tremendous amount about yourself, your site, and the various organisms now or potentially in and around your garden. The exciting part is about to begin. It is time to start the design phase.

1. Dave heard this quote from Judith Gregory, who read it in *Harvard Magazine* as part of a service for people looking for the authors of quotes. However, she never found out who said it, nor has Dave.

2. Thanks to Dan Earle for this summary of the essence of design process!

3. Thanks to Walt Cudnohufsky of the Conway School of Landscape Design for this saying.

4. Thanks again, Walt Cudnohufsky.

5. And again, thanks to Walt Cudnohufsky and the staff at the Conway School of Landscape design for these ideas.

6. This practice has numerous useful implications in other arenas of human activity, as well, which we'll let you ponder on your own.

7. Yeomans, 1958, pages 22–28.

8. Mollison and Holmgren, 1978, page 36.

9. Please read the background on niche analysis in "Desired-Species Niche Analysis" earlier this chapter (page 159), if you haven't already.

10. Subsoil nutrient testing is not a common practice. According to Will Brinton of Woods End Lab in Maine, subsoil testing may require special techniques, and your testing service may give you inappropriate recommendations if they don't know that it is subsoil they are testing. Consult with your soil-testing service; they should tell you whether they can do it. If they think you are crazy, either educate them or go somewhere else. This is cutting-edge stuff!

⚬4⚬

Design Processes 2:
The Design Phase

Successful woodland gardens depend on the sympathetic interpretation of the site's possibilities and an awareness of appropriate plant associations.

—SAMUEL JONES, JR., AND LEONARD FOOTE, *Gardening with Native Wildflowers*

Forest gardening attempts to take ecology from being primarily a descriptive science to being a prescriptive or predictive science. Up to this point in the design process, we have focused on describing the realities we face as human beings seeking to garden in a particular space and time. Though all the work laid out in chapter 3 may not seem like "design," it is a remarkably critical part of effective ecological design. If we are to have any chance of predicting—that is, designing—a future ecological reality, we must fully understand the current reality, including both our goals and the site with all its inhabitants. When we get impatient and jump into the design phase too early, we inevitably find ourselves struggling to make reasonable decisions; retracing our steps to put a solid foundation under our ideas, get unstuck, or resolve conflicts; or failing miserably at achieving our desired ends. When we patiently prepare the ground, the design phase has a better chance of being like riding downhill on a bicycle—exhilarating, fun, and, sometimes, a rush of ideas falling into place with relative ease. Of course, that analogy doesn't convey the fact that there is work involved; it's just that it usually isn't as grueling as the earlier stages can be. The higher you climb uphill through goals articulation and site analysis and assessment, the more momentum and understanding you will have for the downhill run. That

rush of wind in your face, and the higher-quality outcome, makes the preparation worth the effort.

This chapter completes our explication of the forest-garden design process with a focus on the most interesting, stimulating, and occasionally exasperating part: the design phase. As we've said before, forest gardening is, at its essence, the simple act of choosing what plants to place where and when in the garden. Though it sounds straightforward, this simple work must have the full weight of in-depth understanding behind it if it is to generate the kinds of ecosystems we desire. While volume 1 provided vital theoretical background for design, here we must integrate the myriad ecological theories and realities into a practical design-phase process.

The first section of this chapter reviews and further develops the crucial ideas needed to successfully complete a forest-garden plan. We begin by sketching out the four stages of the design-phase process—design concept, schematic design, detailed design, and patch design—to give you an overview of where we are headed. We then discuss the four realms of forest garden design—garden infrastructure, vegetation architecture, succession, and social structure or guild and polyculture design. We talk about each of the four realms individually because it is essential to understand each realm separately before we mix them together. Of the four realms, we emphasize fleshing out the most complex aspects of forest gardening, succession design and guild and polyculture design. Throughout these discourses, we briefly discuss how to design each realm in the context of the four stages of the design phase. We end the first section by presenting a synthesis of the four realms with each other and with the four design-phase stages as one flow of work.

The bulk of the chapter offers detailed guidance for working through each of the four stages of the design phase while dealing with all four realms of forest garden design. Here we offer specific guidance, building on the work we did in the last chapter, to make a sympathetic interpretation of the site's possibilities and to develop appropriate plant associations with awareness. This work helps us apply ecological theory directly to our gardens—with all the fascinating variables that entails.

THE FOUR STAGES OF THE DESIGN PHASE

Let's begin by developing and reviewing the theoretical background that will guide the design-phase process. What are the threads we must weave together into an integrated forest garden design? What processes must we use to weave these threads together, and which threads do we entwine at what stages? We'll discuss the process of weaving first, and then the threads and how to weave them together.

Einstein definitely had his finger on an important pulse when he said, "Imagination is more important than knowledge." However, we must not throw out the baby with the bathwater. Both imagination and knowledge are critical resources in design. Indeed, the principal task of the design phase is to integrate our imagination of what could be with the self-knowledge and site knowledge gained through our efforts in chapter 3. Central to this task is the integration of our knowledge and our imagination in such a way that the big picture of what we achieve harmonizes with the details of

what we do to achieve it. The four stages of the design phase help us achieve both these core tasks, creating integration of imagination and knowledge at both large and small scales. What follows is a very brief explanation of each of the four stages of the design phase (see also table 4.1). Each will be discussed in greater detail in the how-to section.

The first stage of the design phase is the formation of the design concept. The design concept is

---

TABLE 4.1. The four stages of the design phase and their main purposes.

Design Concept:
- Summarizes the organizing idea or site-specific vision for the design.
- The "seed" of the design; integrates all aspects of the design and guides schematic and detailed design.
- ➤ A written statement of up to three sentences with a thumbnail sketch.

Schematic Design:
- Expands seed of design concept to a sketchy but more specific level; can also help you discover your design concept.
- Focuses on overall layout, patterning, and relationships between functions and elements, as well as approximate sizes, shapes, and locations.
- Generates many options and permutations that you can select from among, refine, and recombine; "graphic brainstorming."
- ➤ Rough bubble diagrams with notes, evaluations, brainstorms, possible design directions, and other such comments on them.

Detailed Design:
- Takes chosen scheme to a more refined and defined level of design.
- Deals with exact sizes, shapes, locations, and architecture of features, elements, and patches.
- ➤ Clean line drawings and construction diagrams (plus bubble diagrams at a closer-in scale) with notes, species and materials lists, timelines, design intentions, and commentaries.

Patch Design:
- Final integration of all forest-garden design issues at their most detailed level.
- Patch-by-patch planting diagrams with species lists that fulfill the design criteria laid out in the detailed design stage.
- Construction detailing: gets into species, materials, construction, edges, colors, and textures.
- ➤ Accurate and detailed drawings, sometimes at an enlarged scale, often accompanied by written documents and lists of specifications, species, and so on.

the "big idea" or organizing notion of the whole design for our site. Our goals statement tells us our mission, and our base map and site analysis and assessment tell us the context within which we will achieve that mission. The design concept defines our vision for achieving that mission in that specific context in its most essential or fundamental aspect. Ideally, all the design details flow from this vision and harmonize with it, support it, and manifest it. The design concept is the seed that has all the instructions for articulating the vision in complete detail implicit within its core. It takes the form of a written statement of three sentences or less accompanied by a thumbnail sketch. Finding the design concept is not an easy task, and it cannot be forced. Sometimes it comes before we even get to the design phase; other times we have to work on the following stage of design before it becomes clear.

The next stage of the design phase involves working at a schematic level to solve the problems, answer the questions, and manifest the intentions laid out in the goals within the site context. Schematic design expands the seed of the design concept to see how it manifests in somewhat greater detail—and it sometimes represents a process of seeking to find the pattern that will ultimately make the design concept clear. Schematic design is sketchy, relational, and unspecific, but clear. We typically use bubble diagramming to play with different patterns and options for the size, shape, and location of design elements and the relationships between them—that's the sketchy and relational part. The clarity comes from working out the relationships, locations, and rough shapes and sizes of each major design element until it feels right, bright, and lucid. We must sometimes develop many options and even variations on the options before we find the best fit. This is why we use sketchy bubble diagrams—so we don't get too invested in a particular scheme until we know that it gets our design where we want it to be in a rough way. The spotlight here is on function, purpose, and relationships, with rough physical characteristics attached to them.

Once we have a solid scheme that resolves all the basic design issues, we work at a more detailed level. The detailed-design stage is where we take our chosen scheme and make it more exact, specifying the physical details in harmony with the big picture. Our drawings become more hard-edged here, less rough and sketchy. We focus less on function at this level and more on how to serve those functions in the physical world. We may zoom in and use sketchy bubble diagrams for a while at that scale, but we are always driving toward drawings with exact dimensions so we can specify materials and quantities and locate things exactly in space and time. Some people prefer to do detailed design on-site rather than on paper (see the discussion in the "Basic Mapping for Landscape Design" section of chapter 3), and this is fine, but design on paper still plays into that work on a frequent basis.

In typical landscape architecture, planting design is part of detailed design. Choosing how many of each species go where follows the detailing of purpose in bubble diagramming at the schematic stage. In forest-garden design, however, we have chosen to distinguish the design of vegetation patches from detailed design because the design of plant polycultures is the essence of forest gardening and is not necessarily a quick and easy affair. The careful and conscious design of each patch is the final integration of the four realms of forest garden design, and it deserves special attention.

The above overview of the four stages of the design phase should be enough to go on for now. Obviously, many details of each stage need to be laid out for you to be able to complete each stage well. We will save that for the last section of this chapter. In the meantime, let us deepen our understanding of the four realms of forest gardening, plugging them into the four stages as separate strands before we weave them together into a complete model for the design phase.

THE FOUR REALMS OF FOREST GARDEN DESIGN

The four realms of forest garden design encompass the design issues unique to forest gardens as well as those typical of garden design. The realms are:

- infrastructure: garden features, functions, and elements, including beneficial-animal habitat elements;
- vegetation architecture: habitat design;
- vegetation dynamics: succession design; and
- social structure: guild and polyculture design.

Three of these correspond to the major facets of forest ecosystems discussed in volume 1—architecture, social structure, and succession. Infrastructure deals with typical garden and landscape design issues as well as animal habitat elements.

These four realms interrelate. When you design, they all need to come at once, in tandem, in a way. In this section, though, we will discuss each separately so we know which specific issues fall into each realm. Because succession design and guild and polyculture design are such new aspects of design for which this book offers new understandings and theories, we will spend more effort laying out the considerations for these two realms than for the others, including more detail on their design processes. We will, however, address them in the order presented above.

INFRASTRUCTURE: GARDEN FEATURES, FUNCTIONS, AND ELEMENTS

Gardens are for people. The infrastructure realm provides a place to consider and design all the garden elements that people need or want to meet their own needs or to manage the garden for its practical, social, or aesthetic functions. Since beneficial animals also have infrastructure needs, we include them in this realm, too. Features include garden art and architecture like benches, tables, swings, hammocks, sculpture, arbors, trellises, fences, patios, and the like.

Elements are physical things like features, only they tend to fade into the background to help the garden work well or they provide habitat for beneficial animals. They include things like pathways, sheds, irrigation lines, water tanks, cold frames, and greenhouses, as well as rock piles, brush piles, standing dead trees, water elements, and the like. The boundary between features and elements is vague, the former being more aesthetic and prominent, and the latter more invisible or practical, but an arbor or garden pond, for example, may fall in either or both of the categories. Functions are abstract compared to features and elements, often representing the purposes that the physical things serve, such as social gathering; organic matter storage and processing; visual screening; access and circulation; water management, collection, and distribution; and overwintering habitat for invertebrates.

Your goals are likely to include many things that fall into this realm of forest garden design, particularly if your forest garden has purposes beyond food production. Seeing your forest garden as an outdoor living room, as discussed in pattern #6 (chapter 2), should get you thinking about the social and aesthetic functions of the garden space, and what features it will need to make it feel comfortable and encourage you to use and, indeed, to live in the space. Even if your garden's main purpose is more practical, however, you need to design your infrastructure well, whether it be pathways, irrigation works, mulch storage and management, critter control, or other issues your goals and site analysis and assessment have raised. Good infrastructure design is essential to minimizing maintenance, maximizing productivity, and providing habitat for beneficial animals.

Infrastructure elements may define the core design concept or underlie it. For example, in one forest garden a social gathering space and path system may define the feel, purpose, and organization of the garden. In another the paths may serve only to make the forest garden as efficient, easy to use, and practical as possible—social spaces are a side issue if they are present at all. In any case, it is usually best to design the infrastructure functionally and schematically before getting into too much detail. In the schematic stage, determine the functions and the rough size, shape, and location of the elements that perform those functions, as well as the relationships between given functions or elements and the other parts of the garden. Many of these choices may already be defined in your goals statement or they will arise from your site analysis and assessment work. You may need to go back to your goals statement to articulate criteria for these functions in more depth. When everything is in the right pattern and relationship conceptually and schematically, you can move into detailed design to define the exact size, shape, and location of any physical features and elements and choose their materials, construction, colors, textures, and edge treatments.

Since this book focuses on forest garden design, we will not offer many specifics about the design of particular kinds of infrastructure here. General permaculture and garden design books have plenty to offer you in this regard. We will, however, give you some guidance about how to design infrastructure in each stage of the design phase later in the chapter.

VEGETATION ARCHITECTURE: HABITAT DESIGN

Volume 1 laid out the five elements of forest architecture as vegetation layers, soil horizons, vegetation density, vegetation patterning, and ecosystem diversity. These architectural elements define the characteristics of any habitat or community in its most concrete, basic, and designable terms. When we say "habitat design," we mean defining these architectural elements in your forest garden's vegetation.

We can characterize habitats or plant communities as a whole by names such as shrubland, woodland, forest, oldfield mosaic, and so on. We can also define these habitats in more detail by describing the density, patterning, and diversity of species in each vegetation layer and each patch (the soil horizon structure can sometimes be definitive as

well). This means that we can design such habitats in a similar way, working from the general to the specific, that is, from the habitat to the patch and from broad habitat descriptions to the five elements of architecture. Habitat design, then, involves designing the architecture of the habitat as a whole, the pattern of patches that together form the habitat, and the architecture of each patch, in that general order.

In chapter 3 we discussed variations in the design process based on whether you are designing from ecosystem to plants or from plants to ecosystem. The essential forest-garden design process of designing the habitat overall and then the layers and patches applies to either of these basic design approaches. If you are designing from plants to ecosystem, you need to make sure you have completed your desired-species niche analysis as discussed in the "Clear Intentions: Articulating Your Gardening Goals" section of chapter 3 before beginning the design phase. This niche analysis work will help you determine what kinds of site conditions your desired species require or prefer. Your site analysis should tell you where such site conditions exist, where and how to create the right conditions through site preparation, and whether you should abandon certain species. Then you can begin making design decisions by specifying the habitats you need to meet your desired species' requirements. If you are working from ecosystem to plants, the basic process outlined below fits right into your design flow.

Clearly, a brief and broad description of the habitat type is appropriate in the design concept stage. The habitat type will be central to the design concept for many forest gardens, though not necessarily all, but your design concept should specify the habitat type(s) in any case. Begin to spell out the implications of that habitat choice in the schematic-design stage by characterizing the habitat or habitats in terms of the five elements of architecture for the overall garden and by sketching bubble diagrams depicting the pattern of patches within the habitat. This patch-pattern diagram should roughly characterize the location, size, shape, function, architecture, and site conditions of each patch in concert with the infrastructure layout. You can also specify some of the plants each patch contains and roughly where they go if these are central to the patch function or they define the patch's architecture.

Once you get into detailed design, design and characterize each patch in more detail as part of the foundation for your final species-selection process, which is discussed in the guild and polyculture design subsection later. In the patch-design stage, you decide which species go where in each patch based in part on the site conditions and architectural design criteria you have listed. In this way, you generate the habitat you want patch by patch.

The fact that diversity is one of the five elements of architecture but species selection is discussed in social structure design may create some confusion. There is overlap here, and we have to draw the line somewhere. However, as discussed in volume 1, chapter 3, we have to consider diverse forms of diversity: compositional, structural, and functional. In habitat design, we focus on characterizing these three kinds of diversity in general terms. Habitat design helps guide the design of the social structure realm during the latter stages of the design phase.

In addition, it is impossible to separate space and time in the real world. This means that habitat design and succession design go hand in hand. We must design our habitats in the context of a successional scheme and timeline, thinking through the growth and development of our habitats over time. Let's discuss this next.

Vegetation Dynamics: Succession Design

Vegetation dynamics or succession design deals with the design of community transformations over time, including designed disturbances (such as site preparation) and planned changes in species dominance through planting, establishment, and varied plant performance. These topics cover some of the most challenging territory in forest-garden design, as well as the most interesting. As we said earlier, forest gardening attempts to take ecology from description to prediction; succession design is right at the cutting edge of this effort. Both excitement and dread arise from that fact: excitement at the possibilities, at the fun we can have, and at what we can learn from this work; dread because of the complexity of the topic and because we have so many mistakes to make before we really know what is going on. Luckily, there are enough variations on the succession-design theme to suit almost anyone's tastes and tolerance for convolution. We hope this subsection clarifies your understanding, options, and choices in the face of this newness and intricacy.

While we expect that most people will use the simplest succession-design model we offer, the variations on the theme require a more substantive discussion of this realm than of the previous two. Briefly reviewing relevant concepts is appropriate here; see chapter 6 in volume 1 for more depth if what we outline below is unfamiliar. This volume's chapter 7 and the "Directed Succession" section of chapter 1 (page 39) discuss the management and guidance of succession. Here we shall focus on design.

Key Concepts and Models

Six basic ideas underlie the succession-design process we outline in this chapter (see table 4.2). These ideas bring together habitat design and succession design by describing the ecosystem as a whole in time and space.

Our exploration of patch dynamics theory in volume 1 showed us that the patch is the basic spatial unit of ecosystems, and therefore of ecosystem

TABLE 4.2. Six keys to succession design.		
	Time	Space
Temporary Endpoint:	Horizon	Habitat
Pattern That Connects:	Scenario	Pattern
Basic Unit of Design:	Phase	Patch

design. The pattern of patches connects the individual patches to generate the habitat as a whole. We can describe and design that habitat by defining the pattern of patches and the architecture of each patch, as presented above.

Patch dynamics theory also tells us that each patch in an ecosystem has its own unique successional pathway wherein the architecture of the patch changes over time. We can define phases of succession in a patch or a habitat by describing the architecture of a patch or the habitat as a whole during a given period. Therefore, the basic unit of ecosystem design in time is the phase.

Since disturbance is an integral part of successional processes and succession is therefore never-ending, no final endpoint or climax exists to which we can design. Consequently, we design to a temporary endpoint at the furthest reach of our timeline and vision, which we call the horizon. The horizon habitat is thereby the habitat that exists at a given time and place in the future. Each patch in a habitat succeeds from its current condition to the horizon habitat through a pattern of phases called a successional scenario. That last sentence said "from its current condition to the horizon habitat," and this means that the successional scenario includes any designed disturbances that occur for site preparation prior to planting, as well as the planting and establishment process itself. The four models of succession outlined in volume 1, chapter 6, offer us a range of successional scenarios we can play with in our forest gardens.

Linear Succession to a Horizon

The simplest scenario to design and use is linear succession to a horizon, which mimics linear succession to a climax. Linear successions relate most directly to people's individual perceptions of successions in nature, where a disturbed patch of ground succeeds from barren to herbs, then shrubs, then pioneer trees, and then shade-tolerant trees, for example. We have dropped the word *climax* from use in forest garden design because the theory

has been dropped by most succession researchers and because, even if it were valid, the time it takes to reach climax conditions is so long that it is unreasonable to consider attempting. We therefore design to a horizon habitat as discussed above.

You can set your horizon at any time in the future, but setting it too far ahead may be unrealistic—unless you have a clear inheritance plan and heirs that are up for continuing the vision into the far future (for example, see box 2.1, page 115)! Most people designing forest gardens will design to a horizon habitat defined by the size and age of their mature trees, making the process little different than what most people do when designing gardens. We can get more complex and interesting than that, though. *Instant Successions* (#31), *Nuclei That Merge* (#32), and *Relay Plantings* (#33) are patterns from chapter 2 that relate most directly to this kind of scenario, and they offer possibilities for interplay and combination that can make linear successions more fun than the typical garden design approach. Typical garden design timelines are fine too, though, if they meet your needs, interests, and capabilities. The basic design process we outline later is ideally suited to the linear-succession model.

Rotational Mosaics

The shifting-mosaic steady state model offers the most challenging succession-design possibilities. It holds potential for stable yields of all crops in the most diverse forest-garden ecosystem possible while still allowing for continuous directed change and, in theory, minimal maintenance work. Shifting-mosaic mimics will be similar to the rotational systems typical of organic farms and annual vegetable gardens, except that the varied life spans of the crop trees, shrubs, and herbs in forest gardens make the design process more thought-provoking. Rotational mosaics are most suited to larger-scale gardens. See pattern #18 in chapter 2 for more discussion of these ideas.

To design rotational mosaics, you will need to creatively use the basic design process we outline, estimating the spans of each phase carefully to see how the phases fit together in a complete rotational cycle that exists in different phases simultaneously in different patches. Balancing the spatial and temporal aspects of the scheme will be the most difficult challenge, as most of the long-lived species take up large areas while the short-lived and earlier-succession species are smaller plants. Since this is an activity for the large-scale, the hard-core, and the experimental, we won't go into much detail in this book, but many of the information resources you need are here for you (see especially the "Estimated Useful Life Spans of Selected Woody Species" table in appendix 2). Have fun if you try it!

Gap Successions

Gap succession is one of the internal ecosystem dynamics that drives the shifting-mosaic steady state model (see pattern #16 in chapter 2). Yet gap succession has broader applications in design and can fit into other successional scenarios. It will probably play a central role in rotational mosaics, but it also applies as a linear succession—especially to forest gardens within existing wooded areas or older forest gardens where you replant gaps created in the existing fabric. Gap-succession design involves first getting clear on the size, shape, severity, and intensity of disturbance you want to create for what purposes; designing the disturbance carefully is key to achieving your aims (see volume 1, chapter 6, for details on disturbances and gaps). The strategy of habitat co-optation in the discussion of the social structure realm below holds more ideas relevant to this successional scenario.

Patch Dynamics: The Ever-Present Now

The patch-dynamics succession model provides inspiration for free-form approaches to succession design, where each patch goes its own way and you disturb and redirect the patch's succession at will or on a whim. You can use this model in a wide variety of ways, either planning the successions in each patch using the basic succession-design process or doing minimal if any planning. Thinking of the horizon as lying in the very near term will help you connect to the process we discuss in the rest of this chapter. Your habitat—that is, the system your patches create as a whole—may consist of patches of varying character that do not add up to a specific habitat per se but compose a mosaic of patches. The potential difficulty with this approach is that you may be tempted to throw out the other pieces of the design process we discuss and thereby make the same mistakes others have already made, especially in the area of plant spacing. Letting go of succession design and living in the "ever-present now" does not mean that plant spacing and other design principles do not apply!

As we said, succession design is at the cutting edge of ecology as a predictive science. Some kinds of scenarios discussed above may require alterations to the design process we present in this chapter. You will need to be creative and flexible as you work through the design phase if you decide to do anything besides linear succession to a horizon. Since you will choose your successional scenario in the first stage of the design phase, you will be able to keep your eye out and adapt as you work your way through.

A Succession Design Process

Let's briefly discuss a general succession-design scheme you can adapt to each kind of succession scenario above and your own circumstances. This scheme aims at the most intensively designed scenarios (except rotational mosaics).

First, as mentioned earlier, your design concept should briefly but clearly characterize the horizon habitat, for example by stating that the garden is a savanna mimic or a woodland garden. The design concept should also state what kind of successional scenario you foresee. This sets the context for everything else that follows and will help you choose your succession-design process.

In the schematic design stage, further define the successional scheme for the garden as a whole.

How far in the future is your successional horizon? Most people should sketch out the site preparation and establishment schemes you have in mind for the garden. If you have a complex or long-term successional scenario, create a timeline to sketch out the phases of the scenario for the habitat overall, at least in chronological order if not in terms of rough time frames, and describe the architectural character of each phase.

During detailed design the focus is on refining your horizon habitat scheme, so most of you will have to do little succession planning. Those with complex or long-term successional scenarios have some additional work, though. Choose one or two critical successional phases from your timeline and make a bubble diagram of these earlier phases characterizing the functions and site conditions of each patch. This will help you select all of the species you need for your species palette.

If you are planning a shifting-mosaic or rotational scheme, planning one successional sequence and then just repeating it with different starting times is the easiest way to do it. If that doesn't work for your production goals, then you'll have to figure out a way to start that either lets your different patches mature at different rates or ensures that they get disturbed at certain times to get the right rhythm going between the patches.

During patch design, make sure you consider specific site preparation and establishment schemes for each patch. It may help to make a succession timeline for any patches that have complex successional scenarios to assist you in choosing species and pondering disturbance and maintenance regimes. Reality-check your patch-succession timeline against what you know and can find out about growth rates and sizes at different ages of the species you are siting, adjusted for your site conditions (see the "Estimated Useful Life Spans of Selected Woody Species" table in appendix 2).

All this sounds complex, and it can be. The trick is designing the future and thinking through the implications of that for the present and nearer term. Keeping your future sketches sketchier, focusing on the woody plants for that time frame, helps keep it simple enough to grasp and work with. Besides, we expect most people will be using the simple linear-succession scenario and can forgo the harder aspects of succession design.

SOCIAL STRUCTURE: GUILD AND POLYCULTURE DESIGN

The core of social structure design lies in guild and polyculture design, and guild and polyculture design lies at the very core of forest gardening. A firm grip on this realm increases our ability to realize our most fundamental forest-gardening goals. As we said earlier, at its simplest forest garden design involves choosing plants and deciding when and where to place them in the garden. Through these seemingly straightforward acts, we must generate the forestlike structures and functions we wish to mimic to achieve our ends. Our plantings must generate architectures, social structures, and successional sequences similar to those of our forest models as appropriate to our goals. Therefore, in forest gardening we select appropriate plants (as well as other habitat elements) and arrange them in patterns, spacings, and sequences that result in healthy plants growing in effective guilds and polycultures.

Effective Guilds and Polycultures: Review and Definitions

Let's briefly review a few key points. In chapter 4 of volume 1 we distinguished between two kinds of guilds: resource-partitioning guilds and mutual-support guilds. Resource-partitioning guilds (or resource-sharing guilds) include species at the same level of the food web with the same or similar community niches partitioning a shared resource to avoid competition. These guilds create redundancy of community function in the ecosystem. Mutual-support guilds, on the other hand, involve species from different community niches at the same or different levels of the food web. Their niche characteristics interact such that the inherent products of each guild member meet the inherent needs of other guild members, forming a web of functional relationships. These functional interconnections help the community regulate and maintain itself and reduce the amount of work and external input the ecosystem requires. Some guilds require interacting individuals to grow in the same space, though some do not; not all guilds are polycultures, but all effective polycultures consist of guilds.

Effective polycultures are mixtures of plants and other organisms that:

- as a whole yield more than comparable monocultures (additive yielding or overyielding);
- require fewer labor, energy, and materials inputs;
- minimize stress, competition, and herbivory;
- maximize harmony and cooperation;
- generate self-renewing fertility;
- live within a sustainable water budget; and
- remain stable (i.e., have a relatively constant structure and composition) with little or no maintenance, or exhibit an intended or otherwise useful successional pathway with little or no maintenance.

In other words, effective polycultures result from the creation of resource-partitioning guilds that reduce competition and increase redundancy and mutual-support guilds that maximize cooperation and reduce work. Specifically, we want these guilds to:

- increase the supply of vital nutrients, especially those in high demand (typically N, P, K, Ca) or those in short supply;
- exploit more niches in the ecosystem more completely (e.g., shade-tolerant plants under sun-loving plants, mixing deep- and shallow-rooting plants);
- support diverse and balanced populations of animals, insects, and microbes (e.g., insectary plants, diverse perennials providing varied, year-

round root exudates to a healthy soil food web);
- resist pest and disease epidemics due to their species and genetic diversity;
- stabilize microclimate conditions above- and belowground (by layering vegetation and covering the ground surface); and
- prevent the invasion and establishment of unwanted plant species and foster the growth and performance of desired species in a desired sequence of prominence (by providing ground covers and mulch-producing plants, selecting species based on their growth habits and time to maturity, and so on).

Therefore, designing effective guilds and polycultures requires clear, site-specific objectives, an understanding of the resource conditions and limiting factors in our garden environment, and knowledge of the weed, pest, and disease populations we confront. The design processes outlined here address these requirements.

As you can see when reading through the goals above, guild and polyculture design pulls together all the ecology discussed in volume 1, as well as most of the issues and strategies discussed in chapter 1 of this volume. The simple choice of which plant to place where and when is not as simple as it seems! Effective guild and polyculture design requires coordinating the design of patches, guilds, and polycultures. How you get there varies depending on the approach you choose, but at some point in every approach you will need to design the patch structure of the forest garden and select a full complement of species, taking account of guild relationships while you do both. This is followed by the design of polycultures that include the larger guilds. Let's discuss some of these guild relationships a bit more so we understand the spatial relationships that govern the effectiveness of guilds and polycultures.

Patch Guilds and Garden Guilds
In the forest garden, we want to optimize guild functioning so we can achieve our design objec-

TABLE 4.3. Spatial design guidelines for some specific guild functions. "Patch guilds" are those functions requiring guild members to grow together within a patch. "Garden guilds" can function when members are spread over larger areas, operating throughout the garden or neighborhood. It appears that all garden guilds can also work as patch guilds.

Guild Function	Patch or Garden Guild?	Patterning Guidelines
Beneficial insect nectary plants	Either	• Throughout garden, especially near plants needing herbivore protection. Maximum distances from nectary plants to protected crops, and between nectary plants, vary greatly from species to species of beneficial insect. These distances are unknown for most beneficials. • Provide flowers at all times of growing season. • Some researchers recommend whole patches, clusters, scatters, drifts, or linked clusters, a.k.a. archipelagos, of insectary plants. However, these may at times become a "sink" of beneficial insects rather than a source for surrounding crop areas. • Overwintering sites may be in protected microclimates somewhat away from summer habitat.
Honey plants	Either	• Large patches, linked patches, or linked clusters reduce bee searching time and energy, increasing honey yield. • Early- and late-season flowers are critical for spring gear-up and winter survival of colonies.
Pollinator support plants	Either	• Linked or scattered clusters, scatters, drifts. • Few noncrop plants should be flowering during crop flowering periods, if possible. This will maximize pollination of crop plants.
Aromatic pest-confusing plants	Patch optimal	• Best planted around plants needing protection. • Can disperse them everywhere, especially in prevailing wind sectors (as a garden guild).
Fertility plants (nitrogen fixers, dynamic accumulators)	Patch optimal	• Best in scatters, drifts, or regular patterns in the root zones of crops needing the nutrients. • Can create distinct fertility patches for cut-and-carry mulch (but this garden guild makes work).
Ground cover	Patch	• Dense ground-covering mats or patches.
Weed barrier	Patch	• Encircling or walling off patches from adjacent rhizomatous weeds or vigorous ground covers.
Soil-profile partitioning	Patch	• Mix plants with different rooting patterns and depths in regular or random patterns, or mix them in drifts, scatters, or small clumps.
Light partitioning	Patch	• Place sun-loving plants in the canopy, with shade-tolerant plants increasing in number and degree of shade tolerance in successively lower layers. • Also consider light coming into the patch from the sides; in this case, lower-layer species may not have to be as shade tolerant.

tives. To optimize their functioning, we must understand that some guilds work only when their members grow together within a patch, while others can function across the whole garden or neighborhood, weaving patches together. We call these two ways guilds express themselves in space patch guilds and garden guilds, respectively.

Effective polycultures, by definition, require that the plants in each patch constitute a resource-partitioning guild so competition within the patch is minimized. However, not all resource-partitioning guilds express themselves as patch guilds. While many mutual-support guilds work as garden guilds, not all can or must; one polyculture patch may constitute a complete mutual-support guild. The specific function of a guild determines whether it must take one of these spatial forms or can express itself as either one (see table 4.3). For example, plants partitioning soil resources vertically because of their root structure won't partition the soil unless they grow in polyculture (a patch guild). Species that partition pollinators by flowering at different times of the year need to grow not necessarily in the same patch, only within the same general area (a garden guild). On the other hand, dynamic accumulators in a mutual-support guild with a crop plant must grow in the same patch as the crop (a patch guild), unless you want to cut and carry mulch (a garden guild that includes you as a member).

Guild-Member Patterning

As table 4.3 points out, whether or not guild members are in the same patch, guild-member patterning also affects whether or how well each of these specific guild functions works. We can imagine that some guild-member distribution patterns will work more effectively than others, depending on the function. For example, beneficial-insect nectary plants should be near the crop plants we want the beneficials to protect, though we don't know specific distances for most beneficial insects. Since we want these beneficials to cruise everywhere looking for prey or hosts, we probably want to scatter nectary plants all over, mixing them right in with crops. There is some speculation that we can use aromatic plants, such as the *Alliums* (onions), to mask or confuse the scents pests use to locate their hosts. Placing these companions in the same patch as, and all around, the plants needing protection would be optimal. However, on a garden-wide basis, you could also focus them up- and downwind of the garden in the prevailing wind directions. On the other hand, when providing nectar for honeybees you probably want to minimize the bees' time and energy spent searching for flowers; thus, planting generalist nectary flowers in clumps, clusters, or drifts would be most advantageous.

So we should consider whether a guild function should express itself as a patch or garden guild while schematically designing the patch structure of the forest garden as a whole. In some cases, the details of guild-member patterning will also influence the garden's overall pattern of patches and the functions we want each patch to perform, not to mention the planting patterns within a patch.

Guild and Polyculture Design Strategies

Numerous ways to design guilds and polycultures exist; more are waiting to be invented. We can only begin to cover the gamut here by briefly laying out a few obvious and reasonable approaches. Each strategy has its advantages and disadvantages and is appropriate for some people or projects and not others. Here we will briefly discuss the main features of six strategies, but we will focus our attention on the two with which we have the most experience and that most people are likely to use: guild-build and habitat mimicry. This conversation again places us at the cutting edge of ecology as a predictive science, so we have much to learn and explore.

The question of whether you are working from ecosystem to plants or from plants to ecosystem arises again in guild and polyculture design. The guild and polyculture design strategies discussed below fall roughly into these two approaches: plants-to-ecosystem strategies include guild-build, crops-only polycultures, and random assembly, while habitat mimicry, habitat invention, and habitat co-optation are ecosystem-to-plants strategies. Of course, if you want to live life a little more fully you can combine these approaches and strategies, too.

While each guild and polyculture design strategy has a different set of design tools at its core, these tools perform similar functions. *Patch characterization* provides the species-selection criteria you need, *species selection* winnows your species choices to those most effective for your purposes, and *polyculture design* assembles the species in effective groupings. The differences between strategies lie in how you undertake each of these three basic processes using the tools mentioned in the discussion below (see table 4.4) and described in detail later in this chapter. The early stages of guild and polyculture design follow the paths described in the previous discussions of the other realms.

The important thing to remember through all the following is that this discourse relates only to how we *design* guilds and polycultures. Once we design them, we have to plant and observe them to

TABLE 4.4. Species selection and polyculture design tools and how they are used in different guild and polyculture design strategies. N/N Species = native and naturalized species; X = core tools used in the strategy; • = may be used in the strategy; − = minimally or not used in the strategy. None of the tools are mutually exclusive; the only question is which are core to the strategy and whether or how you use the others.

Basic Forest Garden Approaches	Guild and Polyculture Design Strategies	Species Selection Tools					Polyculture Design Tools		
		Desired-Species Selection	Guild-Species Selection	Ecological Analogs	Existing-Species Selection	N/N Species Selection	Polyculture Build	Polyculture Analogs	Random Assembly
Plants to ecosystem	guild-build	X	X	•	•	•	X	•	−
	crops-only	X	•	−	−	−	X	•	−
	random assembly	X	•	•	•	•	−	−	X
Ecosystem to plants	habitat mimicry	−	−	X	•	•	•	X	−
	habitat invention	X	X	•	•	•	•	X	−
	habitat co-optation	X	•	X	X	•	•	•	−

see what happens. By understanding and applying ecological theory we increase our chances of achieving our design objectives, but this is no guarantee. Trial, error, and observation will always play an important role. Each polyculture design essentially represents a test of the theory and knowledge we have available and an opportunity to improve our theory and knowledge. The reality in the field will ultimately guide us. If we watch closely and ponder skillfully, we'll learn a lot along the way.

Our discussion will begin with the three strategies that fall into the plants-to-ecosystem approach and then turn to the ecosystem-to-plants strategies.

Guild-Build

The guild-build process may provide the most assurance of meeting our forest garden goals and objectives. It is the most design-oriented, front-end-loaded approach to polyculture and guild design discussed here, and it is based on what we know or guess about plants, their species niches, and how they interact. As a result, it applies our theories and knowledge more robustly than any other method. It appears to be the best approach to designing polycultures with the unique, wide-ranging set of plants that the forest-garden palette has to offer. If we are creating completely new species mixtures using plants from around the world, how else would we go about designing effective polycultures in a rational way? Guild-build offers us the opportunity to learn the most about how to build a better mousetrap in the shortest time, with the lowest risk of complete failure.

The guild-build method involves the following steps:

1. Niche-analyze all the species you want to grow using desired-species niche analysis, as laid out in the goals articulation discussion of chapter 3. Thin this list based on your site analysis and assessment work.

2. Design and characterize the functions, conditions, and architecture of the garden's patches during schematic and detailed design, as discussed in the previous subsections. For guild-build, you should characterize the patches in great detail. This prepares you for species selection.

3. The core tool for species selection in this strategy is what we call guild-species selection,

though other techniques can play a support role. In guild-species selection, you list all of the ecological functions you want your garden ecosystem to perform in all of the different patch conditions your garden has or will have during its successional sequence. You then select species to perform those functions in all the conditions you have specified to create a master species list or species palette.

4. During the patch-design stage, build polycultures for each patch using your species palette. Built polycultures consist of compatible plants that form resource-partitioning guilds within the patch while they simultaneously fulfill your desired uses and functions and create mutual-support guilds within the patch and across the garden as desired. Your knowledge of plant-species' niches forms the foundation of the polyculture-build process.

We'll provide the details of each of the above steps as we go through the design-process how-to later.

Since guild-build can create novel plant combinations from species that may never have grown together before, it presents some risk of creating unintended negative interactions. However, creating novel plant combinations randomly, without using guild-build, has an even higher risk of this. Consequently, we recommend using as many native-species associations in the mix as possible, or at least grouping species by native region to some degree. In any case, the polyculture-build technique is an attempt to minimize negative and maximize positive interactions through conscious design.

The biggest challenge is that guild-build is a lot of work, and it represents only the design part. Afterward you have to plant what you design, and then see what happens. Is it worth the effort? We think so. Our limited understanding of plants and their interactions hampers the guild-build process, yet guild-build gives us a clearer understanding of our polyculture designs. We can use that under-

standing to observe and evaluate our polycultures more effectively. The guild-build process should therefore shorten the time it takes to develop various regionally appropriate "standard" effective polycultures for a range of sites and growing conditions using the broadest range of plants. Once we do that, the need for doing guild-build will diminish greatly; we will have developed useful polyculture patterns that we can take "off the shelf" when needed. Even then, though, the need for this somewhat grueling process will still exist for unusual sites, unusual species, and interesting people with unusual goals.

Crop-Only Polycultures

This guild and polyculture design strategy limits plant selections to only those species that yield products for direct human use. Simplifying the system to crop-plant-only polycultures should maximize yields and still confer some ecosystem benefits, while simplifying design. Whether it will simplify management compared to the wider species palettes generated by the guild-build strategy is a question that only experimentation will reveal for sure. Indeed, this is one of the drawbacks of the crops-only strategy—we can theoretically expect our workload and the need for external inputs to increase compared to guild-build because the ecosystem will take on fewer functions itself. If the garden is more vegetationally complex, yet we still do much of the maintenance work, it may not be worth it. If the garden is more vegetationally complex, but it takes on more self-maintaining qualities, the additional complexity is more likely to be worth it. Consequently, the goal in crop-only polycultures should be to maximize the numbers of multiple-function crop plants, so we can get our functions and eat them too.

The design process for crops-only polycultures follows that of guild-build, except that the only required species-selection technique is desired-species selection. Undertaking guild-species selection to seek additional crops that also perform ecosystem functions is certainly worthwhile. In any case, it behooves you to select a wide variety of multifunctional crop plants from the beginning to give you the most options in your polyculture-build process. The polyculture design process for crops-only polycultures is exactly like that of guild-build, just with a more limited species palette. Crops-only polycultures may work optimally as patches within a more diverse forest garden matrix to maximize beneficial animal habitat and the garden's compositional diversity. However, you can also design your whole forest garden using this strategy.

Random and Semi-Random Mixtures

At the opposite end of the spectrum from the intensive guild-build process we find an approach that many forest gardeners seem to have taken: select a group of interesting plants with useful characteristics, throw them together in more or less random mixtures, and see what happens. They seem to assume the plants will work it out themselves, eventually. There is definitely some wisdom in this way of going about things, yet it has its drawbacks, too.

The other guild and polyculture design strategies discussed here provide opportunities to apply and test theories likely to offer us numerous gardening benefits. Nonetheless, they can also limit our thinking and blind us to possibilities. Throwing out those theories and playing with random groupings of plants may offer us clues and discoveries that theories would never provide. It's also a lot easier on the front end of the process, since you don't have to do so much thinking and decision making. On the other hand, leaving your gardening goals to chance is much less likely to give you the results you want. Our guess is that, compared to the other methods, throwing plants together at random is more likely to lead to lackluster performance, complete failure, competitive exclusion by one or a few species, or the work of preventing one of those outcomes.

Most forest gardeners using this "throw it together" approach have improved upon complete randomness by planting random mixtures of species chosen from groups of plants with similar tolerances and site preferences. This at least gives the plants a fighting chance of surviving the conditions, regardless of the social circles in which they find themselves. Then the random polycultures at least provide clues about how plants with similar tolerances compete or partition resources. We can organize our randomness in other ways, too.

Assuming we'll plant between two and seven species in each polyculture patch, we can try planting various patches with different mixtures of species with similar site tolerances and see what happens. Using the same species in different random combinations will offer us interesting information about the behavior of each species. Based on those results, we can test different mixtures to see how species grow together and how well they yield or perform. Such rote empirical methods will probably take much work and time to yield effective polycultures. However, even the design-oriented methods will require this work at the back end of the process to fine-tune the polycultures and guilds. It won't be easy work necessarily, but it should be fun and interesting, and somebody has to do it.

All in all, we recommend using random assembly in at least some patches in your garden just to spice things up and provide some relief from planning everything out. You can carefully select your species for their uses, functions, and site tolerances and then randomly mix them in the patch-design stage, or you can randomly assemble your species palette and randomly assemble your polycultures, or both in different places. Either way, you will have fun and learn some worthy things if you pay attention. We do not recommend putting your whole garden together this way, however, unless you have absolutely no attachment to the outcome. Just remember to pay attention to the spacing guidelines covered later in the chapter so you don't make the same mistakes many others have made before you.

Habitat Mimicry

Habitat mimicry is the first of our guild and polyculture design strategies that represents the ecosystem-to-plants design approach. The strategy rests on two assumptions. The first is that evolutionary forces have forged functioning guilds in native ecosystems and native plant polycultures over time. The second is that mimicking these natural guilds and polycultures will increase the chances of creating low-competition, high-cooperation forest gardens.

The challenge here is that the theory of coevolution is somewhat controversial (see volume 1, page 152), and the ability to make good species analogies is not well tested. In addition, evolutionary forces won't necessarily have filled all the gaps in the ecological fabric of temperate plant communities, potentially leaving some guild functions unfulfilled. However, the habitat-mimicry design approach could provide interesting polyculture and guild combinations to test that other methods would not generate, and we can use the guild-build process as a supplement to fill in any guild gaps that do exist if we desire.

The core work of habitat mimicry takes place through architectural design, species selection, and polyculture design:

1. Use model ecosystem analysis (see chapter 3, page 164) to help you create architectural design criteria for the mimic habitat and its patches and to list species from the model community and its polycultures.
2. Use those criteria to design the layers, density, patterning, and diversity of the mimic habitat and its patches during schematic and detailed design as discussed in earlier subsections.
3. Mimic the model habitat during species selection by directly using species from the model habitat that offer beneficial functions and uses and by using ecological analogs of model species that have fewer known benefits for you or your garden. You can also use existing-species niche analysis and native-

and naturalized-species niche analysis to help you with species selection.

4. Imitate the model community in the patch-design stage by creating structural and functional analogs of the model habitat's polyculture patches. If you are unable to observe patches in an example of the model community, then you may need to use the polyculture-build process instead, as in the guild-build strategy.

The ecological-analog species-selection process involves niche-analyzing a model species and looking for taxonomically, structurally, and functionally similar species that may have more benefits for us or our gardens than the model. We discuss the theory behind the idea in volume 1, chapter 4, and the practical application of the theory later in this chapter.

Making polyculture analogs is similar to making species analogs in concept. If possible, you should observe or find data on the kinds of polyculture patches found in the model habitat during model ecosystem analysis or later on as necessary. Substitute species from your palette of selected species for those in the model polyculture to create a patch with similar architecture.

Habitat Invention

Habitat invention provides the designer with a little more room to play than in habitat mimicry. It works on the assumption that structural mimicry of model ecosystems can provide functional benefits that we want but also allows us to base the design on species we want to grow more so than does habitat mimicry. It also builds guilds more consciously, providing greater assurance of good guild functioning.

As an ecosystem-to-plants design approach, this guild and polyculture design strategy still relies on model ecosystem analysis to develop architectural design criteria. However, the intention is to use novel combinations of desired and selected guild species to structurally mimic a broad habitat type.

Habitat invention therefore uses desired-species niche analysis and guild-species selection as its core species selection techniques; ecological analogs and the other species selection techniques work as supplements. Polyculture design takes place through creating structural mimics of model patches using the polyculture analog process described above.

Habitat Co-optation: Aikido

To co-opt something is to divert it to a use or application different from its original purpose. Prime examples include the co-opting of pagan symbols and rituals by Christian churches that resulted in Christmas trees, Easter bunnies, and so on. In the forest-gardening context, co-optation means taking an existing ecosystem and redirecting its successional path and species composition to your own ends. This usually involves following the lead of the system you are co-opting by substituting desired but ecologically analogous species for those that exist or are establishing themselves as succession proceeds. It can also involve setting back succession and redirecting the community's development, such as by creating a series of gaps in an existing woodland or forest and planting trees that will grow to eventually create a nut forest. Habitat co-optation does not include the wholesale removal of an existing plant community and replacement of it with other species, however. Co-optation respects and includes the preexisting community to at least some extent, attempting to blend with and "aikido" the existing system.

As a result of the above intentions, habitat co-optation blends the methods of habitat mimicry and habitat invention:

1. Desired-species niche analysis provides important fodder for habitat co-optation, helping guide both your site analysis and your design of the interventions needed to co-opt the existing ecosystem. Model ecosystem analysis may also be helpful if you want to significantly alter the existing community to mimic something different than what is there, like a gap or clearing succession created within existing woods.

2. Existing-species niche analysis during site analysis and assessment is also fundamental to habitat co-optation. It allows you to pick which species to keep in your co-opted system, as well as to gather data for ecological-analog species selection. Your basic vegetation analysis and assessment should help you understand the nature of the existing ecosystem's architecture so you can work effectively with it.

3. The species selection process for habitat co-optation varies depending on exactly what you are doing. Various combinations of desired-species selection, existing-species selection, and ecological-analog selection seem to apply to most of the design projects we can think of in this strategy. Guild-species selection and native- and naturalized-species selection can also play significant roles depending on your druthers.

4. The polyculture design process for habitat co-optation also depends on your situation and your druthers. Making polyculture analogs is ideal if you have the information on model polycultures you need to do it. Building polycultures from scratch is also a reasonable option.

The guild and polyculture design strategies described above are the most practical and obvious possibilities we have used, heard about, or thought of so far.

Guild and polyculture design is the forest-garden design realm that carries the design process to its final and most detailed synthesis. All of the considerations discussed in the other three realms—infrastructure, vegetation architecture, and succession design—come to rest in the design of individual polycultures and individual patches. We have discussed each realm separately. Now let us discuss how we integrate them with each other and with the four stages of the design phase.

INTEGRATING THE FOUR REALMS AND THE FOUR STAGES

The connections between the four realms have been coming to the surface as we moved through the accounts above. How do we integrate all of this? Table 4.5 presents a summary of a complete forest garden design-phase process that incorporates all four realms into the four design-phase stages outlined earlier. This table says almost everything that needs to be said about how the four realms and the four stages come together. The theme of integration needs a little bit of conversation, though. Our attempt in forest gardening is to design an integrated ecosystem, so where does this integration occur in the design process?

The integration of the forest garden realms occurs at two design scales: the design concept and patch design. The design concept sums up the design as a whole entity. It is the seed of the design, and as such it pulls together all of the designer's key ideas and intentions and relates them to a specific piece of earth that the designer knows quite well by that time. Ideally, all the schemes and details flow

---

TABLE 4.5. A scheme for integrating the four realms of forest garden design with each other and with the four stages of the design phase.

Design Concept:

- Characterize your site-specific vision for the forest garden and its main organizing idea or features; characterize the horizon habitat(s) and overall successional scenario in a few words.

Schematic Design:

- Develop bubble diagrams to play with infrastructure layout—rough sizes, shapes, locations, and relationships between infrastructure features, elements, and functions.
- Characterize the architecture of the horizon habitat(s) on a very general bubble diagram. If working from plants to ecosystem, define habitats based on the niche requirements of desired species. If working from ecosystem to plants, base these choices on your model or imagined ecosystem.
- Select habitat-defining species, such as large trees and shrubs and essential desired species, using the species selection processes appropriate for your guild and polyculture design strategy.
- Integrate the horizon habitat, the key species, and the infrastructure on a sketchy overall-layout diagram. The diagram should also characterize the pattern of patches that generates the horizon habitat(s): roughly define patch size, shape, main function, architecture, and site conditions of each patch and, if you already know it, the key species in the patch.
- Define the horizon time in years from the present. Work out basic site preparation and establishment schemes (what, how, when, where). If you have a complex or long-term successional scenario, characterize the phases of the habitat's overall successional scenario on a rough timeline and create patch-pattern diagrams of earlier successional phases as needed.
- Rough out your budget for establishment, and begin estimating costs.

Detailed Design:

- Refine your schematic design: create an accurate layout diagram coordinating patches, planting beds, paths, and other infrastructure layout and functions. Accurately design the sizes, shapes, and locations of infrastructure, patches, and essential species already chosen. Characterize architecture, guild functions, management needs, and site conditions of each patch in more detail.
- Refine and further develop budget estimates based on your detailed design plan.
- If you have a long or complex succession, select one or two critical successional phases prior to the horizon from your schematic timeline. Use your detailed layout diagram for the horizon time as a base to create overlays depicting the patch patterns and characteristics of the earlier successional phases you chose.
- Complete your species palette. First, summarize species selection criteria based on the characteristics of the patches as defined in your design plan. Then select additional species for the patch purposes and guild functions left unfulfilled by your initial species selections in schematic design.

Patch Design:

- Design each patch: species, patterning, and spacing; successional timeline if needed; site preparation and establishment scheme; specific maintenance requirements; and so on. Use the polyculture design tools appropriate to your guild and polyculture design strategy.
- Complete final infrastructure construction details if needed: exact size, shape, color, texture, materials, construction, and edge treatments.
- Finalize site preparation and establishment staging plans for the whole garden once all patches are designed.
- Compile a master list of plants and other materials needed to establish the garden. Finalize budget estimates

or should flow from that seed. The design of individual patches and their polycultures is the most detailed articulation of the information contained in that seed, however. For the intended design concept to come into manifestation, each patch must contain within it the patterns of plants and plant sequences that will build the whole system the design concept envisions. All of the work between the concept and the patch is simply a way of clarifying your design intentions in more and more detail so the concept can express itself in its clearest fashion where the rubber meets the road: in the design of each little piece of the garden and the plants and animal-habitat elements you choose to place there.

It seems like a lot of work for something so seemingly straightforward as putting plants in the ground at a particular place and time. But again, you get to choose how much design intensity you want to engage with and how far you want to go. We offer the most intensive process we can imagine so those who want to take it to the maximum can go there with our guidance. If you want to back off, map out a simpler plan for yourself and have a blast in both the design and the implementation that comes afterward!

DESIGN PHASE HOW-TO

So, how do we go about actually designing a forest garden? Let's find out. We'll start with a few basic strategies that apply throughout the process, and a few questions to keep in mind as you go. Then we'll work through the four stages of the design phase in logical sequence, even though we know that this "rational, intuitive, and messy" process doesn't always follow a logical sequence in practice.

BASIC DESIGN STRATEGIES AND QUESTIONS

Keep the following thoughts in mind as you work through the design processes discussed from here on. These basic strategies come in handy at any stage of design and run as an undercurrent through much of the discussion that follows.

Design Is Rational, Intuitive, Messy, and Nonlinear
While the design exercises we offer in the rest of this chapter are logical and mostly orderly, we want to remind you of what we said at the beginning of the previous chapter: design is rational, intuitive, and messy, as well as nonlinear. There are several places in the design process flow that follows where we will discuss several sets of exercises or streams of information that you must work to integrate in a way unique to you and your project. Don't be afraid to read ahead or go back if you feel stuck, because sometimes the process we outline won't work for you in the order in which we present it. Follow your own star. Use what we offer as guidelines and reference points along your way, not a rigid plan.

Solve It Schematically First
If you get caught up in design details too early in your work flow, unresolved larger-scale problems may make your detailed solutions worthless. Resolve the basic patterns and large-scale issues first. Where should the various primary functions, patches, and activity areas go? Do the general sizes, shapes, locations, and relationships of the spaces and functions work? Should the pathways be linear, rectangular, looped, branching, or something else? What will be your basic implementation and establishment strategies? Based on this principle, plant placement is one of the last kinds of design choices we make, because it is one of the most detailed decisions. This principle lies behind the whole design-phase process outlined in this chapter, and it applies within each stage of the design phase, too. Get the big picture right, then work into more detailed issues.

Theoretically, then, the design work flows from guiding design concept to schematic design to details to specific plant placements in patch design. In practice, however, it doesn't always work that way. Sometimes the schematics or details sink the more general design patterns, or we can't figure out the broad patterns without working on the details. Most of the time, though, setting the overall placements of and relationships between functions, elements, circulation, and character at a general, schematic level is the best place to start.

This principle also applies to each of the little chunks of the design process. For example, when designing a particular patch in the last stage of the design phase you might want to use schematic bubble diagrams to initially sketch out the patch's functions or zones of use. Then you can choose species for each zone within the patch.

Iteration and Evolution

Design is an iterative process, meaning you cycle through a set of actions again and again. By repeating the cycle of generate, evaluate, select, generate, evaluate, select, you evolve better designs. You can apply this process at different stages of the design phase, using different design techniques each time (bubble diagrams, sandbox design, wild design, on-site design, and so on). Here's one way to do it. This example assumes you are working in the schematic design stage, but the principles discussed apply at any stage.

Generate Design Options

Generate a set of options for your schematic design. Either brainstorm on paper to generate many different option plans in a short time, or more slowly and consciously develop different options. How many ways can you organize the site or the garden? Locate and give things a general size and shape. Use bubble diagrams, sections/elevations, and ideas from chapter 2. Bubble out spaces, functions, paths, flows, character, and vegetation patches. Generate five to seven options—a few variations on a theme or two, as well as a few radically different ones. Note the positives and negatives of each option, and write down the intent behind each scheme, right on the sketches.

Don't always limit yourself to sensible and reasonable ideas. "Silly" ideas often have interesting implications if you follow them to their logical conclusions—on paper at least! Intentional mistakes, bold departures from convention, and random choices can be good learning experiences and can get your thinking outside the box.

Evaluate and Winnow the Options

Use your goals statement, your site analysis summary, and your gut sense to assess the options. Walk the site, imagining each scheme. Write down your questions and problems, what works and what doesn't, in each scheme. Find good and bad things about every one: things you like and don't like, goals met and not met, unexpected problems and benefits created by how you might lay things out. Then select the best two or three schemes overall, as well as any ideas you like from the others. You may need to hop to a more detailed level of design to make sure the schemes work at that level. That's okay—just don't get caught up in detailed design until you've settled on the best scheme at a larger scale.

Regenerate Design Options; Pick the Best and Leave the Rest

Improve the best schemes and see what new ideas you can generate based on your evaluations. Redraw and resketch these new or recombined ideas. Generate a new batch of options as well, and evaluate and winnow them along with your improved ideas.

Always start this iterative process by generating options dealing with fundamental choices and problems, laying out the bones of the site: the locations of key elements, pathways, and functions; choosing form families (that is, will you use primarily organic, curvilinear, or rectilinear lines and geometric or natural forms?); symmetry; and so on. As you design, evaluate, and winnow, you will probably find yourself gravitating toward one or two choices. At some point, you will have to make a basic choice between options before you invest in much more design. This may be when you have one or more options you are happy with, or when you run out of time to keep going. Stop iterating and make the choice.

Once you settle on a scheme, make sure the infrastructure, architecture, social structure, succession, and concept all align and that the scheme meets all or most of your goals and fits the site. Then work at a more detailed level. You can use the iteration and evolution process to design the various details you must decide upon in detailed design—and then use it again when you get into patch design, generating options for each patch, evaluating, winnowing, and generating new options as necessary to get a good result.

Design the Overstory, Then Work Down

The overstory garners the most sun, produces the most, and largely determines the underlying growing environment. In most cases, therefore, you'll want to design the overstory first, placing your most productive crops there. There may be cases where designing the overstory first doesn't make sense, such as when the understory plants are the main crop. You might then design the understory crop system first, fitting the overstory in around them.

Use Overlays to Coordinate Design Realms, Schemes, and Details

Tracing-paper overlays with different vegetation layers or site factors on each overlay help coordinate all the aspects of the design plan, such as grading and drainage; proposed zones of use; site preparation, implementation, and succession planning; schematic layout; and so on. Overlays are especially critical for succession planning and for coordinating the various layers of vegetation as you design. Make sure you have a roll or sheets of tracing paper on hand so this technique is available to you. It makes design much easier.

When Should I Drop the Paper and Design On-Site?

Each person will answer this question differently. Some will jump to on-site design after completing only a schematic design, if they even go that far on paper. Others will go into great detail on paper, playing with polyculture patterns for various patches, scheming out the zones of use in each planting area, and thinking through other odd details and conundrums before doing anything in the physical world. Ultimately, the choice is yours. There are a number of factors to balance in making this decision, and designing in the field doesn't mean you never sketch again, either!

The more accurate your base plan, the more worthwhile detailed on-paper design becomes. Even with an accurate base plan, always refer back to the ground when designing, and use the map primarily to store information and "think out loud." We often go back and forth between on-site design and paper design during the detailed-design stage. The site plan eventually becomes less useful anyway, since it's easier to design a garden bed on graph paper at a scale of 1 inch equals 4 feet (1:50 in the metric system).

Another factor is how you think and make decisions. Designing perennial beds on paper feels ridiculous to some people. Once they get to this level, such folks find it easier to lay out the plants in their pots and rearrange them until it looks good—quite a valid approach. Then again, sketching complex food-producing polycultures in plan and section views might help you think through the kinds of interactions the possible polyculture partners will have. It can therefore help you avoid mistakes that require taking the patch apart and putting it back together again differently. It also helps you estimate how many plants you will need for a given space so you can procure them.

The key thing to remember is that you never stop designing! Even as you put plants in the ground you will make adjustments, get insights, and so on—keep pencils and paper handy. Design detailing helps you clarify what you are doing, make sure the key pieces get put in place rather than getting lost in the shuffle, estimate your materials needs appropriately, and prevent at least some avoidable mistakes (such as those listed in table 4.6). Whether you

TABLE 4.6. Common forest garden design mistakes to avoid.

- Not articulating goals, or not setting clear or reasonable goals.
- Starting too big—planting more than you can reasonably water the first year or take care of from there on out. Start small and grow from there.
- Planting a forest garden as an icon, rather than a living space.
- Not analyzing the site enough to avoid site-specific problems.
- Not accounting for the possibility of vandalism in urban or suburban situations.
- Not checking for lead or other contamination in soils.
- Planting in poor microclimates (frost pockets, wind tunnels).
- Unwillingness to think through the design in many or all of its aspects: physically, biologically, socially, logistically, financially.
- Not selecting species or varieties resistant to diseases common to your area or common to the crop that may come to your area within the life span of the planting.
- Planting sun-loving plants in shady situations, and expecting them to perform well just because it's a forest garden.
- Spacing plants too close together; assuming that because it's a forest garden, we don't need to worry about proper spacing.
- Not providing sufficient space to move carts or other materials or equipment in or through the garden.
- Being impatient and not preparing the ground well enough.
- Lack of clear management oversight or accountability, especially in community, nonprofit, or demonstration garden situations.
- Assuming "low maintenance" or "largely self-maintaining" means you have nothing to do to manage the system.
- Not thinking through succession plans so that the horizon habitat develops naturally from the initial planting with minimal human input.

design in detail on paper or with stakes, string, and powdered lime on-site, keep envisioning your desired future right through planting and aftercare, making sure you manifest on the ground the goals that you have articulated for yourself.

How to Know When You Are Finished

This question is different from the previous one, though related. Even when designing on-site, you need to ask, "How much design is enough?" Your goals and your gut are the best guides. Does the design achieve the essential goals? (Check your design against your goals statement.) Does it work well with the site? (Check your design against your site analysis and assessment.) Does it feel right?

Can you implement it without major questions arising during installation? Do you have more energy to put into designing? Are you ready to begin implementation no matter where the design stands? Is the implementation strategy clear? Have you checked for mistakes or run it by one or two folks with a stake in the outcome or knowledge of the subject? At minimum, your design should allow you to place at least the major infrastructure elements and any woody plants with the confidence that you haven't made avoidable or large-scale conceptual mistakes. Others may design in much more detail to ponder possibilities and work through design issues. It all depends on how much fun you are having designing, how excited you are to get things in the ground and growing, and what time of year it is!

With these general comments in mind, let's begin exploring how to design, starting with the visionary seed: the design concept.

DESIGN CONCEPT: THE ORGANIZING IDEA

The design concept is the big idea that integrates the site, the goals, and the garden inhabitants in a unified whole, resolving the key issues and challenges this integration presents. It expresses the essence, not only of what the design will achieve once built, but also of the *means* of that achievement on your particular site. The design concept organizes all the elements of the design and gives them meaning, so they pull in the same direction. It guides the designer while creating schemes and details. A good design concept is a challenging ideal, not always achieved, but always worth pursuing. A unifying idea is what gives any landscape design or piece of art its juice.

Let's step back from the grandiose to give a relatively simple example of a design concept:

A small, crescent-shaped forest-edge garden sweeps around the northwest corner of the yard, forming a cozy, protected outdoor space with morning sun and afternoon shade. It provides fruits and berries for fresh eating and flowers for the table, while blocking unsightly views and leaving play space for the children. Having grown from the lawn through an instant succession, the garden's full-size fruit trees, shrubs, and diverse perennials now provide a lush, secluded getaway for relaxing in a comfy chair or eating in peace at the picnic table.

It brings images to mind, doesn't it? Design concepts intentionally use "image" and "action" words to evoke the reality you seek to create and the benefits it brings. Design concepts connect to motivating values, making them real and achievable. The statement above tells you what kind of garden it is, how it fits the site, and which goals it achieves. You can almost read the thought process behind its development. This design concept resolves conflicts (unsightly views, play space versus forest-garden space), achieves goals (fruits and berries for fresh eating, flowers for the table, secluded getaway), and offers guidance for schematic and detailed design (small, crescent-shaped, northwest corner, morning sun and afternoon shade, in addition to the above)—all in three full but complete sentences. It also provides just the guidance one needs to design the horizon habitat and successional scenario by describing the garden as a forest-edge and an instant succession growing out of the lawn.

How, Where, and When You Find One

To find or develop your design concept, you have to conceptually solve the design problem(s) in front of you. The main question to ask is, "What big idea integrates my forest-gardening goals with my site?" Maybe this idea arose already as you worked on goals articulation and site analysis. On the other hand, you may not get your concept until you mess around with the design at the schematic stage. Sometimes a unifying idea never comes. Discovering the organizing idea is one of those mysterious events that can be difficult, if not impossible, to arrange or explain. Make your offerings to the muse now! We can't necessarily control the insight or its timing, but we can

create fertile ground for the insight to sprout, take root, and grow. If you've done the work discussed so far, you've improved that intellectual soil. Whether you ultimately get one or not, working toward a unifying idea is essential to coherent design.

Design concepts sometimes arise from the goals or site analysis and assessment (A&A) work, especially the A&A summary—look back at that work and see whether you can find it lurking there. If an organizing idea hasn't arisen from this early work, then seek it early in the design phase. This may mean getting into schematic design, but start by looking directly for your organizing idea. Sometimes you can see, feel, or hear the design concept in response to a question you ask the land, either silently or out loud. Sometimes organizing ideas come in quiet moments on the site when all the thinking and questioning in your mind dies down. Some people get the big idea in meditation, from dreams or memories, from images in books, or by visiting other people's gardens.

Design concepts can also arise directly out of the site's existing character. For instance, Dave once noticed a spiral shape in the landform around an educational center in western Massachusetts. He didn't see it until late in the game, but once he saw it, it wouldn't let go of him and it became the basis for the design. The more Dave pursued the concept, the clearer its multiple benefits became. Enhancing this spiral form resolved all of the water-flow, pedestrian-circulation, social-space, microclimate, planting, and symbolic needs of the project. You know you have a good concept when it won't let go of you, and when it resolves all or most of the details with which you have to contend without forcing things. Sometimes multiple design concepts arise; in that case, you have to develop each one enough so you can evaluate and choose between them.

The design process itself should help you discover a good idea. At some point, though, if a concept does not arise naturally from the design work you may need to make a bold decision that organizes the design and ties things together. If all else fails, simply use an arbitrary element to organize the site and all of its elements—a path, a function, a shape, a pattern from a book, an archetypal geometry, a pattern from the site, or a habitat you choose to mimic. That arbitrary element serves the purpose of unifying the whole design. At the very least, make sure your concept describes the horizon habitat(s) and the overall successional scenario(s) of the garden. You need these two pieces of information to move ahead with your forest garden design.

Get Your Design Concept Down, and Get It Good

The goal of this exercise is that you have a written design concept three sentences or less in length accompanied by a clear, simple, site-specific diagram. The ideas in these two documents must organize the whole design and provide clear direction for the forest garden in terms of characterizing the horizon habitat and the successional scenario. Organizing ideas usually don't arrive in that form. Instead, we have to catch them in whatever form they arise and hone them as much as we can in the time we have available so they become the clearest touchstone we can get to guide our design.

If you are designing a simple forest garden with few social or aesthetic complications, discovering and defining your design concept may be a straightforward process of choosing your horizon habitat, your successional scenario, and a site-specific pattern for the garden. What we discuss below relates to more complex designs—thin or expand the process to meet your needs. Again, you may need to work on your schematic design before you can choose or discover your design concept, but start by seeing whether you can find it from the beginning. Design is often a nonlinear process, so you may need to come back to this exercise later.

Record Your Initial Thoughts

Begin by reviewing your goals and site analysis summary. Do your goals and solution-directions all head your design in a particular direction? Do they point in more than one direction? At some moment along the way did you have a flash of insight that tied it all

together and told you where to take the design? Do your best to summarize your thinking in pithy written statements and small "back-of-the-envelope" sketches. The sketches don't have to be accurate and to scale—they just need to represent the site and how the goals live there in a clear enough manner that the concept is comprehensible. Figure 4.1 shows three forest-garden design concepts to give you a sense of where you are headed.

You may need to iterate and evolve more than one option, but try to narrow your options to one before moving on if you can. If you haven't come up with anything reasonable in your first try, continue through the following steps. Even if you have an initial attempt down, you may want to go through these steps to check what you have done and to see whether you can improve your concept. If you feel you have a good draft of your design concept, you can go to the end of the exercise to test, refine, and revise your work. In fact, whenever you feel like you've "got it" as you move through the following steps, you can skip to the last step to finalize your work.

Review the Pattern Language for Inspiration

Patterns #9 through #22 in chapter 2 represent possible overall patterns of the forest garden that might suit your situation. Review these to see whether they have any bearing for you and your garden, either alone or in combination. Do you want a more or less formal layout (patterns #9 and #10) or a garden that mimics natural vegetational architecture (#11 through #18), or do you want to use the theory behind forest gardening to co-opt a more "classic" landscape pattern (#19 through #22)? These patterns are great for helping you decide upon your horizon habitat. Patterns #30 through #34 can help you think about succession and establishment, as can #16 and #18 and the discussion of succession design in the first section of this chapter. Establishment patterns such as these may fundamentally alter or affect your design planning, so make sure to consider them early.

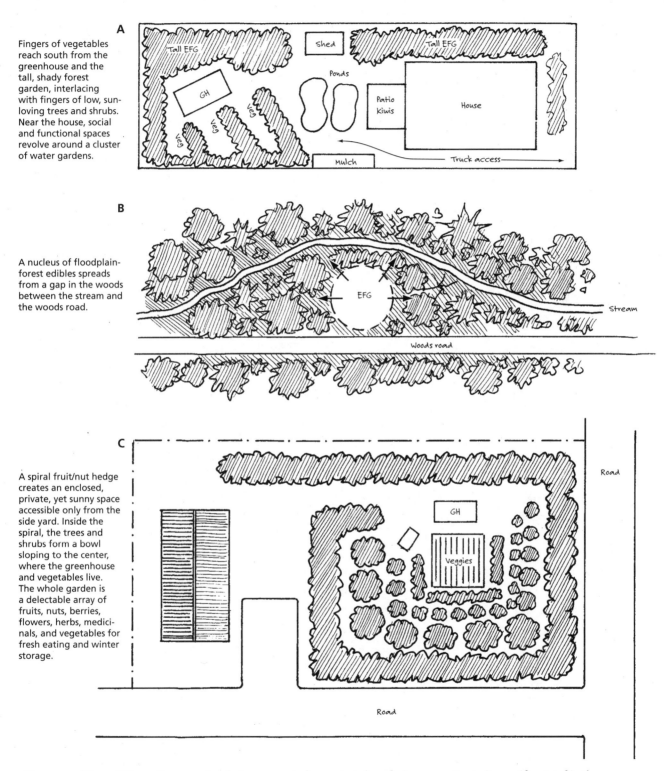

Fingers of vegetables reach south from the greenhouse and the tall, shady forest garden, interlacing with fingers of low, sun-loving trees and shrubs. Near the house, social and functional spaces revolve around a cluster of water gardens.

A nucleus of floodplain-forest edibles spreads from a gap in the woods between the stream and the woods road.

A spiral fruit/nut hedge creates an enclosed, private, yet sunny space accessible only from the side yard. Inside the spiral, the trees and shrubs form a bowl sloping to the center, where the greenhouse and vegetables live. The whole garden is a delectable array of fruits, nuts, berries, flowers, herbs, medicinals, and vegetables for fresh eating and winter storage.

FIGURE 4.1. Three different forest-garden design concepts demonstrate how design concepts are site specific, stated in three sentences or less, and easily sketched "on the back of an envelope." Design concept A expresses the essence of the scheme for our case study of Eric Toensmeier's and Jonathan Bates's forest garden design in Holyoke, MA. GH = greenhouse; EFG = edible forest garden.

Choose a Design-Concept "Seed Crystal"

Seed crystals for design concepts are categories of ideas or things that often organize and unify a site plan. If you have yet to discover your design concept, or if you want to refine what you've generated so far, it may help to consider whether your design's central idea may build on one of these seed crystals.

Forest-garden design concepts often crystallize around one or more of the following kinds of elements[1]:

- Horizon habitat or ecosystem character: "almost a thicket," "rich floodplain forest"
- Successional scenario: "a nut-tree clearing growing up within rich woods," "a rotational mosaic of vegetables, oldfield, shrubland, and woodland"
- Site use or function: "a gathering place for small groups"
- Relationships: "hidden behind," "towering over"
- Feelings: "peaceful," "mysterious"
- Character (of the space or object): "woodsy," "an intimate, leafy garden"
- Layout (2-D, its form on the ground): "circular," "linear"
- Space or volume (3-D): "a narrow gap surrounded by tall trees"
- Materials (usually less important, but potentially a theme): stone, brick

For example, is the core concept of your design that your backyard is an open shrubland surrounded by deep forest? Is there a feeling you want your forest garden to engender that is the main focus of your design? Does a single use or function determine the arrangement of all your garden features or elements?

Find Inspiration in Pictures or Other Gardens

Another option to help you find your concept is to look through both volumes of this book to see whether any of the pictures or illustrations give you the germ of an idea. Can they provide the unifying principle you need? You may need to look through gardening, ecology, or travel books or to wander in wild places, botanical gardens, or other people's places to gain your revelation. Try to abstract from the image that strikes you what seed crystal speaks to you and your site. Then write and sketch a concept that applies that idea to your circumstances.

If You Still Cannot Discover Your Design Concept

As we said before, sometimes the design concept does not make itself known until later in the design process, or it never does. You may need to go out on site, empty your mind, and listen. You may need to talk it out with someone else, either a friend, a family member, or a design professional. Sometimes a design concept is hiding in plain sight and you just can't see it because you are too close to the process or too attached to a particular outcome or way of seeing things. If you are stuck and short on time you may need to choose an arbitrary element to build your design around, but do this as a last resort.

If you decide not to develop a design concept yet, move into schematic design. Lightning may strike as you work on the schemes or details. Make sure you step back later to see whether a design concept has developed naturally in response to the further work. If you "get the concept" while doing some other task, make sure to take the time to write it down and draw a simple, no-nonsense diagram to represent it. Then come back to this section to refine, revise, and test it.

Test, Refine, and Revise Your Design Concept

To proceed with the following piece of work, you should have at least a first draft of a three-sentence-or-less concept statement and a thumbnail sketch. Now it is time to sharpen it up and make sure it is a viable concept. It takes time and effort to develop a crisp, clear statement that integrates and organizes all the essential ingredients outlined in your goals statement with the most influential characteristics of your site. Give yourself the time to do it well.

Read your design-concept statement out loud to yourself. Does it feel and sound clear as a bell? Read it to someone else, and get his or her response. Consider each word and whether it is the right one, or whether your body is telling you something is off. Use a thesaurus if needed to hone the wording. Make sure your design concept is in present tense and active voice, as in your goals articulation work.

Once you have a workable statement, ask yourself the following questions:

- If you succeeded in implementing your design concept as written and drawn, would you have achieved all the goals you set out in goals artic-ulation? Will the garden as conceived satisfy you? Reread your goals statement to help you answer this question.
- Will all the significant challenges identified in your site analysis and assessment have been addressed or resolved if the concept comes to pass? Will the site's needs have been met? Does it take advantage of the site's key oppor-tunities? Does the concept build on the solu-tion-directions that arose from your site A&A? Compare the concept to your site A&A work to help you decide.
- Does the concept "marry" the goals and the site? Does it embody your goals on your site in a way that reflects and honors both? Is the con-cept site-specific?
- Does the concept give you clear guidance for schematic and detailed design? Does it get all the elements you need to integrate pulling in the same direction? Does it clearly define the horizon habitat and the successional scenario? Think a bit about where you are going to go with the concept in schematic design to answer this for now. You'll get the full answer soon enough.
- Finally, and perhaps most importantly, does your design concept evoke the essence of the forest garden you want to create? Does reading it or looking at the sketch give you a good feeling in your body, bring a smile to your eyes and face, or create a lift in your heart?

Hone, rewrite, and resketch your design concept until the answer to all of the above questions is "yes." Pay attention to your body's signals as you ponder these questions and your concept, for if you feel discomfort about the ideas you have on paper, something is likely to be "off" in the concept. The clearer you can make this touchstone, the better it will guide your decisions later. Remember, you should be able to quickly and simply sketch the design concept, as well as write it in no more than three sentences. That way you can call it to mind without referring to a piece of paper stashed some-where. Once you have achieved that, pat yourself on the back, jump for joy, and then move into schematic design.

SCHEMATIC DESIGN: ROUGHING IT

The main purpose of schematic design is to work out the garden's rough layout, focusing on the rela-tionships among major garden features, elements, functions, vegetation architecture, and successional development. This prevents hard-to-fix strategic errors that can cause long-term irritation involving the whole design, not just a small area. For example, placing your mulch and compost piles in the wrong place can cause unnecessary extra miles of travel over your gardening lifetime. Strategic schematic thinking can significantly reduce the labor required to run a garden. If you have not yet worked out your design concept, schematic design also serves to help you find your concept. You may need to jump back and forth from schemes to details a little to ensure things fit, but focus on schematic design until your scheme works.

Specifically what do you design at the schematic stage? Four things, in a rough way: (1) the size, shape, and relative location of garden infrastruc-ture (landscape spaces, functions, features, and ele-ments); (2) the forest garden's horizon habitat architecture, both overall and in terms of the key

species and the pattern of patches that it contains;
(3) the habitat's overall successional scenario; and
(4) your budget for establishing the garden. Any
one or more of these topics may be the definitive
aspect of your design—for different projects the
most defining aspect of the schematic phase will
be different. For example, infrastructure patterning
may be the most critical and defining part of one
person's garden, while the canopy polyculture pattern may set the pace for another person's design.
Sometimes you'll need to work out infrastructure
and habitat patterning in tandem, while other
times the habitat is more flexible and can work
within the parameters that infrastructure sets. And
so on. It is hard to know up front which aspect of
the design will be most critical to you, though your
goals and concept will give you some guidance.
You mainly just have to dive in to find out.

Again, schematic design is not necessarily a linear
process. Iteration and evolution is a key strategy in
this phase. As you mess around with design options
you will discover which pieces have the fewest limitations and which have the most, which choices
have the most consequences for other design
choices, and which are most flexible. You simply
have to sketch things out and think through their
implications to figure it out. This means jumping
back and forth between the four schematic design
topics listed above as you go, because they all have
to come at once.

Starting Points and Key Ideas

The next subsections discuss the details of the
schematic design process and how to work with
these four topics of schematic design. However,
people often don't know where to begin putting
pencil to paper, which problems to solve first, or
generally where to start. We'll therefore begin with
a few ideas on that subject.

Start in the Most Difficult Place

When we avoid the most challenging design problems and design the easy things first, we often find
that the easy answers have to change to accommodate a good solution to the difficult challenges.
Which parts of your design are the hardest to penetrate, the thorniest to grapple with, the slipperiest
to grab onto? Get clear on that, and start there.
Which functions or elements have the most restrictive design criteria? Locate them first. The biggest
design challenges are the hardest to solve but are
more demanding of their context. Crack the tough
nuts first and leave the easy pickings for later.

Perhaps your site assessment revealed shallow-
to-hardpan soils that stay soaked in cool seasons
but get droughty in summer, while the plants you
most want to grow are deep-rooted or drought-
and wet-intolerant. What preparatory work can
break up the hardpan, adding more rooting depth
and soil water storage? The nature of that work will
influence the layout patterns, species selection,
polyculture design, and successional trajectory of
your forest garden. For example, deep chisel-
plowing and a series of taprooted green-manure
rotations before planting offer different layout
options than double-digging or raised beds. Your
irrigation-system choices will influence planting
patterns as well. Can you see how skipping over
these issues could lead you down a primrose path
you'd just have to walk back up anyway?

Begin with the Essentials

If no thorny problems stand in your way, consider
which goals are the most essential to achieve, which
design questions are most central to your design, or
which problems are the most important to solve.
Which plants or other design elements are most
critical to your happiness? Your early decisions
need to anchor these most essential elements of
your design. If you haven't done it already as part of
your goals articulation, prioritize the key goals and
design criteria to help you focus.

The Scale of Permanence

The scale of permanence can organize your design
thinking as well as your site analysis (see box 3.4).

Since landform and water-flow patterns are more difficult to change than vegetation, for example, think about how the grading and drainage affect other aspects of the design early on. Remember, though, that the scale of permanence is not a hard-and-fast rule, since in designed landscapes landform and water must respond to vegetation, zones of use, buildings, and so on, too, if the latter are more important to the design than the former. However, if you find you don't know what to consider next, the scale can help you think that through.

These starting points apply generally throughout the design process and within each of the four key aspects of schematic design, but especially in working out the basic patterns of the infrastructure and garden overall. Use your goals statement and your inner sense to guide you in choosing with which of the four topics of schematic design you should begin. We think most people will need to begin with infrastructure layout or habitat design or both in tandem, and so we lead our discussion with these two topics.

Play with Infrastructure Layout

Landform, water, and access issues come early in the scale of permanence because they are less ephemeral than vegetation. The key physical features and infrastructure elements usually relate directly to these landscape components and normally have more exacting design requirements than most plants as well, especially in terms of any necessary grading and drainage work. They also tend to cost the most money. For these reasons we should design grading, drainage, irrigation, circulation, and other infrastructure elements early in the process. Where are the paths and nodes going to be? What about the shed, the compost and mulch piles, the fences, the visual screen, and the patio? How will the irrigation system work in general, what kind of drainage and grading features must you have, where will the dry soil mound that provides habitat for native bees go, and so on? If you already have a clear concept, these decisions may be easy. If you don't, then you may have much more work to do. Even in the former case, though, you may find your concept shifting some as you work through the schematics.

Begin with the most difficult, important, or permanent issues, features, functions, or elements of the garden, as discussed above. Make sure you are clear about the design criteria for these items, that is, the size, shape, location, and relationship each item requires. In fact, keep an ongoing list of the design criteria for the different elements, because they may change or you may realize you have other criteria as you work on your design.

Lay tracing paper over your base plan, and get out your pencil and scale. Sketch options for the locations of the various elements on your list. Where are the logical places they might go? Sketch them on the plan one at a time in rough bubble-diagram format at the approximate size and shape they need to be. Some of these items will have more stringent location criteria than others and therefore may have fewer possible locations. Try to get and remain clear about the knowns and the variables. Play with many possible alternatives, using a fresh piece of tracing paper each time, and write on each sketch your evaluations and other thoughts as you go to help you keep your thinking clear. Iterate and evolve options. These sketches do not have to be nice and neat—in fact, we encourage messy drawings at this stage (see figure 4.2). Consider patterns from chapter 2 that apply to your situation, especially patterns #23 through #29, as well as #8, *Zones of Water Use*. Assess which design elements have the most influence on other choices for your project. Assess your options by comparing each one with your design goals and your site analysis. Looking at your goals and site A&A work is one way of staying on track or getting unstuck.

Expand the number of options and then narrow them, and do this several times until either you run out of time or energy or you find one that works well enough for your gut to feel satisfied. Somewhere along the line, it is good to run your

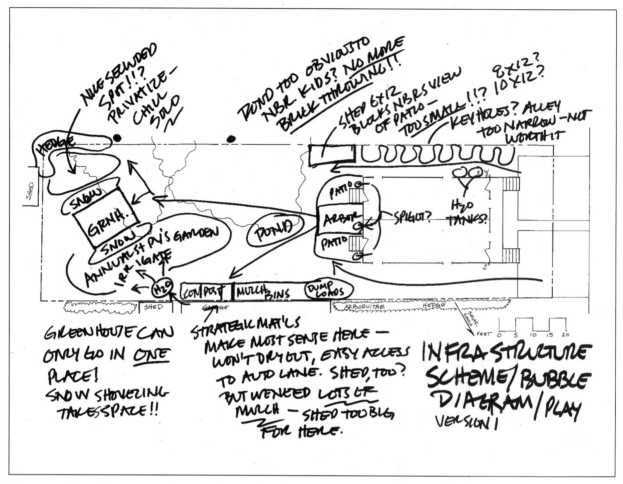

FIGURE 4.2. This schematic bubble diagram of a possible infrastructure layout for our design-process case study shows you that messy sketches are perfectly acceptable in this stage of design. Use very generalized bubbles, circles, arrows, and other symbols to help you graphically brainstorm, test various patterns, think through implications, and generate and evaluate options. Make sure you write your thoughts on the drawing, too! This keeps both sides of the brain engaged. *Field sketch by Dave Jacke.*

top options through the other topics of schematic design to see what implications each of your best options has for other aspects of the design. The overall question to ask is "Which pattern of elements creates the most harmonious design, meets the highest number of most important criteria, or generates the best set of relationships in the site plan?" When you have an answer to that question, you have the beginnings of a scheme to go on. Of course, this infrastructure scheme will have to be reconciled with a few other streams of design information, including vegetation architecture design.

Define the Horizon Habitat

As discussed earlier, you first characterize the kind of horizon habitat or habitats you want your forest garden to have during the design-concept stage using simple descriptors like "shrubland," "open woods," and so on. In schematic design, you get more specific by defining the spaces the different habitats will occupy and describing the density, patterning, and diversity of each vegetation layer for the habitat as a whole. If you are working from plants to ecosystem, define these habitat characteristics primarily based on the

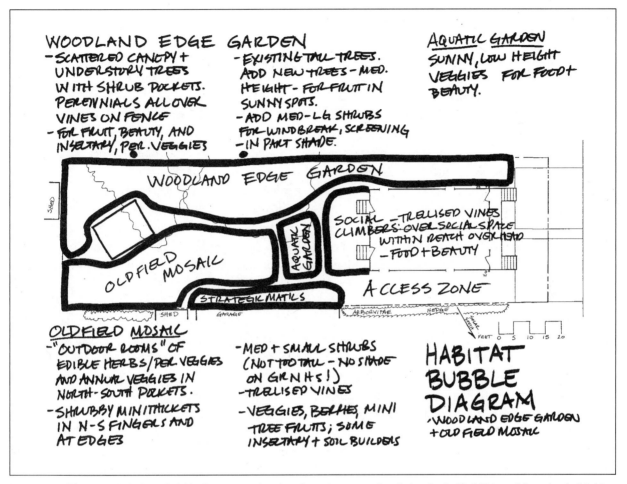

FIGURE 4.3. This simple habitat bubble diagram took only a few minutes to sketch, but it clarified Eric and Jonathan's thinking about how to organize their garden tremendously and gave them permission to move forward on their design with confidence. Sometimes sketching the obvious validates and grounds your work, freeing you from vague uncertainty that slows down your thought process. *Field sketch by Dave Jacke.*

needs and characteristics of your desired species—you may need to jump to the next exercise ("Select Habitat-Defining Species") before doing this one in that case. If you are working from ecosystem to plants, you should have some sense from your model ecosystem analysis of what kinds of habitat architecture will mimic your model habitat. Let's hope your model ecosystem analysis yielded overall habitat architecture descriptions, as well as patch patterns and polyculture groupings. If not, you may have to invent as you go along, but that's okay.

Begin defining your horizon habitat(s) by creating a very quick bubble diagram laying out the rough size, shape, and location of your main habitat areas (see figure 4.3). If your forest garden will consist of only one horizon habitat, then you don't need to bubble-diagram as long as you know where the edges of the habitat will be. In the latter case, simply begin to spell out the architecture in writing on a sheet of paper or one of your other schematic drawings. In the former case, write your thoughts about the basic architecture of each habitat on the bubble diagram. In either case, include in your notes at least the density and patterning of each vegetation layer. If you have an idea already, name the dominant species or kinds of plants in the overstory and outline your intentions for the diversity of the layers. For example, one habitat might be a "mixed fruit-tree woodland with a low, unevenly spaced canopy; scattered fruiting-shrub clumps in small canopy openings; and useful and functional herbs forming a diverse, continuous ground cover," while another could be an "open nut savanna over perennial vegetable patches and multifunctional ground-covering herbs."

This bubble diagram should be very quick and simple. Go into more detail than your design concept, but avoid getting too detailed—you will have an opportunity to define the patches within each habitat later in the process. Clearly you will need to integrate these thoughts with decisions about infrastructure, successional scenarios, and patch patterns. With some brief written descriptions and very rough sketches or bubble diagrams of the habitats, you can work with some of the other pieces you need to take your habitat design to a deeper level.

As you work on this, remember to check out relevant patterns in chapter 2 and use those that relate to your situation and strike your fancy. These include #38, *Three-Layer Minimum*, and #39, *Lumpy Texture*, among others.

Select Habitat-Defining Species

Habitat-defining species are those that characterize or determine the structure or function of the plant community. In the phrase *apple orchard*, for example, *orchard* denotes the pattern and purpose of the habitat, and *apple* the dominant and defining species. Ecologists consider species that individually or collectively cover more than 50 percent of an overstory the *dominant* species and give the habitat their name(s), as in oak-hickory forest. Habitat-defining species may also be those that most directly fulfill the planting's primary purpose, even if they are understory plants (a ginseng plantation,

for example), for we design the habitat around them.

The fact that we design the habitat around such essential desired species is why we select them this early in the design process. Their niche characteristics will affect many design factors, including planting-bed or patch sizes and locations, shade and sun, water and maintenance needs, and other issues relevant to patch patterning. For most forest gardeners, defining species will include essential trees and larger shrubs from your desired-species niche analysis or overstory large tree- and shrub-layer plants from the ecological-analog process, depending on which selection strategy you intend to use. The size of plants that are significant in defining the habitat and its patch patterns depends in part upon the scale at which you are designing.

This is one of the first tests of your design: if you find that many of your most-desired species do not fit your habitat plan for some reason, you need to reconsider your direction. Do you need to do more site preparation or to change your habitat specifications to accommodate your favorite plants, or are things working out just right? Do you need to drop some species from your list because they are unsuited to your situation? It may behoove you to look over all of your desired species and make sure that you understand what kind of habitat needs they have so you can make sure to accommodate them in your schematic design.

We discuss species selection processes in the detailed-design stage later in this chapter (page 274). Of those discussed there, desired-species and ecological-analog selection are the most relevant. Please go to that section for details on these selection processes. Come back to this section when you have created an initial master list or species palette containing only habitat-defining species using primarily desired-species or ecological-analog selection or both. You will need the design data for these keystone species during the next part of schematic design.

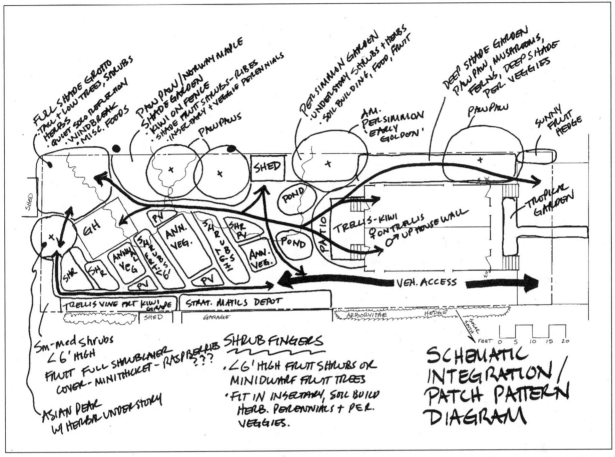

FIGURE 4.4. This bubble diagram roughs out the integrated layout of infrastructure, patch patterns, and key plants for our design-process case study. Patches and planting beds are mostly synonymous and are roughly sized to fit typical or key shrubs or vegetable gardens. Path patterns are shaping up, and the specific architecture of patches is getting more defined. Some species have landed in their approximate locations, and options for the pond(s) are developing. This diagram is not completely settled, but it is good enough to go on for now. More iteration will occur in detailed design to refine it further. *Field sketch by Dave Jacke.*

Pattern Patches and Integrate the Layout

The patterning of the patches within a habitat—patch patterning—usually follows work developing the placement of major garden features and elements, the size and location of habitat areas, and the selection of primary habitat-defining species. Patch patterning typically forces you to integrate these three themes—we'll focus our comments here on patch patterning, but you will find that the sizes of key plants will affect the sizing of planting beds and the locations of paths, and that patches tend to be synonymous with planting beds. Refer back to

your infrastructure schemes, goals, and site A&A along the way so you can keep clear on the various issues you are trying to resolve. Think about solar access, views, social spaces, practical management issues, and the like. Look through patterns #23 through #52 in chapter 2 for ideas and inspiration, too. This plan should start pulling all the pieces together in an approximate way.

The final drawing from this work can be a quick and dirty bubble diagram like figure 4.4: a rough sketch that lays out the basic pattern and structure of the garden's infrastructure and describes the approximate size, shape, location, main functions, architecture, and site conditions of each patch. However, you may find that you need to iterate and evolve to get to the final sketch because of the number of things you are attempting to synthesize. You may also have to pop back to one of the other pieces of the puzzle as a separate issue to get there. Overlays of tracing paper are often helpful for relating the various pieces of work to each other.

Start patch patterning by defining the patches in the canopy or overstory layer. Your habitat bubble diagram should tell you whether the canopy will be mostly evergreen or deciduous, dense or more open, dominated by fruit trees or by nuts. Here you will define the patterns within those general prescriptions. For example, if there will be variations in canopy density you should now decide where the open and dense areas will be. If there will be patches of varying species composition, where will they be, how big will they be, and what species will they contain? How do these overstory types relate to the underlying site conditions and to the other garden functions you have in mind, such as wind protection, visual screening, social gathering spaces, views, and so on? Define the characteristics of each patch as listed in the previous paragraph. Clarifying these characteristics for each patch greatly helps you determine what plants to select and place in each patch for your guilds to work. What kinds of patches lie within the habitats you've laid out? Which vegetation layers exist in which patches? How big should they be?

Once you have chosen reasonable placements for the larger-scale elements and the overstory patches in bubble-diagram fashion, you can develop a pattern for the understory vegetation patches using bubble diagrams that are more specific. You may want to design your overstory polycultures using the habitat-defining species you have already chosen before designing the understory patches, but you can also wait to do that until you have done more species selection later.

Define the purpose(s) of each patch. What purposes you choose for a patch will depend on your goals, the patch location, the growing conditions, and whether or how you want to apply ideas such as zones of use or planting-bed zones to your garden. Remember to think through your patch and garden guilds as discussed in the guild and polyculture design section earlier this chapter (page 239). What guild functions should be in which patches for the guilds to work properly? Will a particular patch be a beneficial-insect polyculture, a pocket of monoculture production, or a polyculture including crops, insectary plants, and dynamic accumulators? A temporary soil-improvement patch, or a permanent living fixture? Do you intend it mostly for insectary habitat and privacy screening, with a few nibbles mixed in, or is it primarily for crop production? If so, which crop(s)?

As you can see, these patch characteristics interrelate, so you may not know where to start. In most cases, the purposes should govern, but this varies from situation to situation. Sometimes you can't figure out all of these characteristics for every patch. So don't get too caught up in defining patch characteristics in detail; focus on defining purposes and architecture enough to guide you into the next steps. Your site analysis and goals, as well as patterns from chapter 2, should help greatly in defining the patch patterns and purposes. See especially patterns #44, *Polyculture Patches*, and #45, *Pockets of Production*. You will have additional chances to define the patches in greater detail during successional scheming and in detailed design.

Naming or numbering each patch will help you later in the process, especially if the name relates to the "theme" or purpose of the patch. We have created patches consisting of "all edible leafy greens" and "the three perennial sisters," as well as "all insectary" and "edible roots" patches, and so on.

It is a relief to remember that it is hard to eat all of the perennial vegetables that you can grow in a forest garden of even moderate size. You will therefore probably have large areas of primarily soil-building, ground-covering, and insectary polycultures whose

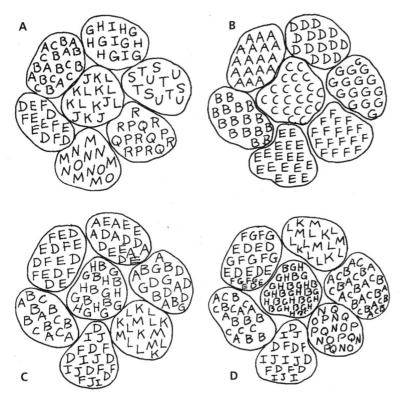

FIGURE 4.5A–D. There is more than one way to make a polyculture. Here are four variations, each with seven patches: (a) all seven patches are polycultures, each patch has different species, and each species occurs in only one patch—very high diversity; (b) seven monoculture patches—low diversity; (c) each patch has different mixtures of species, but some species are in more than one patch; (d) some plant combinations are repeated in different patches. The implications for design time, management ease, learning about plants and plant combinations, and potential species interactions vary for each of these examples.

design does not have to be as intensive or detailed as for crop or mixed crop-and-functional-plant polycultures. Yet by designing in patches, you set up clearer design detailing, species selection, and management. With a sense of the purposes, management, architecture, and conditions of each patch, you can compile a list of all the guild functions that must occur in which growing conditions in what vegetation layers. This clarity will greatly assist you during detailed design in selecting species for your garden and in selecting species from your species palette for each patch.

When patterning your patches, remember that patches and polycultures occur at several scales simultaneously; most tree patches are larger than herb patches, for example, simply because of the size of the plants involved. Yet even for herbaceous perennials, you can have polycultures at different scales, though their levels of diversity and usefulness to us vary. Unless you choose otherwise for

your own reasons, we suggest that each polyculture patch contain between two and seven species to help you keep things manageable and understandable. This means that the pattern of patches will be critical in creating diversity and functional interconnection between many guild members.

Designing your patch patterns does require you to think about your detailed design a little bit, especially with regard to the planting patterns and functions. Consider a garden area consisting of seven patches (see figure 4.5). You could design a maximum-diversity polyculture where all seven patches are polyculture patches, each patch contains a unique mixture of plants, and each species occurs in only one patch (figure 4.5a). At the other extreme, you could create seven monoculture patches where each patch consists of only one species, but the species is different from that of the others (we call such monopatches "pockets of production" when the species grown is a crop;

figure 4.5b). Taken as a whole, we could still consider these seven monopatches a polyculture, though one that is far less diverse and interactive than the seven polyculture patches mentioned previously. In between these extremes, you could design a set of patches where each contains a unique combination of species, but some species occur in more than one patch (figure 4.5c), or a polyculture where some combinations of plants get repeated in several patches (figure 4.5d).

Each of these kinds of polycultures has different uses. If you want to grow crops singly to keep things simple for yourself but still have a somewhat diversified system, the monopatch design makes sense. Many vegetable gardens end up in such a pattern. However, this pattern offers pests easy pickings since their hosts are still concentrated. The different polyculture patches of the first example offer the most diversity in the smallest space but may present problems of insufficient pollination and difficult management and harvesting for some crops. We would also need to design each patch separately, increasing the design workload. Repeated polyculture patch designs offer opportunities to save on design time and to observe how the polyculture works in more than one case. This may reveal more information to the gardener than if only one version of each mixture gets planted. Thinking about your patch functions and character in these terms will help you design your patch pattern and your species mixtures later on in design.

Once you have a rough diagram that seems to pull together the key species, the infrastructure, and the habitat and patch design, you have done the biggest part of the integration you will need for schematic design. You aren't quite done with schematic design, though. We still have to take a stab at succession design and look at budget issues to some degree.

Scheme Your Succession

The other core task of schematic design is further defining the successional scenario of the habitat overall, including at least defining the horizon time and working out site preparation schemes. For those with complex or long-term successional scenarios, it may also entail a successional timeline. This involves thinking through the key phases of the successional scenario, estimating each phase's life span, and characterizing the architecture of the whole habitat in each phase in general terms.

Set Horizon Time

Most of you should set your horizon time using your canopy or overstory species. You will most likely want to set these plants at spacings that relate to their mature crown diameter. Therefore, try to estimate how many years it takes for the various species to reach that size, and how long-lived they are (see page 528). If the ages to maturity of the various canopy plants varies by many years or some live much shorter lives than others, it would behoove you to plan accordingly. You could set your horizon time at the maturity of the longer-lived species, include the shorter-lived species in the horizon habitat, and assume you will replant the shorter-lived species somewhere during your successional scenario. On the other hand, you could use the same horizon time, not include the shorter-lived species in the horizon habitat, plant the longer-lived species closer together, and assume you will cut out the shorter-lived species as they die and let the longer-lived species fill in the holes. For example, fruit trees such as apricots are estimated to have a useful life of 25 to 30 years, while peaches may yield for even less time. On the other hand, mulberries and persimmons may yield for 150 years or more, and persimmons begin their maximum bearing phase in 25 to 50 years (see the "Estimated Useful Life Spans of Selected Woody Species" table in appendix 2). You could therefore plant apricots, peaches, and other shorter-lived fruits with mulberries and persimmons among them so that as the latter begin their long maximum bearing period the former are getting shaded out and it doesn't matter because the former are getting old anyway.

Ponder Site Preparation

Site preparation can be a tough nut to crack, or it may be a cinch. Read chapter 5 in depth to help you reckon what to do. Your site analysis should have identified the site conditions that may be limiting. Now evaluate the options for how to deal with them. Your goals work should have helped you set a "policy" on whether to adapt to site conditions or modify them to suit your plant's needs. If you have done desired-species niche analysis, it should help you understand how to proceed if you want to grow those species. Let these data guide you.

Map out your strategy on tracing paper: where you will do broadscale cultivation and cover crops, where you will do double-dug beds, and where you will simply sheet-mulch, for example. These choices may be a major factor in determining your horizon habitat, or they may not—it depends on your site and your willingness to invest in modifying it. Your budget and your horizon habitat scheme will also influence your site preparation plans—work back and forth on all these aspects. If your site conditions are complex, you may need to work out specific site preparation plans and sequences both in writing and on your site plan. Think it through well; the effort is definitely worth it over the long run. If your site preparation strategies are complex, you may need to do one or more bubble diagrams to work these out. For example, you might decide to do a series of cultivations and cover crops starting in one area and expanding to other areas as you plant your forest garden in stages.

Create a Successional Timeline and Patch Diagrams?

Not every forest gardener must do these steps, though you may choose to. Those of you with challenging successional scenarios have the greatest need to create a successional timeline, and perhaps even to bubble-diagram the pattern of patches in a phase or two between the horizon and the initial planting. This is particularly true if your horizon is far in the

TABLE 4.7. A sample successional timeline for a forest garden habitat on a site where a fruit-tree orchard already exists. The goal is that a small fruit patch succeeds to a fruit/nut woodland over time. The site has many soil improvers early in succession and then gradually shifts to a focus on insectary-habitat plants later on.

Approx. Year	Phase: Notes
2006	
2008	**Site Prep:** Deep tillage to reduce compaction. Series of cultivations and cover crops over two growing seasons for soil improvement.
2010	**Establishment:** Phased planting over two to three years: sheet mulch and dense planting of nuclei of sun-loving herbs and young shrubs for small fruit. Herbs are mostly soil improvers and ground covers, with some insectary plants and perennial vegetables.
2015	**Oldfield Habitat:** Herbs dominate as shrubs grow. Soil improves. Harvest perennial vegetables and cut flowers; nurture ground covers for weed control.
2025	**Shrubland:** Minithickets of small-fruit-bearing shrubs dominate, with patches of herbs in and around them. Harvest fruits, perennial vegetables, cut flowers. As herbs age and decline, begin to shift species functions to insectary plants from soil improvers. Maintain ground covers as needed. Plant clumps of fruit and nut trees in herb pockets among shrubs at end of phase or as existing orchard declines.
2030	**Shrub-Tree Mosaic:** Trees start shading out sun-loving herbs and shrubs. Replace sun-loving species with shade-tolerant species piecemeal as shade deepens, shifting sun shrubs to shade herbs. Maintain shrubs in sunny patches.
2050+	**Fruit/Nut Woodland:** Trees dominate, but wide spacing and clumping leave sunny patches for shrubs and herbs. Replace aging shrubs as necessary to maintain small-fruit production

future and there are several distinct phases in between or you are working on a rotational scenario.

A timeline can be a simple affair or a complex one. Simply draw a straight line down the left edge of a piece of paper and break it into segments to denote the phases of succession. Make a column along the line to estimate the time from the present to the beginning and end of each segment. Then write notes about each segment next to the line, such as the site conditions, disturbances required, dominant plants or plant types, and main functions or purposes of each phase (see table 4.7). For example, you may want the early phases of your succession to focus on soil improvement with beneficial-animal habitat secondary, while those priorities may flip in later succession. In what phase might that switch occur, what conditions will be present when it does, and will you need to intervene to make the switch happen?

A timeline may be all you decide to play with at this stage of the design phase, but if you are interested or feel a need, you can also bubble-diagram some earlier phases of succession as overlays on top of your schematic design plan. Your timeline should help you decide which phase or phases to diagram—pick something in the middle when the architecture is significantly different from that of the horizon. Then make a bubble diagram of what you expect your patch patterns and conditions will be for that time period.

Successional considerations may affect your overall layout scheme and patch patterning. You may need to revisit this work after thinking through some of the implications of the timing issues.

Rough Out Your Budget

The final task of schematic design is to begin getting a handle on how you will pay for all this and what it will cost. How much can you afford to pay in the establishment phase? Can you pay for all the plants and site preparation at once, or will you have to plant the garden in stages so you don't break the bank account? At first, the main thing is to look over your finances and settle on a realistic figure for your implementation budget on a yearly basis, if you haven't done that as part of goals articulation. As you get further into the schematic design process, you can jump back to the budget issues and estimate costs for various site preparation strategies, for example, or the cost of the canopy species or infrastructure you select (table 4.8 provides a list of possible budget categories to consider as you develop your estimates). This will

---

TABLE 4.8. Possible categories of budget items needed to develop and maintain a forest garden.

Site Preparation
  seed
  soil amendments (compost, fertilizers)
  mulch
  equipment rental
  hired labor (e.g., for tillage or clearing)

Infrastructure
  sheds, buildings, arbors
  fencing, trellis
  irrigation
  pathways, patios, and so on
  furniture
  sculpture and ornament

Establishment
  plants
  mushroom inoculum
  soil amendments
  mulch
  tools and equipment (e.g., hoses, shovels, wheelbarrow)
  labor
  food for laborers

Upkeep
  mulch
  soil amendments
  plants and seed
  management tools and equipment
  harvest and storage equipment
  iced-tea glasses
  hammock repair

---

shape your sense of how to establish your garden as you design, and it may change your sense of your establishment or successional scenario. For example, if you find you have high site preparation costs, you might decide to establish using nuclei that merge rather than a broadscale instant succession that would require buying and planting large quantities of plants all at once.

As you can see, even schematic design can be a complex business. Working with the infrastructure, horizon habitat, canopy design, successional scenario, and budget so they all tie together requires following your nose, trusting your instincts, and working back and forth from one topic area to another. Given the nonlinear and idiosyncratic nature of each person and each project, we can't tell you what to do in a strict order. It is a rational, intuitive, and messy process, but it is fun, an intellectually challenging puzzle, and worth it in the end. Clearly, it is good to work out how all of these schematic design topics relate to one another. If you are lucky and have a simple set of goals and a simple site, the process will be a breeze. If not, tough it out and persist. The more clarity you get at the schematic level, the easier it will be when you get to detailed design.

You want to end the schematic stage with a single set of tracing paper overlays depicting and coordinating the rough infrastructure layout; the horizon habitat architecture with its patch pattern and functions and perhaps some of the key species located in a sketchy way; and one or more sketches of earlier phases of succession for the habitat overall (if needed). You may also need one or more drawings portraying your site preparation and garden establishment phasing. All of these should have notes on them helping explain the drawings. In addition, you should have the beginnings of your species palette with a list of habitat-defining species and a rough budget for the project, including the ballpark costs of infrastructure and site preparation. You may also need a timeline and other documents estimating and characterizing the successional scenario of the habitat at large.

DETAILED DESIGN: NITTY GRITTY

Schematic design begins the integration of your goals, site, and garden inhabitants and prevents major strategic mistakes. You must now get more specific about all the features and characteristics you laid out roughly there, bringing your design ideas to a state of concrete clarity.

The boundaries between the schematic and detailed design phases are not always clear, but the distinction is useful. The kinds of drawings you do in the two phases are different. Schematic drawings are sketchy and not very accurate, mainly taking the form of bubble diagrams. They primarily deal with relationships between functions and spaces, generate large-scale options for you to choose between, and help you work out the coordination of infrastructure, habitat, canopy, succession, and budget. Detailed design drawings are harder-edged, clearer, crisper, and drawn with as much accuracy as you can muster. They take the chosen scheme and make it more accurate and more buildable. During detailed design, you make a host of decisions about the garden's myriad particulars. You can make such detailed decisions now that you have an overall scheme that you know works, that achieves your goals in the larger sense.

During the detailed-design stage you should:

- refine your overall schematic design plan to create a more accurate layout, resolve outstanding issues, accommodate new information from late in the schematic stage, precisely locate principal species already chosen, and characterize patches in greater detail;
- summarize criteria for further species selection;
- finalize plant species composition of the garden overall, that is, complete your species palette;
- determine the exact size, shape, location, color, texture, materials, construction, and edge treatments of all major garden infrastructure, "hardscape" elements, and landscape features, including especially finalizing any grading issues; and
- refine and further develop your budget estimates.

The order of this to-do list provides a good general guide for the order of events in the detailed-design stage. However, this will certainly vary depending on your goals, your site, and the succession and polyculture design schemes you intend to use. As in schematic design, begin with the most difficult, important, or permanent elements. This usually means the infrastructure but may also include larger trees and shrubs or the canopy as a whole.

At this stage, some of you may decide to jump to design on-site, at least to some degree (see "Designing on Paper versus Designing On-Site" on page 170). However, while you may choose to work out your design on the ground with stakes or other tools, you must still characterize the patches you designate and use that information to select species. It is usually also beneficial to accurately draw what you work out on the ground so you have a record and can use the drawing to help you make budget estimates.

Refine Overall Layout and Horizon Patches

Now take your schematic plan to the next level. Again, you will be working with the integration of infrastructure, key species, and habitat design, so it is hard to give you exact design-process sequences. It usually works best to go through area by area or patch by patch and make decisions about how to accommodate all the needs and opportunities each space presents. The goal is to end up with a hard-line drawing depicting accurate design intentions

for each square foot of the garden. You should depict your intentions both graphically and in writing, as always.

Accurately define the locations, sizes, and shapes of the infrastructure features and elements, and, if these thoughts come to mind, note down their possible materials, construction, colors, textures, and edge treatments. By the time you finish refining your overall layout plan there should be little need to move these features later in the process, but you are likely to erase and move things around a lot during the detailed design stage. You may need to enlarge drawings or draw more detail in one or more areas. You can start out with sketchy drawings as you work on details, but ultimately you should aim to create hard-line drawings detailing the exact size, shape, and location of every element (see figure 4.6).

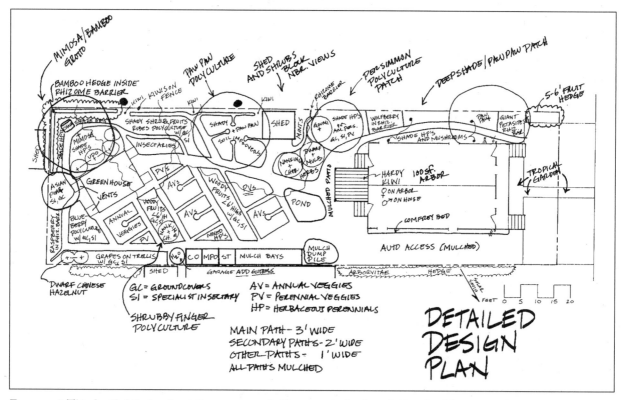

FIGURE 4.6. This detailed-design sketch for our case study illustrates the harder-edged style of drawing used in this stage of design. Use medium-hard pencil rather than marker or soft pencil; use your engineer's scale often to get accurate paths, beds, trellises, and so on; a circle-drawing template will help you draw accurate plant crowns quickly. Notice the similarities and differences between this and figure 4.4 and you will begin to understand the shift in design thinking that happens from schematic to detailed design. Notes on the drawing include species names and more details on proposed guild functions in understory layers. *Sketch by Dave Jacke.*

For patch design, the key thing that must emerge from this refinement process is a set of design criteria for each patch. These criteria will help you select species for your species palette and choose species from your species palette to put in each patch. You already accomplished much of this work in schematic design, but now you have an opportunity to look at what you did, think it through in more detail, double-check your assumptions, make changes, and fill out the longer list of patch characteristics below more completely. Remember to consider the garden-wide guild functions of the habitat when refining the patch patterns and functions, integrating garden and patch guilds into your patch characterizations as appropriate. If you have a complex succession, you will need to do some of this work for earlier successional phases (see "Characterize Midsuccession Patches If You Must," below), but start working with the horizon for now.

Make sure that each patch (or set of patches) has attached to it graphic depictions or descriptors for the following characteristics:

- accurate size, shape, and location;
- primary purpose or guild functions, as well as secondary ones;
- architecture in terms of plant sizes and forms (tree, shrub, herb) or density of the various layers, as well as their patterning and plant species or kind;
- site conditions, especially sun/shade, moisture, and soil fertility, *at the horizon time*; and
- management needs or regime.

You can note these patch characteristics right on the drawing or make a separate list.

Note that here we mention defining the primary and secondary purposes of each patch. While fruit production may be the primary purpose of one patch, you need to decide whether the other plants in the patch should be soil improvers, beneficial-insect habitat, both, or something else. Or perhaps the purpose changes from early to late succession, from soil improvers as the crops get started to insectary plants as they reach peak production. Obviously, you are likely to favor plants that can do more than one of these functions, but it is good to think through your priorities.

Define architecture in terms that are the easiest for you to design. Generally this means you must think about the actual sizes and forms of the plants you want in the patch, such as "small to medium shrubs" or "large herbs." You can use table 4.9 to coordinate your architectural specifications with the terms we use to describe the height categories of plants in the Plant Species Matrix in appendix 1. If you want to use the layer definitions instead because they are easier for you to envision or give you more latitude, you can use the data in table 4.10 to keep your language consistent and relate the layer definitions to the plant sizes in table 4.9.

None of these patch qualities are independent of each other. Coordinate the patch purpose with the

TABLE 4.9. Plant forms, height categories, and the height symbols used for them in the Plant Species Matrix (appendix 1). These relate directly to the layer definitions in table 4.10.

Form	Height	Category	Symbol
Tree	100+ ft./30+ m	Very large	vl
	50–100 ft./15–30 m	Large	l
	25–50 ft./8–15 m	Medium	m
	12–25 ft./4–8 m	Small	s
	0–12 ft./0–4 m	Dwarf	d
Shrub & Bamboo	25+ ft./8+ m	Extra large	xl
	12–25 ft./4–8 m	Very large	vl
	6–12 ft./2–4 m	Large	l
	3–6 ft./1–2 m	Medium	m
	6–36 in./15–100 cm	Small	s
	0–6 in./0–15 cm	Prostrate	p
Vine	12+ ft./4+ m	High	h
	0–12 ft./0–4 m	Low	l
Herb	6+ ft./2+ m	Very large	vl
	3–6 ft./1–2 m	Large	l
	18–36 in./50–100 cm	Medium	m
	6–18 in./15–50 cm	Small	s
	0–6 in./0–15 cm	Prostrate	p

		TABLE 4.10. Forest-garden vegetation layers defined.

TABLE 4.10. Forest-garden vegetation layers defined.

Layer	Height	Definition / Plant Forms Included
Relative		
Overstory	any	The topmost layer of any two or more layers of vegetation
Canopy	12–150+ ft./4–45+ m	Any overstory higher than 12 feet (4 m): trees, shrubs, vines
Understory	any	Any layer of vegetation under an overstory
Absolute		
Tall Tree	50+ ft./15+ m	Trees and vines
Low Tree	12–50 ft./4–15 m	Trees, large shrubs, and high vines
Shrub	6–12 ft./2–4 m	Trees, shrubs, vines, and very large herbs
Herb	0.5–6 ft./0.15–2 m	Herbs, shrubs, trees, and scrambling vines
Ground	0–0.5 ft./0–15 cm	Any plants, woody or herbaceous, plus the current year's leaf litter or mulch
Vine	0.5+ ft./15+ cm	Woody or herbaceous climbing vines

management regime, architecture, and growing conditions. Patch size may depend on the size of the defining plants for the patch. You may need to think about the specific needs of your desired crops to define some of these purposes. If the patch lies under a fruit tree, perhaps you want low-growing ground covers that double as fertility or insectary plants there, so you can easily pick up dropped fruit or get in to prune, spray, or check for pests. You probably won't want to dig up the soil under the tree every year to harvest root crops or to mow under the tree every week or two. Architecture plays into these considerations, too. Is the fruit tree going to have low or high branches? The size and kind of tree, and whether you will prune it, will create different shade conditions for the patch underneath it. How will these conditions affect your choice of plants in the patch below? You may want to create patches of tall herbaceous insectaries to help perform aesthetic functions such as privacy

screening, but that won't work well under a low-hung dwarf or semidwarf fruit tree. And so on.

All of the patch characteristics discussed above guide the selection of the plant species that go in each patch in each successional phase. Creating a table of all the patches and their characteristics in each phase may be useful, especially for larger projects, and especially if you are doing guild-species selection during the species selection exercise. Final species selection is a necessary prerequisite for final patch design and successional planning, but the more you can sketch out your intentions, the easier it will be to select species. Again, though, if you have a long-term horizon or a complex succession, you probably need to do more succession design before you finish selecting species.

Refine Cost Estimates

Take another stab at your cost estimates now that you have a detailed design plan with accurate sizes, shapes, and materials. At this point you will have to focus on the infrastructure, since you don't have much plant-species data to go on yet. That is fine. Can you afford the infrastructure you have proposed? If not, what changes might you make to the plan? How might the cost estimates affect your site preparation and establishment scheme? Ponder these questions and make any changes to your plan before you move on.

Characterize Midsuccession Patches If You Must

Most forest gardeners will not have to think too much about characterizing patches from successional phases earlier than the horizon time. Simple linear successions with relatively near-term horizons can work without going into too much detail, though opportunities for elegant design, multiple functions, and early-succession yields may be lost. This piece of work can lead to a feeling of being overwhelmed—if that's the case, don't do it, and skip to the next subsection. Do this exercise if you are stout of heart, passionate, and intrigued with succession design or must think through your successional schemes more thoroughly because of the task you have set yourself. The purpose of this exercise is to generate additional species selection criteria so you can include species for early stages of succession, and to help you work out your initial planting plans and later interventions for instant successions, nuclei that merge, rotational mosaics, slow-growing tree crops, and other complex or lengthy successions. This exercise assumes you did at least a successional timeline during the schematic stage. You may find that the schematic bubble diagrams you already did provide you with enough data for species selection criteria, in which case you can skip this exercise. Then again, you may want to take your succession planning to the next level. If you did not do successional bubble diagrams earlier *and* you have a long-term or complex succession, then this exercise is more likely to be for you.

Use your final detailed-design drawing of the horizon habitat patches and infrastructure as a base layer for this effort. You will also need your schematic succession timeline. If you did bubble diagrams of earlier successional phases, they will come in handy, too. Choose which of the successional phases in your timeline seem most critical to map out (if you already did schematic diagrams, you should probably choose the same phases unless your plans have changed). These will be phases where you expect to intervene or replant or where the overstory vegetation radically shifts from the horizon or from preceding phases. You might want to illustrate the habitat just *before* you make a major disturbance to alter the species composition, for example. Such a situation is like a horizon, for you must work out the patch patterns and species placements and work backward from there to figure out your planting scheme. Don't choose too many phases to diagram; just pick one, two, or perhaps three key phases. Start with the phase closest in time to the horizon and then work backward.

Lay tracing paper over your horizon design. Retrace the overall layout pattern of the garden, leaving the plants off the tracing for now.

Determine the time difference between the horizon and the phase you are now sketching. Mark and label the stem locations of habitat-defining plants that you expect will be present in the current phase that are also shown in the horizon phase. Estimate the height and crown sizes of those species at the earlier phase, draw in the crowns, and write inside each crown the estimated height of each plant as you do so.

With that step complete, look over the drawing and try to imagine the habitat as it will stand in the condition you have drawn. Characterize the patch conditions in the habitat at that phase of succession. Consider whether you want additional species to fill in the spaces you have at that point, and what they might do for you. Will the patch purposes vary between that phase and the horizon? List the kinds of functions and site conditions you see in that phase plan, and compare them to the list of patch characteristics you made for the horizon. If there are different conditions from those of the horizon, add them to your table of species selection criteria. Then lay another sheet of tracing paper over your previous one, and repeat the same process for an even earlier phase of succession if you want. Add to your list of species selection criteria for each phase of succession until you have drawn all the phases you wanted to envision.

Make sure when designing your succession that you think through the natural implications of the later phases for the earlier phases and vice versa. If you do not link the phases in a sensible way, your plans will go awry or you will have to put in work to follow the plan. The intention is to design a succession that will happen of its own accord once planted. If you envision a certain kind of canopy thirty years from now, then design a planting that will naturally create that system as long as the plants perform as expected.

Design more sketchily for the far-future phases of succession and in greater detail for the closer-in phases. For example, for the horizon time you may design only the canopy patches in detail, with general purposes and architecture for the understory layers. In midsuccession, you may want to design the shrub layers more fully in addition to the canopy, with rough sketches for the herb and ground layers. However, you are likely to design the herb layers in much more detail for the initial planting and other early phases of succession.

Species Selection: The Core of Guild Design

Species selection is one of the primary tasks of detailed design. It is also the most vital part of guild design because the niche characteristics of species determine the kinds of interactions possible between them. Which species selection tools you use depends on which guild and polyculture design strategy you follow (see table 4.4, page 243).

You may have laid groundwork for choosing your plants when articulating your goals by analyzing the niches of desired species, and you may have continued to do so when analyzing the niches of the species already existing on your site. Desired-species selection and existing-species selection are two strategies that arise from these earlier exercises. The two niche concepts discussed at length in chapter 4 of volume 1—species niches and community niches—provide two additional species selection strategies. Guild-species selection, based on species niches, works from the plants to the ecosystem. The selection of ecological analogs, based on community niches, works from the ecosystem to the plants. Finally, you can use the niche analysis technique to find and select from among any useful local native and naturalized species you find in your region.

We'll briefly present these species selection tools in approximate order of most to least frequently used: desired-species selection; guild-species selection; ecological-analog selection; existing-species selection; and native- and naturalized-species selection. All of these selection tools have two common requirements, however: they all work best when you have clear selection criteria, and you will need to create a master list or species palette where you will store all the key design information you need for each species.

Species Selection Criteria

Species selection criteria help us sort through the many species available to pick those that will best serve our purposes. As a rule, the selection process works best if you use a set of filters to sort through all the possible species (see table 4.11). Different circumstances will determine which of these filters to use first. In extreme environments (i.e., the far north or very wet or dry sites), site tolerances and preferences will limit the possible species the most, so that's the best place to start (see the Plant

---

TABLE 4.11. Categories of plant search criteria and plant selection filters. Define the criteria for your project based on your goals and site analysis and assessment.

1. Plant Uses and Functions

Direct Human Uses:
- Food, fuel, fiber, "farmaceuticals"

Ecosystem Functions:
- Fodder: insectary, wildlife food, livestock food
- Fertilizer: dynamic accumulators, nitrogen fixers, mulch producers
- Habitat: shelter, nesting, building materials, etc. (wildlife, birds, insects)
- Ground covers

2. Plant Tolerances and Preferences
- Climate: plant hardiness zone, other factors if important
- Soil moisture (dry, moist, wet)
- Light (full sun, part shade, full shade)
- Soil food web (fungal:bacterial balance)
- Native region
- Successional stage
- Soil fertility
- Soil pH
- Soil texture

3. Nuisance Factors
- Opportunists, rate and means of dispersal and expansion
- Persistence
- Poisons
- Irritants: thorns, stinging, rash producers, allergies, etc.

4. Plant Availability
- Where you can get them
- Quality of stock
- Quantity available
- Cost

Species Matrix for this information). In less extreme environments, specific functions and uses may be the main factors determining which species to use (use the species-by-use and species-by-function tables in appendices 2 and 3 for this). Define for yourself what level of plant opportunism you will tolerate, and do the same for poisonous plants and other nuisances. Will you plant opportunist species if they are already in your neighborhood but not introduce new ones, or will you not plant any known opportunists? Will you shy away only from deadly poisonous plants or also from those that can cause illness?

If you have followed the design process outlined so far you have already begun to develop your plant selection criteria. How? By bubble-diagramming the patch patterns of your horizon habitat (and perhaps earlier successional phases), characterizing each patch, and making a table or checklist of patch characteristics. Your goals and site A&A should have already provided you with information you need for your selection criteria by influencing your patch design and characterization, but it would be good to double-check that. Make sure you know your climate factors, including plant hardiness zone, and the kinds of crops you want and perhaps when you want to harvest them, for example. Working with table 4.11 and your list of patch characteristics, summarize your own selection criteria so you have a checklist handy.

Your Master List

One of the most basic tools we have for species selection is the master list or species palette (see worksheet 3). This is where you will list your selected species and the niche information about them that is relevant to your design. We intend you to photocopy this worksheet out of the book, enlarging it to 8.5-inch x 14-inch paper as you do so. Make several copies so you can have one sheet for each vegetation layer and a set of such sheets for each habitat. This way you will have room to add species as you work through the species selection

process without things getting too mixed up. You may also choose to type this data into your computer so it is easier to copy and move data on species from one place to another. A portion of a sample master list for our Holyoke, Massachusetts, case study is shown in table 4.12.

With your selection criteria clear and a blank set of master-list sheets at the ready, let us begin our review of the five possible species selection tools.

Desired-Species Selection

Desired-species selection is the primary species selection tool in forest gardening. It plays a key role in all of the guild and polyculture design strategies we discuss in this book, with the exception of habitat mimicry. It comes into play during schematic design as well as in detailed design. We'll discuss desired-species selection from the beginning so you understand how all the parts of the tool work together.

You lay the foundation for desired-species selection in goals articulation by listing your desired species. Put your brainstormed list of desired species from your goals statement onto worksheet 1 (page 161) and niche-analyze them on the form to guide site A&A, assess the plants' suitability to your site, and understand their functions and uses. At the end of site analysis you may prune the list of those species unsuited to your land and prioritize the remaining species by suitability as well as into desirability categories of essential, important, and nice. With this work done, you are ready for the actual selection work.

During schematic design we suggest that you choose habitat-defining species (see page 262) to help you design your habitat patches. So look over your desired-species niche analysis form and pick out the most essential plants, the ones you cannot live without. Also pick out those that are essential or important and the largest (usually trees and shrubs); any that you want to grow in large quantities that must be in an overstory layer; and must-have species that have very specific growing requirements. Make a separate list of these species,

Worksheet 3: Species-Selection Master List for _____

Habitat (sun, moisture, etc): _____

Page _____

Latin	Common	Form	Ht x Wdth	Habit	Root	Uses:					:Functions				Notes / Patch	Qty	Avail Y / N

Enlarge 137% when copying to fit on an 8.5-inch x 14-inch sheet of paper. This form may also be found on the Web at www.edibleforestgardens.com.

TABLE 4.12. A portion of the master species list for the case-study forest garden in Holyoke, MA. This table includes only some of the species for the polyculture patch designs shown later in this chapter; we dropped some columns from the master list due to space limitations. Organizing your species by size and habit helps you find them when you are searching for species for your patch designs. You may want to have separate lists for each habitat type in your garden.

Latin	Common	Ht x Wdth	Light	Uses: Ed	GC	N2	:Functions DA	Nectar	Notes / Patch
Running Trees 12+'									
Diospyros virginiana	American persimmon 'Early Golden'		○	Fr					pers
Clumpers 6–12'									
Eleagnus multiflora	goumi	6–8 x 6–8	○◐	Fr		X			pers
Morus x hybrid	'Geraldi dwarf' mulberry	8 x 6–8	○	Fr					pers
Prunus tomentosa	Nanking cherry	6–10 x 6–8	○	Fr				G	pers, finger
Clumpers 3–6'									
Malus pumila	minidwarf apple	4–6 x 4–6	○	Fr				G	finger
Symphytum x uplandicum	Russian comfrey	1–4 x 3	○◐				X	G	pers1
Runners 3–6'									
Matteuccia struthiopteris	ostrich fern	2–6 x indf	◐●	Sht					shade
Petasites japonicus giganteus	giant fuki	5–6 x indf	◐●	Sht				S	shade
Polygonatum biflorum commutatum	giant Solomon's seal	3–5 x 4+	○●	Sht					shade
Clumpers 1.5–3'									
Agastache foeniculum	anise hyssop	2–4 x 1–2	○◐	Lvs				G	pers2
Bunium bulbocastanum	earth chestnut	2 x 1–2	○	Rt				S	pers1, pers2
Chenopodium bonus–henricus	good King Henry	1–3 x 1–1.5	○◐	Lvs					pers1
Cichorium intybus	chicory	1–4 x 1–2	○◐	Lvs			X	G	pers1
Crambe maritima	sea kale	2–3 x 3	○◐	Lvs				G	pers2
Eryngium maritimum	sea holly	2 x 2	○	Lvs Rt				S	pers2
Indigofera decora	Chinese indigo	1.5 x 6–8	○		X	X			pers1
Melissa officinalis	lemon balm	1–2 x 2+	○◐	Lvs	X		X	G	pers2
Myrrhis odorata	sweet cicely	3 x 3	○◐	Lvs Rt				S	pers2
Sium sisarum	skirret	3 x 1–2	○	Rt				S	pers1
Solidago odora	sweet goldenrod	2–4 x 2–4	○◐	Lvs				S	pers2
Runners 1.5–3'									
Laportaea canadensis	wood nettle	1–3 x 1–3	◐●	Lvs					shade

and ponder that list. Does it feel good and right or a bit overbearing and weighty? Is the list too long or just about right? Which species are least essential, if any? Do any fall out the bottom, or do they all hang together? Think about them in the context of your schematic design work so far and see whether any seem unrealistic. Those species that survive these questions are your first-round picks, and your habitat definers. Put them on your master list as your initial core of selected species. The rest of the species on your list may get included later.

During detailed design, look over your desired-species list again in the context of what you now know about your design and its patch characteristics. Use your species selection criteria to pick out species that fit the site conditions, architectural needs, functions, and uses you have laid out in your design plan. Focus on multifunctional species and on single-use species of high value to you that are well adapted to the site conditions you have specified. You may not accommodate all of your desired species in your design plan. This is why you prioritized them after site A&A. Any that do fit your design criteria can go on your master list on the appropriate sheet for its layer and habitat.

Guild-Species Selection

In the second species selection tool, guild-species selection, we build ecosystem social structure from the ground up, from the parts to the whole. Along with desired-species selection, this process lies at the core of the guild-build and habitat invention strategies for guild and polyculture design. Guild-species selection rests upon a foundation of a detailed design providing plant selection criteria for each patch and a clear sense of the ecological functions needed for the ecosystem to work well under all the growing conditions in the garden.

That last point is the key. We select guild species based on our understanding of the ecological functions needed throughout the forest garden. Typically, these include food production, the gathering and retention of specific nutrients, beneficial-insect nectary plants, and ground covers for weed control. You can add other guild functions to this list, such as beneficial-insect overwintering plants, bee plants, butterfly plants, rooting patterns, light requirements, and so on, based on your specific goals or ecological situation. Consider how to partition the most scarce or limiting resources on your site, and what forms of support key members of your forest garden will need. Some functions may have critical seasons, which you should identify if possible (e.g., early-season nectar for bees greatly influences the hive's ability to thrive during the summer).

You need to select species to perform each of these guild functions in every forest garden habitat where your design plan indicates the function is needed. Your patch design estimates the conditions in which the guild members will have to grow. To keep the selection process and goals clear, we suggest you use the guild-selection forms in worksheets 4 through 7 to select species for each guild, or you can create your own way of working with your functions and conditions. The forms provide a place to

write down species under consideration for each function, including where you see them fitting into your design. With the forms in hand, modified as necessary to fit your circumstances, you can look for species to fit your guild-design objectives. Look first among your desired- and existing-species niche analyses. You can also find some of this information in the "Functions" columns of the Plant Species Matrix and the species-by-use and species-by-function tables in appendices 2 and 3. Look, too, in other gardening books, plant catalogs, and so on.

Add species to your guild-selection forms, but do not make final selections until you have compiled a good set on your guild forms. Once you have gotten a good array of species for one guild function, go through and select those that have the most different functions and uses or the highest value for your garden. When you decide a plant should be in your garden, put it on your master list and mark it on the guild form so it is easier to find amid the other candidate species.

You will find that some species participate in more than one guild. Therefore, when you add a species to the master list, you should also add it to the other guild forms you are using to help you keep it straight. As you go through this process, it's also helpful to note in which patches each species might go (based on the purposes and growing conditions you expect in each patch), if such thoughts arise.

You might imagine that this can be complex and grueling work, but it's fun to see what plants you can find to meet the design requirements, and it does help you learn the species and their characteristics. Guild-species selection also offers the best chance of fulfilling all the ecological functions we know of in the forest garden.

Ecological Analogs

An ecological analog is a species or variety substituted for another ecologically similar species or variety for a specific reason. The degree of similarity between the analog and the model depends on the purposes of the designer and the species

Worksheet 4: Crop Guild Selection Form for _____

Habitat _____   **Main** _____   **Minor** _____   **Really Minor** _____

Do separate sheets for, or cluster species as, Main Crops, Minor Crops, and Really Minor Crops. e = early; m = mid; l = late

Species	Variety	Tolerances			Product	Years to Bearing	Season of Yield								
		sun	water	soil			Spring			Summer			Fall		
							e	m	l	e	m	l	e	m	l

Enlarge 137% when copying to fit on an 8.5-inch x 14-inch sheet of paper. This form may also be found on the Web at www.edibleforestgardens.com.

Worksheet 5: Soil-Builders Guild Selection Form for _____

Habitat _____ Page _____

Species	N2	Other Nutrients (P, K, Ca . . .)						Tolerances		
								sun	water	soil

Worksheet 6: Nectary-Guild Flowering Calendar for _____

Habitat _____   **Page** _____

Spec = specialist nectary; Gen = generalist nectary; Poll = provides pollen for insects; Hum = hummingbird plant.
Other functions: Butterfly (F) or aesthetics (E), for example.

Species	Function:					Months of Bloom							
	Spec	Gen	Poll	Hum	Other	M	A	M	J	J	A	S	O

Worksheet 7: Ground-Covers Guild Selection Form for _____

Clumpers ____ **Runners** ____ **Mat Formers** ____ Do separate sheets for clumpers, runners, and mat formers.

Habitat _____

Page ____

Species	Common Name	Density	Rate	Height	Width				

Enlarge 137% when copying to fit on an 8.5-inch x 14-inch sheet of paper. This form may also be found on the Web at www.edibleforestgardens.com.

available for substitution. Most people use ecological analogs as the foundation of a habitat-mimicry approach for guild and polyculture design, but finding analogs also forms the core species selection tool for habitat co-optation. You can also use it simply to select additional species for your guild-build process if, for example, one of your existing or desired species won't work on your site and you want to find something similar.

We begin building the foundations for ecological-analog species selection in goals articulation with the model ecosystem analysis exercise. There you identify the model ecosystem you want to mimic in your forest garden, as well as its member species. You develop habitat design criteria based on observations or inferences about the model's architecture. You also niche-analyze the model species to help you do site A&A, set initial directions for which species you will use directly and which you want to mimic, and support developing the architectural criteria.

In schematic design, you need to make an initial selection of habitat-defining species to help you develop your schematic design (see page 262 for that discussion). Do this by looking through your model-species niche analysis and the architectural criteria from your model habitat and looking for the overstory dominants and the most common and largest species in the understory. Then go through the analogy-making process described below to make your analogies. In detailed design you can go through the rest of the model species and make analogies for them.

In choosing analogous species, you will have to decide the relative importance of ecological mimicry and its potential benefits against your design goals. For example, if you want a substitute for an existing exotic weed that grows on your forest garden site, the ecological similarity of the analog may be less important than its usefulness. On the other hand, if you are trying to mimic a native habitat species by species, ecological similarity may hold more importance for your design. We'll take

the latter case as the basis for most of our discussion below, since you can always relax your selection criteria from the hard ecological line we'll take for the sake of that argument.

The most ecologically essential aspect of making an analogy is that the two species *should fill similar community niches in similar habitats*. This means you need to understand the species niches and ecology of model and candidate species, at least a little. Is the model species a canopy tree of late succession on acid, dry soils; a suckering pioneer shrub with broad tolerances; or a wet-tolerant climax-forest spring ephemeral? Find a useful species that fills the same niche and your purposes, and you're on your way.

Remember, though, that when the environmental conditions and habitat in which the model and the analog grow or grew are the same or highly similar, the community niches will be more similar in ways that we don't even know about. Hence the species niches will match more effectively, as well. For example, warm spells frequently punctuate the extreme cold of eastern North American winters. Many people do not know that this is not so in many other temperate-forest environments. These warm spells can fool nonnative trees into thinking spring has arrived, resulting, for example, in apricot trees breaking dormancy too early. The following cold snap can then kill a tree, its flowers, or its flower buds if it is not adapted to deal with these temperature extremes. Given such environmental variations between regions, you might want to start looking for analogous species within the local or regional flora before going further afield. When you start looking at plants from more distant ecosystems, look first in ecosystems with climate, site, and successional conditions the most similar to your own. In this way, the analog is most likely to adapt well to your own climate and site.

Taxonomic similarity *can* indicate similarity of niche and function. However, it isn't the best guide by itself, because closely related species can fill quite different niches and have different characteristics.

For example, different native oak species may have quite different rooting patterns: some grow taproots, some grow heart roots, while others are shallow rooted. Therefore, taxonomic similarity is secondary to niche and habitat similarity in making species analogies; however, it may be important for meeting our direct needs, such as for fruit, nuts, or other products.

Combining all three factors—similar niches, similar habitats, and closely related species—will most likely help you find similar ecosystem structure and function in your ecological analog. So, as with habitat, look for analogous species starting with closely related taxonomic groups first, and then widen the net if you cannot find something suitable. Some examples, from most to least similar, might include:

- *Same habitat, niche, and species, different variety.* Using 'Patriot' highbush blueberries (*Vaccinium corymbosum*) in a northern hardwoods-conifer forest mimic rather than wild highbush blueberries. Note that the niche will be somewhat different since the analog is a hybrid cultivar developed for high fruit production in full sun. It may not tolerate shade as well as the model species.
- *Same genus, different community niche or habitat.* Substituting a saskatoon cultivar (*Amelanchier alnifolia* 'Smoky', for example) in place of running serviceberry (*Amelanchier stolonifera*) or Allegheny serviceberry (*Amelanchier laevis*). These multistemmed, fruiting woodies come from moist to dry habitats in North America. However, Allegheny serviceberry is a multistemmed tree in eastern wooded environments, while running serviceberry and saskatoon are suckering shrubs that create thickets on rocky ground, stream banks, and open fields. Running serviceberry evolved in the eastern deciduous forest, while saskatoon grows in the western prairies. Smoky's high production of tasty berries recommends itself over the other two

unimproved species. Another example: exchanging northern pecan (*Carya illinoinensis*) selections for shagbark hickory (*Carya ovata*). Though both provide nuts, grow taproots, and create thin canopies, shagbark is more an upland species while pecan is more of a floodplain species. Pecan also has better varieties for nut production.
- *Same family, similar niche and habitat, different climatic origins.* Using pear (*Pyrus communis*) or apple (*Malus pumila*) cultivars instead of native hawthorns (*Crataegus* spp.). All three genera contain small pioneer trees in the rose family, or Rosaceae, though the hawthorns are native to North America and the domesticated pears and apples hail from Eurasia.
- *Same climatic region, similar community niche, different taxonomy.* If you cannot find a suitable analog in a taxonomic relative, then look for suitable substitutes from any family. For example, say you want a highly productive nut and timber substitute for American chestnut (*Castanea dentata*, a taprooted, straight-stemmed, canopy nut producer in the beech family, Fagaceae), but you don't want to risk chestnut blight or use the more branching Chinese chestnut. You may decide that pecan or a shagbark hickory selection would be good, since they are also North American taprooted, straight-stemmed canopy nut producers, though in the walnut family (Juglandaceae).

Information in the Plant Species Matrix that you can use to make analogies include the family and habitat columns, plant form and habit, and functions and uses. You will likely need additional references to gather such information for native model species (see appendix 7).

You can also create analogs by grafting cultivars onto existing wild stock. This certainly works within a species, such as grafting apple cultivars onto wild apples you discover on your site. However, you can sometimes graft different species from the same genus onto each other, such as various cherries or plums on native cherries or plums (*Prunus* spp.) or Korean nut pine on white pine (*Pinus koraiensis* and *Pinus strobus*, respectively). You can even sometimes graft different genera, such as medlar on hawthorn (*Mespilus* on *Crataegus*), pear on hawthorn (*Pyrus* on *Crataegus*), or pear on chokeberry (*Pyrus* on *Aronia*). The more taxonomically distant two species are, however, the less likely the graft will work well for the long haul.

Start by selecting model species you will use directly in a manner similar to selecting desired species. Add these chosen species to your master list. With the above principles in mind, go through your model-species lists and make analogies for the remaining species. Your model-species niche analysis should help you make your choices. You may need to use a blank desired-species niche analysis form (worksheet 1, page 161) to write down candidate mimics and then to select between them. Use your species selection criteria to help you choose. Place the chosen analogs on your master list. Make sure you keep the connection between the model and the mimic species clear by noting which species you are substituting for which. That will help you make polyculture analogies during the patch design stage.

Existing-Species Selection

Virtually every forest garden site has at least a few plants already growing on it. The fourth species selection tool, existing-species selection, involves identifying these species and researching their characteristics so you can decide whether to use them in your garden or not. The technique rests upon existing-species niche analysis, which we discuss in the site analysis phase of design. It is one of the core tools of the habitat co-optation guild and polyculture design strategy. You can use it as an adjunct species selection technique for virtually any guild design strategy (see table 4.4, page 243).

Worksheet 2 (page 209) provides existing-species niche analysis forms that provide space for observing the growing conditions, habitat, and health of the plant in question as well as possible functions, uses, and problems. With this information in hand, you can decide whether to include the existing plant in your garden. Compare the data on each existing species with your species selection criteria to help you decide. Add any you choose to use to your master list.

Native- and Naturalized-Species Selection

Local native and naturalized ecosystems are another valuable source for possible forest garden species. Locally native species presumably have adapted to the conditions present in your locale, at least in undisturbed environments. Naturalized nonnative species, those that have migrated to your area and are reproducing on their own without human support, are obviously also adapted to your region's conditions. Naturalized species usually do best in human-influenced habitats. In the site analysis phase of design you may have researched such species in your locale to find out which are useful in what ways. In native- and naturalized-species selection, we use our species selection criteria to choose which, if any, of these plants will go in our forest garden. Besides using the local species directly in your garden, you can also use the native and naturalized species you find as models for ecological analogs.

This species selection technique is similar to model ecosystem analysis, except that it deals only with species, not habitat architecture, and it looks for potential species in many habitats, not just one, thereby casting a wider net. It also follows essentially the same process as the existing- and desired-species selection described earlier. You just have to be careful not to select opportunist species that could be a problem in your garden or neighborhood. Find local sources for lists of "invasives" in your region. Our "Watch List" (appendix 4) includes useful and functional species that have some characteristics of which we should be wary, such as opportunism or toxicity. Check your local species against these lists before putting them on your master list.

Put these five species selection strategies into your designer's toolbox, and use them as part of your guild and polyculture design strategies or just go crazy and use them in whatever creative way you wish. Each one can help you create a palette of species on which you can draw in the next stage of the design phase. If you have completed all of the above work, you are ready to proceed to that next stage: patch design.

PATCH DESIGN: FINAL INTEGRATION

In the patch design stage, you determine the species composition, patterning, and spacing of your garden plantings patch by patch to a high degree of specificity. This work is based on the purposes and characteristics expressed in your detailed design plan, your species palette, and any successional scheming you have done. Also consider crop yields (see table 7.9, page 437). Patch design integrates all of your previous work into those seemingly simple choices of which plants go where, when. However, designing the plantings is not the only task you must do for your design to be complete—you also need to think through a few construction details.

This section begins by exploring three design techniques you can use to assemble polycultures in accord with your guild and polyculture design strategy, as well as a feature article on ground-cover polycultures. A quick trip into designing patch succession follows, and then a discussion of plant spacing that offers guidelines to help you negotiate this most important and all-too-often overlooked aspect of forest garden design. You will need to work through and synthesize the above topics for each patch you design until you have planting plans for every piece of your garden. Then you should check that you have used all the plants on your species palette, or at least enough of them to make sure your garden has fully functioning guilds.

With your patch designs settled, you can and must puzzle out how to build what you have wrought. Finalizing your plans for site preparation and establishment is therefore on the agenda. If you have infrastructure to install, work out its construction details. Then, of course, there is that budget you can finish once you know how you will prepare the ground, what you will plant when, and what you will build. Let us remind you again, though, that we are presenting a full-blown design process here, and you need not do all of these steps. Choose your own path and follow your own star.

Patch design often requires that we jump to a closer-in scale of design thinking, enlarging our drawings as we narrow our focus. Worksheet 8 provides a form to help you design each patch. It will help you think about the conditions in each patch and keep track of the species you intend to use, and why, as well as their architecture, their spacing, and how many you need for that patch. Alternatively, enlarge relevant portions of your design plan to a workable scale on a photocopier and go to it. You can start with your most important or difficult patches and work to the least important or easiest ones, or go the other way around to help you build your confidence before you get to the hard stuff.

In any case, all your previous work comes to a finely honed point here. Keep your focus and passion going for one more round of design—for then you can begin making your fully-imagined creation!

Polyculture Design Techniques

Not every forest garden patch must or will contain polycultures. However, for those that will, a clear and rational polyculture design process comes in handy. We offer below three methods for your choosing, each one appropriate under different circumstances and used in different guild and polyculture design strategies. However, you can use all three techniques in different patches in your garden if you want, or you can even combine them in different ways. All of that is up to you. We recommend that you reread the presentation of guild and polyculture design earlier in the chapter to refresh your memory about what is an effective polyculture

Worksheet 8: Polyculture Patch Worksheet for _____

Habitat _____   Patch _____   Phase _____   Page _____

Polyculture Purposes / Functions / General Description & Concept:

Patch Conditions (soil, moisture, light, successional stage, disturbance regime, etc):

Species	Form	Ht x W	Habit	Root	Uses & Functions:							Spacing	Approx # plants

Enlarge 137% when copying to fit on an 8.5-inch x 14-inch sheet of paper. This form may also be found on the Web at www.edibleforestgardens.com.

(see page 239) and the components of the different guild and polyculture design strategies.

We also want to remind you here that for most polycultures you should limit the number of inter-mixed species to between two and seven. More will complicate dynamics and probably lead to competi-tive exclusion of one or more species unless you maintain it. Even seven-species polycultures will be challenging to design well. However, note that we said "intermixed" species. You may design a patch with subpatches within it, each subpatch containing from two to seven species well mixed with each other, but not mixing much with the other subpatches. It is the mixing that counts in the complexity, not where you draw the line around the patch.

Polyculture-Build

If we are using unique sets of plants to create new and interesting polycultures, then we have few models we can use for direct mimicry. We therefore need a tool to help us create effective polycultures from scratch, applying our ecological theories in a direct and meaningful way. The polyculture-build method is that tool. An extension of guild-species selection, polyculture-build is the final movement of the guild-build and crops-only design strategies. You can also use it as an adjunct tool for any of the other approaches to guild and polyculture design. The basic idea of polyculture-build is to plant com-plementary plants together to form resource-parti-tioning guilds within patches while simultaneously selecting species that form mutual-support guilds within and between patches. It is difficult to use this technique to its utmost if you have not done guild-species selection beforehand, but the process can help you find resource-partitioning guilds within species palettes that are more limited.

In most cases you will by now have a detailed design plan that shows the size and shape of spe-cific patches as well as their purposes (ecological functions and human uses), proposed management regime, expected growing conditions, and overall architecture. This design plan should express your desired patterning for both garden guilds and patch guilds across the designed habitats. You should also have a species palette that includes plants you want to grow as crops for human uses and plants that form all the ecosystem support guilds shown in your design plan. These two prerequisites lay the foundation for proper guild functioning in your garden. Now, how do we design polycultures?

Fulfill Critical Purposes First

In polyculture-build, you start by selecting the species that are the most critical components of each patch—those that fulfill the main intended purpose of the patch most directly. You may have already chosen habitat-defining species for a partic-ular patch during schematic design, or your patch may not have a species located in it yet. Pick this or these species now, making sure their site tolerances and preferences match the patch conditions. Most often, but not necessarily, these will be crop species, and we would hope you can choose species that perform multiple functions. Look to your detailed design plan to see what patch purposes you decided on earlier, and then go through your species lists to choose one or two, perhaps more, species and con-sider the optimal locations for them in the patch.

The next step is to see what other uses and func-tions you have designated for this patch, and to compare that to the uses and functions of the species already selected. Find the gaps, and then seek plants to fill them. This is where it starts to get tricky, though—you need to select plants that are complementary to those you have already chosen for the patch.

Plant Complementary Plants Together

For a patch with defined purposes, conditions, and architecture, select complementary plants that fit the desired patch characteristics. How do we know which plants are complementary?

- **Tolerance to Conditions.** Obviously, you want to match the plants for a patch with the growing conditions in the patch to maximize survival and yield. Beyond that, though, mixing plants with equal tolerance to the patch conditions will reduce competitive exclusion. If one species in a patch fits the growing conditions much more closely than the others do, it is more likely to outcompete the others to extinction. This could be either bad or good from your perspective. If you want the patch succession to go somewhere, you could pick better-adapted and more vigorous plants for the later stages and less well-adapted plants for the earlier stages. Look to the Plant Species Matrix or your own research as shown on your niche-analysis and guildspecies selection forms to find out what tolerances the plants listed there have.

• **Architecture.** By definition, compatible plants grow in different physical spaces with different forms, heights, rooting patterns, and so on. If plants have the same size, form, and habit, then proper spacing between them is an absolute must, or they are more likely to compete with each other. Plants with different aboveground architectures may be able to grow closer to each other without competing. They may also have different belowground architectures, but this isn't always the case. You can find information on aboveground architecture in the "Form" column of the Plant Species Matrix. The matrix also offers information on root patterns for as many species as we could find that data.

Not all plant forms work well in polycultures.[2] Trees with very dense canopies (especially evergreens) or with dense surface roots may prevent understory layers from developing successfully. The same goes for compact, exclusionary, dense-canopied, evergreen, or shallow-rooted shrubs. According to some folks, these "unsociable" plants would include things like apples, plums, cherries, and other common fruit trees, as well as lavender (*Lavandula* spp.), rosemary (*Rosmarinus officinalis*), and bay (*Laurus nobilis*), though not

all agree on these species, including us. If necessary, you can plant such trees and shrubs in clumps and plant around them, train them to a high canopy, or prune out canopy branches or multistemmed trunks for more light. Of course, we might like to avoid the work such measures require, unless pruning is part of harvesting coppice or managing for other products.

So-called sociable shrubs grow upright and have thin canopies, thin foliage, and deep roots. They are usually deciduous. Sociable trees have similar characteristics. These include such plants as serviceberries (*Amelanchier* spp.), pawpaw (*Asimina triloba*), mulberries (*Morus* spp.), redbud (*Cercis canadensis*), persimmons (*Diospyros* spp.), kousa dogwood (*Cornus kousa*), chaste tree (*Vitex agnus-castus*), angelica tree (*Aralia elata*), and rose of Sharon (*Hibiscus syriacus*). Hickories (*Carya* spp.), honey and black locusts (*Gleditsia triacanthos* and *Robinia pseudoacacia*), and walnuts (*Juglans* spp.) also have open crowns, though walnuts have allelopathic compounds to consider (see the "Species Known to Tolerate Juglone" table in appendix 3 to see what plants are compatible with walnuts).

In the root zones of shallow-rooted crop trees, plant densely shading, deep-rooted herbs and shrubs, along with bulbs and mild-mannered runners to fill gaps. The dense shade in that list is intended to limit competition by shallow-rooted weeds from getting in the shallow-rooted tree's way. In the root zones of deeply rooting trees you can have a more diverse understory. The richest understory layers will be possible under a high, thin canopy of deeply rooted trees (walnuts, persimmons, hickories). With clusters of upright, thin-crowned, deep-rooted shrubs underneath, you'd have more room and light for a variety of herb and ground-layer species. Around trees planted in clusters, you could add light-filled edge zones to increase the possible diversity in the lower layers.

Also consider architecture when thinking about successional design for a patch. The usual herbs-shrubs-trees succession pattern reflects architectural change in the patch over time. You can plan this into the patch architecture even if you plant everything at once, since most shrubs and trees take longer to grow than most herbs.

• **Behavior (Growth Habit).** Mix clumpers, runners, and mat formers, especially for ground covers. Note that extremely vigorous runners, such as mints, need to be planted with much larger clumpers or restrained with rhizome barriers or they overrun other plants (see #52, *Expansive Plant Containers,* in chapter 2). For plants of similar size and growth habit, mix those of equal vigor, or else competitive exclusion will reign unless you prune periodically. Suckering trees and suckering or stoloniferous shrubs may also cause problems in polycultures, especially those thicket-forming shrubs usually growing in extensive communities over large areas, such as raspberries and blackberries (*Rubus* spp.). Don't forget time niches, too; bulbs and spring ephemerals can mix in with summer-green and evergreen herbs nicely. Mixing annuals, biennials, and perennials at the start of a succession often works well, since many perennials are slow to establish. Partitioning the flowering times or annual timing of maximum plant size within a patch may help minimize competition for water in droughty sites. The "Habit" column of the Plant Species Matrix provides behavior information for each species listed.

• **Management Regime.** Put plants with compatible management regimes in the same patch. For example, putting yearly-dug root crops in a polyculture with ginseng plants needing seven years to mature makes no sense. However, a polyculture of root crops dug every year along with self-sowing annuals or vigorous perennials might work—e.g., annual chickweed (*Stellaria media*), violets (*Viola* spp.), and the like. You can mix management needs in one patch if the management varies from layer to layer and there are no conflicts between layers.

• **Species Interactions.** The discussion of two-species interactions in volume 1, chapter 4, has implications for selecting patch partners. Do you want a plant to facilitate or cooperate with a particular patch member? Are you looking for a competitive or inhibitive ground cover for a specific preexisting weed challenge in this patch? Think about the needs and offers of species you have already chosen for a patch, then look for other species that can help meet those needs or make use of those offers.

As you can see, finding complementary plants is not necessarily an easy prospect, and the more plants you already have in the polyculture, the harder it gets, but we do what we can. Keep cycling through the process of comparing the intended functions and uses of the patch with the functions and uses of the plants you have selected until you have filled all the "purpose niches" in the patch. Also look at the architectural niches available, and make sure you have covered all the ground you can with the different species you have selected. It makes sense for many patches to include low, shade-tolerant running species to fill gaps between the other plants as a last resort. And, as you select each species, you also need to consider the patterns in which you will plant the plants.

Within-Patch Patterns

When selecting plants for a patch, consider the pattern in which you will plant them. Determine this by the plants' architecture, uses, functions, and behavior, by the purpose of the patch and its size, shape, and accessibility, and by aesthetic concerns.

• Create zones in planting beds and patches according to accessibility—the plants used least often being behind the plants used most frequently.

- Use geometric patterns, organic patterns, or whatever meets your goals. Organic planting patterns include drifts, clumps, and scatters. Grouping an uneven number of plants together with varied distances between them makes plant clusters look most natural.
- Mix plants of one species amid other species for disease and insect reductions. Also scatter insectary plants all over to get the beneficial insects spread around (see patterns #36, *Extraordinary Edibles Everywhere*; #50, *Drifts, Clumps, and Scatters*; and #51, *Functional Plants Throughout*, in chapter 2).
- Cluster plants that need to cross-pollinate at a distance from each other no greater than the maximum recommended cross-pollination distance. This is usually 50 to 100 feet (15 to 30 m) for insect-pollinated crops. To avoid planting blocks of the same species, which will maximize pests and diseases, you can mix several species in overlapping patterns of cross-pollinating trees 50 or so feet (15 m) apart. We call these *Cross-Pollination Clusters* (pattern #48).
- Put plants accumulating needed nutrients in the root zones of plants with high demand for those nutrients.
- Not all patches need to be polyculture patches, even though such patches might have pest- and disease-reduction benefits. Monoculture crop patches (*Pockets of Production*, pattern #45) fit well into a matrix of diverse plantings if that simplifies management or harvest.
- When designing crop polycultures, create *Layers of Harvest* (pattern #40) by constructing each layer of the planting from species that have similar habits, forms, and crop characteristics. Imagine you have a ground layer of violets and miner's lettuce (*Montia* spp.), along with taller crop plants in the herb and shrub layers. It will be relatively easy to harvest the ground layer because the crops there are harvested in the same way, at the same time, for the same use (with scissors, for greens). However, trying to

harvest edible berries from one crop that is mixed into the same layer as a medicinal leaf crop might get troublesome.
- *Ground-Cover Carpets* (pattern #49; see feature article 3) are essential in almost every patch as weed controls. They can also serve other functions, such as insect nectary or fertility improvement.
- *Three-Layer Minimum*, pattern #38, applies to the whole forest garden, rather than to patches per se, but keep it in mind. If it doesn't have three layers or more, it isn't a forest garden!

Use a circle-drawing template, your engineer's scale, your design plan, and tracing paper to help you sketch as you consider all these factors, select your species, and play with patterns for their layout in the patch. Use worksheet 8 to assist you also (page 287). If you have the need, energy, or interest, consider patch succession (discussed later this section) as you go through this process. Eventually, you will come to realize that you have selected all the species you need and found places for them in the patch design. Then you can repeat the whole process with every other patch in your garden.

Keep track of which species you are selecting for each patch as you go, so you can monitor your progress at creating all the guilds on your guild-species selection forms (the master list provides some space for this). Tracking how many of which species you intend to use in each patch will also speed your plant acquisitions and help you work on your budget.

Polyculture Analogs

Polyculture analogs provide the final step of the guild and polyculture design strategies of habitat mimicry and habitat invention. The intention is to mimic the effective polycultures we find in natural ecosystems, whether these ecosystems contain only native or both native and naturalized species. Polyculture analogs are similar to species analogs in concept. The theory is that we can receive the

Feature Article 3:
Ground-Cover Polycultures

This article originally appeared in *Agroforestry News*,[3] a publication of the Agroforestry Research Trust in Devon, England, and is revised and reprinted here with permission. The author, Martin Crawford, is director of the trust and the author of other books and articles on forest gardening in the English climate (see the case study of his forest garden in volume 1, page 291). We have adapted this article to our climate and the terms we use in this book. We have also replaced the original species Martin used in the examples with species from our own ground-cover table in appendix 3.

Introduction

Just as any collection of different species growing together tends to use available resources more efficiently, ground-cover polycultures tend to:

- utilize the soil space and available nutrients more efficiently by having root systems of different character;
- utilize the available sunlight more efficiently by having shoot and leaf systems of different character, usually interweaving and intercepting a higher total of light—thus making a better ground cover by reducing the amount of light reaching the soil surface; and
- be less susceptible to major damage from pests and diseases, since usually only one species is affected at a time.

As with all polycultures, there may be disadvantages as well, particularly with ease of harvesting; gathering fruits, leaves, and the like will take longer and thus be more labor-intensive than in monocultures. There are ways of getting around this, however, particularly by planting ground covers of different heights. Occasionally, one plant may be detrimental to another and restrict the other's growth (e.g., by chemical exudates from the roots), but this seems to be rare and the exception.

One special case of beneficial interaction is when one species is a nitrogen-fixing plant. Though there are not many ground-cover species that are nitrogen fixers, these are well worth considering as they will help feed the whole ground-cover layer and reduce the decline in density that can occur when some ground-cover plants are unfed for years on end.

Ground-Cover Plants

For the purposes of this discussion, only species below 18 inches (45 cm) in mature height are considered ground covers. The guidelines below are, however, certainly useful for designing with larger species as well. Ground-cover plants fall into four natural categories (see table 4.13 for examples):

- **Clumping perennials.** These may be deciduous (i.e., die down to the ground each winter) or evergreen. They grow in a fairly well-behaved clump, perhaps spreading slowly via rhizomes or seed.
- **Running perennials.** Again, these may be deciduous or evergreen. Their habit is to spread rapidly, usually via rhizomes or stolons. They tend to weave among other plants and quickly fill gaps between plants where there is more bare soil and/or light.
- **Clumping shrubs.** These may be deciduous (losing their leaves in winter but retaining woody shoots) or evergreen. They tend to be slow-spreading, though there are exceptions. Clumping shrubs do not spread by runners, and they spread to a certain width and no further. They may be multistemmed, thicket forming, or mat forming in habit.
- **Running shrubs.** Similar to running perennials but with woody stems. Running shrubs spread indefinitely and may be thicket forming or mat forming.

TABLE 4.13. The top forty ground covers. Running species spread indefinitely; clumping and mat-forming species stay in one place. Density: thickness of plant cover; M is medium, H is high. Rate: the speed at which the plant grows; S is slow, M is medium, F is fast. Light: light preference; ○ is full sun, ◐ is part shade, ● is full shade. DA = dynamic accumulator, N2 = nitrogen fixer.

Latin Name / Common Name	Density	Rate	Form	Height	Width	Light	Notes
Running Species							
Antennaria plantaginifolia / pussytoes	M–H	M	Herb	8–10″	indef	○◐	native, insectary
Asarum canadense / wild ginger	H	S	Herb	6–10″	indef	◐●	native, edible roots
Campanula portenschlagiana / Dalmatian bellflower	H	F	Herb	6–9″	indef	○◐	edible leaves and flowers
Conoclinium coelestinum / hardy ageratum	H	F	Herb	12–20″	indef	○◐	native, insectary
Coreopsis rosea / pink tickseed	M–H	F	Herb	6–24″	indef	○◐	native, nectary
Fragaria chiloensis / beach strawberry	M–H	F	Herb	6″	indef	○	delicious berries
Galax urceolata / galax	H	M	Herb	6–12″	indef	○●	native, evergreen
Houttuynia cordata / tsi, hot tuna	M	F	Herb	12–15″	indef	○◐	edible leaves, culinary
Mentha longifolia / horse mint	H	F	Herb	24–36″	indef	○◐	edible tea
Mentha suaveolens / apple mint	H	F	Herb	24–36″	indef	○◐	edible tea
Mentha x villosa / Bowles's mint	H	F	Herb	18–36″	indef	○◐	edible tea
Montia spp. / miner's lettuce	M–H	M–F	Herb	4–12″	indef	◐●	delicious leaves, self-seeding
Potentilla anserina / silverweed	M–H	F	Herb	3–14″	indef	○	native, DA, edible roots
Rubus tricolor / creeping raspberry	H	F	Shrub	18″	indef	○◐	edible berries, zone 7
Stachys affinis / Chinese artichoke	M–H	M–F	Herb	12–18″	indef	○◐	edible tubers
Tiarella cordifolia / foamflower	H	M	Herb	6–12″	indef	◐●	native, nectary
Viola canadensis / Canada violet	M–H	F	Herb	6–12″	indef	○●	native, edible leaves and flowers
Viola tricolor / Johnny jump-up	M	M	Herb	6–10″	indef	○◐	delicious leaves and flowers
Waldsteinia fragarioides / barren strawberry	H	M	Herb	4–8″	indef	○◐	native
Woodwardia areolata / netted chain fern	M–H	M	Herb	12–18″	indef	◐●	native

(continued next page)

(table 4.13, continued)

Latin Name Common Name	Density	Rate	Form	Height	Width	Light	Notes
Clumping & Mat-Forming Species							
Astragalus glycyphyllos milk vetch	M	F	Herb	6–12"	1–2'	○◐	N2
Athyrium filix-femina lady fern	H	M	Herb	18–36"	18–24"	◐●	native
Callirhoe involucrata purple poppy-mallow	M–H	M	Herb	3–10"	4–5'	○◐	native, edible roots and leaves
Ceanothus prostratus mahala mat	H	F	Shrub	3–6"	10'	○	N2, zone 7
Chrysogonum virginianum green and gold	H	M	Herb	2–8"	18"	○◐	native, insectary
Coreopsis verticillata thread-leaved coreopsis	M–H	F	Herb	18"	3'	○◐	native, nectary
Genista pilosa cv. 'Vancouver Gold' silky-leaf woodwaxen	H	M	Shrub	6"	3–4'	○	N2, sterile seeds
Genista pilosa procumbens silky-leaf woodwaxen	H	M	Shrub	2"	3'	○	N2
Genista sagittalis arrow broom	H	M	Shrub	4–18"	2–3'	○	N2
Hemerocallis fulva daylily	M–H	F	Herb	1–2'	2–3'	○◐	edible roots, flowers, more
Heuchera americana alum root	H	S	Herb	6–24"	1–3'	◐	native
Indigofera incarnata Chinese indigo	H	M	Shrub	4–18"	6–8'	○◐	N2
Lotus corniculatus 'Plena' prostrate bird's-foot trefoil	H	M	Herb	1"	1–2'	○◐	N2, sterile
Oxalis oregana red wood sorrel	H	M	Herb	10"	2–3'	◐●	edible leaves
Phlox subulata moss pink	M–H	M	Herb	4–6"	2'	○◐	native
Polygonum bistorta bistort	M–H	M	Herb	18–24"	18–24"	○●	edible leaves
Rosmarinus officinalis cv. 'Huntington Carpet' rosemary	H	S–M	Shrub	1'	4'	○	culinary herb
Rubus x stellarcticus all-fieldberry	M–H	M	Herb	4–6"	2–3'	○	delicious berries
Rumex scutatus buckler-leaved sorrel	H	M	Herb	6–12"	12"	○◐	edible leaves, DA
Symphytum grandiflorum large-flowered comfrey	H	F	Herb	8–12"	18"+	○◐	DA extraordinaire
Vaccinium crassifolium creeping blueberry	H	M	Shrub	6"	6'	○◐	native, berries, evergreen

Mixing Ground-Cover Plants

Any of the above types of plants can be mixed together in a ground-cover layer. In terms of efficiency of ground cover, evergreen plants tend to do a better job, and mixing at least one running perennial species among clumping perennial or shrub species makes a big difference. In mixing different types of plants together, the different habits necessitate some consideration of their relative heights, light requirements, spread, and planting time/distance/pattern; these are discussed in the list of different combinations below. This list considers just two different types at a time, but there is no reason why more species should not be added, though the increase in benefits (in terms of efficiency of cover and resource use) slows as more species are added. Please note that "planting distance" here means the standard recommended planting distance for a single species to form a ground cover within one to two years.

When mixing plant species together, planting patterns become relevant. For plants with a clumping habit, this is easy when they have a similar spread and planting distance—this planting distance is retained and the plants merely mixed in the even pattern (figure 4.7). For clumping plants with different spreads, though, the only efficient ways to

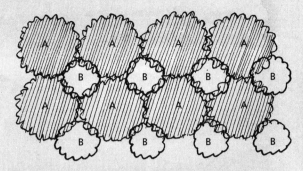

FIGURE 4.8. With clumping ground covers of radically different size, we run into problems if we use the same numbers of plants: species B covers much less area than A—one-quarter the area if A is twice as big as B. This pattern also reduces the interactions between species, making the patch more of a monoculture.

cover the ground are either to have similar numbers of each species with the smaller taking much less area (figure 4.8) or to have many more of one species than the other per unit area (figure 4.9). Increasing the number of the smaller species may mean having to plant in patches of single species, which somewhat negates the point of mixing species in the first place. Mixing clumping plants with running plants is much easier, though—the planting distances are not

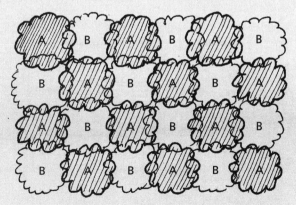

FIGURE 4.7. A ground-cover polyculture of two clumping species (A and B) with similar crown diameters and recommended planting distances is easy to interplant. Evenly mixing the two species provides plenty of species interaction. Of course, you can also plant them randomly or in other patterns.

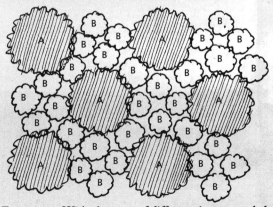

FIGURE 4.9. With clumpers of different size we can balance the area covered by each species by using four or five times as many plants of species B than of A, and planting species A at twice its standard planting distance. A smaller species-A planting distance is impractical because then it would be difficult to fit species B in the gaps efficiently.

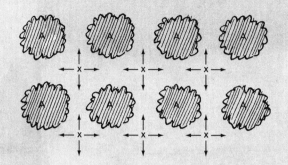

FIGURE 4.10. Mixing clumping and running plants is much easier than mixing different-size clumpers. Since runners will fill gaps, planting distances are less critical. In this example, species A is planted at its typical planting distance, but alternate staggered rows of A are replaced with the running species X at the same spacing. If X were a vigorous runner, widening the spacing of A would let X fill more area.

so critical because the running plants will quickly spread to fill all the bare areas (figure 4.10).

Clumping Perennial with Clumping Perennial

Planting. Best planted at the same time, otherwise one may well overpower the other. If the plants share similar height and spread, plant at the standard planting distance, mixing the plants in rows or randomly.

Habits. Best if both are deciduous or both are evergreen.

Heights. Easiest if roughly the same height and spread.

Light. If the same height, they should have the same light requirements. If one is smaller than the other, the smaller should have lower light requirements (i.e., be more shade tolerant).

Example. Lemon balm (*Melissa officinalis*) and giant chickweed (*Stellaria pubera*). Lemon balm is somewhat taller, at 1 to 2 feet (30 to 50 cm) tall, while giant chickweed grows only 6 to 12 inches (15 to 30 cm) high. However, both are spaced at 12 inches (30 cm), and the chickweed can tolerate quite a bit of shade. This is a fine polyculture for partial shade, with both species also serving as generalist nectaries and sources of edible greens.

Clumping Perennial with Clumping Shrub

Planting. If the shrub is quite vigorous, they can be planted at the same time. Many shrubs are less vigorous than perennials, though, in which case the shrubs can be planted a year before the perennials. If the spreads are similar, plant at the standard planting distance, mixing in rows or randomly; if the spreads are dissimilar, it is best to have a lot more of the smaller species than the larger to fill the space efficiently.

Habits. The shrub can be evergreen or deciduous, as can the perennial.

Heights. Best if the shrub is larger than the perennial, otherwise it may get swamped. This is especially important if the shrub is deciduous and the perennial evergreen.

Light. Should have similar requirements, or the perennial can have slightly more shade tolerance (depending on the height difference).

Example. Chinese indigo (*Indigofera incarnata*) and large-flowered comfrey (*Symphytum grandiflorum*). Both species are vigorous, dense, and fast-growing. Chinese indigo fixes nitrogen and grows 18 inches (45 cm) high. Ordinarily indigo bushes are spaced at 3 to 4 feet (1 to 1.3 m) apart. The comfrey species is an excellent low ground cover, reaching 12 inches (30 cm) high and spaced the same distance apart. You will need to use extra comfrey plants to fill in the gaps. This polyculture is a great low-maintenance way to build soil fertility.

Clumping Perennial/Shrub with Running Perennial/Shrub

Planting. Best planted at the same time, or the clumper can be planted a year before. Plant the clumper at slightly more than its usual planting distance (1.2 to 2 times, depending on the vigor of the runner), and interplant with a similar number of the runners spread throughout.

Habits. Either plant can be deciduous or evergreen. The one combination that may cause problems is evergreen clumper with deciduous runner, since the runner may get swamped.

Heights. Clumpers should quickly grow taller than the runners in this polyculture.

Light. The runner should have similar or slightly lower light requirements than the clumper.

Example. Marginal wood fern (*Dryopteris marginalis*) with Labrador violet (*Viola labradorica*). The ferns are slow-growing but, at 18 inches (45 cm) tall, are not in danger of being outcompeted by the fast-growing but low (4 inch/10 cm) violets. Both species are evergreen and shade tolerant. This is a fine native ground-cover polyculture, though offering little by way of food (the violet flowers are the only food worth eating). Figure 4.11 shows a similar polyculture from the Smith College botanical garden in Northampton, Massachusetts. Figure 4.12 shows another polyculture from Martin Crawford in England.

Clumping Shrub with Clumping Shrub

Similar in most respects to the clumping perennial with clumping perennial example above.

Example. Arrow broom (*Genista sagittalis*) and creeping blueberry (*Vaccinium crassifolium*). Creeping blueberry is a wonderful evergreen mat former (to 6 inches/15 cm high) with edible fruit. Arrow broom is a clumping nitrogen fixer growing up to 18 inches (45 cm) high. Both will grow in pH 5.5 to 6.0 and can be spaced at 12 inches (30 cm). Allowing additional space for the blueberries will result in better fruiting.

Running Perennial/Shrub with Running Perennial/Shrub

Planting. Should be planted at the same time. Plant at the standard planting distances for both species, in patches or randomly.

Habits. Best if both deciduous or both evergreen. If there is one of each, and the evergreen species forms a dense cover, then it will probably shade out the deciduous species.

Heights. Can differ or be similar.

Light. Similar requirements if similar heights, otherwise the lower should have lower light requirements.

(continued next page)

FIGURE 4.11. This ground-cover polyculture of ferns and Labrador violet (*Viola labradorica*) demonstrates how different plant architectures can make a good polyculture. Low, mat-forming violets and taller, arching, but clumping ferns cover the ground well and make for a ground layer of simple beauty. While the flowers are the only decent edible from these particular violets, substituting another violet species and replacing these ornamental ferns with a species with edible fiddleheads can make this polyculture much more effective for our purposes. *Photo by Eric Toensmeier.*

FIGURE 4.12. This ground-cover polyculture uses a clumping perennial with a running shrub. The clumper in this case is the ornamental flowering onion (*Allium neopolitanum*) growing through the evergreen raspberry runner *Rubus pentalobus*. We could easily substitute any other more useful *Allium* for the ornamental onion. The raspberry shown offers only fair-quality fruit best for wildlife, but it provides medicinal uses and nectar for generalist insects, and its low, evergreen habit makes it an excellent ground cover. *Photo by Martin Crawford.*

(feature article 3, continued)

Example. Wild ginger (*Asarum canadense*) and mayapple (*Podophyllum peltatum*). Both of these runners tolerate quite deep shade. Wild ginger forms a slowly spreading, low, dense carpet 4 to 8 inches (10 to 20 cm) high. Mayapple spreads quickly by rhizomes and sends up numerous sprouts like umbrellas on a busy beach, but these umbrellas are only 12 to 18 inches (30 to 50 cm) high. Both are native, and the mayapple produces an edible fruit even in shade. Together they make a good combined cover. Plant the wild ginger 8 to 12 inches (20 to 30 cm) apart, and the mayapple 12 inches (30 cm) apart.

Minimizing Harvesting Complications

Having a mixture of species in a ground-cover layer obviously complicates any harvesting of plant parts. Remember that in many cases, if your goal is a weed-suppressing ground cover, overharvesting leaves will thin the ground cover too much.

The most useful method of reducing the complications of harvesting is to mix species that grow at distinctly different heights. This could even allow for quite intensive production, for example by growing a larger perennial herb like garlic chives (*Allium tuberosum*) with a low-growing running cover like sheep sorrel (*Rumex acetosella*). A variation on the height-difference scheme is to have the taller species deciduous in habit, with a summer "crop" to harvest, along with an evergreen lower species with an autumn or winter "crop"; both species will be easily accessible and visible when they are required.

functional benefits of natural polycultures by mimicking the structure of the model using species placed in analogous planting patterns. The species so planted may or may not be selected using the ecological-analog species selection process. In fact, it is the variation in species selection techniques that distinguishes habitat mimicry from habitat invention as design strategies: habitat mimicry uses ecological analogs for species selection, while habitat invention uses desired-species selection and guild-species selection as primary tools. Both, however, use polyculture analogs for the polyculture design part.

The foundation of polyculture analogs is model ecosystem analysis conducted during goals articulation. There we strongly urged you to gather data about and, if possible, to actually observe the architecture of the model community, especially natural groupings of plants growing in the same space. This data and these observations are critical to being able to use the polyculture analog process. Without them, it will be rather difficult to mimic the natural polycultures! Luckily, we can go observe old-growth forests if we do our homework (see appendix 7), and we can also read writers such as E. Lucy Braun, whose 1950 book *Deciduous Forests of Eastern North America* provides good descriptions of many forest types in the biome.

Yet even if you are able to make observations of the model ecosystem, you must be careful, for natural plant groupings do not necessarily represent effective polycultures. Plant distributions are strongly influenced by chance events. We must beware of competition in natural ecosystems and look for signs of stress within members of natural plant groups, which may indicate that competition is taking place. We should also look for recurring groupings of healthy plants that may indicate beneficial interactions.

In addition, our intention is to *mimic* the natural polycultures, not to *imitate* them. Just because plants may often grow in certain combinations in nature does not mean we should automatically recreate that pattern. Try to understand the dynamics of such polycultures and see which aspects of the assembly serve your purposes and which do not—take the best and leave the rest. If your purpose is to recreate the natural ecosystem, then by all means imitate, but that is more likely to be restoration work, not forest gardening.

Assuming you have done the design work we proposed earlier, you will have on hand both your detailed design plan with patch patterns defined and a list of species selected for your purposes. You should have defined your patch patterns based on your observations of or data on the model ecosystem and therefore selected species based on criteria derived from the model habitat to some degree.

After species selection, use your model ecosystem analysis to find natural plant groupings to mimic. If you can, it would probably be beneficial to revisit the model community to look at these groupings again. Think about the architecture of the various species in each model plant assembly. What is their form (tree, shrub, herb) and height? What kinds of growth habits and root patterns do they exhibit (see the introduction to appendix 1)? Which species on your master list are similar? If you used ecological analogs for species selection the substitutions should be easy at this stage, as long as you kept track of which mimic species you selected as analogs for which models. If you didn't do ecological analogs, keep your eye on architectural features in the model polyculture when making analogies, but also consider the ecological functions of the two species. You may have to combine your niche analysis of model species with your natural polyculture observations or data and niche analyses of your species palette to decide how to make the analogies.

There is no guarantee that this process will work entirely to your satisfaction—the underlying theory is tenuous, not all of us have access to model ecosystems to observe, and even if you can observe you may not quite know what to look for or how to interpret it. Therefore, you may want to supplement the polyculture analog process with polyculture-build or random assembly as needed to get your juices flowing about the results.

Random Assembly

Random assembly is an easy polyculture "design" process to understand, for its name describes the basic approach. This polyculture design tool applies primarily to the random-assembly guild and polyculture design strategy. There are many variations on the theme, however, so let us describe a few of them. At one extreme, you could build indiscriminate polycultures by picking species completely randomly from a species list for wide-ranging habitats such as the Plant Species Matrix in appendix 1 (this is unlikely to have good results). You could narrow the species palette using any number of simple criteria (such as hardiness zones and soil moisture or shade tolerance) and then randomly choose from the resulting list. You can assemble a more rational species palette using one of the organized approaches we presented earlier and then choose species randomly for one or more polycultures in your garden from that palette. At the other extreme, you could throw a random species or two into a polyculture you design using the organized techniques we described above. Random assembly has even more possible permutations than these— we encourage you to use the technique in whatever ways suit your fancy and your design. We also urge you to pay attention to plant spacing even if you randomly assemble the species for your polyculture, and to observe your random assemblies to see what you can learn from them. For more discussion of this topic, see page 245.

No matter which polyculture design tool or tools you use, you need to both select species for each patch and map out where you will place them in relation to each other. This latter raises the issue of plant spacing, which we shall deal with later. At the same time, you may also need to consider your successional plans as you design your polycultures. How to work with this is what we will discuss next.

Patch Succession

If you have put in the time to work out your succession plans for the reasons we have mentioned before, then now is the time to take it to the final step. Dealing with succession in the patch design stage involves making a patch-specific succession timeline with species attached to it, and making an extra patch design drawing or two once you have drawn your horizon patch plan.

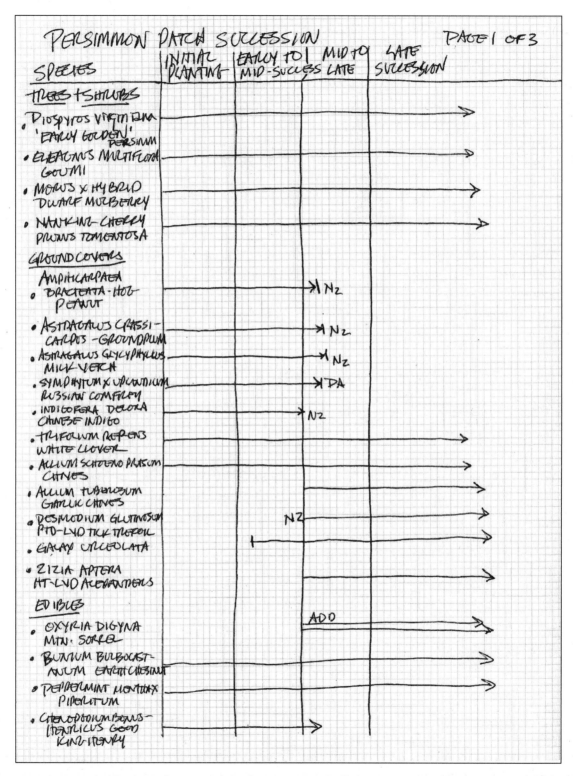

FIGURE 4.13. Patch-succession timelines can be simple and quite clarifying. They help you think through which species will last how long in the successional sequence, determine points where disturbance might be needed, and select species for the polyculture. *Sketch by Dave Jacke.*

A patch-succession timeline can be pretty simple and quite clarifying. It takes off from the overall habitat timeline you probably developed in schematic design and puts species into it to fill out the specifics of how the vegetation changes over time. This work is most critical for instant successions, since you have to plant everything for the whole successional sequence all at once. If your succession will have phases where you expect to disturb and replant the herb layer while the shrubs and trees keep growing, then you really have to design only the initial herb-layer planting now. You can wait to design the subsequent phases of the herb layer until later if you want. However, looking ahead can help you plan purchases or propagation activities, as well as have contingency plans in place if something unexpected happens.

Basically all you need to do is make a timeline across the top of a piece of paper and break that line into segments representing your patch's phases of succession (see figure 4.13). Then you can make a list of species down the edge of the page and project their expected life spans onto the timeline. Doing this while you are selecting species during polyculture design will help you understand the temporal implications of your polyculture design choices as you go, and it can guide your species selection choices as well.

While the diagramming is simple, however, the thinking behind it is not likely to be so. Think through the implications of your choices in time and space and in terms of patch purposes and maintenance. It is easy to put plants into your timeline without realizing that doing so implies you will have to disturb and replant the patch, for example. The more you know about the plants, the better your choices and thinking will be, and this is currently the biggest limitation to good succession design. Still, making a timeline can focus our attention on what we need to know, help us observe better, and give us theories to test, revise, and refine. It's a process, and part of the adventure of forest gardening in its infancy.

Making overlay drawings of the patch at different phases of succession is similar to what we discussed in both schematic and detailed design, only here we are getting to specific plants at specific locations at not-so-specific times (see figures 4.14 and 4.15 and table 4.14). Coordinate your sketching with your timeline to help you get it clear. Imagine the site conditions as they are likely to change through time, and choose and place the plants in anticipation of those changes. Our experience is that this work can be quite exciting as we envision the garden's future. This is especially true for small gardens where we gardeners often feel depressed by how few of the plants we want seem able to fit onto our site. Imagining the successional future gives us hope for the new plant friends we can welcome into our lives down the road.

The hardest part of this is being realistic about the future conditions in our gardens and making decent choices about what plants to use at those times. This is why we design more sketchily for the future and in greater detail in the near term, especially for the herb layer.

Plant Spacing

Overly dense spacing is the biggest, most common mistake we've seen in forest garden design in all our travels. People seem to think we want to mimic forests in all ways, including their high density, but this isn't necessarily true. Dense spacing leads to high competition for light, water, and nutrients. Only late-succession plants are adapted to such high-stress environments. These plants put more energy into protecting themselves from stress, and less into reproducing or growing rapidly, than we might like. Many forest gardeners have planted midsuccession species (i.e., fruit trees) at late-succession density, and this does not work for long.

Plant spacing is the design of vegetation density and pattern through the selection of the distances between plants. Plant spacing is certainly key in the design and planting phase of forest gardening, when we decide how many plants go in what space at

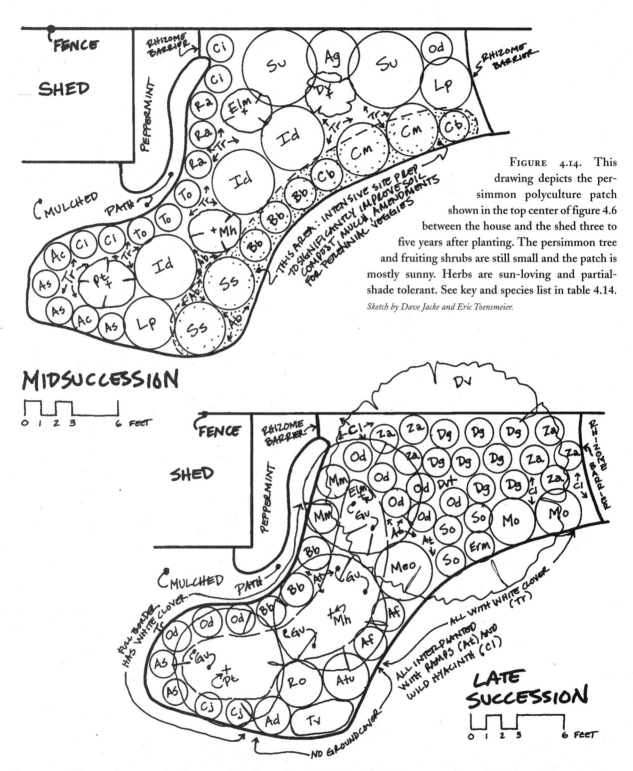

FIGURE 4.14. This drawing depicts the persimmon polyculture patch shown in the top center of figure 4.6 between the house and the shed three to five years after planting. The persimmon tree and fruiting shrubs are still small and the patch is mostly sunny. Herbs are sun-loving and partial-shade tolerant. See key and species list in table 4.14. *Sketch by Dave Jacke and Eric Toensmeier.*

FIGURE 4.15. The persimmon polyculture patch in figure 4.14 at the successional horizon consists of fruiting shrubs and a persimmon tree with a shade- and partial-shade-tolerant herb understory. This successional plan requires replanting as the sun-loving herbs get shaded out. The space on the corner near the house and patio now has culinary herbs after having been a root-crop zone in early succession. *Sketch by Dave Jacke and Eric Toensmeier.*

TABLE 4.14. Species from two successional phases of the persimmon polyculture patch illustrated in figures 4.14 and 4.15 and their main functions. Symbols mark plants on drawing. T = tree; SH = shrub; HP = herbaceous perennial; cul = culinary; plant parts listed are edible; N2 = nitrogen fixer; GC = ground cover; GN = generalist nectary; SN = specialist nectary; DA = dynamic accumulator; APC = aromatic pest confuser.

Symbol	Latin Name	Common Name	Form: Main Functions
Throughout Succession *Tree & Shrub Layers*: Dv, Pt sun-loving; Elm, Mh take part shade.			
Dv	*Diospyros virginiana*	American persimmon 'Early Golden'	T: fruit, beauty, self-pollinating
Elm	*Eleagnus multiflora*	goumi	SH: fruit, N2, beauty, screen
Mh	*Morus x hybrid*	'Geraldi dwarf' mulberry	SH: fruit, beauty, screen
Pt	*Prunus tomentosa*	Nanking cherry	SH: fruit, beauty, screen
Throughout Succession *Herb Layer*: mostly sun to part-shade tolerant.			
As	*Allium schoenoprasum*	chives	HP: greens, GC, GN, APC
Bb	*Bunium bulbocastanum*	earth chestnut	HP: tubers, SN
Mp	*Mentha x piperita*	peppermint	HP: cul, tea, GC, GN, DA
Od	*Oxyria digyna*	mountain sorrel	HP: greens, DA
Tr	*Trifolium repens*	white clover	HP: N2, GC, GN, DA
Midsuccession *Herb Layer*: mostly sun-loving, will get shaded out.			
Ab	*Amphicarpaea bracteata*	hog peanut	HP: tubers, N2, GC
Ac	*Astragalus crassicarpus*	groundplum milk vetch	HP: pods, N2, GC
Ag	*Astragalus glycyphyllos*	milk vetch	HP: N2, GC
Cb	*Chenopodium bonus-henricus*	good King Henry	HP: greens
Ci	*Cichorium intybus*	chicory	HP: greens, DA, GN
Cm	*Crambe maritima*	sea kale	HP: greens
Id	*Indigofera decora*	Chinese indigo	SH: N2, GC, GN
Lp	*Lupinus perennis*	lupine	HP: N2, GN, beauty
Ra	*Rumex acetosa*	sorrel	HP: greens, DA
Ss	*Sium sisarum*	skirret	HP: tubers, SN
Su	*Symphytum x uplandicum*	Russian comfrey	HP: GC, GN, DA
To	*Taraxacum officinalis*	dandelion	HP: greens, SN, DA
Late Succession *Herb Layer*: mostly part-shade or shade tolerant; relay planted.			
Af	*Agastache foeniculum*	anise hyssop	HP: cul, GN
At	*Allium tricoccum*	ramps	HP: greens, APC, ephemeral
Atu	*Allium tuberosum*	garlic chives	HP: greens, GC, GN, APC
Ad	*Artemisia dracunculus v. sativa*	'Licorice' tarragon	HP: cul, SN, APC
Cl	*Camassia leichtlinnii*	wild hyacinth	HP: tubers, ephemeral
Cj	*Cryptotaenia japonica*	mitsuba	HP: greens, SN
Dg	*Desmodium glutinosum*	pointed-leaved tick trefoil	HP: N2, GC
Erm	*Eryngium maritimum*	sea holly	HP: roots, SN
Gu	*Galax urceolata*	galax	HP: GC, evergreen
Mm	*Malva moschata*	green gumbo, gumbo leaf	HP: greens
Meo	*Melissa officinalis*	lemon balm	HP: cul, DA, GC, GN, APC
Mo	*Myrrhis odorata*	sweet cicely	HP: greens, SN
Ro	*Rosmarinus officinalis*	'Arp' rosemary	HP: cul
So	*Solidago odora*	sweet goldenrod	HP: greens, SN
Tv	*Thymus vulgaris*	thyme	HP: cul, GC, GN
Za	*Zizia aptera*	heart-leaved alexanders	HP: GC, SN

what distances. However, spacing is central to ongoing management and maintenance concerns, too. Plant growth, yields, weed management, pest and disease control, and harvesting all affect plant spacing, and vice versa. Remaining clear about the issues and dynamics of plant spacing is fundamental to knowing how to manage vegetation: whether and when to prune, shear, pull, sow, thin, or plant.

Guidelines for plant spacing exist, but spacing is not as simple as people like to think. Such conventions provide good starting points, offering basic initial guidance. While forest gardening breaks old conventions in important ways, plant spacing is a place where we must tread carefully. To paraphrase the Dalai Lama, "one must know how to break the rules if one is to break them properly." Many factors influence plant-spacing decisions, including your design goals, site characteristics, and the characteristics of your desired plant species and varieties. Each of these three factors has many components to consider. Your design goals influence spacing decisions because of issues like these:

- desired crops and yields;
- desired garden character, including vegetation texture and pattern, whether hedgelike (dense, linear) vs. orchardlike (dense, regular, broadscale) vs. wildish woodland (varied density and pattern) vs. savanna-like (open, less than 40 percent tree cover, varied spacing);
- desired microclimate in and around the forest garden—shade, wind, frost protection, height of bottom of canopy;
- desired rapidity of closure and self-maintenance of canopy or other vegetation layer;
- need for harvesting and management access;
- desired plant form—vertical, limbless vs. widespreading, branching trees;
- patch and polyculture characteristics—species composition and compatibility, patch size, and characteristics of surrounding patches; and

- succession planning—the need to shade out unwanted plants early on; your willingness to thin densely planted individuals; the desired longevity of the successional phase; and the mix of species in instant-succession planting.

Site characteristics affect plant spacing through features like:

- climate;
- microclimate;
- limiting factors such as light and soil fertility, moisture, and depth; and
- preexisting unwanted plants—their species, vigor, and behavior.

Desired plant species' and varieties' characteristics also shape plant spacing, such as:

- plant form and habit (for woody plants, whether they are suckering, multistemmed, or standard; for herbaceous species, whether they are runners, clumpers, mat formers, or sprawlers; and the root system patterns of all species);
- growth rate;
- ability to self-propagate, tolerance of division and transplanting; and
- ultimate plant size.

In turn, the ultimate sizes of plants are affected by factors such as species, rootstocks, cultivar vigor, site conditions (especially sun, soil fertility, and soil texture), and cultural regime. Cultivar vigor may significantly increase or decrease the size of a tree from what you would expect based on your rootstock choice. The cultural regime factors that affect plant size include irrigation, fertilizer, competition from other plants, pruning, and fruit thinning. Fruit thinning is an interesting one. Plants allowed to bear early in their life or that give heavy yearly crops will be smaller than those prevented from early bearing or allowed light crops in alternate years.

Given all these factors, we can see that plant spacing can be a complex matter. We have plenty of reasons to break any rules that might exist, or at least to bend them. Nonetheless, a few guidelines follow.

Articulate Your Goals and Assess Your Site

Our design goals and site conditions are key to understanding what rules we should break, if we break any. Most of us, in most situations, should follow normal plant spacing guidelines, because the guidelines help create healthy plants with minimal pest, disease, and competition problems. However, there are also a good number of situations where we should at least modify the guidelines, if not drop them. Only being clear on our goals and site conditions can tell us when that is the case. For example, planting linden (*Tilia* spp.) for coppice production of edible leaves means we should plant the trees only a few feet, rather than dozens of feet, apart. If you want to grow black walnut trees for straight timber, you will want to induce rapid upward growth and limit side branching by planting them close together. On the other hand, most orchard trees produce more fruits or nuts and have fewer diseases with wider spacing and more side branches. Similar issues and considerations arise for herbaceous plants.

Planting Distances Depend on Plant Type

Planting distances depend on the kind of plants involved and the purposes of the planting. We'll mention a few general points before getting into specific guidelines.

We can broadly separate plants into either clumping or running growth habits. As classified in the "Habit" column of the Plant Species Matrix, clumpers include:

- standard trees, shrubs, and vines;
- sprouting trees and multistemmed shrubs;
- clumping thicket-forming and mat-forming shrubs; and
- mat-forming or just plain clumping herbs.

Runners include:

- suckering trees and vines;
- running mat-forming and thicket-forming shrubs; and
- plain running or running mat-forming herbs.

We design spacing for clumpers using the "crowns-touching rule" and its variations, discussed below. Spacing for runners is covered following that.

Persistent plants, that is, those that are difficult to move or remove once established, need the most careful attention to planting distances, as well as planting location. These include woody plants as well as persistent perennial herbs (the latter are noted in the "Nuisance" column of the Plant Species Matrix).

Perennials that do not tolerate division and transplanting need more space to allow a longer period before division and transplanting are necessary. You can plant species that divide and transplant easily more tightly, since you can open up space as they grow.

Rooting patterns influence the amount of competition between species, so planting distances can vary depending on the plants in polycultures. Plants with varied rooting depths are more likely to thrive in close spacing than plants that compete for the same vertical soil space. The same goes for species that exhibit their major growth periods at different times during the growing season, such as spring ephemerals, summer-green herbs, and fall bulbs.

The Crowns-Touching Rule: Foundation of Clumping-Plant Spacing

The crowns-touching rule says to space plants at a distance such that their crowns will just touch when they are mature (figure 4.16). Estimate the expected mature crown diameter for each plant,

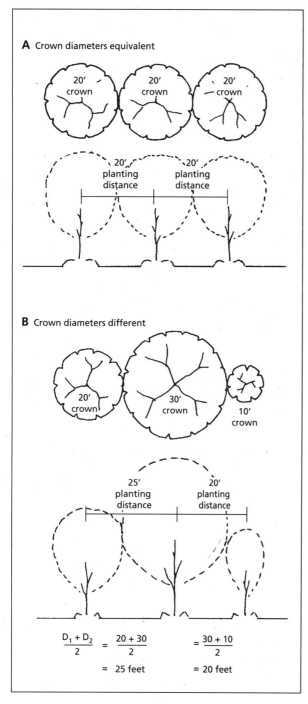

A Crown diameters equivalent

20'
crown

20'
crown

20'
crown

20'
planting
distance

20'
planting
distance

B Crown diameters different

20'
crown

30'
crown

10'
crown

25'
planting
distance

20'
planting
distance

$$\frac{D_1 + D_2}{2} = \frac{20 + 30}{2} \qquad = \frac{30 + 10}{2}$$

$$= 25 \text{ feet} \qquad = 20 \text{ feet}$$

FIGURE 4.16. The crowns-touching rule suggests that we place plants so their crowns just touch each other at their expected mature crown diameter. For plants with equivalent crown diameters (a), use the expected crown diameter as the planting distance. For two plants with different mature crown diameters (b), the planting distance between them is the average of the two crown diameters.

and place individuals of the same species and variety the expected crown diameter apart; for two trees with a crown diameter of 40 feet (12 m), plant trunks 40 feet apart.

When planting different species or varieties next to each other, average the expected diameters to find the planting distance; that is, $(\text{Dia.}_1 + \text{Dia.}_2) \div 2 =$ spacing distance. In this way, the crowns of the plants should just touch when mature. You can do this graphically on your design plan using a circle-drawing template or circle-drawing compass to draw circles at scale with the circles just touching each other.

Generally, we should provide enough space for plants to grow to their full form to minimize stress to them. The crowns-touching rule allows this to happen. Using this rule as the foundation means that we start here and vary our spacing from the crowns-touching basis depending on a variety of factors.

Estimating Crown Diameters

Estimating the expected crown diameter of a plant can be tricky. The Plant Species Matrix provides expected crown diameters for all plants listed. These crown size estimates generally represent the genetic maximum for a species growing in ideal conditions. Use them as guides only. Modify the estimates based on specific variety information, rootstocks, climate, site, and management conditions.

Because the crown size estimates are the genetic maximum under ideal conditions, most modifications to estimated crown size will be to make them smaller based on less-than-ideal conditions. However, genetic variation and exceptional growing conditions can increase the ultimate size of a plant. For example, particularly vigorous varieties may grow larger than others on the same rootstock; nursery catalogs usually tell you the projected size of a variety, or sometimes the percentage of dwarfing or enlargement from standard sizes. If your soils are fertile, moist, well drained, and deep, your climate and microclimates are good, and you intend to care for the plants well, you might assume full crown diameters 10 to 20 percent larger than the appendix 1 estimates. On the other hand, poor site conditions cause plants to grow more slowly and to reach a smaller ultimate size, sometimes 25 percent smaller or more. Some fruit tree varieties grow as much as 40 percent smaller than the expected size based on rootstock selection. You will have to use your site analysis and assessment information and your gut sense to estimate the percentage variation in plant size, unless you have much experience to go on. *Always modify your plant size estimate based on genetics (variety and rootstock selection) before modifying your estimate based on site and then cultural factors.*

Use the Crowns-Touching Rule When . . .

- *Planting clumping species.* Running plants have different considerations (see below).
- *Light is the primary limiting factor on your site.* Crowns-touching spacing assumes that soil fertility, moisture, and depth are not limiting factors in the planting.
- *Individual plant productivity is a primary goal, not weed exclusion.* See the discussion immediately below.
- *You desire shady understory conditions, but not 100 percent shade.* Crowns-touching spacing provides a maximum cover value of 90 percent when all individuals have the same crown size and they are planted diagonally, and 78 percent when planted in squares. Crowns-touching spacing therefore leaves significant opportunities for other species, wanted or unwanted, to grow between the plants thus planted. To exclude unwanted species, we must either grow additional species (such as ground covers or other crops) in the understory or plant closer than crowns-touching.
- *You are working with thin-canopied trees.* Trees with thin foliage provide more sunlight to lower layers, so you can plant them with crowns touching and still have significant light below them for partial-shade-tolerant species. Of

course, even with thin-crowned trees, if you want sun-loving herbs in the understory you will probably have to spread things out a bit.

Plant Wider than Crowns-Touching When . . .

- *Soil conditions are limiting.* Expand the plant spacing to reduce competition for limiting resources. The more severe the limitations, the further apart the woodies should be spaced. Maximum distances may be about three times the crown diameter in the most limiting soils: dry, infertile, *and* shallow.
- *You are planting species with the same or similar rooting patterns.* Plants using the same soil horizons will compete more, especially in limiting soils. Crowns-touching or wider spacing may be necessary between plants that share the same soil space.
- *You want more sunlight for underlying plants.* In England, Martin Crawford added an additional 30 percent of the crown diameter around *each* woody plant in his forest garden for this reason. That is, he provided an additional 9 feet (3 m) around each tree with a 30-foot-diameter (9 m) crown, for a total planting distance between two 30-foot trees of 48 feet (15 m). This means that to calculate the planting distance between two trees you would use the formula:

Planting distance = $(Dia_1 + Dia_2)$ x P + $[(Dia_1 + Dia_2) \div 2]$

where P = the additional spacing percentage, stated as a decimal (30% = 0.3).

This formula works for trees of different mature crown diameters, too (see figure 4.17). For example, if you had trees with 20- and 30-foot (6 and 9 m) mature crown diameters and you wanted 30 percent space around them, the planting distance between them would be:

$$\begin{aligned} \text{Distance} &= (20 + 30) \times 0.3 + [(20 + 30) \div 2] \\ &= 50 \times 0.3 + [50 \div 2] \\ &= 15 + 25 \\ &= 40 \text{ feet} \end{aligned}$$

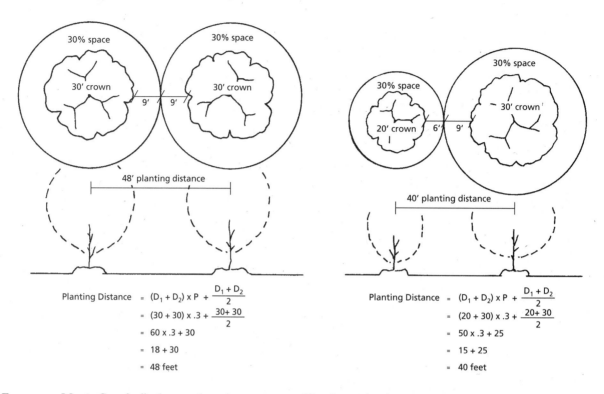

$$\text{Planting Distance} = (D_1 + D_2) \times P + \frac{D_1 + D_2}{2}$$
$$= (30 + 30) \times .3 + \frac{30 + 30}{2}$$
$$= 60 \times .3 + 30$$
$$= 18 + 30$$
$$= 48 \text{ feet}$$

$$\text{Planting Distance} = (D_1 + D_2) \times P + \frac{D_1 + D_2}{2}$$
$$= (20 + 30) \times .3 + \frac{20 + 30}{2}$$
$$= 50 \times .3 + 25$$
$$= 15 + 25$$
$$= 40 \text{ feet}$$

FIGURE 4.17. Martin Crawford's plant spacing scheme suggests adding from 25 to 50 percent additional space around each canopy tree to provide more sun for understory plants. These examples use 30 percent space, adding 9 feet (3 m) on all sides of each of two 30-foot (9 m) trees, creating a planting distance of 48 feet (15 m) between them. For trees of varying diameters, use the formula shown to figure the planting distance.

Such planting distances result in even spacing with plenty of room for understory plants. Martin now recommends adding from 25 to 50 percent additional space around each tree: 25 percent to provide light to understory plants; 50 percent to retain the feel of a woodland but provide plenty of sun for sun-loving understory crops. Note that by the standards discussed in volume 1, chapter 3, 25 percent space by Martin's definition is equal to 40 percent coverage, because the space between the trees will equal the average radius. This means that Martin is recommending planting savannas, not woodlands. Remember, though, that Martin's garden in England is at a high latitude, and this reduces the amount of sun the ground receives in his garden. At lower latitudes we can probably achieve similar results with somewhat closer spacing.

- *You need to prevent plant disease problems in humid climates.* This applies particularly in southern areas. Good air circulation prevents or slows the spread of a number of fungal and bacterial diseases. Preventing crowns from touching can reduce pest and disease transmission from one tree to another. Research your local pest and disease problems and consider this information in the process.
- *You are planting suckering woodies or rhizomatous or stoloniferous herbs.* These usually fill in to become denser than the planted spacing, and they may require thinning to maintain the designed spacing. Hence, you might want to plant them farther apart than the rule suggests and let them fill in on their own. This can save money on plant stock, but it will take longer to get a full stand, and the stand will have variable spacing due to the suckers. Suckering plants provide little habitat for understory plantings unless you thin them.

• *You are planting standard trees or shrubs with a low branching habit.* Standard woodies (single-stem specimens) may or may not provide understory habitat depending on the height of the bottom of the canopy and the crown density of individual plants. You may need to plant dense-crowned or low-limbed canopy trees farther apart to provide light for the understory than you would plant thin-crowned or high-limbed plants.

Plant Closer than Crowns-Touching When . . .

• *You are mixing plants with different root patterns.* Plants that use different portions of the soil profile will compete for soil resources less than if their main absorbing roots share the same soil horizons. Shallow- and taprooted trees planted near each other are less likely to compete than are two shallow-rooted trees, for example. We should therefore be able to plant mixed species more closely together. However, light will still limit some species, so crowns-touching spacing is still necessary unless one or both species are shade tolerant.

• *You want faster canopy closure, such as for weed control.* This is the case for many ground-cover plants but may also apply in other situations. The "Ground Covers" table in appendix 3 provides planting distances for ground-cover species.

• *You are willing to thin plants as they mature.* Sometimes we plant seedling plants at a close spacing and thin them as we learn the qualities of the resulting plants. This is one way to reduce the cost of planting, since seedling stock is usually much cheaper than are named varieties. However, to get decent plants we must be able to select those that fit our needs. So, we can plant fifty seedling persimmons, for example, and select the strongest and fastest growing in the early stages by cutting out the slow and weak ones. We can then select for fruit quality later on, eliminating the plants we don't

want and working toward reasonable spacing at the same time.

• *You intend the planting as a screen, hedge, or thicket, or you want to induce strong vertical growth without side branches for coppice or timber production.* For screening, hedging, or to induce vertical growth with few or no side branches, reduce the crowns-touching planting distance by one-third to one-half. For coppice species, see appendix 3 as a guide for species listed there or for close relatives. For other species, no coppice-spacing data is available as far as we know. Until further research takes place, we will have to guess at coppice spacings for other species based on the information we provide.

Vary Planting Distances for Structural Diversity and a Natural Look

Standardizing all the spacing distances we use will generate less lumpy texture and structural diversity than might be optimal. Therefore, we should consider varying the planting distances we use, even if we are placing species that all have the same spacing distance. Hence, in some areas the crowns would touch, in others there would be wider or narrower spacing, and in still others there would be gaps and meandering openings through the forest garden (in chapter 2, pattern #14, *Woodland Gardens*, and figure 2.14 offer a few examples). Not only would this create more lumpy texture, but it would also look more natural and be much more interesting. Planting in drifts, clumps, and scatters varies plant spacing. When you plant in intersecting drifts, clumps, and scatters, you get many beautiful, interesting, and highly naturalistic patterns (see chapter 2, pattern #50, and figure 2.57).

Space Runners Based on Growth Rate and Time to Complete Coverage

If you want to create a solid thicket of shrubs or a solid stand of suckering trees such as persimmons, pawpaws, and so on, simply plant the plants at a wider than crowns-touching spacing and let them fill in.

Obviously, faster-growing plants will probably spread faster than slow-growing species. Unfortunately, we do not have good information on how fast most of the species over 2 feet (60 cm) tall will start suckering. The Plant Species Matrix offers growth rate information for some of these species, and you'll have to guess from there. For shrubs less than 2 feet (60 cm) tall, see the "Ground Covers" table in appendix 3 for recommended planting distances.

Many of the larger suckering woodies are desirable plants; however, it is hard to imagine wanting a solid stand of most of them. You can plant them at a reasonable spacing using the crowns-touching rule and simply prune out suckers to a reasonable spacing when they appear, as few of these species are vigorously suckering (except black locust, *Robinia pseudoacacia*). In any case, many suckering trees need to have the older stems pruned out occasionally, with younger suckers taking over in their stead. This keeps fruit production at its highest.

We generally recommend planting running herbs at a distance such that they will fill the spaces between themselves and their neighbors within one to one and a half growing seasons (twelve to eighteen months). Their spacing therefore depends upon the size of plants you start with and the species' growth rate, which in turn depends upon plant genetics and site conditions. The "Ground Covers" table (appendix 3) provides approximate planting distances for many of these plants. Desire for complete ground cover sooner than that may push you to plant closer together.

Planting even moderately sized areas with ground covers takes large numbers of plants (table 4.15), and this can cost large amounts of money if you buy them all. Money or plant shortages may therefore induce you to plant farther apart or to cover a smaller area. Propagating your own stock from seed, cuttings, or divisions is cheaper and more fun, though more time-consuming. Just remember that if you propagate from seed, the plants may perform differently than you expect because of genetic variation.

Vigorous running plants, such as running bamboos and black locust, can become a major nui-

TABLE 4.15. The number of ground-cover transplants needed to plant different areas for different planting distances. Use these figures to calculate how many ground-cover plants you need to fully stock a given area with ground covers by multiplying the appropriate number from the second column by how many square feet you must cover. *From* Perennial Ground Covers *by David S. MacKenzie, published in 1997 by Timber Press, Inc. Used by permission.*

Inches between plants	Plants needed per			Square feet covered by each plant
	1 square foot	100 square feet	1,000 square feet	
3	16.000	1,600.0	16,000	0.06
4	9.000	900.0	9,000	0.11
5	5.750	575.0	5,750	0.17
6	4.000	400.0	4,000	0.25
7	2.930	293.0	2,930	0.34
8	2.250	225.0	2,250	0.44
9	1.780	178.0	1,780	0.56
10	1.440	144.0	1,440	0.69
12	1.000	100.0	1000	1.00
14	0.730	73.0	730	1.37
16	0.560	56.0	560	1.78
18	0.440	44.0	440	2.27
20	0.360	36.0	360	2.77
24	0.250	25.0	250	4.00
30	0.160	16.0	160	6.25
36	0.110	11.0	110	9.09
48	0.060	6.0	60	16.70
72	0.028	2.8	28	35.70
96	0.015	1.5	15	66.70
120	0.010	1.0	10	100.00

sance. Therefore, the most important issue for plants such as these is limiting their spread in some way. We recommend some form of rhizome barrier to do this. See "Minimal Competition" in chapter 1 (page 35) and pattern #52 for a more complete discussion. If you want to slow down a plant that grows too fast, you can also plant it in poor conditions: dry, infertile, shady, or cool. This will not, however, stop it from spreading completely.

Respect the limits to plant density

Each piece of land has a maximum amount of vegetation that it can support. If our gardens exceed these limits, plant health will suffer, productivity will drop, and some plants will die until balance is reestablished. Since spacing deals directly with plant density, we must address this issue, despite the difficulty in measuring plant density or knowing what the limits are for any given piece of land.

Only well-watered sites with deep and fertile soils will be able to provide enough resources for every layer of the forest garden to be completely full of vegetation. On less well-endowed sites, we must reduce the number of vegetation layers we design into our garden ecosystem. This is where lumpy texture comes in; we can vary the density of the layers throughout the garden to achieve structural diversity and diversity of plant species and community niches, while at the same time keeping the total plant density in any one area to a reasonable limit. In places where soils are poor, shallow, or dry, we may have to go below the

three-layer minimum needed for forest garden status and plant prairie, scrub, or savanna mimics instead.

Design Your Patches One by One

With all the information above in mind, design your patches one by one. If you want polycultures in some patches, use the polyculture design tools we discuss. If you want some patches of monoculture, go for it, but ponder proper plant spacing and surround the monocultures with diverse plantings. If you want to do some succession design but not do it everywhere, that sounds great. Or if you want to do the full-on succession thing everywhere, more power to you. Trust your own design process, skills, and heart to lead you the right way, and make use

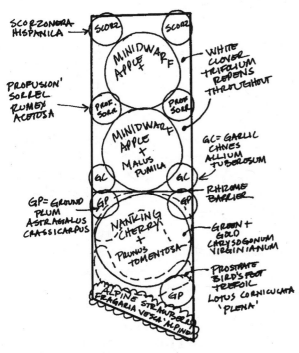

FIGURE 4.18. This polyculture patch design specifies the plantings for the finger of shrubs extending south from the southeast corner of our case study's greenhouse in figure 4.6. The patch is intended to stay sunny and be maintained as a fruiting shrub patch in perpetuity. Two minidwarf apples and a Nanking cherry compose the overstory, with a mix of multifunctional edibles and soil-improving ground covers underneath. *Sketch by Dave Jacke.*

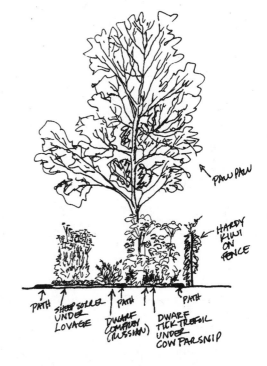

FIGURE 4.19. Schematic cross sections are a useful tool for envisioning polycultures of plants that you do not know very well. This patch will live under the right-hand (eastern) Norway maple canopy along the north edge of our case study's property. The polyculture consists of a pawpaw understory tree layer with herbs of various sizes underneath. The main functions of the herb layer include soil improvement and attracting beneficial insects. Notice how the various plants occupy radically different architectural niches. *Sketch by Dave Jacke.*

of the tools we offer to help you through. Work through all the pieces and accommodate them to each other and things should turn out fine. Figures 4.18 and 4.19 offer glimpses of some additional patch designs for different circumstances.

Check Your Design: All Plants Used?

By specifying the required functions and conditions in the garden through schematic patch patterning, and by carefully selecting a species palette to meet these requirements, the patch design process helps ensure that all desired garden functions get fulfilled. Don't stop there, though. Once you complete your patch designs, check to make sure your patch designs use all those species you selected, or at least enough to make sure the guild functions get performed. Otherwise, you may not be making full use of all your earlier guild-design efforts. Keeping track on your master list of which species you use in which patches should make this task easier.

Plan for Construction, Site Preparation, and Establishment

If your garden design includes infrastructure elements or features, you may need to work out construction details of those elements so you can build or buy them. Now is the time to do this. This may involve creating accurate, site-specific construction detail drawings or searching the Web, books, stores, or catalogs for the arbor, bench, or preformed pond just right for your needs. Many resources are out there to help you successfully negotiate these decisions. If your budget is an important piece of the design puzzle, work on these things now to help you at least estimate costs, if not nail them down. Besides, many infrastructure elements and features have to get built before planting day arrives. You may as well figure these things out early so you can hop on them and get them done. The sooner they are in place, the sooner you can get your forest garden going.

We have raised the issue of designing your site preparation and establishment processes before, but now that your patch designs are complete you can make final decisions. Take all of the work you have done and create a simple bubble diagram of the garden area that depicts your best thinking about the patterns and types of site preparation you will use in both time and space. Will you deal with the whole site similarly, or will specific patches get different treatments? In what order will you do things in which places? These may be simple questions to answer, or they may not. Use chapter 5 as a guide, along with your detailed- and patch-design plans. Site preparation may also play into your budget work.

Establishment planning may be something you need to do before proceeding further, as well. How much time, energy, labor, and money do you have available for planting? How will this influence your sequencing of site preparation and of planting? You can think this through now or take a break and think it through later.

Finalize Budget Estimates

Finally, we come to filthy lucre yet again. If you listened to our advice, you did rough estimates of your budget along the way, mainly based on infrastructure design. This should have affected the design plans you created. With your patch designs complete, you can now estimate the cost of planting, if not site preparation in addition. As you develop these numbers, you may need to feed the implications back to your design. As we have said before, all these factors must come to an accommodation with each other through the design process. When everything is in sync, you can consider your design process complete. Congratulations!

CHAPTER SUMMARY

At the beginning of chapter 3 we wrote about design as a process of discovery. We hope that you have found this to be the case, that you have discovered things about yourself, your landscape, and your future forest garden and its inhabitants that you couldn't have imagined before beginning. The process we laid out in this and the preceding chapter appears highly rational, but we trust you have experienced the intuitive aspects of it as you have worked, and we expect that the messiness has made itself known! You have consciously worked through four of the six fundamental actions of design we discussed in chapter 3: goals articulation, site analysis and assessment, design concept, and design proper. That leaves two that we should at least touch on in this summary—evaluation and implementation.

Evaluation is a key piece of the design process, and indeed, it is happening at least unconsciously all the time, especially during the design phase. It is a good idea to make it explicit, however. We recommend you look over the work you have done and acknowledge, weigh, and value it. Give yourself a few pats on the back. Think about how you would do it differently next time, what you have learned, and what you still want to learn. Review your design in light of your goals statement to see how it stacks up. How does it feel to you? Does it meet your goals? Where does it exceed them, and where does it fall short? How have your goals changed, and how does the plan reflect those changes? You don't have to modify anything in light of these observations. Simply notice, take it in, and acknowledge your efforts and intentions. We hope you have had fun during the design process. Now is when the fun really begins!

Implementation is the next phase of your work, and the last piece of the design process. Site prepa-ration usually comes first, followed by staking out the design on the ground and making final adjustments. Then you can plant. Chapters 5 and 6 cover these steps in detail.

We have only begun a long process of developing and evolving effective polycultures and forest garden designs. Our forest garden designs represent our best guesses about what will work given what we know, surmise, and have observed about our sites and about the ecology of forest mimics. Once we have planted the polycultures we design, we need to watch them carefully, to observe how they change and grow, to see who leaves, who sticks around, and who crashes the party. How does the polyculture work for us when we plant, harvest, manage, or maintain our garden? What needs to change? How might we do it differently? We can and should alter our polycultures to reflect our learning and test new ideas. Add or subtract species, rip out a patch and start over, disturb two similar patches differently to see what happens. Through such observations and ponderings as we play, we will improve our ability to design effective polycultures and excellent forest gardens.

When we get hundreds (or even thousands) of people designing, planting, and perfecting guilds, polycultures, and plants in an array of environments, we will begin to see forest gardening blossom into the fullness of its potential. We have much to learn. These ideas are just the beginning. Now enjoy preparing and planting your garden, and living, growing, and evolving with it.

1. Again, thanks to Walt Cudnohufsky at the Conway School of Landscape Design for this "handle."
2. Much of this and the next paragraph come from Crawford, 1999.
3. Crawford, 1997c.

5

Site Preparation

Although you are probably impatient to get your trees in the ground and growing, a little bit of time spent now in proper preparation will pay you back handsomely in healthier, more productive trees and less work in the future.

—STELLA OTTO, *The Backyard Orchardist*

Soils must usually be prepared and amended prior to planting. The extra effort will be worthwhile since perennial wildflowers live for many years in the same spot. . . . Developing good garden soils from undesirable soils may seem to pose a real problem, but with patience, energy, and planning, wonders can be accomplished. . . .

—SAMUEL JONES, JR., AND LEONARD FOOTE,
Gardening with Native Wildflowers

Planting a forest garden can take much hard physical labor. In addition, most of you will have invested significant time and energy in your garden design. If you're going to invest that much in design and planting, taking the time to prepare the ground is worthwhile, even if it takes one or two years. "One or two years?!" we hear you say. Yes, perhaps.

It is easy to allow our enthusiasm (and impatience) to override what we know will be best in the long run, and to skip site-preparation work. Obviously, we feel these issues are important enough to have devoted a whole chapter to them. As you read the following, you will see some of the problems you may face and understand why they are important to address. The fact that much of this information is not well known indicates that most people are into the quick fix. Well, forest gardening is about slowing down, looking at the big picture and the long term, and preparing the ground well before acting. Proper site preparation will build a solid foundation under your garden. It will enable all of your hard work to

pay off to its utmost. This chapter provides you with comprehensive information on site preparation challenges you may face and strategies you can use to meet those challenges—perhaps even turning them to your own advantage.

SITE PREPARATION

When selecting plants, two basic choices define the ends of a continuum: select species adapted to the site conditions you have, or alter the site to suit the desired species. Clearly, selecting species suited to the site requires the least energy investment and minimizes ecological damage. However, if you don't modify the site to create favorable conditions, it may narrow the range of species you can choose. Sometimes that's a good thing, but it may also reduce the chances of success for your chosen species or reduce the returns in food quality or quantity. Therefore, people often alter the site before planting. We humans usually go overboard in this direction

TABLE 5.1. Comparison of ability to modify site conditions before and after planting. *Adapted by permission of Pearson Education, Inc., Upper Saddle River, NJ, from Richard W. Harris, James R. Clark, and Nelda P. Matheny,* Arboriculture: Integrated Management of Landscape Trees, Shrubs, and Vines, *3rd edition, © 1999.*

Site Characteristics	Ability to Modify	
	Preplant	Postplant
Soil Texture		
Increase coarseness	Low	Low
Increase fineness	Low	Low
Replace	Good	Moderate to low
Increase organic content	Good*	Low
Soil structure		
Reduce compaction	Moderate*	Low
Increase aeration	Moderate*	Low
Soil moisture		
Increase water-holding capacity	Moderate*	Low
Increase water percolation	Good to moderate	Moderate to low
Increase surface drainage	Good	Good to low
Increase internal drainage	Good to low	Moderate to low
Lower water table	Good to low	Good to low
Soil chemical characteristics		
Raise pH	Good	Moderate
Lower pH in alkali soil	Good to moderate	Moderate to low
Lower pH in calcareous soil	Low	Low
Lower salinity	Good to moderate	Good to moderate
Lower boron	Moderate	Moderate
Reduce herbicide residue	Good to low	Moderate to low
Reduce heavy metals	Low	Low

*Effects usually short-term.

and frequently overlook side effects of the site work we do. This section focuses on effective, low-investment, ecologically sound site-preparation strategies for forest gardeners, though we'll consider a few more extreme measures as well.

We cannot easily modify all unfavorable site conditions (see table 5.1). Those we can modify we must deal with before planting, almost without exception. Otherwise, improving the site significantly disturbs existing plants. Therefore, thoroughly assess the site early on to find all potential problems before planting your forest garden.

Thinking of site preparation as designed disturbances raises a couple of key issues. First, we should treat site preparation as another design problem. In other words, articulate goals and objectives, analyze and assess the situation, discover a guiding concept, and scheme and design the solution. This section won't walk through this process, but it will offer information you need to make choices. Chapters 3 and 4 discuss integrating site preparation into the design process. Second, this idea connects site preparation to the succession dynamics discussed in volume 1, chapter 6. Site preparation directly affects the subsequent successional pathway: what niches are available, what plants are available to those niches, and which plants perform best under the conditions the disturbance creates. The patterning, kind, intensity, and timing of the disturbance should all mesh with your successional plans, species selections, and garden design.

Every site-preparation action affects at least one of the following aspects of the site, each of which helps define what kind of habitat the site becomes:

- vegetation composition and its successional pathway;
- soil architecture, the soil food web, and fertility; and
- water supply, flow, and storage.

Naturally, most site-preparation work affects several or all of these, even if you intend the action to influence only one of them. Knowing you want to create a specific habitat or habitats and that each action affects more than one of these factors should help you decide what site-preparation actions to take. Try to avoid unintended side effects and to choose actions with multiple benefits. Ponder site preparation carefully, choosing the strategies that meet the most objectives with the least time, work, or cost, depending on your priorities.

SITE-PREPARATION GOALS AND OBJECTIVES

Ultimately, improving plant performance and reducing long-term maintenance are the whole point of site preparation for forest gardeners. This usually means creating specific conditions to grow specific desired species successfully, creating specific habitat types, or diversifying habitat conditions. Habitat diversification is the opposite of what most site-preparation strategies usually intend. Most farmers want a uniform site. Most forest gardeners want to create intentionally varied habitats. This difference alters site-preparation strategies to some degree. In any case, clarity on your goals and objectives forms the first step in site preparation.

You should have articulated your goals during the design process. These goals will have guided your analysis and assessment of the site. That site assessment should provide you with specific site-preparation objectives you want to achieve to meet your articulated goals. These might include:

Managing vegetation by:
- redirecting existing successional trends;
- creating specific habitats;
- minimizing/eliminating competition: "weed" control;
- maximizing desired plant performance; and
- diversifying or improving microclimates or community types.

Improving soil conditions by:
- altering moisture regime;
- improving horizon profile structure;
- relieving compaction;
- improving nutrient status and pH;
- optimizing soil organic-matter content;
- enlivening the soil food web; and
- matching fungal-bacterial balance to desired crops.

Improving water regime by:
- optimizing topography and grading;
- altering soil drainage;
- improving infiltration;
- improving water supply; and
- creating aquatic or wetland habitat.

The list above suggests only topic areas to consider. You should go through that list, and your site-analysis observations, to define specific desired conditions for each topic area. These objectives may differ for different habitats in your forest garden. What kind of moisture regime do you have, and what kind do you want? Specifically what compaction or consistence conditions do you want to create for your plants, at what depth? What nutrients do you want at what supply levels in what layers? What specific weeds do you want to control, and what level of control do you want? And so on. As with goals articulation in the overall design process, don't worry here about how you will achieve these objectives—just define the objectives themselves.

Typically, we would like a prepared forest garden site to exhibit the following desired conditions or contain the following legacies:

- only desired plant species remain alive;
- ideally, remaining undesirable species are easily controlled or eliminated (try to eliminate potential persistent or competitor-strategist weeds prior to planting; at minimum, have a long-term control strategy or find uses for them);
- propagules (seeds, roots, stumps) remaining on-site should be only those of desired or useful species or should be easily controllable;
- the soil contains abundant organic matter (3 to 5 percent);
- there are adequate and balanced nutrient supplies in the topsoil and subsoil (especially in terms of typical limiting nutrients such as N, P, K, Ca);
- no toxins should be present in the soil, as either petrochemicals, toxic quantities of micronutrients, undesirable plant allelochemicals, or microbes;
- there is a vibrant soil food web (abundant and balanced organism populations);
- the soil profile has good structure and drainage, allowing for deep root penetration, good soil aeration and moisture retention, and prevention of waterlogging, unless a poorly drained habitat is desired;
- the topsoil exhibits healthy aggregation (crumb structure); and
- the topography and surface drainage characteristics should suit the design goals.

Obviously, you should modify these typical desired conditions to suit your design. Once you know your goals, assess the site using your goals as a guide.

Choosing Site-Preparation Strategies and Techniques

With your objectives clear and your site conditions assessed, choose which techniques and strategies to use to prepare the site for planting based on:

- your goals and objectives (including crop species);
- site conditions;
- your garden design patterns;
- your establishment strategy, including the kind of plant stock you will use (seeds, balled and burlapped, potted, bare root, etc.; see chapter 6);
- the tools and equipment available; and
- time factors, costs, and labor availability.

Often just being clear on these factors will make certain techniques or strategies jump out at you. Sometimes you will have to consider more carefully, review options, and piece a plan together.

Many sites will probably need fairly simple site preparation, including a year or two of cover cropping to control weeds and improve soil, some adjustment of soil organic-matter content, amendments for nutrition, perhaps compaction or drainage work, and a good sheet mulch for weed control during establishment. These will form the core of site preparation for most of you. However, many sites have one or more challenges that go beyond the basic prescription and require more thought and action. The site analysis discussed in chapter 3 should identify these challenges for you. The following sections will guide your actions and choices.

Some site-preparation techniques involve large-scale or intensive interventions, yet even subtle approaches may have a large impact. What is the least you can do to significantly move the ecosystem in the direction of increasing health? How fast do you need or want change to occur, and how much time, money, and energy can you afford to invest? What other actions will your project force you to take, and how can you piggyback site modification onto those? For example, maybe you need to build a new septic system and so will have equipment on-site. For not much extra money, while it's there the backhoe could loosen hardpan in your garden, dig swales, or make pits and mounds for you. Just remember that these actions will have other consequences to which you may have to respond, such as soil compaction.

Remember to consider the principles discussed throughout the book when making these choices, too. For instance, the principle of multiple functions suggests that your site-preparation strategy should serve multiple purposes, and that you should carefully consider the implications of each option so you can minimize or take advantage of possible negative consequences. For example, on a droughty site with thick hardpan starting 2 feet (60 cm) below the surface, you could coordinate irrigation-line trenches and tree-planting patterns, with deep-rooted trees over or near the trenches and shallow-rooted species planted elsewhere.

Sequencing Site Preparation

Once you have chosen your site-preparation strategies and techniques, you must decide in what order to undertake them. Generally, you should work from the broad scale to the details, from deep soil layers to surface treatments. When altering existing vegetation, it often works best ecologically to make canopy alterations first and then work your way down to the ground layer, but for practical reasons you usually need to open access through the shrub and herb layers first. Of course, each situation will be unique, and you will have to think through the specifics to make them work optimally for your goals and site. Just remember to think long-term; a one-year delay in planting is probably worth the time if it means the difference between good soil drainage and mediocre soil drainage, or good control of vigorous rhizomatous weeds like quackgrass and poor control of them. Wisdom beats impatience and impulsiveness in the end every time, and often sooner than that. We have seen or experienced the consequences of inadequate site preparation too many times: poor performance and productivity; a need for extremely high maintenance; greatly increased difficulty of weed control from working around desired plants; or loss of the initial investment completely. Choose your site preparation wisely, plan it well, and carry it out carefully and faithfully. It's definitely worth it!

A ROGUE'S GALLERY OF CHALLENGING SITE CONDITIONS

The discussions below flesh out details of the issues listed in the first column of table 5.2 and follow that order of presentation. The site-preparation techniques and strategies follow in alphabetical order in the next subsection.

Climate

Low rainfall, strong winds, and frost can damage or kill plants if not dealt with skillfully. Some regions experience predictable dry months, while others experience drought infrequently or unpredictably. We should expect and prepare for such extremes to increase, or at least for patterns to shift, as global warming gathers momentum. Strong winter winds can dry plants just as much as, if not worse than, the hot winds of summer. Frozen ground means essentially that plants experience drought because water is not available. Reducing winter winds keeps woody plants vital, healthy, and productive. Early fall or late spring frosts challenge us to observe and adapt to our site's microclimates. Even if such events do not kill plants, they can kill flowers or damage fruit, reducing the harvest considerably.

Landform

Land sloping too steeply erodes easily, especially with bare, fine-textured, or poorly aggregated soils. Mechanically mowing slopes steeper than 25 percent (a 5-foot rise in 20 feet of run, or a 2.5 m rise in 10 m of run) is difficult and unsafe. Flat sites drain poorly, causing puddling or long-term wetness. When slopes fall below 2 percent (¼ inch per foot; 2 cm per m), runoff moves slowly, if at all. This can cause root stress in wet-intolerant plants and kill soil life. Wet soils also increase the chances and severity of compaction. Sites with low topographic diversity have lower habitat, microclimate, and soil diversity. Hence they have lower potential species diversity.

TABLE 5.2. Site conditions indicating the need for adaptive design or site modification. Capitalized phrases without numbers refer to solutions in the Hero's Gallery. Parenthetic terms such as (#23) following italicized phrases refer to patterns in chapter 2, where the ideas are discussed. OM = organic matter.

Site Condition	Adaptive Design	Planting-Site Modification
Climate		
Low rainfall/drought (seasonal or overall)	• Plant deep-rooted, drought-tolerant species or species dormant in dry seasons. • Increase soil aggregation and water-holding capacity by increasing soil OM content and improving soil biology: Mulch, Compost and Compost Tea.	• Pre-plant Cover Crops to increase soil OM. • Infiltration Swales. • Irrigation Systems.
Strong winds (cold, drying, damaging)	• Choose wind-tolerant plants. • Plant in less exposed locations.	• Plant windbreaks or install wind fences. • Use Mounds as windbreaks.
Frost in late spring or early fall	• Choose tolerant plants. • Avoid planting in frost pockets, find warmer microclimates: midslope positions, good cold-air drainage. • Plant sensitive plants in cold zones to delay flowering: north slopes, north side of house, etc.	• Install ponds and stone or black surfaces to absorb and hold heat in the garden. • Modify cold-air "dams" in the landscape: cross-slope fences, hedges, etc.
Landform		
Too steep	• Permanent vegetative cover, especially woodies • Unmown, hand-mown, or grazed. • Contour planting. No paths or contour paths.	• Check Logs. • Infiltration Swales (for infiltration, erosion control). • Regrading, terracing, retaining walls.
Too flat	• May need wet-tolerant species in puddle zones.	• Regrading, *Pits and Mounds* (#23), Raised Beds, Mound Planting. • French drains or Subsurface Drainage may be necessary.
Low topographic/habitat diversity	• Varied vegetation types. • Varied disturbance regimes. • Varied *Zones of Water Use* (#8).	• Regrading. • *Pits and Mounds* (#23). • Put in a pond.
Soil		
Soil Structure/Profile		
Surface compaction (in topsoil)	• Select deep-rooted plants. • Select wet-tolerant plants if needed. • Mulch, Native Fungi Transplants. • Mycorrhizal Inoculation, Soil Inoculation. • PREVENTION is the best approach: see "Compaction," page 324.	• Deep-rooted Cover Crops. • Amend with OM and till: "thoroughly incorporate organic matter through depth of compaction."[1] Compost and Compost Tea. • Deep Ripping or Chisel Plowing. Soil Staking • Infiltration Swales. • Double Digging or hand-loosening of compaction.
Restrictive layer near surface less than 2 feet (0.6 m) thick with permeable soil below it (e.g., plowpan)	• Select deep-rooted or wet-tolerant plants. • Mulch. • Penetrate Restrictive Layer at planting. • Use butterfly planting (chapter 6).	• Deep-rooted Cover Crops. • Deep Ripping or Chisel Plowing. • Radial Trenching with soil replacement. • Double Digging. Infiltration Swales. Soil Staking.
Restrictive layer near surface thicker than 2 feet (0.6 m), with permeable soil below it	• Select deep-rooted plants, maybe wet-tolerant plants. • Mulch. • Penetrate Restrictive Layer at planting. • Use butterfly planting (chapter 6).	• Radial Trenching. • Backhoe Loosening. Double Digging. • Infiltration Swales. • Mounds and Mound Planting, Raised Beds.

(continued next page)

(table 5.2, continued)

Site Condition	Adaptive Design	Planting-Site Modification
Soil: *Soil Structure/Profile* continued		
Restrictive layer less than 4 feet (1.2 m) from the surface with no permeable soil below it, e.g., shallow over hardpan	• Select shallow-rooted or wet-tolerant plants. • Some sites may be wet in fall, winter, and spring and droughty in summer: select plants appropriately. • Use butterfly planting (chapter 6).	• Deep Ripping or Chisel Plowing. Double Digging. Backhoe Loosening. Radial Trenching. • Import topsoil. Mounds and Mound Planting, Raised Beds. Subsurface Drainage if needed. • If droughty: Infiltration Swales, Irrigation Systems.
Restrictive layer more than 4 feet (1.2 m) from surface, no permeable soil below (deep over hardpan)	• Select flat- and heart-rooted trees, not tap-rooted. Select wet-tolerant plants if needed.	• Backhoe Loosening. • Install Subsurface Drainage if needed.
Shallow over bedrock (< 4 ft./1.2 m in depth)	• Select shallow-rooted species. Some sites and bedrock types may require wet-tolerant species; others may require drought tolerants. • Seek bedrock fractures and deep pockets for deep-rooted species. • Use butterfly planting (chapter 6). • Mulch.	• Deep-Mulch soil creation. • Mounds and Mound Planting, Raised Beds. • Irrigation Systems. • In extreme cases, import topsoil.
Abrupt soil texture boundaries (most common at filled sites).	• Mulch. Do not amend planting holes with organic matter. • Select deep-rooted species.	• Thoroughly mix soil layers with a backhoe or through Double Digging.
Too clayey	• Select deep-rooted, clay- and wet-tolerant plants. Some clay soils are also droughty. • Mycorrhizal Inoculation, Soil Inoculation.	• Add organic matter: Mulch, Compost and Compost Tea, Cover Crops, Soil Staking. • Raised Beds, Mound Planting. Radial Trenching. • DO NOT ADD SAND.
Too silty	• Select adapted plants. • Mycorrhizal Inoculation, Soil Inoculation.	• Add organic matter: Mulch, Compost and Compost Tea, Cover Crops. • DO NOT ADD SAND.
Too sandy	• Select deep-rooted, drought-tolerant, and sand-adapted plants. • Use dynamic accumulators and nitrogen fixers to improve fertility and reduce leaching. • Mycorrhizal Inoculation, Soil Inoculation.	• Add organic matter: Mulch, Compost and Compost Tea, Cover Crops, green and brown manures. • Install Irrigation Systems, Infiltration Swales. • DO NOT ADD CLAY.
Too rocky	• Select adapted plants (from rocky habitats). • Minimize digging and cultivation. • Mycorrhizal Inoculation, Soil Inoculation.	• Add soil; Raised Beds, Mounds and Mound Planting. • Mulch heavily. • Use rocks (to create snake-habitat piles, stone walls, etc.).
Too humusy	• Select adapted plants (acid, wet tolerant). • Mycorrhizal Inoculation, Soil Inoculation, Native Fungi Transplants.	• May require high levels of lime and nutrients. • Soil replacement.
Soil Moisture Conditions		
Droughty/low water-holding capacity	• Usually caused by very sandy, gravelly, or rocky soils. See "Too Sandy," above.	
Excess water-holding capacity	• Usually caused by excessively clayey, silty, or humusy soils. See sections of table relevant to cause.	
Low percolation/infiltration rate	• May be caused by steep slopes, fine texture, low OM content, compaction, high salinity, or poor soil biology. Oiling of urban and suburban soils is also an issue. See relevant sections of table.	

Site Condition	Adaptive Design	Planting-Site Modification
Soil: *Soil Moisture Conditions* *continued*		
Poor surface drainage (puddling, saturated soil at surface)	• May be caused by flat slopes, fine texture, low OM content, compaction, restrictive layers, high water table, high salinity, or poor soil biology. Oiling of urban and suburban soils is also an issue. See relevant sections of table. • Diverting uphill runoff may reduce surface puddling or wetness.	
Poor internal drainage (saturated soil beneath surface)	• Caused by flat slopes, fine texture, compaction, restrictive layers, high salinity, or high water table. See sections of table relevant to cause.	
Excessive internal drainage	• Usually caused by sandy or gravelly soils in deep layers. See sections of table relevant to cause.	
High water table	• Select wet-tolerant plants. • Use butterfly planting (chapter 6). • Highly evaporative plants (e.g., willows) may lower the water table.	• Raised Beds, Mounds and Mound Planting. • Install Subsurface Drainage system. • Lower elevation of nearby surface waters.
Soil Chemical Characteristics		
High pH (alkaline soil)	• Select adapted plants. • Apply micronutrient fertilizers as needed to reduce deficiencies.	• Apply sulfur at recommended rates based on soil testing results. • Use acidifying chemical fertilizers.
Low pH (acid soil)	• Select adapted plants. • Avoid acidifying chemical fertilizers. • Foster a healthy soil food web, especially mycorrhizas, to increase nutrient uptake by plants.	• Apply lime, wood ashes at rates based on soil test. • Prescribed Burning. • To maintain low pH but add calcium, use gypsum ($CaSO_4$).
High salinity (e.g., road salt)	• Select salt-tolerant plants. • Mulch. • Use Leaching Irrigation. • Select a different site. • Mycorrhizal Inoculation, Soil Inoculation.	• Modify site to maximize soil drainage if necessary, incorporate gypsum, and apply Leaching Irrigation. • Alter drainage to keep salty runoff out of garden. • Use a fence, wall, or hedge to stop salt spray.
Heavy-metal contamination (arsenic, lead, cadmium, etc.)	• Don't use tires, pressure-treated wood, etc. in garden. • Select a different site for edible crops. • Mulch or maintain dense ground cover to stop contaminated dust and reduce child/animal exposure and soil erosion. • Grow hyperaccumulators to reduce soil concentrations of metals. • Chelate metals: add abundant organic matter, Compost and Compost Tea, Mycorrhizal Inoculation, Soil Inoculation, Native Fungi Transplants. • Grow crops that do not concentrate metals in edible parts.	• Raised Beds or Mounds and Mound Planting using clean soil; use shallow-rooted crops. • Replace soil. • Block car exhaust. • For cationic metals: raise pH above 6.5, add phosphorus to reduce bioavailability. • For anionic metals: lower pH to reduce bioavailability, avoid adding phosphorus. • Drain wet soils to oxidize metals and reduce bioavailability (except for chromium, which is less mobile in wet soils).
Infertility/nutrient imbalance	• Select adapted plants, nitrogen fixers, or dynamic accumulators. • Use Mulch high in required nutrients. • Improve soil biology for better plant nutrient capture: Compost and Compost Tea, Native Fungi Transplants, Mycorrhizal Inoculation, Soil Inoculation.	• Amend the Soil: Compost and Compost Tea, powdered or liquid soil fertilizers, foliar feeding.

(continued next page)

(table 5.2, continued)

Site Condition	Adaptive Design	Planting-Site Modification
Soil *continued*		
Soil Biology Imbalances		
Soil bacteria too dominant (need more fungi)	• Choose plants adapted to bacterial soils. • Plant pioneer woody plants to shift bacterial soils to fungal dominance. • Avoid soil disturbance. • Mulch, especially with carbonaceous material.	• Inoculate: Native Fungi Transplants, fungal Compost and Compost Tea, Mycorrhizal Inoculation, Soil Inoculation. • Soil Staking. • Prescribed Burning.
Soil fungi too dominant (need more bacteria)	• Change choice of plants. • Fertilize with nitrogen.	• Till the soil to kill fungi and foster bacteria. • Incorporate organic matter into the soil, especially green. • Apply good bacterial Compost and Compost Tea.

Pest and disease organisms prevalent, slow decomposition, no or minimal soil aggregation, slow infiltration, surface puddling (insufficient soil organism diversity or lack of specific functional groups)	• Strengthen root-zone food web:
	  - Mycorrhizal Inoculation, Soil Inoculation;
	  - use Compost-Plug Planting;
	  - maintain diverse plant cover.
	• Strengthen decomposer food web:
	  - provide diverse dead organic matter;
	  - inoculate with decomposers: Compost and Compost Tea, Native Fungi Transplants.
		• Improve soil aeration and drainage.
		• Provide food resources for specific missing organisms.
		• Minimize soil disruption: no chemical fertilizers, pesticides, herbicides, tilling.
		• Soil solarization: in summer, cover bare soil with a layer of clear or black plastic, weighting the edges. Allow sun to "cook" the soil for several weeks.

Vegetation		
Unwanted aggressive rhizomatous, persistent perennials or tenacious propagules (roots, stumps, tubers, etc.) within site	• Place garden elsewhere. • Find a use for the plants, e.g., use as mulch. • Cut plants and Mulch heavily (sheet-mulch; see chapter 6). • Use competitive exclusion: plant and favor competitors, disfavor unwanted species. • Alter habitat conditions: change light or water regime, soil food web, pH, etc.	• Till and use Cover Crops for two years. • Repeatedly chop, pull, mow, graze heavily, burn, or cut back plants until roots are exhausted. • Grub out roots: by hand or using pigs. • Apply weighted heavy black plastic, plywood, or other robust light-limiting coverings for up to a year, maybe more, to kill plants. • Woody Weed Extraction. • Prescribed Burning. • Some especially difficult species and circumstances may require Herbicides.
Unwanted aggressive rhizomatous perennials invading from around site	• Place garden elsewhere. • Plant barrier plants (e.g., comfrey). • Create a mown strip barrier. • Mycorrhizal Inoculation, Soil Inoculation.	• Install plastic or masonry Rhizome Barriers. • Create a barrier pond or water-filled moat. • Create a chicken moat (chapter 1, figure 1.3).
Unwanted woody plants	• Place garden elsewhere. • Plant shade-tolerant understory species.	• Cut, turn into mushrooms, firewood, chips, etc. • Create *Gaps and Clearings* (#16) in stages to replace existing species over time. • Woody Weed Extraction. • Repeatedly cut plants until roots are exhausted. • Some especially difficult species and circumstances may require Herbicides.

Site Condition	Adaptive Design	Planting-Site Modification
Vegetation *continued*		
Prolific seed bank of unwanted species	• Place garden elsewhere. • Avoid soil disturbance. • Mulch heavily, especially sheet mulch. • Establish complete ground cover. • Never fertilize sites with large weed seed banks!	• Cover Crop. • Soil solarization: in summer, cover bare soil with a layer of clear or black plastic, weighting the edges. Allow sun to "cook" the soil for several weeks. • Repeatedly tilling, allowing weed seeds to sprout, then tilling again sometimes works.
Periodic heavy seed pressure from outside site	• Place garden elsewhere. • Avoid soil disturbance. • Mulch heavily. Time sheet-mulch applications to minimize sprouting. • Establish complete ground cover.	• Eliminate seed-producing neighbors. • Install windbreaks or other barriers to seed movement. • Well-timed Prescribed Burning.
Poison ivy or other nuisance species	• Place garden elsewhere. • Increase shade. • Avoid soil disturbance. • Establish complete ground cover with vigorous useful species. • Eternal vigilance is the price of freedom: catch and pull new plants early.	• Till and use Cover Crops for two or more years. • Grub roots by hand. • Pigs eat poison ivy roots. • Repeatedly pull, mow, graze heavily (goats), or cut back plants until roots are exhausted. • Apply weighted heavy black plastic, plywood, or other light-limiting coverings until plants die. • Rhizome Barriers prevent root spread from outside. • Cut back plants outside garden just after flowering to prevent seed spread by birds. • Some especially difficult species and circumstances may require Herbicides. Cut plants, then flail into small pieces, while wearing lots of protective gear. Spot-treat resprouts with translocating herbicide. • Alter the environment to reduce favorable growing conditions: deep Mulch or vigorous heavily shading plants.

1 Harris, Clark and Matheny, 1999, page 181.

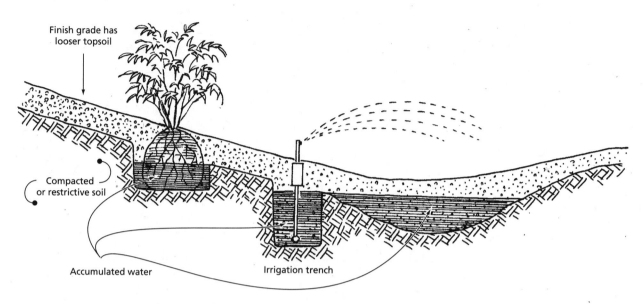

Finish grade has looser topsoil

Compacted or restrictive soil

Accumulated water

Irrigation trench

FIGURE 5.1. Typical construction practices often result in loose imported soils sitting atop soils compacted during construction. The underlying compaction restricts water movement and root growth, which results in water ponding below the surface of the looser soil layers. This can kill trees and other plantings. Similar effects occur when planting trees into natural dense or fine-textured soils, leaving the plant in a water-collecting bowl.

COMPACTION

Compaction results when soils bear heavy or concentrated weight and the pore space between soil particles decreases. Wetness lubricates the motion of soil particles and increases the damage. Compaction reduces water infiltration, drainage, and movement, as well as soil aeration, the ease of root penetration, and mycorrhizal activity. It kills off beneficial fungi and aerobic bacteria and fosters disease-causing anaerobic bacteria. Construction equipment, cars, and even lawn tractors, bicycles, and human feet can cause soil compaction; compression results from a high weight per unit area, not the total weight of the object. For example, a 200-pound person on a 30-pound bicycle (a total of 104 kg) with 8 square inches (52 sq. cm) of footprint yields about 29 pounds per square inch of pressure (2 kg per sq. cm). Meanwhile, a 12,000-pound (5,443 kg) bulldozer on two 6-foot-long by 18-inch-wide tracks (180 by 45 cm) creates around 5 pounds per square inch (0.3 kg per sq. cm).

Since compactive force spreads as it moves down into the soil profile, damage from feet and cars usually stays in the top 4 inches (100 mm) of soil, with the worst compression occurring about ¾ inch (20 mm) from the surface. The worst compaction from heavy equipment, trucks, and tractors usually remains in the top 6 to 8 inches (150 to 200 mm) but can go much deeper if the soil is wet or it squeezes out from under tires.[1] Agricultural tillage often creates a layer of compacted soil called a "plowpan" just below the depth of tillage, usually 6 to 12 inches (150 to 300 mm) from the surface. On construction sites, topsoil or other material may loosely cover one or more deep intentionally or unintentionally compacted layers, impeding water movement and root penetration (see figure 5.1). You may find intentional compaction near buildings, roads, sidewalks, and other infrastructure as shown in table 5.3. Always dig below the surface to see what's going on!

Compaction is hard to remedy, especially after planting. Many of the soil-loosening techniques in

TABLE 5.3. Areas and depths of soil normally compacted during site development and construction. Compaction depth and intensity differ with soil texture, soil moisture at the time of impact, compactive pressure, and other factors. Note that compactive pressure is the weight per area: a lightweight object with a small footprint may generate more pressure than a heavy object with a large footprint. *Adapted from Harris, Clark, and Matheny, 1999, page 113.*

Near buildings	5–10 ft./1.5–3 m wide
Near road edges	5 ft./1.5 m wide
Under roads	2–3 ft./0.6–1 m deep
Under sidewalks	8–12 in./0.2–0.3 m deep
Near bottom of a fill slope	1–12 ft./0.3–4 m wide
Any area of fill	throughout fill plus 6 in./0.15 m
Utility trenches	throughout depth of backfill
Areas driven over by vehicles or equipment	up to 2–3 ft./0.6–1 m deep

table 5.2 and the following section have not received adequate scientific scrutiny or have given mixed results. *Preventing compaction is the best approach.* Here are some ways to do that:

- Avoid cultivation, landscape work, and travel over the site when the soil is wet or after you have loosened or cultivated it. Minimize tillage generally.
- Loosen soil only when it is dry.
- Minimize travel over the site, even on foot. Stay on defined paths and away from tree roots.
- Vehicles traveling over soil should have smooth, wide, low-pressure tires and be lightweight. Narrow or knobby tires concentrate weight. This includes carts, bicycles, and the like.
- Thick, coarse mulch helps spread weight over the soil.
- Well-aggregated, biologically active soils resist compaction more effectively and spring back some once the weight is removed. However, they have more pore space to lose and can compact more dramatically than poorly aggregated soils. The activities of soil organisms can recreate pore spaces if compaction has not gone past the point of no return. If it has, the organisms will need help to return to work.

RESTRICTIVE LAYERS

A restrictive layer is any soil horizon with certain combinations of soil texture, structure, and consistence that limit water and air movement or root growth (see feature article 2). Soil compaction also creates restrictive layers (see above). Some soils naturally have very tight hardpan horizons due to their natural history or fine texture. Depths and thicknesses of such layers vary tremendously from place to place. For example, soils formed where ancient lakes used to exist can have clay layers with highly permeable sand and gravel above or below them. Other soils developed in materials mixed together and compacted by tons of glacial ice, creating a restrictive layer from the surface all the way to bedrock. Hundreds more variations exist, each with implications for water movement, seasonal high water tables, droughtiness, soil fertility, rooting depth, plant health, and productivity.

Since the possible variations overwhelm the space available here, you will have to do specific on-site research to understand your soil-profile situation and its implications for growing conditions. Lean heavily on your county soil surveys and your own soil-pit observations. Chapter 3 and feature article 2 include pointers on soil assessment.

ABRUPT SOIL-TEXTURE BOUNDARIES

Radical shifts in soil texture from one soil horizon or area to another can restrict water movement and root penetration. Abrupt changes in pore size create restrictions to water movement due to the surface tension of water within the soil. Why roots will not cross such abrupt soil boundaries is unclear. For example, researchers once noted that pear tree roots did not grow into or through a naturally occurring coarse sand horizon from overlying loamy soils, even though the sand was underlain by a moist silty clay loam. In such a case, we might expect roots to easily move down through the more freely draining layer to the moister soil below, yet they would not. Mixing the three layers with a backhoe resulted in deeper soil penetration by the pear roots.[2] Similarly, some people place a few inches of crushed stone in the bottom of tree planting holes to assist planting-hole drainage. In reality, the crushed stone does not begin to fill with water until the soil above, around, and *under* the crushed stone saturates, so the stone layer fills from below. Adding stone to the bottom of the planting hole actually waterlogs the plant *more*, not less!

Abrupt shifts in soil texture occur most frequently on filled sites. However, such shifts occur naturally where flowing water sorted sand and gravel into layers, or where sediments accumulated before and after changes in climate or flooding regime. Abrupt soil-texture boundaries also occur when we amend planting holes with organic materials or completely surround *and cover* the root-ball of potted or balled-and-burlapped plants with soil of a finer texture than the root-ball has. Both of these conditions can cause plant failure due to inadequate drainage or lack of root-ball saturation, respectively (figure 5.2).

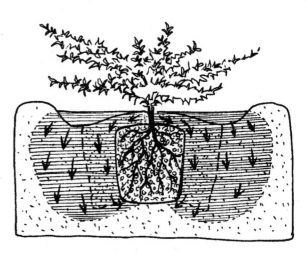

FIGURE 5.2. Never cover the root-ball of a transplant with soil whose texture is finer than that of the soil in the root-ball. If you do, the abrupt soil-texture boundary between the root-ball and the surrounding soil will cause the water to flow around the root-ball, not into it. The root-ball will begin to soak in water only when the water rises from below. Instead, leave the root-ball surface exposed and water it directly.

SOIL TEXTURE EXTREMES

Soils exhibiting any texture extreme may be problematic for crops or may limit species selection. Clayey soils tend to hold many nutrients, yet they compact easily and in wet seasons frequently lack sufficient oxygen for healthy roots. Some clays expand and contract dramatically as they absorb water and dry out, thereby cracking and destabilizing plants, walkways, building foundations, and other structures. Sandy soils cannot hold much water against the pull of gravity, so they tend to drain too easily and often end up droughty. They also hold fewer nutrients.

Extremely silty soils tend to aggregate poorly and squish out from under heavy objects when wet. They can also hold large amounts of water, leading to oxygen stress for roots. However, they usually hold large amounts of nutrients as well. Soils with high amounts of humus or organic matter have similar properties, except they frequently contain high acidity and few nutrients or hold onto nutrients too tightly for plants to gain access to them unless aided by mycorrhizas.

*Do **not** try to alter soil texture by adding sand to silt or clay.* Adding sand to clay only makes matters worse, essentially turning your soil to concrete as the small particles fill the voids between the large particles. This actually *reduces* the soil's pore space until a large percentage of the soil consists of the amended material. Even adding clay or silt to sandy soils is problematic. The quantities of materials required to properly balance textures is huge, the cost for significant change is usually prohibitive, and the logistics of obtaining an even mixture are overwhelming. Lumps of clay in a sand matrix won't do much for your soil texture. *Always use organic matter and soil biology (especially mycorrhizal and other fungi) to alter soil texture, not sand, clay, or silt.* Soil staking can also help in tight soils (see "Soil Staking" in the Hero's Gallery section of this chapter for details).

LOW PERCOLATION/INFILTRATION RATE

Slow infiltration arises from a number of factors. Steep slopes increase runoff and decrease the amount of rain that seeps into soil. Fine-textured soils percolate slowly because of small soil pore spaces. Compacted or low-organic-matter soils have less pore space and poor aggregation. High salt content destroys aggregates, and biologically poor soil doesn't have the organisms to create them, leading to the same condition: few and small soil pores that limit infiltration. Many urban and suburban soils resist wetting and infiltration,[3] presumably because oily air pollutants cover the soil surface, so water beads up rather than soaking in. Slow infiltration reduces the effectiveness of irrigation and natural rainfall. More water runs off, leaving the soil drier, or it puddles on the surface.

As you can imagine, many of these factors interrelate to create a vicious cycle of soil-quality decay: slow infiltration causes puddling, which makes compaction more likely. Compaction harms soil biology and destroys aggregates, reducing aeration and pore space, further reducing infiltration. Slow infiltration therefore often indicates other problems, even though it is a problem in itself.

Poor Surface Drainage

Puddling on the soil surface or saturated surface soil indicates poor surface drainage. Poor surface drainage is usually an indicator of other problems, such as compaction, restrictive layers, or slow infiltration and its causes (see above). Excessively flat site topography or a high water table can also cause puddling.

High Water Table

The water table is the interface between saturated and unsaturated soil, the top of the pool of water held in the ground. The water table moves up and down with season and rainfall but has a typical range at each site given average climate conditions. The seasonal high water table is the highest average water-table elevation at a given site, usually occurring in the spring. When the water table comes near the surface, it can kill plants and soil organisms by depriving the soil of oxygen. This lack of oxygen also alters the color of the soil, with iron taking red, oxidized forms in unsaturated soils and gray, reduced forms in soil saturated for long time periods. "Mottled" soil color helps us estimate the seasonal high water table. Water tables may be "perched" on top of restrictive layers, even when the soil below the restrictive layer is unsaturated. Water tables may also extend down to the bedrock and may be strongly influenced by nearby water bodies.

High water tables can severely limit plant growth by limiting rooting depth, even when the high water table lasts for only a few days and the soil is otherwise droughty. Some plants will die if their roots are flooded for only a few hours; others can take extended periods of wet soils. Use your county soil survey and soil-pit observations to help you determine the estimated seasonal high water table so you can either adapt to or modify your conditions.

High pH

Excessively alkaline soils (over pH 7) can cause deficiencies of phosphorus, iron, zinc, manganese, copper, and cobalt in plants. A few crops adjust well to high-pH soils, but most require neutral or slightly acid conditions. High pH can be a problem in urban sites or anywhere near intact concrete or mortar or concrete rubble. High pH values can also arise from high salinity (see page 328).

Low pH

Excessively acid soil causes deficiencies of all of the most critical plant nutrients—nitrogen, calcium, magnesium, phosphorus, potassium, sulfur, molybdenum, and boron. Acidity below pH 5.5 begins reducing availability of most of these nutrients and limits the survival of bacteria and actinomycetes. Fungi can survive throughout all pH ranges. They become more dominant in acid soils, buffering the soil in a slightly acid range that many native plants prefer (see volume 1, chapter 5, "Fungal-Bacterial Balance"). However, in urban and suburban areas in the early twenty-first century, we must account for acid rain, more broadly known as acid deposition, which significantly alters this stable, naturally buffered acidity.

Acid deposition includes acid rain and snow, as well as dry deposition of acid particles falling from the atmosphere. Acid deposits can break the soil out of the healthy fungi-buffered pH range, making plant nutrients unavailable, increasing nutrient leaching, and increasing the availability of toxic elements such as aluminum and heavy metals. Long-term research in New Hampshire's relatively pristine Hubbard Brook Experiment Station shows that thirty years of acid deposition reduced soil calcium levels by over one-half. "The trees have nearly stopped growing" there, according to one report, and "depleted and leached soils have weakened root systems in the Allegheny National Forest" in Pennsylvania as well.[4] Again, the burden shifts to the intervenor; an end to acid deposition, adding lime and fertilizer, fences against deer, and time may be all that can renew these forests. If you live anywhere in the eastern, downwind half of North America, especially in urban or suburban areas, or in sites with low-calcium parent materials, check your soils for acidity, nutrients, and heavy metals to determine how badly acid deposition has damaged your soils. Conserve energy, drive less, buy less, and buy locally to help cut down on acid pollution.

SALINITY

The term *salinity* describes the concentration of salts in the soil or in water. The most common salts include sodium chloride, calcium chloride, and potassium chloride, but magnesium, aluminum, bromine, and other reactive metal ions count as salts, too. High soil salinity damages the soil food web. Many plants cannot grow, or cannot grow well, in highly or even moderately saline soils. Sodium in particular breaks down soil aggregates, reducing soil aeration, drainage, and infiltration.

Most naturally salty soils occur in arid regions and along seashores, but human activities also influence soil salinity. Many chemical fertilizers have salts in them. Some groundwater sources contain enough

salt that irrigating with them can damage soils and plants. Recycling household wastewaters makes sense in many cases, but we need to consider salinity from household contaminants in that regard. Some municipal governments apply calcium chloride to dirt roads to keep dust down. However, throughout most of the temperate-forest region, the most common culprits are winter road-deicing agents. Sodium chloride is the most common and damaging deicer. Potassium chloride is an infrequently used, more expensive, less damaging substitute.

The conventional wisdom about deicing salts says that as long as you get enough rainfall during the growing season, soils and plants are relatively unaffected, except in areas very close to the roads in question. The fact that Milwaukee, Wisconsin, dumped 11 pounds of sodium chloride per running foot (16 kg/m) on its streets in 1989 should give us pause, though.[5] Eighteen years of road salting in Maine resulted in high salt levels in the top 6 to 8 inches (15 to 20 cm) of soil up to 45 feet (14 m) from the road. Salt levels were half as high at 45 feet as they were at 6 feet (2 m).[6] Clearly, older roads with more traffic and a longer history of salting will have broader, more intense impacts than newer roads with less intensive ice-clearing programs.

We must also consider road runoff: low-lying areas near roads can get very high exposure to salty runoff. In addition, salt spray from roads can damage evergreens or burn emerging leaves in spring if not washed off. Many plants tolerant of salty soils will not tolerate salt spray. The reverse is also true: many plants that tolerate salt spray do not tolerate salty soils.

While it is true that "a good soil can become saline in one season,"[7] in most areas of temperate forest, current climate conditions do not favor this possibility. However, the presence of road salt or highly evaporative or droughty conditions combined with the use of salty irrigation water can stress sensitive or even moderately sensitive plants. This is especially true on clayey or poorly drained soils where less salt leaching occurs. Shallow soils, planters, and containers are also more vulnerable. If your garden site is within 50 feet (15 m) of a heavily salted road, you might want to check the salt levels in your soil. In addition, as global climates warm, we can expect changes that may affect the ability of soils to cleanse themselves of salt by natural rainfall. Finally, please note that if you have road-salt problems, you should also test your soil for lead from the old leaded gasolines.

HEAVY METALS

Heavy metals are metallic chemical elements that become toxic to plants or their herbivores (i.e., us) at sufficient soil concentrations. As elements—that is, basic atoms found in the periodic table of the elements—heavy metals cannot biodegrade. They also generally do not leach very far or very fast. Once they land somewhere they tend to stay there. Their behavior and management depend partly on whether they are positively or negatively charged atoms. Positively charged or cationic metals include lead, cadmium, nickel, copper, mercury, zinc, chromium, and manganese. Negatively charged or anionic metals include arsenic, molybdenum, selenium, and boron.

Heavy metals occur most frequently as pollutants from industrial culture, though some occur at significant concentrations in specific types of rock. For example, most automobile tires contain cadmium and zinc, so areas near roads, tire dumps, or garden tire sculptures may contain elevated levels. Cadmium also occurs in superphosphate fertilizer, and chemically fertilized lands may have elevated levels of it.[8] In fact, recent evidence indicates that many chemical fertilizers contain materials, including heavy metals, that we would otherwise consider hazardous waste![9] The manufacturers call them "inert ingredients" instead.

Copper sulfate is often used to kill algae in ponds and lakes, so sediments and irrigation water from these sources may be suspect. Acid rain releases mercury and aluminum from soil storage. Mercury may be the most toxic heavy metal for humans. Even breathing the gases from or handling the

contents of a broken thermometer can cause symptoms of toxicity! Recent studies suggest that pressure-treated lumber containing copper, chromium, or arsenic leaches these metals far more than previously recognized, so don't use this material anywhere, but especially not near food plants. However, you never know where someone might grow food in the future, and heavy metals never decay. Chromium and arsenic migrate in soils more easily than other elements. Heavy metals may be present in the soil from industrial operations, such as leather tanning, that took place even in colonial times. Many old orchards have become housing developments in recent decades; orchard soils may contain high arsenic or lead levels from the insecticides used in olden times.

Lead, probably the most ubiquitous heavy metal, was a component of house paint and auto fuel until banned late in the past century. Though some people consider less than 500 parts per million (ppm) of lead in the soil a "low" lead concentration, no safe level of lead exists. As a potent neurotoxin, lead harms human biology at the smallest concentrations, causing learning disabilities, reduced intelligence, and immune-system damage. Some urban soils contain over 2,000 ppm of lead from demolished buildings and traffic exhaust. Of course, now that lead is illegal (at least in paint, though not in "fertilizer"), house paint frequently contains mercury to reduce mildew!

Soil acidity makes cationic heavy metals more available to plants. Neutral to alkaline soils and high soil organic-matter levels help bind these metals and prevent uptake. The opposite is true of anionic metals: lower pH reduces their availability to plants. Different plants take up different metals at different rates, and different metals tend to concentrate in specific plant parts. For example, lead tends to concentrate in leafy vegetables but not in fruiting vegetables. Hence, tomatoes, peppers, strawberries, squash, and so on are the safest crops to grow in high-lead soils. Kale and collards do not take up much lead and are among the safer leafy greens to grow in high-lead soil. Root crops concentrate moderate amounts of lead, and the soil clinging to the crop may also contaminate them.[10] We have not found information regarding heavy-metal uptake by perennial crops at this time. Frequently, however, the worst ingestion of soil-borne heavy metals comes from breathing dust, not eating food, so keep contaminated soils moist, mulched, and vegetated.

If your site is urban, within 100 feet (30 m) of a road, or within 50 feet (15 m) of a building built before 1978, test the soil for lead. On filled or reclaimed sites, different soil horizons may have different lead concentrations. For other metals, decide whether to test based on the site's and the neighborhood's history.

The newly emerging field of phytoremediation offers hope for metal-contaminated soils. Some plants, called hyperaccumulators, have demonstrated the ability to concentrate certain heavy metals up to 10,000 parts per million in their tissues. In the course of several years of cropping these plants, soil concentrations of heavy metals can decline significantly.[11]

INFERTILITY AND NUTRIENT IMBALANCE

Infertility, the overall lack of a number of important nutrients, reduces plant productivity and species selection options. It commonly arises in excessively sandy soils, soils low in organic matter and soil life, and geologically old, abused, or overexploited soils. Some parent materials tend to lack a wide range of nutrients, producing infertile soils as a result.

Nutrient imbalances are defined relative to the needs of desired crop plants. Such imbalances can take several forms. Urban and suburban soils may experience excessive nitrogen input from atmospheric pollution, while other nutrients leach away at high rates due to acid rain. Agriculture may have depleted specific nutrients, but not others, if the soils had the same crop grown on them for many years in a row. Nutrient imbalances may also arise from imbalances in the mineral content of soil parent materials. We must address each of these or other causes of nutrient imbalances in a unique way for each site. As discussed in volume 1, chapter 5, we must consider the fertility of the topsoil, the subsoil, and the parent materials to determine our self-renewing-fertility development strategies.

SOIL BIOLOGY IMBALANCES

Consciously managing the soil food web, a new and potentially powerful aspect of gardening, offers many gifts to the wise gardener (see volume 1, chapter 5). Ensuring the formation of proper mycorrhizas on your plants is a fundamental component of this work, as is creating a soil fungal-bacterial balance appropriate to your crops. Mycorrhizas offer numerous benefits, but most often we don't need to do anything to help them form. When a soil lacks the right fungi, though, inoculation can make a huge difference. Bacteria-dominated soils foster earlier-succession grasses, annuals, and perennials, and vice versa. Fungi-dominated soils foster pioneer trees and shrubs and later-succession perennial herbs, and vice versa. The wrong balance will severely limit the health, competitiveness, and productivity of your crops.

Even if you have the right fungal-bacterial balance, sufficient diversity of organisms, in both the decomposer web and the root-zone web, is essential to gain the benefits of healthy soil food webs. Signs of insufficient diversity include prevalence of disease organisms, slow decomposition, minimal or no soil-particle aggregation, and slow infiltration or surface puddling. Each of these may signal other problems besides or in addition to an unhealthy soil food web.

UNWANTED VEGETATION

The nature of the existing unwanted plants in and around the garden site, their vigor, and their means of propagation should significantly influence your site-preparation strategies. Your ability to direct succession down your desired path depends on preplanting site preparation to a large degree. This is especially true when dealing with prolific seed banks of ruderal species, vigorous rhizomatous plants, persistent perennials with tenacious propagules, and heavy seed pressure from neighboring individuals. Such plants can create increased workloads or threaten the garden with inundation if they are vigorous competitors. Incomplete eradication of vigorous rhizomatous plants (e.g., quackgrass, *Agropyron repens*) can lead to an overwhelming weed problem two or three years down the line, when controlling the weed is much more difficult around your established or establishing herbs.

If your unwanted plants are woody species, you may need to clear a space for your desired species. Do this clearing with due consideration to minimizing negative consequences for native plants and wildlife. As we've said elsewhere, cutting existing forests to make a forest garden makes little sense, especially if the forest is already healthy. Use the principle of site repair in this regard (pattern #5). If you do decide to cut down trees or shrubs, though, consider the fact that you can grow mushrooms in the stumps and logs left over. You will need to inoculate the logs or stumps when they are fresh, so find out more about this before cutting so you can be prepared (see pattern #37).

A HERO'S GALLERY OF SITE-PREP STRATEGIES AND TECHNIQUES

We use the word *hero* with tongue firmly planted in cheek here. Heroism implies a "silver bullet" approach to solving problems, which often only creates more problems. We're looking instead to "solve for pattern" and intervene the least to do the most. Solving for pattern means understanding the whole system and discovering which conditions play the largest role in creating a less-than-optimal site for your purposes. Knowing this, you can then decide which one, two, or three interventions will most significantly affect all the challenges your site offers, while minimizing damage to the site's good qualities.

We list the site-preparation strategies and techniques below in alphabetical order to help users of

table 5.2 find them. Their order of appearance has nothing to do with their usefulness or desirability.

AMENDING THE SOIL: NUTRIENTS AND pH

Soil testing is the obvious precursor to any soil amendment program, including understanding both parent-material and topsoil nutrient levels. Your parent materials may indicate a need for long-term nutrient amendments, or they may not. Make sure your nutrient needs are clear, since different crops will require nutrients in different amounts. In addition, add your nutrients in a form the ecosystem can handle, and make sure the ecosystem can absorb them with minimal nutrient leaching. You can find details on specific amendments and when, where, and how to use them in other references (see appendix 7).

In most cases, add nutrients either as rock powders or in organic form. Chemical fertilizers usually have highly available constituents that tend to burn plants and soil organisms, tend to leach away before they can be absorbed by the ecosystem, and often contain unwanted acids or other constituents, including hazardous waste! They may still be useful in some situations, such as extremely poor soils needing immediate help just to get vegetative cover established, but you can usually find good organic amendments for almost any circumstance. Soil containing plenty of organic matter will absorb chemical fertilizers with less leaching, though the fertilizers will also tend to burn up some of that organic matter.

Rock powders tend toward stability and leach minimally. Though less immediately available to plants, their nutrients stick around for the long haul. This puts the onus on you to stimulate healthy soil biology to make those nutrients available to your green allies. The same goes for organic amendments, such as bonemeal, dried blood, leather meal, and organic blends; they leach less easily, stick around longer, and generally require healthy, living soil to be effective. Compost and compost tea, of course, provide not only nutrients and organic matter but also the soil life to make those nutrients work. Mulch is perhaps the slowest method of applying nutrients, but it works well, minimizes soil disturbance, and fosters fungi-dominated soils. Rock powders and organic amendments are typically a site-preparation nutrition strategy, while mulch is a maintenance nutrition strategy, as are dynamic accumulators and nitrogen fixers.

Applying organic amendments to the soil surface mimics natural processes but delays their taking effect. Incorporating amendments into the soil takes energy, disturbs the soil and established plants, and favors bacterial soil conditions, but it speeds nutrient uptake by plants. You can also apply nutrients as foliar sprays or mix them into irrigation water.

The standard approach to raising pH (making soil less acid, or more alkaline) involves adding limestone to the soil. Soil testing will tell you how much lime to apply to raise pH the required amount. However, beware of recommendations for typical crops, for they may raise pH too high for your plants, which may be acid-tolerant species. A rough guide is that 80 pounds of ground lime per 1,000 square feet or 1.5 tons per acre (390 kg/1,000 sq. m, or 3.4 metric tons/ha) will temporarily raise pH one point,[12] but this varies by soil texture, cation exchange capacity, and so on. Pelletized lime creates less dust than regular lime, easing lung congestion and minimizing waste.

For excessively alkaline soils, incorporating sulfur into the soil lowers pH, yet this can be expensive. It may not be economical to acidify soils with calcareous parent materials for this reason. Soil testing will tell you how much sulfur to apply to neutralize excess alkalinity. One author states that applying 7 pounds of sulfur per 1,000 square feet or 300 pounds per acre (34 kg/ 1,000 sq. m. or 335 kg/ha) will drop pH by one point. Again, however, this varies by soil texture and calcium content. Pelletized sulfur is preferable to powdered sulfur, which requires you to wear protective gear to apply it because the dust can severely damage lungs, eyes, or skin. Plants need protection, too. On sites with existing plants, even if you use pelletized sulfur, apply only half the required amount, and only when plants are dormant, to minimize shock and burning.[13] Pity the poor soil microbes!

BACKHOE LOOSENING

This technique uses a backhoe to break up restrictive layers, ideally without mixing topsoil and subsoil. You can either dig whole beds this way or dig trenches through the planting area linking tree-planting locations.

Backhoes remain a commonly available piece of equipment for hire, usually with an operator, in most regions of North America. They can do much work and much damage in very short order, so choose your backhoe operator carefully. A skilled operator is well worth the extra money, if he or she costs more. Our experiences with uncommunicative, domineering, or less-skilled operators demonstrate that fixing equipment-induced site problems can easily cost double what it cost to create the problem in the first place! Even good operators will cause some negative impacts on your site, such as compaction. Therefore, use backhoe loosening only as a last resort, or to deal with deep-seated restrictive layers that handwork cannot reasonably remedy. Remember the following if you proceed:

- Keep topsoil and subsoil separate as the digging progresses. One good way to do this is to mimic the double-digging technique (see figure 5.5): dig the topsoil from a section at one end of a bed or trench and place it in a pile near the other end. The backhoe can then reach into the hole or trench, scoop the hardpan layer into the bucket, shake it, and place it back into the trench in the same location. The operator then removes the topsoil from the next trench section, placing it on top of the just-loosened subsoil, loosens the newly exposed subsoil, and moves on. In this way, the topsoil moves progressively toward the initial end of the trench,

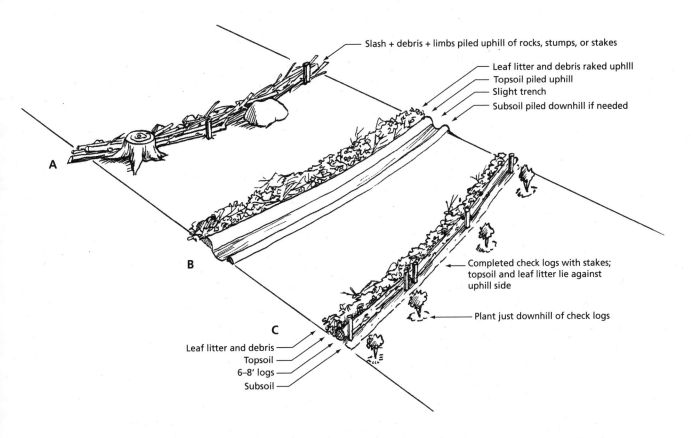

Slash + debris + limbs piled uphill of rocks, stumps, or stakes

Leaf litter and debris raked uphill
Topsoil piled uphill
Slight trench
Subsoil piled downhill if needed

A

B

Completed check logs with stakes;
topsoil and leaf litter lie against
uphill side

Plant just downhill of check logs

C

Leaf litter and debris
Topsoil
6–8' logs
Subsoil

FIGURE 5.3. Check logs help stop erosion on steep, compacted, or unvegetated slopes by retaining a small amount of surface moisture in the soil and preventing the erosion of leaf litter and debris. (a) The simplest method is to lay limbs and brush along the contour uphill of rocks, stumps, or stakes. (b) You can also rake surface litter uphill of the check log site, excavate a shallow trench along the contour, and then stake logs in the trench. (c) Backfill uphill of the logs with the topsoil and leaf litter.

without having to lie on the soil surface next to the trench. The operator can then place the first topsoil removed into the trench at the far end to fill the topsoil gap left over.

- Do your best to loosen the hardpan without mixing subsoil and topsoil. Mixing subsoil into topsoil reduces the topsoil's health and productivity. Mixing topsoil into subsoil represents a loss of productive soil from where it has the most benefit and may lead to anaerobic subsoil conditions as organic matter attempts to decompose in deep horizons.

CHECK LOGS

Steep slopes erode more easily, generate more runoff, and soak up less rainfall than gentle slopes. In addi-

tion, they cannot hold mulch or a litter layer as well as they might. Check logs simply and cheaply reduce all these problems (figure 5.3) and add structural and compositional diversity to a site. They can stop limited and dispersed slope erosion, but they cannot stop severe or concentrated erosion. As the logs decompose, they provide habitat for soil critters, fungi, and small wildlife, as well as becoming storehouses of water themselves. Check logs are usually placed just above or below a tree or shrub planting site to assist in capturing rainfall for the planting. They are best used when there is "waste" wood that can be put to good use. If you need to infiltrate water and stop erosion but do not have wood to play with, see "Infiltration Swales" (below). Here are some pointers for using check logs:

- Lay logs and long limbs 1 to 4 inches (2 to 10 cm) in diameter on the ground along the slope contour. Place them against the uphill sides of stumps, rocks, or other stabilizing features, or drive stakes just below them to hold them in place.
- Make sure not to lay the check logs in long lines or in patterns that concentrate runoff in one area. Instead, create many small, scattered catchments to disperse runoff so it soaks into the ground to rejuvenate soil and plants.
- Mulch the uphill side of the check logs a little bit so they catch more water.
- Plant uphill of a check log if you want to use the log as part of the watering "dish" around the plant or as a terrace. Plant downhill of the check log to let the log soak water into the ground uphill of the plant and help water it.
- For greater stability, more effective catchment of runoff water, and more work, use logs up to 6 or 8 inches (15 to 20 cm) in diameter. Rake loose surface organic materials away from either side of the log's final resting place, depositing them uphill of the log site. Dig a shallow contour trench, piling some of the soil (preferably subsoil) just downhill of the trench and firming it with your feet. Keep litter-layer or mulch materials and topsoil separate from any mineral subsoil by piling them uphill of the trench. The trench should be just deep enough that the log will lie firmly in it on undisturbed soil, supported by the pile of diggings, and will not roll. If there is a lot of runoff, bury the log deeper to ensure the water seeps into the ground rather than collecting and washing out the log. Replace the organic materials and topsoil uphill of the log and on any disturbed soil showing below it. You may also want to stake these bigger logs to hold them in place.
- Also consider inoculating your check logs with edible mushrooms for tasty added benefits and faster log decomposition.

COMPOST AND COMPOST TEA

Compost and compost tea are vital soil amendments. They provide nutrients in organic form, inoculate and nurture soil food webs, and improve soil aggregation, structure, and consistence. They can help decrease surface soil compaction and balance any problematic soil texture. The active organic matter that compost provides can help make heavy metals less available to plants by chelating them. Composts with a high bacterial content can help improve the soil fungal-bacterial balance for early-succession plants, while fungi-dominated composts can improve the soil fungal-bacterial balance for later-succession plants. Compost and compost tea are both good inoculants for a wide range of soil organisms that can improve overall soil-food-web structure and function, which affect many other soil qualities. Methods for creating good fungal compost, bacterial compost, and compost tea are covered in other references.[14]

COMPOST-PLUG PLANTING

Compost-plug planting provides a strong root-zone food web for perennial herb or small tree and shrub transplants. This helps the plants withstand transplant shock and fight off disease organisms in unhealthy soil, increasing transplant survival rates, health, and growth. It also inoculates the planting site with beneficial soil organisms without the need to amend the whole area with compost. This reduces the cost and effort of improving soil-food-web conditions on large sites. Dr. Elaine Ingham used this technique to rapidly improve strawberry-crop root-zone biology, plant health, and yields on extremely sick California soils. Here are the basic steps to follow:

- Produce or acquire enough healthy, biologically active compost with the right fungal-bacterial balance for your projected needs.
- Transplant small plants into plugs of healthy compost in seedling trays or plant pots of

appropriate size. You can try planting seeds directly into compost plugs, but some seeds rot easily before germination if the starting medium is not sterile.

- Allow the plants to grow in the compost for at least several weeks. Care for them as you normally would, with watering, temperature control, and light. Additional fertilizer may not be necessary depending on the quality of the compost, the length of time the plants are growing in it, and the plant species. If you apply additional fertilizer, use organic fertilizer to preserve the health of the compost organisms.

- Transplant plants when the time is right. The plants should have a diverse, healthy, and balanced root-zone food web that will spread as their roots grow into the surrounding soil. Care for the transplants as normal. Beware of overwatering, which can kill root-zone organisms.

- The biggest caution with this method is the potential for the plants to remain rootbound in the nice compost of the planting hole, rather than spreading their roots out of the planting hole into the native soil. It may be advisable to gently knock some of the loose compost off the roots before planting to minimize the amount of planting hole filled with compost rather than native soil, while keeping some compost in contact with the plant roots for inoculation purposes. Also, mulch and maybe even fertilize the surface around the planting hole to encourage roots to grow beyond the hole. You can also use the butterfly planting method, especially for herbaceous perennials. Read the full discussion of planting techniques in chapter 6 so you understand all of these issues well before using compost-plug planting.

COVER CROPS

A cover crop is a planting of annual or perennial herbs intended to improve soil fertility, build soil organic matter, prevent erosion, loosen compacted soils, outcompete weeds, alter insect or disease conditions in the soil, or create some combination of these benefits. Cover crops usually grow for a set time and then get tilled in to improve the soil, but they may be a permanent orchard feature. Cover cropping as a site-preparation technique for soil improvement and weed management works best for tillable sites with no existing permanent perennial plants. However, you can use cover crops in a number of ways, a few of which are outlined below. Many other references provide information on specific cover crop species for different soil conditions and regions of the world (see appendix 7). Use these references to develop the specifics of the ideas discussed below.

Green and Brown Manuring

Green manuring occurs when you grow a cover crop for a time and then till it into the soil as green matter. Tilling usually takes place when the plant begins flowering (its time of maximum size and nutrient concentration) but may take place earlier or later. If you wait until the plant dies and turns brown before tilling it in, the crop is a brown manure. Green manures break down rapidly in the soil (usually a few weeks), build soil fertility more than soil organic matter, and foster bacterial soils more strongly than brown manures. Brown manures break down more slowly (weeks to months), add more organic matter than nutrients to the soil, and favor fungi slightly more than bacteria. Choose dynamic-accumulator or nitrogen-fixing species for fertility improvement and allelopathic species such as rye or buckwheat for weed control. You can sow and till green or brown manures either a patch at a time or over a whole field at once before planting.

This practice has shown demonstrated benefits for orchard- and landscape-tree survival, health, and productivity. A series of preplanting green manure crops can radically improve soil tilth and fertility and reduce weed dominance. Deep-rooted cover crops increase soil organic-matter content

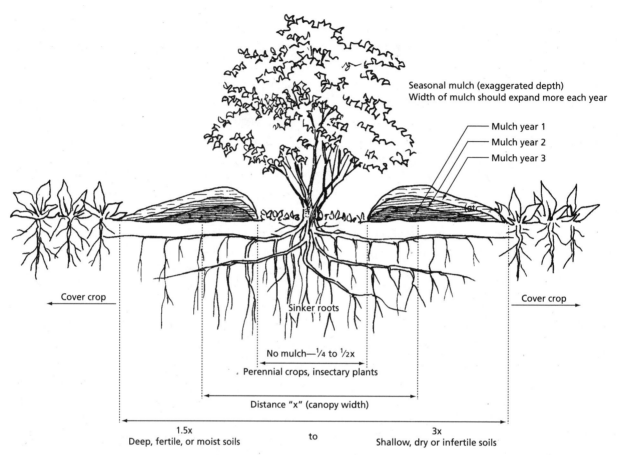

Seasonal mulch (exaggerated depth)
Width of mulch should expand more each year

Mulch year 1
Mulch year 2
Mulch year 3

Cover crop

Cover crop

Sinker roots

No mulch—¼ to ½x

Perennial crops, insectary plants

Distance "x" (canopy width)

1.5x
Deep, fertile, or moist soils

to

3x
Shallow, dry or infertile soils

FIGURE 5.4. You can use soil-improving cover crops as the leading edge of an expanding mulch doughnut around trees. Grow the cover crops outside the root zone, which is one and a half to three times the crown area (depending on soils). As the root zone expands, expand the mulch area over the top to cover the cover crops. Leave the area near the trunk free of mulch to prevent crown rot; grow ground covers there to control weeds.

more deeply than any other method and can break up deep hardpan or plowpan layers, though this takes some time. Some reports suggest that up to two years of green manuring improves soil sufficiently for later-planted trees to overtake the growth of trees on un-cover-cropped soils within five years. While most of us do not plan that far in advance, even one year's worth of deep-rooted green manuring is significant.

Rolling Cover Crops
Using cover crops as the leading edge of an expanding nucleus allows you to have your cover crops and eat them too (figure 5.4). You can plant small trees or tree clumps and surround them with mulch doughnuts sufficient for the first year of root growth. Outside the mulch doughnuts, plant soil-improving cover crops. Expand the mulch doughnuts as the trees grow by sheet-mulching over the cover crops. This encourages tree roots to grow outward into the cover-cropped soil as it improves over time.

Permanent Cover Crops
Permanent perennial cover crops offer continuous soil improvement, erosion control, beneficial insect habitat, and a source of mulch, depending on the species chosen. This, essentially, is what forest gar-

dening is all about, except the cover crops include edibles and medicinals as well as insectary plants. Some orchardists till their cover crops into the soil every year and resow. If you do this, till near trees very carefully, for you will hit tree roots at a greater distance than you might suspect. Some experiments have shown that cutting various cover crops at the right time encourages beneficial insects to climb into walnut or apple trees to control specific pests. Which cover-crop species are used, when they are cut, and the pests controlled vary from region to region. Contact your local cooperative extension service or organic growers' association for details.

DEEP RIPPING OR CHISEL PLOWING

Most chisel plows, soil rippers, slip plows, or subsoilers consist of a simple plow frame with sturdy tines that stick straight down into the soil like a knife.[15] Dragging the tines through the soil breaks up compacted earth to whatever depth the plow can go. This broadscale strategy requires at least a tractor. Deeper ripping and more compacted soils require more powerful equipment, such as a bulldozer. Obviously, this technique is best for extreme situations or when the equipment is readily available. It is viable only on sites without trees or shrubs.

However, typical chisel plows or subsoilers leave the soil more prone to resealing and recompaction than backhoe loosening, even when equipment does not drive over the site afterward, and especially in clay soils.[16] Resealing is less likely if you can find and use a Yeomans plow instead. Yeomans plows were specially designed for soil loosening in difficult Australian soils. Their forward-curved tines and "bat's-wing" foot not only split the soil but lift it from below to crack overlying compacted layers and reduce friction on the main shaft of each tine. Also, the Yeomans shakerator vibrates the tines as they move through the soil, reducing the power required to run the plow through deep or compacted soil. Key points to consider when chisel-plowing follow:

- Deep-rip or chisel-plow only when the soil is moist to dry.
- Run the subsoiler or slip plow in two or more directions diagonal (*not* perpendicular) to each other at a depth below the restrictive layer, or at least 1 to 2 inches (2.5 to 5 cm) below the topsoil horizon. The right equipment can go as deep as 5 to 7 feet (1.5 to 2 m), but this requires a lot of pulling power. Make sure the tines follow in the tractor's tracks to reloosen tire compaction. Run the last rip along the contours to minimize erosion and maximize runoff capture.
- Irrigate several times to settle the soil, or allow natural rainfall to do this over time.
- Avoid using heavy equipment to final-grade the site afterward.
- Ideally, the site will have deep-rooted perennial cover crops growing before deep ripping takes place. Closely grazing or mowing the plants before ripping causes plant-root dieback, providing abundant organic matter to feed decomposer organisms. Subsoiling adds oxygen to the mix, speeding decomposition and nutrient release. Irrigating deeply after ripping further stimulates that decomposition and urges plant roots to fill the newly created voids in the soil, preventing the voids from collapsing. P. A. Yeomans, inventor of the plow and the "keyline" technique, calls this combination of events a "soil climax." Soil climaxes deepen the topsoil and rooting depth, increase soil organic matter, foster vigorous soil biology, and maximize soil storage of nutrients, carbon, and water.[17]

DOUBLE DIGGING

Double digging provides optimal soil-profile conditions in garden planting beds by loosening the topsoil and the subsoil, adding compost to the topsoil, and maintaining natural soil-profile structure. Research has shown that double digging can radically increase vegetable yields and allow much closer plant spacing, though its effects on woody plants have been less well documented. Its main drawback is the amount of work it takes, and the possible consequences of that work on one's back.

Double digging works best on a small scale. It is most appropriate for heavy or compacted soils, for soils with significant restrictive layers, for high-value crops with a reasonably small root spread, and for people who understand how to use their body and hand tools with minimum strain. Double digging is less appropriate for large areas, for large crops, and in sandy, free-draining soils. If you have a large area to cover, use an army or give yourself a reasonable time frame. In areas with hot summers, double digging can increase organic-matter decomposition rates and may be contraindicated. However, with perennial or tree crops, a one-time, preplanting double digging is unlikely to destroy much organic matter and may have major benefits for long-term productivity, especially if you prevent recompaction forever afterward by using designated paths.

The discussion below summarizes how to double-dig garden beds (see figure 5.5). However, Robert Kourik's and John Jeavons's books provide excellent, in-depth discussion of double-digging theory and methodology.[18] Before undertaking double digging in earnest, please see one or both of these works. Here's the basic process:

- Lay out your planting bed with stakes or hose to mark the edges. Design your beds so that you can care for them without stepping on them if possible. Double digging is a lot of work. Don't waste that effort by designing a garden that requires you to compact with your feet what you just loosened with your back!

- Find a piece of plywood or other material to help spread your weight as you stand on the garden bed to work. You'll need a square shovel, a spading fork, a wheelbarrow, and enough compost to cover the whole planting bed to a depth of about 1 inch (2.5 cm).

- Prepare the bed for digging by irrigating it for up to two hours, letting it rest until slightly moist (up to two days), loosening the surface,

and weeding out plants. You may need to gently reirrigate briefly after weeding and let the water soak in for a day to make sure the soil is slightly moist before digging.

- Place up to 1 inch (2.5 cm) of compost evenly across the surface of the planting bed. You may also add lime or other rock powders at this time if you want.

- Starting at one end of the bed, and standing on your digging board, remove the top 12 inches (30 cm) or so of soil from a trench about 12 inches (30 cm) wide across the bed. Place it in the wheelbarrow or on a piece of plastic, plywood, or drop cloth at the opposite end of the planting bed for use later.

- Stand in the trench with the square shovel. Loosen and aerate the soil in the bottom of the trench *without inverting it* by lifting a shovelful at a time and letting it slide back into the hole from which it came. In more compacted subsoil, you can drive the spading fork into the subsoil and wiggle it back and forth to loosen the subsoil instead. If you are vigorous, in a highly compacted subsoil you can use a spading fork to lift out sections of the subsoil and break it up on the tines of the fork as it falls back into the hole it came from. Dig at an angle into the subsoil at the bed edges so the loosened subsoil is wider than the bed surface, giving the roots more room to grow.

- Move your digging board back a foot-length. Stand on the digging board and cut a new trench 1 foot (30 cm) deep and wide across the bed, throwing the topsoil onto the loosened subsoil in the previous trench. This will mix the compost into the topsoil and leave loose, enriched topsoil on top of loosened subsoil. It also reveals a new trench of subsoil you can then loosen as before.

- Work your way across the planting bed a trench at a time, throwing the topsoil over the just-loosened subsoil as you go. Stay on your digging board to minimize compaction of the soil you are about to double-dig. Do not walk on the soil you have already loosened, which should stick up

1. Loosen soil, remove weeds and rocks

2. Add compost

3. Remove soil to the depth and width of the spade

4. Loosen subsoil

5. Move topsoil from second trench into first

6. Loosen subsoil

7. Last trench— refill with soil from first

FIGURE 5.5. Double digging offers an intensive way to decompact soils in growing beds, providing more root space for plants. It is only necessary in compacted soils or soils of fine texture that need more pore space. Sandy soils benefit from it less. See the text for a full explanation.

higher than the surrounding ground. When you get to the far end and have loosened the subsoil in the last trench, use the topsoil you removed from the first trench to fill the last trench.

- Rake to shape the bed surface. Leave the surface level, with a little lip around the edges to catch rainfall and soak it in. Gently hand-irrigate to settle the soil.
- Plant and mulch the bed as soon as possible to minimize erosion and compaction from rainfall.

HERBICIDES: FLAMES, HOT WATER, AND CHEMICALS

For many people, *herbicide* is a dirty word, and for good reason. Any well-informed person with a decent memory should have plenty of reason not to trust the chemical companies' claims that a chemical, even a "safe" or "biodegradable" chemical, really meets the safety test. For this reason alone, as well as others, the reflexive, unthinking use of chemical herbicides is a travesty when it comes to good land management. Luckily, this seems less typical in our culture than it used to be. Notice, however, the words *reflexive*, *unthinking*, and *chemical* above. Herbicides are not necessarily a bad thing.

An "herbicide" is any agent used to kill or inhibit plants or plant growth.[19] When we hear the term, we usually think of chemical herbicides, but it actually covers a broader range of materials. This section briefly discusses flame weeding, hot-water weeding, and a variety of chemical herbicides, both approved organic and nonorganic. However, all of these materials can be used either reflexively and unthinkingly or skillfully and appropriately.

Flame or thermal weeding involves passing a torch flame over plant leaves to rupture their cell membranes. Since it works without actually burning the tissues (burning the plants can actually stimulate growth), you can walk with your flame weeder at a reasonable pace. As long as the tissues reach 201° to 212°F (94° to 100°C) for at least 1/10 second, the leaves will turn limp and darken immediately and will die and dry up in a few days. Flame-weeder

torches cost under $100, plus the fuel and fuel tank (see appendix 7 for suppliers). They leave no harmful residues in the soil if you use LPG (liquefied petroleum gas) for fuel.[20] Flame weeding kills plant tops but not roots, and it has obvious fire and human-harm risks associated with it. It works best when plants are young (two to four leaves) and have few reserves in their roots. Perennial weeds require several treatments. The technique is unreliable against grasses. Never use a flame weeder against poison ivy or poison oak, or you may end up inhaling the irritant oils and find yourself in the hospital!

Nurseryman Steve Breyer created a very effective hot-water weeding system using commonly available, off-the-shelf components.[21] He mounted a 40-gallon (150 l), two-element electric water heater onto a large-capacity garden cart (400-pound/180 kg load rating) along with an air compressor to keep up the water pressure. He stands the garden cart and tank on end, fills the tank with water, and plugs it in to heat. Once it's boiling, he closes a valve to let the tank build up to about 20 pounds (1.4 kg/sq cm) of pressure as the water gets hotter than atmospheric boiling temperature. By adding a 30-pound (2 kg/sq cm) pressure-relief valve to the 100-pound (7 kg/sq cm) valve the tank came with, he keeps the tank at a safe, low pressure and has two levels of pressure safety. After unplugging the tank, he moves the cart around, stands it on end again, and distributes the boiling water and steam through 50 feet (15 m) of high-temperature pressure hose with an attached wand and trigger.

Superheating the water and keeping it under pressure makes the water boil as it leaves the nozzle. It can kill plant tops and roots to about 1 inch (2.5 cm) deep in the soil, and the residue irrigates the remaining plants in the garden. The whole setup weighs in at around 400 pounds (180 kg) when full and requires a few hundred dollars in up-front costs (cheap when used over many years). He times his hot-water applications to stay ahead of the weeds and does little other weed management in his nursery except maintaining vigorous ground covers or mulch when possible. We should note, however, that Steve has a nursery business at stake, so he is motivated to create and consistently use such a tool. Rumors have circulated that someone is building these units to sell, so perhaps those of us with smaller gardens may find such a system worth our while.

In recent years, some certified-organic herbicides have hit the market.[22] These include corn gluten and herbicides based on ethanoic or acetic acid (vinegar) and potassium salts of fatty acids (soap). Corn gluten is a preemergent herbicide preventing root development on seedlings of a number of mostly annual weeds and grasses, clover, dandelion, crabgrass, creeping bentgrass, orchardgrass, and giant foxtail. It provides nitrogen and phosphorus as a slow-release fertilizer (9-1-0) and is nontoxic to people, pets, and wildlife. Its preemergent nature limits its forest garden uses, but it's good to know about. Ethanoic and acetic acid–based herbicides (e.g., Burnout) and herbicidal soaps (e.g., Concern or Scythe) work within hours of contact on plant tissues but do not translocate to kill roots. As broad-spectrum herbicides, they will top-kill and set back almost any annual or perennial, but completely killing perennials requires repeated applications. Some soap products require mixing with water, and hard or alkaline water will reduce or eliminate their effectiveness.

All the above products and techniques are generally regarded as safe and nontoxic to humans and animals. They are great tools to have in our toolbox. They all work best on young plants and seedlings, having less effect on older, more established perennials. Repeated use of these safer methods works on older plants similarly to repeated cutting, with the roots eventually dying of exhaustion. Even if you don't try to kill the weeds, setting them back can give desirables the chance they need to outcompete, making further maintenance unnecessary. Setting back unwanted plants may also allow us to get our mulch systems in place to suppress the weeds permanently. Consequently, these herbicides are worth a try as part of a total system of vegetation management. Yet their inability to translocate to roots and

kill the whole plant limits their value against vigorous, persistent, deeply rooted, and especially well-established perennial plants.

Having been diehard organic landscapers and gardeners most of our lives, we are now convinced there are times and places where limited, skillful, nonorganic chemical herbicide use *may* be appropriate, or at least more appropriate. We have even recommended their use to clients in a few cases. These have been situations where a highly competitive, persistent, extremely vigorous plant, such as Japanese knotweed (*Reynoutria japonica*, formerly *Polygonum cuspidatum*), Oriental bittersweet (*Celastrus orbiculatus*), or our native poison ivy (*Toxicodendron radicans*), completely overwhelms a landscape and defies all viable nonchemical means of control. Then a carefully chosen nonorganic chemical herbicide becomes a useful tool, usually as a last resort after attempting other options.

The potential negative effects of nonorganic chemical herbicides include groundwater contamination, adverse health effects on the applicator (both known and unknown), toxicity to fish and other animals, and damage to soil food webs as well as neighboring plants. Mycorrhizal fungi in particular may be hurt by nonorganic chemical herbicides. Some reports of herbicide moving through mycorrhizas to other plants have surfaced, but this appears rare.

Therefore, if you decide to use nonorganic chemical herbicides, use a rapidly biodegradable herbicide that adsorbs to soil particles tightly so it won't leach into groundwater much. Soil-applied herbicides tend to stick around longer, affect soil microbes more, are harder to target to specific plants, and get into groundwater more easily, so choose a foliar-applied chemical. The herbicide should have low mammalian toxicity and little or no toxicity to fish, amphibians, reptiles, or insects. To deal with the persistent, established plants for which these herbicides are most appropriate, the chemical should translocate, that is, move through the whole plant before killing it. Otherwise, you may as well use one of the safer organic contact herbicides discussed above.

Few herbicides can meet all of the above selection criteria. So far, glyphosate—a broad-spectrum, nonselective herbicide—appears the best match (e.g., Roundup or, if you dislike giving money to Monsanto, Touchdown). However, some people have expressed concerns about the "inert ingredients" being more of a contamination problem than the herbicides themselves. Since inert ingredients are usually not specified on labels, it is hard to tell whether these additives are truly safe. In addition, many herbicides require applicators to have certified training before commercial use but are also registered for home use. Be forewarned: just because it is registered for home use does not necessarily mean a chemical is safe.

When applying a chemical herbicide, apply it at the highest safe concentration to minimize the need for repeat applications. Three methods minimize your own contact with the chemical and reduce the effects of spray drift on nearby desirable plants: using a wick applicator (like a sponge) to apply it to leaves, injecting it into the plant stem, or painting it on freshly cut stumps (less than thirty minutes after cutting). If you must spray, use low pressure to create larger droplets less likely to drift onto nearby plants, and apply it on a windless day. Inform yourself about the possible effects of the herbicide on humans and other species (fish, amphibians, insects, and so on) as well as how to safely mix and apply the herbicide. Read and follow the label instructions. Wear adequate protective gear, and wash your hands before touching your face, other people, plants, or food. Wash contaminated clothing separately from other clothes. Keep children and pets from entering herbicided areas until the time you expect the herbicide to have fully degraded. Dispose of containers and wash equipment properly, whatever that means. Once you've done the dirty work, get the cat back in the bag to decrease your temptation to use the quick fix again.

All the herbicides discussed above have advantages: they are relatively cheap (in monetary terms, anyway; we don't know all of their true costs), they can be effective, and, if used skillfully, their effects can be quite focused. Most other vegetation-management techniques have broad impacts on the plant community, rather than focused effects on specific plants. This is often okay or even desired, but herbicides can allow fine-tuned guidance of a plant community without setting back succession on a broad scale. It's like removing a runner from a race, or setting the runner back, without starting the whole race over again.

However, if we aren't careful, using any kind of herbicide can shift the burden to the intervenor, creating reliance on herbicides as an ongoing management tool, rather than using them as a one-time or initial-phase intervention to set the system on a desired track. This is perhaps the greatest danger, for then the other risks (groundwater contamination, human harm, and so on) can become institutionalized and chronic. Getting the cat back in the bag once it has escaped is no easy task.

Herbicides are, therefore, just like any other designed disturbance; see them in the context of the current and following successional process. Include them only as a small part of a larger strategy to direct the plant community somewhere in particular. Envision what happens after herbiciding to keep the target species under control. How will site conditions change once the herbicides have done their job? What must you do to create conditions favoring the desired species and inhibiting the undesirables so the system manages itself? For example, what vigorous ground-cover plants might fill the same niche as, and outcompete, poison ivy? By seeing the system as a whole and understanding how to use herbicides in this context, we avoid unthinking and reflexive action and build considered responses and healthy ecosystems. We can then use herbicides once, or at worst infrequently, as a tool to guide the plant community to greater self-maintenance and less reliance on herbicides in any form.

INFILTRATION SWALES

In many local regulations governing storm-water system design in the United States, the word *swale*

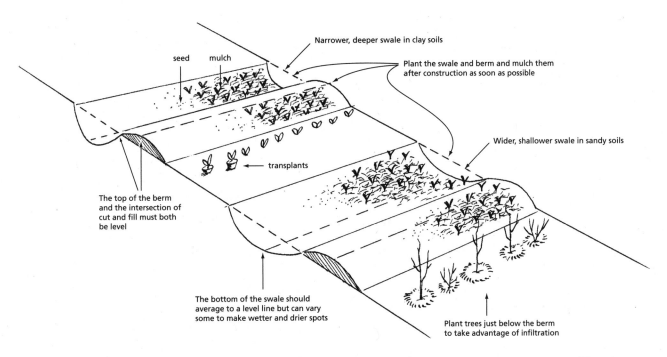

seed   mulch

Narrower, deeper swale in clay soils

Plant the swale and berm and mulch them
after construction as soon as possible

Wider, shallower swale in sandy soils

transplants

The top of the berm
and the intersection of
cut and fill must both
be level

The bottom of the swale should
average to a level line but can vary
some to make wetter and drier spots

Plant trees just below the berm
to take advantage of infiltration

FIGURE 5.6. Infiltration swales stop erosion and increase the infiltration of runoff water into the soil on sloping land. They always run along the contour so that water sits in the dug trench and soaks into the soil. The top of the berm and the intersection of the cut and fill must be dead level to prevent the swale from washing out, but the bottom of the swale can vary a little to make wetter and drier areas inside. Seed and mulch disturbed soil as soon as possible after construction. Plant trees downhill of the berm to make use of the infiltrated water.

denotes a sloping ditch dug into the ground that conveys water from one place to another. In permaculture parlance, *swale* denotes a ditch that lies level, not at a slope, with a berm on the downhill side. Water collects in these swales and soaks into the ground along their whole length, rather than running to one end and out. To avoid confusion of terms, we will call the latter an "infiltration swale," and let everyone else use the term *swale* as they will. In the meantime, the word *ditch* will here mean a sloping water-conveying trench. Mollison provides an overview of infiltration swales and many creative ideas for their use in *Permaculture: A Practical Guide for a Sustainable Future*.

Infiltration swales soak runoff water into the ground as a way of reducing runoff and erosion, improving groundwater recharge, and establishing nearby trees and other plants. They are most useful on sloping sites with fine-textured, droughty, compacted, or eroding soils, in arid or semiarid climates, or below impervious surfaces such as parking lots

and large roofs. The intent is to replace the swales with the natural infiltration of loose, living soils and good vegetative cover. Planting trees on or just below the berm takes advantage of the infiltrated water, improves tree survival, stabilizes the berm, and eventually makes the swale obsolete because of soil improvements by the trees. The swales eventually fill with mulch and eroded soil, but this only improves tree nutrition, and the trees have usually taken over the swale's functions by then anyway. When infiltration swales lie below impervious surfaces they should be maintained, since the runoff often exceeds what a healthy soil can absorb without harm. Infiltration swales can also take the overflow from cisterns, graywater systems, diversion ditches, garden ponds, and so on, if properly designed and, in the case of graywater, if legal.

For the structure to remain stable, you must dig the infiltration swale in undisturbed soil. Use the excavated material to make the berm on the downhill side (figure 5.6). *Infiltration swales always run along the contour.* The downhill edge of the excavation *and* the top of the berm should be level so water will pond and infiltrate. While the swale bottom may vary in slope somewhat to create wetter and drier areas, it should average to a level line over middle and long distances. You might want to make a larger, deeper, wider spot in the swale just uphill of a grove of trees and let adjacent parts of the swale drain into it. In tight soils, you can rip or loosen the bottom. You can even excavate a deeper spot and put in a pond liner to create frog habitat.

Infiltration swales may have V-shaped cross sections, but infiltration improves if they have flat bottoms. The bottom width depends on the kind of soil you have and the multiple functions of the swale system. In clay soils water infiltrates slowly, so dig deep swales to provide more water storage and vertical-wall surface area. Build wider and shallower swales in sandy soils, since the water absorbs more readily and sand is less stable when wet. You can make the swale bottom a specific width if you want to mow it or if you want to collect and use the silt and mulch that collect there with a tractor or front-end loader. The berm top can serve as a location for fences, pathways, or cart paths, among other things.

Long slopes usually have a series of swales to reduce the amount of runoff any one swale must deal with. The distance between swales depends upon the amount of rainfall: closer together in high rainfall areas and farther apart in drier regions. According to Mollison, "The distance between swales can be from three to twenty times the average swale width," for areas with rainfall of over 50 inches (127 cm) per year or with less than 10 inches (25 cm) per year, respectively.[23] Assuming a linear relationship between annual precipitation and interswale distance, then, in sites with rainfall of between 30 and 40 inches (75 and 100 cm) per year, swales should be from twelve to seven times the swale width apart. Mollison offers no specific guidelines for determining swale width based on soil conditions or climate. We have been unable to confirm or deny these figures with reputable designers, so use them at your own risk, or consult with your county soils agency.

A few comments about infiltration swale design are in order:

- Design your swales schematically first. Think through how the swales relate to pathways and water flows as well as planting patterns on your site. See Mollison's book for a number of design ideas that integrate swales with tree crops, animal systems, and so on.
- Stake out your swales on-site. Use a leveling device to keep your stakes on the contour (figure 5.7). Transits or builder's levels are the most accurate tools, but lower-tech alternatives can work if used with care. However, the consequences of laying out a swale at a pitch without realizing it are potentially dire. Dave and some students once laid out and dug infiltration swales on a sloping field using an A-frame level. They forgot to account for the constant slight error of placing the stakes on the downhill side of the level each time they installed them, while placing the level on the downhill side of the stakes every time they checked levels. A serious gully developed in short order during a thunderstorm when the "swales" concentrated the field's runoff in one spot. Oops.
- Dig the trench uphill of the stakes, piling the excavated material downhill of the stakes. This keeps the junction between the native soil and the berm level. This junction is usually a weak spot, as water can seep under the berm at the seam between undisturbed and excavated ground. Mattocks or two-person shovels move the most material most easily by hand (figure 5.8). The resulting cut bank in the undisturbed soil and the side slopes of the berm should be no steeper than 1:3 (rise to run) to minimize erosion and soil collapse.
- Plant and mulch the berm and the swale itself immediately after digging. This prevents erosion and stabilizes the disturbed soil.

Irrigation Systems

Irrigation systems provide one of the most important nutrients plants need—water. As our climate

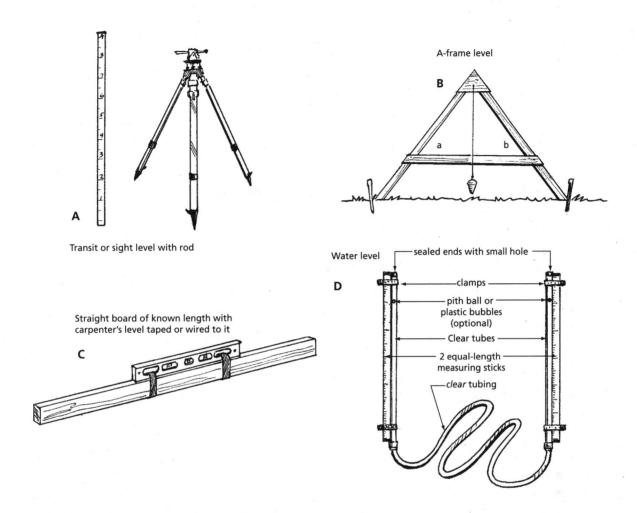

FIGURE 5.7. We present a few different leveling devices you can use for marking out swales or estimating slopes from highest to lowest accuracy. (a) Transits and sight levels are highly accurate tools for setting elevations, but they are not cheap and they require at least two people. (b) A-frame levels are lightweight and simple and cheap to build, and they can be quite accurate if you are careful using them. Get the geometry right: the two legs should be of equal length, angles a and b should be equal, the plumb bob should hang from the center of the top, and the crosspiece should be level when the legs are on a level surface. Mark where the plumb-bob string meets the crosspiece with the tool on a level surface, and you are ready to roll. (c) A long, straight piece of lumber with a regular carpenter's level taped or wired to it works quickly and easily, though it can be clumsy. (d) Water levels consist of two upright measuring sticks with a clear plastic tube filled with water attached. The tube must be clear so you can make sure no air bubbles throw off the water levels. When the two sticks stand at the same elevation, the water will be at the same height on each measuring stick.

changes over the coming years, irrigation may become more important for stabilizing our gardens and food supply. In droughty soils or droughty times, a good irrigation system pays off handsomely. However, the irrigation method affects how much water is used, its effectiveness, the cost of the system, and plant health, weed competition, and successional processes.

Plants differ in their ability to respond to increased water supplies. Competitor- and ruderal-strategy species respond more rapidly than stress tolerators, so that irrigation, especially broadcast or spray irrigation (sprinklers and their ilk), can push succession backward. Broadcast irrigation can cause mildew by wetting leaves or collar rot by sending cascades of water down tree trunks. It also wastes large quantities of

Mattock, two heavy blades,
one parallel to handle, one perpendicular

The two-person shovel

FIGURE 5.8. Mattocks and two-person shovels make for the easiest swale digging. Each allows you to pull excavated material out of the trench in one motion, the mattock when working alone, the two-person shovel for pairs.

water through evaporation, runoff, wind, or hitting the ground away from crop plants. Broadcast irrigation is, however, better than losing your plants to a drought! If you use broadcast irrigation or water by hand, make sure to water deeply and infrequently, rather than shallowly and often. This encourages plant roots to grow down into the soil where they can find more water. If they stay near the surface, they'll be more susceptible to drought or lack of watering while you're on vacation.

Drip irrigation is the preferred irrigation method. It conserves water, puts it into the ground where your plants need it, reduces disease problems, and can reduce weeding, too, by putting the water right on the plants you want to water. Drip irrigation saves time and labor over the long run, provides precise water control for optimum soil moisture and productivity, and preserves and improves soil structure by preventing puddling and compaction. Precise supply control and distribution allows you to direct succession more effectively. On the other hand, a drip system has a high up-front cost and takes time to design and create. The benefits are worth it, though, if you do it well.

Irrigation-system design goes well beyond the scope of this book. Robert Kourik has written an excellent guide to drip irrigation systems, as have other authors (see appendix 7).

LEACHING IRRIGATION

When you irrigate to remove excess salt, boron, or other micronutrients, you must irrigate far more than you normally would.

- Test the soil to determine the nature and extent of the problem. If excess sodium is present, the soil lab should tell you how much gypsum ($CaSO_4$) to apply before leaching to help get the salt out. Also test your irrigation water for excess salts.
- Before leaching irrigation, make sure the soil drains well enough for the water to carry away the unwanted constituents. Deal with any restrictive layers or a high water table first. See table 5.2, "Soil Structure/Profile," for guidance.
- If you are trying to leach out sodium, apply gypsum and incorporate it into the soil using a tiller or other equipment.
- Apply several leaching irrigations. The more saline the irrigation water is, or the more salt-sensitive the plants, the more you'll have to use. The faster the soil drains, the faster you can apply the water. The goal is to leach the salts or other toxins below the root zone of the plants (3 feet/1 meter deep or deeper). The following chart offers an approximate guide for irrigation

quantity and salt reduction, using good-quality water. Finer soils require more water, and coarser soils less.

For each 4 inches (100 mm) of medium-textured soil:

This much good irrigation water:	Removes about this much salt:
2 inches (50 mm)	50%
4 inches (100 mm)	80%
8 inches (200 mm)	90%

MOUNDS, MOUND PLANTING, AND PITS AND MOUNDS

Mounding diversifies soil habitats by offering various microclimates in a small space—sunnier, shadier, drier, and wetter. While similar to raised beds, mounds provide greater habitat variation and design freedom. You can create mounds of virtually any size, shape, height, or steepness to achieve different effects. Mounds increase the planting surface area available by 5 to 20 percent or more, depending on their height. On wet sites or those with shallow soils over bedrock or hardpan, mounding provides additional rooting depth while reducing the amount of imported material required compared to filling the whole area. Root crowns are the most critical parts of plant root systems to keep dry: if they rot the whole plant is lost, whereas if root tips get too wet, the plant can replace them. By raising the root crown of trees and shrubs above wet soils, mound planting can make the difference between success and failure for some species on some sites.

Mounds have a few challenges, however. First, the material you use has to come from somewhere. When you excavate an area on-site to build a mound, this can create pits and mounds similar to those that develop in old-growth forests. Carefully think through the design of both the pit and the mound before moving any soil. If material comes from off-site, pay attention to the nature, texture,

and quality of the soil and the impacts on the off-site landscape. Move earth responsibly and economically by trucking soil the minimum distance possible, and make sure that obtaining the soil will not contribute to the destruction of valuable off-site habitats. Acquire contaminant-free fill of reasonable fertility whose texture meets your design objectives. Very sandy soil may be fine if you want to grow Mediterranean herbs, but not if you want moisture-loving plants.

Second, carefully consider how the mound will affect water flows in, under, on, and around it. Use soil of a consistent texture within the mound. Abrupt soil texture boundaries can prevent the mound from absorbing, holding, and wicking moisture; saturate downhill areas; and limit the success of plants. The mound's soil texture should resemble the underlying soil texture. This maximizes capillary connection between the mound and its foundation, allowing plants in the mound to draw water from the native soil.

The shape, surface roughness, and steepness of the mound also influence its moisture regime. Steep, convex shapes with smooth surfaces absorb less water. Flatter, rougher, more concave, or undulating shapes absorb more. Laying the mound across a slope may periodically create very wet conditions on the uphill side, but it will help the mound absorb water. Laying the mound directly up and down a slope will allow runoff to flow around it, leaving the mound much drier. Following is a proposed series of steps for mound design and construction:

- Consider your mound design objectives. Think about the plants you want to grow, the growing conditions you want to create, and the effects of the mound on the physical space and site aesthetic. Decide on the height, shape, and size of the mound(s). Sketch out your ideas.
- Outline the mound's shape on the ground using rope, hose, powdered lime, or sand. You can drive and mark stakes to show the mound's height at key points such as peaks or valleys. If

you need help visualizing the mound further, tie string or rope from the stakes to the ground to outline the slopes. Change the outline or heights to suit your goals or your aesthetic tastes.

- Estimate the amount of material you will need, and think about what mound soil texture you want based on your site conditions and design objectives.[24] Remember to account for topsoil removal under the mound, and for soil shrink and swell when excavating and compacting it (see below).

- Remove all organic material and topsoil from the mound site before building it. This prevents decomposing material under the mound from creating an anaerobic layer and provides useful organic matter and topsoil for the mound surface or other areas. It also improves capillary connection to the ground.

- Build the mound. Fill from the center to the edges or from one side to the other. Avoid excessive walking on, or driving full wheelbarrows or equipment over, the soil as you place it. This prevents excessive compaction and its consequent restriction of rooting and water movement. Some packing is necessary to stabilize and consolidate the material in preparation for planting, however. If your fill is subsoil, place the topsoil on top! Overfill the mound by 5 percent or so to allow for settling.

- If you are removing material from a pit on-site, remember that the soil will expand because you add pore spaces when you dig it up. Sand swells by about 10 percent and "common earth" by 25 percent. Clay can swell as much as 43 percent! While sand under moderate compaction can shrink to virtually its original volume, common earth will leave you with about 10 percent more volume after moderate compaction. Clay compacts only enough to leave you with about 30 percent more volume than you started with! Those of you with fine-textured soils should take account of this in your design.

- Shape the mound with a rake after all of the fill is in place. Leave a rough surface unless you want drier growing conditions in the mound. Create miniswales (see "Infiltration Swales," above) to increase runoff infiltration.

- Water the mound before planting to settle the soil further, if possible without creating too much erosion. Otherwise, you may need to settle the soil with your feet if you succeeded in leaving the mound really fluffy during construction. If the soil settles too much after planting it can leave plant roots high and dry. Let the mound dry out a bit before planting.

- Plant woody and large herbaceous plants. Mulch. Plant small plants after mulching. Water the mound and the plants fairly heavily.

MULCH

Mulch takes the cake as the number-one landscape problem solver, for site preparation as well as plant establishment and ongoing maintenance and management.

Table 5.2 shows mulch as an adaptive-design or site-modification response to fourteen site conditions, including droughty soils, salinity, heavy metals, compaction in upper soil horizons, excess soil bacteria, infertility, shallow soil, and weed problems of various kinds. While each of these conditions may require a specific kind of mulch or way of applying it, the basic act remains the same: lay some kind of material on the soil surface to alter conditions above and below the material. The conditions listed above need nothing fancy (see feature article 4, below, for an overview). A few specifics on using mulch for the more challenging site conditions follow.

Mulch helps deal with droughty soils by conserving moisture and increasing the organic-matter content of the soil. It decreases salinity by conserving moisture, and thereby increasing the rate of salt leaching. Heavy metals become chelated, or attached, to organic molecules in soils with high proportions of organic matter. Chelated metals are

TABLE 5.4. Relative abundance of soil nutrients in leaf litter of southern New England trees (by rank from high to low). *From Jorgensen, 1978, used by permission.*

Calcium	Magnesium	Potassium	Phosphorus	Nitrogen
basswood	basswood	shagbark hickory	pin cherry	hemlock
bitternut hickory	bitternut hickory	tulip tree	black birch	basswood
tulip tree	tulip tree	sugar maple	shagbark hickory	shagbark hickory
pin cherry	pin cherry	black birch	white ash	quaking aspen
quaking aspen	red maple	beech	white oak	black birch
shagbark hickory		red oak	basswood	white pine
sugar maple				

less likely to be taken up by plants. How mulch loosens compacted soils is somewhat of a mystery. It probably results from improved conditions and energy sources for soil organisms, who loosen up the soil as a matter of course. This takes time and may not reach as deeply as needed. Organic matter on the soil surface supports soil fungal populations more effectively than bacteria populations, since fungi can grow into the litter layer to gather energy and nutrients, while bacteria cannot do so easily.

If you have soil-infertility problems, choose your mulches partly based on their nutritional content if you can. Mulch leaches nutrients into the underlying soil, and its decomposition releases nutrients and energy. Table 5.4 shows the relative abundance of various nutrients in common eastern forest tree leaves, for example. Table 5.5 provides the nutrient content and carbon to nitrogen ratios (C:N) of some other mulch materials. The nutrients the mulch releases can leach out of the soil if too few plants exist to soak them up, so apply mulch judiciously.

Obviously, for shallow soils you will want to rapidly increase the depth of topsoil. This may require 6 to 9 inches (15 to 23 cm) of mulch at a time, or more, depending on how fast you want to increase soil depth. Note, however, that you will increase the organic-matter content of the site, not the mineral-particle content, if you only mulch. Mulching for soil creation has its limits. Too much organic matter in the soil can cause wetness and oxygenation problems, among other things. If the soil is very shallow, importing soil may be advisable, too. Digging soil out of pathways to add to planting beds is one way to do this. In addition, excessive mulch may starve plant roots of oxygen and slow plant growth by keeping soils too cool.

Finally, for weed problems, we have special applications. The basic laying on of organic matter definitely inhibits many weeds. Some species require more determined efforts, though, such as smother mulches and soil solarization.

Smother mulching involves laying a heavy light-blocking material over the soil surface to starve plants of light until they die. It works for vigorous rhizomatous perennials and prolific soil seed banks. Depending on the problem species and their root reserves, this can take weeks to months, even more than one year. We have used cardboard with no mulch on top (so it doesn't rot as fast) for this, as well as very thick plastic, and have at times considered using plywood on tough customers, though we've yet to do it. All of these need weights on them to prevent wind lift.

Soil solarization is similar to the above but uses clear or black plastic on a tilled soil surface to fumigate the soil by capturing the sun's heat. Obviously, it must be done in sunny locations and seasons for it to work. When it works, though, it works: "summer temperatures under clear plastic can be lethal to plant roots to a depth of 300 mm (12 inches)."[25] The process may take a whole growing season, though it can kill soil pests and diseases, as well as weed seeds in the soil. The problem is that if the weather doesn't cooperate you're stuck. We prefer black plastic to help limit weed growth even if the sun doesn't shine enough.

TABLE 5.5. Nutrient content and carbon:nitrogen ratios of various organic materials. Nutrient content is stated as percent composition, so multiply the weight of material by the percent to find the absolute amount of nutrient you are working with. For example, 500 pounds of grass hay contains from 100 to 130 pounds of nitrogen (N), 25 to 55 pounds of phosphate (P_2O_5), and 125 to 175 pounds of potash (K_2O). Ca = calcium. *From Gershuny and Smillie, 1986, and Gershuny, 1993.*

Material	C:N ratio	N	P_2O_5	K_2O	Ca
sawdust	300–500:1	1	0.2	1	
sugarcane fiber	200:1	0.25	0.04	0.02	
straw	75–150:1	12–20	3–6	20–30	
grass hay	80:1	20–26	5–11	25–35	
corn stalks	60:1				
leaves	30–50:1	16	7	3	
beef & dairy cattle manure	+25:1	10–14	5–9	10–11	2.4–5
horse manure	+25:1	10	4	10	
swine manure	+25:1	10	6.3	9.1	11.4
sheep manure	+25:1	28	9.7	24	11.7
poultry manure	+25:1	25	25	12	36
cow manure & bedding	15–25:1	6	1.5	5	
legume hay	12–24:1	45–60	10–15	35–45	
seaweed	19:1	1.5	0.75	5	
vegetable wastes	12:1				
humanure	5–10:1	5–7	3–5	1–2	
mixed slaughterhouse waste	2:1	7–10			
fish scrap		3–7	2–6		
alfalfa meal		5	1	2	
rabbit manure		2.4	1.4	0.6	
steamed bonemeal		1	11	0	24
duck manure		0.6	1.4	0.5	
grass clippings		0.5	0.2	0.5	

MYCORRHIZAL INOCULATION

Seventy percent of plants depend on mycorrhizal fungi to thrive, and another 12 percent sometimes form these partnerships. The numerous significant benefits to both plants and soils make it obvious that we should foster this mutualism. However, inoculating our plants or soils with mycorrhizal fungi in some way is worthwhile only if *all* of the following conditions exist:

- you want to grow obligate mycorrhizal plants in any situation, or facultative mycorrhizal plants in poor soils;
- the site has insufficient native fungi to inoculate your plants;
- the plants will not receive ongoing maintenance (e.g., fertilizer, irrigation, soil-borne pest and disease control, weeding), or you want to minimize the need for such maintenance; and
- the available inoculum is the proper kind and quality to do the job.[26]

Do Your Plants Form Mycorrhizas?

Table 5.6 lists the plant groups that depend upon or sometimes associate with mycorrhizal fungi, and with what types of fungi they associate. Use this list to help you assess the first and fourth items listed above. When in doubt, assume that the plant in question is obligate mycorrhizal, and that it associates with arbuscular mycorrhizal fungi, for these are the most common situations.

TABLE 5.6. Plants and their mycorrhizal fungi partners.[1] **Seventy to 80 percent of plants form mycorrhizas, most with arbuscular mycorrhizal (AM) fungi. Some plants partner with ectomycorrhizal (EM) fungi. A few form specialized mycorrhizas such as ericoid, arbutoid, or other mycorrhizas. See volume 1, chapters 4 and 5, for more information and descriptions of the kinds of mycorrhizas.**

Nonhost Plants:

"Nonhosts" do not associate with mycorrhizal fungi. Mycorrhizal fungi can suppress or kill some nonhost plants. *Healthy soil food webs can therefore suppress or kill many "weed" species.*

- Plants adapted to wetlands or saturated soils.
- Many perennial and annual ruderal "weeds" of disturbed sites, native or exotic.
- Most members of the following families: Brassicaceae (mustard family), Amaranthaceae (amaranth family), Chenopodiaceae (goosefoot family), and Bromeliaceae (bromeliads).
- Some to most species in the following genera: *Dudleya, Lupinus, Mimulus, Penstemon, Sambucus.*
- Any plant with fine, highly branched roots may be a nonhost or facultative mycorrhizal.

Facultative Mycorrhizal Plants:

Facultative mycorrhizal plants compose about 12 percent of flowering plants and do not depend on fungi, so they may or may not form mycorrhizas. They are more likely to partner with fungi in poor soils.

- A few miscellaneous shrubs and trees, mostly ruderal and competitor-strategist species.
- Some annual species in the following groups: Poaceae (grasses), Apiaceae (composite or aster family), and Fabaceae (legumes).
- A few perennial Poaceae (grasses) and Apiaceae (umbels), especially those with fine, well-branched roots.
- Any plant with fine, highly branched roots may be facultative mycorrhizal or a nonhost.

Obligate Mycorrhizal Plants:

Obligate mycorrhizal plants compose about 70 percent of flowering plants and include many nonflowering plants. They depend on mycorrhizal fungi to thrive, or even to survive. Some obligate species do not develop fine roots and require the fungi for that role. Mycorrhizas come in several forms. Specific plants partner with each form of fungal associate, usually in a diffuse, rather than pairwise, mutualism.

Arbuscular Mycorrhizal (AM) Plants:

By far the most common form of mycorrhiza in plants, though only several hundred fungi species form them.

- Plants not mentioned elsewhere in this table are most likely obligate AM plants.
- Most trees and shrubs, including most fruit and nut trees and all small fruits; most perennial and annual herbs; bulbs; some ferns; most legumes; most grasses, including bamboos. See below for exceptions.
- The only AM evergreens include redwoods, cedars, and junipers. All others are EM.

Ectomycorrhizal (EM) Plants:

Though more rare among plant species, thousands of fungal species form EM.

- Plants in the following families: Betulaceae (birches, alders, etc.), Corylaceae (hazels and filberts), Fagaceae (oaks, chestnuts, beeches, etc.), Pinaceae (pines, hemlocks, spruces, firs, true cedars, larches, etc.), Myrtaceae (myrtles), and Cistaceae (rock rose family, including *Helianthemum* and *Cistus* species).
- Family Salicaceae (willows and poplars) and alders form EM as adults, but young plants may be more AM.
- A few Rosaceae (rose family) plants form EM, but most, including all the useful species, form AM.
- Hickories, including pecans (*Carya* species), form EM, while others in Juglandaceae (the walnut family) form AM.
- Some heath family (Ericaceae) plants form EM, especially some *Arbutus* (strawberry tree) and *Arctostaphylos* (bearberry) species. The rest form ericoid or arbutoid mycorrhizas.

Ericoid Mycorrhizal Plants:

Few species form these types of mycorrhizas.

- Ericoid fungi partner with most members of the Ericaceae (heath family, also known as ericads), including the following genera: *Azalea, Epigaea, Gaultheria, Gaylussacia* (huckleberries), *Kalmia* (mountain laurels), *Rhododendron*, and *Vaccinium* (blueberries and cranberries).
- Some ericads form EM, especially some *Arbutus* (strawberry tree) and *Arctostaphylos* (bearberry) species. Manzanitas (*Arctostaphylos* spp.) and madrone (*Arbutus menziesii*) form arbutoid mycorrhizas, not ericoid or EM.
- These fungi are currently not propagated. Inoculate with soil from under wild members of the group, preferably within the same genus or species.

Other Specialized Obligate Mycorrhizas:

- Orchids and "parasitic" nongreen plants have other special partners.

1 Sources: St. John, 1996; various inoculant company Web sites.

Feature Article 4:
Mulch

Mulch is a many-splendored thing. The benefits of its use are so numerous, and the challenges so few and mostly so manageable, that mulch makes sense in almost every circumstance (see tables 5.7 and 5.8). Mulch can aid in site preparation, though it is most commonly used in plant establishment and garden maintenance and management. Though in essence mulching is a simple act, the details of how it's done significantly influence its effects. We must therefore be clear about our intentions, as usual. The many kinds, benefits, and uses of mulch make this a bit difficult, but let's give it a go. The discussion below will cover the general principles behind mulching, with a focus on site-preparation issues. Chapter 6 provides details relevant to the plant-establishment uses of mulch.

Mulching is one of the last steps in establishing a garden, though people sometimes mulch as a site-preparation technique. The vast majority of times, you should complete all your other grading, soil improvements, amending, and landscape construction before mulching. Otherwise, the mulch just gets in the way. Once your garden is planted, mulching will likely be necessary for a number of years for weed control and soil improvement, if not for aesthetics. You can usually stop mulching or reduce the amount significantly when the ground covers fill in and take over weed control. Also, as the forest garden begins generating its own leaf litter, the need for additional mulch declines. Two main factors influence the effects of mulch, and these are mulch type and mulch depth.

Mulch materials range from plastic sheeting, fabric, cardboard, newspaper, and even plywood to various kinds of stone and organic matter including hay, straw, grain hulls of various kinds, leaves, shredded bark, wood chips, sawdust, and the like. In addition, each type of wood product has different qualities depending on the tree species from which it is made.

TABLE 5.7. Benefits of mulch.[1]

- Conserves soil moisture by reducing soil temperatures, evaporation, evapotranspiration from weeds, and contact between the wind and the soil. Increases capture of dewfall. Decreases need for irrigation.
- Reduces salt buildup, aids salt leaching. Reduces shrink/swell of clay soil.
- Eliminates or reduces soil erosion.
- Improves soil structure. Conserves soil aggregates by reducing wet-dry cycles.
- Decompacts soil due to increased soil life.
- Prevents compaction by traffic and rainfall.
- Supports natural soil-horizon structure and functions by feeding soil from above.
- Increases soil fertility by leaching from mulch and by decomposition. Feeds the soil energy and nutrients at a rate it can handle without nutrient loss to groundwater.
- May decrease or eliminate the need for supplemental fertilizers. .
- Fertilizes soil without favoring early-succession plants (ruderals, competitors).
- Improves nutrient uptake in apples, chestnuts, and peaches compared to grass or bare soil.[2] This is probably true for other species, too.
- Increases fine root growth in plants. Allows surface root feeding with minimal weed competition. Meanwhile, plants under mulch root as deeply or *more deeply* than unmulched plants, contrary to some reports.[3]
- Increases soil-food-web health. Increases fungal biomass in the soil.
- Provides habitat for beneficial predators, including spiders, mites, snakes, toads, salamanders, etc.
- Reduces diseases by reducing soil splash onto plants.
- Reduces weed competition.
- Moderates soil temperatures. Prevents frost heaving of plants. Reduces root winterkill. Allows root growth later in fall or even through winter.
- Improves traffic surface and safety on wet soil.

1 Derived from Harris, Clark, and Matheny, 1999, pages 202–6, and other sources.

2 Atkinson, 1980.

3 Harris, Clark, and Matheny, 1999, page 208.

TABLE 5.8. Challenges of mulch and their solutions.[1]

Mulch may cause excessive soil moisture in fine-textured or poorly drained soils.	Improve drainage, mulch thinly, or don't mulch at all.
Sheet mulch (weed-barrier layers covered by mulch) may limit rainfall infiltration.	Cardboard and newspaper overlaps allow some infiltration; water heavily before mulching with them to make up for reduction. Install drip irrigation. You can also use pervious materials (Typar #3301 or #3401, spun-bonded polyester, etc.), though we discourage the use of plastics if you can avoid it.
Mulch may cause nitrogen deficiency, but only if using small, high-carbon particles (e.g., sawdust), if the mulch rots easily, or if it is incorporated into the soil.	Use chunky, slow-rotting materials. Don't incorporate them into soil. Fertilize with nitrogen if deficiency occurs. If deficiency symptoms continue, soil may be too wet for proper nitrogen metabolism.
Radiant heating and cooling can cause extreme mulch-surface air temperatures. This can kill small plants in summer and accentuate cold in spring, fall, and winter.	Create a plant canopy or shade structure to limit radiational heating and cooling. Thin mulches allow some soil heat absorption and re-radiation. Remove mulch in spring and fall so soil warms and reduces frost. Use dark or stone mulch.
Warm mulched soil keeps plant growth vigorous later in the season. Plants may harden off slowly in fall, causing winterkill of the current year's growth.	Plant hardier species. For less hardy species, minimize nitrogen fertilizing, especially after midsummer; use thin mulch, summer-only mulch, or no mulch.
Mulch may favor some pests and diseases: slugs, rodents, *Armillaria* root rot, collar rot (*Phytophthora*). Fungal diseases may travel in mulch (fireblight, *Armillaria*).	Use slug traps. Gravel mulch and mesh tubes around trunks stop rodents. Use disease-free or composted mulch. Keep organic mulch 4 inches (10 cm) away from woody stems to prevent fungal diseases. If *Armillaria* or *Phytophthora* are already present, use no mulch, apply compost tea, or otherwise improve the soil food web. Avoid mulches made from susceptible species, e.g., apple chips may have fireblight.
Weed seeds in the mulch.	Avoid hay or straw unless low in seeds (e.g., second and third hay cuttings), laid under weed barrier, or gleaned by chickens. Avoid mulches from small-fruited trees or with ruderal seeds (e.g., hackberry, privet, Siberian elm, Oriental bittersweet).
Fire hazard.	Use dense, moisture-retaining or nonflammable materials. Sawdust, dry straw, and peat are most dangerous. Wood chips, bark, and stone mulches are safer.
Some mulches are toxic, especially to young plants, due to allelopathy or chemicals.	Avoid mulch from eucalyptus, larch, spruce, Douglas fir, redwood, cedar, Norway maple, and walnuts, all of which are allelopathic. Leach mulch, especially from the above species, before use: heavy sprinkling or several months of rain. Use composted materials. Avoid materials from herbicided areas. Some plastics release PVC.

1 Adapted from Harris, Clark, and Matheny, 1999, pages 206–8.

The mulch universe is big! When choosing materials for mulch, consider the following factors:

- Cost, both for the material and for trucking.
- Availability (quantity and timing).
- Nutrient content and rate of decomposition. Each kind of organic matter has a unique nutrient profile. Oak bark, for example, reputedly contains high calcium levels. Straw has a higher carbon content and fewer nutrients than hay. Fast-decomposing materials are usually smaller in size or have less lignin. These may suck nitrogen out of the soil initially, causing deficiencies in plants, especially if mixed with the soil (there is much dispute over the contention that mulching sucks nitrogen out of the soil; the best information we have indicates that

it does so only in the top ½ inch/1 cm or so of soil, unless mixed in). Slowly decomposing materials do not have this problem, and your mulch investment lasts longer, but they offer fewer nutrients and less energy to the soil.

- Weed potential. Bark mulch usually has few, if any, weed seeds in it, while hay has many, and straw has some. However, straw seeds are usually from grains such as oats or wheat, while hay contains seeds from many perennials, including quackgrass and other challenging species. If you use manure for mulch, consider that ruminants (cows, sheep, and goats) tend to digest weed seeds far more thoroughly than do horses, for example.

- Permeability. Wet leaves can pack densely and inhibit air and water movement through them. Sheet plastic will prevent rain infiltration. Mulches thicker than 4 inches (10 cm) may suffocate soils, roots, and soil life. Permeable fabrics can clog with particles if organic mulch lies on top of them, whereas stone mulch on top keeps the fabric pores clearer.

- Thermal effects. Stone mulches absorb or reflect light and heat, depending on their color, and this affects the aboveground microclimate and soil temperatures. Fluffier materials insulate the soil more effectively than dense materials.

- Mulch stability. Rice and buckwheat hulls are beautiful, but they blow around in the wind. Hay and straw can blow around until they mat down. You can mat them down by watering them. Once fungi start growing into the mulch it should stay put.

- Aesthetics. The look of the mulch may be important in some projects, while not in others. Color and texture both count.

Table 5.8 also illustrates factors to consider when choosing mulch materials, such as toxicity, fire hazard, and the like. Some plant species produce chemicals that inhibit the growth of other plants. Heavily irrigate mulches made from these species or let them sit in the rain for a few months to leach out the toxins before placing them. Use fresh wood chips, bark mulch, and tree leaves only if you know the species they came from are safe, or if you are inoculating your mulch with edible mushroom spores.

Which materials you mulch with depends on what you want to accomplish, what's available at the right price, and how the factors above match your purpose. For example, stone mulches are permanent landscape features offering beauty, permeability, and some heat storage in frost season, but they cost a considerable amount up front. Organic materials cost less and feed the soil, but they need renewal as they decompose. As usual, variety is good, even in your mulches. Using a variety of mulches on your planting beds should help diversify the soil food web. Using different mulch materials for the pathways and the planting beds helps keep distinctions and feet in place.

Determining the optimum mulch depth is a bit trickier than selecting what materials to use. While opportunism may rule in the materials selection, intentions matter more in the depth department. Plan your plantings around a reasonable mulch depth. Plant health can suffer if the plants are mulched too deeply. You may have more weeds than you'd like if it isn't deep enough. To complicate matters, the depth you need to achieve a certain purpose varies by soil type, mulch material, weed species, and even weather conditions. All in all, mulching gets down to the fine art of continuous trial, error, and observation. Here are a few guidelines, though.

One-half to 1 inch (1 to 2 cm) of organic debris or crushed stone will reduce erosion, rainfall compaction, puddling, and disease caused by soil splashing onto plants. It will also reduce evaporation and moderate soil temperatures some. Two to 3 inches or more (5 to 8 cm), depending on the material, is necessary to minimize compaction from foot traffic, insulate the soil, and strongly limit weed populations. Sheet mulching offers virtually total weed control, at least initially. Rather than depending only on mulch depth to control weeds, you should install a barrier layer below or in the middle of the mulch and cover the soil surface over a broad area (see "Sheet Mulching," page 403, for details). The barrier allows you to reduce the depth of mulch necessary to control weeds. Some species, such as quackgrass (*Agropyron repens*) and bindweed (*Convolvulus* spp.), can eventually grow through even sheet mulch, but they are set back strongly and become more easily controlled if you stay on top of things.

For fertility purposes, consider this: mature eastern deciduous forests drop up to 4,500 pounds of organic litter per acre each year (5,000 kg/ha; dry weight).[27] That's about 10 pounds per 100 square feet per year (0.5 kg/sq m), or less than 2 ounces per square foot, or a layer perhaps ½ to ¾ inch deep (1 to 2 cm). It isn't much, really, but it's enough to keep the nutrient cycle and soil food web going in such nutrient-hoarding mature ecosystems. Our forest gardens will not achieve "mature" status for many years. Nutrient losses remain significant for ten to twenty years after disturbance in a rapidly succeeding forest ecosystem. Therefore, just to maintain an earlier-succession system we'll need to lay on more than 10 pounds dry weight of mulch per 100 square feet per year (5 kg/10 sq m). Forest leaves and grass hay are nutritionally comparable (except in K; N-P-K of leaves: 16-7-3; grass hay: 23-8-30). Ten pounds of hay dry weight is about ⅓ of a bale, which will cover 100 square feet about ¾ inch deep (9 sq m about 2 cm deep). A minimum of 1 to 2 inches (2 to 5 cm) per year of mulch seems about right, with greater amounts building nutrient reserves in the soil faster.

For rapid soil building, you may apply many inches of organic mulch, even to the point of placing a solid layer of unopened hay bales across an area to let them rot. Make sure to lay them with the hay fibers running vertically so the bales absorb more rainfall and rot faster. Within one or two years this can result in thick, beautiful topsoil. If you don't have many plants taking up the nutrients, though, many will leach away in the ensuing years. A slow buildup may be better, unless you have extremely shallow soils over bedrock, for example.

Beware of extremely deep mulch for three reasons. First, you can suffocate the soil with excessively deep mulch, especially on fine-textured soil. Organic landscaping standards call for a maximum mulch depth of 4 inches (10 cm) to prevent anaerobic conditions in the soil from harming plants and soil life.[28] We've never had this problem with deep mulch, but not all mulch materials or soils are created equally. Sandy soils breathe rather well, and fine soils less well. Wet leaves can pack down tightly in just a couple of inches, while bulkier or looser materials may allow more air exchange through twice the depth or more.

The second reason to avoid excessive mulch depth is to maximize plant growth. One study showed that oak and pine transplants grew faster over their first two years with 3 inches (8 cm) of mulch than with 0, 6, or 9 inches (0, 15, or 25 cm) of mulch. The spring growth spurt of deeply mulched trees was delayed by several weeks because of cold soil temperatures.[29]

Finally, try to stay reasonable for your own sake as well. The volume of material needed to cover an area rises rapidly, particularly if you want lots of depth, and this can get expensive and takes more work. Each inch of mulch spread across 100 square feet equals one-third of a cubic yard, or about half a bale of straw. If bark mulch costs $12 per cubic yard, and you want 3 inches of mulch, that's $12 per 100 square feet, which adds up fast. Very deep mulch is useful once in a while to build soil or protect plants from weather, but don't keep it deep forever.

On a more detailed level, mulch should be thinner or absent within 4 inches (10 cm) or more of woody plant stems and trunks, especially if you have a history of collar rot or other fungal diseases. Account for the mulch depth when planting your trees, shrubs, and perennials so their crowns aren't swamped. Plant plants higher when you're using mulch to keep their heads above water. If rodents are a problem, place wire-mesh tubes around woody plants, and embed this tube in 3 inches (8 cm) of gravel mulch that extends at least 6 inches (15 cm) around the plant.

Finally, mulch is a great substrate for growing mushrooms! Not only do mushrooms taste great and provide excellent nutrition, but they also require little or no attention. They will probably increase yields of other species in your garden by breaking down the mulch and improving soil nutrition more rapidly. A number of mushroom species are easily cultivated in mulch.

Does Your Site Have Enough Natural Inoculum for Rapid Colonization?

As stated in volume 1, *most sites should not need mycorrhizal inoculation* (the same is true for nitrogen fixers). Don't let anyone trying to sell you something tell you otherwise. However, sites with the characteristics or disturbance histories listed in volume 1, chapter 5 ("Managing Mycorrhizas"), probably lack sufficient native fungi to colonize your plants properly and rapidly. Rapid colonization is key, especially when planting seeds or transplants. When properly inoculated, the mycorrhizas go to work within days seeking out water and nutrients, improving soil structure, reducing pest and disease susceptibility, and minimizing competition around vulnerable young plants. Particularly if you cannot do much after-planting care, some form of mycorrhizal inoculation is good insurance when site conditions are in doubt or nonhost plants threaten to outcompete your plantings.

What Kind and Quality of Inoculum Is Available?

This relates to the kinds of fungi your plants need and whether you will use commercial or natural inoculum. One of the first questions to ask when you've decided to inoculate is which kind of fungi you need. This depends on the plants involved (see table 5.6). Once you know what kind of mycorrhizal fungi your plants need, then you must decide how to inoculate. Consider soil inoculation (see below) before purchasing commercial mycorrhizal fungi, or if you need ericoid fungi. Commercial inoculants currently cover only arbuscular mycorrhizal and ectomycorrhizal fungi. If you choose commercial inoculum, you must choose the company, an application method, and the fungi mix in the product.

The number of companies selling commercial mycorrhizal inoculants has grown rapidly in recent years. A modern-day equivalent of the Wild West, this market often lacks quality product information, and few rules and regulations protect consumers. Watch out for snake oil! To select mycorrhizal inoculant companies or products, use the following tips, and appendix 7:

- Inform yourself about mycorrhizas before making your purchase.
- If a company and its literature cannot speak intelligently on the subject, or if a company representative is not available to answer questions, go elsewhere. Beware of hype, including photos depicting huge growth increases from use of the company's products—this *may* indicate profiteering with cheap unwanted fertilizer in the inoculum rather than expensive desired fungi. On the other hand, studies have frequently demonstrated significant growth increases from inoculum use, particularly on degraded sites. Just remember to measure your results based on all the multiple benefits from mycorrhizas, not just growth increases.
- Has the company's product been tested by third parties to evaluate its colonization success? At least 25 percent colonization after thirty days is the absolute minimum the product should achieve under controlled conditions; 30 to 40 percent is considered good. More is better. Ask for documentation of the test results. Does the company give a money-back guarantee?
- Ask about the product's ingredients. Beware if the company will not disclose them. If it contains fertilizers, especially chemical fertilizers, you should generally avoid the product. Some products do contain other ingredients, such as gelling agents and perhaps humic acids, for good reason. Unscrupulous manufacturers include fertilizers to boost growth while lowering fungal content in the product. Some ingredients actually *prevent* colonization or kill fungi. Ask why the ingredients are there if you don't understand the reasoning.
- Find out how many active propagules of what kind the product contains. *The Instant Expert's Guide to Mycorrhizas*[30] tells how to evaluate and use the numbers. The form of propagule

(mycelium, spores, or fragments of colonized roots) influences viability (spores last longer), infectivity (spores colonize more slowly), storage, handling, and application. Arbuscular mycorrhizal fungal spores are relatively large and will not withstand grinding, so if you are buying a powder, ask how the powder was made.

- When you receive the product, it should not have a putrid odor. Most products should be dry when received. As live organisms, the product has a shelf life of about twelve months. Check the expiration date and, if you can, the manufacture date.

- Bone up on specific storage, handling, and application requirements, both from the manufacturer and in the general literature.

These tips make it sound like a lot of work, and it can be. However, for forest gardening, you should only have to apply the inoculum once. Since you won't be generating intense disturbances as in conventional agriculture, the fungi should stick around.

Which Application Method?

When applying mycorrhizal inoculants, the key is to get viable propagules in contact with roots as soon as possible. The faster the fungi reach the roots, the faster mycorrhizas will form. The faster mycorrhizas form, the faster the plant will receive the benefits and the fungi will spread into the soil to do their work. Timing is important: plant survival is often determined in the first few days or weeks, and the faster the mycorrhizas fill the soil around the plant, the more resources they will gather and the less competition the plant will experience with ruderal or competitor-strategist weeds, many of which are nonmycorrhizal.

The application method you choose should therefore get the inoculum into the root zone of the plant, ideally right onto the roots, and not leave it on the soil surface. Mycorrhizas form mainly on fine roots, so you want to inoculate the ends of the roots, not near the trunks of trees or shrubs. Which method works best depends on the kind of plant stock you will plant.

- Root dips of bare-root stock work best, getting the fungi right onto the roots. A gel solution is the optimum dip, as the gel keeps the propagules suspended in solution rather than sinking to the bottom of the bucket. Most gels contain added ingredients, so read labels and ask questions to make sure you are getting a high propagule count.

- Adding inoculum to the planting hole at the time of planting also works, though you need more inoculum than with root dips. Some manufacturers make tablets or pellets you can insert into the root-ball of containerized or balled-and-burlapped plants before they go into the ground. This would seem a faster and easier way to colonize than dusting or gel-coating the root-ball, especially if you can place the tablet next to some fine roots. It also means you breathe less dust, and this is good, especially for those allergic to molds.

- Broadcasting inoculum and mixing it into the soil before seeding works if the inoculum has high propagule density and the application rate is high enough. However, placing inoculum at high density near the seeds, preferably below them, increases positive outcomes compared to broadcasting the inoculum everywhere. Some folks have had great results using modified farm equipment or land imprinters to inject powdered inoculum below the surface in line with seed-drill rows.

- Injection of inoculated water into the soil at root level can work, as long as you inject near the fine roots of the plant. This can be guesswork on established trees, but most established trees should already be colonized anyway. In any case, injections should occur at the drip line of the crown, if not farther out, if you want to find the fine roots. Where to inject is clearer with just-planted containers or balled-and-burlapped specimens.

- Drenches (irrigating the soil surface with inoculum mixed in water) have a low success rate, probably because arbuscular mycorrhizal fungal propagules are large relative to soil pore spaces in all except sandy soils. Drenches are more viable with ectomycorrhizal fungi because the spores are much smaller.

Fungal Species in the Inoculum

Most products currently contain mixtures of mycorrhizal fungi species, based on the thought that if the site doesn't work very well for one species, some other fungus in the mix will find the site hospitable. Some even mix arbuscular and ectomycorrhizal fungi in one product, so you have to buy only one bottle of tablets, for example, for all your trees and shrubs, and you don't have to think about what you're doing. Sounds logical and easy, but there's a problem.

You will have a lower density of arbuscular fungi in a product that mixes arbuscular and ectomycorrhizal species than in a pure arbuscular mycorrhizal product. So when a mixed powder gets dusted onto an apple root-ball, for example, the density of arbuscular fungi spores is lower, so the colonization probability is lower. Hence the effectiveness and speed of colonization drops. The same principle holds at the level of fungal species: the more species in the mix, the lower the density of any one species. The shotgun approach is more likely to hit the target, but less likely to knock it down effectively.

We will not recommend that you try to select the one or two "right" fungal species for your site, as this goes too far for most of us, even were the information available and accurate. We do recommend that you not buy a product that mixes arbuscular and ectomycorrhizal fungi if you can help it. You might also choose products with fewer different fungi, selected from the most adaptable generalist species, such as the arbuscular mycorrhizal fungus *Glomus intraradices.*

Consult and follow the manufacturer's instructions for applying specific products once you have made your choices. And remember: evaluate the success or failure of the inoculation based on all of the benefits mycorrhizas offer, not just dramatic plant growth.

Native Fungi Transplants

Research has demonstrated that inoculating soils and plants with commercial mycorrhizal inoculants improves the performance and yield of many crops, annual and perennial, especially in highly disturbed, infertile, or acid soils. However, just as we might want to be wary of introducing exotic plant species to healthy landscapes, we should probably beware of casually introducing exotic fungi to soils (even though scientists have yet to observe "invasive exotic fungi" taking over inoculated soils). At the same time, mining soils from healthy ecosystems to inoculate our gardens with their microbes can only add stress to the few remaining healthy ecosystems (see "Soil Inoculation," below). We need to husband these biological resources and draw what we need from them renewably and sustainably with minimal disturbance. The following way to transplant locally native fungi (and probably other critters) from healthy woodland to your garden should achieve these objectives, at least for some fungal species.[31]

While this method will mainly transplant decomposer fungi and some of their associates, this alone has value in developing forest-garden soil food webs. Some of these decomposers will also be mycorrhizas, particularly ectomycorrhizal fungi, which are known decomposers. Some may be edible mushrooms. Some may be disease fungi—there is no way to know except to identify the organisms you collect, which few people can do unless and until they fruit. There is some risk, and probably some benefit, though these are both hard to measure. However, it seems worthwhile since more fungi are beneficial than not. Here are some steps to follow:

- Find a healthy native ecosystem at a successional stage similar to that of your garden. "Healthy native ecosystem" may be an oxymoron, but you can figure something out. Look for habitats with diverse native species, minimal pollutants and unnatural disturbances, and healthy, vigorous, disease-free plants.
- Lay a thin blanket of clean wood chips or other mulch material, ½ to 1 inch (1.5 to 3 cm) thick, over an area of the forest floor where it will remain moist, mostly shaded, and undisturbed for a period of weeks. Beware of carrying unwanted guests in the material you bring to the native ecosystem: wood chips from sick trees may spread disease to the healthy ecosystem!
- Come back a few weeks later (two to six or more, depending on mulch material, site, and season). The wood chips are ready to move when a fungal network has colonized the surface so densely that they bind the chips together and you can pick up the chip mat in large pieces. Shake off the majority of the soil, and carry the mats away to your garden. Keep the mats cool, moist, and dark as they travel. Bagging the mats in plastic or paper bags may help ensure that other critters that came along for the ride don't escape en route. Remulch the colonization site with local material so you leave no trace of your presence!
- Scatter the mats or mat pieces in favorable habitats in your garden and cover thinly, ideally with mulch of similar nature to the initial transplant substrate. Keep the inoculated material in good-size pieces so there is a "critical mass" at each inoculation site. Place them near plants you particularly want to inoculate. Make sure each inoculation site has other substrates for the inoculum to grow into, such as more wood chips, for example.
- Different kinds of mulch (leaves, chips, bark, twigs, or branches from different tree species, straw, and so on) will attract different species of fungi and other organisms at each stage of decomposition in the healthy ecosystem. Experiment with different ecosystems and sites, different materials, and different colonization times to get the highest diversity of organisms to your site.

Penetrating Restrictive Layers

Try this when (and only when) permeable soil underlies a restrictive or impervious layer, but broadscale treatments are unavailable or impractical. No experimental evaluation of this technique has been published that we know of, but it is fairly commonly used and should work if done carefully. Pay attention to soil-texture boundary issues when using this technique.

- After digging the planting hole, bore a hole from the bottom of the planting hole through the restrictive layer to the permeable material. A hole 4 to 6 inches (100 to 150 mm) in diameter is fine for drainage, while larger holes work better for rooting. Power augers work well for this task.

For Drainage Only

- Fill the borehole with medium or coarse sand, fine gravel, or soil of a similar texture to that of the permeable soil above the restrictive layer (figure 5.9). If the restrictive layer is silty or clayey, the coarsest material you should use is medium sand, since coarser material will plug. If the soil is fluid when saturated, wrap a perforated pipe with geotextile or filter fabric and place the pipe into the borehole. The fabric will prevent the pipe from filling with particles. Extend the pipe to at or near the surface, but leave it empty. Cap the pipe to prevent soil and debris entry. You can then back-flush the pipe with water if it appears to clog.
- One hole per tree should work best for most situations, but if the soils overlying the hardpan are highly permeable, a clump of trees can be drained by one borehole. For planting-bed drainage use multiple boreholes in each bed. No

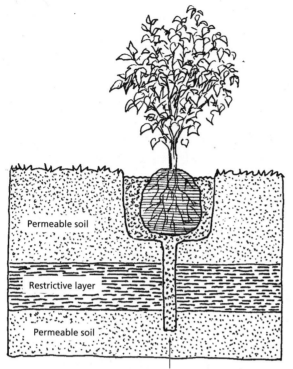

Borehole, 4–6″ (10–15 cm) in diameter for drainage, larger for rooting

FIGURE 5.9. When a restrictive layer lies near the surface and is underlain by a permeable soil, bore a hole from the bottom of the planting hole through the restrictive layer into the permeable soil below. For drainage only, make the borehole 4 to 6 inches (10 to 15 cm) in diameter; for rooting below the restrictive layer, make it one-third to one-half the diameter of the planting hole. Fill the borehole with soil of similar texture to that of the soil above the restrictive layer and plant your tree with the same soil around it.

studies have yet determined optimal spacing of boreholes; however, one researcher recommends one hole for every 6 feet (2 m) of planting bed. You could install one bed with an observation well (a perforated pipe you can look into and measure water levels in) and watch water levels after repeated heavy irrigation to see whether your spacing provides adequate drainage. Water levels should drop at least 0.1 inch (2 mm) per hour, or the plants will likely suffer.[32]

For Rooting Below the Hardpan Layer
- Make the borehole diameter larger (up to one-third to one-half the planting-hole diameter).

Fill the borehole with soil of similar or slightly coarser texture than that of the planting-hole backfill soil. This will offer fewer barriers to root penetration than if the roots have to cross one or two major soil-texture boundaries.[33] If the plants can root into underlying layers, they will resist drought better and require less irrigation.

PRESCRIBED BURNING

We can use fire as a management tool, even in suburban areas, if we design our sites to accommodate the practice and know when and how to burn properly. Well-managed burning can improve nutrient cycling, vegetation composition and diversity, crop productivity, and soil-food-web health, as well as help with pest, disease, and opportunist plant control. Though fire is most commonly used to manage meadows, prairies, and savannas, some forest ecosystems also benefit. Fire is an especially appropriate management tool in forested regions where it was commonly used by native peoples or largely defined the precolonial landscape.

This rich topic deserves far more attention than we can give it here. The Nature Conservancy is working with prescribed burning in many of its local land management programs, has an online fire management manual, and sometimes offers trainings and workshops, as well as volunteer opportunities to help with prescribed burns.[34] Make sure you know what you're doing and why, get whatever permits you need from local authorities, and enlist the cooperation of your local fire department before trying it!

RADIAL TRENCHING

Radial trenching works well in severely compacted or dense, fine-textured soils that restrict rooting from top to bottom, or when trees already exist or have already been planted on your site. It is less labor-intensive than double digging and causes less plant disturbance than chisel plowing. It can also work well if the surface is compacted or restrictive but underlying layers are more permeable, especially if you can trench deeply enough to break into the

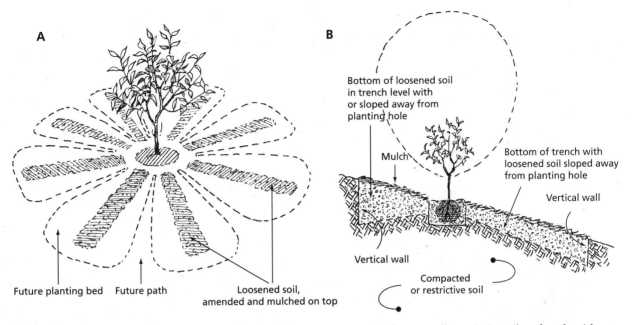

A

Future planting bed   Future path   Loosened soil, amended and mulched on top

B

Bottom of loosened soil in trench level with or sloped away from planting hole

Mulch

Bottom of trench with loosened soil sloped away from planting hole

Vertical wall

Vertical wall

Compacted or restrictive soil

FIGURE 5.10. Radial trenching improves tree growth and health in very compacted or naturally restrictive soils and works with pre-existing or newly planted trees. You can either replace the soil in the trenches with high-quality materials or simply loosen what is there but amend and mulch on top. (a) Six to eight trenches radiating from the tree in all directions to at least the tree's expected crown diameter, if not more, is the optimal design. Plan your planting beds and paths so the paths do not go over the loosened soils. (b) On sloping sites, make sure the trenches do not lead underground water toward the planting hole. Make sure the trench surface area is equal to or less than the bottom surface area to reduce water concentrating in the belowground space. In other words, make the trench walls vertical.

permeable underlying layers. In some situations it pays to backfill the trenches with higher-quality soil and organic material; in others, backfilling with the loosened trench soil works fine. Radial trenching helps trees and shrubs spread their root systems out of their planting holes for greater stability and to gather more resources. Research has demonstrated improved tree growth and root density using the technique when preexisting soils are heavily compacted or naturally restrictive.[35] Design radial trenches to work with your pathway patterns to minimize compaction over tree roots (figure 5.10a). An alternative to trenching that achieves a similar effect is to make radial raised beds (see below).

Here's how to go about using radial trenching:

- Dig six to eight trenches radiating from the planting hole or existing tree by hand or by using a backhoe, soil trencher, or other equipment. For existing trees, orient the trenches

between large roots. You can also excavate with water or compressed-air equipment to limit root damage to existing trees, or you can simply use a spading fork to loosen the topsoil in lines radiating from the planting site. Trenches can be 1 to 2 feet (30 to 60 cm) wide and up to 2 feet (60 cm) deep. They can extend up to three times the crown diameter away from the tree but should extend at minimum to the expected mature-crown drip line. In clay or hardpan soils, orient the slope of the trench bottoms to drain water away from the planting hole. On sloping sites, you may want more trenches radiating downhill than up for this reason. However, make sure to trench uphill, too, for this will help the tree anchor itself in that direction. Take care that the surface area of the trenches is equal to or smaller than the area of the trench bottoms to reduce the likelihood of waterlogging the loosened soil; vertical-sided trenches or trenches with the walls sloping outward as they descend are best (figure 5.10b).

- Backfill with either the loosened trench soil or high-quality material. Experiments showed that backfilling with 100 percent aged hardwood leaf compost resulted in higher root density after one year than did a 50:50 compost and soil mixture.[36] However, the quantities of material required for complete soil replacement are enormous, so replacing only the topsoil layer may be more efficient, even if the trenches run deeper. Overfill the trenches to allow for settling, and avoid running equipment and feet over them afterward.
- Irrigate several times to settle soil, or allow natural rainfall to do this over time.
- Mulch at least the crown area of existing trees, if not all of the trenches themselves.
- Place planting beds over the radial trenches, and fill them with diverse plantings to make the most of the loosened soil you have created.

RAISED BEDS

One of the main reasons to build raised beds is to increase rooting depth or the depth of topsoil over hardpan, bedrock, or wet soils. Raised beds are also easier for some elders and many disabled people to maintain, if the beds are high enough. Most people know about raised garden beds these days, for they have become a common garden strategy. However, thinking through the rooting depth and properly building the soil horizons within raised beds is not as common as it should be, though these strongly affect plant growth and health.

Consider the issue of rooting depth when you design your beds. Ideally, forest gardens will have at least 3 feet (1 m) of rooting depth. Obviously, importing 3 feet of soil to a site is expensive, so we do what we can. What kinds of plants will your beds accommodate? This question is especially important when you are building beds over bedrock or dense, thick hardpan. For smaller, shallow-rooted plants, including plants grown in quart and gallon (1 l and

4 l) pots before being transplanted to the garden, 12 to 18 inches (30 to 45 cm) of soil is a reasonable minimum, but this will limit the water and nutrient resources available to them. For larger, deep-rooted plants, or those grown in containers larger than 1 gallon (4 l) or arriving balled-and-burlapped, deeper beds may be necessary. You can also create deeper pockets for these specimens.[37] If the native topsoil is reasonably loose, include that in your calculations.

People often build raised beds right over existing topsoil and vegetation, without considering what happens when organic matter gets buried and goes anaerobic. Such anaerobic layers impede water movement and root growth, limit the normal transfer of gases and nutrients in the soil profile, and produce toxic by-products such as ammonia and alcohol that reduce plant and soil organism health. The topsoil and organic matter should always stay on top, or your garden will drag a hidden weight behind it, slowing its performance for many years.

You can create raised beds in a number of ways, including double digging, importing soil, or simply using topsoil from the pathways to build up the height of the planting beds. You can construct bordering walls to hold the beds in place using wood, concrete blocks, ferrocement, stone, slabs of broken concrete, logs, or what have you, or you can simply mound the soil, slope it gently, and mulch it. Following are a few other points to bear in mind:

- Consider site drainage issues before doing anything. The preexisting landform will exert strong influence over water movement, especially if the raised-bed soils have a dramatically different texture from that of the existing soils. For example, with sandy-loam planting beds on top of dense hardpan, the hardpan will control water flow below the beds. Some beds may saturate if they stand in low areas, while others will be high and dry. You may need to regrade or fix drainage problems before building beds on top of them.

• The orientation and shape of the raised beds also influence drainage patterns. Pathways may become streams or ponds if you aren't careful, even becoming erosive gullies in the worst cases! Think this through and adapt your bed design to preempt or take advantage of such situations. Dave once inadvertently created a great automatic watering system in his garden by laying a bed across the slope below a runoff pathway. When it rained hard the runoff ponded in the path uphill of the bed and quickly soaked into the fine sandy loam. This bed required far less irrigation than other parts of the garden, though the pond was an occasional and temporary inconvenience.

• Lay out the outlines of your raised bed(s) on the site using rope, garden hose, stakes, lime, or other means. Design your pathways well, using the pathway patterns discussed in chapter 2.

• When building walls around the beds, in most cases it is best to build the walls before bringing in the soil to minimize construction hassle and planting-bed compaction. If the beds are large and there is space, you can bring in soil before building the walls if there will be room to work on the walls around the piles. Remember to include mulch depth when calculating wall height and soil depth.

• If your raised beds will be deep, strip the topsoil and organic material from the bed area before placing the new soil in the beds. How deep is too deep depends on soil texture; fine soils cause low oxygen only a few inches below the surface, whereas sandy soils may allow sufficient oxygen to prevent anaerobic decomposition many inches deep.

• Loosen the native soil in the bed before backfilling using a spading fork. You might want to work mineral (not organic) fertilizers into the subsoil before filling if the soil is particularly poor in nutrients. Leave the native soil surface rough to maximize surface contact between the native soil and the bed fill and to assist in water infiltration.

• Consider the soil horizon structure you will create when you select soil materials. Use lessfertile soil in the lower layers of deep beds if you can, and leave the best-quality soil for the top. This can save considerable expense if you are buying and importing materials, as topsoil is usually rather expensive. Six to 8 inches (15 to 20 cm) of topsoil is great; more is better. However, the added benefits diminish as the topsoil gets deeper, while the costs increase at a constant rate.

• Overfill your beds by 5 to 10 percent to allow for settling to your desired final grade. Again, remember to account for the depth of mulch when filling the beds.

RHIZOME BARRIERS

Vigorous rhizomatous plants can spread far and wide underground unnoticed, suddenly popping out of nowhere in places we don't want them. They are hard enough to eliminate from the garden site that preventing them from spreading back into the garden from outside becomes a critical task. Also, we may want to plant vigorous rhizomatous crops such as bamboo that we need to keep in bounds. Rhizome barriers physically wall off one area from another belowground, keeping rhizomatous plants where we want them. Consider the following points when using rhizome barriers:

• Ideally, rhizome barriers consist of a longlasting, continuous, solid material that roots cannot penetrate. Many plants will eventually find and penetrate any seams or laps in noncontinuous materials if they are not well sealed. Heavy-gauge high-density polyethylene (HDPE) plastic *at least* 60 mils (1.5 mm) thick is probably the material of choice. It is light, flexible, easily installed, and easily removed and can be bought in rolls of various widths and cut to a desired length. Though hard to remove, and more expensive and labor-intensive to build, poured concrete, mortared stone walls, ferrocement, and other masonry materials work well for this purpose, too. Ferrocement yields thin but very strong walls of virtually any size and shape, taking less space and allowing more creativity than the other masonry options. It is made from a 2-inch (5 cm) or so thickness of mortar plastered from both sides onto a frame made from expanded metal mesh or chicken wire attached to ½-inch (1 cm) iron reinforcing rods driven into a trench in the ground or anchored in poured concrete (figure 5.11). Rolls of aluminum flashing work, but they may conduct enough heat to cause greater freeze damage to plant roots. Avoid fiberglass sheeting, which cracks and breaks, leaving a mess, and wood, which has seams and eventually rots so rhizomes get through. Especially avoid pressure-treated wood products containing toxic chemicals and heavy metals. If you can, go for plastic or ferrocement.

- The rhizome barrier should extend about 2 inches (5 cm) above the mulch surface. Most perennial herbs and grasses will not overcome a 12- to 18-inch-deep (30 to 45 cm) barrier. Brambles such as raspberry need at least a 2-foot-deep (60 cm) barrier. Most bamboos require 30 to 36 inches (75 to 90 cm) of barrier depth.[38] Deep-rooted bamboos, or those planted in deep, soft, fertile, well-watered and well-drained soils, require more.
- Ideally the rhizome barrier will tilt slightly away from the plants we intend it to contain. This induces roots to go up rather than down when they hit the barrier and reduces the chances of a vigorous plant, such as a bamboo, piercing the barrier.
- The barrier should surround the contained area in graceful curves lacking sharp corners, particularly with bamboos and plastic barriers. Bamboos have sharp root tips, so a corner in the barrier may allow the plants to build up enough pressure to puncture any plastic, especially those less than 60 mils (1.5 mm) thick. Also keep the

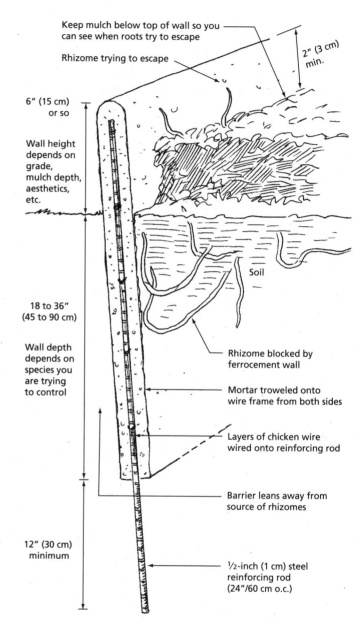

FIGURE 5.11. Any rhizome barrier should extend at least 2 inches (5 cm) above the mulch layer and a minimum of 12 to 18 inches (30 to 45 cm) below grade, or deeper, depending on the species you need to control. Ideally, the top of the barrier will tilt away from the species you want to control to encourage roots to go up when they hit the barrier, not down. A ferrocement barrier like that shown here consists of ½-inch (1 cm) steel reinforcing rods on 24-inch (60 cm) centers with chicken wire or expanded metal mesh wired to them. Mortar is then troweled onto the mesh frame from both sides to a thickness of about 2 inches (5 cm). This makes a very strong, long-lasting, and seamless barrier to rhizomes.

barrier away from jagged objects (e.g., rocks) that may puncture it under root pressure.

- When you have a seam, lap the joint by at least 1 foot (30 cm). Roll the joint if you can. Seal it with glue or caulk, make sure it has no gaps, and clamp, bolt, or rivet it together. Place such seams in strategic locations where a loss of containment will be obvious, will be easily managed, and will cause the least harm to desired crops or a neighbor's property.

- Visually inspect the barrier each fall and spring to ensure it still works. Keep mulch from covering the top of the barrier or roots will grow through the mulch and over the containment. Look for signs of containment loss around the whole perimeter, especially near the seams. You don't have to dig up the barrier unless you think there is a problem somewhere.

- If you are contemplating growing running (as opposed to clumping) bamboo, read up on bamboo containment in more depth. These vigorous plants are extremely useful and beautiful if you keep them where you want them. Otherwise they can be a major nuisance!

SOIL INOCULATION

Sites with barren soils or that have experienced major disturbance often lack many critical soil-food-web critters, including mycorrhizal fungi. Soil inoculation is a simple process of transferring soil and duff (partially decomposed litter) from an appropriate healthy native ecosystem to your site to inoculate the roots of newly planted plants with native fungi, nitrogen-fixing and plant-growth-promoting bacteria, pathogen-suppressing microbes, soil-structure-building organisms, and whatever other critters come along for the ride. This means you risk bringing disease or pest organisms along with you, as well as the multitude of beneficials that usually overwhelm the bad guys in healthy ecosystems. It differs from native fungi transplants (above) by the fact that you are moving a quantity of actual soil from a natural site to your garden, rather than just a substrate for decomposer organisms. Soil transfers will probably bring a wider variety of organisms than will colonized substrate transfers. Bear the following in mind when using soil inoculation:

- Determine whether your site qualifies as a candidate for soil inoculation. Sites that may need soil inoculation are those listed in volume 1, chapter 5, "Managing Mycorrhizas." These tend to be disturbed sites in one form or another. Extremely clayey, sandy, or silty soils may also benefit from soil inoculation if they lack adequate aggregation. Soil inoculation may help where slow infiltration, puddling, slow decomposition, poor aggregation, or the prevalence of pest and disease organisms indicates an imbalanced soil food web. Plants in salty, compacted, or infertile soils or in soils with heavy metals may also benefit from additional soil-food-web members. Soil inoculation may also help plants that need arbuscular mycorrhizal fungi to survive in sites where previously only ectomycorrhizal plants grew, or vice versa. Most sites will not need soil inoculation, as most of the critters your garden needs either are already there or will show up relatively soon once you create good conditions for them. Soil inoculation is probably not worth the risk of transferring disease organisms if your site does not exhibit the need or if you are growing plants or crops for sale.

- Fully evaluate your soil conditions for drainage problems, chemical imbalances, compaction, and so on. Improve these limiting conditions before planting or inoculating, if possible, or the time, effort, and impact of soil transfers on the native ecosystem will be wasted. Make sure you have a hospitable environment for the organisms you transplant to call home.

- Select an appropriate donor site for your transplant. Think about soil types, drainage, slope aspect, and vegetation cover. Consider the kinds of plants you are planting: do they need arbuscular mycorrhizal fungi, ectomycorrhizal fungi, or some other special kind of mycorrhizal fungi (see table 5.6)? Finding a donor site that has similar mycorrhizas to what your site has or will need will help you build the entire soil food web appropriate to your crops. We discuss donor-site criteria further below.

- Estimate the amount of donor soil you need. Soil is a weak inoculum, so a fair amount is needed, especially to inoculate mycorrhizal fungi. How many plants do you have to inoculate? Each plant will need at least one or two handfuls of soil, but one-half bucket is a more reliable amount. Either way, that adds up quickly, so try to inoculate as few plants as possible to minimize damage to the donor site. You can inoculate every second, third, or fourth plant in a planting, expecting that the critters will travel from place to place.
- Once you've chosen a donor site and estimated the amount of soil you will need from it, choose and acquire your return gift to the donor site: clean mulch, good-quality compost, rock powder fertilizers, or some other material in an amount comparable to what you remove. Make sure the gift is appropriate to the donor site. Don't carry diseases and pests to the donor site in return for its favor to you!
- Harvest your donor soil no more than a day or two before inoculating your plants during planting. If you keep the donor soil in buckets too long, its value as an inoculum will deteriorate.
- Take partially decomposed litter, topsoil, and especially *fine roots* (for mycorrhizal fungi) from several spots in the donor area. Take material from at least two or three spots, even for a small quantity of soil. This not only spreads the impact of your extraction but also should give you a better range of critters. You can mix the soil from the different spots in one container. Replace what you take with your gift, and offer thanks and blessings! Keep the donor soil cool, moist but not wet, and shaded or dark until planting time. Try to keep your extraction sites unobtru-

sive, and cover them with local or brought-in mulch to blend them to the rest of the landscape. Mulching the donor sites is especially important, as disturbed soil in an otherwise healthy ecosystem may invite opportunist species.

- When planting your new plants at your garden, add inoculum from the donor site to the planting hole. Work it in as closely around the roots of the plants as possible to maximize contact between the roots and the inoculum.
- If you use this technique, do it with great restraint, respect, responsibility, and caring. Our species has done so much damage to natural areas already, it would be a shame and a sham to do even more harm in the name of ecological gardening!

One of the most important factors to consider in using soil inoculation is selecting your donor site. Here are a few tips:

- Always avoid using weedy soils as donor sites. Weedy soils tend to have weed seeds and also usually lack the right mycorrhizal fungi for almost any more mature ecosystem. They tend to contain more pathogens and pests and fewer beneficial organisms.[39]
- Forests high in diversity are usually dominated by arbuscular mycorrhizal (AM) fungi. Low-diversity forests, especially evergreen forests, tend to be dominated by ectomycorrhizal (EM) or arbutoid fungi. Also, forests that have a continual buildup of organic matter on the soil surface tend to have EM fungi, because EM fungi strip nitrogen out of leaf litter rapidly to feed their hosts, and this slows decomposition.[40]
- Environmental conditions at the donor site should match those at your planting site as closely as possible with respect to soil type, drainage regime, slope aspect, and, ideally, vegetation cover. The less environmental change the soil goes through, the better an inoculum it will be.

- Examine the trees and other plants at the donor site carefully. Look for shelf fungi and other signs of disease on living trees. Are the tree crowns full and healthy, or do many trees have ratty foliage or dead branches? Look for opportunist exotic plants: do you see Oriental bittersweet, poison ivy, garlic mustard, or other problem plants whose seeds or roots you might transfer to your site if you take soil from there?
- Consider the families or genera of the plants you intend to inoculate. A donor site with related species could be optimal; that way you will most likely transfer appropriate fungi and other critters for your plants. However, you are also more likely to transfer pests and diseases of your crops. Research the local wild diseases and pest of your crops to see what could be a problem. It is unwise for nurseries or commercial orchard operations to even consider soil inoculation as an option for this reason. It is also probably unwise to consider orchards as donor sites for this reason.
- You should also consider ethics and legalities. Do you have or can you get permission to take soil from the site as long as you replace it with a similar volume of clean mulch material? Is the site on public land? If the latter, it's probably best to avoid using it as a donor site. Not only is it illegal, but if everyone took soil from public lands they would be destroyed in short order.

SOIL STAKING

This technique loosens soil and increases infiltration, aeration, and soil fungal biomass, while preserving the stability of steep slopes. You can install soil stakes around existing plants with minimal damage, thereby minimizing chances of erosion on steep sites. The stakes are meant to decompose, mimicking the rotting of roots, which act as long "pipes" conveying water, nutrients, and gases through the soil after a tree dies. Here's how to do soil staking:

- Determine the depth of compaction you want to treat, the area you want to cover, the density of stakes you want to use, and how much stake you want to have showing above the soil surface. Leaving some showing helps capture and hold mulch on steep slopes, though it makes the site less safe should someone trip and fall into the staked area. Placing stakes 6 to 12 inches (15 to 30 cm) apart is reasonable for heavily compacted soils. Stakes over 2 feet (60 cm) long are harder to drive and harder to acquire in sufficient numbers.
- Cut stakes from deadwood, brush, or branches that are of the required length. Solid wood, not decayed material, is necessary when driving stakes into compacted soil. Cut the stakes at an angle or sharpen one end to make driving easier. Minimum stake diameter will vary by species, stake length, and soil firmness; smaller-diameter stakes will not drive into hard soil before breaking. However, smaller stakes decompose more quickly, which can be an advantage. Beware of using live branches of willows or other easily propagated plants, or you may unwittingly plant a grove!
- Plant any plants you want on the site before staking.
- Drive the stakes vertically into the ground at the spacing and in the pattern you designed, leaving the desired amount showing.
- Mulch if desired.

SUBSURFACE DRAINAGE SYSTEMS

Sites with a high water table can sometimes be made drier using subsurface drainage systems. These usually consist of perforated pipe or drainage tiles installed in rows at least 4 feet (1.2 m) below finish grade. The distance between pipes varies depending on soil texture, with finer soils requiring closer spacing for proper drainage to occur. Pipes need at least a 1 percent slope toward an outlet where water can drain by gravity to a stream, ditch, or other surface waterway. Hence, the land must slope to the outlet enough to make up for the depth of the pipes below the drained site's final grade, plus the slope of the drainage pipe. Consult with an engineer or your county Natural Resources Conservation Service for design and installation assistance.

WOODY WEED EXTRACTION

When removing unwanted woody plants—vines, shrubs, and small trees—we usually either cut the plants down or dig them out. Some people use herbicide on them. Unfortunately, many species simply resprout when cut to the ground, either from the stump or from root suckers. Digging takes a tremendous amount of work, and the resulting soil disturbance can lead to greater weed problems or damage to desirable plants nearby. Herbicides have their problems, too, though they have their time and place when used carefully (see "Herbicides," above). Few people know about woody-weed-pulling tools and their many advantages for removing opportunist plants or just woody plants in the wrong place at the wrong time.

Woody-weed pullers come in a number of forms, each with advantages and disadvantages. All use lever action to yank woodies out of the ground with at least some of their roots, yet with minimal soil disturbance and effort. The two with the best reputations are the Weed Wrench and the Root Jack.

The Weed Wrench comes in four sizes for different-size stems. As you pull down on the handle, it grasps the stem in question. The tool's design makes wrenching even large shrubs or saplings relatively easy. Made from steel, it is heavy, but very strong and effective.

The Root Jack works similarly but comes in one size. Some folks feel it clamps stems more effectively, but that its wooden handle is more likely to break, though the tool is lighter. It has a flat hoe built in for clearing away soil and mulch to get the best grasp on the stem.

Weed extraction works like this:

- Select a subject to yank out of the ground. Clear a suitable space to work in so you can lever the tool without injuring either yourself or nearby desired plants. Find a good spot on the stem to clamp the tool onto. You may need to prune off a few lower branches to get access to the stem, so keep your pruners or loppers handy.
- Clamp the tool onto the stem and lever the handle toward the ground.
- You may need to reposition the tool for a second or third yank to pull out the plant by the roots completely. Follow the roots as they pull out of the ground and try to get as much root as possible, leaving the minimum in the ground to resprout.
- Some plant species can reroot or resprout when you discard them. Chip such plants, or let them dry completely in the sun before piling them or using them as mulch. Beware of plants with seeds on them, even unripe seed. Once the plant is out of the ground it will put all its remaining energy into ripening seed in hopes some will survive to the next generation. You may need to burn such plants, or hot-compost them, especially if they are an opportunist species.
- As with any disturbance, it pays to replant or mulch soon after disturbance to maximize your ability to direct the following succession. Have some seed, mulch, or plants on hand to begin the healing process right away, or you may have to contend with another weed problem later.

CHAPTER SUMMARY

As you can see, a multiplicity of challenging site conditions and possible responses to them exist. This chapter offers guidance for working with many of them. The biggest challenge comes in figuring out what to do when you have more than one of these challenges, or you want or need to use more than one strategy—as many folks will. You will then need to figure out what strategies to use together, for what reasons, and in what order.

If you follow the principles of design laid out in this book, you will seek strategies that have multiple functions. For example:

- hot-water weeding will kill unwanted plants and irrigate the garden;
- raised beds may help you avoid a high water table, build soil fertility, and deal with an unhealthy soil food web;
- installing subsurface drainage pipes can lower water tables and may also help you create deeper soil pockets for taprooted trees in a clay soil; and
- extracting woody weeds can help you gather the materials you need for soil staking.

Making your site preparation activities do double or triple duty for you is simple common sense—site preparation can be a lot of work!

When it comes to which strategies to use in what order, in most cases you'll want to work from the deeper layers of soil up—it makes little sense to mulch before you double-dig, for example. However, it may make sense to plant cover crops before chisel plowing—that way you can create the "soil climax" discussed in the "Deep Ripping or Chisel Plowing" subsection.

Ultimately, each one of us just has to work out the details of the strategies and order of events we will use given our unique goals and circumstances. One thing is sure, though. If you skip site preparation, you are likely to regret it for a long time to come.

1. Harris, Clark, and Matheny, 1999, page 110.
2. Harris, Clark, and Matheny, 1999, page 189.
3. Sauer and Andropogon Associates, 1998, page 81.
4. Sauer and Andropogon Associates, 1998, page 79.
5. Harris, Clark, and Matheny, 1999, page 200.
6. Harris, Clark, and Matheny, 1999, page 200.
7. Harris, Clark, and Matheny, 1999, page 196.
8. Mollison, 1990, page 194.
9. Williams and Williams, 2002, pages 37–39.
10. Roxbury Community School, Inc., 1983, page 31.
11. Soil Quality Institute, 2000, pages 4–7. For more information, see the "Urban Technical Notes" at the USDA's Soil Quality Institute Web site: soils.usda.gov/sqi/publications/utn.html.
12. Sauer and Andropogon Associates, 1998, page 261.
13. Sauer and Andropogon Associates, 1998, page 262.
14. See *The Compost Tea Brewing Manual* available at www.soilfoodweb.com, and tools and equipment available at www.growingsolutions.com.
15. Much of the following information comes from Harris, Clark, and Matheny, 1999, page 181.
16. Nelda Matheny, personal communication.
17. See *Water for Every Farm* by P. A. Yeomans (1981) for more information.
18. Kourik, 1986, and Jeavons, 1995.
19. *Webster's New Collegiate Dictionary*. Springfield, MA: Merriam Co., 1981.
20. Harmony Farm Supply, 2002, page 90.
21. Breyer, personal communication, May 2002. For more information, contact Tripple Brook Farm plant nursery, 37 Middle Road, Southampton, MA 01073, www.tripplebrook farm.com.
22. NOFA Organic Land Care Committee, 2001, page 35.
23. Mollison, 1990, page 168.
24. The volume of a pyramid or cone = 1/3 x base area x height; the volume of a prismoid = the average of the area of its two ends times its length, or (area 1 + area 2)/2 x length.
25. Harris, Clark, and Matheny, 1999, page 206.
26. This list adapted from St. John, 1996, page 3.
27. Yahner, 1995, page 37.
28. NOFA Organic Land Care Committee, 2001, page 37.
29. Harris, Clark, and Matheny, 1999, page 205.
30. *The Instant Expert's Guide to Mycorrhizas* by Ted St. John, PhD, 2000. You can download this at www.mycorrhiza.org.
31. Adapted from Sauer and Andropogon Associates, 1998, page 157.
32. Harris, Clark, and Matheny, 1999, page 191.
33. Harris, Clark, and Matheny, 1999, page 190.
34. Visit www.tncfire.org.

35. Harris, Clark, and Matheny, 1999, page 184.
36. Harris, Clark, and Matheny, 1999, page 184.
37. Lovejoy, 2001, page 33.
38. Meredith, 2001, page 156.
39. St. John, personal communication, 2002.
40. St. John, personal communication, 2002.

6

Garden Establishment

The planting of a tree is a sacred act. . . . Each time we break open
the earth, layer out the developing roots, and tamp the soil back in
place we embrace our mutual destiny with trees.

—MICHAEL PHILLIPS, *The Apple Grower*

He had pursued his plan, and beech trees as high as my shoulder,
spreading out as far as the eye could reach, confirmed it. . . . When
you remembered that all this had sprung from the hands and soul of
one man, without technical resources, you understood that men could
be as effectual as God in other realms than that of destruction.

—JEAN GIONO, *The Man Who Planted Trees*

Now the rubber meets the road! With all your planning and preparation complete, you should be in an excellent position to create a largely self-maintaining forest garden. It all depends now on the skill with which you put it into the ground. Before we get into nitty-gritty details, though, let us remember the reality of which the two quotes above remind us.

In these times of what many consider a decline in civilized society and planetary health and well-being, we nonetheless have the power to act creatively for the benefit of all—while meeting our own needs, too. We share a mutual destiny with trees, and with all those living beings that share the landscape and the planet with us. Our understanding of this functional interconnection with our interspecies compatriots is what leads many of us to plant our forest gardens. We hope that, at the very least, your enlightened understanding of your own true self-interest drives you to behave in such a manner. Either way, the very specific ways in which we physically plant our trees, shrubs, herbs,

ferns, and mushrooms manifest our spiritual connections to these other beings, and to the ecosystem as a whole. Let these insights, values, and feelings inform your approach to the very physical act of planting your garden.

Digging a "ten-dollar hole for a one-dollar tree" can seem excessive, but it truly does make a difference for the tree. It therefore makes a difference in the quality of how we express the sacred act of tree planting. Mindfulness takes many forms and always leads toward more skillful action. This chapter aims to increase the mindfulness with which you embody your already-thoughtful forest garden design—to increase the skillfulness of your planting work. The ideas that follow represent ideals in this effort of mindful planting. We encourage you to focus on progress, not perfection, in this regard.

Staking out your design on the ground before planting helps you faithfully translate your design into physical reality. It also provides you the opportunity to "test" and revise that design before creating the real thing. Proper planting and aftercare head the garden down the right successional path, reduce maintenance, and build productivity for the long run. This chapter discusses these skills, and the tools and techniques they require. With that in mind, let's think about a reasonable flow of work to create the forest garden, so you can minimize backtracking and redoing earlier work.

THE ORDER OF EVENTS

Every construction project has at least one logical work sequence that makes the construction process go smoothly, efficiently, and effectively. Landscape construction and planting are no different. Of course, the logical sequence may be quite different for specific projects and situations, but most projects follow a typical order of events. Forest garden construction includes tasks such as site preparation, staking out, planting, mulching, and aftercare, in roughly that order. In most cases, due to the nature of the work, we must break some of these steps into pieces and move them around, so site preparation occurs in two stages, for example, as might staking out and planting.

The items listed in table 6.1 represent a more robust sequence than you might use. The steps and stages could vary significantly; you may add extra

---

TABLE 6.1. A typical forest-garden construction sequence.

- Broadscale site preparation:
  - Grading and drainage, chisel plowing, etc.
  - Irrigation infrastructure.
  - Tilling, cover-cropping, large-scale amendments, etc.
  - Site clearing, Brush Hogging, patch clearing, etc.
- Staking out, stage one: paths and beds, woody plant locations.
- Bed-by-bed site preparation (e.g., double digging, soil staking, amending, etc.).
- Planting woodies.
- Sheet mulching.
- Staking out, stage two: patches.
- Planting herbs and mushrooms.
- Aftercare (watering, weeding, etc.).

---

steps. Pick and choose what to do when, depending on your circumstances. For example, you may need to stake out some garden features before installing irrigation pipes, and others afterward. Use table 6.1 as a rough guide, and develop your construction sequence from there. The balance of this chapter explains details of the construction process in more or less chronological order, beginning with staking out the design on-site.

STAKING OUT

Staking out your design on the ground translates your on-paper design to full-scale reality. It also culminates the design process and, for some people, will be where they do much of their design thinking. Even while staking out, however, continuing to sketch things out on paper can help you visualize what you're doing and see the big picture. Bounce back and forth between paper and site as necessary to get the design well in hand. Keep your goals and objectives in mind, if not in hand. They will help you get out of impasses more than almost anything else.

This brief section discusses the practicalities of staking-out strategy and techniques.

STAKE-OUT STRATEGY

Staking out your design is a bit like making a drawing. When drawing, you find reference points and lines and sketch them in roughly and lightly at first to define the outlines. You continue working in light pencil to fill in a few key details until you are sure the outline works well as a composition and reasonably approximates what you are drawing. Only when you have sketched the whole picture in rough fashion do you start making the lines darker, committing to a specific line in a certain place, making firm strokes and giving depth and color. Working this way allows you to evaluate your choices along the way, to feel your way into the reality you are creating, and to correct mistakes and distortions before building on them too far.

Similarly, when staking out your design, create your on-the-ground outline by locating objects or features that have the strictest size, shape, and location requirements or that determine the overall character of the design most strongly. Stake out these things first, and then fill in around them with everything else. Tree locations, pathways, water lines, ditches, swales, and windbreaks usually have the most exacting spacing, slope, or location requirements, though patios, parking areas, and other hard features qualify. Sometimes a view from a particular spot, a sweep of the eye as you move through space, or some other intangible is the most important feature defining the garden. Whatever the key things are, stake them out using tape measures, colored flagging, and markers or paint, and walk around getting a feel for the space you are creating. Review your design goals; look over your design sketches or plans. Does it all fit together so far? Don't stake out too much before evaluating how it works, how it feels, and how it looks. Stake and evaluate, stake and evaluate, stake and evaluate. Once you have the key items located with confidence, you can move into staking out features that are more flexible or more detailed. Use the stakes to "sketch" at first, then pound them in more firmly once you want to commit to your decisions.

If you aren't sure what is most important in your design, you can also start at one edge and work across the landscape. You may end up moving more stakes around that way, but no matter: the key is simply to begin defining your design on the ground, trying it out, and modifying it before you actually build anything. You'll learn as you go, as long as you work with awareness and often refer back to your goals.

STAKE-OUT TECHNIQUES

Some of the following techniques can help you translate from paper to the ground, while others help you check or refine your design in physical reality. For some techniques, we're talking basic geometry: two points define a line, a minimum of three points define a curve or a triangle. Other techniques essentially use a slightly more sophisticated game of make-believe than what kids do. Have fun! This discussion assumes you have already made a base plan using the tools and techniques discussed in the "Basic Mapping for Landscape Design" section of chapter 3. Look there for details on triangulation and extensions with offsets.

Triangulation

To review what we learned and used to make our base plan: Triangles are the most stable geometries. We can use them to accurately locate anything on our plan or on the ground, as we use them in mapping. This is mapping in reverse, though! We can use triangles to stake out our design plan on the ground.

If you have two points of known location and distance from each other (called benchmarks) that appear on both the map and the ground, you can accurately locate any other point on the ground or on the map by measuring from each of the two known points to the third point. The benchmarks should be prominent, central points accessible to many or most places on the property, and often they will be the points that you used during mapping for the same purpose.

On the map, use your engineer's scale to measure the distance from each benchmark to a key object in your design, for example, a tree or a path intersection. Then measure those distances on-site with tape measures. Having two tape measures and three people makes this much faster and easier. You can tie or hook two tape measures to a stake at each benchmark to substitute for the two other people. You can use a piece of rope or string with cloth or flagging tied to it to mark the desired distance as a substitute for one tape measure. While triangulation may be accurate, it is time-consuming. Use it to define a few key points, and then use other methods to stake out the rest of the features if you can.

Triangulating is like using a drawing compass to find a desired point at the intersection of two circles. Be careful that you have the angles right: two circles virtually always overlap in more than one place, and those two intersections can sometimes lie near each other. Always double-check your found point by eyeballing or measuring to another known point, or by estimating or measuring to evaluate where the other intersection of the circles would fall. Patience, double-checking, and a methodical approach pay off with this method. Carpenters say, "Measure twice, cut once." We say, "Measure twice, stake once."

Extensions and Offsets

To review: If you have a building or other angular object near the garden site and on your map, you can use extensions and offsets to find and mark points on the ground. An extension line essentially extends the wall of the building so you can use that line to find points on the ground. Again, this is the reverse of the mapping process. Extensions and offsets are easier and faster than triangulation and take fewer people, but they aren't as accurate.

Hook your 100-foot (33 m) tape measure to the building corner. Lay the tape measure on the ground as an extension of and in line with the building wall, following the instructions discussed in chapter 3. You can then extend the wall line on the design plan, measure distances to specific features on that line, and translate them to the ground with your tape measure and stakes.

Sometimes you'll want to stake a point that does not intersect the extension line. To do so, draw a line on your design plan from the point you want to stake to the extension line such that the intersecting line is 90 degrees to the extension line. Measure the distance on the map from the building corner to the intersection of those two lines, and from the intersection to the object or point you want to stake. Then recreate those lines and distances on the ground to mark the point. It is best to have two tape measures for this, one marking the line off the building wall, and the other for the 90-degree offset line. Gauging an accurate right angle is difficult in the field, though, so the offset line adds significant error in staking out, especially as the point gets far-

ther from the extension line. Use a framing square or similar tool to help you gauge the 90-degree angle. Avoid using the offsets if you can, especially if accuracy in locating a point is critical.

Rope, Hose, Lime

When laying out pathways, planting-bed edges, and the like, we often want to create nice curves, rounded corners, odd shapes, and so on. Stakes rarely do such geometries justice, at least in laying them out and playing with them. Using rope or hose to lay out such lines greatly aids in rapidly shaping them to our liking, feeling the space they create, following the lines of sight and sweeps of the eye they engender, and changing our minds.

After laying out one area with rope or hose, you may need some way of marking the lines so you can remove the hose to mark out another area. Placing stakes periodically along the line is good, but you can also use ground limestone, rock phosphate, or another mineral fertilizer powder to do this. Even old Portland cement or mortar mix that has gone bad but still crumbles can work well. Make sure the powder has a strongly contrasting color to the ground, or you won't see it easily! Simply pour out enough powder to leave a solid line that will resist a few rainfalls. If you don't have much powder, you can make piles every few feet to mark the line. A light dusting will disappear too soon to give you time to follow the guides. If by chance a lime line ends up in the wrong place, you can simply scratch it out with your feet and fertilize your soil at the same time! A bag of lime provides far more line marking per dollar than a bundle of stakes.

Stakes, Color Schemes, Grades

If you're staking out a large area with a complex set of paths, trees, shrubs, and other features, it helps to develop a color scheme for your stakes to help you see the patterns the stakes mark out. Use colored flagging for this, or paint the stake tops to distinguish path stakes from plants, trees from shrubs, even fruit trees from nut trees. Color-coding the stakes will help you keep your stake layout straight, so when laying out the trees you measure the spacing pattern from tree stake to tree stake, not tree stake to path stake by accident. You can also label each plant stake with a particular species to avoid confusion on planting day, either by color-coding or with an actual written label. This also helps you space the plants the proper distance apart, since different species are different sizes. A friend of ours had a multicolor code on his stakes for his orchard, where one color denoted the rootstock, another the interstem, and a third the kind of tree he planned to place there. This allowed him to ponder the conditions at each spot, decide what rootstock would fit best, and stay clear during planting. He could also look over the scene and see patterns, count how many of each rootstock he needed, and so on.

You can also use stakes to set grades for cuts and fills of soil in different places. Use a marking pen or red crayon to show the height above existing grade to which you want to fill a bed along a path, for example, or to write "–6" to denote a cut of 6 inches (15 cm) on the uphill side of a path to make it level. As mentioned in the "Mounds, Mound Planting, and Pits and Mounds" section in chapter 5, you can even tie string from stake to stake to help you imagine and adjust the end product and to estimate the quantity of material needed.

Test Runs

After staking out an area of pathways, planting beds, or what have you, pretend you are going about your business in the garden once it is complete. Walk through the paths with your garden cart to see whether the paths are wide enough and you have enough turnarounds. Fill the cart with mulch and try walking around with it. Maybe you should move the path to make it easier or put the strategic materials depot somewhere else? Imagine the crowns of trees when they are fully mature, and how they will affect your travels. Can you reach all parts of the planting beds from the paths, or might you want to narrow the beds some? How will moving hose around in the garden work? Do you need another faucet or more hose? Check the width of your mower and how it will be to mow certain areas. You can cut saplings the height of the mature trees and stick them in place to see whether you think they'll affect the views negatively or screen an ugly view well enough. With clients, I've even gone so far as to put saplings in the corner locations of a future house and get people up on step ladders with a simple "window frame" to see whether they like the view from proposed window locations. Play with your staked-out design; put it through its paces, challenge it with imagined floods or a large garden party to see whether you think it should change before you build it. Now isn't your last chance to change the design, but it may be your last best chance. Inhabit the space as best you can. Besides being useful, it's fun!

Another thing to try once you've staked out the garden is to look out the attic window or to get up on the roof or into a tree and get a bird's-eye view. Such a change in perspective can help you see the site whole and may add to your deliberations or confirm what you've decided. Just don't fall!

Last Checks and Details

We can't emphasize enough that the biggest mistake most forest gardeners make is the improper spacing of their plants, especially woody plants. You can always move herbs to give them more space if they're too dense, but woody plants get more difficult to move with age, and you often don't realize they're too close together until they are mature. Staking out your woody plants is one of the best preventives for this error, after designing things well on paper. It forces you to think through the plan at full scale, to translate your paper design faithfully to reality, and to adapt it carefully if the design and the reality are at odds. Making spacing decisions when you're in the thick of planting day will often lead to mistakes or quick, less-than-optimal judgments. Trees and shrubs grow and produce best when uncrowded. Don't put yourself in the position of having to cut down every second tree because you didn't think it through beforehand.

Once you've staked out your site, you can revise or create your estimates for construction and planting materials. How many square feet of cardboard do you need for sheet-mulching? How many yards of compost or wood chips? Does your plant list need revision? Do you need more hose? How much fertilizer do you need? Does the design as staked out work within your budget? What might you change in the design as a result of these questions?

ACQUIRING PLANTS

Extra attention to details before and during planting will pay dividends for decades, but errors made at the beginning can haunt you for just as long.

—Bart Hall-Beyer, *Ecological Fruit Production in the North*

Need we say more? We'll present many details worth your extra attention in the next few sections, from plant purchasing and evaluation of stock, through planting techniques based on the latest research, to after-planting care.

Planting-stock selection has a huge influence on the health, productivity, and longevity of your trees, shrubs, and perennials. The two most important aspects of plant selection are finding the plants you want and evaluating the stock you find. Here are some important things most folks don't know.

Finding What You Want

Knowing what kinds of plants you want and finding them can represent a challenge in forest gardening. This challenge has several facets, including what form and size of planting stock to acquire, finding unusual plants, and whether to use wildlings or nursery-propagated natives.

Containers, B-and-B, or Bare Root?

Woody plants usually come in one of three forms: container plants, balled-and-burlapped (B-and-B), or bare root. Perennials usually come in containers or as seed, though cuttings or divisions aren't unusual when you have gardening buddies. Each form has its advantages and disadvantages for the grower, the purchaser, and the planet.

Container plants are easily stored, moved, and cared for, and they allow the use of sterile bulk potting soils, which is why so many nurseries use them. Container plants have all of their roots intact, including their fine roots. Little root damage occurs when planting out a container plant, at least in theory. Therefore, you can plant potted plants almost any time in the growing season as long as they receive reasonable care. This gives the gardener and the salesperson the most flexibility.

However, container growing usually involves pampering plants with chemical fertilizers and pest controls, which can leave plant roots microbiologically impoverished, make them poor foragers, and leave them unprepared for the vagaries of the landscape jungle, not to mention container growing's environmental impacts. Such fertilization also often results in a poor root-to-shoot ratio, with plants having very large tops relative to their roots. This makes the plant more dependent on high maintenance inputs once it's in the ground. In addition, many nurseries pay little attention to healthy root form. This can leave potted plants with circling or pot-bound roots that can girdle and kill the stem as the tree matures, leave the plant prone to breakage, or reduce root spread into surrounding soil after planting. Methods to detect and treat these conditions follow shortly. Well-grown potted woody plants can make fine specimens. Poorly grown potted woodies can cost more than what you pay for them in time and trouble. Container-grown perennials usually have fewer problems and are much more consistently viable as long as you treat bound roots properly when planting.

Balled-and-burlapped woody plants grow in the field. The nursery then prunes the roots and wraps the root-ball in burlap, and sometimes a wire cage to help keep the root-ball together during transport.

Size is the major advantage of B-and-B stock; you can't get large trees or shrubs for immediate landscape effect unless you get a B-and-B specimen. B-and-B plants are usually not pampered as much as container-grown species. They've had to fend for themselves in the field for a number of years, though they probably received fertilizer and other inputs. B-and-B plants are less likely to have circling roots than container-grown plants, but this may still be a problem if the field stock originally grew in containers. In addition, the transplanting process cuts off a large portion of the plant's root system, leaving the B-and-B plant with a low root-to-shoot ratio, like its container-grown cousins. However, the container-grown plants at least still have their fine roots, while B-and-B plants probably don't. This makes B-and-B plants more likely to experience water stress after planting, so they need much care and feeding for a long time once they are in the ground. Meanwhile, we should recognize the impact of digging soil from a field somewhere when the plants are balled and trucked away, not to mention the extra fuel from shipping the extra weight. The biggest challenge with B-and-B plants, though, is the same as their major advantage: their size.

Even a "small" B-and-B plant can weigh 200 pounds (90 kg) or more. Equipment becomes necessary for planting quickly as plant size increases. Nurseries mostly use the B-and-B method for plants larger than a 3- to 5-gallon (12 to 20 l) container, so you usually pay a significantly higher price for them. Finally, research has shown that smaller plant stock recovers from transplant shock more rapidly. Trees half the size of their neighbors at planting can be 50 percent larger than those neighbors within five years, even when both are planted at the same time.[1] Clearly, large B-and-B trees and shrubs are called for only when you need an immediate landscape effect, and if you have money to burn on higher prices, labor, equipment, and maintenance.

Deciduous woody plants and evergreen seedlings often come as bare-root stock. They usually grow in the field for one or more years, then get dug up, have the soil washed off their roots, and get stored over winter. Sometimes they are dug when ordered and shipped immediately. Bare-root plants should be dormant when they arrive. Put them in the ground as soon as possible, certainly before they leaf out. This means early spring or fall planting *only*.

Bare-root stock is usually inexpensive both in price and in shipping cost. This means you can buy more plants for your money. The plants are small, a major advantage in terms of transplant-shock recovery speed, as well as ease of planting. Small plants mean smaller holes, which is a big deal, especially in rocky New England! You can see the plants' roots, so you won't have any hidden root problems and usually only good-quality plants get shipped. Bare-root plants create fewer environmental impacts because they leave their home soil behind, and they require few or no potting soils or peat (with the consequent mining impacts) for production. We can more easily and effectively inoculate bare-root plants with mycorrhizal fungi than any other type of stock. They also need less afterplanting care because they get their roots right into the soil and get growing. If a plant does die, at least your investment in the plant was minimal.

The main disadvantages of bare-root plants include their small size and the limited planting season. We discussed the relative growth of small and large trees and shrubs above, so the small size can actually result in larger plants five or ten years down the line. However, the quick-fix satisfaction of seeing a large plant appear all of a sudden doesn't exist with bare-rooters. Instead, you get the slow joy of watching the kids grow up over time. As for planting season, well, that's just one of those facts of life. It can limit your choice of plants if you have to plant in a certain time frame.

Growing plants from seed is fun, though it can get tricky, too. However, it's often not that hard, and it can generate a large number of plants. The cost of seed varies widely by species, but it can be very low. Sometimes you can even gather the seed yourself locally. Growing from seed gives you the highest within-species genetic diversity possible, whereas many container-grown, B-and-B, and bare-root plants are genetically identical. Some species are available only as seed, so if you want that specific plant you'll have to try it. Different woodies and perennials have different, sometimes very complex and specific germination requirements, so you'll have to research the details (see appendix 7). Find out the germination requirements before you buy seed! Make sure you are up to the task for each species, or you may find yourself in over your head. Growing perennial or woody plants from seed takes the most time, attention, and patience of any of the methods discussed.

In contrast, planting divisions of perennials or taking cuttings and growing them out can be fast, easy, and cheap. One of Dave's brothers once worked at a greenhouse propagating houseplants. Over the course of a few months, he pirated enough cuttings to fill his room literally to overflowing, until the plants spilled out into the rest of the house. Propagating perennials is a blast! Many woodies, such as currants (*Ribes* spp.) and raspberries (*Rubus* spp.), propagate easily, too, by layering, cuttings, or a number of other methods. Perennials often grow to a point that we must divide them to keep them healthy. These divided pieces quickly fill new spaces. If friends or neighbors give you such plants, check them carefully to make sure they are pest and disease free, pick through the root-ball to look for vigorous weed rhizomes, and make sure you know the plant's name and niche.

If you have to plant in the summer, container-grown stock is your best choice. If you're planting in the fall or spring, go with bare-root plants if you can. It's cheaper, the plants require less aftercare, and ultimately they yield a better return on your investment even if you have to wait a year or two more for the fruits or nuts to start popping out. Bare-root stock requires preplanning, though, while container plants can be more of an impulse buy. Maybe that's another reason the nursery trade

likes them. Resort to B-and-B stock only when the money is available, you need large plants for immediate effect, and a commitment to long-term care exists.

Hard-to-Find Species

Forest gardeners face an interesting chicken-and-egg challenge: Many of the species we'd like to plant are hard to find, because there is little demand for them in the nursery trade. Yet the demand doesn't exist at least partly because they aren't available. Sometimes you can find the species, but not in the form you might like. Some species, for example, are available only as seed (such as ramps, *Allium tricoccum*) or from only one nursery as a large, expensive, container-grown plant, when you want something small and inexpensive. This is simply part of the challenge and excitement of forest gardening at this time in history.

The nursery lists in appendix 7 provide some of the sources we have found that carry the plants of interest. Numerous other nurseries lie unobtrusively tucked away in the nooks and crannies of the world. More and more of these businesses are available on the Internet. Simply typing a plant's Latin name into a search engine and hitting return will provide you vast quantities of information on a plant and the people who propagate it. Unfortunately, many nurseries are not on the Web, and not all nurseries are created equal. Keep looking—eventually you'll find what you're looking for—but also buy cautiously. Look for inspection certificates that state that the stock is disease free, and make sure there is a money-back guarantee, for example. Even consider buying one or two plants initially to evaluate quality before making a big purchase from an unknown operation.

Wildlings and Nursery-Propagated Natives

As forest gardeners, many of us will be on the lookout for useful native plants. It can be tempting to go out in the woods looking for, and taking, plants for our gardens. *Please do not transplant natives from healthy or even unhealthy wild ecosystems into your garden*. This can be and has been a major cause of native-plant decline. Leave the native plants where you find them, unless you know the site where they are growing is about to be destroyed or developed. Then, by all means, rescue as many plants as you can and find a good home for them.

Questions surround even the harvesting of seed from wild plants, especially from rare plants. Don't take seed from rare species unless you are a skilled propagator committed to making sure the seed you take grows to maturity. For less-rare plants, take only a small portion of the seed available from any one place or stand of plants. This makes sense both for you and for the plant. Getting seed from diverse areas will ensure higher diversity in your population, with greater chances that some of the seeds will adapt to your garden's conditions. Leaving most of it where it belongs will help keep the plants going in their natural setting.

When buying native species, make sure the nursery is reputable and honest. Some nurseries sell plants taken from the wild as "nursery-grown" stock because they took it from the woods somewhere, grew it in their nursery for a little while, and then potted it up to sell. Make sure what you buy is "nursery-propagated" and not "nursery-grown" or of unnamed origin.

Smaller Plants Are Better

The point that smaller plants are better is worth reiterating, because it goes against our cultural conditioning. Smaller woody plants often grow to full size faster than larger transplants because small plants recover from transplant shock much faster. Smaller plants require less after-planting care for the same reason. Larger plants need more care for a longer period because they lose proportionately more roots in the process of getting to you. Also, smaller potted or B-and-B plants are more likely to have a balanced root-to-shoot ratio. This reduces plant stress because the roots are better able to meet the demands of the shoots for water and nutrients.

EVALUATING STOCK

Whether you buy plants at a local garden center or order them by mail, evaluating stock quality is a frequently overlooked step in the process that can improve the results of your planting labors significantly. Good-quality plants will grow more vigorously and require less maintenance than poor-quality stock. Here's how to tell the difference.

Root-to-Shoot Ratio

Stand back and evaluate the relative size of the shoots and roots of any plants you are thinking of buying. Plants with a moderate amount of top growth relative to their root-ball usually grow more vigorously and require less initial maintenance than those with a large top.[2] Most nurseries fertilize and water their plants aggressively to get the most top growth they can, because top growth sells plants. However, this practice can actually increase stress on the plants and reduce growth and survival once they get in the ground because the roots can't serve the top adequately without all the inputs. "High initial maintenance must be provided even if the top is thinned to reduce evapotranspiration."[3] *Root-to-shoot ratio is a key factor in creating a low-maintenance landscape!* Small is beautiful.

For bare-root trees and shrubs, the root spread should be at least one-sixth the plant height for specimens up to 10 feet (3 m) tall. For B-and-B stock, see table 6.2 for size recommendations from the American Nursery and Landscape Association. Not all nurseries follow these guidelines, so let the buyer beware! Root-balls larger than shown may be desirable. The root-ball sizes in this table are probably too large for container-grown stock since they have more fine roots, but no other clear guidelines exist for potted plants.

Form and Branching

The topic of plant form and branching relates more to larger tree and shrub stock than to small stock of the same species, since you can shape the form of small stock as it grows. Do the trees and shrubs you

TABLE 6.2. Recommended minimum root-ball sizes for different types of field-grown trees. Note: Trees having a coarse or wide-spreading root system or that are moved out of season require a root-ball in excess of the recommended sizes. We have rounded metric equivalents. *Adapted from* American Standard for Nursery Stock, *© 2004 American Nursery and Landscape Association. Used by permission.*

Standard and Slower-Growing Shade (Types 1 and 2) Trees			
Caliper (in)	Minimum ball diameter (in)	Caliper (mm)	Minimum ball diameter (cm)
0.5	12	13	30
0.75	14	19	36
1	16	25	41
1.25	18	32	46
1.5	20	38	50
1.75	22	40	56
2	24	50	61
2.5	28	63	71
3	32	76	81
3.5	38	90	97
4	42	100	107
4.5	48	110	122
5	54	130	137

Small Upright and Small Spreading (Types 3 and 4) Trees			
Height (ft.)	Minimum ball diameter (in.)	Height (m)	Minimum ball diameter (cm)
2	10	0.6	20
3	12	0.9	30
4	14	1.2	35
5	16	1.5	40
Caliper (in.)		Caliper (mm)	
0.75	16	19	41
1	18	25	46
1.25	19	32	48
1.5	20	38	50
1.75	22	40	56
2	24	50	60
2.5	28	63	70
3	32	76	80
3.5	38	90	95
4	42	100	105
4.5	48	110	120
5	54	130	135

or open center form, make sure the plant has that potential form. You can always prune out low branches if you want more light to reach the ground layer, but if you need screening at a low height and your plant doesn't have branches there, it won't fulfill your purposes.

Trees and shrubs should have one-half or more of their foliage on branches growing from the bottom two-thirds of their trunk (figure 6.1).[4] Trees shaped like lollipops have a higher likelihood of breaking in the wind, since they take most of their wind stress at a concentrated spot just below the lowest branch, high on the trunk. Woodies with their foliage weighted more toward the bottom two-thirds of the trunk will have a more even distribution of stress. Trees should be able to stand on their own without staking or support. If pulled out of an upright position by wind or a hand, they should return to upright on their own.

Pests, Disease, Nutritional Status, Injuries, Overall Vigor

If a plant shows signs of pests, disease, major injuries, or poor nutrition or vigor, reject it immediately and get your money back. Don't import pests or diseases to your garden; quarantine stock you receive through the mail so existing plants don't get exposed. Look for spotting on the leaves, sticky substances that may indicate mites or aphids, small holes in stems or trunk, fuzzy gray or white powder, and other signs. Dig a little into the soil at the base of the stem to look for collar rot and other fungal diseases. Any plant with pest or disease problems may also have nutrient deficiencies.

If a plant has leafed out, check the leaf color. Color should be green to dark green for most species and varieties, and the leaves large and the foliage dense. Yellow, bronze, reddish, or purple coloring in various patterns may indicate poor nutrition, though some plants have natural color variations that mimic these symptoms. Especially check the lower leaves and growing tips for color changes or dieback. Thin and brittle leaves, or thin foliage overall, are other signs of poor nutrition.

are buying have the right form for your purposes? Will they adapt well to wind stresses? For example, if you plan to prune a fruit tree to a central leader

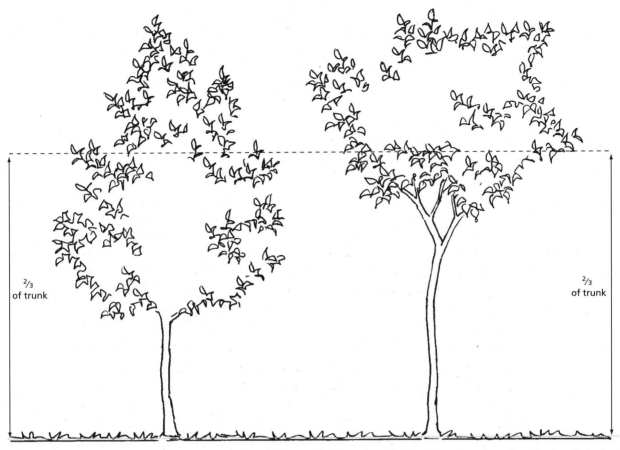

2/3
of trunk

2/3
of trunk

FIGURE 6.1. Trees and shrubs resist wind stresses best when one-half or more of their foliage is on branches growing from the bottom two-thirds of their trunk. Lollipop-shaped trees like the one at right are much more likely to break in the wind.

Look for injuries to the trunk, stems, and roots, either current or healed over. Distinguish between normal and healthy pruning wounds and other wounds. Look for injuries due to poor staking practices, labels, wires, and weed-whip damage around the base of trees. If the trunk was ever girdled by a label or tie, even if the tie is now removed, the tree may never recover its full vigor, and the trunk may be weak at that point. Check the condition and strength of any graft unions. The bark at the graft should have little or no cracking between the two varieties, and the union should withstand firm pressure on the top of the tree (as in wind) without the crack increasing in size.

Inspect the health and vigor of the roots, if you can. This is easy for bare-root stock but nearly impossible for B-and-B stock. You can usually lift container-grown plants out of their pots. Just be

careful not to damage the stock; if a tree stem lifts more than 1 inch (0.5 cm) before the root-ball starts to lift, don't lift any farther. That plant may have kinked or circling roots, poorly developed roots, or other problems. Roots should flex without breaking easily in most species. Healthy roots on most plants are a light color. A few blackened or dead roots are okay, but more than a few are not. Large, dark-colored roots may indicate low vigor or a plant that has been pot-bound too long.

Young trunks and branches should have smooth, bright bark color. Though some species have rough, dull, cracked, or dark bark, these may also indicate poor vigor. Use a thumbnail to check stems for green tissues below the bark if the plants are dormant. For most perennials, stems should be vibrant and flexible, not dull, ratty, and easily broken.

Most trees will grow 1 foot (30 cm) per year, and some more, when healthy. Look for bark markings indicating the beginning and end of the year's growth to check this indicator. All growth should have a good taper, however, meaning that the trunk and branches should be thicker near the base than at the ends. Long, spindly growth may be weak, may not withstand wind stress, and may indicate overfertilization. Plants with good taper may not be as tall as those without it, but they will be stronger and unlikely to need staking.

Root-Ball Strength

If the root-ball of a B-and-B woody has fallen apart or the plant wobbles relative to the root-ball, its survival is in question and you shouldn't buy or plant it. You may need to partially peel apart the burlap to inspect for this. Wobbling is easy to test for—just wriggle the trunk of the plant and see whether it moves independently of the root-ball. You can also try lifting the stem. If the stem rises an inch or two (3 to 5 cm) without causing the root-ball to begin lifting, reject the plant. When the root-ball falls apart, the roots dry out and die in fairly short order. Intensive irrigation can keep the top looking healthy, but once on-site, the plant will begin to flag.

Kinked and Circling Roots

Root defects caused by poor nursery transplanting practices are hard to uncover in all but bare-root woodies, but they can severely affect a woody plant's long-term health and growth. Properly formed root systems branch symmetrically, extending out and down to support the main trunk. Kinked and circling roots leave woodies, especially future large trees, vulnerable to poor growth, breaking of the trunk at the ground, or death by self-strangling (figure 6.2). Kinked roots are sharp bends in the main or taproots, or both. Circling roots usually run horizontally around the trunk or other roots and can girdle the trunk or root as they grow in diameter. Both conditions often occur together. Such root defects most

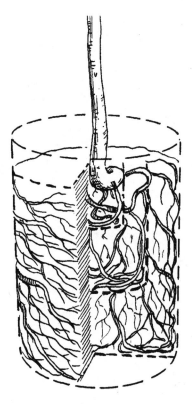

FIGURE 6.2. Kinked and circling roots from poor transplanting practices can severely limit the long-term health and life span of woody plants. One tree may have several layers of kinking from each time it was planted into a larger pot. If one of the main roots circles the root crown, the tree will strangle itself as the trunk and roots both grow in diameter.

commonly affect container-grown plants. B-and-B plants may also have root defects if they grew in containers before field planting. This is yet another reason for buying smaller plants or bare-root stock: it's easier to find and correct, or reject, any root defects at planting time. Top growth can look great even while the root structure is severely defective.

The main roots near the trunk surface and in the center of the root-ball need to be radial and well structured. Attempting to correct these core roots by pruning would severely weaken or kill the plant. The only way to deal with this is to prevent it at the nursery when transplanting. Reject any stock that has problems in the trunk surface area or the root-ball center. Circling peripheral roots are not a problem, as you can correct them at planting time.

Inspect for these conditions by releasing the plant from any stakes holding it up. If the plant falls over by bending at the soil surface, it probably has kinked or circling roots. If it falls over by bending along its whole trunk, the roots are probably fine, though it may not have developed enough taper in its stem and will need *proper* staking (see "To Stake or Not to Stake?" on page 398). You can also gently lift the plant by the stem. If the stem lifts up 1 to 2 inches (3 to 5 cm) before the root-ball starts to lift, suspect circling or kinked roots or simply poor root development. Such plants are unworthy of your money and time.

If the plant passes the above tests, gently dig or wash away soil at the top of the container or root-ball to 3 inches (75 mm) deep and within 2 inches (50 mm) of the trunk (you can replace the removed soil later and the plant should be fine). This should show you any kinked or circling roots from when the plant was in its first small pots. If no main roots show up at this depth, the plant was probably planted too deeply and could get collar rot: don't buy it. If the root structure looks fine at that level, there's a good chance the plant was properly potted up later, too, though it's no guarantee. The only way to tell for sure is to wash away soil from the whole root-ball to see what's going on. Obviously, you can't do this "destructive testing" at a garden center, but if you have received plants by mail or already bought them and you have indications of problems, go ahead. It will kill the plant, but any problems you find are grounds for return of the merchandise and your money back. If one or more plants in a shipment have such problems, you might be wise to reject the whole shipment.

PREPLANTING PLANT CARE

Once you have received your plants and they've passed inspection, you need to care for them well before planting day. Place potted perennials and woodies in a semishady to shady spot and water them regularly. If they must sit in the sun, *mulch or cover the pots to keep the sun off the root-ball*. Direct sunlight can heat plant pots severely, drying out and even killing roots. In fact, planting day sometimes reveals potted plants with roots growing on only one side of the pot for just this reason! B-and-B plants have similar requirements, though the need for water is even more critical. If you have the plants for an extended period, you may need to fertilize them once or twice if the growing medium appears composed mainly of peat or some other infertile material. Go light on the nitrogen and medium on the phosphorus and potassium. Liquid seaweed is a good product for this purpose, as long as it has no fish emulsion in it. Fish emulsion contains too much nitrogen; this spurs top growth, when we want the plant to focus on root growth after transplanting. Liquid seaweed has growth hormones, trace minerals, and other goodies that plants love and that help them overcome transplant shock.

Keep bare-root stock in a moist, cool environment (even a fridge), with moist peat moss, newspaper, or mulch around the roots. Plant bare-rooters within days of their arrival if you can, especially if they begin leafing out. If you can't get them in the ground soon, you can "heel them in" by temporarily planting bundles of them in a shady area in loose, moist soil or deep mulch, usually at an angle rather than upright. Since water stress is the biggest factor in survival, especially for bare-root stock, we like to soak the plants overnight in a seaweed emulsion solution (again, no fish emulsion!) the night before planting day. The plants then get to absorb all the growth hormones, nutrients, and water they can before they go in the ground. You can then carry the plants around the planting site in these buckets of solution to keep the roots from drying out before planting.

ORGANIZING TOOLS, MATERIALS, AND HELPERS

In your enthusiasm, it's easy to order more plants than you can plant yourself in a reasonable amount of time. Even if you successfully avoid this pitfall, getting all the materials together before planting day makes planting go more smoothly, which reduces stress not only on you, but on the plants, too.

Tools and Materials

Table 6.3 lists the tools and materials necessary for planting and immediate after-planting care. This list assumes you have finished all other site preparation and staking out beforehand. If that assumption is incorrect, you will need other tools and materials, too.

It's easy to waste much time looking for a lost tool, especially a small tool, amid holes, soil, mulch, and vegetation. We like to have a bucket, box, or crate to keep all the essential tools and materials in one place while we work in the field. This includes a hand trowel and hand fork, gloves, a tape measure, labels and markers, flagging, inoculants for nitrogen fixers and for mycorrhizas, small bags of fertilizer, the planting plan (a copy, not the original), a retractable knife, hand pruners, drinking water and snacks, and perhaps a portable phone. Sometimes we will have a cart dedicated to the key tools and materials, including the tool bucket, stakes, the bucket(s) of plants in seaweed solution, and larger digging tools. Get into the habit of placing every tool back in its bucket or cart after use. This keeps the work flowing smoothly without unnecessary hitches. It saves money on replacing lost tools, too.

Friends and Helpers

Planting goes much faster with help, and it's more fun, too. Here are a few suggestions about estimating labor needs and planting time and laying the groundwork for working together.

Estimating Labor Needs and Planting Time
Estimating how much time it will take to plant your trees, shrubs, and perennials is not an easy task. The planting rate varies depending on the size of the holes you have to dig and the soil conditions you're digging into, as well as the vigor and compe-tence of the crew. Obviously, harder digging, bigger holes and trees, and a less organized, enthusiastic, or focused workforce will slow things down.

For example, on one project it took five people about twenty-five person-hours to plant 140 small bare-root and potted trees, in 6- to 8-inch-deep (15 to 20 cm) paper pots, into firm sandy loam over the course of two days, including breaks, training, jaw-boning, and fixing mistakes. That's an average of five or six trees per hour per person. Four of us working for less than an hour were able to minimally mulch about thirty of those trees, not including acquiring the mulch and cardboard. The site was compact, well staked out, and easily accessible, and water was easily available. The weather was ideal. We had a relaxed but productive pace most of the time. The digging was easy since the holes were so small, and the soil was free of stones and roots. We had a good time; there was a fair amount of banter along the way. Two of those twenty-five hours involved one of us going around after the planting rush to make sure all the trees were planted at the right depth and had proper "dishes," labels, and stakes. Dave was able to properly plant about seven or eight trees per hour working on his own under similar conditions but with no dis-tractions and at a more vigorous but still relaxed pace. Martin Crawford, who planted a 2-acre (0.8 ha) forest garden by himself, got thirty to forty trees planted per day.[5] At the other extreme, it can take an hour or more for two young, buff guys to plant a single large B-and-B tree, digging in firm, rocky soil and maneuvering the root-ball into the hole by hand.

In general, perennials take less time because they are smaller than most trees and shrubs. They tend to require smaller tools. However, there are usually many more of them in a given area, and the greater amount of bending involved can stress people's back more, requiring more breaks.

Laying the Groundwork
When you have a number of people coming to help on planting day, laying the groundwork well makes

---

TABLE 6.3. Planting and aftercare tools and materials.

Materials:

- Planting plan and engineer's scale.
- Plants, with sun/wind protection, especially for roots.
- Water: enough hose to reach all areas of the site, plus watering cans or buckets; some sort of diffuser to break flow into droplets is good.
- Inoculant (as needed).
- Fertilizers: seaweed emulsion, rock powders (lime, rock phosphate, greensand, etc.) as needed.
- Permanent plant labels, preferably filled out before planting day.

- A tarp, piece of plywood, or more cardboard upon which to temporarily place soil from your planting holes.
- Cardboard, newspaper, or other sheet-mulch material, in quantity.
- Mulch in quantity: compost, wood chips, straw, leaves, etc.
- Animal protection: wire cages, netting, or plant tubes.
- Self-care items: water, sunscreen, bug repellent, hat, gloves, food, etc.

Tools:

- Extra stakes.
- Flagging, markers, etc.
- Measuring tape.
- Spading fork.
- Square shovel.
- Round-point shovel.
- Mattock or pick-mattock.
- If your site is rocky, a pry bar or other rock-removal tools.
- Hand trowel.
- Three-pronged hand fork.

- Hand pruners (bypass type).
- A knife for cutting root-balls.
- Wheelbarrow or cart(s).
- Buckets for plants and tools.
- Retractable knife to cut cardboard.
- Pitchfork for mulch.
- Iron rake.
- Whatever tools your animal protection needs: wire cutters, hammer, staple gun, etc.

---

all the difference. Staking everything out ahead of time is essential, or people waste much time waiting for the next steps to become clear. Label the stakes so people can move ahead without asking too many questions. If you'll have many helpers on planting day, it may be wise to explain everything to a trusted friend ahead of time so you can delegate. Have all the tools together beforehand, create your tool buckets, sort your plants, have all the materials handy and organized, and make sure you have enough hose.

Some people dig planting holes before planting day, but besides being an injury risk from the possibility of stepping into them unawares, it is best to dig the hole with the plant in hand so you can dig it the appropriate size. In addition, the hole will dry out over time, and this will decrease plant survival and increase the need for watering later. Also, if rain falls into the hole, it may collapse and need redigging.

ORGANIZING

The theme of thinking ahead continues with getting organized before planting, and staying that way during it. Think through your strategic materials depots, water supplies, the flow of work, and weather-related considerations.

Strategic Materials Depots

Designate one or more strategically placed depots for bulky materials, especially mulch, both in your garden plan and as part of your pre-planting-day setup. It's amazing how much time and energy you can save by dumping mulch piles in the right place, preferably uphill of most of the planting site. Food is another strategic material. Stock up on goodies and real meals before planting day—a well-fed workforce is a happy workforce, even if it's a workforce of one.

Water

You will need a tremendous amount of water on planting day, and for some time thereafter, to keep your plants alive and happy. Putting plants in the ground without enough water available to get the plants established, and a decent means of delivering it to them, will be a waste of time, money, and energy. You will lose many more plants if you don't water sufficiently than if you do. Successfully establishing container-grown woodies requires watering each one every day or two for at least a week (preferably longer) after planting.

Each small woody plant will need at least a gallon (4 l) of water each time you irrigate. Larger plants could need as many as 20 gallons (75 l) to thoroughly soak the root-ball. Perennials could use as much as a gallon, too. At 8 pounds per gallon (1 kg/l), the weight adds up fast. Think it through ahead of time. How much water will you need each day, and how will you get it there?

Plan the Work

Following a reasonable pattern of planting will speed the work and make after-planting care more efficient. Finish planting one area before moving to another if you can. Minimize moving your operations from one area to another and then back again. When planting one zone, think about the most effective way to do it before starting in willy-nilly. For example, if plants are to be planted very close to each other, moving the hose among just-planted plants can do quite a bit of damage. Maybe you should start on the side of the space away from the hose, and plant your way out toward the hose connection. If the species pattern is very complex, you may decide that planting one species at time to keep it straight is the most sensible approach. It's up to you to determine the optimal strategy for each situation. The point is to create and follow a strategy to organize your work, both over the whole garden area and within each area you are planting.

FIGURE 6.3. Keep your bare-root plants in a bucket of water while you work on-site on planting day. This keeps them fully hydrated and reduces transplant shock. Adding seaweed emulsion to the water provides them with nutrients and growth hormones, too. *Photo by Dave Jacke.*

Mind the Weather

The best planting weather is cool and overcast, with maybe even a scattered light shower here and there, but not a heavy downpour, with the soil moist but not wet. This keeps the plants from drying out, while the workers avoid overheating or sliding around in mud compacting the soil. If the sun is out or it's hot, windy, or dry, take extra precautions to keep your plants and yourselves hydrated. Carry small batches of well-watered plants around with you while planting (figure 6.3), and keep the rest in the shade and out of the wind. Water heavily after planting, perhaps more than once. If you can, avoid planting in the heat of the day. Late afternoon and evening are best under these conditions, giving the plants time to put out some root hairs and new roots overnight before getting exposed to the blast furnace.

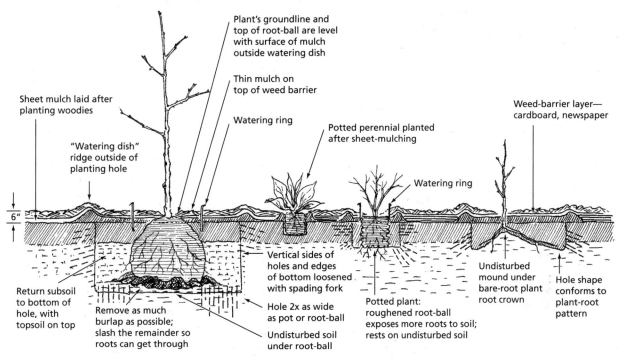

Plant's groundline and top of root-ball are level with surface of mulch outside watering dish

Thin mulch on top of weed barrier

Watering ring

Potted perennial planted after sheet-mulching

Weed-barrier layer—cardboard, newspaper

Sheet mulch laid after planting woodies

"Watering dish" ridge outside of planting hole

Watering ring

6"

Vertical sides of holes and edges of bottom loosened with spading fork

Return subsoil to bottom of hole, with topsoil on top

Remove as much burlap as possible; slash the remainder so roots can get through

Hole 2x as wide as pot or root-ball

Undisturbed soil under root-ball

Potted plant: roughened root-ball exposes more roots to soil; rests on undisturbed soil

Undisturbed mound under bare-root plant root crown

Hole shape conforms to plant-root pattern

FIGURE 6.4. The result of your planting and mulching labors should look something like this "forest-garden layer cake."

Ideally, if it's raining heavily or has just rained a lot, stop work to avoid unsafe conditions and soil compaction. When the soil is wet, it compacts easily, and this may affect soil health and plant success for many years. If you must work in these conditions for some reason, at least beware of safety issues when swinging wet tools and moving laden carts, for example. Take special care that you break up the smearing of wet soil around the edges of planting holes, or you may box in your plants (see "Scarify the Hole," below). Stay on designated paths as much as possible. Consider laying a piece of plywood over wet soil to spread your weight while you work in planting beds.

PLANTING DAY

You're finally ready to put plants in the ground! However, you may be wondering what's the best technique. You will hear different versions of the optimal planting technique from everyone to whom you talk. What follows is our take based on the latest research and our own experience, starting with a brief primer on the essentials, including a vision of the ideal end product.

THE END RESULT: A FOREST-GARDEN LAYER CAKE

In most cases, your completed planting should look something like figure 6.4. The goal, by the time you finish the planting process, is this: you have created niches and planting sites through disturbance (site preparation), your desired plants are in the ground at ideal spacing for your goals, and little or no spaces or resources are available for unwanted plants. Create that desired condition by firmly establishing desired species to fill all the available niches and smothering the rest with sheet mulch. By the end of planting, the initial floristic composition should be strongly biased toward your preferred species, giving them a major head start over the competition in the successional race. The planting should be fairly dense, and the sheet mulch should give your plants time to get established and spread before the surviving weeds can get through the sheet layer. If you've designed, prepared your site, planted, and cared for your garden well, your plants will grow into all the vegetation layers and soil horizons far ahead of any weeds.

Once you've set up your garden this way, your maintenance work should be minimal for a significant period of time, if not forever more. Persistent weeds like quackgrass or bittersweet may still stick out their heads, but a sweep-through every few days with a little pulling action should keep these under control as long as you are observant, consistent, thorough, and determined in your weeding. A stitch in time saves nine! Now let's talk about how to get there, starting with the planting principles you need to apply for optimal success.

PLANTING TECHNIQUE PRIMER: WE DO WHAT WE CAN

Please understand that while the principles outlined below will increase your establishment success, nobody's perfect. You'll get better at planting the more you do it. The principles run through the detailed planting instructions that follow.

If you've never created a garden this way before, it may behoove you to go through the complete process in a small space once before doing a large area. This will give you a sense of the time and effort it takes and help you work out some of the bugs in the details, such as at which phase to plant perennials, how much mulch to place and how that affects planting depth, and so on. Make your mistakes in a small area so you can avoid them on a larger scale when the stakes are higher.

Plant Woodies, Sheet-Mulch, Then Plant Perennials

In almost all cases, you should use sheet mulch to control weeds after planting, at least around trees and shrubs, if not on a broad scale. The question then becomes, when do you mulch, before or after planting? The answer is both.

Woody plants generally require much digging to get into the ground, especially if they are B-and-B or container-grown. Obviously, mulching before digging big holes would be a hassle. On the other hand, perennials usually get planted rather densely, and establishing a solid sheet-mulch weed barrier around them is difficult. Since most perennials are small, you can plant them through the sheet mulch more easily. Some perennials and most seeded crops can be planted on top of the sheet-mulch barrier and they will grow fine. Plant perennials that are already large before you sheet-mulch, however.

Maintain the Soil Profile

Keeping the topsoil on top and the subsoil below maintains healthy soil structure and prevents anaerobic conditions from developing deep in the soil. Whenever you dig, separate the soil by horizons, and put it back in the hole in the proper order. Amending planting holes with organic matter can cause anaerobic conditions, too. It also encourages roots to stay in the planting hole rather than searching out nutrients elsewhere. In addition, you need to fertilize the soil while respecting the soil profile. Most fertilizers should go up top, preferably spread around and over the planting hole, if not mixed into the whole topsoil horizon.

Set the Groundline

Planting a plant too high or too low is a common and sometimes fatal mistake. Always look for the original groundline of a tree, shrub, or perennial, and plant it so the final grade meets that line. Make sure to account for the depth of mulch on top of the soil: you can plant the plant the right depth relative to the *soil* and then kill it with mulch if you don't think it through. Digging the hole to the right depth for the plant is an essential part of this, as backfilled soil settles significantly after watering. This can leave a plant with roots out of the ground or settle the plant too deeply. *Always set the root-ball on undisturbed soil to prevent settling of the plant.* Obviously, if you dig the hole too deeply you cannot do this. Dig carefully! We will deal with the too-deep-a-hole scenario later in the chapter.

Spread the Roots

Most plants grown in pots become pot-bound and need their roots spread for them. B-and-B plants rarely have that problem, but it's easy to forget to spread the roots even with bare-root plants. Spreading the roots will increase the volume of soil the plant explores more rapidly than any other technique. It saves the plant time and work and increases survival, even if spreading the roots seems to damage the roots drastically. Digging a big enough hole is step one in this process. From there, several techniques apply, depending on the circumstances.

Spreading the roots also means making sure roots can get out of the planting hole easily. You make that possible by loosening the soil on the sides of the planting hole and at the bottom of the hole around the root-ball (not under it), especially in fine or wet soils that smear when you dig the hole. You also encourage that by fertilizing properly.

PLANTING WOODIES: STEP-BY-STEP DETAILS

The above four basic goals weave through the details of the planting process. Each goal affects each step of planting, from digging the hole to after-planting mulching. Let's discuss the key points of each step of planting in order. The following discussion is oriented primarily toward woody plants, but many of the points also apply to perennials.

Find the Plant's Groundline

For optimum results, custom-dig each planting hole for each specific plant. Finding the groundline of each plant and estimating hole depth is the first task. Therefore, before digging a hole, select the plant for the hole and assess its root-ball or root structure to see what size and shape of hole to dig.

For container and B-and-B plants, do not assume the current soil depth is the proper planting depth. Always look for the change in bark texture and color that denotes the plant's desired soil line. This is easy for bare-root stock. For B-and-B plants, remove any unnecessary nursery field soil on top of the root-ball before measuring the root-ball and

digging the hole. People sometimes plant container plants too deeply, sometimes too shallowly, and sometimes just right. Figure out where the optimum soil line is, then measure the soil depth in the container and add or subtract as necessary. You may want to keep a clipboard, pencil, and scrap paper handy so you can write down depths to prevent having to refigure while you dig. *Keep the plant roots moist while you dig the hole.*

Orient the Plant for Optimum Presentation

Before digging the hole, decide how you want to orient the plant. This is especially important for bare-root stock, because the shape of the roots will affect the shape of the hole you dig. Even with potted or B-and-B plants, though, it is good to decide on the orientation early. It is easy to forget to do when in the thick of the physical labor of getting plants in the ground.

We must weigh a number of factors to determine the best orientation of a plant. On windy sites, prevailing winds should prevail as a factor. Bare-root stock should have the largest root pointing into the winds that prevail when the tree is in leaf, since plants naturally grow their largest roots in that direction for maximum stability. The side of the plant with the most branches should face prevailing growing-season winds, as the winds will encourage growth on the downwind side. If a tree has a bud graft union, it usually forms a crook in the trunk. Sunburn can damage the upward-facing surface of this crook if it faces the afternoon sun. The bud side of the bud graft should face the afternoon sun. Obviously, the above factors may tell you to orient the plant in different directions. You will have to make the best choice given the situation.

If wind and sun aren't critical factors, look at the plant's aboveground form. Imagine the plant as it grows and consider activities around the plant. You may want low branches facing away from paths to minimize future pruning, or you may want them to screen a certain view, for example. Also consider aesthetics. If you will see the plant mainly from one

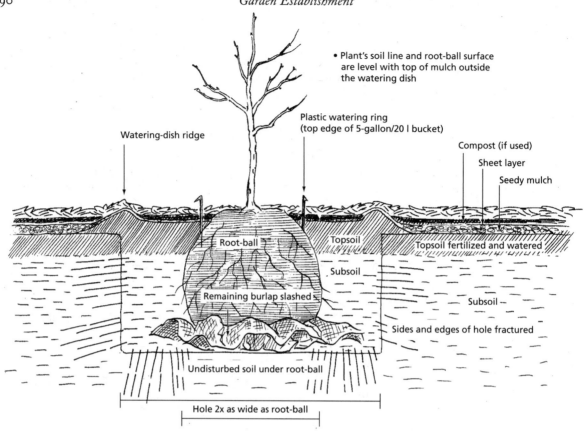

- Plant's soil line and root-ball surface
  are level with top of mulch outside
  the watering dish

Watering-dish ridge

Plastic watering ring
(top edge of 5-gallon/20 l bucket)

Compost (if used)

Sheet layer

Seedy mulch

Root-ball

Topsoil

Topsoil fertilized and watered

Subsoil

Remaining burlap slashed

Subsoil

Sides and edges of hole fractured

Undisturbed soil under root-ball

Hole 2x as wide as root-ball

FIGURE 6.5. Detail of final grade and planting cross section for a B-and-B plant. Final grades of all woody plants should be similar: the soil line on the plant and the top of the root-ball should be level with the top of the mulch surface outside the watering dish. With deep-mulch systems this will necessitate raising the watering dish above the existing soil. The future soil level will rise as you add mulch over the years, even when you take mulch decomposition into account.

or two directions, orient the plant so the best side faces the primary view.

Ten-Dollar Hole, One-Dollar Tree

Old-timers used to say "dig a ten-dollar hole for a one-dollar tree." By this, they meant dig a bigger hole than you think you might need. Bigger holes aren't necessarily better, though. A ten-dollar hole is a quality hole, not a big one, and quality depends on good information. As mundane as it may seem, the details of how you dig the hole are a major factor in planting success. Hole-digging criteria follow, with explanations.

Hole Width

For container or B-and-B plants, dig a hole twice as wide as the root-ball diameter. This should give you room to work around the plant (to remove burlap, for example), to spread pot-bound roots, and to pack soil properly around the root-ball to avoid air pockets without unduly increasing the amount of digging necessary.

For bare-root plants, the hole should be wide enough to accommodate the roots without crowding, even after you spread them to their optimum form. This means that holes for bare-root stock will probably be smaller than for container plants, because it is easier to pack soil properly and avoid air pockets with bare-root stock than with root-balls. Holes for bare-root stock may not be circular, though! Create a hole appropriate for the shape of the roots, whatever that means. Make sure you shape the hole so the plant is oriented how you want it, as discussed above.

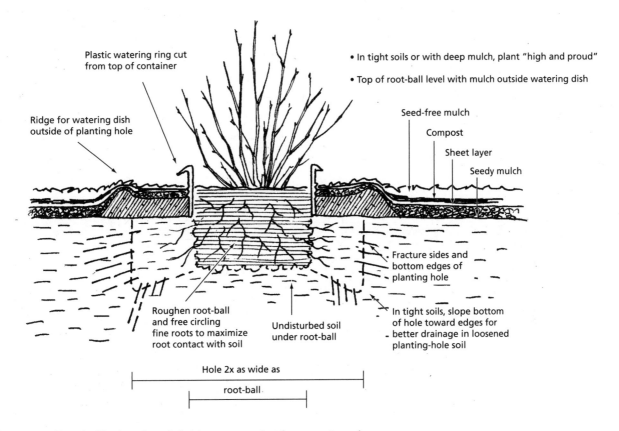

Plastic watering ring cut
from top of container

Ridge for watering dish
outside of planting hole

• In tight soils or with deep mulch, plant "high and proud"

• Top of root-ball level with mulch outside watering dish

Seed-free mulch

Compost

Sheet layer

Seedy mulch

Fracture sides and
bottom edges of
planting hole

Roughen root-ball
and free circling
fine roots to maximize
root contact with soil

Undisturbed soil
under root-ball

In tight soils, slope bottom
of hole toward edges for
better drainage in loosened
planting-hole soil

Hole 2x as wide as

root-ball

FIGURE 6.6. Detail of final grade and planting cross section for a container plant.

Vertical Sides

The hole should have vertical sides. Some people recommend sloping the sides so the top is wider than the bottom, but this can increase waterlogging dramatically, especially in tight soils. If the surface area of loosened soil is greater than that of the hole's bottom, a larger surface area will contribute rainfall to a smaller area of root zone. The resulting pool of water can kill your plant.

Hole Depth and Final Grade

Plant "high" or "proud" in all but sandy soils[6] to help prevent crown rot. In fine or tight soils, the groundline of the plant should be ½ to 1 inch (13 to 25 mm) above *final grade* for bare-root stock, plants in 1-gallon (4 l) or smaller containers, or root-balls less than 8 to 10 inches (20 to 30 cm) in diameter. For larger containers or root-balls in fine soils, the plant's groundline should be 1 to 2 inches

(25 to 50 mm) above final grade. In sandy soil, the groundline of the plant should be at final grade or 1 to 2 inches (25 to 50 mm) deeper to reduce root drying. Consider also whether you will need to modify the root-ball to deal with root defects or whether you will use butterfly planting (see "Prune the Roots" and "Set the Plant and Spread the Roots," below). These will influence hole depth.

Final grade is the surface of the *mulch* placed after planting, *including any compost layer* (see figures 6.5, 6.6, and 6.7). If you intend to place a layer of compost on the soil after planting or to mulch heavily, reduce hole depth accordingly. If you intend to mulch heavily, reduce the depth of mulch near the stems of trees and shrubs so that they don't end up sticking out of the soil too far. You may need to regrade the area around the trees and shrubs some to make this work. One inch (25 mm) of mulch near a tree stem, with a weed barrier under it, should

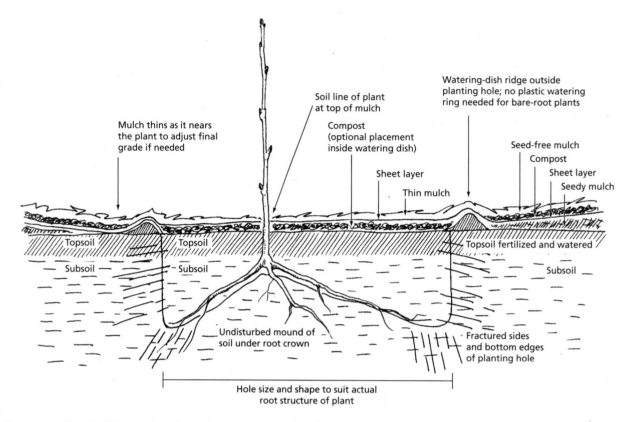

Mulch thins as it nears the plant to adjust final grade if needed

Soil line of plant at top of mulch

Compost (optional placement inside watering dish)

Sheet layer

Thin mulch

Watering-dish ridge outside planting hole; no plastic watering ring needed for bare-root plants

Seed-free mulch
Compost
Sheet layer
Seedy mulch

Topsoil

Topsoil

Topsoil fertilized and watered

Subsoil

Subsoil

Subsoil

Undisturbed mound of soil under root crown

Fractured sides and bottom edges of planting hole

Hole size and shape to suit actual root structure of plant

FIGURE 6.7. Detail of final grade and planting cross section for a bare-root plant. You can place compost under the sheet layer inside the watering dish if you want (it usually goes on top of the sheet layer).

work well in most circumstances. We recommend that you sketch a cross-section of your intended soil lines and mulch depth to work out the details.

In all cases, the root-ball should rest on undisturbed soil. Do not dig the hole too deep. If the plant rests on disturbed soil, even if it is tamped, it will likely settle after watering, which can lead to crown rot as the planting hole surface fills with water after rains, and with mulch and soil over time. Always measure the plant roots to determine planting depth, and figure out hole depth using the guidelines below. Check the hole's depth as you dig so you don't go too far.

For bare-root plants, dig the bottom of the hole to conform to the shape of the roots, so the crown of the plant sits on undisturbed soil, if possible. This means the bottom of the hole is likely to have a mound in the middle, underneath the stem, and the bottom will slope down from that point. We recognize that most holes are deeper in the middle, and that digging a

hole deeper at the edges is more difficult, but this will keep the plant at the elevation you want, rather than having it settle into the muck later on.

For B-and-B plants, always remove unnecessary nursery-field soil on top of the root-ball before measuring the root-ball and digging the hole. Digging and wrapping a tree or shrub usually alters the location of the root-ball surface relative to the soil line on the plant's trunk; you have to check each plant to find the true soil line.

General Points

It's important to dig with a square shovel, not a round-pointed shovel. Square shovels provide greater accuracy in shaping the bottom of your planting hole. You should also keep handy some cardboard, plywood, or tarps on which to pile the soil from the hole as you dig. An amazing amount of soil gets lost when laid on grass, leaves, or dead twigs and branches, so you can end up short on backfill material. This one factor can make a big difference in how well you shape the soil after planting, and hence how effectively your watering works. Finally, dig the hole one soil horizon at a time if you can, keeping topsoil piles separate from subsoil piles on the tarp or cardboard. Then you can replace them in the appropriate parts of the hole, more or less.

Scarify the Hole

This is no Halloween joke! When we dig, the soil around the inside of the hole smears into a thin but solid layer that roots have a hard time penetrating. Soils that are wet or that have significant silt and clay fractions are most susceptible, but even sandy loams smear significantly. Digging planting holes with power screw augers can compact the hole sides even more. Scarifying the hole means scraping or poking the sides and bottom to break up this solid layer so roots can get into undisturbed soil.

In small holes or sandy soils, raking the hole bottom and sides with a hand fork works fine. In bigger holes, in finer-textured soils, or when there are restrictive layers or compaction, forcefully jab the inside of the hole with a spading fork and wiggle the fork around to loosen the soil around the hole and break up the smearing. *Avoid doing this directly under the root-ball*, though, to avoid the settling discussed earlier.

Prune the Roots

Before the plant goes in the hole is the last chance you'll get to correct root defects or remove dead or diseased roots. Take the opportunity.

Prune Broken or Diseased Roots

Especially for bare-root plants, check the root system for broken, dead, diseased, or twisted roots. Check the outside of the root-balls of container or B-and-B plants for the same. Make clean cuts back to healthy tissue to reduce disease possibilities where roots have broken or died. Also remove moldy roots, but be cautious here. Plants part-

nering with ectomycorrhizal fungi may have beneficial fungi visible on their roots that you would not want to remove, though seeing this on nursery stock is rare. These usually congregate near the root tips. See volume 1, figure 1.1, or check the Web sites listed in appendix 7 for pictures of ectomycorrhizal fungi if you want to know what you're looking at. Arbuscular mycorrhizal fungi are invisible to the naked eye, so remove any roots with visible fungi on AM plants.

Roughen the Root-Ball

Before cutting circling roots (below), straighten any roots circling the outer edge of the root-ball or matted on the bottom of container plants if you can, and roughen the outside of the root-ball if the plant is pot-bound. Roughening the root-ball and straightening peripheral roots can increase the volume of soil the roots fill immediately after planting by up to two times. This eases the extension of new roots from the root-ball and thereby increases plant survival. "Removing one-fourth to one-half the roots in the outer 25 mm (1 inch) of a root ball should set back none but the most sensitive plants. Most plants will in fact be stimulated."[7] This applies to both woody and herbaceous plants.

Cut Circling Roots

For woody container plants, you may have to slice into the root-ball with a knife or pruners to cut circling roots that could choke the plant as it grows in diameter. Some people cut the root-ball vertically on two opposite sides of the ball, half the distance from the periphery to the trunk, to cut hidden circling roots as a standard practice. Butterfly planting (below) does little or nothing to prevent circling roots near the crown from girdling woody plant stems.

Set the Plant and Spread the Roots

Recheck the orientation of the plant and the size and shape of the hole relative to the plant's roots. If the plant is large and hard to move, check these with the plant still on the ground outside the hole.

Before placing a plant in its hole, relocate the groundline on the stem, and measure the distance from the groundline to the bottom of the root-ball. Check the depth of the hole, including the compost and mulch you'll lay on afterward, to see whether it seems about right. Adjust the planting hole if necessary. If you must backfill the hole because you dug too deeply, tamp the backfill soil firmly to minimize settling. If you dig further, make sure to scarify the hole again, too.

Besides roughening the root-ball (above), spreading the roots takes several forms depending on the kind of stock you have. Spreading the roots includes both physically spreading the roots when you plant and making sure the roots can spread unobstructed on their own.

Bare Root: Leave or Build a Cone

As stated earlier, for bare-root stock, try to leave a cone of undisturbed soil in the middle of the hole for the plant crown to rest upon. If you haven't done this, or if the cone is less than perfect, build a cone out of soil to support the plant. Tamp the soil in the cone to reduce settling. The cone should hold the plant slightly high to allow for settling. Set the plant and spread its roots over the cone, using soil to hold the roots in place if they won't stay where you want them. Make sure the trunk is vertical, and keep checking the groundline to make sure the planting depth is right. Step back and look at the plant once or twice to make sure it is well placed and oriented before inoculating and backfilling.

Container Plants: Roughen the Root-Ball and Straighten the Roots

Once you have roughened the root-ball and, if necessary, pruned the roots, set the plant in the hole and spread out the roots. Check the groundline again, and make sure the plant is vertical and oriented properly. Use backfill soil to hold the plant upright and keep the roots spread if necessary. Step back and look at the plant once or twice to make sure it is well placed and oriented before inoculating and backfilling.

If the plant is in a papier-mâché or peat pot, remove the pot to maximize root growth. In no case should you leave the peat or papier-mâché sticking aboveground, for it will wick water out of the root-ball and kill the plant by drought. Dave killed many plants this way on one of his first solo planting jobs; the soil outside the peat pots was nice and moist, but the root-balls were bone dry within days and resisted wetting when watered.

B-and-B: Remove Burlap and Cage

Place B-and-B stock into the hole and check for proper depth and orientation. Adjust for uprightness by tipping the plant and pushing soil under one side.

Ideally, you will get most of the cage, burlap, and twine out of the planting hole, including out from under the root-ball, but in practice this is difficult to do without damaging the root-ball, especially for large plants. Wire baskets threaten the long-term stability of trees, making them more susceptible to blowing over in strong winds, even ten years after planting. They can weaken roots by constriction or wounding as they enlarge. Green-colored twine or burlap contains toxic compounds to prevent rotting. If left around the root-ball, they can constrict the enlarging roots as they grow through the mesh. Besides, who wants toxins in the soil around their plants, anyway? Yet the root-ball must stay together or the plant will likely fall over or die. Do not attempt to remove the burlap, twine, and cage before the plant is in the hole!

Once the plant is at the right depth and in position, before removing the burlap and twine, remove the wire cage if there is one. If the root-ball is fragile and threatens to fall apart (which is often the case), judicious cutting of the cage's lower half may allow you to partly backfill, make some further cuts, and pull the wire out. The same goes for the burlap. So, cut the twine and cage around the bottom of the root-ball, and make large gashes in or remove pieces of the bottom of the burlap. Backfill around the root-ball to one-third to one-half of its depth to hold it together. Inoculate with mycorrhizas at this stage if you must (see below). Then remove the rest of the cage and burlap by cutting them into pieces. If the piecemeal approach is too difficult, simply cut and remove as much burlap, twine, and wire as you can without threatening the integrity of the root-ball. Make as many slashes as you can in the burlap to allow root egress. Try to remove the cage and burlap from at least the top 8 to 12 inches (20 to 30 cm) of the root-ball, if not more. The risk of plant death is high if the root-ball falls apart, especially if the plant has leafed out.

Butterfly Planting

In shallow soils over bedrock, restrictive layers, or high water, or in very clayey or compacted soils, butterfly planting may be in order. In these situations, the vast majority of root growth in the first three years occurs in the top 5 inches (13 cm) of soil. When the water table is high, roots planted deeper may get killed. Placing all the roots in those top 5 inches maximizes plant health and growth. Butterfly planting will not prevent circling roots near the stem from girdling a woody plant, however.

To use this technique, split the root-ball of a container plant in half from the bottom up to about two-thirds of the way to the top. Spread the two halves apart and place the plant on a mound in a shallow hole (figure 6.8). You can use this technique on both woody and herbaceous container plants. It is not appropriate for B-and-B stock.

Inoculate

See the discussions on "Mycorrhizal Inoculation" and "Soil Inoculation" in chapter 5 and the discussion of inoculation for nitrogen fixers in volume 1, chapter 5. Remember, only the most damaged sites will need inoculation at all. If you need to inoculate bare-root stock, you may actually inoculate before setting the plant and spreading the roots, using a root dip. Otherwise, inoculate after spreading the roots using a powder, tablet, or drench or by

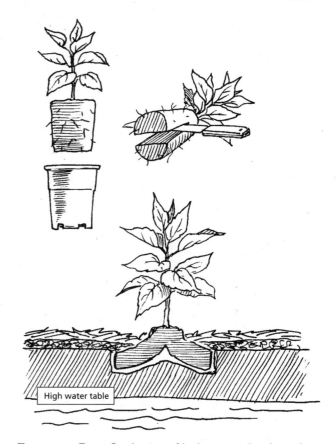

FIGURE 6.8. Butterfly planting of both perennial and woody potted stock may be advisable for shallow soils over high water tables, bedrock, or restrictive layers (but not for B-and-B stock). Split the root-ball of the container plant in half, starting at the bottom, for about two-thirds of its depth. Spread the two halves apart and plant them on a mound in a shallow hole.

applying soil from a healthy ecosystem. For container plants and B-and-B plants, inoculate after setting the plant and before backfilling, using the latter methods.

Backfill, Puddle In, and Straighten

Never amend the planting-hole backfill soil. Do not add crushed stone to the bottom of the hole; it actually makes drainage worse, not better. Altering the backfill texture with sand, clay, or soil from elsewhere creates a root-growth barrier due to soil-texture changes. Organic matter and fertilizer are out, too. Research has demonstrated that amendments in the hole have inconsistent positive effects, and often have negative consequences. They prevent

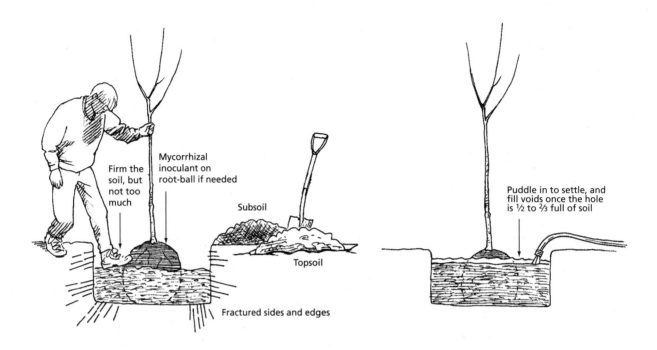

Firm the soil, but not too much

Mycorrhizal inoculant on root-ball if needed

Subsoil

Topsoil

Fractured sides and edges

Puddle in to settle, and fill voids once the hole is ½ to ⅔ full of soil

FIGURE 6.9. Inoculate the roots or root-ball before filling the hole if needed. Firm the soil every 3 inches (8 cm) of backfilled depth or so, making sure to fill all voids. You can add small amounts of mineral fertilizers such as rock phosphate and greensand to the subsoil if your soils are deficient. Once the hole is ½ to ⅔ full, start puddling in with water and your hands to help settle the backfill. Keep an eye on the final grade of the plant and lift it as you go if necessary.

roots from reaching out of the planting hole to look for resources, and organic matter can go anaerobic and thereby thwart root growth. Backfill with the soil that came out of the hole, minus any rocks or boulders, in the reverse order it came out—subsoil in the bottom, topsoil on top. If you run short, make up the difference with compost, or with topsoil from another area of the site with similar texture.

Backfill in layers, firming the soil every 3 inches (8 cm) or so. Avoid pushing the roots together as you backfill; keep them spread apart. Fill carefully, making sure to fill all the voids so no air pockets can block root growth. Step back and assess the plant's straightness as you go.

Once the hole is about one-half to two-thirds full, "puddle in" the plant by filling the hole with water and jiggling it and the soil in the hole with your hands (figure 6.9). This helps remove air pockets and settles the soil. It may also weaken B-and-B root-balls, so you may want to do this with

more soil in the hole. If your soils are tight, you may want to water only after you've finished filling the hole so things don't get too wet. In sandier soils, we water two or three times on planting day if we can to charge the ground around each plant with water.

Check the groundline again. If the plant settles too much after puddling in, you may need to get a shovel or spading fork under the root-ball to lift it while someone else pushes soil underneath. Never lift by the stem alone! For bare-root plants, water the soil in the hole well, and you may be able to get your hands into the mud to lift the plant from below or gently tug the plant up by the stem. Lift the plant higher than you want it, then settle it back lower with a little downward pressure. Once things are set, finish filling the hole with soil, topsoil on top. Remember that the surface of the root-ball or the groundline of the bare-root plant should be "high" or "proud" by up to 1 to 2 inches (3 to 5 cm) above final grade in all but sandy soils.

Make a Dish and Water It

Surround each plant with a small ridge of tamped soil to hold water like a bowl (figures 6.5, 6.6, and 6.7). For large plants, the soil "watering dish" should be at least 30 inches (75 cm) in diameter; for smaller plants it can be smaller. Ideally, the ridge will sit outside the edge of the hole so it doesn't disappear as the hole settles. Water the plant after making the dish to test the ridge's stability. If "final grade" includes compost, add it after making the dish and watering it. Don't add mulch until after you've checked for settling and finished staking and installing critter protection as applicable.

Container and B-and-B plants should also have a watering ring (figure 6.10) to ensure adequate water reaches the root-ball in the early days after planting—if the root-ball soil texture is radically different from that of the surrounding soil, the root-ball may not soak up *any* water until the surrounding soil is completely saturated. You can make watering rings from the top 4 to 5 inches (10 to 12 cm) of plastic plant pots or buckets, such as those the plants came in. You may need to cut the ring vertically to get it around the plant. If so, duct tape the cut before pushing the ring 1 to 2 inches (3 to 5 cm) into the soil. Water the ring to check for leaks, then add compost if necessary. Mulch placed inside the ring will prevent scouring when you add water later. Don't add mulch, and perhaps don't place the watering ring, until after you've checked the plant for settling.

Labeling

Label each tree with a permanent tag *immediately* after planting it. Otherwise, you are more likely to make labeling mistakes. The best labels are soft metal tags that you write on with a ballpoint pen to make an imprint that won't wear off. These usually attach to the plant with thin wires. On windy sites with small plants, it may be advisable to put the tag on a stake nearby rather than on the plant itself to minimize bark damage.

FIGURE 6.10. A plastic watering ring is helpful for container-grown and B-and-B plants, in addition to the watering dish. Made from the top 4 to 5 inches (10 to 12 cm) of the container the plant came in or a large bucket, watering rings direct water right to the root-ball. Without a watering ring, the root-ball may not soak up sufficient water from surrounding soils, and plant survival decreases. The seam that results when you cut the ring in order to fit it around the plant (shown here) should be taped shut.

Check for Settling

Let the plant sit for a while after watering it and go plant something else. At least an hour later, go back through and check plants for settling. Lift any that seem too deep using a shovel or spading fork under the root-ball. You can also change the grades around the plant if the root-ball is fragile and grade changes are feasible.

To Prune or Not to Prune?

Research has shown that if sufficient water is available, severely pruning the tops of trees and shrubs after planting usually *decreases* the speed of plant recovery and growth. Such pruning simply adds more trauma on top of the transplanting trauma. Little or no pruning is better. Some remedial pruning to begin correcting or shaping the basic branch structure is desirable, as long as you don't go very far. Also, if you have a weak-stemmed tree planted in a windy area, prune to decrease the risk of wind damage. Otherwise, let the plant settle into the ground without further ado.

On the other hand, if you expect the tree or shrub *not* to receive sufficient water, some top-pruning to reduce water demand *may* be beneficial.

To Stake or Not to Stake?

Staking used to be common practice but is often unnecessary and can damage or weaken plants, besides costing time and money. Trees that do not bend and move in the wind do not grow tapered trunks. Tapered trunks, that is, those with a stem thicker at the bottom than at the top, distribute bending forces along the whole stem, while untapered trunks concentrate these forces at one point and break. Hence, rigidly staked trees do not grow tapered trunks, become reliant on stake support, and more often blow over after stake removal. They grow fewer roots and more top, too, which may be good in the short run, but not in the end. Poor staking can also girdle or wound bark, trunk, and branches from rubbing or constriction. Excessively high staking can focus wind stress at a single point just above the stake, leading to breakage even on trees with tapered trunks. Most shrubs and trees need no staking at all, especially if they are small or have many lower branches to keep people and equipment away from the trunk.

Valid reasons to stake include protecting the plant from vehicles, mowing equipment, and vandals; anchoring the roots and root-ball of a large tree or shrub while roots grow into undisturbed soil; and supporting trunks of trees unable to stand alone or return upright after being pushed over. Improper, excessively rigid staking often creates the latter case. Some minidwarf and dwarf fruit and nut trees require permanent support staking because the rootstocks that cause dwarfing also have low rooting vigor. You will find details on this last situation in other references.

Protective staking usually requires only two or three stakes 20 to 30 inches (50 to 75 cm) tall set

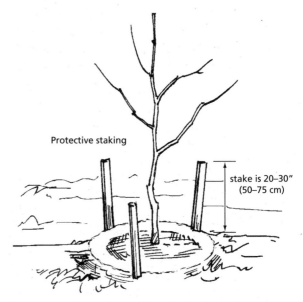

FIGURE 6.11. Protective staking shields plants that can stand on their own from mowers, string trimmers, or hoses being pulled along nearby. Place two or three 20- to 30-inch-high (50 to 75 cm) stakes away from the tree trunk, with no wires or ties connected to the plant.

away from the trunk, with no ties or wires connected to the plant (figure 6.11). Anchor stakes for trees with strong trunks but small or fragile root systems should also stay short and should focus on anchoring the root-ball, not the trunk. If the tree has a firm root-ball that threatens to turn in its hole, you can drive three or four stakes into the ground tight to the edge of the root-ball 1 foot (30 cm) into undisturbed soil *below* the root-ball (figure 6.12a). Leave the stake tops 1 inch (3 cm) above the top of the root-ball. Tie 12-gauge (2 mm) galvanized wire in a loop around the stakes at the root-ball surface. Twist the wire ends together to snug the stakes against the root-ball and hold it in place (figure 6.12b). If the root-ball is firm in its hole but the tree is unstable in its root-ball, use two or three short stakes as above with flexible figure-eight loops between each stake and the trunk to anchor the tree in the root-ball and allow the trunk to flex (figure 6.12c).

Only trees that cannot stand on their own or cannot return to upright after bending require support staking. These plants usually were improperly

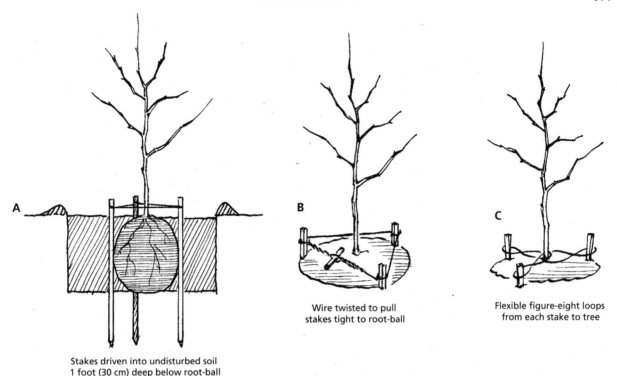

Stakes driven into undisturbed soil
1 foot (30 cm) deep below root-ball

Wire twisted to pull
stakes tight to root-ball

Flexible figure-eight loops
from each stake to tree

FIGURE 6.12. Anchor staking can be used to stabilize weak or wiggly root-balls or trees that are not stable within their root-balls. (a) In both cases, drive three stakes about 1 foot (30 cm) into undisturbed soil below the root-ball, leaving the tops about 1 inch (3 cm) above the top of the root-ball. (b) For wiggly or weak root-balls, run a wire between all three stakes and twist the wire to draw the stakes toward each other and against the root-ball. (c) For unstable trees, loop flexible figure-eight loops between each stake and the base of the trees.

staked or overfertilized in the nursery. Ideally, you would not have selected such specimens when choosing your planting stock. If you did somehow end up with such trees, determine the lowest height at which you can hold the trunk steady and the top will return to upright after being bent over (figure 6.13a and b). Support the tree about 6 inches (15 cm) higher than this point. Place one stake on either side of the tree so the line between the two stakes lies perpendicular to prevailing winds. Make figure-eight loops from each stake to the tree at the height determined, using ties made of elastic webbing, cloth, polyethylene tape, flexible tubing, or similar material. Put a solid cross-tie between the two stakes on the downwind side of the stakes near the ground (figure 6.13c). The cross-tie will keep the stakes upright and help them resist wind, especially when the soil is wet. This setup allows the

tree to sway in the wind and begin developing its trunk taper.

Support staking isn't the only alternative for weak trees, however. You can cut off most young (less than 2 inches/5 cm in diameter) deciduous trees 1 foot (30 cm) above the ground or the graft union and allow them to regrow without support. Many species will regrow rapidly without any support and may reach their precutting height within a year if you select one sprout to keep and prune out the rest. The resulting tree will likely be strong faster than will a similarly weak, staked companion planted at the same time.

Critter Protection

You aren't finished planting until you've protected your babies from herbivores, at least the big damaging ones. What kind of protection your plants

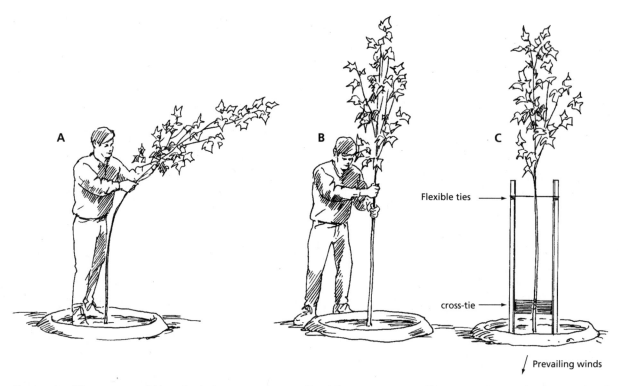

Flexible ties

cross-tie

Prevailing winds

FIGURE 6.13. Use support staking *only* when a tree cannot stand upright on its own or will not return to upright when you bend it over (a and b). Support the tree about 6 inches (15 cm) higher than the lowest point on the trunk where you can hold the trunk steady and the top of the tree will return upright after being bent down. (c) Place two stakes on either side of the tree so a line between them is perpendicular to prevailing winds. A cross-tie near the bottom will stabilize the stakes. Use flexible ties to support the tree at the proper height.

need depends on what critters you have. Rabbits, rodents, and deer are the most common problems, though dogs and porcupines can also do major damage. While fencing the whole garden makes the most sense, it isn't cheap. If that's your choice, you should already have your fencing up by now! Temporary patch-by-patch fencing until plants are established may be a useful alternative. Plant-by-plant protection may include galvanized wire or plastic mesh tubes tied to stakes around each tree, various plastic tree shelters, or chemical repellents. Let's briefly discuss each plant-by-plant method.

Mesh tubes allow water and air movement around the trunks, and they are easy to make and install. However, weeds can grow into and through the mesh, which can be a hassle. Worse, the plant's branches can be hard to extricate if they grow through the mesh. This means we should keep

mesh tubes short, which means they are most effective against rabbits and rodents. Rodents can also burrow through the ground, so a good strategy is to bury the mesh tube in the soil 2 to 3 inches (5 to 8 cm) deep, and surround it with a circle of crushed stone mulch the rodents will find hard to burrow through (figure 6.14).

Plastic tree shelters are solid plastic tubes of various heights that create a "minigreenhouse" environment favoring tree survival and growth while offering protection from critters and mowers. However, the increased height growth usually comes at the cost of thinner tops, fewer roots, and untapered trunks needing support staking for two or three years after shelter removal. In deer country, they may be indispensable for unfenced plantings, but you have to use the 6-foot (2 m) tubes, which aren't cheap and look bad in the landscape.

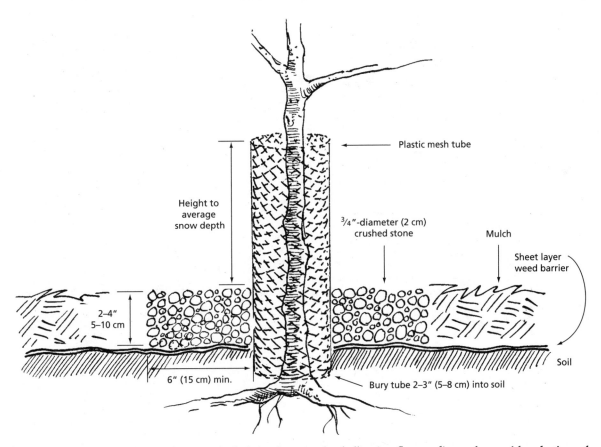

Plastic mesh tube

Height to average snow depth

¾″-diameter (2 cm) crushed stone

Mulch

Sheet layer weed barrier

2–4″
5–10 cm

Soil

6″ (15 cm) min.

Bury tube 2–3″ (5–8 cm) into soil

FIGURE 6.14. Protecting trees from rodents, particularly in winter, can be challenging. Surrounding each tree with a plastic mesh tube stuck into the ground 2 to 3 inches (5 to 8 cm) up to the height of the average snow depth helps greatly. Placing a 6-inch-wide (15 cm) circle of ¾-inch-diameter (2 cm) crushed stone mulch 2 to 4 inches (5 to 10 cm) deep around the plastic mesh discourages burrowing rodents even further. You can mulch with regular mulch materials outside the gravel ring.

Chemical deer repellents have received mixed results from what research we've seen. Some people swear by one brand, while others swear *at* the same brand. A friend has had great success repelling deer from his orchard for years by hanging mesh bags in each tree full of Dial or Irish Spring soap and gobs of human hair from the barber shop—at least until this past winter, when he had major deer damage. For others we know, the soap-and-hair strategy has never worked. For deer, fencing or a dog is really the best option.

Fertilize and Water

Water heavily on planting day to charge the soil around the plant with water and to settle the soil in the hole more quickly. Then you are more likely to catch plants that settle too deeply before mulching. Of course, in poorly drained or tight soils or soils with a restrictive layer, you can't water as much as in sandy, well-drained soils. You'll have to judge how much watering to do. Don't leave the soil waterlogged and anaerobic by any means, but give the plant everything it needs and a bit more. Once you lay down sheet mulch, less water will get into the ground easily, so it's worth getting as much water in there as you can beforehand.

We like to fertilize each plant with liquid seaweed solution on planting day, usually during the final watering of each plant that day (this minimizes leaching of the fertilizer). Seaweed extract contains growth hormones, trace minerals, and small amounts of macronutrients and appears to

FIGURE 6.15. The cardboard goes on top of the watering dish after trees are planted, checked for settling, staked if needed, and labeled. In this case we put compost only within the watering dish for each tree because of limited compost resources and the huge numbers of trees we planted. We placed cardboard only directly around each tree for the same reasons. Ready for mulch! *Photo by Dave Jacke.*

FIGURE 6.16. And the mulch goes on. These semidwarf apple trees were doubtless planted too deeply and mulched too heavily, but they did fine nonetheless. They probably did not experience crown-rot problems because the soils were well-drained sandy loams and fine sandy loams. *Photo by Dave Jacke.*

greatly help plants overcome transplant shock. You can also spread lime, rock phosphate, greensand, or other mineral or organic fertilizers around each woody plant now, if you haven't incorporated them into the soil before planting. Water these into the ground around each plant before mulching. Avoid feeding newly planted plants nitrogen, however, for it will spur shoot growth when you want to support root growth (this includes seaweed extracts that contain fish emulsion). Nitrogen fertilizer will also spur weed growth, and we don't want that! Phosphorus supports root growth, but applying highly available phosphorus can reduce the formation of mycorrhizas, so use rock phosphate or

another slowly available form, and let the fungi get the phosphorus to the plants.

After watering and fertilizing, you're finished planting! If this completes only the woodies, fertilize the broader area if you haven't already, before you mulch.

Mulching: Now or Later?

As discussed above, we usually plant woody plants, then sheet-mulch and plant perennials through the sheet mulch. If that is what you plan to do, then sheet-mulch next. Mulching does not have to take place on planting day, but it should happen as soon as possible afterward to prevent weed competition and reduce water loss from the soil.

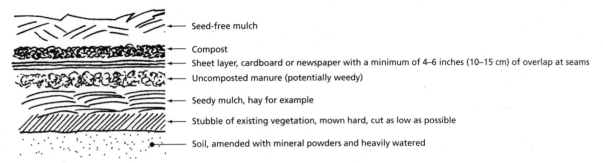

Total depth = 3 to 9 inches (8 to 23 cm) or more initially. Rots down quickly

— Seed-free mulch

— Compost
— Sheet layer, cardboard or newspaper with a minimum of 4–6 inches (10–15 cm) of overlap at seams
— Uncomposted manure (potentially weedy)

— Seedy mulch, hay for example

— Stubble of existing vegetation, mown hard, cut as low as possible

— Soil, amended with mineral powders and heavily watered

FIGURE 6.17. The specifics of sheet mulching vary depending on the materials you have available, but a few key principles apply. Mow existing vegetation, apply mineral fertilizers, and water heavily before mulching. Always use a sheet or weed-barrier layer unless the site is weed free. Weedy or seedy mulches, including uncomposted manure, go under the weed barrier; compost and weed-free mulches go on top. Never leave compost exposed to the sun; mulch over it with weed-free materials. Total mulch depths can range from 3 to 9 inches (8 to 23 cm) when first applied, with deepest mulches on extreme sites.

You may have done enough site preparation that you will use just mulch to exclude weeds, and not sheet mulch, because few weeds survive. In that case, you can mulch after planting the perennials. If you aren't going to mulch the whole site at all, you should probably still mulch at least around the woody plants you have just put in the ground (see figures 6.15 and 6.16). Weed growth near the trunks of woody plants can severely limit transplant survival and growth. You should mulch at least 1 to 2 feet (30 to 60 cm) from their trunks for this reason. Make sure not to overmulch; more than 4 inches (10 cm) of mulch is excessive near plants. Pay attention to the groundline of each plant as you mulch near it to prevent crown rot.

SHEET MULCHING

In most cases, when we make a new garden somewhere, we use sheet mulch to get things started. In sheet mulching, you use whatever organic materials you have, plus a weed barrier, to build up the organic matter on the site and smother weeds, covering a wide area completely. The word *sheet* denotes both mulching the whole area with a sheet of mulch and using a weed barrier under the mulch. If carefully applied, these two features can eliminate unwanted plants from a large area. This is especially useful when densely planted woodies and perennials make it difficult even to see the weeds, much less pull them out without hurting other plants.

When creating a sheet-mulched garden, you separate your mulch into two kinds, weed free and weedy or seedy, and lay the weedy mulches down first. You then cover them with a layer of corrugated cardboard, newspaper, or other biodegradable sheet material to prevent weed growth and put the weed-free mulches on top (figure 6.17). The sheet layer is critical to the success of the enterprise, for it prevents—or at least greatly slows—the growth of any weeds surviving in the ground or sprouting in the seedy mulch. That's the basic idea. Now for the details.

Complete area-wide coverage may not be possible if you have existing plants you want to keep on the site. This can leave holes in your mulched area, but often you can just mulch right up to the desired plants, leaving them surrounded. If your site has no perennial weeds, you can dispense with the weed-barrier layer and just use mulch. Sometimes your weeds are too vigorous for even sheet mulch to handle, and you have to create more intense disturbances to deal with the problem first, followed by sheet mulch later. Usually though, just sheet mulching works great. We have taken old garden sites full of vigorous perennial weeds and quickly transformed them back into gardens without tilling and with little other labor, while improving the soil in the process.

Hay, some leaves, seedy straw, and uncomposted manures fall in the weedy mulch category. Fully composted material, leaf mold, some leaves, most lawn clippings, wood chips, bark mulch, and relatively seedless straw fall in the weed-free category. Ultimately, you'll have to judge the relative weediness of your mulches. The key thing is to have enough weed-free mulch to cover the sheet layer by at least 1 inch (3 cm). If you have to, you can put weedy mulches on top, but it creates more work later on. Placing mulch under the sheet layer is optional. Getting the sheet layer covered is more critical in most cases.

We prefer cardboard or newspaper or both for the weed-barrier layer, since they are cheap, readily available, biodegradable, and easy to cut to fit odd shapes and objects in the landscape. Newspaper works well for less vigorous weeds, while cardboard is required for persistent species such as quackgrass. Colored newspaper used to have inks with heavy metals in them. Safe, nontoxic soy-based inks have supposedly replaced these. Many people use plastic or fabric barriers to control weeds, but we haven't had good experiences with them. They are expensive and nonbiodegradable, and they ultimately end up in a landfill or incinerator somewhere. We like a biodegradable barrier, because once the weeds are under control, the barrier isn't needed anymore. Once it's gone, the soil is easier to work, the plants can move around at will, and the soil absorbs water and breathes more effectively.

Before sheet mulching (or planting), always finish all your site grading and soil preparation work. If the site is full of grass or weeds, cut them hard, right to the ground, to shock them and reduce their reserves for resprouting. Plant woody plants and large perennials before sheet mulching to get the big holes out of the way. Small plants and seeds can go in after sheet mulching. Also, always make sure to add all the soil amendments you want before sheet mulching. If you aren't going to till the

FIGURE 6.18. Always charge the soil with water before laying down sheet mulch to aid decomposition and make up for reduced infiltration under the weed barrier. In this garden we laid the cardboard on the paths before we mulched the beds to reduce dirtying of feet and minimize compaction. *Photo by Dave Jacke.*

soil, spread the powders after mowing and irrigate heavily to wash the amendments into the soil. In fact, in almost all cases you should irrigate heavily before sheet mulching to charge the soil with water (figure 6.18). Once the weed-barrier layer is down, infiltration will fall sharply. Charging the soil with water beforehand helps balance this out and will help begin mulch decomposition.

Once you've done these preparatory steps, lay down the weedy mulch. Our experience is that it works best to lay uncomposted manures on top of carbonaceous material, rather than the other way around, at least in humid climates. The hay and carbon below the manure will more readily mix with and absorb the manure without going anaerobic that way. If the manure is on the bottom, it won't mix with the other stuff as much and may go anaerobic. Once you've laid down the first layer or two of mulch, water it to help begin the rotting. As usual, you'll have to judge how much water to apply given your soil types and how wet the mulch is already. Again, though, adding water is key, since these layers will have a weed barrier over them that may limit infiltration. Be careful not to get too much mulch around plants, especially if it's hot manure that may burn them.

Next, lay down your weed barrier (figure 6.19). If you can, go to the local furniture or appliance store to get cardboard, because large sheets have fewer seams. Every seam between pieces of cardboard or newspaper should overlap by at least 4 inches (10 cm), if not 6 inches (15 cm) or more. This makes it more difficult for plants to wend their way to the surface before their energy runs out. If you're using cardboard, you'll need newspaper too, to help cover seams and holes. Lay any newspaper at least six sheets thick for weed prevention, plus overlaps. It disappears fast, so gather plenty!

One layer of corrugated cardboard usually lasts about a year in New England's climate, though it will degrade faster farther south. Newspaper degrades in the space of weeks or months. Even if we're mulching planting beds with newspaper, we usually mulch paths with cardboard so we get the whole garden space under control and have to worry only about weeds coming in from the edges of the garden. Getting good coverage of paths and at the edges between paths and beds makes weed control much easier.

It's easy to fit newspaper around plants, rocks, oddly shaped paths, and so on. Cardboard demands a little more creativity and a knife, preferably a retractable utility knife for safety. Never place cardboard directly against a plant stem. The cardboard can abrade the stem when it moves as you walk. Keep the cardboard at least an inch or two (2 to 5 cm) away from stems to prevent this and provide some breathing room. You can cut a slice from the edge of a piece of cardboard to the middle and then cut out a triangle to go around the stem. Pull the slice apart, place the cardboard around the plant with the stem inside the triangle, and flatten the sheet to the ground. Cover the seam with newspaper and you've got a pretty solid weed barrier around that plant.

Soak the newspaper in water buckets before spreading so it doesn't blow around. Spray the card-

FIGURE 6.19. In this sheet-mulch project we were short on mulch materials, so we put no mulch under the weed barrier. We used newspaper under the growing beds because the existing weeds were few and easily smothered. Wetting the newspaper before laying it prevents wind-lift. Lay the sheets like shingles from one side of the space to another, always leaving the same edge free each time you lay a piece. This allows you to throw on the next mulch layer like rain, so the mulch presses the seams closed to seal out weeds. Use at least six sheets of thickness, and at least 4 inches (10 cm) of overlap at the seams, more if possible. *Photo by Dave Jacke.*

board with water to weigh it down if necessary. Wetting the cardboard also helps you mold it to the land's contours, but it can make it more vulnerable to ripping. If so, lay some newspaper over the rip and keep on trucking! You may need to keep spraying things as you lay down the sheets if the weather is dry or windy.

Lay weed barriers over a whole area at once before laying weed-free mulch on top if you can. This way you can make sure you've covered all the

FIGURE 6.20. You can see the keyhole-bed design for this vegetable garden taking shape here. We had lots of compost for this garden and used it lavishly on top of the weed barrier. With the compost down, the top mulch goes on several inches thick. *Photo by Dave Jacke.*

though, burying all that bad news to make something beautiful, fruitful, and life enhancing.

PLANTING PERENNIALS AFTER SHEET MULCHING

A few tips follow for those of you planting perennials after planting woodies and then sheet mulching. First, lay out your potted perennials on top of the mulch in the pattern you want to plant them, area by area. This helps make sure you have enough plants in the right pattern. Step back and survey the pattern and spacing. Make adjustments as necessary.

For each plant, take the plant out of its pot, if needed, so you can estimate the depth and width of hole you'll need. Decide whether you want to butterfly-plant or not (see the discussion on page 395). Pull back the mulch from the planting spot, and use a hand trowel or knife to cut an **X** in the sheet layer. If the root-ball of the plant must go below the sheet layer, pull up the cut sheet layer or fold it under itself to get it out of the way. If not, you can just plant right on top of the **X**. Roughen the root-ball, or otherwise spread the roots in the root-ball, as discussed earlier. Perform whatever surgical operations on the roots you must, and then dig the hole as appropriate. Make sure to consider the proper planting depth relative to final grade, including mulch. Place the plant in the hole. Firm the soil around the roots, and water the plant deeply. You may need additional soil or compost to backfill around the root-ball to prevent voids or air pockets from drying out the plant's roots. Pull the sheet layer snugly around the root-ball, adding more newspaper if needed to cover any gaps or holes. Pull the mulch back around the plant, and voilà! Finished! Move on to the next plant (figures 6.21 and 6.22).

You can also plant seeds into sheet mulch by pulling back the top mulch, laying compost or topsoil on top of the weed barrier, and seeding into it (figure 6.22). If you want, you can slice or punch through the weed barrier and fill the space with

seams and holes for the best weed control possible. If you mulch as you go, mulch an area at a time, and keep the mulch edge away from the sheet edge. Try not to toss mulch into the seams, but use it to push the sheet layers tight against each other for a better seal; it's like laying a roof and getting all the overlaps facing down the roof slope so water can't run under the shingles. If mulch gets into the seams between sheets, you've lost weed containment.

If your weed-free mulch includes compost, place the compost on top of the sheet layer, with the straw or leaves or other material on top (figure 6.20). The compost will then stay moist and help break down the sheet layer. Sometimes you have to water the hay or straw to mat it down so it won't blow away. With that your sheet mulching is finished. You can move on to planting perennials or seeds, if that's in your plans.

The great thing about sheet mulching is how fast it goes, once you've gathered all the materials. It's pleasant work, and it saves many hours and much hassle in pulling weeds later on. Just try not to read the newspaper too much while you're laying it down, it's not good for your head. It is refreshing,

FIGURE 6.21. Planting transplants into the sheet mulch is easy. Pull back the top mulch, right down to the sheet layer, to make a small pocket. Cut an X in the weed barrier with a knife and fold back the edges. Dig a hole to an appropriate depth, pop in your plants, and backfill with additional compost if necessary. Snug the mulch around the plant and water. Done! *Photo by Dave Jacke.*

compost or soil to place the seeds. This depends on what you are seeding, what kind of weed barrier you have, and how intense the weeds are that you just buried under the sheet mulch.

Tables 6.4 and 6.5 summarize the planting techniques discussed above. Feel free to photocopy these pages and take them out in the field to help you remember the details.

"Planting" Mushrooms

We offered an introduction to mushroom cultivation in chapter 1 and in pattern #37. If you plan to cultivate mushrooms in your mulch, now is the time to inoculate your mulch. If you are using log or stump culture, you should have inoculated right after cutting down the trees, when the stump or logs were fresh. You can get more detailed information on mushroom cultivation in mushroom supply catalogs and in the references mentioned in appendix 7.

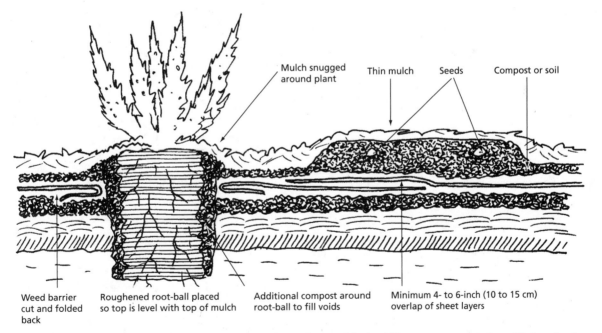

FIGURE 6.22. A container-propagated perennial herb planted into sheet mulch should have root access to the soil below the sheet layer. Any spaces around the root-ball should be filled with compost or soil, and the mulch should be snugged up against the plant to prevent weed growth (left). Seeding into sheet mulch is also easy (right). Pull back the top mulch to expose the compost layer, if you have one, or the sheet layer if you don't have a compost layer, in the whole area where you intend to plant the seed. Fill the void with compost or weed-free topsoil up to the level of the mulch surface. Plant your seeds in that bed of compost or soil, cover thinly with mulch, and water.

TABLE 6.4. Woody-plant planting sequence.

1. Stake out locations of woody plants.
2. Find the plant's groundline.
   - For container or B-and-B plants, check whether current root-ball surface is the proper groundline; adjust top of root-ball as needed.
   - Keep the plant roots moist while you dig the hole.
3. Orient the plant for optimum presentation.
   - Consider wind, sun, access to the plant, and primary views of the plant.
4. Ten-dollar hole, one-dollar tree.
   - Figure the hole depth so the groundline of the plant is at the surface of mulch; plant "high" or "proud" in all but sandy soils.
   - Dig the hole soil horizon by soil horizon; keep topsoil piles separate from subsoil piles on tarps or cardboard.
   - For container or B-and-B plants, dig a hole twice as wide as the root-ball.
   - For bare-root plants, dig the hole a shape and width that will accommodate the roots without crowding, even after you spread them to their optimum form.
   - The hole should have vertical sides.
   - In all cases, the root-ball or root crown should rest on undisturbed soil, either on a flat space (container, B-and-B) or on an undisturbed mound (bare root).
5. Scarify the hole.
   - Rake or poke the hole's sides and bottom outside edges (not under the roots or root-ball) to break up smearing of hole surface.
6. Prune the roots.
   - Prune broken or diseased roots.
   - Roughen container-plant root-ball and straighten roots to increase surface area.
   - Cut circling roots.
7. Set the plant and spread the roots.
   - For B-and-B, remove burlap and cage.
   - Use butterfly planting in shallow soils.
   - Orient the plant for optimum presentation.
   - Recheck depth of groundline, including mulch, before backfilling; adjust as necessary.
8. Inoculate.
   - Inoculate with mycorrhizas, nitrogen-fixing bacteria, or actinomycetes.

9. Backfill, puddle in, and straighten.
   - Backfill with the soil that came out of the hole, minus any rocks or boulders, in the reverse order it came out—subsoil in the bottom, topsoil on top.
   - Backfill in layers, firming the soil every 3 inches (8 cm) or so.
   - Once the hole is one-half to two-thirds full, "puddle in" with water to remove voids.
   - Remember that the surface of the root-ball or the ground-line of the bare-root plant should be "high" or "proud" by up to 1 to 2 inches (3 to 5 cm) above final grade in all but sandy soils.
10. Make a dish and water it.
    - Surround each planting hole with a small ridge of tamped soil to hold water like a bowl.
    - Container or B-and-B plants should also have a watering ring.
11. Label each tree with a permanent tag immediately after planting it.
12. Check for settling.
13. To prune or not to prune?
    - Little or no pruning after planting is usually better.
    - If you expect the tree or shrub not to receive sufficient water, some top-pruning to reduce water demand may be beneficial.
14. To stake or not to stake?
    - Staking is often unnecessary and can damage or weaken plants.
    - Only trees that cannot stand on their own or cannot return to upright after being bent require support staking.
    - Protective staking usually requires only two or three short stakes set away from the trunk.
15. Provide critter protection.
    - What kind of protection your plants need depends on what critters you have.
16. Fertilize, water, and mulch.
    - Water heavily on planting day, and frequently thereafter until establishment.
    - Fertilize each plant with liquid seaweed solution as the last watering on planting day.
    - Mulch after checking for settling; water before mulching if you mulch later.

TABLE 6.5. Herbaceous perennial planting sequence; planting into sheet mulch.

1. Sheet-mulch.
   - Sheet-mulch after planting woodies, but before planting all but the biggest perennials.
2. Lay out perennials.
   - Lay the perennials on top of the mulch in the planting pattern you want; adjust as necessary to suit your goals and your tastes.
3. Prepare the hole.
   - Take the perennial out of its pot or otherwise get a look at its root-ball; judge the hole's depth and width.
   - Decide whether you want to butterfly-plant the plant; if so, slice and bend the root ball as required.
   - Pull back the mulch from the planting spot, and use a hand trowel or knife to cut an X in the sheet layer in the spot where the perennial will go.
   - If the root-ball must be planted deeper than the sheet layer, fold the cut sheet material under itself to get it out of the way.
   - Roughen the root-ball or otherwise spread the roots in the root-ball.
   - Dig the hole to an appropriate depth and width; consider the proper planting depth relative to final grade, including mulch.
4. Insert the plant.
   - Place the plant in the hole, checking for final grade.
   - Firm the soil around the root-ball, making sure to fill voids under and around the root-ball with soil or compost to prevent drying of the roots.
   - Water the plant deeply and check for settling.
5. Remulch.
   - Pull the sheet layer snugly around the root-ball, adding more newspaper if needed to cover any gaps or holes. Pull the mulch back around the plant.
6. Water frequently until fully established.

AFTERCARE: PROACTIVE PLANT ESTABLISHMENT

With your plants properly in the ground and labeled, staked, pruned, or protected from critters as necessary, you can do the pleasant chores that help establish the plants you've planted. Proper planting lays the foundation of speedy plant establishment. Aftercare builds on top of that foundation to nurture the plant's own healing and growth so it can quickly assume its roles in the garden

FIGURE 6.23. A planted and sheet-mulched forest garden bed with irrigation system in place. Here the drip irrigation system is on the mulch surface; if you intend to have a permanent drip system, laying it under the mulch will be more effective. Central Rocky Mountain Permaculture Institute, Basalt, CO. *Photo by Dave Jacke.*

ecosystem. Monitoring, watering, fertilizing, mulching, and weeding constitute the primary aftercare activities. These activities gradually give way to management and maintenance activities once establishment is assured.

Monitoring

Monitoring forms the basis of both proactive establishment and garden management. During the establishment phase, frequently check each newly planted plant to see how it's doing. This will give you the best sense of what the plants need at any given moment, whether it's water, mulch, weeding, or foliar feeding to help a struggling plant get on its feet. As the plants establish more fully you can cut back on the individual attention, looking more generally at what's going on in the garden. Never completely stop looking over individual plants, though. A private interview is in order every once in a while. Establish your monitoring habits early, so you can carry them on for the long term.

Watering

Water is the most important physical element of proactive establishment, yet excess water can do much damage. One old saw we used for years says you should water transplanted woodies at least once a day for a week, once a week for a month, and once a month for a year, with natural rainfall included in that amount. Unfortunately, this easily remembered guideline doesn't do the topic or your plants justice, even though it has some merit. How much to water depends on factors such as kind of planting stock, soil type, the plant's root-to-shoot ratio, temperature, humidity, wind, sunshine, season of planting, the plant's drought and wetness tolerance, the availability of water and time, and so on.

Bare-root deciduous woody stock often needs no irrigation after planting unless the soil or the season is unusually dry or irrigation is normally given to plants in your climate—as long as the stock is dormant. As long as the soil remains moist, these plants don't really need irrigation until two to four weeks after they start active shoot growth. Bare-root stock will actively grow roots after planting if the soil is moist and the shoots are still dormant when planted. Excessive watering can harm roots during this period due to lack of oxygen in the soil.

Unlike bare-root stock, deciduous or evergreen container plants or B-and-B stock may need regular irrigation after planting, especially if planted in full leaf, but even when dormant. This depends on those factors listed above, and then some. Many of these plants have a low root-to-shoot ratio, so stress can occur rapidly when the roots can't support the shoots. Wind, low humidity, dry soils, and sunny weather make this problem worse. In addition, capillary action can suck water out of the root-ball when the surrounding soil texture is finer than that of the root-ball, which it often is. This occurs even if the surrounding soil is near its water-holding capacity, with up to 80 percent of the water in a 1-gallon (4 l) root-ball drawn out within twenty-four to thirty-six hours.[8] This necessitates watering every day for the first few weeks unless it rains, and sometimes even when it does rain. The challenge is that daily watering can leave the surrounding soil extremely wet, which will limit root growth.

Therefore, when caring for container or B-and-B plants, check the moisture level of the *root-ball* every day, as well as the moisture level of the surrounding soil. Every day for the first week or so, water directly onto the root-ball using a plastic watering ring (as described in "Make a Dish and Water It," above), and supply only enough water to wet the root-ball and maybe a bit of the soil outside it. Once every two or three weeks, or if the surrounding soil is also dry, fill the larger soil dish outside the ring as well. A plastic watering ring is critical for this situation, as it allows you easily to water only the root-ball zone. After the first week, decrease the watering frequency some, but keep the plant from wilting. Always check the soil's and the root-ball's moisture level before watering so you know what to do. After a few more weeks, you can cut watering of container or B-and-B stock to a minimum unless you have a dry season or dry soil.

If you have drip irrigation installed, all the better. For bare-root stock, place the emitters around the plant to encourage root growth away from the stem and prevent crown rot. Do the same for containers and B-and-B stock, but also place an emitter over the root-ball to keep it well supplied for the first few weeks. Then turn it on and let it drip, but keep checking to make sure the watering rate is right. After the plant is well established, remove the emitter from the root-ball area, but leave the others.

Herbaceous perennials usually need more frequent irrigation to establish than woodies do. Three months of watering should be the maximum needed, hopefully less. Again, check the soil and root-ball moisture levels, or use wilting as the signal for action. Since most perennials come as container plants, capillary action can have the same effects as for woody container plants. Try specifically to water the root-balls in the early going.

For all plant types in later stages, water deeply enough so the water penetrates to a few inches (8 cm) below the bottoms of the roots to encourage deeper root penetration. Shallow rooting increases a plant's drought sensitivity and irrigation dependency. Only add as much water as the soil can absorb, though. You can always add more water if the soil is dry, but you can't do much if it's too wet. It's always better to underwater a little than to overwater. Avoiding anaerobic soil is paramount!

Fertilizing

In most cases, fertilizing carries less importance for plant establishment than watering and weed control. It comes second in the list, though, because you should amend the soil before you mulch. Many of you will have amended the soil during site preparation, but if not, fertilize now. If you're using powdered fertilizers, spread them over the ground and water them in before mulching. Though not as effective as mixing them into the whole topsoil horizon, this does the job with less muss and fuss, leaves the soil food web less traumatized, and helps charge the ground with water before you mulch it. The earthworms and plants will mix the nutrients into the topsoil eventually.

No matter what you do, in the first year after planting focus on phosphorus, potassium, and calcium, not nitrogen, to help roots grow. Feeding nitrogen stimulates shoot growth, which can stress the plant if shoots grow too much before roots are well established. If you have inoculated with mycorrhizal fungi, do not fertilize with highly available phosphorus, or you will prevent mycorrhiza formation. Use slowly available forms such as rock phosphate. Foliar feeding gets nutrients to plants directly, especially right after planting, with little nutrients going to potential competitors. Foliar or liquid fertilizers are about the only way to fertilize specific plants once you have mulched in earnest. Look to other references and your soil-test results for information about specific amendments to use. In all cases, use organic amendments only. This helps feed and care for the soil food web.

Other Points

Keep an eye on the mulch levels in the garden. Wind and heavy rains can move mulch around, leaving bare spots, particularly where the mulch is thinner near the stems of woody plants. Always have extra mulch on hand to top-dress over the weeks and months as needed.

After lack of water, weed competition is the major factor preventing desired-plant establishment. Early, vigorous weed control is critical, especially if you haven't done much site preparation. This is one reason we mulch! If you aren't mulching, then mow or pull weeds near your plants, but by all means, manage the weeds or you may lose your plants.

Remember that most things in your forest garden are not set in concrete, though a few of them may literally be so. Right after planting is your last best chance to make revisions to your design as it is expressed on the ground. After acknowledging yourself for the work you have done, take the time to walk around your garden and soak in the experience of the ecosystem that you are cocreating. If anything jumps out at you that you might want to change, take note of it and do something about it. If not, you have something else for which to acknowledge yourself.

1. Harris, Clark, and Matheny, 1999, page 163.
2. Harris, Clark, and Matheny, 1999, page 170.
3. Harris, Clark, and Matheny, 1999, page 170
4. Harris, Clark, and Matheny, 1999, page 169.
5. Crawford, 2003, personal communication.
6. Harris, Clark, and Matheny, 1999, page 221.
7. Harris, Clark, and Matheny, 1999, page 223.
8. Harris, Clark, and Matheny, 1999, page 240.

7

Management, Maintenance, and Coevolution

> While establishment of the project has involved a lot of digging and other hard labor, maintenance, as I have said, has been minimal. In fact it grows less from year to year, as the trees and other perennial plants which have decided to stay grow stronger, more deeply rooted, more stable and secure, and thus better able to withstand the onslaughts of pests, disease germs and weeds.
>
> —ROBERT HART, *Forest Gardening*

Our forest gardens live simultaneously in the realms of ecological and evolutionary time. In ecological time, plant populations grow, stabilize, and decline as the plant community wanders down its successional pathway. Daily and seasonal events influence how individual plants fare along the way, and hence where the community goes in these wanderings. In evolutionary time, species evolve, adapting to changing conditions through natural selection. We forest gardeners participate in these processes through our gardening activities with varying degrees of awareness. This chapter intends to help you "take the reins" more consciously, guiding both ecological and evolutionary changes through management, maintenance, and coevolution.

Management involves shaping ecological forces and guiding change in your backyard ecosystem by monitoring ecosystem dynamics, envisioning future possibilities, directing succession, and determining the nature and timing of maintenance activities. Management never ends, as long as you have a sense of what you want and the will to create it. We often think we're managing something when we

are, in fact, maintaining it. Understanding that distinction is crucial in forest gardening.

Maintenance is the grunt labor of running the garden—mulching, pruning, fertilizing, harvesting, and so on. As Robert Hart found, the work of maintaining your forest garden should decrease as the garden develops. Good management, continual learning, and plant breeding should help decrease maintenance even further, while keeping yields as high as possible. Maintenance is an ecological and evolutionary force. It needs careful guidance, or it can push succession and evolution in unintended directions.

Coevolution involves learning, cultural evolution (that is, changes in human belief systems, social and economic structures, technologies, and resource choices), and species improvements through selection and breeding, as well as other interactions. When we coevolve we adapt ourselves to the plants and animals in our gardens, and to the garden as a whole, while they in turn adapt to us. Though it is a long-term process, we can speed evolution up, creating shifts in form and function for the mutual benefit of our ourselves and our gardens.

Management, maintenance, and coevolution interweave as we nudge our garden ecosystem toward meeting our goals, both in the present and for the future. The boundaries between these three processes are necessarily fuzzy, but for the sake of argument we'll discuss them separately. First, though, let's talk about the tools we might need to accomplish these tasks.

TOOLS OF THE TRADE

Our tools say a lot about who we are, what we do, and how we think about what we do. Some folks have said that the only five tools Robert Hart used to manage his Shropshire forest garden were a harvest bucket, hedge shears for pruning, a sickle for cutting back grasses and herbs, a bag of mulch, and a wheelbarrow to carry the rest around in. The simplicity of this list indicates the simplicity of the basic tasks Robert undertook in his forest garden every day: cutting back plants, mulching, and puttering about observing, pondering, and foraging here and there. A profoundly simple man, and a profoundly simple plan. Surely this means the forest garden achieves our goal of self-maintenance, doesn't it? It's a nice myth.

In reality, Robert also used a chipper, a helper to run it, and tools besides the sickle and shears for cutting the coppice he chipped. He used a spading fork to prepare soil and a mattock, a shovel, and a trowel to plant. He used cans for watering and pitchforks for moving seaweed, straw, and manure. He used ladders for harvesting and gloves to avoid getting stuck by the brambles. There were probably tools in his shed we didn't see when we visited. However, even this more complete list is relatively short and "low-tech" compared to our possible needs in North America. In addition, the most important forest-garden management tools are missing from the list altogether.

The relative lack of pests and diseases in Robert's native Shropshire compared to North America means that we North Americans will likely need more pest- and disease-monitoring and management equipment than Robert did. The lack of decent tree pruning in Robert's garden indicated some other lack, whether it was one of knowledge, interest, tools, or skill, or simply the failing agility of old age. Hedge shears just don't cut it for many pruning jobs. We'll probably want the tools to do a better job there. If you use just one-quarter of the design process offered in chapters 3 and 4 (which would still be more than Robert did), you will need a few additional tools for that, and for staking out your design before you plant. That way you are more likely to get your tree spacings right. All this is still not to mention any specialized tools or equipment your particular site may need as part of the site-preparation process, for drip irrigation, or whatever else.

You may need only a small number of tools for everyday maintenance and management, depending on your crops, but you will need more for establishment and periodic disturbances. Most gardeners probably possess most of the needed tools or can easily gain access to them. However, you already possess the most essential tools you'll need. Their proper use will make your gardening life a lot easier.

The first of these lie within you: your brain, heart, and senses. Keep these tools well tuned. The ability to observe carefully, think clearly, listen to his heart's leadings, and marshal the information at his disposal led Robert Hart to invent his temperate-climate forest garden in the first place. Basic horticultural and sophisticated ecological knowledge are the main things Robert lacked. His limited horticultural knowledge led to his worst mistakes, while his lack of ecological sophistication limited his success. What he had, though, was vision, and heart, and intuitive sense. These latter qualities made all the difference, allowing Robert's garden to shine despite his limitations. The knowledge and ideas this book offers provide leverage to overcome the other lacks. Add your experience and inner resources to the many outer resources available and you will have much to go on.

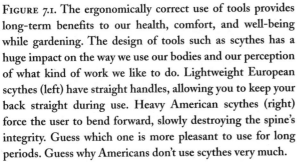

FIGURE 7.1. The ergonomically correct use of tools provides long-term benefits to our health, comfort, and well-being while gardening. The design of tools such as scythes has a huge impact on the way we use our bodies and our perception of what kind of work we like to do. Lightweight European scythes (left) have straight handles, allowing you to keep your back straight during use. Heavy American scythes (right) force the user to bend forward, slowly destroying the spine's integrity. Guess which one is more pleasant to use for long periods. Guess why Americans don't use scythes very much.

FIGURE 7.2. A proper shoveling stance keeps your back straight at all times and uses your legs, your arms, and the levering action of the shovel to do the work. When working in a deep hole or with a D-handled shovel, squatting is the best position, as shown here. Long-handled shovels should be used when standing fully upright.

The second most essential tool, related to the first, is your body. Forest gardening is a physical activity, especially during establishment. Caring for your body in the process is key. Robert Hart started his forest garden at least partly because he had a physical disability, he was aging, and he wanted a less demanding garden than annual vegetables allowed. With the establishment phase out of the way, he could ride the garden's growth and development over time to the end of his life with decreasing labor requirements and increasing yields. Even so, it pays to use well-designed tools, and to use them properly, even if you aren't approaching the end of your years.

Ergonomically correct tools keep our bodies healthy and happy, singing with the work rather than cringing at it. For instance, typically heavy, curvy-handled American scythes force the user's back to bend to swing the scythe properly (figure 7.1). This posture and the weight of the cheap American blades stresses the spinal discs and back muscles mightily. European-style scythes, on the other hand, have light, hand-forged blades with longer, straighter handles and an extension for the second hand. This allows the user to maintain an upright posture while using a lighter tool, which are always concerns when doing hard or repetitive labor. Consequently, scything weeds and grasses for mulch becomes a joy, allowing longer, more productive work periods. One can awake the next day with minimal ache or strain, if any. Quality tools properly used will make your body last longer.

We should learn to use even standard tools ergonomically, such as long-handled shovels. Most people shovel by bending over, again putting stress on the spine, especially the lower back. Bending the knees and keeping the back upright while shoveling strengthens the legs, opens the pelvis, and keeps the spine healthy and happy (figure 7.2). It takes a while to tone the body and acclimate to shoveling this way, but it definitely saves the back.

So, while the complete list of tools forest gardening requires is fairly long, keep the emphasis on the tools that make the most difference: your smarts and your body. The wise manager finds ways to reduce the need for grunt labor whenever possible and, if grunt labor is necessary, takes the time to figure out how to make it the most efficient and effective labor possible. If you have excess growth of one plant and need to cut it back, how can that serve some other need in the garden? Where can you use the "waste" matter as mulch? If you need to dig up a bed to harvest roots, how can you turn that disturbance to advantage in your successional scheme for the patch? If there's no way to avoid digging up a large rock, figure out how to get it out of the ground with the least effort and trauma possible. Using such thinking tools in your day-to-day garden activities makes whatever work you do doubly or triply effective, and a lot more fun, too.

With all that in mind, let's begin our consideration of managing, maintaining, and coevolving with the forest garden.

MANAGEMENT

Essentially, management entails observing what is, envisioning what might be, determining how to get from point A to point B, and doing what it takes to get there. As an ongoing design process, it begins with monitoring the garden, not only as the foundation of envisioning and creating a future condition, but also to make sure that appropriate maintenance gets done.

MONITORING: THE KEY
TO EFFECTIVE MANAGEMENT

Monitoring forms the basis of good garden establishment, management, and maintenance. Walking through, hanging out in, and observing your garden each day will give you the best sense of what it needs at any given moment, whether it's water, mulch, weeding, or fertilizing. Only by knowing what's going on in your garden can you effectively decide where you'd like it to go in the future. Live in your garden and it will live in you. Give it time, attention, and direction and it will reward you tenfold. Spend time communing with your plants. You'll better hear and see their needs, and they'll respond, if you do.

Monitoring can take many forms, from undirected observation to formalized directed observations, documentation, and measurement. Both kinds of monitoring have value. Undirected observation can lead to unique realizations, while photos and records offer perspective and information you may need or find of interest years later. A few thoughts on how to monitor for management follow.

Making Daily Rounds

The habit of making a daily round is a basic monitoring practice. Besides being enjoyable and relaxing (hopefully), it will give you the clearest sense of what's going on in your garden on a continual basis. It will help you see what work needs doing, which plants need help, and what food is ready to harvest. If you've placed your garden "in the way," you'll be walking through it as a matter of course in your daily life. If not, make a point of doing daily rounds, so it becomes a habit, so your day doesn't feel complete without it. We doubt you'll regret it.

Your daily rounds can be undirected or directed observation sessions, or both. Recording daily high and low temperature measurements, or biological events such as the development of flowers and fruits (phenology), can form the core of your daily rounds. Build around that with whatever time and attention you can offer. Paths lined with fragrant flowers or plants that bear every few days through the season, such as alpine strawberries or perennial broccoli, can also help motivate you. Once you're out, take the time to notice what's going on.

Periodically Poke and Prod More Deeply

Besides the daily round, more serious poking and prodding is also in order once in a while. Check out a few plants up close, inspecting tops and bottoms of leaves, stems, and even the root crown. Make random sweeps with an insect-collecting net. Dig a soil pit to see how it's going down there. Get off the beaten path to see your garden from a different per-

---

TABLE 7.1. Monitoring tools.

- rain gauge
- max/min thermometers
- growing-degree-day recorder to monitor pest outbreak timing
- journal, notebook
- identification books: plants, mushrooms, insects, birds, amphibians, reptiles, etc.
- entomologist and botanist friends
- insect sweep net, kill jar, mounting kit
- pest monitoring traps: pheromone traps, sticky cards, sticky balls
- hand lens (10x)
- plans of garden beds or patches to monitor changes in plant patterns
- camera and film
- shovel, soil core probe
- tensiometer to monitor soil moisture
- eyes, ears, nose, tongue, skin, mind

---

spective every so often. Poking and prodding regularly will add depth to the breadth that daily rounds give you. These can be random-access excursions or organized inquiries, or both.

What to Watch

The possible range of observations to make in even a small forest garden is infinite. The essentials are much fewer. Here's what you might need to monitor, at least informally, to manage your forest garden effectively.

Climate

Keeping track of climatic factors such as precipitation, temperatures, and so on used to be a common activity of early settlers, whose lives and livelihoods depended on knowing local weather conditions. Many people recorded these observations in journals of one kind or another for later reference. Such information may help you understand why one species isn't performing as well this year as last, or at least to hypothesize about it. Over time, you'll see patterns and be able to make better management and maintenance decisions if you have this information. Written observations aren't necessary, but they are quite useful.

Max/min thermometers are a fun way to gather such information. They record the high and low temperatures over whatever period you choose. Dave likes to place several of these thermometers in different microclimates so he gets a sense of the variations over time and space. A rain gauge is another cheap climate-monitoring tool. Combining rain-gauge data with soil observations can improve your decisions about when to irrigate and how much. Simple notes in a journal about frost timing and patterns, sunny and cloudy weather, and so forth can also help you stay in touch with your garden and your world.

Plant Health, Performance, Behavior, and Production

How healthy do the plants look? Learn to recognize the difference between the glossy leaves and vibrant color of a well-watered plant and the dullness of a water-stressed plant. Water well before plants wilt, for wilting is a sign you've let things go too far and damage has already occurred.

The color, gloss, and vibrancy typical of a plant provided with adequate moisture also indicate a plant with good nutrition. Look at the older leaves on the plants. Are the plants robbing from Peter to pay Paul, leaving the older leaves yellowing and dying to keep their growth going? Do unusual colors show in the leaves, whether the leaf as a whole, along the edges, or in the leaf veins? Reddish, purple, or yellowing leaves may indicate nutrient deficiencies.

Notice how the various plant species perform and behave in the garden and how productive they are. What percentage have survived and established themselves? Is the plant a vigorous competitor-strategist? Does it spread rapidly? Is it tightly bunching or more spread out? How's the yield? The flavor? How do these compare to last year? To other patches or garden sites? Relating this information to climate records can help you choose species and varieties to keep, expand, or eliminate. It can help you design or refine your polycultures, too.

Keep an eye out for mushrooms in your garden, and identify the ones you find. Keep track of how your planted mushrooms are doing. Is the mulch wet enough? How punky are the logs or stumps? Is it time to start a new log so you don't lose continuity of mushroom production?

Polyculture Behavior and Successional Trends

Observe how plants interact in polycultures. If you have the same polyculture design in several patches, compare how the patches behave. Does one species dominate? Do the different patches act the same or differently? Why? Do particular weeds tend to come up in one patch but not others? Can you think of unfilled niches in a polyculture, and species that might fill them usefully? How much disturbance does the polyculture need to stay balanced? Does the patch seem to be heading in the successional direction you intended?

Insect Populations

Monitoring insect populations is an obvious need in a crop system. Many books discuss the pests of specific crops you'll need to watch for (see appendix 7). Hopefully you informed yourself about these during the design process (see "Site Analysis and Assessment," chapter 3). Check above and below leaves and on stems for insect eggs, aphid masses, and so on. Look for holes in tree stems with goo oozing out or small bits of wood piled up below. Slug trails, holes in leaves, and so on are also indicators—but so are increased populations of ground beetles who eat slugs. Useful tools here include an insect sweep net, a kill jar, an entomologist friend, field guides, and a hand lens. Specific pests may require specific monitoring tools, such as pheromone traps, sticky balls, sticky paper, and so on. However, don't limit yourself to monitoring pests. Watch the diversity of the whole system of which the pests are a part. This may give you clues about pest dynamics, such as why a pest was worse at one time and not another, what some of the predators might be, and, if you watch carefully, how you can encourage these allies.

The more you know and learn, the better you can observe. Your varmint, pest, and disease analysis and assessment should help you learn where and when to look and what to look for, so you can take action in a timely fashion if necessary.

Other Animals

Keep your eyes peeled for the other animals in the garden, or their signs, including birds, amphibians, reptiles, and mammals. Notice where you see them and what they're doing. Look for tracks, scat, holes, or chew marks. Listen for songs and sounds night and day. Research to find out more about the ones you find there. Ponder how you can encourage the ones you want and discourage the ones you don't.

Soil Quality

Last but not least, there's the soil. At least half of your plants live down there, so dig soil pits at least once every year or two or three to check on soil conditions. Take samples for soil tests at least every two or three years, too, if not annually. This will help you amend the soil as necessary or know whether your dynamic accumulators are doing their job. Observe water movements to see whether your site-preparation work took effect. Does the soil drain faster than it used to? How is the soil's aggregation, structure, consistence, and color? How deep do the roots go? Is the profile changing? Is the topsoil deeper? Is the subsoil looser?

Just to give you a little encouragement, Martin Crawford's experience has been that the soil under his permanent vegetative cover is becoming very friable and high in organic matter after less than ten years of growth. His soil pH "appears to be stable after the initial application of calcified seaweed as a liming material." In addition, he has found that after five or six years, almost everything clearly began growing faster and had greater health—at least partly due to the soil improvements he has noticed in the ecosystem, as well as improved microclimates.[1]

Beyond these basics, you can propose questions to answer and theories to test in your garden and monitor specific things in response. Monitoring what's going on in your garden should be one of the most fun parts, besides eating the fruits of your labors. We encourage you to watch carefully throughout the development process in your own garden. The more you look, the more you will see, and the more you will learn and find inspiration in what is going on around you. Garden ecology is endlessly fascinating. Just watch out you don't spend all your time hanging out there. All play and no work makes Jack a poor boy.

MANAGING SUCCESSION AND POLYCULTURES: DANCING WITH DYNAMIC VEGETATION

Like any intelligent animal, we humans can be trained to react in specific ways to a given stimulus. Our parents, school, television, and childhood environment create powerful habits of thought and behavior within us. Yet we are more than simple Pavlovian reactors. We can inquire, think, and intuit. In the sometimes tiny gap between stimulus and reaction, we always have a choice.

Most of us have habitual reactions to vegetation change. The grass gets long, we mow it. A "weed" pops up, we yank it. A flower goes to seed, we deadhead it. We can even react to the reactions: the grass gets long and we rebelliously let it grow. Many of our culture's vegetation-management habits simplify systems and prevent change, controlling plants and vegetation. To forest-garden well, we need to step into the gap after the stimulus—breathe, observe, consider, and choose. We must respond to vegetation change and dance with it, not react and control. Our feet may be clumsy and slow at first, but we'll catch on and get into the flow eventually. The dance may be a free-form, moment-to-moment improvisation, a disciplined and formal sequence of steps, or a fluid, choreographed expression of changing desires and intent. That's up to us and our plant and animal partners. Either way, the unified oldfield theory will be our dance instructor.

Succession Guidance Questions

A good instructor helps us learn by asking us good questions. The unified oldfield theory (chapter 1 and volume 1, chapter 6) helps us ask such questions and make keener observations in any vegetation-design or management situation. The three causes of plant succession—site or niche availability, differential species availability, and differential species performance—provide a solid basis for these questions and observations.

For example, if you have a weed problem, ask the following questions (once you have determined that indeed you don't want a particular plant around):

- Why does the weed have a site or niche available? What niche does it fill?
- How did it make itself available to fill that space? How did it get there?
- Why is it performing so well compared to other plants?

If you want to establish a plant or plants, ask:

- What is the best way to make an appropriate site available to this/these plants, and no others? What kind of site or niche do these plants need?
- What is the best way to bring the plant(s) to the site (i.e., by seed, cuttings, bare-root or container-grown stock, etc.), and when? How can I foster the plants' own self-propagation activities?
- How can I ensure that the desired plant(s) establish and perform optimally?

If you want to slow or stop plant succession, ask:

- Will new sites reverse, stop, or speed succession? How can I prevent new sites or niches from becoming available, if that is appropriate? What kinds of disturbance, if any, will maintain the current species?
- How can I minimize the availability of unwanted species to the site?

• How can I reduce the performance of invading plants? How can I improve the performance of established plants?

And so on. The "Contributing Processes or Conditions" and "Defining Factors" in table 1.6 suggest more detailed lines of inquiry behind each of the above questions. For example, in the weed situation above, you could consider, among other things:

• the size of the site the weed occupies;
• when disturbance last occurred and the characteristics of that disturbance;
• the size, nature, and viability of the propagule pool that generated the weed;
• how the landscape patterns or dispersal agents may have aided dispersal or created the pattern of the weed you found;
• the resources available to the weed and its life strategy, architecture, and other niche characteristics; and
• the strategies, architecture, and niches of neighboring plants, animals, and other organisms to discern interactions between them, such as herbivory, competition, mutualism, and so on.

Each situation will require its own particular set of questions, determined by your goals and situation. Such questions, based on the three causes of succession, will guide the selection of succession-guidance strategies and techniques. Table 1.8 lists various techniques for each management strategy.

Site selection, species selection, community design, and site preparation will determine most of the dynamics of your designed successions. Once you have planted your garden, though, you may need to nudge things in the direction you intended using one or more succession-management techniques. Let's look in more detail at the most common succession-management techniques used in forest gardening.

The Top Four Succession-Management Disturbances

Mulching, trimming, weeding, and clearing make up the bulk of the designed disturbances most people will use to manage succession in their forest gardens. The first three of these can also function as maintenance activities, though the intent and perhaps the specifics of the practices will vary as a result. This means we need to keep our wits about us to avoid slipping into maintenance, as discussed below.

Mulching guides succession primarily by limiting site and light availability. This inhibits many unwanted plants, at least temporarily, and for some mulching methods and species (e.g., annual weeds in the soil seed bank) for as long as the mulch stays in place. Inhibiting unwanted plants gives preferred species the opportunity to take control of the site and its succession. Mulch also affects plant performance in numerous ways, as discussed in feature article 4. Please note that mulch can add nutrients to the soil while fostering later-succession plant and soil microbe species, especially fungi. In contrast, soluble chemical fertilizers foster bacteria-dominated soils as well as the ruderal and competitor-strategist plants characteristic of early succession.

Trimming in its various manifestations can direct plant performance as well as site and propagule availability. Pruning and thinning within reason can maintain the pruned plant's performance in the successional marathon. It may also improve light conditions for underlying plants. You can discourage a plant with intense pruning or thinning or by shearing or cutting the plant. Pruning fruit trees in midsummer reduces the amount of energy the trees store for the following year, slowing their growth. Coppicing not only yields useful material for mulch or construction projects but sets succession back. The frequency of cutting, the spacing of the plants, and their growth rate determine how long the understory layers remain exposed to sunlight and how long they stay in the shade. This influences the diversity and cyclic successional pattern of the sun-loving and shade-loving understory plants in turn.

Weeding alters species availability and makes new sites available for occupancy. It should be necessary primarily before and during garden establishment. Once preferred species get established, unwanted plants should appear only to tell you that a vegetation patch contains a niche you could fill with a useful species or two, or that your maintenance or disturbance regimes need rethinking. Digging, pulling, hoeing, grubbing, and woody-weed extraction all tend to make new sites available for more weeds. Consequently, we should follow these practices with mulching or planting desired species when necessary to continue the intended succession. Herbicides (flame weeding, hot water, or chemicals) usually eliminate unwanted plants without much soil disturbance. This can make it easier to remove unwanted plants while allowing preferred plants to establish dominance with minimal upset. Girdling (cutting through a tree's bark all the way around its trunk to cut off fluid circulation) kills trees with minimal soil disturbance but can result in a dangerous tangle if large trees aren't cut down before they fall on their own.

Clearing usually occurs infrequently in forest gardens and is used mainly as a means of resetting the successional clock or establishing a new successional path by making new sites available. It takes many forms. Sometimes we'll need to clear a large area, sometimes just a spot or patch for relay plantings as the garden shifts from a sunny environment to a shadier one during succession. Clearing can involve all vegetation layers or just one or two. It may or may not include soil disturbance. Its size, shape, timing, nature, and intensity depend on your goals. All the designed-disturbance techniques lie at your disposal. In any case, as suggested elsewhere in this work, we need to consider such a disturbance an integral part of the following succession. This means designing the clearing operation carefully, and proactively planting soon afterward. What legacies do you want to leave behind? What species and propagules do you want to remove? What resources and conditions do you want to alter? What species do you intend to plant in the space left over, and why?

Many of the designed disturbances discussed above alter the availability of resources, and this may lie at the core of their effectiveness in guiding succession. So let's look at resource-management techniques as well.

Directing Plant Performance through Resource Management

Resource availability directly determines plant performance and also influences competition between plants. Plants most urgently need water and light resources to survive. Water-management techniques are fairly straightforward. Mostly we irrigate if we can when the garden has too little water, though cutting back vegetation will also reduce water demand. Otherwise there isn't much we can do to manage water availability once site preparation is complete. We manage light availability mainly using designed disturbances such as pruning, thinning, mowing, burning, grazing, and the like. This leaves nutrients as the major plant-performance resource that we can manage.

Design approaches such as installing dynamic nutrient-accumulating and nitrogen-fixing plants take time to improve soil quality. Nutrient-rich mulches take less time, especially if you mulch with compost. Directly amending soils or foliar feeding have the most rapid results, but unless necessary for initial plant establishment, these do not build ecosystem function as well as the other approaches. Often some combination is needed, with amendments used first and an increasing reliance on mulches and plant-based self-renewing fertility later on. This depends partly on the nutrient status of your topsoil and subsoil, as well as your crop's nutrient needs.

Pruning and shearing, harvesting, and thinning fruits and flowers all direct plants' stored energy and alter plant performance. Thinning fruits before they fully develop can increase the size and quality of the remaining fruit. Removing flowers reduces stress on newly planted plants and improves establishment success by directing plant growth to roots and shoots. Delaying gratification in the first year or two can therefore increase long-term tree health and productivity and help lead your succession where you want it to go.

Proactive Planting

Proactive planting plays a minor role in the management of successions once they're started. It mainly takes the form of relay plantings as conditions shift during succession, or spot-planting if a plant dies or gets moved for some reason or you want to alter a polyculture mix. Sometimes a natural disturbance will necessitate replanting to establish control and prevent weeds after the event.

Soil-Food-Web Management

In most forest gardens, managing the soil food web for succession-guidance purposes is a simple affair or nonevent. If you've prepared the soil well and inoculated at planting time as necessary, the lack of ongoing soil disturbance in forest gardens should allow the soil food web to manage itself most of the time. Sometimes, though, soil-borne pests or diseases threaten to overwhelm your plants and your succession plans, or the soil and plants just don't seem to be functioning at their best. Specific pests such as root nematodes may require action. Establish whether poor soil moisture or aeration conditions, for example, are contributing to the pest or disease problem. If not, simply applying healthy compost or compost tea will help many of these situations. You can also supply the soil with specific foods for specific organisms or even supply the beneficial organisms yourself.

Manage Polycultures, Don't Maintain Them

As Martin Crawford has written, a self-maintaining polyculture "is encouraged to form via positive management, not just by planting and walking away. Put simply, plants which are not wanted are discouraged and plants wanted are encouraged. This is achieved by manipulating conditions so that the wanted plants can outcompete . . . the unwanted."[2]

Ideally, the polycultures we design will maintain themselves and follow the successional path we desire without much effort on our part. Practically speaking, few of us yet have the skills and knowledge about forest garden plants for our polyculture designs to work well most of the time. This will take experimentation and careful observation to develop. In the meantime, we may need to coax our polycultures into a self-maintaining balance or along our desired successional path.

Nonetheless, a fine line distinguishes intervention to nudge the system into self-maintenance and ongoing disturbance as a crutch to maintain the polyculture's balance or successional direction. Watch for signals indicating when you've crossed this line. If you need to repeatedly cut back one plant species in a polyculture because it outcompetes the others or to prod another into more vigorous growth, your polyculture mix isn't working. You are maintaining the polyculture, not managing it. Either change the species mix or let go and see what happens, taking note of what you're learning.

For example, one of Dave's garden patches contains the edible mint-family ground cover Chinese artichoke (*Stachys affinis*), along with a mix of other plants. Large, clumping herbs that waken early in spring (e.g., *Valeriana officinalis*, *Lathyrus venetum*, *Sanguisorba canadensis*) shade out the later-sprouting but vigorous artichoke, causing few competition problems. The perennial onions (particularly *Allium fistulosum*, *A. cepa proliferum*, and *A. schoenoprasum*) seem to grow fine with the artichoke, because their early-spring growth habit and upright or clumping forms mix well with the dense but upright mint-family habit. However, Dave recently planted some heart-leaved alexanders and golden alexanders (*Zizia aptera* and *Z. aurea*) in that bed to see whether these partial-shade-tolerant native nectaries can coexist with the exotic artichoke. The new little plants need some help getting established in the midst of the vigorous preexisting artichoke, so he weeds once in a while to give them space and light. If Dave must always pull the artichoke to keep the alexanders going, though, he will move the alexanders elsewhere.

This maintenance-reduction rule does not apply to harvesting, at least not directly. We don't want to reduce the harvesting (it is the point, after all), but we also don't want the harvesting to create maintenance needs beyond that. For example, cutting sorrel (*Rumex acetosa* or *R. scutatus*) leaves for food will tend to reduce the plant's vigor. If you've chosen polyculture associates well, the sorrel's neighbors will not outcompete it as a result. Otherwise, you may need to give the sorrel extra fertilizer to keep the polyculture in balance or to change the polyculture mix. We must carefully observe the plants, the polyculture system, and our own behavior to develop the most self-maintaining plant combinations.

A Word on Weeds

Having placed "weeds" in their proper successional context is all well and good, but let's get very practical about this. The people with whom we have spoken who have the longest experience with forest gardens all say they have few weed problems at all. This is the good news: the practice appears to bear out the theories. On the other hand, when we begin forest gardening, we often deal with "weeds" of a different nature than those we'll deal with later on. Most gardeners probably know the weed species from the earlier successional stages. Let us speak here of those from later stages. Since we are creating a different situation from that with which most of us are familiar, perhaps we could use a few tips on what to look for. So, let's see what someone with direct experience has to say about it. Each of us is likely to have a different suite of weeds, given our varying ecological contexts, but we'll likely deal with many of them in similar ways.

Martin Crawford says that spring and early summer weeding is the biggest maintenance job in his ten-year-old Devon, England, forest garden. His main weeds are trees, however, such as ash, willow,

birch, and sycamore maple, along with brambles, nettles (*Urtica dioica*), and cleavers (*Galium aparine*). The trees seed in from the adjacent woods and are easily pulled when small. The brambles in particular are very important to manage, for they can swamp a forest garden quickly (this is probably true anywhere). Nettles are ubiquitous in Britain, so Martin doesn't need more, despite their usefulness. The cleavers scramble over young trees and shrubs and can distort them as they grow. He pulls out all of these perennials by the roots if he can, so they won't come back to haunt him.

Another vigorous herbaceous plant problem Martin deals with is creeping buttercup (*Ranunculus repens*). This plant is a problem only where his ground covers are thin or where they are deciduous. British winters are getting warmer (not surprisingly); the buttercup can now sometimes grow all winter and thereby get ahead of his nonevergreens. He is working to replace his deciduous ground covers to adapt to this situation. Most other undesirable plants Martin cuts with shears, because, he says, he is "happy for these to regrow, as this increases their nutrient-pump value." Turning our weed problems into opportunities is the name of the game, when possible.

All of the above sounds like a lot, but really it isn't that bad. Martin spends about six days per month in April, May, and June and two days per month in July and August on "weeding patrols." Other than that, he says, self-maintenance has really begun to take shape.[3] For a young, 2.1-acre (0.8 ha) forest garden, 22 days of weeding in a 240-day growing season (USDA hardiness zone 9) isn't bad at all. In the meantime, Martin's desired plants are growing larger and denser all the time, and his weed problems should further decline. It's a good thing, too, because Martin planted and now manages the whole 2 acres (0.8 ha) all by himself. One of his biggest lessons is that timing is critical: "If you don't get the timing right, you can easily double the work."[4] Now that's succession and polyculture design in action!

The Horizon Always Moves:
Ongoing Succession Design

When we design forest garden successions, we envision the horizon habitat and the patterns and phases of the patches that will get there. After planting our garden, we tweak the vegetation to keep each patch on its successional path. We avoid slipping into maintenance mode, doing our best to keep that burden on the vegetation itself. Meanwhile, as each patch develops we can stand back and see it whole in time and space, with an eye to the future. We can keep the intended horizon habitat and patch-phase scheme in mind, see how things are developing, and revise our plans when necessary. As the horizon recedes ahead of us, we can think further ahead, get more specific about the phases and patches we designed only vaguely to begin with, and think about what lies at the new horizon. Ongoing design is a significant part of forest garden management.

For example, let's say you designed and planted a large instant-succession forest garden. An array of nut trees will compose the horizon-habitat canopy, for both nuts and timber. You also put in some hazels (*Corylus* spp.), saskatoon serviceberries (*Amelanchier alnifolia*), and jostaberries (*Ribes nigridolaria*) as the primary shrub-stage crops, with numerous multifunctional perennials to dominate the earliest phases. Your initial scenario was that the herbs would dominate first, and the shrubs would climb over them to come to prominence in four to six years' time. You expected the jostaberries to mature sooner than the taller hazels and saskatoons, which would eventually dominate the jostaberries and shade a few out. You surrounded the nut trees with your tallest saskatoons to induce the nut trees to grow with few lower branches up to about 15 feet (5 m) for better timber quality. Since the saskatoons are an experimental crop, you'll let them be the first to get shaded out by the nuts. In fifteen or twenty years the nut trees would start to get big, and the shrub crops would slowly decline as the nut trees came into production and achieved full size. You did not intend any relay plantings or substitutions until after the nut trees began closing the canopy. Having planted everything at once as an instant succession, this scenario depends completely on plant performance to unfold as expected.

Let's pretend that, four years down the line, the above succession plan doesn't seem to be working out as you thought it would. Though the nut trees appear healthy and strong, they haven't made much top growth. For some unknown reason, the saskatoons did not take well to your site. They did eventually establish, but they haven't grown very fast. The jostaberries did the opposite, exploding out of the ground and bearing large quantities of fruit sooner than you'd expected. The hazels are coming along, but a few died because deep wind-blown snow allowed rodents to get over your trunk protection and chew their bark. What to do?

Return to the basic design process outlined in chapters 3 and 4. First, go back to your original goals. Are they still valid? What has changed and what hasn't? Revise and restate as necessary. Then assess the situation relative to those goals. You have some gaps in your shrub canopy, and the shrub layer is less diverse than you had hoped. At least the nut trees won't get shaded out by the saskatoons, since both are growing slowly. Some of the hazels may resprout from the stump. Slower nut-tree growth may give you more time to plant other fast-growing berry crops. And so on.

After assessing the situation, you can brainstorm various ideas for redesign or management. For example, you could improve nut-tree nutrition to see whether that helps them grow faster; replace the dead hazels with raspberries, black currants, or maybe some native *Amelanchier* species to see how they do compared to the saskatoons; or sit back and see what happens. Imagine these three scenarios in more detail, and consider where the succession would lead. How would your goals be affected by each option? Are there any locations where weeds could become a problem if you don't maintain vegetative cover? Should you redesign the patch or manage it to alter plant performance, or both, and how? Ongoing design is not all that complicated in most cases and grows out of good monitoring. Sometimes, though, drastic things happen that alter our plans dramatically.

In one project we were involved in, labor always came in periodic summer bursts, with minimal maintenance otherwise. The original forest garden plan had gotten planted, but many of the plants subsequently died due to drought and the lack of consistent establishment care. Insufficient site preparation also led to a resurgence of quackgrass. A few beds remained fairly free of it, while most succumbed completely. The herbaceous perennials never even had a chance to cover the ground. The broadscale instant-succession strategy was left tattered and was still threatened. In addition, in the two years since the garden had been planted, the designers realized that the fruit trees they had planted would yield during a period when students would not be present. Clearly the tune had to change. The losses created an opportunity to shift the focus of the horizon habitat.

Since most of the resources available for the project had already been spent, we shifted to a new plan using the "nuclei that merge" succession strategy. The gardeners will secure the remaining weed-free beds with rhizome barriers and thoroughly weed them. They will consolidate the surviving plants in these beds, transplanting carefully to make sure no quackgrass comes with them. The intention is to establish firm control over the remaining open patches, letting the surviving, more competitive plants grow and self-propagate. In the meantime, adjacent patches will receive intensive site preparation to eliminate quackgrass and improve the soil. Once the remaining plants fill the existing patches, relay plantings of less vigorous, later-succession species will go into the established patches, and the true-grit survivor plants will go into the newly established patches to secure them.

On a broader scale, the intended horizon habitat also shifted focus. To better match the yields to the timing of demand, the gardeners will plant summer-ripening berries where fruit trees have died. Creating the "nuclei that merge" strategy means that the forest garden patches will mature at different times, not the same time. This will create more "lumpy texture" in the design than would have been the case in the original plan, which is good. It also allows the gardeners to calibrate the size of the garden to what they can truly maintain under their available labor regime. Finally, the new strategy allows them to build the garden in a more sustainable manner, focusing their maintenance efforts on establishing new beds only after the older beds have become more self-maintaining. This means the gardeners can improve the design of new patches as they learn along the way.

As the above examples illustrate, people make mistakes in their designs, and in their follow-through, and things often don't work out as planned. Rather than dispense with the planning, we can use these opportunities to learn. Sometimes these situations end up working out for the better anyway.

From Sun to Shade and Back Again

Natural forest successions often go through a phase called *understory repression* just after the tree canopy closes. The canopy in this phase usually consists of numerous young pioneer trees at very dense spacing, all competing for light. As a result, the understory becomes quite dark, and any shrub or herb species left from the oldfield stage die out. The canopy begins to open up again as canopy losers fade and canopy winners emerge. Hence, light levels increase in the understory, and shade-tolerant plants can move in and survive. The understory-repression phase clears the understory of sun-loving oldfield plants and prepares the ground layer for colonization by woodland plants.

Designed forest gardens are unlikely to experience understory repression. We don't usually plant our trees so densely, for one thing. We're not likely to want our gardens to go through the high-competition, low-yield period this implies. Besides,

FIGURE 7.3. A ring of shade-loving plants can grow outward as your trees grow over time.

we will probably have grown fond of our sun-loving plants, so we won't want to see them totally disappear. Instead, we'll probably substitute some kind of disturbance to clear the ground layer, followed by relay plantings of preferred shade-tolerant species. We can also gradually shift to shade tolerants by transplanting out the sun lovers and putting shade lovers in their place or by self-propagating an expanding "ring" of shade lovers from the trunks of trees outward as the trees grow (figure 7.3). By the time the tree crowns touch, we'll have an understory dominated by shade-loving plants. In the meantime, the sun lovers can be establishing new forest garden patches elsewhere. Alternatively, you can thin or coppice the maturing dominants to reestablish sunny patches in the developing forest garden. These could be short-lived trees that you can kill without guilt or that die of their own accord.

No matter what you decide to do, you need to decide how you'll deal with this shift from a primarily sunny environment to a primarily shady environment. Most forest gardens will eventually go through this shift or will present the option of this shift to you. Hopefully you've thought it through in your design process. If not, think about it now, at least a little.

GRUNT LABOR AND ITS FRUITS: MAINTENANCE AND HARVESTING

Despite all our efforts to design and build a self-maintaining garden ecosystem, we will still have work to do. It's hard to completely escape grunt labor when gardening. Pruning, watering, fertilizing, mulching, weeding, pest control, and propagation still have roles to play in the forest garden. Our design, site-preparation, and establishment efforts will reduce the ongoing effort required if we did them well. As the plants grow and mature, attracting animal and other allies, our grunt labor quotient should decrease further, as yields go up. Still, maintenance work will remain, as long as we want the garden a certain way.

Learning to do less maintenance and still achieve our gardening goals challenges us technically, biologically, and ecologically, to be sure. It also challenges us to look at ourselves, to change our perceptions, values, and habits of thought and behavior. This is what the following subsection on mindful maintenance is all about, even as we discuss the work we will have to do as the seasons roll through their cycles. Then we'll address the prime focus of forest gardening: harvesting the bounty.

MINDFUL MAINTENANCE: LEARNING TO DO LESS

What is the minimum we must do to keep our forest garden running and yielding well? Masanobu Fukuoka spent thirty years asking himself this question and trying out his answers. He eventually found a way to grow rice achieving competitive yields with many fewer inputs and minimal intervention in the ecosystem.[5]

All maintenance techniques are a form of intervention. The principle of shifting the burden to the intervenor reminds us to remain wary of these, lest we assume more burdens than we can or want to carry. In contrast, if we design multifunctional, functionally interconnected polyculture successions, letting things go once we set them up should be our primary approach. We should at least restrain ourselves from acting until we've undertaken protracted and thoughtful observation.

Observing and pondering before acting will teach us much. Watch yourself wanting to take or maintain control of the ecosystem, but don't take it or maintain it. Don't react. Act. Respond. Step into the gap after the stimulus, and take a deep breath. Consider your purposes, consider the context, consider timing, consider methods, and consider consequences. Play with the ecosystem. Try something new, including doing nothing. If we keep doing what we've always done, we'll keep getting what we've always gotten. The wise manager knows when to sit and watch, as well as when and how to act responsibly. The better we get at designing forest gardens, the less we'll have to do. The more we watch what happens when we do less, the better we'll get as designers and managers. As Fukuoka said in his landmark book *The One-Straw Revolution*, "The ultimate goal of farming is not the growing of crops, but the cultivation and perfection of human beings."[6] Acting with more consideration, wisdom, and forethought, and less reactivity, is part of this cultivation, and central to forest gardening.

Even so, we will learn that we still have chores to do. The ecosystem dynamics we create in the forest garden should minimize these chores and perhaps change the way we do them, but the remaining work still falls into the same old categories of weeding, trimming, mulching, watering, fertilizing, pest control, propagation, and harvesting. What needs doing in the garden each season? The following discussion summarizes the common tasks, at least as far as we understand them based on our current experience. With more forest gardeners out there playing with mindful maintenance, we may learn ways to reduce these tasks further.

THE SEASONAL MAINTENANCE CYCLE

Each season has typical garden chores. Forest gardens are no different. Tables 7.2 through 7.6 pro-

TABLE 7.2. Maintenance tools.
• drip-irrigation equipment
• hoses, sprinklers, rain gauge
• hoe, stirrup hoe
• Weed Wrench, Root Jack
• broadcast seeder
• planting tools: square shovel, spading fork, etc.
• pitchfork, shovel, rake
• wheelbarrow, cart
• loppers, pruning saw, hand pruner, pole pruner, chainsaw
• chipper
• mower, scythe, sickle
• backpack sprayer
• 5-gallon (20 l) buckets
• hammock

vide a comprehensive catalog of the maintenance tools we might require and the tasks we might perform in the forest garden in each season. Notice the word *might*. As a comprehensive list, it seems pretty long. On the other hand, many of these tasks won't be necessary every year, or in every garden, or in every patch. Use the tables to keep yourself organized and clear about what you may need to do, but use your own judgment. After your garden is established, the need to weed will decline drastically, for example, but you should still keep a lookout for weeds every spring regardless.

Most of the entries in these tables are self-explanatory. We'll delve more deeply into two topics, however, because they contain more complex issues than the tables can discuss.

Watering Tips

We discussed watering during the establishment phase in chapter 6. Here the discussion focuses on watering after establishment.

Once your plants are firmly established the need for supplemental watering should decrease. In most of the eastern United States, assuming that the global climate doesn't change too much, little or no irrigation should be needed most of the time. Dry spells can wreak havoc, however, especially if they come at the wrong time. Chances are that dry spells

TABLE 7.3. Possible spring maintenance activities.

Activity	Spring
Propagation & Planting	• Most seeds are best started in early to late spring indoors or out. • Plant woody plants before dormancy breaks, but after the soil thaws, especially bare-root stock. • Replant any holes in your ground covers. • Graft in early to late spring, depending on species. • Take stem or root cuttings of perennials in spring, but not during bloom. • Divide most perennials in spring before they bloom. Divide early bloomers just after flowering.
Fertilizing & Watering	• Minimize nutrient leaching by fertilizing only after the soil has warmed and plants are growing. • Irrigate in early spring only if drought conditions prevail or you are establishing new plants. Once plants start actively growing, water more often as needed.
Mulching	• Pull back mulch to warm soil or uncover mulch-protected plants as weather warms and stabilizes. • Once soil warms, sheet- or deep-mulch for establishment or weed control. Add maintenance mulch after spring weeding, but before plants have fully leafed out and get in the way. • Build your mulch stockpiles. Look for mulch-gathering opportunities in the neighborhood.
Weeding	• Weed problems can double or triple if not caught early, especially in the case of perennial weeds. It's easier to see weeds before desired perennials fill out. Some weeds will resprout if buried in mulch. Leave them in the sun or rot them in a water barrel and then fertilize with the water. • Mulch after weeding. • Begin monitoring garden edges, rhizome barriers, and along pathways for rhizomatous weed ingress. Prevent mulch or vegetative growth from covering or breaching rhizome barriers.
Trimming	• Stop harvesting coppice before sap begins to rise or before the ground thaws and becomes too wet to work on. • Prune fruit trees before dormancy breaks, preferably in late winter, but early spring is OK, too. • Prune nut trees shortly after they break dormancy or a few weeks after a late frost. • Inspect all trees and shrubs for winterkill after they have leafed out. Prune out dead wood and crossing branches. • Remove flowers from newly planted woodies to focus their energy on establishment. • Thin or divide overcrowded perennials in early spring to increase vigor, bloom, and density. • Begin regularly cutting surrounding grassy or weedy areas to prevent their seed from spreading into the garden.
Food Web Management: Pests & Beneficials	• Watch for slug damage in mulched gardens. Seedlings, newly planted plants, and just-sprouting perennials are most susceptible. Make beer traps for area-wide control. A few sensitive plants can be protected using rings of diatomaceous earth on the ground, cloches, or collars of copper flashing. Slugs won't crawl on copper. • Start monitoring varmints, diseases, and insect pests as appropriate to the herbivore and the weather. • Watch for gaps in your nectary-plant flowering season. Find species to fill the gaps.
Harvesting	• Spring brings greens, shoots, flowers, mushrooms, and root crops.

TABLE 7.4. Possible summer maintenance activities.

Activity	Summer
Propagation & Planting	• You can plant container plants right through the summer as long as they get watered enough. • Replant any holes in your ground covers up into the hot season. • Do your budding in midsummer. • Monitor spring grafts and unwrap as they mature.
Fertilizing & Watering	• Stop providing fertilizer to woody plants by midsummer to ensure proper hardening off in the fall. • Cut dynamic accumulators and mulch with them. • Take tissue samples for nutrient analysis at the proper stage of a plant's growth for the nutrient being measured. • Monitor rainfall and soil moisture. Irrigate as necessary.
Mulching	• Add mulch as necessary for weed control and fertility. • Stop adding high-nitrogen mulches by midsummer to slow plant growth and aid hardening off for winter. • Build your mulch stockpiles. Look for mulch-gathering opportunities in the neighborhood.
Weeding	• Keep after perennial weed sprouts all summer. If you kill them to the ground often enough you will exhaust their resources and they'll die. • Any weeds you pull now may still be able to pollinate and ripen seed. Move them to a designated place, compost them, burn them, or let them rot in a water barrel and use the water as fertilizer. • Watch out for weed dispersion. Pay attention to the flowering and dispersal of problem plants in or near the garden. Cut or mow nearby weeds before they set seed. If you cannot do this, then time mulching activities to deal with seed drop. • Continue monitoring garden edges, rhizome barriers, and along paths for rhizomatous weed ingress. Prevent mulch or vegetative growth from covering or breaching rhizome barriers.
Trimming	• Thin excess developing fruit on fruit trees to ensure larger, higher-quality yields. Insects will help you do this if your pest controls aren't working well. • Shear or trim perennials that appear to be outcompeting wanted neighbors or that function as dynamic accumulators. Use the prunings as mulch around nutrient-hungry crops. • Summer pruning of fruit trees (before mid-July) helps stunt the tree by reducing the amount of energy stored for the following year's growth. • In midsummer, check growth of limbs on fruit and nut trees. Widen narrow crotch angles by spreading the branches. • Prune or thin berry plants as necessary after fruiting is completed. • Thin perennials that appear overcrowded and weak. • Continue regular cutting of nearby weedy or grassy areas that could contribute seeds or rhizomes to your weed problems.
Food-Web Management: Pests & Beneficials	• Keep slug watch, especially on sensitive species or if the weather stays moist. • Stay on top of pests and diseases with careful monitoring and by enacting your pest managment plan. • Pick up fruit drops as they occur to prevent insects from completing their life cycles. You can also run chickens or sheep through your garden to do this, but control them carefully to limit damage. • Notice which plants tend to have disease or pest problems the most often. Find a more suitable spot for them where they can really thrive, or take them out of your garden completely. • Watch for gaps in your nectary-plant flowering season. Find species to fill the gaps.
Harvesting	• Harvest berries, flowers, medicinals, mushrooms, early tree fruits, and some perennial vegetables. As summer deepens, most greens will be less tasty than earlier on.
Miscellaneous	• In urban or suburban areas with poor air quality, you may occasionally need to wash dust and dirt off the leaves of plants with a fast-moving stream of water to maintain optimum health and productivity.

TABLE 7.5. Possible autumn maintenance activities.

Activity	Autumn
Propagation & Planting	• Begin stratifying seeds of hard-to-germinate perennials at the appropriate time for spring planting. • Plant woody stock after dormancy, before ground freeze-up.
Fertilizing & Watering	• Take soil samples for nutrient testing in the fall. • Water ground covers heavily in late fall before the ground freezes. Charging the soil with water now will help the plants survive drought stress induced by frozen soil.
Mulching	• If plant growth appears too vigorous in early fall, remove mulch to let soil cool. • Once plants are dormant, replace mulch to prevent freeze-thaw, to keep soil from freezing too deeply, and to support ongoing root growth. Deeply mulch marginally hardy plants. • In warm winter areas, do not cover crowns of plants susceptible to rot during wet weather. • Build your mulch stockpiles. Look for mulch-gathering opportunities in the neighborhood.
Weeding	• Any weeds you pull now may still ripen seed they've set. Carefully move them to a designated place, compost them, burn them, or let them rot in a water barrel and use the water as fertilizer.
Trimming	• Begin coppicing woodies after leaves are off and the sap is down. • Avoid cutting dead flower stalks and vegetation in the fall. See below.
Food-Web Management: Pests & Beneficials	• Fall and winter are prime deer, rabbit, and rodent damage seasons. Renew deer repellents and rabbit and rodent protection around trees. • Avoid deadheading perennial flower stalks and cutting dead vegetation in the fall. These provide excellent overwintering habitat for many beneficial insects and spiders. Cut them in spring instead, before new growth occurs, but after temperatures have risen and insects are active. • Watch for gaps in your nectary-plant flowering season. Find species to fill the gaps.
Harvesting	• Prime harvest season for fruits, nuts, mushrooms, some berries, and root crops. Can, dry, root-cellar, pickle, cook, and eat away!
Miscellaneous	• Some ground covers may not allow leaves to fall through their foliage in the fall and become matted and smothered. Remove leaves from on top of these species or they may rot over winter.

TABLE 7.6. Possible winter maintenance activities.

Activity	Winter
Propagation & Planting	• Peruse catalogs and drool. Order plant stock early to make sure you get what you want.
Fertilizing & Watering	• Prevent freeze damage: make sure your irrigation system is shut down properly and your hoses are emptied and stored. • Ponder results of fall soil tests. Make plans for spring fertility tasks and rites.
Mulching	• Build your mulch stockpiles. Look for mulch-gathering opportunities in the neighborhood.
Weeding	• Observe wind patterns and watch for weed seeds blowing in from the neighborhood.
Trimming	• Harvest coppice as long as soil is frozen or firm to minimize soil damage. • Prune fruit trees starting in late winter.
Food-Web Management: Pests & Beneficials	• Research the pests and diseases you had this past year and plan strategies for the coming year. • Purchase or prepare any traps, baits, or other control strategies you will need. Make a calendar of what problems to watch for when, and which strategies to deploy when for optimum protection.
Harvesting	• Set up for maple sap collection. Collect sap and boil in late winter. • Dig root crops as weather permits.
Miscellaneous	• Sharpen and oil your garden tools. Dream of your garden while you and it sleep. • Consider how you might want to garden differently this year.

will increase in frequency as the climate warms, at least in some areas.

Herbaceous perennials need the most water when they are growing most actively, usually in the first half of the growing season. Woody crops need adequate moisture throughout flowering and fruit development for optimal yield, as well as during their most active growth in the spring. For some crops, such as juneberries, this means that late summer and fall watering can drop greatly compared to spring and early summer. Late-ripening crops such as most nuts and many tree fruits need adequate moisture throughout the entire growing season. In general, though, gardens as a whole need the most water in mid- to late summer. Spring rains and snowmelt decrease irrigation needs in spring and often into early summer. Demand decreases in the fall due to both the plants' needs (unless they are ripening fruit) and cooling weather conditions. Monitoring plant color and soil moisture, and using a rain gauge, will tell you whether plants are suffering or happy, and when to water and how much.

One common guideline says to provide your garden with 1 inch (3 cm) of water each week, which equals about 60 gallons per hundred square feet (25 l/sq. m). If your rain gauge shows you received less rainfall than that, you might consider watering. However, soil depth, texture, and water-holding capacity, recent weather history, air temperature, humidity, and windiness also affect how much irrigation a garden needs. Shallow and sandy soils need more frequent watering. If you just came through a rainy period, the ground may have plenty available for a while. Hot, dry, or windy weather increases water demand. Use the guideline above, but look at the overall moisture level of the soil at various depths, the plant color, and the weather history and forecast to make your decision. Plants should have a nice gloss and color. Dullness indicates water stress. Wilting means things have gone too far and that damage is already occurring.

Most of the water that perennial and woody plants use comes from the top foot or two (30 to 60 cm) of soil. Sixty to 80 percent of the water plants use comes from the top 4 feet (1.2 m). Unless you have the equipment to measure soil moisture (called a soil tensiometer) or take soil samples at depth, you will have to use the topsoil as a guide. For unmulched or thinly mulched perennials, if the top inch (3 cm) of soil is dry, you can water, or not. Once the soil is dry to 1½ to 2 inches (4 to 5 cm), watering is definitely necessary. In mulched systems, it's often a little harder to tell because the soil dries out more evenly with depth, and less from the top down. You never want the soil to get powder-dry, because it absorbs water less readily then. Keep the soil evenly moist, but not wet.

It's always better to water less frequently and deeply than to water every day a little bit. Plant roots respond to the water regime. Watering deeply sends roots deep and helps inoculate your plants against drought or forgetfulness. It's good to check the effectiveness of your irrigation as you go. If the mulch has become dry as well as the soil, the mulch can absorb large amounts of water before the soil and the plant roots get a drop. This is another good reason to use a drip irrigation system, which you can place under the mulch.

Water in the early morning if you use spray irrigation so leaves can dry off during the day to decrease chances of disease. Spray irrigating in the heat of the day leads to high evaporation losses and can burn leaves, as droplets focus sunbeams like a lens.

Drip irrigation is useful anywhere rains are not dependable. You can set up the system with a timer so it goes on and off automatically each week, but this does not adjust to the weather. Some soil tensiometers not only measure soil moisture but can turn on or off the water supply for more accurate and timely irrigation. Human senses and judgment work just fine if you don't want to get fancy, though. You can set drip systems to maintain constant moisture, or you can cycle them on and off to water deeply once a week or so. A number of good books and catalogs provide design information and equipment for drip irrigation (see appendix 7).

Water quality is another important issue. Well water can be high in salts, so you might want to test your water, particularly if you live in an arid or semi-arid area (see "Salinity" in chapter 5 for more information). Most cities and towns have chlorinated water, and this is less than ideal for gardens. Fluoridation of your water supply may also be an issue. If your water is fluoridated, you may want to research the effects of fluoride on gardens so you can make informed choices. Spray irrigating does allow some of the chlorine to evaporate before it gets into the ground, but that leaves the sodium in place. If you can, use nonchlorinated water to irrigate. Roof runoff collection is a great idea, but storing enough water to make a difference in even a medium-size garden gets expensive fast. If you have chlorinated water, consider a filter, both for your drinking water and for your garden. Your body and your plants will thank you. You'll need a filter for drip irrigation anyway, so you can just upgrade it to remove chlorine as well.

In all cases, make sure you don't overwater. Waterlogged soil loses oxygen fast, and this kills the soil food web as well as plant roots. There's little you can do in this case except wait for the soil to drain and dry, whereas underwatering is easily remedied. Fine-textured soils have this problem much more frequently than sandy soils. Always err on the side of too little water.

Supporting Beneficials and Controlling Pests and Diseases

The range of activities involved in supporting beneficials and monitoring and controlling pests and diseases makes writing about these subjects comprehensively in the space available here nearly impossible. Each crop has its particular pests, with its particular monitoring techniques, natural enemies, and other means of control. This is why chapter 3 suggests researching varmints, pests, and diseases for your specific region and crops. Appendix 7 lists useful books and catalogs for more information to help you in this effort. What follows is a brief overview of some key topics and issues.

Prevention of problems is the best approach, so start there. Forest gardening leans heavily on the selection of resistant varieties, scattering and mixing crops to make pests work harder to find hosts, providing habitat for diverse predators, and "lumpy" vegetation texture as the foundation of pest and disease management. These strategies are all discussed elsewhere in this volume. Ongoing research suggests that good-quality compost tea can prevent many major diseases by improving the microbial food web on leaf and fruit surfaces, among other places.

Supporting beneficial critters is an ongoing effort. Don't expect to get all the habitat elements built into your garden at the beginning. Fine-tune your array of flowering plants for beneficial insects as time goes on. Once you have things planted and growing, take note of which nectary plants flower in your garden when. Watch neighbors' gardens and nearby wild areas to see which flowers attract what insects at what times. You might choose to bring some of these to your garden to diversify your array or fill gaps in your flowering sequence. Observe which beneficials your garden attracts, and use appendix 5 to research their food habits. Figure out what gaps your garden might have, and how you can fill them.

For some plants, especially most fruit trees, good sanitation makes good sense for disease or pest control. This includes raking up and burning fallen leaves and prunings. Organic apple orchardists sometimes apply lime, then flail-mow, and they place compost on top of leaves after the trees go fully dormant in the fall. This alters the pH of the leaves to discourage scab fungi, and the compost decomposes the scab spores and leaves. Some research indicates that spraying fallen leaves with healthy compost tea can do just as good a job of reducing disease problems as removing the leaves and burning or composting them. The fruits that fall off the trees through the summer contain pest larvae that will pupate and leave the fruit before long. Feeding these "drops" to pigs, sheep, or chickens, hot-composting them, or drying them in the sun kills the larvae and stops the pest from completing its life cycle. Research the above and other practices further in other references.

While good sanitation is essential for maintaining many fruit species, that doesn't mean "tidiness" has to go along with it. Let go of the need for order and neatness. Maintenance patterns have a big impact on beneficials, as well as pests and diseases. Luckily, the less of some kinds of maintenance you do, the better off beneficials are. Disturbances in general disrupt the food web's self-development. Make sure you leave at least some areas of the garden wild and messy. Let sleeping logs lie. Leave brush in place or pile it somewhere out of your way (as long as it doesn't threaten to spread disease, as fruit-tree prunings do). Stay on paths so the soil doesn't compact, or you might be stepping on a salamander that's working for you. Avoid deadheading flowers, especially fall flowers, since they provide overwintering habitat. Some dead flower heads can be quite beautiful in winter.

To monitor pests and diseases, learn what to look for, where to look for it, and when, based on your varmints, pests, and diseases assessment. Learn the life cycles and niches of each of these garden inhabitants so you can identify them at each stage and intervene when and where they are most vulnerable. Decide upon a *threshold level* for each. A threshold level is the level of observed damage or the population level at which you intervene to prevent a significant loss of crop yield. Rarely should we seek to completely eliminate a pest or disease from our garden. Doing so destroys the livelihoods of the critters we depend on to keep the pests and diseases in check. What we want is for the problem species' populations to stay low, so they aren't a major problem, but we let them remain to keep the food web intact.

Remember that ecosystems sometimes exhibit a lag time between when a pest population reaches a damaging level and when the pest's predators can respond to control the population. Fukuoka and a number of forest gardeners have talked about seeing a pest population exploding one day, and a few days or a week later they observe a predator response and the pest population dies back. Such events are like the normal illnesses all children get. Some doctors consider such events critical to a child's maturation, and the same may be true of forest-garden food webs. Without such testing, the immune system weakens and stops working. Patience and careful observation during a pest outbreak can minimize your workload and help the ecosystem develop its own internal balancing mechanisms. Intervening at the wrong time could leave you with the tasks of control you don't want. Setting threshold levels helps you sit back and watch what's going on without reacting reflexively, giving the system time to take care of itself.

On the other hand, some pests and diseases can grow out of control rapidly, making balancing the population more difficult. As you research pests and diseases, try to assess the potential for explosive population growth. For example, fireblight is a fast-spreading bacterial disease that demands instantaneous response and extremely careful prevention. It infects apple, pear, and hawthorn trees, as well as other rose-family plants, and can kill whole branches or even trees in short order. Even if you've seen no signs of the disease, when pruning susceptible species in the warm, humid regions where it can occur, you should disinfect your pruning tools *after each cut* with a 5 percent chlorine bleach solution.

How quickly you intervene also depends on what kind of damage a pest does. You can probably give the ecosystem more time to respond to an insect attacking the leaves of a fruit tree than one that directly attacks the ripening fruit itself. Aphid populations, for example, often explode quickly because the females can give birth to live nymphs without mating. They usually go after the leaves and twigs of young shoots, particularly on woody crops. In blocks of bearing apple trees, as Michael

Phillips says, "just look upon any aphids you find on watersprouts as your summer pruning crew."[7] However, young trees consisting mostly of the green shoots aphids love can be overwhelmed rapidly, before beneficials can respond. In such times, a dormant oil spray or insecticidal soap is probably advantageous. Check the aphids for parasitism and predation by beneficials first, though, for the balancing forces may have already begun their work (check field guides and garden insect books to help you identify parasitized aphids and aphid predators, as well as other insects you may have problems with). Sometimes plant nutrition impacts pests and diseases, too. Aphids prefer plants rich in nitrogen. Overfertilizing can lead to problems.

Once you know how to monitor the population and determine a threshold level, decide how you will maintain that balance when you must intervene. Many control techniques exist, many of which apply to specific pest species. Each technique has side effects varying from minor to broad-spectrum food-web disruption. Pick your techniques carefully, and monitor their effects on the ecosystem as best you can. Often it is wise to use more than one technique, or to have backup techniques in case one control method or another does not work as it should. This is particularly true for the most damaging pests or diseases and the most important crops.

Different control techniques also have different timing implications. Some act more quickly than others or prevent outbreaks rather than control them when they occur. Passive devices such as sticky traps, sticky balls, and pheromone traps may take longer to achieve control than handpicking or direct spraying, though they are more selective than most sprays. You may decide to apply the former strategies as a matter of course, or at least sooner in the game than the more intensive, faster-acting interventions that have broader impacts on the food web. Some people are beginning to use compost tea to treat diseases, not just as a preventive. It works by inoculating above-ground plant parts with a full spectrum of food-web microbes that rebalance the leaf, fruit, or stem surface ecosystem.

Harvesting

Harvesting takes the cake as the most enjoyable kind of maintenance. Whether you're grazing on tidbits as you make your daily rounds or filling baskets with fruit for storage, harvesting is where it's at. How do you know when to harvest? How much food will you get, and what should you do with it? What tools do you need? How does harvesting affect forest garden ecology?

What to Harvest

Many gardeners lack familiarity with many forest garden plants, particularly as edible or medicinal crops. Make sure you know your plants and plant parts well. For example, the common perennial vegetable rhubarb (*Rheum rhabarbarum*) has poisonous leaves. Not everyone knows that, but everyone eats only the petioles, or leaf stems. Elderberries (*Sambucus canadensis*) produce berries that taste excellent (when properly prepared), and the fully opened flowers make decent fritters. The rest of the plant and the unripe fruit, however, can cause nausea, vomiting, and diarrhea. Don't mistake horse chestnuts for edible chestnuts, like Dave once did as a naive young person. Horsechestnuts contain a dangerous glycoside, and the bitterness won't leave your mouth for many unpleasant hours. A number of delicious, nutritious, even medicinal edible mushrooms easily grow in forest gardens, but most of us have heard the horror stories about people sickening or dying from eating the wrong toadstool.

Some wild native plants that we should watch out for, too, can spread into our forest gardens. The most dangerous ones include poison hemlock (*Conium maculatum*)—no relation to the hemlock tree, but an herbaceous perennial naturalized from Europe that is a relative of parsley, Queen Anne's lace, dill, caraway, and fennel (family Apiaceae). It is most famous as the herb used to kill Socrates when the Athenians condemned him for his teachings. At least it causes a painless death, unlike the other parsley-family plants to watch out for. One small mouthful of one of our native water hemlocks (*Cicuta maculata* and *C. bulbifera*) can kill a full-grown human quickly and violently. The water hemlocks' delicious odor and flavor, and their similarity to carrots or parsnips, has led more than one person to greatly relish their dying meal. As their name implies, they prefer wet soils, but they will grow in moist garden soil, as will poison hemlock. Parsley-family plants are often hard to tell apart, especially when dormant. It is up to you to make sure you know what you are harvesting and eating! You do so at your own risk. Knowledge is power. Teach yourself and your children well.

On a lighter note, when we know what's edible and what's not, the options available expand considerably. Many people have yet to experience the explosive aroma of eating apple blossoms, the sweet tang of fresh ramps (*Allium tricoccum*), or the soft, cucumber flavor of salad burnet leaves (*Sanguisorba minor*). Many gardens contain Johnny-jump-ups (*Viola tricolor*), but not everyone knows that all parts of the plant are edible, and pretty good tasting, too. Isn't it great that you can keep these vigorous, self-sowing plants from taking over your garden while filling your salad bowl at the same time?

When to Harvest

In harvesting, timing is everything. Each crop has its seasons of yield and best harvesting time for your purposes. For example, catching the filberts before the squirrels and jays takes excellent timing and observation. If you're off by a little, you won't harvest much. Getting optimum nutrition from your crops depends on timing too. Vitamin-C levels in fruits and berries tend to peak in the afternoon. Herbs and leaf crops contain maximal nutrients and phytochemicals just before the plants flower. The heat of the day and hours of sunshine also deplete some constituents, so harvesting in the morning after the dew dries is the best time for many crops. See table 7.7 for more rough

TABLE 7.7. When to harvest.

What	Ideal Harvest Times
Roots	Usually when dormant; fall, winter, spring. Peak potency for medicinals usually occurs in fall. Some edibles taste better after freezing during winter.
Shoots	Spring, as rising out of the ground, before leaves unfurl. Harvest after dew dries, before heat of day.
Greens & Leaves	Harvest after dew dries, before heat of day. However, recent research indicates that greens store longer when harvested late in the day. *Edibles*: Perennial greens usually taste best in spring and early summer. You can harvest some plants' growing tips all season (e.g., nettles) or cut back plants for fresh growth. *Medicinals*: Peak potency usually occurs just before flowering.
Flowers	Most have highest flavor, potency, and nutrition at peak scent shortly after opening. Harvest after dew dries, before heat of day.
Fruits	Highest vitamin-C content occurs in afternoon. Ripe fruits usually separate easily from the plant; show proper color; feel firm but yielding; and taste excellent. Taste-testing will teach you the look and feel of ripe fruits. Pick some fruits slightly or very unripe and allow to soften (pawpaw, pears, persimmon). Never eat a persimmon until fully softened! Beware of bruising fruits after picking.
Nuts	Harvest promptly upon maturity. Shake out of trees or gather from ground when they fall. Some nuts mature before husks or burs, so picking can thwart squirrels (e.g., chestnut). Research proper handling and storage to prevent fungal decay after harvest. Most should be husked or hulled promptly, then cured by air-drying to prevent spoilage and improve flavor. Store under proper conditions.
Seeds	Most seeds ripen at about 40% moisture content but get harvested at 20% or less moisture as the plant browns. If seed heads threaten to shatter when dry, harvest as maturing, before drying. Harvest during dry weather, after dew dries, before heat of day.
Teas	As for culinaries, leaves, flowers, or roots, as appropriate.
Culinaries	Virtually any time for immediate use. Flavors and oil content are often strongest in the morning, especially just before flowering. Mediterranean herbs are most flavorful during hot, dry weather.
Mushrooms	Harvest periods vary by species, weather conditions, inoculation timing, and substrate quality. Mushrooms mature and fade quickly, so check logs or beds frequently when they are producing. Allow cap to open fully. Harvest before insects or rot set in. Make sure you can identify your edible fungus and any similar potentially toxic species.

TABLE 7.8. Harvesting tools.

- harvest bucket, baskets, crates
- berry buckets to hang around neck
- wheelbarrow, cart, truck
- ladder, stepladder, stool
- long-handled fruit picker
- blueberry rake
- scissors, hand pruners, shears, sickle
- gloves for thorny crops
- sun hat
- friends, songs

guidelines. Table 7.8 lists some of the most important harvesting tools you might need.

Each crop has different indicators of ripeness, as well. It would be difficult to catalog all of these in one place given the diversity of crops we're interested in. As you learn your plants, you will learn how to tell when things are ready to harvest. Often this demands taste-testing for a period to see how the flavors develop along with the colors and the "feel" of a fruit, for example. Be careful, though. As stated earlier, elderberries are poisonous until ripe. Persimmons taste incredibly awful until completely soft, when they taste heavenly. Research your particular crops well in the abundant information resources available in our age. A number of books explain how to tell when a crop is ready to harvest in more detail than we can go into here.

Quality and Quantity

Yield quantities from various crops can vary dramatically from place to place and time to time. This results not only from variation in soils and weather, but also from planting associates, spacing, and management and maintenance practices. Nonetheless, table 7.9 offers some clue about what kinds of yields you may expect from selected forest garden plants with good fertility, weather, and management. In overly dense plantings like many we have seen, you can expect these figures to drop as a result of competition, shading, and the like. Even so, most forest gardeners have been amazed at the yields they get,

both in quantity and diversity. With proper spacing and sophisticated management, you may exceed the figures given. Hopefully, you've planned enough yield to meet your needs while leaving some for pests, diseases, and varmints, and accounting for bad weather. Then, even if you have a bad year, you should still come out okay. By overdesigning, you can also relax a bit about how intensively you have to manage pests and diseases.

Another way to reduce the intensity of pest and disease management is to lower your standards for fruit perfection. In Western countries we've gotten used to seeing perfect fruit; no bug holes or worms here, on account of the all the pesticides and other chemicals we pour onto the land. So what if an apple has a little scab? It doesn't make the fruit less tasty or nutritious. If there's a worm in the fruit, plenty of edible flesh may still remain. If it came out of your own backyard, it's probably fresher and has more vitamins than many commercially grown products on the market. Changing our cultural biases is a form of work, but maybe we should consider it a viable option compared to at least some of the spraying, trapping, handpicking of pests, and so on.

Finally, yields in polyculture may decrease for a particular crop on a per-acre basis, perhaps even a per-plant basis. Let us remember to measure the yields of forest gardens as a whole rather than piecemeal. If we've done our homework well, and the theories discussed in volume 1 are correct, the total yield from the forest garden should be higher than the sum of yields from monoculture crops grown separately. Even if not, diverse yields provide critical insurance in the system. You can count on some crops yielding better under one season's conditions than other crops. The next year, under different conditions, different sets of crops will do well and poorly, but you're still more likely to get your needs met.

Getting Around While Harvesting

Most orchards have a grassy or bare-earth surface, which eases maintenance and harvesting operations.

TABLE 7.9. Approximate yields of selected forest garden fruits, nuts, and berries. Yields per plant vary by age, cultivar (cv.), and rootstock. Updated and expanded versions of this table with complete references are available at www.edibleforestgardens.com. *Sources: Smith, 1994; NNGA, 1979, among many others.*

Species Name	Common Name	Harvest Season	Approx. Yield per Plant
Actinidia arguta	hardy kiwi	fall	5–10 gal/20–40 l; 125 lb/57 kg
Actinidia kolomikta	superhardy kiwi	fall	5–10 gal/20–40 l; 125 lb/57 kg
Asimina triloba	pawpaw	Aug–Sep	1–3 bu/35–105 l; average 9 lb/4 kg at 5 years old
Carya illinoinensis	pecan	Oct–Jan	10-year-old trees: 50 lb/23 kg; 15–20-year-old trees: 75–100 lb/34–45 kg
Carya laciniosa	shellbark hickory	fall	10 bu/35 l (crops every two years)
Carya spp.	hickories	fall	best cvs. at 25 yrs old: 50–75 lb/23–34 kg
Castanea spp.	chestnuts	fall	20–40 lb/9–18 kg; up to 240 lb/109 kg
Corylus spp.	filberts, hazelnuts	late Aug–mid-Oct	20–25 lb/9–11 kg; up to 123 lb/58 kg
Cydonia oblonga	quince	Sep–Oct	1 bu/35 l; up to 220-330 lb/100–150 kg
Diospyros kaki	kaki persimmon	Sep–Oct	1–2 bu/35–70 l
Diospyros virginiana	American persimmon	Sep–Oct	1 bu/35 l; 25–100 lb/11–45 kg
Fragaria vesca 'Alpine'	alpine strawberry	Jun–Sep	0.25 pint/0.1 l
Fragaria x ananassa	garden strawberry	Jun–Jul, Jun–Sep	June bearing, day neutral: 1 pint/0.5 l
Juglans nigra	black walnut	Sep–Oct	trunk dia. <10 in/25 cm: 20 lb/9 kg; 15–26 in/38–66 cm: 47 lb/21 kg; >26 in/66 cm: 100 lb/45 kg; up to 160 lb/73 kg or more
Juglans regia	English walnut	late Aug–mid-Sep	8–10 lbs/4–5 kg at age 10; large trees: 6 bu/210 l
Malus pumila	apple	late Jul–late Oct	10–30 bu/350–1,060 l
Prunus armeniaca	apricot	Jul–Aug	dwarf: 1–2 bu/35–70 l; standard European cvs.: 3–4 bu/105–140 l
Prunus avium	sweet cherry	early–late Jul	dwarf: 0.75 bu/26 l; semidwarf: 1 bu/35 l; standard: 2 bu/70 l
Prunus cerasus	sour cherry	mid-Jul–early Aug	1–2 bu/35–70 l
Prunus domestica	European plum	Jul–Sep	dwarf: 0.5–1 bu/18–35 l; standard: 1–2 bu/35–70 l
Prunus dulcis	almond	late Aug–Oct	10–40 lb/5–18 kg
Prunus persica	peach	late Jul–early Sep	dwarf: 1–2 bu/35–70 l; standard: 2–3 bu/70–105 l
Prunus persica nucipersica	nectarine	late Jul–early Sep	dwarf: 1–3 bu/35–105 l; standard 3–5 bu/105–175 l
Prunus salicina	Japanese plum	Jul–Sep	dwarf: 0.5–1 bu/18–35 l; standard: 1–2 bu/35–70 l
Pyrus bretschneideris	Asian pear	Aug–early Oct	dwarf: ±1 bu/35 l; semidwarf: 1–2 bu/37–70 l; standard: 3–8 bu/105–280 l
Pyrus communis	pear	Aug–Oct	dwarf: ±1 bu/35 l; standard: 2–4 bu/70–140 l
Ribes hirtellum	smooth gooseberry	midsummer	4–6 qt/4–6 l
Ribes nigrum	black currants	midsummer	3–5 qt/3–5 l
Ribes silvestre	red currant	midsummer	3–5 qt/3–5 l
Ribes uva-crispa	gooseberry	midsummer	4–6 qt/4–6 l
Ribes x culverwellii	jostaberry	midsummer	4–6 qt/4–6 l
Rubus occidentalis	black raspberry	midsummer, fall	2–6 qt/2–6 l (everbearing: two crops)
Rubus x hybrids	blackberry	late summer	1–2 qt/1–2 l
Rubus x hybrids	boysenberry	late summer–fall	4–8 qt/4–8 l
Rubus x hybrids	dewberry	Jul–early Aug	2–4 qt/2–4 l
Rubus x hybrids	raspberry	midsummer, fall	2–6 qt/2–6 l (everbearing: two crops)
Sambucus canadensis	elderberry	early Aug–mid-Sep	12–15 lb/5–7 kg
Vaccinium angustifolium	lowbush blueberry	late summer–fall	3–8 qt/3–8 l
Vaccinium ashei	rabbiteye blueberry	late summer–fall	3–8 qt/3–8 l
Vaccinium corymbosum	highbush blueberry	late summer–fall	3–8 qt/3–8 l
Vitis labrusca	fox grape	mid-Aug–fall	10–15 lb/5–7 kg
Vitis rotundifolia	muscadine grape	late summer–fall	8–16 qt/8–15 l
Vitis vinifera	European grape	late summer–fall	10–15 lb/5–7 kg

In complex polycultures, getting around the garden while harvesting is likely to be a bit trickier. There will be herbaceous plants of all kinds all over, and perhaps some shrubs or vines here or there. These could make getting around with a ladder more challenging, for example, or finding a place to put down a box for the pears you're harvesting more difficult. Hopefully you've thought these things through ahead of time. If you plan it right, you could scythe or otherwise mow the work area around the trees before harvest season without damaging the herbs below. Perhaps these herbs are going dormant at the time, or perhaps they will get harvested first. This way you can maximize access without sacrificing multiple functions and mutual-support guilds.

Testing Tastes, Changing Diets, Putting Food By

When we start exploring the diversity of foods available in forest gardens, several things will happen. We'll find ourselves either enjoying or feeling challenged by the new flavors we have in our mouths; our bodies may react to the new foods in pleasant or unpleasant ways; and the way we cook and eat may change.

Many of the plants discussed in this book taste great. Some wild, or less-developed, foods have more intense, or just plain different, flavors than our cultured mouths find comfortable. They can have more bitter, pungent, sour, or astringent constituents and fewer sugars than the tamed and pampered foods we normally eat, or their flavors have more subtlety than we can detect. With our culture's addiction to refined sugars and the widespread use of artificial flavorings to make hamburgers taste more hamburger-like and chocolate more chocolatey, we've lost our ability to detect subtle nuances of gustatory experience. Our sense of what is sweet and what isn't is way out of whack. Fast food has to have strong flavors; we eat it so fast we don't chew it to release the food's deeper textures. If you do chew fast food thoroughly, it doesn't taste very good. On the contrary, chewing natural foods thoroughly usually releases more and more flavors.

Sometimes when eating one of the seemingly less delicious wildlings, what at first tastes somewhat bitter or astringent, or even just bland, becomes sweet the more you chew. If it doesn't become sweet, at least the initial taste usually dies down and other flavors come to the fore. Chewing familiarizes our bodies with a food, so we know whether to swallow it. Plant chemicals soak into the bloodstream, and our bodies respond. If we listen, we get a sense of yes or no. This is a great way to test a known edible plant for the first time. In our toxified world, many people have food allergies or other problems. Test new foods before swallowing to make sure you don't react negatively. *Always make sure, though, that you have identified it properly, know it to be an edible plant and plant part in the proper season, and have prepared it correctly.*

Make major dietary changes slowly. Many perennial greens and flowers taste quite satisfactory, and you'll need little adjustment. Add some new ones into your salads along with the usual lettuce and tomatoes. You can increase the proportion of new greens over time as you get used to them, going farther afield into more unusual flavors. You'll quickly be making salads exclusively from perennial vegetables without batting an eye.

For the most odd flavors or unusual foods, try one new thing at a time, perhaps, and pay attention to your body's response over the next few hours or day or so. Adding a whole mix of new foods at once can overwhelm your system and dissuade you from eating any of them again, even if it was only one of them that caused a problem. Some people, for example, get gassy after eating Jerusalem artichokes, while others eat them like there's no tomorrow with nary a hint of trouble. Whether and how you cook the harvest can make a big difference, too. The aforementioned elderberries don't taste that great raw, though they'd do in a pinch. But make them into jelly, juice, wine, or baked goods, and they're excellent.

Some flavors are simply unfamiliar. The British love their currants and gooseberries (*Ribes* spp.). In the United States these fruits are hardly known, and if they are, they aren't that popular. It's not that they taste bad, they're just different, and we all have our habits. Lovage (*Levisticum officinale*) has a very strong celery-parsley flavor that takes some getting used to. Once you're used to it, know how to use it, and prepare it properly, it's delightful. Don't use it like lettuce—it's too strong. Use the seeds like celery seed. The tender young leaves and stalks are fantastic in spring soups, particularly combined with one of any number of sorrels (*Oxyria digyna*, *Rumex* spp., or *Oxalis* spp.). You can cut lovage's hollow midsummer stalk for use as a straw. This is reputedly the best way to drink a Bloody Mary, but perhaps it would work well with pureed fresh tomato soup or gazpacho. If you're going to try something, commit to eating it more than once, and try different ways of doing it. First impressions aren't necessarily accurate.

As for changing our ways of cooking and eating, this comes down to having the right kitchen equipment and storage facilities and collecting and creating good recipes. All these topics are beyond the scope of this book (see appendix 7). Nevertheless, the abundant diversity produced by forest gardens provides plenty of opportunities to practice the fine arts of cooking, putting food by, and acting with generosity toward our fellow human beings. As Miranda Smith says in her excellent little book *Backyard Fruits and Berries*, "Friends and neighbors react very differently to a basket of strawberries than they do to offerings of extra tomatoes and zucchini."[8] The same is true of baskets of tree fruits, nuts, interesting vegetables, edible flowers, and fresh shiitake mushrooms!

Harvesting as Designed Disturbance
Harvesting disturbs some plants more than others, depending on what you harvest, how intensively you harvest, and when. Picking leaves obviously can set back plant performance significantly, usu-

ally much more than harvesting fruit or flowers. Digging root crops requires disturbing the soil and plants in a whole patch, or at least spots within a patch. This sets up a successional dynamic that needs consideration. In most cases, gathering the yield alters the performance primarily or only of the plant you're cropping, though it may alter the performance of neighboring plants as well. Let's think through some implications and strategies.

Leaf and stem harvesting reduces a plant's ability to gather energy, and hence its ability to grow and compete. It may set a plant back in the successional marathon, allowing others to take the lead and direct the successional sequence. Intensive harvesting may spur growth of new or neighboring plants by giving them more sun or water or open up sites for weeds to establish. Some crops can respond to cutting quickly, barely skipping a beat. Such fast-recovering plants include mints (*Mentha* spp.), comfreys (*Symphytum* spp.), and stinging nettle (*Urtica dioica*), for example. All these have extensive root systems they can draw upon to recover. Not all fast-recovering plants are equal, though. Rhubarb and asparagus both bounce back from their respective harvesting regimes, but asparagus is a weaker competitor than rhubarb and can't take as much abuse without losing steam for the long haul. Perhaps the size of their respective root systems has something to do with this, as might their foliage architecture and density. In addition, some fast-recovering plants recover via self-sowing because they have adapted to frequent disturbance. Miner's lettuce (*Montia perfoliata*) and Johnny-jump-ups (*Viola tricolor*) are perfect examples. Notice, though, that most of the above species are sun-loving plants.

Most woodland plants have less resilience in the face of leaf and stem harvesting. They tend to grow more slowly and often have smaller root systems simply because they have adapted to sites with less light available. We cannot crop these species as intensively without consequences we might not like. Ramps have a short growing season, and each plant puts out only two leaves each year. We usually harvest only one leaf off each plant so it can still store energy for next year and produce flowers and seed. Our patches of ramps are too small and too young to determine whether this is the best harvesting strategy, but so far, so good. Perhaps we should be harvesting patches more heavily every other year, giving them a rest in between to gather strength. Only time and experimentation will tell. Similarly, the woodland plants rosy bells (*Streptopus roseus*), twisted stalk (*Streptopus amplexifolius*), and sessile bellwort (*Uvularia sessilifolia*) may establish slowly and recover slowly from the harvesting of their small asparagus-like shoots in spring. Under garden conditions they will probably build more reserves and recover more quickly. We have yet to try it and see.

Root crops are sometimes a whole different story. Unlike leaf harvesting, plucking roots can take away all or most of the dormant plant, leaving little or nothing behind to replace it. Root harvesting also disturbs the soil, increasing the possibilities of weed problems. For fast-growing plants with multiple tubers such as Jerusalem artichoke (*Helianthus tuberosus*), groundnut (*Apios americana*), and Chinese artichoke (*Stachys affinis*), this is of little consequence. It is easy to leave behind some tubers to grow for the following year. The slowest growers, such as the woodland plants ginseng (*Panax quinquefolius*), goldenseal (*Hydrastis canadensis*), and Indian cucumber root (*Medeola virginiana*), will have the most weed-control issues, not to mention reestablishment challenges. These plants do not readily self-propagate and need help if harvested intensively. As for woodland leaf crops, lower rates of harvest are appropriate, along with facilitated propagation.

The effects of harvesting on neighboring plants and successional sequencing is hard to predict without specific circumstances in front of us, and even then it's tricky. Certainly when harvesting leaf or root crops we must be mindful of the possibility of providing openings for unwanted plants to establish in. When gathering roots, fruits, or flowers, we interrupt the possibility of the plant self-propagating and so must propagate the plant ourselves. There would seem little way around these impacts of our activities, except by wisely limiting ourselves and supporting the plants' growth and propagation by how we harvest: leaving the strongest individuals to set seed or send out runners; replanting a portion of the tubers we dig; and cutting leaves and flowers just enough for our needs, while leaving enough for the plant to take care of itself. If we're willing to go beyond such self-limitation by fertilizing, weeding, watering, and so on, we should measure that additional work against the additional yield we achieve. Are we simply acting reflexively, or are we thinking things through, testing ideas, and discovering the truth? The extra work may not be worth it in the long run. Again, only playing with it will tell for our own particular circumstances at a given time. Even if we come full circle back to a more intensive maintenance approach, we will be smarter for it, and probably will do a better job of it for having taken the journey.

COEVOLUTION: THE FUTURE OF FOREST GARDENING

I had a vision of mini-forests in millions of back-gardens.

—Robert Hart

Never can we garden in isolation. Even when we think we're disconnected from society, from its ills and its benefits, we get proven wrong. Our neighbor's actions affect our air, our water, our soil—whether it's our neighbor next door or our neighbor across the ocean. The plants, microbes, insects, birds, amphibians, and reptiles with whom we share our gardens know few or no bounds. We need them, and they need us. We're all in this together.

How we garden is a reflection of our worldview. When we acknowledge our interdependence at a deep level, it changes that worldview. The information this book provides should help you understand that interdependence in a more grounded and sophisticated fashion than you did before. Designing your forest garden using the involved process described here, or even a scaled-back version of that process, should help you recognize specific ways that interdependence manifests in your garden, and in your life. So begins, or continues, your own evolution as a human being, as a gardener, as a designer, as an ecologist. That personal evolution must be ongoing if you are to guide your forest garden, and for it to guide you, to a higher and clearer realization of that interdependence, of the mutual support and cooperation within and between species that is our birthright. This interdependence and that evolution lie at the heart of forest gardening.

At the same time, the plants and animals in our gardens will evolve, even if we simply go about our business and pay no attention to selecting and breeding them. Simply planting seeds in your garden and seeing which survive and thrive is itself a form of selection and breeding. We've heard it said that "if you aren't killing plants on a regular basis, you aren't learning anything." In that case, the plant species aren't evolving much either. Anything that survives and reproduces in your garden, and anything that dies, represents part of the evolutionary process. With a little more attention and intention, we can speed this evolution and direct it in ways that will greatly benefit ourselves, our species, and our garden companions. There's plenty of this work needed to take forest gardening closer to its true potential.

Personal evolution and plant evolution don't necessarily have to go together, but imagine if they do happen at the same time, in a deep and conscious way. They will feed on each other, support each other, build and grow and change in ways we could never predict. That is coevolution, the plants changing us and us changing the plants; neither forcing the other to violate their intrinsic character, but each supporting the other to meet their needs

and express their purposes in the world, and finding themselves changed through the interaction. This silently powerful experience is a tangible expression of the beauty and cooperation manifested in mycorrhizas, for example, and in a thousand other interactions between beings acting according to their true nature.

Such human-plant coevolution can work just fine for each of us in our own individual gardens, but just imagine what could happen when we add the social and cultural dimension to it. With many of us playing, the interchange will occur that much faster. Not only can we learn how to forest-garden better when we share information, but we can cross-fertilize in more ways than one, trading experiences, strength, hope, labor and plants, and stories and songs. If we change our worldview deeply, at the core, and find ways to build that experience in others through a tangible physical activity that is fun, healthy, and life-promoting for all concerned, where could that go? What kind of cultural evolution is possible? How can we get there?

PERSONAL EVOLUTION: LEARNING AND GROWTH

> Except as ye become like little children, ye shall not enter the Kingdom of Heaven.
>
> —MATTHEW 18:3

Children, by their very nature, learn and grow all the time. Not only that, but they learn by playing. Sometimes they organize their play, while other times they play freely, roaming the realms of their senses and imagination. Despite the intensely organized approach to design and management taken in this book, you are each free to play with what this book presents in whatever way works for you. Each of us has our own ways of learning, our unique background, perspectives, questions, and dreams. We hope the organization and detail presented support you in choosing what you need to do in your way. The few simple ideas that follow may contribute to your own learning process.

Observation

Paying attention is a foundational skill and learning process. The observation exercises and agendas presented for site analysis and assessment (chapter 3) and monitoring (earlier this chapter) will certainly add to your learning and growth. The question we would ask here, though, is "What does what you observe in the forest garden tell you about yourself?" This question applies at a very practical level, in terms of how your behavior affects the plants and animals in the garden and the successional path of the ecosystem you have cocreated. It also applies at a more fundamental level. If you can see how each living thing in the garden acts according to its true nature, then where does the anger and hatred toward pests and diseases or toward "invasive" plants come from? If we can see this wide diversity, and how these diverse life forms paradoxically bind themselves together into a functional system by being true to themselves, what does that mean about our own assumptions concerning how we relate to other humans, or even animals? There are many deep lessons here.

The challenge in all of this is that "we see things not as they are, we see things as we are."[9] What do we see reflected back to us in the mirror of the garden? Are you willing to own all the things you see as yourself? If not, which ones will you own, and which will you not? Why?

Clearly the kind of self-observation we are talking about here is not a common thing in our culture. Nor is it absolutely necessary to forest gardening. We would submit, however, that without this kind of self-reflection we will miss the opportunity the forest garden offers us to see ourselves whole, as well as to learn how to let the garden manage itself. Our habitual intervention in business that is not ours is hard to see, but the garden can help us see these habits. If we watch ourselves and our actions and measure the consequences with skillful observation, we can reduce our workload, receive our yields, offer our thanks and our caring back, and enjoy the quiet adventure of the lives within and around us.

Documentation

On a more technical level, we can record our observations of the garden in ways that will assist our learning over long time periods. Memory is less than accurate. Causes and effects play out over multiple time frames. Just how old is that tree now? Which variety was the one that tasted so good last year? What were our intentions for this patch when we planted it six years ago? Plans, goals, sketches, drawings, journal notes, photographs—these and other records are invaluable tools in recollecting the past so you can make decisions for the future.

You could take pictures from the same vantage point each year so you can catalog the growth of the garden. You could photograph particular polyculture patches as they develop through the season or the years so you can better observe plant dynamics. A graph-paper sketch plan of the "as planted" beds or patches can form the basis for similar sketches over several years showing how the planting pattern has evolved. As mentioned already, regular journal entries with rainfall and temperature readings, dates of harvest, flowering times, and random observations and events are fun to read in later years and can help you solve mysteries. They also provide a simple structure to get you noticing and taking in your observations, as well as pondering them "out loud" on the page. You could also keep a large-format calendar on the wall to note some of the basic weather data or other time-sensitive information. Any or all of these can be fun and interesting, and that's fine, but they are most useful when you have a clear idea of why you want the information so you can design your documentation to help you answer specific questions.

Testing Theories

If you want to get really serious about this field, you can develop theories to test or questions to answer and organize yourself to follow through on them.

Backyard and on-farm research has a long and honored history in the world. It can be fun, too. You could find a local high school teacher or college professor to help you develop your theory or question and develop a method to research it. You might even be able to get money for the project and the equipment needed to really find out what's going on.

Think about replications of the same polyculture design with different management regimes, or variations on polyculture mixtures to see what grows best together, and how the combinations affect yields of useful products. Which combinations overyield, and which don't? Study insect populations in your garden. Where are they when? What species come to which nectary flowers, and what pests do they parasitize or eat? How does that change when you alter the flower populations in the garden by cutting some, but not others? How many of which insects overwinter under, on, in, or around various plants? How many rodents have you got living there, from which species? What happens to yields of a crop or a polyculture when you stop a certain maintenance practice in one part of the garden, but keep doing it in another? How long does it take for the soil to warm up in spring under different mulches compared to under various ground covers? If you're willing to dig up some of your plants, it would be really neat to see some documentation of the root patterns of various forest garden plants under various forest garden conditions. Are the plants partitioning the soil profile or not?

The possibilities are endless. Some of us are rubbing our hands in anticipation of this kind of play. Some of us aren't.

Creative Play

"Who cares about all that scientific stuff anyway? I just want a beautiful, productive landscape. I don't care whether it yields more or less, really, I just want the joy of playing in the forest garden and eating its fruits, following my fancy and my inspiration." If that sounds like you, great! Have fun. Nobody says it has to be all technical and exact. You can still learn

from or simply just enjoy your garden by playing with it, finding plant combinations that are pleasing to your eye and palate, as well as being low-maintenance. There is much to be said for the free-form, intuitive way of gardening. This is how Robert Hart did his. When we visited him and his garden, he said to us over and over, "I don't know much about plants." Not in his head anyway. But his intuitive sense guided him to create a garden so beautiful that Dave cried when he first walked into it. Robert loved his garden, and it fed him well. Though his garden wasn't technically perfect, it fulfilled its purposes for him, and that's what mattered most.

So if creative play and intuitive flow are your style, go with that. Use this book as a reference when you have a question or an observation you want background on. We need information sometimes to help our intuitions become clear or to manifest our intuitions in the world with a decent level of skill. When we follow that inner guidance, listen to that inner voice, and pay attention to those visions, we never know what might come out. For Robert, it was a vision of miniforests in millions of backyards. If he hadn't paid attention and followed through, even though he "didn't know much about plants," where would we be now? With a little more information in your hands, how far can you go?

SELECTING AND BREEDING SPECIES

One of the current limitations to forest gardening is the paucity of plants selected and bred for this way of gardening *relative to the potential*. Don't get us wrong: many good plants already exist (see "Forest Gardening's Top 100 Species" in volume 1, appendix 1). It's just that the potential is so much greater, and gaps in the fabric of good multipurpose plants need filling. For example, the ramp (*Allium tricoccum*) is already elegantly suited to life in polycultures, *and* it is a mighty tasty plant. Wild ginger (*Asarum canadense*), another native shade-tolerant edible, is also well suited to life in polycultures. It makes a beautiful ground cover, but its roots could use significant flavor improvement. The story is similar for many other species. However, given the structure of the nursery and landscape industries, corporate dominance of research and breeding institutions (with their tunnel-vision focus on genetic engineering), and the novelty of forest gardening, we can't expect the industry to do all this plant development for us. As they say, we are the ones we've been waiting for. Indeed, through the vast majority of human history, farmers and gardeners did all the plant breeding.

We can't cover the topic of plant breeding and selection in great detail here. We can, however, offer pointers and stimulate your sense of the potential for you (yes, you) to take part in this fun and fascinating endeavor. Even if you don't think you could ever be a plant breeder, the fact is that just by gardening you participate in this evolution. Once you realize that, and how it works, you can more consciously direct plant development as you go about your business. At the very least you can keep your eyes peeled and your tongue testing for better plants that may cross your path.

How Selection and Breeding Work

Dave once lived in a small "solar cabin" in New Hampshire whose whole south face consisted of a greenhouse providing both heat and food to its occupant. You might say that the ratio of glass area to interior air volume was a bit out of whack. On a sunny day in February when it was below zero outside, the cabin could top 100°F (38°C) if he didn't leave a window open when he went to work. Needless to say, the greenhouse environment was kind of intense.

Most of us know that lettuce tends to go bitter when the weather turns hot. In the time Dave lived in that cabin, he developed a lettuce variety that could produce sweet leaves over a long harvest season in the greenhouse's desert conditions. Starting with Buttercrunch as the base variety, Dave grew successive generations from seed, letting the plants that resisted the heat best cross-pollinate and continue on to the next generation. In two

years of year-round development, he doubled the nonbitter productive life of the plants. He called it "Cabin Crunch" lettuce. Too bad he let the seed go after he moved out. It was good stuff.

The above example represents both selection and breeding. Selection is a process of choosing plants with desirable traits from among a range of plants available to you. Breeding involves choosing the parents you want to cross-fertilize, expecting that some of their offspring will have the desirable traits of both parents. Breeding work is always followed by selection. Selection does not have to involve breeding, at least not by you—and it can happen anywhere you encounter plants, not just in your garden.

Genetic change takes place in plant species when sexual reproduction occurs. Clearly, annuals can evolve fairly quickly. Perennials take more time to breed because they don't always flower their first year, and it may take several growing seasons to evaluate all their characteristics. Still, in a relatively short period we can shift the genetic character of an herbaceous plant in a chosen direction by selecting parents, cross-pollinating them, planting the seed, and selecting from among the resulting plants those that best meet our criteria. Anyone with a reasonable level of intelligence can do this. It just takes persistence, commitment, clear goals, and good observation. You have to be willing to grow plants from seed, too, but for most perennial herbs, at least, this is little problem. For woodies it may take special procedures and more time, but we can still speed things up. The advantage perennials have, though, is that once a variety has been selected or developed, it is easy to propagate and maintain, whereas annuals take more work in that regard.

We once heard a story of some folks developing tree crops, we believe it was hazelnuts, using a mass-selection strategy that went something like this. First, they take seed from multiple parents and sow it thickly in a large bed, resulting in thousands of seedlings in a relatively small area. After one or two growing seasons, the bed is a tangle of heavily competing plants. Many individuals die under these conditions, leaving the strongest behind. They then weed out the weaker individuals, leaving the stronger at a reasonable spacing for the next phase. Some of the remaining plants grow faster than the rest, and more thinnings occur every year or two. When the plants begin bearing, the breeders evaluate their nut size, yield, and flavor. They cut out some plants, cross-pollinate others, and start the process over again. They also clonally (asexually) propagate some for further evaluation. This process greatly speeds the evaluation of many seedlings. The early going selects for strong germination, stress and disease resistance, vigorous growth, and competitiveness. The later cullings select for bearing at an early age or for nut size, quality, and yield. They were doing this work to create a *whole population* of developed hazelnuts—not just a few varieties. In this way, they would have genetic diversity in their main crop, while still achieving the yields they desired. We could use a similar process for herbaceous perennials.

On the other hand, not everyone who wants to select and breed plants wants to work that intensively on it. Those of you with a more idle interest can play a role, too, with less work, as long as you have room to spare and like to experiment a bit. In fact, all gardeners select plants without quite realizing it, and some even breed them unconsciously.

Selection the Easy Way

The simple act of planting plants in our gardens and seeing which survive, which thrive, and which we prefer is itself a process of selection. If you start a bunch of good King Henry plants from seed, transplant them all into your garden, and some don't make it, selection has occurred. When plants begin bearing or enter maturity, we all usually evaluate the plants based on what we want out of them. Sometimes we get rid of plants we don't like. We favor the plants we do like, often propagating them to increase their population—or they propagate on their own. This is all plant selection in a basic, and passive, sense. Active selection takes several forms:

- evaluating and selecting varieties that have already been developed that best fit your purposes and your site;
- selecting among seedlings we buy or grow those that have the best characteristics and propagating them; and
- evaluating and selecting wild plants for propagation based on their characteristics and usefulness.

Evaluating and selecting existing cultivars is selection only in the sense of choosing what works best for us, not in terms of improving what is available in cultivation. We could stand to do quite a bit of work in this way, however. Which named yarrow cultivars work best as insectaries and dynamic accumulators? Which apple varieties have the best-tasting flowers, as well as fruit? Which maypop (*Passiflora incarnata*) varieties flower best and produce the most fruit? It would be good to answer questions such as these, and more. The Seed Savers Exchange is a great source for finding heirloom and rare seeds and plant material that you might want to try out, as are the Northern Nut Growers Association (NNGA) and the North American Fruit Explorers (NAFEX; see appendix 7).

To turn this selection process into a means of finding a new plant variety that exhibits specific characteristics, you have to add more variation to the mix, which means sexual reproduction. We therefore need to plant or select from among seedlings. So, if you're interested in selecting improved varieties, either grow plants from seed yourself or buy seedlings someone else has germinated. Evaluate the seedlings based on your selection criteria. Cuttings, tissue culture, division, layering, and every other propagation technique result in genetically uniform plants. We need and want the diversity of sexually propagated material, both as a base for selection and to help guard against diseases and pests in our garden.

Selection also includes testing fruits of wild juneberries (*Amelanchier* spp.) in the woods of your

region, for example, and propagating those that
have the best flavor or other characteristics. Many
new plant varieties have been found and named in
this manner. For woody crops, especially native
fruit and nut trees, this is one of the fastest ways to
improve the stock we have available for cultivation.
Breeding and evaluating woody crops takes
decades. Meanwhile, the genetic diversity of temperate tree species is quite high. Only a tiny percentage of this diversity has been evaluated. Many
of the best varieties of bur oak, northern pecan,
American persimmon, and pawpaw, for example,
are nothing more than grafted selections of unusually good wild plants. Taste-testing native fruits and
evaluating the size, crackability, and flavor of native
nuts are great fun and could result in a real find.
Just make sure you properly identify what you're
eating before taking a bite! If you want to do this
kind of work with other like-minded people, get in
touch with either NNGA or NAFEX, which
organize field trips to do just this every year.

Basic Breeding

We cannot call the above selection processes
breeding unless we take the selected plants, intentionally cross-fertilize them, plant the seedlings,
and continue the process. Obviously breeding is
more work. It's not as difficult as it might seem,
though, at least for some crops. In her indispensable book *Breed Your Own Vegetable Varieties*, Carol
Deppe explains the whole process in simple, understandable terms. She includes information on
domesticating wild edibles and breeding perennial
vegetables. The book also includes charts with pollination and other key breeding information on
several hundred plant species. If you're interested in
breeding vegetables and flowers, this is the place to
go for information. If you want to breed woody
crops, get in touch with NNGA and NAFEX.

Characteristics to Select and Breed For

The plant characteristics we desire for forest gardening differ in significant ways from those most

people breed into plants. Certainly, we seek plants
with high yields of tasty fruits and nuts, solid cold
hardiness, and good pest and disease resistance like
everyone else. We also want plants that can produce
those yields in at least partial shade, grow well in
polycultures, attract beneficial insects better than
the average plant, and so on (table 7.10). Some of
these characteristics are things most breeders
haven't even thought of, much less have a desire to
breed for. Who but a forest gardener would be
interested in developing a densely growing prostrate perennial legume with sweet pods, or a sweet
cicely (*Myrrhis odorata*) with maximum nectar production for beneficials? Low-maintenance perennial crops are not on the radar screen of most
professional breeders. Luckily, there are notable
exceptions, including recent work to domesticate
pawpaws and groundnuts.

Edible species grown in forest gardens tend to
fall in the following categories:

- "Overbred" crops that, at least in our climate,
  are highly dependent on humans. Peaches and
  apples, for example, require a great deal of
  attention to grow successfully. For the forest
  garden, we prefer either resistant varieties of
  apple and peach or species with less susceptibility. Back-crossing such species to wilder
  strains might make some sense.
- Domesticated low-maintenance species that make
  excellent main crops for forest gardens. Most of
  the food plants listed in "Forest Gardening's Top
  100 Species" (volume 1, appendix 1) fall in this
  category. Crops such as gooseberries and pears
  yield well, but without nearly as much work as
  the overbred species. This group also includes
  crops that, while somewhat domesticated, retain
  much of their feral nature, like Jerusalem artichokes, pawpaws, American persimmons, and
  hardy kiwis. This group of plants still could use
  breeding and selection for improved and diversified flavors, better production in shade, more variation in timing of harvest, storability, and so on.

TABLE 7.10. Qualities and characteristics that we want to enhance through selection and breeding.

- Higher yields in partial and full shade for partially or fully developed crops (e.g., good King Henry, Turkish rocket, sorrels, raspberries, blueberries).
- Improved flavor, nutrition, or yield of undeveloped crops (e.g., maypop [*Passiflora incarnata*], pawpaw, persimmon, eastern juneberries, running serviceberry, native hickories, oaks).
- Disease and pest resistance.
- Hardiness, early ripening, and late flowering for northern areas (e.g., hardier persimmons and pawpaws; late-flowering almonds and apricots; early-ripening pecans).
- Sociability in polycultures: selecting and breeding plant groups to enhance niche separation and reduce competition.
- Useful habits and behaviors, such as:
  - perennialism in developed annual crops (e.g., broccoli and other Brassicaceae, sunflowers, peas and beans);
  - dwarfing and prostrate forms of crops to aid multilayer plantings (e.g., low-growing nitrogen fixers, dynamic accumulators, and insectary plants; dwarf nut trees; improved hardiness, flavor, and yield in ground-covering raspberries);
  - strongly competitive ground covers (e.g., a densely ground-covering strawberry would be great);
  - more or less suckering habit (e.g., less or nonsuckering pawpaw, black locust, *Eleagnus*);
  - seedlessness or sterility in especially useful opportunist species (e.g., goumi and other *Eleagnus*, sea buckthorn).
- Increased or varied time of harvest (e.g., earlier- and later-fruiting varieties of any crop; there is a nonflowering sorrel species that you can harvest all season).
- Nectary attractiveness and flowering times (e.g., maximum nectar production; we also especially need early-season and long-season bloomers).
- Improved ability to accumulate nutrients from deeper soil layers.
- Beauty: color, form, flower size, and length of bloom.

- Finally, a large number of forest garden plants have received little or no breeding attention. Some, like ramps and ostrich fern, are already fine foods. Many others, however, are excellent raw material but have too strong a flavor for most people, such as Turkish rocket (*Bunias orientalis*), or are not very productive, like Indian cucumber root (*Medeola virginiana*).

Breeders have particularly neglected herbaceous perennial crops in general. We should place a high priority on developing cold-hardy perennial brassicas—there are many delicious perennial varieties, but few are hardy even in zone 7 (crossing with hardier biennial kales should do the trick). In other cases, improved varieties exist but are hard to come by, such as skirret plants (*Sium sisarum*) with tender roots.

Another intriguing prospect is breeding plants for improved function. Ground covers have received some attention; we know that certain varieties within a species make better ground covers by growing at a higher density and with a more prostrate habit, for example. But there is much more to do, especially in selecting ground covers for edibility and multifunctionality. We also know that some legume varieties fix more nitrogen than their species in general, so we should be able to develop improved nitrogen fixation for many species. The same may be true for dynamic accumulators. Nectary plants show special promise in this regard. Ornamental-flower breeders can greatly alter flowering periods—earlier, later, shorter, longer. We also know that ornamental breeding tends to decrease the amount of useful nectar in flowers. What if we selected in the opposite direction, for increased nectar, and for longer flowering periods? Perhaps we could create a suite of "supernectary" plants.

Perhaps one of the most interesting and challenging pieces of this is to consider breeding plants in a polyculture context. Most plants are bred and selected when growing in monoculture and for monoculture. If we want our plants to perform well in polycultures and to maximize the yields and performance of those polycultures, we should breed the plants in polycultures, or at least breed them for characteristics that will suit them to polyculture performance. Do some individuals of a species tend to grow more taprooted or shallow-rooted than others? Might we select for these traits to aid us in designing polycultures that partition the soil profile and minimize competition? We could select and breed plants that grow taller or shorter, so they mix more effectively with others of complementary architecture, or trees that have thinner canopies. Selecting and breeding for higher yields in polyculture is an obvious task. Perhaps we could coax some of the useful opportunists to put more of their "invasive" vigor into producing edible fruit, and less into dispersion and expansion? Native American breeding of corn, beans, and squash successfully achieved such polycultural objectives in the past. Let us do such work again, with a wider array of plants and a broader set of goals.

So, you can see we have our work cut out for us. The needs are there, and the plants are out there evolving away. All it will take is for a bunch of us to engage in the serious play of selecting and breeding the plants we're looking for, if they don't already exist—that, and sharing our results through organizations like the Seed Savers Exchange, the Northern Nut Growers Association, and North American Fruit Explorers. Within a few decades of work by a network of amateur gardeners, we can dramatically increase the potential of forest gardening to provide for our needs in a sustainable fashion. Your experiments, or even just your keen eyes and testing tongue, can and will make a significant difference in the development of this new form of food production—as long as we spread the fruits of our labors.

SEEDS ON THE WIND

The forest garden is far more than a system for supplying mankind's material needs.

—ROBERT HART

When the European colonists came to North America, they brought with them a large number of plants foreign to this land. Their way of making a living—their cultural paradigm—included these plants from back home: how they grew them; how they cooked, stored, and ate them; and how they used them for fuel, fiber, fodder, and farmaceuticals. This cultural paradigm had land-use implica-

tions. They created the conditions needed for these plants to grow, cutting down forests and plowing the soil because that was what they knew how to do to survive. Once the land was modified, many of their plants naturalized, reproducing and spreading on their own. These plants were seeds on the wind, spreading the culture of Europe across the North American continent.

Plants influence the development of culture. Culture influences the development of landscapes, and plant evolution, too. As we grow, use, and further develop forest garden plants, our culture will change. So will the landscapes around our habitations. Our thoughts and feelings will change. Our sense of who we are will change, of what is right and wrong, of our place in the scheme of things. The forest garden is far more than a system for supplying our material needs.

So far we have discussed coevolution on a small scale, with individual people and plants. How can we take that coevolution to the next level? How can a larger context support and encourage our own evolution and that of our plants and our gardens? How can forest gardening support and encourage the evolution of our culture to a more ecologically harmonious way of living? How can we, and our plants, become seeds on the wind, reproducing and spreading a new culture across the face of the temperate parts of the planet?

Cross-Fertilizing and Propagating

As you go about creating and managing your forest garden, don't forget to reach out to other people. If our plants are not isolated entities in space and time, disconnected from the world around them, then neither are we. We need our own mutual-support and resource-sharing guilds in society to help us become better forest gardeners. The more of us there are out there doing this kind of thing, the better off we'll all be. How can we cross-fertilize with others and propagate the forest garden idea?

Formal gardener networks and support structures certainly apply to this question to at least some degree. You can get answers to many basic questions about growing fruits and nuts from your state's cooperative extension service. Organic farming and gardening organizations have sprung up all over the place, and they are usually full of helpful and interesting people with wide experience. Garden clubs, botanical gardens, botany expeditions, seminars, and conferences offer opportunities to learn from others and to share what you're trying and learning with them. Visit other people's gardens to see what they have going.

If you want to know what a plant that you're considering bringing to your garden looks like, it's best to see it in the flesh. Botanic gardens are great for this purpose, but some native species aren't commonly found in cultivation. Contact native plant societies or botanists from local colleges who might know where to find it. Get together with friends and visit some old-growth forest or other healthy habitat in your region. This has been invaluable to us, for we have met a number of plants that we hadn't seen before by doing this. It has helped us understand forest ecology better, too.

One great way to get the heavy lifting (or digging) done early in your forest gardening life is to form a "worknet." A worknet is a network of people who commit to spending a day at each other's homes to do together what each would otherwise have to do alone. We each get repaid for our time at everyone else's place when they show up at our place to clear a planting site, dig holes and plant, or mulch like heck. Dave once had as many as thirty people involved in a worknet at his place shingling the house, building terraces, planting apple trees, and having a grand old time. In return he helped one friend prune her orchard, mulched someone else's garden, and moved rocks to make way for a garden at a third site, among other things. This worknet helped build his network of friends. He got to share his skills and knowledge with others and to learn from them in turn. It's also fun to help build a number of gardens from the ground up that you can watch develop over time.

Share plants with other gardeners. Most gardeners are inherently generous. When we have surplus, we share it with others, even if it isn't really surplus. Perennial plants support this by multiplying themselves in numerous ways and requiring division every so often. When you have too many forest garden plants around, start giving them away. As long as they aren't opportunist species, you may be starting someone on a new career that could change his or her life. If you have enough plants propagating themselves, you could start a small nursery. We need nurseries where people can get access to plants used specifically in forest gardening. There aren't many out there yet.

Once your own garden is going strong, open it up to other people. The neighborhood where Dave used to homestead had several open-house days over the years. These not only were fun but gave him contacts and brought people who could answer his questions, while he answered theirs and showed off his place. He had valuable plants given to him on more than one occasion and learned some neat things. People gave him gardening ideas that came in quite handy.

These forms of social cross-fertilization and idea propagation have supported our experiments with forest gardening and ecological design and have supported others in their experiments, too. As more of us engage in such activities, let us hope they support, deepen, and expand a shift in our culture's way of seeing the world.

Cultural Evolution, Cultural Revolution

The most essential challenge for humanity is to learn to eat from nature's bounty without destroying it in the process, to find our appropriate niche within nature.

—JUDITH SOULE AND JON PIPER,
Farming in Nature's Image

As we mimic forest ecology in our gardens, we learn at a visceral level the reality of the ecological principles that govern our lives. How can this not change us irrevocably? We are a species with significant power and authority over other living things. What is the role of a beneficial authority? Is it not to foster the growth, development, health, and well-being of those for whom and to whom we are responsible? When we intervene and attempt control, we bear the burden of maintaining that which we cannot fully understand. As we learn to interact with our gardens wisely, respectfully, and consciously, to let the gardens take care of their own business, perhaps we will be learning about our appropriate niche in nature. As we learn to mimic the forest in our gardens, and to find our appropriate niche there, perhaps we can learn to mimic the forest in our society, and our society will find its appropriate niche in nature. Such cultural evolution would truly be a cultural revolution.

Indeed, as David Perry said, "The community is a unique form of biological system in which the individuality of the parts . . . acts paradoxically to bind the system together."[10] How can we mimic in human society the mycorrhizas that sustain the forest, linking its members into a single functional unit? Neither the fungus nor the plant dominates the other. Each is true to its nature, doing what comes naturally. Each offers its particular talents for the benefit of the other, ensuring their mutual survival through mutual aid. Can we free ourselves from the culturally created and self-imposed limitations of monoculture mind so we can know ourselves truly for the first time? If we don't, how can our individuality act paradoxically to help us forge true human communities, built on mutual aid, mutual respect, and the functional interconnection of diverse, multifaceted beings?

Can we clear our eyes and see that cooperation is truly what holds ecosystems and societies together? Mycorrhizal links in the forest floor transform the relationship between two trees from competition to cooperation by assisting the sharing and distribution of scarce resources. What structures can we create that will induce the canopy dominants of our culture to share their abundant resources, through the lowest of the low, for the benefit of all society and, ultimately, themselves? Need we grab so much, once we learn to pluck the fruits of nature's bounty that she freely offers to us? We have created a "dog eat dog" world out of the belief that that's what the world is like. Can we not create a different world, if we but believe we can, and act in that knowledge and faith?

We are powerful beings in our glory, made in the Creator's image, if you will. The idea, the belief, the promise of low-maintenance abundance is waiting. Let us test that promise, shall we? It requires of us a paradigm shift, a transformation of our own consciousness. The metaphysics are out there in the Garden. So is dinner. Welcome to the adventure.

"Use your imagination constructively. An *idea*, a *small yard* and one tree may be made to produce astounding results."

—J. Russell Smith, *Tree Crops: A Permanent Agriculture*

1. Crawford, 2003, personal communication.
2. Crawford, 1999, page 38.
3. Martin Crawford, 2003, personal communication.
4. Martin Crawford, 2003, personal communication.
5. See Fukuoka, 1978.
6. Fukuoka, 1978, page 119.
7. Phillips, 1998, page 104.
8. Smith, 1994, page 66.
9. This quote came to Dave from a friend and is attributed to the Talmud. It has changed his life.
10. Perry, 1994, page 250.

EPILOGUE

A Story of Robert

He sat by his coal stove, knees shaking from age, or from cold. "Would you like some more black currant crumble?" he asked, a gleam in his eye, half a smile on his lips. Eric and I looked at each other askance, smiled knowingly, and silently groaned. I took a drink from my glass of water.

"No thanks, Robert," I said. "I've had my fill of jacket potatoes." Eric decided to be polite and humor the eighty-four-year-old gentleman with yet another helping. I remembered a quote from the *Let's Go Guide to Britain*: "English cooking, like the English climate, is a training for life's unavoidable hardships." My stomach ached. Very sweet baked beans over half of a half-baked potato didn't go down too well, even when heated a second time.

We sat in Church Stretton, Shropshire, England, on the evening of the fourth straight day of cold rain in September 1997. I was sick with a sore throat. Robert's "eco-house," a dark, cramped stone hut, was the only warm place around, but being there meant training ourselves for life's unavoidable hardships. Robert was a dedicated vegan who had little talent for cooking, and even if he did, he seemed to be getting past his ability to care for himself, or manage his dingy kitchen in the farmhouse across the terrace. Our accommodations were another little hut down below the garden. It was just big enough for the two of us to stretch out

on the floor side by side in our sleeping bags, with two hand-widths between us and room for our backpacks at our feet. At least the rain didn't come in much. We were thankful just to be there.

We had arrived in our rental car still giddy both from trying to learn British driving and from realizing our dream of coming to England to study forest gardens. The highlight of our trip: four days with Robert A. de J. Hart, author and visionary elder of the forest garden idea, originator of the oldest temperate-climate forest garden in the world. We were to interview Robert, study his garden, make the first accurate map of the garden that he or we knew of, and write a critique for publication in our book. We were determined to be clearheaded and hard-nosed, but fair; balanced, but no holds barred. We expected a gold mine of information.

When I first passed through the gate of Robert's garden, I cried. It was beautiful. Something hit me deep in my gut and opened my heart. After years of reading about these things, after having started my own forest garden only to lose it to divorce before it was fully born, and after more years trying to find a place to start over, here I was. These things were real. It looked just like a forest, but we could find so many food plants in it. Amazing.

By now, though, a different reality had set in. Steady rain had washed off whatever patina of glory I'd seen. As the patriarch of an idea spreading rapidly throughout Britain and gaining a foothold in other countries, Mr. Hart had become somewhat of a mythic figure made frail, and real, and more than a little quirky. I didn't think I had him on a pedestal, but even this jaded thirty-something-year-old ecological designer didn't expect to hear the world-renowned Mr. Hart exclaim, "I really don't know much about plants." He was serious. He never spoke the word *design* during our visit—it wasn't part of his usual vocabulary, much less one of his regular activities. It showed in his gardens.

Pears and apples grew so close together they were crooked and stunted in a forlorn attempt to get out of each other's way. The thicket of currants and gooseberries, among other things, made it difficult to get around in the garden on foot, much less with a wheelbarrow. Imagine trying to find the food to harvest in here? The dense shade and close vegetation, plus the humid, cool climate, made the garden interior rank and a near-perfect breeding ground for disease. The plant diversity seemed high at first glance, but in reality the species palette was rather limited. Nothing was labeled, and Robert couldn't remember the names of most of the varieties and some of the species he had planted over the years. As we mapped the garden, we began to see that there was little rhyme or reason for the placement of most of the plants we found growing in it. Robert said he had planted the garden "by intuition." It seemed more like chance to me.

As we spent more and more time with him I began to see that Robert had very clear ideals, a lot of determination, and little sense of practicality. One night I did Reiki healing work on him, as he seemed to be in pain much of the time. He asked me to stop at one point and reached down into his shirt to adjust something. I could feel the adjustment he made in the pit of *my* stomach as I heard a gurgle, followed by a sigh of relief. Mr. Hart explained that he had gotten a hernia forty years prior while working the farm but had refused medical treatment, aiming for a spiritual healing instead. It seemed most of his pain was due to this untreated wound in his abdomen. He had started his forest garden, dug the holes and planted the trees, with his intestines sloshing in and out of his stomach cavity.

I went through at least a half day of euphoria, and at least two days of depression. Was our whole mission and project a sham? Was this nutty professor onto something? Or were he and I and all the urbanite ecology buffs too committed to our ideals and too far removed from practical reality to know the difference? If this really worked, why had no one thought of it before? Self-doubt tore at me as sharply as my ragged throat. It kept raining and it stayed cold.

What slowly dawned on me through the fog of flu and indigestion, however, was the ingenuity behind Robert's humble idea. Here was a man who knew "nothing" about horticulture, an inveterate idealist and a dreamer at heart, who had an insight that made sense, and then went about making almost all the mistakes you could make in creating a forest garden. And it still worked. Eighteen years later, Robert had eaten out of his garden, sold fruits and vegetables out of his garden, and gotten tremendous joy out of his garden. He even spawned a movement and became world-famous from his crazy 40-foot by 80-foot plot of ground. The gift of this simple philosopher-fool is an idea that may be almost foolproof. It's up to us to learn from Robert's genius and from his mistakes, and to make it work better than Robert could ever have imagined.

FIGURE E.1. Robert Hart—idealist, dreamer, visionary philosopher, and horticulturist for the love of it—in his forest garden, September 1997. *Photo by Dave Jacke.*

APPENDICES: DETAILED TABLE OF CONTENTS

Introduction to the Appendices

The two volumes of this book have covered the vision, ecology, design, establishment, and management of forest gardens. In the following seven appendices we provide information on critical component parts—that is, plant, mushroom, and animal species that you will assemble in your design. We also offer a bit of climate data and a compendium on publications, organizations, and suppliers of tools, organisms, and materials that are useful for forest gardeners. This introduction gives you an overview of what the appendices contain, explains how we chose the plant and mushrooms species, and makes a few suggestions for how to use what these pages hold in store. We also discuss the taxonomic references used for this book.

OVERVIEW

The Plant Species Matrix (appendix 1) summarizes niche information on 626 plant species and varieties in table form, arranged by Latin name. Here you can search for the right species for your design. You can develop species palettes by identifying plants suited to your climate, soils, and levels of sunlight. In addition to the wide range of information about the tolerances, preferences, behavior, and architecture of plants, the matrix will tell you about the functions and uses of plants. The Plant Species Matrix also provides information on the form and habit of plants to help you design effective guilds and polycultures. Finally, the matrix notes potential nuisances and lets you know whether you should

check out the "Poisonous Plants" table (appendix 4) for more information on possible toxicity.

The species-by-use tables (appendix 2) and species-by-function tables (appendix 3) organize additional information on the plant species that appear in the matrix (and a few others) and allow access to the plant data from the entry point of uses and functions instead of plant species. The twelve species-by-use tables in appendix 2 relate to species characteristics directly useful to humans, including edible fruits, nuts, leaves, roots, and tea and culinary plants; superfoods and medicinals; and coppicing species from Britain and North America. The "Edible Fruits and Berries" table, for example, provides information on the flavor and uses of edible fruits and berries, along with information on pollination requirements. Appendix 2 also includes tables on the niche characteristics of selected cultivable, edible mushrooms and on the estimated useful life spans of many of the woody crop species in the Plant Species Matrix.

The eight species-by-function tables in appendix 3 are similar to those in appendix 2, but they relate to ecosystem support functions, not direct human uses. These tables cover nitrogen fixers and their inoculants; dynamic accumulators; food, shelter, and nectar plants for beneficial insects and wildlife; ground covers; aromatic pest-confuser plants; and plants tolerant of or susceptible to juglone, the allelochemical that walnuts release to reduce competition from other species. The "Ground Covers" table, for example, lists density, spacing, growth rates, and other useful information for ground-cover selection. Where possible we have categorized the species-by-function tables by form and habit, to assist you in finding a good match for your niches.

The two tables in appendix 4, "Species of Concern," cover plants with drawbacks. The "Poisonous Plants" table lists toxicity concerns about a range of plants that *are* included in the Plant Species Matrix, including even common edible species like apples, rhubarb, and asparagus. The "Watch List" table discusses useful and functional species that we chose *not* to include in the Plant Species Matrix because of toxicity, vigorous vegetative spread, or a tendency to disperse into the surrounding community.

Appendix 5, "Niche Requirements of Beneficial Animals," provides three tables detailing everything we could find about the niches and habitat requirements of vertebrates and invertebrates beneficial for the garden. The first two tables approach the subject from the perspective of the animals, while the third table approaches it from the perspective of the habitat elements and which animals they support. The last two appendices include maps of US Department of Agriculture (USDA) hardiness zones for North America and for Europe (appendix 6) and listings of the best publications, organizations, and suppliers of tools, plants, fungi, and testing that we know about (appendix 7).

HOW WE CHOSE THE SPECIES

The Plant Species Matrix puts a palette of 626 plants in your hands, of which a staggering 490 are edible and all but four are perennial! Until now, forest gardeners have had to cross-reference books, online databases, and nursery and seed catalogs to find the information they needed. We have pulled together information from all of those sources and more to provide you with a powerful tool for species selection and design.

The plant species included here are essentially a "superguild" selected for the eastern deciduous

forest region from USDA plant hardiness zones 4 through 7 (see the range map, figure 0.2, in volume 1's introduction). All are adapted to our climate, and there are plenty of species for sun and shade and for wet, dry, acid, and alkaline soils. Of course, these species will also do well in most of Earth's other temperate climates.

We have emphasized delicious, multifunctional, and low-maintenance plant species. We have included native species wherever possible (just over half of the species in the matrix are native to eastern North America). Finally, we strove to include as broad a sampling of omega-level diversity as possible—that is, we have worked to include a broad sampling of diversity at the higher taxonomic levels such as family, order, and superorder.

There were literally thousands more species that we might have included, but we limited ourselves to roughly six hundred. You can, of course, plant any other species you choose. Use the existing- and desired-species niche analysis forms in chapter 3 to help you design polycultures with other species. Just keep in mind that many common ornamentals, like daffodils, are quite poisonous.

USING THE APPENDICES TO SELECT SPECIES

Chapter 4 covers species selection in detail. Here are a few reminders and tips for effective use of these appendices:

- If you have good soils and a reasonable climate, you can begin species selection by browsing "Forest Gardening's Top 100 Species" (volume 1, appendix 1) or the species-by-use and species-by-function tables. Your lack of limiting factors means that your goals and interests can guide you more so than for those who are not so fortunate.
- Use the species-by-use tables to find the most delicious or productive fruits, nuts, and vegeta-

bles. You can then look them up in the Plant Species Matrix to make sure they are suited to your conditions. The matrix also provides basic ratings for most species for most of their uses or functions (see "Key to the Plant Species Matrix" in appendix 1).

- If you are looking for standout plants to perform specific ecosystem functions, start with the species-by-function tables. There you will find lists of nitrogen fixers, ground covers, and more.

- If your site is challenging due to extreme cold, wet or acid soils, heavy shade, or other factors, you will probably want to start by searching through the Plant Species Matrix to find species that prefer or tolerate your site and climate. Then you can look them up in the species-by-use and species-by-function tables to evaluate how well they will perform your desired functions and generate a list of candidates on a desired-species niche analysis form (chapter 3).

- If you are looking for a species to fill a specific niche, like an edible nitrogen-fixing ground cover for partial shade, run your fingers down the relevant columns in the Plant Species Matrix for the functions and uses you want, and write down the species that meet your multiple-function goals.

- If you want to screen out species that are vigorously expansive or dispersive, check the nuisance column of the Plant Species Matrix. The nuisance column also lets you know whether species are thorny and stinging. The poison column and the "Poisonous Plants" table (appendix 4) can help you avoid planting poisonous species.

- The Plant Species Matrix is designed to help you with polyculture design and guild building. It provides information on tolerances to soil, light, and moisture conditions, as well as architecture (form) and behavior (habit)—a great help in analyzing plant niches and building guilds (see chapters 3 and 4).

TAXONOMIC REFERENCES USED

Taxonomists occasionally revise classification of plants at all levels, from species to superorder. We have endeavored to use the most widely accepted contemporary references in our work on *Edible Forest Gardens*. The foundation of the taxonomy used here is the Royal Horticultural Society's *Index of Garden Plants* (Griffiths, 1994). For natives not covered there, we used Kartesz's *Synonymized Checklist of the Vascular Flora of the United States, Canada, and Greenland* (1994).

Family names have been updated to reflect changes since that time (Compositae to Asteraceae, Cruciferae to Brassicaceae, Graminae to Poaceae, Leguminosae to Fabaceae, and Umbelliferae to Apiaceae). The lily alliance has been revised in accordance with *Flora of the Northeast* (Magee and Ahles, 1999).

APPENDIX 1

Plant Species Matrix

KEY TO THE
PLANT SPECIES MATRIX

The Plant Species Matrix can help you analyze and assess the niches of 626 useful and functional plants. We compiled the information in the Plant Species Matrix from books, online databases, interviews, and personal observation and experience. Many of these sources are in apparent conflict with each other. We have done our best to reconcile these conflicts through interviews and direct observation. For some species, we have been unable to obtain sufficient information. Thus, there are some gaps in the matrix. Also, don't be surprised if your plants seem not to have read this table. Please consider everything here to be only rough estimates for how these plants will perform for you. Test the limits of hardiness, pH, and the other categories.

To learn more about these plants, check out the resources listed in appendix 7. Visit local nurseries, botanical gardens, pristine old-growth areas, and urban waste areas to see these plants in action. Seeing a plant in person is often more valuable than any amount of reading or research. Later revisions of this table will be able to incorporate the gardening experience of our readers, providing a far more valuable resource for future gardeners.

TAXONOMY

The Plant Species Matrix and the other tables list species alphabetically by Latin name (see "Introduction to the Appendices" for information on the sources of Latin names used here). This aligns the information in the tables with the taxonomic relationships of the plants. Taxonomy relates plants to each other by their evolutionary and structural similarity. This helps us understand the ecological similarities between plants. You can also use taxonomic information when searching for ecological analogs or when trying to maximize compositional diversity (see chapter 4 for details).

Genus and Species: Unlike the case with common names, there is one and only one accepted Latin name for any species at any time. This ensures that the plants you read about here are the same as the ones you are thinking about, particularly when multiple common names apply to the same species, or when the same common name applies to different species. You also often need a species' Latin name to order it from a catalog. The abbreviation "cv." after a species name indicates the following data relates to a specific cultivar of the species, whose name is given under the common name. Unfortunately, Latin names do change at times. See the index of Latin synonyms (page 627) for out-of-date Latin names that are still in use in nursery catalogs and gardening books.

Common Name: Many species have multiple common names. We have tried to choose the most-common common name for each species in the matrix. We cannot list multiple common names here due to space limitations, but do not be surprised to see these species listed under other common names in nursery catalogs and gardening books. Always use Latin names to be certain. Use the index of common and Latin names (page 629) to help you find the Latin names for plants you know only by common name.

Family: Knowing the plant family to which the genus belongs is important for a number of reasons. These include ecological similarities, similarity of usefulness and function, and the sharing of pests and diseases within the plant families. For example, rose-family plants tend to share diseases and pests. Understanding that Oregon grape (*Mahonia aquifolium*) is in the family Berberidaceae along with Canada barberry (*Berberis canadensis*) helps you understand the similarity in their medicinal uses: both have roots containing berberine, a powerful antibacterial, antifungal, and antiseptic agent and liver tonic.

Tolerances

This section of the Plant Species Matrix can help you select species well suited to your current or desired site conditions.

Hardiness Zones: The US Department of Agriculture hardiness zones listed in this column (see the zone maps in appendix 6) are only a basic guide; many other factors influence plant hardiness and success. In addition, individual varieties and plants vary. A single number indicates the coldest zone the plant can tolerate. A range indicates extremes of warm and cold the species can tolerate where we could find this information: some plants cannot survive without sufficient chilling.

Light: Plant preferences encompass many fine gradations of light and shade. However, because of the basic level of information available in our research, we have used only three basic categories.
- ○ Full Sun means the plant prefers or tolerates total sunlight for at least six hours of the day.
- ◑ Part Shade can mean many things—dappled or thin shade all day, full sun for three hours followed by full shade for three hours, and so on.

You will have to experiment to see what the plant can tolerate.
- ● Full Shade means the plant prefers or tolerates complete shade almost all day. Plants on this list can grow in the understory of forests with closed canopies.

Moisture: This is really a combination of two different but related factors: drainage and wetness tolerance. However, as most of the references we used did not distinguish between these two factors, we were unable to do so.
- ◌ Xeric means plants are drought tolerant and may hail from desertlike areas. Note that these plants still need watering during establishment.
- ◖ Mesic covers a broad range of medium soils, from moist to somewhat dry. Plants preferring this range should not be planted where they will have seasonal wet feet. They will most likely need supplemental watering during dry periods.
- ● Hydric species, as used here, can grow in wet or seasonally wet spots, but not necessarily standing water.

Soil pH: Soil pH is the acidity or alkalinity in the soil. Many commonly grown plants thrive in the pH range of 6 to 7. Many of the less common crops thrive in strongly acid or alkaline conditions; consider using these species as one of several strategies to adapt to extreme pH soils. The sources from which we drew this research vary widely in how they list a plant's pH tolerances. Some list the widest range a species can tolerate, while others list only its preferred range. Dare to stretch the boundaries a bit—this information is not the final word on plant pH tolerances. The scale works as follows:

Strongly Acid	Acid	Garden	Alkaline
3.5–5.0	5.1–6.0	6.1–7.0	7.1–8.5

Each column has room for two blocks. If only one block is shaded, that indicates that the plant tolerates only a portion of the range.

ARCHITECTURE: FORM AND HABIT

Understanding these factors is key to polyculture design. This understanding offers you guidance on the plant's suitability for polycultures and its potential roles and associates. See chapter 4 for ideas on using this information to design successful polycultures.

Form: This column indicates the plant's aboveground "architecture": tree, shrub, bamboo, vine, or herb. Within those categories, plants are grouped by size (see table below for details). The dividing line between categories can be fuzzy. For example, certain very tall multistemmed sumacs and juneberries could be seen as either shrubs or trees. We have tried to assign each plant to the optimal category, but such choices are arbitrary in certain cases.

Tree: A woody plant tending to have a single trunk, but including suckering species where each sucker has a treelike form. Usually taller than shrubs.

Shrub: A woody plant with multiple stems or forming thickets.

Bamboo: Woody relatives of grasses, often growing quite tall.

Vine: Woody or herbaceous plants that cannot support themselves but instead climb or sprawl on other plants, trellises, or other supports. Some will form good ground covers if given nothing to climb. Woody vines resprout from buds on the stem each year. Herbaceous vines die back to the ground each winter and resprout from the roots.

Herb: Nonwoody plants including ferns, grasses, and wildflowers.

Habit: The growth habit, or "behavior," of the species. It is important to know whether a plant will sit still or spread by runners, for example, or whether it is an evergreen, ephemeral, or annual. Perennial herbs generally die back to the ground every winter and come back in spring, with the exception of evergreen species. The Plant Species Matrix lists a few self-seeding annual species as well.

Plant habit categories and symbols	
Form	**Habit**
Tree	
E	Evergreen.
std	Standard. Single-trunked and nonsuckering.
skr	Suckering. Sending up shoots at a distance from the trunk from roots, rhizomes, or stolons.
spr	Sprouting. A standard tree that sends up shoots from the base.
Shrub & Bamboo	
E	Evergreen.
ms	Multistemmed. Multiple shoots arising from the crown.
Ctkt	Clumping thicket former. Forming a colony by sending up shoots at a distance from the crown, but not spreading beyond a certain size.
Rtkt	Running thicket former. As above, but spreading indefinitely.
Cmat	Clumping mat former. Makes a dense prostrate carpet that does not spread beyond a certain size.
Rmat	Running mat former. As above, but spreading indefinitely.
Vine	
w	Woody.
r	Herbaceous.
E	Evergreen.
vine	Ordinary vine sending a single shoot or multiple shoots from a crown.
v/skr	Suckering vine. Sends up suckers at a distance from the parent plant from roots, rhizomes, or stolons.
Herb	
a	Annual. There are very few annuals in the Plant Species Matrix, and all are self-seeding.
e	Ephemeral. Emerging in spring and dying back by summer every year.
E	Evergreen.
clmp	Clumper. Spreading to a certain width and no wider.
run	Runner. Spreading indefinitely by stolons or rhizomes.
Cmat	Clumping mat former. Makes a dense prostrate carpet that does not spread beyond a certain size.
Rmat	Running mat former. As above, but spreading indefinitely.

Root Pattern: We do not have root information for all species in the Plant Species Matrix. However, this information is helpful in designing resource-sharing guilds, so we have included what we have. See chapter 5 in volume 1 for more background on plant root patterns and behavior.

Woody Plant Root Patterns

F: Flat. Mostly shallow roots forming a "plate" near the soil surface. May also develop vertical "sinkers" or "strikers" in various places.

Fb: Fibrous. Dividing into a large number of fine roots immediately upon leaving the crown.

H: Heart. Dividing from the crown into a number of main roots that both angle downward and spread outward.

T: Tap. A carrotlike root (sometimes branching) driving directly downward.

With the modifiers:

Sk: Suckering. Sending up new plants from underground runners (either rhizomes or root sprouts) at a distance from the trunk or crown.

St: Stoloniferous. Rooting from creeping stems above the ground.

Herbaceous Root Patterns

B: Bulb. Modified leaves forming a swollen base. Onions and garlic are bulbs.

C: Corm. A thick swelling at the base of the stem.

Fb: Fibrous. Dividing into a large number of fine or fleshy roots immediately upon leaving the crown.

R: Rhizomatous. Underground stems that send out shoots and roots periodically along their length. They can travel great distances, or stay close to the crown.

T: Tap. A carrotlike root (sometimes branching) driving directly downward.

Tu: Tuberous. Producing swollen potato-like "roots" (actually modified stems).

With the modifiers:

Fl: Fleshy. Thick or swollen, usually a form of fibrous or tap roots.

St: Stoloniferous. Rooting from creeping stems above the ground.

Height: The approximate height achieved by a mature plant of the given species. Quotation marks (") mean inches, and apostrophes (') mean feet. In the case of herbaceous plants, this indicates the height of the flowers, though the majority of the foliage may be lower. Some species have a range of heights (e.g., 3–6'), while others have single figures (e.g., 4'). This reflects the information available in the different resources we consulted in preparing the Plant Species Matrix. Of course, all plants grow to a range of heights depending on genetic and site-specific factors.

Due to space limitations the matrix provides height and width data only in English measurements. To convert feet to meters, multiply by 0.3048. To convert inches to centimeters, multiply by 2.54.

Width: The approximate horizontal spread of a mature plant from the given species. Quotation marks (") mean inches, and apostrophes (') mean feet. "Indef" indicates indefinite spread, as the plant spreads by runners or other means. As with height, numbers may be single or a range based on the information source. Of course, all plants grow to a range of widths depending on genetic and site-specific factors.

Growth Rate: The rate at which the plant grows and/or spreads. These rates are highly subjective and based on the reports of a variety of authors, as well as personal observation. Growth rates are substantially affected by climate and resource availability. This data is not available for all of the plants in the Matrix.

F: Fast.

M: Medium.

S: Slow.

Form	Height	Height (metric)	Category	Symbol
Plant forms, height categories, and height symbols				
Tree				
	100+ ft.	30+ m	Very large	**vl**
	50–100 ft.	15–30 m	Large	**l**
	25–50 ft.	8–15 m	Medium	**m**
	12–25 ft.	4–8 m	Small	**s**
	0–12 ft.	0–4 m	Dwarf	**d**
Shrub & Bamboo				
	25+ ft.	8+ m	Extra large	**xl**
	12–25 ft.	4–8 m	Very large	**vl**
	6–12 ft.	2–4 m	Large	**l**
	3–6 ft.	1–2 m	Medium	**m**
	6–36 in.	15–100 cm	Small	**s**
	0–6 in.	0–15 cm	Prostrate	**p**
Vine				
	12+ ft.	4+ m	High	**h**
	0–12 ft.	0–4 m	Low	**l**
Herb				
	6+ ft.	2+ m	Very large	**vl**
	3–6 ft.	1–2 m	Large	**l**
	18–36 in.	50–100 cm	Medium	**m**
	6–18 in.	15–50 cm	Small	**s**
	0–6 in.	0–15 cm	Prostrate	**p**

HABITATS

This section of the Plant Species Matrix can help you select species that grow wild in the vegetation types and successional stages that you currently have or plan to have in your forest garden. In this context, *habitat* means the vegetation types or stages of succession within which the plant tends to naturally occur in the wild. There is a reasonable correlation between the habitat or successional stage and the plant strategies discussed in volume 1, chapters 4 and 6 (ruderal, competitor, or stress tolerator, or RCS).

Native Region: Knowing a plant's region of "origin" can help you select native species, if that is one of your concerns. It may also help you understand the adaptations and tolerances of various species, or, combined with habitat information, it may help you find possible polyculture associates that have similar evolutionary histories and may have similar adaptations. Remember that plants are always on the move. These regions of "origin" or "nativity" merely reflect a species' home range as of an uncertain date of "discovery"—most likely just prior to the great global plant migrations that began with global human travel about five hundred years ago.

This column denotes the regions of the world where the plant is "native." We strongly encourage the planting of species native to your region wherever possible. To find out whether a species is native to your state or province, and not just to the eastern forest region, consult a local flora guide or talk to your nearest botanical garden.

ASIA: Eastern Asia, notably the temperate parts of China, Japan, and Korea.
AUST: Australia.
CULT: Of cultivated or hybrid origin. This includes hybrids developed by gardeners as well as a few naturally occurring hybrids.
ENA: Eastern North America. The region covered by this book, ranging from zones 4 to 7 and from the coast to the edge of the prairie. Many of these species are also native beyond this region, but they are not so marked in this column.
EUR: Europe, including some Mediterranean species that also grow in northern Africa.
EURA: Eurasia. This includes species that grow in central Eurasia (i.e. Kazakhstan), as well as many that range throughout the continent.
PRAI: Native to the North American prairies, but not the eastern forest region.
SAM: South America.
WNA: Western North America.

Disturbed: Areas recently disturbed, whether by human or natural causes. Many of these plants can be observed as urban or garden "weeds" or roadside plants. Often characterized by annuals and other ruderals, perennial ruderal-competitors, and opportunistic ("invasive") species.

Meadows: Open habitat usually dominated by plants using the competitor and ruderal-competitor strategies, most often grasses, with nongrassy herbs (also known as forbs) mixed in. Usually managed by humans to keep it in meadow condition.

Prairies: Permanent grasslands, often maintained by fire and low rainfall. Depending on the disturbance regime and resource availability, virtually any of the plant strategies may operate in these habitats.

Oldfields: Old fields in the process of becoming forest. Generally dominated by perennial herbaceous species like grasses and forbs, but also including a mix of pioneer shrubs and trees of mostly competitor species, with a mix of stress-tolerant competitors and RCS strategists.

Thickets: Dense vegetation, dominated by shrubs, but also featuring a diversity of trees and herbaceous plants. Again, these are mainly competitors and stress-tolerant competitors.

Edges: Boundaries between two habitats, here generally indicating the boundary between forest and more open fields. Species growing in these environments use strategies similar to those used in oldfields and thickets until the edge becomes part of the forest.

Gaps/Clearings: Gaps or clearings in forests: temporary sunny niches in the otherwise shady forest. Though gaps are similar to edges, thickets, and oldfields, more stress tolerators play roles in this habitat, depending on the size of the gap. See chapter 6 in volume 1 for a discussion of gap dynamics.

Open Woods: Woods with scattered trees and significant sun, often due to dry conditions or fire. Includes prairie savannah habitats. Humans may also maintain such systems. Dominated by stress-tolerant competitors and stress tolerators, unless regularly disturbed by humans or fires, in which case competitors, RCS strategists, and even ruderals may be included.

Forest: Deciduous or mixed deciduous and coniferous forest. Stress tolerators dominate here.

Conifer Forest: Very shady. Stress tolerators dominate here, too.

Other Habitats: This includes wetlands, beaches, riverbanks, deserts, alpine areas, and a wide range of other habitat types where a range of plant strategies may dominate.

USES AND FUNCTIONS

These columns help you select species to provide the human uses or ecosystem functions you desire for your forest garden. You can then look them up in the species-by-use and species-by-function tables to learn more.

Uses: In this book, the term *uses* denotes direct human uses of crop plants or mushrooms. We focus on presenting edible species; we have not selected for the matrix species whose primary use is as a fuel, fiber crop, or farmceutical, for example. Uses other than edibility are extra benefits of the species discussed here, increasing their value for the forest gardener. However, more work is needed before we can create matrices of forest garden species specifically for uses other than food. In these columns, E = excellent; G = good; F = fair; Y = has the particular use but is unrated for flavor or quality.

Edible Fruit: See the species-by-use "Edible Fruits and Berries" table (page 497) for details.

Edible Nuts/Mast: See the species-by-use "Edible Nuts and Mast" table (page 502) for details.

Edible Greens, Etc.: See the species-by-use "Edible Leaves, Stalks, and Shoots" table (page 505) for details.

Edible Roots: See the species-by-use "Edible Roots" table (page 509) for details.

Culinary: Used as a culinary herb or spice. See the species-by-use "Culinary Herb and Spice Plants" table (page 511) for details.

Tea: Used to make teas or other beverages. See the species-by-use "Tea and Beverage Plants" table (page 513) for details.

Edible Other: Edible flower buds, flowers, pods, saps, seeds and grains, twigs, or other edible parts. See the species-by-use "Other Edible Parts" table (page 515) for details.

Medicinal: Used as a medicinal plant or a superfood (S). See the species-by-use "Superfoods and Best Medicinal Plants" table (page 519) for details on superfoods or species rated as excellent medicinals. The medicinals data here and in appendix 2 describes the farmaceutical uses of species included only because of their edible uses or ecosystem functions. We did not select species for this matrix primarily for medicinal uses.

FUNCTIONS: *Functions* in this book denotes plant characteristics and behaviors that support ecosystem self-maintenance. Each column has specific symbols, as described below.

N$_2$ Fixer: If a **Y** appears in this column, the species fixes nitrogen. See the species-by-function "Nitrogen Fixers" table (page 531) for details. The associated "Nitrogen-Fixer Inoculants" table (page 534) will tell you which bacterial groups inoculate the nitrogen-fixing plants in question.

Dynamic Accumulator: If a **Y** appears in this column, the species acts as a dynamic accumulator. See the species-by-function "Dynamic Accumulators" table (page 535) for details.

Wildlife: Provides food or shelter for beneficial birds or other vertebrates. **F** indicates food, **S** is shelter, and **B** is both. See the species-by-function "Food and Shelter Plants" (page 536) table for details.

Invrt. Shelter: If a **Y** appears in this column, the species provides shelter for beneficial invertebrates: insects and other arthropods. See the species-by-function "Food and Shelter Plants" table (page 536) for details.

Nectary: Provides nectar or pollen for beneficial insects. **G** indicates generalist nectaries. **S** indicates specialist nectary plants. Other flowering plants may also provide nectar resources but either are not documented as such or do not provide significant quantities. See the species-by-function "Nectary Flowering Calendar" and "Food and Shelter Plants" tables (pages 545 and 537) for details.

Ground Cover: If a **Y** appears in this column, the species acts as a weed-suppressing ground cover. See the species-by-function "Ground Covers" table (page 550) for details.

Other Uses/Functions: At this time, this includes only plants with potential use as aromatic pest confusers or for coppice management. **A** indicates strong-scented aromatic plants that may confuse pests and prevent them from finding their desired food plants. See the species-by-function "Aromatic Pest Confusers" table (page 555) for details. **C** indicates species known to coppice. See the species-by-use "British Coppice Species" and "North American and Other Coppice Species" tables (pages 523 and 524) for details.

DRAWBACKS

You may choose not to select otherwise promising plants due to the drawbacks listed here.

Nuisances:

All: Allelopathic. Can poison neighboring plants. See the species-by-function "Juglone Susceptibility and Tolerance" table for details.

D: Dispersive. Annoyingly successful at spreading by seed, whether in the garden or in the neighborhood. May be dispersed by any method, including wind and animal vectors.

E: Expansive. Spreading very vigorously, usually by rhizomes; may need to be contained by a rhizome barrier.

H: Hay fever. Windblown pollen can cause allergies in susceptible people.

P: Persistent. Very difficult to remove once planted, often resprouting from even tiny pieces of root.

S: Sprawling vigorous vine.

St: Stings (nettles).

T: Thorny or spiny.

Poison: Some or all parts of the plant are poisonous. Please note that even apples are listed as poisonous, because their seeds are toxic. See the species-of-concern "Poisonous Plants" table (page 557) for details.

| Taxonomy | | | | Tolerances | | | Soil pH | | | | Architecture | | |
Genus	Species	Common Name	Family	Hardiness Zones	Light	Moisture	Strongly Acid	Acid	Garden	Alkaline	Form	Habit	Root Pattern
Acacia	angustissima	prairie acacia	Fabaceae	7-10	○◑	◊◊			■■	■■	m Shrub	ms	
Acacia	angustissima hirta	dwarf prairie acacia	Fabaceae	7-10	○◑	◊◊			■■	■■	s Shrub	ms	
Acer	saccharinum	silver maple	Aceraceae	3b	○◑	◊●		■■	■		l Tree	std	F
Acer	saccharum	sugar maple	Aceraceae	3-7	○●	◊			■■	■	l Tree	std	F, H
Acer	saccharum var. nigrum	black maple	Aceraceae	3b	○●	◊			■■	■	l Tree	std	F
Achillea	millefolium	yarrow	Asteraceae	3-10	○	◊◊	■■	■■	■■	■■	m Herb	run	Fb, R
Achillea	ptarmica	white tansy yarrow	Asteraceae	3-7	○	◊◊	■■	■■	■■		s Herb	run	R
Actinidia	arguta	hardy kiwifruit	Actinidiaceae	4-8	○	◊	■■	■■	■■		h Vine	w vine	H
Actinidia	kolomikta	superhardy kiwifruit	Actinidiaceae	3-8	○◑	◊	■■	■■	■■		h Vine	w vine	
Actinidia	purpurea	purple hardy kiwifruit	Actinidiaceae	4-8	○	◊	■■	■■	■■		h Vine	w vine	
Adiantum	pedatum	maidenhair fern	Adiantaceae	3-8	◑●	◊	■■	■■	■■		m Herb	clmp	R
Agastache	foeniculum	anise hyssop	Lamiaceae	3-8	○◑	◊			■■		m-l Herb	clmp	F
Alcea	rosea	hollyhock	Malvaceae	4	◑	◊		■■	■■		vl Herb	clmp	
Allium	ampeloprasum	perennial sweet leek	Alliaceae	6-9	○	◊			■■		s-m Herb	clmp	B
Allium	canadense	wild garlic	Alliaceae	3-9	○◑	◊◊			■■		s-m Herb	clmp	B
Allium	cepa aggregatum	potato onion, shallot	Alliaceae	5-9	○	◊			■■		s Herb	clmp	B
Allium	cepa proliferum	Egyptian walking onion	Alliaceae	5-10	○	◊			■■		m Herb	clmp	B
Allium	cernuum	nodding wild onion	Alliaceae	3-8	○◑	◊	■	■■	■■	■■	s-m Herb	clmp	B
Allium	fistulosum	Welsh onion	Alliaceae	4-10	○	◊			■■	■	m Herb	clmp	B
Allium	schoenoprasum	chives	Alliaceae	2-10	○◑	◊			■■	■■	s-m Herb	clmp	B
Allium	tricoccum	ramps	Alliaceae	4-8	◑●	◊		■	■■		s Herb	e clmp	B
Allium	tuberosum	garlic chives	Alliaceae	3-10	○	◊		■■	■■	■■	s-m Herb	clmp	B
Alnus	cordata	Italian alder	Betulaceae	6	○◑	◊◊●		■■	■■	■■	m Tree	std	
Alnus	incana	gray alder	Betulaceae	2-6	○◑	◊◊●		■■	■■	■	m-l Tree	std	
Alnus	rugosa	speckled alder	Betulaceae	2-6	○◑	●		■■	■■	■	vl-xl Shrub	ms	F
Alnus	serrulata	smooth alder	Betulaceae	5-8	○◑	●		■■	■■		vl Shrub	ms	F, Sk
Althaea	officinalis	marsh mallow	Malvaceae	3-7	○	◊◊●			■■		m-l Herb	clmp	T
Amelanchier	alnifolia	saskatoon	Rosaceae	2	○	◊		■■	■■	■■	m-vl Shrub	ms	St
Amelanchier	bartramiana	Bartram's shadblow	Rosaceae	4-7	○	◊◊	■	■■	■■		s-l Shrub	ms	
Amelanchier	lamarkii	juneberry	Rosaceae	3	○	◊			■		xl Shrub	ms	F, Sk
Amelanchier	obovalis	southern juneberry	Rosaceae	6-8	○	◊		■	■■		l Shrub	ms	
Amelanchier	stolonifera	running juneberry	Rosaceae	4	○	◊◊		■■	■■		m Shrub	Rtkt	St
Amorpha	canescens	leadplant	Fabaceae	3	○	◊◊				■■	s Shrub	ms	T, Sk
Amorpha	fruticosa	false indigo	Fabaceae	3	○	◊◊			■■	■■	l-vl Shrub	ms	F, Sk
Amorpha	nana	fragrant false indigo	Fabaceae	3-6	○	◊◊		■	■■	■	s Shrub	ms	
Amorphophallus	riveri var. konjac	konjac	Araceae	6-10	○◑	◊			■■		l Herb	clmp	C
Amphicarpaea	bracteata	hog peanut	Fabaceae	3-9	○●	◊		■■	■■		l Vine	a r vine	Fb
Andropogon	gerardii	big bluestem	Poaceae	3	○◑	◊◊		■■	■■		vl Herb	clmp	Fb
Antennaria	dioica	pussytoes	Asteraceae	3-9	○◑	◊◊		■■	■■		p-s Herb	E clmp	St
Antennaria	plantaginifolia	pussytoes	Asteraceae	3-10	○◑	◊◊		■■	■■		p-s Herb	run	St
Apios	americana	groundnut	Fabaceae	3-10	○◑	◊		■■	■■		l Vine	r v/skr	Tu
Apios	fortunei	Fortune's groundnut	Fabaceae	U	○◑	◊	■■	■■	■■	■	l Vine	r vine	Tu
Apios	priceana	Price's groundnut	Fabaceae	6	○◑	◊		■■	■■		l Vine	r vine	Tu
Aquilegia	canadensis	columbine	Ranunculaceae	3-8	○●	◊		■■	■■	■■	s-m Herb	clmp	T

Groups: **Architecture** (Height–Growth Rate) · **Habitats** (Native Region–Other Habitats) · **Uses** (Edible Fruit–Medicinal) · **Functions** (N_2 Fixer–Other Uses/Functions) · **Drawbacks** (Nuisances, Poison)

Height	Width	Growth Rate	Native Region	Disturbed	Meadows	Prairies	Oldfields	Thickets	Edges	Gaps/Clearings	Open Woods	Forest	Conifer Forest	Other Habitats	Edible Fruit	Edible Nuts/Mast	Edible Greens, Etc.	Edible Roots	Culinary	Tea	Edible Other	Medicinal	N_2 Fixer	Dynamic Accumulator	Wildlife	Invert. Shelter	Nectar	Ground Cover	Other Uses/Functions	Nuisances	Poison
3-6'	3-6'	F	ENA			✓				✓	✓			✓									Y		F			G			P
1-3'	1-6'	F	ENA			✓				✓	✓			✓									Y		F			G	Y		P
75-100'	75-100'	F	ENA									✓		✓							G			Y				G	C	D	P
75-100'	50-75'	S-M	ENA								✓			✓							E	F		Y				G	C	D	P
75-100'	50-75'	S-M	ENA								✓										G			Y				G	C	D	P
2-3'	indef	F	EURA	✓	✓		✓							✓								E		Y			Y	S	A	D	P
6-12"	indef	F	EURA	✓	✓		✓							✓								Y					Y	S	A	D	P
20-100'	20-100'	F	ASIA						✓		✓	✓	✓		E							S								S	
20-100'	20-100'	M-F	ASIA	✓					✓	✓	✓	✓	✓	✓	E							S								S	
20-100'	20-100'	M-F	ASIA					✓							E							S								S	
18-24"	3-5'	S	ENA									✓		✓							Y							Y		
2-4'	1-2'	M	WNA		✓			✓		✓	✓			✓						E	E					Y	G	A		
7'	2'	F	EURA	✓										✓		G					F	S						G			
1-2'	1'	M	EUR											✓		E	G					S						G	A		
6-24"	1'	F	ENA	✓	✓	✓	✓				✓			✓		G	G	G	F			S						G	A	P, D	P
1'	1'	M	EURA											✓		G	E	E				S						G	A		
2'	2-5'	M-F	EURA	✓										✓		G	G	G				S						G	A		
1-2'	1-2'	S	ENA		✓	✓			✓					✓		G		G				S						G	A		
2-3'	1-2'	S-M	ASIA											✓		E	E	E				S						G	A		
6-20"	6-20"	S-M	ASIA	✓	✓											E		E			G	S			Y		Y	G	A		
6-10"	indef	S	ENA										✓			E	E	E				S						G	A		
18"	12"	S-M	ASIA					✓						✓		E		E			G	S					Y	G	A		
30-50'	20-35'	F	EUR											✓								G	Y						C		
40-60'	25-40'	F	EUR				✓	✓		✓	✓			✓								G	Y						C		
20-35'	20-35'	F	ENA					✓				✓		✓								G	Y		S			G	C		
12-20'	12-20'	F	ENA					✓						✓								G	Y		S			G	C		
2-4'	2-4'		EURA		✓			✓												G	G		E									
5-15'	5-15'	M	WNA				✓	✓		✓	✓	✓		✓	E							S			F			G			P
2-8'	2-8'		ENA					✓			✓			✓	E							S			B			G			P
35-50'	20-35'	M	ENA					✓		✓	✓			✓	E							S			F			G			P
8-10'	8-10'	M	ENA					✓						✓	E							S			F			G			P
4-6'	indef	M	ENA				✓	✓						✓	E							S			B			G			P
3'	3-6'	M	PRAI		✓	✓			✓	✓	✓			✓									Y				Y	G			P
6-20'	12-20'	M	ENA	✓	✓			✓		✓	✓			✓									Y				Y	G			P
3'	3'	M	PRAI		✓	✓								✓									Y				Y	G			P
4-5'	3-4'	S	ASIA								✓			✓						Y		G									P
1-3'	1-3'	M-F	ENA				✓	✓		✓	✓	✓								G	Y	Y				Y		Y		
5-6'	3-4'	M	ENA		✓	✓	✓																			Y	G		H	
2-10"	12"	S	EURA		✓	✓					✓										F					Y	S	Y		
2-10"	indef	M	ENA		✓				✓		✓			✓							F					Y	S	Y		
4-8'	indef	M-F	ENA		✓			✓	✓					✓							E		Y			Y	G	Y	S	
3-6'	3-6'	M-F	ASIA					✓						✓							E		Y			Y	G			
3-6'	3-6'	M-F	ENA					✓						✓							E		Y			Y	G			
1-2'	1-2'	S	ENA						✓	✓	✓			✓											F		G			

Taxonomy				Tolerances			Soil pH				Architecture		
Genus	Species	Common Name	Family	Hardiness Zones	Light	Moisture	Strongly Acid	Acid	Garden	Alkaline	Form	Habit	Root Pattern
Arabis	caucasica	rock cress	Brassicaceae	4-10	○	◊◊		■	■■	■■	s Herb	clmp	
Aralia	cordata	udo	Araliaceae	4b	○◐	◊	■■	■	■■		vl Herb	clmp	
Aralia	elata	angelica tree	Araliaceae	4b	○○	◊	■■	■	■■		vl Shrub	Ctkt	Sk
Aralia	hispida	bristly sarsaparilla	Araliaceae	3	○○	◊◊	■■	■	■		s Shrub	Ctkt	Sk
Aralia	nudicaulis	wild sarsaparilla	Araliaceae	3	○◐	◊	■■	■	■		s Herb	run	R
Aralia	racemosa	spikenard	Araliaceae	4	○●	◊		■	■■		m Shrub	ms	Sk
Araucaria	araucana	monkey puzzle tree	Araucariaceae	6-8	○	◊			■■		l Tree	E std	
Arbutus	unedo	strawberry tree	Ericaceae	8	○	◊			■■		l-vl Shrub	ms	
Arctostaphylos	uva-ursi	bearberry	Ericaceae	2	○	◊◊	■	■■	■		p Shrub	E Rmat	F
Armoracia	rusticana	horseradish	Brassicaceae	2-8	○◐	◊	■■	■	■■	■■	l Herb	run	T
Arnoglossum	atriplicifolia	pale Indian plantain	Asteraceae	4	○◐◐	◊		■■	■		l Herb	clmp	
Aronia	arbutifolia	red chokeberry	Rosaceae	4b	○○	◊◊	■■	■			l Shrub	ms	F, Sk
Aronia	melanocarpa	black chokeberry	Rosaceae	3	○○	◊◊	■■	■			s-m Shrub	Ctkt	F, Sk
Artemisia	dracunculus var. sativa	French tarragon	Asteraceae	5	○	◊		■■	■■		l Herb	clmp	R
Artemisia	frigida	fringed sagebrush	Asteraceae	2	○○	◊◊	■■	■	■		s Herb	clmp	Fb
Artemisia	stelleriana	beach wormwood	Asteraceae	3-9	○○	◊◊		■■	■		m Herb	clmp	R
Arundinaria	gigantea	canebrake bamboo	Poaceae	6-9	○○	◊◊		■	■■	■	l-vl Bamboo	E run	R
Arundinaria	gigantea tecta	dwarf canebrake	Poaceae	6-9	○○	◊◊		■	■■	■	m Bamboo	E run	R
Asarum	canadense	wild ginger	Aristolochiaceae	3-8	○●●	◊		■■	■■		p-s Herb	run	R
Asarum	shuttleworthii	Shuttleworth's ginger	Aristolochiaceae	6-9	○●	◊		■■			p-s Herb	E clmp	R
Asarum	splendens	Chinese evergreen wild ginger	Aristolochiaceae	5-9	◐●	◊		■■	■		p-s Herb	run	R
Asclepias	incarnata	swamp milkweed	Asclepiadaceae	3-9	○	◊◊◊	■■	■■	■		l Herb	clmp	R
Asclepias	syriaca	milkweed	Asclepiadaceae	3-8	○	◊◊		■■	■		l Herb	run	R
Asimina	triloba	pawpaw	Annonaceae	5b-7	○●	◊			■■	■■	s-m Tree	skr	T, H, Sk
Asparagus	officinalis	asparagus	Asparagaceae	2-9	○	◊			■	■	l Herb	clmp	R
Asphodeline	lutea	yellow asphodel	Asphodelaceae	6-9	○○	◊			■■		m Herb	clmp	Tu
Aster	divaricatus	white wood aster	Asteraceae	4-8	○●	◊		■■	■		m Herb	clmp	Fb, St
Aster	novae-angliae	New England aster	Asteraceae	3-9	○○	◊◊		■	■■		l Herb	clmp	R
Astragalus	canadensis	Canadian milk vetch	Fabaceae	3-8	○◐	◊◊			■■		s-l Herb	run	
Astragalus	crassicarpus	groundplum milk vetch	Fabaceae	3-8	○	◊◊					s Herb	clmp	R
Astragalus	glycyphyllos	milk vetch	Fabaceae	4-8	○	◊◊		■■	■■		s Herb	clmp	
Astragalus	membranaceous	huang-qi	Fabaceae	5	○	◊◊		■■	■■		m Herb	clmp	
Athyrium	filix-femina	lady fern	Dryopteridaceae	3-8	○●●	◊◊		■■	■		m-l Herb	clmp	R
Atriplex	halimus	saltbush	Chenopodiaceae	7	○	◊◊		■■	■		m Shrub	ms	
Balsamorhiza	sagittata	balsamroot sunflower	Asteraceae	4	○◐	◊◊		■	■		s-m Herb	clmp	T
Baptisia	australis	wild blue indigo	Fabaceae	4-8	○◐	◊◊	■■	■	■		m-l Herb	clmp	T
Baptisia	tinctoria	yellow wild indigo	Fabaceae	4-9	○◐	◊◊		■	■■		m Herb	clmp	T, Fb
Bellis	perennis	English daisy	Asteraceae	4-10	○●	◊			■■		p Herb	clmp	Fb, R
Berberis	canadensis	Canada barberry	Berberidaceae	4-8	○◐	◊◊		■■	■■		m Shrub	ms	
Beta	vulgaris maritima	sea beet	Chenopodiaceae	7	○◐	◊		■■	■■	■■	m Herb	clmp	T
Betula	alleghaniensis	yellow birch	Betulaceae	3-7	○●	◊	■■	■	■		l Tree	std	F, H
Betula	lenta	black birch	Betulaceae	3	○◐	◊◊	■				l Tree	std	H
Blephilia	ciliata	downy wood mint	Lamiaceae	4-7	◐	◊◊	■■	■	■		s-m Herb	clmp	
Blephilia	hirsuta	hairy wood mint	Lamiaceae	4-7	◐	◊	■■	■	■		s-m Herb	clmp	
Borago	officinalis	borage	Boraginaceae	3	○	◊		■■	■		a Herb	a clmp	

Architecture			Habitats												Uses								Functions							Drawbacks	
Height	Width	Growth Rate	Native Region	Disturbed	Meadows	Prairies	Oldfields	Thickets	Edges	Gaps/Clearings	Open Woods	Forest	Conifer Forest	Other Habitats	Edible Fruit	Edible Nuts/Mast	Edible Greens, Etc.	Edible Roots	Culinary	Tea	Edible Other	Medicinal	N_2 Fixer	Dynamic Accumulator	Wildlife	Invert. Shelter	Nectary	Ground Cover	Other Uses/Functions	Nuisances	Poison
6-12"	18"	M-F	EURA											✓			F					G					G	Y			
6-9'	6-9'	F	ASIA					✓			✓			✓			E					E					S			P
15-30'	15-20'	S-M	ASIA					✓			✓	✓		✓			Y									S	S			P
1-3'	1-3'	M	ENA						✓	✓	✓								F	F		F				S	S		T	P
12-18"	indef	M	ENA						✓		✓	✓		✓						F		F				F	S	Y		P
3-6'	3-6'	M	ENA					✓						✓					F	F		E					S			P
100'	50'	S	SAM										✓	✓	E												S			
6-20'	6-9'	S-M	EUR						✓		✓			✓	G												F			
2-6"	indef	S-M	ENA							✓	✓	✓		✓	F				F			E				F		G	Y	
3'	indef	F	EURA	✓			✓							✓			F		E			E							A	P	P
3-6'	3'		ENA	✓				✓		✓	✓			✓								F					S			
6-12'	3-6'	S	ENA		✓			✓	✓		✓			✓	F							F					F	G			
1.5-6'	6-10'	S-F	ENA				✓		✓		✓			✓	G							F				B		G	Y	
4'	4'	S	EURA	✓	✓									✓					E			G				Y	S		A	H	P
18"	18"	S-M	ENA	✓	✓	✓								✓								F				Y	S	Y	A	H	P
2'	3'	S	ENA	✓										✓								G				Y	S	Y	A	H	P
10-20'	indef	F	ENA								✓	✓		✓					G								S			E	P
6'	indef	F	ENA								✓	✓		✓					G			Y					S			E,H	P
4-8"	indef	S	ENA									✓		✓					F			F						Y			P
4-8"	14"	S	ENA									✓		✓					F									Y			P
4-8"	indef	S	ASIA									✓		✓					F									Y			P
3-5'	1-2'	M	ENA		✓			✓						✓								F						G			P
3-4'	indef	F	ENA				✓	✓						✓					G		F	F						G		E,P,D	P
20-35'	20-35'	S-M	ENA					✓			✓			✓	E							F				S			C		P
3-5'	18-36"	M	EURA	✓	✓	✓	✓							✓					E			G						G		D	P
2-3'	2-3'	M	EURA											✓					G	G	E	F									
2'	2'	M-F	ENA						✓		✓	✓															Y	S			
4-5'	4-5'	F	ENA	✓	✓			✓						✓													Y	S			
1-4'	indef	M	ENA		✓				✓		✓			✓						Y			Y				Y	G			P
6-15"	1-2'	S	PRAI		✓					✓	✓			✓								G	Y				Y	G			P
8-12"	3-5'	F	EUR	✓	✓		✓	✓	✓					✓								Y	Y				Y	G	Y		
2-3'	2-3'		ASIA					✓	✓					✓							G	E	Y				Y	G			P
18-36"	18-24"	M	ENA		✓								✓	✓								F						Y			
6'	9'		EUR											✓			E					F								H	P
1-2'	1-2'	M	WNA			✓					✓			✓			Y	Y									Y	S	Y		
2-4'	2-5'	S-M	ENA	✓		✓		✓		✓	✓			✓									Y				Y	G			P
2-3'	2-5'	S-M	ENA		✓	✓				✓	✓			✓								G	Y				Y	G			
6"	1-2'	S	EUR	✓	✓									✓			G					G					Y	S	Y	D	
5'	3-5'	M	ENA						✓	✓	✓	✓		✓	F							E				F		G		T,D	P
3'	2'	S	EUR	✓										✓			E					G						G		H	P
50-75'	35-50'	M	ENA										✓	✓						E	G	G			Y			G	C	D	
50-75'	35-50'	M	ENA					✓						✓						E	G	G			Y			G	C	D	
1-2'	1-2'		ENA	✓	✓			✓											G	G							Y	G	A		
1-2'	1-2'		ENA								✓								G	G							Y	G	A		
1-2'	9-12"	F	EURA	✓															G		G	F					Y	G		D	

Genus	Species	Common Name	Family	Hardiness Zones	Light	Moisture	Strongly Acid	Acid	Garden	Alkaline	Form	Habit	Root Pattern
Brassica	*oleracea*	wild cabbage	Brassicaceae	7	○	◊		■	■		m Herb	clmp	F
Brassica	*oleracea (acephala* group)	tree collards	Brassicaceae	7	○	◊		■	■		l-vl Herb	clmp	F
Brassica	*oleracea (botrytis* group) cv.	perennial broccoli 'Nine Star'	Brassicaceae	7	○◐	◊		■	■		m Herb	clmp	F
Bunias	*orientalis*	Turkish rocket	Brassicaceae	4	○◐	◊◊		■	■		m Herb	clmp	
Bunium	*bulbocastanum*	earth chestnut	Apiaceae	5	○	◊			■	■	m Herb	clmp	Tu
Calamintha	*nepeta*	calamint savory	Lamiaceae	6-10	○	◊		■	■	■	m Herb	run	St
Callirhoe	*involucrata*	purple poppy-mallow	Malvaceae	4	○◐	◊◊	■	■	■	■	p-s Herb	clmp	T
Calycanthus	*floridus*	Carolina allspice	Calycanthaceae	5	○●	◊◊		■	■		l Shrub	Ctkt	F, Sk
Camassia	*cusickii*	Cusick's camass	Hyacinthaceae	5-8	○◐	◊◊					m Herb	clmp	B
Camassia	*leichtlinnii*	wild hyacinth	Hyacinthaceae	5-8	○◐	◊◊			■		s-m Herb	e run	B
Camassia	*quamash*	camass	Hyacinthaceae	4	○	◊◊	■	■	■		s-m Herb	e run	B
Campanula	*carpatica*	Carpathian bellflower	Campanulaceae	3-8	○◐	◊		■	■	■	s Herb	clmp	Fb
Campanula	*glomerata*	clustered bellflower	Campanulaceae	3	○◐	◊			■		m Herb	clmp	
Campanula	*portenschlagiana*	Dalmatian bellflower	Campanulaceae	3-7	○◐	◊		■	■	■	p-s Herb	run	
Caragana	*arborescens*	Siberian pea shrub	Fabaceae	2-7	○	◊◊	■	■	■	■	l-vl Shrub	ms	
Caragana	*frutex*	Russian pea shrub	Fabaceae	2-7	○	◊◊	■	■	■	■	l Shrub	ms	
Caragana	*pygmaea*	pygmy pea shrub	Fabaceae	3-7	○	◊◊		■	■	■	m Shrub	ms	
Cardamine	*bulbosa*	spring cress	Brassicaceae	4-8	○◐	◊◊			■		s-m Herb	clmp	Tu
Cardamine	*diphylla*	toothwort	Brassicaceae	3-8	◐●	◊			■		s Herb	e run	R
Cardamine	*pratensis*	cuckoo flower	Brassicaceae	3-7	○◐	◊◊			■		s-m Herb	clmp	R
Carex	*pensylvanica*	Pennsylvania sedge	Cyperaceae	4-8	○●	◊◊		■	■		s Herb	E clmp	
Carya	*illinoinensis*	pecan	Juglandaceae	6-9	○	◊			■	■	l-vl Tree	std	T
Carya	*laciniosa*	shellbark hickory	Juglandaceae	6	○	◊◊			■	■	l Tree	std	T
Carya	*ovata*	shagbark hickory	Juglandaceae	4-7	○◐	◊◊			■		l Tree	std	T
Carya	x hybrids	hican	Juglandaceae	5	○	◊			■		l Tree	std	T
Castanea	*dentata*	American chestnut	Fagaceae	4	○◐	◊◊	■	■			l-vl Tree	std	T
Castanea	*mollissima*	Chinese chestnut	Fagaceae	5	○	◊◊	■	■	■		m Tree	std	
Castanea	*pumila*	chinquapin	Fagaceae	5b	○	◊◊	■	■			l-vl Shrub	ms	H, F, Sk
Ceanothus	*americanus*	New Jersey tea	Rhamnaceae	3b	○◐	◊◊	■	■	■		s Shrub	ms	F
Ceanothus	*prostratus*	mahala mat	Rhamnaceae	7-10	○◐	◊◊		■	■	■	p Shrub	E Cmat	F
Celtis	*laevigata*	sugarberry	Ulmaceae	6	○	◊◊		■	■	■	l Tree	std	F
Celtis	*occidentalis*	hackberry	Ulmaceae	3-7	○◐	◊◊			■	■	l Tree	std	H
Centranthus	*ruber*	red valerian	Valerianaceae	6	○◐	◊			■		m Herb	clmp	
Cephalotaxus	*harringtonia*	plum yew	Cephalotaxaceae	6	○●	◊			■		l-vl Shrub	E ms	
Cercis	*canadensis*	redbud	Fabaceae	5-9	○●	◊◊			■	■	s-m Tree	std	T
Cercocarpus	*montanus*	mountain mahogany	Rosaceae	6	○	◊			■	■	l-vl Shrub	ms	
Chaenomeles	*speciosa*	flowering quince	Rosaceae	4-8	○	◊		■	■		l Shrub	ms	
Chamaemelum	*nobile*	chamomile	Asteraceae	5-8	○	◊◊		■	■	■	p Herb	Cmat	
Chasmanthium	*latifolium*	northern sea oats	Poaceae	5	○◐	◊		■	■		l Herb	clmp	
Chenopodium	*bonus-henricus*	good King Henry	Chenopodiaceae	3-9	○◐	◊			■	■	s-m Herb	clmp	T, Fb
Chimaphila	*maculata*	pipsissewa	Pyrolaceae	4-7	◐	◊◊		■			p Herb	E run	R
Chimaphila	*umbellata*	pipsissewa	Pyrolaceae	4-7	◐	◊◊		■			p-s Herb	E run	R
Chrysogonum	*virginianum*	green and gold	Asteraceae	5-9	○◐	◊			■		p Herb	E clmp	R
Chrysosplenium	*americanum*	golden saxifrage	Saxifragaceae	3-8	○●	◊◊	■	■	■	■	p Herb	Cmat	Fb, St
Cichorium	*intybus*	chicory	Asteraceae	3	○◐	◊	■	■	■	■	s-l Herb	clmp	T

Height	Width	Growth Rate	Native Region	Disturbed	Meadows	Prairies	Oldfields	Thickets	Edges	Gaps/Clearings	Open Woods	Forest	Conifer Forest	Other Habitats	Edible Fruit	Edible Nuts/Mast	Edible Greens, Etc.	Edible Roots	Culinary	Tea	Edible Other	Medicinal	N2 Fixer	Dynamic Accumulator	Wildlife	Invert. Shelter	Nectary	Ground Cover	Other Uses/Functions	Nuisances	Poison
3'	2'	F	EUR											✓			G				Y	S		Y			Y	G			P
3-9'	3-5'	F	CULT											✓			G					S		Y			Y	G			P
18-36"	18-36"	F	CULT											✓			G		G			S		Y			Y	G			P
18-36"	1-2'	F	EURA	✓	✓	✓								✓			G				G										P
2'	1-2'	M	EUR		✓									✓						E	F							Y	S			
2'	indef	M	EUR	✓	✓		✓			✓	✓	✓	✓	✓					Y	G	G								Y	A		
3-10"	4-5'	M	WNA			✓								✓	F	G													Y			
6-12'	6-12'	S-M	ENA							✓	✓			✓						Y			F				S					P
1-2'	1'		WNA		✓									✓				Y											G			P
18-28"	18-28"		WNA		✓	✓				✓	✓			✓			G											G			P
1-2'	1-2'		WNA		✓				✓	✓			✓	✓			G											G			P
8-10"	18"	S	EURA		✓									✓			G				Y							G	Y		
3'	2'	F	EURA	✓	✓		✓							✓			G				Y							G			
6-9"	indef	M-F	EURA	✓										✓			G				Y							G	Y	E	
8-20"	12-18'	M-F	ASIA	✓				✓		✓				✓							F	Y		F	Y	G		T	
6-10'	6-10'	S	ASIA				✓	✓			✓	✓		✓								Y		F	Y	G		T	
4'	4'	S-M	ASIA		✓	✓								✓								Y		F	Y	G		T	
8-20"	8-20"		ENA		✓					✓	✓			✓		G	G	G			F									
8-16"	indef	M	ENA								✓			✓					G		F									P
8-20"	8-20"		EUR		✓						✓	✓		✓			E				F								D	P
10"	12"	S-M	ENA							✓	✓	✓		✓												G	Y		
75-120'	75-120'	S	ENA								✓			✓		E					S		Y			G	C	H	
70-85'	30-50'	M	ENA						✓		✓	✓		✓		E					S		Y			G	C	H	
70-85'	30-50'	S	ENA	✓				✓			✓	✓		✓		E					S		Y			G	C	H	
75'	50'	S	CULT											✓		E					S		Y			G	C	H	
75-100'+	50-75'	M-F	ENA								✓	✓		✓		E					S					G	C		
25-35'	25-35'	S-M	ASIA					✓			✓	✓		✓		E					S					G	C		
6-20'	6-20'	M	ENA	✓				✓		✓	✓	✓	✓	✓		E					S					G	C		
3'	3-6'	S-M	ENA			✓	✓			✓	✓			✓						E	E	Y		F		G			
3-6"	10'	S-M-F	WNA								✓	✓		✓								Y				G	Y		
60-100'	60-100'	M-F	ENA								✓	✓		✓	F									F		G	C	H	
75-100'	75-100'	M-F	ENA		✓			✓		✓	✓		✓	F									F		G	C	H	
3'	3'		EURA	✓										✓					G										
10-15'	10-15'	S	ASIA					✓			✓			✓	F	Y									S				
20-35'	20-35'	S-M	ENA					✓		✓	✓			✓					G		E	F			F		G		
6-20'	6-20'	S	WNA					✓		✓				✓								Y				G			P
6-10'	6-10'	M-F	ASIA											✓	G						F					G			P
3-6"	1'	M	EURA	✓										✓						E	E	Y				Y	S	Y		
3'	2-3'	M	ENA		✓	✓	✓				✓			✓											Y	G		H	
1-3'	12-18"	M	EUR	✓			✓		✓					✓			E			G	F							D, H	P
4"	indef	S	ENA									✓		✓							E						Y		
6-10"	indef	S	ENA							✓	✓	✓	✓	✓							E						Y		
3-6"	18"	M-F	ENA					✓			✓			✓											Y	S	Y		
2-5"	2'+	S-M	ENA								✓			✓			Y										S	Y		
1-4'	1-2'	F	EURA	✓			✓		✓					✓					G	E	G			Y	Y	G		D	

| Taxonomy | | | | Tolerances | | | Soil pH | | | | Architecture | | |
| | | | | Hardiness Zones | Light | Moisture | Strongly Acid | Acid | Garden | Alkaline | | | |
Genus	Species	Common Name	Family								Form	Habit	Root Pattern
Claytonia	caroliniana	Carolina spring beauty	Portulacaceae	4-8	◑●	◊		■■			p-s Herb	e Rmat	C
Claytonia	megarhiza	alpine spring beauty	Portulacaceae	2	○	◊					p Herb	clmp	T
Claytonia	virginica	spring beauty	Portulacaceae	4-8	◑●	◊◊		■■	■■		p-s Herb	e run	C
Clinopodium	glabellum	smooth-leaved satureja	Lamiaceae	6	○◑	◊		■■			m Herb	E clmp	Fb
Clintonia	borealis	bluebead lily	Convallariaceae	3-7	◑●	◊	■■	■■			s Herb	clmp	R
Clitoria	mariana	butterfly pea	Fabaceae	6-9	○◑	◊◊					l Vine	r vine	
Colocasia	esculenta	taro	Araceae	7-10	○◑	◊◊		■■	■■		l Herb	clmp	C
Colutea	arborescens	bladder senna	Fabaceae	5-7	○	◊◊			■■	■■	l-vl Shrub	ms	
Commelina	erecta	Virginia dayflower	Commelinaceae	6-9	○◑	◊		■■			m-l Herb	clmp	R
Comptonia	peregrina	sweetfern	Myricaceae	2-6	○◑	◊	■	■■	■		s Shrub	Ctkt	F, Sk
Conoclinium	coelestinum	hardy ageratum	Asteraceae	6-10	○◑	◊◊		■■			s-m Herb	run	R
Conopodium	majus	pig nut	Apiaceae	6	○◑	◊		■■			s Herb	clmp	Tu
Coptis	trifolia var. groenlandica	goldthread	Ranunculaceae	2-7	◑●	◊◊	■■				p Herb	E run	R
Coreopsis	auriculata	dwarf tickseed	Asteraceae	5-9	◑	◊	■■	■■	■■		s Herb	clmp	Fb, St
Coreopsis	rosea	pink tickseed	Asteraceae	4-9	○	◊◊		■■	■		m Herb	run	Fb, St
Coreopsis	verticillata	thread-leaved coreopsis	Asteraceae	3-9	○	◊◊		■■	■		m Herb	clmp	Fb, St
Cornus	canadensis	bunchberry	Cornaceae	2	○●	◊	■	■■			p-s Shrub	E Rmat	Sk
Cornus	florida	flowering dogwood	Cornaceae	5b-9	○●	◊		■	■		m Tree	std	F, H
Cornus	kousa	kousa dogwood	Cornaceae	5	○◑	◊		■■	■■		m Tree	std	
Cornus	mas	cornelian cherry	Cornaceae	4	○	◊		■■	■■		s Tree	std	
Cornus	paniculata	gray dogwood	Cornaceae	3	○◑	◊◊		■■	■■		l Shrub	Ctkt	F, Sk
Cornus	sericea	red osier dogwood	Cornaceae	4	○	◊◊		■■	■		l Shrub	ms	Sk
Corylus	americana	American hazel	Corylaceae	3	○●	◊		■■	■		l Shrub	Ctkt	F, Sk
Corylus	avellana	European filbert	Corylaceae	4	○	◊		■■	■■	■■	vl Shrub	Ctkt	Sk
Corylus	chinensis	Chinese tree hazel	Corylaceae	7	○	◊		■■	■■		vl Tree	std	
Corylus	colurna	tree hazel	Corylaceae	5	○	◊		■	■■		l Tree	std	
Corylus	cornuta	beaked hazel	Corylaceae	3	○	◊		■■	■■		l Shrub	Ctkt	F, Sk
Corylus	x colurnoides	trazel	Corylaceae	5	○	◊		■■	■■		l Tree	std	
Corylus	x hybrids	filazel, hazelbert	Corylaceae	3	○	◊		■■			vl Shrub	Ctkt	Sk
Crambe	maritima	sea kale	Brassicaceae	4-8	○◑	◊◊		■	■		m Herb	clmp	T
Crataegus	aestivalis	mayhaw	Rosaceae	6-9	○	◊●	■■	■■			m Tree	std	
Crataegus	mollis	downy hawthorn	Rosaceae	3b	○	◊◊		■■	■■		m Tree	std	T
Crataegus	pinnatifida	Chinese haw	Rosaceae	6	○	◊◊		■■	■■		s Tree	std	T
Crataegus	punctata	dotted hawthorn	Rosaceae	4b	○	◊◊		■■	■■		s-m Tree	std	T
Crocus	sativus	saffron crocus	Iridaceae	6	○◑	◊		■	■■	■■	p Herb	run	C
Cryptotaenia	canadensis	honewort	Apiaceae	3-7	◑●	◊		■■			s-m Herb	clmp	Fb, R
Cryptotaenia	japonica	mitsuba	Apiaceae	5	◑●	◊		■■	■■	■	s-m Herb	clmp	T, F
Cudrania	tricuspidata	che fruit	Moraceae	5-10	○	◊◊		■■			s Tree	spr	
Cunila	origanoides	Maryland dittany	Lamiaceae	4-9	◑	◊	■■	■			s Herb	clmp	
Cydonia	oblonga	quince	Rosaceae	5-9	○	◊		■■			d-s Tree	std	F
Cymopterus	newberryi	corkwing	Apiaceae	7	○	◊					m Herb	clmp	T
Cymopterus	purpurascens	gamote	Apiaceae	6	○	◊					m Herb	clmp	T
Cytisus	decumbens	prostrate broom	Fabaceae	6-8	○	◊◊		■■	■■	■■	p-s Shrub	Cmat	
Darmera	peltata	Indian rhubarb	Saxifragaceae	5-7	○◑	◊●		■■	■■	■■	l Herb	clmp	R
Darmera	peltata nana	dwarf Indian rhubarb	Saxifragaceae	5-7	○◑	◊●		■■	■■	■■	s-m Herb	clmp	R

Architecture				Habitats											Uses								Functions							Drawbacks	
Height	Width	Growth Rate	Native Region	Disturbed	Meadows	Prairies	Oldfields	Thickets	Edges	Gaps/Clearings	Open Woods	Forest	Conifer Forest	Other Habitats	Edible Fruit	Edible Nuts/Mast	Edible Greens, Etc.	Edible Roots	Culinary	Tea	Edible Other	Medicinal	N_2 Fixer	Dynamic Accumulator	Wildlife	Invert. Shelter	Nectary	Ground Cover	Other Uses/Functions	Nuisances	Poison
3-6"	indef		ENA								✓						G	G									G			
4"	4"		WNA											✓			G	G									G			
3-12"	indef		ENA									✓		✓			G	G									G			
1-2'	4'	F	ENA	✓										✓								Y					G	Y	A	
6-18"	6-12"	S	ENA									✓	✓	✓			F					F								
2-3'	2-3'		ENA					✓	✓	✓	✓			✓									Y				Y			
4-5'	4-5'	S	ASIA											✓			G	E				F								P
6-15'	6-9'	M-F	EUR	✓				✓	✓		✓			✓								F	Y				Y			D	P
18-36"	18-36"	F	ENA		✓			✓		✓		✓	✓	✓			F													
3'	4-8'	S-M	ENA	✓			✓	✓		✓	✓		✓	✓						G		G	Y			S				H	
12-30"	indef	M-F	ENA					✓			✓	✓		✓													Y	G	Y	E	
1'	1'		EUR		✓				✓					✓						G						Y	S			
2-4"	indef	S	ENA					✓				✓	✓	✓							E						Y			
6-12"	1+	M	ENA						✓		✓	✓													S	Y			
4-9"	indef	S	ENA		✓					✓		✓	✓	✓	G						F			F	Y			
18"	3'	M-F	ENA		✓			✓	✓	✓																S	Y			
35'	35'	S-M	ENA									✓		✓							F		Y	F			C		
30'	20'	S	ASIA					✓						✓	G									F					
20'	20'	M	EURA											✓	G						Y			F					
6-12'	6-12'	S-M	ENA				✓	✓	✓					✓										B		S			
6-12'	6-12'	F	ENA	✓				✓				✓		✓										B		S			
6-12'	6-20'	M-F	ENA	✓				✓	✓		✓	✓		✓			G								S	S	G	C	H	
12-25'	25'	M-F	EUR				✓				✓	✓		✓			G								S		G	C	H	
120'	75'		ASIA									✓					G								S		G	C	H	
80'	30'	M	EURA									✓		✓			G								S		G	C	H	
6-12'	6-12'	M	ENA	✓			✓	✓	✓		✓	✓		✓			G								S	S	G	C	H	
60'	40'		CULT											✓			G								S		G	C	H	
12-20'	12-15'		CULT											✓		E								S	S	G	C	H	
2-3'	3'	M-F	EUR											✓			E			G	G					G			P
27'	27'		ENA											✓	E							E		F		G	C	T	
35-50'	35-50'	S-M	PRAI		✓				✓		✓				F							E		F		G	C	T	
21'	21'		ASIA			✓	✓							✓	G							E		F		G	C	T	
20-35'	20-35'	S-M	ENA		✓			✓	✓			✓		✓	F							E		F		G	C	T	
6"	6"		EURA											✓							E	F				G			P
1-3'	1-2'	M	ENA					✓			✓			✓			G		Y						Y	S		
1-3'	1-2'	M	ASIA								✓			✓			E		Y		E				Y	S		
15-25'	15-25'	S	ASIA											✓	G						F			S				
8-16"	6-12"		ENA					✓		✓	✓								Y	G	G				Y	G	A	
10-20'	10-20'	M	EURA					✓	✓					✓	E							F				G			P
1'	1'		WNA			✓								✓						E					Y	S		
1'	1'		WNA			✓								✓						E					Y	S		
4-8'	3'+	M	EUR											✓								Y				Y	G	Y	P
3-6'	3-6'		WNA								✓	✓		✓			Y									G		
12-28"	12-18"	S-M	WNA								✓	✓		✓			Y									G	Y	

Taxonomy				Tolerances			Soil pH				Architecture		
Genus	Species	Common Name	Family	Hardiness Zones	Light	Moisture	Strongly Acid	Acid	Garden	Alkaline	Form	Habit	Root Pattern
Decaisnea	fargesii	blue bean	Lardizabalaceae	7	○◑	◊			■■		vl Shrub	ms	
Dennstaedtia	punctilobula	hay-scented fern	Dennstaedtiaceae	3-8	○●	◊		■	■■		s-m Herb	run	R
Desmodium	canadense	showy tick trefoil	Fabaceae	3-6	○◑	◊◊	■	■■	■■	■■	m-l Herb	clmp	T
Desmodium	glutinosum	pointed-leaved tick trefoil	Fabaceae	3-9	○◑	◊					s-m Herb	clmp	
Dicentra	eximia	dwarf bleeding heart	Fumariaceae	3-9	◑	◊		■■	■■		s Herb	clmp	Fb, R
Dioscorea	batatas	Chinese yam	Dioscoreaceae	5-10	○◑	◊			■■		l Vine	r vine	T, Fl
Dioscorea	japonica	jinenjo	Dioscoreaceae	4-10	○	◊			■■		l Vine	r vine	Tu
Diospyros	kaki	kaki persimmon	Ebenaceae	7-10	○	◊			■■	■■	m Tree	std	T
Diospyros	virginiana	American persimmon	Ebenaceae	5-9	○	◊◊		■	■■	■■	l Tree	skr	T, Sk
Diplotaxis	muralis	sylvetta arugula	Brassicaceae	7	○	◊◊		■■	■■		s Herb	clmp	
Diplotaxis	tenuifolia	sylvetta arugula	Brassicaceae	7	○	◊◊		■■	■■		s Herb	clmp	
Dryas	octopetala	mountain avens	Rosaceae	2-4	○◑	◊◊		■	■■	■	p Shrub	E Cmat	Fb
Dryopteris	marginalis	marginal wood fern	Dryopteridaceae	3-9	◑●	◊		■■	■■		m Herb	E clmp	R
Echinacea	purpurea	purple coneflower	Asteraceae	3-8	○◑	◊			■■		l Herb	clmp	T
Eleagnus	commutata	silverberry	Eleagnaceae	2-6	○	◊◊		■■	■■	■■	l Shrub	ms	F, St
Eleagnus	multiflora	goumi	Eleagnaceae	5-8	○◑	◊◊		■■	■■	■■	l Shrub	ms	
Epigaea	repens	trailing arbutus	Ericaceae	2	○◑	◊◊	■	■■			p Shrub	E Rmat	T, H
Epilobium	angustifolium	fireweed	Onagraceae	1-8	○◑	◊◊			■■		p-s Herb	clmp	Fb, R
Epilobium	latifolium	river beauty	Onagraceae	1-4	○	◊◊					l Herb	run	Fb
Equisetum	scirpoides	dwarf horsetail	Equisetaceae	1-9	○◑	◊◊		■■	■■	■	s Herb	E run	R
Equisetum	sylvaticum	woodland horsetail	Equisetaceae	1-5	◑●	◊◊		■	■■	■	s-m Herb	E run	R
Erigenia	bulbosa	pepper and salt	Apiaceae	4-7	◑●	◊			■■		p-s Herb	clmp	Tu
Erigeron	pulchellus	Robin's plantain	Asteraceae	4	○◑	◊		■■	■■		s-m Herb	clmp	St
Eryngium	maritimum	sea holly	Apiaceae	4b	○	◊◊		■■	■	■■	m Herb	clmp	T
Erythronium	americanum	trout lily	Liliaceae	4-7	◑●	◊		■■	■■		p-s Herb	e clmp	C, St
Eucalyptus	gunnii	cider gum	Myrtaceae	7	○◑	◊◊					l Tree	std	
Fagus	grandifolia	American beech	Fagaceae	3b-8	○●	◊		■	■		l Tree	skr	F, H, Sk
Fagus	sylvatica	European beech	Fagaceae	5	○●	◊		■■	■■	■■	l Tree	skr	Sk
Foeniculum	vulgare	fennel	Apiaceae	6	○	◊◊			■■		l Herb	clmp	
Fragaria	chiloensis	beach strawberry	Rosaceae	4-9	○	◊		■	■■		p Herb	E run	Fb, St
Fragaria	moschata	musk strawberry	Rosaceae	5	○◑	◊		■	■■		p-s Herb	E run	Fb, St
Fragaria	vesca	woodland strawberry	Rosaceae	5-10	○◑	◊		■	■■		s Herb	E run	Fb, St
Fragaria	vesca alpina	alpine strawberry	Rosaceae	5-10	○◑	◊		■	■■		s Herb	E clmp	Fb, St
Fragaria	virginiana	wild strawberry	Rosaceae	4-9	○◑	◊		■	■■		p-s Herb	E run	Fb, St
Fragaria	x ananassa	garden strawberry	Rosaceae	3-10	○	◊		■	■■		s Herb	E run	Fb, St
Fritillaria	camschatcensis	Kamchatka lily	Liliaceae	3	○◑	◊		■	■■	■	m Herb	clmp	B, R
Galax	urceolata	galax	Diapensiaceae	5-9	◑●	◊		■	■■	■	s Herb	E run	Fb, St
Gaultheria	hispidula	creeping snowberry	Ericaceae	3	◑●	◊	■	■■			p Shrub	E Rmat	F, St
Gaultheria	procumbens	wintergreen	Ericaceae	3	◑●	◊◊	■	■■	■		p Shrub	E Rmat	F, St
Gaultheria	shallon	salal	Ericaceae	6-8	○◑	◊	■	■■	■		s-m Shrub	E Rtkt	F, St
Gaylussacia	baccata	black huckleberry	Ericaceae	3	○◑	◊		■	■■		s Shrub	Rtkt	Sk
Gaylussacia	brachycera	box huckleberry	Ericaceae	5-9	○◑	◊	■	■			p-s Shrub	E Rmat	
Genista	pilosa	silky-leaf woodwaxen	Fabaceae	6-8	○◑	◊◊		■	■■	■■	s Shrub	ms	
Genista	pilosa procumbens	trailing silky-leaf woodwaxen	Fabaceae	6-8	○◑	◊◊		■	■■	■	p Shrub	Cmat	
Genista	sagittalis	arrow broom	Fabaceae	3-8	○◑	◊◊		■	■■	■■	p-s Shrub	Cmat	

Architecture			Habitats												Uses								Functions							Drawbacks	
Height	Width	Growth Rate	Native Region	Disturbed	Meadows	Prairies	Oldfields	Thickets	Edges	Gaps/Clearings	Open Woods	Forest	Conifer Forest	Other Habitats	Edible Fruit	Edible Nuts/Nest	Edible Greens, Etc.	Edible Roots	Culinary	Tea	Edible Other	Medicinal	N$_2$ Fixer	Dynamic Accumulator	Wildlife	Invert. Shelter	Nectary	Ground Cover	Other Uses/Functions	Nuisances	Poison
15'	10-15'	M	ASIA					✓				✓		✓	Y																
1-2'	indef	F	ENA		✓				✓	✓	✓	✓		✓															Y		E	
2-6'	1-3'	M-F	ENA		✓	✓		✓			✓			✓									Y			Y				D	
2-3'	2-3'	M-F	ENA								✓			✓									Y			Y				D	
12-18"	12-18"	S-M	ENA								✓	✓		✓														Y			P
10'	10'	M-F	ASIA	✓	✓			✓			✓	✓		✓			E					E								S, D	
9'	9'	M-F	ASIA						✓		✓			✓						G	E	G									
25-40'	25-40'	S-M	ASIA											✓	E							G						G			P
50-75'	35-50'	S-M	ENA		✓		✓	✓	✓	✓	✓	✓			E							G				F		G	C		P
1'	1'		EUR	✓										✓			G					Y									
1'	1'		EURA	✓										✓			G					Y									
3-6"	2'	M	ENA	✓										✓	Y					Y			Y					Y			
18"	36"	S	ENA									✓		✓														Y			P
3-4'	1-2'	M-F	ENA		✓	✓					✓			✓					F			E					Y	G			
6-12'	6-12'	M-F	WNA			✓								✓	F								Y		F			G		D	
6-8'	6-8'	M-F	ASIA					✓			✓			✓	G								Y		F			G		D	
4-6"	indef	S	ENA						✓	✓	✓	✓	✓	✓							G	G						G	Y		
4-16"	2-6'	F	ENA	✓	✓				✓	✓		✓		✓			G					F				F		G		D	
4-6'	4-6'+		ENA											✓			G														
6-8"	indef	S	ENA					✓			✓			✓								F		Y				Y			P
10-20"	indef	M	ENA		✓			✓			✓			✓								F		Y				Y			P
4-9"	4-5"		ENA								✓									Y							Y	S		
12-20"	12-20"	M-F	ENA		✓						✓			✓													Y	S		
2'	2'	M	EUR											✓			G	G									Y	S		
5-10"	5"	S-M	ENA					✓				✓		✓				F	G			F									P
80'	25'	M-F	AUST								✓			✓						E	E	Y							A		P
75-100'	50-75'	S-M	ENA									✓		✓		F	G				F			Y			G	C		P
80'	80'	S-M	EUR									✓		✓		F	G				F			Y			G	C		P
3-5'	1-3'	M-F	EUR	✓	✓	✓														E	G	E					Y	S		D	
6"	indef	F	WNA											✓	E							G			Y	F		G	Y		
6-12"	indef	M-F	EUR						✓						E							G			Y	F		G	Y		
8"	indef	M-F	EUR	✓				✓	✓	✓				✓	E							G			Y	F		G	Y		
10"	10"	M-F	EUR					✓						✓	E							G			Y	F		G			
4-12"	indef	F	ENA		✓			✓			✓			✓	E							G			Y	F		G	Y		
6-12"	indef	M-F	CULT	✓											E							G			Y	F		G	Y		
1-3'	6"	M	WNA		✓						✓			✓					G												
6-12"	indef	M	ENA								✓																Y			
1-4"	indef	S	ENA									✓	✓	✓	G									Y	F		Y			
2-6"	indef	S	ENA						✓	✓	✓	✓	✓		E					E	F			Y	F		Y			
1-6'	indef	M	WNA										✓	✓	G						F					B	G	Y		
3'	indef	S	ENA					✓		✓		✓		✓	G										F		G			
6-8"	indef	S	ENA									✓		✓	G										F		G	Y		
1'	3-4'	S-M	EUR											✓								Y				Y	G	Y		P
2"	3'	S-M	EUR											✓								Y				Y	G	Y		P
4-18"	2-3'	S-M	EUR											✓								Y				Y	G	Y		P

| Taxonomy | | | | Tolerances | | | Soil pH | | | | Architecture | | |
Genus	Species	Common Name	Family	Hardiness Zones	Light	Moisture	Strongly Acid	Acid	Garden	Alkaline	Form	Habit	Root Pattern
Genista	tinctoria	dyer's greenwood	Fabaceae	4-7	○	◊◆		■	■■	■■	s Shrub	ms	
Geranium	maculatum	wild geranium	Geraniaceae	3-8	○○	◆	■	■■			s-m Herb	clmp	R
Geum	rivale	water avens	Rosaceae	3	○○	◊◆			■■		m Herb	clmp	R
Geum	urbanum	clove root	Rosaceae	7	○○	◊◆			■■		m Herb	clmp	R
Ginkgo	biloba	maidenhair tree	Ginkgoaceae	5	○	◆			■■	■■	vl Tree	std	
Gleditsia	triacanthos	honey locust	Fabaceae	4b-9	○	◊◆			■■	■	l Tree	std	T, H, F
Glycyrrhiza	glabra	licorice	Fabaceae	6	○○	◆			■■	■	l Herb	run	St
Glycyrrhiza	lepidota	American licorice	Fabaceae	3-8	○○	◊◆			■■■	■	m Herb	run	R
Glycyrrhiza	uralensis	Chinese licorice	Fabaceae	5-9	○○	◆			■■	■	m Herb	run	R
Gymnocarpium	dryopteris	oak fern	Dryopteridaceae	2-7	◐●	●		■	■■■	■	s Herb	run	R
Halesia	tetraptera	silverbell	Styracaceae	4	○●	◆	■■	■■			s-m Tree	clmp	
Hedysarum	boreale	sweet vetch	Fabaceae	3	○	◆			■■		s-m Herb	clmp	T
Helianthus	decapetalus	thin-leaved sunflower	Asteraceae	2-8	○○	◆		■	■■		l Herb	run	R
Helianthus	giganteus	giant sunflower	Asteraceae	2-9	○○	◊◆		■■	■■		l-vl Herb	run	R
Helianthus	giganteus var. subtuberosum	Indian potato	Asteraceae	2-9	○●	◊◆		■■	■■		l-vl Herb	run	R
Helianthus	maximilianii	Maximilian sunflower	Asteraceae	2	○○	◊◆		■	■■		m-vl Herb	run	Tu, R
Helianthus	tuberosus	Jerusalem artichoke	Asteraceae	2-10	○○	◆		■■	■■	■	vl Herb	run	Tu
Helianthus	x laetiflorus	showy sunflower	Asteraceae	4	○○	◊◆		■■	■■		l-vl Herb	run	Tu
Heliopsis	helianthoides	oxeye sunflower	Asteraceae	4	○○	◆					l Herb	clmp	
Hemerocallis	fulva	tawny daylily	Hemerocallidaceae	2-9	○○	◊◆		■■	■■	■■	m-l Herb	clmp	Tu, R
Hemerocallis	hybrids	daylily	Hemerocallidaceae	3-9	○○	◊◆		■■	■■	■■	s-l Herb	clmp	Fb, Fl
Hemerocallis	lilio-asphodelus	yellow daylily	Hemerocallidaceae	3-9	○○	◊◆		■■	■■	■	m-l Herb	clmp	Tu, R
Heracleum	sphondylium	cow parsnip	Apiaceae	2-9	○○	◆		■■	■■		l-vl Herb	clmp	T
Heuchera	americana	alum root	Saxifragaceae	4-9	◐	◆		■■			p-s Herb	E clmp	R
Hibiscus	syriacus	rose of Sharon	Malvaceae	5-9	○○	◆			■■		l Shrub	ms	
Hieracium	venosum	rattlesnake weed	Asteraceae	3	○○	◆	■	■■			s-m Herb	clmp	
Hippophae	rhamnoides	sea buckthorn	Eleagnaceae	3-7	○○	◊◆		■	■■	■	l-vl Shrub	Ctkt	Sk
Hippophae	rhamnoides cv.	sea buckthorn 'Dorana Dwarf'	Eleagnaceae	3-7	○○	◊◆		■	■■	■	m Shrub	Ctkt	Sk
Houttuynia	cordata	hot tuna	Saururaceae	5-8	○○	◊◆		■■	■■	■	s Herb	run	R
Hovenia	dulcis	Japanese raisin tree	Rhamnaceae	6-9	○	◆			■■	■■	m Tree	std	
Humulus	lupulus	hops	Cannabidaceae	4	○	◆			■■		h Vine	r vine	R
Hydrophyllum	virginianum	Virginia waterleaf	Hydrophyllaceae	4-7	◐●	◆		■■	■■		s-m Herb	clmp	R
Hylotelephium	telephium	orpine	Crassulaceae	3-9	○○	◊◆		■■	■■	■	s Herb	E clmp	Tu
Ilex	glabra	inkberry	Aquifoliaceae	5	○○	◆		■■	■■		l Shrub	E Ctkt	
Illicium	floridanum	Florida star anise	Illiciaceae	6b-10	○●	◊◆		■■	■■		l Shrub	E Ctkt	Sk
Indigofera	decora	Chinese indigo	Fabaceae	5	○	◆		■■	■■	■	s Shrub	ms	
Ipomoea	leptophylla	bush morning glory	Convolvulaceae	4-7	○	◊◆			■■		s-l Herb	clmp	Tu
Ipomoea	pandurata	wild potato vine	Convolvulaceae	6-9	○○	◆			■■		l Vine	r vine	T, Tu
Iris	cristata	dwarf crested iris	Iridaceae	4-8	○●	◆		■■	■■	■	p-s Herb	Rmat	R
Jeffersonia	diphylla	twinleaf	Berberidaceae	5-8	○●	◆			■■	■	s Herb	clmp	Fb
Juglans	ailantifolia var. cordiformis	heartnut	Juglandaceae	5	○	◆			■	■■	l Tree	std	
Juglans	cinerea	butternut	Juglandaceae	3	○	◆		■	■■	■	l Tree	std	T
Juglans	nigra	black walnut	Juglandaceae	4b-7	○	◊◆		■	■■	■	l Tree	std	T
Juglans	regia	Carpathian walnut	Juglandaceae	5-7	○	◆		■■	■		l Tree	std	

Height	Width	Growth Rate	Native Region	Disturbed	Meadows	Prairies	Oldfields	Thickets	Edges	Gaps/Clearings	Open Woods	Forest	Conifer Forest	Other Habitats	Edible Fruit	Edible Nuts/Mast	Edible Greens, Etc.	Edible Roots	Culinary	Tea	Edible Other	Medicinal	N$_2$ Fixer	Dynamic Accumulator	Wildlife	Invert. Shelter	Nectary	Ground Cover	Other Uses/Functions	Nuisances	Poison
2-3'	2-3'	S	EUR		✓			✓	✓			✓	✓	✓								F	Y				Y	G			P
1-2'	2-3'	F	ENA				✓	✓				✓		✓								G						G			
2'	1-2'	F	ENA									✓		✓						F		F						G			
2'	1-2'	S	EURA					✓				✓		✓			F		Y	Y		F						G			
130'	10-30+	S-M	ASIA											✓		G				F		E								C		P
50-75'	50-75'	F	ENA				✓				✓	✓		✓	F							F						G		C	T	
3-6'	indef	S-M	EURA			✓								✓					G	E	E	E	Y	Y			Y	G		P	
1-3'	indef	F	PRAI	✓	✓	✓	✓							✓				F	G	G	E	E	Y	Y			Y	G		E, P	
2'	indef	F	ASIA		✓	✓						✓		✓					G	E	E	E	Y	Y			Y	G		P	
8-11"	indef	S	ENA						✓	✓	✓	✓		✓														Y			
20-40'	15-30'	M	ENA								✓				Y															C		
10-24"	20"		ENA											✓			G						Y			Y					
3-5'	indef	F	ENA		✓			✓			✓			✓								F					Y	S			P
5-12'	indef	F	ENA		✓			✓		✓	✓										Y	S					Y	S			P
5-12'	indef	F	ENA		✓			✓		✓	✓								G		Y	S					Y	S			P
2-12'	indef	F	ENA	✓	✓	✓													G		Y	S					Y	S		E, All	P
6-12'	indef	F	ENA	✓	✓			✓											E			S					Y	S		E	P
4-8'	indef	F	ENA	✓	✓	✓		✓			✓			✓					G			S					Y	S			P
4-5'	3-5'		ENA	✓	✓			✓	✓		✓			✓													Y	S			
2-6'	3-5'	F	ASIA	✓	✓			✓				✓		✓		F	F				E	G			F			Y	E, P	P
1-4'	2-5'	S-F	EURA											✓		F	F				E	G			F			Y	E, P	P
3-5'	3'	F	ASIA	✓	✓			✓			✓	✓		✓		F	F				E	G			F			Y	P	P
4-10'	4-8'	M-F	ENA	✓	✓			✓	✓		✓			✓		F	G	Y				F					Y	S			P
3-12"	1'	S	ENA									✓										F			F		S	Y		
6-12'	6-10'	M	ASIA					✓						✓		F				F	Y				F					
1-3'	1-2'	F	ENA		✓			✓	✓	✓	✓										F						S			
10-20'	10-20'	M	EURA											✓	G							S	Y		B				D	
4'+	4'	M	EURA											✓	G							S	Y		B				D	
12-15"	indef	F	ASIA											✓						G	G	E					Y	E	
30-45'	30-45'	M	ASIA			✓			✓					✓							E	F							E	
15-30'	15-30'	M-F	ENA	✓				✓		✓	✓			✓			G				E	E			E				S	
1-3'	1-2'	M	ENA							✓		✓					G				F						G			
12-18"	18-24"	M	EURA	✓				✓	✓					✓			F				F							D	
10'	10'	M	ENA					✓						✓										B	G			P
6-10'	4-6'	M	ENA						✓		✓	✓								G		G			S			
18"	6-8'	F	ASIA											✓									Y			Y	Y		P
1-4'	1-4'		PRAI		✓												F				G					G		P
4-6'	4-6'		ENA		✓		✓	✓	✓		✓			✓			F				G					G		P
4-8"	indef	M-F	ENA								✓	✓		✓							Y			F		Y		P
10-12"	16"	S	ENA							✓	✓	✓									G					Y		
60'	60'	M	ASIA									✓		✓		E					S		Y			G		
50-75'	50-75'	M-F	ENA									✓		✓		E					S		Y			G		C	
75-100'	75-100'	F	ENA							✓	✓	✓		✓		E					S		Y			G		C	All
100'	75-100'	M-F	EURA									✓		✓		E					S		Y			G		

Genus	Species	Common Name	Family	Hardiness Zones	Light	Moisture	Strongly Acid	Acid	Garden	Alkaline	Form	Habit	Root Pattern
Juglans	regia	English walnut	Juglandaceae	7-9	○	◊			■■	■	vl Tree	std	
Juglans	x bixbyi	buartnut	Juglandaceae	4	○	◊			■■	■	l Tree	std	
Lactuca	perennis	perennial lettuce	Asteraceae	5	○○	◊			■■		m Herb	clmp	
Laportaea	canadensis	wood nettle	Urticaceae	3-8	○◐	◊		■	■■	■	s-m Herb	run	
Lathyrus	japonicus maritima	beach pea	Fabaceae	3b-7	○	◊◊			■■		l Vine	r v/skr	R
Lathyrus	latifolius	everlasting pea	Fabaceae	4-9	○○	◊◊		■	■■	■	l Vine	r v/skr	R
Lathyrus	linifolius var. montanus	bitter vetch	Fabaceae	6b	○○	◊◊		■■	■■		l Vine	r vine	
Lathyrus	tuberosus	earth-nut pea	Fabaceae	6b	○◐	◊			■■	■	l Vine	r v/skr	Tu
Lespedeza	bicolor	bush clover	Fabaceae	4-7	○	◊◊		■■	■■	■■	l Shrub	ms	
Lespedeza	capitata	round-headed bush clover	Fabaceae	4-8	○○	◊◊			■■		m-l Herb	clmp	
Levisticum	officinale	lovage	Apiaceae	4	○○	◊		■	■■	■	l-vl Herb	clmp	R
Ligusticum	canadense	Canada ligusticum	Apiaceae	6	○●	◊					l Herb	clmp	
Ligusticum	canbyi	osha	Apiaceae	3	○●	◊					l Herb	clmp	T
Ligusticum	scoticum	Scotch lovage	Apiaceae	4	○	◊◊		■■	■■	■■	m Herb	clmp	T
Lilium	brownii	Hong Kong lily	Liliaceae	7	○◐	◊			■■		l Herb	clmp	B
Lilium	canadense	Canada lily	Liliaceae	3-7	○○	◊		■■			l-vl Herb	clmp	B, St
Lilium	lancifolium	tiger lily	Liliaceae	5	○○	◊		■■	■		l Herb	clmp	B
Lilium	longiflorum	white trumpet lily	Liliaceae	7	○○	◊			■■		m Herb	clmp	B
Lilium	philadelphicum	wood lily	Liliaceae	4-7	○○	◊	■■	■■			s-m Herb	clmp	B, St
Lilium	superbum	Turk's-cap lily	Liliaceae	4-8	○○	◊◊		■■	■		l-vl Herb	clmp	B, St
Lindera	benzoin	spicebush	Lauraceae	5-8	○●	◊◊	■	■■	■		l Shrub	ms	H
Linnaea	borealis	twinflower	Caprifoliaceae	3-7	◐	◊	■■				p Shrub	E Rmat	Fb, Sk
Lobelia	cardinalis	cardinal flower	Lobeliaceae	4-10	○○	◊◊	■■	■■	■■		m Herb	clmp	Fb
Lomatium	cous	biscuit root	Apiaceae	5	○	◊◊			■■	■■	m-l Herb	clmp	T
Lomatium	dissectum	fern-leaved biscuit root	Apiaceae	5	○	◊◊			■■		m-l Herb	clmp	T
Lomatium	macrocarpum	large-fruited biscuit root	Apiaceae	5	○	◊◊			■■	■■	m-l Herb	clmp	T
Lomatium	nudicaule	biscuit root	Apiaceae	5	○	◊◊					m-l Herb	clmp	T
Lonicera	caerulea var. edulis	edible honeysuckle	Caprifoliaceae	3	○	◊		■■	■■		m Shrub	Cthk	
Lonicera	kamschatica	honeyberry honeysuckle	Caprifoliaceae	3-8	○○	◊			■■	■	m Shrub	ms	
Lonicera	sempervirens	trumpet honeysuckle	Caprifoliaceae	4	○○	◊			■■		l-h Vine	w vine	
Lonicera	villosa	northern fly honeysuckle	Caprifoliaceae	3	○	◊◊		■■	■■		s Shrub	ms	
Lotus	corniculatus cv.	prostrate bird's-foot trefoil 'Plena'	Fabaceae	5	○○	◊◊		■■	■■	■■	p Herb	Cmat	
Lupinus	hybrids	hybrid lupine	Fabaceae	3	○	◊	■	■■			m Herb	clmp	
Lupinus	perennis	lupine	Fabaceae	3-9	○	◊◊	■■	■■			s-m Herb	clmp	F
Lycopodium	clavatum	running club moss	Lycopodiaceae	1-8	◐	◊◊		■■	■■		s Herb	E run	
Lycopus	uniflorus	northern bugleweed	Lamiaceae	3-7	○○	◊◊		■■	■■		s-m Herb	clmp	Tu, R, St
Maackia	amurensis	Amur maackia	Fabaceae	3-7	○●	◊◊		■■	■■	■■	s-m Tree	std	
Magnolia	virginiana	sweet bay magnolia	Magnoliaceae	5b-9	○●	◊◊		■■	■		s-l Tree	E std	H
Mahonia	aquifolium	Oregon grape	Berberidaceae	5	○●	◊		■■	■■	■■	m Shrub	E ms	F, St
Mahonia	repens	creeping mahonia	Berberidaceae	5-9	○○	◊◊		■■	■		s Shrub	E Ctkt	St
Maianthemum	canadense	false lily-of-the-valley	Convallariaceae	2-8	○●	◊	■■	■■			p Herb	run	R
Malus	baccata	Siberian crabapple	Rosaceae	3	○	◊		■■	■		s-m Tree	std	
Malus	ioensis	prairie crabapple	Rosaceae	2	○	◊		■■	■■	■	s-m Tree	std	F
Malus	pumila	apple, minidwarf	Roseaceae	4-9	○	◊			■■		d Tree	std	F
Malus	pumila	apple, dwarf	Rosaceae	4-9	○	◊			■■		d Tree	std	F

Height	Width	Growth Rate	Native Region	Disturbed	Meadows	Prairies	Oldfields	Thickets	Edges	Gaps/Clearings	Open Woods	Forest	Conifer Forest	Other Habitats	Edible Fruit	Edible Nuts/Mast	Edible Greens, Etc.	Edible Roots	Culinary	Tea	Edible Other	Medicinal	N_2 Fixer	Dynamic Accumulator	Wildlife	Invert. Shelter	Nectary	Ground Cover	Other Uses/Functions	Nuisances	Poison
100'+	75-100'	M-F	EURA								✓	✓		✓	E							S		Y				G			
60'	60'	M-F	CULT											✓	E							S		Y				G			
2'	1'	F	EURA	✓										✓			F					E					Y	G		D	
1-3'	1-3'	M	ENA									✓		✓			E				E	F								St	P
1-2'	indef	M	ENA	✓										✓						Y			Y					Y	G	Y		P
6'	indef	F	EUR	✓	✓			✓	✓					✓									Y					Y	G	Y		P
1-2'	1-2'		EUR					✓	✓		✓	✓							G		Y		Y					Y	G			P
3-4'	indef	M-F	EUR		✓				✓					✓					G				Y					Y	G			P
6-9'	6-9'		ASIA		✓	✓		✓	✓	✓	✓	✓					F			Y	Y		Y					Y	G			
2-4'	2-4'		ENA		✓	✓		✓			✓			✓								F	Y					Y	G			
4-8'	4-8'	M-F	EURA	✓	✓				✓					✓			G			G		F						Y	S			
3-6'	3'		ENA								✓	✓		✓														Y	S			
4'	3'		WNA									✓							G	Y	G							Y	S			
2'	2'		ENA											✓					G	Y		F						Y	S			
4'	2'	S	ASIA		✓			✓	✓		✓			✓					G			F				F						
3-8'	3-4'	S	ENA		✓						✓								F			F				F						
6'	2-4'	S	ASIA	✓	✓			✓						✓					G							F						
3'	1'	S	ASIA											✓					G							F						
1-3'	1-3'	S	ENA		✓	✓				✓	✓			✓					F			F				F						
3-8'	4-8'+	S	ENA		✓			✓		✓	✓	✓							F							F						
6-12'	6-12'	S-M	ENA					✓			✓			✓						G	G	G				F						
1-3"	indef	M	ENA					✓			✓	✓	✓	✓								F							Y			
3'	2-3'		ENA								✓			✓								G				F		G				P
18-36"	18-36"		WNA											✓		F	G											Y	S			
18-36"	18-36"		WNA											✓			G											Y	S			
18-36"	18-36"		WNA			✓								✓			G											Y	S			
18-36"	18-36"		WNA								✓			✓		F	G											Y	S			
5'	5'		ASIA					✓							G											F		G		D	P
5'	5'		EURA											✓	G											F		G		D	P
4-15'	4-15'	M-F	ENA					✓	✓																B		G	Y	D	P
1-3'	1-3'		ENA		✓						✓			✓	G											F		G		D	P
1"	1-2'	M	EUR	✓				✓	✓													Y					Y	G	Y		P
3-4'	2-3'	F	CULT											✓								Y	Y				Y	G			P
1-2'	1-2'	M	ENA	✓	✓	✓				✓	✓		✓	✓								Y	Y				Y	G	Y		P
5-12"	indef	S	ENA				✓	✓		✓	✓											G							Y		
6-24"	6-24"	M	ENA		✓			✓						✓					G								Y	G			
20-30'	20-35'	S	ASIA		✓			✓	✓					✓									Y				Y				P
12-70'	12-25'	M-F	ENA								✓	✓		✓						Y					B		G	C		
3-6'	3-6'	S	WNA					✓			✓		✓	✓	F						E				B		G		T	P
1-2'	4-5'	S	WNA		✓			✓			✓	✓	✓	✓	F										B		G	Y	T	P
2-4"	indef	M-F	ENA						✓		✓	✓									F						Y			
20-50'	20-50'	M	ASIA	✓										✓	F						F		Y	F		G	C		P
20-35'	20-35'	M	ENA	✓	✓				✓		✓			✓	F						F		Y	F		G	C		P
4-6'	4-6'	M	EURA											✓	E						F		Y	F		G	C	D	P
5-12'	5-12'	M	EURA											✓	E						F		Y	F		G	C	D	P

Genus	Species	Common Name	Family	Hardiness Zones	Light	Moisture	Strongly Acid	Acid	Garden	Alkaline	Form	Habit	Root Pattern
Malus	*pumila*	apple, semidwarf	Rosaceae	4-9	○	◊			■■		s Tree	std	F
Malus	*pumila*	apple, standard	Rosaceae	4-9	○	◊			■■		m Tree	std	F
Malva	*alcea*	mallow	Malvaceae	5	○◐	◊◊		■■	■■	■■	m Herb	clmp	T
Malva	*moschata*	musk mallow	Malvaceae	4	○◐	◊		■■	■■	■■	m Herb	E clmp	
Matteuccia	*struthiopteris*	ostrich fern	Dryopteridaceae	2-8	○●	◊◊	■■	■■	■■		l Herb	run	R
Medeola	*virginiana*	Indian cucumber root	Convallariaceae	3-8	●	◊	■■■				s Herb	clmp	R
Medicago	*sativa*	alfalfa	Fabaceae	3	○	◊			■	■■	s-m Herb	clmp	T
Melissa	*officinalis*	lemon balm	Lamiaceae	5	○◐	◊			■■■	■	s-m Herb	clmp	Fb, St
Mentha	*arvensis*	American field mint	Lamiaceae	3-8	○◐	◊◊		■	■■■	■	s-m Herb	run	R, St
Mentha	*requienii*	Corsican mint	Lamiaceae	6-10	○●	◊◊		■	■■■	■	p Herb	Cmat	R, St
Mentha	*spicata*	spearmint	Lamiaceae	4-10	○◐	◊◊		■	■■■	■	s-m Herb	run	R, St
Mentha	*suaveolens*	apple mint	Lamiaceae	6	○◐	◊◊		■	■■■	■	s Herb	run	R, St
Mentha	*x piperita*	peppermint	Lamiaceae	3-10	○◐	◊◊		■	■■■	■	m Herb	run	R, St
Mentha	*x villosa*	Bowles' mint	Lamiaceae	6	○◐	◊		■■	■■		m Herb	run	R, St
Mertensia	*maritima*	oyster plant	Boraginaceae	2-7	○	◊			■■		s Herb	clmp	T
Mespilus	*germanica*	medlar	Rosaceae	5-8	○	◊		■	■■■	■	s Tree	std	
Mitchella	*repens*	partridgeberry	Rubiaceae	4-8	○●	◊◊	■■	■■			p Shrub	E Rmat	Fb, St
Mitella	*diphylla*	miterwort	Saxifragaceae	4-8	○●	◊◊			■■		s Herb	clmp	R
Monarda	*didyma*	bee balm	Lamiaceae	4-9	○◐	◊		■■	■■■		l Herb	run	R
Monarda	*fistulosa*	wild bergamot	Lamiaceae	3-9	○◐	◊◊		■■	■■■		m-l Herb	run	R
Montia	*perfoliata*	miner's lettuce	Portulacaceae	4	○	◊			■■		s Herb	a Rmat	Fb
Montia	*sibirica*	Siberian miner's lettuce	Portulacaceae	4	○●	◊◊		■■	■■		s Herb	mat	Fb
Morus	*alba*	white mulberry	Moraceae	5	○◐	◊◊		■	■■■	■	m Tree	std	
Morus	*nigra*	black mulberry	Moraceae	6	○◐	◊		■	■■■	■	m Tree	std	
Morus	*rubra*	red mulberry	Moraceae	5b-9	○◐	◊◊			■■■	■■	m Tree	std	T, H
Morus	*x hybrid cv.*	'Geraldi Dwarf' mulberry	Moraceae	5	○◐	◊◊			■■■	■	d Tree	std	
Morus	*x hybrids*	hybrid mulberry	Moraceae	5-9	○	◊			■■■	■	m-l Tree	std	
Myrica	*cerifera*	southern bayberry	Myricaceae	6b-9	○◐	◊◊	■■	■■■	■■		l-xl Shrub	E ms	St
Myrica	*gale*	sweet gale	Myricaceae	1-6	○	◊◊	■■	■■			s-m Shrub	ms	St
Myrica	*pensylvanica*	northern bayberry	Myricaceae	2-7	○	◊◊		■■	■		l Shrub	Ctkt	H, F, St
Myrrhis	*odorata*	sweet cicely	Apiaceae	4	○◐	◊		■	■■■	■	m Herb	clmp	T, F
Nasturtium	*officinale*	watercress	Brassicaceae	2-10	○◐	◊◊			■	■	s Herb	run	Fb
Onoclea	*sensibilis*	sensitive fern	Dryopteridaceae	3	○◐	◊◊	■■				s-m Herb	run	R
Opuntia	*compressa*	prickly pear cactus	Cactaceae	5-9	○	◊		■■	■■	■■	p-s Shrub	Cmat	Fb
Origanum	*vulgare hirtum*	oregano	Lamiaceae	4-9	○	◊◊			■■	■	s-m Herb	clmp	R
Osmorhiza	*claytonii*	sweet cicely	Apiaceae	4	○●	◊		■■	■■		s-m Herb	clmp	Fb, Fl
Osmorhiza	*longistylis*	anise root	Apiaceae	4	○●	◊		■■	■■		s-m Herb	clmp	Fb, Fl
Oxalis	*grandis*	great wood sorrel	Oxalidaceae	5	○●	◊					s-m Herb	run	R
Oxalis	*montana*	wood sorrel	Oxalidaceae	3	○●	◊		■■	■■		p Herb	run	R
Oxalis	*oregana*	red wood sorrel	Oxalidaceae	7-10	○●	◊		■■	■■		s Herb	clmp	R
Oxalis	*violacea*	violet wood sorrel	Oxalidaceae	3	◐	◊		■■	■■		p-s Herb	clmp	B
Oxyria	*digyna*	mountain sorrel	Polygonaceae	2-8	○◐	◊		■■	■■		s Herb	clmp	R
Pachysandra	*procumbens*	Allegheny spurge	Buxaceae	5-8	○●	◊			■		s Herb	clmp	R
Panax	*quinquefolius*	American ginseng	Araliaceae	4-7	○●	◊		■■	■■		s Herb	clmp	T, Fl
Panax	*trifolius*	dwarf ginseng	Araliaceae	4	○●	◊		■■	■		p Herb	run	Tu

Column groups: **Architecture** (Height–Growth Rate) · **Habitats** (Native Region–Other Habitats) · **Uses** (Edible Fruit–Medicinal) · **Functions** (N_2 Fixer–Other Uses/Functions) · **Drawbacks** (Nuisances–Poison)

Height	Width	Growth Rate	Native Region	Disturbed	Meadows	Prairies	Oldfields	Thickets	Edges	Gaps/Clearings	Open Woods	Forest	Conifer Forest	Other Habitats	Edible Fruit	Edible Nuts/Mast	Edible Greens, Etc.	Edible Roots	Culinary	Tea	Edible Other	Medicinal	N_2 Fixer	Dynamic Accumulator	Wildlife	Invert. Shelter	Nectary	Ground Cover	Other Uses/Functions	Nuisances	Poison
12-20'	12-20'	M	EURA											✓	E							F		Y	F			G	C	D	P
25-35'	25-35'	M	EURA		✓		✓	✓			✓			✓	E							F		Y	F			G	C	D	P
3'	2'		EUR	✓	✓				✓					✓			G				G	G					Y	G		D	
3'	2'	F	EUR	✓	✓									✓			G				G	G					Y	G		D	
2-6'	indef	M-F	ENA								✓	✓		✓	E																
8-12"	6"	S	ENA								✓			✓						E												
1-3'	1-3'	M	EURA	✓	✓									✓						G	E	S	Y	Y			Y	G		D	
14-24"	2'+	M	EURA	✓							✓			✓							E	E		Y			Y	G	A	D	
6-20"	indef	F	ENA							✓	✓			✓							E	G		Y			Y	G	A	E	
1"	1'	S	EUR					✓			✓	✓		✓							E	G		Y			Y	G	A		
8-24"	indef	F	EURA	✓	✓									✓							E	G		Y			Y	G	A	E	
12-18"	indef	M-F	EURA	✓										✓							E	G		Y			Y	G	A	E	
1-2'	indef	F	EURA	✓			✓							✓							E	E		Y			Y	G	A	E	
2'	indef	F	EURA											✓							E	G		Y			Y	G	A	E	
1'	3'		ENA											✓					G	G											P
20'	20'	M	EURA				✓	✓			✓			✓	G														G			
1-2"	indef	S-M	ENA								✓		✓	✓	F							G				F		Y			
6-12"	8-12"	F	ENA								✓	✓															S	Y			
3-4'	2-6'	M-F	ENA				✓			✓	✓			✓					G		E	G	G				F	Y	G	A	E	
2-4'	2-6'	F	ENA	✓	✓	✓	✓	✓	✓		✓			✓					G	E						F	Y	G	A		
6-12"	indef	M-F	WNA	✓	✓		✓				✓	✓		✓			E												Y		D	
8-12"	indef	M-F	WNA		✓		✓				✓	✓		✓			G												Y		D	
40'	40'	F	EURA	✓		✓	✓	✓						✓	G							G			F					C	D, H	P
30'	50'	F	EURA											✓	G							G			F					C	D, H	P
35-50'	35-50'	F	ENA				✓				✓	✓		✓	G							G			F					C	D, H	P
8'	6-8'	F	CULT					✓	✓					✓	E							G			F					C	D, H	P
30-60'	30-60'	F	CULT											✓	E							G			F					C	D, H	P
10-30'	10-30'	M-F	ENA				✓				✓			✓						Y		G	Y			B			G		H	
2-6'	2-6'	S-M	ENA				✓							✓						Y		G	Y			B			G		H	
6-12'	6-12'	M-F	ENA				✓				✓		✓	✓						Y			G	Y			B			G		H	
3'	3'	M	EUR		✓				✓		✓	✓		✓			E	G	E	E								Y	S	A	D	
6-12"	indef	M-F	EURA											✓			E		E			G						Y			D	P
1-2'	indef	F	ENA		✓		✓	✓			✓			✓															Y		E	P
4-8"	3'	S	ENA		✓						✓		✓	✓	F		F				F	G							G		T	
1-2'	1-4'	M-F	EURA	✓							✓	✓		✓							E	E		Y			Y	G	A		
1-3'	1-2'		ENA				✓				✓	✓		✓					G			E						Y	S			
1-3'	1-2'		ENA								✓	✓		✓				G	G			E						Y	S			
8-36"	indef		ENA								✓	✓		✓					G		G	G										
2-6'	indef	M-F	ENA								✓	✓							G		G	G							Y			
10"	2-3'	M	WNA	✓							✓	✓		✓					G		G	G							Y			
4-8"	1-2'	F	ENA									✓							G		G	G									D	
2-12"	12"	M	ENA	✓										✓					E			G									D	P
6-12"	6-10'	S-M	ENA								✓	✓	✓	✓															Y			
6-16"	1'	S	ENA								✓	✓		✓								G	E						S			
6"	6"	S	ENA		✓					✓	✓	✓									G	G							S			

Taxonomy				Tolerances			Soil pH				Architecture		
Genus	Species	Common Name	Family	Hardiness Zones	Light	Moisture	Strongly Acid	Acid	Garden	Alkaline	Form	Habit	Root Pattern
Parthenium	integrifolium	wild quinine	Asteraceae	4	○◐	◌◌					s-l Herb	clmp	Fl
Passiflora	incarnata	maypop	Passifloraceae	6-10	○	◌◌		■	■	■	h Vine	r v/skr	St
Perideridia	gairdneri	yampa	Apiaceae	5	○◐	◌			■	■	m-l Herb	clmp	Tu
Persea	borbonia	red bay	Lauraceae	6-9	○◐	●	■	■	■		m-l Tree	E std	
Petasites	japonicus	fuki	Asteraceae	4-9	◐	◌			■	■	m-l Herb	run	R
Petasites	japonicus giganteus	giant fuki	Asteraceae	4	◐●	◌◌		■	■	■	l Herb	run	R
Phaseolus	polystachios	wild bean	Fabaceae	6-10	○◐	◌◌	■	■	■		l Vine	r vine	
Phlox	divaricata	wild blue phlox	Polemoniaceae	4-9	○◐	◌	■	■	■		s Herb	E clmp	Fb
Phlox	nivalis	trailing phlox	Polemoniaceae	6-9	○◐	◌◌	■	■	■		s Herb	clmp	Fb
Phlox	stolonifera	creeping phlox	Polemoniaceae	4-9	○◐●	◌	■	■	■		p-s Herb	E run	Fb, St
Phlox	subulata	moss pink	Polemoniaceae	4-9	○	◌◌	■	■	■	■	p Herb	E clmp	Fb
Phyllostachys	dulcis	sweetshoot bamboo	Poaceae	7	○◐	◌			■	■	vl-xl Bamboo	E run	R
Phyllostachys	nuda	stone bamboo	Poaceae	7	○◐	◌			■	■	vl-xl Bamboo	E run	R
Phyllostachys	viridi-glaucescens	blue-green glaucous bamboo	Poaceae	7	○◐	◌			■	■	vl-xl Bamboo	E run	R
Physalis	heteropylla	ground cherry	Solanaceae	3	○	◌		■	■		s-m Herb	clmp	Fb, R
Phytolacca	americana	pokeweed	Phytolaccaceae	3-9	○	◌		■	■	■	l-vl Herb	clmp	T
Pimpinella	saxifraga	burnet saxifrage	Apiaceae	5	○◐	◌◌		■	■	■	m Herb	clmp	Fb
Pinus	albicaulis	whitebark pine	Pinaceae	3	○	◌		■	■		m Tree	E std	T
Pinus	armandii	Chinese white pine	Pinaceae	5	○	◌					l Tree	E std	T
Pinus	cembra	Swiss stone pine	Pinaceae	4-7	○	◌			■		m-l Tree	E std	H
Pinus	cembra var. sibirica	Siberian stone pine	Pinaceae	3	○	◌●		■	■		vl Tree	E std	T
Pinus	edulis	pinyon pine	Pinaceae	5	○	◌			■		m Tree	E std	T
Pinus	flexilis	limber pine	Pinaceae	3-7	○◐	◌◌		■	■		m-l Tree	E std	T
Pinus	jeffreyi	Jeffrey pine	Pinaceae	6	○	◌					vl Tree	E std	T
Pinus	koraiensis	Korean pine	Pinaceae	4-7	○	◌◌		■	■		m-l Tree	E std	F, T
Pinus	pumila	Japanese stone pine	Pinaceae	4	○	◌		■	■		d Tree	E std	H
Platycodon	grandiflorus	balloon flower	Campanulaceae	5	○	◌			■		s-m Herb	clmp	T
Podophyllum	peltatum	mayapple	Berberidaceae	3-8	◐●	◌	■	■	■		s Herb	run	Fb, R
Polygonatum	biflorum	Solomon's seal	Convallariaceae	3-7	○●	◌◌	■	■	■		s-m Herb	run	R
Polygonatum	biflorum var. commutatum	giant Solomon's seal	Convallariaceae	3-7	○●	◌◌	■	■	■		m-l Herb	run	R
Polygonum	bistorta	bistort	Polygonaceae	4-8	○●	◌		■	■	■	m Herb	clmp	R
Polygonum	bistortoides	western bistort	Polygonaceae	2	○	◌●	■	■	■		s-m Herb	clmp	R
Polygonum	viviparum	alpine bistort	Polygonaceae	1-8	○◐	◌			■		s Herb	clmp	R
Polypodium	glycyrrhiza	licorice fern	Polypodiaceae	6	◐●	◌			■		s Herb	E clmp	R
Polypodium	virginianum	rock polypody	Polypodiaceae	3	◐●	◌		■			s Herb	E clmp	R
Polystichum	acrostichoides	Christmas fern	Dryopteridaceae	4-7	○◐●	◌		■	■	■	m-l Herb	E clmp	R
Polytaenia	nuttallii	prairie parsley	Apiaceae	4	○◐	◌◌					m-l Herb	clmp	
Polytrichum	commune	common haircap moss	Polytrichaceae	2-10	◐●	◌	■	■			p Herb	Rmat	
Potentilla	anserina	silverweed	Rosaceae	3-7	○	◌◌		■	■	■	p-s Herb	run	T, St
Prosopis	glandulosa	honeypod mesquite	Fabaceae	7	○	◌◌			■	■	vl Shrub	ms	Sk
Prunus	alleghaniensis	Allegheny plum	Rosaceae	5	○	◌			■		s Tree	spr	
Prunus	americana	American plum	Rosaceae	3-8	○	◌◌		■	■		m Tree	skr	F, Sk
Prunus	americana var. nigra	Canada plum	Rosaceae	3	○	◌			■		d-s Tree	skr	Sk
Prunus	angustifolia	Chickasaw plum	Rosaceae	5	○	◌			■		l Shrub	Ctkt	Sk
Prunus	angustifolia var. watsonii	sandhill plum	Rosaceae	5	○	◌			■		m Shrub	Rtkt	Sk

Architecture			Habitats												Uses								Functions							Drawbacks	
Height	Width	Growth Rate	Native Region	Disturbed	Meadows	Prairies	Oldfields	Thickets	Edges	Gaps/Clearings	Open Woods	Forest	Conifer Forest	Other Habitats	Edible Fruit	Edible Nuts/Mast	Edible Greens, Etc.	Edible Roots	Culinary	Tea	Edible Other	Medicinal	N_2 Fixer	Dynamic Accumulator	Wildlife	Invert. Shelter	Nectary	Ground Cover	Other Uses/Functions	Nuisances	Poison
1-4'	1-3'		ENA	✓		✓		✓			✓			✓								G						S			P
10-30'	indef	F	ENA	✓	✓			✓	✓		✓			✓	G					G		E			F					E, S	
18-36"	12-18"		WNA		✓				✓		✓	✓						E	Y								Y	S			
40-70'	40'	M	ENA								✓			✓					G	Y						S		G			
2-4'	indef	F	ASIA							✓	✓	✓					G					F				Y	S	Y		E, P	
5-6'	indef	F	ASIA								✓	✓					G					F				Y	S			E	
1-3'	1-3'	M	ENA					✓			✓	✓	✓							Y			Y		F	Y	G	Y			
12-16"	18-36"	M-F	ENA								✓	✓		✓											F			Y			
12"	18"	M	ENA					✓			✓	✓	✓											F			Y			
3-12"	indef	M-F	ENA								✓	✓		✓											F			Y			
4-6"	2'	M-F	ENA		✓						✓	✓		✓											F			Y			
20-40'	indef	F	ASIA					✓	✓		✓						E								S					E	
20-35'	indef	F	ASIA					✓	✓		✓						E								S					E	
20-35'	indef	F	ASIA					✓	✓		✓						E								S					E	
1-3'	1-3'	M-F	ENA	✓	✓		✓		✓		✓	✓		✓	F							F			F					E	P
5-9'	5-9'	F	ENA	✓	✓					✓				✓			E					G			F					P, D	P
3'	2'		EURA	✓	✓				✓				✓	✓			E					F				Y	S			D	
32'	20'		WNA								✓	✓	✓	✓		Y				Y	G			S					
65'	30-40'	S-M	ASIA								✓	✓	✓	✓	Y					Y	Y			S					
30-65'	15-25'	S	EURA								✓		✓	✓	Y					Y	Y			S					
110'	50'	S	ASIA										✓	✓	Y					Y	Y			S					
50'	35'	S-M	WNA								✓	✓	✓	✓	E					Y	Y			S					
30-75'	15-50'	S	WNA								✓		✓	✓	Y					Y	Y			S					
100-200'	50-100'	M	WNA										✓	✓	Y					Y	Y			S					
30-100'	15-50'	S	ASIA	✓							✓	✓	✓	✓	E					Y	Y			S					
1-7'	1-7'	Š	ASIA											✓	Y					Y	Y			S					
1-3'	1-3'	M	ASIA		✓									✓					G		E					G			
12-18"	indef	F	ENA		✓						✓	✓		✓	G						F					Y			P
1-3'	2'+	S-M	ENA					✓	✓			✓		✓			E	F			E					Y			
3-5'	4'+	S-M	ENA					✓	✓			✓		✓			E	F			E								
18-24"	18-24"	F	EURA		✓			✓	✓	✓				✓			E				G					Y		D	
8-28"	8-28"	M	WNA		✓									✓			G	G											
1'	1'		ENA		✓									✓			F	G											
6-8"	2-5'	S-M	WNA											✓				G											
10"	5'	M	ENA								✓	✓		✓							G					Y			
18-36"	3-4'	S	ENA									✓		✓							F					Y			
18-36"	12-18"		ENA			✓		✓	✓					✓										Y	S				
1-2"	indef	S	ENA								✓	✓	✓													Y			
3-14"	indef	F	ENA	✓										✓					G	Y	F	Y					G	Y	D	
12-25'	30'	M	WNA	✓		✓								✓		G						Y				G		T, D, H	
12-20'	12-20'		ENA					✓	✓		✓			✓	G						F			F		G		T	P
20-35'	20-35'	F	ENA		✓			✓	✓		✓	✓		✓	E						F			B		G		T	P
6-20'	6-20'	M	ENA					✓	✓					✓	E						F			F		G		T	P
8-10'	8-10'		ENA	✓	✓	✓		✓	✓					✓	G						F			B		G		T	P
3-6'	5-70'		ENA		✓	✓		✓	✓					✓	F						F			B		G		T	P

Taxonomy				Tolerances			Soil pH				Architecture		
Genus	**Species**	**Common Name**	**Family**	**Hardiness Zones**	**Light**	**Moisture**	**Strongly Acid**	**Acid**	**Garden**	**Alkaline**	**Form**	**Habit**	**Root Pattern**
Prunus	armeniaca	"alpricot"	Rosaceae	5-9	○	◐			■	■■	s-m Tree	std	
Prunus	armeniaca	apricot, dwarf	Rosaceae	5-9	○	◐			■	■■	d Tree	std	
Prunus	armeniaca	apricot, semidwarf	Rosaceae	5-9	○	◐			■	■■	s Tree	std	
Prunus	armeniaca	apricot, standard	Rosaceae	5-9	○	◐			■	■■	s-m Tree	std	
Prunus	avium	sweet cherry, dwarf	Rosaceae	5-9	○	◐			■■		d Tree	spr	
Prunus	avium	sweet cherry, semidwarf	Rosaceae	5-9	○	◐			■■		d-s Tree	spr	
Prunus	avium	sweet cherry, standard	Rosaceae	5-9	○	◐			■■		m Tree	spr	
Prunus	cerasifera	myrobalan plum	Rosaceae	5	○	◐	■	■■	■■	■■	s-m Tree	spr	
Prunus	cerasus	sour cherry	Rosaceae	4-8	○	◐			■■		s Tree	spr	
Prunus	cerasus var. frutescens	dwarf sour cherry	Rosaceae	4-8	○	◐			■■		d Tree	spr	
Prunus	domestica	European plum, dwarf	Rosaceae	4-9	○	◐			■■		d Tree	spr	
Prunus	domestica	European plum, standard	Rosaceae	4-9	○	◐			■■		s Tree	spr	
Prunus	domestica var. institia	damson plum	Rosaceae	4	○	◐			■■		s Tree	spr	
Prunus	dulcis	almond, dwarf	Rosaceae	6-9	○	◐			■■		d Tree	std	
Prunus	dulcis	almond, semidwarf	Rosaceae	6-9	○	◐			■■		d-s Tree	std	
Prunus	dulcis	almond, standard	Rosaceae	6-9	○	◐			■■		s-m Tree	std	
Prunus	fruticosa	Mongolian bush cherry	Rosaceae	2	○	◐			■■		s Shrub	ms	
Prunus	hortulana	hog plum	Rosaceae	5	○	◐◐			■■	■	s-m Tree	spr	F
Prunus	japonica var. nakai	Japanese bush cherry	Rosaceae	4	○	◐			■■		l Shrub	Ctkt	F
Prunus	mandschurica	Manchurian apricot	Rosaceae	3-9	○	◐			■■		vl Shrub	ms	F
Prunus	maritima	beach plum	Rosaceae	3	○	◐			■■		l Shrub	Ctkt	Sk
Prunus	munsoniana	wild goose plum	Rosaceae	5	○	◐			■■		l Shrub	Ctkt	Sk
Prunus	persica	peach, dwarf	Rosaceae	5-9	○	◐			■■		d Tree	std	
Prunus	persica	peach, semidwarf	Rosaceae	5-9	○	◐			■■		d-s Tree	std	
Prunus	persica	peach, standard	Rosaceae	5-9	○	◐			■■		s Tree	std	
Prunus	persica nucipersica	nectarine, dwarf	Rosaceae	5-9	○	◐			■■		d Tree	std	
Prunus	persica nucipersica	nectarine, semidwarf	Rosaceae	5-9	○	◐			■■		d-s Tree	std	
Prunus	persica nucipersica	nectarine, standard	Rosaceae	5-9	○	◐			■■		s Tree	std	
Prunus	pumila	eastern dwarf cherry	Rosaceae	3b	○	◐◐		■■	■■		m Shrub	ms	
Prunus	pumila var. besseyi	sand cherry	Rosaceae	3	○	◐◐			■■		m Shrub	Ctkt	Sk
Prunus	salicina	dwarf Japanese plum	Rosaceae	6-10	○	◐			■■		d Tree	spr	
Prunus	salicina	Japanese plum	Rosaceae	6-10	○	◐			■■		s Tree	spr	
Prunus	tomentosa	Nanking cherry	Rosaceae	3-7	○	◐◐			■■		l Shrub	ms	T, F
Prunus	virginiana	chokecherry	Rosaceae	2	○◐	◐◐			■■	■	m Tree	skr	F, Sk
Prunus	x gondouinii	duke cherry	Rosaceae	4-8	○	◐			■■		s Tree	spr	
Prunus	x hybrid cv.	'Hall's Hardy Almond'	Rosaceae	5-9	○	◐			■■		d-s Tree	std	
Prunus	x hybrids	hybrid plum	Rosaceae		○	◐			■■		d-s Tree	spr	
Prunus	japonica x jacquemontii cvs.	dwarf bush cherry 'Jan', 'Joy', 'Joel'	Rosaceae	3-8	○	◐			■■		m Shrub	ms	
Pseudostellaria	jamesiana	tuberous chickweed	Caryophyllaceae	4	◐●	◐					s-m Herb	clmp	Tu
Psoralea	esculenta	prairie turnip	Fabaceae	3-7	○	◐◐					s-m Herb	clmp	Tu
Pycnanthemum	flexuosum	hyssop-leaved mountain mint	Lamiaceae	5-9	○◐	◐◐			■■		s-m Herb	clmp	R
Pycnanthemum	virginianum	Virginia mountain mint	Lamiaceae	4-9	○◐	◐◐			■■		s-m Herb	clmp	R
Pyrus	bretschneideris	Asian pear	Rosaceae	4-9	○	◐			■		m Tree	std	
Pyrus	communis	European pear, minidwarf	Rosacea	4-9	○	◐			■		d Tree	std	
Pyrus	communis	European pear, dwarf	Rosaceae	4-9	○	◐			■		d-s Tree	std	

Architecture				Habitats											Uses								Functions							Drawbacks	
Height	Width	Growth Rate	Native Region	Disturbed	Meadows	Prairies	Oldfields	Thickets	Edges	Gaps/Clearings	Open Woods	Forest	Conifer Forest	Other Habitats	Edible Fruit	Edible Nuts/Mast	Edible Greens, Etc.	Edible Roots	Culinary	Tea	Edible Other	Medicinal	N_2 Fixer	Dynamic Accumulator	Wildlife	Invert. Shelter	Nectary	Ground Cover	Other Uses/Functions	Nuisances	Poison
20-30'	20-30'	M	EURA											✓	E	G						E					G				P
4-8'	4-8'	M	EURA											✓	E							E					G				P
12-15'	12-15'	M	EURA											✓	E							E					G				P
20-30'	20-30'	M	EURA											✓	E							E					G				P
6-8'	8-15'	M	EURA											✓	E							F			F		G		C	D	P
10-15'	18-20'	M	EURA											✓	E							F			F		G		C	D	P
25-35'	35-40'	M	EURA	✓				✓						✓	E							F			F		G		C	D	P
15-30'	15-30'	F	EURA											✓	G							F			F		G			T	P
20'	25'	M	EURA	✓		✓		✓	✓					✓	E							F			F		G				P
10'	12'	M	EURA											✓	E							F			F		G				P
10-12'	10-15'	M	EURA											✓	E							F					G				P
15-20'	15-20'	M	EURA					✓	✓					✓	E							F					G				P
15-25'	15-25'	M	EURA					✓	✓					✓	E							F					G			T, D	P
8'	8'	M	EURA											✓		E						S					G				P
8-20'	8-20'	M	EURA											✓		E						S					G				P
20-30'	20-30'	M	EURA					✓	✓					✓		E						S					G				P
3'	3'	M	ASIA			✓		✓			✓			✓	G							F				B	G				P
12-30'	12-30'	F	PRAI					✓	✓		✓	✓		✓	G							F					G				P
8'	8'		ASIA		✓							✓			G							F				B	G				P
12-15'	12-15'	M	EURA											✓	G							F					G				P
8'	8'	M-F	ENA					✓						✓	G							Y				B	G			T	P
10'	10'		PRAI	✓		✓		✓	✓					✓	G							F				B	G				P
2-5'	2-5'	M	EURA											✓	E							G					G				P
10-14'	10-14'	M	EURA											✓	E							G					G				P
15-20'	20-25'	M	EURA					✓	✓					✓	E							G					G				P
2-5'	2-5'	M	EURA											✓	E												G				P
10-14'	10-14'	M	EURA											✓	E												G				P
15-20'	20-25'	M	EURA					✓	✓					✓	E												G				P
3-6'	3-6'		ENA	✓				✓		✓				✓	G							F				B	G				P
3-6'	3'		WNA			✓								✓	G							F				B	G			T	P
8-12'	10-15	M	ASIA											✓	E							F					G				P
15-18'	15-20'	M	ASIA									✓			E							F					G				P
6-10'	6-8'	M	ASIA											✓	G							F			F		G				P
35-50'	20-35'	F	ENA	✓			✓	✓	✓						G							F				B	G		C	D	P
20'	25'		CULT											✓	E							F					G				P
10-15'	10-15'		CULT											✓		G						F					G				P
10-25'	10-25'		CULT											✓	E							F					G				P
3-4'	3-4'		CULT											✓	E							F				B	G				P
8-20"	8-20"		WNA					✓			✓	✓					G	G				S					G				
6-20"	6-20"	S	PRAI			✓				✓	✓			✓			G						Y			Y	G				P
1-3'	indef	M-F	ENA		✓			✓		✓									E			F				Y	G	Y	A		
1-3'	indef	F	ENA	✓				✓				✓		✓							E	F				Y	G	Y	A		
25-30'	25'	M	ASIA											✓	E												G				P
4-6'	4-6'	M	EURA	✓				✓						✓	E												G		C		
8-15'	10-15'	M	EURA	✓				✓						✓	E												G		C		

Taxonomy				Tolerances			Soil pH				Architecture		
Genus	Species	Common Name	Family	Hardiness Zones	Light	Moisture	Strongly Acid	Acid	Garden	Alkaline	Form	Habit	Root Pattern
Pyrus	communis	European pear, semidwarf	Rosaceae	4–9	○	◆			■		s Tree	std	
Pyrus	communis	European pear, standard	Rosaceae	4–9	○	◆			■		m Tree	std	
Pyrus	communis	perry pear	Rosaceae	4–9	○	◆			■		l Tree	std	
Quercus	acutissima	sawtooth oak	Fagaceae	5	○	◆		■	■		m Tree	std	
Quercus	alba	white oak	Fagaceae	4–8	○◐	◇◆			■	■	l Tree	std	T
Quercus	bicolor	swamp white oak	Fagaceae	4	○◐	◇◆			■		l Tree	std	F
Quercus	fruticosa	fruticosa oak	Fagaceae	4b	○	◆			■		l Tree	std	
Quercus	gambelii	Gambel oak	Fagaceae	6	○	◇◆					vl Shrub	Ctkt	Sk
Quercus	ilex var. rotundifolia	holly oak	Fagaceae	7	○	◇◆					l Tree	std	
Quercus	macrocarpa	bur oak	Fagaceae	2–8	○	◇◆	■	■	■	■	l Tree	std	T
Quercus	meuhlenbergii	chinkapin oak	Fagaceae	4b	○	◇◆			■	■	m Tree	std	H
Quercus	michauxii	swamp chestnut oak	Fagaceae	6	○	◇◆		■	■		l Tree	std	
Quercus	prinoides	dwarf chinkapin oak	Fagaceae	5b	○	◇◆	■	■	■		l Shrub	ms	H, Sk
Quercus	prinus	chestnut oak	Fagaceae	5	○◐	◇◆			■		l Tree	std	T
Quercus	x hybrid	Compton's oak	Fagaceae	5	○	◇◆		■	■		l Tree	std	
Quercus	x schuettei	Schuette's oak	Fagaceae	4b	○	◇◆			■		l Tree	std	
Rheum	australe	Himalayan rhubarb	Polygonaceae	5–8	○◐	◆		■	■		vl Herb	clmp	
Rheum	palmatum	turkey rhubarb	Polygonaceae	4	○◐	◆		■	■		vl Herb	clmp	
Rheum	x cultorum	rhubarb	Polygonaceae	1–9	○◐	◆			■		l Herb	clmp	Fb
Rhexia	virginica	meadow beauty	Melastomataceae	4	○◐	◇◆	■	■			s–m Herb	clmp	Tu
Rhodiola	rosea	roseroot	Crassulaceae	2	○◐	◇◆			■		p–s Herb	E clmp	R
Rhododendron	pericylmenoides	pinxter flower azalea	Ericaceae	4b–8	○●	◇◆	■	■			l Shrub	ms	F, Sk
Rhus	aromatica	fragrant sumac	Anacardiaceae	4–8	○	◆			■	■	s–l Shrub	Ctkt	F, Sk
Rhus	aromatica cv.	fragrant sumac 'Gro-Low'	Anacardiaceae	4–8	○	◇◆			■	■	s Shrub	Ctkt	F, Sk
Rhus	copallina	winged sumac	Anacardiaceae	5	○	◇◆			■		xl Shrub	Rtkt	F, Sk
Rhus	glabra	smooth sumac	Anacardiaceae	2	○	◇◆			■		l–vl Shrub	Rtkt	F, Sk
Rhus	hirta	staghorn sumac	Anacardiaceae	3	○	◇◆			■		xl Shrub	Rtkt	F, Sk
Ribes	americanum	American black currant	Grossulariaceae	3	○◐	◇◆			■	■	m Shrub	ms	F, Sk
Ribes	aureum	golden currant	Grossulariaceae	3	○◐	◆			■		m–l Shrub	ms	H, Sk
Ribes	hirtellum	smooth gooseberry	Grossulariaceae	3	○◐	◆		■	■		m Shrub	ms	
Ribes	missouriense	Missouri gooseberry	Grossulariaceae	4	○◐	◇◆			■	■	m Shrub	ms	F, Sk
Ribes	nigrum	black currant	Grossulariaceae	4	○◐	◆		■	■		m Shrub	ms	
Ribes	odoratum	clove currant	Grossulariaceae	3b	○◐	◇◆			■	■	l Shrub	ms	H, Sk
Ribes	silvestre	red currant	Grossulariaceae	3	○◐	◆			■		m Shrub	ms	
Ribes	triste	American red currant	Grossulariaceae	3	○◐	◇◆		■	■		m Shrub	ms	
Ribes	uva-crispa	gooseberry	Grossulariaceae	3	○◐	◆		■	■		m Shrub	ms	Sk
Ribes	x culverwellii	jostaberry	Grossulariaceae	3	○◐	◆		■	■		m–l Shrub	ms	
Ribes	x hybrids	gooseberry hybrids	Grossulariaceae	3	○◐	◆		■	■		m Shrub	Ctkt	Sk
Robinia	hispida	bristly locust	Fabaceae	4–8	○	◇◆			■	■	l Shrub	Ctkt	St
Robinia	pseudoacacia	black locust	Fabaceae	3b	○	◇◆		■	■		l Tree	skr	F, Sk
Robinia	viscosa	clammy locust	Fabaceae	5–8	○	◇◆			■	■	l–vl Shrub	Rtkt	F, Sk
Rosa	carolina	pasture rose	Rosaceae	4b–8	○	◇◆			■	■	s Shrub	Rtkt	F, Sk
Rosa	palustris	marsh rose	Rosaceae	3–9	○	◆					l Shrub	Ctkt	St, Sk
Rosa	rugosa	rugosa rose	Rosaceae	2–7	○	◇◆		■	■		m Shrub	Rtkt	Sk
Rosa	setigera	prairie rose	Rosaceae	4b–7	○	◇◆			■	■	l Shrub	Ctkt	F, Sk

Height	Width	Growth Rate	Native Region	Disturbed	Meadows	Prairies	Oldfields	Thickets	Edges	Gaps/Clearings	Open Woods	Forest	Conifer Forest	Other Habitats	Edible Fruit	Edible Nuts/Mast	Edible Greens, Etc.	Edible Roots	Culinary	Tea	Edible Other	Medicinal	N_2 Fixer	Dynamic Accumulator	Wildlife	Invert. Shelter	Nectary	Ground Cover	Other Uses/Functions	Nuisances	Poison
15-20'	15'	M	EURA	✓				✓						✓	E													G	C		
25-40	25	M	EURA	✓				✓						✓	E													G	C		
70'	15-55'	M	EURA											✓	G													G	C		
50'	50'	M-F	ASIA								✓	✓	✓	✓	F							F						G	C	D, H	P
75-100'	75-100'	S-M	ENA							✓	✓			✓	F							E		Y				G	C	H	P
75-100'	50-75'	M-F	ENA									✓		✓	F													G	C	H	P
60'	60'	F	CULT											✓	F													G		H	P
15-25'	15-25'	S	WNA								✓	✓	✓	✓	F												S	G		H	P
75'	75'	S-F	EUR					✓						✓	G												S	G		H	P
75-100'	75-100'	S	ENA			✓					✓	✓		✓	F													G	C	H	P
35-50'	35-50'	S-M	ENA					✓			✓	✓		✓	F													G	C	H	P
75-100'	75-100'	M	ENA								✓	✓		✓	F													G	C	H	P
12'	12-20'	S	ENA			✓		✓	✓		✓		✓		F													G		H	P
50-75'	75-100'	S-M	ENA								✓	✓		✓	F													G	C	H	P
60'	60'	F	CULT											✓	F													G		H	P
70'	70'	F	CULT											✓	F													G		H	P
6-10'	6'		EURA		✓									✓			E					E								P
6'	6'		ASIA		✓									✓			E					E								P
3-5'	3-5'	F	ASIA	✓										✓			E					E							P	P
1-2'	1'	M-F	ENA											✓			G	G													
5-10"	5-10"	S-M	ENA	✓										✓			Y	Y				F						G	Y		
6-12'	6-12'		ENA					✓			✓	✓		✓												Y					P
2-8'	6-10'	M-F	ENA	✓	✓	✓	✓	✓	✓		✓			✓							E	Y			B			G			P
2'	8'	M-F	ENA	✓	✓	✓	✓	✓	✓		✓			✓							E	Y			B			G	Y		P
20-35'	20-35'	F	ENA	✓	✓			✓	✓	✓	✓			✓							E	Y			B			G		E, D	P
10-20'	20-35'	F	ENA			✓	✓	✓	✓	✓	✓			✓							E	Y			B			G		E, D	P
35-50'	35-50'	M-F	ENA				✓	✓	✓					✓							E	Y			B			G		E, D	P
3-6'	3-6'	M	ENA					✓			✓	✓		✓	F							F			B			G			
3-8'	3-6'		WNA					✓						✓	G										B			G			
3-5'	3-5'		ENA			✓		✓		✓	✓	✓		✓	G										B			G		T	
3-6'	3-6'	F	ENA				✓	✓			✓			✓	G										B			G		T	
3-5'	3-5'	M-F	EURA					✓	✓		✓			✓	E							G			B			G			
6-12'	6-12'+	F	ENA			✓	✓	✓			✓			✓	E										B			G			
3-5'	3-5'	M	EURA					✓	✓		✓	✓		✓	E										B			G			
3-5'	3-5'		ENA								✓	✓		✓	G										B			G			
3-5'	3-5'	M	EURA					✓	✓		✓	✓		✓	E							F			B			G		T	
4-8'	4-8'	F	CULT											✓	E										B			G			
3-5'	3-5'		CULT											✓	E										B			G		T	
6-12'	3-6	F	ENA	✓			✓	✓			✓			✓									Y		B		Y	G		E, T	P
50-75'	35-50'	F	ENA	✓			✓	✓	✓		✓	✓		✓								G	Y		Y	F	Y	G	C	E, T, D	P
6-20'	6-20'	F	ENA				✓	✓			✓	✓		✓									Y		B		Y	G		E, T	P
3'	6-12'+	F	ENA	✓		✓	✓	✓	✓		✓			✓	F							G			B			G			
5-7'	5-7'	F	ENA					✓			✓			✓	F							G			B			G			
4-6'	4-8'+	F	ASIA	✓										✓	G							G			B			G		E, D	
6-12'	12-30'	F	PRAI		✓	✓	✓	✓	✓	✓	✓			✓	F							G			B			G		E	

Genus	Species	Common Name	Family	Hardiness Zones	Light	Moisture	Strongly Acid	Acid	Garden	Alkaline	Form	Habit	Root Pattern
Rosa	*villosa*	apple rose	Rosaceae	3-7	○	◆			■	■	m Shrub	ms	
Rosmarinus	*officinalis*	rosemary	Lamiaceae	7-9	○	◊◆		■	■■	■	s-m Shrub	E ms	
Rosmarinus	*officinalis* cv.	rosemary 'Arp'	Lamiaceae	5-9	○	◊◆		■	■■	■	s-m Shrub	E ms	
Rosmarinus	*officinalis* cv.	rosemary 'Huntington Carpet'	Lamiaceae	7-9	○	◊◆		■	■■	■	s Shrub	ms	
Rubus	*allegheniensis*	Allegheny blackberry	Rosaceae	3b	○	◊◆	■	■■	■		m Shrub	Rtkt	F, Sk
Rubus	*chamaemorus*	cloudberry	Rosaceae	2-4	○	◊◆◆	■■	■■	■■	■■	p-s Herb	clmp	R
Rubus	*flagellaris*	prickly dewberry	Rosaceae	4	○◐	◆			■■		s Shrub	Rtkt	Sk
Rubus	*fruticosus*	blackberry	Rosaceae	6	○	◆		■	■		m-l Shrub	Rtkt	Sk
Rubus	*idaeus*	raspberry	Rosaceae	3-9	○	◆		■	■		m Shrub	Rtkt	Sk
Rubus	*idaeus* var. *strigosus*	American red raspberry	Rosaceae	2-6	○	◊◆		■	■		m Shrub	Rtkt	Sk
Rubus	*illecebrosus*	strawberry-raspberry	Rosaceae	6b	●	◆			■■		s Shrub	E Rtkt	Sk
Rubus	*occidentalis*	black raspberry	Rosaceae	4	○	◊◆	■	■■	■		m Shrub	Rtkt	F, Sk
Rubus	*odoratus*	purple-flowering raspberry	Rosaceae	4	○◐	◆		■■	■		m Shrub	ms	Sk
Rubus	*parviflorus*	thimbleberry	Rosaceae	4-9	○●	◆			■■		m Shrub	ms	Sk
Rubus	*pentalobus* cv.	'Emerald Carpet' raspberry	Rosaceae	7	○◐	◆		■■	■■	■■	p Shrub	E Cmat	Sk
Rubus	*spectabilis*	salmonberry	Rosaceae	6	○	◆		■■	■		m Shrub	Ctkt	Sk
Rubus	*tricolor*	creeping bramble	Rosaceae	7b	○●	◆			■■		s Shrub	Rmat	Sk
Rubus	x hybrids	boysenberry, et al.	Rosaceae	6	○	◆		■	■		m Shrub	Rtkt	Sk
Rubus	spp.	dewberry	Rosaceae	7	○	◆		■	■		m-l Shrub	Ctkt	Sk
Rubus	x *stellarcticus*	all-fieldberry	Rosaceae	2-8	○	◆		■■	■■		s Herb	Cmat	
Rumex	*acetosa*	French sorrel	Polygonaceae	3-9	○◐	◆		■■	■■	■	s-m Herb	clmp	Fb
Rumex	*acetosella*	sheep sorrel	Polygonaceae	3	○	◊◆	■■	■■	■		p Herb	Rmat	St
Rumex	*scutatus*	buckler-leaved sorrel	Polygonaceae	3-9	○◐	◊◆		■■	■■	■■	s Herb	clmp	
Salvia	*officinalis*	broadleaf sage	Lamiaceae	5-9	○	◊◆		■	■■	■	s Shrub	E ms	H
Sambucus	*canadensis*	elderberry	Sambucaceae	3-10	○◐	◊◆			■■	■	l Shrub	ms	F, Sk
Sanguisorba	*canadensis*	American great burnet	Rosaceae	3-8	○◐	◊◆		■■	■■	■■	l Herb	clmp	R
Sanguisorba	*minor*	salad burnet	Rosaceae	5	○◐	◆				■■	s-m Herb	clmp	R
Sanguisorba	*officinalis*	great burnet	Rosaceae	4	○◐	◆		■	■■		m Herb	clmp	R
Sasa	*kurilensis*	chishima-zasa bamboo	Poaceae	7	○◐	◆			■■	■■	m-l Bamb	E run	R
Sassafras	*albidum*	sassafras	Lauraceae	5b	○◐	◊◆		■■	■■		m Tree	skr	T, Sk
Satureja	*douglasii*	yerba buena	Lamiaceae	5-9	○◐	◆		■■	■		p Herb	E clmp	R
Saxifraga	*stolonifera*	strawberry saxifrage	Saxifragaceae	7-10	◐●	◆			■■		p-s Herb	E Rmat	St
Schisandra	*chinensis*	magnolia vine	Schisandraceae	4b	○◐	◆		■	■■		h Vine	w vine	
Scorzonera	*hispanica*	scorzonera	Asteraceae	4-9	○◐	◆			■■		s-m Herb	clmp	T
Secale	*cereale* cv.	rye 'Varimontra'	Poaceae		○	◆			■■		s-l Herb	clmp	
Sedum	*album*	white stonecrop	Crassulaceae	6	○◐	◊◆		■■	■■	■	p Herb	E run	
Sedum	*reflexum*	stonecrop	Crassulaceae	3	○◐	◊◆		■■	■■	■	s Herb	E run	
Sedum	*ternatum*	wild stonecrop	Crassulaceae	3-8	○●	◆				■■	p Herb	E run	
Semiarundinaria	*fastuosa*	temple bamboo	Poaceae	6b	○◐	◆			■■		l-xl Bamboo	E run	R
Senecio	*aureus*	golden groundsel	Asteraceae	4	○◐	◊◆		■■	■		s-m Herb	clmp	R
Senecio	*obovatus*	round-leaved ragwort	Asteraceae	4	◐	◆		■	■		s-m Herb	clmp	St
Shepherdia	*canadensis*	Canadian buffaloberry	Eleagnaceae	2	○	◊◆			■■	■■	l Shrub	ms	H
Silphium	*laciniatum*	compass plant	Asteraceae	4	○◐	◊◆					l-vl Herb	run	
Silphium	*perfoliatum*	cup plant	Asteraceae	4	○◐	◆					l-vl Herb	run	R
Silphium	*trifoliatum*	whorled rosinweed	Asteraceae	4	○◐	◆					l-vl Herb	run	

Column groups: Architecture (Height, Width, Growth Rate) · Habitats (Native Region → Other Habitats) · Uses (Edible Fruit → Medicinal) · Functions (N$_2$ Fixer → Other Uses/Functions) · Drawbacks (Nuisances, Poison)

Height	Width	Growth Rate	Native Region	Disturbed	Meadows	Prairies	Oldfields	Thickets	Edges	Gaps/Clearings	Open Woods	Forest	Conifer Forest	Other Habitats	Edible Fruit	Edible Nuts/Mast	Edible Greens Etc.	Edible Roots	Culinary	Tea	Edible Other	Medicinal	N$_2$ Fixer	Dynamic Accumulator	Wildlife	Invert. Shelter	Nectary	Ground Cover	Other Uses/Functions	Nuisances	Poison
4'	4'	F	EURA				✓		✓		✓				G				·			G			B		G			D	
3-4'	3-4'	S	EUR	✓										✓					E	G		E			F		Y	G		A	
3-4'	3-4'	S	EUR	✓										✓					E	G		E			F		Y	G		A	
1'	4'	S-M	EUR	✓										✓					E	G		E			F		Y	G	Y	A	
3-6'	6-12'+	F	ENA	✓			✓	✓	✓	✓	✓			✓	E		F			G		S			B		G			E	
3-8"	3-8"	S	ENA											✓	E							S			F		G				
1'	indef	M	ENA	✓	✓	✓	✓	✓	✓		✓			✓	Y					G		S			F		G				
4-8'	4-8'	F	CULT											✓	E					G		S			B		G			E	
4-6'	4-6'	F	CULT											✓	E		F			G		S			B		G			E	
3-6'	6-12'+	F	ENA	✓			✓	✓		✓	✓			✓	E		F			G		S			B		G			E	
1-2'	indef	M-F	ASIA	✓				✓						✓	G							S			F			G	Y			
3-6'	6-12'+	F	ENA	✓	✓			✓	✓	✓	✓			✓	E		F			G		S			B		G			E	
6'	6'	F	ENA					✓	✓		✓			✓	F							S			B		G				
4-6'	4-6'	M	WNA	✓					✓	✓	✓			✓	G		F					S			B		G				
2-4"	3'	M	ASIA											✓	F							S			F			G	Y			
4-5'	4-5'	M-F	WNA	✓				✓	✓				✓	✓	E		F			G		S			B		G			E	
18"	7'	F	ASIA					✓						✓	F							S			F			G	Y			
4-6'	4-6'	F	CULT											✓	E						G	S			B		G			E	
4-8'	4-8'	F	CULT											✓	E						G	S			B		G			E	
1'	2'+	M-F	CULT											✓	E							S			F			G	Y			
1-3'	10-12"	M	EURA		✓						✓			✓			E					F		Y					D	P
6"	indef	F	EURA	✓	✓												E					F		Y				G	Y	D, E, H	P
1'	1-2'	M	EURA			✓											E					F		Y					Y		P
18-30"	30-36"	M	EUR	✓										✓					E	G		G			F		Y	G		A	
6-12'	6-12'	F	ENA				✓	✓	✓		✓	✓		✓	G					G		E			B		S				P
4-5'	4-5'	M	ENA		✓	✓					✓	✓		✓					G								Y	G			
1-2'	1'	M	EUR	✓	✓									✓					G							Y	Y	G		D	
3'	2'	M-F	EUR		✓			✓						✓					G		F						Y	G		D	
5-10'	indef	F	ASIA					✓						✓					E							S				E	
35-50'	35-50'	M-F	ENA	✓			✓		✓		✓			✓						F	E	F			B			G		C	
2"	3'	M	WNA					✓				✓	✓	✓						Y	E	Y			Y		Y	G	Y	A	
6-8"	indef	F	ASIA											✓						Y								S	Y		
20'	20'	M	ASIA								✓	✓	✓	✓	G						Y	E				S				S	
1-3'	1-2'	M	EUR					✓						✓					E	E							Y	S			
1-4'	1-2'	M	EURA											✓								E					Y	G		H	P
2-5"	indef	F	EURA											✓			F					F						G	Y			P
8-10"	indef	M	EUR	✓										✓			F		·			F						G	Y			P
2-6"	indef	S-M	ENA											✓			F					F						G	Y			P
10-35'	indef	S-M	ASIA								✓			✓	E											S				E	
1-3'	18"	M-F	ENA		✓	✓		✓			✓	✓		✓								G					Y	S			P
6-24"	1-2'	M-F	ENA		✓							✓		✓													Y	S			P
6-12'	6-12'	S-M-F	ENA					✓	✓		✓			✓	F								Y			F		G				
4-10'	indef	F	ENA			✓	✓		✓	✓	✓			✓							F	F			F	Y	S			E	
4-8'	indef	F	ENA	✓	✓	✓		✓				✓		✓							Y	F			F	Y	S			E	
3-7'	indef	F	ENA			✓		✓	✓	✓		✓									Y				F	Y	S			E	

| Taxonomy | | | | Tolerances | | | Soil pH | | | | Architecture | | |
Genus	Species	Common Name	Family	Hardiness Zones	Light	Moisture	Strongly Acid	Acid	Garden	Alkaline	Form	Habit	Root Pattern
Sium	sisarum	skirret	Apiaceae	5–9	○◑	◊◊		■	■■	■■	m Herb	clmp	Tu
Smallanthus	uvedalia	leafcup	Asteraceae	4	◑	◊		■■	■■		s–l Herb	clmp	
Smilacina	racemosa	false Solomon's seal	Convallariaceae	2–8	○●	◊◊		■■	■		s–m Herb	run	R
Smilax	herbacea	carrion flower	Smilacaceae	4	○◑	◊		■■	■■		l Vine	r vine	
Solidago	flexicaulis	zig-zag goldenrod	Asteraceae	4	○●	◊◊		■■	■■		s–m Herb	clmp	R
Solidago	missouriensis	Missouri goldenrod	Asteraceae	4	○◑	◊◊					s–m Herb	clmp	R
Solidago	odora	sweet goldenrod	Asteraceae	3–9	○◑	◊◊	■	■■	■		m–l Herb	clmp	Fb
Sophora	japonica	Japanese pagoda tree	Fabaceae	4–8	○	◊◊			■■		l Tree	std	
Sorbus	americana	American mountain ash	Rosaceae	2	○	◊		■■	■■		s–m Tree	std	
Sorbus	aucuparia	rowan	Rosaceae	3–7	○	◊		■■	■■		s–m Tree	std	
Sorbus	decora	showy mountain ash	Rosaceae	2–5	○	◊◊		■■	■■		s–m Tree	std	F
Sorbus	domestica	service tree	Rosaceae	4	○	◊			■■		m Tree	std	
Sorghum	x hybrid	perennial sorghum	Poaceae	7–10	○	◊			■■		l Herb	run	
Stachys	affinis	Chinese artichoke	Lamiaceae	5–9	○	◊			■■		s–m Herb	run	R
Stachys	hyssopifolia	hyssop hedge nettle	Lamiaceae	6–9	○	◊◊		■■	■■		s–m Herb	clmp	St
Stachys	palustris	woundwort	Lamiaceae	3	○◑	◊◊		■■	■■		s–l Herb	clmp	R
Stellaria	media	annual chickweed	Caryophyllaceae	4	○◑	◊			■■		s Herb	a Rmat	Fb
Stellaria	pubera	giant chickweed	Caryophyllaceae	5–8	◑●	◊			■■		s Herb	clmp	
Streptopus	amplexifolius	twisted stalk	Convallariaceae	3–8	◑●	◊			■		s–m Herb	clmp	Fb, R
Streptopus	roseus	rosybells	Convallariaceae	3–8	◑●	◊			■		s–m Herb	clmp	R
Strophostyles	umbellata	wild bean	Fabaceae	6–9	○◑	◊◊					l Vine	r vine	
Stylosanthes	biflora	two-flowered pencil flower	Fabaceae	5	○◑	◊◊					s–m Herb	clmp	
Symphytum	grandiflorum	large-flowered comfrey	Boraginaceae	4–8	○◑	◊◊		■	■■	■■	s Herb	clmp	R
Symphytum	officinale	comfrey	Boraginaceae	4	○◑	◊		■	■■	■■	l Herb	clmp	Fb, Fl
Symphytum	x uplandicum	Russian comfrey	Boraginaceae	6–8	○◑	◊		■	■■	■■	s–l Herb	clmp	Fb, Fl
Taenidia	integerrima	yellow pimpernel	Apiaceae	4	○◑	◊					s–m Herb	clmp	T
Taraxacum	officinale	dandelion	Asteraceae	3	○◑	◊			■■	■	s–m Herb	clmp	T
Thaspium	barbinode	meadow parsnip	Apiaceae	4	○◑	◊					s–l Herb	clmp	T
Thaspium	trifoliatum	woodland thaspium	Apiaceae	4	◑	◊					s–l Herb	clmp	T
Thelypteris	noveboracensis	New York fern	Thelypteridaceae	2	◑●	◊◊		■	■■		s–m Herb	run	R
Thermopsis	villosa	Carolina bush pea	Fabaceae	5–8	○◑	◊◊		■■			l Herb	clmp	
Thymus	vulgaris	thyme	Lamiaceae	4–10	○	◊◊			■■	■■	p–s Shrub	Cmat	T
Tiarella	cordifolia	foamflower	Saxifragaceae	3–8	◑●	◊		■■	■		p–s Herb	run	St
Tilia	americana	American basswood	Tiliaceae	3	○●	◊			■■		l Tree	spr	T, F
Tilia	x vulgaris	linden	Tiliaceae	4	○◑	◊◊		■■	■■		l Tree	spr	Sk
Toona	sinensis	fragrant spring tree	Meliaceae	5	○	◊		■■	■■	■■	m–l Tree	skr	Sk
Tradescantia	virginiana	Virginia spiderwort	Commelinaceae	4–9	○◑	◊◊		■■	■■	■	s–m Herb	run	
Trifolium	pratense	red clover	Fabaceae	3	○	◊		■■	■■	■	s–m Herb	clmp	T
Trifolium	repens	white clover	Fabaceae	4	○◑	◊		■	■■		p–s Herb	clmp	St
Trillium	grandiflorum	white trillium	Trilliaceae	3–7	◑●	◊		■■	■■	■	s Herb	e run	R
Tripsacum	dactyloides	eastern gamma grass	Poaceae	3–9	○◑	◊		■■	■■		vl Herb	clmp	
Triteleia	grandiflora	blue dicks	Alliaceae	6	○◑	◊◊			■■		s–m Herb	e clmp	C
Triticum	x aestivum	perennial wheat	Poaceae		○	◊			■■		m–l Herb	clmp	
Ulmus	rubra	slippery elm	Ulmaceae	3–9	○	◊			■■	■	m–l Tree	std	
Urtica	dioica	stinging nettle	Urticaceae	4–8	○◑	◊		■	■■	■	s–l Herb	run	Fb, R

Height	Width	Growth Rate	Native Region	Disturbed	Meadows	Prairies	Oldfields	Thickets	Edges	Gaps/Clearings	Open Woods	Forest	Conifer Forest	Other Habitats	Edible Fruit	Edible Nuts/Mast	Edible Greens, Etc.	Edible Roots	Culinary	Tea	Edible Other	Medicinal	N_2 Fixer	Dynamic Accumulator	Wildlife	Invert. Shelter	Nectary	Ground Cover	Other Uses/Functions	Nuisances	Poison
3'	1-2'	M	EUR											✓							E							Y	S			
18"-5'	1-3'		ENA					✓			✓			✓								G					Y	S			
1-3'	indef	S	ENA						✓	✓		✓	✓	✓	F		G														P
6-10'	4-6'	M-F	ENA				✓	✓	✓		✓				Y		G									F						
1-3'	1-3'	M-F	ENA					✓				✓		✓						Y	Y	E					Y	S			P
1-3'	1-3'	F	ENA	✓			✓	✓	✓		✓			✓						Y		Y	E					Y	S			P
2-4'	2-4'	F	ENA	✓				✓		✓	✓			✓			G			G	E	E					Y	S	A		P
50-75'	50-75'	M-F	ASIA											✓			G						Y				Y	G			P
10-30'	10-30'		ENA								✓	✓	✓	✓	F							F			F			G	C		P
20-40'	15-35'	M	EURA	✓				✓	✓		✓	✓	✓	✓	G							F			F			G	C	D	P
20-35'	20-35'	M	ENA								✓			✓	F										F			G	C		P
30-35'	30-35'	M	EUR					✓			✓			✓	G										F			G	C	D	P
6'	indef	F	CULT											✓							E									E, D, H	
18"	indef	M-F	ASIA											✓			E										Y	G	Y	P	
6-30"	1'		ENA		✓									✓			G										Y	G			
1-3'	1'		ENA	✓	✓	✓								✓			G					G					Y	G			
6-12"	1-2'	F	EURA	✓	✓				✓					✓			E					S				Y	Y	G	Y	D	
6-12"	1'	M-F	ENA								✓			✓			G					S					Y	G	Y		
1-2'	1-2'	S-M	ENA					✓		✓		✓		✓	F		G		G												P
1-3'	1-3'	S-M	ENA		✓					✓		✓		✓	F		G														P
1-3'	1-3'		ENA		✓			✓		✓	✓	✓		✓									Y				Y				
6-20'	6-10'		ENA		✓	✓		✓		✓	✓	✓											Y				Y				
8-12"	18"+	F	EURA	✓			✓	✓						✓								E		Y		Y	Y	G	Y	P	P
3-5'	3-5'	F	EURA	✓			✓	✓						✓								E		Y		Y	Y	G		P, D	P
1-4'	3'	F	EURA	✓			✓	✓						✓								E		Y		Y	Y	G		P	P
1-3'	1-2'		ENA			✓		✓			✓	✓		✓													Y	S			
6-24"	6-24"	F	EURA	✓	✓									✓			E	F	G	F	S				Y		Y	G		D	
1-4'	8-24"		ENA					✓			✓			✓													Y	S			
1-4'	1-2'		ENA					✓		✓	✓	✓		✓													Y	S			
12-24"	indef	M	ENA					✓			✓	✓	✓	✓														Y			
4-5'	2-3'	S	ENA		✓				✓	✓	✓			✓									Y				Y				P
6-18"	3-4'	S-M	EUR	✓	✓			✓						✓					E	G		E					Y	G	Y, A	D	
6-12"	indef	M-F	ENA									✓										F					S	Y			
75-100'	50-75'	M-F	ENA								✓	✓		✓			E			E		G			Y			G	C	D	
75-100'	40'	M	EUR	✓							✓	✓		✓			E			E		G			Y			G	C	D	
30-70'	30-45'	M-F	ASIA							✓				✓			G			G		F							C	D	
1-2'	indef	M-F	ENA	✓	✓			✓			✓			✓			F					F						G	Y		P
6-16"	6-16"	M	EURA	✓	✓				✓		✓			✓						G	F	E	Y	Y			Y	G	Y	D	
4-10"	6-36"	M	EURA	✓	✓				✓					✓						G	F		Y	Y			Y	G	Y	D	
12-18"	indef	S-M	ENA								✓	✓		✓			F					G						G	Y		
6'	5-6'	M-F	ENA		✓	✓	✓															F					Y	G		H	
1-2'	1'	S	WNA		✓						✓	✓	✓	✓										Y							
2-4'	2-3'	M	EURA											✓								E					Y	G		H	P
40-60'	40-60'	M-F	ENA	✓				✓			✓			✓								Y	E							C	
1-5'	indef	F	EURA	✓	✓		✓	✓	✓		✓			✓			E			E		S			Y		Y			St, E, D	P

Taxonomy				Tolerances			Soil pH				Architecture		
Genus	Species	Common Name	Family	Hardiness Zones	Light	Moisture	Strongly Acid	Acid	Garden	Alkaline	Form	Habit	Root Pattern
Urtica	dioica var. gracilis	native nettle	Urticaceae	3	○	♦			■■		l Herb	run	Fb, R
Uvularia	sessilifolia	bellwort	Convallariaceae	3-8	○●	♦		■■	■■		s Herb	clmp	R
Vaccinium	angustifolium	lowbush blueberry	Ericaceae	2-6	○	♦♦	■■	■■			s Shrub	Ctkt	F, St
Vaccinium	ashei	rabbiteye blueberry	Ericaceae	7b	○	♦	■	■■			m-vl Shrub	ms	Sk
Vaccinium	corymbosum	highbush blueberry	Ericaceae	4b-8	○	♦♦	■■	■■			l Shrub	ms	F, St
Vaccinium	crassifolium	creeping blueberry	Ericaceae	7-9	○◐	♦	■■	■■			p Shrub	E Cmat	
Vaccinium	macrocarpon	cranberry	Ericaceae	3	○	♦	■■	■■			p Shrub	E Rmat	F, St
Vaccinium	vitis-idaea	lingonberry	Ericaceae	4-7	○	♦♦	■	■■			s Shrub	E Cmat	Sk
Vaccinium	x hybrids	half-high blueberry	Ericaceae	3-7	○	♦	■■	■■			s-m Shrub	ms	
Verbena	canadensis	rose verbena	Verbenaceae	5-9	○○	♦♦		■	■■	■	p-s Herb	clmp	
Vernonia	noveboracensis	New York ironweed	Asteraceae	4	○	♦		■■			l-vl Herb	clmp	
Veronica	officinalis	speedwell	Scrophulariaceae	4	○◐	♦		■■			s Herb	E run	
Viburnum	cassinoides	witherod viburnum	Caprifoliaceae	2-8	○◐	♦♦		■■	■		l Shrub	ms	F
Viburnum	lentago	nannyberry	Caprifoliaceae	2	○◐	♦♦			■■	■	vl-xl Shrub	ms	F
Viburnum	trilobum	highbush cranberry	Caprifoliaceae	2	○	♦♦			■■		l Shrub	ms	F
Vicia	americana	American vetch	Fabaceae	3-7	○	♦					l Vine	r vine	R
Vicia	caroliniana	wood vetch	Fabaceae	3-9	○●	♦					l Vine	r vine	
Vicia	cracca	tufted vetch	Fabaceae	6	○○	♦			■■		l Vine	r vine	R
Viola	canadensis	Canada violet	Violaceae	4	○○	♦			■■		s Herb	run	R
Viola	labradorica	Labrador violet	Violaceae	3	○●	♦		■■	■■	■	p Herb	E run	
Viola	odorata	sweet violet	Violaceae	6	○○	♦		■■	■■		s Herb	E run	R, St
Viola	sororaria	blue violet	Violaceae	4-8	○○	♦			■■		s Herb	run	R
Vitex	agnus-castus	chaste tree	Verbenaceae	6-8	○	♦♦			■■		l-vl Shrub	ms	
Vitis	labrusca and hybrids	fox grape	Vitaceae	3-9	○	♦♦		■	■■	■	h Vine	w vine	
Vitis	riparia	riverbank grape	Vitaceae	2-6	○	♦♦			■■	■■	h Vine	w vine	
Vitis	rotundifolia	muscadine grape	Vitaceae	7-10	○	♦			■■		h Vine	w vine	
Vitis	vinifera and hybrids	grape	Vitaceae	6-9	○	♦♦			■		h Vine	w vine	
Waldsteinia	fragarioides	barren strawberry	Rosaceae	4-7	○●	♦♦		■	■		p-s Herb	E run	R
Wisteria	floribunda	Japanese wisteria	Fabaceae	4-9	○	♦		■	■■	■■	h Vine	w vine	
Wisteria	frutescens	American wisteria	Fabaceae	5	○○	♦		■■			h Vine	w vine	
Wisteria	macrostachya	Kentucky wisteria	Fabaceae	5-9	○○	♦♦			■■	■	h Vine	w vine	H
Woodwardia	areolata	netted chain fern	Blechnaceae	4-9	◐	♦♦		■■	■■		s Herb	run	R
Woodwardia	virginica	Virginia chain fern	Blechnaceae	3-10	◐	♦♦		■■	■■		m Herb	run	R
x Sorbaronia	hybrid	aronia x mountain ash	Rosaceae	3	○	♦			■■		d Tree	std	
x Sorbocrataegus	hybrid	haw x mountain ash	Rosaceae	3	○	♦			■■		d Tree	std	
x Sorbopyrus	hybrid	pear x mountain ash	Rosaceae	3	○	♦			■■		d-s Tree	std	
Xanthoceras	sorbifolium	yellowhorn	Sapindaceae	5-7	○	♦		■	■■	■■	s Tree	std	
Yucca	baccata	banana yucca	Agavaceae	5	○	♦♦			■■	■■	s-m Shrub	E ms	T
Zanthoxylum	americanum	prickly ash	Rutaceae	3	○	♦♦			■	■■	s-m Tree	skr	Sk
Zanthoxylum	piperitum	Japanese pepper tree	Rutaceae	7	○○	♦			■■	■■	m Shrub	Ctkt	Sk
Zizia	aptera	heart-leaved alexanders	Apiaceae	4	○○	♦		■■	■■		m Herb	clmp	Fb
Zizia	aurea	golden alexanders	Apiaceae	4	○○	♦		■■	■■		s-m Herb	E clmp	
Ziziphus	jujuba	jujube	Rhamnaceae	6-9	○	♦♦			■■	■■	s-m Tree	skr	T, Sk

Height	Width	Growth Rate	Native Region	Disturbed	Meadows	Prairies	Oldfields	Thickets	Edges	Gaps/Clearings	Open Woods	Forest	Conifer Forest	Other Habitats	Edible Fruit	Edible Nuts/Mast	Edible Greens, Etc.	Edible Roots	Culinary	Tea	Edible Other	Medicinal	N_2 Fixer	Dynamic Accumulator	Wildlife	Invert. Shelter	Nectary	Ground Cover	Other Uses/Functions	Nuisances	Poison
3-4'	1-3'	F	ENA	✓	✓		✓	✓	✓			✓		✓			E		E			Y			Y		Y			St, E, D	P
8-12"	8-12"	S	ENA					✓				✓		✓			G	F							F						
2'	3'+	S	ENA							✓	✓	✓		✓	E							S			F			Y			
4-18'	4-18'	S	ENA								✓		✓	✓	E							S			F						
6-12'	6-12'	S	ENA				✓	✓			✓	✓		✓	E							S			F						
2-6"	5'+	S-M	ENA								✓		✓	✓	E							S			F			Y			
6"	indef	S-M	ENA											✓	E							S			F			Y			
6-12"	2'	S-M	ENA											✓	E							S			F			Y			
2-4'	2-4'	S	CULT											✓	E							S			F						
4-12"	18"	M-F	ENA		✓	✓				✓	✓			✓											F		G	Y			
5-8'	3-4'	M-F	ENA		✓			✓						✓													G				P
12"	indef	M-F	ENA		✓						✓			✓						Y		F			F		G	Y			
6-12'	6-12'	M	ENA				✓	✓				✓		✓	F					Y					F		S				P
20-35'	10-20'	M-F	ENA	✓	✓			✓	✓					✓	F										F		S				P
6-12'	6-12'	M	ENA		✓		✓					✓		✓	G										F		S				P
3'	3'	M-F	ENA		✓			✓			✓			✓			Y						Y	Y		Y	G			P
1-5'	1-5'		ENA					✓			✓	✓		✓						Y			Y	Y		Y	G			P
5'	5'		EURA	✓	✓			✓		✓	✓			✓			Y				Y		Y	Y		Y	G			P
6-16"	indef	M-F	ENA							✓		✓	✓	✓			G				G	F		Y			Y			
4"	indef	F	ENA	✓				✓		✓		✓		✓			F				G			Y			Y			
6-8"	indef	F	EURA	✓	✓					✓		✓		✓			G				G	G		Y			Y			
6-12"	indef	F	ENA	✓	✓						✓	✓		✓			F				G			Y			Y		D	
8-20'	8-20'	M-F	EUR									✓		✓					Y			E				G			D	
35'+	20-35'+	F	ENA					✓	✓		✓			✓	E		G					S			F		G		S	
35'+	20-35'+	F	ENA					✓	✓			✓		✓	E		G					S			F		G	Y	S	
12-20'	12-20'	F	ENA					✓	✓			✓		✓	E							S			F		G		S	
12-20'	12-20'	F	EUR							✓	✓			✓	E		E					S			F		G		S	
4-8"	indef	M-F	ENA						✓	✓				✓														Y			
30-50'	30-50'	F	ASIA					✓			✓	✓		✓								Y	Y			Y	G		S, E	P
30-40'	30-40'	F	ENA					✓	✓		✓			✓									Y			Y	G		S	P
20-35'	12-20'	F	PRAI			✓						✓		✓									Y			Y	G		S	P
12-18"	indef	M	ENA								✓			✓														Y			
18-24"	indef	S-M-F	ENA								✓	✓		✓														Y		E	
10'	10'	M	CULT											✓	F														P
10'	10'	M	CULT											✓	F														P
10-25'	10-25'	M	CULT											✓	G														P
18-24'	18-24'	S	ASIA					✓						✓		Y	Y				Y								T	
3-4'	3-4'	S	WNA			✓								✓	G		F				Y	G			F				T	
20-35'	20-35'	F	ENA				✓	✓			✓	✓		✓					Y			E				S		G	T	P
6'	6'		ASIA					✓	✓					✓						E		E				S		G	T, D	
2'	2'	M-F	ENA		✓	✓		✓		✓	✓	✓		✓													Y	S		
12-30"	12-24"	M-F	ENA		✓	✓		✓		✓	✓	✓		✓							G	F					Y	S		
15-30'	15-30'	F	EURA	✓		✓								✓	G							E						G	T, D	

APPENDIX 2

Species–by–Use Tables

CAUTIONS AND GUIDELINES FOR SAFE EATING

When dealing with edible and medicinal plants and mushrooms it is of utmost importance to exercise caution. Most gardeners will find many of the foods listed in these appendices new or unfamiliar. The following guidelines will keep you safe and healthy as you explore the diverse world of your edible forest garden. Don't let these guidelines scare you—we have sampled a diversity of species in research for this book, and while some have tasted terrible, neither of us has ever gotten sick from any plant *while following these guidelines*. After some years of experimentation, neither of us can imagine a spring without eating nettles and ramps, or a fall without the luscious flavor of hardy kiwifruit—experiences we never even imagined previously. Please note that the following guidelines apply only to plants. For information on the safe consumption of mushrooms refer to the books listed in appendix 7.

- If a plant is not specifically listed as edible (in this book or elsewhere), assume it is poisonous. If *any part* of a plant listed in this book is not listed as edible, assume the unlisted plant part is poisonous. Apple seeds and rhubarb leaves are two examples of poisonous parts of commonly eaten plants. Eric once tasted the leaves of clearly labeled wild ginger (*Asarum canadense*), a plant that does have edible roots. He remembered that there was a ginger-flavored ground cover with edible leaves and thought wild ginger must be it. Unfortunately, he was

thinking of *Houttuynia cordata*. Eric became very ill, throwing up within about half an hour (not an experience he would like to repeat!). Now he always refers back to the literature before trying any new plants, and so should you.

- **Make sure children and visitors know that not everything in the "edible" forest garden is edible.** Remind children and guests (as well as yourself!) that, as in any garden, you should never just pop something in your mouth without knowing what it is.
- **This book is not a guide to wild edibles.** Please do not use it as such. Correct identification of wild plants can be difficult and is often possible only during the brief period when the plant is in flower. Consult a field guide like those listed in the appendix 7. Do not harvest wild members of the parsley family (Apiaceae, formerly Umbelliferae), as there are many deadly look-alikes, some that even taste delicious!
- **Check the "Poisonous Plants" table in appendix 4 when indicated in the Plant Species Matrix.** When using the Plant Species Matrix you can check the "poison" column to see whether the plant has any toxic parts. Then look up the species in the "Poisonous Plants" table to learn more. You may be surprised to learn of the toxic potential of many edible and ornamental plants you already grow in your garden.
- **Read the species-by-use tables carefully.** Appendix 2 lists the edible uses of many plants. Read them carefully. If a plant is listed as being eaten cooked, do not eat it raw. Many edible plants contain toxins that cooking deactivates.

Also, make sure to eat the plants during the proper season—fruits when ripe, greens only when young, or whatever is indicated in the tables.

- **Consider planting only nontoxic plants.** You may choose to plant only nontoxic species. However, this will severely limit the species you can choose, particularly in the case of legumes, which are often poisonous. It would, however, be easy to exclude those plants that can cause a strong reaction from eating a small amount.

- **Consider creating "all edible" polyculture beds.** Polycultures made up entirely of plants with edible leaves allow for safe grazing, for example. The same could be done with polycultures of other foods. Keep an eye out for weeds or unwelcome species seeding or creeping in, however.

- **Make sure to label plants with which you are not familiar.** Until you know your plants well, we recommend labeling them. In time, you will know them intimately, but until then, labeling will provide you with the chance to look them up and make sure you have the right species. Mapping, labeling, and getting to know your plants is not only good for safety but fun!

- **Remain wary of misidentification, even by reputable nurseries.** Generally, plants you order from a nursery or seed company will be the species you requested. Occasionally nurseries or seed companies accidentally mislabel plants or have themselves purchased and propagated mislabeled plants for sale. In flower gardens this may be an annoyance, or indeed you may never notice at all. However, with edible species, you could potentially be getting a similar but nonedible—or even poisonous—species. If you are ordering from a company that lists the species as edible (like a fruit-tree nursery), you can be confident that you can eat what you receive from them. However, when ordering obscure edibles from a company specializing in native wildflowers (for example), you may want to let them know you are planning to eat the plant, and make sure there is no possibility of misidentification or of other species being mixed in with the batch. To be completely safe, verify the identity of your plants by using a field guide or a resource like the Royal Horticultural Society's *Index of Garden Plants.*

- **Always double-check before eating an unfamiliar species for the first time.** Your forest garden may contain a bewildering array of species, and it can be hard to remember which of those legumes have edible pods and which are poisonous. Make sure to refer back to the tables in this book (or other sources) before trying new species, or any species with which you are not well acquainted.

- **Look out for food allergies.** Many people have allergies, often strong ones, to even common cultivated plants. You never know whether you might be allergic to a new food plant you are trying for the first time. Some people can go into anaphylactic shock from eating a single almond or peanut; their allergic reactions can vary by season, depend on other foods eaten recently, and so on. Such folks should be understandably very cautious in sampling new edible plant species. You should be, too. Be particularly cautious about plants in the same family as plants to which you know you are allergic.

- **Follow a first-try protocol.** Responsible edible wild plant guides give guidelines for trying any new plant species—these should also be used when trying any new cultivated foods. First, try a tiny bit. Does it taste "mediciny," "poisonous," or somehow toxic? How does your body react to it? Even if this or another book says it is edible, if it tastes terrible or you get uncomfortable symptoms from eating it, don't eat any more. Go back to your references to make sure you are eating the right plant part at the right time of year, with the right preparation, or try another cautious experiment when the plant is in a different life stage. If a tiny bit seems all right, try a few bites in another hour. Give your body time to react. Then try more even later if things seem okay. Work the new food into your diet slowly, refraining from gorging on it and mixing it with other foods until it is familiar to you. This is probably partly how our ancestors learned how to eat new wild plants.

- **Cautious experimentation brings great rewards.** By following the guidelines above, you will be sure of safety as you sample new species. Don't be intimidated by the need to proceed in a deliberate and thoughtful manner. You may soon find that you become an avid promoter of American persimmon, good King Henry, groundnut, and jostaberry. A fascinating world of new food plants awaits you in your own backyard!

EDIBLE FRUITS AND BERRIES

One of the biggest appeals of forest gardening is the opportunity to forage in your own backyard for an incredible array of edible fruits and berries. With judicious species selection, you can enjoy fresh fruit from late spring through late fall. With so many species from which to choose, it is important to clarify your goals (unless you have enough room to plant a few of every species listed here). Perhaps you have limited space and you want only the best high-quality fruit for fresh eating. You may want low-maintenance species like kiwis and persimmons, or you may be willing to put in the extra work to get apples and peaches. Do you like to make jams and jellies to preserve food for winter? Many species with fruit of poor fresh-eating quality make fantastic jam.

In most cases, named varieties have substantially better fruit than seedlings, particularly in highly bred fruits like apples and pears, where you should use only named varieties. Remember that almost all of these species require full sun to fruit well. Notable exceptions include pawpaw, Oregon grape, goumi, mulberry, and superhardy kiwi.

Poll: Pollination. Remember that you must pay attention to pollination to get fruit! Pollination codes are as follows:

A   Self-pollinating, i.e., one lone plant can produce fruit.

B   Requires cross-pollination, i.e., you need at least two different cultivars and both will set fruit.

B1 Some cultivars are self-fertile, some require cross-pollination. Most set better fruit with cross-pollination.

C   Like B above, but not all varieties pollinate all other varieties. See catalogs for listings of compatible varieties.

D   Have male and female plants; females need males to fruit. Ten females to one male is a good ratio.

E   Like D above, but some cultivars have both male and female flowers.

Cvs?: Improved cultivars (from breeding or selection from wild plants) are available if this column is checked.

Rating: A subjective flavor classification: E = excellent; G = good; F = fair; and U = unknown to authors. For species marked as having cultivars, this column is a general rating for the cultivars as a group, not the wild unimproved species. Flavor quality varies greatly between cultivars and within species.

Notes: Information on flavor and uses. "Cooked" indicates that the fruit should be used only when cooked. The flavor may be poor when raw, or the fruit may actually be toxic when raw.

EDIBLE FRUITS AND BERRIES: TREES

Latin Name	Common Name	Poll.	Cvs?	Rating	Notes
Amelanchier lamarkii	juneberry	A	✓	E	berry with blueberry-almond flavor
Asimina triloba	pawpaw	B	✓	E	our largest native fruit; custard-pineapple-mango flavor; creamy
Celtis laevigata	southern hackberry	A		F	berry; sweet
Celtis occidentalis	hackberry	A		F	berry; sweet
Cornus kousa	kousa dogwood	B		G	fruit, some good; skins inedible
Cornus mas	cornelian cherry	B1	✓	G	tart, cherrylike fruit
Crataegus aestivalis	mayhaw	B	✓	E	prized for jelly; also raw
Crataegus mollis	downy hawthorn	B		F	fruit cooked; similar to crabapple
Crataegus pinnatifida	Chinese hawthorn	B	✓	G	prized for jelly; also raw
Crataegus punctata	dotted hawthorn	B		F	fruit cooked; similar to crabapple
Cudrania tricuspidata	che fruit	D		G	mild strawberry-fig-melon flavor
Cydonia oblonga	quince	A	✓	E	large aromatic fruit; cooked; excellent
Diospyros kaki	kaki persimmon	E***	✓	E	very popular Asian fruit; large, very sweet; eat only when superripe and soft
Diospyros virginiana	American persimmon	E***	✓	E	delicious, rich, sweet flavor; eat when super-ripe; highly astringent when unripe
Halesia tetraptera	silverbell	Unknown		U	unripe fruit is tart
Malus baccata	Siberian crabapple	B	✓	F	tart fruit; cooked
Malus ioensis	Iowa crabapple	B		F	tart fruit; cooked
Malus pumila	apple	C	✓	E	popular; delicious fruit
Mespilus germanica	medlar	A	✓	G	spicy applesauce flavor once allowed to soften fully indoors
Morus alba	white mulberry	B1	✓	G	sweet, but a bit insipid
Morus hybrids	hybrid mulberry	B1	✓	E	sweet, a bit tart, and delicious
Morus nigra	black mulberry	B1	✓	G	sweet, but a bit insipid
Morus rubra	red mulberry	B1	✓	G	sweet, but a bit insipid
Prunus alleghaniensis	Allegheny plum	B*		G	native plum; good flavor
Prunus americana	American plum	B*	✓	E	native plum; good flavor
Prunus americana var. nigra	Canada plum	B*	✓	E	native plum; good flavor
Prunus angustifolia	Chickasaw plum	B*		G	native plum; good flavor
Prunus armeniaca	"alpricot"	B1	✓	E	tasty fruit plus almondlike nut inside
Prunus armeniaca	apricot	B1	✓	E	common delicious fruit
Prunus avium	sweet cherry	C	✓	E	delicious
Prunus cerasifera	myrobalan plum	B	✓	G	good-flavored plum
Prunus cerasus	sour cherry	A	✓	E	excellent tart cooking cherry
Prunus domestica	European plum	B	✓	E	delicious common plum; damson similar
Prunus hortulana	hog plum	B*		G	native plum; good flavor
Prunus mandschurica	Manchurian apricot	B	✓	G	small, sweet-tart fruit; nongrafted varieties often of poor quality
Prunus maritima	beach plum	B*	✓	G	native plum; good flavor
Prunus munsoniana	wild goose plum	B*		G	native plum; good flavor
Prunus persica	peach	B1	✓	E	delicious common fruit
Prunus persica nucipersica	nectarine	B1	✓	E	"fuzzless" peach
Prunus salicina	Japanese plum	B	✓	E	delicious common plum

EDIBLE FRUITS AND BERRIES: TREES *continued*

Latin Name	Common Name	Poll.	Cvs?	Rating	Notes
Prunus virginiana	chokecherry	B	✓	G	small, sour-bitter fruit; improved varieties have better quality
Prunus x *gondouinii*	duke cherry	B	✓	E	intermediate sweet-sour cherry
Prunus x *hybrids*	hybrid plums	B	✓	E	most commercial plums are European and Asian hybrids; delicious
Pyrus bretschneideris	Asian pear	C**	✓	E	tasty apple-pear flavor
Pyrus communis	European pear	C**	✓	E	delicious common fruit
Pyrus communis	perry pear	C**	✓	G	hard fruit excellent for making "perry" pear cider; not good raw
Sorbus americana	American mountain ash	B		F	berries cooked
Sorbus aucuparia	rowan	B		G	fruit for cooking
Sorbus decora	showy mountain ash	B		F	berries cooked
Sorbus domestica	service tree	B1	✓	G	fruit small; somewhat pearlike
x *Sorbaronia*	(mtn. ash x chokeberry)	B	✓	F	cooking fruit
x *Sorbocrataegus*	(mtn. ash x hawthorn)	B	✓	F	sweet-tart cooking berry
x *Sorbopyrus*	(mtn. ash x pear)	B	✓	G	rose-flavored 1.5" (4 cm) fruit; seedless; tasty fresh
Ziziphus jujuba	jujube	B1/C	✓	G	eat fresh like an apple or dried like a date

*Many wild plums will pollinate any cultivated plum. European plums will pollinate only Europeans, Asian plums only Asians, etc. Consult your catalog for compatibility.

**Most Asian and European pears will pollinate each other, but some varieties will not. Check your catalogs.

***Some persimmon females will set fruit without pollination. Persimmon pollination can be complicated; there are even reports that they can be pollinated by chestnuts! Refer to a catalog or Reich's *Uncommon Fruits for Every Garden* (2004) for more information.

EDIBLE FRUITS AND BERRIES: SHRUBS

Latin Name	Common Name	Poll.	Cvs?	Rating	Notes
Amelanchier alnifolia	saskatoon	A	✓	E	delicious blueberry-almond flavor
Amelanchier bartramiana	Bartram's shadblow	A		E	as above, with pear-shaped berries
Amelanchier obovalis	southern juneberry	A	✓	E	as above
Amelanchier stolonifera	running juneberry	A		E	as above
Arbutus unedo	strawberry tree	A	✓	G	sweet and juicy but mealy
Aronia arbutifolia	red chokeberry	A		F	berry, cooked; high pectin
Aronia melanocarpa	black chokeberry	A	✓	G	berry, cooked; high pectin
Berberis canadensis	Canada barberry	A		F	acid berry; cooked
Cephalotaxus harringtonia	Japanese plum yew	D		F	sweet, piney fruit
Chaenomeles speciosa	Japanese flowering quince	B	✓	G	fruit cooked; tart
Decaisnea fargesii	blue bean	A		U	metallic blue pods with tapioca-like edible goo inside
Eleagnus commutata	silverberry	B1		F	dry, mealy berries; cooked
Eleagnus multiflora	goumi	B1	✓	G	sweet berries
Gaultheria shallon	salal	A		G	sweet berries
Gaylussacia baccata	black huckleberry	B		G	sweet berries; blueberry-like, but a bit drier; Thoreau's favorite.
Hippophae rhamnoides	sea buckthorn	D	✓	G	acid fruit; very nutritious
Lonicera caerula var. *edulis*	edible honeysuckle	B		G	sweet berries

EDIBLE FRUITS AND BERRIES: SHRUBS *continued*

Latin Name	Common Name	Poll.	Cvs?	Rating	Notes
Lonicera kamschatica	honeyberry honeysuckle	B	✓	G	sweet honey-flavored berries
Lonicera villosa	northern fly honeysuckle	B		G	blueberry-like
Mahonia aquifolium	Oregon grape	A		F	acid berry; cooked
Malus pumila	minidwarf apple	C	✓	E	popular; delicious fruit
Morus spp.	mulberry	B1	✓	E	sweet, a bit tart, and delicious
Prunus angustifolia watsonii	sand plum	B		F	cooking plum
Prunus cerasus var. *frutescens*	dwarf sour cherry	B	✓	E	sour cherry
Prunus fruticosa	bush cherry	B		G	acid fruit
Prunus japonica nakai	Japanese bush cherry	B		G	sweet-sour cherries
Prunus pumila	eastern dwarf cherry	B		G	the largest-fruited native wild cherry
Prunus pumila var. *besseyi*	sand plum	B	✓	G	native plum; less flavorful
Prunus tomentosa	Nanking cherry	B	✓	G	small sweet cherries
Prunus japonica x *jacquemontii* cvs	hybrid dwarf cherry	B	✓	E	sweet-sour cherries
Pyrus communis	minidwarf pear	C**	✓	E	delicious common fruit
Ribes americanum	American black currant	A		F	musky; cooked only
Ribes aureum	golden currant	A	✓	G	large, tasty berry
Ribes hirtellum	American gooseberry	A	✓	G	berries fresh or cooked
Ribes missouriense	Missouri gooseberry	A	✓	G	berries fresh or cooked
Ribes nigrum	black currant	A	✓	E	berries cooked; esteemed in Europe; 'Consort' resists white pine blister rust
Ribes odoratum	clove currant	A	✓	E	sweet-tart fruits; delicious
Ribes silvestre	red and white currant	A	✓	E	popular European cooking-juice berry
Ribes triste	American red currant	A		G	similar to above
Ribes uva-crispa and hybrids	gooseberry	A	✓	E	delicious; most cultivars are hybrids
Ribes x *culverwellii*	jostaberry	A	✓	E	delicious; sweet-tart; blight resistant
Rosa carolina	pasture rose	A	✓	F	fruit (hips) cooked; high in vitamin C
Rosa palustris	marsh rose	A		F	hips cooked; tart
Rosa rugosa	rugosa rose	A	✓	G	sweet and fleshy fruit eaten fresh or cooked
Rosa setigera	prairie rose	A		F	hips cooked; tart
Rosa villosa	apple rose	A	✓	G	fleshy sweet hips to 1"(3 cm); fresh or cooked
Rubus allegheniensis	Allegheny blackberry	A		E	delicious blackberry
Rubus flagellaris	prickly dewberry	A		F	small blackberry-like, low yields
Rubus fruticosus	blackberry	A	✓	E	the cultivated blackberry
Rubus idaeus	red raspberry	A	✓	E	the commercial red raspberry
Rubus idaeus var. *strigosus*	American red raspberry	A	✓	E	the commercial red raspberry
Rubus illecebrosus	strawberry-raspberry	A		G	cooked fruit: strawberry and raspberry flavor
Rubus occidentalis	black raspberry	A	✓	E	the common "blackcap"
Rubus odoratus	purple-flowering raspberry	A		G	a drier, seedier raspberry
Rubus parviflorus	thimbleberry	A		G	berries fresh or cooked; bears well in shade
Rubus pentalobus cv.	'Emerald Carpet' raspberry	A		F	berries; poor quality
Rubus spp.	dewberry	A	✓	E	the commercial trailing blackberry
Rubus spectabilis	salmonberry	A		E	excellent raspberry
Rubus x hybrids	boysenberry, loganberry, etc.	A	✓	E	raspberry x blackberry
Sambucus canadensis	elderberry	B	✓	G	small berries for cooking
Shepherdia canadensis	buffaloberry	D		F	bitter; contains soapy saponins

EDIBLE FRUITS AND BERRIES: SHRUBS *continued*

Latin Name	Common Name	Poll.	Cvs?	Rating	Notes
Vaccinium ashei	rabbiteye blueberry	A*	✓	E	southern heat-loving blueberry; delicious
Vaccinium corymbosum	highbush blueberry	A*	✓	E	delicious berries
Vaccinium x hybrids	half-high blueberry	A*	✓	E	delicious berries
Viburnum cassinoides	witherod viburnum	B		F	poor fruit; for cooking only
Viburnum lentago	nannyberry	B		F	poor fruit; for cooking only
Viburnum trilobum	highbush cranberry	A	✓	G	sour; for cooking

*Vacciniums are self-fertile but produce more fruit if a different cultivar is present.

**Most Asian and European pears will pollinate each other, but some varieties will not. Check your catalogs.

EDIBLE FRUITS AND BERRIES: VINES

Latin Name	Common Name	Poll.	Cvs?	Rating	Notes
Actinidia arguta	hardy kiwifruit	D	✓	E	cultivated; delicious, sweet kiwi flavor
Actinidia kolomikta	superhardy kiwifruit	D	✓	E	cultivated; delicious, sweet kiwi flavor
Actinidia purpurea	purple kiwifruit	D	✓	E	purple colored
Passiflora incarnata	maypop	B		G	native passionfruit; good for juices
Schisandra chinensis	magnolia vine	E	✓	G	berries; sweet-tart; reputed to contain all five flavors; cultivated
Smilax herbacea	carrion flower	D		U	some sources say the ripe fruits can be eaten raw or cooked
Vitis labrusca and hybrids	fox grape	A	✓	E	sour; Concord-type flavor
Vitis riparia	riverbank grape	A	✓	E	sour; Concord-type flavor
Vitis rotundifolia	muscadine grape	E*	✓	E	delicious sweet and sour flavor
Vitis vinifera and hybrids	grape	A	✓	E	cultivated; sweet for fresh, others for wines

*Most muscadines are self-pollinating. Some are female only and need the company of a self-pollinating variety.

EDIBLE FRUITS AND BERRIES: SUBSHRUBS AND PROSTRATE SHRUBS

Latin Name	Common Name	Poll.	Cvs?	Rating	Notes
Arctostaphylos uva-ursi	bearberry	A		F	small, dry, bland berry
Cornus canadensis	bunchberry	A/B		G	somewhat bland berries; mild wintergreen flavor
Gaultheria hispidula	creeping snowberry	A		G	sweet wintergreen flavor
Gaultheria procumbens	wintergreen	A	✓	E	sweet wintergreen flavor
Gaylussacia brachycera	box huckleberry	B		G	similar to blueberry but a bit drier
Mahonia repens	creeping mahonia	A		F	acid berry; cooked
Mitchella repens	partridgeberry	A/B		F	tasteless berry
Rubus tricolor	creeping bramble	A		F	decent raspberry; not productive
Rubus x *stellarcticus*	all-fieldberry	A	✓	E	sweet red raspberry
Vaccinium angustifolium	lowbush blueberry	A*	✓	E	delicious wild blueberry
Vaccinium crassifolium	creeping blueberry	A*		E	delicious wild blueberry
Vaccinium macrocarpon	cranberry	A*	✓	E	sour fruit for sauces
Vaccinium vitis-idaea	lingonberry	A*	✓	E	similar to cranberry

*Vacciniums are self-fertile but produce more fruit if a different cultivar is present.

EDIBLE FRUITS AND BERRIES: HERBACEOUS SPECIES

Latin Name	Common Name	Poll.	Cvs?	Rating	Notes
Fragaria chiloensis	beach strawberry	A/B1		E	wild strawberry flavor
Fragaria moschata	musk strawberry	A/B1	✓	E	musky strawberry flavor
Fragaria vesca alpina	alpine strawberry	A/B1	✓	E	wild strawberry flavor; everbearing
Fragaria vesca americana	American wood strawberry	A/B1	✓	E	wild strawberry flavor
Fragaria virginiana	wild strawberry	A/B1	✓	E	delicious; small fruit
Fragaria x ananassa	strawberry	A/B1	✓	E	large, delicious fruit
Opuntia compressa	prickly pear cactus	B1		F	de-spine fruits and eat
Physalis heterophylla	ground cherry	A		F	wild tomato relative; golden berries in paper husks; unripe fruit very poisonous.
Podophyllum peltatum	mayapple	A/B		G	lemon-flavored fruit; poisonous until ripe
Rubus chamaemorus	cloudberry	A		E	delicious red raspberry
Smilacina racemosa	false Solomon's seal	A/B		F	berry; bittersweet; possibly cathatic in quantity
Streptopus amplexifolius	twisted stalk	A/B		F	berry; cucumber flavored; possibly cathatic in quantity
Streptopus roseus	rosybells	A/B		F	berry; cathartic in quantity
Yucca baccata	banana yucca	hand*		G	young fleshy fruits eaten

*Outside of their native range banana yuccas must be pollinated by hand. They are ordinarily pollinated by a yucca moth that does not exist in eastern North America.

EDIBLE NUTS AND MAST

Nut trees produce tasty, nutritious, and easily stored foods. Mast includes the nuts of beech, chestnut, oak, and other forest trees eaten by livestock and wild animals. Nuts and mast are key sources of protein, carbohydrates, and fats. The difference between grafted and seedling walnuts, pecans, and hickories is critical to understand: seedlings begin bearing later and tend to have nuts that are difficult to remove from their shells. For many other species seedlings are perfectly acceptable. However, grow improved varieties whenever possible. Some species listed here, notably the oaks, are not eaten as nuts but are roasted and ground to make a nutritious and tasty flour or meal. Eating raw or even cooked acorns of most species is a bitter experience, but exceptions to this rule exist.

Poll: Pollination. Most nuts are wind pollinated. Pollination codes are as follows:

A   Self-fertile species, i.e., one lone plant can produce fruit.

B   Requires cross-pollination, i.e., you need at least two different cultivars and both will set fruit.

B1 Some cultivars are self-fertile, some require cross-pollination (via the wind). Most set better fruit with cross-pollination.

B2 Like B above, but insect-pollinated.

C   Like B above, but not all varieties pollinate all other varieties. See catalogs for listings of compatible varieties.

D   Have male and female plants; females need male plants to fruit. Ten females to one male is a good ratio.

Cvs? If this column is checked, improved varieties (from breeding or selection from wild plants) are available.

Rating is a subjective flavor classification: E = excellent; G = good; F = fair; and U = unknown to authors. For species with cultivars, the quality of ungrafted seedlings is shown in parentheses.

EDIBLE NUTS AND MAST: LARGE & VERY LARGE NUT TREES

Latin Name	Common Name	Poll.	Cvs?	Rating	Descripton
Araucaria araucana	monkey puzzle tree	D		E	bears huge cones with large, tasty nuts
Carya illinoinensis	pecan	B	✓	E(f)	superdelicious nuts; often hard to crack out
Carya laciniosa	shellbark hickory	B	✓	E(f)	very tasty; large nuts; often hard to crack out
Carya ovata	shagbark hickory	B	✓	E(f)	very tasty; large nuts; often hard to crack out
Carya x hybrids	hican	B	✓	E(f)	large and tasty; less productive than pecan
Castanea dentata	American chestnut	B		E	tasty; small nuts; chestnut blight currently prevents successful production in eastern North America
Corylus chinensis	Chinese tree hazel	B		G	small nuts
Corylus colurna	Turkish tree hazel	B	✓	G	small nuts
Corylus x *colurnoides*	trazel	B	✓	G	tree form; resistant to eastern filbert blight
Fagus grandiflora	American beech	B	✓	F	very small; flavorful; cook if eating in quantity
Fagus sylvatica	European beech	B		F	very small; flavorful; cook if eating in quantity
Ginkgo biloba	maidenhair tree	D	✓	G	"fruit" surrounding seed smells terrible and causes rashes; cultivar 'Mother Lode' does not smell and is very productive; seeds must be cooked (toxic raw); overconsumption of even cooked nuts can deplete the body of vitamin B_6; consume with caution!
Gleditsia triacanthos	honey locust	D	✓	F	young pods and seeds cooked; sweet mature pods nibbled or ground; excellent livestock fodder
Juglans ailantifolia var. *cordiformis*	heartnut	B1	✓	E(f)	excellent walnuts; easy to crack out
Juglans cinerea	butternut	B1	✓	E(f)	flavorful; some good crackers, some tough to crack
Juglans nigra	black walnut	B1	✓	E(f)	excellent flavor; good cultivars available; most tough to crack out
Juglans regia	English walnut	B1	✓	E(f)	great flavor and cracking; not hardy
Juglans regia	Carpathian walnut	B1	✓	E(f)	good nut and hardier than species
Juglans x *bixbyi*	buartnut	B1	✓	E(f)	heartnut x butternut; productive; some hard to crack out
Pinus armandii	Chinese white pine	A		U	pine nuts
Pinus cembra	Swiss stone pine	A		U	pine nuts
Pinus cembra var. *sibirica*	Siberian pine	A		U	pine nuts
Pinus flexilis	limber pine	A		U	pine nuts
Pinus jeffreyi	Jeffrey pine	A		U	pine nuts
Pinus koraiensis	Korean pine	A		E	pine nuts; commercial
Quercus alba	white oak	B*		F	"sweet" acorns ground for meal
Quercus bicolor	swamp white oak	B*		F	"sweet" acorns ground for meal
Quercus fruticosa	fruticosa oak	B*		F	"sweet" acorns ground for meal
Quercus ilex rotundifolia	Holm oak	B*		G	perhaps the best acorns; some have almond-like flavor; can eat straight or grind for meal
Quercus macrocarpa	bur oak	B*	✓	F	large, "sweet" acorns ground for meal
Quercus michauxii	swamp chestnut oak	B*		F	"sweet" acorns ground for meal
Quercus prinus	chestnut oak	B*		F	"sweet" acorns ground for meal

EDIBLE NUTS AND MAST: LARGE & VERY LARGE NUT TREES *continued*

Latin Name	Common Name	Poll.	Cvs?	Rating	Descripton
Quercus x hybrid	Compton's oak	B*		F	"sweet" acorns ground for meal
Quercus x *schuettei*	Schuette's oak	B*		F	"sweet" acorns ground for meal

*Oaks require cross-pollination, but not necessarily from the same species. There is usually another oak around the neighborhood.

EDIBLE NUTS AND MAST: MEDIUM & SMALL NUT TREES

Latin Name	Common Name	Poll.	Cvs?	Rating	Descripton
Castanea mollissima	Chinese chestnut	B	✓	E	larger nuts; less flavor than *C. dentata*; commercial
Castanea x hybrids	hybrid chestnut	B	✓	E	select varieties for ideal flavor and size; various crosses between a number of species
Pinus albicaulis	whitebark pine	A		U	pine nuts
Pinus edulis	pinyon pine	A		E	pine nuts
Prunus armeniaca	"alpricot"	B2	✓	G	apricot with almondlike kernel
Prunus dulcis	almond	B2	✓	E(g)	commercial; tasty; cold-tender trees
Prunus x hybrid cv.	'Hall's Hardy Almond'	B2	✓	G	smaller kernel; hardy tree
Quercus acutissima	sawtooth oak	B*	✓	F	"sweet" acorns; 125 lbs (57 kg) per tree!; ground for meal
Quercus meuhlenbergii	chinkapin oak	B*		F	"sweet" acorns; ground for meal; high oil content
Xanthoceras sorbifolium	yellowhorn	A/B		U	reportedly with macadamia flavor

*Oaks require cross-pollination, but not necessarily from the same species. There is usually another oak around the neighborhood.

EDIBLE NUTS AND MAST: LARGE & VERY LARGE SHRUBS

Latin Name	Common Name	Poll.	Cvs?	Rating	Descripton
Castanea pumila	Allegheny chinquapin	B	✓	E	tasty; small nuts
Cephalotaxus harringtonia	Japanese plum yew	D		U	nuts edible
Corylus americana	American hazel	B	✓	G	small and hard shelled
Corylus avellana	European filbert	B	✓	G	large, tasty, easy to crack; susceptible to filbert blight
Corylus cornuta	beaked hazel	B		G	small and hard shelled; shell has irritating bristles
Corylus x hybrids	filazel, hazelbert	B	✓	E	good nut size and cracking; resistant to filbert blight
Pinus pumila	Japanese stone pine	A		U	pine nuts; fastest-bearing nut pine: only ten years
Prosopis glandulosa	honeypod mesquite	A/B		G	sweet, caroblike pods; nibble raw or grind for meal
Quercus gambelii	Gambel oak	B*		F	"sweet" acorns ground for meal
Quercus prinoides	dwarf chinkapin oak	B*		F	"sweet" acorns ground for meal

*Oaks require cross-pollination, but not necessarily from the same species. There is usually another oak around the neighborhood.

EDIBLE LEAVES, STALKS, AND SHOOTS

If you wish to grow the many plants with edible leaves, stalks, and shoots in the forest garden primarily as food plants, make sure to select species with flavor ratings of "excellent" or "good." Species rated as "fair" are used primarily for other uses or functions and offer a minor side benefit of edible greens, stems, or shoots. Such species are best mixed with other, more palatable vegetables when used. Unless otherwise noted, leaves on these species become much less palatable after flowering (just like lettuce). The flavor ratings are E = excellent; G = good; F = fair; and U = unknown to authors.

EDIBLE LEAVES, STALKS, AND SHOOTS: TREES, SHRUBS, BAMBOOS, AND WOODY VINES

Latin Name	Common Name	Rating	Description
Aralia elata	Chinese angelica tree	U	young leaves; cooked
Arundinaria gigantea (incl. ssp. *tecta*)	canebrake bamboo	G	cooked bamboo shoots; somewhat bitter
Atriplex halimus	saltbush	E	leaves salty, spinachlike; delicious
Cercis canadensis	redbud	G	leaf buds
Fagus spp.	beech	G	young leaves; surprisingly tender
Hibiscus syriacus	rose of Sharon	F	young leaves
Lespedeza bicolor	bush clover	F	young leaves
Phyllostachys spp.	running bamboos	E	young shoots; the *Phyllostachys* species listed in the matrix are among the best and can all be eaten raw or cooked
Rubus allegheniensis	Allegheny blackberry	F	young shoots
Rubus idaeus	raspberry	F	young shoots
Rubus idaeus var. *strigosus*	American red raspberry	F	young shoots
Rubus occidentalis	black raspberry	F	young shoots
Rubus parviflorus	thimbleberry	F	young shoots
Rubus spectabilis	salmonberry	F	young shoots
Sasa kurilensis	chishima-zasa bamboo	E	bamboo shoots; cooked
Semiarundinaria fastuosa	temple bamboo	E	bamboo shoots; sweet even when raw
Tilia americana	basswood	E	mildly mucilaginous young leaves; very nice
Tilia x europaea	linden	E	mildly mucilaginous young leaves; very nice
Toona sinensis	fragrant spring tree	G	young leaves; roasted-garlic flavor; cultivated
Vitis spp.	grapes	G	leaves pickled and stuffed
Vitis vinifera	grape	E	leaves pickled and stuffed
Xanthoceras sorbifolium	yellowhorn	U	young leaves

EDIBLE LEAVES, STALKS, AND SHOOTS: FORBS AND HERBACEOUS VINES

Latin Name	Common Name	Rating	Description
Alcea rosea	hollyhock	G	young leaves; good thickener for soups
Allium ampeloprasum	salad leek	E	onion flavor; cultivated as a leaf crop
Allium canadense	wild garlic	G	strong onion flavor; can cause digestive upset in children
Allium cepa aggregatum	potato onion, shallot	G	onion flavor

EDIBLE LEAVES, STALKS, AND SHOOTS: FORBS AND HERBACEOUS VINES *continued*

Latin Name	Common Name	Rating	Description
Allium cepa proliferum	Egyptian onion	G	onion flavor
Allium cernuum	nodding wild onion	G	onion flavor
Allium fistulosum	Welsh onion	E	onion flavor; a cultivated scallion
Allium schoenoprasum	chives	E	onion flavor; cultivated
Allium tricoccum	ramps	E	onion flavor; sweet; broad leaves
Allium tuberosum	garlic chive	E	onion flavor; cultivated
Althea officinalis	marsh mallow	G	leaves cooked; good thickener
Arabis spp.	rock cress	F	cress flavored
Aralia cordata	udo	E	blanched shoots like asparagus; cultivated in Japan; boil in salted water or slice and soak in salted water to remove unpleasant flavor; crisp, tender, and lemony
Armoracia rusticana	horseradish	F	young leaves; strong horseradish flavor
Asclepias syriaca	common milkweed	G	young shoots, young leaves, or young pods cooked in two or three changes of water; poisonous raw; use with caution
Asparagus officinalis	asparagus	E	young shoots; cultivated
Asphodeline lutea	yellow asphodel	G	young shoots
Balsamorhiza sagittata	balsamroot sunflower	U	young leaves and shoots; slight pine flavor
Bellis perennis	English daisy	G	young leaves
Beta vulgaris maritima	sea beet	E	perennial ancestor of chard and beets; leaves eaten like chard
Borago officinalis	borage	G	young leaves; hairy; mild minty flavor when cooked
Brassica oleracea	wild cabbage	G	perennial wild ancestor of cabbage, kale, broccoli, and many more; eaten like kale
Brassica oleracea acephala	tree collards	G	tasty and productive perennial collard
Brassica oleracea botrytis cv.	'Nine Star' perennial broccoli	G	leaves similar to collards
Bunias orientalis	Turkish rocket	G	very potent mustard flavor when raw; usually cooked; minor cultivated vegetable
Callirhoe involucrata	purple poppy-mallow	F	young leaves mucilaginous; thickener
Campanula carpatica	Carpathian bellflower	G	young leaves; slightly sweet
Campanula glomerata	clustered bellflower	G	young leaves; slightly sweet
Campanula portenschlagiana	Dalmatian bellflower	G	young leaves; slightly sweet
Cardamine bulbosa	spring cress	G	young leaves; cresslike
Cardamine pratensis	cuckoo flower	E	delicious; watercress flavor
Centranthus ruber	red valerian	G	leaves edible
Chenopodium bonus-henricus	good King Henry	E	spring shoots like asparagus; excellent; greens somewhat bitter and good when cooked
Chrysosplenium americanum	golden saxifrage	U	young leaves; spicy
Cichorium intybus	chicory	E	bitter young leaves; cultivated
Claytonia caroliniana	Carolina spring beauty	G	mild cooking green
Claytonia megarhiza	alpine spring beauty	G	mild cooking green
Claytonia virginica	spring beauty	G	mild cooking green
Clintonia borealis	corn lily	F	young leaves are cucumber flavored
Colocasia esculenta	taro	G	leaves and stems cooked at least 45 minutes; some varieties (like 'Celery Stem') for less time; ornamental varieties are poisonous; eat only food varieties

EDIBLE LEAVES, STALKS, AND SHOOTS: FORBS AND HERBACEOUS VINES *continued*

Latin Name	Common Name	Rating	Description
Commelina erecta	Virginia dayflower	F	young leaves
Crambe maritima	sea kale	E	cultivated for blanched shoots; young leaves also eaten
Cryptotaenia canadensis	honewort	G	young leaves and stems cooked
Cryptotaenia japonica	mitsuba	E	young leaves and blanched stems; cultivated
Darmera peltata, incl. *nana*	Indian rhubarb	U	peeled leafstalks; raw or cooked
Dioscorea japonica	jinenjo	G	young shoots
Diplotaxis spp.	sylvetta arugula	G	spicy; potent arugula flavor
Epilobium angustifolium	fireweed	G	young shoots
Epilobium latifolium	river beauty	G	young shoots
Eryngium maritimum	sea holly	G	blanched young shoots
Erythronium americanum	yellow trout lily	F	young leaves
Geum urbanum	clove root	F	young leaves
Hemerocallis spp.	daylilies	F	young shoots; can cause digestive upset
Heracleum sphondylium	cow parsnip	F	young leaves and leafstalks
Humulus lupulus	hops	G	young shoots cooked
Hydrophyllum virginianum	Virginia waterleaf	G	cooked greens excellent with one change of water
Hylotelephium telephium	orpine	F	succulent young leaves
Lactuca perennis	perennial lettuce	F	young blanched leaves
Laportaea canadensis	wood nettle	E	cooked young greens excellent; very nutritious; caution: stings before cooked!
Levisticum officinale	lovage	G	blanched stems like celery; young leaves
Ligusticum canbyi	osha	G	young leaves, shoots, stems; like strong celery
Ligusticum scoticum	Scotch lovage	G	blanched stems like celery
Lomatium cous	biscuit root	F	young leaves and stems
Lomatium nudicaule	biscuit root	F	stems and leaves like celery
Malva alcea	mallow	G	young leaves and shoots; mucilaginous
Malva moschata	musk mallow	G	young leaves and shoots; mucilaginous
Matteuccia struthiopteris	ostrich fern	E	young fiddleheads; excellent
Mertensia maritima	oyster plant	G	leaves fleshy; oyster flavored
Montia perfoliata	miner's lettuce	E	excellent raw; lettuce flavor; cultivated
Montia sibirica	Siberian miner's lettuce	G	good raw in spring; terrible once flowers
Myrrhis odorata	sweet cicely	E	leaves; delicious with sweet anise flavor
Nasturtium officinale	watercress	E	the cultivated watercress; delicious
Opuntia compressa	prickly pear cactus	F	de-spined pads eaten as a vegetable
Oxalis spp.	great wood sorrel	G	a tart nibble
Oxyria digyna	mountain sorrel	E	tasty tart leaves; good through fall
Petasites japonicus, incl. *giganteus*	fuki	G	peeled, cooked leafstalks eaten like celery
Phytolacca americana	pokeweed	E	young shoots; a popular wild edible; use only green shoots below 8″ (20 cm) tall, remainder of plant poisonous; peel, and do not use any pink portions; cook in several changes of water
Pimpinella saxifraga	burnet saxifrage	E	leaves and shoots; cucumber flavor
Polygonatum biflorum	Solomon's seal	E	young shoots excellent

EDIBLE LEAVES, STALKS, AND SHOOTS: FORBS AND HERBACEOUS VINES *continued*

Latin Name	Common Name	Rating	Description
Polygonatum biflorum var. *commutatum*	giant Solomon's seal	E	young shoots excellent; very asparagus–like
Polygonum bistorta	bistort	E	excellent potherb
Polygonum bistortoides	American bistort	G	potherb; tart
Polygonum viviparum	alpine bistort	F	potherb; tart
Pseudostellaria jamesiana	tuberous chickweed	G	lettucelike greens
Rheum australe	Himalayan rhubarb	E	apple-flavored rhubarb stalks; cook only; cultivated; leaves and roots poisonous
Rheum palmatum	turkey rhubarb	E	enormous rhubarb stalks; excellent; cook only; cultivated; leaves and roots poisonous
Rheum x cultorum	rhubarb	E	leafstalks cooked; tart; leaves and roots poisonous
Rhexia virginica	Virginia meadow beauty	G	young leaves; slightly sweet and tart
Rhodiola rosea	roseroot	U	succulent leaves, stems, and shoots
Rumex acetosa	French sorrel	E	excellent fresh or cooked; tart; cultivated
Rumex acetosella	sheep sorrel	E	leaves tart; raw or cooked
Rumex scutatus	buckler-leaved sorrel	E	tart, tasty leaves; cultivated
Sanguisorba canadensis	American great burnet	G	young leaves
Sanguisorba minor	salad burnet	G	young leaves; cucumber flavor; cultivated
Sanguisorba officinalis	great burnet	G	young leaves; cucumber flavor; cultivated
Saxifraga stolonifera	strawberry saxifrage	U	leaves cooked
Scorzonera hispanica	scorzonera	E	raw leaves similar to lettuce
Sedum album	white stonecrop	F	succulent young leaves
Sedum reflexum	stonecrop	F	succulent young leaves
Sedum ternatum	wild stonecrop	F	succulent young leaves
Smilacina racemosa	false Solomon's seal	G	young shoots
Smilax herbacea	carrion flower	G	young shoots
Solidago missouriensis	Missouri goldenrod	U	young leaves
Solidago odora	sweet goldenrod	G	nibble; sweet anise flavor
Stellaria media	annual chickweed	E	lettucelike greens excellent raw
Stellaria pubera	great chickweed	G	lettucelike greens
Streptopus amplexifolius	twisted stalk	G	young shoots; cucumber flavor
Streptopus roseus	rosybells	G	young shoots; cucumber flavor
Taraxacum officinale	dandelion	E	young leaves; sometimes blanched; cultivated
Tradescantia virginiana	Virginia spiderwort	F	young leaves
Trillium grandiflorum	white trillium	F	young unfolding leaves; sunflower flavor
Urtica spp.	stinging nettle	E	cooked young greens excellent; very nutritious; caution: stings before cooked!
Uvularia sessilifolia	sessile bellwort	G	young shoots
Vicia americana	American vetch	U	young shoots
Vicia cracca	tufted vetch	U	young shoots
Viola labradorica	Labrador violet	F	young leaves; slightly fuzzy
Viola sororaria	woolly blue violet	F	young leaves; slightly fuzzy
Viola spp.	violets	G	young leaves
Yucca baccata	banana yucca	F	young flower stalk; peeled

EDIBLE ROOTS

A great many species with edible tubers, taproots, corms, bulbs, rhizomes, and other underground parts can grow in forest gardens. If edibility is your primary concern, select species with "excellent" or "good" flavor ratings. The flavor ratings are E = excellent; G = good; F = fair; and U = unknown to authors. We based these on a subjective combination of flavor and productivity. For example, hog peanut (*Amphicarpaea bracteata*) has tiny underground beans that taste great but are hard to find and not very productive.

EDIBLE ROOTS

Latin Name	Common Name	Rating	Description
Allium canadense	wild garlic	G	onion flavor; can cause digestive upset in children
Allium cepa aggregatum	potato onion, shallot	E	outstanding onion flavor; excellent keepers; productive
Allium cepa proliferum	Egyptian onion	G	onion flavor
Allium fistulosum	Welsh onion	E	onion flavor
Allium tricoccum	ramps	E	onion flavor
Althaea officinalis	marsh mallow	G	roots candied
Amorphophallus riveri var. *konjac*	konjac	U	large roots eaten; also used as thickener; cook at least 45 minutes; eat only food types, not ornamental varieties; cultivated in Asia
Amphicarpaea bracteata	hog peanut	G	underground beans; nutty flavor
Apios americana	groundnut	E	high-protein staple; improved varieties available; delicious
Apios fortunei	Fortune's groundnut	E	many tubers strung along rhizomes; delicious
Apios priceana	Price's groundnut	E	single large tuber; delicious
Asphodeline lutea	yellow asphodel	G	lots of small, nutty edible roots
Astragalus canadensis	Canadian milk vetch	U	roots cooked
Balsamorhiza sagittata	balsamroot sunflower	U	roots raw or cooked; some say tastes "piney," others say very tasty
Bunium bulbocastanum	earth chestnut	E	sweet chestnut flavor
Callirhoe involucrata	purple poppy-mallow	G	sweet, starchy roots
Camassia cusickii	Cusick's camass	U	cooked bulbs have sweet, anise-squash flavor; pressure-cook at 250°F for nine hours; this species has larger bulbs than the others do, though some reports indicate that the flavor of this species is poor
Camassia spp.	camass, wild hyacinth	G	cooked bulbs have sweet, anise-squash flavor; pressure-cook at 250°F for nine hours
Cardamine bulbosa	spring cress	G	horseradish flavor
Claytonia caroliniana	Carolina spring beauty	G	excellent but tiny tubers
Claytonia megarhiza	alpine spring beauty	G	good flavor, large roots
Claytonia virginica	spring beauty	G	excellent but tiny tubers
Colocasia esculenta	taro	E	edible corms are starchy and sweet; take two or more years to mature in zone 7; must cook at least 45 minutes, poisonous otherwise; eat only food types, not ornamental varieties
Conopodium majus	pignut	G	chestnut/hazelnut flavor with radish aftertaste
Cryptotaenia canadensis	honewort	U	roots cooked
Cryptotaenia japonica	mitsuba	U	roots cooked

EDIBLE ROOTS *continued*

Latin Name	Common Name	Rating	Description
Cymopterus newberryi	corkwing	E	roots very sweet in spring
Cymopterus purpurascens	gamote	E	roots sweet, tender, parsniplike
Dioscorea batatas	Chinese yam	E	cultivated; large, starchy 2' to 3' (60–90 cm) taproots eaten cooked; also pea-size edible aerial tubers
Dioscorea japonica	jinenjo	E	cultivated; clusters of large, starchy tubers; also pea-size edible aerial tubers; cooked
Erigenia bulbosa	pepper and salt	U	tiny edible tubers
Eryngium maritimum	sea holly	G	roots have chestnut-parsnip flavor
Erythronium americanum	yellow trout lily	G	tiny bulbs are delicious
Fritillaria camschatcensis	Kamchatka lily	G	roots eaten raw or cooked; sometimes bitter
Glycyrrhiza lepidota	American licorice	F	roots sometimes cooked as a vegetable; flavor varies from bitter to sweet
Hedysarum boreale	sweet vetch	G	carrot-licorice flavor
Helianthus giganteus var. *subtuberosum*	Indian potato	G	edible tubers
Helianthus maximilianii	Maximilian sunflower	G	edible tubers
Helianthus tuberosus	Jerusalem artichoke	E	edible tubers; cultivated; productive and very sweet; raw or cooked
Helianthus x laetiflorus	showy sunflower	G	edible tubers
Hemerocallis spp.	daylily	F	productive; very strong flavor; can cause gas
Heracleum sphondylium	cow parsnip	G	rutabaga flavor
Ipomoea leptophylla	bush morning glory	F	enormous roots (up to 5'/150 cm long and 2'/60 cm wide); cooked; sometimes bitter and causing stomach upset, sometimes like its relative sweet potato; use with caution
Ipomoea pandurata	wild potato vine	F	enormous roots (up to 5'/150 cm long and 2'/60 cm wide); cooked; sometimes bitter and causing stomach upset, sometimes like its relative sweet potato; use with caution
Lathyrus linifolius montanus	bitter vetch	G	sweet chestnut flavor; nutritious
Lathyrus tuberosus	earthnut pea	G	sweet and starchy; occasionally cultivated
Ligusticum canbyi	osha	U	strong celery flavor
Ligusticum scoticum	Scotch lovage	U	roots chewed, candied
Lilium brownii	Hong Kong lily	G	bulbs cooked; thickener; sweet and starchy
Lilium canadense	Canada lily	F	bulbs used as thickener
Lilium lancifolium	tiger lily	G	bulbs cooked; parsnip flavor
Lilium longiflorum	white trumpet lily	G	bulbs mild, slightly sweet
Lilium philadelphicum	wood lily	F	bulbs used as thickener
Lilium superbum	Turk's-cap lily	F	bulbs used as thickener
Lomatium spp.	biscuit root	G	roots cooked or dried and used as flour; fresh strong celery-peppery flavor; former Native American staple; whole genus reported edible
Lycopus uniflorus	bugleweed	G	crisp tubers raw or cooked
Medeola virginiana	Indian cucumber root	E	small tubers; delicious cucumber flavor
Mertensia maritima	oyster plant	G	oyster-flavored roots
Myrrhis odorata	sweet cicely	G	roots eaten cooked; sweet anise flavor

EDIBLE ROOTS *continued*

Latin Name	Common Name	Rating	Description
Osmorhiza longistylis	sweet cicely	G	anise-flavored roots
Perideridia gairdneri	yampa	E	nutty flavor; former Native American staple; small
Platycodon grandiflora	balloon flower	G	raw or cooked; crunchy
Polygonatum biflorum	Solomon's seal	F	rootstocks cooked; starchy
Polygonatum biflorum var. commutatum	giant Solomon's seal	F	rootstocks cooked; starchy
Polygonum bistortoides	American bistort	G	nutty, excellent
Polygonum viviparum	alpine smartweed	G	like *P. bistortoides* above, but smaller
Polypodium glycyrrhiza	licorice fern	G	licorice-flavored rhizomes
Potentilla anserina	silverweed	G	large numbers of small roots; parsniplike; formerly cultivated in Scotland
Pseudostellaria jamesiana	tuberous chickweed	G	tasty tubers
Psoralea esculenta	prairie turnip	G	staple; starchy; turnip flavor
Rhexia virginica	Virginia meadow beauty	G	small tubers; nutty flavor
Rhodiola rosea	roseroot	U	crisp tubers; cooked
Scorzonera hispanica	scorzonera	E	carrotlike; sweet, nutty flavor; cultivated
Sium sisarum	skirret	E	delicious; productive; cultivated
Stachys affinis	Chinese artichoke	E	cultivated; excellent crisp, minty tubers; raw or cooked; productive
Stachys hyssopifolia	hyssop hedge nettle	G	crisp tubers; excellent
Stachys palustris	woundwort	G	as above
Streptopus amplexifolius	twisted stalk	G	cucumber-flavored rootstocks
Taraxacum officinale	dandelion	F	roots cooked
Triteleia grandiflora	blue dicks	U	roasted corms are sweet
Uvularia sessilifolia	sessile bellwort	F	rootstocks cooked

CULINARY HERB AND SPICE PLANTS

A number of interesting herb and spice plants can grow in forest gardens. Note that many culinary herbs can also be added to salads of mixed greens. Also, assume that the part used is the foliage unless otherwise indicated. The flavor ratings are E = excellent; G = good; F = fair; and U = unknown to authors.

CULINARY HERB AND SPICE PLANTS: TREES AND SHRUBS

Latin Name	Common Name	Rating	Description
Aralia hispida	bristly sarsaparilla	F	roots for tea and root-beer flavor
Aralia racemosa	spikenard	F	roots for tea and root-beer flavor
Calycanthus floridus	Carolina allspice	U	dried bark is used as a substitute for cinnamon; other parts, especially the fruit, are very toxic
Illicium floridanum	Florida star anise	G	wild relative of star anise; seed pod and seeds have strong anise flavor
Lindera benzoin	spicebush	G	dried, powdered fruits used like allspice; need male and female plants to set fruit; the leaves are also used
Magnolia virginiana	sweet bay magnolia	U	used like bay leaf

CULINARY HERB AND SPICE PLANTS: TREES AND SHRUBS *continued*

Latin Name	Common Name	Rating	Description
Myrica cerifera	wax myrtle	U	used like bay leaf; eucalyptus-like
Myrica gale	sweet gale	U	used like bay leaf; aromatic
Myrica pensylvanica	bayberry	U	used like bay leaf; citruslike
Persea borbonia	redbay	G	leaves are excellent bay leaf substitute
Rosmarinus officinalis	rosemary	E	cultivated culinary herb
Salvia officinalis	broadleaf sage	E	cultivated culinary herb
Sassafras albidum	sassafras	F	dried leaves used as a thickener, the "filet" in gumbo; consumption has been linked to cancer
Toona sinensis	fragrant spring tree	G	young leaves; roasted-garlic flavor
Vitex agnus-castus	chaste tree	U	seeds a mild pepper substitute; leaves are also used as a spice
Zanthoxylum americanum	prickly ash	U	dry fruit a pepper substitute; related to Szechuan pepper; need male and female to set fruit
Zanthoxylum piperitum	Japanese pepper tree	E	dry-roasted "fruit" (dry husk around seed) similar to related Szechuan pepper; mildly pungent with lemon flavor; need male and female plants to set fruit; intensely fragrant young leaves eaten raw or cooked

CULINARY HERB AND SPICE PLANTS: HERBACEOUS SPECIES

Latin Name	Common Name	Rating	Description
Allium ampeloprasum	sweet leek	G	onion-flavored leaves
Allium canadense	wild garlic	G	garlic-flavored roots; can cause digestive upset in children
Allium cepa aggregatum	shallot	E	magnificent; a blend of red onion and garlic
Allium cepa proliferum	Egyptian onion	G	scallion
Allium cernuum	nodding wild onion	G	onion-flavored greens
Allium fistulosum	Welsh onion	E	scallion
Allium schoenoprasum	chives	E	popular culinary; edible greens and flowers
Allium tricoccum	ramps	E	mild oniony leaves; bulbs potent!
Allium tuberosum	garlic chive	E	onion-garlic flavor
Armoracia rusticana	horseradish	E	roots are the source of horseradish
Artemisia dracunculus var. *sativa*	French tarragon	E	delicious culinary herb
Asarum spp.	wild ginger	F	gingerlike rhizome; used as a flavoring; potent
Blephilia spp.	wood mints	G	minty leaves
Bunium bulbocastanum	earth chestnut	F	leaves used like parsley, seeds like celery seed
Calamintha nepeta	calamint savory	U	strong pennyroyal-like minty flavor
Cardamine bulbosa	spring cress	G	horseradish-flavored root
Cardamine diphylla	toothwort	G	mildly horseradish-flavored rhizomes
Crocus sativus	saffron crocus	E	flower styles (delicate red parts) are the source of cultivated saffron
Cryptotaenia japonica	mitsuba	E	leaves used like parsley, seeds like celery or dill seed
Cunila origanoides	Maryland dittany	U	mintlike flavor
Foeniculum vulgare	fennel	E	anise-flavored stems, leaves, and seeds
Geum urbanum	clove root	U	clove/cinnamon-flavored root; used as spice

CULINARY HERB AND SPICE PLANTS: HERBACEOUS SPECIES *continued*

Latin Name	Common Name	Rating	Description
Glycyrrhiza spp.	licorice	G	dried, powdered roots used for licorice flavor
Heracleum sphondylium	cow parsnip	U	seeds used like celery seed
Houttuynia cordata	hot tuna	G	young leaves have unique spicy ginger/fish flavor; used in Asian cooking
Levisticum officinale	lovage	G	roots used for celery-like flavor; seeds use like celery seed; leaves have lemon-parsley flavor
Ligusticum canbyi	osha	G	leaves, seeds, roots; strong celery flavor
Melissa officinalis	lemon balm	E	lemony mint flavor
Mentha spp.	mints	E	minty flavor for cooking or salads
Monarda spp.	bee balm	G	minty flavor
Myrrhis odorata	sweet cicely	E	delicious leaves and fresh green seeds; sweet, anise flavor
Nasturtium officinale	watercress	E	pungent, peppery taste
Origanum vulgare hirtum	oregano	E	cultivated herb
Osmorhiza claytonii	sweet cicely	G	anise-flavored leaves
Osmorhiza longistylis	aniseroot	G	anise-flavored leaves and roots
Perideridia gairdneri	yampa	U	seeds used like caraway
Satureja douglasii	yerba buena	U	wild savory relative
Solidago odora	sweet goldenrod	G	anise-flavored leaves and flowers
Thymus vulgaris	thyme	E	cultivated culinary herb

TEA AND BEVERAGE PLANTS

Many of the finest hardy tea plants are ideally suited for forest gardens, sometimes producing larger leaves in dim light. Describing the variety of different flavors, especially from the different mints and their relatives, is difficult. Suffice it to say that you must try them all to appreciate their subtle and not-so-subtle differences. Blending them can result in sublime satisfaction. Develop your own favorite tea blends—icy peppermint with lemon balm, winter-green with honey, sweet goldenrod (once known as blue mountain tea) with the pink lemonade of sumac, and more. The flavor ratings are E = excellent; G = good; F = fair; and U = unknown to authors. Use first-try protocols as described on page 496. Check the medicinals list in the Plant Species Matrix and the "Superfoods and Best Medicinal Plants" table (later in this appendix), and research plants' pharmaceutical uses, too, as many of these are medicinal herbs. The part used is the dried foliage unless otherwise indicated.

TEA AND BEVERAGE PLANTS

Latin Name	Common Name	Rating	Description
Agastache foeniculum	anise hyssop	E	delightful licorice-mint tea
Aralia hispida	bristly sarsaparilla	F	roots for tea and root-beer flavor
Aralia nudicaulis	wild sarsaparilla	F	roots for tea and root-beer flavor
Aralia racemosa	spikenard	F	roots for tea and root-beer flavor
Arctostaphylos uva-ursi	bearberry	F	leaves and fruits for tea
Astragalus membranaceous	huang-qi	G	roots used for tea

TEA AND BEVERAGE PLANTS *continued*

Latin Name	Common Name	Rating	Description
Betula alleghaniensis	yellow birch	E	twigs, root bark, and dried leaves; wintergreen flavor
Betula lenta	black birch	E	twigs, root bark, and dried leaves; wintergreen flavor
Blephilia spp.	wood mint	G	minty
Calamintha nepeta	calamint savory	G	pungent pennyroyal aroma
Ceanothus americanus	New Jersey tea	E	flavor like true tea; used during US Revolutionary War
Chamaemelum nobile	chamomile	E	popular soothing tea
Cichorium intybus	chicory	G	dried roots roasted for coffee substitute
Comptonia peregrina	sweetfern	G	sweet, aromatic
Cunila origanoides	Maryland dittany	G	aromatic, minty
Dryas octopetala	mountain avens	U	unknown
Echinacea purpurea	purple coneflower	F	bad taste; popular medicinal
Eucalyptus gunnii	cider gum	E	sap used to make a beverage remarkably like apple cider
Foeniculum vulgare	fennel	G	anise flavor
Fragaria spp.	strawberry	G	leaves make a mild tea
Gaultheria hispidula	creeping snowberry	U	leaves for tea
Gaultheria procumbens	wintergreen	E	wintergreen flavor; leaves and fruits
Geum rivale	water avens	F	roots used for chocolate-like beverage
Geum urbanum	clove root	U	cinnamon-clove flavor
Ginkgo biloba	maidenhair tree	F	leaves used for tea
Glycyrrhiza lepidota	American licorice	G	sweetness variable in different seedlings; some excellent
Glycyrrhiza spp.	licorices	E	root is source of licorice; cultivated
Humulus lupulus	hops	E	cones are a component of beer; cones and leaves for tea
Laportaea canadensis	wood nettle	E	dark, rich, nutritious tea
Lespedeza bicolor	bush clover	U	leaves used for tea
Lindera benzoin	spicebush	G	leaves, twigs, and bark; spicy
Medicago sativa	alfalfa	G	nutritious; not supertasty
Melissa officinalis	lemon balm	E	delightful lemony mint
Mentha requienii	Corsican mint	E	strong pennyroyal mint
Mentha spp.	mints	E	delicious mint
Monarda spp.	bee balm, wild bergamot	E	strong minty flavor
Myrica cerifera	wax myrtle	G	robust
Myrica gale	sweet gale	G	delicate and palatable
Myrrhis odorata	sweet cicely	E	sweet anise flavor
Origanum vulgare	oregano	U	leaves used for tea
Panax quinquefolius	American ginseng	G	roots used in tea and medicine
Panax trifolius	dwarf ginseng	G	roots used in tea and medicine; also to nibble
Passiflora incarnata	maypop	G	leaves used; soothing
Persea borbonia	redbay	U	bay-leaf flavor
Pinus spp.	pines	U	chopped young needles; rich in vitamins A and C
Potentilla anserina	silverweed	U	leaves used for tea
Pycnanthemum spp.	mountain mint	E	very strong mint flavor
Rhus spp.	sumacs	E	all species listed in this book can make "pink lemonade": put fruit heads in water in the sun to make a sun tea—very delicious; do not boil (releases bitter tannins)
Rosmarinus officinalis	rosemary	G	leaves used for tea

TEA AND BEVERAGE PLANTS *continued*

Latin Name	Common Name	Rating	Description
Rubus spp.	raspberry, blackberry	G	leaves used for mild tea
Salvia officinalis	broadleaf sage	G	leaves used for tea
Sambucus canadensis	elderberry	G	flowers used for mild tea
Sassafras albidum	sassafras	E	roots used in tea as root-beer flavoring; strong
Satureja douglasii	yerba buena	E	minty, camphor taste
Schisandra chinensis	schisandra	U	dried fruit for tea and as medicinal
Solidago flexicaulis	zigzag goldenrod	U	leaves used for tea
Solidago missouriensis	Missouri goldenrod	U	dried leaves and flowers used for tea
Solidago odora	sweet goldenrod	E	dried leaves and flowers; anise/tarragon flavor
Taraxacum officinale	dandelion	G	roots roasted for coffee; flowers used for wine
Thymus vulgaris	thyme	G	leaves used for tea
Tilia spp.	linden, basswood	E	flowers are sweet and well flavored
Trifolium spp.	red and white clover	G	leaves and flowers
Urtica spp.	stinging nettle	E	rich, very nutritious
Veronica officinalis	speedwell	U	leaves used for tea
Viburnum cassinoides	witherod viburnum	U	leaves used for tea

OTHER EDIBLE PARTS

These plants produce a myriad of edible parts. While many are only novelties, some are truly useful food plants. The flavor ratings are E = excellent; G = good; F = fair; and U = unknown to authors.

Most of the species with edible seeds and grains have low yields of small seeds and are difficult to harvest. With breeding work they might become interesting new crops.

EDIBLE SAPS

Latin Name	Common Name	Rating	Description
Acer saccharinum	silver maple	G	sap for syrup and sugar
Acer saccharum	sugar maple	E	sap for syrup and sugar
Acer saccharum var. *nigrum*	black maple	G	sap for syrup and sugar
Betula alleghaniensis	yellow birch	G	sap for sweet wintergreen syrup
Betula lenta	black birch	G	sap for sweet wintergreen syrup
Eucalyptus gunnii	cider gum	E	sap tapped in Australia; flavor very much like apple cider; used fresh or fermented; does not need to be boiled down like other saps

EDIBLE BROCCOLI-LIKE FLOWER HEADS AND FLOWER BUDS

Latin Name	Common Name	Rating	Description
Brassica oleracea	wild cabbage	U	small broccoli-like heads
Brassica oleracea botrytis cv.	'Nine Star' perennial broccoli	G	delicious small broccoli heads; the plant dies if seed matures; cut all heads and it can live for several years
Bunias orientalis	Turkish rocket	G	small broccoli-like heads; like broccoli raab

EDIBLE BROCCOLI-LIKE FLOWER HEADS AND FLOWER BUDS *continued*

Latin Name	Common Name	Rating	Description
Crambe maritima	sea kale	G	small broccoli-like heads
Hemerocallis spp.	daylilies	E	flower buds eaten as a vegetable, common in Asian cooking

EDIBLE FLOWERS

Latin Name	Common Name	Rating	Description
Alcea rosea	hollyhock	F	somewhat waxy
Allium canadense	wild garlic	F	strong onion flavor
Allium schoenoprasum	chives	G	strong chive flavor
Allium tuberosum	garlic chives	G	strong onion/garlic flavor
Asclepias syriaca	common milkweed	U	boiled 1 minute, then made into fritters
Asphodeline lutea	yellow asphodel	E	flowers said to be sweet and delicious
Borago officinalis	borage	G	cucumber-flavored, but has hairy bracts
Campanula spp.	bellflower	U	slightly sweet
Cercis canadensis	redbud	E	sweet, pealike flower
Epigaea repens	trailing arbutus	G	flower tubes (corollas) edible; sweet and sour
Hemerocallis spp.	daylilies	E	fresh or dried
Hibiscus syriacus	rose of Sharon	F	somewhat waxy
Houttuynia cordata	hot tuna	G	ginger-fish flavor; culinary
Lespedeza bicolor	bush clover	U	flowers edible
Monarda didyma	bee balm	G	flowers sweet and minty
Opuntia compressa	prickly pear cactus	F	waxy
Oxalis spp.	wood sorrels	G	tart
Robinia pseudoacacia	black locust	G	sweet flowers cooked in fritters
Taraxacum officinale	dandelion	F	flowers in fritters and wine
Trifolium pratense	red clover	F	flowers edible
Trifolium repens	white clover	F	flowers edible
Viola spp.	violets	G	flowers edible; sometimes candied
Xanthoceras sorbifolium	yellowhorn	U	flowers edible
Yucca baccata	banana yucca	U	flowers edible
Zizia aurea	golden alexanders	G	flowers edible

EDIBLE PODS

Latin Name	Common Name	Rating	Description
Asclepias syriaca	common milkweed	F	flower buds boiled in several changes of water; poisonous when raw
Astragalus crassicarpus	groundplum milk vetch	G	1" (3 cm) pods; sweet and pealike
Cercis canadensis	redbud	F	young pods eaten
Lathyrus japonicus maritima	beach pea	U	young pods like snow peas
Malva alcea	mallow	G	small pods; mucilaginous
Malva moschata	musk mallow	G	small pods; mucilaginous
Yucca baccata	banana yucca	U	young pods eaten as a vegetable

EDIBLE SEEDS AND GRAINS

Latin Name	Common Name	Rating	Description
Amphicarpaea bracteata	hog peanut	U	small aboveground seeds edible
Arundinaria gigantea ssp. *tecta*	dwarf canebrake bamboo	U	seeds, produced every 3 or 4 years, used as a grain; watch for poison purple fungus on grains!
Caragana arborescens	Siberian pea shrub	F	beans cooked; small and troublesome to harvest
Chenopodium bonus–henricus	good King Henry	G	seeds used as a grain (quinoa relative)
Helianthus giganteus (incl. var. *subtuberosum*)	giant sunflower	U	seeds like small sunflower seeds
Helianthus maximilianii	Maximilian sunflower	U	seeds like small sunflower seeds
Lathyrus japonicus maritima	beach pea	U	seeds like fresh or dried peas; can be poisonous if eaten in great quantity for too long
Lathyrus linifolius montanus	bitter vetch	U	seeds cooked; can be poisonous if eaten in great quantity for too long
Lespedeza bicolor	bush clover	U	seeds cooked like beans
Medicago sativa	alfalfa	E	seeds sprouted
Phaseolus polystachios	wild bean	U	seeds fresh or dried like beans; same genus as kidney bean
Secale cereale cv.	'Varimontra' perennial rye	E	grain used like annual rye; watch for poison purple fungus on grains!
Solidago flexicaulis	zigzag goldenrod	U	seeds edible
Sorghum x hybrid	perennial sorghum	E	grain used like annual sorghum
Tripsacum dactyloides	eastern gamma grass	F	tastes like corn, but each seed has woody hull
Triticum x *aestivum*	perennial wheat	E	grain used like annual wheat; varieties incl. 'Jefferson'; watch for poison purple fungus on grains!
Vicia cracca	tufted vetch	U	seeds edible

Most of these species have low yields of small seeds and are difficult to harvest. With breeding work they might become interesting new crops.

EDIBLE TWIGS

Latin Name	Common Name	Rating	Description
Betula alleghaniensis	yellow birch	G	wintergreen flavored for chewing
Betula lenta	black birch	G	wintergreen flavored for chewing
Hovenia dulcis	Japanese raisin tree	E	swollen twig tips are sweet and chewy like raisins

MISCELLANEOUS EDIBLE PARTS

Latin Name	Common Name	Rating	Description
Eucalyptus gunnii	cider gum	G	exudes a sweet, thick edible gum
Rhododendron periclymenoides	pinxter flower azalea	U	stem galls (fungal growths) are crisp and sweet
Silphium laciniatum	compass plant	F	resin from cut flowers used as chewing gum
Silphium spp.	cup plant, rosinweed	U	may produce a resin like *Silphium laciniatum*
Ulmus rubra	slippery elm	U	sweet, mucilaginous inner bark is chewed

EDIBLE MUSHROOMS

We can grow many mushrooms in forest gardens, some truly of gourmet quality. This table presents only a small portion of those you can grow. CAUTION! All mushrooms should be cooked before being eaten. Similar-looking mushrooms may be toxic. All mushroom cultivators must learn to accurately identify mushrooms before attempting cultivation. This book cannot cover identification and potential toxicity and allergies from fungi (for example, some mushrooms cause illness if consumed with alcohol but are otherwise fine). Read Paul Stamets's *Growing Gourmet and Medicinal Mushrooms* or field identification guides for more information, or review the mushroom catalogs listed in appendix 7.

Niche: D = decomposer; FP = facultative parasite (attacks the sick).

Natural Culture Medium: Techniques for growing outdoors.

Preferred Substrate: Materials mushrooms grow upon; HW = hardwoods (many hardwoods coppice; see British and North American coppice species tables later this appendix).

Native Range: Where native; may have naturalized elsewhere.

EDIBLE MUSHROOMS

Species Common Name	Niche	Natural Culture Medium	Preferred Substrate	Native Range	Notes
Agrocybe aegerita black-poplar agrocybe	D	chips, stumps	HW, esp. cottonwood, box elders, willow, poplar, maple	se US, Far East, s Europe	mild porklike flavor
Auricularia auricula Auricularia polytricha wood ear	D	logs, maybe stumps	conifer or HW, esp. oak, willow, locust, mulberry; woody soils	temperate HW forests worldwide	gelatinous texture; mild flavor
Coprinus comatus shaggy mane	D	chips, rich soils, manure, etc.	HW sawdust, cow or horse manure with straw or sawdust, soils with manure	temperate climates worldwide	tender; delicious; decomposes rapidly once ripe
Grifola frondosa hen-of-the-woods, maitake	D, FP	stumps, logs	oaks, elm, maple, beech, blackgum; occasionally larch, rarely pine	n temperate decid. forests, ne US	excellent but tough; cook long and slowly
Hericium erinaceous lion's mane	D, FP	stumps, logs	oak, walnut, beech, elm, maple, sycamore, other HW	North America, Europe, Asia	excellent; when fresh resembles lobster
Hypholoma sublateritium chestnut mushroom, kuritake	D	logs, stumps, sawdust	oak and chestnut	Europe, e North America, temperate Asia	good quality; similar to oyster mushroom
Hypholoma tessulatus = *Hypholoma marmoreus* beech mushroom	D, FP	chips, logs, stumps	elm, beech, cottonwood, maple, willow, oak, other HW	n temperate forests worldwide	good quality; similar to oyster mushroom
Hypsizygus ulmarius garden oyster mushroom	D	straw, garden debris, logs, stumps, maybe sawdust	straw, garden debris, elm, beech, cottonwood, maple, willow, oak, other HW	n temperate forests worldwide	good quality; similar to oyster mushroom

EDIBLE MUSHROOMS *continued*

Species Common Name	Niche	Natural Culture Medium	Preferred Substrate	Native Range	Notes
Laetiporus sulphureus chicken of the woods	D	stumps, logs	oak, other HW	North America	excellent; really tastes like chicken breast!
Lentinula edodes shiitake mushroom	D	logs	broadleaf trees, esp. oak, sweetgum, poplar, alder, cottonwood, ironwood, beech, birch, willow	Far East	nutty, rich, delicious
Lepista nuda blewit mushroom	D	wood chips, compost piles, grass clippings	garden debris	temperate North America and Europe	rich; flavor resembles button mushroom
Morchella spp. black, yellow, white, and other morels	D	inoculated burn sites, orchard inoculation	burn sites, sandy HW-forest soils, apple orchards, apple, elm, cottonwood, oak, fir	temperate climates worldwide	nutty flavor; delectable; prized by mushroom lovers
Pleurotus cystidiosus abalone, maple oyster	D, FP	chips, logs, stumps	maple, cottonwood, beech, oak, elm, sweetgum, poplar	e and se US, Asia, s Africa	tender; flavor resembles that of oysters
Pleurotus eryngii king oyster	FP	logs, stumps, straw	buried HW roots	s Europe, c Asia, n Africa	tender; flavor somewhat resembles that of oysters
Pleurotus euosmus tarragon oyster	D	chips, logs, stumps	elm stumps and logs	British Isles	tender; flavor somewhat resembles that of oysters
Pleurotus ostreatus THE oyster mushroom, straw mushroom	D, FP	logs, stumps	HW, esp. cottonwood, oaks, alder, maple, aspen, ash, beech, birch, willow, elm, poplar, occasionally conifers	temperate and tropical forests worldwide	tender; flavor somewhat resembles that of oysters
Pleurotus pulmonarius Indian oyster	D	chips, straw, logs, stumps	conifers, HW, esp. alder, poplar, cottonwood, oak, elm, aspen	North America, Europe	tender; flavor resembles that of oysters
Stropharia rugoso–annulata king stropharia, garden giant	D	chips, straw, soil, compost	HW forests, HW debris, soils high in woody matter	North America	firm; flavor of potatoes soaked in red wine

SUPERFOODS AND BEST MEDICINAL PLANTS

We made little effort to include in this book plants with primarily medicinal uses. However, many of the species in the Plant Species Matrix have medicinal qualities. This table lists species from the matrix that are superfoods or that our medicinals consultants rated as excellent medicinals. Many other species in the matrix have lesser medicinal qualities; they are not included here. For more information on the other medicinals listed in the Plant Species Matrix, see the medicinals references in appendix 7. Superfoods are foods so nutritious or containing such high amounts of a specific nutritional factor that they can be used medicinally. Superfoods are marked with an S, while medicinals are rated as excellent (E), good (G), or fair (F). Thanks to Chris Marano of Clearpath Herbals in Wendell, Massachusetts, and to Peter Buhl, student of Chinese medicine, for their help in preparing this table. Chinese medicinal uses are derived from *Oriental Materia Medica: A Concise Guide*, by Hong-Yen Hsu, PhD, and associates, 1986. Medical terms used here are defined in the glossary.

IMPORTANT: This table does not substitute for good references on the use of medicinal plants. Proper plant identification, growing conditions, proper preparation of the right plant parts at the right time of year, proper diagnosis, and proper dosage all combine to influence the potency and effects of medicinal plants, as do the specific circumstance of each person's body and interactions with other herbal medicines and conventional drugs. Some of these substances may be toxic when improperly used and may not be noted as such here. Use these substances only under the supervision of trained medical personnel of your choosing.

SUPERFOODS AND BEST MEDICINAL PLANTS

Species	Common Name	Superfood	Medicinal	Notes
Achillea millefolium	yarrow		E	leaf, stem, flower: antihemorraghic, anti-inflammatory, tonic
Actinidia spp.	hardy kiwis	S	G	fruit: superfood—very high in vitamin C and potassium, high enzyme content; dissipates heat and fever with restlessness, invigorates blood, diuretic; root: similar uses
Agastache foeniculum	anise hyssop		E	leaf: diaphoretic, heart tonic, used to treat fevers
Allium spp.	perennial onions	S	G	leaf, bulb: superfood—best land-plant sources of selenium, nutritive to mucous-membrane tissues, some spp. similar to garlic in medicinal properties
Althaea officinalis	marsh mallow		E	leaf: tea; flower: edible emollient, demulcent, nutritive; root: mucilaginous, and used to treat cough, laryngitis, gastrointestinal problems
Amelanchier spp.	juneberry, saskatoon	S	G	fruit: pemmican ingredient, female tonic, pregnancy tonic
Aralia cordata	udo		E	dried root: anti-arthritic, tranquilizer, analgesic, promotes circulation, expels wind-dampness, used to treat headache from common cold and knee and loin pain
Aralia racemosa	spikenard		E	root: female reproductive tonic, alterative, tonic
Arctostaphylos uva-ursi	bearberry		E	leaf: excellent urinary antiseptic, astringent, toner; WARNING: internal use may cause toxicity; use with care.
Armoracia rusticana	horseradish		E	root: stimulant, aperient, antiseptic, rubefacient
Astragalus membranaceous	huang–qi		E	root: nutritive, adaptogen, tonic, anticancer, premier chi tonic in Chinese medicine
Berberis canadensis	Canada barberry		E	root: antibacterial, liver tonic, antiseptic
Brassica spp.	perennial broccoli, kale, etc.	S	G	seed, flower: detoxification, anticancer; leaf: superfood for same reasons, especially when juiced
Carya spp.	pecan, hickories	S		nut: high-quality protein and high in omega fatty acids
Castanea spp.	chestnuts, chinkapin	S		nut: high-quality protein and high in omega fatty acids
Ceanothus americanus	New Jersey tea		E	root: lymphatic remedy, blood purifier, astringent
Chamaemelum nobile	chamomile		E	flower: calmative, anti-anxiety, carminative
Chimaphila maculata *Chimaphila umbellate*	pipsissewa		E	leaf: antiseptic, diuretic, astringent, tonic for urinary tract, kidney, and prostate
Coptis trifolia var. *groenlandica*	goldthread		E	root contains berberine: antibacterial, antifungal, antiseptic, bitter tonic

SUPERFOODS AND BEST MEDICINAL PLANTS *continued*

Species	Common Name	Superfood	Medicinal	Notes
Corylus spp.	hazelnuts, filberts	S	F	nut: superfood—high in protein, omega fatty acids; bark: astringent
Crataegus spp.	hawthorns		E	berry, leaf, flower: excellent heart and cardiovascular tonic, hypotensive, anti-arrhythmia, joint and digestive tonic, promotes digestion, expels phlegm, supports connective tissue; coppice these species to keep leaves within reach
Dioscorea batatas	Chinese yam		E	dried, peeled rhizome: superior herb in Chinese medicine, supplements the spleen and stomach, tonifies lungs and kidneys, used to treat diarrhea due to spleen deficiency, chronic dysentery, cough due to general debility, overactive bladder, diabetes
Echinacea purpurea	purple coneflower		E	flower, root, leaf, stem juice: immune stimulant, lymphatic, blood purifier
Foeniculum vulgare	fennel		E	seed: carminative, galactagogue
Ginkgo biloba	maidenhair tree		E	leaf: cardiovascular, eye, and cerebral tonic, increases circulation and oxygenation; coppice this species to keep leaves within reach
Glycyrrhiza glabra *Glycyrrhiza lepidota* *Glycyrrhiza uralensis*	licorice American licorice Chinese licorice		E	root: powerful adaptogen for general debility; strengthens core, antihepatoxic, antiviral, immune and female reproductive tonic, anti-allergenic, builds weak stomach, lungs, and intestines
Helianthus spp.	sunflowers	S		seed: protein, omega fatty acids
Helianthus tuberosus	Jerusalem artichoke	S	G	tuber: pancreatic tonic, balances blood sugar
Hippophae rhamnoides	sea buckthorn	S		berry: very high in vitamin C and bioflavonoids
Houttuynia cordata	hot tuna		E	leaf, entire plant: antibacterial, antiviral, used to treat lung ailments, urinary antiseptic, diuretic, antifungal, antispirochete (Lyme disease), insect toxin; CAUTION: slightly toxic—not for consistent long-term use
Humulus lupulus	hops		E	"cone": sedative, diuretic, bitter tonic, cholagogue, antibacterial, inhibits some fungi and yeast, powerful growth inhibitor of gram positive bacteria, used to treat lung diseases, general anti-inflammatory, antimalarial
Juglans ailantifolia var. *cordiformis*	heartnut	S		nut: high-quality protein, omega fatty acids
Juglans cinerea *Juglans nigra*	butternut black walnut	S	E	root bark: laxative, relieves liver congestion; hull: antifungal, anti-parasitic; nut is superfood (see heartnut above)
Juglans regia and varieties	English and Carpathian walnuts	S	G	nut: protein, oils; also prostate tonic
Lactuca perennis	perennial lettuce		E	latex: nerve tonic, sedative, pain reliever
Mahonia aquifolium	Oregon grape		E	root: antibacterial, antifungal, liver tonic, cholagogue, antiseptic, relieves diarrhea
Medicago sativa	alfalfa	S	E	leaf: mineral-rich nutritive, diuretic, antioxidant, phytoestrogenic, high in vitamin K (bones), antiviral, detoxifier
Melissa officinalis	lemon balm		E	leaf: antiviral, antidepressant, antioxidant, antihyperthyroidic, carminative, antiseptic, calmative
Mentha x *piperita*	peppermint		E	leaf: antiviral, antidepressant, antioxidant, antihyperthyroidic, carminative, antiseptic, calmative
Origanum vulgare hirtum	oregano		E	leaf: carminative, antibacterial, diaphoretic
Osmorhiza claytonii *Osmorhiza longistylis*	sweet cicely anise root		E	root: adaptogenic, tonic for debility of all kinds; leaf as tea is tonic also

SUPERFOODS AND BEST MEDICINAL PLANTS *continued*

Species	Common Name	Superfood	Medicinal	Notes
Panax quinquefolius	American ginseng		E	root: premier adaptogen, tonic for debility of all kinds, the only cooling form of ginseng, can be used long-term, primarily a respiratory/lung tonic, used to treat TB and related conditions
Passiflora incarnata	maypop		E	flower and leaf: anti-anxiety, antidepressant, sedative
Platycodon grandiflorus	balloon flower		E	root: a superior lung remedy, expectorant, tonic, ventilates and soothes the lungs, resolves phlegm, drains pus, tranquilizer, analgesic; some toxicity, but first remedy of choice in China
Polygonatum biflorum	Solomon's seal		E	rhizome: excellent tonic for debility and lung ailments, strengthens joint and connective tissue, nerve tonic
Prunus armeniaca	apricot		E	kernel: in Chinese medicine frequently used for shortness of breath, expectorant, antitussive, lubricates the intestines; CAUTION: slightly toxic, not for extended use
Prunus dulcis	almond	S	G	nut: nutritive; oil used for mucous-membrane health
Pseudostellaria jamesiana	tuberous chickweed	S	E	herb: mineral rich, demulcent, healing to all tissues, lung tonic, skin tonic, anti-inflammatory, vulnerary
Quercus alba	white oak		E	inner bark: astringent, mucous-membrane toner, used to treat prolapse and diarrhea, styptic, tonic; coppicing may increase inner bark production
Rheum spp.	rhubarbs		E	root: astringent, tonic, stomachic, aperient, laxative, part of Essiac formula, very strong antibacterial, inhibits DNA and protein synthesis in bacteria (especially staph and strep), anti-carcinogen, cathartic, cools blood, purges fire, stimulates bile and pancreas secretions, purgative, relieves constipation due to excess heat, delirium, mania, stuffiness, sensation of fullness, incipient diarrhea; SHORT-TERM USE ONLY
Rosmarinus officinalis	rosemary		E	herb: carminative, antimicrobial, antiseptic, liver tonic, clears mind, brain tonic, important antioxidant
Rubus spp.	raspberries, etc.	S	E	root, leaf: excellent astringent, tonic; fruit: various antioxidants, low glycemic index, vitamin C, fiber, cancer preventive, detoxifier
Sambucus canadensis	elderberry		E	berry, flower, inner bark: antimicrobial, antiviral, diuretic, anti-catarrhal, many more uses
Schisandra chinensis	magnolia vine		E	fruit: superior adaptogen, tonic, immune builder, thyroid tonic, brain tonic, liver tonic, main use as respiratory tonic in Chinese medicine, relieves shortness of breath and cough, helps almost every organ system, antidiarrheal
Solidago spp.	goldenrods		E	herb, leaf, flower: diuretic, diaphoretic, carminative, antimicrobial, expectorant, anticatarrhal
Stellaria spp.	chickweeds	S	E	herb: mineral rich, demulcent, healing to all tissues, lung tonic, skin tonic, anti-inflammatory, vulnerary
Symphytum spp.	comfreys		E	herb, root: internal and external vulnerary par excellence, demulcent, mucous-membrane tonic, lung tonic; CAUTION: contains pentacyclic alkaloids—cumulative toxicity to liver, not for long-term internal use
Taraxacum officinale	dandelion	S	E	leaf: diuretic par excellence, antibacterial, also a superfood; root: superior liver tonic, super blood balancer, kidney tonic, aperient, digestive tonic, antibacterial
Thymus vulgaris	thyme		E	herb: superior antibacterial, antiviral, antifungal, antiseptic, diaphoretic, carminative, anticatarrhal

SUPERFOODS AND BEST MEDICINAL PLANTS *continued*

Species	Common Name	Superfood	Medicinal	Notes
Trifolium pratense	red clover		E	flower: lymphatic, blood purifier, anticancer, expectorant, antispasmodic, vulnerary
Ulmus rubra	slippery elm		E	inner bark: demulcent, digestive remedy, mucous-membrane healer, digestive aid, nerve tonic, nutritive, lung tonic; coppicing may increase inner bark production
Urtica dioica	stinging nettle	S	E	leaf: mineral rich, diuretic, tonic for general debility, builder of blood, bone, connective tissue, kidneys
Vaccinium macrocarpon	cranberry	S	E	berry: antiseptic, diuretic, used in cases of urinary tract infections—acidifies the urinary tract and vagina to dispel yeast infections, inhibits bacterial adhesion to cell walls
Vaccinium spp.	blueberries	S	E	berry: eye and vision tonic, superfood, high in antioxidants, minerals, enzymes, etc.; leaf: blood-sugar balancer, blood purifier, used in diabetes
Vitex agnus-castus	chaste tree		E	berry: female reproductive tonic par excellence
Vitis spp.	grapes	S	E	fruit and seed: strengthen blood vessels, antioxidant, support collagen; seed: especially antimicrobial, antiviral
Zanthoxylum americanum *Zanthoxylum piperitum*	prickly ash Japanese pepper tree		E	bark: circulatory stimulant, diaphoretic, analgesic, carminative, anti-inflammatory, expectorant, used externally as a rubefacient
Ziziphus jujuba	jujube		E	fruit: nutritive, tonic, restorative for debility, tonifies spleen, moistens heart and lungs, nourishes spirit, a superior herb in Chinese medicine; seed: calmative, anti-anxiety, nourishes liver, calms heart and spirit, sedative, high-grade drug in Chinese medicine

BRITISH COPPICE SPECIES

This table lists British coppice species and their spacing and uses. North American species are probably similar. "Age" is age of coppice shoots at harvest. Our information is drawn from the discussion in Raymond Tabor's *Traditional Woodland Crafts: A Practical Guide* (B.T. Batsford, Ltd., London, 1994).

BRITISH COPPICE SPECIES

Species	Spacing	Age (Years)	Some Traditional Uses
Acer campestre *A. pseudoplatanus* Maple and sycamore	11 ft./3.4 m	7–12 12–25	• bean rods, hedge and fence stakes • turnery, furniture, small carved objects, firewood, charcoal
Alnus glutinosa Alder	"not too far apart"	12–25 20–40	• kindling, scythe handles, broom handles and heads, small turnery, river revetments, river piles, charcoal • clogs, charcoal
Betula pendula *Betula pubescens* Birch	"not too far apart"	5–10 10–20	• broom heads, horse jumps, kindling, withes • broom and rake handles and heads, small turnery, firewood, charcoal
Carpinus betulus Hornbeam	not stated	20–30	• gear teeth and pulleys, firewood, charcoal

BRITISH COPPICE SPECIES *continued*

Species	Spacing	Age (Years)	Some Traditional Uses
Castanea sativa Sweet chestnut	8 ft./2.4 m	12–18	• hop poles, bean rods, pea sticks, posts, pale and wire fencing, paling, gates, lathes, fruit props, charcoal
Corylus avellana Hazel	7 ft./2 m	6–12	• pea sticks, garden stakes, bean rods, thatching, fences, barrel hoops, fascines, clothes props, pegs, pheasant traps, withes and bonds (like stiff rope)
		12–15	• gates, rake handles, rustic poles, hedging stakes, etc.
		>15	• firewood, charcoal
Crataegus monogyna Hawthorn	used when found	not stated	• turnery, gear teeth, mallet heads, aromatic firewood, charcoal
Fraxinus excelsior Ash	11 ft./3.4 m	7–12	• rake handles, scythe handles, gates, bean rods, garden stakes, barrel hoops, broom handles, broom heads, pegs
		12–25	• handles, tent pegs, turnery, furniture, rake heads and teeth, fence rails, wedges, charcoal, firewood
Populus tremula Aspen	suckers; spacing variable	6–12	• withes, broom handles
		12–25	• clog soles, firewood
Prunus avium Wild cherry	not stated	not stated	• "always valued for the color and quality of its wood"
Prunus padus Bird cherry	used when found	not stated	• turnery, gear teeth, mallet heads, aromatic firewood, charcoal
Quercus robur *Quercus petraea* Oak	11 ft./3.4 m	7–12	• basket making, garden stakes, sticks
		12–20	• gates, hedge stakes, lathes, wedges
		20–30	• baskets, stakes, bark for tanning, turnery, roof shingles, posts, firewood, charcoal
Salix caprea *Salix cinerea* Sallow / willow	7 ft./2 m	6–12	• withes, bean rods, pegs, thatch, gates, scythe handles, clothes pegs, barrel hoops, hedge stakes, fascines, tool handles, rake handles and heads
		12–25	• firewood, charcoal
Sorbus aucuparia Rowan	used when found	not stated	• turnery, gear teeth, mallet heads, aromatic firewood, charcoal
Sorbus terminalis Service	used when found	not stated	• turnery, gear teeth, mallet heads, aromatic firewood, charcoal
Tilia cordata Lime / pry / linden	8 ft./2.4 m	10–15	• pea sticks, bean rods, broom handles, bast (tough rope)
		15–25	• hop poles, turnery, charcoal, bast
Ulmus procera Elm	11 ft./3.4 m	7–12	• tree stakes, hedge stakes, gates, bean rods, pea sticks, withes
		12–25	• turnery, stakes, firewood, charcoal

NORTH AMERICAN AND OTHER COPPICE SPECIES

The species listed here are documented coppice plants: they resprout from the stump or from roots when cut down. The table includes Plant Species Matrix or native eastern deciduous forest species that we have seen coppicing, or that references document as such. (References include Beresford-Kroeger, 2003; B & T World Seeds, 2004; Ron Yaple, forestry consultant and arborist, Sheffield, MA, personal communication; Pratt, 1959, pages 118–19; Kricher and Morrison, 1988, pages 57, 59, and 101; Tilth, 1982, pages 152–69; US Forest Service, 1990.)

Most hardwood trees and shrubs will coppice to some degree, if cut young enough. However, some species are better for coppice forestry than others. There is wide experience with coppice forestry in Europe, particularly Britain (see the previous table for a list of British species and their uses). Little work appears to have been done using North American species—references are rare. Therefore, this area is rife with opportunities for research and empirical trials. This list is only the merest of beginnings. We show here only uses for which we have a reference, either known coppice uses or timber uses that may be relevant to coppice uses. Other uses are possible. Check the "Edible Mushrooms" table (earlier in this appendix) for information on which of these species may work for mushroom production.

NORTH AMERICAN AND OTHER COPPICE SPECIES		
Latin Name	**Common Name**	**Notes / Known Uses**
Acer spp.	maples	most species coppice; fuel; probably similar to British species
Alnus spp.	alders	fuel, stakes, poles, fence posts; probably similar to British species
Asimina triloba	pawpaw	can use bark of coppiced material to distill numerous active chemical constituents for farmaceuticals, insecticides, etc.
Betula alleghaniensis	yellow birch	seedlings and saplings sprout well; older stumps sprout poorly; fuel, furniture, woodenware; distillation: wood alcohol, charcoal, tar, oils
Betula lenta	black birch	reproduces well from small stumps; fuel, furniture, woodenware, pulp; distillation: birch oil
Betula papyrifera	paper birch	prolific coppicer, esp. when young; fuel, pulp, mulch
Betula spp.	birches	fuel; coppicing varies among spp.
Carpinus caroliniana	American hornbeam	may be similar to British species; tool handles, levers, wedges, mallets
Carya aquatica	water hickory	stumps under 2 ft/60 cm in diameter sprout readily; fuel, stakes, tool handles, poles, fence posts
Carya cordiformis	bitternut hickory	stump, crown, and root sprouting common and prolific; charcoal, fuel, smoking meats, dowels, tool handles, ladders, stakes, poles, posts; calcium accumulator
Carya glabra	pignut hickory	vigorous stump and root sprouting common, but not prolific; fuel, stakes, posts, poles, tool handles
Carya illinoinensis	pecan	vigorous stump sprouts common; fuel, stakes, posts, poles, tool handles; timber used for furniture, machining
Carya laciniosa	shellbark hickory	coppices readily; coppice management recommended by US Forest Service; fuel, stakes, posts, poles, tool handles; timber used for furniture, tool handles, sporting goods, fuel, charcoal
Carya ovata	shagbark hickory	almost all stumps <10 in/24 cm sprout; older stumps root-sucker more and coppice less; fuel, stakes, posts, poles, tool handles; timber used for furniture, flooring, tool handles, ladder rungs, dowels, gym equipment, athletic goods, fuel, charcoal, smoking meats
Carya tomentosa	mockernut hickory	prolific; more sprouts on younger stumps; fuel, stakes, posts, poles, tool handles; timber used for pulp, fuel, charcoal, tool handles, ladder rungs, athletic goods, farm implements, dowels, gym equipment, poles, shafts, well pumps, furniture, smoking meats
Castanea dentata	American chestnut	fuel, stakes, posts, tool handles, poles, fence posts; see British species
Castanea mollissima	Chinese chestnut	fuel, stakes, poles, fence posts; probably similar to British species
Castanea pumila	Allegheny chinkapin	fuel, stakes, poles, fence posts; probably similar to British species
Celtis laevigata	sugarberry	sprouts from small stumps; fuel
Celtis occidentalis	hackberry	sprouts from small stumps, rarely from large ones; fuel, furniture

NORTH AMERICAN AND OTHER COPPICE SPECIES *continued*

Latin Name	Common Name	Notes / Known Uses
Cornus florida	flowering dogwood	cut in late winter; coppice grows higher on larger stumps; also layers; spools, pulleys, mallet heads, weaver's shuttles; calcium accumulator
Corylus americana	American hazel	probably similar to British species
Corylus colurna	tree hazel	probably similar to British species
Corylus cornuta	beaked hazel	probably similar to British species
Crataegus spp.	hawthorns	fuel, stakes, poles, fence posts; probably similar to British species
Diospyros virginiana	American persimmon	coppices readily, root-suckers; timber used for turnery, shoe lasts, shuttles, golf club heads, plane stocks; inner bark medicinal; indelible ink from fruits
Fagus grandifolia	American beech	sprouts well off < 4 in/10 cm stumps, but not larger; suckers from roots; fuel; timber used for furniture, baskets, pulp, turnery, charcoal, creosote
Fraxinus americana	white ash	coppices sparsely; fuel, tool handles, steam bending, baskets, baseball bats
Fraxinus pennsylvanica	green ash	coppices readily; fuel, tool handles, steam bending, basketry, baseball bats
Fraxinus spp.	ashes	probably similar to British species; fuel; snowshoes, hockey sticks, tennis rackets, basketry
Ginkgo biloba	maidenhair tree	coppicing is used to produce leaves for commercial herbal preparations
Gleditsia triacanthos	honey locust	coppices freely; fodder, fence posts; little used due to scarcity, but wood is dense, heavy, hard, strong, stiff, shock resistant, durable
Halesia tetraptera	Carolina silverbell	coppices readily; timber for carving, turnery, crafts, woodenware, pulp
Juglans cinerea	butternut	timber used for furniture, novelties, toys, and more
Juglans nigra	black walnut	sprouts near root collar best—sprouts higher on older stumps often get heart rot; timber used for furniture, gunstocks, and more
Liriodendron tulipifera	tulip poplar	coppices prolifically; best sprouts near base of stump; fuel, pulp, furniture
Magnolia virginiana	sweetbay	coppices, but usefulness unknown
Malus spp.	apples	fuel, scion wood
Morus spp.	mulberries	root-suckers, layers, coppices; fuel, structural material, plaiting
Nyssa aquatica	water tupelo	prolific coppicer; timber used for boxes, crates, baskets, furniture
Ostrya virginiana	eastern hop hornbeam	coppicing common, esp. on higher stumps; fuel, tool handles; slow grower
Oxydendron arboreum	sourwood	coppices prolifically and persistently; tool handles, fuel
Pinus rigida	pitch pine	one of the only conifers that coppices; useful for biomass energy, paper, creosote, pitch, turpentine
Platanus occidentalis	sycamore	coppices readily from sapling or polewood stumps, esp. late dormant-season cutting; commercially coppiced for biomass energy, pulp, fuel
Populus balsamifera	balsam poplar	coppices, root-suckers, layers, sprouts from broken roots or stems; pulp, core stock, boxes, crates, fodder; can be dispersive and expansive
Populus deltoides	eastern cottonwood	sprouts on low-cut stumps up to 25 years old; high yields in coppice management; furniture, pulp, energy biomass, windbreaks, cattle feed
Populus grandidentata *Populus tremuloides*	bigtooth aspen quaking aspen	these species function and are used similarly; they root-sucker and rarely coppice; mulch, chips, browse, pulp, wildlife habitat, fodder; timber used for shingles, novelty items, sauna benches, playground structures

NORTH AMERICAN AND OTHER COPPICE SPECIES *continued*

Latin Name	Common Name	Notes / Known Uses
Prunus pensylvanica	pin cherry	root-suckers readily; rootstock for sour cherry, fuel, fiber, biomass
Prunus serotina	black cherry	coppices readily, even from large, old stumps; furniture, fuel, fruit
Prunus spp.	cherries, plums, etc.	many *Prunus* spp. coppice; fuel, scion wood, woodworking
Pyrus communis	European pear	fuel, stakes, poles, fence posts
Quercus alba	white oak	particularly vigorous coppicer; uses as below
Quercus spp.	oaks	most spp. coppice well; best coppice on stumps <10–12 in/25–30 cm in diameter; fuel, stakes, poles, fence posts, shiitake logs, cooperage, farm implements, basketry (*Q. michauxii*); see British species
Robinia pseudoacacia	black locust	vigorous coppice and root suckers; fuel, stakes, poles, fence posts; timber used for ship timbers, tree nails, boxes, crates, pegs, novelties, biomass energy; heartwood highly rot-resistant: lasts up to seventy years in ground as a post
Salix alba	white willow	fuel, stakes, poles, fence posts
Salix spp.	willows	coppice or root suckers, depending on spp.; weaving, basketry, artist's charcoal, fuel, biomass, mulch; timber used for turnery, cooperage, pulp, boxes, novelties
Sassafras albidum	sassafras	root suckers; coppices prolifically from young stumps; root-bark oil is medicinal and a perfume; timber used for cooperage, buckets, posts, furniture, chew sticks for tooth care
Sorbus spp.	mountain ashes	probably similar to British species
Syringa vulgaris	common lilac	fuel
Tilia americana	American basswood	prolific sprouter; fuel, stakes, poles, fence posts, edible leaves; soft wood works well for carving, crafts, turnery, baskets, mats, rope, bast; coppicing keeps edible leaves low and tender
Toona sinensis	fragrant spring tree	edible leaves; coppicing keeps edible leaves near at hand
Ulmus americana	American elm	coppices vigorously; probably similar to British species; timber used for hockey sticks, furniture, baskets, boxes, crates, pulp
Ulmus rubra	slippery elm	coppices readily; timber used for furniture, paneling, containers; inner bark medicinal
Ulmus thomasii	rock elm	root-suckers and coppices, but uncommonly; wood highly valued for its strength, quality, bendability; bent furniture, crates, ship timbers.

ESTIMATED USEFUL LIFE SPANS OF SELECTED WOODY SPECIES

This table provides data on the estimated years to bearing and useful life spans of various woody crop species. The useful life of a woody plant varies tremendously depending on rootstock, soil, climate, care, and nutrition. Though a general guide, this table offers you some ability to sketch scenarios for successions and long-term rotations. Dashes indicate that data was not found before publication.

"Approximate Years between Major Crop Years" indicates whether the species is alternate or multi-year bearing; a "1" indicates consistent yearly bearing. Data is from Friends of the Trees, 1992; Hall-Beyer and Richard, 1983; NNGA, 1979; Jeavons, 1995; Kourik, 1986; Logsdon, 1981; Otto, 1993; Reich, 1991; St. Pierre, 1992; and Young and Young, 1992, among others. Updated and expanded versions of this table with complete references are available at www.edibleforestgardens.com.

ESTIMATED USEFUL LIFE SPANS OF SELECTED WOODY SPECIES

| Latin Name | Common Name | Approximate Years: | | | Estimated Useful Life (Years) |
		To Begin Bearing grafted/seedling	To Max. Bearing	Between Major Crop Yrs.	
Actinidia arguta	hardy kiwi	3—8	11—16	—	30
Amelanchier alnifolia	saskatoon	3—5	12—15	1	30—50
Amelanchier spp.	juneberry/serviceberry	2—4	—	—	—
Araucaria araucana	monkey puzzle	15—40	—	—	—
Aronia spp.	chokeberry	2	—	1—2	—
Asimina triloba	pawpaw	3—6/8—12	—	—	—
Asparagus officinalis	asparagus	3	6—7	—	15—20
Carya illinoinensis	pecan	10—20	—	1—2	up to 150
	grown in south	3—6	15—20	—	up to 150
	grown in north	8—10	20—25	—	up to 150
Carya laciniosa	shellbark hickory	8—10	—	1—2	100—350
Carya ovata	shagbark hickory	40	—	1—3	100—350
Carya spp.	hickories	3—4+/—	—	—	100—350
Castanea crenata	Japanese chestnut	3+	—	—	—
Castanea mollissima	Chinese chestnut	2—10/4—16	10	—	50—400+
Celtis laevigata	hackberry	15	—	—	—
Cercis canadensis	redbud	5	—	2	—
Cornus mas	Cornelian cherry	6—13	—	—	150—200
Corylus spp.	filbert/hazel	2—3/4—6	8	—	30—50
Cydonia oblonga	quince	3—4	—	—	—
Diospyros americana	American persimmon	2—3/6—8	25—50	—	20—300
Diospyros kaki	Oriental persimmon	2—3/6—8	25—50	—	300—600
Fagus grandifolia	American beech	40	—	2—3	—
Ficus spp.	fig	3—6	—	—	17
Fragaria hybrids	strawberries	<1—2	—	—	4
Ginkgo biloba	maidenhair tree	30—40	—	—	—
Gleditsia triacanthos	honey locust	10	—	—	10—100
Hovenia dulcis	raisin tree	7—10	—	—	—

ESTIMATED USEFUL LIFE SPANS OF SELECTED WOODY SPECIES *continued*

Latin Name	Common Name	Approximate Years: To Begin Bearing grafted/seedling	To Max. Bearing	Between Major Crop Yrs.	Estimated Useful Life (Years)
Juglans ailantifolia var. *cordiformis*	heartnut	2—4/10—14	—	1—3	40+
Juglans cinerea	butternut	20	—	2—3	—
Juglans nigra	black walnut	3—6/10—16	—	—	30—200+
Juglans regia	English walnut	2—5/4—8	—	—	—
Malus pumila	apple:				
	standard	5—8	10	—	35—50—100
	semidwarf	4	10	—	—
	dwarf	3	5	—	10—30
Morus alba	white mulberry	5—10	—	—	150
Morus nigra	black mulberry	—	—	—	300 +
Morus rubra	red mulberry	2—3/8—12	—	—	30—125
Pinus albicaulis	whitebark pine	20—30	—	3—5	—
Pinus armandii	Chinese white pine	20	—	—	—
Pinus cembra	Swiss stone pine	25—30	—	6—10	—
Pinus cembra var. *sibirica*	Siberian stone pine	25—35	—	3—8	—
Pinus edulis	pinyon pine	25—75	—	2—5	—
Pinus flexilis	limber pine	20—40	—	2—4	—
Pinus jeffreyi	Jeffrey pine	8	—	2—4	—
Pinus koraiensis	Korean nut pine	4—6/12—40	—	3—5	—
Prunus alleghaniensis	Allegheny plum	—	—	1	—
Prunus americana	American plum	—	—	1—2	—
Prunus armeniaca	apricot	2—5	5—7	1	12—30
Prunus avium	sweet cherry	6—7	—	1	—
	standard	4—5	10—20	—	15—20
	dwarf	2—3	5—6	—	—
	bush	3	—	—	—
Prunus cerasifera	Myrobalan plum	—	—	2—3	—
Prunus cerasus	sour cherry	6—7	—	1	—
	standard	4—5	10—20	—	15, 20—25
	dwarf	3	—	—	15—20
	bush	3	—	—	—
Prunus domestica	European plum	3—4	4—6	—	—
Prunus dulcis	almond	6—7	—	1	—
Prunus persica	peach	3—8	4—9	1—2	—
Prunus persica nucipersica	nectarine	3—5	8—12	—	8—12
Prunus pumila var. *besseyi*	sand cherry	2—3	—	—	—
Prunus serotina	black cherry	5	—	1—5	—
Prunus tomentosa	Nanking cherry	2—3	—	1—2	15
Prunus x hybrid	'Hall's Hardy' almond	2—3/6—8	—	—	—
Pyrus bretschneideris	Asian pear	3—7	—	—	100—300
Pyrus communis	European pear	2—3/6—8	8—10	—	15+, 50—75

ESTIMATED USEFUL LIFE SPANS OF SELECTED WOODY SPECIES *continued*

Latin Name	Common Name	Approximate Years: To Begin Bearing grafted/seedling	To Max. Bearing	Between Major Crop Yrs.	Estimated Useful Life (Years)
Quercus acutissima	sawtooth oak	5	—	1	—
Quercus alba	white oak	20	—	4—10	—
Quercus bicolor	swamp white oak	20	—	3—5	—
Quercus macrocarpa	bur oak	35	75—150	2—3	400
Quercus michauxii	swamp chestnut oak	20	—	3—5	—
Quercus prinus	chestnut oak	20	—	2—3	—
Quercus x schuettei	Schuette's oak	4—8/8—12	—	—	—
Rheum x cultorum	rhubarb	2—3	—	—	10—15+
Ribes nigrum	black currant	2—3	4—6	—	10—20
Ribes spp.	gooseberries, currants	2—3	4—6	2—3	15—20
Ribes x culverwellii	jostaberry	—	4—6	—	10—20
Rosa rugosa	rugosa rose	3	—	—	—
Rubus hybrids	blackberries	1—2	3—4	—	6—25
Rubus hybrids	boysenberries	1—2	—	—	6—10
Rubus hybrids	raspberries	1—2	3—4	—	6—10
Sambucus canadensis	elderberries	2—4	3—4	—	—
Sorbus aucuparia	rowan	15	—	1	—
Vaccinium hybrids	blueberries	3—5	8	—	10—15, 50 +
Vaccinium macrocarpon	cranberry	2—3	—	—	100+
Vaccinium vitis-idaea	lingonberry	2—3	—	—	20+
Viburnum cassinoides	witherod viburnum	—	—	1	—
Vitis spp.	grapes	2—3	4—5	—	50 +
Ziziphus jujuba	jujube	—	—	1	—

APPENDIX 3

Species-by-Function Tables

NITROGEN FIXERS

Research has shown *Alnus* and *Hippophae* species to be particularly good at fixing nitrogen. Other than that, we know little about the relative efficiency of nitrogen fixers; until more research is performed, assume they all fix about the same amount of nitrogen. Thus, choose nitrogen fixers by finding the best form, habit, height, and width to fit your design. Nitrogen fixers can also perform multiple functions. Edible species include goumi (*Eleagnus multiflora*) and groundnuts (*Apios* spp.). *Genista* and *Cytisus* make excellent ground covers. Outstanding ornamentals include *Wisteria* spp., *Lathyrus latifolius*, and *Sophora* spp. Most nitrogen fixers are also fine generalist nectary plants, and many provide habitat for parasitic wasps. We present them in broad size categories. Abbreviations: "exp" = expansive; "skr" = suckering; "indef" = indefinitely spreading; "herb." = herbaceous.

NITROGEN FIXERS: TREES

Latin Name	Common Name	Form & Habit	Height	Width
Alnus cordata	Italian alder	standard	30–50'	20–35'
Alnus incana	gray alder	standard	40–60'	25–40'
Maackia amurensis	Amur maackia	standard	20–30'	20–35'
Robinia pseudoacacia	black locust	suckering	50–75'	35–50'
Sophora japonica	pagoda tree	standard	50–75'	50–75'

NITROGEN FIXERS: LARGE TO VERY LARGE SHRUBS

Latin Name	Common Name	Form & Habit	Height	Width
Alnus rugosa	speckled alder	multistemmed	20–35'	20–35'
Alnus serrulata	smooth alder	multistemmed	12–20'	12–20'
Amorpha fruticosa	false indigo	multistemmed	6–20'	12–20'
Caragana arborescens	Siberian pea shrub	multistemmed	8–20'	12–18'
Caragana frutex	Russian pea shrub	clumping	6–10'	6–10'
Cercocarpus montanus	mountain mahogany	multistemmed	6–20'	6–20'
Colutea arborescens	bladder senna	multistemmed	6–15'	6–9'
Eleagnus commutata	silverberry	multistemmed	6–12'	6–12'
Eleagnus multiflora	goumi	clumping	6–8'	6–8'
Hippophae rhamnoides	sea buckthorn	thicket former	10–20'	10–20'
Lespedeza bicolor	bush clover	clumping	6–9'	6–9'
Myrica cerifera	wax myrtle	multistemmed	10–30'	10–30'
Myrica pensylvanica	bayberry	thicket former	6–12'	6–12'

NITROGEN FIXERS: LARGE TO VERY LARGE SHRUBS *continued*

Latin Name	Common Name	Form & Habit	Height	Width:
Prosopis glandulosa	honeypod mesquite	multistemmed	25′	30′
Robinia hispida	bristly locust	thicket former	6–12′	3–6′
Robinia viscosa	clammy locust	thicket former, exp	6–20′	6–20′
Shepherdia canadensis	buffalo berry	multistemmed	6–12′	6–12′

NITROGEN FIXERS: SMALL TO MEDIUM SHRUBS

Latin Name	Common Name	Form & Habit	Height	Width
Acacia angustissima	prairie acacia	clumping	3–6′	3–6′
Acacia angustissima hirta	dwarf prairie acacia	clumping	1–3′	1–6′
Amorpha canescens	leadplant	multistemmed	1–3′	3–6′
Amorpha nana	fragrant indigobush	multistemmed	3′	3′
Caragana pygmaea	pygmy pea shrub	clumping	4′	4′
Ceanothus americanus	New Jersey tea	clumping	4′	3–6′
Comptonia peregrina	sweetfern	thicket former, exp	3′	4–8′
Genista pilosa	silky leaf woodwaxen	clumping	1′	3–4′
Genista tinctoria	dyer's greenwood	clumping	2–3′	2–3′
Hippophae rhamnoides cv.	sea buckthorn 'Dorana Dwarf'	thicket former, exp	4′	4′
Indigofera decora	Chinese indigo	clumping	18″	6–8′
Myrica gale	sweet gale	multistemmed	2–6′	2–6′

NITROGEN FIXERS: PROSTRATE SHRUBS

Latin Name	Common Name	Form & Habit	Height	Width
Ceanothus prostratus	mahala mat	mat former, exp	3–6″	10′
Cytisus decumbens	prostrate broom	mat former	8″	3′
Dryas octopetala	mountain avens	mat former	3-6″	2′
Genista pilosa procumbens	prostrate woodwaxen	mat former	2″	3′
Genista sagittalis	arrow broom	mat former	4–18″	2–3′

NITROGEN FIXERS: VINES

Latin Name	Common Name	Form & Habit	Height	Width
Amphicarpaea bracteata	hog peanut	herb. vine	1–3′	1–3′
Apios americana	groundnut	herb. vine	4–8′	4–8′
Apios fortunei	Fortune's groundnut	herb. vine	3–6′	3–6′
Apios priceana	Price's groundnut	herb. vine	3–6′	3–6′
Clitoria mariana	butterfly pea	herb. vine	2–3′	2–3′
Lathyrus japonicus maritima	beach pea	herb. vine, skr	1–2′	1–2′
Lathyrus latifolius	everlasting pea	herb. vine, skr	6′	6′
Lathyrus linifolius montanus	bitter vetch	herb. vine	1–2′	1–2′
Lathyrus tuberosus	earthnut pea	herb. vine, skr	3–4′	3–4′
Phaseolus polystachios	wild bean	herb. vine	1–3′	1–3′
Strophostyles umbellata	wild bean	herb. vine	1–3′	1–3′

NITROGEN FIXERS: VINES *continued*

Latin Name	Common Name	Form & Habit	Height	Width:
Vicia americana	American vetch	herb. vine	3′	3′
Vicia caroliniana	wood vetch	herb. vine	1–5′	1–5′
Vicia cracca	tufted vetch	herb. vine	5′	5′
Wisteria floribunda	Japanese wisteria	woody vine	30–50′	30–50′
Wisteria frutescens	American wisteria	woody vine	30–40′	30–40′
Wisteria macrostachya	Kentucky wisteria	woody vine	20–35′	12–20′

NITROGEN FIXERS: MEDIUM TO LARGE HERBS

Latin Name	Common Name	Form & Habit	Height	Width
Astragalus canadensis	Canada milkvetch	running, exp	1–4′	indef
Astragalus membranaceous	huang-qi	clumping	2–3′	2–3′
Baptisia australis	blue wild indigo	clumping	2–4′	2–5′
Baptisia tinctoria	yellow wild indigo	clumping	2–3′	2–5′
Desmodium canadense	showy tick trefoil	clumping, exp	2–6′	1–3′
Desmodium glutinosum	pointed-leaf tick trefoil	clumping	2–3′	2–3′
Glycyrrhiza glabra	licorice	running, exp	2–6′	indef
Glycyrrhiza lepidota	American licorice	running	1–3′	indef
Glycyrrhiza uralensis	Chinese licorice	running	2′	indef
Hedysarum boreale	sweet vetch	clumping	10–24″	20′
Lespedeza capitata	round-headed bush clover	clumping	2–4′	2–4′
Lupinus perennis	wild lupine	clumping	1–2′	1–2′
Lupinus hybrids	hybrid lupines	clumping	2–4′	2–3′
Medicago sativa	alfalfa	clumping	1–3	1–3′
Thermopsis villosa	Carolina bush pea	clumping, exp	4–5′	2–3′
Trifolium pratense	red clover	clumping	6–16″	6–16″

NITROGEN FIXERS: PROSTRATE TO SMALL HERBS

Latin Name	Common Name	Form & Habit	Height	Width
Astragalus crassicarpus	groundplum milk vetch	clumping	6–15″	1–2′
Astragalus glycyphyllos	milk vetch	clumping	8–12″	3–5′
Lotus corniculatus cv.	prostrate bird's-foot trefoil 'Plena'	mat former	1″	1–2′
Psoralea esculenta	prairie turnip	clumping	6–20″	6–20″
Stylosanthes biflora	pencil flower	clumping	6–20″	6–10″
Trifolium repens	white clover	clumping	4–10″	6–36″

NITROGEN-FIXER INOCULANTS

See the discussion in volume 1, chapter 5, for background on this table. This table lists only nitrogen-fixing species from the Plant Species Matrix. For more information see Martin Crawford's *Nitrogen-Fixing Plants for Temperate Climates* (1998), from which this table was adapted.

NITROGEN-FIXER INOCULANTS

Latin Name	Type	Inoculation Groups
Acacia angustissima	leguminous	cowpea
Alnus spp.	actinorhizal	alder, bayberry; promiscuous
Amorpha spp.	leguminous	cowpea
Amphicarpaea bracteata	leguminous	cowpea
Apios spp.	leguminous	cowpea
Astragalus spp.	leguminous	alfalfa, bean, clover
Baptisia spp.	leguminous	cowpea
Caragana spp.	leguminous	clover, cowpea, lupine, soybean
Ceanothus spp.	actinorhizal	promiscuous
Cercocarpus montanus	actinorhizal	promiscuous
Clitoria mariana	leguminous	cowpea
Colutea arborescens	leguminous	clover, cowpea, pea
Comptonia peregrina	actinorhizal	promiscuous
Cytisus decumbens	leguminous	cowpea
Desmodium spp.	leguminous	cowpea
Dryas octopetala	actinorhizal	promiscuous
Eleagnus spp.	actinorhizal	eleagnus, bayberry; promiscuous
Genista spp.	leguminous	cowpea
Glycyrrhiza spp.	leguminous	several
Hedysarum boreale	leguminous	unknown
Hippophae rhamnoides	actinorhizal	eleagnus, bayberry; promiscuous
Indigofera decora	leguminous	cowpea
Lathyrus spp.	leguminous	pea
Lespedeza spp.	leguminous	cowpea
Lotus corniculatus 'Plena'	leguminous	lupine
Lupinus spp.	leguminous	lupine
Maackia amurensis	leguminous	unknown
Medicago sativa	leguminous	alfalfa
Myrica spp.	actinorhizal	bayberry, eleagnus, alder
Phaseolus polystachios	leguminous	bean
Prosopis glandulosa	leguminous	unknown
Psoralea esculenta	leguminous	cowpea, others
Robinia spp.	leguminous	black locust
Shepherdia canadensis	actinorhizal	eleagnus, bayberry; promiscuous
Sophora japonica	leguminous	cowpea
Strophostyles umbellata	leguminous	mealybean
Stylosanthes biflora	leguminous	unknown
Thermopsis villosa	leguminous	cowpea, others
Trifolium spp.	leguminous	clover
Vicia spp.	leguminous	pea
Wisteria spp.	leguminous	unknown

DYNAMIC ACCUMULATORS

Dynamic accumulators have received little research attention; this table represents only the species for which we could find information. Many more forest garden species probably fill this role. Perhaps we could select and breed plants for improved accumulation of subsurface minerals, yielding improved fertilizer sources for forest gardens.

The most important nutrients to provide for woody species are nitrogen, potassium, phosphorous, and calcium (N, K, P, Ca), because they most frequently limit plant growth. A separate table deals with nitrogen fixers (N_2 fixers), though a few also appear here. We rate the dynamic accumulators below based on their purported ability to accumulate these primary nutrients, as follows:

★★★ Excellent = 3 of N, K, P, Ca

★★ Good = 2 of N, K, P, Ca

★ Fair = 1 of N, K, P, Ca

Some species accumulate three or more nutrients other than N, K, P, and Ca.

To select dynamic accumulators for your forest garden, first test both your topsoil and your subsoil to determine nutrient deficiencies (if any; subsoil testing may require special methods, so talk to your testing service). If the subsoil is deficient in nutrients, add fertility from off-site, but plant dynamic accumulators for scarce nutrients to minimize leaching losses. If the topsoil is deficient but the subsoil is not, select species from the list below that will slowly replenish the topsoil with nutrients lacking in the topsoil. You will probably also want to select species from this table that will catch and recycle all critical nutrients, particularly in high-rainfall areas. You will likely also want some good general dynamic accumulators, like comfrey and sorrel, to keep general fertility high.

DYNAMIC ACCUMULATORS

Latin Name	Common Name	Rating	K	P	Ca	S	Co	Cu	Fe	Mg	Na	N_2 Fixers
Acer saccharum	sugar maple	★★	K		Ca							
Acer spp.	maples	★	K									
Achillea millefolium	yarrow	★★	K	P				Cu				
Allium schoenoprasum	chives	★★	K		Ca							
Betula lenta	black birch	★★★	K	P	Ca							
Betula spp.	birches	★		P								
Brassica spp.	perennial brassicas	★		P		S						
Carya ovata	shagbark hickory	★★★	K	P	Ca							
Carya spp.	hickory and pecan	★★	K		Ca							
Chamaemelum nobile	German chamomile	★★★	K	P	Ca							
Cichorium intybus	chicory	★	K		Ca							
Cornus florida	flowering dogwood	★★★	K	P	Ca							
Equisetum spp.	horsetails	★			Ca		Co		Fe	Mg		
Fagus spp.	beeches	★	K									
Fagus sylvatica	European beech	★★	K		Ca							
Fragaria spp.	strawberry								Fe			
Gaultheria procumbens	wintergreen									Mg		
Glycyrrhiza spp.	licorices	★★		P								N_2
Juglans nigra	black walnut	★★★	K	P	Ca							
Juglans spp.	walnuts	★★	K	P								
Lupinus spp.	lupines	★★		P								N_2

Latin Name	Common Name	Rating	K	P	Ca	S	Co	Cu	Fe	Mg	Na	N₂ Fixers
DYNAMIC ACCUMULATORS *continued*												
Malus spp.	apples	★	K									
Medicago sativa	alfalfa								Fe			N₂
Melissa officinalis	lemon balm	★		P								
Mentha x piperita	peppermint	★	K							Mg		
Nasturtium officinale	watercress	★★★	K	P	Ca	S			Fe	Mg	Na	
Potentilla anserina	silverweed	★★	K		Ca			Cu				
Quercus alba	white oak	★		P								
Robinia pseudoacacia	black locust	★★★	K		Ca							N₂
Rumex spp.	sorrels and docks	★★★	K	P	Ca				Fe		Na	
Sanguisorba minor	salad burnet								Fe			
Satureja spp.	savory	★		P								
Stellaria media	chickweed	★★	K	P								
Symphytum spp.	comfreys	★★★	K	P	Ca			Cu	Fe	Mg		
Taraxacum officinale	dandelion	★★★	K	P	Ca			Cu	Fe			
Tilia americana	basswood	★★		P	Ca					Mg		
Tilia spp.	linden	★★		P	Ca							
Trifolium spp.	clovers	★		P								
Urtica dioica	stinging nettle	★★	K		Ca	S		Cu	Fe		Na	
Vicia spp.	vetches	★★★	K	P								N₂
Viola spp.	violets	★		P								

FOOD AND SHELTER PLANTS FOR BENEFICIALS

These plant species provide food or shelter for beneficial organisms, including nesting by birds, invertebrate oviposition (egg laying) and overwintering sites, cover (protection from weather and predators), or preferred resting, roosting, and "hanging out" sites (see appendix 5 for the habitat requirements of specific organisms). Of course, simply by virtue of being plants, all plant species provide habitat for beneficial organisms. In particular, the dried flower heads and stems of herbaceous perennials provide important overwintering habitat for a wide range of beneficial invertebrates. However, those listed here are known to provide additional or special benefits.

The studies undergirding this table are surely just a tiny window into the preferences of the tens of thousands of beneficial organisms. They do, however, provide a starting point, and they make certain otherwise unremarkable plant species become more prominent by revealing their role as food or shelter providers. Importantly, the table below illuminates the multifunctionality of plants and their intense relationships with animals—realities that we are only beginning to unravel.

BIRDS

Food: These columns show seasonal availability of fruit for omnivorous birds that also eat insects. "Hum nectar" indicates hummingbird nectar plants; see the "Nectary Calendar" table for flowering times.

Shelter: Thicket formers provide cover for birds and other beneficials, including nesting sites. Woody evergreens also provide cover from climate and predators, especially in the winter and early spring months.

INSECTS AND SPIDERS

Food: Specialist nectary plants provide food for parasitoid wasps and specialist predatory insects. These plants also offer good nectar sources for all pollinators and any other nectar-using beneficials. Generalist nectary plants provide food for various native pollinators and some predatory and other beneficial insects (such as beneficial true bugs, green lacewings, ladybird beetles, some wasps, hover flies, and parasitic flies). While virtually any flower is of some use as a nectary, the literature notes those listed here as particularly good for this purpose. No doubt many other species are also of use. Most generalist nectary plants do not work for specialist insects. "Pollen" indicates species that provide pollen, an important protein source for some animals, especially when rearing young or producing eggs.

Shelter: Oviposition plants provide preferred egg-laying sites. Insects and spiders prefer overwintering species for hibernation, either in soil under the plant or in the dead stems, flower heads, or foliage. Insects and spiders appear to prefer foliage plants as habitat for resting or other purposes.

FOOD AND SHELTER PLANTS FOR BENEFICIALS

| | BIRDS | | | | | | INSECTS & SPIDERS | | | | | |
| | Food | | | | Shelter | | Food | | | Shelter | | |
PLANT SPECIES	Summer Fruit	Fall Fruit	Winter Fruit	Hum Nectar	Thicket	Evergreen	Spec. Nectary	Gen. Nectary	Pollen	Oviposition	Overwintering	Foliage
Acacia angustissima				•				•				
Acer spp.								•				
Achillea spp.							•	•		lacewings	parasitoid wasps, ground beetles, spiders	parasitoid wasps, lacewings, spiders
Agastache foeniculum								•		lacewings		wide range of invertebrates
Alcea rosea								•				
Allium spp.								•				
Alnus rugosa and *serrulata*				•			•					
Amelanchier bartramiana	•			•				•				
Amelanchier stolonifera	•			•				•				
Amelanchier spp.	•							•				
Amorpha spp.								•		lacewings		parasitoid wasps
Amphicarpaea bracteata										lacewings		parasitoid wasps
Andropogon gerardii									•		ground beetles	
Antennaria spp.							•	•				parasitoid wasps
Apios spp.								•		lacewings		parasitoid wasps
Aquilegia canadensis				•				•				
Arabis caucasica								•				
Aralia cordata							•	•				
Aralia elata				•			•	•				
Aralia hispida				•			•	•				

FOOD AND SHELTER PLANTS FOR BENEFICIALS *continued*

PLANT SPECIES	BIRDS						INSECTS & SPIDERS					
	Food				Shelter		Food			Shelter		
	Summer Fruit	Fall Fruit	Winter Fruit	Hum Nectar	Thicket	Evergreen	Spec. Nectary	Gen. Nectary	Pollen	Oviposition	Overwintering	Foliage
Aralia nudicaulis	•						•	•				
Aralia racemosa							•	•				
Araucaria araucana						•						
Arbutus unedo	•											
Arctostaphylos uva-ursi		•						•				
Arnoglossum atriplicifolia							•	•				
Aronia arbutifolia			•					•				
Aronia melanocarpa			•		•			•				
Artemisia spp.							•	•				parasitoid wasps
Arundinaria gigantea				•	•							
Asclepias spp.								•				
Asimina triloba					•							
Asparagus officinalis								•				
Aster spp.							•	•				parasitoid wasps
Astragalus spp.								•		lacewings		parasitoid wasps
Balsamorhiza sagittata							•	•				parasitoid wasps
Baptisia spp.								•		lacewings		parasitoid wasps
Bellis perennis							•	•				parasitoid wasps
Berberis canadensis		•						•				
Betula spp.									•			
Blephilia spp.								•		lacewings		
Borago officinalis								•		lacewings		spiders, damsel bugs, ground beetles, parasitoid wasps
Brassica spp.								•				parasitoid wasps
Bunium bulbocastanum							•	•		lacewings		parasitoid wasps
Calycanthus floridus					•							
Camassia spp.								•				
Campanula spp.								•				
Caragana spp.				•				•		lacewings		parasitoid wasps
Carex pensylvanica									•			
Carya spp.									•			
Castanea spp.									•			
Ceanothus americana				•				•				
Ceanothus prostratus								•				
Celtis spp.			•					•				
Cephalotaxus harringtonia						•						

FOOD AND SHELTER PLANTS FOR BENEFICIALS *continued*

PLANT SPECIES	BIRDS Food — Summer Fruit	Fall Fruit	Winter Fruit	Hum Nectar	Shelter — Thicket	Evergreen	INSECTS & SPIDERS Food — Spec. Nectary	Gen. Nectary	Pollen	Shelter — Oviposition	Overwintering	Foliage
Cercis canadensis				•				•				
Cercocarpus montanus								•				
Chaenomeles speciosa								•				
Chamaemelum nobile							•	•				parasitoid wasps
Chasmanthium latifolium									•		ground beetles	
Chrysogonum virginianum							•	•				parasitoid wasps
Chrysosplenium americanum							•	•				
Cichorium intybus								•		hover flies	spiders	parasitoid wasps
Claytonia spp.								•				
Clinopodium glabellum								•				
Clitoria spp.										lacewings		parasitoid wasps
Colutea arborescens										lacewings		parasitoid wasps
Comptonia peregrina				•								
Conoclinium coelestinum								•				parasitoid wasps
Conopodium majus							•	•		lacewings		parasitoid wasps
Coreopsis spp.							•	•				
Cornus canadensis		•										
Cornus florida		•										
Cornus kousa		•										
Cornus mas	•											
Cornus paniculata		•		•			•	•				
Cornus sericea		•		•			•	•				
Corylus spp.				•					•			
Crambe maritima								•				
Crataegus spp.			•					•				
Crocus sativus								•				
Cryptotaenia spp.							•	•		lacewings		parasitoid wasps
Cudrania tricuspidata				•								
Cunila origanoides								•		lacewings		
Cydonia oblonga								•				
Cymopterus spp.							•	•		lacewings		
Cytisus spp.								•		lacewings		parasitoid wasps
Darmera peltata								•				
Desmodium spp.										lacewings		parasitoid wasps
Diospyros virginiana			•					•				
Echinacea purpurea								•				parasitoid wasps
Eleagnus spp.			•					•				
Epigaea repens								•				

FOOD AND SHELTER PLANTS FOR BENEFICIALS *continued*

PLANT SPECIES	BIRDS — Food — Summer Fruit	Fall Fruit	Winter Fruit	Hum Nectar	BIRDS — Shelter — Thicket	Evergreen	INSECTS & SPIDERS — Food — Spec. Nectary	Gen. Nectary	Pollen	INSECTS & SPIDERS — Shelter — Oviposition	Overwintering	Foliage
Epilobium angustifolium				•				•				
Erigenia bulbosa							•	•		lacewings		parasitoid wasps
Erigeron pulchellus							•	•				parasitoid wasps
Eryngium maritimum							•	•		lacewings		parasitoid wasps
Fagus spp.									•			
Foeniculum vulgare							•	•		lacewings		parasitoid wasps, spiders
Fragaria spp.	•							•				
Gaultheria shallon	•				•	•		•				
Gaultheria spp.		•	•									
Gaylussacia spp.	•							•				
Genista spp.								•		lacewings		parasitoid wasps
Geum spp.								•				
Gleditsia triacanthos								•				
Glycyrrhiza spp.								•		lacewings		parasitoid wasps
Hedysarum spp.										lacewings		parasitoid wasps
Helianthus spp.							•	•				parasitoid wasps
Heliopsis helianthoides							•	•				parasitoid wasps
Hemerocallis spp.				•								
Heracleum sphondylium							•	•		lacewings		parasitoid wasps
Heuchera americana				•			•	•				
Hibiscus syriacus				•								
Hieracium venosum							•	•				
Hippophae rhamnoides		•	•		•							
Hydrophyllum virginianum								•				
Ilex glabra		•			•	•		•				
Illicium floridanum					•	•						
Indigofera decora										lacewings		parasitoid wasps
Ipomoea spp.								•				
Iris spp.				•								
Juglans spp.									•			
Lactuca perennis								•				parasitoid wasps
Lathyrus spp.								•		lacewings		parasitoid wasps
Lespedeza spp.								•		lacewings		parasitoid wasps
Levisticum officinale							•	•		lacewings		parasitoid wasps
Ligusticum spp.							•	•		lacewings		
Lilium spp.				•								
Lindera benzoin		•										

FOOD AND SHELTER PLANTS FOR BENEFICIALS *continued*											
	BIRDS						INSECTS & SPIDERS				
	Food				Shelter		Food			Shelter	
PLANT SPECIES	Summer Fruit	Fall Fruit	Winter Fruit	Hum Nectar	Thicket	Evergreen	Spec. Nectary	Gen. Nectary	Pollen	Oviposition	Overwintering	Foliage
Lobelia cardinalis				•				•				
Lomatium spp.							•	•		lacewings		parasitoid wasps
Lonicera sempervirens			•			•		•				
Lonicera spp.				•				•				
Lotus corniculatus 'Plena'												parasitoid wasps
Lupinus spp.								•		lacewings		parasitoid wasps
Maackia amurensis										lacewings		parasitoid wasps
Magnolia virginiana		•				•						
Mahonia spp.			•			•		•				
Malus spp.			•					•				
Malva spp.								•		lacewings		spiders
Medicago sativa			•					•		lacewings		parasitoid wasps, damsel bugs, ladybird beetles, ground beetles
Melissa officinalis								•		lacewings		
Mentha spp.								•		lacewings		
Mespilus germanica								•				
Mitchella repens			•									
Mitella diphylla							•	•				
Monarda spp.				•				•		lacewings		
Morus spp.	•											
Myrica pensylvanica		•		•				•				
Myrica gale and *cerifera*		•				•		•				
Myrrhis odorata							•	•		lacewings		parasitoid wasps
Opuntia compressa								•				
Origanum vulgare								•		lacewings		
Osmorhiza spp.							•	•		lacewings		parasitoid wasps
Panax quinquefolius							•	•				
Panax trifolius							•	•				
Passiflora incarnata				•								
Perideridia gairdneri							•	•		lacewings		parasitoid wasps
Persea borbonia						•		•				
Petasites japonicus							•	•				parasitoid wasps
Phaseolus spp.				•				•		lacewings		parasitoid wasps
Phlox spp.				•								
Phyllostachys spp.					•	•						
Physalis spp.		•										

FOOD AND SHELTER PLANTS FOR BENEFICIALS *continued*

| PLANT SPECIES | BIRDS | | | | | | INSECTS & SPIDERS | | | | | |
| | Food | | | | Shelter | | Food | | | Shelter | | |
	Summer Fruit	Fall Fruit	Winter Fruit	Hum Nectar	Thicket	Evergreen	Spec. Nectary	Gen. Nectary	Pollen	Oviposition	Overwintering	Foliage
Phytolacca americana		•										
Pimpinella saxifraga							•	•		lacewings		parasitoid wasps
Pinus spp.						•						
Platycodon grandiflorus								•				
Polytaenia nuttallii							•	•		lacewings		parasitoid wasps
Potentilla anserina								•				
Prosopis glandulosa								•				
Prunus americana, angustifolia, pumila, var. besseyi, japonica, maritima, munsoniana, and *virginiana*	•				•			•				
Prunus spp.	•							•				
Psoralea spp.								•		lacewings		parasitoid wasps
Pycnanthemum spp.								•		lacewings		
Pyrus spp.								•				
Quercus gambelii				•					•			
Quercus ilex						•			•			
Quercus spp.									•			
Rhus spp.			•		•			•				
Ribes spp.	•			•	•			•				
Robinia hispida, R. viscosa				•	•			•		lacewings		parasitoid wasps
Robinia pseudoacacia				•				•		lacewings		parasitoid wasps
Rosa spp.		•	•	•	•			•				
Rosmarinus officinalis				•				•		lacewings		
Rubus spp. (ground covers)	•							•				
Rubus spp. (all others)	•				•			•				
Rumex acetosella									•			
Salvia spp.				•				•		lacewings		
Sambucus canadensis	•			•	•		•	•				
Sanguisorba spp.									•	lacewings		
Sasa kurilensis					•	•						
Sassafras albidum		•			•			•				
Satureja douglasii								•		lacewings		
Saxifraga stolonifera							•	•				
Scorzonera hispanica							•	•				parasitoid wasps
Secale cereale									•		ground beetles	
Sedum spp.								•				
Semiarundinaria fastuosa					•	•						

FOOD AND SHELTER PLANTS FOR BENEFICIALS *continued*

PLANT SPECIES	Summer Fruit	Fall Fruit	Winter Fruit	Hum Nectar	Thicket	Evergreen	Spec. Nectary	Gen. Nectary	Pollen	Oviposition	Overwintering	Foliage
	BIRDS						INSECTS & SPIDERS					
	Food				Shelter		Food			Shelter		
Senecio spp.							•	•				parasitoid wasps
Shepherdia spp.		•						•				
Silphium spp.			•				•	•				parasitoid wasps
Sium sisarum							•	•		lacewings		parasitoid wasps
Smallanthus uvedalia							•	•				parasitoid wasps
Smilax herbacea		•										
Solidago spp.							•	•				parasitoid wasps, ambush bugs
Sophora japonica								•		lacewings		parasitoid wasps
Sorbus spp.		•	•					•				
Stachys spp.								•		lacewings		
Stellaria media								•		hover flies		
Stellaria spp.								•				
Strophostyles umbellata										lacewings		parasitoid wasps
Stylosanthes biflora										lacewings		parasitoid wasps
Symphytum spp.								•		lacewings	spiders	parasitoid wasps, spiders
Taenidia integerrima							•	•		lacewings		parasitoid wasps
Taraxacum officinale								•				parasitoid wasps
Thaspium spp.							•	•		lacewings		parasitoid wasps
Thermopsis spp.										lacewings		parasitoid wasps
Thymus spp.								•		lacewings		
Tiarella cordifolia							•	•				
Tilia spp.								•				
Tradescantia virginiana								•				
Trifolium pratense								•		lacewings		parasitoid wasps
Trifolium repens								•		lacewings		parasitoid wasps, spiders, ground beetles
Trillium grandiflorum								•				
Tripsacum dactyloides									•		ground beetles	
Triticum aestivum									•		ground beetles	
Urtica dioica										lacewings		ladybird beetles
Vaccinium spp.	•											
Verbena spp.				•				•				
Vernonia noveboracensis								•				
Veronica spp.				•				•				
Viburnum acerifolium			•				•	•				
Viburnum cassinoides			•				•	•				

FOOD AND SHELTER PLANTS FOR BENEFICIALS *continued*

| | BIRDS | | | | | | INSECTS & SPIDERS | | | | | |
| | Food | | | | Shelter | | Food | | | Shelter | | |
PLANT SPECIES	Summer Fruit	Fall Fruit	Winter Fruit	Hum Nectar	Thicket	Evergreen	Spec. Nectary	Gen. Nectary	Pollen	Oviposition	Overwintering	Foliage
Viburnum dentatum		•					•	•				
Viburnum lentago			•				•	•				
Viburnum trilobum			•				•	•				
Vicia spp.								•		lacewings		parasitoid wasps
Vitex agnus-castus								•				
Vitis riparia		•						•				
Vitis spp.		•						•				
Wisteria spp.								•		lacewings		parasitoid wasps
Yucca spp.				•								
Zanthoxylum americanum					•			•				
Zanthoxylum piperitum					•			•				
Zizia spp.							•	•		lacewings		parasitoid wasps
Ziziphus jujuba								•				

NECTARY CALENDAR

Use this chart to ensure that you choose a variety of nectar plants that will bloom throughout the season, just as you would use an ordinary bloom calendar to ensure ornamentals all season. The dates come from numerous sources, including personal observation. These flowering times are intended to provide a rough guide only. Expect earlier flowering in southern gardens and later in cold, short-season climates. Keep track of times in your own garden, and those of nearby neighbors, nurseries, and botanical gardens.

We have made a special effort to include a diversity of specialist nectary plants, with a number of species available for a range of soil, water, and shade conditions. Many are also edible or otherwise useful. A great many species listed here function as generalist nectaries, many of which the literature specifically mentions as good bee fodder plants. Presumably, this means they are good fodder for other insects as well. No doubt many other species in the Plant Species Matrix work well as generalist nectaries.

Specialist Nectary: Indicates plants forming clusters of tiny flowers easily accessible to the short mouthparts of specialist predatory and parasitoid insects.

Generalist Nectary: Indicates plants providing nectar to a wider range of beneficial insects, including predators, native pollinators, and nonnative honeybees. Many beneficial invertebrates eat pollen. Those plants that provide only pollen (but no nectar) are marked "pollen."

Hummingbird: Plants that provide nectar to hummingbirds. This is a partial list. Many nurseries have more detailed information. Hummingbirds undoubtedly visit other species on this list. Species marked "E" (excellent) make the finest hummingbird foods.

NECTARY CALENDAR

Latin Name	Specialist Nectary	Generalist Nectary	Humming-bird	Apr	May	Jun	Jul	Aug	Sept	Oct
Acacia angustissima and *hirta*		●	●			■	■	■	■	■
Acer spp.		●		■	■					
Achillea spp.	●	●				■	■	■	■	■
Agastache foeniculum		●					■	■	■	
Alcea rosea		●				■	■	■		
Allium spp.		●			■	■	■			
Alnus spp.		pollen		■						
Amelanchier spp.		●		■	■					
Amorpha spp.		●				■	■			
Andropogon gerardii		pollen						■	■	■
Antennaria spp.	●	●		■	■					
Apios spp.		●					■	■	■	
Aquilegia canadensis		●	● E	■	■	■				
Arabis caucasica		●		■	■					
Aralia cordata	●	●					■	■		
Aralia elata	●	●					■	■		
Aralia hispida	●	●				■	■	■		
Aralia nudicaulis	●	●			■	■	■			
Aralia racemosa	●	●				■	■	■		
Arctostaphylos uva-ursi			●	■	■					
Arnoglossum atriplicifolia	●	●					■	■	■	
Aronia spp.		●			■	■				
Artemisia spp.	●	●					■	■	■	
Asclepias spp.		●				■	■	■		
Asparagus officinalis		●				■	■			
Aster spp.	●	●						■	■	■
Astragalus spp.		●				■	■	■		
Balsamorhiza sagittata	●	●				■	■			
Baptisia spp.		●				■	■			
Bellis perennis	●	●		■	■	■				
Berberis canadensis		●			■	■				
Betula spp.		pollen		■						
Blephilia spp.		●				■	■	■		
Borago officinalis		●				■	■	■	■	
Brassica spp.		●		■	■					
Bunium bulbocastanum	●	●				■	■	■		
Camassia spp.		●			■	■				
Campanula spp.		●				■	■	■		
Caragana spp.		●	●	■	■					
Carex pensylvanica		pollen		■	■					
Carya spp.		pollen			■					
Castanea spp.		pollen				■	■			

NECTARY CALENDAR

Latin Name	Specialist Nectary	Generalist Nectary	Humming-bird	Apr	May	Jun	Jul	Aug	Sept	Oct
Ceanothus americana		•	•			■	■			
Ceanothus prostratus		•				■	■	■		
Celtis spp.		•			■					
Cercis canadensis			•	■						
Cercocarpus montanus		•			■	■				
Chaenomeles speciosa		•		■	■					
Chamaemelum nobile	•	•				■	■	■	■	
Chasmanthium latifolium		pollen					■	■	■	
Chrysogonum virginianum	•	•		■	■					
Chrysosplenium americanum	•	•		■						
Cichorium spp.		•					■	■	■	■
Claytonia spp.		•		■						
Clinopodium glabellum		•					■	■		
Conoclinium coelestinum		•						■	■	
Conopodium majus	•	•			■	■				
Coreopsis spp.	•	•				■	■	■		
Cornus paniculata	•	•			■	■				
Cornus sericea	•	•			■	■				
Corylus spp.		pollen		■						
Crambe maritima		•			■	■				
Crataegus spp.		•			■					
Crocus sativus		•							■	
Cryptotaenia spp.	•	•				■	■			
Cunila origanoides		•					■	■		
Cydonia oblonga		•			■					
Cymopterus spp.	•	•		■	■					
Cytisus spp.		•			■	■				
Darmera peltata		•		■	■					
Diospyros spp.		•			■	■				
Echinacea purpurea		•				■	■	■		
Eleagnus spp.		•			■	■				
Epigaea repens		•		■						
Epilobium angustifolium		•	•			■	■	■	■	
Erigenia bulbosa	•	•		■						
Erigeron pulchellus	•	•			■	■				
Eryngium maritimum	•	•				■	■	■		
Fagus spp.		pollen			■					
Foeniculum vulgare	•	•				■	■	■		
Fragaria spp.		•			■	■				
Gaultheria shallon		•			■	■				
Gaylussacia spp.		•			■	■				
Genista spp.		•				■	■	■		

NECTARY CALENDAR *continued*

Latin Name	Specialist Nectary	Generalist Nectary	Humming-bird	Approximate Flowering Times						
				Apr	May	Jun	Jul	Aug	Sept	Oct
Geum spp.		•			■	■	■			
Gleditsia triacanthos		•			■					
Glycyrrhiza spp.		•				■	■			
Helianthus spp.	•	•						■	■	■
Heliopsis helianthoides	•	•					■	■	■	
Hemerocallis spp.			•	■	■	■	■			
Heracleum sphondylium	•	•		■	■	■				
Heuchera americana	•		•	■	■					
Hibiscus syriacus			• E				■	■	■	
Hieracium venosum	•	•			■	■	■	■		
Hydrophyllum spp.		•			■	■				
Ilex glabra		•			■	■				
Ipomoea spp.		•					■	■	■	■
Iris spp.			•	■						
Juglans spp.		pollen			■					
Lactuca perennis		•					■	■	■	
Lathyrus spp.		•			■	■	■			
Lespedeza spp.		•							■	■	■
Levisticum officinale	•	•				■	■			
Ligusticum spp.	•	•				■	■	■		
Lilium spp.			• E			■	■	■		
Lobelia cardinalis		•	• E					■	■	
Lomatium spp.	•	•		■	■	■				
Lonicera sempervirens		•	• E	■	■	■	■	■		
Lonicera spp.		•	•	■	■	■				
Lupinus spp.		•			■	■	■			
Lycopus uniflorus		•					■	■	■	
Magnolia virginiana		•			■	■	■			
Mahonia spp.		•		■	■					
Malus spp.		•		■	■					
Malva spp.		•				■	■	■	■	
Medicago sativa		•		■	■	■	■	■	■	■
Melissa officinalis		•					■	■	■	
Mentha spp.		•					■	■		
Mespilus germanica		•			■					
Mitella diphylla	•	•		■	■	■				
Monarda spp.		•	• E			■	■	■		
Myrica spp.		•		■	■					
Myrrhis odorata	•	•			■	■				
Opuntia spp.		•				■	■			
Origanum vulgare hirtum		•					■	■		
Osmorhiza spp.	•	•				■	■			

NECTARY CALENDAR *continued*

Latin Name	Specialist Nectary	Generalist Nectary	Humming-bird	Approximate Flowering Times						
				Apr	May	Jun	Jul	Aug	Sept	Oct
Panax quinquefolius	•	•		▓	▓	▓				
Panax trifolius	•	•		▓						
Passiflora incarnata			•				▓	▓	▓	▓
Parthenium integrifolium	•	•				▓	▓	▓	▓	
Perideridia gairdneri	•	•		▓	▓					
Persea borbonia		•		▓	▓					
Petasites japonicus	•	•		▓						
Phaseolus polystachios		•	•				▓	▓	▓	▓
Phlox spp.			•	▓	▓	▓	▓			
Pimpinella saxifraga	•	•		▓	▓	▓	▓			
Platycodon grandiflorus		•					▓	▓		
Polytaenia nuttallii	•	•		▓	▓	▓				
Potentilla anserina		•			▓	▓	▓			
Prosopis glandulosa		•		▓	▓	▓				
Prunus spp.		•			▓					
Pseudostellaria jamesiana		•			▓	▓				
Psoralea esculenta		•			▓	▓	▓			
Pycnanthemum spp.		•					▓	▓	▓	
Pyrus spp.		•			▓					
Quercus spp.		pollen		▓	▓					
Rhodiola rosea		•			▓	▓	▓			
Rhododendron spp.			•	▓	▓	▓	▓	▓		
Rhus spp.		•			▓	▓	▓			
Ribes spp.		•	•	▓	▓					
Robinia hispida and *R. viscosa*		•	•	▓	▓	▓				
Robinia pseudoacacia		•	•	▓	▓	▓				
Rosa spp.			•			▓	▓			
Rosmarinus officinalis			•	▓	▓	▓	▓	▓	▓	▓
Rubus spp.		•				▓				
Rumex acetosella		pollen			▓	▓	▓			
Salvia spp.		•	• E				▓	▓	▓	
Sambucus canadensis	•	•	•			▓	▓			
Sanguisorba spp.							▓	▓		
Sassafras albidum		•			▓	▓				
Satureja douglasii		•				▓	▓	▓		
Saxifraga stolonifera	•	•				▓	▓	▓		
Scorzonera hispanica		•				▓	▓			
Secale cereale		pollen			▓	▓				
Sedum spp.		•				▓	▓	▓		
Senecio spp.	•			▓	▓	▓				
Shepherdia canadensis		•		▓						

NECTARY CALENDAR *continued*

Latin Name	Specialist Nectary	Generalist Nectary	Humming-bird	Apr	May	Jun	Jul	Aug	Sept	Oct
Silphium spp.	●	●	●			■	■	■	■	
Sium sisarum	●	●				■	■			
Smallanthus uvedalia	●	●						■	■	
Solidago spp.	●	●						■	■	■
Sophora japonica		●					■	■		
Sorbus spp.		●			■	■				
Stachys spp.		●				■	■	■		
Stellaria spp.		●		■	■					
Symphytum spp.		●				■	■			
Taenidia integerrima	●	●		■	■	■				
Taraxacum officinale		●		■						
Thaspium spp.	●	●		■	■					
Thymus spp.		●				■	■			
Tiarella cordifolia	●	●		■	■					
Tilia spp.		●				■	■			
Tradescantia virginiana		●			■	■	■			
Trifolium pratense		●			■	■	■	■	■	
Trifolium repens		●			■	■	■	■	■	
Trillium grandiflorum		●		■	■					
Tripsacum dactyloides		pollen						■		
Triticum aestivum		pollen			■	■				
Vaccinium spp.			●	■	■					
Verbena canadensis		●	●			■	■	■	■	
Vernonia noveboracensis		●						■	■	
Veronica officinalis		●	●		■	■	■			
Viburnum cassinoides	●	●				■	■			
Viburnum lentago	●	●			■	■				
Viburnum trilobum	●	●			■	■				
Vicia spp.		●			■	■	■	■		
Vitex agnus-castus		●							■	■
Vitis spp.		●				■	■			
Wisteria spp.		●				■				
Yucca spp.			●			■	■			
Zanthoxylum spp.		●		■	■					
Zizia spp.	●	●		■	■					
Ziziphus jujuba		●		■	■					

Approximate Flowering Times

GROUND COVERS

Ground covers suppress the germination or spread of weeds. They can also offer beauty and complete the visual appearance of a forest (ferns in particular are good for this), as well as perform almost any of the other functions we might want in the forest garden. We define ground-cover plants as less than 24 inches (60 cm) tall and dense enough to be at least somewhat effective. From the great diversity of ground covers available, we have chosen those that are multifunctional, native, or both. Feel free to incorporate your favorite ornamental ground covers in your forest garden—just don't eat them!

We categorize ground-cover species by form and habit (e.g., prostrate woody plants, indefinitely spreading herbaceous perennials, sprawling vines). To select ground-cover species, first determine the form and habit that will best fit your polycultures. Then review the species in that part of the table, consider how fast you want your ground cover to fill in, and find the right ones for you. To learn a species' multiple functions, see the Plant Species Matrix.

KEY

Rating:
★★ = high-density (deciduous or evergreen) or medium-density evergreens. These make the best ground covers.
★ = moderately or less effective ground covers.

Density: Ground-cover density. H = high, M = medium, L = low, U = unknown. The denser the ground cover, the more effectively it will suppress weed germination and growth. However, even an extremely dense ground cover such as pachysandra will permit some tree seedlings to grow each year. You can combine lower-density species in polycultures to make effective covers (see feature article 3, page 292).

Rate: Growth rate under good conditions. S = slow, M = medium, and F = fast. Faster plants fill in more quickly and compete more effectively but can get out of hand. Slow-growing plants, once established, require little care.

Habit: r = runner, c = clumper, mf = mat former, s = sprawler, hc = herbaceous climber, wc = woody climber.

Height: The height of mature plants; " = inches, ' = feet. To convert feet to meters multiply by 0.3048. To convert inches to centimeters multiply by 2.54.

Spacing: The planting distance required for plants to create complete cover within 12 to 18 months; " = inches, ' = feet. This is different from width, which can be much greater, or indefinite in the case of runners. These are not optimal spacings for the plant to reach its full size or have spacious room to grow. If you want to grow these to their full potential as crop plants or for other reasons, use their width as listed in the Plant Species Matrix, not the spacing figures below. Of course, rate of growth, and therefore spacing for full ground cover within 12 to 18 months, will vary depending on plant health and growing conditions.

Notes: Evergreen and semi-evergreen (evgrn and semi-ev) ground covers are more effective, as they provide a cover even in early spring and late fall, when some weeds are sometimes otherwise able to get established. You can use foot-tolerant (ft tol) species in areas receiving some foot traffic, although of the species listed here only white clover is suitable for heavily used pathways.

GROUND COVERS: INDEFINITELY SPREADING LOW SHRUBS

Latin Name	Common Name	Rating	Density	Rate	Habit	Height	Spacing	Notes
Gaultheria shallon	salal	★	L–M	M	r	1'/6'*	1–2'	evgrn
Gaylussacia brachycera	box huckleberry	★★	H	S	r	6–8"	2–3'	
Rubus illecebrosus	strawberry-raspberry	★	M	M–F	r	2'	2–3'	semi–ev
Rubus tricolor	creeping raspberry	★★	H	F	r/mf	18"	3–5'	

*Salal grows to 1' in sun and to 6' in shade.

GROUND COVERS: CLUMPING LOW SHRUBS

Latin Name	Common Name	Rating	Density	Rate	Habit	Height	Spacing	Notes
Acacia angustissima hirta	prairie acacia	★	U	F	c	1–3'	4–6'	
Aronia melanocarpa	black chokeberry	★	M	F	c	1–3'	3–4'	
Genista sagittalis	arrow broom	★★	H	M	c	4–18"	8–12"	
Indigofera decora	Chinese indigo	★	M	F	c	18"	3–4'	
Mahonia repens	creeping mahonia	★	M	S	c	1–2'	12–16"	semi-ev
Rhus aromatica cv.	fragrant sumac 'Gro-Low'	★	M	M	c	2'	3–5'	
Rosmarinus officinalis cv.	rosemary 'Huntington Carpet'	★★	H	S–M	c	1'	2–3'	
Vaccinium angustifolium	lowbush blueberry	★	L–M	S	c	6–24"	12–18"	
Vaccinium vitis-idaea	lingonberry	★	M	M	c	6–12"	12–18"	
Vaccinium vitis-idaea minor	dwarf lingonberry	★	M	M	c	8"	6–8"	

GROUND COVERS: INDEFINITELY SPREADING PROSTRATE SHRUBS (UNDER 6")

Latin Name	Common Name	Rating	Density	Rate	Habit	Height	Spacing	Notes
Arctostaphylos uva-ursi	bearberry	★★	M	S–M	mf/r	2–6"	1–2'	evgrn
Cornus canadensis	bunchberry	★★	M	S	r	4–9"	8–12"	evgrn
Epigaea repens	trailing arbutus	★	L	S	mf/r	4–6"	6–10"	evgrn
Gaultheria hispidula	creeping snowberry	★★	H	S	mf	3–6'	4–6"	evgrn
Gaultheria procumbens	wintergreen	★	L–M	S	r	3–5"	10–14"	evgrn, ft tol
Linnaea borealis	twinflower	★	M	M	r	1–3"	6–8"	evgrn, ft tol
Mitchella repens	partridgeberry	★	M	S–M	mf	1–2"	6–8"	evgrn, ft tol
Vaccinium macrocarpon	cranberry	★	L	S–M	mf	1–4"	10–14"	evgrn

GROUND COVERS: CLUMPING PROSTRATE SHRUBS (UNDER 6")

Latin Name	Common Name	Rating	Density	Rate	Habit	Height	Spacing	Notes
Ceanothus prostratus	mahala mat	★★	H	F	mf	3–6"	3–5'	evgrn
Cytisus decumbens	prostrate broom	★	M	M	c	4–8"	16–24"	
Dryas octopetala	mountain avens	★★	M	M	mf/c	3–6"	8–12"	evgrn, ft tol
Genista pilosa cv.	silky leaf woodwaxen 'Vancouver Gold'	★★	H	M	c	6"	18–24"	sterile seed
Genista pilosa procumbens	trailing silky leaf woodwaxen	★★	H	M	c	2"	18–24"	
Rubus pentalobus cv.	raspberry 'Emerald Carpet'	★★	M	M	r	2–4"	16–30"	evgrn
Thymus spp.	thymes	★	M	M	mf	1–6"	8–12"	ft tol
Vaccinium crassifolium	creeping blueberry	★★	H	M	mf	6"	12–18"	evgrn

GROUND COVERS: INDEFINITELY SPREADING HERBACEOUS PERENNIALS

Latin Name	Common Name	Rating	Density	Rate	Habit	Height	Spacing	Notes
Achillea millefolium	yarrow	★	M	F	r	18–36″	8–16″	
Achillea ptarmica	yarrow	★	M	F	r	18–24″	8–16″	
Antennaria plantaginifolia	pussytoes	★	M	M	mf	8–10″	10–14″	
Aralia nudicaulis	wild sarsaparilla	★	L	M	r	1–2′	10–14″	
Asarum canadense	wild ginger	★★	H	S	r	8–10″	8–12″	
Asarum splendens	Chinese evergreen wild ginger	★★	H	S	r	4–6″	8–12″	semi-ev
Calamintha nepeta	calamint savory	★	M	M	r	2′	12–18″	
Campanula portenschlagiana	Dalmatian bellflower	★★	H	F	r	6–9″	8–12″	
Chimaphila maculata	pipsissewa	★	M	S	r	4″	6–14″	evgrn
Chimaphila umbellata	pipsissewa	★	M	S	r	6–10″	6–14″	evgrn
Conoclinium coelestinum	hardy ageratum	★★	M–H	F	r	12–30″	12–18″	
Coptis trifolia var. *groenlandicum*	goldthread	★★	M	S	r	2–4″	4–8″	evgrn, ft tol
Coreopsis rosea	pink tickseed	★	M–H	F	r	6–24″	12–18″	
Dennstaedtia punctilobula	hay-scented fern	★	L–M	F	r	1–2′	18–24″	
Equisetum scirpoides	dwarf horsetail	★	M	S	r	6–8″	10–18″	semi-ev
Equisetum sylvaticum	wood horsetail	★	L	M	r	10–20″	10–18″	evgrn
Fragaria chiloensis	beach strawberry	★★	M–H	F	r	6″	8–14″	evgrn, ft tol
Fragaria moschata	musk strawberry	★★	M	F	r	12″	8–14″	evgrn
Fragaria vesca	wood strawberry	★	M	F	r	8″	8–14″	evgrn
Fragaria virginiana	wild strawberry	★	M	F	r	4–12″	8–14″	evgrn
Fragaria x *ananassa*	cultivated strawberry	★	L–M	M–F	r	6–12″	8–14″	evgrn
Galax urceolata	galax	★★	H	M	r	6–12″	12–16″	evgrn
Gymnocarpium dryopteris	oak fern	★	M	S	r	8–11″	8–10″	
Houttuynia cordata	hot tuna	★	M	F	r	12–15″	8–10″	ft tol
Iris cristata	dwarf crested iris	★	L	M	mf	7″	10–14″	
Lycopodium clavatum	club moss	★	M	S	r	1–3″	10–14″	evgrn
Maianthemum canadense	false lily of the valley	★	L–M	F	r	2–6″	10–14″	
Mentha arvensis	field mint	★	M–H	F	r	1–3′	10–14″	
Mentha requienii	Corsican mint	★	L–M	S	mf	1″	6–10″	ft tol
Mentha spicata	spearmint	★	M–H	F	r	12–24″	12–16″	
Mentha suaveolens	apple mint	★★	H	F	r	24–36″	10–14″	
Mentha x *piperita*	peppermint	★	M–H	F	r	12–24″	10–14″	
Mentha x *villosa*	Bowles's mint	★★	H	F	r	18–36	10–14″	
Montia perfoliata	miner's lettuce	★	M	M–F	r	4–12″	6–8″	self-seeds
Montia siberica	Siberian miner's lettuce	★	M	M–F	r	4–12″	6–8″	self-seeds
Onoclea sensibilis	sensitive fern	★	M	F	r	12–24″	14–20″	
Oxalis montana	wood sorrel	★	M	M–F	r	4″	10–14″	
Petasites japonicus	fuki	★★	M–H	F	r	2–4′	2–4′	ft tol
Phlox stolonifera	creeping phlox	★	L–M	F	mf	6–12″	10–12″	evgrn
Podophyllum peltatum	mayapple	★	L–M	F	r	12–18″	12″	
Polygonatum biflorum	Solomon's seal	★	L–M	M	r	1–3′	8–12″	
Polytrichum commune	common haircap moss	★	L–M	S	mf	2–4″	3–6″	evgrn
Potentilla anserina	silverweed	★	M–H	F	r	3–14″	10–14″	ft tol

GROUND COVERS: INDEFINITELY SPREADING HERBACEOUS PERENNIALS *continued*

Latin Name	Common Name	Rating	Density	Rate	Habit	Height	Spacing	Notes
Rumex acetosella	sheep sorrel	★★	M	F	r	4–8"	10–14"	
Saxifraga stolonifera	strawberry saxifrage	★★	H	F	r	6–8"	10–16"	evgrn
Sedum album	white stonecrop	★★	H	F	r	2–5"	6–10"	evgrn
Sedum reflexum	stonecrop	★★	M–H	M	r	8–10"	6–10"	evgrn
Sedum ternatum	wild stonecrop	★★	H	S–M	mf/r	2–6"	6–10"	semi-ev
Stachys affinis	Chinese artichoke	★★	M–H	M–F	r	12–18"	10–14"	
Stellaria media	annual chickweed	★	M	F	mf/r	3–8"	10–14"	self-seeds
Thelypteris noveboracensis	New York fern	★	M	M	r	1–2'	12–18"	
Tiarella cordifolia	foamflower	★★	H	M	r	6–12"	10–16"	
Tradescantia virginiana	spiderwort	★	M	M	r	1–3'	12–18"	
Veronica officinalis	common speedwell	★★	M	M	r	12"	8–12"	evgrn
Viola canadensis	Canada violet	★	M	F	r	6–12"	8–12"	
Viola labradorica	Labrador violet	★★	M	F	r	4"	8–12"	evgrn
Viola odorata	sweet violet	★★	H	F	r	6–8"	8–12"	evgrn
Viola sororaria	blue violet	★	M–H	M	r	6–8"	8–12"	
Waldsteinia fragarioides	barren strawberry	★★	M–H	M	r	4–8"	10–16"	evgrn, ft tol
Woodwardia areolata	netted chain fern	★	M–H	M	r	12–18"	12–18"	
Woodwardia virginica	Virginia chain fern	★★	H	F	r	1–3'	18–24"	

GROUND COVERS: CLUMPING HERBACEOUS PERENNIALS

Latin Name	Common Name	Rating	Density	Rate	Habit	Height	Spacing	Notes
Adiantum pedatum	maidenhair fern	★	M	S	c	18–24"	12–14"	
Allium schoenoprasum	chives	★	M–H	M	c	1'	6–10"	
Allium tuberosum	garlic chives	★	M	M	c	1–2'	6–10"	
Antennaria dioica	pussytoes	★	M	S	c	2–6"	10–14"	semi-ev
Arabis caucasica	rock cress	★	M	M	c	6–12"	8–12"	
Artemisia frigida	fringed sagebrush	★	M	M	c	18"	8–12"	
Artemisia stelleriana	beach wormwood	★	M	M	c	2'	3'	
Asarum shuttleworthii	Shuttleworth's wild ginger	★★	H	S	c	8"	8–12"	
Astragalus glycyphyllos	milk vetch	★	M	F	c	6–12"	1–2'	
Athyrium filix-femina	lady fern	★★	H	M	c	1.5–3'	10–14"	
Balsamorhiza sagittata	balsamroot sunflower	★	M–H	M	c	1–2'	12–18"	
Bellis perennis	English daisy	★	L–M	S	c	3–6"	8–12"	ft tol
Callirhoe involucrata	purple poppy-mallow	★	M–H	M	c	3–10"	2–3'	
Campanula carpatica	Carpathian bellflower	★★	H	S	c	8–10"	8–12"	
Carex pensylvanica	Pennsylvania sedge	★	L–M	S–M	c	10"	8–14"	semi-ev, ft tol
Chamaemelum nobile	chamomile	★	M	M	c	3–6"	10–14"	ft tol
Chrysogonum virginianum	green and gold	★★	H	M	mf	2–8"	6–12"	semi-ev, ft tol
Chrysosplenium americanum	golden saxifrage	★	L–M	S–M	c	4"	6–12"	
Clinopodium glabellum	smooth-leaved satureja	★★	M	F	c	1–2'	10–16"	evgrn, ft tol
Coreopsis auriculata	dwarf tickseed	★	M	M	c	6–12"	1–2'	
Coreopsis verticillata	thread-leaved coreopsis	★★	M–H	F	c	18"	10–14"	
Darmera peltata nana	dwarf indian rhubarb	★	M	M	c	12–28"	12-18"	

GROUND COVERS: CLUMPING HERBACEOUS PERENNIALS *continued*

Latin Name	Common Name	Rating	Density	Rate	Habit	Height	Spacing	Notes
Dicentra eximia	wild bleeding heart	★	M	M	c	12–18"	12–16"	
Dryopteris marginalis	marginal wood fern	★★	M	S	c	15–18"	18–24"	evgrn
Geranium maculatum	wild geranium	★	L–M	F	c	1–2'	2–3'	
Hemerocallis fulva and *hybrids*	tawny daylily	★★	M–H	F	c	2'	14–30"	
Hemerocallis lilio-asphodelus	yellow daylily	★	M	F	c	2–3'	14–30"	
Heuchera americana	alum root	★★	H	S	c	6–24"	12–14"	evgrn
Jeffersonia diphylla	twinleaf	★★	M	S	c	10–12"	10–14"	
Lotus corniculatus cv. 'Plena'	prostrate bird's-foot trefoil	★★	H	M	mf	1"	1–2'	ft tol
Lupinus perennis	wild lupine	★★	M–H	M	c	1–3'	10–14"	
Melissa officinalis	lemon balm	★★	M–H	M	c	1–2'	8–12"	
Mitella diphylla	miterwort	★★	M	F	c	6–12"	6–10"	
Origanum vulgare hirtum	oregano	★★	M	M	c	1–2'	10–12"	
Oxalis oregana	redwood sorrel	★★	H	M	c	10"	10–14"	
Pachysandra procumbens	Allegheny spurge	★	L–M	M	c	6–12"	6–10"	
Phlox divaricata	blue phlox	★	M	M	c	8–12"	10–12"	
Phlox nivalis	trailing phlox	★	M	M	c	12"	10–12"	
Phlox subulata	moss pink	★★	M–H	M	mf	4–6"	10–12"	evgrn, ft tol
Polygonum bistorta	bistort	★	M–H	M	c	18–24"	12–18"	
Polypodium virginianum	rock polypody	★★	M	M	c	10"	12–18"	evgrn
Polystichum acrostichoides	Christmas fern	★★	M	S	c	18–30"	18–24"	evgrn
Pycnanthemum flexuosum	hyssop-leaved mtn. mint	★	M	M–F	c	1–2'	10–14"	
Rhodiola rosea	roseroot	★★	H	S–M	c	6–16"	6–10"	
Rubus x *stellarcticus*	all-fieldberry	★	M–H	M	c	6"	6–10"	
Rumex scutatus	buckler-leaved sorrel	★	M–H	M	c	6–12"	6–12"	
Satureja douglasii	yerba buena	★★	M	M	mf	2"	10–16"	evgrn, ft tol
Stellaria pubera	star chickweed	★★	M–H	M	mf	6–12"	8–10"	
Symphytum grandiflorum	large-flowered comfrey	★★	H	F	c	8–12"	10–14"	
Trifolium pratense	red clover	★	M	M	c	12–18"	6–12"	
Trifolium repens	white clover	★	M	M	c	4–8"	6–12"	very ft tol
Trillium grandiflorum	white trillium	★	M	M	c	12–18"	10–14"	
Verbena canadensis	rose verbena	★	M	M	mf	4–6"	12–18"	

GROUND COVERS: SPRAWLERS & CLIMBERS*

Latin Name	Common Name	Rating	Density	Rate	Habit	Height	Spacing	Notes
Amphicarpaea bracteata	hog peanut	★★	M–H	M–F	hc	1–3'	10–14"	
Apios americana	groundnut	★	M	M–F	hc	2–6'	12–18"	
Lathyrus japonicus maritima	beach pea	★	M	M	hc	2–5'	10–14"	
Lathyrus latifolius	everlasting pea	★	M	F	hc	24"	18–24"	
Lonicera sempervirens	evergreen honeysuckle	★	M	M–F	wc	8–16"	1–3'	semi-ev
Phaseolus polystachios	wild bean	★	M	M	hc	1–3'	10–14"	
Vitis riparia	riverbank grape	★★	H	F	wc	6–12"	3–5'	

*Heights and widths as ground covers; these plants perform differently as trellised climbers; see Plant Species Matrix.

AROMATIC PEST CONFUSERS

Some growers and researchers speculate that these strong-scented plants, when mixed in polycultures, confuse pests and reduce their ability to find and eat your crops. Note that many aromatic species are fine culinary, spice, or otherwise edible plants.

AROMATIC PEST CONFUSERS	
Latin Name	**Common Name**
Achillea spp.	yarrow
Agastache foeniculum	anise hyssop
Allium spp.	onions and allies
Armoracia rusticana	horseradish
Artemisia dracunculus sativa	French tarragon
Artemisia spp.	wormwoods and sagebrushes
Blephilia spp.	wood mints
Calamintha nepeta	calamint savory
Clinopodium glabellum	smooth-leaved satureja
Cunila origanoides	Maryland dittany
Eucalyptus gunnii	cider gum
Melissa officinalis	lemon balm
Mentha spp.	mints
Monarda spp.	bee balm, bergamot
Myrrhis odorata	sweet cicely
Origanum vulgare hirtum	oregano
Pycnanthemum spp.	mountain mint
Rosmarinus officinalis	rosemary
Salvia officinalis	broadleaf sage
Satureja douglasii	yerba buena
Solidago odora	sweet goldenrod
Thymus vulgaris	thyme

JUGLONE SUSCEPTIBILITY AND TOLERANCE

Juglone is a chemical produced by black walnuts (*Juglans nigra*) that can poison some plants. This strategy helps black walnuts eliminate certain competitors. Black walnuts exude juglone from their roots, rain washes it off their leaves, and the roots, leaves, and nut husks release it when they decompose. Juglone most strongly affects the area directly under the canopy, but smaller amounts arise in the soil wherever the walnut's roots grow, which can be quite a distance beyond the canopy. Fortunately, the chemical does not affect many forest garden species. Improving your soil drainage can mitigate the effectiveness of this natural herbicide. Do not use black walnut leaves as mulch on sensitive plants.

JUGLONE SUSCEPTIBILTY AND TOLERANCE: SPECIES KNOWN TO BE NEGATIVELY AFFECTED BY JUGLONE	
Latin Name	**Common Name**
Alnus spp.	alder
Aronia spp.	chokeberry
Asparagus officinalis	asparagus
Baptisia spp.	wild indigos
Brassica spp.	perennial brassicas
Castanea spp.	chestnuts
Celtis spp.	hackberry
Lespedeza spp.	bush clovers
Lilium spp.	lilies
Malus pumila	apple
Medicago sativa	alfalfa
Physalis heterophylla	clammy ground cherry
Prunus spp.	some cherries (mostly ornamentals)
Pyrus spp.	pear, Asian pear
Rheum x cultorum	rhubarb
Rubus spp.	blackberry
Tilia spp.	basswood, linden
Vaccinium spp.	blueberry
Viburnum spp.	a few viburnums
Vitis spp. (probably *V. vinifera*)	cultivated grapes

SPECIES KNOWN TO TOLERATE JUGLONE	
Latin Name	**Common Name**
Acer spp.	maples (most)
Alcea rosea	hollyhock
Allium spp.	onions and allies
Asarum spp.	wild ginger
Asimina triloba	pawpaw

SPECIES KNOWN TO TOLERATE JUGLONE *continued*

Latin Name	Common Name
Carya spp.	pecan and hickory
Cercis canadensis	redbud
Claytonia spp.	spring beauty
Corylus spp.	hazel and filbert
Crataegus spp.	mayhaw and hawthorn
Crocus sativus	saffron crocus
Cydonia oblonga	quince
Dicentra eximia	dwarf bleeding heart
Diospyros virginiana	American persimmon
Echinacea purpurea	purple coneflower
Erythronium spp.	trout lily
Gleditsia triacanthos	honey locust
Helianthus tuberosus	Jerusalem artichoke
Hemerocallis fulva	daylily
Hibiscus syriacus	rose of Sharon
Hydrophyllum virginianum	Virginia waterleaf
Lindera benzoin	spicebush
Monarda spp.	bee balm and wild bergamot
Morus alba	white mulberry
Myrrhis odorata	sweet cicely
Onoclea sensibilis	sensitive fern
Phlox subulata	creeping phlox
Podophyllum peltatum	mayapple
Polygonatum biflorum var. *commutatum*	giant Solomon's seal
Polystichum acrostichoides	Christmas fern
Prunus spp.	some edible cherries
Quercus spp.	oaks
Robinia pseudoacacia	black locust
Rosa spp.	roses (at least wild species)
Rubus occidentalis	black raspberry
Sambucus canadensis	elderberry
Sedum spp.	stonecrop
Stellaria media	chickweed
Taraxacum officinale	dandelion
Tradescantia virginiana	Virginia spiderwort
Trifolium repens	white clover
Trillium grandiflorum	white trillium
Ulmus rubra	slippery elm
Viburnum spp.	most viburnums
Viola canadensis	Canada violet
Vitis spp. (but not *V. vinifera*)	wild grapes

APPENDIX 4

Species of Concern

POISONOUS PLANTS

Poisons are an important plant defense against herbivory. Just the thought of it keeps many people from sampling unfamiliar edible plants. However, you have nothing to worry about if you identify a plant correctly, eat only the right parts at the right time, and follow the instructions at the beginning of appendix 2. Nonetheless, it is good to know potential toxins in your garden. This is just as true if you grow only ornamentals—children often put all kinds of things in their mouths.

Generally speaking, legumes are very often toxic, presumably because they are trying to protect their high-nitrogen foliage from herbivory. Likewise, many in the Apiaceae (umbel family) are highly toxic, with one bite from some species causing death. On the other hand, many important food crops and spices are from this family (carrots, parsnips, parsley, celery, cilantro, dill, cumin, and so on). When dealing with any plant from either of these two families as a potential edible, make *very sure* you know you have the right plant in your hands before it goes into your mouth! In all cases, for plants in this table, assume that all parts of the plant are toxic unless listed as edible in appendices 1 and 2. If for any reason you think you or someone you know has been poisoned, contact a poison control center immediately, and keep a sample of the plant in question handy to help properly identify the potential toxin.

POISONOUS PLANTS

Latin Name	Common Name	Poisonous Parts and Effects
Acacia angustissima	prairie acacia	Has toxic relatives.
Acer spp.	maples	Toxic foliage; can cause serious circulatory system problems.
Achillea spp.	yarrow	All parts. Can cause digestive disturbance.
Allium canadense	wild garlic	Can give young children severe digestive upset.
Amelanchier spp.	juneberry	Leaves contain cyanide. Excessive consumption can cause vomiting, coma, and even death.
Amorpha spp.	false indigo, leadplant	No parts of the plants are edible; presumably they are toxic. *A. fruticosa* is used as an insecticide.
Amorphophallus riveri var. *konjac*	konjac	All parts contain calcium oxalate. Raw or undercooked roots, stems, and leaves cause painful burning in mouth and throat. Eat only food (not ornamental) varieties.
Aralia spp.	aralias	Raw berries are toxic.
Armoracia rusticana	horseradish	Large quantities of members of the brassica family, eaten raw, can cause nausea and diarrhea, especially in small children.
Artemisia spp.	sagebrushes	Foliage toxic (not tarragon).
Arundinaria gigantea	canebrake bamboo	Toxic ergot fungus often grows on seeds. Watch for pink to dark purple fungi resembling grains, of grain size or larger.
Asarum spp.	wild ginger	Leaves toxic.
Asclepias incarnata	swamp milkweed	Many relatives are highly poisonous (see *A. syriaca* below).

POISONOUS PLANTS *continued*

Latin Name	Common Name	Poisonous Parts and Effects
Asclepias syriaca	common milkweed	All parts. Can cause digestive upset and heart problems. Nonetheless a popular wild edible. Make sure to boil thoroughly in several changes of water. Has killed livestock.
Asimina triloba	pawpaw	Everything but fruit is toxic. Foliage and woody parts are used as an insecticide and presumably are toxic. Seeds also poisonous. Some people get rashes as an allergic reaction to eating or handling the fruit.
Asparagus officinalis	asparagus	Eating raw shoots can cause rashes.
Astragalus spp.	milk vetch	Leaves. Some species cause "locoism," a nervous-system poisoning of livestock. One must eat large amounts over a long time to produce this effect. While roots of *A. canadensis* are reportedly edible, consume them with caution. *A. membranaceous* is a poisonous medicinal and should be used only with advice from a medical professional.
Atriplex halimus	saltbush	Contains oxalic acid; excessive consumption of raw foliage over long periods can decrease blood calcium.
Baptisia spp.	wild indigo	All parts toxic; has caused death in livestock.
Berberis canadensis	Canada barberry	Leaves and roots. Large quantities can cause digestive upset and confusion.
Beta vulgaris	sea beet, beet, chard	Contains oxalic acid; excessive consumption of raw foliage over long periods can decrease blood calcium.
Brassica oleracea	kales, cabbages, broccolis, etc.	Large quantities of members of the brassica family, eaten raw, can cause nausea and diarrhea, especially in small children.
Bunias orientalis	Turkish rocket	Large quantities of members of the brassica family, eaten raw, can cause nausea and diarrhea, especially in small children.
Calycanthus floridus	Carolina allspice	Fruits and seeds. Excessive consumption can cause convulsions. Overconsumption of fruits has killed livestock.
Camassia spp.	camass, wild hyacinth	Edible species look similar to toxic death camass (*Zigadenus* spp.) when not flowering. Make sure your nursery has not confused the two!
Cardamine spp.	toothwort, etc.	Large quantities of members of the brassica family, eaten raw, can cause nausea and diarrhea, especially in small children.
Cercocarpus montanus	mountain mahogany	Foliage toxic to livestock.
Chaenomeles speciosa	flowering quince	Leaves contain cyanide. Excessive consumption can cause vomiting, coma, and even death.
Chenopodium bonus-henricus	good King Henry	Contains oxalic acid; excessive consumption of raw foliage over long periods can decrease blood calcium.
Colocasia esculenta	taro	All parts contain calcium oxalate. Raw or undercooked roots, stems, and leaves cause painful burning in mouth and throat. Eat only food (not ornamental) varieties.
Colutea arborescens	bladder senna	Seeds toxic.
Crambe maritima	sea kale	Large quantities of members of the brassica family, eaten raw, can cause nausea and diarrhea, especially in small children.
Crocus sativus	saffron	Excessive consumption (5 gm/0.175 oz or more) can cause illness or death (that would be an awful lot of saffron!).
Cydonia oblonga	quince	Leaves contain cyanide. Excessive consumption can cause vomiting, coma, and even death.
Cytisus decumbens	prostrate broom	Can cause paralysis or death in extreme cases.
Dicentra eximia	dwarf bleeding heart	Can cause convulsions; can be fatal in large quantities.
Diospyros spp.	persimmon	Underripe fruits. Can (very rarely) form "bezoars" or balls of undigested fruit in stomach and intestines. Extremely excessive consumption of ripe fruit can also cause this, particularly if seeds are swallowed. Bezoars cause digestive problems and may even require surgery. Previous stomach surgery makes bezoar formation more likely.
Dryopteris marginalis	marginal wood fern	Has toxic relatives.

POISONOUS PLANTS *continued*

Latin Name	Common Name	Poisonous Parts and Effects
Equisetum spp.	horsetail	Foliage toxic.
Erythronium americanum	trout lily	Foliage toxic if eaten in large quantities.
Eucalyptus gunnii	cider gum	Foliage toxic.
Fagus spp.	beech	Overconsumption of raw nuts can cause digestive upset, especially in children.
Genista spp.	brooms	All parts toxic to nervous system. Usually mild, occasionally fatal.
Ginkgo biloba	maidenhair tree	Do not eat the flesh of the "fruit," which can cause rashes. Wear gloves for harvest and processing. The roasted seeds are a popular edible in Asia, but raw seeds can deplete the body of Vitamin B_6 and are particularly toxic to children.
Helianthus spp.	sunflower	Young foliage. Can occasionally cause nervous system toxicity in livestock.
Hemerocallis spp.	daylilies	Overconsumption of tubers and leaves can cause diarrhea.
Heracleum sphondylium	cow parsnip	Contact with leaves can cause photodermatitis—a skin rash caused by chemicals from the leaves interacting with sunlight.
Ilex glabra	inkberry	Has toxic relatives.
Indigofera decora	Chinese indigo	Has toxic relatives.
Ipomoea leptophylla	bush morning glory	Seeds may cause vomiting and hallucinations. Leaves may be toxic. Roots may cause digestive upset in some people—use with caution.
Ipomoea pandurata	wild potato vine	Seeds may cause vomiting and hallucinations. Leaves may be toxic. Roots may cause digestive upset in some people—use with caution.
Iris cristata	dwarf crested iris	Has toxic relatives.
Laportaea canadensis	wood nettle	Causes stinging from contact with leaves, stems, and roots.
Lathyrus spp.	beach pea, earthnut pea	Beans. Large amounts consumed over long periods can cause nervous-system problems, including long-term paralysis.
Lobelia cardinalis	cardinal flower	All parts. Contains nervous-system toxins, can cause convulsions, some relatives have killed livestock.
Lonicera spp.	honeysuckle	Has highly toxic relatives.
Lotus corniculatus cv.	prostrate bird's-foot trefoil 'Plena'	All parts poisonous; contains cyanogenic glycosides (cyanide).
Lupinus spp.	lupine	Some species cause convulsions, coma, and liver damage.
Maackia amurensis	Amur maackia	All parts toxic.
Mahonia spp.	Oregon grape	Leaves and roots. Large quantities can cause digestive upset.
Malus spp.	apple and crabapple	Seeds and leaves contain cyanide. A cup of seeds can be fatal.
Mertensia maritima	oyster plant	All parts. Possible risk of long-term liver damage from excessive consumption.
Morus spp.	mulberry	In some species, unripe fruits and leaves cause intense digestive upset and hallucinations.
Nasturtium officinale	watercress	Large quantities of members of the brassica family, eaten raw, can cause nausea and diarrhea, especially in small children.
Onoclea sensibilis	sensitive fern	All parts toxic.
Oxyria digyna	mountain sorrel	Contains oxalic acid; excessive consumption of raw foliage over long periods can decrease blood calcium.
Parthenium integrifolium	wild quinine	Has toxic relatives.
Physalis heterophylla	clammy ground cherry	Leaves and green (unripe) fruit poisonous. Can be fatal to children. Tomatoes have the same toxins.
Phytolacca americana	pokeweed	All but cooked young shoots are toxic. Can cause intense vomiting, diarrhea, and nervous-system poisoning. Use with caution, and follow preparation instructions in "Edible Leaves, Stalks, and Shoots" in appendix 2 or a wild edible guide.
Podophyllum peltatum	mayapple	All but ripe fruit toxic. Causes intense digestive upset. Consume fruit in moderation.

POISONOUS PLANTS *continued*

Latin Name	Common Name	Poisonous Parts and Effects
Prunus spp.	cherry, plum, peach, nectarine, apricot	Pits (seeds) and leaves contain cyanide. Can cause vomiting, coma, and even death.
Psoralea esculenta	prairie turnip	Contact with leaves can cause photodermatitis—a skin rash caused by chemicals from the leaves interacting with sunlight.
Quercus spp.	oak	Do not consume raw acorns in quantity.
Rheum spp.	rhubarb	Leaves and roots toxic, can cause serious kidney damage.
Rhododendron periclymenoides	pinxter flower azalea	Foliage of many azaleas and rhododendrons can cause vomiting, convulsions, and coma if eaten.
Rhus spp.	sumacs	Sap. Occasionally causes rashes. Do not boil fruit when making tea, as this releases intensely bitter tannins.
Robinia spp.	locust	Bark, seeds, and leaves can cause vomiting and diarrhea.
Rumex spp.	sorrel	Contains oxalic acid; excessive consumption of raw foliage over long periods can decrease blood calcium.
Sambucus canadensis	elderberry	Leaves can cause digestive upset and nervous-system poisoning. Raw fruits can cause digestive upset in some people.
Secale cereale	rye	Toxic ergot fungus can grow on seeds. Watch for pink to dark purple fungi resembling grains, of grain size or larger.
Sedum spp.	stonecrop	All parts. Occasionally causes digestive upset.
Senecio spp.	ragworts	Some species are very toxic; do not eat any of them. Can cause liver damage. Possible carcinogen.
Smilacina racemosa	false Solomon's seal	Berries edible in small quantities, but may be cathartic.
Solidago spp.	goldenrods	Some species are toxic in excessive amounts. Sweet goldenrod is fine in moderate amounts.
Sophora japonica	Japanese pagoda tree	Foliage and seeds toxic.
Sorbus spp.	mountain ash	Leaves contain cyanide. Excessive consumption can cause vomiting, coma, and even death.
Streptopus spp.	twisted stalk, rosybells	Berries edible in small quantities, but may be cathartic.
Symphytum spp.	comfrey	All parts. Possible long-term liver damage from excessive long-term use or extremely excessive short-term use.
Thermopsis villosa	Carolina bush pea	Foliage toxic.
Tradescantia virginiana	Virginia spiderwort	Some related species cause rashes.
Triticum x *aestivum*	wheat	Toxic ergot fungus can grow on seeds. Watch for pink to dark purple fungi resembling grains, of grain size or larger.
Urtica spp.	stinging nettle	Causes stinging from contact with leaves, stems, and roots.
Vernonia noveboracensis	New York ironweed	Has highly toxic relatives.
Viburnum spp.	viburnum	Excessive consumption of fruit, leaf, or bark from some species can cause vomiting. Highbush cranberry, at least, is safe to consume in quantity when cooked.
Vicia spp.	vetch	Some species have toxic seeds.
Wisteria spp.	wisteria	All parts toxic.
x *Sorbaronia*, x *Sorbocrataegus*, and x *Sorbopyrus*	mountain ash hybrids	Leaves contain cyanide. Excessive consumption can cause vomiting, coma, and even death.
Zanthoxylum americanum	prickly ash	Leaves toxic.

THE WATCH LIST

This table includes a number of species whose intense toxicity or noxious weediness precludes their use in edible forest gardens despite their potential uses or functions. While they may have a role to play, you should watch out for them because they pose a danger to your health and well-being, your garden, or your ecological neighborhood.

Opportunist species are supercompetitive in the garden or in the ecosystem (and are called "invasive" by others). They are noted as native or exotic.

Expansive opportunists spread vegetatively by rhizomes, by runners, or by sprawling and smothering. These species are generally too "unsociable" to make good companions in forest gardens.

Dispersive opportunists spread by seed, often dispersed by birds, other animals, or wind over long distances. Some dispersive opportunists make fine neighbors in forest gardens but naturalize too vigorously in surrounding areas. Note that if these species have already established well in your area, there is not much harm in planting them in your garden—depending on who you talk to.

Persistent species are extremely difficult to eliminate once planted.

Highly poisonous species are very toxic, and some are deadly. Note that many species that *are* in the Plant Species Matrix are highly poisonous but offset this characteristic with other qualities. See the preceding table of poisonous plants.

Disease vectors are alternate carriers of diseases that affect important wild or crop plants. If the crop or wild plant is in your garden or area, avoid planting these species.

Look-alikes are plants that look like useful plants from the same family. *Some of these in the umbel family (Apiaceae) are deadly poisonous.* We note here only *a few* of the poisonous look-alikes of edible plants listed in the matrix.

THE WATCH LIST			
Latin Name	**Common Name**	**Issue of Concern**	**Uses & Functions**
Aegopodium podagraria	goutweed, bishop's weed	opportunistic (exotic): expansive, dispersive, and persistent; Apiaceae look-alike	excellent ground cover, edible leaves, specialist nectary
Aethusa cynapium	fool's parsley	highly poisonous; Apiaceae look-alike	specialist nectary
Akebia quinata	five-leaved akebia	opportunistic (exotic): expansive and dispersive	edible fruit, ground cover
Albizia julibrissin	mimosa	opportunistic (exotic): dispersive	nitrogen fixer, outstanding hummingbird plant, beautiful
Alliaria petiolata	garlic mustard	opportunistic (exotic): dispersive	excellent edible leaves
Anthriscus sylvestris	woodland chervil	opportunistic (exotic): dispersive; Apiaceae look-alike	specialist nectary, edible leaves, good-quality edible roots
Artemisia vulgaris	mugwort	opportunistic (exotic): expansive and dispersive	specialist nectary, tea plant, some varieties selected for edible leaves
Berberis spp.	exotic barberries	opportunistic (exotic): dispersive	edible fruit, some quite good
Campanula rapunculoides	creeping bellflower	opportunistic (exotic): expansive, dispersive, and persistent	ground cover, edible roots
Cicuta maculata	water hemlock	highly poisonous; Apiaceae look-alike	specialist nectary
Conium maculatum	poison hemlock	highly poisonous; Apiaceae look-alike; opportunistic (exotic): dispersive	specialist nectary
Cytisus scoparius	Scotch broom	opportunistic (exotic): dispersive	nitrogen fixer
Dioscorea bulbifera	air potato	opportunistic (exotic): dispersive and expansive	edible "aerial tubers" borne on vines aboveground, highly productive

THE WATCH LIST *continued*

Latin Name	Common Name	Issue of Concern	Uses & Functions
Eleagnus angustifolia *Eleagnus umbellata*	Russian olive autumn olive	opportunistic (exotic): dispersive	nitrogen fixer, edible fruit
Eupatorium rugosum	white snakeroot	highly poisonous	specialist nectary
Juniperus communis *Juniperus virginiana*	juniper	disease vector: cedar apple rust, affecting many rose family fruits, especially apples	outstanding beneficial wildlife cover and food plants; attract up to 60 species of birds
Laburnum anagyroides	golden chain tree	highly poisonous	nitrogen fixer
Lactuca pulchella	blue lettuce	opportunistic (native): expansive, dispersive, and persistent	edible leaves
Lamium galeobdolon formerly *Lamiastrum galeobdolon*	yellow archangel	opportunistic (exotic): expansive	edible leaves
Menispermum canadense	Canada moonseed	highly poisonous	excellent native ground cover
Pachysandra terminalis	pachysandra	(exotic) tacky, overused	ground cover
Polygonum cymosum, formerly *Fagopyrum cymosum*	perennial buckwheat	opportunistic (exotic): expansive	edible shoots
Polygonum japonicum, formerly *Polygonum cuspidatum, Reynoutria japonica,* or *Fallopia japonica*	Japanese knotweed	opportunistic (exotic): expansive, dispersive, and persistent	edible shoots, excellent generalist nectary
Ribes nigrum	black currant	disease vector: white pine blister rust, a serious white pine disease; some varieties, like 'Consort', don't carry the disease	edible fruit
Smilax bona-nox *Smilax laurifolia* *Smilax rotundifolia*	greenbriars	opportunistic (native): expansive	young shoots excellent; rootstocks used to make gelatin substitute
Sonchus spp.	sow thistle, milk thistle	opportunistic (exotic): dispersive	edible young leaves, excellent generalist nectary and spider food and cover plants
Thladiantha dubia	red hailstone vine	opportunistic (exotic): expansive, dispersive, and persistent	edible young leaves and shoots, edible fruit
Toxicodendron radicans	poison ivy	highly poisonous	excellent native ground cover, excellent wildlife food plant
Tussilago farfara	coltsfoot	opportunistic (exotic): expansive, dispersive, and persistent	specialist nectary, ground cover, edible leaves and stems
Zanthoxylum simulans	Szechuan pepper	disease vector: alternate host for serious citrus disease	important cultivated spice plant
Zigadenus spp.	death camass	deadly look-alike for edible *Camassia* spp.	none known

APPENDIX 5

Niche Requirements of Beneficial Animals

We intend this set of tables to offer you as much information as possible on the niche requirements and characteristics of vertebrate and invertebrate animals considered beneficial or potentially beneficial for forest gardeners. We have attempted to assemble this information so it is useful to designers but is also based in ecological reality. We hope these tables will allow you to more consciously design, or at least influence, your forest garden's food web.

The first two tables provide data on the guilds, behaviors, food preferences, habitat needs, and special niche requirements of beneficial vertebrates and invertebrates. They are designed to help you learn which animals you may want in your garden; maximize the desirability of your garden for those you want or know you have; and understand how much influence you may have over their habitat. Some vertebrates, for example, may need territories larger than what you directly control. Therefore, evaluating your neighborhood's potential as habitat for such species is critical—and the tables should help you do this well. For species with smaller territories, these tables should help you provide all the habitat elements needed for them to live happily in your garden. Obviously, we do not know everything about the animals listed in these tables, and we have little or no direct control over their behavior. Hence, we offer no guarantees that the animals you desire will reside in your garden even if you offer everything these tables say they need. We are dealing with probabilities here, and are attempting to stack the deck in our own, our animal allies', and our garden's favor.

The last table in this appendix lists which animals benefit from which habitat elements, and how they benefit, based on the data in the previous two tables. This will help you consider which habitat elements have the most benefits for your garden's food web and which species your garden already has elements to support. Please realize, however, that each beneficial animal has a whole suite of niche requirements that the garden must meet for it to thrive over successive generations. If you provide good bird perches, birds still may not inhabit your garden if they have inadequate nesting sites. Therefore, use both sets of tables together as you design your beneficial animal habitats. The third table will help you make your most multifunctional moves, but the first two tables will help you design habitats for specific species and species groups.

NICHES AND HABITAT NEEDS OF BENEFICIAL VERTEBRATES

This table focuses on species and groups from the eastern United States, listing them in taxonomic order as shown in DeGraaf and Yamasaki, 2001. Species are diurnal (daytime active) unless otherwise noted. Territories listed are for breeding pairs and are not necessarily exclusive; they may overlap with others of the same species. Thanks to Jonathan Bates for his first round on this table. References include Beal, McAtee, and Kalmbach, 1927; Behler and King, 1979; DeGraaf and Rudis, 1983; DeGraaf and Yamasaki, 2001; Forbush, 1927; Forbush, 1929; Griggs, 1997; Henderson, 1987; Martin, Zim, and Nelson, 1951; Schutz, 1970; Sibley, 2000.

NICHES & HABITAT NEEDS OF BENEFICIAL VERTEBRATES: AMPHIBIANS

Species	Guild/Niche Strategies	Animal Foods
Salamanders: ORDER Caudata		
Mole Salamanders: FAMILY Ambystomatidae		
• spotted salamander, *Ambystoma maculatum* • blue-spotted salamander, *Ambystoma laterale* • marbled salamander, *Ambystoma opacum*	Juvenile aquatic: insectivorous water gleaner. Adult terrestrial: insectivorous ground gleaner; nocturnal; fossorial; terrestrial hibernator; aquatic breeder with pool fidelity. Spotted may live 20 years.	Juveniles eat aquatic organisms. Adults eat earthworms, other annelids, centipedes, snails, slugs, spiders, insects, especially beetle adults and larvae.
• tiger salamander, *Ambystoma tigrinum*	Omnivorous ground gleaner. Aquatic breeder. Up to 13 in/40 cm long.	Voracious consumer of earthworms, large insects, small mice, amphibians.
Newts: FAMILY Salamandridae		
• red-spotted newt (adult), red eft (juvenile), *Notophthalmus viridescens viridescens*	Juvenile terrestrial for 2–7 years: carnivorous ground gleaner; burrows under logs and debris to hibernate. Adult aquatic: carnivorous water gleaner.	Snails important to diet of red eft. Also eat insects and their larvae, tadpoles, frog eggs, mollusks, crustaceans, spiders, mites, occasionally small minnows.
Lungless Salamanders: FAMILY Plethodontidae		
• northern redback salamander, *Plethodon cinereus*	Completely terrestrial: insectivorous ground gleaner. May forage in trees and shrubs in wet weather. Lays eggs in or under rotted logs, stumps, rocks, crevices. Hibernates 1–3 ft/0.3–1 m deep.	Mites, insects, and insect larvae 65–75% of prey. Also snails, slugs, spiders, sow bugs, millipedes.
Frogs and Toads: ORDER Anura		
Toads: FAMILY Bufonidae		
• *Bufo* spp.	Insectivorous ground ambushers. Most active during evening. Hibernate in burrows 1–3 ft/0.3–1 m deep. Aquatic breeders.	Eat terrestrial arthropods—insects, spiders, centipedes, and millipedes—as well as slugs, snails, and earthworms.

Plant Foods	Habitats	Key Habitat Requirements
N/A	Moist woods, stream banks, beneath stones, logs, boards. Deciduous or mixed woods in or near floodplains, wetlands, depressions, or on dry or rocky hillsides with nearby breeding pools.	Moist woods containing water (permanent, semipermanent, ephemeral) with no fish. Man-made ponds must be >50 yrs. old for breeding to occur. Travel range up to 1/4 mile/400 m from breeding pools.
N/A	Wide-ranging midwestern/western species in diverse habitats: arid sagebrush plains, pine barrens, mountain forests, damp meadows; to 11,000 ft/3,353 m elevation.	Other animal burrows or soil that is easily burrowed into.
N/A	Boreal to subtropical moist, deciduous, coniferous, or mixed forests with clean semipermanent or permanent water for breeding.	Adult newts: stable, clean water with aquatic vegetation. Juvenile efts: moist leaf litter, brush piles, logs and stumps in woods, for cover and hibernation. Prefer old growth over disturbed stands, deciduous over conifer.
N/A	Forest litter in mixed deciduous or coniferous woods, inside logs or stumps, under stones, leaf litter, and bark. Prefers well-drained habitats, or dry habitats with moist micro-habitats. Avoids wet or very moist places. To 5,600 ft/1,707 m elevation.	Logs, stumps, rocks, woody debris piles. Sensitive to forest disturbance: takes 50–60 years to recover to precutting populations. Home ranges of 150–250 sq ft/14–23 sq m.
Accidental ingestion of plant matter only	Native to moist upland woods, but found anywhere there is cover, damp soil, and food: yards, gardens, etc. Sea level to mountains.	Need shallow water areas to lay eggs; good ground cover; sandy alluvial or loose soils. Home ranges within 100 ft/30 m. May move 200–700 ft/60–210 m to water to breed.

NICHES & HABITAT NEEDS OF BENEFICIAL VERTEBRATES: AMPHIBIANS *continued*

Species	Guild/Niche Strategies	Animal Foods
Tree Frogs: FAMILY Hylidae		
• gray tree frog, *Hyla versicolor*	Insectivorous bark ambusher. Aquatic breeding sites highly variable. Hibernates under tree roots and leaves. Most active during evening.	Forages for small insects, aphids, plant lice, mites, and snails in vegetation and on the ground.
• northern spring peeper, *Pseudacris crucifer crucifer*	Insectivorous riparian ambusher. May move far from water, though. Terrestrial hibernator, aquatic breeder.	Eats small nonaquatic insects, mostly ants, flying bugs, beetles, flies, springtails, spiders, mites, ticks, and small snails. Prey taken depends mainly on catchability and availability, not preferences.
True Frogs: FAMILY Ranidae		
• wood frog, *Rana sylvatica*	Insectivorous ground ambusher. Hibernates under moist forest floor debris or flooded meadows. Aquatic breeder.	Eats insects, especially beetles, flies, ants, bees, but also spiders, snails, slugs, various worms.

NICHES & HABITAT NEEDS OF BENEFICIAL VERTEBRATES: REPTILES

Species	Guild/Niche Strategies	Animal Foods
Lizards, Skinks, and Snakes: ORDER Squamata		
Iguanids: FAMILY Iguanidae		
• eastern fence lizard, *Sceloporus undulatus*	Arboreal or terrestrial insectivore. Egg layer. Diurnal. Hibernates in winter.	Eats any insect, spider, centipede, or snail. Prefers beetles.
Anguid Lizards: FAMILY Anguidae		
• slender glass lizard, *Ophisaurus attenuatus* • eastern glass lizard, *Ophisaurus ventralis*	Terrestrial or burrowing carnivores. Lay eggs. Diurnal.	Insects, small mammals, other lizards.
Racerunners: FAMILY Teiidae		
• racerunner, *Cnemidophorous sexlineatus*	Terrestrial carnivore. Lays eggs.	Insects, other invertebrates.
Skinks: FAMILY Scincidae		
• five-lined skink, *Eumeces fasciatus* • southeastern five-lined skink, *E. inexpectatus* • broad-headed skink, *E. laticeps* • ground skink, *Scincella lateralis*	Insectivorous ground ambushers. *E. inexpectatus* and *E. laticeps* also arboreal. Lay eggs in rotted stumps, loose soil, under logs and rocks.	Eat primarily insects, insect larvae, and spiders; also grubs, snails, beetles, flies, crustaceans, young mice.
Colubrid Snakes: FAMILY Colubridae		
• common garter snake, *Thamnophis sirtalis*	Carnivorous ground ambusher. Hibernates and lays eggs belowground. Sometimes active at night.	Earthworms 80% of diet, but also eats slugs, toads, frogs, salamanders. Not as beneficial to gardens as believed.
• eastern milk snake, *Lampropeltis triangulum triangulum*	Carnivorous ground ambusher. Nocturnal. Hibernates in rock piles or belowground. Lays eggs in loose soil, litter, sawdust, manure piles.	Eats mice (75% of diet), other small mammals, slugs, lizards, birds and bird eggs, and snakes. Beneficial near farm buildings, etc., where mice are abundant.

Plant Foods	Habitats	Key Habitat Requirements
N/A	Common in forested areas with small trees and shrubs in or near shallow water. Likes moss and lichens. Inhabits moist areas under rotted logs and loose bark or inside hollow trees.	Still or slow-moving water for breeding: ditches, temporary or permanent pools, ponds, swamps, and bogs. Small rees,shrubs,moss, and liche. Moist areas on, in, and around trees: rotted logs, tree roots, leaf litter.
N/A	Marshy, wet, or second-growth deciduous woods, bogs, open lowlands, fields, and coniferous woods; on the ground or burrowed into soil. Breeds in temporary or permanent water. Sea level to 2,000 ft/610 m.	Needs temporary or permanent pools, with emergent vegetation, preferably in wooded areas for breeding. Hibernates on land under moss or leaves. Home range 4–18 ft/ 1.2–5.5 m in diameter around forest debris and vegetation.
N/A	Terrestrial. Ubiquitous from sea level to 3,800 ft/1,158 m in moist woods, or dry woods with moist microhabitats.	Prefers woods with small breeding ponds, temporary pools, slow stream backwaters. Uses brush, hummocks, etc. for cover. Average home range 77 sq yd/66 sq m.

Plant Foods	Habitats	Key Habitat Requirements
N/A	Sunny locations; prefers rotting logs, open woodlands, open grassy dunes, prairies.	Prefers dry, open forest of pine or hard-woods. Needs sunny sites for basking.
N/A	Dry or moist grassland, oldfields, sand prairies, and open woods.	Use mammal burrows for refuge or hibernation.
N/A	Dry, sunny areas; grasslands, open woods.	Prefers well-drained soils.
N/A	Steep, rocky, patchy woods with logs, slash, abundant leaf litter; moist woods with ground cover; near old buildings; in damp spots. Some spp. may inhabit drier areas.	Rocks, rock piles, old stumps, slash, logs, leaf litter. Need areas to sunbathe. Hibernate under rocks, in rotten logs, underground. *E. fasciatus* home range 30–90 ft/9–27 m in diameter.
N/A	Ubiquitous. Damp environments of all kinds: river bottoms to mountains; forest and stream edges, fencerows, swamps, overgrown lots; to 8,000 ft/2,450 m.	Takes cover under rock and straw-bale piles, etc., on hot days. Home range about 5 acres/2 ha, up to 35 acres/14 ha.
N/A	From sea level to 8,000 ft/2,450 m in brushy or woody cover; farmlands, woods, barns, meadows, outbuildings, disturbed areas, rodent runways.	Logs, stones, boards for cover. Resembles venomous copperhead, but don't kill it! Home range about 50 acres/20 ha.

NICHES & HABITAT NEEDS OF BENEFICIAL VERTEBRATES: REPTILES *continued*

Species	Guild/Niche Strategies	Animal Foods
• eastern worm snake, *Carphophis amoenus amoenus*	Insectivorous ground gleaner. Nocturnal, fossorial, extremely secretive. Hibernates and rests belowground. Lays eggs in shallow depressions under logs, etc.	Earthworms, soft-bodied insects and larvae, grubs, slugs.
• northern brown snake, *Storeria dekayi dekayi*	Insectivorous ground ambusher. Nocturnal. Hibernates and lays eggs belowground.	Slugs, snails, earthworms, insects, minnows, occasionally small frogs. Can extract land snails from thin shells.
• northern redbelly snake, *Storeria occipitomaculata occipitomaculata*	Insectivorous ground ambusher. Hibernates and lays eggs belowground. Nocturnal in hot weather.	Eats slugs, earthworms, soft insects and larvae, sow bugs, occasionally salamanders.
• racer, *Coluber constrictor*	Carnivorous ground ambusher. Good climber. Lays eggs belowground. Not actually a constrictor.	Eats large insects, frogs, lizards, snakes, small rodents, birds.
• rough green snake, *Opheodrys aestivus*	Arboreal insectivore, graceful and mild tempered. Lays eggs twice per year.	Grasshoppers, crickets, caterpillars, spiders.

NICHES & HABITAT NEEDS OF BENEFICIAL VERTEBRATES: BIRDS

Species	Guild/Niche Strategies	Animal Foods
Goatsuckers: ORDER Caprimulgiformes, FAMILY Caprimulgidae		
• nighthawk, *Chordeiles minor*	Insectivorous air screener. Mainly eats at night and twilight, sometimes in daytime. Tropical migrant.	Eats flying mosquitoes, grasshoppers, leaf chafers, June beetles. Eats night-flying moths that damage fruit trees. Sometimes eats crickets, ants, and beetles off the ground. 100% insect diet.
nightjars: • whip-poor-will, *Caprimulgus vociferus* • chuck-will's-widow, *Caprimulgus carolinensis*	Insectivorous air screeners. Ambush from perches, sometimes ground forage. Nocturnal. Tropical migrants.	Same as above.
Swifts and Hummingbirds: ORDER Apodiformes		
Swifts: FAMILY Apodidae • *Chaetura, Cypseloides,* and *Aeronautes* spp. • chimney swift, *Chaetura pelagica*	Insectivorous air screeners. Cannot perch, must hang on vertical surfaces. Migratory (tropics).	Feed exclusively on flying insects such as flies and beetles.
Hummingbirds: FAMILY Trochilidae • ruby-throated hummingbird, *Archilochus colubris*	Omnivorous: floral hover-gleaner, insectivorous air ambusher. Tree branch nester. Migratory (tropics).	Pollinator. Eats many tiny insects, especially when breeding and raising young: flies, gnats, mosquitoes. Bringer of great joy in the garden.
Woodpeckers: ORDER Piciformes, FAMILY Picidae		
• downy woodpecker, *Picoides pubescens* • hairy woodpecker, *Picoides villosus*	Insectivorous bark gleaners. Nest in tree cavities and crevices. Year-round residents.	Eat wood-boring ants, caterpillars, beetle larvae, codling moth larvae, borers, aphids, scale, weevils, and plant and bark lice; 70–85% of diet.

Plant Foods	Habitats	Key Habitat Requirements
N/A	Dry to moist forests, often near streams; in loose soil of gardens, pastures; under debris. Prefers loose, porous, sandy soils. To 4,300 ft/1,300 m.	Needs loose, porous, sandy soils for hiding and hibernating. Also uses decayed logs, stones, leaves, other debris to hide. Home range less than 1/4 acre/1,000 sq m.
N/A	Ubiquitous. Urban and rural areas, dry or moist, disturbed and successional. Rare in old-growth forests.	Stones, leaf piles, banks, logs, brush piles. Needs anthills, mammal tunnels for hibernation. Goes belowground in hot weather. 10–15 ft/3–5 m average daily movement.
N/A	Prefers woodlands and upland woody ridges but uses many habitats, including moist and wet areas; to 5,600 ft/1,700 m. Under surface debris.	Woodland debris: bark, rotting wood.
N/A	Oldfields, grasslands, grassy streams, brush, open woodland, rocky wooded hillsides, mountain meadows; to 7,000 ft/2,150 m.	Lays eggs in rotting stumps, sawdust, under rocks, in small mammal tunnels. Hibernates in groups in rocky hillsides.
N/A	Up to 20 ft/6 m high in vines, bushes, trees near or overhanging water; to 5,000 ft/1,500 m.	Lush green vegetation overhanging water.

Plant Foods	Habitats	Key Habitat Requirements
N/A	Grasslands, cultivated fields, clearings, prairies. Always in open areas.	Lays eggs directly on well-drained ground; prefers gravel roofs in urban areas. Territory averages 26 acres/11 ha in Detroit, MI.
N/A	Dry, open, deciduous or mixed woods, early successional forests. Prefer stands near large clearings and brushy field edges.	Need perches to ambush flying insects. Lay eggs directly on well-drained ground in open or under brush. Kansas whip-poor-will territories average 7–25 acres/3–10 ha.
N/A	Chimney swifts mainly inhabit built areas with nearby brush or woods. Others found mainly in open and wooded habitats.	Nest in vertical cavities in cliffs, hollow trees, or buildings: chimneys, silos, wells, walls, etc.
Tubular nectar-bearing flowers, e.g., trumpet vine, honeysuckle.	Various wooded habitats, dense to open, deciduous to coniferous, orchards, edges, gardens, parks.	Needs tubular nectary flowers. Prefers red flowers. Nests on down-sloping tree branches, frequently over running water, sheltered overhead by leaves. Feeding territory 0.25 acres/1,000 sq m.
Small fruit and berries; acorns, hazelnuts; 15–30% of diet.	Downy: deciduous, mixed, or urban forests, orchards, forest edges, farmyards. Hairy: all forest types, but prefer mature bottomlands.	Need living or dead trees a minimum of 6 in/15 cm (downy) or 10 in/25 cm (hairy) in diameter for nesting. Downy prefers trees 10–22 in/25–56 cm in diameter with many saplings nearby. Territories average 2–10 acres/0.8–4 ha (downy) and 6–25 acres/2–10 ha (hairy).

NICHES & HABITAT NEEDS OF BENEFICIAL VERTEBRATES: BIRDS *continued*

Species	Guild/Niche Strategies	Animal Foods
Perching Songbirds: ORDER Passeriformes		
Tyrant Flycatchers: FAMILY Tyrannidae		
• flycatchers, *Empidonax* spp. • pewees, *Contopus* spp. • kingbirds, *Tyrannus* spp.	Insectivorous air salliers, some leaf gleaning. Nest sites vary by spp.: ground, shrubs, and tree twigs, branches, and cavities. Migratory (mainly to the tropics).	Eat mostly mosquitoes and other true flies, also other small flying insects. Help control agricultural pests such as curculios. Kingbirds: 90% insect diet, mainly pests.
• phoebes, *Sayornis* spp.	Insectivorous air salliers. Nest in rock outcrops, upturned tree roots, human habitats. Migratory (tropics, s. US).	89% flying insect diet: bees, wasps, ants, beetles, grasshoppers, crickets, flies, true bugs, spiders, and curculios!
Vireos: FAMILY Vireonidae		
• *Vireo* spp.	Insectivorous gleaners: upper, middle, or lower canopy and canopy interior or fringe, depending on spp. All species nest on tree twigs. Migratory (tropics, s. US).	Eat mostly caterpillars, leaf rollers, beetles, moths, true bugs, ants, flies, snails; also spiders, bees, wasps. Most vireos over 90% insect diet.
Chickadees and Titmice: FAMILY Paridae		
• chickadees, *Poecile* spp. • titmice, *Baeolophus* spp.	Insectivorous lower-canopy gleaners, omnivorous in winter. Tree cavity and crevice nesters. Resident.	Caterpillars, ants, aphids, scale, plant lice, sawfly larvae, weevils, leafhoppers, flies, etc. (summer); dormant insects and eggs (winter). 50–70% of diet.
Nuthatches: FAMILY Sittidae		
• *Sitta* spp.	Insectivorous bark gleaners, omnivorous in winter. Cavity and crevice nesters. Mainly resident. May winter in s. US.	Eat weevils, scales, borers, gypsy moth and tent caterpillars, cankerworms, insect eggs. All of summer diet, 60% of yearly.
Creepers: FAMILY Certhiidae		
• brown creeper, *Certhia americana*	Insectivorous bark gleaner. Tree crevice and cavity nester. Resident and migrant. May move to s. US for winter.	Insects: small beetles, ants, true bugs, caterpillars, spiders.
Wrens: FAMILY Troglodytidae		
• several genera and species	Insectivorous ground and lower-canopy gleaners. Mainly tree cavity and crevice nesting. Some species resident, some migrate to s. U.S.	Primarily (95%) eat many kinds of insects gleaned from ground litter, tree trunks, shrub branches, leaves: ants, flies, millipedes, spiders, etc.
Thrushes: FAMILY Turdidae		
• blue bird, *Sialia sialis*	Omnivorous ground gleaner. Low tree cavity and crevice nester. Resident in s. US, also winters in tropics.	Insects 70% of diet: grasshoppers, beetles, crickets, caterpillars; also moths, borers, weevils, aphids, bugs, snails, spiders.
Wood Warblers: FAMILY Parulidae		
• numerous genera and species	All insectivorous gleaners, mostly in upper or lower canopies, some on bark or ground. Diverse nesting habits. Mainly tropical migrants.	Eat ants, aphids, cankerworms, locusts, plant lice, borers, beetles, bugs, caterpillars, scale, mosquitoes, eggs of many insects, etc.

Plant Foods	Habitats	Key Habitat Requirements
Small amounts of small fruit and berries.	Varies by species: all kinds of woodlands and forests; edges; urban, suburban, and agricultural areas; parks; swamps; etc. High, low, and midelevation.	Perches from which to sally forth. Each species has specific habitat requirements. Some spp. benefit from forest fragmentation, others don't. Territories vary widely: <1–10 acres/0.4–4 ha depending on species and habitat.
11% small fruits and berries.	Prefer open areas near water. Also partially open woods, edges, wooded ravines, and agricultural and suburban areas.	Sheltered nesting ledges. Low, conspicuous perches to sally forth from; usually have favorite perches. Territories 0.7–3.5 acres/0.3–1.4 ha.
Small amounts of fruit and berries.	Various successional and forest types, from brushy tree–scrub mosaics to extensive unbroken mature forest, depending on species. Few prefer coniferous forest.	Habitat types most determinant, each spp. with own preferences. Most territories 1–3 acres/0.4–1.2 ha, but range from <1–12.5 acres/0.4–5 ha. Yellow-throated and red-eyed need min. 250 acres/100 ha for viable populations.
Small berries, seeds, mast important in winter. 30–50% of diet.	Woodlands, thickets, orchards, urban areas. Chickadees inhabit all forest types. Titmice prefer broadleaf trees.	Chickadees: standing dead trees >4 in/10 cm in diameter for nesting and feeding. Titmice: nesting cavities in deciduous or mixed woods. Territories: 2–17 acres/0.8–7 ha.
Berries, seeds, pine nuts, and mast bulk of winter diet, 40% of yearly.	Mature to open mixed, deciduous, or coniferous forest, depending on spp. Some prefer forest edges, parks, suburbs, etc.	Cavities in live or dead trees, preferably >12 in/30 cm in diameter. Territories 17–50 acres/7–20 ha!
A small amount of vegetable material, esp. mast. Suet.	Dense, mature forests and forested wetlands with standing dead trees with loose bark. Upland forests within 200 ft/61 m of water. Winter: open woods, parks, suburbs.	Nest sites critical to creeper success: builds behind loose bark flaps on live, dead, or dying trees. May use rotted knotholes or old woodpecker cavities.
Berries and wild fruits a small portion of diet, if at all.	Upland species like brushy areas, whether within or outside of woodlands. Various spp. prefer coniferous, mixed, or deciduous woods.	Low brushy vegetation, alone or within wooded areas. House wren: nesting cavities in trees >10 in/25 cm in diameter. Winter wren will nest in stumps, logs, other low cavities. Territories <1–10 acres/0.4–4 ha for upland species.
Fleshy fruits and berries compose about 30% of diet.	Fields, orchards, farmland, shelterbelts, suburbs, riparian woods, forest clearings.	Birdhouses, low cavities for nesting. Feeds in areas of bare soil or sparse ground cover. Starlings outcompeting it in many areas. Home range: 5 acres/2 ha.
Most don't eat plant matter. Eat berries and seeds only if insects scarce, if ever.	Virtually all are forest, brush, and forest-edge dwellers. Each species has specific habitat preferences.	Special needs vary tremendously by species, mainly based on preferred habitat types. Viable warbler populations need minimum areas from 25–750 acres/10–300 ha depending on species.

NICHES & HABITAT NEEDS OF BENEFICIAL VERTEBRATES: BIRDS *continued*

Species	Guild/Niche Strategies	Animal Foods
Tanagers: FAMILY Thraupidae • scarlet tanager, *Piranga olivacea*	Insectivorous upper-canopy gleaner: gleans twigs, leaves, dead branches. Tree twig nester. Tropical migrant.	86% of diet is animals; prefers caterpillars, bugs, moths, beetles, ants, bees, wasps. Also eats leaf rollers and borers.
Icterids: FAMILY Icteridae • orchard oriole, *Icterus spurius* • Baltimore oriole, *Icterus galbula*	Insectivorous upper-canopy gleaners. Tree twig and branch nesters. Tropical migrants.	Insects gleaned from foliage 80–90% of diet. Eat caterpillars, locusts, grasshoppers, leaf miners, rose chafers, cabbage worms, curculios.

NICHES & HABITAT NEEDS OF BENEFICIAL VERTEBRATES: MAMMALS

Species	Guild/Niche Strategies	Animal Foods
Bats: ORDER Chiroptera		
Plain-Nosed Bats: FAMILY Vespertilionidae • small brown bats, *Myotis* spp.	Insectivorous air hawkers. Nocturnal. Breeding sites include tree cavities, crevices, buildings. Hibernate in winter, usually in caves.	Feed on flying insects: flies, moths, flying ants, mosquitoes, bugs, ground beetles.
Insectivores: ORDER Insectivora		
Shrews: FAMILY Soricidae • mainly *Sorex* spp.	Mainly insectivorous ground gleaners. Nocturnal and diurnal. Generally active year-round. Breed belowground.	Eat adult and larval stages of beetles, ants, moths, and flies; also eat snails, slugs, spiders, mice, voles, grasshoppers.
Moles: FAMILY Talpidae • hairy-tailed mole, *Parascalops breweri* • eastern mole, *Scalopus aquaticus*	Insectivorous ground gleaners. Nocturnal aboveground, but active day and night all year. Tunnels aerate soil.	Eat grubs, insects, insect larvae, slugs, and snails. 82–97% animal-food diet.

Plant Foods	Habitats	Key Habitat Requirements
14% of diet is fruits, including cherry, mulberry, raspberry, elderberry.	Inhabits many successional stages. Prefers mature deciduous or mixed forest. Wooded parks and suburbs, orchards, roadsides, power-line cuts.	Most nests occur in trees >9 in/23 cm in diameter. Territories 4–7 acres/2–3 ha. A viable tanager population requires about 250 acres/10 ha minimum.
Small fruit and berries under 10–20% of diet. Baltimore oriole drinks juice from grapes.	Orchards, farmlands, gardens, suburban shade trees, rural roads, riparian zones, floodplains, open woods, open areas with scattered trees.	Avoids heavy forest. Orchard oriole nests usually 10–20 ft/3–6 m high, on a forked tree or shrub twig. Baltimore oriole usually nests 25–30 ft/8–9 m high on long, drooping deciduous branches. Territories 3–10 acres/1–4 ha.

Plant Foods	Habitats	Key Habitat Requirements
N/A	Forage over water, in open woods, along forest trails, at forest edges, and at different heights in forest depending on species. Prefer to roost in larger trees and in larger tree stands.	Need day and night roosting areas: under loose bark of live or dead trees >16 in /41 cm in diameter, in hollow trees or tree cavities, in caves, on cliffs, under stones, and in out-buildings, attics, and bathouses. Home ranges mostly unknown.
N/A	Damp deciduous or coniferous woodland or meadows; bogs or moist swales.	Need ground cover: leaves, leaf mold, rotten logs, rocks, stumps, herbaceous vegetation. Some spp. like crevices, rubble, stone walls, tunnels of other animals, woody debris. Known home ranges vary from 0.1–2.5 acres/400 sq m–1 ha, with most under 1 acre/0.4 ha.
Will eat some plant matter.	Uplands; open woods, meadows. Use surface tunnels for foraging and deep tunnels for nesting.	Require loose, well-drained, loamy soils, free of rocks, heavy clay, or gravel. Home ranges from 0.1–0.4 acres/400–1,600 sq m.

NICHES AND HABITAT NEEDS OF BENEFICIAL ARTHROPODS

This table focuses on species and groups from the eastern United States, though most go beyond that range. Species are diurnal (daytime active) unless otherwise noted, and are listed in taxonomic order.

Thanks to Jonathan Bates for his first round on this table. References: Arnett, Jr., 2000; ATTRA, 1999a; Borror and White, 1970; Delaplane and Mayer, 2000; The Green Spot, Ltd., 2003; Olkowski, Daar, and Olkowski, 1991; Pickett and Bugg, 1998; Yepsen, Jr., 1984.

NICHES & HABITAT NEEDS OF BENEFICIAL ARTHROPODS: ARACHNIDS		
Species	**Guild/Niche Strategies**	**Animal Foods**
Spiders: ORDER Araneae; 38,834 recorded species in US and Canada		
	Generalist, venomous, insectivorous web builders, running foragers, and ambushers on the ground and in all vegetation layers. Different species specialize in different habitats, foraging times, places, and styles. Hibernate in soil, mulch, crevices, and dead plant parts.	Flying and crawling insects, insect eggs, also other small animals. They catch and eat whatever is most abundant, thereby preventing pest explosions.
Mites: ORDER Acari		
Predatory Mites: FAMILY Phytoseiidae	Specialist foraging predators or parasites of insect or arachnid eggs, larvae, or adults.	Pest mites, thrips, scale, grasshoppers, other organisms. Used to control spider mites in orchards, greenhouses, indoor plants.

NICHES & HABITAT NEEDS OF BENEFICIAL ARTHROPODS: CENTIPEDES: 2,500 recorded species in the world		
Species	**Guild/Niche Strategies**	**Animal Foods**
Centipedes: CLASS Chilopoda	Generalist, venomous ground-foraging insectivores. Primarily nocturnal. May live as long as six years.	Small insects and arthropods, slugs, other organisms.

NICHES & HABITAT NEEDS OF BENEFICIAL ARTHROPODS: INSECTS: 87,107 recorded species in US and Canada		
Species	**Guild/Niche Strategies**	**Animal Foods**
Dragonflies and Damselflies: ORDER Odonata (chewing mouthparts); 407 recorded species in US and Canada		
	Adults: insectivorous air hawkers. Larvae: carnivorous aquatic foragers. Eggs laid in water.	Adults: mosquitoes and other flying insects; Larvae: aquatic insects, any prey small enough for them to catch and eat.

Plant Foods	Habitats	Key Habitat Requirements
N/A	Virtually all terrestrial and wetland habitats. More abundant in moist, well-vegetated environments. 64,000–2,265,000 spiders per acre in temperate meadow sites!	*Sensitive to both mechanical and chemical disturbances.* Their soft bodies need high humidity and moderate temperatures. Mulch, especially grass-legume hay, is critical for spider habitat. Need plants and interstices for web placement. Overwintering sites: dead seed heads, hollow stems, plant clumps, leaf litter, crevices, in soil under specific plant species, e.g., yarrow, comfrey, tansy, chicory. Trunk bands and trunk traps increase winter survival and spring populations. Preferred foliage to rest on includes yarrow, borage, *Malva* spp., fennel, comfrey, *Trifolium repens*.
Pollen is alternative food source, particularly grass pollen.	Soil, litter, humus, manure, bark, leaves, animal skin and hair, aquatic ecosystems.	*Sensitive to both mechanical and chemical disturbances.* Moderate air temperatures, not too dry. Can wipe out prey species and then die out; must have stable source of food to survive: provide grasses for pollen. Trunk bands and trunk traps can increase winter survival and spring populations.

Plant Foods	Habitats	Key Habitat Requirements
N/A	Soil, under debris, in rotting wood, leaf litter, under bark, protected places.	Moist, protected places: soil, litter, debris.

Plant Foods	Habitats	Key Habitat Requirements
N/A	Adults usually found near water, but some spp. can range for many miles. Larvae live in ponds and streams in various microhabitats: plant stems, mud, rocks, bottom surface.	Even small ponds attract these beneficials. They like relatively open areas but also go into woods.

NICHES & HABITAT NEEDS OF BENEFICIAL ARTHROPODS: INSECTS *continued*

Species	Guild/Niche Strategies	Animal Foods
Earwigs: ORDER Dermaptera (chewing mouthparts); 20 recorded species in US and Canada		
	Omnivorous generalist foragers. Nocturnal. Most die in fall; some survive in soil, mulch, protected crevices. Lay eggs in damp places. Larvae similar to adults.	Eggs, young, and adults of mites, insects, psyllids, nematodes; shown effective as biocontrol for aphids on apples.
Mantids and Cockroaches: ORDER Dictyoptera (chewing mouthparts); 69 recorded species in US and Canada		
Praying Mantids: FAMILY Mantidae; 20 spp. in US and Canada		
	Generalist insectivorous stalkers and ambushers. Larvae overwinter in egg cases; adults may hibernate through southern winters.	Small insects when young, larger as they grow. Adults can eat small salamanders, shrews, and frogs. Often cannibalistic. More iconic than effective biocontrol agent.
True Bugs: ORDER Hemiptera (sucking mouthparts); 3,834 recorded species in US and Canada		
Stink Bugs: FAMILY Pentatomidae; 260 spp. in US, and Canada		
• Tribe Discocerini mostly predaceous, including spined soldier bug, *Podisus maculiventris*	Generalist insectivorous predators (other tribes herbivorous). Disperse by flying.	Only some spp. eat animals: caterpillars, beetle larvae, bedbugs. Spined soldier bug eats larvae, caterpillars, especially Colorado potato beetle, Mexican bean beetle. Cannibalistic.
Seed Bugs: FAMILY Lygaeidae; 318 spp. in US and Canada SUBFAMILY Geocorinae • big-eyed bugs, *Geocoris* spp.; 25 species in US and Canada	Omnivorous, generalist ground predators. Lay eggs on the ground and in dried plant matter. Disperse by flying.	Mites, fly larvae, aphids, leafhoppers, cabbage loopers, flea beetles.
Ambush Bugs: FAMILY Phymatidae; 27 spp. in US and Canada		
	Generalist insectivorous flower and foliage ambushers. Disperse by flying.	Wide insect and mite food range; insects as large as bumblebees.
Assassin Bugs: FAMILY Reduviidae; 157 spp. in US and Canada		
	Mainly generalist insectivorous foliage foragers. Lay eggs in soil and under rocks. Disperse by flying. Some spp. blood-sucking.	Predators of aphids, fly larvae, caterpillars, bedbugs, leafhoppers, tomato hornworms, bees.
Damsel Bugs: FAMILY Nabidae; 34 spp. in US and Canada		
(Especially *Nabis* spp.)	Generalist insectivorous and nectari-vorous predators, foliage foragers. Disperse by flying.	Aphids, leafhoppers, thrips, treehoppers, mites, caterpillars.
Minute Pirate Bugs, Flower Bugs: FAMILY Anthocoridae; 89 species in US and Canada		
(Especially *Orius* spp.)	Generalist insectivorous foliage or ground predators. Disperse by flying.	Eat corn earworms, pear psyllas, codling moths, thrips, mites, caterpillars, aphids, leafhopper nymphs, insect eggs.
Plant Bugs: FAMILY Miridae; 1,930 spp. in US and Canada		
• Species in SUBFAMILY Isometopinae (7 spp.) and GENUS Deraeocoris (64 spp.), among others, are mostly predacious	Generalist insectivorous foliage predators. Disperse by flying. Many plant bugs are herbivorous, specializing on particular plant species.	Eat aphids, fly larvae, stinkbugs, scale.

Plant Foods	Habitats	Key Habitat Requirements
Algae, fungi, plant seedlings. Often blamed for plant damage caused by other animals.	Upper layers of soil, mulch, leaf litter. Hide in damp cracks and crevices, in small spaces, under rocks, boards, in rolled-up newspapers, etc.	Gather earwigs by placing plant pots stuffed with hay or straw upside down on the soil at night. Next day hang pot in aphid-infested trees. Corrugated bands on trees and hibernation boxes increase winter survival and spring populations.
N/A	Not native to N. America. Oldfields, meadows, thickets, hedgerows, roadside borders; sometimes attracted to lights to catch insects.	Egg cases must remain off the ground through winter and early spring to prevent waterlogging.
Most other spp. in family are plant feeders and damage fruit trees, vegetables, etc.	Widespread.	Overwinter in weeds, garden debris, and tree bark. Need ground cover for overwintering.
Adults feed on pollen, nectar, and seeds.	Throughout the US. Moist or dry sites, mostly on the ground, especially in sandy places, in woods, near streams; under weed clumps, sparse grass.	Dried leaves, dried stems, hollow stems for laying eggs. Ground cover for overwintering: logs and vegetation. Cool season cover crops.
N/A	Tall weeds, dense woods, along streams, alluvial areas. Prefer goldenrods, but hide in any vegetation, especially flowers.	Ground cover for overwintering.
N/A	Throughout US, various habitats in all vegetation layers.	Ground cover for overwintering: vegetation, logs, stones, loose bark, etc.
Adults feed on nectar.	Very common throughout US. Mainly on low herbaceous vegetation.	Nectar-bearing flowers to attract adults. Ground cover for overwintering. Preferred plants include *Borago officinalis* and *Medicago sativa*.
Nymphs feed on pollen.	Common. Found on flowers, under bark, in leaf litter, or in fungi, from field crops to trees.	Weeds and leaf litter. Maintain permanent plantings. Provide flowers with a rich supply of pollen and nectar, i.e., clover, daisies, goldenrod, yarrow.
Most other members of this family are herbivores and can be major pests.	Very common. In all vegetation layers. Often abundant.	Hedgerows and flowers. Ground cover for overwintering. Different species specialize in different habitats or prey on insects only on certain plant species.

NICHES & HABITAT NEEDS OF BENEFICIAL ARTHROPODS: INSECTS *continued*

Species	Guild/Niche Strategies	Animal Foods
Jumping Ground Bugs: FAMILY Dipsocoridae; 6 spp. in US and Canada		
	Generalist insectivorous ground predators. Disperse by flying.	Wide insect and mite food range.

Lacewings and Allies: ORDER Neuroptera (chewing mouthparts); 349 recorded species in US and Canada

Species	Guild/Niche Strategies	Animal Foods
Green Lacewings: FAMILY Chrysopidae; 87 spp. in US and Canada		
Brown Lacewings: FAMILY Hemerobidae; 60 spp. in US and Canada		
	Insectivorous foliage predators specializing in soft-bodied insects. Adults nocturnal. Lay eggs on undersides of leaves.	Adult brown and larvae of both groups eat soft-bodied insects: aphids, caterpillars, mites, scales, thrips, insect eggs, mealybugs.

Beetles: ORDER Coleoptera (chewing mouthparts); 23,701 recorded species in US and Canada

Species	Guild/Niche Strategies	Animal Foods
Ladybird Beetles: FAMILY Coccinellidae; 399 spp. in US and Canada		
	Insectivorous foliage foragers. Some spp. migrate to hibernation sites in late spring after gorging.	Adults and larvae are predators of aphids, whiteflies, scales, mealybugs, psyllids, mites, and insect eggs.
Ground Beetles: FAMILY Carabidae; 2,271 spp. in US and Canada		
	Running ground and foliage predators, some carrion eaters and parasites. Mostly generalists, but some specialists. Mostly nocturnal. Most larvae also predaceous.	Mites, snails, slugs, earthworms, nematodes, many insects, including cutworms, fly eggs and larvae, cabbage root maggots, Colorado potato beetles, aphids, and other soil organisms. Some eat gypsy moths, cankerworms, and tent caterpillars.
Rove Beetles: FAMILY Staphylinidae; 3,187 spp. in US and Canada		
	Mainly omnivorous running ground and foliage scavengers; some parasites.	Most common species are carrion eaters. Predaceous species eat various insects and mites, ants, termites, mainly in decaying organic matter.

Bees, Wasps, and Ants: ORDER Hymenoptera (chewing mouthparts); 17,777 recorded species in US and Canada

Species	Guild/Niche Strategies	Animal Foods
Braconid Wasps: FAMILY Braconidae; 1,937 spp. in US and Canada		
	Larvae: specialist insect-larva parasitoids. Adults: nectarivorous. Adults 1/16–1/2 in/2–15 mm in length. Solitary, not social wasps. Eggs laid in or near host; larvae pupate in host.	Parasitoids mainly of larvae, especially of moths and butterflies, but also beetles, flies, wasps, spiders, cabbage worms, codling moths, gypsy moths, Oriental fruit moths, tent caterpillars, strawberry leaf rollers, European corn borers, cutworms, tomato hornworms, sawflies, wood-boring beetles, aphids.

Plant Foods	Habitats	Key Habitat Requirements
N/A	In moist places on the ground. Moss, leaf litter, ant nests, along margins of streams and lakes.	Moist environment, leaf litter. Ground cover for overwintering.
Adults of some green spp. feed on pollen and nectar.	Brown tends toward wooded habitats. Green prefers more open habitats: grass, weeds, shrubs.	Preferred egg-laying sites include the undersides of large or hairy leaves of spp. such as *Achillea millefolium, Ajuga reptans, Anthriscus silvestris, Borago officinalis, Malva moschata, Oenothera biennis, Symphytum officinale, Trifolium pratense, Urtica dioica.* Provide nectar and pollen all season. Artificial hibernation sites increase winter survival and spring populations for better pest control. Lacewings overwinter well in forests.
Adults feed on pollen and nectar.	Abundant, widely distributed.	Garden mulch for overwintering. Prefer to hang out on *Urtica dioica, Medicago sativa, Symphytum officinale,* among others. Hibernate in perennial bunchgrasses, under leaves, under mullein.
N/A	Larvae develop in upper soil horizons. Adults mainly on the ground, but also may tunnel or climb plants, even into trees. Spring or autumn breeding. Overwinter in weedy, brushy areas. Like logs, rocks, grassy ground, stream and pond shores.	Provide ground cover, mulch, and permanent plantings such as clumping grasses. Preferred herbs for carabids to rest on include *Borago officinalis, Medicago sativa, Trifolium repens.* Preferred overwintering sites for carabids include the soil under *Achillea millefolium,* among others.
Many species eat fungi.	In decaying vegetable matter, compost piles, moss, fungi, dung, carrion; under stones; near creeks; under bark; in caves and animal nests; on flowers.	Provide mulch, rotting vegetable matter, debris, fungi.
Adults: nectar from small, short-throated flowers. May also feed on pollen.	Widely distributed, found almost everywhere.	Small flowering plants rich in nectar, i.e., dill, yarrow, mustard, fennel—umbels and asters in general. Seem to prefer the foliage of alfalfa, borage, brassicas, umbels, asters, Papilionoideae (a subfamily of legumes). Prefer overwintering in soil under *Achillea millefolium* and *Symphytum officinale,* among other "weeds" in European studies. Small size increases susceptibility to wind; use windbreaks. Braconids are most active at high temperatures and low humidity.

NICHES & HABITAT NEEDS OF BENEFICIAL ARTHROPODS: INSECTS *continued*

Species	Guild/Niche Strategies	Animal Foods
Ichneumonid Wasps: FAMILY Ichneumonidae; 7,775 spp. in US and Canada		
	Larvae: specialist or generalist insect-larva or insect-pupa parasitoids. Adults: nectarivorous and pollenivorous. Adults 1/8–1.5 in/3–40 mm long.	Parasitoids of moth and butterfly caterpillars, sawflies, wood-boring beetles and their larvae, aphids.
Chalcid Wasps: SUPERFAMILY Chalcidoidea; 2,223 spp. in US and Canada		
The most beneficial families include Chalcididae, Encyrtidae, Eulophidae, Eurytomidae, Mymaridae (fairyflies), Pteromalidae, Torymidae, Trichogrammatidae	Larvae: mostly specialist parasitoids of insect pupae, larvae, and eggs. Adults: nectarivorous. Adults rarely over 1/8 in/4 mm long.	Parasitoids of scales, aphids, mealybugs, beetles, moths, butterflies, flies, true bugs, wasps, ants, weevils, thrips, leafhoppers, psyllids, mites, spruce budworms, tomato hornworms, cotton bollworms, corn earworms, corn borers, codling moths.
True Wasps: FAMILY Vespidae		
Potter Wasps: SUBFAMILY Eumeninae; 70 spp. in US and Canada		
	Solitary or social. Larvae: insect larvae, nursery fed. Adults: predatory nectivores. Mud-nest builders, as "pots" on ground surface, in burrows, or on twigs, branches, etc. Generally docile.	Adults provision their nests with paralyzed (stung) caterpillars, beetle larvae, other larvae for their own larvae to eat.
Hornets and Yellow Jackets: SUBFAMILY Vespinae; 18 spp. in US and Canada		
	Mostly social. Larvae: mostly insectivorous, nursery fed. Adults: opportunist predatory omnivores. Hornets nest aboveground, yellow jackets below. Fertilized queens hibernate over winter. Generally aggressive.	Adults feed their larvae both immature and adult paralyzed (stung) soft-bodied insects, spiders, and small animals of many kinds, alive or dead. *Vespa crabro*, the European hornet, eats grasshoppers, horseflies, flies, bees, yellow jackets.
Paper Wasps: SUBFAMILY Polistinae; 19 spp. in US and Canada, mostly in south		
	Usually social. Larvae: insect larvae, nursery fed. Adults: insectivorous. Make a paper nest with no outer covering hanging by a thread in a protected place. Generally docile.	Adults predaceous, mainly insectivorous, eating caterpillars of tobacco hornworm, cabbage butterfly, etc., and other soft-bodied insects, such as aphids. One colony may kill over 2,000 caterpillars per year.
Digger Wasps: FAMILY Sphecidae; 1,139 spp. in US and Canada		
(Especially mud dauber wasp, *Pepsis mildei*)	Usually solitary. Larvae: nursery fed, insectivorous, some specialized. Adults: generally nectarivorous. Build mud nests in cavities, often in soil.	Adults provision larvae or feed them daily: caterpillars, beetle grubs, thrips, crickets, katydids, cockroach larvae, spiders, aphids, cutworms, true bugs, stinkbug larvae, flies, ants, leafhoppers.

Plant Foods	Habitats	Key Habitat Requirements
Same as above.	Same as above. Ichneumonids disperse readily over large distances.	Same as above. Ichneumonids are most active at moderate temperatures and high relative humidity. Some studies indicate they may be more active in shade than in full sun.
Same as above.	Same as above.	Same as above.
Adults eat nectar and pollen.	Widely distributed. Woody, brushy habitats for some species.	Nearby mud or damp soil for nest building.
Some adults girdle stems or twigs to drink sap and go after sweets and other foods, including meat.	Widely distributed. Both make paper nests with an outer covering. Hornets may nest in high or low forest canopies or in or on buildings.	A cavity or protected place to hang their nest, or loose, dry soil in which to burrow and make their nest. Water and dead wood for nest making.
N/A	Widely distributed.	A protected place to hang their nest. Sources of water and dead wood to make paper. Artificial nesting locations increase number of wasp colonies in a garden, and their predation rates.
Adults feed on nectar and pollen.	Widely distributed. Nest sites vary by spp.: belowground (various soils); inside hollow branches, twigs, grass stems, wood-borer sites, etc.; under bark. Some attach mud cells to various objects.	Water, mud to build nests. Brushy, weedy habitat. Loose, dry soil. Some species prefer specific flowers, e.g., umbels, sumac, elderberry, milkweed, *Ceanothus* spp.

NICHES & HABITAT NEEDS OF BENEFICIAL ARTHROPODS: INSECTS *continued*

Species	Guild/Niche Strategies	Animal Foods
Bees: SUPERFAMILY Apoidea; 3,547 species in US and Canada		
Yellow-faced Bees: FAMILY Colletidae; 153 spp. in US and Canada		
	Pollenivorous and nectarivorous. Wood or soil nesting.	N/A
Sweat Bees: FAMILY Halictidae; 502 spp. in US and Canada		
	Pollenivorous and nectarivorous. Ground nesting. Solitary, but some nest in groups.	N/A
Leaf-cutting and Mason Bees: FAMILY Megachilidae; 682 spp. in US and Canada		
• leaf cutter bees, *Megachile* spp.; 130 spp. in US and Canada	Pollenivorous and nectarivorous. Solitary; wood or soil nesting. 150 leaf-cutters do the pollination work of 3,000 honeybees. Docile.	N/A
• orchard mason bees, Osmia spp.; 140 species in US and Canada, including blue orchard bee, *Osmia lignaria*, and hornfaced bee, *Osmia cornifrons*	Pollenivorous and nectarivorous. Solitary or gregarious. Wood nesting.	N/A
Digger Bees: FAMILY Anthophoridae, SubFAMILY Anthophorinae; 321 spp. in US and Canada		
(Especially shaggy fuzzyfoot bee, *Anthophora pilipes villosula*)	Pollenivorous and nectarivorous. Solitary, ground nesting. May nest in dense aggregations. Shaggy fuzzyfoot native to Japan; active for 6 weeks in spring; will pollinate in the rain.	N/A
Bumblebees: FAMILY Apidae; 55 spp. in US and Canada		
(Especially *Bombus* spp.)	Pollenivorous and nectarivorous. Social, ground nesting. Annual: only fertilized queens hibernate; all workers die each year.	N/A
Honeybees: FAMILY Apidae		
• *Apis mellifera*	Pollenivorous and nectarivorous. Social. Aboveground cavity nesting.	N/A

Plant Foods	Habitats	Key Habitat Requirements
Pollen and nectar.	Widespread. Prefer midsuccession or other sunny, open habitats with diverse nectar and pollen plants.	Nest in plant stalks, insect burrows, and similar cavities, or in bare or lightly vegetated soil.
Pollen and nectar.	Common. Prefer midsuccession or other sunny, open habitats with diverse nectar and pollen plants.	Prefer dry, south-facing, sandy banks free of vegetation for nesting. Also nest in clay, stream banks, other locations.
Pollen and nectar.	Very common. Prefer midsuccession or other sunny, open habitats with diverse nectar and pollen plants. Most active in midsummer in temperatures above 70°F/21°C.	Nest in wood cavities, hollow plant stems, drilled wood blocks, or in earth. Prefer legume blossoms.
Pollen and nectar.	Prefer midsuccession or other sunny, open habitats with diverse nectar and pollen plants. Use existing holes in wood, straw, foam, etc., or build earthen cells on twigs or in plant galls or decaying wood. Some spp. construct small earthen cells on or under stones or in burrows.	Nests need to be near water so they can gather mud for nesting. Also, nests should be placed so they get morning sunlight. Eggs hatch at 50–55°F/10–13°C. Extreme cold and early thaws may kill hibernating bees. Excellent apple pollinators, much more efficient than honeybees. Rarely fly >300 ft/ 90 m from nests.
Pollen and nectar. All spp. store honey and pollen in nests for larvae.	Prefer midsuccession or other sunny, open habitats with diverse nectar and pollen plants. Shaggy fuzzyfoot: moist, warm climates; survives mild winters only.	Prefer cliff faces, earthen banks, adobe walls, etc. for nesting. Prefer sunny, open habitats with diverse nectar and pollen plants. Shaggy fuzzyfoot: pollinates blueberries, apples, other crops, mid-March to early June.
Pollen and nectar.	Undisturbed meadows, barns, woodlots. Prefer midsuccession or other sunny, open habitats with diverse nectar and pollen plants. Form small colonies of 100–500 workers. Work harder and faster at cooler temperatures and in windier and rainier weather than honeybees.	Prefer dry, south-facing, sandy banks with no vegetation for nesting. Need grassy thatch, unused rodent burrows to build nests. Nesting sites undisturbed for long term build populations over the years. Pollinate raspberries, blackberries, strawberries, cranberries, blueberries, and many others. The only pollinators of potatoes. Prefer red clover forage. Prefer to forage within 164–2,070 ft/50–63 m from their nest!
Pollen and nectar.	Cultivated, native to Eurasia, Africa. Widely naturalized, but parasites have now reduced viable hives.	Human-made hives, natural woodland cavities, buildings. Prefer to forage close to their nest, but will go several miles if necessary.

NICHES & HABITAT NEEDS OF BENEFICIAL ARTHROPODS: INSECTS *continued*

Species	Guild/Niche Strategies	Animal Foods
Flies: ORDER Diptera (sucking mouthparts); 16,914 recorded species in US and Canada		
Hoverflies (Syrphids): FAMILY Syriphidae; 874 spp. in US and Canada		
	Larvae: insectivorous foliage foragers or litter feeders. Adults: nectarivorous flying pollinators.	Larvae of many spp. eat aphids, thrips, leafhoppers, mealybugs, caterpillars, scale. Some scavenge in dung, carrion, rotting vegetation.
Robber Flies: FAMILY Asilidae; 883 spp. in US and Canada		
	Adults: insectivorous aerial predators. Larvae: predaceous ground or litter foragers.	Adults attack butterflies, moths, beetles, wasps, bees, and grasshoppers on the wing. Subterranean or litter-layer larvae eat grubs and grasshopper eggs.
Parasitic Flies: FAMILY Tachinidae; 1,277 spp. known in US and Canada, plus many other spp. undescribed		
	Larvae: insectivorous larval parasites, usually specialized. Adults: nectarivorous. Considered key to regulating pests in most terrestrial ecosystems.	Adults feed on insect honeydew. Larvae parasitize caterpillars and grubs, including European corn borers, cutworms, tent caterpillars, armyworms, gypsy moths, Japanese beetles, Mexican bean beetles, sawflies, bug and grasshopper larvae and adults.

Plant Foods	Habitats	Key Habitat Requirements
Adults feed on pollen and nectar. Pollen provides protein for egg laying.	Many habitats, usually on flowers.	Plant diverse nectary and pollen-bearing flowers to attract adults. Avoid spraying; they are sensitive to chemicals. Prefer to lay eggs on *Stellaria media*, *Viola arvensis*, *Cichorium intybus*, *Tanacetum vulgare*, among others. Tend to concentrate in wind-protected areas.
N/A	Adults in various habitats. Larvae in soil, in leaf litter, under bark, or in decaying wood. Adults rest on dead twigs and weeds or open ground.	Rotting wood, leaf litter, loose soil.
Adults feed on nectar.	Ubiquitous; in most terrestrial habitats. Adults look like houseflies or bees but stay near flowers.	Tend to benefit from plant intercrops and polycultures.

BENEFICIAL-ANIMAL HABITAT ELEMENTS

This table lists beneficial-animal habitat elements, the animals they support, and how the animals use them. It is based on the data in the previous tables in this appendix. Please use this as a rough guide only; more data is needed to confirm it.

BENEFICIAL-ANIMAL HABITAT ELEMENTS

| HABITAT ELEMENT | ANIMALS THAT USE THE HABITAT ELEMENT FOR: | |
	Feeding	Resting
Vegetation: ground layer/ground covers	spiders, mites, praying mantids, dragonflies, big-eyed bugs, assassin bugs, damsel bugs, flower bugs, plant bugs, ground beetles, braconid wasps, ichneumonid wasps, chalcid wasps, hornets, yellow jackets, shrews, moles, nighthawks, nightjars, wrens, thrushes, bluebirds, wood warblers, skinks, snakes, toads, frogs, tree frogs, salamanders	big-eyed bugs, assassin bugs, damsel bugs, flower bugs, plant bugs, ground beetles, braconid wasps, ichneumonid wasps, chalcid wasps, shrews, skinks, snakes, frogs, salamanders
Vegetation: herb layer	spiders, mites, praying mantids, dragonflies, big-eyed bugs, assassin bugs, damsel bugs, flower bugs, plant bugs, ground beetles, braconid wasps, ichneumonid wasps, chalcid wasps, hornets, yellowjackets, wrens	big-eyed bugs, assassin bugs, damsel bugs, flower bugs, plant bugs, ground beetles, braconid wasps, ichneumonid wasps, chalcid wasps, robber flies
Vegetation: shrub layer	spiders, mites, dragonflies, assassin bugs, flower bugs, plant bugs, hornets, yellowjackets, bats, vireos, wrens, tree frogs, northern redback salamanders	assassin bugs, flower bugs, plant bugs, robber flies, bats, vireos, wrens, tree frogs, northern redback salamanders
Vegetation: low tree layer	spiders, mites, dragonflies, assassin bugs, flower bugs, plant bugs, bats, woodpeckers, vireos, chickadees, titmice, wrens, wood warblers, tanagers, orioles, tree frogs, northern redback salamanders	assassin bugs, flower bugs, plant bugs, hornets, bats, woodpeckers, vireos, chickadees, titmice, wrens, wood warblers, tanagers, orioles, tree frogs
Vegetation: tall tree layer	spiders, mites, dragonflies, assassin bugs, flower bugs, plant bugs, hornets, bats, nighthawks, swifts, woodpeckers, vireos, wood warblers, tanagers, orioles, tree frogs	assassin bugs, flower bugs, plant bugs, bats, nighthawks, swifts, woodpeckers, vireos, wood warblers, tanagers, orioles, tree frogs
Trees > 4 in/10 cm in diameter standing dead	chickadees	
Trees > 6 in/15 cm in diameter living or dead		
Trees > 10–12 in/25–30 cm in diameter living or dead		
Moss	jumping ground bugs, rove beetles, tree frogs	jumping ground bugs, rove beetles, tree frogs

Nesting/Egg Laying	Overwintering
spiders, flower bugs, digger wasps, hoverflies, shrews, nighthawks, nightjars, flycatchers	spiders, stinkbugs, big-eyed bugs, ambush bugs, assassin bugs, damsel bugs, flower bugs, plant bugs, jumping ground bugs, lacewings, ladybird beetles, ground beetles, shrews
spiders, praying mantids, flower bugs, digger wasps, hoverflies, flycatchers	spiders, praying mantids, stinkbugs, ambush bugs, ground beetles
spiders, potter wasps, hornets, digger wasps, flycatchers, vireos	spiders, chickadees, titmice
spiders, potter wasps, hornets, hummingbirds, flycatchers, vireos, tanagers, orioles	woodpeckers, chickadees, titmice
spiders, potter wasps, hornets, flycatchers, vireos, tanagers, orioles	woodpeckers, chickadees, titmice
chickadees	
downy woodpecker	
hairy woodpecker, nuthatches, wrens, tanagers	

BENEFICIAL-ANIMAL HABITAT ELEMENTS *continued*

	ANIMALS THAT USE THE HABITAT ELEMENT FOR:	
HABITAT ELEMENT	**Feeding**	**Resting**
Fungi	flower bugs, rove beetles	flower bugs, rove beetles
Manure or dung	mites, rove beetles	mites, rove beetles
Nectar-bearing flowers	green lacewings, ladybird beetles, braconid wasps, ichneumonid wasps, chalcid wasps, potter wasps, digger wasps, bees (all), hover flies, parasitic flies, hummingbirds	
Pollen-bearing flowers	mites, flower bugs, green lacewings, ladybird beetles, chalcid wasps, potter wasps, digger wasps, bees (all), hoverflies	
Summer berries and fruits (small amounts)	flycatchers, phoebes, vireos, chickadees, titmice, nuthatches, wrens, thrushes, bluebirds, wood warblers, tanagers, orioles	
Summer seeds and nuts (mast)	woodpeckers, chickadees, titmice, nuthatches, creepers	
Autumn fruits (high in fat, nutrients)	woodpeckers	
Autumn seeds and nuts (mast)	woodpeckers	
High-carbohydrate winter berries	nuthatches	
High-carbohydrate winter seeds and nuts (mast)	woodpeckers, chickadees, titmice, nuthatches, creepers	
Suet	woodpeckers, creepers	
Airborne insects	bats, nighthawks, nightjars, swifts, flycatchers, hummingbirds	
Caves, rock crevices		
Buildings	spiders, centipedes, earwigs	spiders, centipedes, earwigs, bats, swifts
Cliffs, rock outcrops		swifts
Sheltered ledges		
Perches: high	nightjars, flycatchers	
Perches: low	flycatchers, phoebes	
Trunk bands		
Bark crevices	woodpeckers, nuthatches, creepers, wrens, wood warblers	
Cavities under bark, bark flaps	rove beetles, robber flies, woodpeckers	flower bugs, rove beetles, robber flies, bats
Tree cavities, hollow branches	woodpeckers	swifts
Insect/borer/drilled holes in wood	woodpeckers	

Nesting/Egg Laying	Overwintering
swifts	bats
spiders, hornets, paper wasps, honeybees, bats, swifts, phoebes	spiders, centipedes, earwigs, ladybird beetles
swifts, phoebes	
phoebes	
	spiders, mites, earwigs
woodpeckers, chickadees, titmice, nuthatches, creepers	spiders, mites, centipedes, earwigs, stinkbugs
digger wasps, bats, creepers	centipedes, earwigs, assassin bugs
hornets, paper wasps, digger wasps, yellow-faced bees, leafcutting bees, honeybees, bats, swifts, woodpeckers, flycatchers, chickadees, titmice, nuthatches, creepers, wrens, bluebirds, thrushes	
digger wasps, yellow-faced bees, leafcutting bees, mason bees (also in other materials: foam blocks, etc.)	

BENEFICIAL-ANIMAL HABITAT ELEMENTS *continued*

HABITAT ELEMENT	ANIMALS THAT USE THE HABITAT ELEMENT FOR:	
	Feeding	**Resting**
Protected overhangs		swifts
Straw-stuffed plant pots		earwigs
Plant clumps (dead or dormant)		ground beetles, robber flies, frogs
Dead seed heads		
Hollow stems, plant galls		
Leaf litter	soil organisms (especially fungi), spiders, jumping ground bugs, ground beetles, robber flies, shrews, skinks, snakes, salamanders	flower bugs, ground beetles, robber flies, shrews, skinks, snakes, frogs, salamanders
Mulch (diverse materials)	soil organisms (especially fungi), spiders, jumping ground bugs, ground beetles, rove beetles, robber flies, shrews, skinks, snakes, salamanders	flower bugs, ground beetles, rove beetles, robber flies, shrews, skinks, snakes, frogs, salamanders
Space on top of rocks		skinks, snakes (sunning)
Space under rocks, rock piles	shrews, skinks, snakes, salamanders	ground beetles, rove beetles, shrews, skinks, snakes, salamanders
Space under soil surface debris	rove beetles, robber flies, shrews, moles, skinks, snakes, salamanders	ground beetles, robber flies, shrews, skinks, snakes, salamanders
Brush piles	skinks, snakes, salamanders	skinks, snakes, frogs, tree frogs, salamanders
Dead logs, rotting wood, old stumps	soil organisms, rove beetles, robber flies, shrews, moles, skinks, snakes, salamanders	shrews, skinks, snakes, frogs, tree frogs, salamanders
Soil surface	big-eyed bugs, ground beetles, rove beetles, robber flies, skinks, snakes	big-eyed bugs, ground beetles, skinks, snakes
Loose, undisturbed soil	soil organisms, robber flies, shrews, moles	soil organisms, robber flies, shrews
Insect or animal burrows	shrews, moles	shrews, moles
Soil near surface	ground beetles, shrews, moles	ground beetles, shrews
Deep soil		shrews, moles
Dry soil	shrews, moles	shrews, moles
Sandy banks		
Damp soil, mud	garter snakes	garter snakes, tree frogs
Near ponds, streams	dragonflies, garter snakes, toads, frogs, tree frogs	garter snakes, toads, frogs, tree frogs
On water surface		
In water	dragonflies (nymphs), salamanders	dragonflies (nymphs)

Nesting/Egg Laying	Overwintering
hornets, paper wasps, bats, swifts	
	earwigs
big-eyed bugs, flower bugs	spiders, praying mantids, big-eyed bugs, stinkbugs, assassin bugs, flower bugs, lacewings, ladybird beetles, ground beetles
big-eyed bugs	spiders
big-eyed bugs, digger wasps, yellow-faced bees, leafcutting bees, mason bees	spiders, big-eyed bugs
big-eyed bugs, flower bugs	spiders, centipedes, earwigs, stinkbugs, big-eyed bugs, assassin bugs, flower bugs, plant bugs, jumping ground bugs, lacewings, ladybird beetles, ground beetles
flower bugs	soil organisms, spiders, centipedes, earwigs, stinkbugs, assassin bugs, flower bugs, plant bugs, jumping ground bugs, lacewings, ladybird beetles, ground beetles
mason bees	
mason bees, skinks	centipedes, earwigs, assassin bugs, ground beetles, skinks, salamanders
skinks, snakes, salamanders	centipedes, earwigs, stinkbugs, assassin bugs, jumping ground bugs, ground beetles, skinks, tree frogs, salamanders
skinks, snakes, salamanders	salamanders
hornets, yellowjackets, paper wasps (for nest making), mason bees (nest inside), wrens, skinks, snakes	soil organisms, centipedes, skinks, snakes, tree frogs, salamanders
potter wasps	
soil organisms, potter wasps, digger wasps, skinks	soil organisms, toads, salamanders
yellow-faced bees, mason bees, shrews	shrews, northern brown snake
potter wasps, digger wasps, digger bees, bumblebees, shrews, snakes	spiders, centipedes, earwigs, ground beetles, shrews, skinks, snakes, toads, salamanders
shrews, moles	shrews, moles, snakes, toads
yellowjackets, digger wasps, bumblebees, shrews, moles, snakes	shrews, moles, snakes
sweat bees, bumblebees, snakes	snakes
potter wasps, digger wasps, mason bees (for making nests)	
hornets, yellowjackets, paper wasps, digger wasps, mason bees (need water for nest making), hummingbirds, phoebes	
dragonflies	
toads, frogs, tree frogs	dragonfly eggs/nymphs

Plant Hardiness Zone Maps

Please note: Full-color versions of these maps are available in volume 1, appendix 2.

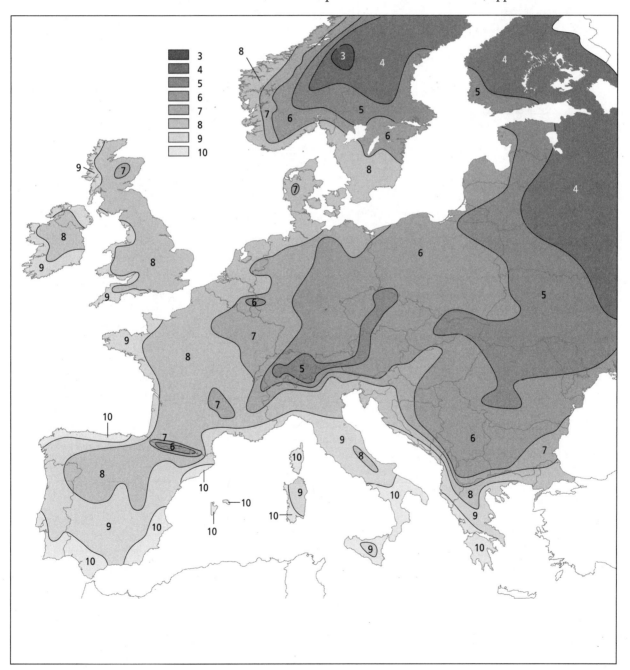

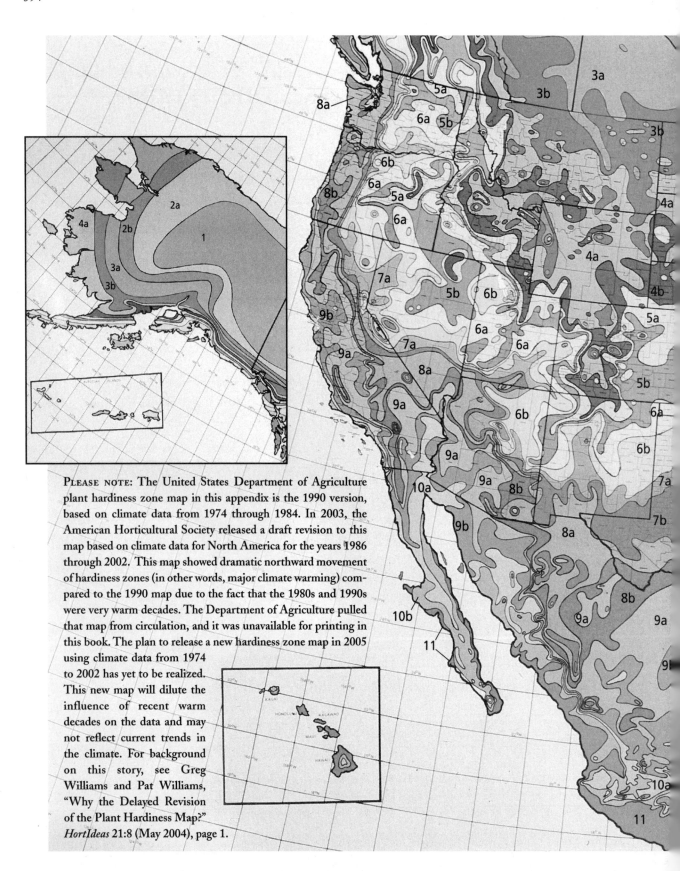

PLEASE NOTE: The United States Department of Agriculture plant hardiness zone map in this appendix is the 1990 version, based on climate data from 1974 through 1984. In 2003, the American Horticultural Society released a draft revision to this map based on climate data for North America for the years 1986 through 2002. This map showed dramatic northward movement of hardiness zones (in other words, major climate warming) compared to the 1990 map due to the fact that the 1980s and 1990s were very warm decades. The Department of Agriculture pulled that map from circulation, and it was unavailable for printing in this book. The plan to release a new hardiness zone map in 2005 using climate data from 1974 to 2002 has yet to be realized. This new map will dilute the influence of recent warm decades on the data and may not reflect current trends in the climate. For background on this story, see Greg Williams and Pat Williams, "Why the Delayed Revision of the Plant Hardiness Map?" *HortIdeas* 21:8 (May 2004), page 1.

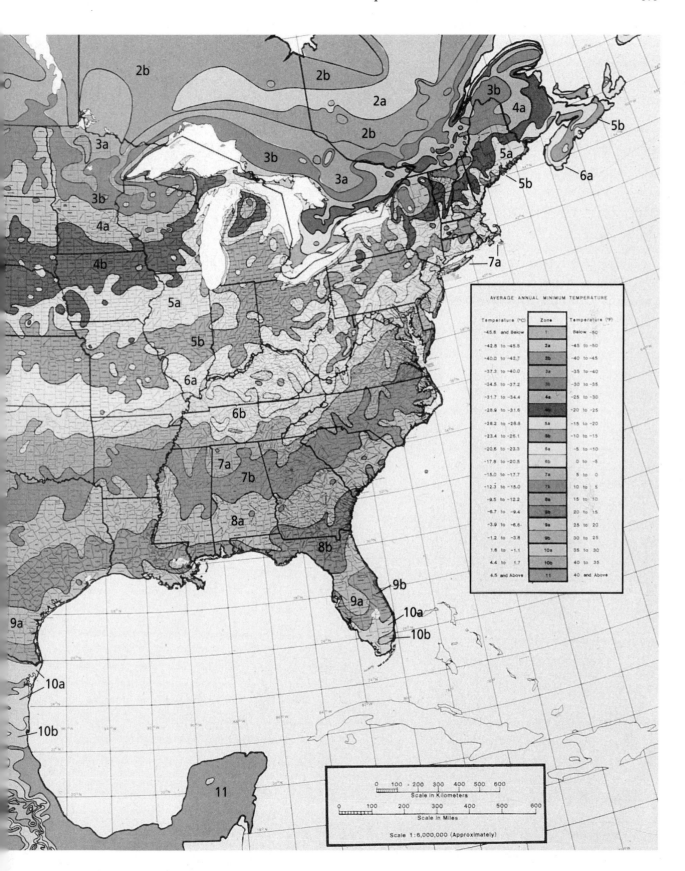

APPENDIX 7

Resources

PUBLICATIONS

FOREST GARDENING & PERENNIAL POLYCULTURES

Agroforestry News.
A quarterly magazine from the Agroforestry Research Trust featuring articles on forest garden design and profiles of useful plants for Britain. Available from the Agroforestry Research Trust (see under "Organizations"), and through the *Permaculture Activist* (see below).

Apios Institute for Regenerative Perennial Agriculture online database
Online resource featuring user-generated reports on forest garden species, polycultures, and garden designs. Online at www.apiosinstitute.org.

Creating a Forest Garden: Perennial Crops for a Changing Climate. MARTIN CRAWFORD.
Guide to forest gardening by director of the Agroforestry Research Trust, an international leader in temperate-climate perennial polycultures.

Designing and Maintaining Your Edible Landscape Naturally. ROBERT KOURIK.
A critical reference for forest gardeners, covering design, site preparation and planting, pest control, fertility, mulching, and more. Excellent. Definitely worth pursuing.

Farming in Nature's Image. JUDITH SOULE AND JON PIPER.
An important work on the science of perennial polycultures. Chapters 4 and 5 are required reading! They discuss the authors' work with the Land Institute to develop perennial polycultures modeled on the prairie ecosystem.

Forest Gardening. ROBERT HART.
The book that started it all, describing Hart's experiments in adapting the tropical forest polyculture model to his temperate climate. Inspirational, but not terribly informative.

How to Make a Forest Garden. PATRICK WHITEFIELD.
Fills in much of the practical information that Hart's book lacks. A useful handbook for forest gardening in the British climate.

Tree Crops: A Permanent Agriculture. J. RUSSELL SMITH.
Written in 1927, this classic book is one of the foundations of permaculture. Describes a tree-based agricultural model to provide food for humans and livestock.

A Year in a Forest Garden. MARTIN CRAWFORD.
Video presenting four seasons in Martin Crawford's forest garden, demonstrating species, theory, and practices like coppicing and harvesting.

USEFUL PLANTS & FUNGI

Cornucopia: A Source Book of Edible Plants. STEPHEN FACCIOLA.
Describes over three thousand species of edible plants, with sources to order each and every one! A powerful tool in the hands of an adventurous gardener.

Edible Wild Plants of Eastern North America. LEE ALLEN PETERSON.
Describes many plants that might be included in forest gardens. Particularly useful are the tables in the back describing useful plant species for a range of habitats and successional stages.

Growing Gourmet and Medicinal Mushrooms. PAUL STAMETS.
The bible of mushroom production. Though focused on indoor culture techniques, it includes information on the outdoor cultivation of mushrooms on logs, stumps, compost piles, and mulch.

Growing Unusual Vegetables. SIMON HICKMOTT.
Provides growing and use information on interesting vegetables, including many perennials. Focuses on British climate.

A Guide to Nut Tree Culture in North America, volume 1. DENNIS FULBRIGHT, EDITOR.
Comprehensive tome on nut production. Covers most hardy nut species, except walnuts (which will be covered in the forthcoming second volume).

Landscaping With Fruit: Strawberry Ground Covers, Blueberry Hedges, Grape Arbors, and 39 Other Luscious Fruits to Make Your Yard an Edible Paradise. LEE REICH.
Mouth-watering guide to cold-climate edible-landscaping fruits, with great information of productivity and level of maintenance.

Mycelium Running: How Mushrooms Can Help Save the World. PAUL STAMETS
Guide to growing and using mushrooms for food, forestry, and remediation of environmental problems from clear-cuts to oil spills.

Nitrogen-Fixing Plants for Temperate Climates. MARTIN
CRAWFORD.
Excellent reference for selecting nitrogen-fixing plants. A
British focus, but very relevant to eastern North America.

Perennial Ground Covers. DAVID MACKENZIE.
By far the best guide to ground covers we have seen.

*Perennial Vegetables: From Artichoke to "Zuiki" Taro, a Gardener's
Guide to Over 100 Delicious, Easy-to-Grow Edibles.* ERIC
TOENSMEIER
Detailed profiles of perennial vegetable crops including many
temperate species, with design and management strategies.

Plants for a Future. KEN FERN.
Remarkable guide to useful plants from an author with over
one thousand useful species in his collection. Focus on British
climate. Beware: Ken Fern enjoys plant flavors that we find dis-
tasteful.

Plants for a Future online database.
Information on over seven thousand useful species for temperate climates, with wild habitat, propagation, edible and
medicinal uses, and much, much more. Incredibly useful and
free! Online at http://www.pfaf.org.

Uncommon Fruits for Every Garden. LEE REICH.
Well-written guide to low-maintenance, delicious, hardy fruits.

Wild Edible Plants of Western North America. DONALD KIRK.
Covers the full range of edible plants of the West, from the
Sonoran desert to the Yukon Territory.

NATIVE PLANTS

Gardening with Native Wildflowers. SAMUEL JONES AND
LEONARD FOOTE.
An excellent guide to growing southeastern natives.

*Growing and Propagating Native Wildflowers of the U.S. &
Canada.* WILLIAM CULLINA.
Beautiful and informative, with hard-to-find propagation infor-
mation from Cullina's years of experience with the New
England Wildflower Society.

Native Trees, Shrubs, & Vines. WILLIAM CULLINA.
Another fantastic reference from Cullina.

*Native Trees, Shrubs and Vines for Urban and Rural America: A
Planting Design Manual for Environmental Designers.* GARY
HIGHTSHOE.
This mind-blowingly comprehensive book is for the hard-core
designer. A remarkable range of information about each
species, including rooting type, pollution tolerance, and native
range by county! A great investment.

COOKBOOKS FOR FOREST
GARDEN PLANTS & FUNGI

Billie Joe Tatum's Wild Foods Field Guide and Cookbook. BILLIE
JOE TATUM.
Features great recipes for many wild edible plants and mush-
rooms. Also a good field guide.

*Edible Wild Mushrooms of North America: A Field-to-Kitchen
Guide.* ALAN BESSETTE, ARLEEN BESSETTE, AND DAVID
FISCHER.
Useful field guide with mouthwatering photos and recipes.

Native Harvests: American Indian Wild Foods & Mushrooms. E.
BARRIE KAVASCH.
This is an expanded twentieth anniversary edition of Kavasch's
earlier celebrated book. Contains many great recipes for many
native wild edibles.

Vegetables from Amaranth to Zucchini: The Essential Reference.
ELIZABETH SCHNEIDER.
Information and recipes, including many for forest garden veg-
etables and mushrooms.

ECOLOGY AND EASTERN NORTH
AMERICAN ECOSYSTEMS

1491: New Revelations of the Americas Before Columbus.
CHARLES MANN.
Mind-opening information on the complex and populous pre-
Columbian societies in the New World. Much coverage of
agriculture and land-management practices.

*Changes in the Land: Indians, Colonists, and the Ecology of New
England.* WILLIAM CRONON.
Fascinating history of the New England forest. Provides
insights on the broader history of the eastern forest region in
the past millennium.

Deciduous Forests of Eastern North America. E. LUCY BRAUN
This classic 1950 book is one of the most comprehensive surveys
of the vegetation of the eastern deciduous forest. It relates vegetation to climate and landform and gives species lists and relative
abundances to help describe the plant communities. A great
source for model ecosystem information.

Ecology. PAUL COLINVAUX.
This textbook provides an excellent in-depth review of the full
breadth of the science of ecology as it stood in the mid-1980s.
Colinvaux believes strongly in Gleason's individualistic view of
plant communities.

Ecology of Eastern Forests. JOHN KRICHER AND GORDON
MORRISON.
This Peterson guide packs much useful information into a
field-guide-size reference.

The Eternal Frontier: An Ecological History of North America and Its People. TIM FLANNERY.
An engaging natural and social history of the last 65 million years of North America that underlines the fluid nature of ecosystems as they change over time. We recommend reading this before taking on Theodoropoulos's *Invasion Biology: Critique of a Pseudoscience* (page 345).

Forest Ecosystems. DAVID PERRY.
This book was a key reference for *Edible Forest Gardens*. Perry provides solid scientific footing and a well-integrated systems view of both the big picture of forest ecosystems and the critical details.

The Forgotten Pollinators. STEPHEN BUCHMANN AND GARY PAUL NABHAN.
A groundbreaking book for lay readers. Elucidates the importance of pollination in ecosystems and the effects of the loss of pollinators due to human disturbance.

Ghosts of Evolution: Nonsensical Fruit, Missing Partners, and Other Ecological Anachronisms. CONNIE BARLOW.
Illuminates the botanical aftermath from the evolutionarily "recent" loss of the giant sloth, mammoth, mastodon, and other "megafauna" from the eastern forest region. It changed our thinking about "native" ecosystems. Another prerequisite for Theodoropoulos's *Invasion Biology*.

Landscape Restoration Handbook. DONALD HARKER, SHERRI EVANS, MARC EVANS, AND KAY HARKER.
Lists native "climax" species for all regions of the continental U.S. Very helpful for ecological analog design.

New England Wildlife: Habitat, Natural History, and Distribution. RICHARD DeGRAAF AND MARIKO YAMASAKI.
An excellent reference on the ecology of the region's native birds, mammals, reptiles, and amphibians. The earlier version (by DeGraaf and Rudis and published by the US Forest Service) is out of print but is available online as a download at http://www.fs.fed.us/ne/newtown_square/publications/popular-publications.shtml

Old Growth in the East: A Survey. MARY BYRD DAVIS.
Describes the characteristics of eastern old growth. Documents numerous existing stands and fragments of old growth you can visit for each state east of the Mississippi.

Soil Biology Primer. NATURAL RESOURCES CONSERVATION SERVICE (NRCS).
This short handbook describes the basics of soil food web ecology and the roles of various organisms in the soil ecosystem. A good introduction, and the online version is free. Visit http://www.soils.usda.gov/sqi/soil_quality/soil_biology/soil_biology_primer.html. For hard copies go to http://www.swcs.org/en/publications/books/soil_biology_primer.cfm.

Some Ecological Aspects of Northeastern American Indian Agroforestry Practices. KARL DAVIES.
This article was ahead of its time in describing the sophisticated eastern North American Indian agroforestry practices, particularly prescribed burning to encourage nut, berry, and wildlife production. More evidence that there has not been a "primeval forest" in our region for thousands of years. Online at http://www.daviesand.com.

Tending the Wild: Native American Knowledge and the Management of California's Natural Resources. M. KAT ANDERSON.
Details sophisticated indigenous land management of California over a 12,000 year period before European arrival. Fantastic models for long-term sustainable ecosystem management.

NATIVES AND EXOTICS

Invasion Biology. MARK DAVIS.
This scientific text is a skeptical review of invasion biology, questioning assumptions in a less polemical style than Theodoropoulos.

Invasion Biology: Critique of a Pseudoscience. DAVID THEODOROPOULOS.
Proposes that the "invasive species" movement is based on bad science, and that it misses the true causes of the environmental crisis. Raises many, many important questions. It truly changed the way we think and see. Required reading, but read the following first to prime you well: *The Eternal Frontier* (Flannery); *Guns, Germs, and Steel* (Diamond); and *Ghosts of Evolution* (Barlow).

The Once and Future Forest: A Guide to Forest Restoration Strategies. LESLIE JONES SAUER AND ANDROPOGON ASSOCIATES.
This is a good book by a recognized authority in ecological design and restoration, but it is also alarmist in tone. Many good strategies, and decent information on the ecological health of the eastern forest, but beware of the invasion biology.

Stalking the Wild Amaranth. JANET MARINELLI.
Along with Sauer's book above, this one is a good contrast to David Theodoropoulos. Raises good questions about how we might garden "in the age of extinction."

FIELD GUIDES

Field Guide to Trees and Shrubs. GEORGE PETRIDES.
A guide to eastern woody plants. One of the few field guides that includes both trees and shrubs. The botanical keys are usually helpful to those who know the lingo, but the drawings could be better.

Garden Insects of North America: The Ultimate Guide to Backyard Bugs. WHITNEY CRANSHAW.
This is a good identification guide to the herbivores, predators, and pollinators in your garden, but it provides minimal information on the ecology and management of the pests described. Use along with *The Organic Gardener's Handbook of Natural Insect and Disease Control* (Ellis and Bradley).

Insect, Disease, and Weed ID Guide. JILL CEBENKO AND DEB MARTIN.
A welcome overview of unwelcome organisms.

Mushrooms of Northeastern North America. ALAN BESSETTE, ARLEEN BESSETTE, AND DAVID FISCHER.
An excellent field guide to eastern mushrooms, including edibility.

Newcomb's Wildflower Guide. LAWRENCE NEWCOMB.
Our favorite wildflower and flowering-shrub identification guide for the eastern region.

Weeds of the Northeast. RICHARD UVA, JOSEPH NEAL, AND JOSEPH DiTOMASO.
Excellent guide to annual and perennial weeds (including many useful species).

PERMACULTURE

Gaia's Garden: A Guide to Home-Scale Permaculture. TOBY HEMENWAY.
A good introduction for North American gardeners.

Introduction to Permaculture. BILL MOLLISON AND RENY MIA SLAY.
Mollison's most readable overview of permaculture.

Permaculture: Principles and Pathways beyond Sustainability. DAVID HOLMGREN.
Larger view of permaculture and humanity's post-petroleum future, within a framework of practical principles for design.

The Permaculture Activist.
Quarterly magazine for North American permaculture enthusiasts. Articles on forest gardens, useful plants, and more. Available from http://www.permacultureactivist.net.

Permaculture Magazine.
This British permaculture magazine includes articles on forest gardens, useful plants, et cetera. Available from http://www.permaculture.co.uk.

Water for Every Farm: Using the Keyline Plan. P. A. YEOMANS.
The basic book on keyline planning, one of the foundations of permaculture.

GARDENING AND FARMING IN THE FOREST

The American Woodland Garden: Capturing the Spirit of the Deciduous Forest. RICK DARKE.
The author of this book undertook a photo essay following one specific patch of forest through twenty years. The book also describes many ornamental aspects of woodland gardening in the eastern forest and provides a catalog of numerous woodland natives and their ornamental uses.

Beth Chatto's Woodland Garden: Shade-Loving Plants for Year-Round Interest. BETH CHATTO.
For the ornamental woodland gardener, especially in Britain, this book is wonderful. Great pictures, good information, and an engaging style.

Ecoforestry: The Art and Science of Sustainable Forestry. ALAN DRENGSON AND DUNCAN TAYLOR, EDITORS.
A wealth of essays on the scientific, philosophical, economic, and practical issues of sustainable forestry, from researchers, practitioners, and theorists.

Restoration Forestry: An International Guide to Sustainable Forestry Practices. MICHAEL PILARSKI.
A wide-ranging collection of essays, contacts, and information for using forestry as a means of ecological healing.

The Silvicultural Basis of Agroforestry Systems. MARK ASHTON AND FLORENCIA MONTAGNINI, EDITORS.
The contributors put some solid scientific footing under agroforestry, examining plant-environment interactions, plant-plant interactions, nutrient dynamics, and so on.

Temperate Agroforestry Systems. ANDREW M. GORDON AND STEVEN M. NEWMAN, EDITORS.
Reviews the status of agroforestry systems used in temperate climates throughout the world. An excellent global overview.

The Woodland Way: A Permaculture Approach to Sustainable Woodlot Management. BEN LAW.
How to make a living from the woods while living in and caring for it. Based on Ben's life cutting coppice, making charcoal, and building crafts in rural Britain.

ECOLOGICAL GARDENING, FARMING, AND LANDSCAPING

American Horticultural Society Plant Propagation: The Fully Illustrated Plant-by-Plant Manual of Practical Techniques. ALAN TOOGOOD, EDITOR.
An easy-to-use, comprehensive guide to the full range of propagation techniques.

Arboriculture: Integrated Management of Trees, Shrubs, and Vines. RICHARD HARRIS, JAMES CLARK, AND NELDA MATHENY.
An excellent reference on the subject, with solid footing in research and practice. Highly recommended.

Biotechnical Slope Protection and Erosion Control. DONALD GRAY AND ANDREW LEISER.
An excellent technical manual on using plants and other means besides concrete to stabilize slopes. A must-see for anyone with a challenging site or doing professional design.

Breed Your Own Vegetable Varieties: The Gardener's and Farmer's Guide to Plant Breeding and Seed Saving. CAROL DEPPE.
Crucial guide to backyard breeding for vegetables and more. Includes information on domesticating wild edibles.

Building Soils for Better Crops. FRED MAGDOFF.
Good overview of ecological soil care.

Drip Irrigation for Every Landscape and All Climates. ROBERT KOURIK.
As the title suggests, this book tells all.

How to Grow More Vegetables (and Fruits, Nuts, Berries, Grains, and Other Crops) Than You Ever Thought Possible, On Less Land Than You Can Imagine. JOHN JEAVONS.
The bible of intensive gardening and mini-farming, with lots of information on double-digging techniques.

The Instant Expert Guide to Mycorrhiza: The Connection for Functional Ecosystems. TED ST. JOHN.
The best summary we've found so far on mycorrhizas. Available in .pdf format at http://www.mycorrhiza.org.

Lasagna Gardening. PATRICIA LANZA.
A manual on sheet-mulch gardening.

Northeast Cover Crop Handbook. MARIANNE SARRANTONIO.
Very nice guide to cover cropping for the eastern forest region.

The Organic Gardener's Handbook of Natural Insect and Disease Control. BARBARA ELLIS AND FERN MARSHALL BRADLEY.
Identification and organic remedies for pests and diseases.

Start with the Soil. GRACE GERSHUNY.
Excellent introductory guide to soils.

Soil Foodweb, Inc.
www.soilfoodweb.com
Great online resource for soil biology information.

Rainwater Harvesting for Drylands and Beyond Volume One. BRAD LANCASTER.
Practical overview to capturing rainwater and using it productively in the home and landscape.

CLIMATE INFORMATION

Climatological Summaries—Climatography of the U.S. National Oceanic and Atmospheric Administration. 1950–present. No. 20, NATIONAL CLIMATE DATA CENTER, Asheville, NC.

Annual Degree Days to Selected Bases Derived from 1951–1980 Normals. Supplement 1 to *Climatography of the U. S. no. 81.* NATIONAL OCEANIC AND ATMOSPHERIC ADMINISTRATION. 1982. National Climate Data Center, Asheville, NC.

Climatic Atlas of the United States. NATIONAL OCEANIC AND ATMOSPHERIC ADMINISTRATION. 1980. National Climate Data Center, Asheville, NC.

ORGANIZATIONS

Agroforestry Research Trust
46 Hunters Moon
Dartington, Totnes
Devon TQ9 6JT
United Kingdom
(++44) (0)1803 840776
www.agroforestry.co.uk
The world's leading temperate forest garden research institution. Excellent publications, including *Agroforestry News.*

American Bamboo Society
750 Krumkill Rd.
Albany, NY 12203-5976
www.americanbamboo.org
Amateur and professional bamboo enthusiasts.

American Chestnut Foundation
469 Main Street, Suite 1
PO Box 4044
Bennington, VT 05201-4044
(802) 447-0110
www.acf.org
Dedicated to restoring the American chestnut through breeding and other efforts.

Apios Institute for Regenerative Perennial Agriculture
www.apiosinsitute.org

Promoting development of edible forest gardens and other perennial production systems. Projects include online user-generated profiles of species, polycultures, and site designs.

Association for Temperate Agroforestry
203 ABNR Bldg.
University of Missouri
Columbia, MO 65211
(573) 882-9866
www.aftaweb.org
Promoting agroforestry including forest farming.

Ecological Agriculture Projects
McGill University (Macdonald Campus)
Ste-Anne-de-Bellevue, QC H9X 3V9
Canada
(514) 398-7771
Fax: (514) 398-7621
Email: info@eap.mcgill.ca
www.eap.mcgill.ca
One of the world's best collections of materials on sustainable food and agriculture systems, probably the best in North America. Many of the materials are unpublished or out of print, or otherwise difficult to obtain. Check out their virtual library online!

Edibleforestgardens.com
www.edibleforestgardens.com
The place for updates, networking, and additional information on forest gardens. Hosted by the authors of the tome you are reading.

The International Ribes Association
PO Box 428
Booneville, CA 95415
(707) 895-2811
Information and networking for professional and backyard growers of *Ribes* fruits (currants, gooseberries, and jostaberries).

The Land Institute
2440 E. Water Well Rd.
Salina, KS 67401
(785) 823-5376
www.landinstitute.org
Researching "natural systems agriculture," perennial polycultures modeled on prairie vegetation. Breeding new perennial grain and legume crops. Awesome!

North American Fruit Explorers (NAFEX)
1716 Apples Rd.
Chapin, IL 62628
www.nafex.org
Association of fruit enthusiasts. Their journal *Pomona* reports on members' experiences with breeding, hardiness trials, and work with rare or unusual species and varieties.

North American Mycological Association
6615 Tudor Ct.
Gladstone, OR 97027-1032
(503) 657-7358
www.namyco.org
Amateur and professional mushroom enthusiasts. Can connect you with one of the many regional mycological associations. For both wild collectors and growers of mushrooms.

North American Native Plant Society
PO Box 84, Station D
Etobicoke, ON M9A 4X1
Canada
(416) 680-6280
www.nanps.org
Native plant enthusiasts from the U.S. and Canada. Can connect you with one of the many regional native plant associations.

Northern Nut Growers Association
PO Box 427
648 Oak Hill School Rd.
Townsend, DE 19734-0427
www.icserv.com/nnga
Network of researchers, commercial producers, and backyard enthusiasts growing nut trees (plus persimmon and pawpaw).

The PawPaw Foundation
c/o Pawpaw Research
147 Atwood Research Facility
Kentucky State University
Frankfort, KY 40601
www.pawpaw.kysu.edu/ppf/default.htm
Work to popularize the pawpaw (*Asimina triloba*).

Plants for a Future
Blagdon Cross
Ashwater, Beaworthy
Devon EX21 5DF
United Kingdom
01208 872 963
Organization promoting useful perennial plants, especially edibles. Their Web site, including their indispensable database, is a fantastic resource.

Seed Savers Exchange
3076 North Win Rd.
Decorah, IA 52101
(563) 382-5990
www.seedsavers.org
Remarkable organization whose members exchange seeds and plant material of vegetables, fruits, nuts, herbs, and flowers.

Society for Ecological Restoration
285 W. 18th Street, Suite 1
Tucson, AZ 85701
(520) 622-5485
www.ser.org
Organization dedicated to repairing damaged ecosystems. Many of their techniques are of interest to forest gardeners.

United Plant Savers
PO Box 400
East Barre, VT 05649
(802) 479-9825
www.unitedplantsavers.org
Encourages preservation and restoration of native medicinal plants.

PLANT, TOOL, AND SUPPLIES SOURCES

SOURCES OF PLANTS

Your local nursery will doubtless have a selection of apples, peaches, blueberries, and some common ground covers. This list focuses on sources for hard-to-find plants, including fruit and nut trees and shrubs, perennial vegetables, natives, and functional plants like nitrogen fixers, ground covers, and nectary plants. There are many more nurseries and seed companies offering good plants; please just use this list as a place to start.

Several resources can help you track down specific plants:

Cornucopia II: A Sourcebook of Edible Plants by STEPHEN FACCIOLA is a remarkable work listing 3,000 edible species and thousands of cultivars, and which nurseries and seed companies offer them. Also includes sources of edible fungi. Published by Kampong Press in 1998.

The Fruit, Berry, and Nut Inventory lists sources for 6,000 commercially available varieties from 280 nurseries. Available from Seed Savers Exchange.

The Seed Search, compiled by Karen Platt, is an international listing of 43,000 species and varieties with sources. Available from www.seedsearch.demon.co.uk/books.html.

The Andersen Horticultural Library Plant Information Online service offers an online subscription service to its database of plant sources. For $39.95 a year you get access to the database, with sources for 88,000 species and varieties, from over 700 sources. The database can be found online at http://plantinfo.umn.edu.

Agroforestry Research Trust
46 Hunters Moon
Dartington, Totnes
Devon TQ9 6JT
United Kingdom
(++44) (0)1803-840776
www.agroforestry.co.uk
Nursery and seed company featuring useful plants for cool temperate climates.

Arrowhead Alpines
PO Box 857
1310 N. Gregory Road
Fowlerville, MI 48836
(517) 223-3581
www.arrowheadalpines.com
Wide selection of interesting plants.

Badgersett Research Corporation
Rt. 1, Box 141
Canton, MN 55922
(507) 743-8570
www.badgersett.com
Breeders of unique hazel and chestnut varieties.

B&T World Seeds UK
Little Whitnell
Nether Stowey, Bridgewater
Somerset TA5 1JE
United Kingdom
01278 732-748
www.b-and-t-world-seeds.com
Unbelievable catalog with 35,000 listings.

Bamboo Garden Nursery
1507 SE Alder Street
Portland, OR 97214
(503) 647-2700
www.bamboogarden.com
Hardy bamboos.

Cook's Garden
PO Box 1889
Southampton, PA 18966
(800) 457-9703
www.cooksgarden.com
Gourmet vegetables, with an especially good selection of chicories.

Edible Landscaping
361 Spirit Ridge Lane
Afton, VA 22920
(434) 361-9134
www.eat-it.com or www.ediblelandscaping.com
Very nice collection of unusual fruits, nuts, and berries. Good quality stock, all container plants, shipped all over.

Evergreen YH Enterprises
PO Box 17538
Anaheim, CA 92817
(714) 637-5769
www.evergreenseeds.com
Asian vegetable seeds, many perennials.

Fedco Trees
PO Box 520
Waterville, ME 04903
(207) 873-7333
www.fedcoseeds.com/trees.htm
Fruits, nuts, berries, and some perennial vegetables. Great antique apple variety selection.

Forest Farm
990 Tetherow Road
Williams, OR 97544
(541) 846-7269
www.forestfarm.com
Enormous selection of plants, a great source for unusual nitrogen fixers.

Future Foods
Luckleigh Cottage
Hockworthy, Wellington
Somerset TA21 0NN
United Kingdom
01398-361-347
www.futurefoods.com
Many perennial vegetables. Also offer their book *Growing Unusual Vegetables*.

F. W. Schumacher
36 Spring Hill Road
Sandwich, MA 02563-1023
(508) 888-0659
www.treeshrubseeds.com
Fantastic selection of woody plant seeds.

G & N Ramp Farm
Box 48
Richwood, WV 26261
(304) 846-4235
Sell ramps and ramp products.

Gardens North
5984 Third Line Rd N.
North Gower, ON K0A 2T0
Canada
(613) 489-0065
http://gardensnorth.com
Many useful plants including hard-to-find Canadian natives.

Gardens of the Blue Ridge
PO Box 10
Pineola, NC 28662
(828) 733-2417
www.gardensoftheblueridge.com
Appalachian natives and other interesting species.

Green Mountain Transplants
2290 Vermont Rte. 14 North
East Montpelier, VT 05651
(802) 454-1533
www.gmtransplants.com
Perennials shipped in multispecies flats, an inexpensive way to get large numbers of plants.

Grimo Nut Nursery
979 Lakeshore Rd., RR 3
Niagara-on-the-Lake, ON L0S 1J0
Canada
(905) YEH-NUTS
www.grimonut.com
Grafted nuts, persimmons, and pawpaws.

Herb Garden & Historical Plants Nursery
Pentre Berw
Gaerwen
Anglesey LL60 6LF
United Kingdom
01248-422208
www.historicalplants.co.uk
Rare plants including wild cabbage and saltbush.

Hidden Springs Nursery
170 Hidden Springs Lane
Cookeville, TN 38501
(931) 268-9889
Great selection of unusual fruiting plants.

J. L. Hudson, Seedsman
Star Route 2, Box 337
La Honda, CA 94020
www.jlhudsonseeds.net
Fascinating collection of native plants from around the world. Also wrote and offer *Invasion Biology: Critique of a Pseudoscience*.

John Gordon Nursery
1385 Campbell Boulevard
Amherst, NY 14228
(716) 691-9371
www.geocities.com/nuttreegordon/0Kgordon.htm
Grafted persimmon, pawpaw, and nut trees.

Johnny's Selected Seeds
955 Benton Avenue
Winslow, ME 04901
(207) 861-3900
www.johnnyseeds.com
Wide range of conventional vegetables, flowers, and herbs, including many useful perennials.

John Scheepers, Inc.
23 Tulip Drive
PO Box 638
Bantam, CT 06750
(860) 567-0838
www.johnscheepers.com
Good source for camass species and other useful bulbs.

Mountain Gardens
546 Shuford Creek Road
Burnesville, NC 28714
(828) 675-5664
www.mountaingardensherbs.com
Large collection of useful plants, many perennial vegetables, natives, and ground covers.

New England Wildflower Society
Garden in the Woods
180 Hemenway Road
Framingham, MA 01701
508-877-7630
www.newfs.org
Collection of native wildflowers.

Nolin River Nut Tree Nursery
797 Port Wooden Road
Upton, KY 42784
(270) 369-8551
www.nolinnursery.com
Grafted nut trees, fantastic selection.

North American Fruit Explorers (NAFEX)
1716 Apples Road
Chapin, IL 62628
www.nafex.org
Members exchange rare fruit seeds, cuttings, and grafting wood.

Oikos Tree Crops
PO Box 19425
Kalamazoo, MI 49019
(269) 624-6233
www.oikostreecrops.com
Astounding selection of oaks, including hybrids. Also many other useful woody and perennial crops, such as hickory and northern pecan selections.

One Green World
28696 S. Cramer Road
Molalla, OR 97038
(877) 353-4028
www.onegreenworld.com
Unusual fruit crops, including many interesting introductions from the former Soviet Union. Excellent place.

Perennial Pleasures
PO Box 147
East Hardwick, VT 05836
(802) 472-5104
www.antiqueplants.com
Offers an excellent clone of skirret with no noticeable woody core, and many other functional and useful perennials.

Peters Seed and Research
PO Box 1472
Myrtle Creek, OR 97457
www.pioneer-net.com/psr
Perennial grains and brassicas; genius plant breeders.

Prairie Moon Nursery
Route 3, Box 1633
Winona, MN 55987
(866) 417-8156
www.prairiemoon.com
Wide selection of native prairie plants.

Raintree Nursery
391 Butts Road
Morton, WA 98356
(360) 496-6400
www.raintreenursery.com
Great selection of fruit, nuts, and bamboos.

Richters Herbs
357 Highway 47
Goodwood, ON L0C 1A0
Canada
(905) 640-6677
www.richters.com
Fantastic catalog offering many perennial vegetables. Some species available in bulk for low cost.

St. Lawrence Nurseries
325 State Highway 345
Potsdam, NY 13676
(315) 265-6739
www.sln.potsdam.ny.us
Hardy fruits, nuts, and berries.

Seed Savers Exchange
3076 North Win Road
Decorah, IA 52101
(563) 382-5990
www.seedsavers.org
Grassroots organization listing over 12,000 vegetable varieties, plus a miscellaneous section full of interesting perennials. Also has exchanges for fruits, nuts, flowers, and herbs.

Shooting Star Nursery
444 Bates Road
Frankfort, KY 40601
(502) 223-1679
www.shootingstarnursery.com
Eastern natives.

Southern Exposure
PO Box 460
Mineral, VA 23117
(540) 894-9480
www.southernexposure.com
Excellent collection of perennial onions.

Thomas Etty Esq.
45 Forde Avenue
Bromley
Kent BR1 3EU
United Kingdom
www.thomasetty.co.uk
Heirloom and unusual vegetables.

Tripple Brook Farm
37 Middle Road
Southampton, MA 01073
(413) 527-4626
www.tripplebrookfarm.com
Great selection of cold-hardy useful plants including fruit, bamboos, and perennial vegetables and a fantastic selection of ground covers.

Under A Foot Plant Company
5326 72nd Avenue SE
Salem, OR
(503) 581-8915
www.stepables.com
Nursery specializing in foot-tolerant prostrate ground covers. Features many multifunctional species.

Woodlanders
1128 Colleton Avenue
Aiken, SC 29801
(803) 648-7522
www.woodlanders.net
Great selection of woody and perennial plants.

Sources of Edible Mushroom Spawn

Fungi Perfecti
PO Box 7634
Olympia, WA 98507
(800) 780-9126
www.fungi.com
THE source for gourmet mushrooms for outdoor culture. Wrote *Growing Gourmet and Medicinal Mushrooms.*

L. F. Lambert Spawn Co.
PO Box 407
Coatesville, PA 19320
(610) 384-5031
Offers spawn for many species and strains.

Mushroompeople
PO Box 220
Summertown, TN 38483
www.thefarm.org/mushroom
Shiitake specialists.

Northwest Mycological Consultants
702 NW 4th Street
Corvallis, OR 97330
(541) 753-8198
www.nwmycol.com
Shiitake and other mushroom spawn.

Sylvan Spawn
87 Lakes Boulevard
Dayton, NV 89403
www.sylvaninc.com
Oyster and shiitake spawn.

SOURCES OF LEGUME AND MYCORRHIZAL INOCULANTS

The mycorrhizal inoculant companies listed here include only those tested by the International Culture Collection of (Vesicular) Arbuscular Mycorrhizal Fungi (INVAM) at West Virginia University and shown to have an infectivity of over 30 percent on an average basis. For testing methods and results, see http://invam.caf.wvu.edu under "Other Info: Commerce."

AgBio
9915 Raleigh Street
Westminster, CO 80031
(877) 268-2020 or (303) 469-9221
www.agbio-inc.com
Mycorrhizal inoculants.

Becker Underwood, Inc.
PO Box 667
801 Dayton Avenue
Ames, IA 50010
(515) 232-5907
www.beckerunderwood.com
Maker of Rhizanova mycorrhizal inoculant products. Also has offices in Canada, Britain, and France.

BioOrganics Mycorrhizae Inoculants
53606 Bridge Drive
La Pine, OR 97739
(888) 332-7676 or (541) 536-1583
www.bio-organics.com
Mycorrhizal inoculants.

Johnny's Selected Seeds
955 Benton Avenue
Winslow, ME 04901
(207) 861-3900
www.johnnyseeds.com
Legume inoculants.

Lipha Tech
3101 W. Custer Avenue
Milwaukee, WI 53209
(414) 462-7600
Legume inoculants.

Urbana Laboratories
PO Box 1393
St. Joseph, MO 64502
(800) 821-7666
Legume inoculants.

SOURCES OF BENEFICIAL INSECTS AND OTHER ORGANISMS

Extremely Green Gardening Co.
49 Lincoln Boulevard PMB 113
Abington, MA 02351
(781) 878-5397
www.extremelygreen.com
Wide range of beneficial insects and other organisms.

The Green Spot, Ltd.
93 Priest Road
Nottingham, NH 03290-6204
(603) 942-8925
www.greenmethods.com
Beneficial insects and other organisms, as well as integrated pest management supplies (sticky traps, etc.).

Harmony Farm Supply
3244 Highway 116 North
Sebastopol, CA 95472
(707) 823-9125
www.harmonyfarm.com
Beneficial insects and integrated pest management supplies.

Peaceful Valley Farm Supply
PO Box 2209
Grass Valley, CA 95945
(530) 272-4769
www.groworganic.com
Source of beneficial insects, bird- and bathouses, and integrated pest management and growing supplies.

Planet Natural
1612 Gold Avenue
Bozeman, MT 59715
(800) 289-6656
www.planetnatural.com
Beneficial insects and integrated pest management and garden supplies.

TESTING SERVICES

Harmony Farm Supply
3244 Highway 116 North
Sebastopol, CA 95472
(707) 823-9125
www.harmonyfarm.com
Soil and water testing, including tests for harmful soil organisms.

Soil Foodweb, Inc.
1128 NE 2nd Street, Suite 120
Corvallis, OR 97330
(541) 752-5066
www.soilfoodweb.com
Soil-food-web testing.

Woods End Research Laboratory, Inc.
PO Box 297
Mt. Vernon, ME 04352
(207) 293-2457
www.woodsend.org
Compost and soil testing services. A leader in organic and unconventional testing. Talk to them about subsoil testing.

TOOL & SUPPLY SOURCES

DripWorks, Inc.
190 Sanhedrin Circle
Willits, CA 95490
(800) 522-3747
www.dripworksusa.com
Drip irrigation supplies.

Extremely Green Gardening Company
49 Lincoln Boulevard, PMB 113
Abington, MA 02351
(781) 878-5397
www.extremelygreen.com
Organic growing supplies.

Fedco
PO Box 520
Waterville, ME 04903
(207) 873-7333
www.fedcoseeds.com
Organic growers' supplies including drip irrigation.

Harmony Farm Supply
3244 Highway 116 North
Sebastopol, CA 95472
(707) 823-9125
www.harmonyfarm.com
Drip irrigation, organic growing supplies, wide selection.

Johnny's Selected Seeds
955 Benton Avenue
Winslow, ME 04901
(207) 861-3900
www.johnnyseeds.com
Organic growers' supplies including drip irrigation.

Market Farm Implements
257 Fawn Hollow Road
Friedens, PA 15541
(814) 443-1931
www.marketfarm.com
US distributor of the Yeoman's Plow.

Peaceful Valley Farm Supply
PO Box 2209
Grass Valley, CA 95945
(530) 272-4769
www.groworganic.com
Wide array of organic growing tools and supplies.

Planet Natural
1612 Gold Avenue
Bozeman, MT 59715
(800) 289-6656
www.planetnatural.com
Wide range of organic growing supplies.

Root Jack
Michael Giacomini
PO Box 726
Ross, CA 94957
(415) 454-0849
Sells a woody-weed removal tool.

Tripple Brook Farm
37 Middle Road
Southampton, MA 01073
(413) 527-4626
www.tripplebrookfarm.com
A nursery offering a low-tech tree-digging system.

The Weed Wrench Co.
PO Box 512
Grants Pass, OR 97528
(877) 484-4177
www.weedwrench.com
Sellers of a great heavy-duty woody-weed removal tool.

GLOSSARY

adaptogen: an agent that helps the human organism adapt to stressful conditions.

additive yielding: also called *overyielding*; when the yield of two or more crops grown in polyculture is more than that of equivalent areas of the two crops grown in monoculture; in some contexts, additive yielding also includes the *system yield*, that is, when yields of one or more crops are lower than when they are grown in monoculture, but the diverse yields of the polyculture add together for a higher total yield.

adventitious roots: roots growing from a stem or other upper part of a plant, rather than the root crown or another root.

aggrade: to build biological capital within an ecosystem during succession; the opposite of *degrade*.

agroforestry: the growing of agricultural products using trees and other woody plants, often in combination with typical annual crops or other common agricultural systems; specifically includes systems such as *alley cropping*, nut and fruit orchards, forest gardening, animal fodder systems (a.k.a. *silvopastoral* systems), windbreaks, etc. Different from forestry in that agroforestry integrates agricultural production, whereas forestry is concerned specifically with growing trees for lumber, pulp, or other wood products.

allelochemicals: chemicals produced by plants, animals, or microbes not for metabolic functioning but serving ecological purposes such as defense against herbivores or competitors.

allelopathy: the inhibition of one plant by another through the use of chemical compounds, usually as a means of defense against competition.

alley cropping: growing annual crops between widely spaced rows of tree crops.

alterative: an agent that gradually and favorably alters the condition of the body; also known as a blood purifier.

analgesic: an agent taken to relieve pain without causing loss of consciousness.

anti-allergenic: an agent that reduces or relieves allergies.

anti-arrhythmia: an agent that helps restore rhythmic beating of the heart.

antibacterial: an agent that kills or inhibits bacteria.

anticatarrhal: a substance that eliminates or counteracts the formation of mucus.

antifungal: an agent that kills or inhibits fungi.

antihemorraghic: an agent that reduces bleeding from broken blood vessels.

antihepatoxic: a substance that helps detoxify the liver and protects the liver from damage due to toxicity.

antihyperthyroidic: an agent that reduces or rebalances thyroid gland overactivity.

anti-inflammatory: an agent that reduces swelling of tissues.

antimalarial: an agent that relieves or reduces malaria.

antiparasitic: an agent that kills or inhibits intestinal parasites.

antioxidant: an agent that prevents oxidation; a preservative; also a substance that removes oxidizing agents from within the human body, thereby reducing aging and free radical damage.

antiseptic: a substance that can be applied to the skin to prevent the growth of bacteria.

antispasmodic: an agent that prevents or relieves spasms or cramps.

antispirochete: an agent that inhibits or kills spiral bacteria, such as syphilis or Lyme disease bacteria.

antitussive: an agent that prevents or relieves cough.

antiviral: a substance that kills or inhibits viruses.

aperient: a substance used to relieve constipation.

aspect: the direction a site, slope, or *microclimate* faces relative to the sun.

astringent: a substance that has a constricting or binding effect.

base map: a proportionally scaled, bird's-eye-view plan of a site in its current state that forms the basis for site analysis and design drawings.

between-patch guild: a guild that does not require its plant members to grow within the same patch for the guild to function.

biogeochemical cycles: cycles of chemical elements, including nutrients, through the ecosystem, transforming the elements into living (bio), mineral (geo), and chemical forms as they go.

biomass: literally "life matter"; living or dead tissues, chemicals, or other organic material produced by plants, animals, microbes, or other living things; when dead, it becomes organic matter (OM).

bulb: a short underground stem with fleshy leaves or scales; actually a modified leaf bud serving as a storage organ.

calmative: an agent with mild sedative or calming effects.

canopy: the uppermost spreading branchy layer of a forest; the topmost of any vegetative layer overhead, usually with more or less continuous cover. The canopy can be very high, or it can be relatively low, as long as it is above the shrub layer (12 feet/3.7 m).

carminative: an agent that relieves and removes gas from the digestive system.

carnivores, primary and secondary: organisms that gain their needed energy from other nonproducer organisms; primary carnivores eat *herbivores*, secondary carnivores eat primary carnivores.

cathartic: a powerful purgative or laxative, causing severe evacuation, with or without pain.

cation exchange capacity: the quantity of cations the soil can hold; the relative number of cation exchange sites within a soil; the higher the cation exchange capacity, the more cationic nutrients the soil can hold for nutrient uptake by plants and other organisms.

chelate: to form a compound consisting of a metal atom surrounded by a molecule, usually an organic molecule; chelation makes many toxic metals less toxic.

cholagogue: an agent that increases the flow of bile to the intestines.

circulation: the patterns of movement of people, animals, vehicles, and materials around and through a site.

clearing: a vertical open space within a forest matrix extending through the vegetation layers from the canopy to the top of the herb layer (6 feet or 2 meters high), with a diameter to height ratio between 2 and 4.

climax: the "endpoint" of a successional sequence, usually thought of as a specific forest type for each part of eastern North America. See chapter 6 in volume 1 for a more thorough explanation.

codominant: those fewest species whose combined cover value composes the majority of the vegetation for their layer or, for the community as a whole, the overstory; to be codominant, species must usually have a cover value of at least 20 to 30 percent.

community niche: an ecological role within a community, e.g., "canopy foliage herbivore," "lignin decomposer," "late-succession understory tree"; community niches may be filled by numerous species.

competitor: in the context of the core strategies of species niches, a competitor species allocates most of its resources toward growth and competition, rather than reproduction or stress tolerance.

consistence: see *soil consistence*.

consumers: organisms that must gain their needed energy from another organism and cannot obtain it directly from a nonbiological source; contrast with *producers*.

coppice: "COP-iss"; a.k.a. stump sprouts; the woody material regrowing from the stump or roots of a tree or shrub after it has been cut down; as a verb, "to coppice" is to cut so as to cause a renewal of sprouting from a stump.

corm: an enlarged, fleshy, but solid, bulblike base of a stem, lacking the fleshy leaves of a true bulb; not a modified leaf bud but part of the stem, serving as a storage organ.

corridor: a long, narrow plant and animal community surrounded by an area with a dissimilar community structure and composition.

coverage, cover value, or **percent cover:** the amount of area covered by the canopy of a given species or set of species.

cross-inoculation groups: groups of nitrogen-fixing plants that can inoculate each other with the proper bacteria for nitrogen fixation; named for the kinds of plants in the group, e.g., the cowpea group or the pea group.

crown density: the concentration of opaque matter in a tree, shrub, or herb crown as it affects the transmission of light to the vegetation layers below.

deciduous: denotes plants that drop their leaves for a period of each year, such as during the winter in temperate climates or the dry season in the tropics.

decomposers: organisms that gain their needed energy by breaking down biomass lost as waste from other organisms or left over from other already-dead organisms.

demulcent: an agent that is locally soothing and softening; often *mucilaginous*; usually taken internally to help protect damaged or inflamed tissue.

diaphoretic: an agent that induces sweating.

diffuse mutualism: a mutualist strategy in which a species can cooperate with an array of potential partners; the opposite of *pairwise mutualism.*

dispersive: denotes plants that spread rapidly and far by seed, borne by either animals or wind; we use this value-neutral term rather than words like *invasive*, which both is inaccurate and presumes that invasiveness is a behavior resulting only from plant characteristics, not the interaction between the plant and its environment.

disturbance: any relatively discrete event in time that disrupts ecosystem, community, or population structure and changes resources, substrate availability, or the physical environment.

diuretic: an agent that induces or increases urination.

dominant: the dominant species of a community is that overstory species that contributes the most cover to the community, compared to other overstory species; dominance usually occurs when the species has a cover value of over 50 percent. The term may also refer to the dominant species within a particular vegetation layer. The community or layer is often named for the dominant species. Many people object to the term *dominant* for political/ideological reasons. We use the term despite its problems because we want to maintain an interface with concepts from vegetation ecology.

ecological analogs: species or groups of species selected by humans for specific reasons to perform a function, fill a niche, create a habitat, or exhibit a form similar to that of a model species or species group.

ecological equivalents: species or groups of species that evolved to perform a function, fill a niche, create a habitat, or exhibit a form similar or equivalent to that of a species or species group in an ecologically similar or equivalent habitat.

ecological time: time scales at which ecosystems change, but evolutionary change is a minimal influence; for forest ecosystems, ecological time is on the order of years, decades, and centuries. Beyond that we get into the realm of evolutionary time.

edge environments: transition zones between two distinct habitats, where the edge contains species from both neighboring habitats as well as species specifically adapted to the transition zone.

eluviation: "ee-LOO-vee-AY-shun"; the transportation of dissolved or suspended material within the soil by the movement of water when rainfall exceeds evaporation; a.k.a. *leaching.*

emergent property: a characteristic, quality, or behavior that emerges from the interactions between elements, such that the property can be said to belong only to the interacting elements as a whole system, not to the elements themselves.

emollient: an agent that softens, protects, or soothes the skin when applied locally.

endophytes: organisms, typically fungi, living within the leaves and stems of plants, usually within the plant cells, as plant mutualists gaining sugars from the plant in return for protecting the plant from pests and diseases.

environment niche: a suite of ecological conditions within which a given species can exploit an energy source effectively enough to reproduce and colonize similar conditions; the mirror image of the *species niche.*

ephemeral: a plant that leafs out, flowers, fruits, and then goes dormant for the rest of the growing season; this strategy is most common in spring, hence the name *spring ephemeral.*

exotic: a plant that arrived in North America after European contact, either as a self-propelled or accidental immigrant or imported intentionally by humans.

expansive: denotes particularly vigorous plants that spread vegetatively by rhizomes, stolons, or other means; we use this value-neutral term instead of words like *rampant*, *aggressive*, or *invasive*, especially the latter, which presumes that "invasiveness" is a characteristic residing only within plants when instead it results from the interaction between plants and their environment.

expectorant: an agent that induces the coughing up of mucous secretions from the lungs.

facilitation: an ecological interaction between two species where one species is unaffected by the fact that it benefits the other.

facultative: not obligated to use a typical niche strategy, lifestyle, or behavior, but may use it under some conditions; e.g., facultative mycorrhizal plants associate with mycorrhizal fungi when soil nutrients are limited.

facultative parasite: a organism that parasitizes hosts that are already sick or dying.

farmaceutical: homegrown or farm-grown medicinal crops; this is the opposite of, and does not include, anything involving genetically engineered plants for producing chemical drugs, which the pharmaceutical industry calls "pharming."

floristics: relating to the study of the distribution of plants within an area.

fodder: coarse food fed to domestic animals, especially cattle, horses, and sheep, but also other animals such as goats, rabbits, chickens, llamas, ostriches, yaks, and water buffalo. Fodder is cut and fed directly or stored for later use.

forb: any nongrassy herbaceous plant, such as ferns, perennial flowers, wildflowers, bulbs, herbaceous vines, etc.

forest: a stand of trees with 100 percent canopy coverage and interlocking crowns.

friable: literally "spongy"; with reference to *soil consistence*, it means easily crumbled or pulverized.

galactagogue: a substance that increases the flow of milk in breast-feeding women.

gap: a vertical open space within a forest matrix extending through the vegetation layers from the canopy to the top of the herb layer (6 feet or 2 meters high), with a diameter to height ratio less than 2.

gap dynamics: the successional processes that occur when trees die within a forest matrix, leaving a gap, clearing, or glade.

garden guild: a guild of plants that can or must function with plants and other organisms spread across more than one patch within a garden, habitat, or neighborhood; contrast with *patch guild*.

generalist herbivores: herbivores that eat whatever plant foods they can find that are palatable; contrast with *specialist herbivores*.

girdling: cutting through the living parts of a tree's or shrub's bark into the older, nonliving wood around the stem's whole circumference, but not cutting the plant down; girdling allows the plant to remain standing for a time but kills it.

glade: a vertical open space within a forest matrix extending through the vegetation layers from the canopy to the top of the herb layer (6 feet or 2 meters high), with a diameter to height ratio greater than 4.

gross primary production: the total amount of solar energy captured in photosynthesis by a plant or ecosystem; compare to *net primary production (NPP)*.

guilds: groups of species that partition resources or create networks of mutual support.

habit: a plant's behavior as it is reflected architecturally; determined by the pattern the plant produces as it reproduces and spreads, e.g., mat forming, standard tree, clumping herb, etc.

habitat: a place or type of place that provides food, water, or refuge to a species or individual; usually characterized by vegetation type or other dominant ecosystem features.

herbivores: organisms that gain their needed energy from the products of producers, that is, plants, by either eating, parasitizing, or forming mutualistic relationships with them.

hydric: wet or very wet; containing plenty of moisture; compare to *mesic* and *xeric*.

hypotensive: causing a lowering of blood pressure.

inhibition: an ecological interaction between two species where one species either benefits from or is unaffected by its suppression or limiting of the establishment, growth, reproduction, or activities of the other.

initial floristic composition: the theory that the flora of a community undergoing succession changes due only to variation in which species are dominant at a given time, not because the different species arrive as conditions change. This theory stands on the idea that all or most of the site's flora is present at the beginning of the successional sequence, and that the successional pathway is influenced primarily by that initial flora, not by recruitment during the sequence.

insectary plant: a plant providing food or shelter to beneficial insects.

insectivorous: insect eating.

intensity (of disturbance): the amount of energy expended during a disturbance.

invasive: denotes a plant, animal, or other species considered a threat to ecosystem integrity or human values due to its expansive or dispersive behavior within certain environmental contexts; this term is usually used in a way that indicates the user believes the species so-named is the source of the threat; we do not use this term to describe plants because it ascribes to plants characteristics that are not properly resident only in the plants; see *opportunist*. Volume 1 of this work offers more discussion of this topic in several feature articles.

landform: in design, the shape and slope of the earth's surface, as well as the composition and pattern of its bedrock and surficial geology.

laxative: a mild *purgative*.

layering: a means of propagation or plant dispersal where the plant forms roots along a branch or stem that is placed in a small trench by humans or that touches the ground of its own accord.

leaching: the transportation of dissolved or suspended material within the soil by the movement of water when rainfall exceeds evaporation; a.k.a. *eluviation*.

legacy: a biological, mineral, or chemical inheritance passed down from one ecosystem to the next; usually refers to legacies remaining after disturbance resets the successional clock.

light saturation: the intensity of light (usually expressed as percent of full sun) at which a plant's rate of photosynthesis can no longer increase.

macronutrients: the nine nutrients that constitute the vast majority (99.5 percent) of plant biomass: carbon, oxygen, hydrogen, nitrogen, phosphorus, sulfur, potassium, calcium, and magnesium (C, O, H, N, P, S, K, Ca, Mg).

mesic: containing a moderate amount of moisture; compare to *hydric* and *xeric*.

microclimate: the climate of a small site, area, or habitat; a microclimate can be as small as a kitchen table or as large as the side of a mountain, as long as its conditions are essentially uniform and significantly different from the overall climate and neighboring microclimates.

micronutrients: the nine plant nutrients that are required by plants to function but make up only 0.5 percent of plant biomass: chlorine, iron, manganese, boron, zinc, copper, molybdenum, cobalt, and nickel (Cl, Fe, Mn, B, Zn, Cu, Mo, Co, Ni).

mimicry: the close external resemblance of an animal or plant (or part of one) to another animal or plant or an inanimate object; in forest gardening, the structural and functional resemblance of a designed garden to a model ecosystem.

monoculture: in agriculture, the growing of one species or crop variety in one area; in culture, the homogenization of cultural expression to a single or narrow set of values, behaviors, social structures, and ways of being; in psychology, the limiting of perspective such that one sees the world as composed of elements that have only one purpose, function, feature, or value.

mottles: spots or patches of soil color significantly different from the color of surrounding soil; usually an indicator of the estimated seasonal high water table.

mucilaginous: pertaining to, resembling, or containing mucilage; slimy.

multistemmed: describes a shrub with more than one stem arising from the crown; in trees this habit is called *sprouting*.

mutual-support guild: a group of species from different *trophic levels* that interact in such a way as to support each other; these species meet each other's intrinsic needs by using each other's intrinsic by-products, that is, they functionally interconnect.

mutualism: an ecological interaction between two species where both species benefit from the interaction; may be *obligate* or *facultative* and *diffuse* or *pairwise*.

mycorrhiza: (plural: mycorrhizas); a mutualistic relationship between a plant and a fungus, where the plant gives the fungus sugars in return for water, nutrients, and, often, protection from soil-borne pests.

native: a species that established itself on the North American continent before European contact.

nectary plant: a plant providing nectar to beneficial insects as a source of calories; may be divided into specialist nectary and generalist nectary, depending on the kinds of insects that use the nectary—generalists or specialists, which each have different kinds of mouthparts.

net primary production (NPP): the amount of energy captured by plants during photosynthesis that is not used for respiration; NPP represents the amount of solar energy converted into *biomass*.

neutralism: an ecological relationship between two species where neither species affects the other.

niche: a general term denoting "ecological space"; see definitions for the three kinds of niches: *species niche*, *community niche*, and *environment niche*.

niche analysis: enumerating the characteristics of a species, community, or environment niche as far as is possible by breaking it into its component parts, such as, for a *species niche*, needs, products, behaviors, intrinsic characteristics, evolutionary history and associates, and so on.

nodulation: the formation of nodules caused by the mutualism between nitrogen-fixing bacteria (*Rhizobium* spp. or *Frankia* spp.) and their plant hosts.

nodules: small, round beads or balls containing nitrogen-fixing bacteria that grow on the roots of nitrogen-fixing plants. If they are pink or red inside when you cut them open, nitrogen fixation is happening.

nonnative: see *exotic*.

NPP: *net primary production*.

nutritive: providing nourishment; nutritious.

obligate: restricted to one niche strategy or particularly characteristic mode of life or behavior, e.g., obligate mycorrhizal fungi can survive only as mutualists of plants.

oldfield: a former agricultural field, pasture, hayland, meadow, or lawn that has been abandoned and is undergoing *succession*; usually refers to the middle stages of succession, when the ecosystem consists of a patchy mosaic of herbs, shrubs, trees, and vines.

OM: organic matter.

omnivores: organisms that gain their needed energy from more than one *trophic level*.

opportunist: formerly known as *invasive*; a species that exhibits highly *dispersive* and/or *expansive* behavior. Some of these, especially *exotic* species, are perceived by humans as a threat to ecosystem integrity. We use this term rather than *invasive* to include the environment as a component of the dynamic called "invasion," because opportunistic species take advantage of resources and opportunities available in the environment. Volume 1 of this work offers more discussion of this topic in several feature articles.

overstory: the topmost layer of a plant community; usually called a canopy unless the overstory is under 12 feet (3.7 m) high.

overyielding: see *additive yielding*.

oviposition: "egg-laying location"; usually refers to insect egg location requirements; each insect species has different oviposition requirements, which can be quite specific as to substrate or plant host, microclimate, and location on the host plant or substrate.

pairwise mutualism: a mutualistic relationship between two species where they can cooperate only with each other, and not with any other partners; the opposite of *diffuse mutualism*.

parasitoid insects: insects whose adults lay their eggs in or on host insects (usually pests), and whose young eat the host when they hatch.

parent material: the underlying rock or other mineral material within and upon which soils develop; forms the "constitution" of the overlying soil, strongly influencing the *soil texture*, *soil structure*, *soil consistence*, and nutrient content.

patch: a plant and animal community surrounded by an area with a dissimilar community structure or composition.

patch guild: a guild that can function as a guild only when the plants or other organisms live or grow within the same patch; contrast with *garden guild*.

percent cover: see *coverage*.

perennial: a plant growing back every year without starting from seed.

permaculture: the conscious design and cocreative evolution of human cultures, settlements, and agricultural systems, using ecological principles and indigenous wisdom to mimic the diversity, stability, and resilience of natural systems; a contraction of *permanent agriculture* and *permanent culture*, coined by David Holmgren and Bill Mollison in Australia in the late 1970s.

phenology: the study of cyclic and seasonal natural phenomena, especially in relation to climate, plants, and animal life.

phytoestrogenic: an herb that contains plant-produced estrogen compounds that mimic those produced by humans; often used to treat various conditions in women.

pioneer: the first plants to colonize a new site or to begin the change from one successional stage to another; pioneer trees are the first to invade a grassland, for example.

pollarding: cutting a woody plant so it coppices, but cutting it well above ground level to keep fresh shoots out of reach of livestock.

polyculture: the growing of more than one species or crop variety in a patch or space at one time; contrast with *monoculture*.

predatory insects: insects whose adult or larval stages directly catch and eat other insects; contrast with *parasitoid insects*.

primary succession: succession that begins with bare soil or rock, with no biological legacies from the predisturbance ecosystem.

producers: organisms that transform energy from sunlight (or, rarely, some other nonbiological source) into biomass.

propagule: any plant part that can produce a new individual of the species, such as a seed or a viable root or stem fragment or bud.

purgative: an agent that causes cleansing or watery evacuation of the bowels, usually with painful cramps.

relay floristics: the theory that the flora of a site undergoing succession changes as conditions shift due to the recruitment of new species to the community and the dying out of existing ones; that is, that the species arrive and depart in waves as conditions change; contrast with *initial floristic composition*.

resource-partitioning guild: see *resource-sharing guild*.

resource-sharing guild: a group of species from the same *trophic level* that use the same resource in a similar way but avoid competition by specializing and differentiating when, where, or how they use the resource.

rhizomatous: a plant that spreads by means of *rhizomes*.

rhizome: a rootlike structure, actually a modified stem, that spreads through the soil and from which shoots and roots grow to form new, interconnected "plants."

rhizosphere: the root zone of the soil; primarily refers to the very thin layers of soil adjacent to roots that is influenced by root exudates and full of microbial life; some authors use the term to describe the soil horizons where roots primarily live, that is, the O, A, and B horizons.

richness, species richness: the total number of species in a given area; richness is different from diversity, in the ecologist's sense of the word, which also measures the relative abundance of the species, not just how many species there are.

root: the part of a plant that grows in the opposite direction from the stem, usually underground, lacking nodes.

root density: the concentration of roots in a given area of soil.

root sucker: a shoot arising from a true root, not a *rhizome* or *stolon*, at a distance from the plant's main stem.

root suckering: a plant that grows *root suckers*.

root zone: the area of intensive microbial activity and diversity within a few millimeters or centimeters of plant roots; this activity is caused in great part by root exudates.

rubefacient: an agent that causes reddening or irritation when applied to the skin.

ruderal: literally from Latin, "rubble"; in the context of the core strategies of species niches, a ruderal species allocates most of its resources toward reproduction and dealing with disturbance, rather than stress tolerance or growth and competition.

savanna: a transition plant community between prairie and forest consisting primarily of prairie plants and deep-rooted trees, with tree cover generally below 40 percent.

secondary succession: succession that begins after a disturbance to a preexisting ecosystem, so that the direction of the following succession is influenced by the biological legacies from the previous ecosystem.

sedative: an agent that strongly quiets the nervous system.

seed bank: the total inventory of viable seeds stored in the soil, leaf litter, streambed, or lakebed of an ecosystem, some old and decay resistant, some newer and not as long-lasting; the seed bank may contain literally millions of seeds per acre, including numerous plant species; these numbers accumulate in forest soils and litter as well as in agricultural and suburban soils.

self-maintenance: when an entity or system maintains itself, performing all the work needed to run the system, such as providing nutrients and water, mulching, and so on.

self-management: when a system or entity envisions its future, and marshals the forces needed to achieve that vision; includes guiding succession and evolution.

self-regulation: part of self-maintenance, wherein an entity or system regulates itself; in the garden this includes keeping populations of insects, animals, diseases, and plants in balance.

severity (of disturbance): the actual level of impact a disturbance has on a given species or community.

shifting-mosaic steady state: a theoretical ecosystem condition where each patch of the landscape is constantly cycling from gap disturbances to mature forest and back again, while at the larger scale the landscape exhibits relative stability in its vegetation characteristics.

shrub: a woody plant of limited height with multiple stems arising at or near the ground. Usually shorter than a tree; however, some dwarf trees are smaller than some large shrubs.

shrubland: a shrub-dominated plant community where shrub layer coverage is greater than 40 percent but less than 100 percent, and there is little or no tree cover above it.

silvopastoral systems: agroforestry systems integrating tree crops with grazed pasturelands. The trees provide food, fuel, fiber, fodder, and fertilizer production, as well as benefits such as wind reduction, soil salinity control, humidification of the air, shade, and improved grazing-animal weight gain due to microclimate improvements.

sinkers: roots that grow downward from a location along a horizontal root, rather than from the root crown.

soil consistence: the relative firmness or looseness of the soil in its undisturbed condition, ranging from loose to very firm.

soil horizon: a generally horizontal stratum of soil with uniform and distinct characteristics, including texture, structure, consistence, and color, and a dominant or predominant ecological function or characteristic, such as organic matter accumulation and decomposition, assimilation, leaching, etc.

soil profile: the vertical pattern of soil horizons: their depth, texture, structure, consistence, and color.

soil structure: the shape, alignment, and patterning of soil particles, e.g., blocky, platy, massive, or granular.

soil texture: the fineness or coarseness of a soil, determined by the percentage of different particle sizes (sand, silt, and clay) composing the soil.

specialist herbivores: herbivores that will eat only specific plant species or plant parts.

species niche: the relationship of an organism to food and enemies; its core strategy for making a living, and its multiple inherent needs, products, characteristics, functions, and tolerances.

species strategy: the core of the *species niche*; a genetically coded pattern or suite of adaptations evolved by a species that allows it to make a living in a certain way under certain conditions.

spring ephemeral: see *ephemeral*.

sprouting: when used as a class of plant habit or behavior in this book, denotes a tree that forms shoots at the base of the stem or trunk; these shoots may arise from rhizomes, buds on the crown, or root suckers, but they are nonetheless at the base of the plant.

stimulant: an agent that causes increased activity of another agent, cell, tissue, organ, or activity.

stolon: a modified stem that grows horizontally above the ground, from which a plant forms new shoots and roots as a means of expansion.

stoloniferous: a plant that spreads by means of *stolons*.

stomachic: a tonic that promotes digestion or improves appetite.

stool: a tree stump that grows regularly cut coppice.

stress tolerator: in the context of the core strategies of species niches, a stress tolerator allocates most of its resources toward resisting stress, rather than reproduction or growth and competition.

strikers: see *sinkers*.

structure: see *soil structure*.

styptic: an agent that checks bleeding by constricting blood vessels.

succession: the progressive change from one ecosystem or habitat type to another by natural processes of soil and community development and colonization; in the eastern United States, usually refers to the transformation of bare soil or disturbed lands back to forest, but in other climates and circumstances succession can mean other outcomes. See chapter 6 in volume 1.

suckering: describes plants that spread by means of *rhizomes* or *root suckers*, with stems or shoots arising at a distance from the main stem or trunk.

superfood: a foodstuff extremely rich in nutrients or beneficial compounds, so that eating it produces healing effects.

texture: see *soil texture*.

thicket: a shrub-dominated plant community with little or no tree cover where the crowns of the shrubs interlock and cover 100 percent of the area.

threshold level: the pest population level at which you will take a specific pest management action; the threshold level and the management action should be determined in advance, and you should have a monitoring program that will help you determine the population size and tell you when the threshold is reached.

toner: an astringent substance applied to the skin to reduce oiliness and improve its condition.

tonic: an ambiguous term referring to substances thought to have an overall positive medicinal effect of an unspecified nature; often paired with adjectives denoting which organs or physiological systems the substance affects.

trophic level: one of the different levels of the food web, e.g., producer, herbivore, primary carnivore, and so on; *trophic* literally means "nursing" in Greek; each species on the same trophic level operates on a common feeding plan.

tuber: a fleshy, thickened part of a rhizome, usually at the end, serving as a storage organ. Most often bears buds, or "eyes," as on potatoes.

umbel: numerous tiny flowers that, taken together, compose a flower that forms a flattened, umbrella-shaped disk.

understory: any layer of vegetation underlying the canopy or overstory. Ecologists also use the term to describe a specific ecological niche of trees adapted to grow and reproduce in the shade of the canopy, e.g., "understory trees."

understory repression: a stage of succession where dense pioneer tree saplings shade out sun-loving shrubs and herbs, and the understory often becomes barren. Understory repression is followed by the development of a shade-loving herbaceous layer and a more varied canopy structure as competition between the saplings kills off some of their number, and shade-tolerant trees, shrubs, and herbs colonize and grow below them.

varmint: a vertebrate animal, usually wild, that competes for the crops we grow or otherwise causes trouble in our garden ecosystem.

vulnerary: an agent used for healing wounds.

weathering: the physical disintegration and chemical decomposition of materials at or near the earth's surface.

within-patch guild: a set of plants that must grow together in a patch for the guild to become operative.

woodland: a tree-dominated plant community where tree cover is greater than 40 percent but less than 100 percent.

xeric: dry; containing little water; compare to *hydric* and *mesic*.

yield: useful product; in a forest garden context, *yield* is usually defined as the yield of the whole system (system yield), not just one species or plant within the system.

BIBLIOGRAPHY

Alexander, Christopher. 1979. *The Timeless Way of Building*. New York: Oxford University Press.

Alexander, Christopher, Sara Ishikawa, and Murray Silverstein, with Max Jacobson, Ingrid Fiksdahl-King, and Shlomo Angel. 1977. *A Pattern Language: Towns, Buildings, Construction*. New York: Oxford University Press.

Allen, O. N., and Ethel Allen. 1981. *The Leguminosae: A Sourcebook of Characteristics, Uses, and Nodulation*. Madison, WI: University of Wisconsin Press.

American Nursery and Landscape Association. 2004. *American Standard for Nursery Stock: ANSI Z60.1–2004*. Washington, DC: American Nursery and Landscape Association. Available free at www.anla.org.

Arnett, Ross H., Jr. 2000. *American Insects: A Handbook of the Insects of North America North of Mexico*. 2nd edition. Boca Raton, FL: CRC Press.

Art, Henry W. 1986. *A Garden of Wildflowers: 101 Native Species and How to Grow Them*. Pownal, VT: Storey Communications.

Atkinson, David. 1980. "The growth and activity of fruit tree root systems under simulated orchard conditions." In *Environment and Root Behavior*, ed. David N. Sen, 171–85. Jodhpur, India: Geobios International.

ATTRA. 1998. "Integrated pest management." Prepared by Rex Dufour and Janet Bachman. Fayetteville, AR: US Department of Agriculture, Appropriate Technology Transfer for Rural Areas, Fundamentals of Sustainable Agriculture Series.

ATTRA. 1999a. "Alternative pollinators: Native bees." Prepared by Jane Greer. Fayetteville, AR: US Department of Agriculture, Appropriate Technology Transfer for Rural Areas, Horticultural Technical Note. Available as a .pdf download at www.attra.org.

ATTRA. 1999b. "Principles of sustainable weed management for croplands." Prepared by Preston Sullivan. Fayetteville, AR: US Department of Agriculture, Appropriate Technology Transfer for Rural Areas, Agronomy Systems Guide. Available as a .pdf download at www.attra.org.

Baker, Harry. 1980. *Fruit: The Simon & Schuster Step-by-Step Encyclopedia of Practical Gardening*. New York: Simon & Schuster.

B & T World Seeds. 2004. "Trees for coppicing." www.b-and-t-world-seeds.com/a1.asp?title=Trees+for+Coppicing&list=172 (accessed January 28, 2004).

Beal, F. E. L., W. L. McAtee, and E. R. Kalmbach. 1927. *Common Birds of Southeastern United States in Relation to Agriculture*. United States Department of Agriculture Farmers' Bulletin no. 755. Washington DC: USDA.

Behler, John L., and F. Wayne King. 1979. *National Audubon Society Field Guide to Reptiles and Amphibians*. New York: Alfred A. Knopf.

Bell, Michael. 2003. *The Gardener's Guide to Growing Temperate Bamboos*. Portland, OR: Timber Press.

Bender, Steve, ed. 1998. *The Southern Living Garden Book*. Birmingham, AL: Oxmoor House.

Beresford-Kroeger, Diana. 2003. *Arboretum America: A Philosophy of the Forest*. Ann Arbor, MI: University of Michigan Press.

Bessette, Alan, Arleen Bessette, and David Fischer. 1997. *Mushrooms of Northeastern North America*. Syracuse, NY: Syracuse University Press.

Borror, Donald J., and Richard E. White. 1970. *A Field Guide to the Insects of America North of Mexico*. The Peterson Field Guide Series, no. 19. Boston: Houghton Mifflin.

Bowling, Barbara L. 2000. *The Berry Grower's Companion*. Portland, OR: Timber Press.

Brentmar, Olafur, and Alan Kapuler. 1988. *A Coevolutionary Structure for the Plant Kindom*. Corvallis, OR: Peace Seeds.

Brooks, R. R. 1972. *Geobotany and Biogeochemistry in Mineral Exploration*. New York: Harper & Row.

Brown, Emily. 1986. *Landscaping with Perennials*. Portland, OR: Timber Press.

Brown, Lauren. 1979. *Grasses: An Identification Guide*. New York: Houghton Mifflin.

Buchman, Stephen L., and Gary Paul Nabhan. 1996. *The Forgotten Pollinators*. Washington DC: Island Press/Shearwater Books.

Burrell, C. Colston. 1997. *A Gardener's Encyclopedia of Wildflowers*. Emmaus, PA: Rodale Press.

Burrows, George E., and Ronald J. Tyrl. 2001. *Toxic Plants of North America*. Ames, IA: Iowa State University Press.

Carpenter, I. W., and A. T. Guard. 1954. "Anatomy and morphology of the seedling roots of four species of the genus *Quercus*." *Journal of Forestry* 52 (April): 269–74.

Cebenko, Jill, and Deb Martin. 2001. *Insect, Disease, and Weed ID Guide*. Emmaus, PA: Rodale Press.

Clausen, Ruth Rogers, and Nicolas H. Ekstrom. 1989. *Perennials for American Gardens*. New York: Random House.

Cranshaw, Whitney. 2004. *Garden Insects of North America: The Ultimate Guide to Backyard Bugs*. Princeton, NJ: Princeton University Press.

Crawford, Martin. 1993. *Bee Plants*. Dartington, Totnes, Devon, UK: Agroforestry Research Trust.

Crawford, Martin. 1994. "Nut pines." *Agroforestry News* 3(1): 28–35.

Crawford, Martin. 1995a. "Fertility in agroforestry and forest gardens: Nitrogen." *Agroforestry News* 3(3): 18–23.

Crawford, Martin. 1995b. "Fertility in agroforestry and forest gardens: Phosphorus." *Agroforestry News* 3(3): 35–37.

Crawford, Martin. 1995c. "Fertility in agroforestry and forest gardens: Potassium." *Agroforestry News* 3(3): 32–35.

Crawford, Martin. 1995d. "Fertility in agroforestry and forest gardens: Soil pH and calcium." *Agroforestry News* 3(3): 38–40.

Crawford, Martin. 1995e. "Forest gardening: Edges." *Agroforestry News* 3(2): 12–16.

Crawford, Martin. 1995f. *Hazelnuts: Production and Culture*. Dartington, Totnes, Devon, UK: Agroforestry Research Trust.

Crawford, Martin. 1996. *Plums: Production, Culture and Cultivar Directory*. Dartington, Totnes, Devon, UK: Agroforestry Research Trust.

Crawford, Martin. 1997a. *Cherries: Production and Culture*. Dartington, Totnes, Devon, UK: Agroforestry Research Trust.

Crawford, Martin. 1997b. *Currants and Gooseberries: Production and Culture*. Dartington, Totnes, Devon, UK: Agroforestry Research Trust.

Crawford, Martin. 1997c. "Forest gardening: Groundcover polycultures." *Agroforestry News* 6(1): 5–12.

Crawford, Martin. 1997d. *Groundcover Plants*. Dartington, Totnes, Devon, UK: Agroforestry Research Trust.

Crawford, Martin. 1998. *Nitrogen-fixing Plants for Temperate Climates*. Dartington, Totnes, Devon, UK: Agroforestry Research Trust.

Crawford, Martin. 1999. "Forest gardening: Polycultures and matrix planting." *Agroforestry News* 7(2): 37–40.

Crossley, D. I. 1940. "The effect of a compact subsoil horizon on root penetration." *Journal of Forestry* 38: 794–96.

Cullina, William. 2000. *The New England Wildflower Society Guide to Growing and Propagating Wildflowers of the United States and Canada*. New York: Houghton Mifflin.

Cullina, William. 2002. *Native Trees, Shrubs and Vines: A Guide to Using, Growing, and Propagating North American Woody Plants*. New York: Houghton Mifflin.

Daar, Sheila. 1993. "Designing weeds out of urban landscapes." *The IPM Practioner* XV(8). Berkeley, CA: Bio-Integral Resource Center.

Davies, K. M., Jr. 1990. "Microclimate evaluation and modification for northern nut tree plantings." In *Annual Report of the Northern Nut Growers Association*, volume 81. Also available at www.daviesand.com.

Davies, K. M., Jr. 1995. "Non-traditional tree crops for northern climates." Can be found at www.daviesand.com.

Davis, P. H., ed. 1965. *Flora of Turkey and the East Aegean Islands*. Edinburgh, UK: Edinburgh University Press.

DeGraaf, Richard M., and Deborah D. Rudis. 1983. *New England Wildlife: Habitat, Natural History, and Distribution*. US Department of Agriculture, Forest Service, Northeast Forest Experiment Station, General Technical Report NE-108. Out of print, but available online as a .pdf download at www.srs.fs.usda.gov/pubs.

DeGraaf, Richard M., and Mariko Yamasaki. 2001. *New England Wildlife: Habitat, Natural History, and Distribution*. Hanover, NH: University Press of New England.

Delaplane, K. S., and D. F. Mayer. 2000. *Crop Pollination by Bees*. Cambridge, MA: CAB Publishing. Available as a .pdf download at www.cabi-publishing.org.

Deppe, Carol. 2000. *Breed Your Own Vegetable Varieties: The Gardener's and Farmer's Guide to Plant Breeding and Seed Saving*. White River Junction, VT: Chelsea Green.

Dirr, Michael A. 1975. *Manual of Woody Landscape Plants: Their Identification, Ornamental Characteristics, Culture, Propagation and Uses*. 4th edition. Revised 1990. Champaign, IL: Sterling.

Dramstad, Wenche E., James D. Olson, and Richard T. T. Forman. 1996. *Landscape Ecology Principles in Landscape Architecture and Land-Use Planning*. Washington DC: Island Press.

Elias, Thomas S., and Peter A. Dykeman. *Edible Wild Plants: A North American Field Guide*. New York: Sterling.

Elliott, Douglas B. 1976. *Roots: An Underground Botany and Forager's Guide*. Old Greenwich, CT: Chatham Press.

Ellis, Barbara, and Fern Marshall Bradley. 1996. *The Organic Gardener's Handbook of Natural Insect and Disease Control.* Emmaus, PA: Rodale Press.

Ettema, C. H., and R. A. Hansen. 1997. "Nematode diversity in litter of varying complexity." *Soil Ecology Society Abstracts.*

Eyre, Suzanne Normand, ed. 1997. *The Sunset National Garden Book.* Menlo Park, CA: Sunset Books.

Facciola, Stephen. 1990. *Cornucopia: A Sourcebook of Edible Plants.* Vista, CA: Kampong Publications.

Facciola, Stephen. 1998. *Cornucopia II: A Sourcebook of Edible Plants.* Vista, CA: Kampong Publications.

Fern, Ken. 1997. *Plants for a Future: Edible and Useful Plants for a Healthier World.* Hampshire, UK: Permanent Publications.

Fernald, Merrit Lyndon. 1970. *Gray's Manual of Botany: A Handbook of the Flowering Plants and Ferns of the Central and Northeastern United States and Adjacent Canada.* 8th edition. New York: Van Nostrand.

Fischer, David, and Alan Bessette. 1992. *Edible Wild Mushrooms of North America: A Field-to-Kitchen Guide.* Austin, TX: University of Texas Press.

Flint, Harrison L. 1983. *Landscape Plants of Eastern North America Exclusive of Florida and the Immediate Gulf Coast.* New York: John Wiley & Sons.

Forbush, Edward Howe. 1927. *Birds of Massachusetts and Other New England States, Part II: Land Birds from Bob-Whites to Grackles.* Massachusetts Department of Agriculture. Norwood, MA: Norwood Press.

Forbush, Edward Howe. 1929. *Birds of Massachusetts and Other New England States, Part III: Land Birds from Sparrows to Thrushes.* Massachusetts Department of Agriculture. Norwood, MA: Norwood Press.

Foster, Steven. 1984. *Herbal Renaissance.* Salt Lake City, UT: Gibbs-Smith.

Foster, Steven, and James A. Duke. 1990. *A Field Guide to Medicinal Plants: Eastern and Central North America.* Peterson Field Guide Series, no. 40. Boston: Houghton Mifflin.

Friends of the Trees. 1992. *Kiwi Fruit Enthusiast's Journal,* volume 6. Ed. Michael Pilarski. Tonasket, WA: Friends of the Trees.

Fukuoka, Masanobu. 1978. *The One-Straw Revolution: An Introduction to Natural Farming.* Emmaus, PA: Rodale Press.

Fulbright, Dennis, ed. *A Guide to Nut Tree Culture in North America,* volume 1. Townsend, DE: Northern Nut Grower's Association.

Futuyma, Douglas J., and Montgomery Slatkin, eds. 1983. *Coevolution.* Sunderland, MA: Sinauer Associates.

Gerritsen, Henk, and Piet Oudolf. 2000. *Dream Plants for the Natural Garden.* Portland, OR: Timber Press.

Gershuny, Grace. 1993. *Start with the Soil.* Emmaus, PA: Rodale Press.

Gershuny, Grace, and Joseph Smillie. 1986. *The Soul of Soil: A Guide to Ecological Soil Management,* 2nd edition. St. Johnsbury, VT: Gaia Services.

Giono, Jean. 1985. *The Man Who Planted Trees.* White River Junction, VT: Chelsea Green.

Glenn, D. M., and W. V. Welker. 1993. "Root development patterns in field grown peach trees." *Journal of the American Horticultural Society* 118(3): 362–65.

Gordon, Andrew M., and Steven M. Newman, eds. 1997. *Temperate Agroforestry Systems.* New York: Center for Agriculture and Biosciences International.

The Green Spot, Ltd. 2003. *The Green Methods Catalog: The Official Catalog of the Green Spot, Ltd.* Nottingham, NH: The Green Spot.

Griffiths, Mark. 1994. *Index of Garden Plants: The New Royal Horticultural Society Dictionary.* Portland, OR: Timber Press.

Griggs, Jack L. 1997. *All the Birds of North America: American Bird Conservancy's Field Guide.* New York: Harper Collins.

Grubov, V. I. 1999. *Plants of Central Asia: Plant Collections from China and Mongolia.* Enfield, NH: Science Publishers.

Hall-Beyer, Bart, and Jean Richard. 1983. *Ecological Fruit Production in the North.* Trois-Riviéres, Quebec: Jean Richard.

Halpin, Anne. 1981. *Gourmet Gardening: 48 Special Vegetables You Can Grow for Deliciously Distinctive Meals.* Emmaus, PA: Rodale Press.

Häni, Fritz J., Ernst F. Boller, and Siegfried Keller. 1998. "Natural regulation at the farm level." In *Enhancing Biological Control,* ed. Charles H. Pickett and Robert C. Bugg, 161–210. Berkeley, CA: University of California Press.

Harker, Donald, Sherri Evans, Marc Evans, and Kay Harker. 1993. *Landscape Restoration Handbook.* Boca Raton, FL: Lewis Publishers.

Harmer, R., and G. Kerr. 1995. "Creating woodlands: To plant trees or not?" In *The Ecology of Woodland Creation,* ed. Richard Ferris-Kaan, 113–28. New York: John Wiley & Sons.

Harmony Farm Supply. 2002. *Harmony Farm Supply Growers Resource Guide: 2002 Catalogue.* Graton, CA: Harmony Farm Supply.

Harper & Row Publishers, Inc. 1981. *Harper & Row's Complete Field Guide to North American Wildlife, Eastern Edition*. New York: Harper & Row.

Harrington, H. D. 1967. *Edible Native Plants of the Rocky Mountain*. Albuquerque, NM: University of New Mexico Press.

Harris, Charles W., and Nicholas T. Dines. 1988. *Time-Saver Standards for Landscape Architecture*. New York: McGraw-Hill.

Harris, Richard N., James R. Clark, and Nelda P. Matheny. 1999. *Arboriculture: The Integrated Management of Landscape Trees, Shrubs and Vines*. 3rd edition. Upper Saddle River, NJ: Prentice-Hall.

Hart, Robert A. de J. 1991. *Forest Gardening*. Totnes, Devon, UK: Green Books.

Hemenway, Toby. 2001. *Gaia's Garden: A Guide to Home-Scale Permaculture*. White River Junction, VT: Chelsea Green.

Henderson, Carroll L. 1987. *Landscaping for Wildlife*. St. Paul, MN: Minnesota's Bookstore, Minnesota Department of Administration, Print Communications Division.

Hickmott, Simon. 2003. *Growing Unusual Vegetables: Weird and Wonderful Vegetables and How to Grow Them*. Bristol, UK: Eco-Logic Books.

Hightshoe, Gary L. 1988. *Native Trees, Shrubs and Vines for Urban and Rural America: A Planting Design Manual for Environmental Designers*. New York: Van Nostrand-Reinhold.

Hill, Lewis. 1977. *Fruits and Berries for the Home Garden*. Charlotte, VT: Garden Way.

Hills, Lawrence. 1976. *Comfrey: Past, Present, and Future*. London: Faber and Faber.

Holch, A. E. 1931. "Development of roots and shoots of certain deciduous tree seedlings in different forest sites." *Ecology* 12(2): 259–98.

Holmgren, David. 2002. *Permaculture: Principles and Pathways beyond Sustainability*. Hepburn, Victoria, Australia: Holmgren Design Services.

Hsu, Hong Yen, PhD. 1986. *Oriental Materia Medica: A Concise Guide*. New Canaan, CT: Keats.

James, Theodore, Jr. 1983. *How to Grow Fruits, Berries and Nuts in the Midwest and East*. Tucson, AZ: HP Books.

Jean, Frank C., and John E. Weaver. 1924. *Root Behavior and Crop Yield under Irrigation*. Washington DC: Carnegie Institute of Washington.

Jeavons, John. 1995. *How to Grow More Vegetables Than You Ever Thought Possible on Less Land Than You Can Imagine*. 5th edition. Berkeley, CA: Ten Speed Press.

Jelitto, Leo, and Wilhelm Schacht. 1990. *Hardy Herbaceous Perennials*, volumes 1 and 2. Portland, OR: Timber Press.

Johnson, Lorraine. 1999. *100 Easy-to-Grow Native Plants for American Gardens in Temperate Zones*. Buffalo, NY: Firefly Books.

Jones, Samuel B., Jr., and Leonard E. Foote. 1990. *Gardening with Native Wildflowers*. Portland, OR: Timber Press.

Jorgensen, Neil. 1978. *A Sierra Club Naturalist's Guide: Southern New England*. San Francisco: Sierra Club Books.

Kallas, John. 1999. *The Wild Food Primer*. Portland, OR: Wild Food Adventures.

Kartesz, John. 1994. *A Synonymized Checklist of the Vascular Flora of the United States, Canada, and Greenland*. Portland, OR: Timber Press.

Kavasch, Barrie. 1999. *Native Harvests: Recipes and Botanicals of the American Indian*. 2nd edition. New York: Vintage Books.

Kershaw, Linda, Andy MacKinnon, and Jim Pojar. 1998. *Plants of the Rocky Mountains*. Renton, WA: Lone Pine.

Kindscher, Kelly. 1987. *Edible Wild Plants of the Prairie: An Ethnobotanical Guide*. Lawrence, KS: University Press of Kansas.

Kirk, Donald. 1975. *Wild Edible Plants of Western North America*. Happy Camp, CA: Naturegraph.

Kirkland, A. H. 1904. *Usefulness of the American Toad*. Farmer's Bulletin no. 196. Washington DC: United States Department of Agriculture.

Komarov, V. L., ed. 1998. *Flora of the USSR*. Translated from the Russian. Washington DC: Smithsonian Institute Libraries.

Kourik, Robert. 1986. *Designing and Maintaining Your Edible Landscape, Naturally*. Santa Rosa, CA: Metamorphic Press.

Kricher, John C., and Gordon Morrison. 1988. *Ecology of Eastern Forests*. Peterson Field Guides, no. 37. Boston: Houghton Mifflin.

Kruckberg, Arthur. 1992. *Gardening with Native Plants of the Pacific Northwest*. Seattle, WA: University of Washington Press.

Lampe, Kenneth. 1985. *AMA Handbook of Poisonous Plants*. Chicago, IL: American Medical Association.

Lanza, Patricia. 1998. *Lasagna Gardening*. Emmaus, PA: Rodale Press.

Laycock, William A. 1967. *Distribution of Roots and Rhizomes in Different Soil Types in the Pine Barrens of New Jersey*. Professional Paper 563-C. Washington DC: US Geological Survey.

Lemmon, J. G. 1900. *Handbook of West-American Conebearers.* Oakland, CA: Lemmon Herbarium.

Li, Fumin, D. Jordan, Felix Ponder, Jr., Edwin Berry, Victoria Hubbard, and Kil Yong Kim. 1997. "Earthworm and microbial activity in a central hardwood forest after compaction and organic matter removal." *Soil Ecology Society Abstracts.*

Liberty Hyde Bailey Hortorium. 1976. *Hortus III: A Concise Dictionary of Plants Cultivated in the United States and Canada.* New York: MacMillan General Reference.

Little, Elbert L. *National Audubon Society Field Guide to North American Trees: Eastern Region.* New York: Alfred A. Knopf.

Logsdon, Gene. 1981. *Organic Orcharding: A Grove of Trees to Live In.* Emmaus, PA: Rodale Press.

Lovejoy, Ann. 2001. *Ann Lovejoy's Organic Garden Design School.* Emmaus, PA: Rodale Press.

Luken, James O. 1990. *Directing Ecological Succession.* New York: Chapman & Hall.

Lutz, Harold F., Joseph Ely, Jr., and Silas Little, Jr. 1937. *The Influence of Soil Profile Horizons on Root Distribution of Eastern White Pine.* Bulletin 44. New Haven, CT: Yale University School of Forestry.

Lynch, Kevin, and Gary Hack. 1984. *Site Planning.* 3rd edition. Cambridge, MA: MIT Press.

Mabey, Richard. 1989. *Food for Free.* London: Harper Collins.

MacKenzie, David S. 1997. *Perennial Groundcovers.* Portland, OR: Timber Press.

Magdoff, Fred. 2000. *Building Soils for Better Crops.* Washington DC: Sustainable Agriculture Network.

Magee, Dennis W., and Harry E. Ahles. 1999. *Flora of the Northeast: A Manual of the Vascular Flora of New England and Adjacent New York.* Amherst, MA: University of Massachusetts Press.

Martin, Alexander C., Herbert S. Zim, and Arnold L. Nelson. 1951. *American Wildlife and Plants: A Guide to Wildlife Food Habits.* New York: Dover Publications.

McGary, Jane, ed. 2001. *Bulbs of North America.* Portland, OR: Timber Press.

Meredith, Ted Jordan. 2001. *Bamboo for Gardens.* Portland, OR: Timber Press.

Mollison, Bill. 1979. *Permaculture Two: Practical Design for Town and Country in Permanent Agriculture.* Stanley, Tasmania, Australia: Tagari Books.

Mollison, Bill. 1988. *Permaculture: A Designer's Manual.* Tyalgum, Australia: Tagari Publications.

Mollison, Bill. 1990. *Permaculture: A Practical Guide for a Sustainable Future.* Washington DC: Island Press.

Mollison, Bill, and David Holmgren. 1978. *Permaculture One: A Perennial Agriculture for Human Settlements.* Melbourne, Australia: Corgi Books, Transworld Publishers.

Mollison, Bill, with Reny Mia Slay. 1994. *Introduction to Permaculture.* 2nd edition. Tyalgum, Australia: Tagari Publications.

Morrison, Susan Dudley. 1989. *The Passenger Pigeon.* Gone Forever Series, Crestwood House. New York: MacMillan.

Mueller, Oscar P., and Marlin G. Cline. 1959. "Effects of mechanical soil barriers and soil wetness on rooting of trees and soil mixing by blowdown in central New York." *Soil Science* 88(2): 107–11.

National Oceanic and Atmospheric Administration (NOAA). 1974. *Climates of the States.* Port Washington, NY: Water Information Center.

Nentwig, Wolfgang. 1998. "Weedy plant species and their beneficial arthropods: Potential for manipulation in food crops." In *Enhancing Biological Control,* ed. Charles H. Pickett and Robert L. Bugg, 49–71. Berkeley, CA: University of California Press.

Newcomb, Lawrence. 1977. *Newcomb's Wildflower Guide.* New York: Little, Brown.

NHWSPCC and NHSCC. 1984. *Soil Manual for Site Evaluations in New Hampshire.* 3rd printing. Concord, NH: New Hampshire Water Supply and Pollution Control Commission and New Hampshire State Conservation Commission.

NNGA. 1976. *Nut Tree Culture in North America.* Ed. Richard A. Jaynes. Hamden, CT: Northern Nut Growers Association.

NOFA Organic Land Care Committee. 2001. *Standards for Organic Land Care: Practices for Design and Management of Ecological Landscapes.* Northeast Organic Farming Association (NOFA), Connecticut Chapter, P.O. Box 386, Northford, CT 06372.

Olkowski, William, Sheila Daar, and Helga Olkowski. 1991. *Common-Sense Pest Control: Least-toxic Solutions for Your Home, Garden, Pets and Community.* Newtown, CT: Taunton Press.

Otto, Stella. 1993. *The Backyard Orchardist.* Maple City, MI: Otto Graphics.

Peattie, Donald Culross. 1953. *A Natural History of Western Trees.* Boston: Houghton Mifflin.

Pellett, Frank. 1976. *American Honey Plants, Together with Those Which Are of Special Value to the Beekeeper as Sources of Pollen.* Hamilton, IL: Dadant and Sons.

Perry, David A. 1994. *Forest Ecosystems*. Baltimore, MD: Johns Hopkins University Press.

Peterson, Lee Allen. 1977. *A Field Guide to Edible Wild Plants: Eastern and Central North America*. Peterson Field Guide Series, no. 23. Boston: Houghton Mifflin.

Peterson, Roger Tory, and Margaret McKenny. 1968. *A Field Guide to Wildflowers of Northeastern and North-central North America*. Peterson Field Guide Series, no. 17. Boston: Houghton Mifflin.

Petrides, George A. 1972. *A Field Guide to Trees and Shrubs*. 2nd edition. Peterson Field Guide Series, no. 11. Boston: Houghton Mifflin.

Phillips, Michael. 1998. *The Apple Grower*. White River Junction, VT: Chelsea Green.

Pickett, Charles H., and Robert L. Bugg, eds. 1998. *Enhancing Biological Control: Habitat Mangement to Promote Natural Enemies of Agricultural Pests*. Berkeley, CA: University of California Press.

Pickett, S. T. A, and M. J. McDonnell. 1989. "Changing perspectives in community dynamics: A theory of successional forces." *Trends in Ecology & Evolution* 4:241–5.

Plants for a Future online database. www.ibiblio.org/pfaf/D_search.html.

Platnick, Norman I. 2005. *World Spider Catalog, Version 5.5*. American Museum of Natural History. http://research.amnh.org/entomology/spiders/catalog/ COUNTS.html. Accessed July 26, 2005.

Platt, Karen. 1998. *The Seed Search*. Sheffield, UK: self-published.

Point Foundation. 1980. *The Next Whole Earth Catalog: Access to Tools*. Ed. Stewart Brand. New York: Random House.

Pojar, Jim, and Andy McKinnon. 1994. *Plants of the Pacific Northwest Coast: Washington, Oregon, British Columbia, and Alaska*. Renton, WA: Lone Pine.

Polunin, Oleg, and Martin Walters. 1985. *A Guide to the Vegetation of Britain and Europe*. New York: Oxford University Press.

Pratt, Rutherford. 1959. *1,001 Questions Answered about Trees*. New York: Dodd, Mead.

Proctor, Michael, Peter Yeo, and Andrew Lack. 1996. *The Natural History of Pollination*. Portland OR: Timber Press.

Rackham, Oliver. 1993. *Trees and Woodland in the British Landscape: The Complete History of Britain's Trees, Woods, and Hedgerows*. London: Weidenfield & Nicolson.

Reich, Lee. 1991. *Uncommon Fruits Worthy of Attention: A Gardener's Guide*. Reading, MA: Addison-Wesley.

Reich, Lee. 2004. *Uncommon Fruits for Every Garden*. Portland, OR: Timber Press.

Robinson, Raoul. 1996. *Return to Resistance: Breeding Crops to Reduce Pesticide Dependence*. Davis, CA: agAccess.

Rodwell, J. S., and G. S. Patterson. 1995. "Vegetation classification systems as an aid to woodland creation." In *The Ecology of Woodland Creation*, ed. Richard Ferris-Kaan, 63–74. New York: John Wiley & Sons.

Roxbury Community School, Inc. 1983. *Urban Permaculture Project: An Agricultural Landscape Design for the Inner Cities*. Report to the National Endowment for the Arts, Grant 22-4230-209. June 1983. Project Director Michael Talbot. Boston: Roxbury Community School.

St. John, Ted. 1996. "Mycorrhizal inoculation: Advice for growers and restorationists." *Hortus West* 7(2): 1–4. Available in .pdf format at www.mycorrhiza.org.

St. John, Ted. 2000. *The Instant Expert Guide to Mycorrhiza: The Connection for Functional Ecosystems*. Available in .pdf format at www.mycorrhiza.org.

St. Pierre, Richard G. 1992. *Growing Sasktoons: A Manual for Orchardists*. Saskatoon, Saskatchewan, Canada: Department of Horticultural Science, University of Saskatchewan.

Sarrantonio, Marianne. 1994. *Northeast Cover Crop Handbook*. Emmaus, PA: Rodale Press.

Sauer, Leslie Jones, and Andropogon Associates. 1998. *The Once and Future Forest: A Guide to Forest Restoration Strategies*. Washington DC: Island Press.

Schneider, Elizabeth. 2001. *Vegetables from Amaranth to Zucchini: The Essential Reference*. New York: Morrow Cookbooks.

Schutz, Walter E. 1970. *How to Attract, House and Feed Birds*. New York: Collier Books.

Sibley, David Allen. 2000. *The Sibley Guide to Birds*. New York: Alfred A. Knopf.

Smith, J. Russell. 1950. *Tree Crops: A Permanent Agriculture*. New York: Harper & Row.

Smith, Miranda. 1994. *Backyard Fruits and Berries*. Emmaus, PA: Rodale Press.

Soil Quality Institute. 2000. *Heavy Metal Soil Contamination*. Soil Quality—Urban Technical Note no. 3, September 2000. Auburn, AL: US Department of Agriculture, Natural Resources Conservation Service, Soil Quality Institute.

Soule, Judith D., and Jon K. Piper. 1992. *Farming in Nature's Image*. Washington DC: Island Press.

Spirn, Anne Whiston. 1998. *The Language of Landscape*. New Haven, CT: Yale University Press.

Sprackling, John A., and Ralph A. Read. 1979. *Tree Root Systems in Eastern Nebraska*. Nebraska Conservation Bulletin no. 37. Lincoln, NB: University of Nebraska–Lincoln, Institute of Agriculture and Natural Resources, Conservation and Survey Division.

Stamets, Paul. 1993. *Growing Gourmet and Medicinal Mushrooms*. Berkeley, CA: Ten Speed Press.

Stamets, Paul, and J. S. Chilton. 1983. *The Mushroom Cultivator*. Olympia, WA: Agarikon Press.

Stephens, H. A. 1973. *Woody Plants of the North Central Plains*. Lawrence, KS: University of Kansas Press.

Steyermark, Julian A. 1963. *Flora of Missouri*. Ames, IA: University of Iowa Press.

Sweet, Muriel. 1962. *Common Edible and Useful Plants of the West*. Healdsburg, CA: Naturegraph.

Tabor, Raymond. 1994. *Traditional Woodland Crafts: A Practical Guide*. London: B. T. Batsford.

Tatum, Billie Joe. 1976. *Billie Joe Tatum's Wild Foods Field Guide and Cookbook*. New York: Workman.

Tilford, Gregory. 1997. *Edible and Medicinal Plants of the West*. Missoula, MT: Mountain Press.

Tilth. 1982. *The Future Is Abundant: A Guide to Sustainable Agriculture*. Arlington, WA: Tilth.

Thompson, Peter. 1997. *The Self-Sustaining Garden: A Gardener's Guide to Matrix Planting*. London: B. T. Batsford.

Tierra, Michael. 1990. *The Way of Herbs*. New York: Pocket Books, Simon & Schuster.

Tilford, Gregory. 1997. *Edible and Medicinal Plants of the West*. Missoula, MT: Mountain Press.

Toensmeier, Eric. Forthcoming. *Perennial Vegetables*. White River Junction, VT: Chelsea Green.

Toogood, Alan, ed. 1999. *American Horticultural Society Plant Propagation: The Fully Illustrated Plant-by-Plant Manual of Practical Techniques*. New York: Dorling Kindersley.

Turner, Nancy, and Adam Szczawinski. 1991. *Common Poisonous Plants and Mushrooms of North America*. Portland, OR: Timber Press.

UNESCO. 1973. *International Classification and Mapping of Vegetation*. Paris: United Nations Educational Scientific and Cultural Organization.

United States Forest Service. 1990. *Hardwoods*. Volume 2 of *Silvics of North America*. Technical Coordinators Russel M. Burns and Barbara H. Honkala, Timber Management Research. Agriculture Handbook 654. Washington DC: Forest Service, United States Department of Agriculture.

Uva, Richard H., Joseph C. Neal, and Joseph M. DiTomaso. 1997. *Weeds of the Northeast*. Ithaca, NY: Cornell University Press.

Vilmorin-Andrieux, M. M. 1885. *The Vegetable Garden: Illustrations, Descriptions, and Culture of the Garden Vegetables of Cold and Temperate Climates*. London: John Murray.

Weaver, John E. 1919. *The Ecological Relations of Roots*. Publication no. 286. Washington DC: Carnegie Institute of Washington.

Weaver, John E. 1920. *Root Development in the Grassland Formation*. Publication no. 292. Washington DC: Carnegie Institute of Washington.

Weaver, John E., and William E. Bruner. 1927. *Root Development of Vegetable Crops*. New York: McGraw-Hill.

Westbrooks, Randy, and James Preacher. 1986. *Poisonous Plants of Eastern North America*. Columbia, SC: University of South Carolina Press.

Whealy, Kent. 2001. *Fruit, Berry, and Nut Inventory*. Decorah, IA: Seed Savers Exchange.

Willard, Terry. 1992. *Edible and Medicinal Plants of the Rocky Mountains and Neighboring Territories*. Alberta, Canada: Wild Rose College of Natural Healing.

Williams, Greg, and Pat Williams. 2002. "Hazardous materials contaminate some fertilizers." *HortIdeas* 19(4): 37–39.

Woodruff, J. G., and Naomi Woodruff. 1934. "Pecan root growth and development." *Journal of Agricultural Research* 49(6): 511–30.

Yahner, Richard H. 1995. *Eastern Deciduous Forest: Ecology and Wildlife Conservation*. Minneapolis: University of Minnesota Press.

Yeager, A. F. 1935. "Root systems of certain trees and shrubs grown on prairie soils." *Journal of Agricultural Research* 51(12): 1085–92.

Yeomans, P. A. 1958. *The Challenge of Landscape: The Development and Practice of Keyline*. Sydney, Australia: Keyline. Out of print. Can be found at the library of the US Department of Agriculture in Washington DC.

Yeomans, P. A. 1981. *Water for Every Farm: Using the Keyline Plan*. Adelaide, Australia: Griffin Press.

Yepsen, Roger B., Jr., ed. 1984. *The Encyclopedia of Natural Insect & Disease Control*. Emmaus, PA: Rodale Press.

Young, James A., and Cheryl G. Young. 1992. *Seeds of Woody Plants in North America*. Portland, OR: Dioscorides Press.

Zheng-Yi, Wu, and Peter H. Raven, eds. 1999. *Flora of China*. St. Louis, MO: Missouri Botanical Garden.

INDEX OF LATIN SYNONYMS

Over the years, Latin names occasionally change. This index will help you find the current synonyms used in this book for a number of outdated names still in use. Consult the introduction to the appendices to see how we arrived at our list of current names. The first table allows you to translate from old names with which you may be familiar to the names we use in this book. The second table allows you to find out what other names have been used, and may still be used, by nurseries and other references for the plants we list in this book. In both tables, the currently accepted names are listed in **bold**.

Outdated Name	Correct Name
Acer nigrum	***Acer saccharum* var. *nigrum***
Amelanchier canadensis	***Amelanchier lamarkii***
Amelanchier laevis	***Amelanchier lamarkii***
Amelanchier x *grandiflora*	***Amelanchier lamarkii***
Amorphophallus konjac	***Amorphophallus riveri* var. *konjac***
Amygdalus communis	***Prunus dulcis***
Amygdalus persica	***Prunus persica***
Amygdalus persica var. *nucipersica*	***Prunus persica* var. *nucipersica***
Armeniaca mandschurica	***Prunus mandschurica***
Armeniaca vulgaris	***Prunus armeniaca***
Arundinaria tecta	***Arundinaria gigantea* var. *tecta***
Azalea nudiflora	***Rhododendron periclymenoides***
Berberis aquifolium	***Mahonia aquifolium***
Berberis repens	***Mahonia repens***
Brodiaea douglasii	***Triteleia grandiflora***
Cacalia atriplicifolia	***Arnoglossum atriplicifolia***
Castanea americana	***Castanea dentata***
Cedrela sinensis	***Toona sinensis***
Chamaenerion angustifolium	***Epilobium angustifolium***
Chamaenerion latifolium	***Epilobium latifolium***
Chasmanthium uniflorum	***Chasmanthium latifolium***
Commelina virginiana	***Commelina erecta***
Coptis groenlandica	***Coptis trifolia* var. *groenlandica***
Cornus racemosa	***Cornus paniculata***
Cornus stolonifera	***Cornus sericea***
Dentaria diphylla	***Cardamine diphylla***
Eupatorium coelestinum	***Conoclinium coelestinum***
Halesia caroliniana	***Halesia tetraptera***
Hedyotis caerulea	***Houstonia caerula***
Heracleum lanatum	***Heracleum sphondylium***
Heracleum maximum	***Heracleum sphondylium***
Indigofera incarnata	***Indigofera decora***
Lathyrus angustifolius	***Lathyrus latifolius***

Outdated Name	Correct Name
Lathyrus maritimus	***Lathyrus japonica* var. *maritima***
Lilium tigrinum	***Lilium lancifolium***
Malus domestica	***Malus pumila***
Malus sylvestris var. *domestica*	***Malus pumila***
Matteuccia pensylvanica	***Matteuccia struthiopteris***
Opuntia humifusa	***Opuntia compressa***
Peltiphyllum peltatum	***Darmera peltata***
Pinus siberica	***Pinus cembra* var. *siberica***
Polygonatum commutatum	***Polygonatum biflorum* var. *commutatum***
Polymnia uvedalia	***Smallanthus uvedalia***
Prunus besseyi	***Prunus pumila* var. *besseyi***
Prunus institia	***Prunus domestica* var. *institia***
Prunus nigra	***Prunus americana* var. *nigra***
Pycnanthemum hyssopifolium	***Pycnanthemum flexuosum***
Rheum rhabarbarum	***Rheum* x *cultorum***
Rhus typhina	***Rhus hirta***
Ribes grossularia	***Ribes uva-crispa***
Ribes nigridolaria	***Ribes* x *culverwellii***
Ribes sativum	***Ribes silvestre***
Rorippa nasturtium-aquaticum	***Nasturtium officinale***
Rosa pomifera	***Rosa villosa***
Rubus calycinoides	***Rubus pentalobus***
Rubus strigosus	***Rubus idaeus* var. *strigosus***
Satureja glabrella	***Clinopodium glabellum***
Sedum rosea	***Rhodiola rosea***
Sedum telephium	***Hylotelephium telephium***
Stachys sieboldii	***Stachys affinis***
Stellaria jamesiana	***Pseudostellaria jamesiana***
Urtica gracilis	***Urtica dioica* var. *gracilis***
Viola papilionacea	***Viola sororaria***

Correct Name	Outdated Name	Correct Name	Outdated Name
Acer saccharum var. nigrum	Acer nigrum	Matteuccia struthiopteris	Matteuccia pensylvanica
Amelanchier lamarkii	Amelanchier canadensis	Nasturtium officinale	Rorippa nasturtium-aquaticum
Amelanchier lamarkii	Amelanchier laevis	Opuntia compressa	Opuntia humifusa
Amelanchier lamarkii	Amelanchier X grandiflora	Pinus cembra var. siberica	Pinus siberica
Amorphophallus riveri var. konjac	Amorphophallus konjac	Polygonatum biflorum var. commutatum	Polygonatum commutatum
Arnoglossum atriplicifolia	Cacalia atriplicifolia	Prunus americana var. nigra	Prunus nigra
Arundinaria gigantea var. tecta	Arundinaria tecta	Prunus armeniaca	Armeniaca vulgaris
Cardamine diphylla	Dentaria diphylla	Prunus domestica var. institia	Prunus institia
Castanea dentata	Castanea americana	Prunus dulcis	Amygdalus communis
Chasmanthium latifolium	Chasmanthium uniflorum	Prunus mandschurica	Armeniaca mandschurica
Clinopodium glabellum	Satureja glabrella	Prunus persica	Amygdalus persica
Commelina erecta	Commelina virginiana	Prunus persica var. nucipersica	Amygdalus persica var. nucipersica
Conoclinium coelestinum	Eupatorium coelestinum	Prunus pumila var. besseyi	Prunus besseyi
Coptis trifolia var. groenlandica	Coptis groenlandica	Pseudostellaria jamesiana	Stellaria jamesiana
Cornus paniculata	Cornus racemosa	Pycnanthemum flexuosum	Pycnanthemum hyssopifolium
Cornus sericea	Cornus stolonifera	Rheum X cultorum	Rheum rhabarbarum
Darmera peltata	Peltiphyllum peltatum	Rhodiola rosea	Sedum rosea
Epilobium angustifolium	Chamaenerion angustifolium	Rhododendron periclymenoides	Azalea nudiflora
Epilobium latifolium	Chamaenerion latifolium	Rhus hirta	Rhus typhina
Halesia tetraptera	Halesia caroliniana	Ribes silvestre	Ribes sativum
Heracleum sphondylium	Heracleum lanatum	Ribes uva-crispa	Ribes grossularia
Heracleum sphondylium	Heracleum maximum	Ribes X culverwellii	Ribes nigridolaria
Houstonia caerulea	Hedyotis caerulea	Rosa villosa	Rosa pomifera
Hylotelephium telephium	Sedum telephium	Rubus idaeus var. strigosus	Rubus strigosus
Indigofera decora	Indigofera incarnata	Rubus pentalobus	Rubus calycinoides
Lathyrus japonica var. maritima	Lathyrus maritimus	Smallanthus uvedalia	Polymnia uvedalia
Lathyrus latifolius	Lathyrus angustifolius	Stachys affinis	Stachys sieboldii
Lilium lancifolium	Lilium tigrinum	Toona sinensis	Cedrela sinensis
Mahonia aquifolium	Berberis aquifolium	Triteleia grandiflora	Brodiaea douglasii
Mahonia repens	Berberis repens	Urtica dioica var. gracilis	Urtica gracilis
Malus pumila	Malus domestica	Viola sororaria	Viola papilionacea
Malus pumila	Malus sylvestris var. domestica		

INDEX OF COMMON AND LATIN NAMES

Common Name	Latin Name	Common Name	Latin Name
fragrant false indigo	*Amorpha nana*	Himalayan rhubarb	*Rheum australe*
fragrant spring tree	*Toona sinensis*	hog peanut	*Amphicarpaea bracteata*
fragrant sumac	*Rhus aromatica*	hog plum	*Prunus hortulana*
French sorrel	*Rumex acetosa*	hollyhock	*Alcea rosea*
French tarragon	*Artemisia dracunculus* var. *sativa*	holly oak	*Quercus ilex* var. *rotundifolia*
fringed sagebrush	*Artemisia frigida*	honewort	*Cryptotaenia canadensis*
fruticosa oak	*Quercus fruticosa*	honeyberry honeysuckle	*Lonicera kamschatica*
fuki	*Petasites japonicus*	honey locust	*Gleditsia triacanthos*
galax	*Galax urceolata*	honeypod mesquite	*Prosopis glandulosa*
Gambel oak	*Quercus gambelii*	Hong Kong lily	*Lilium brownii*
gamote	*Cymopterus purpurascens*	hops	*Humulus lupulus*
garden strawberry	*Fragaria* X *ananassa*	horseradish	*Armoracia rusticana*
garlic chives	*Allium tuberosum*	hot tuna	*Houttuynia cordata*
giant chickweed	*Stellaria pubera*	huang-qi	*Astragalus membranaceous*
giant fuki	*Petasites japonicus giganteus*	hybrid dwarf cherry	*Prunus* X hybrids
		hybrid lupine	*Lupinus* hybrids
giant Solomon's seal	*Polygonatum biflorum* var. *commutatum*	hybrid mulberry	*Morus* X hybrids
		hybrid plum	*Prunus* X hybrids
giant sunflower	*Helianthus giganteus*	hyssop hedge nettle	*Stachys hyssopifolia*
golden alexanders	*Zizia aurea*	hyssop-leaved mountain mint	*Pycnanthemum flexuosum*
golden currant	*Ribes aureum*	Indian cucumber root	*Medeola virginiana*
golden groundsel	*Senecio aureus*	Indian potato	*Helianthus giganteus* var. *subtuberosum*
golden saxifrage	*Chrysosplenium americanum*		
		Indian rhubarb	*Darmera peltata*
goldthread	*Coptis trifolium* var. *groenlandica*	inkberry	*Ilex glabra*
		Italian alder	*Alnus cordata*
good King Henry	*Chenopodium bonus-henricus*	Japanese bush cherry	*Prunus japonica* var. *nakai*
		Japanese pagoda tree	*Sophora japonica*
gooseberry	*Ribes uva-crispa*	Japanese pepper tree	*Zanthoxylum piperitum*
goumi	*Eleagnus multiflora*	Japanese plum	*Prunus salicina*
grape	*Vitis vinifera* and hybrids	Japanese raisin tree	*Hovenia dulcis*
gray alder	*Alnus incana*	Japanese stone pine	*Pinus pumila*
gray dogwood	*Cornus racemosa*	Japanese wisteria	*Wisteria floribunda*
great burnet	*Sanguisorba officinalis*	Jeffrey pine	*Pinus jeffreyi*
great wood sorrel	*Oxalis grandis*	Jerusalem artichoke	*Helianthus tuberosus*
green and gold	*Chrysogonum virginianum*	jinenjo	*Dioscorea japonica*
ground cherry	*Physalis heterophylla*	jostaberry	*Ribes* X *culverwellii*
groundnut	*Apios americana*	jujube	*Ziziphus jujuba*
groundplum milkvetch	*Astragalus crassicarpus*	juneberry	*Amelanchier lamarkii*
hackberry	*Celtis occidentalis*	kaki persimmon	*Diospyros kaki*
hairy wood mint	*Blephilia hirsuta*	Kamchatka lily	*Fritillaria camschatcensis*
'Hall's Hardy Almond'	*Prunus* X hybrid	Kentucky wisteria	*Wisteria macrostachya*
hardy ageratum	*Conoclinium coelestinum*	konjac	*Amorphophallus riveri* var. *konjac*
hardy kiwifruit	*Actinidia arguta*		
hay-scented fern	*Dennstaedtia punctilobula*	Korean pine	*Pinus koraiensis*
hazelbert	*Corylus* X hybrids	kousa dogwood	*Cornus kousa*
heart-leaved alexanders	*Zizia aptera*	Labrador violet	*Viola labradorica*
heartnut	*Juglans ailantifolia* var. *cordiformis*	lady fern	*Athyrium filix-femina*
		large-flowered comfrey	*Symphytum grandiflorum*
hican	*Carya* X hybrids	large-fruited biscuit root	*Lomatium macrocarpum*
highbush blueberry	*Vaccinium corymbosum*	leadplant	*Amorpha canescens*
highbush cranberry	*Viburnum trilobum*	leafcup	*Smallanthus uvedalia*

Common Name	Latin Name	Common Name	Latin Name
lemon balm	*Melissa officinalis*	nodding wild onion	*Allium cernuum*
licorice	*Glycyrrhiza glabra*	northern bayberry	*Myrica pensylvanica*
licorice fern	*Polypodium glycyrrhiza*	northern bugleweed	*Lycopus uniflorus*
limber pine	*Pinus flexilis*	northern fly honeysuckle	*Lonicera villosa*
linden	*Tilia* x *vulgaris*	northern sea oats	*Chasmanthium latifolium*
lingonberry	*Vaccinium vitis-idaea*	oak fern	*Gymnocarpium dryopteris*
lovage	*Levisticum officinale*	oregano	*Origanum vulgare hirtum*
lowbush blueberry	*Vaccinium angustifolium*	Oregon grape	*Mahonia aquifolium*
lupine	*Lupinus perennis*	orpine	*Hylotelephium telephium*
magnolia vine	*Schisandra chinensis*	osha	*Ligusticum canbyi*
mahala mat	*Ceanothus prostratus*	ostrich fern	*Matteuccia struthiopteris*
maidenhair fern	*Adiantum pedatum*	oxeye sunflower	*Heliopsis helianthoides*
maidenhair tree	*Ginkgo biloba*	oyster plant	*Mertensia maritima*
mallow	*Malva alcea*	pale Indian plantain	*Arnoglossum atriplicifolia*
Manchurian apricot	*Prunus mandschurica*	partridgeberry	*Mitchella repens*
marginal wood fern	*Dryopteris marginalis*	pasture rose	*Rosa carolina*
marsh mallow	*Althaea officinalis*	pawpaw	*Asimina triloba*
marsh rose	*Rosa palustris*	peach	*Prunus persica*
Maryland dittany	*Cunila origanoides*	pear	*Pyrus communis*
Maximilian sunflower	*Helianthus maximilianii*	pecan	*Carya illinoinensis*
mayapple	*Podophyllum peltatum*	Pennsylvania sedge	*Carex pensylvanica*
mayhaw	*Crataegus aestivalis*	pepper and salt	*Erigenia bulbosa*
maypop	*Passiflora incarnata*	peppermint	*Mentha* x *piperita*
meadow beauty	*Rhexia virginica*	perennial broccoli 'Nine Star'	*Brassica oleracea botrytis* cv.
meadow parsnip	*Thaspium barbinode*	perennial lettuce	*Lactuca perennis*
medlar	*Mespilus germanica*	perennial sorghum	*Sorghum* x hybrid
milk vetch	*Astragalus glycyphyllos*	perennial sweet leek	*Allium ampeloprasum*
milkweed	*Asclepias syriaca*	perennial wheat	*Triticum* x *aestivum*
miner's lettuce	*Montia perfoliata*	perry pear	*Pyrus communis*
Missouri goldenrod	*Solidago missouriensis*	pig nut	*Conopodium majus*
Missouri gooseberry	*Ribes missouriense*	pink tickseed	*Coreopsis rosea*
miterwort	*Mitella diphylla*	pinxter-flower azalea	*Rhododendron pericylmenoides*
mitsuba	*Cryptotaenia japonica*		
Mongolian bush cherry	*Prunus fruticosa*	pinyon pine	*Pinus edulis*
monkey-puzzle tree	*Araucaria araucana*	pipsissewa	*Chimaphila maculata*
moss pink	*Phlox subulata*	pipsissewa	*Chimaphila umbellata*
mountain avens	*Dryas octopetala*	plum yew	*Cephalotaxus harringtonia*
mountain mahogany	*Cercocarpus montanus*	pointed-leaved tick trefoil	*Desmodium glutinosum*
mountain sorrel	*Oxyria digyna*	pokeweed	*Phytolacca americana*
muscadine grape	*Vitis rotundifolia*	potato onion	*Allium cepa aggregatum*
musk mallow	*Malva moschata*	prairie acacia	*Acacia angustissima*
musk strawberry	*Fragaria moschata*	prairie crabapple	*Malus ioensis*
myrobalan plum	*Prunus cerasifera*	prairie parsley	*Polytaenia nuttallii*
Nanking cherry	*Prunus tomentosa*	prairie rose	*Rosa setigera*
nannyberry	*Viburnum lentago*	prairie turnip	*Psoralea esculenta*
native nettle	*Urtica dioica* var. *gracilis*	Price's groundnut	*Apios priceana*
nectarine	*Prunus persica* var. *nucipersica*	prickly ash	*Zanthoxylum americanum*
		prickly dewberry	*Rubus flagellaris*
netted chain fern	*Woodwardia areolata*	prickly-pear cactus	*Opuntia compressa*
New England aster	*Aster novae-angliae*	prostrate bird's-foot trefoil 'Plena'	*Lotus corniculatus* cv.
New Jersey tea	*Ceanothus americanus*		
New York fern	*Thelypteris noveboracensis*	prostrate broom	*Cytisus decumbens*
New York ironweed	*Vernonia noveboracensis*	purple coneflower	*Echinacea purpurea*

Common Name	Latin Name	Common Name	Latin Name
purple-flowering raspberry	*Rubus odoratus*	sea beet	*Beta vulgaris maritima*
purple hardy kiwifruit	*Actinidia purpurea*	sea buckthorn	*Hippophae rhamnoides*
purple poppy-mallow	*Callirhoe involucrata*	sea holly	*Eryngium maritimum*
pussytoes	*Antennaria* spp.	sea kale	*Crambe maritima*
pygmy pea shrub	*Caragana pygmaea*	sensitive fern	*Onoclea sensibilis*
quince	*Cydonia oblonga*	service tree	*Sorbus domestica*
rabbiteye blueberry	*Vaccinium ashei*	shagbark hickory	*Carya ovata*
ramps	*Allium tricoccum*	shallot	*Allium cepa aggregatum*
raspberry	*Rubus idaeus*	sheep sorrel	*Rumex acetosella*
rattlesnake weed	*Hieracium venosum*	shellbark hickory	*Carya laciniosa*
red bay	*Persea borbonia*	showy mountain ash	*Sorbus decora*
redbud	*Cercis canadensis*	showy sunflower	*Helianthus* x *laetiflorus*
red chokeberry	*Aronia arbutifolia*	showy tick trefoil	*Desmodium canadense*
red clover	*Trifolium pratense*	Shuttleworth's ginger	*Asarum shuttleworthii*
red currant	*Ribes silvestre*	Siberian crabapple	*Malus baccata*
red mulberry	*Morus rubra*	Siberian miner's lettuce	*Montia sibirica*
red-osier dogwood	*Cornus stolonifera*	Siberian pea shrub	*Caragana arborescens*
red valerian	*Centranthus ruber*	Siberian stone pine	*Pinus cembra* var. *sibirica*
redwood sorrel	*Oxalis oregana*	silky-leaf woodwaxen	*Genista pilosa*
rhubarb	*Rheum* x *cultorum*	silverbell	*Halesia tetraptera*
riverbank grape	*Vitis riparia*	silverberry	*Eleagnus commutata*
river beauty	*Epilobium latifolium*	silver maple	*Acer saccharinum*
Robin's plantain	*Erigeron pulchellus*	silverweed	*Potentilla anserina*
rock cress	*Arabis caucasica*	skirret	*Sium sisarum*
rock polypody	*Polypodium virginianum*	slippery elm	*Ulmus rubra*
rosemary	*Rosmarinus officinalis*	smooth alder	*Alnus serrulata*
rose of Sharon	*Hibiscus syriacus*	smooth gooseberry	*Ribes hirtellum*
roseroot	*Rhodiola rosea*	smooth-leaved satureja	*Clinopodium glabrellum*
rose verbena	*Verbena canadensis*	smooth sumac	*Rhus glabra*
rosybells	*Streptopus roseus*	Solomon's seal	*Polygonatum biflorum*
round-headed bush clover	*Lespedeza capitata*	sour cherry	*Prunus cerasus*
round-leaved ragwort	*Senecio obovatus*	southern bayberry	*Myrica cerifera*
rowan	*Sorbus aucuparia*	southern juneberry	*Amelanchier obovalis*
rugosa rose	*Rosa rugosa*	spearmint	*Mentha spicata*
running club moss	*Lycopodium clavatum*	speckled alder	*Alnus rugosa*
running juneberry	*Amelanchier stolonifera*	speedwell	*Veronica officinalis*
Russian comfrey	*Symphytum* x *uplandicum*	spicebush	*Lindera benzoin*
Russian pea shrub	*Caragana frutex*	spikenard	*Aralia racemosa*
rye 'Varimontra'	*Secale cereale* cv.	spring beauty	*Claytonia virginica*
saffron crocus	*Crocus sativus*	spring cress	*Cardamine bulbosa*
salad burnet	*Sanguisorba minor*	staghorn sumac	*Rhus hirta*
salal	*Gaultheria shallon*	stinging nettle	*Urtica dioica*
salmonberry	*Rubus spectabilis*	stone bamboo	*Phyllostachys nuda*
saltbush	*Atriplex halimus*	stonecrop	*Sedum reflexum*
sand cherry	*Prunus pumila* var. *besseyi*	strawberry-raspberry	*Rubus illecebrosus*
sandhill plum	*Prunus angustifolia* var. *watsonii*	strawberry saxifrage	*Saxifraga stolonifera*
		strawberry tree	*Arbutus unedo*
saskatoon	*Amelanchier alnifolia*	sugarberry	*Celtis laevigata*
sassafras	*Sassafras albidum*	sugar maple	*Acer saccharum*
sawtooth oak	*Quercus acutissima*	superhardy kiwifruit	*Actinidia kolomikta*
Schuette's oak	*Quercus* x *schuettei*	swamp chestnut oak	*Quercus michauxii*
scorzonera	*Scorzonera hispanica*	swamp milkweed	*Asclepias incarnata*
Scotch lovage	*Ligusticum scothicum*	swamp white oak	*Quercus bicolor*

Common Name	Latin Name	Common Name	Latin Name
sweet bay magnolia	*Magnolia virginiana*	western bistort	*Polygonum bistortoides*
sweet cherry	*Prunus avium*	whitebark pine	*Pinus albicaulis*
sweet cicely (European)	*Myrrhis odorata*	white clover	*Trifolium repens*
sweet cicely (native)	*Osmorhiza claytonii*	white mulberry	*Morus alba*
sweetfern	*Comptonia peregrina*	white oak	*Quercus alba*
sweet gale	*Myrica gale*	white stonecrop	*Sedum album*
sweet goldenrod	*Solidago odora*	white tansy yarrow	*Achillea ptarmica*
sweetshoot bamboo	*Phyllostachys dulcis*	white trillium	*Trillium grandiflorum*
sweet vetch	*Hedysarum boreale*	white trumpet lily	*Lilium longiflorum*
sweet violet	*Viola odorata*	white wood aster	*Aster divaricatus*
Swiss stone pine	*Pinus cembra*	whorled rosinweed	*Silphium trifoliatum*
sylvetta arugula	*Diplotaxis* spp.	wild bean (edible)	*Phaseolus polystachios*
taro	*Colocasia esculenta*	wild bean (nonedible)	*Strophostyles umbellata*
tawny day lily	*Hemerocallis fulva*	wild bergamot	*Monarda fistulosa*
temple bamboo	*Semiarundinaria fastuosa*	wild blue indigo	*Baptisia australis*
thimbleberry	*Rubus parviflorus*	wild blue phlox	*Phlox divaricata*
thin-leaved sunflower	*Helianthus decapetalus*	wild cabbage	*Brassica oleracea*
thread-leaved coreopsis	*Coreopsis verticillata*	wild garlic	*Allium canadense*
thyme	*Thymus vulgaris*	wild geranium	*Geranium maculatum*
tiger lily	*Lilium lancifolium*	wild ginger	*Asarum canadense*
toothwort	*Cardamine diphylla*	wild goose plum	*Prunus munsoniana*
trailing arbutus	*Epigaea repens*	wild hyacinth	*Camassia leichtlinnii*
trailing phlox	*Phlox nivalis*	wild potato vine	*Ipomoea pandurata*
trailing silky-leaf woodwaxen	*Genista pilosa procumbens*	wild quinine	*Parthenium integrifolium*
trazel	*Corylus* x *colurnoides*	wild sarsaparilla	*Aralia nudicaulis*
tree collards	*Brassica oleracea acephala*	wild stonecrop	*Sedum ternatum*
tree hazel	*Corylus colurna*	wild strawberry	*Fragaria virginiana*
trout lily	*Erythronium americanum*	winged sumac	*Rhus copallina*
trumpet honeysuckle	*Lonicera sempervirens*	wintergreen	*Gaultheria procumbens*
tuberous chickweed	*Pseudostellaria jamesiana*	witherod viburnum	*Viburnum cassinoides*
tufted vetch	*Vicia cracca*	woodland horsetail	*Equisetum sylvaticum*
turkey rhubarb	*Rheum palmatum*	woodland strawberry	*Fragaria vesca*
Turkish rocket	*Bunias orientalis*	woodland thaspium	*Thaspium trifoliatum*
Turk's-cap lily	*Lilium superbum*	wood lily	*Lilium philadelphicum*
twinflower	*Linnaea borealis*	wood nettle	*Laportaea canadensis*
twinleaf	*Jeffersonia diphylla*	wood sorrel	*Oxalis montana*
twisted stalk	*Streptopus amplexifolius*	wood vetch	*Vicia caroliniana*
two-flowered pencil flower	*Stylosanthes biflora*	woundwort	*Stachys palustris*
udo	*Aralia cordata*	yampa	*Perideridia gairdneri*
violet wood sorrel	*Oxalis violacea*	yarrow	*Achillea millefolium*
Virginia chain fern	*Woodwardia virginica*	yellow asphodel	*Asphodeline lutea*
Virginia dayflower	*Commelina erecta*	yellow birch	*Betula alleghaniensis*
Virginia mountain mint	*Pycnanthemum virginianum*	yellow daylily	*Hemerocallis lilio-asphodelus*
Virginia spiderwort	*Tradescantia virginiana*	yellowhorn	*Xanthoceras sorbifolium*
Virginia waterleaf	*Hydrophyllum virginianum*	yellow pimpernel	*Taenidia integerrima*
		yellow wild indigo	*Baptisia tinctoria*
water avens	*Geum rivale*	yerba buena	*Satureja douglasii*
watercress	*Nasturtium officinale*	zigzag goldenrod	*Solidago flexicaulis*
Welsh onion	*Allium fistulosum*		

GENERAL INDEX

The field research for, and writing of, portions of this manuscript were undertaken under the auspices of the New England Small Farm Institute, Inc., Belchertown, Massachusetts. The New England Small Farm Institute was founded in 1978. Its mission is to promote the viability of our region's small farms. It develops and delivers innovative, farmer-guided programs and resources; provides direct assistance to aspiring, new, and developing farmers; and advocates for new farmers and sustainable small-scale agriculture. The Institute manages Lampson Brook Agricultural Reserve—416 acres of public land designated as a National Historic Register heritage landscape—as a small farm demonstration and training center.

New England Small Farm Institute
PO Box 937, Belchertown MA 01007
(413) 323-4531
www.smallfarm.org

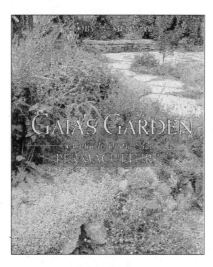